# Advanced Management Accounting

THE ROBERT S. KAPLAN SERIES
IN MANAGEMENT ACCOUNTING
*Robert S. Kaplan, Consulting Editor*

# Advanced Management Accounting

Third Edition

## Robert S. Kaplan
*Harvard Business School*

## Anthony A. Atkinson
*University of Waterloo*

Prentice Hall International, Inc.

**Library of Congress Cataloging-in-Publication Data**

Kaplan, Robert S.
   Advanced management accounting / Robert S. Kaplan, Anthony A.
Atkinson.—3rd ed.
      p.   cm.—(The Robert S. Kaplan series in management
accounting)
   Includes bibliographical references and index.
   ISBN 0-13-262288-2
   1. Managerial accounting.   I. Atkinson, Anthony A.   II. Title.
III. Series.
HF5635.K15 1998
658.15'11—dc21     97-30382
                 CIP

*Editor-in-Chief:*   P. J. Boardman
*Editorial Assistant:*   Jane Avery
*Marketing Manager:*   Deborah Hoffman
*Production Editor:*   Susan Rifkin
*Production Coordinator:*   Cindy Spreder
*Managing Editor:*   Katherine Evancie
*Senior Manufacturing Supervisor:*   Paul Smolenski
*Manufacturing Manager:*   Vincent Scelta
*Design Director:*   Pat Smythe
*Interior Design:*   Donna Wickes
*Cover Design:*   John Romer
*Composition:*   University Graphics
*Cover Art/Photo:*   Ralph Mercer Photography

© 1998, 1989, 1982 by Prentice Hall, Inc.
Upper Saddle River, New Jersey 07458

Printed in the United States of America
10
ISBN 0-13-080220-4

**Prentice-Hall International (UK) Limited,** *London*
**Prentice-Hall of Australia Pty. Limited,** *Sydney*
**Prentice-Hall Canada Inc.,** *Toronto*
**Prentice-Hall Hispanoamericana, S.A.,** *Mexico*
**Prentice-Hall of India Private Limited,** *New Delhi*
**Prentice-Hall of Japan, Inc.,** *Tokyo*
**Prentice-Hall Asia Pte. Ltd.,** *Singapore*
**Editora Prentice-Hall do Brasil, Ltda.,** *Rio de Janerio*

# Contents

# 2 SHORT-TERM BUDGETING, RESOURCE ALLOCATIONS, AND CAPACITY COST   33

# 3 ASSIGNING RESOURCE COSTS TO PRODUCTION COST CENTERS   60

# 4 ACTIVITY-BASED COST SYSTEMS 97

# 5 ACTIVITY-BASED MANAGEMENT 149

# 6 COST BASED DECISION MAKING 222

# 7 DECENTRALIZATION 288

## 8 THE BALANCED SCORECARD: MEASURING TOTAL BUSINESS UNIT PERFORMANCE 367

## 9 FINANCIAL MEASURES OF PERFORMANCE 442

## 10   FINANCIAL MEASURES OF PERFORMANCE: RETURN ON INVESTMENT (ROI) AND ECONOMIC VALUE ADDED (EVA™)   499

# 11 MEASURING CUSTOMER, INTERNAL BUSINESS PROCESS, AND EMPLOYEE PERFORMANCE   551

# 12 INVESTING TO DEVELOP FUTURE CAPABILITIES TECHNOLOGY   593

# 13 INCENTIVE AND COMPENSATION SYSTEMS 673

## 14 FORMAL MODELS IN BUDGETING AND INCENTIVE CONTRACTS   764

# Preface

*Advanced Management Accounting,* third edition, is a major revision from the second edition that was published in 1989. In the preface for the second edition, we were already describing the enormous changes underway for both manufacturing and service operations, and highlighting the rapid evolution in the technology for information processing. These advances created a challenging new environment for management accounting systems. If anything, rapid changes in the theory and practice of management accounting during the past ten years have accelerated, and to keep pace we have introduced significant new coverage and deleted some older material as we wrote the third edition.

The role for management accounting continues to undergo major changes. Management accountants are no longer only scorekeepers of past performance. They have become value-adding members of management teams, creating information vital for enhancing operational excellence, and for formulating and implementing new strategies. A significant development in this new role is a great increase in the importance and use of nonfinancial measures of performance. This book provides extensive coverage of the new management accounting practices being adopted by innovative companies around the world, including activity-based costing, kaizen and target costing, and the Balanced Scorecard.

A research project sponsored by the Institute of Management Accountants and the Financial Executives Institute[1] surveyed U.S. corporate accounting and financial executives about the relative importance of various accounting knowledge and skill areas (AKSAs), and about the extent to which entry-level accountants bring these AKSAs to their initial job. The four AKSAs rated as most important for management accountants were budgeting, product and service costing, control and performance evaluation, and strategic cost management, including activity-based costing. These four AKSAs, how-

---

[1] *What Corporate America Wants in Entry-Level Accountants* (Institute of Mangement Accountants: Montvale, NJ; 1994).

ever, also showed the largest gap between corporate expectations and actual preparation of entry-level accountants. In this third edition, we provide comprehensive treatments of these four highly rated AKSAs.

The book's introduction, surveys the rich historical role for management accounting in the development of large industrial and service enterprises. Chapter 1 provides a comprehensive summary of cost definitions and cost classifications. It uses a comprehensive example to illustrate how traditional notions of fixed and variable costs can be imbedded in a much richer framework of committed and flexible costs. The chapter treats committed costs as arising from managerial decisions to supply capacity to perform anticipated work. It introduces the vital distinction between the costs of resources supplied versus the costs of resources used. It also examines the importance of identifying sustaining costs, at various hierarchical levels and decision points, where managers have the opportunity to make long-term decisions about whether to introduce or continue to support products, lines of business, customers, channels, and market segments. Chapter 2 builds on this framework to address short-term budgeting and decision making with the existing supply of resources. This chapter provides a comprehensive model for short-term budgeting and for optimizing the use of short-term committed resources.

Chapter 3 draws heavily on the treatment of service department costs from the first and second editions, but imbeds this subject in the context of a general treatment of cost system design. Thus, we view the assignment of service and support department costs as the initial assignment stage, from resources to production cost centers, when designing cost systems for operational control and for product and service costing. Chapter 4 extends this framework and introduces activity-based costing, allowing resource costs to flow, not just to production cost centers, but to activities. The chapter builds on this activity framework, to provide a comprehensive introduction to activity-based costing (ABC). It shows how to use a range of different types of activity cost drivers to assign resource costs more accurately to cost objects: products, services and customers. The chapter concludes by summarizing the principal benefits and design trade-offs associated with introducing an activity-based cost system.

Chapter 5, Activity-Based Management (ABM), incorporates material from the pricing chapter in the second edition, and extends this material by describing a full range of strategic and operational decisions that are better informed by the more accurate information drawn from an ABC system. ABM actions include, in addition to re-pricing, decisions about product and customer mix, product design, process improvements, operations strategy, and technology investments. Chapter 6 addresses operational ABM for process improvements and discusses the roles of kaizen costing in continuous improvement, and target costing for influencing future product costs at the design stage.

In summary, we use the conceptual framework of activity-based costing to provide an integrated treatment for these first six chapters. Chapters 1, 4, 5, and 6 are virtually completely new material for *Advanced Management Accounting*, third edition, and Chapters 2 and 3 have been re-written, from the second edition, to fit within this integrated framework.

To accommodate all this new material, we eliminated the two chapters on regression analysis, which were a central feature of the first two editions. The deletion decision was strongly influenced by the theoretical advance that statistical analyses can measure only the results of management decisions (how much capacity to provide, and how quickly managers adjust resource capacity to changes in the demands for resources). Of more relevance for managers is not estimates of the cost of supplying resources, but the cost of the actual demands (the costs of resources used) that activities make on most organizational resources. This role is now accomplished through ABC systems, not statistical analysis. We have also deleted the chapter on joint costs, recognizing that this issue is more a cost accounting topic (for inventory valuation) rather than one that facilitates managerial decision-making and control. And the linear programming section from the second edition has been replaced by Excel's Solver algorithm used to solve the short-term resource allocation example in Chapter 2.

Chapter 7, Decentralization, introduces the second half of the book. Rewritten slightly from the second edition to reflect the impact of ABC and the Balance Scorecard, this chapter remains highly relevant for communicating the challenges of motivating, controlling, and evaluating decentralized organizational units. Chapter 8, the Balanced Scorecard, provides a new comprehensive framework for strategic and operational control. The chapter summarizes the advances in the 1990s of translating strategy into an integrated set of financial and non-financial performance measures tied to customers, innovation and operational processes, and enhanced employee and system capabilities.

Chapters 9 and 10, on profit centers and investment centers, are drawn from the second edition, but repositioned in the third edition to portray the measures for the financial perspective of the Balanced Scorecard. In a major semantic change, the residual income approach, described in the first two editions, has been updated to reflect the surge in interest and application of economic value added. Chapter 11, an enhanced version of the quality and just-in-time chapters in the second edition, summarizes the expanded measurement possibilities from the other three Balanced Scorecard perspectives. It includes quality and cycle time operational measures, but it adds the vitally important measures relating to customer outcomes, the value propositions required to succeed with targeted customers, product and service development, and measures of employee and system capabilities.

Chapter 12, Investments in New Technologies, expands on the second edition's coverage of investment possibilities to include enhanced organizational capabilities. Thus, what had previously been a stand-alone chapter on advanced capital budgeting has now become integrated in the management control framework. Investment decisions are made to achieve outstanding performance in the critical, strategic measures in the four Balanced Scorecard perspectives. Financial payoffs remain important, but investment payoffs also include enhanced performance for customers, for critical internal processes, and for enhancing organizational capabilities.

Chapters 13 and 14, on incentive compensation plans and on formal models for budgeting and incentives, draw from the comparable chapters in the second edition. They have been updated to incorporate new insights from recent research and experience. They also develop the frictions that arise in conventional contract theory research in a more detailed and intuitive manner.

Each chapter, with the possible exception of Chapter 14, contains material that is immediately applicable to contemporary organizations and that has been, in fact, already successfully put to work in practice. Our extensive use of case material reinforces this emphasis on practice in actual organizations. Moreover, we have selected assignment material to illustrate how the concepts in each chapter have been or can be applied not just in somewhat mechanical and idealized situations, but in the context of actual business situations. There may be no simple answers to some of the cases we present, but we believe they will help students come to understand and be able to apply the relevant concepts in the actual organizations they will encounter after leaving the academic setting.

## ACKNOWLEDGMENTS

We have benefited from the contributions of many of our colleagues. We appreciate the helpful reviews and comments about how to improve the Second Edition that were provided by Professors Germain Boer, Vanderbilt University; William D. J. Cotton, SUNY—Geneseo; Michael W. Maher, University of California—Davis; Dale C. Morse, University of Oregon; Vaughan S. Radcliffe, Case Western Reserve University; and Raafat R. Roubi, Brock University. Professor Bill Cotton of SUNY—Geneseo contributed several new cases for the Third Edition. New cases were also provided by Professors Kavasseri V. Ramanathan of University of Washington, Chris Ittner of Wharton, University of Pennsylvania, and Paul Dierkes of Wake Forest University. We appreciate the permission of the Institute of Management Accountants for allowing us to use several cases from various volumes in their Cases in Management Accounting Practice, IMA/AAA Management Accounting Symposium series, and the American Institute of Certified Public Accountants for cases from their AICPA Case Development Program (which included cases written by Professor Paul Foote of California State University at Fullerton and Professor Lawrence Carr). And we wish to thank current and former Harvard Business School Professors Bob Anthony, George Baker, Bill Bruns, Robin Cooper, John Dearden, Bill Fruhan, David Hawkins, Ken Merchant, Jim Reece, Bill Sahlman, Bob Simons, and David Upton for use of their HBS cases.

At Prentice Hall, our editor, PJ Boardman, provided us with continual encouragement and support to complete this revision before the decade ended. Jane Avery and Katherine Evancie facilitated the editing and production process. Susan Rifkin was excellent in overseeing production of the book under tight deadlines. We are grateful for their efforts.

Finally, as always, we appreciate the patience and forbearance of our wives, Ellen and Anne, who gave use the space (both physical and time) for this project.

Robert S. Kaplan
Anthony A. Atkinson

# Introduction

Management accounting systems provide information to assist managers in their planning and control activities. Management accounting activities include collecting, classifying, processing, analyzing, and reporting information to managers. Unlike the financial accounting information prepared for external constituencies, such as investors, creditors, suppliers, and tax and regulatory authorities, management accounting information should be designed to help decision making *within* the firm. Therefore, the scope of management accounting extends beyond traditional measures of the costs and revenues from the transactions that have already occurred to include also information on sales backlogs, unit quantities, prices, demands on capacity resources, and extensive performance measures based on physical or nonfinancial measures.

Because the information to aid internal planning and control activities is not constrained by external reporting requirements, the management accounting system can use data that are less objective and less verifiable than the data used in the financial accounting system. Greater use can be made of future-oriented data such as forecasts and estimates, as well as measures of opportunity costs from transactions not taken. Ultimately, the test of a management accounting system is whether it motivates and assists managers in attaining their organizational objectives in a timely, efficient, and effective manner. Relevance is valued more than objectivity and auditability, though whatever data are used must be defensible and transparent to organizational participants.

## ORIGINS OF COST MANAGEMENT SYSTEMS[1]

Accounts of the operations of the guilds in medieval England suggest that guild members used detailed information about the cost of materials and labor to certify product quality to prospective customers. But before the nineteenth century, organizations conducted virtually all of their transactions with other independent entities to perform individual functions in the manufacturing process. When the bulk of transactions are carried out with entities external to the firm, and few long-term investments are made within the firm, the financial accounting system—the official recorder of such transactions—provides sufficient information to assess the efficiency and profitability of the enterprise.

The origins of modern management accounting can be traced to the emergence of managed, hierarchical enterprises in the early nineteenth century, such as armories and textile mills.[2] These enterprises were formed to conduct an entire multistage production process within a single organization. The organizations took advantage of the economies of scale from relatively capital-intensive processes to hire groups of workers who manufactured the firm's output. Frequently, the manufacturing facility or factory was located next to a readily available energy source, such as rapidly running water, geographically separated from the urban home office of the owners. Information was needed to replace information formerly available from market transactions so that the efficiency of internal production processes could be measured as products moved internally from stage to stage. Also, the home office wanted an information system to motivate the managers at the remote factory site and to judge the efficiency of the managers and workers at the factory. Thus, for a textile mill, internal measures were developed on cost per yard or cost per pound in the separate processes of carding, spinning, weaving, and blanching fabrics.

Perhaps the largest force for developing management accounting systems came from the emergence and rapid growth of the railroads in the mid-nineteenth century. Railroads were the largest and most complex organizations yet created by human beings, with operations having to be conducted and coordinated over vast geographical distances. Fortunately, the telegraph was invented at roughly the same time, and it provided the capability for rapid, inexpensive communication across these vast distances. Innovative railroad managers developed sophisticated approaches to handle the financial transactions required by their extensive operations. New measures such as cost per gross ton mile, cost per passenger mile, and the operating ratio (the ratio of operating expenses to revenues) were developed to help managers evaluate the efficiency of their operating processes.

Many of the innovative management accounting ideas developed by railroad managers were subsequently adopted and extended by the managers of companies in the steel industry. Andrew Carnegie, in particular, was known for having an obsession with knowing his costs and with continually attempting to improve his cost structure relative to competitors:

> Each department listed the amount and cost of materials and labor used on each order as it passed through the subunit. Such information [was used to prepare] monthly statements and, in time, even daily ones providing data on the costs of ore, limestone, coal, coke, pig iron, spiegel, molds, refractories, repairs, fuel and labor for each ton of rails produced. . . .
>
> These cost sheets were Carnegie's primary instrument of control. Costs were Carnegie's obsession. . . . He was forever asking [department heads] the reasons for

changes in unit costs. Carnegie concentrated . . . on the cost side of the operating ratio, comparing current costs of each operating unit with those of previous months and, where possible, with those of other enterprises. . . . Indeed, one reason Carnegie joined the Bessemer pool . . . was to have the opportunity to get a look at the cost figures of his competitors. These controls were effective. . . . The minutest detail of cost of materials and labor in every department appeared from day to day and week to week in the accounts; and soon every man about the place was made to realize it. The men felt and often remarked that the eyes of the company were always on them through the books.

In addition to using the cost sheets to evaluate the performance of department managers, foremen and men, Carnegie [and his general managers] relied on them to check the quality and mix of raw materials. They used them to evaluate improvements in process and in product and to make decisions on developing by-products. In pricing, particularly nonstandardized items like bridges, cost-sheets were invaluable.[3]

Large merchandisers, such as Sears-Roebuck, Marshall Field, and Woolworth, developed in the late nineteenth century to take advantage of the economies of scale from mass distribution of consumer products. These enterprises also needed measures to assess the efficiency of their internal operations. Traditional manufacturing measures, such as cost per pound or cost per mile, were not relevant for the purchasing, stocking, and selling activities of retail organizations. Instead, these companies used measures such as gross margin (sales revenues less purchases and operating costs) and the stock-turn ratio (the ratio of sales to inventory level) to measure the profitability and speed with which purchased merchandise became converted to sales.

In all these examples—textile mills, railroads, steel mills, and retail distributors— managers were developing measures to motivate and assess the efficiency of internal operating processes. There was little concern with measuring the costs of different products or even the periodic "profit" of the enterprise. These organizations had only to process their relatively homogeneous products efficiently: Convert raw materials into a single final product such as cloth or steel, move passengers or freight, or resell purchased goods. If the basic activity were performed efficiently, the managers believed that the enterprise would be profitable. The measures developed were specific to the type of product and process of the organization but had one common characteristic; they measured the efficiency by which input resources were converted to finished products or sales revenue. Even though the production processes of these organizations were quite complex, involving multiple stages of conversion and processing, the organizations had a narrow product focus that enabled them to use simple summaries of output. Textile mills produced yards of fabric, railroads produced gross-ton miles of freight moved, steel mills produced tons of steel, and retailers produced, simply, revenue dollars. Therefore, product costs could be obtained with the same measures used to motivate and evaluate efficient operating processes.

## THE SCIENTIFIC MANAGEMENT MOVEMENT

Complex metal-machining companies, emerging in the mid-nineteenth century, introduced a new set of challenges for management accounting systems. Metal-forming and metal-cutting shops produced a wide variety of finished products, and the different products consumed resources at widely different rates. Because of the dispersion in demands that the various output products made on the firm's capital, labor, and support resources, simple measures of cost per pound or cost per unit of output were not adequate to summarize the efficiency of the conversion processes. Although an early version of job-order costing could capture actual material and labor costs, such costs would not include the cost of capital resources used to bend, form, and cut the metal, and no standards or even historical trends existed to determine whether the costs actually incurred represented efficient operations.

This void was addressed by a group of mechanical engineers who founded the **scientific management** movement. Frederick Taylor is the best known of this group, but many other individuals played an active role in developing this important new field. The scientific management engineers studied work processes closely in order to redesign material and work flow and to decompose complex processes into a sequence of simpler and more controllable processes. The goals were to simplify the work, make the workers more efficient, and be able to monitor the workers' efforts. Detailed and accurate standards for material and labor usage were developed to control work and to pay workers on a "scientifically determined" piecework basis.

Frederick Taylor was primarily interested in worker efficiency, and he relied heavily on quantity standards for the amount of labor and material that should be used under ideal conditions. Others were more interested in evaluating the commercial (financial) success of the enterprise, not just maximizing the efficiency of individual workers. These engineers and accountants extended the quantity standards of the scientific management engineers to include, as well, a labor cost per hour and a material cost per unit so that labor and material cost standards could be developed for production processes. In this way, the standard material and labor cost of products could be predicted and subsequently compared with the costs actually incurred. By the first decade of the twentieth century, sophisticated systems to record and analyze the variances of actual from standard costs had already been articulated.

Before the advent of metal-working shops and the scientific management movement, management accounting systems had focused on directly measured costs, such as material and labor, that could easily be traced to the output product. Although overhead and capital costs existed in all organizations, the narrow product lines of early manufacturing corporations created little demand to attempt to assign indirect costs to output products. Managers focused on the efficiency with which direct labor and material were consumed in the conversion operations, and they assumed that adequate profits would be produced if such efficiencies were achieved. Also, with focused single-product, processslike organizations, it was easy to get summary measures of total cost per unit of output.

The metal-working shops, however, had both high product diversity and relatively high indirect or support costs. Their engineers and managers searched for ways to assign overhead costs to products, especially when bidding on new jobs. Because information collection and processing costs were quite high a century ago, and overhead costs were still less important than direct material and labor costs, it was not deemed worthwhile to invest large amounts of energy and resources to accurately measure and assign indirect and support department costs to products. Simple rules were adopted, such as marking up direct labor hours or dollars by a percentage that reflected the ratio of indirect and support department expenses (i.e., the overhead costs) to anticipated direct labor quantities. This procedure was inexpensive because direct labor was already being measured both to monitor the efficiency of individual workers and to pay them. Thus, the practice of applying overhead to products on the basis of their direct labor content had its origins in the labor-intensive production processes of a century ago.

This shortcut, or approximation, of attributing the consumption of overhead resources to the quantity of direct labor in a product was criticized even at the time:

> We find that as against $100 direct wages on order, we have an indirect expenditure of $59, or in other terms, our shop establishment charges are 59 percent of direct wages in that shop for the period in question. This is, of course, very simple. It is also as usually worked out very inexact. It is true that as regards the output of the shop as a whole a fair idea is obtained of the general cost of the work. . . . And in the case of a shop with machines all of a size and kind, performing practically identical operations by means of a fairly average wages rate, it is not alarmingly incorrect.

> If, however, we apply this method to a shop in which large and small machines, highly paid and cheap labor, heavy castings and small parts, are all in operation together, then the result, unless measures are taken to supplement it, is no longer trustworthy.[4]

Attempts, however, to use machine hours, multiple labor rates, or material quantities as alternative bases for allocating overhead proved unsuccessful, probably because of the added expense of measuring all these new bases. Machines did not have to be paid for their work, so the only reason for measuring and recording machine hours would have been for a more accurate assignment of overhead costs to products. Apparently, the benefits of more-accurate overhead allocations must have been well below the cost of such supplementary measurement, because the practice did not persist in discrete part production processes. The assignment of overhead costs to products on the basis of machine time, however, had been extensively used in process industries—such as chemicals, glass, and petroleum—in which labor costs were relatively small and processing times had to be measured in order to control the physical conversion process.

A second concern was the treatment of unused capacity costs. H. L. Gantt, a contemporary of Frederick Taylor, addressed his concerns, first dealing with how many allocation bases should be used but then focusing on the assignment of costs to actual output produced:[5]

> There are in common use several methods of distributing [indirect] expense. One is to distribute the total indirect expense . . . according to the direct labor. Another is to distribute a portion of this expense according to direct labor, and a portion according to machine hours. Other methods distribute a certain amount of this expense on the material used, etc. Most of these methods contemplate the distribution of *all* of the indirect expense of the manufacturing plant, however much it may be, on the output produced, no matter how small it is.

> If the factory is running at its full, or normal, capacity, this time of indirect expense per unit of product is usually small. If the factory is running at only a fraction of its capacity, say one-half, and turning out only one-half of its normal product, there is but little change in the total amount of this indirect expense, all of which must now be distributed over half as much product as previously, each unit of product thereby being obliged to bear approximately twice as much expense as previously.

> When times are good, . . . this method of accounting indicates that our costs are low, but when times become bad and business is slack, it indicates high costs due to the

> increased proportion of burden each unit has to bear. . . . In other words, our present systems of cost accounting go to pieces when they are most needed. This being the case, many of us have felt for a long time that there was something radically wrong with the present theories on the subject.

Gantt concluded that to fix this problem

> the indirect expense chargeable to the output of a factory should bear the same ratio to the indirect expense necessary to run the factory at normal capacity as the output in question bears to the normal output of the factory.

Gantt's arguments for basing cost driver rates using normal or practical capacity, unfortunately, fell on largely deaf ears, as did his and others' arguments to use multiple cost drivers that would be more representative of the underlying production process. As we will see, the energy and insight from engineers in the scientific management movement were made subservient to simplicity and to the desire, for financial reporting, to allocate all period factory costs to the products produced during that period. Only a few companies attempted to measure and report on the cost of idle capacity.

## MANAGEMENT CONTROL FOR DIVERSIFIED ORGANIZATIONS

Further innovations in management accounting systems occurred in the early decades of the twentieth century to support the growth of multiactivity, diversified corporations. The DuPont Powder Company, established in 1903 as a combination of previously separate family-run or independent companies, provided the prototype for this new organizational form. The managers of the new DuPont Company faced the problems of coordinating the diverse activities of a vertically integrated manufacturing and marketing organization and of deciding on the most profitable allocation of capital to a variety of activities. DuPont was one of the first entities to have to decide which of several diverse operations should be expanded, not just the appropriate scale of operation for processing a single type of product.

Several important operating and budgeting activities were devised by the senior managers of DuPont to coordinate the activities of and allocate resources to their many operating groups. But the most important and enduring management accounting innovation was the return-on-investment (ROI) measure. The ROI provided an overall measure of the commercial success of each operating unit and of the entire organization. Senior managers used the ROI to help direct the allocation of capital to the most profitable divisions. Donaldson Brown, the chief financial officer, showed how the ROI formula could be decomposed into a product of two efficiency measures—the operating ratio (net income divided by sales) and stock turn (sales divided by assets)—developed and used by nineteenth-century single-activity enterprises. Each of these ratios could be decomposed further (see the discussion in Chapter 10) into the income, expense, asset, and liability accounts under the responsibility of local decentralized managers.

Use of the ROI measure was expanded in the 1920s as the multidivisional form of organization evolved in the DuPont and General Motors corporations.[6] The decentralized multidivisional corporation developed to capture economies of scope—the gains from sharing common organizational functions across a broad spectrum of related products.

But the enormous diversity in the product markets served by these giant corporations demanded new systems and measures to coordinate dispersed and decentralized activities. Division managers became responsible for the profitability and return on capital employed by their divisions and had authority to generate capital requests. Corporate-level departments of marketing, purchasing, and finance could not possibly have all the requisite information to function effectively or efficiently in all the markets served by their organizations. Decentralization was necessary, and central managers' functions shifted to running an efficient internal capital and labor market for the organization and to coordinating, motivating, and evaluating the performance of their divisional managers. The ROI measure played a vital role in permitting the internal markets for managers and capital to function. An impressive array of budgeting and forecasting procedures was also developed to plan and coordinate divisional operations.[7]

In retrospect, the 100-year period from 1825 to 1925 saw the emergence and growth of both giant, successful industrial enterprises and a host of management accounting practices. These two phenomena were not independent of each other. In fact, organizations of the size of DuPont, General Motors, or United States Steel were unlikely to have survived without extensive management accounting systems to provide information on the efficiency and effectiveness of their decentralized operations. Technology innovation in transportation (the railroad), communication (telegraph, telephone) and basic processes (for steel, aluminum, metal cutting and forming, machine tools, chemicals, and the internal combustion engine, among many others) created a demand for large enterprises to capture the potential gains from economies of scale and scope. But these gains would not have been realized had there not been simultaneous innovation in measurement systems. These systems communicated corporate goals clearly to decentralized managers and provided feedback on the efficiency of operations managed within the hierarchy of the corporations. Such information was especially valuable for organizations that integrated vertically back to raw materials acquisition and forward to direct delivery to consumers of their products.

## FROM COST MANAGEMENT TO COST ACCOUNTING

The next sixty years, from 1925 to 1985, were not nearly as productive in the development of management accounting procedures. The exact reasons for the slowdown, even halt, of management accounting innovation are still being debated. But at least part of the reason appears to lie in the demand for product cost information for financial accounting reports. The procedures for valuing inventory for financial reports were executed in an efficient manner. Indirect or support department costs were aggregated into large, plantwide cost pools and were allocated to products using simple and available measures of activity—typically direct-labor hours. The concerns expressed earlier in the century, by engineers such as Church and Gantt, about attempting to be more accurate in cost assignment to individual products were not heeded.

In principle, there was no particular reason why the greatly increased demand for published, objective, audited financial statements, and the increased regulations on the procedures used to prepare those statements, should have had any impact on the development of management accounting systems. Companies could have continued to refine their internal measurement techniques to provide independent and more accurate estimates of individual product costs and timely information on operating performance. Separate financial and management accounting staffs have persisted in companies located in German-speaking countries. For many companies in these countries, financial and cost systems are run independently, with a reconciliation module provided to articulate between the two sets of statements at the end of the year when financial statements are prepared. But most Western companies seem to have decided, early in the century when information costs were high and product line diversity was low, that the benefits of keeping two sets of books—one for external parties and one for internal management decisions—were too costly relative to the benefits.

The high cost of information collecting, processing, and reporting coupled with the relatively low distortion for companies with homogeneous product lines led companies to attempt to manage their internal operations with the same information used to report to external constituencies. Thus, product costs were computed on the basis of aggregate, average allocations of manufacturing overhead, and control procedures used monthly variances computed from general ledger financial accounts.

## RECENT DEVELOPMENTS IN MANUFACTURING AND SERVICE COMPANIES

During the 1980s, major new challenges emerged for management accounting. Companies rediscovered the critical role that manufacturing plays in creating a competitive advantage for their organizations. Examples of the new emphasis on manufacturing operations could be found in the commitment to quality in manufacturing and in product design, in the reduction of inventory levels and manufacturing lead times (as represented by just-in-time production and distribution systems), and by the introduction of computer-controlled manufacturing operations (the CIM, or computer-integrated-manufacturing environment). All of the manufacturing innovations stressed continuous improvement activities: the need to constantly improve operating processes from the levels achieved in prior years.

These new (or, in some cases, rediscovered) manufacturing technologies were different from the stable manufacturing environment of mass production of standardized products for the first seven decades of the twentieth century. In the new environment, many companies found that their traditional cost accounting measures were inhibiting the introduction of innovative manufacturing processes and technologies. For example, measures of individual worker efficiency or machine utilization conflicted with factory goals to improve quality, increase throughput, and reduce inventory levels.[8] Attempting to absorb factory overhead into products by producing items well in advance of when they are needed does absorb fixed manufacturing overhead into inventory and does create increases in reported period income (because of favorable volume variances that shift current operating expenses in future periods), but the practice undermines the company's efforts to reduce inventory levels, eliminate manufacturing defects, speed throughput times, and improve responsiveness to customers.

Today's management accounting systems must be designed to support, not to inhibit, the drive for manufacturing excellence. Measurement systems must evolve to support efforts to increase quality and productivity, move to just-in-time and computer-integrated-manufacturing production systems, and help justify investment in new technologies. These issues are discussed in Chapters 6, 11, and 12.

Our discussion may, at a superficial level, appear to focus exclusively on manufacturing rather than service organizations. Discussions on inventory and manufacturing processes might seem of little relevance to managers in financial service, transportation, health-care, retailing, and telecommunications companies. The extensive use of manufacturing terms should not cause readers interested in service industries to ignore the fundamental messages in this chapter and in the remainder of the book. The distinctions between manufacturing and service industries are not critical for the design of effective management accounting systems. About the only substantive difference between manufacturing and service companies arises from the financial accounting demand on manufacturing companies to allocate periodic production costs to items produced but not yet sold.

Managers in service companies, however, have historically used management accounting information far less intensively than managers in manufacturing companies. Service company managers did use financial information to budget and control spending in their functional departments. But even though service companies are frequently as complex and diversified as manufacturing companies, managers usually knew neither the costs of the services they produced and delivered nor the costs of serving different types of customers. All service industries have products that they produce and deliver to customers; the product may be only a little more difficult to define than it is in a manufacturing organization. The products of service organizations have costs that must be understood and analyzed for a wide variety of planning and control decisions. Capacity costing is critical for service companies because virtually all of their spending is related to providing a capacity to serve customers; very few expenses are variable in the short term with services delivered and customers served.

For performance measurement, employees in service companies have more direct contact with customers than do front-line employees in manufacturing companies. Thus, service companies must be especially sensitive to the timeliness and the quality of the service their employees provide to their customers. Customers of service companies immediately notice defects and delays in service delivery. And the consequences from such defects can be severe as dissatisfied customers choose alternative suppliers after an unhappy experience.

## CONTEMPORARY MANAGEMENT ACCOUNTING DEVELOPMENTS

Since the 1980s, academics and companies have been developing new management accounting procedures to meet the challenges of deregulated industries and vigorous global competition. These new procedures are designed to support rapidly changing technologies and new management processes—such as total quality management; just-in-time supply, production, and distribution systems; and reengineering—and a never-ending search for competitive advantage.

The modern approach of viewing management accounting as reporting on the costs of committed and flexible resources is introduced in Chapter 1. Chapter 2 features the role of cost and resource information for short-term decisions that optimize product mix and for performing near-term cash budgeting. Chapter 3 introduces the structure of cost systems by showing how the costs of indirect and support resources can be assigned to production cost centers. This approach is extended by the activity-based costing approach introduced in Chapter 4, which allows resource costs to be traced to activities and subsequently to products, services, and customers. Chapter 5 shows how improved information about products and customers enables managers to make better decisions about pricing, product mix, product design, and customer relationships. Chapter 6 illustrates how activity-based information can be used to motivate performance improvement; it also features operational control systems that provide timely feedback, using both financial and nonfinancial measures for learning and improvement as well as target and life cycle costing, to influence and manage costs over a product's entire life cycle.

The remainder of the book focuses on control of complex, decentralized organizations, a topic introduced in Chapter 7. Balanced scorecards that deploy both financial and nonfinancial measures to link current decisions and actions to long-term financial benefits are discussed in Chapter 8. The financial measures for performance evaluation are discussed in Chapters 9 and 10. Nonfinancial measures for customer and internal business processes are discussed in Chapter 11. Chapter 12 describes how capital budgeting systems can be adapted to stress the development of organizational capabilities, not just simple net present value cash flow calculations. Chapter 13 features the role for managerial compensation systems to motivate performance aligned with overall company objectives. The book concludes with Chapter 14 on the role for formal models to study important management accounting phenomena, such as budgeting, control systems, and compensation.

The book, in total, provides a comprehensive view of the current state of management accounting. Traditional, but still valuable, material has been embedded in contemporary theory and applications. And much new material has been introduced and made available for study, debate, and learning.

## SUMMARY

Management accounting systems play a vital role in helping the managers of complex, hierarchical organizations to plan and control their operations. A superb management accounting system may not guarantee competitive success, particularly if companies do not have good products, efficient operating processes, or effective marketing and sales activities. But an ineffective management accounting system, producing delayed, distorted, or too highly aggregated information, can easily undermine the efforts of companies with excellent research and development, production, and marketing activities. The challenge is to develop management accounting practices that support the basic managerial tasks of organizing, planning, and controlling operations to achieve excellence throughout the organization. The management accounting system cannot be viewed as a system designed by accountants for accountants. The 100-year history from 1825 to 1925 provides evidence on the necessity for parallel development of new management accounting practices to support the company's innovations in production, marketing, and organizational design.

This book takes a user-oriented approach to the design of management accounting procedures and systems. The book also emphasizes the challenges and opportunities from new information technology and the new technology of modern operating and service processes. And, most important, the book features the innovative management accounting developments since the 1980s that leading companies around the world are now using. Students who complete the book should be rewarded with an increased understanding of how management accounting information creates value in organizations. Management accounting has shifted from being the historical scorekeeper to providing information vital for operational and strategic decisions and for motivating and evaluating organizational performance.

## ENDNOTES

1. The discussion in this section summarizes material in H. T. Johnson and R. S. Kaplan, *Relevance Lost: The Rise and Fall of Management Accounting* (Boston: Harvard Business School Press, 1987). The development of managerial capitalism in the United States is documented in A. D. Chandler, *The Visible Hand: The Managerial Revolution in American Business* (Cambridge: Harvard University Press, 1977). Chandler's work provides an enormously valuable historical perspective on the development of the U.S. corporate organization that has great implications for the modern practice and theory of management accounting.

2. See H. T. Johnson, "Early Cost Accounting for Internal Management Control: Lyman Mills in the 1850s," *Business History Review* (Winter 1972), pp. 466–74; and K. W. Hoskin and R. H. Macve, "The Genesis of Accountability: The West Point Connection," *Accounting, Organizations and Society* (1986), pp. 1–37.

3. Chandler, *Visible Hand*, pp. 267–68.

4. A. H. Church, *The Proper Distribution of Expense Burden* (New York: The Engineering Magazine Co., 1908), pp. 28–29.

5. H. L. Gantt, "The Relation between Production and Costs," presented at the American Society of Mechanical Engineers Spring Meeting (June), reprinted in *Journal of Cost Management* (Spring 1994), pp. 4–11.

6. The developments in these two organizations were not independent of each other. Pierre DuPont rescued General Motors from imminent bankruptcy in 1919, and Donaldson Brown became GM's chief financial officer, serving under the newly promoted president, Alfred Sloan.

7. See Chapters 4 and 5 of Johnson and Kaplan, *Relevance Lost*. One particularly impressive achievement, the GM pricing formula based on ROI control, is described in a problem at the end of Chapter 6 of *Relevance Lost*.

8. For a dramatic illustration of such conflicts, see E. M. Goldratt and J. Cox, *The Goal: A Process of Ongoing Improvement* (Croton-on-Hudson, NY: North River Press, 1986).

# 1

# Understanding Cost Behavior

## THE ROLE OF MANAGEMENT ACCOUNTING

Management accounting information serves several major roles in organizations. It enhances decision making, guides strategy development and evaluates existing strategies, and focuses efforts related to improving organizational performance and to evaluating the contribution and performance of organizational units and members.

One of the most important types of management accounting information is cost information.[1] Organizations use information about costs to make important product feature and product mix decisions. For example, despite industry trends to increase variety and customization, Procter & Gamble announced, in 1996, that it would reduce the number of SKUs (stock-keeping units) it offered by nearly 40%. Senior managers made this decision when they understood the cost of product complexity—to themselves, to their distributors, and to their retailers—caused by producing too many versions of the same product. P&G's improved costing systems showed that the increased cost was far higher than the incremental revenues the SKUs generated and the value they created for customers.

Organizations also use cost information to develop competitive strategies. For example, by 1994 the practice of trade loading was well established in the consumer packaged goods industry. Manufacturers promoted their products heavily in certain periods, leading to a pattern of selling high volumes of product into distribution channels on a periodic basis rather than providing a continuous flow of product. With the advent of improved costing systems, organizations came to recognize the additional production costs caused by highly variable production levels and the huge inventory holding costs[2] imposed on wholesalers and retailers by trade loading. Many organizations are now trying to eliminate this practice and to move to continuous replenishment, with manufacturing decisions triggered by consumer takeaway at the retail level.[3]

As a third application, organizations use appropriate cost information to guide their operations improvement activities. Once managers see the costs associated with various organization activities, they can focus their improvement efforts on activities that are major contributors to organization cost. For example, a hospital identified the activities it undertook to provide services to patients, including all support operations, such as admitting and billing. It then identified the drivers, or causes, of those activities. Hospital personnel then tackled the job of cost reduction by focusing, improving, and eliminating high-cost activities. A major goal was to reduce the patient's time in the hospital, primarily by speeding up the scheduling and evaluation of diagnostic tests. The hospital staff developed improved procedures that eliminated some activities and made many others much less costly. The hospital example illustrates two responses to activities with high costs. A high-cost activity might prompt efforts to redesign or eliminate that activity entirely, a process called **reengineering**, or it might prompt efforts to make the activity more efficient and less costly, a process called **continuous improvement**.

Organizations also use cost information to evaluate performance. Using cost to evaluate performance has two purposes. First, an awareness of the high costs of activities often motivates the type of improvement activities illustrated by the hospital example above. Second, by tying the results of cost improvement activities to rewards, planners use cost information to motivate people to pursue organization improvement.

## UNDERSTANDING COST BEHAVIOR

Costs arise from the acquisition and use of organizational resources, such as people, equipment, materials, outside services, and facilities. Organizations acquire and use resources to perform activities. When organizations use resources to perform activities, the financial system records costs.

There are two broad types of costs. The first type of cost is created when the organization acquires productive capacity. We call resources that are acquired or contracted for in advance of when the actual work is done **committed resources**. The costs associated with these resources are called **committed costs**. Most personnel costs, the costs of computing and telecommunications systems, and depreciation on the organization's buildings and equipment are examples of committed costs. The amount of resource capacity acquired determines the magnitude of a committed cost. Committed costs are unaffected by how much the organization *uses* the committed resource. Therefore, the amount of committed costs is related to the **planned level** of activities and is incurred independent of how much use is made of the committed resource during the period.

The second type of cost, which we will call **flexible costs**, arises from the use of **flexible resources**. Raw materials, electrical power consumed in a factory, labor that is acquired and paid for only in the amounts used, and fuel used in vehicles that deliver products to customers are all examples of flexible resources. The actual level of activities performed to make products and serve customers determines the quantity of flexible resources supplied and used.[4] Flexible resources do not have a capacity defined for them, because their supply, hence capacity, can be adjusted up or down to meet actual demands. The organization pays for only the amount of flexible resources that it needs and uses.

## AN EXAMPLE OF COST STRUCTURE

We illustrate these ideas of committed and flexible costs with an example. We start the example by describing how an organization initially acquires its resources. That is, we begin with an understanding of how costs arise and then estimate the resulting cost function. Management accountants typically work in the opposite direction. They observe costs and make inferences about the underlying cost structure. Chapters 3 and 4 take that path. We should understand how costs arise before learning the management accounting function of estimating a cost structure.

Consider Railstar, a railroad whose sole business is to transport passengers and freight between two cities, Rose Terrace and Whistle Stop. Railstar conducts its business from a head office complex in Rose Terrace. This head office complex contains all Railstar's administrative and marketing personnel.

The cost associated with this head office complex is about $50,000,000 per year. These costs include

1. $25,000,000 of costs relating to resources that support all Railstar's operations. The costs of these resources would be incurred even if Railstar carried no passengers or hauled no freight

2. $15,000,000 of costs relating directly to the passenger business, which, in the long run, could be eliminated if Railstar closed its passenger business

3. $10,000,000 of costs relating directly to the freight business that, in the long run, could be eliminated if Railstar closed its freight business.[5]

This cost behavior exhibits the phenomenon of increasing returns to scale. Head office costs are lower if Railstar operates both businesses than if two similar companies operate the businesses separately because separate companies would have to duplicate the $25,000,000 in head office resources for each to operate.[6]

Railstar has built and maintains a roadbed and track between the two cities. The cost of building the track was $500,000,000. Depreciation of existing track amounts to about $80,000,000 per year. Maintenance costs increase by $200 each time a locomotive travels between the two cities and by approximately $20 each time a railcar carrying either passengers or freight travels between the two cities.

Railstar has built and maintains stations in both Rose Terrace and Whistle Stop. Railstar built these stations in anticipation of annual demand for travel on the line. Stations can be built and operated in three sizes: small, medium, and large. The small size handles up to 50,000 passengers per day, medium up to 100,000 passengers per day, and large up to 200,000 passengers per day. A station's annual depreciation cost is approximately $50 per unit of daily passenger capacity.[7] Flexible station-related cost amounts are respectively $5, $3, and $2 per unit of passenger capacity for the small, medium, and large stations. Railstar has built and maintains medium-sized stations in both Rose Terrace and Whistle Stop.

Every six months Railstar personnel decide how many trains to operate each day for the upcoming six-month period. Railstar then prints the resulting passenger schedule, which is valid for the next six months. Railstar operates each train with three locomotives. Railstar leases five locomotives at a cost of $2,000,000 per locomotive per year. Operating personnel assign three locomotives to each train, which is the minimum number of locomotives required by the regulatory authority. They keep one locomotive at each station[8] to do local yardwork and to provide backup when mechanics perform routine maintenance on the running locomotives. The cost (fuel for the locomotives and crew salaries) for each trip is $10,000. Each locomotive assigned to a train provides a total capacity of 30 cars, passenger or freight. Therefore, with three locomotives, the train capacity is 90 cars.

Railstar does not own any freight cars; it hauls freight cars belonging to other railroads. Railstar leases passenger cars for six-month periods at a cost of $50,000 per car per six-month period. Each passenger car can carry 80 passengers. Railstar estimates that hauling a passenger or freight car from one city to the other increases the total of fuel, supplies, and personnel costs by about $500.

Finally, Railstar incurs costs that are directly related to the number of passengers on the train. These include baggage-handling costs and passenger service costs. These costs amount to $10 per passenger trip.

Exhibit 1-1 summarizes Railstar's cost structure.

**EXHIBIT 1-1**  Railstar—Illustrating the Idea of an Organization's Cost Structure

| COST TYPE | COST ELEMENT | AMOUNT |
|---|---|---|
| Head office–related | Total all costs | $50,000,000 per year |
| Roadbed-related | Depreciation | $80,000,000 per year |
|  | Maintenance | $600 per trip |
|  | Maintenance | $20 per car per trip |
| Station-related | Large | |
|  | Depreciation | $10,000,000 per year |
|  | Other | $2 per passenger |
|  | Medium | |
|  | Depreciation | $5,000,000 per year |
|  | Other | $3 per passenger |
|  | Small | |
|  | Depreciation | $2,500,000 per year |
|  | Other | $5 per passenger |
| Train-related | Locomotive lease—provides a basic capacity of 90 cars per train— additional locomotives added at a cost of $2,000,000 per year and each provides an additional capacity of 30 cars per train | $10,000,000 per year |
|  | Trip costs | $10,000 per trip |
|  | Passenger car rental—car capacity is 80 passengers | $50,000 per six-month period |
|  | Hauling cost | $500 per car per trip |
|  | Passenger cost | $10 per passenger |

## Deriving the Total Cost Function

Decision makers at Railstar use cost information for many purposes. One major purpose is to identify whether the market prices that Railstar must meet[9] cover both the cost of providing that service and a reasonable return on invested capital. If they did not, Railstar would have to redouble its efforts to cut costs or decide to abandon that business.

Note that the information in Exhibit 1-1 is not in a form that can be used to compute the cost per unit of freight or passenger service, and, more important, note that many of Railstar's costs are not proportional to the number of freight or passenger service units provided.

Given the information provided we can write an equation for costs, which we can call the cost function, as follows

Total cost = head office–related costs + roadbed costs + station-related costs
+ train-related costs

We cannot specify this cost function in any more detail until we understand the capacity choices that Railstar personnel have made. Given that Railstar is currently operating both a passenger and a freight business, that it has built two medium-sized stations, and that it plans to operate with five locomotives, we can write the annual cost function as[10]

Total cost = $150,000,000 + ($100,000 * number of passenger cars rented)
+ ($10,600 * number of trips) + ($520 * number of car trips) + ($13 *
number of passengers)                                                    [1]

The cost function in equation [1] reflects choices that Railstar personnel have made about three types of committed resources:

1. The decision to be in both the freight and passenger transport businesses, reflected by the head office–related costs
2. Depreciation expenses resulting from acquiring the head office building and maintaining the rail and roadbed
3. The expenses associated with the size of station (small, medium, or large) chosen

Therefore, once Railstar personnel make commitments to acquire long-lived resources, they determine the part of the cost function that is related to committed costs. Committed costs reflect the amount of capacity acquired rather than the amount of capacity used in operations.

Committed costs arise from a decision to acquire a capacity or capability to perform work. These costs do not vary in proportion to production quantity. Once the decision has been made to acquire the resources, the costs of these resources will remain until managers eliminate those resources.

For example, if Railstar personnel decided to use small stations and to be in only the passenger business, the cost function would become, after the passage of time to allow for the adjustment of capacity resources,

Total cost = $135,000,000 + ($100,000 * number of passenger cars rented)
+ ($10,600 * number of trips) + ($520 * number of car trips)
+ ($13 * number of passengers)                                          [2]

Now consider the effect on the total cost shown in equation [1] when Railstar personnel fix the number of passenger cars to lease. Suppose that Railstar personnel choose to lease 60 passenger cars for the upcoming six-month period. Presumably this decision reflects estimates of the number of passengers who will want to ride the train. The total cost function becomes

Total cost = $156,000,000 + ($10,600 * number of trips)
    + ($520 * number of car trips) + ($13 * number of passengers)          [3]

The effect of making resource commitments by choosing capacity should now be evident. Costs that are variable or flexible before a capacity decision become committed costs after the capacity acquisition decision has been made. The subsequent level of operations will not affect those costs. For this reason, we often call these costs fixed because they are independent of the actual level of operations.

Recall that at the start of every six-month period, Railstar publishes a schedule that commits it to a specified number of trips. Suppose that Railstar decides to offer five round-trips each weekday (a total of 50) and two round trips each weekend day (a total of eight).[11] Therefore the total number of trips per week is 58 and the total trip-related costs are[12] $31,969,600 per year. The total cost function, assuming that this pattern continues for two six-month periods making up the year, becomes

Total cost = $187,969,600 + ($520 * number of car trips)
    + ($13 * number of passengers)          [4]

We now have a total annual cost equation that is a function of two variables: the total number of cars and the total number of passengers that Railstar hauls during the year. We can think of each scheduled train as a group or a batch. The cost of the batch (other than the trip-related costs that Railstar committed when it chose its operating schedule) is $520 and reflects the number of cars in the trip (batch).

Suppose that, for operating reasons, Railstar makes a decision about the number of cars to put in each train for a given week on Saturday of the week preceding. Assume that Railstar is committed to hauling an average of 50 passenger cars on each weekday train and 15 passenger cars on each weekend train. The total number of weekday trips is 50 and the total number of weekend trips is eight, so the total passenger cars that will be hauled is 2,620 and the total cost commitment of this schedule is $70,844,800.[13] The total cost function, assuming that this pattern continues for two consecutive six-month periods, now becomes

Total cost = $258,814,400 + ($520 * number of freight cars hauled)
    + ($13 * number of passengers)          [5]

## Determining the Cost per Unit of Service Provided

### From Short-Run to Long-Run Costs

Equations [1] through [5] are total cost functions. The total cost function in equation [5] is expressed in terms of Railstar's most-primitive decision variables: the units of service demanded by, and provided to, Railstar's customers. Recall that committed costs are captured by the constants in the cost functions. The committed costs reflect the many underlying decisions that Railstar personnel have made to provide a given level of capability (to provide both passenger and freight transport service) and capacity. The variable components in the total cost functions represent the flexible costs. These terms estimate how total cost varies in proportion to the two identified activity levels: (1) number of freight cars hauled and (2) number of passengers. Therefore, we can conclude that as the number of passengers carried increases (or decreases) by one unit, the total cost will increase (or decrease) by $13.[14] Between the times at which Railstar makes decisions to adjust capacity up or down, and assuming that operations remain within the range of capacity provided by Railstar's committed costs, the total cost will increase (decrease) by $520 as the number of freight cars hauled increases (decreases) by one unit.

The time period of committed costs clearly varies by resource type. Railstar can adjust passenger operating costs weekly by determining the number of cars to put on each train. It can adjust passenger car expenses semiannually when it determines the number of trips and the number of passenger cars to supply. Annually, Railstar determines how much it will spend on locomotives. Over somewhat longer time periods, the company can adjust the size of its station, the size and composition of its head office, and the degree of maintenance of the rail and roadbed.

Note that the short-term variability in the cost functions (equations [1] through [5]) arises from the number of passengers carried and the number of freight cars hauled. They reflect none of the committed costs. For this reason, the coefficients ($13 and $520) on the flexible resource parameters do not incorporate any effects on long-run costs from decisions that require changes in the capacity being supplied, say, increasing the number of passengers by 25% or eliminating the freight hauling side of the business.

### Calculating the Costs of Services

Equations [1] through [5] represent the costs of supplying resources. Understanding these costs is extremely important. Managers, in the short run, control expenses and spending by monitoring these costs closely. These costs of resource supply are also important for predicting near-term cash flows and are the basis for cash budgeting and working capital decisions. And when managers are making incremental decisions, such as whether to carry an additional passenger or small group of passengers or whether to accept a new freight order, these resource supply costs provide valuable information.

But these are not the only relevant costs for managerial decisions. Organizations that have many different types of resources and that produce and sell hundreds of products to thousands of customers often want to relate the revenues received from such sales to the costs of resources required to generate the sales. Only in this way can the organization get a signal about the relative profitability or loss of its various products and customers. Computing the cost of resources used by individual products and customers provides managers with signals about how different products and customers consume the organization's available capacity. Take Railstar, for example. First-class passengers require more car space and personnel time than do passengers traveling in tourist or coach class. When different types of passengers use capacity in different amounts, managers need a cost signal to indicate the relative cost of all the resources used by these different types. Such a cost—of resources used—can be compared with the price or revenues received to determine whether that product, class of service, or type of customer is profitable. A product is profitable when the revenues received exceed the cost of the resources used to produce and deliver the product.

An income statement for the entire organization (such as Railstar) provides an aggregate signal whether the revenues generated by operations exceed the costs of supplying all committed and flexible resources that enable operations to occur. But this aggregate signal provides little guidance about large variations in profitability among diverse products, services, and customers.

In virtually all service industries, such as Railstar, but also in an increasingly large number of manufacturing organizations, almost all expenses are determined by commitments to supply given levels of capacity, as reflected by the acquisition of committed resources. Relatively few expenses are determined by the actual quantity of work demanded or performed each day—in Railstar's case, passengers carried and freight cars hauled. Most operating expenses are determined by decisions to acquire and sustain capacity, not by what happens today or tomorrow to produce products and services for customers.

Most managers, however, want to understand the relationship between the resource capacity they supply and how the organization's diverse products and customers use that capacity. For this purpose (and for several others as well, as we will see later in the book), managers find it useful to calculate the costs of resources used by individual products and customers. This calculation requires that accountants determine, for each capacity resource, a unit cost for using that resource.

Consider one of Railstar's committed costs: the cost of a passenger car. The leasing cost of the passenger car is $50,000 for six months. How do we go about translating this cost into the cost per passenger carried? Some companies may wait to find out how many passengers were actually carried. They would divide the $50,000 cost by the actual number of passengers to calculate the actual cost per passenger. Managers advocating this approach argue that such an ex post calculation reflects actual operations. Of course, having to wait until the end of the period to calculate a cost per passenger does not make the cost very useful for decision making before the end of the period. To avoid such a wait, many companies divide the projected cost of the passenger car by the number of passengers that it expected to carry over the six-month period. Whether the cost is calculated ex ante or ex post, the per passenger cost could fluctuate quite widely every six months as the load factor, the ratio of passengers carried to capacity, varies.

Alternatively, we could relate the committed cost to the capacity supplied. In this case, we certainly know that the car capacity is 80 passengers, but what is the capacity for the six-month period? The capacity number will be 80 multiplied by the number of scheduled trips per week multiplied by the number of weeks in the six-month period. Note that, because managers can vary the intensity of usage of this type of resource (by varying the number of scheduled trips from period to period), the car lease cost per passenger can vary from one six-month period to another.[15]

For example, if we assume that Railstar intends to operate 58 trips per week, the lease cost per unit of passenger capacity is about $33.

$$\text{Cost per unit of capacity} = \frac{\$50,000}{58 * 26} = \$33.16$$

Does this mean that if one passenger more shows up that car lease costs will increase by $33? Of course not; car lease costs depend on the number of cars that are leased and the leasing cost per car, not on the number of passengers carried. Does it mean that if the long-run demand for passengers shifts down by one unit that the average lease cost will fall by $33 as Railstar personnel react by leasing fewer cars? Of course not; capacity is acquired in chunks, not in individual units. Moreover, the $33 calculation reflects the assumptions made of car use. Different assumptions would result in a cost different from $33. But the calculation is a component in the total resource cost associated with carrying individual passengers. If Railstar is consistently unable to charge prices that cover the $33 per passenger cost of the railcar plus the cost of all other resources supplied to handle passenger traffic, then the company's managers are getting a signal that the economics of their passenger business does not justify a sustained presence in the marketplace.

In the case of Railstar, where a decision to acquire a supply of passenger cars is made every six months, another basis for assigning car costs arises from examining the authorization decision. At the time the decision is made about how many passenger cars to acquire, Railstar's managers have estimates about the quantity and mix of passengers it expects to carry and the prices they can expect to earn from each passenger of each type. Planners use this information to authorize the acquisition of passenger cars and to configure the cars for the anticipated mix of first-class and coach passengers.

For example, suppose that planners decide to dedicate 15 of the 60 passenger cars acquired to first-class service and configure the remaining 45 for coach service. Therefore, every six months, planners will attribute $750,000[16] of the car rental costs to first-class passenger service and $2,250,000, the balance of the car rental costs, to the coach class business.

Recall that cars configured as coach class carry 80 passengers, and assume that cars configured for first class will carry 40 passengers. Suppose that planners expect that, on average, the first-class cars will be 75% occupied and the coach class cars will be 85% occupied. Using the plan developed above to haul 2,620 cars per week, assume that 25% (15/60) of the cars are first-class and 75% are coach class. Therefore, the total capacity available for the two types of cars is

$$\text{Semiannual coach capacity available} = 2620 * 75\% * 80 * 85\% * 26 = 3,474,120 \text{ seats}$$

$$\text{Semiannual first-class capacity available} = 2620 * 25\% * 40 * 75\% * 26 = 510,900 \text{ seats}$$

Therefore, if car costs were assigned based on the planned level of operations, the car rental cost per passenger for each of the two services would be

$$\text{Car lease cost per coach passenger} = \frac{\$2,250,000}{3,474,120} = \$0.65$$

$$\text{Car lease cost per first-class passenger} = \frac{\$750,000}{510,900} = \$1.47$$

Note that these capacity cost per unit calculations reflect:

1. The cost of the committed capacity
2. The allocation base used to allocate capacity
3. The value or size of the allocation base

It may seem unduly complex to perform such calculations. And, in fact, for this highly simplified example in which the resources are being supplied for only one or two products (passengers: first class and coach), managers can probably get by without such a signal. With one or only a very few products, especially when the demands they make on the organization's resources are relatively homogeneous, knowledge of the total cost function (the cost of supplying resources) will likely be adequate for management's needs.

But suppose that Railstar owned or leased its own freight cars and sold freight-carrying services to shippers. Freight, unlike passengers, can be highly variable. Some shippers may wish to have Railstar carry freight that is extremely bulky (beach balls packed in mesh bags) that use up a great deal of a freight car's volume. Other shippers may contract with Railstar to transport extremely heavy products (such as steel coils) that use up a freight car's (and locomotive's) weight-carrying capacity. Still other shippers may ask Railstar to carry products that are quite difficult to handle, such as uncrated bicycles and mufflers that consume a disproportionate share of the railroad's freight sorting and handling capacity. Railstar must set prices for shippers that are competitive with other transport companies, such as trucks, airfreight, and barges. But for Railstar to remain in the freight business, it wants to know which types of freight are best for it to carry.

For this purpose, its managers want a cost signal that lets them know the cost of resources used by different types of freight (beach balls, steel coils, and uncrated bicycles and mufflers). The managers can then compare the prices it receives for different types of freight, and from different customers, with the costs of the resources it must supply to carry the freight. This information provides guidance for decisions about pricing, order acceptance, and product mix (such as whether to concentrate on compact versus bulky, heavy versus light, easy- or difficult-to-handle freight). For this purpose, managers must estimate the unit costs of its various resources, such as the cost per cubic foot of freight car space (if volume-constrained) or cost per pound of freight car (if weight-constrained) plus the cost associated with handling the freight business and specific customer-related expenses.

In summary, for many decisions, including pricing, product mix, market entry and exit, and customer service and delivery, managers need estimates that identify the costs of resources used by different products, services, and customers. This information is derived from, but also is in addition to, the information about the costs of committed resources.

### Computing the Cost of Resources Used

We will start along the path of estimating the costs of resources used by product groups, such as freight and passenger services, by apportioning the committed costs in equation [3] into three groups:

1. One group for costs related to providing freight services
2. One group for costs related to providing passenger services
3. One group for costs related to providing general capacity that provides both freight and passenger services

Exhibit 1-2 summarizes this apportionment.

**EXHIBIT 1-2**  Railstar—Apportioning Annual Costs into Product Groups

| COST TYPE | PASSENGER | FREIGHT | INDIRECT | TOTAL |
|---|---|---|---|---|
| Head Office–Related | | | | |
| General | | | $25,000,000 | $25,000,000 |
| Passenger-related | $15,000,000 | | | $15,000,000 |
| Freight-related | | $10,000,000 | | $10,000,000 |
| Roadbed-Related | | | | |
| Depreciation | | | $80,000,000 | $80,000,000 |
| Maintenance—trip | | | $1,809,600 | $1,809,600 |
| Maintenance—ps car | $2,724,800 | | $2,724,800 | |
| Maintenance—fr car | | $20 per car | | $20 per car |
| Station-Related | | | | |
| Depreciation | | | $10,000,000 | $10,000,000 |
| Other | $3 per passenger | | | $3 per passenger |
| Train-Related | | | | |
| Locomotive lease | | | $10,000,000 | $10,000,000 |
| Trip costs | | | $30,160,000 | $30,160,000 |
| Car lease | $6,000,000 | | | $6,000,000 |
| Hauling cost—ps car | $68,120,000 | | | $68,120,000 |
| Hauling cost—fr car | | $500 per car | | $500 per car |
| Passenger cost | $10 per passenger | | | $10 per passenger |

## HANDLING INDIRECT (COMMON) COSTS

An indirect cost is the cost of capacity that provides services to more than one product. The $25,000,000 portion of head office costs, the roadbed costs, the station costs, the maintenance costs caused by the locomotives, the locomotive lease costs, and the trip costs are all examples of indirect costs in this problem. The issue that we face is how to assign these costs to the individual businesses, freight and passenger, so that we can compute unit costs for the freight and passenger businesses.

There are two broad types of indirect costs: (1) costs that are entirely independent of the level of capacity and (2) resources acquired and costs that vary somehow with the level of capacity. For example, the total expense of key administrative officers would be incurred independent of the scale or actual level of operations. We call this type of cost **business-sustaining**. Theoretically, all companies in the industry, regardless of size or complexity, should have the same level of business-sustaining expenses. We do not attempt to assign business-sustaining expenses further down the organization. The second type of indirect cost can be related to the capacity level of the organization.

As an example, suppose that $5,000,000 of the indirect head office–related costs is the minimum required to support any level of operations. These costs are business-sustaining and are not assigned to individual products. For the balance of indirect head office–related costs, $20,000,000, we need an estimate of the units of service, say 10,000,000 units, that can be handled by this supply of resources. We can calculate the cost of capacity of the headquarter's resources as $2 per unit of service.

Computing the cost of capacity used to make a product reflects the following causal chain. Most committed costs (other than sustaining costs, defined as the minimum amount required to operate a business, facility, or product line) are incurred to supply a given quantity of to the amount of acquired capacity. This assumption enables the management accountant to calculate a cost for using the units of service provided by the capacity.

## COMPUTING THE COST OF UNUSED CAPACITY

Recall that every week the planners at Railstar fix the number of passenger cars that it will put in each train for the upcoming week. There are many reasons why organizations fix, or commit, capacity ahead of time rather than supplying as flexible a capacity as possible. First, committed capacity is often in the form of buildings or factories that have to be built and whose capacity can be varied only at a great cost. Second, committed capacity is often leased from outsiders, as in the case of railcars in this example, and these outsiders, to minimize their exposure to demand uncertainty, often demand long terms for leases. Third, scheduling requirements often require that some capacity elements be put in place so that short-term scheduling can be undertaken.

Contracting in advance to acquire resources also enables the organization to make enormous savings in transactions costs and to reduce its risk. Without making commitments in advance—for equipment, for personnel, and for other resources—the organization would have to contract daily, in spot markets, for each of its resources. Equipment takes time to get into place, personnel take time to get trained and motivated to achieve organizational goals, and all the resource supply must be linked together in a highly integrated fashion to accomplish work for products and customers. It would be impossible to contract daily for most resources using forecasts for how much work is required to be accomplished that day. Also, spot market contracting would subject the company to short-term price fluctuations that it can avoid by committing to acquire a resource at a fixed price for an extended period of time.

The requirement that capacity has to be fixed before the amount needed is determined has a profound effect on costs and is the basis for differentiating between short-run costs and long-run costs. Consider the passenger railcar capacity. Recall that these passenger cars are leased on a six-month term. Railstar leased 60 of these cars for the current six-month period. Recall that a train propelled by three locomotives can pull up to 90 cars, in any combination of freight or passenger.

Suppose that, through a combination of anticipated passenger and freight traffic, Railstar plans to use the following number of passenger cars each day of the week (beginning Sunday): 10, 50, 50, 45, 50, 55, 20—during the current six-month period: an average of 40 cars per day. Recall that the total cost of leasing these cars was $3,000,000 (60 cars @ $50,000). Suppose that instead of renting for a six-month period, Railstar could lease the cars by the day. This condition amounts to a rate that reflects average use, which, in this case, would amount to $2,000,000 (40 cars @ $50,000). Therefore, Railstar has incurred additional charges of $1,000,000 because it must commit to capacity for the six-month period, and, during that time, it cannot adjust capacity for varying demand. This is a very common problem that becomes more difficult as the proportion of costs that are committed increases. Organizations with this characteristic include airlines, telecommunications companies, electrical utilities, and universities.

We can think of the excess capacity issue as follows

$$\text{Resources supplied} = \text{resources used} + \text{unused capacity}$$

In this case, on average,

$$\text{Passenger cars supplied} = \text{passenger cars used} + \text{passenger cars idle}$$
$$60 = 40 + 20$$

or, in terms of costs

$$\text{Total capacity cost} = \text{capacity cost used} + \text{cost of idle capacity}$$
$$\$3,000,000 = \$2,000,000 + \$1,000,000$$

Note that the capacity, or committed cost (on the left-hand side of the equation), is $3,000,000, which is our focus in this chapter. In Chapter 4, we will discuss activity-based costing, which works on how the cost of capacity (in this case $2,000,000) was used by individual products.

When organizations have unused capacity (of committed resources) they often attempt to get customers to shift their demand patterns. For example, an electrical utility might offer time-of-day discounts to motivate customers to move demand to an off-peak period. Airlines offer incentives to customers to travel on weekends by providing substantial discounts if the traveler stays over a Saturday night. Universities attempt to improve the use of committed resources by moving from two-semester, to three-semester, or even four-semester systems that keep the university open year-round. Railstar might respond by offering customers discounts for weekend service (freight or passenger).

The result of the excess costs attributable to idle, or unused, capacity is to increase the organization's costs. In general, the cost of idle capacity is best treated as a period-related rather than a product-related cost.[17]

## COST-VOLUME-PROFIT ANALYSIS

Recall that in this chapter we have presented Railstar's cost structure as if the planners at Railstar knew it. As we will see in Chapter 4, identifying an organization's cost structure is often a difficult process requiring the application of experience and good judgment. However, once planners have identified the organization's cost structure, they can use the information to develop a financial model of the organization.[18]

To illustrate what a simple financial model of an organization might look like, let us add a few more assumptions to the data that we used to develop Railstar's cost structure. Assume that Railstar's planners expect that Railstar will sell 75% of the passenger seats it makes available and that it will haul 25 freight cars on each weekday trip and 20 freight cars on each weekend trip. Finally, assume that the price for a passenger ticket is $40 and that Railstar charges $1,000 to haul a freight car.[19]

With these assumptions, Railstar would expect to earn (lose) approximately $2,900,000 in the upcoming year,[20] as shown in Exhibit 1-3.

This projected loss would cause planners to revise their projected operating plans in order to develop a plan that is both feasible and profitable. For example, the planners might revisit their capacity-related decisions. However, for the discussion here let us assume that the major operating decisions are related to choosing the number of trips and cars to offer and taking steps to ensure that the freight business is properly priced and managed.

**EXHIBIT 1-3**  Railstar—Projected Financial Results

| | PASSENGER | FREIGHT | COMMON | TOTAL |
|---|---|---|---|---|
| No. of trips each weekday | | | | 10 |
| No. of trips each weekend day | | | | 4 |
| No. of passenger cars on each weekday train | 50 | | | |
| No. of passenger cars on each weekend train | 15 | | | |
| Planned no. of freight cars on each weekday train | | 25 | | |
| Planned no. of freight cars on each weekend train | | 20 | | |
| No. of car trips | 136,240 | 73,320 | 3,016 | |
| Load factor | 75% | 100% | | |
| Passengers carried/no. of freight cars hauled | 8,174,400 | 73,320 | | |
| Segment margin/system profit | $128,864,000 | $25,193,600 | | ($2,912,000) |

DETAILS

| | PASSENGER | FREIGHT | COMMON | TOTAL |
|---|---|---|---|---|
| Revenues | $326,976,000 | $73,320,000 | | $400,296,000 |
| Head office costs | 15,000,000 | 10,000,000 | 25,000,000 | 50,000,000 |
| Roadbed-Related Costs | | | | |
|   Depreciation | | | 80,000,000 | 80,000,000 |
|   Maintenance | 2,724,800 | 1,466,400 | 1,809,600 | 6,000,800 |
| Station-Related Costs | | | | |
|   Depreciation | | | 10,000,000 | 10,000,000 |
|   Other | 24,523,200 | | | 24,523,200 |
| Train-Related Costs | | | | |
|   Locomotive | | | 10,000,000 | 10,000,000 |
|   Fuel and Salaries | | | 30,160,000 | 30,160,000 |
|   Passenger Car Rental | 6,000,000 | | | 6,000,000 |
|   Other Costs | 68,120,000 | 36,660,000 | | 104,780,000 |
|   Passenger Costs | 81,744,000 | | | 81,744,000 |
| Total all costs | 198,112,000 | 48,126,400 | 156,969,600 | 403,208,000 |
| Segment margin | 128,864,000 | 25,193,600 | | |
| System profit | | | | −2,912,000 |

To illustrate, suppose that a market analysis suggests that if the number of weekday trips were cut from 10 to 8, with the number of weekend trips remaining constant, that the proportion of seats sold would rise to 90%. Profit would increase to $3,500,000. In fact, profits are very sensitive to the proportion of seats sold; profits increase approximately $2,400,000 for each 1% increase in occupancy. This relation suggests a huge amount of operating leverage; flexible costs are low relative to committed costs. Another way of seeing this is to observe that, for the original data given in this problem, Railstar will cover its costs in the passenger business when the load factor[21] is just over 31%. Consequently, both the passenger and freight businesses must make huge contributions toward covering the costs (such as depreciation on the roadbed) that are common to both segments of Railstar's business.

It is evident in this situation that flexible cost pricing—that is, pricing designed to just recover flexible costs—in this case $13 per passenger, would be a disaster. Pricing must take place with an understanding of, and must reflect, all costs.

Planners can also use financial models to study the effects of price and volume tradeoffs. That is, how much of a volume increase is required to compensate the organization for a given price increase? For example, starting from the initial setting—when the projected loss was $2,900,000—planners might want to evaluate the effect on profits of a price decrease of $5 per ticket. Suppose that such a price decrease would cause the load factor to increase by 3% from 75% to 78%. Would this change be desirable? The effect would be to decrease profits. In fact, the load factor would have to increase to more than 92% as a result of this price increase for the price decrease to be desirable.

Planners are often interested in the level of operations that will result in zero profits. Profits are determined by the level of both products' sales in a multiproduct firm such as Railstar. Suppose we assume that there are no freight operations and that we can eliminate the $10,000,000 of head office costs that are attributable to the freight operations. If we assumed the current level of trips and passenger cars on each train, what level of occupancy would be required for Railstar to cover all its costs? Exhibit 1-4 shows that the load factor is about 85%.

**EXHIBIT 1-4** Railstar—Breakeven Calculation

|  | PASSENGER | FREIGHT | COMMON | TOTAL |
|---|---|---|---|---|
| No. of trips each weekday |  |  |  | 10 |
| No. of trips each weekend day |  |  |  | 4 |
| No. of passenger cars on each weekday train | 50 |  |  |  |
| No. of passenger cars on each weekend train | 15 |  |  |  |
| Planned no. of freight cars on each weekday train |  | 0 |  |  |
| Planned no. of freight cars on each weekend train |  | 0 |  |  |
| Number of car trips | 136,240 | 0 | 3,016 |  |
| Load factor | 84.6% | n/a |  |  |
| Passengers carried/no. of freight cars hauled | 9,220,723 | 0 |  |  |
| Segment margin/system profit | $157,114,726 | $0 |  | $145,126 |
| DETAILS |  |  |  |  |
| Revenues | $368,828,928 | $0 |  | $368,828,928 |
| Head office costs | 15,000,000 | 0 | 25,000,000 | 40,000,000 |
| Roadbed-Related Costs |  |  |  |  |
| Depreciation |  |  | 80,000,000 | 80,000,000 |
| Maintenance | 2,724,800 | 0 | 1,809,600 | 4,534,400 |
| Station-Related Costs |  |  |  |  |
| Depreciation |  |  | 10,000,000 | 10,000,000 |
| Other | 27,662,170 |  |  | 27,662,170 |
| Train-Related Costs |  |  |  |  |
| Locomotive |  |  | 10,000,000 | 10,000,000 |
| Fuel and Salaries |  |  | 30,160,000 | 30,160,000 |
| Passenger Car Rental | 6,000,000 |  |  | 6,000,000 |
| Other Costs | 68,120,000 | 0 |  | 68,120,000 |
| Passenger Costs | 92,207,232 |  |  | 92,207,232 |
| Total all costs | 211,714,202 | 0 | 156,969,600 | 368,683,802 |
| Segment margin | 157,114,726 | 0 |  |  |
| System profit |  |  |  | 145,126 |

Of course, profit-seeking organizations are not interested in just breaking even; organizations want to earn enough to provide a return to shareholders that is consistent with the risk that they have taken investing in the firm. However, planners often use this type of analysis to estimate the level of risk that the organization faces in covering its costs.

## SUMMARY

In this chapter, we described the cost structure of a simple railroad operation. We saw that the railroad's total cost is a combination of committed and flexible costs. Committed costs reflect the cost of capacity that is locked in place before any production takes place. Flexible costs are those costs that are incurred as production takes place and therefore vary with the level of production. We have also seen that there are two types of committed costs. The first type is costs that vary with increases or decreases in the capacity level. The second type is costs that are fixed and do not change as capacity levels vary. We call the latter form of committed costs business-sustaining costs, and we do not try to attribute those costs to individual units of production. However, we attribute the committed costs that vary with the level of capacity acquired to products proportional to each product's use of that capacity.

Once the organization has its capacity, and therefore its cost structure, in place, it uses that capacity to provide products to customers. Decision makers are often interested in developing a financial model of the organization that they can use to estimate the financial effects of different competitive and operating strategies. This approach provides a broad overview of the general results of different operating strategies on profits. In Chapter 4, we will describe an approach that allows decision makers to estimate costs in more detail. Planners then use these costs to evaluate process efficiency, opportunities for improvement, sourcing decisions, and abandonment decisions.

## ENDNOTES

1. Other types of information that management accounting reports might convey include efficiency indicators such as yield measures (the ratio of output to input), quality measures (conformance to specification), and service measures (ability to meet customer requirements). Later chapters will discuss performance measures that are not cost-based.

2. Inventory holding costs include excess manufacturing costs caused by producing large quantities in cycles, storage and warehouse building and maintenance costs, costs related to damage and obsolescence, insurance costs, and the opportunity cost of funds tied up in inventory.

3. Organizations that moved to eliminate trade loading faced both huge skepticism and huge resistance. Therefore, the organizations that moved first to eliminate trade loading demonstrated considerable courage and confidence in the underlying cost data.

4. In this book, we will use the word *products* to refer to both physical goods, such as a box of cereal, and services, such as a phone call, a bank checking account, a medical procedure, a transport of materials or a person, and professional consulting services.

5. For example, Railstar could operate from a smaller head office complex and the people who manage the freight business would be laid off, reassigned, or not replaced when they left Railstar.

6. Total costs are $50,000,000 versus $75,000,000 if the businesses were operated separately.

7. We are assuming here no economies of scale; that is, the cost of acquiring capacity is proportional to the quantity of capacity acquired. In general, the cost of acquiring capacity increases at a decreasing rate as more capacity is acquired.

8. Note that this means that Railstar can operate only one train at a time.

9. Market prices are influenced by the cost of private automobile or bus travel or the cost of hauling goods by truck between Rose Terrace and Whistle Stop.

10. With these capacity choices, annual committed costs are: head office–related—$50,000,000; roadbed-related—$80,000,000; station-related—$10,000,000 ($5,000,000 for each station), and train-related—$10,000,000 for a total of $150,000,000. Because this is an annual cost function, we will convert costs, such as the cost of leasing passenger cars, from a half-year basis to the whole year by assuming that decisions made in the first half of the year are repeated in the second half of the year.

11. The numbers in this sentence are calculated from:
    50 = 5 round-trips * 2 trips per round-trip * 5 weekdays
     8 = 2 round-trips * 2 trips per round-trip * 2 weekend days

12. 58 trips per week * $10,600 per trip * 26 trips per six-month period = $15,984,800 trip-related costs per six-month period. However, because committed costs are expressed in terms of cost per year, we convert the trip-related costs to an annual amount by multiplying the six-month cost by 2: $15,984,800 * 2 = $31,969,600 in trip-related costs per year.

13. The calculations are: 2,620 = (50 * 50) + (15 * 8); and $70,844,800 = 2,620 * $520 * 52.

14. Note that this conclusion reflects the assumption that the station-related and train costs are flexible. If these costs were not flexible—for example, if they reflected the salaries of personnel who are hired to serve passengers—the flexible passenger-related costs would be zero. Note that the flexible passenger-related costs on an airline would reflect the cost of the meal and the cost of the fuel used to carry the passenger and the passenger's luggage, which would likely be close to zero.

15. The supply (capacity) of resources that are people-intensive are not nearly as upwardly flexible as Railstar's passenger rail cars or as machines that normally operate only one shift (out of a possible three).

16. 15 cars * $50,000 rental per car.

17. That is, in conventional practice none of this cost of idle capacity would be traced to individual products.

18. As we will see in later chapters, cost information can also be used in decision making related to process improvement, product pricing, and organization control.

19. There is a considerable simplification here. Essentially, Railstar is charging by capacity rather than by weight, although there are weight restrictions on freight cars. Also there is only one type of freight service (yard to yard) and only one type of passenger service (coach from station to station). However, the simplicity in the example allows us to make the critical points clearly.

20. The financial results discussed below were obtained with the **amach1.xls** worksheet, which is available to your instructor.

21. Load factor = capacity used/capacity available.

---

## ■ *PROBLEMS*

---

### *1-1    Computing Costs*

Atlantic University has eight schools, 350 faculty members, and 20,000 students. An analysis of the university's cost structure yielded the following annual cost estimates.

The university-sustaining cost level is $20,000,000, which includes basic building costs and administrative salaries such as those of the president and the admissions officers. Committed costs at the university level increase, in the long run, by $20,000,000 for each new school added and by $1000 for each additional student enrolled.

The School of Business is a school in Atlantic University. The school-sustaining cost level is $5,000,000. The area-sustaining cost level is $50,000. Committed costs in the

School of Business increase, in the long run, by $200,000 for each faculty member added and by $500 for each unit of student capacity added. Planners at Atlantic University estimate that the total flexible costs per student amount to $600. (All the costs above are annual costs.)

Each faculty member teaches five courses and each student takes nine courses per year.

The Accounting Area in the School of Business has 30 faculty members and is offering 150 courses with, on average, 60 students in each course. Accounting students only take accounting courses.

### Required

(1)   What is the total annual cost per accounting student?
(2)   What is the total annual cost of the accounting program?
(3)   The dean of the School of Business is considering a shift in faculty workload to provide more incentive for research. The shift will result in each faculty member teaching four courses per year. The number of student course enrollments will be unchanged. How will this change affect the cost per student? How will it affect the cost of the accounting program?

## 1-2    Role of Cost Allocation

The Holiday Hotel provides a recreation center for the use of its guests and employees. The center also sells memberships to people in the local community. The center has squash and racket ball court facilities, showering facilities, and a room with various types of exercise equipment. The courts occupy about 70% of the facility's floor space, the showering area 10%, the exercise room 15%, and the administrative offices 5%. In the long-run the hotel could convert unused facilities to additional lodging units. The center reports the following costs for the most recent year:

1.   Assigned building depreciation and staff costs: $400,000. The depreciation charges amount to $250,000; the salaries of the manager and her staff amount to $150,000. Staff costs are independent of the level of activity in the recreation center.
2.   Depreciation on the exercise equipment that are added as demand grows: $200,000.
3.   Maintenance and electrical charges, which are thought to vary with the number of visitors to the center: $300,000.
4.   Laundry costs: $300,000, comprising $50,000 of depreciation on the machines and $250,000 of supplies costs.
5.   The cost of other supplies, which are consumed equally by all visitors to the center: $200,000.

During the last year, there were 67,000 visits to the physical center. The capacity level of each of the showering, exercise, and court areas is estimated as 80,000, 40,000, and 25,000 visits per year respectively.

### Required

(1)   What is the cost per visit to the physical center?
(2)   In the past, the costs of the physical center were charged to the various hotel departments, guest services, and outside business in the ratio 50%, 40%, and 10%. The idea of

charging back to hotel departments is to recognize that the physical center is an employee-related cost. The idea of charging back to guest services is to provide information to support the calculation of cost per guest visit at the hotel. Costs were assigned to the unit relating to memberships with the expectation of covering out-of-pocket costs under the assumption that the facility was built for the use of the employees and guests. Some of the department controllers have complained about this practice and have argued that the charges to the departments should be based on use rather than on employee numbers. Moreover, some controllers have argued that it is unfair and unreasonable to charge all visitors the same. An audit of the center's use, which is thought to reflect average long-term use, suggests that about 25,000 visits were by employees and that 80% of them only showered; the rest used the exercise and court facilities almost equally and showered. About 15,000 visits were by hotel guests, virtually all of whom showered and used the exercise room. The remaining visits were from paid members, all of whom showered, and who used the exercise and court facilities almost equally. Based on this information, how should the costs of the physical center be assigned to the various groups?

## 1-3 Cost Considerations in Strategic Decisions

Brantford Bat Company (BBC) manufactures popular baseball bats that are prized by professional and amateur players. The current flexible cost of manufacturing the bat is $12 per unit. The cost of operating the lathe that produces the bat is about $600,000 per year. This cost includes maintenance and physical obsolescence costs.

BBC is now evaluating the possibility of purchasing a new lathe to manufacture the bat. The new lathe replaces the mechanical patterns currently used to manufacture lathes and relies instead on direct laser sensing by a computer within the lathe to compare the current size of the wood stock being turned on the lathe with a pattern stored in the computer's memory. Although the new machine would not increase the capacity of the bat-making operation, which is 750,000 bats per year, it would reduce the flexible cost of producing the bats to $10 per unit. The cost of operating the new lathe would be about $1,400,000 per year.

If the current level of production and sales of this bat is 500,000 units, should the new lathe be purchased? Ignore the effect of income taxes in answering this question.

## 1-4 Cost-Volume-Profit Analysis and Pricing in the Airline Industry* (Edward Deakin, Adapted)

Trans Western Airlines is considering a proposal to initiate air service between Phoenix, Arizona, and Las Vegas, Nevada. The route would be designed primarily to serve the recreation and tourist travelers who frequently travel between the two cities. By offering low-cost tourist fares, the airline hopes to persuade persons who now travel by other modes of transportation to switch and fly Trans Western on this route.

In addition, the airline expects to attract business travelers during the hours of 7 A.M. to 6 P.M. on Mondays through Fridays. The fare price schedule, or tariff, would be designed to charge a higher fare during business-travel hours so that tourist demand

---

*© 1982 by CIPT Co. Reproduced with permission.

would be reduced during those hours. The company believes that a business fare of $100 one way during business hours and a fare of $60 for all other hours would equalize the passenger load during business-travel and tourist-travel hours.

To operate the route, the airline would need two 200-passenger jet aircraft. The aircraft would be leased at an annual cost of $10,000,000 each. Other committed costs for ground service would amount to $5,000,000 per year.

Operation of each aircraft requires a flight crew whose salaries are based primarily on the hours of flying time. The costs of the flight crew are approximately $800 per hour of flying time.

Fuel costs are also a function of flying time. These costs are estimated at $1,000 per hour of flying time. Flying time between Phoenix and Las Vegas is estimated at 45 minutes each way.

The flexible costs associated with processing each passenger amount to $5. This amount includes ticket processing, agent commissions, and baggage handling. Food and beverage service cost $10 per passenger and will be offered at no charge on flights during business hours. The airline expects to recover the cost of this service on non-business-hour flights through charges levied for alcoholic beverages.

### Required

(1) If six business flights and four tourist flights are offered *each way* every weekday, and 12 tourist flights are offered *each way* every Saturday and Sunday, what is the average number of passengers that must be carried on each flight to break even?

(2) What is the breakeven load factor (percentage of available seats occupied) on a route?

(3) If Trans Western Airlines operates the Phoenix–Las Vegas route, its aircraft on that route will be idle between midnight and 6 A.M. The airline is considering offering a "Red Die" special, which would leave Phoenix daily at midnight and return by 6 A.M. The marketing division estimates that if the fare were no more than $40, the load factor would be 50% for each Red Die flight. Operating costs would be the same for this flight, but advertising costs of $10,000 per week would be required for promotion of the service. No food or beverage costs would be borne by the company. Management wants to know the minimum fare that would be required to break even on the Red Die special, assuming that the marketing division's passenger estimates are correct.

## 1-5   Multiple-Product Cost-Volume-Profit Analysis (CMA, adapted)

Hewtex Electronics manufactures two products, tape recorders and electronic calculators, and sells them nationally to wholesalers and retailers. The Hewtex management is very pleased with the company's performance for the current fiscal year. Projected sales through December 31, 1998, suggest that 120,000 tape recorders and 190,000 electronic calculators will be sold this year. The projected earnings statement, which follows, shows that Hewtex will not meet its earnings goal of 9% of sales after taxes.

### Required

(1) Assuming that the sales mix in the planning documents is achieved, how many tape recorder and electronic calculator units would Hewtex Electronics have to sell in 1998 to break even?

### HEWTEX ELECTRONICS
### Projected Earnings Statement
### For the Year Ended December 31, 1998

|  | 120,000 UNITS TAPE RECORDERS | | 190,000 UNITS ELECTRONIC CALCULATORS | | TOTAL |
|---|---|---|---|---|---|
|  | *Total Amount (000 omitted)* | *Per Unit* | *Total Amount (000 omitted)* | *Per Unit* | *(000 omitted)* |
| Sales | $1,800 | $15.00 | $4,480 | $28.00 | $6,280 |
| Flexible costs |  |  |  |  |  |
| Materials | 480 | 4.00 | 1,140 | 6.00 | 1,620 |
| Labor | 360 | 3.00 | 1,710 | 9.00 | 2,070 |
| Other | 120 | 1.00 | 570 | 3.00 | 690 |
| Committed costs | 280 | 2.33 | 1,400 | 7.37 | 1,680 |
| Total costs | 1,240 | 10.33 | 4,820 | 25.37 | 6,060 |
| Gross margin | 560 | 4.67 | 500 | 2.63 | 1,060 |
| Facility-sustaining costs |  |  |  |  | 2,000 |
| Net income before income taxes |  |  |  |  | (940) |

(2) What volume of sales is required if Hewtex Electronics is to earn a profit in 1999 equal to 9% of sales after taxes? Hewtex Electronics faces a tax rate of 42%.

(3) Hewtex Electronics now allocates committed costs based on flexible labor costs. A study has determined that committed costs are as follows: (1) supervisory costs for tape recorder production—$500,000; (2) supervisory salaries for electronic calculator production—$600,000; (3) the balance of the committed costs are proportional to the number of batches of production. Hewtex Electronics schedules tape recorders for production in batches of 1000, and electronic calculators are made in batches of 10,000. Finally, $300,000 of what was originally classified as facility-sustaining cost was actually attributable to tape recorders, and $400,000 was attributable to the electronic calculator line. Recast the original financial statements to correct the costing errors due to misclassification.

# 2

## Short-Term Budgeting, Resource Allocations, and Capacity Cost

Chapter 1 introduced the notion of flexible and committed resources. Organizations buy and use flexible resources, such as materials and supplies, in the quantities they require. The cost of flexible resources depends on how much is used, which, aside from loss or waste, equals the amount bought. By contrast, the supplies of committed resources, such as machinery and skilled employees, are not variable in the short run. Committed resources provide the capacity to perform many organization activities. Unlike the cost of flexible resources, the cost of committed resources depends on how much is acquired, not on how much is used.

Because committed capacity is not variable in the short run, short-run planning attempts to use committed capacity in the most productive way. As we will see in this chapter, when a committed resource constrains further short-run expansion (that is, further use of flexible resources), that resource has associated with it an opportunity cost reflecting the lost profits that would otherwise have resulted from further production.

This chapter considers the short-run use of committed capacity and the financial results from using committed capacity effectively. We will use an example that is rich enough to illustrate a full range of important issues. Once we have the example in place, we will explore issues relating to short-run resource allocation to forecast financial results.

## THE EXAMPLE

Shannonville Cabinets manufactures and sells five types of large steel electrical cabinets. Annual sales of cabinet 1 are made uniformly through the first and last four months of the year. Annual sales of cabinet 2 are made uniformly through the last six months of the year. Annual sales of cabinet 3 are made uniformly through the first six months of the year. Annual sales of cabinet 4 are made uniformly throughout the year. Annual sales of cabinet 5 are made in equal amounts in June and December. Production is on a just-in-time basis. That is, the amount produced in any month equals the amount sold in that month. The exception is cabinet 5, for which production occurs uniformly through the year. Shannonville Cabinets maintains a minimum cash balance of $50,000 and finances any short-term working capital requirements with a line of credit. Interest is charged each month at the rate of 0.5% of the opening line of credit balance that month. On average, bad debts amount to 5% of sales revenues.

Workers initiate the production process by removing sheet steel from storage, transporting the steel to the cutting area, and inserting the sheet steel into a programmable cutting machine. After the machine cuts the cabinet parts from the sheet steel, the parts are moved to an assembly area where the cabinets are built. The cabinets are then moved to a shipping area for packaging and shipping.

The following are the characteristics of the five cabinets. The amount of work required by each of the cabinets in each activity area is shown as the number of work units.

| CABINET | SELLING PRICE | MATERIALS & LABOR COST | SCHEDULING RESOURCE UNITS | MOVING RESOURCE UNITS | SETUP RESOURCE UNITS | CUTTING RESOURCE UNITS | ASSEMBLY RESOURCE UNITS | SHIPPING RESOURCE UNITS |
|---|---|---|---|---|---|---|---|---|
| C1 | $14,000 | $1,300 | 2 | 7 | 3 | 3 | 2 | 4 |
| C2 | $20,000 | $1,600 | 4 | 3 | 4 | 6 | 5 | 4 |
| C3 | $19,000 | $1,500 | 5 | 2 | 6 | 4 | 3 | 7 |
| C4 | $15,000 | $1,450 | 3 | 5 | 7 | 2 | 4 | 2 |
| C5 | $22,000 | $1,750 | 6 | 4 | 5 | 6 | 5 | 3 |
| Capacity costs | | | $70,000 | $170,000 | $260,000 | $800,000 | $650,000 | $150,000 |
| Monthly capacity units | | | 2,600 | 3,000 | 3,500 | 2,900 | 2,400 | 3,200 |
| Flexible cost per unit used | | | $180 | $300 | $780 | $900 | $720 | $240 |

## SHORT-TERM PLANNING AND BUDGETING

Note that each resource has a certain capacity that is available for production (measured in appropriate capacity units). In addition, each unit of used capacity also requires a certain amount of flexible resources, principally materials and supplies, whose unit costs are reported in the bottom row of the table. With this information, planners at Shannonville Cabinets can choose a production plan to achieve some objective and then forecast the financial consequences of that production plan.

## ACTIVITIES, RESOURCE USE, AND COSTS

This example illustrates the nature of the issues facing short-run production planners. Each product consumes varying amounts of the six constraining factors of production. Two elements of cost associated with each of the factors of production are: a committed cost, which is fixed in the short run and does not vary with use; and a flexible cost, which varies in proportion to the amount of the factor that is used[1]. Each factor of production, or activity, has a unique flexible cost, which we assume is known to the production planners. The facility-sustaining costs, which are unrelated to activity levels, are $12,000,000 per year and are incurred and paid in equal monthly amounts.

We can develop the following table, which summarizes the calculation for each product's contribution margin (CM, net selling price less flexible cost).[2]

|  | C1 | C2 | C3 | C4 | C5 |
|---|---|---|---|---|---|
| Price | $14,000 | $20,000 | $19,000 | $15,000 | $22,000 |
| Material | 1,300 | 1,600 | 1,500 | 1,450 | 1,750 |
| Scheduling | 360 | 720 | 900 | 540 | 1,080 |
| Moving | 2,100 | 900 | 600 | 1,500 | 1,200 |
| Setup | 2,340 | 3,120 | 4,680 | 5,460 | 3,900 |
| Cutting | 2,700 | 5,400 | 3,600 | 1,800 | 5,400 |
| Assembly | 1,440 | 3,600 | 2,160 | 2,880 | 3,600 |
| Shipping | 960 | 960 | 1,680 | 480 | 720 |
| Total | $11,200 | $16,300 | $15,120 | $14,110 | $17,650 |
| CM | $ 2,800 | $ 3,700 | $ 3,880 | $ 890 | $ 4,350 |

## OPTIMIZING THE USE OF SHORT-TERM RESOURCES
### Equal Sales Objective   — constraint @ resource used @ capacity

Suppose that the initial production plan seeks to make the annual sales of all products equal. This objective results in the following planned level of operations and profit[3].

Shannonville Cabinets
Summary of Optimal Solution
Equal Annual Production Units Objective

| Income | $ 51,903 | | Product | Units |
|---|---|---|---|---|
| | | | C1 | 1,309 |
| Sales (net) | $111,919,500 | | C2 | 1,309 |
| Flexible costs | $ 97,363,420 | | C3 | 1,309 |
| Capacity costs | $ 2,100,000 | | C4 | 1,309 |
| Other costs | $ 12,000,000 | | C5 | 1,309 |
| Interest costs | $ 404,177 | | Total | 6,545 |

*continued*

| Resource | Units Available | Maximum Used |
|---|---|---|
| Scheduling | 2,600 | 2,400 |
| Moving | 3,000 | 2,782 |
| Setup | 3,500 | 3,109 |
| Cutting | 2,900 | 2,673 |
| Assembly | 2,400 | 2,400 |
| Shipping | 3,200 | 2,727 |

In this production plan, the Assembly Department is used to capacity. Since this department constrains any additional production, efforts to expand productive capacity, either through acquiring additional resources or through launching initiatives to improve the efficiency of existing resources, would focus on increasing capacity in the Assembly Department.[4]

## Total Sales Objective

Instead of planning production and sales by projecting past numbers, suppose that the planners at Shannonville Cabinets choose a production plan that maximizes total annual sales given existing capacity. Using this criterion, the planners at Shannonville Cabinets would choose the following production plan.

Shannonville Cabinets
Summary of Optimal Solution
Maximize Total Sales Objective

| | | | Product | Units |
|---|---|---|---|---|
| Income | $2,393,761 | | C1 | 1,826.2 |
| | | | C2 | 1,427.4 |
| Sales (net) | $116,500,278 | | C3 | 1,588.7 |
| Flexible costs | $99,673,341 | | C4 | 568.2 |
| Capacity costs | $2,100,000 | | C5 | 1,355.0 |
| Other costs | $12,000,000 | | Total | 6,745.4 |
| Interest costs | $353,176 | | | |

| Resource | Units Available | Maximum Used |
|---|---|---|
| Scheduling | 2,600 | 2,600 |
| Moving | 3,000 | 3,000 |
| Setup | 3,500 | 3,170 |
| Cutting | 2,900 | 2,884 |
| Assembly | 2,400 | 2,400 |
| Shipping | 3,200 | 3,200 |

## Short-Run Profit Objective _maximizing SR CM ; "Optimization Approach"_

Finally, suppose that the criterion used by the planners at Shannonville Cabinets is to maximize the income provided by the production plan. In this case, the chosen production plan would be as follows.

---

### Shannonville Cabinets
### Summary of Optimal Solution
### Maximize Contribution Margin Objective

| Income | $3,126,478 | | Product | Units |
|---|---|---|---|---|
| | | | C1 | 2,003.6 |
| Sales (net) | $113,876,758 | | C2 | 1,325.8 |
| Flexible costs | $96,253,725 | | C3 | 1,531.5 |
| Capacity costs | $2,100,000 | | C4 | 0.0 |
| Other costs | $12,000,000 | | C5 | 1,645.6 |
| Interest costs | $396,555 | | Total | 6,506.6 |

| Resource | Units Available | Maximum Used |
|---|---|---|
| Scheduling | 2,600 | 2,600 |
| Moving | 3,000 | 2,965 |
| Setup | 3,500 | 2,969 |
| Cutting | 2,900 | 2,900 |
| Assembly | 2,400 | 2,291 |
| Shipping | 3,200 | 3,200 |

---

Note that this approach creates the largest value, about $3,126,000, for short-run profit as reported in the income cell, because the production plan for this approach explicitly took this as the performance measure to maximize. Note also that the optimality of this production plan is based on the planners' understanding of the revenues and materials cost of each of the five products, the flexible costs and availability of each of the resources required for production, and the consumption of each activity by each product. Also we have assumed that there is no opportunity to change the resource supply (that is, the level of committed resources).

## OPPORTUNITY COSTS, CAPACITY COSTS, AND THE THEORY OF CONSTRAINTS

As we have seen in the Shannonville Cabinets example, a production constraint limits an organization's ability to increase its income.[5] In this sense, we can say that the constraining factor of production reflects an opportunity cost for the organization because it prevents further expansion and profits. In theory, we should increase the supply of the constraining factor of production as long as the resulting increase in capacity costs is less than the opportunity costs avoided by further expansion. In the long-run sense, this is a capital-budgeting problem in which the initial cost is the increase in capacity cost and the future cash flows represent the annual increase in incremental profits provided by expanding the constraining factor of production.

In the last 10 years, the management and management accounting literatures have devoted attention to Eliyahu Goldratt's theory of constraints.[6] He claims that most manufacturing organizations have a single binding constraint, whereas the Shannonville example indicates that three resources—scheduling, cutting, and shipping—are binding at the optimal solution when the objective is to maximize the short-run contribution margin. Advocates of Goldratt's theory of constraints believe that such multiple binding constraints arise more in academic examples than in the real world.[7] The theory of constraints is based on identifying which resource at any given time is the primary constraint on additional production. The theory of constraints simplifies the optimization approach but gains considerable focus by encouraging active management of this single constraining factor of production. Theory of constraints practitioners increase throughput, and therefore profit, by relieving the constraining, or bottleneck, factor of production. They do this in two ways.

1. Increase the supply of the constraining factor of production by reducing downtime on this resource through effective scheduling and buffering of this resource and by continuous process improvement

2. Reduce the demand on the constraining factor of production by reengineering products so that they use less of that factor of production, or shift the product mix so that additional resources use less of the constraining resource and more of resources with current excess capacity.

The theory of constraints takes the existing production capacity as given and looks for ways to improve the organization's performance within that capacity endowment. The theory of constraints is a short-run operations strategy that does not consider either where the capacity came from or how or when it might be expanded.[8] The idea is to focus on one bottleneck at a time, eliminate that bottleneck's constraint on throughput, and then turn to the next factor constraining production. Resource management and decisions about process improvements and product mix involve a continuous process of evaluating the impacts on bottleneck resources and striving to continuously eliminate one bottleneck after another to increase production throughput.

## THE ISSUE OF MULTIPLE RESOURCES

The discussion in the preceding section relating to opportunity costs is meaningful when there is a single factor constraining production. However, things get much more complicated, and therefore, less obvious, when there are multiple factors constraining production.

If we consider the production plan associated with the objective of maximizing contribution margin or, equivalently, income, we see that the optimal plan calls for the full use of scheduling, cutting, and shipping resources. The optimal production plan does not call for the full use of either the moving, setup, or assembly resources. The process that is followed when there is a single constraining factor of production—which is to expand production until the constraining factor of production is used up—does not work when there are multiple factors of production. First, an optimal production plan can be found only if all the constraining factors of production are considered simultaneously. Second, if the supply of one resource is increased, the optimal production plan will change, and that change, in turn, may lead to a different group of resources now constraining production.

To illustrate, return to Shannonville Cabinets and study the optimal plan when the objective is to maximize short-term income. Note that the scheduling, cutting, and shipping resources are fully used. Therefore, to expand output and profits, the planners would have to increase one of the constraining factors of production. Suppose that Shannonville Cabinets can rent a cutting machine for one year. The rental cost will be $200,000 and will increase monthly capacity to 3,100. Before we go any further, look back at the existing solution and try to guess whether this project should be undertaken.

Here is the optimal solution when monthly cutting capacity increases to 3,100 units.

## Shannonville Cabinets
## Summary of Optimal Solution
## Maximize Contribution Margin Objective—Increase Cutting Capacity

| Income | $3,463,373 | | | Product | Units |
|---|---|---|---|---|---|
| | | | | C1 | 1,964.1 |
| Sales (net) | $116,258,032 | | | C2 | 1,474.5 |
| Flexible costs | $98,301,383 | | | C3 | 1,551.3 |
| Capacity costs | $2,100,000 | | | C4 | 0.0 |
| Other costs | $12,000,000 | | | C5 | 1,632.5 |
| Interest costs | $393,277 | | | Total | 6,622.4 |

| Resource | Units Available | Maximum Used |
|---|---|---|
| Scheduling | 2,600 | 2,600 |
| Moving | 3,000 | 3,000 |
| Setup | 3,500 | 2,968 |
| Cutting | 3,100 | 3,027 |
| Assembly | 2,400 | 2,400 |
| Shipping | 3,200 | 3,200 |

Notice that the new plan calls for a different production level for every product and that profits increase by $338,440, which is the value of increasing the monthly availability of the cutting resource from 2,900 to 3,100 units for one year.

Study the resource use under the new optimal plan paying particular attention to the use of the cutting capacity. Note that the optimal plan does not call for the full use of the increase in the cutting availability. With the increase in the cutting capacity, other resources are now constraining production. Note, though, that the increased profits of $338,400 provided by increasing the cutting availability far exceeds the $200,000 rental cost of that capacity.

## Effects of Reengineering and Continuous Improvement on Profitability

In addition to decisions about capital investment and expansion, planners can use this type of planning model to predict the effect of reengineering or continuous improvement. For example, suppose that a product design team consisting of marketing, purchasing, design, manufacturing, and accounting personnel undertook to improve the design of cabinet 1 so that it could be manufactured more easily. This design team changed the design of cabinet 1 so that it now requires only 2, 2, 1 (down from a level of 3, 3, 2) units in setup, cutting, and assembly, respectively. We can show that the expected benefit in the first period from this redesign is to increase profits from $3,124,933 to $8,234,070, an increase of more than 160%—and this is the benefit just in the first year. Presumably the benefit would extend beyond the first year.

By studying this example we can see that product and process redesign not only improves profits by reducing the cost of the resources that cabinet 1 consumes, but also, by using fewer resources that are constraining production, the redesign increases profits by freeing up resources that Shannonville Cabinets can use to produce other products. For this reason, management tools that focus on reducing the use of constraining resources have a twofold effect on income.

## THE ROLE OF COST INFORMATION IN ALLOCATING SHORT-TERM RESOURCES

The choice of the optimal allocation of the constraining factors of production depends critically on the estimates of the parameters used in the model. Misestimates of the planning parameters—in this case, selling prices, flexible costs, the use of resources by individual products, and resource availability—will result in opportunity losses as planners make suboptimal resource allocations.

Because we are focusing on information that would likely be provided to the planners by the management accounting system, we will illustrate how errors in cost estimates lead to opportunity losses. Suppose that, because of costing system limitations, the estimated flexible costs of using the resources are different from the actual amounts. For example, suppose that the flexible cost of using scheduling, moving, setup, cutting, assembly, and shipping were estimated as $189, $308, $646, $851, $612, and $204.[9] The following exhibit shows the estimated contribution margins (CM) resulting from those estimates.

If planners use these contribution margins to choose production levels, they will choose the production plan and profits shown in the following exhibit. Note that the resulting profit is $3,071,080, which is $53,853 less than the profit that would have resulted from the production plan that would have been chosen if the actual flexible costs had been known.[10] Therefore, inaccurate cost information creates opportunity losses in production planning.

Organizations are most unlikely to know flexible costs with certainty and therefore are likely to experience opportunity costs from planning with inaccurate cost informa-

Chapter 2 Short-Term Budgeting, Resource Allocations, and Capacity Cost 41

|  | C1 | C2 | C3 | C4 | C5 |
|---|---|---|---|---|---|
| Price | $14,000 | $20,000 | $19,000 | $15,000 | $22,000 |
| Material | 1,300 | 1,600 | 1,500 | 1,450 | 1,750 |
| Scheduling | 378 | 756 | 945 | 567 | 1,134 |
| Moving | 2,156 | 924 | 616 | 1,540 | 1,232 |
| Setup | 1,938 | 2,584 | 3,876 | 4,522 | 3,230 |
| Cutting | 2,553 | 5,106 | 3,404 | 1,702 | 5,106 |
| Assembiy | 1,224 | 3,060 | 1,836 | 2,448 | 3,060 |
| Shipping | 816 | 816 | 1,428 | 408 | 612 |
| Total | $10,365 | $14,846 | $13,605 | $12,637 | $16,124 |
| CM | $ 3,635 | $ 5,154 | $ 5,395 | $ 2,363 | $ 5,876 |

### Shannonville Cabinets
### Summary of Optimal Solution
### Maximize Contribution Margin Objective—Faulty Flexible Cost Data

| Income | $3,071,080 | | | Product | Units |
|---|---|---|---|---|---|
| | | | | C1 | 1,695.1 |
| Sales (net) | $113,583,140 | | | C2 | 1,492.9 |
| Flexible costs | $96,039,106 | | | C3 | 1,685.8 |
| Capacity costs | $2,100,000 | | | C4 | 0.0 |
| Other costs | $12,000,000 | | | C5 | 1,542.8 |
| Interest costs | $372,954 | | | Total | 6,416.6 |

| Resource | Units Available | Maximum Used |
|---|---|---|
| Scheduling | 2,600 | 2,600 |
| Moving | 3,000 | 2,744 |
| Setup | 3,500 | 2,964 |
| Cutting | 2,900 | 2,900 |
| Assembly | 2,400 | 2,311 |
| Shipping | 3,200 | 3,200 |

*Income is computed using the actual values of the flexible cost of using the resources.*

tion. Often this opportunity loss is exacerbated when organizations use crude costing systems.

To illustrate, suppose that Shannonville Cabinets does not maintain detailed flexible cost information by activity but rather includes all flexible factory-related costs in a single cost pool. If you look at the optimal solution from the original problem when the objective was to maximize contribution margin, you will see that the total production cost is $46,247,743. Of the total production cost, $9,900,886 is related to materials, leaving a balance of $86,346,857 related to the flexible cost of using capacity. Given that the total production is 6,504.1, the average flexible cost is about $13,300 per unit. Suppose that, based on past production, the planners at Shannonville Cabinets estimate the production cost as $13,300. If we use this estimate of flexible cost, the following product contribution margin estimates would result.

|          | C1        | C2        | C3        | C4        | C5        |
|----------|-----------|-----------|-----------|-----------|-----------|
| Price    | $14,000   | $20,000   | $19,000   | $15,000   | $22,000   |
| Material | 1,300     | 1,600     | 1,500     | 1,450     | 1,750     |
| Flexible | 13,300    | 13,300    | 13,300    | 13,300    | 13,300    |
| Total    | $14,600   | $14,900   | $14,800   | $14,750   | $15,050   |
| CM       | −$   600  | $ 5,100   | $ 4,200   | $   250   | $ 6,950   |

If this information were used for planning, Shannonville Cabinets would choose the following production plan with the following profits.

**Shannonville Cabinets**
**Summary of Optimal Solution**
**Maximize Contribution Margin Objective—Crude Costing System**

| Income          | $2,576,947    |                |              | Product | Units   |
|-----------------|---------------|----------------|--------------|---------|---------|
|                 |               |                |              | C1      | 0.0     |
| Sales (net)     | $112,298,930  |                |              | C2      | 1,772.8 |
| Flexible costs  | $95,066,768   |                |              | C3      | 1,791.4 |
| Capacity costs  | $2,100,000    |                |              | C4      | 0.0     |
| Other costs     | $12,000,000   |                |              | C5      | 2,214.4 |
| Interest costs  | $555,215      |                |              | Total   | 5,778.6 |

| Resource   | Units Available | Maximum Used |
|------------|-----------------|--------------|
| Scheduling | 2,600           | 2,600        |
| Moving     | 3,000           | 1,625        |
| Setup      | 3,500           | 2,714        |
| Cutting    | 2,900           | 2,880        |
| Assembly   | 2,400           | 2,400        |
| Shipping   | 3,200           | 2,644        |

You can see that using this crude costing system has resulted in an opportunity loss of $547,980 because the cost data are obscuring product contribution margins.

You should not conclude from this example that a costing system that is more detailed—in this case—one that computes the cost of individual activities, will always give better results than a crude costing system, for example one that uses only one cost estimate. First, the cost of a detailed costing system may outweigh the opportunity losses saved by making decisions with that costing system. Second, the more detailed costing system may be incompetently designed and managed, resulting in costs that are even more misleading than those obtained by the crude system. However, in general, one would hope and expect that the value of improved costing will outweigh its costs.

## BUDGETING OPERATIONS
### Production and Resource Use

Once an organization has developed its short-run plan, it can project the operating and financial consequences of that plan over a short-run planning horizon, usually one year. In particular, planners are interested in developing estimates of cash flows and resource requirements so that they can arrange to meet capacity and financing requirements in a systematic way.

Based on the assumptions in this example and that sales will take place uniformly during the year, the table on page 44 shows the production plan chosen when the objective is to maximize short-run profit.

Note how the production plan provides details about resource use that are not obvious from the overall solution. For example, no resource is used to capacity in all months. This fact provides insights to production planners that suggest a possibility of exploring other production or sales patterns that might even out the demand on resources. More generally, detailed production plans provide insights that would guide plans to provide for scheduling machine maintenance and holidays and for hiring and training personnel. Recall, however, that these are estimates based on the planning estimates of resource use and availability. If those estimates prove inaccurate, as inevitably they will, the actual results will differ from the plan.

### Cash Flows

A major item of interest in short-term planning is the projection of cash flows expected to result from the production plan. Planners use cash flow projections to identify when they will have excess cash to invest in short-term income opportunities or when they will have to rely on short-term financing such as a bank loan or line of credit to meet the cash needs from operations.

Suppose that Shannonville Cabinets expects that sales collections will be made as follows:

1. Collected in the month of sale: 65%
2. Collected in the month following the month of sale: 20%
3. Collected in the second month following the month of sale: 10%
4. Never collected: 5%

Total dollar sales in November and December of the previous year were $3,000,000 and $5,000,000, respectively. With these assumptions, we can compute the statement on page 45 of projected (pro forma) cash flows that follow from the optimal production plan.

Note that this cash flow projection and financing plan maintains the minimum cash balance at $50,000, as required. The line of credit balance increases in the period January through May, decreases in June and July, then increases during the period August through November, and then decreases in December. The chronic positive balance in the line of

## SCHEDULE OF MONTHLY RESOURCE USE

| | SCHEDULING | MOVING | SETUP | CUTTING | ASSEMBLY | SHIPPING |
|---|---|---|---|---|---|---|
| Production C1 | 2 | 7 | 3 | 3 | 2 | 4 |
| Production C2 | 4 | 3 | 4 | 6 | 5 | 4 |
| Production C3 | 5 | 2 | 6 | 4 | 3 | 7 |
| Production C4 | 3 | 5 | 7 | 2 | 4 | 2 |
| Production C5 | 6 | 4 | 5 | 6 | 5 | 3 |
| Cost per unit of capacity used | 180 | 300 | 780 | 900 | 720 | 240 |
| Capacity costs | $70,000 | $170,000 | $260,000 | $800,000 | $650,000 | $150,000 |

| | JAN | FEB | MARCH | APRIL | MAY | JUNE | JULY | AUG | SEPT | OCT | NOV | DEC |
|---|---|---|---|---|---|---|---|---|---|---|---|---|
| **Sales and Production Plan** | | | | | | | | | | | | |
| C1 sales | 249.4 | 249.4 | 249.4 | 249.4 | 0.0 | 0.0 | 0.0 | 0.0 | 249.4 | 249.4 | 249.4 | 249.4 |
| C2 sales | 0.0 | 0.0 | 0.0 | 0.0 | 0.0 | 0.0 | 221.7 | 221.7 | 221.7 | 221.7 | 221.7 | 221.7 |
| C3 sales | 256.0 | 256.0 | 256.0 | 256.0 | 256.0 | 256.0 | 0.0 | 0.0 | 0.0 | 0.0 | 0.0 | 0.0 |
| C4 sales | 0.0 | 0.0 | 0.0 | 0.0 | 0.0 | 0.0 | 0.0 | 0.0 | 0.0 | 0.0 | 0.0 | 0.0 |
| C5 sales | 0.0 | 0.0 | 0.0 | 0.0 | 0.0 | 821.4 | 0.0 | 0.0 | 0.0 | 0.0 | 0.0 | 821.4 |
| C1 production | 249.4 | 249.4 | 249.4 | 249.4 | 0.0 | 0.0 | 0.0 | 0.0 | 249.4 | 249.4 | 249.4 | 249.4 |
| C2 production | 0.0 | 0.0 | 0.0 | 0.0 | 0.0 | 0.0 | 221.7 | 221.7 | 221.7 | 221.7 | 221.7 | 221.7 |
| C3 production | 256.0 | 256.0 | 256.0 | 256.0 | 256.0 | 256.0 | 0.0 | 0.0 | 0.0 | 0.0 | 0.0 | 0.0 |
| C4 production | 0.0 | 0.0 | 0.0 | 0.0 | 0.0 | 0.0 | 0.0 | 0.0 | 0.0 | 0.0 | 0.0 | 0.0 |
| C5 production | 136.9 | 136.9 | 136.9 | 136.9 | 136.9 | 136.9 | 136.9 | 136.9 | 136.9 | 136.9 | 136.9 | 136.9 |
| **Resource Use** | | | | | | | | | | | | |
| Scheduling units | 2,600.0 | 2,600.0 | 2,600.0 | 2,600.0 | 2,101.3 | 2,101.3 | 1,708.4 | 1,708.4 | 2,207.1 | 2,207.1 | 2,207.1 | 2,207.1 |
| Moving units | 2,805.2 | 2,805.2 | 2,805.2 | 2,805.2 | 1,059.5 | 1,059.5 | 1,212.8 | 1,212.8 | 2,958.5 | 2,958.5 | 2,958.5 | 2,958.5 |
| Setup units | 2,968.4 | 2,968.4 | 2,968.4 | 2,968.4 | 2,220.3 | 2,220.3 | 1,571.5 | 1,571.5 | 2,319.6 | 2,319.6 | 2,319.6 | 2,319.6 |
| Cutting units | 2,593.4 | 2,593.4 | 2,593.4 | 2,593.4 | 1,845.3 | 1,845.3 | 2,151.9 | 2,151.9 | 2,900.0 | 2,900.0 | 2,900.0 | 2,900.0 |
| Assembly units | 1,951.2 | 1,951.2 | 1,951.2 | 1,951.2 | 1,452.4 | 1,452.4 | 1,793.2 | 1,793.2 | 2,292.0 | 2,292.0 | 2,292.0 | 2,292.0 |
| Shipping units | 3,200.0 | 3,200.0 | 3,200.0 | 3,200.0 | 2,202.5 | 2,202.5 | 1,297.7 | 1,297.7 | 2,295.2 | 2,295.2 | 2,295.2 | 2,295.2 |

| | JAN | FEB | MARCH | APRIL | MAY | JUNE | JULY | AUG | SEPT | OCT | NOV | DEC |
|---|---|---|---|---|---|---|---|---|---|---|---|---|
| **Inflows** | | | | | | | | | | | | |
| This month's sales | 5,430,568 | 5,430,568 | 5,430,568 | 5,430,568 | 3,161,270 | 14,907,101 | 2,882,734 | 2,882,734 | 5,152,033 | 5,152,033 | 5,152,033 | 16,897,865 |
| Last month's sales | 1,000,000 | 1,670,944 | 1,670,944 | 1,670,944 | 1,670,944 | 972,698 | 4,586,800 | 886,995 | 886,995 | 1,585,241 | 1,585,241 | 1,585,241 |
| Sales two months ago | 300,000 | 500,000 | 835,472 | 835,472 | 835,472 | 835,472 | 486,349 | 2,293,400 | 443,498 | 443,498 | 792,620 | 792,620 |
| Total collections this month | 6,730,568 | 7,601,512 | 7,936,984 | 7,936,984 | 5,667,686 | 16,715,272 | 7,955,884 | 6,063,130 | 6,482,526 | 7,180,771 | 7,529,894 | 19,275,726 |
| **Outflows** | | | | | | | | | | | | |
| **Flexible Costs** | | | | | | | | | | | | |
| Materials | 947,717 | 947,717 | 947,717 | 947,717 | 623,531 | 623,531 | 594,369 | 594,369 | 918,555 | 918,555 | 918,555 | 918,555 |
| Other flexible costs | 8,131,828 | 8,131,828 | 8,131,828 | 8,131,828 | 5,663,031 | 5,663,031 | 5,436,382 | 5,436,382 | 7,905,180 | 7,905,180 | 7,905,180 | 7,905,180 |
| Total flexible cost outflows | 9,079,545 | 9,079,545 | 9,079,545 | 9,079,545 | 6,286,562 | 6,286,562 | 6,030,752 | 6,030,752 | 8,823,734 | 8,823,734 | 8,823,734 | 8,823,734 |
| **Committed Costs** | | | | | | | | | | | | |
| Total committed cost outflows | 116,667 | 116,667 | 116,667 | 116,667 | 116,667 | 116,667 | 116,667 | 116,667 | 116,667 | 116,667 | 116,667 | 116,667 |
| **Other Costs** | | | | | | | | | | | | |
| Interest costs | 0 | 17,328 | 30,388 | 41,836 | 53,342 | 62,286 | 16,037 | 12,075 | 17,557 | 34,934 | 48,907 | 61,204 |
| Other costs | 1,000,000 | 1,000,000 | 1,000,000 | 1,000,000 | 1,000,000 | 1,000,000 | 1,000,000 | 1,000,000 | 1,000,000 | 1,000,000 | 1,000,000 | 1,000,000 |
| Total other costs | 1,000,000 | 1,017,328 | 1,030,388 | 1,041,836 | 1,053,342 | 1,062,286 | 1,016,037 | 1,012,075 | 1,017,557 | 1,034,934 | 1,048,907 | 1,061,204 |
| Total outflows | 10,196,211 | 10,213,539 | 10,226,600 | 10,238,048 | 7,456,570 | 7,465,515 | 7,163,456 | 7,159,494 | 9,957,958 | 9,975,335 | 9,989,308 | 10,001,605 |
| Net cash flow | (3,465,643) | (2,612,027) | (2,289,615) | (2,301,064) | (1,788,885) | 9,249,757 | 792,428 | (1,096,364) | (3,475,433) | (2,794,564) | (2,459,414) | 9,274,121 |
| **Financing** | | | | | | | | | | | | |
| Opening cash balance | 50,000 | 50,000 | 50,000 | 50,000 | 50,000 | 50,000 | 50,000 | 50,000 | 50,000 | 50,000 | 50,000 | 50,000 |
| Cash before financing | (3,415,643) | (2,562,027) | (2,239,615) | (2,251,064) | (1,738,885) | 9,299,757 | 842,428 | (1,046,364) | (3,425,433) | (2,744,564) | (2,409,414) | 9,324,121 |
| Opening line of credit balance | | | | | | | | | | | | |
| Money borrowed | 3,465,643 | 2,612,027 | 2,289,615 | 2,301,064 | 1,788,885 | 0 | 0 | 1,096,364 | 3,475,433 | 2,794,564 | 2,459,414 | 0 |
| Money repaid | 0 | 0 | 0 | 0 | 0 | 9,249,757 | 792,428 | 0 | 0 | 0 | 0 | 9,274,121 |
| Ending line of credit balance | 3,465,643 | 6,077,670 | 8,367,286 | 10,668,349 | 12,457,234 | 3,207,477 | 2,415,048 | 3,511,412 | 6,986,845 | 9,781,409 | 12,240,823 | 2,966,702 |
| Ending cash balance | 50,000 | 50,000 | 50,000 | 50,000 | 50,000 | 50,000 | 50,000 | 50,000 | 50,000 | 50,000 | 50,000 | 50,000 |

credit may suggest that Shannonville Cabinets should seek a permanent source of financing for its operating cash needs. The expectation with short-term financing such as a line of credit is that the line of credit balance will be zero at some point during the year.

## SUMMARY

In this chapter we have introduced the notion of short-term planning. We have studied

1. How capacity resources can constrain the short-run operating plan
2. Some planning alternatives that managers might choose
3. The financial and operating results from choosing a short-term operating plan

Choosing and projecting the short-run plan provide planners with several important insights. First, they identify what capacity resources are constraining production and provide a prediction of the increased profits that would result from increasing capacity. In this sense, the short-term production plan provides short-term guidance for focusing on improvement activities, such as reengineering and continuous improvement, and long-term guidance in the capital budgeting process that would project the benefit of acquiring more capacity.

Second, short-run planning provides some insight into the opportunity losses that might result from using inaccurate cost estimates to choose a short-term plan. Computing the opportunity loss from using inaccurate cost information to choose an optimal short-term production plan is impossible because the organization will never know its true costs. However, the sensitivity of the short-run production plan to changes in cost estimates will provide a sense of whether the production plan would change dramatically if cost estimates changed. Combined with the knowledge of the conditions when more accurate costing systems are likely to result in significant changes in estimated costs, a topic that we will consider in Chapter 5, planners can identify situations when cost studies would likely improve short-run profitability.

## ENDNOTES

1. For example, the flexible cost relating to moving would include the cost of fuel for forklifts and the cost of casual labor hired by the hour. The flexible cost associated with shipping would include the cost of packaging materials.

2. For now we are interested only in presenting the optimal plan under different planning assumptions. Later, we will develop the details of where the plan numbers came from and will discuss the spreadsheet, so the interested reader will be able to verify these results.

3. The optimal solutions reported in the table titled Summary of Optimal Solution were found using Excel's solver tool, which finds a noninteger solution. Readers familiar with programming methods will recognize that rounding optimal noninteger solutions to integer solutions will not guarantee optimal integer results. However, we have adopted this approach in the interest of using a programming tool (Excel) that is likely to be available to the greatest number of users. Moreover, it is possible that the solution found by Solver, which uses a searching rather than an optimizing algorithm to find the solution, may not be the optimal solution for the problem.

4. We used the Excel spreadsheet **amach2.xls** to develop this and the other plans described in this chapter. If you are interested in following along with this development you should ask your instructor for a copy of this spreadsheet. To begin, you might open the spreadsheet and try inserting different production values in spreadsheet columns E9 through E13. You need to compare columns C18 through C23 with columns D18 through D23 to verify that your tentative production plan has not violated any capacity constraints.

5.  Although the Shannonville Cabinets example considers only manufacturing constraints, in practice, organizations face constraints in all areas of their operations including supply, logistics, selling, and financing. In addition, organizations may experience subtler, often hidden, constraints relating to people and technological skills. We have chosen to focus on production constraints here because they are the most obvious to observe and the simplest to conceptualize. However, the general issues raised in this discussion regarding production constraints apply equally to all types of constraints.

6.  See Eliyahu M. Goldratt and Jeff Cox, *The Goal: A Process of Ongoing Improvement*, (2nd rev. ed). (New York, NY: North River Press, 1992).

7.  If planners follow the approach of expanding output until the first production constraint is encountered, a single resource will always constrain production.

8.  But, within its assumptions, the recommendations provided by the theory of constraints are both persuasive and defensible.

9.  These values were chosen randomly on the interval of plus or minus 20% of the value used in the previous examples, which we are assuming are the true underlying costs.

10. This damage is compounded when organizations use a cost-based formula—for example, cost-plus—to compute prices.

# ■ *PROBLEMS*

## *2-1    Scheduling a Bottleneck Resource*

The OPT Company produces two products, P and Q. The production processes for the products are shown below:

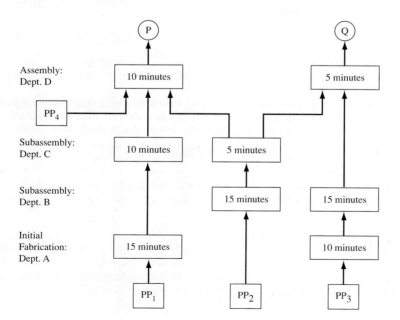

Product P sells for $140 per unit, and product Q sells for $120 per unit. Up to 100 units per week can be sold of P, and up to 50 units per week can be sold of Q. The unit costs of each of the four purchased parts are:

| PURCHASED PART | UNIT COST |
| --- | --- |
| $PP_1$ | $35 |
| $PP_2$ | 40 |
| $PP_3$ | 30 |
| $PP_4$ | 15 |

$PP_2$ is processed through Departments B and C and is required for the final assembly stage of both P and Q. The time (in minutes) required to process each component in each department is shown in the diagram above.

Each department—A, B, C, and D—has one worker, who is paid $18 per hour *worked*. The work in each department is highly specialized, so workers cannot be transferred from one department to another. The plant operates only one shift (40 hours) per week, and no overtime is permitted.

Committed cost is assigned to products at the rate of $36 per direct labor hour.

### Required
(1)  Compute the flexible and committed costs of products P and Q.
(2)  Supposing that productive capacity is allocated based on profit per unit, determine what production plan would apparently yield the highest weekly profits. What are the profits associated with this production plan?
(3)  What production plan maximizes weekly profits?
(4)  How, if at all, would your response to Requirement 3 change if workers were paid whether they worked or not?
(5)  Suppose that a costing study concludes that the committed cost of P is $10 and of Q is $33. How, if at all, would this information change your response in Requirement 3? Does this information have any relevance?
(6)  How, if at all, would your response to Requirement 3 change if workers are cross-trained and can work in any department?

## 2-2    *Scheduling a Production Plan*

Alberton Fisheries Limited (AFL) is an integrated fish products company. AFL operates a small fleet of trawlers. When the trawlers land their catch, AFL can sell the whole (round) fish or process the fish itself.

The processing operation begins by removing the head, tail, skin, bones, and insides of the fish (these byproducts are called offal), leaving two fillets. The fillets represent about 65% of the weight of the whole fish. All the offal is processed into a fertilizer whose net realizable value is zero. In fact, AFL began the fertilizer-manufacturing operation to provide a way of disposing of the offal.

The disposition of the fillets depends on the quality. There are three quality grades used. On average, 40% of the fillets are grade 1, 40% are grade 2, and 20% are grade 3. The grade 1 fillets are sold as fresh fish if there is a market; otherwise they are downgraded to grade 2. The grade 2 fillets are used to prepare gourmet entrées that are sold directly by AFL or, under other names, by other distributors. The process involves cooking the fish and then packing the fillet with other products into a container, which is then frozen. If there is an excess supply of grade 2 fillets, the grade 2 fillets are downgraded to grade 3.

The grade 3 fillets are used either to produce the processed line of products such as breaded fish sticks, or they are frozen into blocks to be stored for future use or sold.

The processing facility can handle a maximum batch of 120,000 pounds of fish. Any trawler load in excess of this amount has to be sold at whatever price it will fetch, because the excess fish would spoil before they could be processed.

The cost of processing a batch of fish has two components. There is a flexible cost of $0.40 per pound of whole fish processed. This cost is related entirely to the unloading and filleting operations and comprises wages paid to the factory workers and other flexible costs. In addition, there is a committed cost of $15,000 per batch processed; this cost is related to factory depreciation, administrative charges, and salaries.

For fish sold fresh, the only other costs beyond filleting are the flexible packaging costs, which average $0.20 per pound, and the flexible shipping and handling costs, which average $1.50 per pound. AFL is currently receiving $5.00 per pound of fresh fish.

The maximum amount of fish that can be cooked and frozen per batch is 50,000 pounds. The flexible cost of cooking and freezing is about $0.35 per pound of fish, irrespective of whether the fish will be sold as an entree or as a processed product.

For the entree products, the average flexible cost of additional items included with the fish is $2.00 per pound of fish packaged, and the flexible packaging cost is $0.40 per pound of fish. Because the entrees, the processed fish products, and the frozen blocks are sold FOB, AFL's factory, there are no shipping costs associated with any of these products. AFL is currently receiving $4.60 per pound of fish sold as an entree.

For the processed products, the average flexible cost of additional material included with the fish is $0.20 per pound of fish package, and the packaging cost is about $0.15 per pound of fish. AFL is currently receiving $2.20 per pound of fish sold as a processed food product.

The flexible cost of freezing the fillets into blocks is about $0.20 per pound. The current market price for frozen blocks is about $1.20. The production manager has advised the marketing manager that she can use about 10,000 pounds of frozen blocks next week and will be willing to pay up to $1.25 per pound for the blocks.

### Required

The captain of one of the trawlers has just radioed in that she will land in two days with about 140,000 pounds of fish. The marketing manager has advised you that he can sell a maximum of 30,000 pounds of whole fish, 25,000 pounds of fresh fish,

28,000 pounds of fish as entrees, 25,000 pounds of fish as processed, and 22,000 pounds of fish sold in frozen blocks. (The last amount does not include the 10,000 that the production manager has offered to take.) The marketing manager has also advised you that whole fish can be sold for $1.25 per pound. What is the optimal disposition of this catch?

## 2-3   *Planning the Conversion of Raw Materials into Finished Products*

Williams Lake Forest Products (WLFP) is an integrated products firm. Planning for the period's activities begins with the wood lot. The maximum amount of raw wood that can be harvested during this period is 12,000,000 units. Wood is harvested in batches of 1,000,000 units. The cost of harvesting is $400,000 per batch plus $3 per unit of wood harvested.

When the raw wood has been harvested, it is graded. On average, about 50% of the raw wood harvested grades out as sawmill-quality wood, 30% grades out as plywood-quality wood, and 20% grades out as pulp-quality wood.

Sawmill-quality wood can be sold, sent to the sawmill for sawing into lumber, or downgraded into plywood-quality wood. Raw sawmill-quality wood can be sold on the open market in batches of 1,000 units for $5,000 per batch.

The sawmill processes wood in batches of 100,000 units. The cost per batch processed in the sawmill is $80,000 plus $2 per unit of wood processed. The availability of saws limits the capacity of the sawmill to 3,000,000 units of wood, or 30 batches. Each 1,000 units of wood processed through the sawmill yields product that can be sold for $7,000.

The plywood-quality wood can be sold, downgraded to pulp-quality wood, or sent to the plywood mill to be made into plywood. Raw plywood-quality wood can be sold in the open market in batches of 1,000 units for $4,000 per batch.

The plywood mill processes wood in batches of 150,000 units. The cost per batch processed in the plywood mill is $90,000 plus $3.10 per unit of wood processed. The capacity of the peeling operation limits the capacity of the plywood mill to 3,750,000 units of wood, or 25 batches. Each 1,000 units of wood processed through the plywood mill yields product that can be sold for $8,000.

The pulp-quality wood can be sold or sent to the paper mill to be made into various paper and cardboard products. Raw pulp-quality wood can be sold in the open market in batches of 1,000 units for $3,000 per batch.

The paper mill processes wood continuously. Therefore, no batching operation occurs in the paper mill. The flexible cost per unit of wood processed in the paper mill is $1.15. The capacity of the paper mill is limited to 4,000,000 units of wood. Each 1,000 units of wood processed through the paper mill yields product that can be sold for $5,000.

The accompanying diagram summarizes the operations of WLFP.

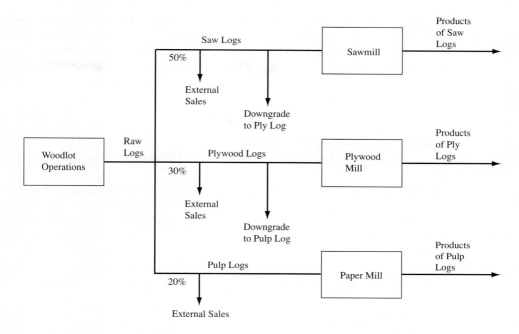

The Marketing Department has advised that the maximum number of 1,000-unit batches that can be sold during the upcoming period of each of the commodities is:

| | |
|---|---|
| Saw logs unprocessed | 600 |
| Plywood logs unprocessed | 700 |
| Pulp logs unprocessed | 500 |
| Saw logs processed | 3,000* |
| Plywood logs processed | 4,000 |
| Pulp logs processed | 5,000 |

*This number represents the maximum amount of sawmill products that can be sold based on processing 3,000 batches of saw logs.*

### Required

Determine the best production plan for the upcoming period.

## 2-4   *Choosing a Product Mix*

Sheet Harbor Chemicals (SHC) manufactures chemicals used in the paint industry. The process involves three departments.

Chemical A, which is purchased for $4 per liter, is processed through Department 1 in batches of 150 liters. Each batch of chemicals processed through Department A produces 100 liters of chemical B and 50 liters of chemical C.

Chemical B is sold for $15 per liter. Chemical C is used in Department 2 to produce chemicals D, E, and F. Department 2 processes chemical C in batches of 200 liters. Each batch processed through Department 2 produces 120 liters of chemical D, 50 liters of chemical E, and 30 liters of chemical F.

Chemical D is sold for $18 per liter. Chemical E is a waste product that is donated to the local municipality to be spread on gravel roads to keep down dust. Chemical F is a hazardous waste product that must be disposed of at a cost of $8 per liter. Alternatively, chemical F can be processed through Department 3 to produce chemical C.

Department 3 processes chemical F in batches of 40 liters. Each batch of chemical F processed produces 20 liters of chemical C. In the past, this operation has had a tendency to build up stocks of chemical C. The maximum storage capacity for chemical C is 1,000 liters.

The accompanying diagram summarizes the production activities at SHC.

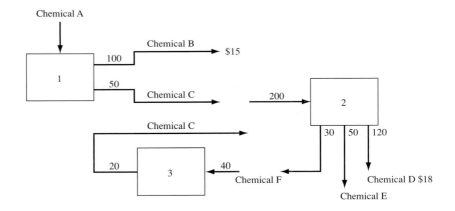

The sales manager indicated that sales of chemical B cannot exceed 40,000 liters in the upcoming period, and sales of chemical D cannot exceed 15,000 liters.

The production manager advised that 8,000 labor hours are available for the upcoming period. Workers are paid $15 per hour worked. The production manager indicates that the labor hours required for each batch in Departments 1, 2, and 3 are 12, 18, and 15, respectively. Moreover, because of constraints related to the mixing vats and storage, the maximum number of batches in Departments 1, 2, and 3 are 700, 120, and 70, respectively. The other flexible costs per batch in Departments 1, 2, and 3 are estimated as $300, $825, and $120.

### Required

Determine the optimal production plan at SHC for the upcoming period.

## 2-5

Yarker Computers manufactures workstations for the graphics design industry. At the moment, the company makes three computers with the following characteristics:

|  | COMPUTER 1 | COMPUTER 2 | COMPUTER 3 |
|---|---|---|---|
| Selling price | $12,000 | $11,000 | $10,000 |
| Flexible costs | $ 7,000 | $ 8,500 | $ 8,000 |
| Contribution margin | $ 5,000 | $ 2,500 | $ 2,000 |

Computers require three major activities during their assembly. These activities consume committed resources. The following table shows the amount of each resource consumed by each computer, the capacity available of that resource, and the cost of each unit of that resource (computed by dividing the total committed cost by capacity).

|  | C1 | C2 | C3 | CAPACITY | PER UNIT COST |
|---|---|---|---|---|---|
| Resource A | 3 | 4 | 6 | 24000 | $ 20 |
| Resource B | 5 | 6 | 2 | 36000 | $200 |
| Resource C | 8 | 3 | 2 | 32000 | $600 |

### Required

(1) Choose a production plan that maximizes the short-run contribution to profits.
(2) Assume that Yarker Computers can adjust capacity levels for the committed resources. What is the optimal production plan?
(3) Assume that Yarker Computers does not keep track of the individual costs of the three resource types. Instead, all committed costs are combined into one account. This costing system estimates the committed cost for each computer by a number that is the average of the committed costs computed for each computer under the more complex costing system. Assume, as in Requirement 2, that committed costs are flexible. What would be the effect on decision making of using the average costing system?

## 2-6

Princess and Division is a firm of professional accountants. The firm consists of 10 partners, 30 associates, and 25 staff members. The firm provides two broad types of service to their clients: consulting and auditing. Each employee can work on either auditing or consulting services. The two types of services differ in terms of the mix of professionals used:

**a.** Auditing work requires two partners, four associates, and four staffpersons for every hour of work demanded by the client.

**b.** Consulting work requires three partners, two associates, and two staffpersons for each hour of work demanded by the client.

Princess and Division treats staff costs as committed costs. Partners earn, on average, $140,000 per year and work about 2800 hours. Associates earn, on average, $50,000 per year and work about 2000 hours. Staff members earn, on average, $20,000 per year and work about 1900 hours.

In addition to staff costs, Princess and Division has other committed costs amounting to $1,000,000 per year. These other committed costs are allocated to jobs based on employee hours worked using a rate equal to the committed cost divided by employee hours available. Princess and Division has other flexible costs, which are estimated as

a. $3 per hour of partner time worked
b. $12 per hour of associate time worked
c. $7 per hour of staff time worked

Princess and Division has developed a blended cost per hour of client time demanded using the following approach:

| ITEM | PARTNER | ASSOCIATE | STAFF | TOTAL |
|---|---|---|---|---|
| Salaries | 140,000 * 10 | 50,000 * 30 | 30,000 * 25 | 3,650,000 |
| Hours worked | 10 * 2,800 | 30 * 2,000 | 25 * 1,900 | 135,500 |
| Flexible costs | 10 * 2,800 * 3 | 30 * 2,000 * 12 | 25 * 1,900 * 7 | 1,136,500 |
| Other costs | | | | 1,000,000 |
| Total costs | | | | 5,786,500 |
| Blended cost per hour | | | | $42.70 |
| Audit cost per hour | 2 * 42.70 | 4 * 42.70 | 4 * 42.70 | $427.05 |
| Consulting cost per hour | 3 * 42.70 | 2 * 42.70 | 2 * 42.70 | $298.93 |

The market rate is $510 per client hour demanded for audit services and $340 per client hour demanded for consulting services.

For the upcoming year Princess and Division expects that demand will exceed capacity for both types of services. Therefore, Princess and Division is faced with the need to decide the optimal mix of jobs to offer.

### Required

(1) Using the blended cost calculation, what is the optimal short-run production mix?
(2) What do you think is the optimal short-run production mix?
(3) Princess and Division has an associated firm—Johnson and Union—that will hire any Princess and Division employee at an hourly rate equal to that employee's annual salary divided by the annual hours worked. The $1,000,000 costs of Princess and Division remain committed. What is the optimal allocation of partner, associate, and staff hours under these conditions?
(4) Continuing the assumptions of Requirement 3, suppose that Princess and Division faces a demand for audit services of 1200 client hours each month in January through April inclusive and 600 client hours each month for the rest of the year. Princess and Division faces a demand for consulting services of 400 client hours each month. Assume also that the maximum amount of time that each person can work each month is 10% of the total annual hours, subject to the condition that total hours worked for the year cannot exceed the indicated number of annual work hours. What is the optimal allocation of partner, associate, and staff hours under these conditions?

# ■ *CASES*

## Choosing a Product Mix* (C. Horngren)

Maria Jones has just earned a university degree in management. She has taken the position of assistant to the president at Roseville Engineering, which manufacturers tungsten carbide drill steels for the gold-mining industry.

Roseville Engineering manufacturers two types of drill steels. One has a steel rod of $\frac{3}{4}$-inch diameter and the other a diameter of 1 inch. The manufacturing takes place in three departments. In the tip-fabricating department, tungsten carbide tips are manufactured from powered wolfram. In the steel-forging department, the steel rods are slotted and prepared for the insertion of the tips. The assembly department puts the tips and steel rods together in a brazing process.

Each department has two severe general capacity limits. The first constraint prohibits further capital expenditure because of a very weak liquid position arising from past losses; the second is the local labor situation, which makes the hiring of more labor, or using overtime, virtually impossible. The capacity of each department is as follows:

Tip fabricating (Dept. A)   200,000 hours
Steel forging (Dept. B)   275,000 hours
Assembly (Dept. C)   350,000 hours

The treasurer has just completed the budget for the forthcoming year. Because of the renewed confidence in gold, the company is expected to operate at full capacity.

The treasurer has produced the following profit analysis of the two products, on which a major production decision was based:

|  | $\frac{3}{4}$-INCH | 1-INCH |
|---|---|---|
| Selling price | $60.00 | $70.00 |
| Flexible Costs |  |  |
| Tungsten carbide | 2.00 | 3.00 |
| Steel | 3.00 | 4.00 |
| Department A Labor | 5.00 | 4.00 |
| Department B Labor | 8.00 | 12.00 |
| Department C Labor | 7.50 | 5.00 |
| Flexible other factory & selling | 4.00 | 6.00 |
| Committed Costs |  |  |
| Committed factory & selling | 19.00 | 22.00 |
| Total costs | 48.50 | 56.00 |
| Profit | $11.50 | $14.00 |

The market survey performed by the sales manager showed that the company could sell as many of either type of rod as it could produce. However, the sales manager urged that the needs of three of the big gold mines must be satisfied in full, even though doing so meant producing a large number of the $\frac{3}{4}$-inch rods, which had less profit than the 1-inch rods. The quantities required by these three gold mines amounted to 200,000 $\frac{3}{4}$-inch rods and 200,000 1-inch rods.

Because the 1-inch rods are more profitable than the $\frac{3}{4}$-inch rods, the treasurer suggested that the remaining capacity be used to produce 1-inch rods. Based on this plan, the treasurer produced the following budgeted income statement for the forthcoming year.

Sales are expected to occur evenly throughout the year.

|  | $\frac{3}{4}$-INCH | 1-INCH |
|---|---|---|
| Sales (in units) | 200,000 | 233,333 |
| Sales (in dollars) | $12,000,000 | $16,333,310 |
| Flexible costs | 5,900,000 | 7,933,322 |
| Committed costs | 3,800,000 | 5,133,326 |
| Total costs | 9,700,000 | 13,066,648 |
| Profit | $2,300,000 | $3,266,662 |

Jones, as her first assignment, is asked by the president to comment on the budgeted income statement. Specifically, the president feels that capacity might be better used with a different sales mix. He wants to know just how much it is costing the company in lost profits to supply the full needs of the three big gold-mining customers. He feels that it might be more profitable to produce only the 1-inch rods.

Jones gathers the following additional information before making her recommendations: Wolfram is purchased at $10 per kilogram (1,000 grams). The $\frac{3}{4}$-inch tips use an average of 200 grams, and the 1-inch tips 300 grams. The special alloy steel costs $4,000 per 2,000 pounds. The $\frac{3}{4}$-inch rods use 1.5 pounds, and the 1-inch rods 2 pounds. Direct-labor costs per hour follow:

| Department A | $20.00 |
|---|---|
| Department B | $16.00 |
| Department C | $10.00 |

Tip fabricating (Department A) is a skilled process. The small tips require detailed work. Owing to the nature of the work, the labor is considered committed because it would be difficult to replace. Committed factory and selling costs have been allocated using the cost drivers thought to explain their behavior.

### Required

If you were Jones, what would be your recommendations to the president?

---

*This problem is adapted from a problem prepared by C. Horngren for *Cost Accounting*, 5th ed. (Prentice Hall, 1982).

# CALIFORNIA PRODUCTS CORPORATION: ANALYZE PRODUCT PROFITABILITY WITH MACHINE CONSTRAINTS AND COMMITTED AND FLEXIBLE COSTS* (F. KOLARITSCH, ADAPTED)

### History

Several members of the Black family started the California Products Corporation in 1985. From 1985 to 1990, Product I was the only product produced, and, although profits were not high, they were sufficient to satisfy the family stockholders.

During 1990, the management of the California Products Corporation, mostly members of the Black family, decided to change from absorption costing to direct costing (flexible costing) upon the advice of a consulting firm. Product J was started into the production line in 1990 and Product K was started in 1994.

Since 1990, the company had losses or very small profits. The profit and loss statement for 1996 (see Table 1), shows that the company broke even during that year. At the board meeting, held shortly after the financial statements for 1996 were released, optimism was voiced concerning the future profit prospects of the company. The reasons given for this optimism were as follows:

1. Products J and K, it was believed, had overcome start-up troubles and finally found acceptance by the public.
2. Products J and K are both high contribution margin products (see Table 4).
3. During 1996 some overtime had been incurred, which it was claimed, cut into profits. It was anticipated that overtime would not be incurred next year.
4. The sales force had finally become convinced of the necessity of pushing Product K because of its high contribution margin.

The profit and loss statement for the year 1997 (see Table 2) was anything but encouraging to the management of the California Products Corporation. The company sustained a loss during that year and, paradoxically, had a considerable backlog of unfilled orders. The overtime was not eliminated, although the overall production in units of output decreased by 80,000 units (see Table 5).

The board meeting that followed the release of the 1997 financial statements was unfriendly, and everyone accused everyone else of incompetence. Without producing any evidence, the vice president in charge of sales accused the production people of gross inefficiency. Evidence was, however, introduced that indicated that sales had to be turned down because production could not supply the goods within the normal delivery time.

The vice president in charge of production accused the salespeople of pushing the wrong product. He pointed out that all the troubles started with the introduction of Product J and Product K. He also accused the vice president in charge of finances of "trickery" and stated that the contribution margin (see Table 4) was nothing except "fancy data" that would mislead everyone.

This meeting resulted in ill feelings among the various functional staff managers. The chairman of the board finally obtained their consent to call in a consulting firm to investigate what had happened and to suggest possible means of making the firm profitable.

An investigation into the flexible expenses, shown in Table 3, confirmed that they were correct and included a charge for normally expected overtime. The prices of the products had not been changed for several years, and there was no expectation that a price change was feasible in the next few years.

An investigation into the $821,000 committed expenses, shown in Table 1 and Table 2, showed that $440,000 was joint committed cost and that $381,000 was a separable committed cost attributable to the company's products as follows:

| | |
|---|---|
| Product I | $71,000 |
| Product J | 200,000 |
| Product K | 110,000 |
| | $381,000 |

An analysis of the joint committed costs of $440,000 showed them to be made up of

| | |
|---|---|
| Manufacturing expenses | $50,000 |
| Selling & administrative expenses | 70,000 |
| Depreciation: | |
| Machine A | 100,000 |
| Machine B | 20,000 |
| Machine C | 200,000 |
| | $440,000 |

Regardless of the above classification, the full amount of $821,000 was committed costs and had been properly classified by the company. Information gathered concerning the production process disclosed that each product had to be worked on by each of the three machines and that each of the three products required different machine times on the various machines. (The average production capacity of the machines is given in Table 6.)

It was estimated that each machine was operated about 1,800 to 2,200 hours during a normal year (practical capacity); that estimate takes into consideration things such as maintenance, repairs, and resetting. The maximum operational time one could expect from each of these machines during a given year without overtaxing them and incurring unreasonably high additional expenses was 2,200 hours.

**TABLE 1**  California Products Corporation Profit and Loss Statement Year 1996

|  | PRODUCT I | PRODUCT J | PRODUCT K | TOTAL |
|---|---|---|---|---|
| Sales | $1,860,000 | $1,584,000 | $412,500 | $3,856,500 |
| Flexible costs | 1,503,500 | 1,232,000 | 300,000 | 3,035,500 |
| Contribution margin | $ 356,500 | $ 352,000 | $112,500 | $ 821,000 |
| Committed expenses |  |  |  | 821,000 |
| Net profit |  |  |  | $ 0 |

**TABLE 2**  California Products Corporation Profit and Loss Statement Year 1997

|  | PRODUCT I | PRODUCT J | PRODUCT K | TOTAL |
|---|---|---|---|---|
| Sales | $1,620,000 | $1,008,000 | $742,500 | $3,370,500 |
| Flexible costs | 1,309,500 | 784,000 | 540,000 | 2,633,500 |
| Contribution margin | $ 310,500 | $ 224,000 | $202,500 | $ 737,000 |
| Committed expenses |  |  |  | 821,000 |
| Net loss |  |  |  | $ (84,000) |

**TABLE 3**  California Products Corporation Variable Product Costs

|  | PRODUCT I | PRODUCT J | PRODUCT K |
|---|---|---|---|
| Materials | $2.50 | $3.20 | $2.90 |
| Labor* | 1.30 | 1.50 | 1.20 |
| Indirect manufacturing expenses | .45 | .50 | .40 |
| Selling & administrative expenses | .60 | .40 | 1.50 |
| Total | $4.85 | $5.60 | $6.00 |

*Includes reasonable allowance for normal overtime.*

**TABLE 4**   California Products Corporation
Contribution Margins

|  | PRODUCT I | PRODUCT J | PRODUCT K |
|---|---|---|---|
| Sales price | $6.00 | $7.20 | $8.25 |
| Cost | 4.85 | 5.60 | 6.00 |
|  | $1.15 | $1.60 | $2.25 |

**TABLE 5**   California Products Corporation
Products Sold (in Units)

|  | PRODUCT I | PRODUCT J | PRODUCT K |
|---|---|---|---|
| 1996 | 310,000 | 220,000 | 50,000 |
| 1997 | 270,000 | 140,000 | 90,000 |

**TABLE 6**   California Products Corporation Average
Product Output Capacity per Machine
Hour* (in Units)

|  | PRODUCT I | PRODUCT J | PRODUCT K |
|---|---|---|---|
| Machine A | 330 | 240 | 150 |
| Machine B | 380 | 215 | 170 |
| Machine C | 540 | 330 | 90 |

*Each machine could work at any given time on one product only.*

### Required

**(1)** Choose the optimal production plan assuming that none of the committed costs is escapable even where there is zero production of one or more products.

**(2)** What is the value of an additional 200 hours of machine C?

**(3)** Determine whether your proposed solution in Requirement 1 remains optimal if the separable committed costs for products I, J, and K are escapable if there is no production of one or more of these products.

---

*Copyright © 1978 by The Ohio State University. Reproduced with permission.

# 3

# Assigning Resource Costs to Production Cost Centers

All cost systems start by assigning resource expenses to cost centers. Data from the organization's financial systems, either the general ledger or the budgeting system, categorize resource expenses by spending code: for example, salaries, fringe benefits, overtime, utilities, indirect materials, travel, telecommunications, computing, maintenance, and depreciation. Expense information from the general ledger is used to assign actual expenses recognized during the period to cost centers and subsequently to products.[1] The ex post assignment of actual costs is used to monitor actual efficiencies and profitability. Expense information from the budgeting system is assigned on an ex ante basis to develop standard costing rates that can be used, during the period, for decision making on consumption of services, pricing, and customer-related decisions. The design and structure of the cost system, however, remain the same whether budgeted or actual resource expenses are being assigned.

Companies organize the recording of resource expenses so that they can be classified by an organizational unit, let us call it a responsibility center, that has direct responsibility for the resource. For example, the expense of providing power would be recorded in the company's utility or power department, the expense of a maintenance worker and supplies and equipment used by the worker would be assigned to the maintenance department, and the expenses of a particular machine would be assigned to the operating department in which the machine is located.

Organizations typically have two types of departments: *production departments*, which directly produce or distribute the firm's outputs, and *service departments*, whose main output is to provide service to other departments. Examples of production departments include machining centers, assembly departments, data transport departments, and check processing departments. Examples of service departments include utilities, maintenance, purchasing, scheduling, production control, stockroom, materials handling, housekeeping, customer order handling, and information systems.

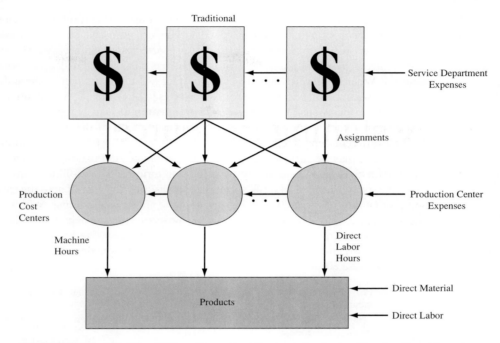

**EXHIBIT 3-1**  Traditional Two Stage Cost System: Assigning Service Department
Costs to Production Centers and Products

Traditional cost systems have the simple two-stage structure shown in Exhibit 3.1.
In the first stage, service department costs are assigned to production or operating departments. In addition, the costs directly arising in these production departments are directly
traced to these departments. Thus, after the first stage, all organizational expenses are assigned, either directly or through assignment from service departments, to production departments. In the second stage, shown in Exhibit 3.1, costs are assigned from production
departments to the products processed through those departments. The first stage of an activity-based cost (ABC) system has the same structure as a traditional cost system, though
instead of assigning service department resource costs to production centers, ABC systems assign resource expenses of both production and service departments to the activities
performed by those resources.

In this chapter, we discuss the first-stage process, the assignment of resource expenses to production departments. In Chapter 4, we expand the discussion to ABC systems, in which many resource expenses get assigned to activities as well as to production
cost centers. We will also discuss, in Chapter 4, the second-stage process, in which production department and activity costs are assigned to products.

## WHY ASSIGN SERVICE DEPARTMENT COSTS?

Service department costs are assigned to production departments for two purposes: (1)
cost control and efficiency and (2) reassignment to products that flow through the produc-

tion departments. For this chapter, we will focus on the cost control and efficiency story. In assigning costs for this purpose, it will be important, as we shall see, to distinguish costs that are short-term variable (these are costs associated with flexible resources) from costs that are fixed in the short term (that is, the costs associated with committed resources). When we turn to activity-based costing (ABC) in Chapter 4, these distinctions become less important because the role for ABC is to direct managers' attention to actions that influence decisions about both flexible and committed resources. Also, systems for cost control and efficiency require accurate measurements of the resources supplied and used by different departments in an organization. For the ABC system, estimates of resources used may be sufficient to guide managerial decision making. In general, companies need both types of systems: systems for monitoring and controlling short-term spending and expenses as well as ABC systems for measuring the cost of activities and the cost and profitability of products, services, customers, and business units.[2] With these differences articulated, we can now concentrate on assigning support department costs for operational control purposes: that is, to promote cost control and efficiency.

The assignment of service department costs to production departments promotes cost control and efficiency by:

1. Providing incentives for efficient performance by the managers of the service departments
2. Motivating prudent use of the outputs from service departments by the managers of production departments

If the costs of using an internal service department are not assigned to user groups, a number of negative consequences can occur. First, more of the service may be demanded by user groups than it is economically reasonable to supply. Without incurring any charge for using a service department's resources, a user could attempt to use the service up to the point at which the marginal benefit is zero. Naturally, this would be well beyond the optimal usage, where the marginal benefit from the service equals the marginal cost of supplying it.

Second, without assigning the cost of the output from a service department, we cannot determine whether the service department is operating efficiently. In the absence of prices charged to profit-conscious departmental managers, the service department must be treated as a discretionary expense center. The budgeted costs, obtained from historical experience, may offer no guarantee that the department is operating efficiently. Also, no signals are available to determine the optimal scale or size of the service department. At times of financial stringency, the size of the service department may be contracted to reduce operating expense. This curtailment of activity may not be desirable if it restricts or downgrades the performance of production departments that would be willing to pay for additional amounts of the service.

Third, if a service department's output is not priced, little guidance exists on whether the firm should continue to supply the service internally. For many service activities, firms have the option to purchase the service externally. For example, utilities, data processing, maintenance, housekeeping, legal, industrial engineering, and security can be either supplied internally or purchased externally. Without a price system to compare relative costs, it may not be obvious when an internal service center is more expensive than external alternatives, because of either internal inefficiencies or an uneconomically small scale of operation.

Finally, if service department costs are not assigned to user departments, managers will have little guidance about the level of service to be provided or demanded. A service department may wish to avoid complaints from users and satisfy them by providing service of excellent quality, based on acquisition of sufficient resources to provide the best and most responsive service possible. If user departments were made to see the cost of receiving this level of service, they might opt for a more economical service level—functional, without frills, and less expensive. But without the incentives and signals emanating from costing the output of a service department, a user department has little opportunity to communicate its preferences on the cost versus service level dimension.

By assigning costs for the output of a service department, we can overcome these four difficulties. Managers of consuming departments who are assigned costs from service departments, based on the quantity and quality of services they receive, will:

1. Exercise more control over the consumption of that output in their departments
2. Compare the costs of using the internal service department with the costs of comparable services purchased outside the firm
3. Attempt to communicate to the service department the quality level of services desired, including showing their willingness to pay more to receive higher-quality service or to accept lower quality in order to pay less

Managers of service departments whose costs are transferred to user departments become aware that the cost assignment will be reviewed critically by profit-conscious departmental and divisional managers; hence, service department managers will be motivated to keep departmental costs down. They may become more entrepreneurial and innovative as they attempt to provide a level and quality of service that will be demanded by user departments. Thus, the service department managers become more responsive to the demands of user groups rather than offering service on a take-it-or-leave-it basis.

We have been focusing on the assignment of service department costs to control the demand and supply of the output from a service department. In principle, the prices could be determined by reference to potential outside suppliers of these services. This possibility will be discussed in Chapter 9 on transfer pricing. Using externally referenced prices would treat service departments as profit centers and, if carried to its logical conclusion, would allow revenue-producing centers the choice of acquiring the service either from the internal service department or from an outside supplier. Typically, however, the charges for use of internal service departments are based on the budgeted or actual costs of these departments, not on market-based prices. We will develop the methods for assigning the **costs** of service departments throughout this chapter. Consideration of a market-referenced pricing system will be deferred to the transfer price discussion in Chapter 9.

## MEASURING COSTS OF USING SERVICE DEPARTMENTS

For cost control and efficiency considerations, service department costs should be *attributed* not allocated to operating departments. **Attribution** is the process of assigning a cost that is unambiguously associated with a particular cost object to that particular cost object. For example, consider the costs of a Power Department that a company maintains to generate its internal power needs. If some department of the company has special power needs, requiring expensive transformers and distribution equipment that are not used by any other unit of the firm, then the costs of those transformers and distribution equipment can be attributed to that department.[3]

Even when an asset is not specifically designated to a particular production department, the output from that asset can still be attributed to operating departments. In this case, we need to choose a measure of activity to cost and charge for a service department's output. In the case of the Power Department, if each production department has a meter that records the consumption of electricity, then the cost of the output supplied by the Power Department can be unambiguously attributed to the production departments on the basis of metered usage. Other examples include the number of purchase orders filled for a purchasing department and hours of maintenance supplied for the labor component of a maintenance department. If a service department provides different kinds of services, then it must define a separate activity for each type of service so that the cost of using of each type of resource can be attributed on the basis of the demands for that resource category; for example, with a centralized computing resource, separate charges could be incurred for central processing unit hours, disk-memory storage, pages of output printed, and connect time.

## AVOID ESTIMATES AND ALLOCATIONS FOR COST CONTROL

Costs that cannot be attributed directly are usually common to several departments and must be *allocated* to cost objects. **Allocation** is the process of assigning a resource cost to a department or a product when a direct measure does not exist for the quantity of the resource consumed by the department or product. Service department costs must be allocated when direct measurement of the output from a production department is not available. Allocation requires the use of surrogate not direct measures: for example, machine horsepower for charging utility expenses to unmetered departments, square footage occupied for housekeeping expenses, total direct costs for a controller's department, or direct-labor hours for many categories of factory overhead costs.

Direct measures may not exist for assigning the costs of these expenses because the cost of obtaining such measures, such as by metering individual production departments or by monitoring the amount of time the housekeeping staff spends in each department, greatly exceeds any potential benefit from using these direct measures. For example, in a site with a central power station and multiple plants on the site, an energy meter may exist only for each factory but not for individual departments within the factories. In this case, we cannot measure or control the usage of energy at the individual production department level. The costs of the central power station could be *allocated* to individual departments, using a surrogate allocation base such as the horsepower of machines within each department multiplied by estimated machine hours worked, but such a process is not valid for cost control or efficiency purposes. It would be like a bowling establishment that could measure only the total number of pins knocked down across all its lanes but not how many were knocked down at each individual lane. The proprietor could report the average number of pins knocked out at each lane, say 8.356, but this number would be of little significance for assessing the performance of individual bowlers.

The assignment of service department costs to producing departments for cost control and efficiency considerations requires an accurate measurement of the consumption of service department resources by each user department. Estimates and allocations can be useful for product costing and inventory valuation, but they are not useful when managers are attempting to control carefully the production and use of a shared resource. Because the assigned cost will be based on a measure unrelated to the demands the production department made on the service department, the cost will not be the direct consequence of actions taken by the manager or workers in the production department. Therefore, the cost signal cannot provide useful feedback on operating performance in the production department during the period.

How might a manager respond to a cost signal based on an arbitrary allocation of costs? First, she might ignore the signal entirely, perhaps the optimal action, recognizing that the signal does not provide any useful information about actions taken in the recent past or likely to be taken in the near future. Two circumstances may prevent the manager from ignoring the signal entirely. First, managers are frequently requested to respond to variances in their periodic operating report and to reconcile the signal with other records, such as from the production control system. Thus, some amount of the manager's time must be committed to responding to reported cost variances, regardless of their source or accuracy.

Second, if the report will be considered when evaluating the manager's performance, the manager will naturally attempt to influence the signal that does get reported. Because the signal, by assumption, cannot be directly affected by the manager's actions in the production department, the manager can influence the signal only by arguing about and negotiating the allocation procedure with other managers, of both production and service departments, or the manager's superiors. These discussions clearly detract from the amount of time the manager has to improve efficiency, productivity, and quality within her own department. By allocating a cost that does not reflect resource consumption by a production department, but continuing to hold managers responsible for such a cost, the company has signaled that managers of such departments should spend some amount of their time discussing and negotiating about allocation percentages with other managers.

## A FUNDAMENTAL COST ACCOUNTING EQUATION

A cost can be decomposed into a quantity and a price component. We can write a cost, $C$, as the product of a quantity, $Q$, of a resource multiplied by the unit price, $P$, of that resource:

$$C = P * Q$$

For example, utility expense can be represented as the product of kilowatt-hours (kWh) consumed (the $Q$ measure) multiplied by the cost per kilowatt-hour (the $P$ measure). When we referred to the existence of a direct measure on service department consumption, we meant that we have an accurate measure of the *quantity*, $Q$, of the service department's output (e.g., the number of kWh) consumed by a production department. Even with such a direct accurate quantity measure, the amount charged to a production department could still include estimates when the price measure, $P$, includes estimated or allocated costs. The price measure could include cost estimates from depreciation, floor space charges, and charges from other service departments.

We believe that the crucial issue, however, is not whether estimates are included in the price measure. More important is whether the quantity $Q$ is measured directly or whether it is a rough estimate based on a surrogate measure. With a good measure of quantity consumed, the price measure would have to be substantially in error before it would adversely affect managerial decisions. As long as operating managers are charged on the basis of an accurate quantity measure, they will probably not spend much time arguing about minor fluctuations in its unit price. Instead, they will act to use the quantity of the resource they consume efficiently and effectively.

If, however, the quantity $Q$ is measured inaccurately, such as when costs of service departments are arbitrarily allocated to operating departments on the basis of headcount, floor space, or direct labor hours, then operating managers are not rewarded or punished for the quantity of the demands they place on service departments. In this case, the use of a surrogate, unrepresentative measure of $Q$ has caused the cost signal to be ineffective in motivating operating efficiencies. Thus, cost attribution to operating departments can be performed when an accurate $Q$ measure exists. But we create an undesirable, perhaps dysfunctional, cost allocation when we use an arbitrary measure for $Q$ that does not represent the actual demands that an operating department makes on a service department.

In recognition of the arguments and distortions that arise when the output of a service department cannot be causally related to actions or demands of individual production departments, many companies divide their indirect and support departments into two categories: traceable and common. The expenses of the traceable service departments—such as maintenance, equipment supplies, setup, tooling, and energy—are assigned to production departments through either direct charging or using an assignment base (e.g., kWh, setup hours) that accurately represents the *quantity* of demands made by a production department on the service or support department. Thus, the expenses that are assigned to a production center include its own expenses (supervision, equipment depreciation and rental) plus directly traceable service and support expenses.

## ASSIGNING SERVICE DEPARTMENT COSTS

Consider a utility department with the following cost characteristics. At its normal activity level of 170,000 kilowatt-hours per month, the utility department has a budget for total operating expenses (including materials and supplies) of $13,600. For fluctuations up to 25% on either side of the normal activity level, the variable cost of the utility department is $0.02/kWh. The utility department provides power to three operating departments, which have the following standard and actual demands for power:

| | OPERATING DEPARTMENT | | | |
| --- | --- | --- | --- | --- |
| | 1 | 2 | 3 | TOTAL |
| Practical capacity (kWh) | 70,000 | 100,000 | 30,000 | 200,000 |
| Normal activity (kWh) | 60,000 | 85,000 | 25,000 | 170,000 |
| Actual activity in January (kWh actually used) | 60,000 | 50,000 | 27,000 | 137,000 |
| Standard kWh allowed for output actually produced in January | 55,000 | 50,000 | 28,000 | 133,000 |

During January, the utility department had actual operating expenses of $13,152.

At least three possibilities arise for assigning the monthly costs of the utility department to the three production departments.

1.   *Standard Average Cost* ($0.08/kWh)

A standard rate system would start by calculating, at the start of the month, an energy rate of $0.08/kWh, obtained by dividing the utility department's budgeted expense of $13,600 by the normal output of 170,000 kWh. The expenses subsequently charged to the departments for the month would be based on the hours actually used by each department multiplied by the standard rate of $0.08:

|  | ACTUAL KWH | ASSIGNED POWER COSTS |
|---|---|---|
| Department 1 | 60,000 | $ 4,800 |
| Department 2 | 50,000 | 4,000 |
| Department 3 | 27,000 | 2,160 |
| Total | 137,000 | $10,960 |

In this situation, the use of a standard rate results in only 80% of the utility department's expenses being charged out to operating departments. Although some of this underabsorption could be due to inefficiencies in the utility department (as we will calculate soon), most of the underrecovery of cost has been caused by Department 2, which demanded 35,000 fewer kilowatt-hours than normal.

To estimate the impact on the utility department's expected costs of working so many fewer hours, we first need to estimate the three departments' monthly fixed cost component. The costs of the committed resources of the service department can be estimated as:

$$\text{Committed costs} = \$13,600 - [\$0.02 * (170,000)] = \$10,200$$

Therefore, at an actual volume level of 137,000 kWh, its expenses should have been:

$$\text{Flexible budget} = \$10,200 + [\$0.02 * (137,000)] = \$12,940$$

The difference between the expected costs ($12,940) that should be incurred at an activity level of 137,000 kWh and the costs charged to departments ($10,960) represents a **volume variance** (unfavorable) of $1980.[4] This volume variance could have been avoided either by working at the normal volume level of 170,000 kWh or, alternatively, if the decline in usage could have been forecasted soon enough, by resetting the overhead recovery rate to:

$$\text{Revised overhead rate} = \frac{\$12,940}{137,000} = \$0.09445/\text{kWh}$$

The remaining part of the utility department's variance between expected and actual costs for January is due to the utility department's not cutting expenses sufficiently given the lower levels of demand during the period. Its actual expenses of $13,152 represents a spending variance of:

$$\text{Spending variance} = 13,152 - 12,940 = \$212 \text{ (unfavorable)}$$

The sum of the volume and spending variance (1980 + 212) equals the $2192 total variance between actual expenses and the amount charged to operating departments:

$$\text{Total variance} = \$13,152 - 10,960 = \$2,192$$

The standard average cost approach has the advantage of having all production and service departments know in advance the costing rate for using the output from the service department. The rate is unaffected by volume fluctuations either in aggregate or by the individual operating departments. The disadvantages are that:

1. Not all the actual expenses are charged out to operating departments
2. It is not obvious how to assign responsibility for the volume variance of $1980
3. The service departments have little information on the short-run incremental cost of using more or less of the service department's output
4. The standard rate is affected by expected utilization of the resource; that is, if expected utilization is far below the capacity of the committed resources, the rate will be biased upward

2. *Actual Average Cost* ($0.096/kWh)

Some companies wait until they know the actual expenses and actual activity levels for the period. They calculate a rate by dividing the actual expense of the service department by its actual output. In this case, the actual rate for January would be $0.096/kWh ($13,152/137,000), and no variance analysis is required because actual expenses are completely assigned to operating departments:

|  | ACTUAL KWH | ASSIGNED POWER COSTS @ 0.096 |
|---|---|---|
| Department 1 | 60,000 | $ 5,760 |
| Department 2 | 50,000 | 4,800 |
| Department 3 | 27,000 | 2,592 |
| Total | 137,000 | $13,152 |

Clearly, however, such a report would produce extensive argument and discussion among several of the operating department managers. First, Department 1 used exactly the hours forecasted for that department, yet the assigned power cost is $5760 rather than the expected (@ $0.08) charge of $4800. Second, Department 3, who worked 8% more hours than expected and therefore helped to consume some of the unused capacity, has a bill more than 20% higher than it would have anticipated. And Department 2, which had it worked at its normal 85,000 hours would have expected a power bill of $6800, actually sees about a 30% reduction in the costs assigned to it. So the department that caused the higher rates for everyone else, because of a 40% reduction in utilization receives a lower bill, and the other two departments, operating at or slightly higher than their normal capacity see sharp increases in the expenses assigned to them. Department 3 has used more than the normal number of kilowatt-hours (which should produce a favorable variance because variable costs are well below full costs) and has actually used less than the standard number of kilowatt-hours for the output it produced; yet it shows an unfavorable variance on power costs.

The manager of Department 3 has been penalized for two factors not ordinarily under that manager's control:

1.  The total amount of power consumed by the other two departments
2.  The unit price and efficiency of the utility department

These two uncontrollable factors produce the unfavorable variance shown for Department 3. Note that if Department 2 had used its normal amount of 85,000 kWh instead of the 50,000 kWh it actually used, the cost per kilowatt-hour would have declined significantly for all departments. The fixed costs of the utility department would have been spread over many more actual hours of service. In effect, by working many fewer hours than normal, Department 2 has generated an unfavorable price variance for itself and an unfavorable total variance for the other two departments.

Also contributing to the unfavorable price variance are the inefficiencies in the utility department amounting to $212, as calculated in the previous section, which is being passed on to the operating departments through a higher average hourly rate. The present scheme charges a manager for the costs of activities and inefficiencies in departments over which the manager has little or no control. The operating departments are also being charged on an average, rather than on a marginal, cost basis. Thus, their managers might be turning down profitable opportunities they might have accepted had they known that incremental power cost them $0.02 to $0.03/kWh rather than the current budgeted figure of $0.08/kWh.

  3.  *Flexible Budget for Short-Run Control of Operating Expenses*
An improved system for attributing service department costs would have the following characteristics:

1.  The level of activity and inefficiency in any single operating department should not affect the evaluation of other operating departments.
3.  Efficiencies or inefficiencies in the service department should be reflected in the evaluation of the service department but not in the evaluation of any operating department.
3.  The evaluation of the service department should not be affected by factors beyond its control, such as unanticipated fluctuations in the quantity of service demanded of it.
4.  The operating departments should be encouraged to expand the use of the service department as long as the incremental benefits to them exceed the company's marginal cost of supplying the service.
5.  The long-term costs of the service department should be paid by the users of its service. Usage of a service department to capacity under the pricing system can be viewed as a reliable signal to expand its capacity. If operating departments balk at paying long-run costs, the service activity can be contracted over time or perhaps made more efficient.

One relatively simple scheme achieves most, if not all, of these benefits. We consider a scheme in which:

1. Each department is charged for the actual quantities of service department output consumed but at a budgeted service department rate not at a rate computed on the basis of actual costs incurred in the service department.

2. Charges are separated into short-run fixed and short-run variable costs. Under this scheme, each operating department would be charged $0.02/kWh actually used. The $0.02 figure is the budgeted variable cost of the service department. Charging at this rate reflects the underlying cost driver (kWh) for the variable cost of the service department.

3. The cost of the committed resources (short-run fixed costs) are calculated on the basis of practical capacity of the resources not the expected utilization of the capacity in the forthcoming period.   ⟶ @ expected levels

The allocation of the $10,200 committed costs to the three operating departments alerts the managers of these departments to the cost of supplying capacity in the power department. It is a reservation price to have access to the relatively low-cost ($0.02/kWh) power on a variable-cost basis. It is also an estimate of the long-run component of marginal cost.

Long-run planning for the service department requires that its long-run costs be considered. For example, if we are estimating the future maintenance costs of a building about to be constructed, then we must consider the long-run maintenance costs. When considering a short-run decision, however, such as whether to undertake a particular maintenance job, we must consider the short-run costs and benefits of the maintenance. The key idea is that different costs are relevant depending on whether we are making a long-run or a short-run demand on maintenance services. These considerations motivated our recommendation that the fixed costs be assigned to production departments on the basis of planned use and that the variable costs in the pool be attributed to departments on the basis of the quantity of output actually used.

Two possibilities for assigning the committed-cost component are (1) proportional to practical capacity and (2) proportional to normal activity levels:

|  | DEPARTMENT | | | |
|---|---|---|---|---|
|  | 1 | 2 | 3 | TOTAL |
| Practical capacity (kWh) | 70,000 | 100,000 | 30,000 | 200,000 |
| Percent of total | 35% | 50% | 15% | 100% |
| Assigned committed costs | $3,570 | $5,100 | $1,530 | $10,200 |
| Normal activity (kWh) | 60,000 | 85,000 | 25,000 | 170,000 |
| Percent of total | 35.3% | 50% | 14.7% | 100% |
| Assigned committed costs | $3,600 | $5,100 | $1,500 | $10,200 |

In this example, little difference exists between the two assignment bases. In practice, however, we should use the base that most closely represents the demand for long-run capacity. This approach avoids the possibility of a death spiral (escalating rates) arising from short-term declines in expected utilization.

Under the proposed scheme, and assigning committed costs on the basis of practical capacity, the power department costs charged to the three operating departments in January would be:

*(Committed costs)*

*% of Practical capacity × 10,200*

→ *these are actual; different from standard*

| | | | | |
|---|---|---|---|---|
| Department 1 | $ 3,570 + | 60,000($0.02) | = | $ 4,770 |
| Department 2 | $ 5,100 + | 50,000($0.02) | = | 6,100 |
| Department 3 | $ 1,530 + | 27,000($0.02) | = | 2,070 |
| Total | $10,200 + | 137,000($0.02) | = | $12,940 |

The only variance recognized in the operating departments arises from using a nonstandard amount of power for the amount of output produced. In Department 1, 60,000 kWh were used instead of the standard allowance of 55,000 kWh. This difference generates an unfavorable usage variance of (5,000)(0.02) = $100. Department 3 shows a favorable usage variance of $20, because it used 1000 fewer kilowatt-hours than the standard allowance (1000 hours at $0.02 = $20). The utility department shows an unfavorable (U) spending (or efficiency) variance of

Actual costs − budgeted costs at actual volume = $13,152 − $12,940 = $212 (U)

→ *b/c based on actual usage*

Note that this method eliminates the influence of rate fluctuations and usage by other departments from the evaluation of services consumed by an individual department. Each production department manager should understand that utility costs being charged to the department are the direct consequences of activities undertaken by and under the control of people in that department. The managers in each operating department will be motivated to use the output from the service department for applications in which the benefit exceeds the $0.02/kWh short-run variable cost. But the operating managers will still see the capacity or longer-run costs of operating the service department through the assigned committed costs. The manager of the service department will be evaluated on a flexible budget so that measured performance will not be affected by fluctuations in demand for the service from the service department. Any inefficiencies in the service department will be reflected in a spending variance for the service department and not passed on as higher charges to the operating departments.

By using standard costs that reflect expected performance, consuming departments have a guideline for short-run planning decisions, and service departments will absorb their own short-run production efficiencies or inefficiencies. If, however, the service department, through its continuous improvement programs, generated sustainable improvements in efficiency and productivity, the users of the outputs from the service department should see these cost shifts so that they can respond to the new cost structure. The implication is that the standard costs should be modified when actual service department costs are known to have shifted, especially when the resource—such as energy—may be critical to the strategic success of the firm.

## SERVICE DEPARTMENTS NOT DIRECTLY SUPPORTING PRODUCTION OUTPUT

Organizations find that the costs of many service and support departments—such as scheduling, product engineering, plant administration, finance, information systems, human resources, purchasing, and materials handling—and plant-level expenses—including property taxes, building depreciation and insurance, and heat and light—cannot be directly assigned to production departments. There are two approaches for dealing with these difficult-to-assign expenses. One approach, unfortunately taken too often by too many companies, is to perform an arbitrary allocation process. The general support expenses are accumulated into a factorywide cost pool, perhaps called general factory overhead, and allocated to production departments using arbitrary measures such as:

- Direct labor hours
- Headcount
- Floor space

associated with each production cost center. We call such cost assignments arbitrary because the costs assigned to a production center may bear no causal relation to the demands by the department on the indirect and support resources. Therefore, decisions made by a production center manager, or employee, such as to reduce direct-labor hours or headcount (the resource drivers used in this arbitrary allocation process) cannot be traced back to a reduction in the demand for the indirect and support resources.

The second and much more preferable approach follows the discipline used to assign the more directly traceable costs to production departments. Each of the resources that are difficult to assign on the basis of the quantity of services demanded by production departments needs to be analyzed to (1) identify the activities performed by the resource and (2) determine the beneficiaries or recipients of the activities. As this process is followed, managers learn that two additional features must be added to the first stage, or resource assignment process:

1. Identify the primary activities, beyond conversion processes, performed for products by organizational resources.
2. Distinguish between primary and secondary activities.

We will discuss the role for activities not directly involved in conversion processes in Chapter 4, when we introduce activity-based cost systems. For the remainder of this chapter, we discuss the distinction between primary and secondary activities.

## PRIMARY AND SECONDARY ACTIVITIES

The examples presented in this chapter have assumed that all activities performed by support departments directly benefited production cost centers. Many support or service departments in companies, however, do not directly support the production of products or delivery of services to customers. These departments provide support to other departments, many themselves service and support departments, as well as to production departments that directly benefit products. For example, consider a human resources or a payroll department that benefits people throughout the organization, in both production and support departments. Or consider the resources that provide space, heat, light, and air-conditioning throughout the plant, to both production areas and support areas. How do we assign these expenses, and do all these expenses eventually find their way to final products?

To illustrate how to handle this situation, let us assume that the Williams Company has two production departments, one primary support department, materials handling, that coordinates the receipt and disbursement of materials to production departments, and several other support departments including plant administration, factory support, security, buildings and grounds, information systems, and human resources. Analysis of the activities provided by these various support departments reveals three principal activities:

- Provide space: for people, machines, materials, and products.
- Provide CPU cycles of information processing.
- Provide employee support (training, advising, etc.).

The resource expenses from various support departments assigned to the activity Provide Space include building depreciation, insurance, taxes, heat, light, air-conditioning, security, internal housekeeping, and maintenance of surrounding grounds outside the factory. The output from this activity is square meters of usable floor space.[5] The cost of this activity would then be assigned to the space occupied by production departments (a primary activity), the space used by the materials handling activity (another primary activity), and the space used by the information systems (IS) equipment and people and the human resources department (secondary activities). After the cost of the Provide Space activity has been assigned, the costs of the IS and Human Resource (HR) departments will include not only their own traceable department costs but also the assignment of occupancy costs. The HR department costs—(associated with the activity Provide Employee Support—have as the cost driver the number of employees.[6] Because the IS department has a significant number of employees, it would receive a cost assignment from HR that would include its pro rata share of HR expenses, which would also include an occupancy charge for HR personnel that it received from the Provide Space activity. Thus two of the secondary activities, Provide Space and Provide Employee Support, would assign some of their expenses to primary departments and some to other secondary activities, such as Provide CPU Cycles. At the final round, the costs in the Provide CPU Cycle activity (which include space and HR costs) would be assigned to production departments and other primary activities on the basis of the number of CPU cycles used by each activity. So, eventually, the expenses of secondary activities will ripple through and find their way to production cost centers.[7]

## ✕ THE NATURE AND PROBLEMS OF RECIPROCAL SERVICES

The next complication arises when reciprocal relationships exist among service departments. For example, a personnel department hires and oversees people for all departments in the organization; a utility department provides heat and light to all departments (including the personnel department and itself), a data processing department provides computer services and output to many service departments, a housekeeping department cleans all areas of a facility, and a maintenance department repairs machinery throughout a facility. With such interactions, an analysis that charges all the costs of each service department directly to production departments and primary activities does not give an accurate picture of cost dependency.

We have already described how to attribute the costs of each service department to all departments, both production and service, that use its output. But once the process begins, just what *the costs* of a service department include is no longer clear. Besides its own traceable costs, each service department will start to accumulate charges from other service departments from which it receives services, and these must be reassigned back to its user departments.

Three major alternatives have been proposed to deal with this interacting, or reciprocal, service department situation:

1. The direct method, in which all service department costs are assigned only to production or primary activities, and the use of service department costs by other service departments and their secondary activities are ignored.

2. The step method, which has the potential of only partially considering the reciprocal services. The step method was illustrated in the preceding section when first the space costs were assigned to human resources and information systems, and then the HR costs were assigned to IS. In this process, we ignored the reciprocal, or feedback, relationship between the secondary activities. For example, we ignored the assignment of IS costs to the HR and Provide Space activities and the assignment of HR costs to the people who participated in the Provide Space activity.

3. The reciprocal method, which models any reciprocal services exactly.

Until the mid-1970s, the direct method was virtually the only method known and used in practice. This situation changed when the Cost Accounting Standards Board (CASB) proposed that the reciprocal method be used instead of the direct method. The proposal instantly legitimized the reciprocal method as the preferred method. Subsequently, the CASB relented when companies complained that they had neither the expertise nor the computing capability to implement the reciprocal method.[8] The CASB then adopted the step method as an acceptable alternative to the preferred reciprocal method and indicated that the direct method was permissible only if it produced costs that approximated those produced by the step method.

During the period when they were reimbursed on the basis of costs incurred, hospitals had elaborate procedures for allocating their support department costs to units that delivered services directly to patients, such as in-patient care, operating rooms, recovery rooms, pharmacy, radiology, and pathology. The traditional step method for allocating support department costs began to be supplanted by the reciprocal method when computing resources became more available to health-care providers. Because the direct and step-down methods are straightforward and illustrated in most introductory textbooks, we will deal only with the reciprocal method, using the Fall River Company as an example.

## Fall River Company: A Numerical Example

The Fall River Company is organized into four units: Power, Water, Division 1, and Division 2. The Power Department supplies power, generated by steam, to the four units using its equipment and consumes water supplied by the Water Department. The Water Department supplies water to the four units from a private reservoir and its water purification equipment. Division 1 and Division 2 are engaged in the primary manufacturing operations of the firm. The firm's management has dictated that all service department costs must be distributed to the two production divisions.

During the past year, the activities of the two service departments (Power and Water) were as follows:

|  |  | UNITS OF SERVICE PROVIDED TO | | | | |
|---|---|---|---|---|---|---|
|  |  | POWER | WATER | DIV. 1 | DIV. 2 | TOTAL |
| Units of service provided from | Power | 20,000 | 30,000 | 80,000 | 70,000 | 200,000 |
|  | Water | 70,000 | 10,000 | 30,000 | 50,000 | 160,000 |

The traceable costs are $3,000,000 in the Power Department and $1,600,000 in the Water Department.

The reciprocal method of cost assignment operates in two steps. The first step considers all service department interactions and computes a charge rate for each service department. In the second step, the charge rate computed in the first step assigns the costs of the service department to each user in proportion to the service levels provided to that user.

The initial objective in the reciprocal method of cost attribution, then, is to find a charge rate for the service departments such that the total charges out of each service department equal the total charges incurred by, and assigned to, each department. In this problem, the required rates are $22.57 for the Power Department and $15.18 for the Water Department. (The details of the calculations are provided in Appendix 3.1.) Exhibit 3.2 demonstrates that these rates have the property of clearing the internal accounts.

The method of finding the charge rates for the two service departments involves constructing a system of simultaneous equations to represent the interactions between the departments and solving the equations to find the appropriate charge rates. The total cost

**EXHIBIT 3-2**   Fall River Company—Service Department Cost Assignment: Reciprocal Cost Method

|  | POWER | WATER | DIV. 1 | DIV. 2 |
|---|---|---|---|---|
| Initial cost | $3,000,000 | $1,600,000 | N/A | N/A |
| Assigned by power* | 451,400 | 677,100 | $1,805,600 | $1,580,000 |
| Assigned by water* | 1,062,700 | 151,800 | 455,400 | 759,000 |
| Assigned out[†] | −4,514,100 | −2,428,900 | 0 | 0 |
| Net cost assigned | 0 | 0 | $2,261,000 | $2,339,000 |

*Total service units consumed (the quantity measure) multiplied by the charge rate per unit.
†Total service units provided (the quantity measure) multiplied by the charge rate per unit.

to be assigned from the Power Department (called the Power Department's reciprocal cost, PDRC) is computed as

PDRC = initial cost incurred + (20,000/200,000) * PDRC + (70,000/160,000) * WDRC

where WDRC is the Water Department's reciprocal cost. Note that the reciprocal cost is computed by adding, to the initial cost incurred in the service department, amounts that reflect the Power Department's share of the reciprocal cost of all the service departments including its own.

The above equation cannot be solved because it contains two unknown variables, PDRC and WDRC. A second, and comparable, equation in the two unknown variables can be written for WDRC:

WDRC = initial cost incurred + (30,000/200,000) * PDRC + (10,000/160,000) * WDRC

In general, we would construct one reciprocal cost equation for each service department. The formulas can be simplified to:

$$(0.9) * \text{PDRC} - (7/16) * \text{WDRC} = 3,000,000$$
$$-(3/20) * \text{PDRC} + (15/16) * \text{WDRC} = 1,600,000$$

When these equations are solved, the reciprocal costs and the indicated charge rates can be computed. Fortunately, computer programs in common spreadsheet languages can solve large systems of simultaneous linear equations so that we do not have to do the calculations by hand.

## The Economic Insights of the Reciprocal Method

So far, we have developed what seems to be just another approach for assigning service department costs to production departments. What remain to be shown are the valuable properties of the reciprocal cost method.

It turns out that the charge rate per unit of service computed by the reciprocal method actually represents the cost of supplying the service to production departments and other service units. In our numerical example, assume initially that all the costs are variable with demand. If the total demand by the production divisions on the Power Department were reduced by one unit, the total costs in the system would fall by $22.57. This charge rate, therefore, represents the marginal cost of providing the service. It provides a reasonable benchmark for comparison with an outside quoted price. Specifically, if an outside utility offered to provide power at the rate of $21 per service unit, the bid could be accepted (because it is less than the inside cost of $22.57 per service unit).[9]

In general, neither the step-down method nor the direct method will compute sufficiently accurate service department costs when extensive interactions exist among service departments. The accuracy and relevance of the reciprocal method derive from its recognition of the reciprocal relationship of costs among service departments. Because the Power Department uses such a large part of the output of the Water Department, the cost of supplying an additional unit of power must reflect not only the direct costs incurred in the Power Department but also the indirect costs incurred in the Water Department.

## The Treatment of Committed Costs

We assumed, initially, that all costs were short-term variable. With the basic model in place, we can now abandon that assumption. But first we must develop two more insights from the information provided by the reciprocal method.

As we argued above, the primary reason for assigning variable and fixed costs separately arises from their different causal factors, or cost drivers. The cost driver for the flexible resources is short-run usage, whereas the cost driver for the committed resources is planned long-run usage. Therefore, to assign service department costs, we require a dual-rate system: one rate for the (variable) costs of flexible resources and one rate for the (fixed) costs of the committed resources. Because variable costs are directly attributable to the user demanding the service, it is economically sound and equitable (if that is a consideration) to attribute variable costs on the basis of the actual quantity consumed.

We assign, as described earlier in the chapter, the costs of the committed resources in proportion to the planned use of capacity they supply. If one division reserves 20% of the output of a facility, then that division should be assigned 20% of the committed costs of the facility. This principle is consistent with activity-based costing (as will be presented subsequently) and with economic arguments (not presented here).[10] This approach, called peak-load pricing, asks users to bear the system costs in proportion to their use of the facility when it is operating at capacity. It has been widely used in utility regulation in North America and Europe.

Thus, even interacting service department costs can be assigned by the approach described in this chapter. The costs of flexible resources in the service department will be assigned on the basis of actual usage, and the cost of committed resources will be assigned on the basis of planned usage.

## Make-or-Buy Decisions and Cost Assignments

If a service department in a reciprocal services situation is shut down, the number of service units purchased externally will be lower than the current production of the internal service department. When the units of service are purchased outside, the current reciprocal pattern of consumption is altered, because the remaining departments do not have to provide service to the external supplier. In the illustration, the Power Department currently supplies power to the Water Department and consumes water provided by the Water Department. Indirectly, then, the Power Department is consuming some of its own output.

The reciprocal method provides information about the number of outside units of a service that would have to be purchased if internal production were discontinued. In this example, if the firm discontinued internal production of power, 166,000 units of power would have to be purchased externally. If water production were discontinued, the firm would have to purchase 138,333 units externally. (Details of these calculations can be found in Appendix 3.1.) We can see, then, that the Power Department consumes 34,000 (200,000 − 166,000) units of its own output. If the power were purchased outside, this indirect consumption would be eliminated.

Another piece of information provided by the reciprocal method is a reciprocal factor for each service department. In this example, the reciprocal factor for the Power Department is 1.2048, and the reciprocal factor for the Water Department is 1.1566. The reciprocal factor for a service department tells us how much the total production of the service department will fall if the external demand on the service department is reduced by one unit.

With the knowledge of the outside units required and the reciprocal factor, we can now evaluate the make-or-buy decision. Kaplan[12] showed that the total variable cost avoided when a service department is shut down can be computed as

$$\text{Variable cost avoided} = \frac{\text{reciprocal cost for the department}}{\text{reciprocal factor for the department}}$$

If we apply this rule to the example, the variable cost avoided if the Power Department is shut down is $3,746,680.[13]

Next we must consider the fixed cost saved if the department is shut down. Suppose the power-generating facilities can be sold, and fixed costs of $2,000,000 are thereby avoided. The total of all costs avoided would be $5,746,680 (3,746,680 + 2,000,000).

Finally, we can compute the maximum price that we would pay to an external supplier. The external number of units required is 166,000, so the maximum price the firm would be willing to pay, per unit provided, to an external supplier is $34.62.[14]

## SPECIAL CASE FOR ARBITRARY ALLOCATIONS

This entire chapter has focused on analytic, causal methods for assigning indirect resource expenses to production departments. We have argued against arbitrary cost allocations that bear little relation between the consumption and supply of resources. One exception to this rule can be noted. Seemingly arbitrary cost allocations may be useful to force periodic managerial discussions and negotiations. For example, some corporations deliberately allocate all corporate overhead expenses to operating departments with allocation bases (such as sales dollars, headcount, or total costs) that have little to do with the consumption or causes of the overhead costs. Senior managers apparently want operating managers to be aware of centrally determined and controlled costs. Perhaps the fully allocated costs are meant to encourage more-aggressive pricing decisions by the decentralized managers (which may or may not be a good idea). But they may also serve to enlist operating managers' support in curtailing the growth of corporate expenses. Only by having all responsible managers see the costs of company planes, corporate headquarters' buildings and furnishings, and other such discretionary expenses may countervailing forces be set in motion to limit the growth and escalation of the costs.

For example, one study[15] examined why a high-tech company (1) assigned marketing expenses and revenues to the managers of product development departments and also (2) assigned product development expenses to marketing managers. The product development managers had no marketing authority and the marketing managers had no product development authority; yet each was held responsible for the actions of the other in a seemingly arbitrary exercise in allocating noncontrollable costs and revenues. The plausible and defensible rationale for this practice was to force active and continual dialogue among product development and marketing managers on the needs of the marketplace and the marketability of proposed products. In this case, the discussions and negotiations that accompanied the arbitrary allocation of costs and revenues were exactly the actions that the senior management of the company wanted to encourage.

To summarize, if we want operating managers to promote efficiencies, improve productivity, and learn more about the characteristics of production processes under their control, then we should send them accurate measures of quantities and good estimates of costs of input resources consumed. If such accurate measures do not exist, then arbitrary quantity measures should not be substituted. Doing so would, in effect, transform a desirable cost attribution into an undesirable cost allocation.

If, however, we want managers to spend much of their time away from their areas of direct responsibility and authority, in discussions and negotiations with other managers about each other's actions, then arbitrary allocations will motivate that behavior. A useful compromise between these conflicting objectives can perhaps be made. Any arbitrary allocation of costs should be done infrequently, say annually, to signal the need for occasional outside discussions and negotiations. Or, alternatively, the company can report to each operating department the total periodic cost of any common or joint corporate resource, without assigning, as the responsibility of individual operating department managers, arbitrarily carved-up pieces of these common or joint costs. The regular periodic operating reports, however, should be left relatively uncontaminated from data that do not accurately reflect actual resource consumption by operating units.

## SUMMARY

Assigning the costs of service departments to production departments sets up an internal market for the supply and demand of internally produced services. By charging for service departments' output, we can:

- Ration demand from user departments
- Provide signals on service department efficiency
- Facilitate comparison with externally supplied service
- Provide opportunities for price-quality tradeoffs

When charges for service department costs are determined, a user department's charges should not be affected by activity levels in other user departments or by inefficiencies in the service department. Also, fluctuations in demand by user departments should be charged on a marginal-cost basis. We have proposed the following scheme:

1. Assign any of the costs of a service department that are directly attributable to a specific organization unit to that unit.
2. Assign the remaining costs in the service department to cost pools based on the factor (the cost driver or quantity measure, as we have referred to it here) that causes each cost to vary in that pool. This approach results in the segregation of costs both by function and by whether they are fixed or variable.
3. Assign the costs in each cost pool to other organization units on the basis of accurate quantity measures of each organization unit's use, or consumption, of the cost driver.

When budgeted rather than actual costs are used to assign service department costs, cost shifts or inefficiencies will be isolated within the service department and not passed on to production departments.

A special problem arises when service departments provide service to each other as well as to production departments. In this case, the costs of the interacting service departments can be assigned using a simultaneous-equation technique (the reciprocal method). The reciprocal method is essential if we want an accurate estimate of the marginal cost of internally supplied service or when attempting to decide whether to replace an internal service department by purchasing the service externally.

## APPENDIX 3.1: THE RECIPROCAL COST PROCEDURE

This appendix provides the algebraic basis for the reciprocal service department assignment procedure described in the chapter. Begin by observing that the reciprocal process can be represented by a system of simultaneous equations defining the reciprocal costs. The equations for the problem discussed in the chapter are repeated here:

$$[(0.9) * PDRC] - [(7/16) * WDRC] = 3,000,000$$
$$[-(3/20) * PDRC] + [(15/16) * WDRC] = 1,600,000$$

These equations can be expressed in algebraic terms as

$$[I - A][B] = [C]$$

where the items in brackets represent matrices or vectors. Thus, in this case:

$$[A] = \begin{bmatrix} 2/20 & 7/16 \\ 3/20 & 1/16 \end{bmatrix} \quad [I] = \begin{bmatrix} 1 & 0 \\ 0 & 1 \end{bmatrix} \quad [B] = \begin{bmatrix} PDRC \\ WDRC \end{bmatrix}$$

$$[C] = \begin{bmatrix} 3,000,000 \\ 1,600,000 \end{bmatrix}$$

The [A] matrix indicates the usage proportions. The element in the $i$th row and $j$th column of this matrix represents the fraction of the total output of service department $j$ consumed by service department $i$. The [I] matrix is an identity matrix. The [B] vector is the vector of reciprocal costs. The [C] vector is the vector of variable costs initially recorded in each of the service divisions. We can solve for matrix [B] by observing that

$$[B] = [I - A]^{-1} [C]$$

where $[I - A]^{-1}$ is the inverse of matrix $[I - A]$, if one exists. This point, incidentally, is where the computer is useful. Functions that compute inverses are provided in most spreadsheet programs. In the case of the example in the chapter:

$$[I - A]^{-1} = \begin{bmatrix} 1.2048 & 0.5623 \\ 0.1928 & 1.1566 \end{bmatrix}$$

and

$$[B] = \begin{bmatrix} 4,514,056 \\ 2,428,915 \end{bmatrix}$$

The numbers on the main diagonal (the line running from the upper left to the lower right) of the $[I - A]^{-1}$ matrix provide the reciprocal factors that are useful for decision making. There is, by construction, one reciprocal factor on the main diagonal for each of the service departments. In the case of our example, the first factor, 1.2048, is related to the Power Department, and the second factor, 1.1566, is related to the Water Department. These are the reciprocal factors.

Dividing the reciprocal (variable) cost of a service department by its associated reciprocal factor yields the cost avoided if that department is shut down. Moreover, dividing the number of units of service currently provided by a service department by the department's reciprocal factor yields the number of units required if the service is acquired externally. The charge rate per unit of service provided by the service department is given by dividing the department's reciprocal cost by the number of units of service provided. Thus, the charge rate for the Power Department equals 4,514,056/200,000 = $22.57.

As we have seen in the example, the cost to be assigned to the production division equals the product of the service department's charge rate and the number of units of service provided to the division. The indicated assignment can also be obtained by extending the algebraic model developed above. Define a matrix $[D]$ such that the element in the $i$th row and the $j$th column represents the fraction of the total output of service department $i$ consumed by production division $j$. Then $[E]$, the vector of service department costs to be assigned to the production divisions, is given by

$$[E] = [B]^T [D]$$

where $[B]^T$ is the transpose of the vector of the reciprocal costs.

In the case of the example:

$$[B]^T = [4,514,056 \quad 2,428,915]$$

$$[D] = \begin{bmatrix} 80,000/200,000 & 70,000/200,000 \\ 30,000/160,000 & 50,000/160,000 \end{bmatrix}$$

$$[E] = [2,261,044 \quad 2,338,956]$$

This means that a total of $2,261,044 of the service department costs is assigned to Division 1, and $2,338,956 is assigned to Division 2.

The analysis can easily be extended to any number of service and production departments.

## ENDNOTES

1. As in Chapter 1, we use the term *products* to refer to all cost objects, which include tangible products (a box of cereal) but also services (a checking account) and customers.

2. R. S. Kaplan, "One Cost System Isn't Enough," *Harvard Business Review* (January–February 1988), pp. 61–66; also, "The Four Stage Model of Cost System Design," *Management Accounting* (February 1990).

3. And, to anticipate concepts that we will discuss in Chapter 10, not only the operating expenses of the assets but also the value of the assets themselves may be assigned to operating departments.

4. We will defer to the problem material at the end of the chapter the alternatives available for assigning this aggregate volume variance back to the individual operating departments.

5. In many factories, not all space is equally costly to supply. For example, in semiconductor wafer fabrication facilities the expense to provide cleanroom space is much higher than the expense to provide normal space. In such cases, the analyst should have at least two activities: Provide Normal Space and Provide Cleanroom Space. The Provide Cleanroom Space activity would incur much higher utility expenses because of the need to recirculate and filter air continuously. Similarly, space provided for warehousing raw materials and finished goods may be less expensive to supply and support than the temperature- and humidity-controlled space required for sophisticated electronics-controlled equipment.

6. Again, this treatment assumes that all employees demand the same time and other resources from the HR department. It would be more realistic, but more complicated, to allow for the HR activities to be more focused on some employees than on others. One could either construct a weighted HR service index to represent the complexity of demands by different individuals, or one could split what is now a homogeneous activity, Provide Employee Support, into two or more separate categories—Provide Complex Support, Provide Average Support, and Provide Basic Support—with employees associated with one of these three mutually exclusive activities.

7. Exactly the same procedure can and should be performed in the activity-based cost (ABC) systems, to be described in Chapter 4. With ABC systems, instead of tracing the costs of support activities just to production cost centers, the costs of support departments will be assigned as well to primary activities, those that directly benefit the production and sales of products.

8. Today, such capability is readily available on common spreadsheet programs running on personal computers.

9. Before outsourcing the power generation to such an outside bidder, the company might first see whether its internal service department can implement process improvements to lower the costs of supplying power below that of the external supplier. Also, the company should check that the quoted price is not artificially low—designed to get the business initially but subsequently to be raised once the company has dismantled its internal power generation department.

10. See, for example W. J. Baumol, "Optimal Depreciation Policy: Pricing the Products of Durable Assets." *Bell Journal of Economics and Management Science* (Autumn 1971), pp. 638–56.

11. R. S. Kaplan, "Variable and Self-Service Costs in Reciprocal Allocation Models," *Accounting Review* (October 1973), pp. 738–48.

12. (4,514,000/1.2048).

13. (5,746,680/166,000).

14. J. Dent, "Tension in the Design of Formal Control Systems: A Field Study in a Computer Company," in *Accounting & Management: Field Study Perspectives,* ed. W. J. Bruns Jr. and R. S. Kaplan (Boston: Harvard Business School Press, 1987), pp. 119–45.

## ■ *PROBLEMS*

### *3-1    Allocating Central Service Department Costs*

"I can't believe it. We just went through a study showing how my department could save money by using the central maintenance department. But the first month using this department shows that my costs are up more than 20 percent." Don Thompson, the general manager of the Delta Division of Ramo Products, had just received his monthly bill for maintenance services and he was obviously upset.

**TABLE 1**

| DIVISION | MAINTENANCE HOURS | PERCENTAGE | ASSIGNED COSTS |
|---|---|---|---|
| Able | 600 | 50% | $ 60,000 |
| Baker | 400 | 33% | 40,000 |
| Carter | 200 | 17% | 20,000 |
| Total | 1,200 | 100% | $120,000 |

**TABLE 2**

| DIVISION | MAINTENANCE HOURS | PERCENTAGE | ASSIGNED COSTS |
|---|---|---|---|
| Able | 600 | 42.9% | $ 55,700 |
| Baker | 400 | 28.6% | 37,100 |
| Carter | 200 | 14.3% | 18,600 |
| Delta | 200 | 14.3% | 18,600 |
| Total | 1,400 | 100% | $130,000 |

Before converting to the in-house department, the Delta Division had used outside suppliers for its maintenance services, at a cost of $15,000 per month. An internal task force, investigating the use of outside services that were also available internally, had found that all the maintenance needs of the Delta Division could be handled internally. At present, the maintenance department had unused capacity, and the additional services required by Delta could be supplied at an incremental cost of $10,000. After some assurance that his division's maintenance services could be supplied at this lower incremental cost, Don Thompson agreed to convert from external to internal supply of services.

After receiving a monthly bill for more than $18,000 for maintenance, Thompson demanded an explanation. Phil Johnson, the manager of the maintenance department, provided the following data. Table 1 shows the allocation of the monthly maintenance department costs of $120,000 to the three other divisions of Ramo Products, before handling Delta's requirements: As Johnson explained, "We have to charge out the costs of our division in some equitable manner. We've decided that an allocation based on hours supplied is as good as any." Johnson then showed (see Table 2) how the allocation to Delta was derived on the basis of incremental costs of $10,000 and the 200 maintenance hours provided to Delta.

### Required

(1) Comment on the method used by Johnson to charge for the use of maintenance in Ramo Products. Why does this method cause Delta's charges to increase from $15,000 to $18,600 per month?

(2) Suggest alternative methods for charging for the use of this internal service department that would provide better incentives for use of this department.

## 3-2 *Allocating Service Department Costs—Fixed and Variable; Actual and Budgeted*

"I get overcharged by the Printing Department each month," declared Bud Perles, the manager of the Greene Company's Advertising Department. "Even though my usage is down during the month, the total amount I have to pay keeps going up. The work done by our Printing Department is certainly high quality, but if these charges keep escalating, I'm going to start taking my business to outside printers."

The Printing Department of the Greene Company provides services to many departments throughout the company. The cost budget for the Printing Department at a normal volume of 800 service hours as well as the actual expenses for September (when 700 hours were actually used) appear below:

| | BUDGET AT 800 HOURS | | ACTUAL IN SEPTEMBER |
| --- | --- | --- | --- |
| | AMOUNT | FIXED (F) OR VARIABLE (V) | |
| Labor | $10,000 | V | $ 9,000 |
| Supervision | 2,000 | F | 2,000 |
| Indirect labor | 3,000 | V | 2,800 |
| Supplies | 11,000 | V | 10,500 |
| Depreciation | 6,000 | F | 6,200 |
| Rent | 4,000 | F | 4,500 |
| Total | $36,000 | | $35,000 |

Depreciation charged each month is a fixed percentage of the original cost of equipment installed in the Printing Department. The rental charge is an allocated share of total monthly building costs. The allocation is proportional to the space occupied by each department.

The cost of the Printing Department is charged to other users on the basis of average *actual* departmental costs during the month multiplied by the number of printing hours used during the month.

The Advertising Department of the Greene Company is a heavy user of the Printing Department's services. Normally, the Advertising Department uses 100 hours each month from the Printing Department, but during September it used 95 hours. The quote at the beginning of the problem was made when Bud Perles received his bill for September usage from the Printing Department.

### Required

(1) Compute the budgeted charge to the Advertising Department at normal volume. Also compute what the budgeted charge would be if the Advertising Department used 95 hours in a month (assume that total demand for the Printing Department remains constant at the budgeted 800 hours).

(2)   Compute the actual charge from the Printing Department to the Advertising Department during September.

(3)   Analyze the difference between what Advertising might have expected to pay at its normal volume of 100 hours and what it actually had to pay for the 95 hours it used during September. Indicate who is responsible for various differences between budgeted and actual costs.

(4)   Comment on any changes you would recommend in charging for the Printing Department.

(5)   Alice Deming, the manager of the Printing Department, responds to Perles's criticism: "We do the best we can in controlling our costs, but it has been difficult because the number of hours we've been working has decreased over the past several years. At the same time, however, we've had to acquire more expensive and sophisticated printing equipment to handle the requests being made by the Advertising Department. That department has been a heavy user of these machines, which the other departments in the company hardly use. If anything, we should charge the Advertising Department more for our services." How did this situation develop, and should a change in the pricing method for the Printing Department's services be made in light of this new information?

## 3-3    *Allocating Fixed Costs of Central Facility*

Belmont Hill Distributors is a decentralized firm specializing in the distribution of consumer products. The firm is divided into three operating divisions along the major product lines: Tru-Fit Hardware Supplies, Mudd Beauty Products, and Atomo Lighting Fixtures.

Three years ago, the company acquired a huge, highly automated regional warehouse. This effort was undertaken as a company project, since no single division had the size to take advantage of the economies of scale attainable by using such a warehouse. At the time of purchase, the three divisions agreed to "share costs on the basis of usage."

The past three years have witnessed large changes in the divisions. Tru-Fit Hardware Division has nearly doubled its volume of operations, whereas the Atomo Lighting Fixtures Division has suffered serious sales setbacks.

Against this background, a meeting took place between the corporate controller and the three divisional controllers. The meeting had been requested by the controller, Art Green, of the Tru-Fit Hardware Division, who was upset about the rapidly increasing warehouse costs being allocated to his division. Green commented: "This business of allocating total warehouse costs to divisions on the basis of actual usage has been prejudicial to our division." Further, Green proposed that "in the future, fixed costs (capital costs) be allocated on the basis of planned usage and *standard* variable cost on the basis of actual usage." Ralph White, the Atomo controller objected, saying, "What if our usage continues to fall? We will end up subsidizing the capital charges associated with the facilities that Tru-Fit uses."

### *Required*

(1)   Comment on this controversy. Do you believe that White's point is valid? If not, why? If so, what would you do to resolve this impasse?

(2)   Assume that all the facts are the same as before with one exception. In this case, the above discussion ends with the following comment from Reg Brown, controller of the Mudd Division: "I'm sick of having to fight about these unreasonable cost allocations all the time. There is an organized market for warehouse space out there that would cost us less than what we pay now. We are taking our business outside."

How, if at all, would this proposal alter your response?

## *3-4      Fort Erie Consumer Products*

Fort Erie Consumer Products manufactured a wide range of consumer products. To support all aspects of its acquisition, manufacturing, distribution, and marketing operations, the company maintained a graphics department. This department, called the Corporate Graphics Department, employed graphics designers and maintained and operated its own printing equipment.

The company was organized on a responsibility basis. The method of evaluating the various responsibility centers varied. Some of the centers were evaluated as cost centers, others as profit centers, and still others as investment centers.

When the Corporate Graphics Department was first established in 1994, there was relatively little interest in, or demand for, the products of the department. To encourage the use of these graphics capabilities, management decided not to charge the services and products of the graphics department to users. By mid-1995, the Corporate Graphics Department was running at capacity and was issuing requests to buy more sophisticated (and very expensive) printing equipment. There was some concern that the graphics department was empire building in the sense that it was acquiring equipment that was technologically elite but had no obvious or legitimate use in the firm.

To provide some control over the Corporate Graphics Department, Maureen Jackson, the vice president of finance, decreed in early 1996 that the Corporate Graphics Department would be run as a cost center. That is, Martin Roy, the manager of the Corporate Graphics Department, would be evaluated on the basis of his ability to control the department's costs relative to budgeted, or standard, costs for the work done. Moreover, to exercise some control on the empire-building inclinations of the graphics department, she declared that the department would be required to charge out all its costs to users. That is, the graphics department was to become customer-driven in the sense that it could not incur any costs that would not be reimbursed by customers.

In response to the vice president's decision, Martin developed a charge rate for his department. Martin decided that there were two classes of costs in his department: materials costs and overhead costs (which consisted of all the costs other than materials costs in the Corporate Graphics Department). In 1995, the graphics department had undertaken 12,736 jobs and had incurred materials costs of $6,704,948 and overhead costs of $5,678,346. There were many components of overhead costs, but the primary components of overhead costs were equipment and equipment-related costs of $3,586,239 and salary costs of $1,408,376.

The decision was made that the charge for any job would be the out-of-pocket materials costs for doing the job, plus an allocation to cover the overhead cost. The materials cost for any job was readily available from the job-cost sheet maintained for each job. The overhead rate for each job was computed by taking the overhead cost per job in the preceding year and adding 10%. Therefore, this rate in 1996 would be $490.44 per job. Martin provided the following rationale for his decision:

> This method is simple and easy to implement. It requires that each job absorb its own materials costs plus bear its fair share of the overhead of the Corporate Graphics Department. The 10% uplift of costs is needed to cover the installation and breaking-in costs of the new equipment that is not yet operational that we feel we ought to

continually acquire in order to provide a full range of printing capabilities. We think of these costs as the research and development costs that we have to incur so that we can educate ourselves and our customers about how to use the state-of-the-art equipment that we are buying.

In 1996, for the first year since the Corporate Graphics Department had been created, demand for jobs fell off. In an attempt to discover what had happened, Maureen Jackson commissioned a special study of users. Although there were many complaints—including dissatisfaction with the timeliness of the work done, the quality of the work done, and the willingness of the Corporate Graphics Department to listen to and meet the customers' needs—the major complaint was cost. The following comment from Paul Tremaine, the manager of the Safety Department, summarized many of the criticisms:

> I'm tired of dealing with these guys. They spend all their time trying to talk us into using their fancy equipment. They have about twelve pieces of printing equipment in there, most of which are doing things that we will never need. We have specific needs, dictated by employee safety standards and requirements, for graphics materials. I do not need graphics consultants and fancy offset printing. I need visibility and coverage provided economically. We know what we want; we just cannot print it ourselves. And their prices—well, they are way out of line. I have a specific budget for printing safety posters and I am going to take my business outside. I can get the same job done outside for about half the cost that I am expected to pay internally.

On the other hand, the comments of some users were very positive. The director of new promotions in the Marketing Department made the following comments:

> I think that their service is great. Their graphics consultants are great—creative and innovative. They take their time and provide outstanding artwork and high-quality graphics. And the cost is next to nothing; we would have to pay almost ten times as much for the same service outside.

In response to these comments, in early 1997 Maureen Jackson directed one of her staff consultants to undertake a preliminary analysis of the situation and provide some alternative approaches to dealing with the problems identified. The gist of the consultant's report was that the cost allocations did not reflect the actual demands and usage of the Corporate Graphics Department. Moreover, the consultant pointed out that conventional cost accounting wisdom required that fixed costs and variable costs be charged and allocated separately. Variable costs should be allocated on the basis of actual usage, and fixed costs on the basis of planned usage. The consultant pointed out that, under the current scheme, materials costs were allocated on the basis of actual cost, whereas fixed and variable overhead costs were allocated on the basis of actual usage. That approach, the consultant pointed out, might create problems.

### Required

(1)   What benefits might accrue from allocating fixed costs on the basis of planned usage and variable costs on the basis of actual usage?

(2) Should standard or actual costs be allocated in a charge-out system such as this?

(3) Explain why the scheme developed by Martin Roy does not fulfill Maureen Jackson's intention that the cost-charging scheme should control the Corporate Graphic Department's empire-building tendencies. What evidence is there of the failure to meet that objective?

(4) What would you recommend to provide the Corporate Graphics Department with a more effective motivation to operate effectively and efficiently?

## 3-5    *Reciprocal Cost Allocations*

Arlington Acoustics manufactures a line of quality speakers. The main production departments are Shipping, Assembly, and Fabrication. These departments are provided with services from centrally maintained facilities: computer; heating and air-conditioning, and power.

The company is organized on a profit-center basis, with the service departments treated as cost centers. Consequently, each period, the costs of computing, heating, and power must be allocated to the production departments.

The company follows the practice of allocating budgeted fixed costs on the basis of planned usage and standard variable costs on the basis of actual usage.

The distribution of actual units of service provided last week is:

|  | COMPUTER | HEATING | POWER | SHIPPING | ASSEMBLY | FABRI-CATION | TOTAL UNITS |
|---|---|---|---|---|---|---|---|
| Computer | 500 | 1,000 | 2,000 | 2,000 | 2,500 | 2,000 | 10,000 |
| Heating | 3,000 | 2,000 | 4,000 | 5,000 | 3,000 | 3,000 | 20,000 |
| Power | 750 | 750 | 250 | 750 | 1,000 | 1,500 | 5,000 |

These service levels corresponded to the amount of planned usage. This week's costs were as follows:

|  | STANDARD VARIABLE COST | BUDGETED FIXED COST |
|---|---|---|
| Computer | $30,000 | $ 50,000 |
| Heating | $60,000 | $100,000 |
| Power | $40,000 | $ 80,000 |

### *Required*

(1) Allocate the fixed and variable costs using the reciprocal allocation method.

(2) What is the variable cost per unit of service provided by the computer facility?

(3) Suppose one-half of the fixed power costs can be avoided if the power unit is shut down:

(a) How many units of power would have to be purchased externally?

(b) What is the maximum price the company would be willing to pay for one unit of service supplied externally?

## 3-6   *Incremental Costs in a Reciprocal Cost System (R. Manes)*

The Darwin Co. has two main products, S and T, each of which is produced in a separate division. In order to produce S and T, the Darwin Co. has two service departments, A and B, which supply intermediate goods and services both to the S and T divisions and to themselves. For the sake of discussion, let A be a materials handling service and B a power generator.

The budget for work to be done by the firm in a coming period is shown in Table 1.

Depreciation expenses are straight-line depreciation of generating equipment in the fifteenth year of an estimated 20-year life, that is to say it is relatively old equipment (although well maintained).

### Required

(1)   Using the reciprocal allocation method, determine the variable costs of service departments A and B allocated to products S and T.

(2)   Choose a basis for allocating the fixed costs of the service departments, and determine the fixed cost allocation to the two products.

(3)   Suppose economic conditions change so that product sales are now expected to be $S = 80$ and $T = 90$. Recalculate Table 1, the production schedule, and the service department budget.

(4)   What are the new sets of allocated variable and fixed service department costs?

(5)   The local utility company offers to sell unlimited amounts of B to Darwin at $130 per unit. Should Darwin accept this offer?

## TABLE 1

| | SOURCE A | SOURCE B | SOURCE S | SOURCE T |
|---|---|---|---|---|
| User of Output | | | | |
| A (materials handling) | 0 | 30 | 0 | 0 |
| B (power) | 20 | 0 | 0 | 0 |
| Division S | 30 | 35 | 0 | 0 |
| Division T | 40 | 55 | 0 | 0 |
| Outside markets | 0 | 0 | 60 | 100 |
| Total (in units of goods and services) | 90 | 120 | 60 | 100 |
| Costs of Service Department | A | B | | |
| 1. Variable labor, overhead, and materials costs | $ 7,200 | $ 4,800 | | |
| 2. Supervision and other out-of-pocket fixed costs | 6,000 | 7,000 | | |
| 3. Depreciation | 4,800 | 8,200 | | |
| | $18,000* | $20,000† | | |

*Plus share of Dept. B's power costs.*
†*Plus share of Dept. A's materials handling costs.*

## ■ *CASE STUDY*

### SELIGRAM, INC.: ELECTRONIC TESTING OPERATIONS*

We put in a piece of automated equipment a year ago that only fits the requirements of one customer. This equipment reduced the direct labor required to test his components and, because of our labor-based burden allocation system, substantially reduced his costs. But putting a $40,000 machine into the general burden pool raised the costs to our other customers. It just doesn't make sense shooting yourself in the foot at the same time you are lowering the company's cost of operations.

*Paul Carte, Manager*

### Introduction

Electronic Testing Operations (ETO), a division of Seligram, Inc., provided centralized testing for electronic components such as integrated circuits. ETO was created as a result of a decision in 1979 to consolidate electronic testing from 11 different divisions of Seligram. ETO commenced services to these divisions in 1983. It was estimated that centralization would save Seligram in excess of $20 million in testing equipment investment over the next five years.

ETO operated as a cost center and transferred products to other divisions at full cost (direct costs plus allocated burden). Although ETO was a captive division, other divisions within Seligram were allowed to use outside testing services if ETO could not meet their cost or service requirements. ETO was permitted to devote up to 10% of its testing capacity to outside customers but chose to work

mainly with other Seligram divisions due to limited marketing resources.

ETO employed approximately 60 hourly personnel and 40 administrative and technical staff members. Budgeted expenses were $7.9 million in 1988 (see Exhibit 1).

### Testing Procedures

ETO expected to test between 35 and 40 million components in 1988. These components included integrated circuits (I.C.s), diodes, transistors, capacitors, resistors, transformers, relays, and crystals. Component testing was required for two reasons. First, if defective components were not caught early in the manufacturing cycle, the cost of repair could exceed the manufacturing cost of the product itself. Studies indicated that a defective resistor caught before use in the manufacturing process cost two cents.

**EXHIBIT 1** Electronic Testing Operations—
1988 Budgeted Expenses

| | | |
|---|---:|---:|
| Direct labor | | $3,260,015 |
| Overhead | | |
|   Indirect labor | 859,242 | |
|   Salary expense | 394,211 | |
|   Supplies and expenses | 538,029 | |
|   Services* | 245,226 | |
|   Personnel Allocations[†] | 229,140 | |
|   Service Allocations[‡] | 2,448,134 | |
|   Total Overhead | | $4,713,982 |
| Total budgeted expenses | | $7,973,997 |

*Includes tool repair, computer expenses, maintenance stores, and service cost transfers from other divisions.*
[†]*Includes indirect and salaried employee fringe benefits, personnel department, security, stores/warehousing, and holidays/vacations.*
[‡]*Includes building occupancy, telephones, depreciation, information systems, and data control.*

---

*This case was prepared by Professor Peter B. B. Turney, Portland State University and Christopher Ittner, Doctoral Student, under the supervision of Professor Robin Cooper.

Copyright © 1988 by the President and Fellows of Harvard College. Harvard Business School case 189-084.

If the resistor was not caught until the end product was in the field, however, the cost of repair could run into the thousands of dollars. Second, a large proportion of Seligram's work was defense related. Military specifications frequently required extensive testing of components utilized in aerospace and naval products. By 1988, ETO had the ability to test 6,500 different components. Typically, however, the division would test about 500 different components each month and between 3,000 and 3,500 per year. Components were received from customers in lots; in 1988, ETO would receive approximately 12,000 lots of components.

ETO performed both electrical and mechanical testing. Electrical testing involved measuring the electrical characteristics of the components and comparing these measurements with the components' specifications. For example, the specifications for an amplifier may have called for a 1-volt input to be amplified into a 10-volt output. ETO would deliver a 1-volt input to the component. By measuring the amplifier's output, ETO gauged its conformance with specifications.

Mechanical testing included solderability, component burn-in, thermal shock, lead straightening, and leak detection. Solderability involved the inspection of components to see if they held solder. Burn-in was the extended powering of components at high temperature. Thermal shock involved the cycling of components between high and low temperatures. Lead straightening was the detection and correction of bent leads on components such as axial components. Leak detection examined hermetically sealed I.C.s for leaks.

Components varied significantly in the number and type of electrical and mechanical testing procedures they required. This variation resulted in about 200 different standard process flows for the division. Process flows were determined by the different combinations of tests and specifications requested by the customer. Based on these combinations,

ETO planners determined the routing of components between testing equipment and the type of tests to be performed at each station. I.C.s, for example, could follow six different flows through the facility. While some I.C.s only required electrical testing at room temperature (solderability and leak detection, for instance), others also required thermal shock and burn-in.

Each type of component required separate software development, and custom tools and fixtures were often required. Software, tools, and fixtures were developed by the engineering group, which was made up of specialists in software development, equipment maintenance, calibration and repair, tooling and fixturing, and testing equipment operation. Software engineers developed programs for specific applications. The programs were then retained in a software library for future use. ETO had 6,500 different software programs on file, of which 1,300 were programs developed in the past year. ETO also had an inventory of 1,500 tools and fixtures, of which 300 had been developed in the past year. The large number of tools and fixtures allowed the testing of components with a wide variety of leads, pin combinations, and mating configurations.

The testing facility was divided into two rooms. The main testing room contained the equipment used for electrical testing. The mechanical room contained the equipment used for mechanical testing, plus incoming receiving and the stockroom. A total of 20 people worked in the two rooms on each of two main shifts, and 10 people worked on the night shift.

### Cost Accounting System

The cost accounting system measured two components of cost: direct labor and burden. Burden was grouped into a single cost pool that included burden costs associated with each

**EXHIBIT 2** Electronic Testing Operations—Calculation of Burden Rate, Based on 1988 Plan

$$\text{Burden rate} = \frac{\text{Total burden \$*}}{\text{direct labor \$} \times 100}$$

$$= \frac{\$4,713,982}{3,260,015} * 100$$

$$= 144.6\%$$

$$\text{Effective rate} = 145\%$$

*Cost breakdown

|  | VARIABLE | FIXED DEPRECIATION | OTHER | TOTAL |
|---|---|---|---|---|
| Total burden | $1,426,317 | $1,288,000 | $1,999,665 | $4,713,982 |

of the testing rooms as well as the engineering burden costs relating to software and tooling development and the administrative costs of the division. Total burden costs were divided by the sum of testing and engineering labor dollars to arrive at a burden rate per direct labor dollar. The division costed each lot of components. Burden was calculated for each lot by multiplying the actual direct labor dollars associated with the lot by the 145% of burden rate. The resulting burden was then added to the actual direct labor costs to determine the lot's total cost. In 1988, the facilitywide burden rate was 145% of each direct labor dollar, of which more than 40% was attributable to equipment depreciation (see Exhibit 2)

### Signs of Obsolescence

Several trends pointed to the obsolescence of the labor-based burden allocation process. Since the founding of the division in 1983, direct labor hours per lot tested had been steadily declining (see Exhibit 3). This trend was aggravated by an increased dependence on vendor certification. Vendor certification was a key component of Just-in-Time (JIT) delivery. With vendor certification, Selig-

ram's suppliers did the primary testing of components. ETO then utilized statistical sampling to verify that the supplier's production process was still in control. Thus, whereas JIT led to an increased number of smaller lots being received by ETO, vendor certification reduced the number of tests performed. Early indications were that JIT deliveries would account for 30% of Seligram's shipments within the next five years.

In addition to declining direct labor content and fewer test lots, the obsolescence of the labor-based allocation system was intensified by a shift from simple inspection services to broader-based test technology. On complex parts requiring screening, environmental conditioning, and testing, the division was consistently cheaper than outside services. Where only elementary testing was required, however, low-technology outside laboratories were often cheaper, especially on large lots. The advantage that the division brought customers over the outside labs was that the latter provided essentially no engineering support, whereas ETO with its resident engineering resources was able to support such service on a rapid and cost-effective basis. The shift to more techni-

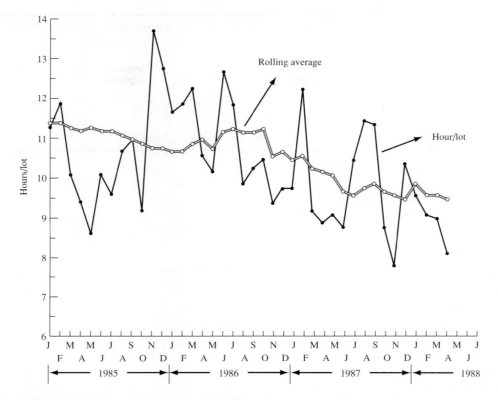

**EXHIBIT 3**  Electronic Testing Operations—Direct Labor Hours per Lot

cally sophisticated services prompted a shift in the labor mix from direct to indirect personnel. The division expected to see a crossover between engineering head count and hourly head count early in the 1990s.

Finally, the introduction of high-technology components created the need for more automatic testing, longer test cycles, and more data per part. Digital components, for example, were currently tested for up to 100 conditions (combinations of electrical input and output states). The new generation of digital components, on the other hand, would be much more complex and require verification of up to 10,000 conditions. These components would require very expensive highly automated equipment. This increase in au-

tomation would, in turn, lead to a smaller base of direct labor to absorb the depreciation costs of this new equipment.

There were fears that the resulting increase in burden rates would drive some customers away. ETO had already noticed an increase in the number and frequency of complaints from customers regarding the rates they were charged for testing.

The division's accounting manager proposed a new cost accounting system to alleviate the problem. Under this new system, burden would be directly traced to two cost pools. The first pool would contain burden related to the administrative and technical functions (division management, engineering, planning, and administrative personnel). This

**EXHIBIT 4** Electronic Testing Operations—Proposed Burden Rates, Based on 1988 Plan

**Machine Hour Rate**

|  | Machine Hours | Burden $* |
|---|---|---|
| Main test room | 33,201 | $2,103,116 |
| Mechanical test room | 17,103 | 1,926,263 |
| Total | 50,304 | $4,029,379 |

Machine hour rate

$$\text{Test room burden } \$ = \frac{\$4,029,379}{50,304} = \$80.10$$
$$\text{Machine hr}$$

Effective machine hour rate = $80.00

**Direct Labor Hour Rate**

Total engineering and administrative burden $ = $684,603

Total direct labor dollars = $3,260,015[†]

Burden rate =

$$\frac{\text{Engr. \& Admin. Burden \$}}{\text{Direct Lbr \$}} \times 100 = \frac{\$684,603}{\$3,260,015} \times 100 = 21\%$$

Effective burden rate per direct labor $ = 20%

*Cost breakdown

|  | VARIABLE | FIXED | | TOTAL |
|---|---|---|---|---|
|  |  | DEPRECIATION | OTHER |  |
| Main test room | $ 887,379 | $ 88,779 | $1,126,958 | $2,103,116 |
| Mechanical test room | 443,833 | 808,103 | 674,327 | 1,926,263 |
| Test Room Burden | $1,331,212 | $ 896,882 | $1,801,285 | $4,029,379 |
| Engineering & admn. | $ 95,105 | $ 391,118 | $ 198,380 | $ 684,603 |
| Total burden | $1,426,317 | $1,288,000 | $1,999,665 | $4,713,982 |

[†]Includes all direct labor costs, including direct labor costs incurred in both test rooms as well as in engineering.

pool would be charged on a rate per direct labor dollar. The second pool would include all other burden costs and would be charged based on machine hours. Exhibit 4 provides the proposed burden rates.

Shortly after the accounting manager submitted his proposal, a consultant hired by Seligram's corporate management prepared an assessment of ETO's cost system. He recommended the implementation of a three-burden-pool system utilizing separate burden centers for each test room and a common technical and administrative pool. Burden would be directly traced to each of the three burden pools. Like the accounting manager's system, burden costs in the test rooms would

then be allocated on a machine-hour basis. Technical and administrative costs would continue to be charged on a rate per direct labor dollar.

To examine the impact of the two alternative systems, ETO management asked that a study be conducted on a representative sample of parts. Exhibit 5 provides a breakout of actual direct labor and machine-hour requirements per lot for the five components selected for the study.

### Technological Future

In 1988, the division faced major changes in the technology of testing that required important equipment acquisition decisions. The

**EXHIBIT 5**  Electronic Testing Operations—Direct Labor
and Machine-Hour Requirements, Actuals for One Lot

| | | MACHINE HOURS | | |
| --- | --- | --- | --- | --- |
| PRODUCT | DIRECT LABOR $ | MAIN ROOM | MECH. ROOM | TOTAL |
| ICA | $ 917 | 8.5 | 10.0 | 18.5 |
| ICB | 2051 | 14.0 | 26.0 | 40.0 |
| Capacitor | 1094 | 3.0 | 4.5 | 7.5 |
| Amplifier | 525 | 4.0 | 1.0 | 5.0 |
| Diode | 519 | 7.0 | 5.0 | 12.0 |

existing testing equipment was getting old and would not be able to keep pace with developments in component technology. Existing components, for example, had between 16 and 40 input/output terminations (e.g., pins or other mating configurations), and ETO's equipment could handle up to 120 terminations. Although the 120-termination limit had only been reached a couple of times in the past few years, a new generation of components with up to 256 terminations was already being developed. Similarly, the upper limit of frequency on existing components was 20 MHz (million cycles per second), whereas the frequency on the next generation of components was expected to be 50 MHz.

The equipment required to test the next generation of components would be expensive. Each machine cost approximately $2 million. Testing on this equipment would be more automated than existing equipment, with longer test cycles and the generation of more test data per part. It was also likely that lot sizes would be larger. The new equipment would not replace the existing equipment but would merely add capabilities ETO did not currently possess. Additionally, the new equipment would only be needed to service the requirements of one or two customers in

**EXHIBIT 6**  Electronic Testing Operations—New Testing Equipment Economics and
Operating Characteristics

| | |
| --- | --- |
| Cost | $2 million |
| Useful life | 8 years |
| Depreciation method | Double declining balance (first-year depreciation costs of $500,000) |
| Location | Main test room |
| Utilization | 10% first year, rising to 60% by third year and in all subsequent years, based on 4,000 hours per year availability (2 shifts × 2,000-hour year) |
| Direct labor requirements: | Approximately five minutes per hour of operation; average labor rate of $30 per hour |
| Engineering requirements: | $75,000 in installation and programming costs in first year |
| Estimated overhead (nonengineering depreciation) | $250,000 ($100,000 variable, $150,000 fixed) |

the foreseeable future. Exhibit 6 provides a summary of the new equipment's economics and operating characteristics.

The impact of this new equipment would be an acceleration in the decline in direct labor hours per lot of components. At the same time, burden would increase with the additional depreciation and engineering costs associated with the new equipment. This would result in a large increase in the burden rate per direct labor dollar. As Paul Carte, manager of ETO, saw it, the acquisition of the new equipment could have a disastrous effect on the division's pricing structure if the labor-based allocation system remained in use:

> We plan on investing $2 million on a large electronic testing machine to test the chips of one or two customers. This machine will be very fast and will require little direct labor. Its acquisition will have a significant effect on our per direct labor dollar burden rate, which will result in an increase in charges to our other customers. It is clear that a number of customers will walk away if we try to pass this increase on. I am afraid that we will lose 25% of our customer base if we don't change our cost system.

# 4

## Activity-Based Cost Systems

Activity-based costing (ABC) developed to provide more-accurate ways of assigning the costs of indirect and support resources to activities, business processes, products, services, and customers. ABC systems recognize that many organizational resources are required not for physical production of units of product but to provide a broad array of support activities that enable a variety of products and services to be produced for a diverse group of customers. The goal of ABC is *not* to allocate common costs to products. The goal is to measure and then price out all the resources used for activities that support the production and delivery of products and services to customers.

ABC attempts to first identify the activities being performed by the organization's support resources. Then it traces the resource expenses of the support resources to the activities, ending up with the total cost of performing each of the organization's support activities. In the next stage, ABC systems trace activity costs to products by identifying a cost driver for each activity (called an activity cost driver), calculating an activity cost driver rate, and using this rate to drive activity costs to products. For each product (or service or customer) the quantity of each cost driver it used during a period is multiplied by the standard cost driver rate. The procedure may sound complicated, but actually it is quite simple to illustrate and even to implement in practice. For example, Exhibit 4-1 shows how a single resource category, *indirect labor*, is decomposed into six different activities performed and then linked, via appropriate activity cost drivers, to cost objects such as products, services, and customers.

We start by extending the discussion in Chapter 3 of assigning the cost of service and support department resources beyond production centers to incorporate activities that support production processes. Subsequently, in this chapter, we describe the second stage of a cost assignment process, in which cost center and activity costs are traced to products.[1]

Activity-based cost systems expand the type of "production cost centers" used to ac-

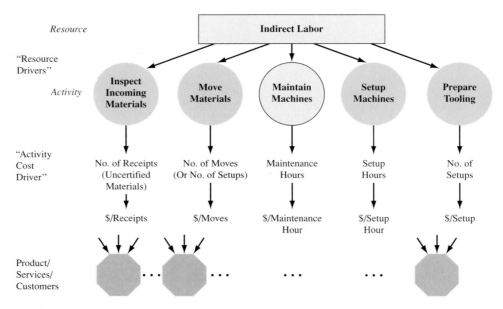

**EXHIBIT 4-1** Activity-Based Costing: Expenses Flow from Resources to Activities to Products, Services, and Customers

cumulate costs. Rather than focus only on the location or organization of responsibility centers, ABC systems focus on the actual activities performed by organizational resources. ABC systems retain, as in traditional systems, activities that convert materials into finished products such as machining products and assembling products within production cost centers. But, in addition, ABC systems recognize that some resources perform work such as setting up machines, scheduling production orders, inspecting products, improving products, and moving materials. These are support activities; they are not directly involved in the physical process of converting raw materials to intermediate and finished products. For service organizations, lacking direct materials and easily traceable direct labor, almost all activities can be considered support: handling customer relationships and enhancing existing services, as well as actually delivering the primary service (a checking account transaction, a phone call, a medical procedure, an airline flight) to the customer.

## ASSIGNING SERVICE DEPARTMENT COSTS TO ACTIVITIES

The costs of many service departments cannot be assigned to production departments via direct charging or a cost driver that reflects a cause-and-effect relationship between the service department and the production department. These untraceable, or "common-cost," service department expenses include scheduling, product engineering, plant administration, information systems, purchasing, materials handling, and plant-level expenses, such as property taxes, building depreciation, insurance, heat, and light. We argued, in Chapter 3, that for cost control and cost responsibility purposes these seemingly common expenses should not be assigned to production centers.

Activity-based cost systems provide a mechanism for establishing causal relationships between expenses that must be treated as common or joint in traditional cost systems. Let us illustrate the ABC resource cost assignment process with a simple example.[2] Consider the materials handling department of the Williams Corporation, which is responsible for receiving raw materials and purchased parts, transporting them to the stockroom, and releasing items to the production floor when they are needed for scheduled production lots. The monthly cost for this department is $50,000. The average number of labor hours worked each month in the plant is 40,000 hours.

In the past, the Williams Corporation had a traditional overhead allocation system in which the costs of indirect support departments were allocated to production departments using direct labor hours (dlh). With this procedure, the burden rate for the materials handling department would be:

$$\text{Materials handling burden rate} = \$50,000/40,000 \text{ dlh}$$
$$= \$1.25/\text{dlh}$$

and a production department that used 6000 direct labor hours in a month would receive an assignment of $7,500 of materials handling expenses. Such an assignment, however, assumes that each hour of direct labor worked in a department requires $1.25 of resources from the materials handling department. Because this assumption is highly unlikely to be even approximately valid, we refer to such an assignment as an allocation; it uses a resource driver, such as direct labor hours, that bears no causal relationship to the demand for or consumption of resources in the materials handling department. For example, one department that does long runs of standard products may make relatively few demands on the materials handling department resources, whereas another department that does many short runs of customized products containing a large number of unique components may make quite heavy demands on the materials handling department. The direct labor resource driver fails to distinguish the large variation in demands for materials handling resources from the two quite different production departments.

In an ABC system, the designer links resource expenses to activities performed. Classifying spending by activities performed accomplishes a 90 degree shift in thinking about expenses (see Exhibit 4-2).

The resource cost drivers collect expenses from the financial system and drive them to the activities being performed by the organizational resources. Thus, after going through this step, organizations learn, usually for the first time, how much they are spending on activities such as purchasing materials and introducing new products.

One does not need extensive time-and-motion studies to link resource spending to activities performed. The goal is to be approximately right, rather than precisely wrong, as are virtually all traditional product costing systems. Many traditional standard cost systems calculate product costs out to six significant digits ($5.71462 per unit), but, because of arbitrary allocation procedures, the first digit is usually wrong. The data to link resource expenses to activities performed can be collected from employee surveys in which individuals, other than the front-line employees who are actually doing production work, are asked to fill in a survey form in which the activity dictionary is listed and they estimate the percentage of time they spend on any activity (in excess, say, of 5% of their time) on the list.

| | Salaries | Energy | Supplies | Equipment |
|---|---|---|---|---|
| Process customer orders | | | | $144,846 |
| Purchase materials | | | | $136,320 |
| Schedule production | | | | $72,143 |
| Move materials | | | | $49,945 |
| Set up machines | | | | $47,599 |
| Inspect items | | | | $45,235 |
| Maintain product information | | | | $27,747 |
| Perform engineering changes | | | | $17,768 |
| Expedite orders | | | | $16,704 |
| Introduce new products | | | | $16,648 |
| Resolve quality problems | | | | $15,390 |

Salaries $371,917

Energy $118,069

Supplies $76,745

Equipment $23,614

Activity-Based Costing

Total  $590,345

Total  $590,345

**EXHIBIT 4-2**   Tracing Organizational Expenses to Activities

Often, cost system designers interview department managers, like Jennifer Cassell, the manager of the materials handling department. An example of an edited and abbreviated transcript of such an interview is presented below:

### Interview with Jennifer Cassell

Q:  How many people work in your department?

A:  Twelve, not counting me.

Q:  What do the people do?

A:  Well, everyone does a little bit of everything; it varies from week to week, even from day to day.

Q:  Sure, but are there some major activities that seem to be done on a regular basis?

A:  I suppose we have three principal activities that would take up at least 90% of our time. The largest is receiving, checking, and logging in incoming shipments of purchased parts. About half our people are involved in this activity, receiving, inspecting a few items in each shipment, updating the documentation, and placing the shipment in the parts storage area.

Another 25% of the people, about three folks, do the same set of activities for raw materials, like steel, aluminum, and plastics.

Q:  What's the other major activity?

A:  Oh, the remaining three people would typically be working with the production control people. My people get copies of the production schedule, and their job is to kit together the purchased parts and raw materials needed for each production run. Then they disburse the parts and materials to the workstation on the floor when and where they are needed.

Q:  Is there anything else?

A:  Each week some new task shows up, perhaps go to quality training, or lend a hand in final goods shipment if they're handling a rush order and are short of help, or even help in process inspection, if needed, since my people are really well trained in statistical process control.

Q:  Cumulatively, are all these special, ad hoc tasks a big time drain?

A:  Not really, it seems like a big bother when it happens, but realistically it's probably 5% or less of our time.

Q:  What about your job. Do you do any direct work with the incoming materials?

A:  Occasionally, if someone is sick or on vacation, but mostly my job is coaching, training, making sure the system is working well, and that we're meeting the needs of our internal customers.

Q:  What determines how long it takes to process an incoming shipment? Does it matter whether it's raw materials or a purchased part, whether it's a large or a small shipment?

A:  Purchased parts are straightforward; just look at one or two, check that they're in conformance, and then take them to the storage area. Almost always, we can get the parts to storage in one trip. Raw materials can come in larger sizes, and some of those big orders can take a while to check and to move into storage. But even that is relatively rare. I would say the time required to process either a shipment of parts or of raw materials depends much more on how many shipments we get than on the size of the shipments.

Q.  What about the activity of disbursing parts and materials to the floor?

A.  Again, volume is not a driver here; work is driven more by how many production runs we have to get ready for than the size of any particular run. For 80% or 90% of production runs, we can handle all parts and materials requirements with one trip to the workstation.

## (2) Identifying Activities and Mapping Resource Costs to Activities

Ignoring the minor activities that are done on an ad hoc basis and that collectively account for less than 5% of the work of the materials handling department, Jennifer Cassell has identified three principal activities performed by people in her department:

- Receiving purchased parts
- Receiving raw materials
- Disbursing parts and material to workstations

We use the information in the interview to map the $50,000 resource cost to the three activities. For simplicity, we will assume that each of the twelve employees (not counting Cassell) is about equally skilled and equally paid. This assumption enables us to use the time percentages for assigning resource costs to the three activities:

| ACTIVITY | PERCENTAGE OF EFFORT | ACTIVITY COST |
|---|---|---|
| Receiving purchased parts | 50% | $25,000 |
| Receiving raw materials | 25 | 12,500 |
| Disbursing parts/materials | 25 | 12,500 |

In this example, we have assumed that all employees' efforts cost the same. If, however, the people doing the materials receiving raw materials activity were more skilled and more highly paid, then we could not use simple percentage assignments. We would have to trace their higher costs to the receiving raw materials activity and use the lower wages for the labor performing the other two activities. Also, if for inspecting purchased parts, a special set of expensive testing equipment had been acquired, then the cost of this equipment should be assigned only to the receiving purchased parts activity. In this case, the percentage assignments of people and their time would be used to assign only the compensation cost of the individuals but not of the equipment they used.

A final consideration is the assumption that we should spread the cost of the department manager, Jennifer Cassell, across all three activities proportional to the time worked by each of the employees under her supervision. This assumption seems reasonable if she provides general coaching and assistance. A more detailed assignment of her costs would be required if she spent disproportionately more of her time with employees performing one of the three activities, or if, for a significant part of her time, she performed one or more of the three activities. We would then assign that portion of her time actually working with parts and materials to the appropriate activity or activities. The remaining time, consisting of general supervision, would then be spread across the three activities using some appropriate metric (such as hours of work or number of activities performed).

This process enables all organizational expenses to be traced to activities performed. And, as the above example clearly shows, many of these newly defined activities are not associated with directly fabricating or assembling the product or servicing a customer. They are support or infrastructure activities. But, as we will see, the costs of these activities can be assigned to products (and services and customers) just as easily as more traditional production costs such as materials, direct labor, and machine production costs.

## Estimates or Allocations?

Earlier we argued against assigning costs to products using allocations—in which the cost driver did not represent actual demands by the product on the resource whose cost was being assigned. At first glance, the process of interviewing Jennifer Cassell and using her approximate estimates of time and effort to assign the resource costs in her department might appear to be an example of an allocation process. In fact, however, the procedure of driving resource costs to activities performed requires an **estimation** process of the underlying quantity variable linking resource supply to activities performed. It is not an **allocation** process that arbitrarily assigns a cost by a measure unrelated to the work being performed. In principle, analysts could install elaborate monitoring and measuring devices to learn exactly the quantity and cost of resources used for the various activities. But such elaborate instrumentation is rarely required, especially to obtain reasonably accurate costs of products, services, and customers. Thus, we use surrogate or approximate measures to obtain data inexpensively since the surrogates are accurate enough for the decisions that will be made using product and customer cost information. The surrogates, such as estimates of time spent in various activities, although reliable enough for these purposes, would not be accurate or precise enough to drive day-to-day productivity improvements and cost reduction. Thus, we see how the data requirements can differ substantially between the two principal uses of costing information: cost control and productivity enhancements versus costing of products, services, and customers.

## ASSIGNING SERVICE DEPARTMENT COSTS: SOME FIXED AND SOME VARIABLE[3]

The resources under the control of Jennifer Cassell's materials handling department were assumed to be "fixed" in the conventional definition of the term. She and the twelve people in her department came to work each day and expected to be paid whether parts and materials shipments arrived or not or whether materials had to be disbursed to the factory floor or not. This situation is typical of many support departments. Commitments to service and support departments are made to acquire personnel, space, equipment, and technology. The supply of these resources will not vary with short-term fluctuations in the demand for services from these service and support departments.

Some support departments, however, may have a mixture of committed resources and resources whose supply may vary with demands for service. Consider the Inspection Department in the Williams Company. This department has some assigned space where work is performed and some specialized equipment. But people are assigned, as needed, to perform inspections. In this case, the resource costs of the inspection department require two different driver rates for assigning inspection costs. The committed expenses for space and equipment will be assigned on the basis of the capacity (or some standard volume measure) provided by these resources, whereas the expenses of the flexible resources, the inspectors, are assigned on the basis of actual demands for their services.

For example, assume that budgeted monthly expenses for the Inspection Department are $80,000. Of this amount, $60,000 represents the cost of the committed resources, and $20,000 represents the cost of the flexible resources. The equipment has a practical capacity of 5,000 inspections per month; the budget for the inspectors reflects an expected volume of 4,000 inspections. The table below shows the calculation of how the cost driver rate for assigning the cost of the Inspection Department is calculated:

| | Inspection Department: Committed and Flexible Resource Costs | | |
|---|---|---|---|
| RESOURCE CATEGORY | BUDGETED EXPENSE | ACTIVITY LEVEL: NO. OF INSPECTIONS | DRIVER RATE |
| Committed | $60,000 | 5,000 (capacity) | $12 |
| Flexible | $20,000 | 4,000 (budgeted) | 5 |
| Total | $80,000 | | $17 |

The $12 rate charges for the cost of resources that are committed (supplied) and are therefore "fixed," independent of the actual demands for services. The $5 rate charges for the resources that are supplied flexibly, as needed, to perform the services demanded of the department.

This distinction, between the costs of committed and flexible resources, can be maintained for all organizational resources. It is quite simple, with today's data bases and systems, to identify which costs assigned to production departments, primary activities, and, eventually, to products are flexible in the short run. This identification will enable information about short-run contribution margin and variable costing to be readily at hand even while the costs of all resources used, whether committed or flexible, by production departments, activities, and products, can be calculated and reported as well.

## ACTIVITY COST DRIVERS

The second stage of an activity-based cost system assigns activity costs to products. This assignment is done by selecting activity cost drivers that link the performance of activities to demands made by individual products. Cost drivers are not unique to ABC systems, of course. Traditional cost systems used simple drivers, such as direct labor dollars, direct labor hours, machine hours, units produced, or materials processed for allocating production cost center costs to products.

Consider the example of a typical German cost system, perhaps the most elaborate and detailed in the world. The number of cost centers in German companies is unusually high. For instance, one German $150 million manufacturing company, producing electric and electronic switches with only three manufacturing stages, uses about 100 cost centers: 15 of them are direct production cost centers, the other 85 are mostly indirect responsibility centers. Big plants of other companies, such as Siemens or Mercedes, can have between 1,000 and 2,000 cost centers. The German companies use such a large number of cost centers so that they can develop flexible budgets that give managers great visibility of cost incurrence at the individual cost center. The large number of cost centers enables them to have individual cost centers with highly homogeneous work processes.

For each cost center, the cost system designer makes a choice about the appropriate cost driver. A cost center doing manual assembly of components would use a direct labor cost driver. A cost center consisting of automatic machines would use machine hours as the cost driver. A cost center doing continuous processing of materials, such as in a chemical process, would use pounds or gallons of materials processed as the cost driver. Thus, a comprehensive cost system could consist of hundreds of different cost centers, each with its own cost driver, chosen to be representative of the nature of work performed at that cost center.

Although these systems are wonderful for providing cost visibility and control at the responsibility and cost center level, they are inadequate for assigning cost center costs to products. The fundamental problem is that many organizational resources are required not for physical production of units of product but to provide a broad array of support activities that enable a variety of products and services to be produced for a diverse group of customers. Despite the use of two or three different types of cost drivers (labor hours, machine hours, materials processed, units produced) in systems with hundreds of cost centers, the cost drivers all share a common and critical characteristic. The quantity of a cost driver used by an individual product is proportional to the physical volume of product produced. That is, if production of a product increases by 10%, then the labor hours, the machine hours, and the materials processed for this product would all increase by 10%. Therefore, the indirect and support costs assigned to this product would increase by 10%.

But many resources of indirect and support departments are not used in proportion to physical volume. Therefore, assigning these costs using cost drivers that are proportional to volume creates significant errors in the costs assigned to individual products. Traditional cost systems, organized around production centers, emphasize work that is proportional to the number of units produced. We call such work *unit-level activities.*

> **Unit-level activities** represent work performed for every unit of product or service produced. The quantity of resources used by unit-level activities is proportional to products' production and sales volumes. Cost drivers for unit-level activities include labor hours, machine hours, and materials quantity processed.

Analysis of many of the activities done by support resources, however, reveals that much of the work they perform is associated with batch, or product-sustaining, activities.[4]

> **Batch-level activities** include setting up a machine for a new production run, purchasing materials, and processing a customer order. The important distinction, between batch and unit-level activities, is that the resources required to perform a batch-level activity are independent of the number of units in the batch (number of components produced after a setup, number of items in a purchase order, or the number of products in a customer shipment).

*[handwritten: independent of volume]*

Traditional cost systems view the expenses of resources performing batch-level activities as *fixed*, because they are independent of the number of units processed in a batch activity. But, of course, as more batch-level activities are demanded (to perform the many setups in a plant producing a wide variety of products and components, to purchase all the components required in a complex product's bill of materials, and to satisfy the many small customized orders for individual customers), the organization must eventually supply additional resources to perform these activities. Thus, one of the advances made by activity-based cost systems over traditional cost systems is the ability to measure and assign the cost of handling production orders, material movements, setups, customer orders, and purchasing to the products, customers, and services that triggered the activity.

> **Product-sustaining activities** represent work performed to enable the production of individual products (or services) to occur. Extending this notion outside the factory leads to **customer-sustaining activities,** which represent work that enables the company to sell to an individual customer but that is independent of the volume and mix of the products (and services) sold and delivered to the customer. Examples of product- and customer-sustaining activities include maintaining and updating product specifications, special testing and tooling for individual products and services, technical support provided for individual products and services, and customer market research and support.

Exhibit 4-3 shows the cost hierarchy of unit, batch, product-sustaining, and customer sustaining activities. It illustrates that costs to sustain a product may not be related

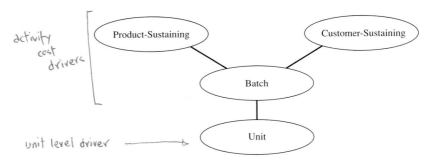

**EXHIBIT 4-3**  ABC Hierarchy of Activities

to individual customers, and, conversely, many customer-related costs may be independent of the products that the organization sustains in its product line.

The costs of product- and customer-sustaining activities are easily traced to the individual products and services for whom the activities are performed, but the *quantity* of resources used in product- and customer-sustaining activities are, by definition, independent of the production and sales volumes for the products and customers. Again, traditional cost systems with their narrow distinction between fixed and variable costs relative to production volumes cannot trace product- and customer-sustaining resources to individual products and customers.

The linkage between activities and cost objects, such as products, services, and customers, is done by **activity cost drivers**. An activity cost driver is a quantitative measure of the output of an activity. Activity-based cost systems require, in addition to traditional unit-level drivers such as labor and machine hours, the use of activity cost drivers that can trace batch, product-sustaining, and customer-sustaining activity costs to products and customers. For each individual activity, the designer selects an appropriate activity cost driver (as shown earlier in Exhibit 4-1).

Examples of activities and associated batch or product-sustaining activity cost drivers are shown in the following table:

| ACTIVITY | ACTIVITY COST DRIVER | BATCH (B) OR PRODUCT-SUSTAINING (P) |
|---|---|---|
| Run machines | Number of machine hours | B |
| Set up machines | Number of setups or setup hours | B |
| Schedule production jobs | Number of production runs | B |
| Receive materials | Number of material receipts | B |
| Support existing products | Number of products | P |
| Introduce new products | Number of new products introduced | P |
| Modify product characteristics | Number of engineering change notices | P |

To assign activity costs to individual products requires knowledge of the *quantity* of the activity cost driver for every individual product. That is, in addition to knowing the materials content, and the direct labor and machine hours required at each production cost center, the ABC system must know, product by product, the quantity of each activity cost driver; for example, for each product, the system must have information on drivers such as:

- Number of setups
- Number of material purchases
- Number of material moves
- Number of engineering change notices

This is a large increase in the amount of information that must be collected. Fortunately, the increased availability of integrated information systems, particularly newly installed enterprisewide systems, enables activity cost driver information to be much more accessible, at low cost, than in the past.

Let us illustrate how to work with activity cost drivers by extending our simple example of the materials handling department in the Williams Corporation. We determined earlier that the materials handling burden rate was $1.25 per direct labor hour ($50,000 department cost per month/40,000 average direct labor hours per month).

Consider a low-volume product, Widget A. About 100 units of Widget A are produced each month. It takes one hour of direct labor to produce each Widget A. With the company's traditional cost system, $125 of materials handling expense were allocated to Widget A each month.

The new ABC system at Williams identified three primary activities done by the materials handling department: receive parts, receive materials, and disburse parts to the production floor. For each of these activities, the ABC system designers chose an appropriate cost driver, and then collected the quantity of the cost driver. They then divided the assigned activity expense by the quantity of the activity cost driver to obtain the activity cost driver rate. The calculations are shown below:

|  | RECEIVE PARTS | RECEIVE MATERIALS | DISBURSE PARTS AND MATERIALS |
|---|---|---|---|
| Activity cost driver | No. of parts receipts | No. of materials receipts | No. of production runs |
| Activity cost | $25,000 | $12,500 | $12,500 |
| Driver quantity | 2,500 receipts | 1,000 receipts | 500 runs |
| Activity cost driver rate | $10/receipt | $12.50/receipt | $25/run |

Widget A is quite a complex product, with more than 50 separate purchased parts and several different types of raw materials required to assemble a finished product. Producing the 100 units of Widget A during the month typically requires one production run, 20 purchased parts shipments, and four raw materials shipments (many shipments are required even for only one production run because of the large number of different parts and materials required to produce Widget A). Using the activity cost drivers to assign materials handling costs to Widget A yields the following computation:

| ACTIVITY | QUANTITY OF ACTIVITY COST DRIVER | ACTIVITY COST DRIVER RATE | ACTIVITY COST |
|---|---|---|---|
| Receive parts | 20 | $10/receipt | $200 |
| Receive materials | 4 | 12.50/receipt | 50 |
| Disburse materials | 1 | 25/run | 25 |
| Total materials handling costs | | | $275 |

The per widget cost of materials handling of $2.75 (= $275/100) is more than twice the $1.25 cost assigned by the traditional direct labor allocation system. The assignment is much higher because of the complexity of Widget A—it requires many different raw materials and purchased parts—and also because production runs are relatively short for this low-volume product.

## Selecting Activity Cost Drivers

The selection of an activity cost driver reflects a subjective tradeoff between accuracy and the cost of measurement. Because of the large number of potential activity-to-product linkages, designers attempt to economize on the number of different activity cost drivers. For example, activities triggered by the same event—prepare production orders, schedule production runs, perform first part inspections, or move materials—can all use the same activity cost driver: number of production runs or lots produced.

ABC system designers can choose from different types of activity cost drivers:

1. Transaction
2. Duration
3. Intensity or direct charging

**Transaction drivers**, such as the number of setups, number of receipts, and number of products supported, count how often an activity is performed. Transaction drivers can be used when all outputs make essentially the same demands on the activity. For example, scheduling a production run, processing a purchase order, or maintaining a unique part number may take the same time and effort independent of which product is being scheduled, which material is being purchased, or which part is being supported in the system.

Transaction drivers are the least expensive type of cost driver but could be the least accurate, because they assume that the same quantity of resources is required every time an activity is performed. For example, the use of a transaction driver such as the number of setups assumes that all setups take the same time to perform. For many activities, the variation in use by individual products is small enough that a transaction driver will be fine for assigning activity expenses to the product. If, however, the amount of resources required to perform the activity varies considerably, from product to product, then more accurate and more expensive cost drivers are required.

**Duration drivers** represent the amount of time required to perform an activity. Duration drivers should be used when significant variation exists in the amount of activity required for different outputs. For example, simple products may require only 10–15 minutes to set up, whereas complex, high-precision products may require 6 hours for setup. Using a transaction driver, such as number of setups, will overcost the resources required to set up simple products and will undercost the resources required for complex products. To avoid this distortion, ABC designers would use a duration driver, such as setup hours, to assign the cost of setups to individual products.

Examples of duration drivers include setup hours, inspection hours, and direct labor hours. They are more accurate than transaction drivers, but they are much more expensive to implement because the model requires an estimate of the duration each time an activity is performed. With only a transaction driver (number of setups), the designer would need to know only how many times a product was set up, information that should be readily available from the production scheduling system. Knowing the setup time for each product is an additional, and more costly, piece of information. Some companies estimate duration by constructing an index based on the complexity of the output being handled. The index would be a function of the complexity of the product or customer processed by the activity, assuming that complexity influences the time required to perform the activity. The choice between a duration and a transaction driver is, as always, one of economics, balancing the benefits of increased accuracy against the costs of increased measurement.

For some activities, however, even duration drivers may not be accurate. **Intensity drivers** directly charge for the resources used each time an activity is performed. In our setup example, a particularly complex product may require special setup and quality control people, as well as special gauging and test equipment each time the machine is set up to produce the product. A duration driver, such as setup cost per hour, assumes that all setup hours on the machine are equally costly, but it does not reflect extra personnel, especially skilled personnel and expensive equipment that may be required on some setups but not on others. In these cases, activity costs may have to be charged directly to the product, on the basis of work orders or other records that accumulate the activity expenses incurred for that product.

Intensity drivers using direct charging are the most accurate activity cost drivers but are the most expensive to implement; in effect they require a job order costing system to keep track of all the resources used each time an activity is performed. They should be used only when the resources associated with performing an activity are both expensive and variable each time an activity is performed.

The choice among a transaction, duration, or direct charging (intensity) cost driver can occur for almost any activity. For example, for performing engineering change notices (to upgrade and support existing products), we could use:

- Cost per engineering change notice (assumes that all engineering change notices consume the same quantity and cost of resources)
- Cost per engineering change hour used for the engineering change notice done for an individual product (allows for engineering change notices to use different amounts of time to perform but assumes that all engineering hour costs are the same)
- Cost of engineering resources actually used (number of engineering hours, price per hour of engineers used, plus cost of equipment such as engineering workstations) on the job

Similarly, for a sales activity, such as support existing customers, we could use either a transaction, a duration, or an intensity driver. For example,

- Cost per customer (assumes that all customers cost the same)
- Cost per customer hour (assumes that different customers use different amounts of sales resource time, but each hour of support time costs the same)
- Actual cost per customer (actual or estimated time and specific resources committed to specific customers)

Often, ABC analysts, rather than actually record the time and resources required for an individual product or customer, may simulate an intensity driver with a weighted index approach. They ask individuals to estimate the relative difficulty of performing the task for one type of product or customer or another. A standard product or customer may get a weight of 1; a medium complexity product or customer may get a weight of 3 to 5, and a particularly complex (demanding) product or customer may get a weight of, say, 10. In this way, the variation in demands for an activity among products and customers can be captured without an overly complex measurement system. Again, the important message is to make an appropriate tradeoff between accuracy and the cost of measurement. The goal is to be approximately right; for many purposes, transaction drivers or estimates of relative difficulty may be fine for estimating resource consumption by individual products, services, and customers.

Activity cost drivers are the central innovation of activity-based cost systems, but they are also the most costly aspects of ABC systems. Often, project teams get carried away with the potential capabilities of an activity-based cost system to capture accurately the economics of their organization's operations. The teams see diversity and complexity everywhere and design systems with upwards of 500 activities. But, in selecting and measuring the activity cost drivers for such a system, a reality check takes hold. Assuming that each different activity requires a different activity cost driver,[5] and that the organization has, say, 5,000 individual products and customers (not an atypically low number for many organizations), then the analyst must be able to enter up to 2,500,000 pieces of information (500 × 5,000): the quantity of each activity cost driver used by each individual product and customer. This is why most ABC systems settle down, for product and customer costing purposes, to having no more than 30–50 different activity cost drivers, most of which can be accessed and traced to individual products and customers relatively simply in their organization's existing information system.[6]

## DESIGNING THE OPTIMAL SYSTEM

Is ABC just a more complex and expensive way to perform cost allocations? No. An activity-based cost system has the capability of tracing back from any cost assignment to underlying economic events. For example, setup costs are assigned on the basis of setups performed for individual products. Product support costs can be traced back to work performed to maintain products in the organization. And customer administration costs can be traced back to handling customer orders, responding to customer requests, and marketing existing and new products to particular customers.

ABC systems may use many **estimates**. For example, a system may use a transaction driver to approximate the resources used each time an activity is performed rather than a detailed cost collection (direct charging, or intensity, driver) for each occurrence of an event. Or the system may estimate the cost of a machine hour by averaging acquisition costs, maintenance costs, and operating costs of the machine over some period of time. These estimates are made, not because actual costs are impossible to trace to particular events, but because the cost of doing a very detailed and actual cost tracing is judged to be greatly in excess of the value or benefits of doing detailed, actual cost tracing. In principle, if more accurate cost attribution were desired, the ABC designer could install a more precise (and much more expensive) measurement system, and the task would be accomplished. So one should not confuse the extensive use of estimates in an ABC cost model (which is a design judgment made, on a cost/benefit basis) from arbitrary allocations, which are absent from a properly designed ABC system. When arbitrary allocations are used, no cause-and-effect relationship can be established between the cost object to which the cost has been assigned and the resources whose cost has been assigned. In an ABC system, every cost assignment to an activity, or a product, service, or customer, should be transparent and traceable, via cause-and-effect relationships, to the demand for resources by the cost object (whether an activity, product, service, or customer).

The goal of a properly constructed ABC system is not to have the most accurate cost system. Consider a target where the bull's-eye represents the actual cost of resources used each time a product is made, a service delivered, and a customer served.[7] To hit this bull's-eye each time requires an enormously expensive system. But a relatively simple system—perhaps 30–50 activities and using good estimates and many transaction drivers, with few intensity drivers or direct charging—should enable the outer and middle rings of the target to be hit consistently; that is, activity and process costs will be accurate to within 5% or 10%. Traditional cost systems virtually never even hit the target, or even the wall on which the target is mounted, as their highly distorted costs approximate firing a shotgun at a barn but shooting directly up in the air or to the sides. Good engineering judgment should be used; 90% or more of the benefits from a more accurate cost system can be obtained with relatively simple ABC systems.

The goal should be to have the best cost system, one that balances the cost of errors made from inaccurate estimates with the cost of measurement (see Exhibit 4-4). Traditional cost systems are inexpensive to operate, but they lead to large distortions in reporting the cost of activities, processes, products, services, and customers. Consequently, managers may make serious mistakes in decisions made on the basis of this information; there is a high cost of errors. But attempting to build an ABC system with 1,000 or more activities, and directly charging actual resource costs to each activity performed for each product, service, and customer would lead to an enormously expensive system. The cost of operating such a system would greatly exceed the benefits in terms of improved decisions made with this slightly more accurate information.

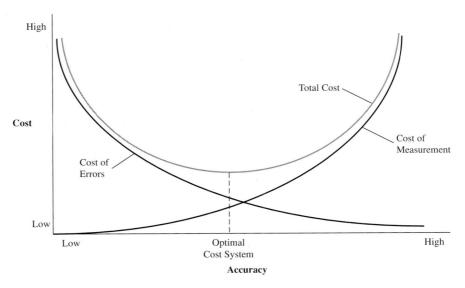

**EXHIBIT 4-4** Activity-Based Costing—Designing the Optimal ABC System

## SUMMARY

Activity-based cost systems provide more accurate cost information about business activities and processes and about the products, services, and customers served by these processes than do traditional cost systems. ABC systems focus on organizational activities as the key element for analyzing cost behavior in organizations by linking organizational spending on resources to the activities and business processes performed by those resources. Activity cost drivers, collected from diverse corporate information systems, then drive activity costs to the products, services, and customers that create the demand for (or are benefiting from) the organizational activities. These procedures produce good estimates of the quantities and the unit costs of the activities and resources deployed for individual products, services, and customers. Just how to use and interpret this more accurate information is the subject of the next two chapters.

## ENDNOTES

**1.** We retain the convention, used in earlier chapters, of using the word *products* to represent not only products produced but also services delivered and customers served. Some people refer to products, services, and customers as *cost objects*. We prefer to use the more familiar word *product* rather than the technical term *cost object*.

**2.** This example is taken from R. Cooper and R. S. Kaplan, "Measure Costs Right: Make the Right Decisions," *Harvard Business Review* (September–October 1988), p. 99.

**3.** See R. S. Kaplan, "Flexible Budgeting in an Activity-Based Costing Framework, *Accounting Horizons* (June 1994), pp. 104–09; and L. F. Christenson and D. Sharp, "How ABC Can Add Value to Decision Making," *Management Accounting* (May 1993), pp. 38–42.

4. The characterization of unit, batch, and product-sustaining activities is due to R. Cooper, "Cost Classifications in Unit-Based and Activity-Based Manufacturing Cost Systems," *Journal of Cost Management* (Fall 1990), pp. 4–14.

5. For product and customer costing purposes, this assumption is correct because any two activities that share a common cost driver (such as number of setups on a particular machine or number of customer requests) can be combined into a single activity without any loss of accuracy. For understanding activity and process costs, however, ABC designers may keep the activities separate even when they share a common cost driver to give visibility to all the individual activities triggered by an incidence of an activity cost driver (a setup or a customer request).

6. With the increased use of integrated, enterprisewide systems, a large number of potential activity cost drivers for ABC systems become automatically available.

7. R. Cooper, "The Rise of Activity-Based Costing—Part Three: How Many Cost Drivers Do You Need and How Do You Select Them?" *Journal of Cost Management* (Winter 1989), p. 34–46.

---

## ■ *CASES*

## THE CLASSIC PEN COMPANY

Jane Dempsey, controller of the Classic Pen Company, was concerned about the recent financial trends in operating results. Classic Pen had been the low-cost producer of traditional BLUE pens and BLACK pens. Profit margins were over 20% of sales.

Several years earlier Dennis Selmor, the sales manager, had seen opportunities to expand the business by extending the product line into new products that offered premium selling prices over traditional BLUE and BLACK pens. Five years earlier, RED pens had been introduced; they required the same basic production technology but could be sold at a 3% premium. And last year, PURPLE pens had been introduced because of the 10% premium in selling price they could command.

But Dempsey had just seen the financial results (see Exhibit 1) for the most recent fiscal year and was keenly disappointed.

The new RED and PURPLE pens do seen more profitable than our BLUE and BLACK

pens, but overall profitability is down, and even the new products are not earning the margins we used to see from our traditional products. Perhaps this is the tougher global competition I have been reading about. At least the new line, particularly PURPLE pens, is showing much higher margins. Perhaps we should follow Dennis's advice and introduce even more specialty colored pens. Dennis claims that consumers are willing to pay higher prices for these specialty colors.

Jeffrey Donald, the manufacturing manager, was also reflecting on the changed environment at Classic Pen:

Five years ago, life was a lot simpler. We produced just BLUE and BLACK pens in long production runs, and everything ran smoothly, without much intervention. Difficulties started when the RED pens were introduced and we had to make more changeovers. This required us to stop production, empty the vats, clean out all remnants of the previous color, and then start the production of the red ink. Making black ink was simple; we didn't even have to clean out the residual blue ink from the previous run if we just dumped in enough black ink to cover it up. But for the RED pens, even small traces of the blue or black ink created quality problems. And the ink for the new PURPLE pens also has demanding specifications, but not quite as demanding as for RED pens.

We seem to be spending a lot more time on purchasing and scheduling activities and just keeping track of where we stand on existing, backlogged, and future orders. The new computer system we got last year helped a lot to reduce the confusion. But I am concerned about rumors I keep hearing that even more new colors may be introduced in the near future. I don't think we have any more capability to handle additional confusion and complexity in our operations.

## Operations

Classic produced pens in a single factory. The major task was preparing and mixing the ink for the different-colored pens. The ink was inserted into the pens in a semiautomated process. A final packing and shipping stage was performed manually.

Each product had a bill of materials that identified the quantity and cost of direct materials required for the product. A routing sheet identified the sequence of operations required for each operating step. This information was used to calculate the labor expenses for each of the four products. All of the plant's indirect expenses were aggregated at the plant level and allocated to products on the basis of their direct labor content. Currently, this overhead burden rate was 300% of direct labor cost. Most people in the plant recalled that not too many years ago the overhead rate was only 200%.

## Activity-Based Costing

Jane Dempsey had recently attended a seminar of her professional organization in which a professor had talked about a new concept,

called activity-based costing (ABC). This concept seemed to address many of the problems she had been seeing at Classic. The speaker had even used an example that seemed to capture Classic's situation exactly.

The professor had argued that overhead should not be viewed as a cost or a burden to be allocated on top of direct labor. Rather, the organization should focus on activities performed by the indirect and support resource of the organization and try to link the cost of performing these activities directly to the products for which they were performed. Dempsey obtained several books and articles on the subject and soon tried to put into practice the message she had heard and read about.

## Activity-Based Cost Analysis

Dempsey first identified six categories of support expenses that were currently being allocated to pen production:

| EXPENSE CATEGORY | EXPENSE |
|---|---|
| Indirect labor | $20,000 |
| Fringe benefits ~ 40% of (DIR+IND) LAB | 16,000 |
| Computer systems | 10,000 |
| Machinery | 8,000 |
| Maintenance | 4,000 |
| Energy | 2,000 |
| Total | $60,000 |

She determined that the fringe benefits were 40% of labor expenses (both direct and indirect) and would thus represent just a percentage markup to be applied on top of direct and indirect labor charges.

Dempsey interviewed department heads in charge of indirect labor and found that three main activities accounted for their work. About half of indirect labor was involved in scheduling or handling production runs. This proportion included scheduling production orders; purchasing, preparing, and releasing materials for the production run; performing a first-item inspection every time the process was changed over, and some scrap loss at the beginning of each run until the process settled down. Another 40% of indirect labor was required just for the physical changeover from one color pen to another.

The time to change over to BLACK pens was relatively short (about 1 hour) since the previous color did not have to be completely eliminated from the machinery. Other colors required longer changeover times; RED pens required the most extensive changeover to meet the demanding quality specification for this color.

The remaining 10% of the time was spent maintaining records on the four products, including the bill of materials and routing information, monitoring and maintaining a minimum supply of raw materials and finished goods inventory for each product, improving the production processes, and performing engineering changes for the products. Dempsey also collected information on potential activity cost drivers for Classic's activities (see Exhibit 2) and the distribution of the cost drivers for each of the

four products. Dempsey next turned her attention to the $10,000 of expenses to operate the company's computer system. She interviewed the managers of the Data Center and the Management Information System departments and found that most of the computer's time (and software expense) was used to schedule production runs in the factory and to order and pay for the materials required in each production run.

Because each production run was made for a particular customer, the computer time required to prepare shipping documents and to invoice and collect from a customer was also included in this activity. In total, about 80% of the computer resource was involved in the production run activity. Almost all of the remaining computer expense (20%) was used to keep records on the four products, including production process and associated engineering change notice information.

The remaining three categories of overhead expense (machine depreciation, machine maintenance, and the energy to operate the machines) were incurred to supply machine capacity to produce the pens. The machines had a practical capacity of 10,000 hours of productive time that could be supplied to pen production.

Dempsey believed that she now had the information she needed to estimate an activity-based cost model for Classic Pen.

## EXHIBIT 1  Traditional Income Statement

|  | BLUE | BLACK | RED | PURPLE | TOTAL |
|---|---|---|---|---|---|
| Sales | $75,000 | $60,000 | $13,950 | $1,650 | $150,600 |
| Material costs | 25,000 | 20,000 | 4,680 | 550 | 50,230 |
| Direct labor | 10,000 | 8,000 | 1,800 | 200 | 20,000 |
| Overhead @ 300% | 30,000 | 24,000 | 5,400 | 600 | 60,000 |
| Total operating income | $10,000 | $ 8,000 | $ 2,070 | $ 300 | $ 20,370 |
| Return on sales | 13.3% | 13.3% | 14.8% | 18.2% | 13.5% |

**EXHIBIT 2** Direct Costs and Activity Cost Drivers

|  | BLUE | BLACK | RED | PURPLE | TOTAL |
|---|---|---|---|---|---|
| Production sales volume (no. of units) | 50,000 | 40,000 | 9,000 | 1,000 | 100,000 |
| Unit selling price | $1.50 | $1.50 | $1.55 | $1.65 | |
| Materials/unit cost | $0.50 | $0.50 | $0.52 | $0.55 | |
| Direct labor hr/unit | 0.02 | 0.02 | 0.02 | 0.02 | 2,000 |
| Machine hour/unit | 0.1 | 0.1 | 0.1 | 0.1 | 10,000 |
| No. of production runs | 50 | 50 | 38 | 12 | 150 |
| Setup time/run (hours) | 4 | 1 | 6 | 4 | |
| Total setup time (hours) | 200 | 50 | 228 | 48 | 526 |
| Number of products | 1 | 1 | 1 | 1 | 4 |

### Required

1. Estimate the costs for the four pen products using an activity-based approach.

2. What are the managerial implications from the revised cost estimates?

## WESTERN DIALYSIS CLINIC (ABC and Healthcare)*

Western Dialysis Clinic is an independent, nonprofit full-service renal dialysis clinic. The clinic provides two types of treatments. Hemodialysis (HD) requires patients to visit a dialysis clinic three times a week, where they are connected to special, expensive equipment to perform the dialysis. Peritoneal dialysis (PD) allows patients to administer their own treatment daily at home. The clinic monitors PD patients and assists them in ordering supplies consumed during the home treatment. The total and product-line income statement for the clinic is shown below:

*This case is adapted from T. D. West and D. A. West, "Applying ABC to Healthcare," *Management Accounting* (February 1997), pp. 22–33.

| CLINIC INCOME STATEMENT | TOTAL | HD | PD |
|---|---|---|---|
| Revenues | | | |
| Number of patients | 164 | 102 | 62 |
| Number of treatments | 34,067 | 14,343 | 20,624 |
| Total revenue | $3,006,775 | $1,860,287 | $1,146,488 |
| Supply costs | | | |
| Standard supplies (drugs, syringes) | 664,900 | 512,619 | 152,281 |
| Episodic supplies (for special conditions) | 310,695 | 98,680 | 212,015 |
| Total supply costs | 975,595 | 611,299 | 364,296 |

*continued*

| CLINIC INCOME STATEMENT | TOTAL | HD | PD |
|---|---|---|---|
| Service costs | | | |
| General overhead (occupancy, administration) | 785,825 | | |
| Durable equipment (maintenance, depreciation) | 137,046 | | |
| Nursing services (RNs, LPNs, nursing | | | |
| administrators, equipment technicians) | 883,280 | | |
| Total service costs | 1,806,151 | 1,117,463 | 688,688 |
| Total operating expenses | $2,781,746 | $1,728,762 | $1,052,984 |
| Net income | $  225,029 | $  131,525 | $   93,504 |
| Treatment Level Profit | | | |
| Average charge per treatment | | $129.70 | $55.59 |
| Average cost per treatment | | 120.53 | 51.06 |
| Profit per treatment | | $  9.17 | $ 4.53 |

The existing cost system assigned the traceable supply costs directly to the two types of treatments. The service costs, however, were not analyzed by type of treatment. The total service costs of $1,800,000 were allocated to the treatments using the traditional ratio-of-cost-to-charges (RCC) method developed for government cost-based reimbursement programs. With this procedure, since HD treatments represented about 61% of total revenues, HD received an allocation of 61% of the $1,800,000 service expenses (approximately $1,100,000).

For many years, the clinics such as West received much of their reimbursement on the basis of reported costs. Starting in the 1980s, however, payment mechanisms shifted, and West now received most of its reimbursement on the basis of a fixed fee not the cost of service provided. In particular, because HD and PD procedures were categorized by the government as a single category—dialysis treatment—the weekly reimbursement for each patient was the same: $389.10. As a consequence, the three HD treatments per week led to a reported revenue per HD treatment of $129.70, and the seven PD treatments per week led to a reported revenue per PD treatment of $55.59. Both procedures appeared to be profitable, according to the clinic's existing cost and revenue recognition system. David Thomas, the controller of Western Dialysis was concerned, however, that the procedures currently being used to assign common expenses may not be representative of the underlying use of the common resources by the two different procedures. He wanted to understand their costs better so that Western's managers could make more-informed decisions about extending or contracting products and services and about where to look for process improvements. Thomas decided to explore whether activity-based costing principles could provide a better idea of the underlying cost and profitability of HD and PD treatments.

### Phase I

In his initial analysis, Thomas decided to focus on the General Overhead category. But rather than continue to use the RCC method for allocating equipment and nursing costs, he asked the clinic staff for their judgments about how these costs should be allocated. On the basis of the staff's experience and judgment, they felt that HD treatments used about 85% of these resources, and PD about 15%.

Thomas decomposed the General Overhead category into four resource cost pools. Then, for each pool, he chose a cost driver that represented how that resource was used by the two treatments. A summary of his analysis is presented below:

| GENERAL OVERHEAD RESOURCE COST POOL | SIZE OF POOL | COST DRIVER |
|---|---|---|
| Facility costs (rent, depreciation) | $233,226 | Square feet of space |
| Administration and support staff | 354,682 | Number of patients |
| Communications systems and medical records | 157,219 | Number of treatments |
| Utilities | 40,698 | Kilowatt usage (estimated) |
| Total | $785,825 | |

Thomas then went to medical records and other sources to identify the quantities of each cost driver for the two treatment types:

| GENERAL OVERHEAD COST DRIVER | HD | PD | TOTAL |
|---|---|---|---|
| Square feet | 18,900 | 11,100 | 30,000 |
| Number of patients | 102 | 62 | 164 |
| Number of treatments | 14,343 | 20,624 | 34,967 |
| Estimated kilowatt usage | 563,295 | 99,405 | 662,700 |

### Required

(1) Prepare the revised set of cost estimates and treatment profit and loss statements for HD and PD, using the information gathered during Phase I. What led to any major difference between the RCC method for allocating cost and the Phase I ABC method?

### Phase II

Thomas was uncomfortable with the consensus estimate that nursing and equipment costs should be split 85:15 between HD and PD treatments, respectively. In particular, he knew that just the nursing resource category contained a mixture of different types of personnel: registered nurses (RNs), licensed practical nurses (LPNs), nursing administrators, and machine operators. He thought it was unlikely that each of these categories would be used in the same proportion by the two different treatments. In the next phase of analysis, Thomas disaggregated the nursing service category into four resource pools and, as with general overhead, selected an appropriate cost driver for each resource pool (see below):

| NURSING SERVICES RESOURCE POOL | SIZE OF POOL | COST DRIVER |
|---|---|---|
| Registered nurses | $239,120 | Full-time equivalents (FTEs) |
| Licensed practical nurses | 404,064 | Full-time equivalents |
| Nursing administration and support staff | 115,168 | Number of treatments |
| Dialysis machine operators | 124,928 | Number of clinic treatments |
| Total | $883,280 | |

| NURSING SERVICES COST DRIVER | HD | PD | TOTAL |
|---|---|---|---|
| RNs, FTE | 5 | 2 | 7 |
| LPNs, FTE | 15 | 4 | 19 |
| Total number of dialysis treatments | 14,343 | 20,624 | 34,967 |
| Number of clinic dialysis treatments | 14,343 | 0 | 14,343 |

Thomas felt that the 85:15 split was still reasonable for the durable equipment use, and, in any case, the relatively small size of this resource expense category probably did not warrant additional study and data collection.

### Required

(2)   Use the information on the distribution of nursing and machine operator resources to calculate revised product-line income statements and profit and loss for individual treatments.

(3)   Analyze the newly produced information and assess its implications for managers at Western Dialysis Clinic. What decisions might managers of the clinic make with this new information that might differ from those made using information from the RCC method only?

(4)   What improvements, if any, would you make in developing an ABC model for Western Dialysis Clinic?

## PAISLEY INSURANCE COMPANY: Activity-Based Costing in a Service Industry* (Bill Cotton)

The Paisley Insurance Company sells a range of insurance products to a variety of residential and commercial customers. The Billing Department (BD) at Paisley provides account inquiry and bill-printing services for the two major classes of customers—residential and commercial. At present the BD services 60,000 residential and 10,000 commercial customer accounts.

The profitability of the company is currently being affected significantly by two factors. First, increased competition in the insurance industry has led to lower insurance premiums being charged by competitors, so Paisley must find ways of reducing

---

*This case is based on an illustration used in "Implementing Activity-Based Costing—The Modeling Approach," a workshop sponsored by the Institute of Management Accountants and Sapling Corporation.

its operating costs. Second, the demand for insurance services will increase in Paisley's main geographic area because of plans for housing developments and commercial construction. The new housing development department estimates that demand from residential customers will increase by almost 20%, and commercial demand will increase by 10% during the next year. Because the BD is currently operating at full capacity, it needs to find ways to create capacity to service the increase in demand. A local service bureau has offered to take over the BD functions at an attractive lower cost (compared with the current cost). The service bureau's proposal is to provide all the functions of BD at $3.50 per account regardless of the type of account.

Exhibit 1 depicts the present traditional costing system in the BD. Note that all the costs associated with the BD are indirect; they cannot presently be traced specifically and exclusively to either customer class in an economically feasible way. The BD used a traditional costing system that allocated all support costs on the basis of the number of account inquiries generated by each of the two customer classes. Exhibit 1 shows that the cost of resources used in the BD in May 1997 was $282,670. BD received 11,500 account inquiries during the month, so the cost per inquiry was $24.58 ($282,670/11,500). There were 9,000 residential account inquiries, 78% of the total. Thus, residential accounts were charged with 78% of the support costs, and commercial accounts were charged with 22%. The resulting cost per account is $3.69 and $6.15 for residential and commercial accounts, respectively.

Management believed that the actual consumption of support resources was much greater than 22% for commercial accounts because of their complexity. For example,

commercial accounts average 50 lines per bill compared with only 12 lines per bill for residential accounts. Management was also concerned about activities such as correspondence (and supporting labor) resulting from customer inquiries, because these activities are costly but do not add value to Paisley's services from the customer's perspective. However, management wanted a more thorough understanding of key BD activities and their interrelationships before making important decisions that would affect Paisley's profitability. The company decided to perform a study of the BD using activity-based costing.

The ABC study was performed by a team of managers from the BD and the chief financial officer from the head office of Paisley. The first task of the ABC team was to determine resources, activities, and related cost drivers. Through interviews with appropriate people, the team identified the following activities and related activity cost drivers.

| ACTIVITIES | ACTIVITY COST DRIVERS |
|---|---|
| Account billing | Number of lines |
| Bill verification | Number of accounts |
| Account inquiry | Number of labor hours |
| Correspondence | Number of letters |

All the resources shown in the indirect cost pool of Exhibit 1 support these four activities. That is, labor, building occupancy, telecommunications, computer, printing machines, and paper are resources supporting account billing, bill verification, account inquiry, and correspondence. Cost drivers were chosen on the basis of two criteria:

1. There had to be a reasonable cause-and-effect relationship between the driver unit and the

consumption of resources or the incurrence of supporting activities.

2. Data on the cost driver units had to be available at reasonable cost.

The second step of the ABC team was to develop a process-based map representing the flow of activities and resources and their interrelationships. This map was developed by interviewing key personnel. Once the linkages between activities and resources were identified and checked, a process map was drawn to provide a visual representation of the operations at the BD. Exhibit 2 is a process map that depicts the flow of activities and resources at the BD. Note that there are no costs on Exhibit 2. The management team focused first on understanding business processes. Costs were not considered until the third step, after the key interrelationships of the business were understood.

In examining Exhibit 2, consider residential accounts. Three key activities support these accounts: account inquiry, correspondence, and account billing. Account inquiry activity consumes the time of personnel who perform this task. The people who perform the account inquiry activity, in turn, use telecommunication and computer resources, occupy space, and are supervised. Correspondence is sometimes necessary as a result of inquiries. The people performing the correspondence activity also require supervision. The account billing activity is performed by billing personnel using printing machines. The printing machines occupy space and require paper and computer resources. The people occupy space, use telecommunications, and are supervised. The costs of each of the resources consumed were determined during Step 3: data collection.

During Step 3, the ABC team collected relevant data concerning costs and the physi-cal flow of the cost driver units among resources and activities. Using the process map as a guide, a member of the accounting staff collected the required cost and operational data. Sources of data included the accounting records, special studies, and, sometimes, "best estimates of managers."

The total indirect costs for May 1997 were split into the new cost pools as follows:

| | |
|---|---|
| Account inquiry | $102,666 |
| Correspondence | 17,692 |
| Account billing | 117,889 |
| Bill verification | 44,423 |
| | $282,670 |

The count of activity cost driver units for the month was determined to be:

| | |
|---|---|
| Number of lines on bills | 1,220,000 |
| Number of commercial accounts | 10,000 |
| Number of labor hours | 1,650 |
| Number of letters | 1,400 |

The consumption of cost driver units by each type of account was as follows:

| | |
|---|---|
| Residential Accounts (60,000) | |
| Labor hours | 900 |
| Letters | 900 |
| Lines | 720,000 |
| Commercial Accounts (10,000) | |
| Labor hours | 750 |
| Letters | 500 |
| Lines | 500,000 |

Bill verification was required for commercial accounts only.

### Required

(1) Prepare an ABC analysis of the BD costs associated with residential accounts and commercial accounts. That is:
 (a) Calculate the cost per driver unit for each activity
 (b) Calculate the cost per account for each customer class
(2) Interpret your results, and recommend how this ABC data can be used by BD management.
(3) What are the benefits and costs of developing an ABC model for this application?

**EXHIBIT 1** Billing Department—Traditional Costing System, May 1997

INDIRECT COST POOL

| | |
|---|---|
| Labor: supervisors | $ 16,800 |
| Labor: Account inquiry | 59,200 |
| Labor: Billing | 33,750 |
| Building occupancy | 23,500 |
| Telecommunications | 29,260 |
| Computer | 89,000 |
| Printing machines | 27,500 |
| Paper | 3,660 |
| Total indirect costs | $282,670 |
| Number of inquiries | 11,500 |
| Cost per inquiry | $24.58 |

$$\text{Cost per residential account} = \frac{9{,}000 \text{ inquiries} * \$24.58}{60{,}000 \text{ accounts}} = \$3.69$$

$$\text{Cost per commercial account} = \frac{2{,}500 \text{ inquiries} * \$24.58}{10{,}000 \text{ accounts}} = \$6.15$$

Process Map of Activities

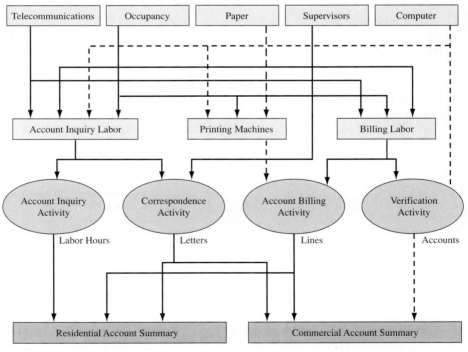

**EXHIBIT 2** The Paisley Insurance Company Billing Department

# BEDFORD MINING (Paul Foote)*

"Good news and bad news!" exclaimed the Director of Research of Bedford Mining. "We have developed a method to produce a new improved product that will provide a net 50% increase in sales measured in volume. But we have no idea if our margins will increase or decrease!" This long-awaited announcement of a new product development immediately riveted everyone's attention on the speaker. The reference to margin changes was a commentary on the inability of the Finance and Marketing departments to provide the research staff with understandable, accurate, and timely costing and marketing information.

"How can I price new products when we do not even know what it costs us to produce our existing products?" questioned the vice president of marketing. The controller retorted, "We can tell you the cost of each product in our Product Line Report!" "Oh, come on," pleaded the vice president of marketing, "you know as well as I those reports are prepared for accountants by accountants and don't tell us anything about the real world. Our customers already think we are overcharging them. Sometimes we worry we are bringing in unprofitable business. Competitors are dropping like flies, and some days we wonder if we are the only sucker left. Most days our bids are too high; on other days no one objects to our price increases, and we wonder if our prices are too low."

"Since we already provide you with every report known to man, what additional information could we possibly provide you?" asked the controller. After thinking for a moment, the vice president of operations stated, "I don't know exactly what I need, but I cer-

tainly know we need a change! And I can tell you that I'll know it when I see it!"

## Manufacturing and Financial Information

At Bedford Mining, the raw ore is exposed in an open pit mine through a continuous stripping process to remove the overburden. The raw ore is then loaded into large dump trucks that drive the ore to a conveyor system. Before being conveyed out of the mine to the refiner, the raw ore is blended to maintain a consistent blend. This practice eliminates adjustments in the refinery and maximizes the different ores and ore grades throughout the mine.

In the refinery, the raw ore is partially crushed and screened and blended with a weak solution of raw ore and water. The mixture is thickened through a series of tanks. After reaching a certain chemical content, the mixture is allowed to dry. Dried product is screened into particular mesh sizes and is either sent to bulk storage, loaded in bulk, or packaged and shipped.

Fifty thousand tons of Product A are expected to be mined, refined, shipped, and invoiced to customers next year. There will be no changes to inventory. The mine and refinery adjust to customers' requests to receive products just-in-time, allowing them to delay cash expenditures and reduce warehouse space requirements. Increased competition, in combination with a generally restrained domestic and international economic outlook, provided the mine and refinery with some unused capacity. Quality programs instituted at the mine and refinery reduced the customers' inspection costs and allowed the mine and refinery to respond quickly to customer orders.

Manufacturing costs are generated by a standard variable cost system that includes

---

*Reprinted with permission from AICPA Case Development Program, Copyright © 1994 by the American Institute of Certified Public Accountants.

**EXHIBIT 1** Cost of Goods Sold: Existing Costing System

|  | COST PER TON | PRODUCT A (50,000 TONS) TOTAL COST | COST PER TON | PRODUCT B (25,000 TONS) TOTAL COST |
|---|---|---|---|---|
| Materials | $150 | $ 7,500,000 | $120 | $3,000,000 |
| Labor and benefits | 75 | 3,750,000 | 75 | 1,875,000 |
| Variable overhead | 35 | 1,750,000 | 40 | 1,000,000 |
| Fixed overhead | 60 | 3,000,000 | 55 | 1,375,000 |
| Total | $320 | $16,000,000 | $290 | $7,250,000 |

the costs of raw materials from the mine and feeds from suppliers. The cost of labor, primarily performing maintenance and operations, is predetermined by a 3-year contract. Variable overhead allocations are based on the consumption of materials and labor. Fixed overhead includes depreciation, amortization of the mine asset, insurance, property tax, and environmental compliance.

Selling costs are related to servicing existing and potential customer accounts. Commissions are paid to distributors who sell the product directly to customers. Shipping costs include the cost of third-party truck and rail delivery. General expenses include the salaries and expenses of support departments such as finance, legal, and administrative.

The finance staff had analyzed the costs for the existing product (A) and the proposed product (B) using the company's existing costing system (Exhibit 1). Profit before tax was calculated using the predictions generated from the current cost system (Exhibit 2). This analysis suggested that Product B would be unprofitable and therefore should not be introduced. After the senior management meeting, discussed above, however, the controller recommended that an activity-based cost analysis be performed and the outcome be compared with the predictions from the existing costing system.

### Activity Analysis

Performing an activity-based analysis provides an entirely different perspective on the assignment of costs between the two products. Rather than use a few large overhead pools, activity-based costing assigns the costs to each activity performed, within a relevant production rate, leaving a much smaller portion of costs to be arbitrarily allocated. The following is a simplification of the results of the workflow analysis:

1. Stripping and mining costs for Product A would be $190 per ton and $110 per ton for Product B.

**EXHIBIT 2** Profit before Tax: Existing Costing System

| STATEMENT OF OPERATIONS | PRODUCT A | PRODUCT B | TOTAL |
|---|---|---|---|
| Sales | $47,000,000 | $13,000,000 | $60,000,000 |
| Cost of goods sold | 16,000,000 | 7,250,000 | 23,250,000 |
| Gross margin | $31,000,000 | $ 5,750,000 | $36,750,000 |
| Selling cost | 6,500,000 | 1,000,000 | 7,500,000 |
| Shipping cost | 14,000,000 | 5,600,000 | 19,600,000 |
| General expenses | 4,000,000 | 500,000 | 4,500,000 |
| Profit before tax | $ 6,500,000 | $(1,350,000) | $ 5,150,000 |

2. Blending costs for both Product A and Product B would be $10 per ton.

3. Crushing costs for Product A and Product B would be $15 per ton.

4. Thickening costs for Product A would be $49 per ton and $0 per ton for Product B. The workflow analysis revealed that thickening was not necessary for the new product, and therefore it assigned no cost for this process. Under the current system, the $49 per ton cost would have been automatically assigned to Product B costs.

5. Drying and sizing costs for Product A would be $76 per ton and $100 per ton for Product B. Because of its chemical properties, Product B would not require sizing, thereby eliminating $100 per ton of cost to the customer.

6. Packaging costs for Product A would be $124 per ton and $20 per ton for Product B.

Customers were expected to take most of Product B in bulk, eliminating most packaging costs.

7. Delivery costs for Product A would be $197 per ton and $106 per ton for Product B. Product B would be sold primarily to existing customers and therefore would use the available room in containers already charged at a flat rate.

8. Commissions for Product A would be $100 per ton and $111 per ton for Product B. Product B costs would be higher because of increased advertising and promotion by the distributors to introduce the new product.

### Required

Should Product B be introduced?

---

# THE ROSSFORD PLANT*
## (Robert Colson and Mark MacGuidwin)

Having heard a professor speak on some of the shortcomings of current cost account systems, I decided to undertake a review of the cost accounting system at our Rossford Plant. I was particularly concerned whether the overhead costs were being allocated to products according to the resource demands of the products. Costing our products accurately has become more important for strategic purposes because of pressures to unbundle sets of original equipment windows for the automakers.

*Mark MacGuidwin, Corporate Controller,*
*Libbey-Owens-Ford Co.*

## Background

Libbey-Owens-Ford Co. (L-O-F), one of the companies in the Pilkington Group, has been a major producer of glass in the United States since the turn of the century. Its Rossford

Plant produces about 12,000,000 "lites" of tempered glass per year. (A lite is a unit such as rear window, which is called a "back lite," or a side window, which is called a "side lite.") The plant makes front door windows, quarter windows, back windows, and sunroofs. About 96% of the lites produced are sold to original equipment (OE) automotive customers; the remaining 4% are shipped to replacement depots for later sale to replacement glass wholesalers. Lite sizes range from 0.73 square feet for certain quarter windows to about 13 square feet for the back lite of a Camaro or Firebird. The average size is approximately 4 square feet.

The Rossford Plant comprises two production processes: float and fabrication ("fab"). The float process produces raw float glass, the raw material for automotive windows. Blocks of float glass are transferred to the fab facility, where lites are cut to size, edged, shaped, and strengthened. The final product is then inspected, packed, and shipped.

*Reprinted with permission from Volume 5 of *Cases from Management Accounting Practice*, from the IMA/AAA Management Accounting Symposium series.

Parts of the Rossford Plant date to the founding of the company. Unlike other L-O-F plants, which were designed around the automated Pilkington float-tank process with computer-controlled cutting and finishing operations, the Rossford Plant was designed for the older process of polishing plate glass to final products. Pilkington float tanks were installed in the plant during the 1970s, and the cutting processes were substantially automated during the 1980s. However, the finishing processes have not yet been automated to the extent that they have been at the other plants.

Mark MacGuidwin, Corporate Controller of L-O-F, and Ed Lackner, Rossford's Plant Controller, became concerned during 1987 about the cost allocation process at Rossford for several reasons. First, the process had not been critically evaluated since the automation of the cutting processes. Second, the overhead cost structure at Rossford differed dramatically from that of other L-O-F plants. A larger pool of indirect costs was allocated to equipment centers. Third, they believed that the cost allocation process at Rossford was not accurately assigning costs to units of product. And fourth, changes in the company's competitive environment were raising strategic issues that demanded accurate product cost information for pricing, product mix, and production scheduling purposes.

### Relationship of Size to Profit

In his investigation, MacGuidwin discovered what he believed were two key observations made by the vice presidents of engineering and manufacturing. Historically, in the automotive glass business, original equipment (OE) customers purchased a complete set of windows for a car model from a single glass manufacturer. Therefore, from the glass manufacturer's perspective, it was only necessary that the markup on cost for the entire set, or bundle, of glass units be adequate for profitability. Despite the buying habits of these OE customers, however, firms in the industry quoted selling prices for individual units of glass within each set. As easy benchmarks, the selling prices were customarily set in proportion to the size in square feet of the units, with smaller lites priced lower than larger lites.

The managers knew, however, that the cost of producing automotive glass is not related proportionately to the size of the unit produced. The production process involves two principal fabricating operations: cutting the unit from a larger block of glass and then bending it to the necessary shape and strengthening it in a tempering furnace. Neither the cutting nor the tempering cost is proportional to the size of the unit produced. Only a limited number of units can be fed into either a cutting machine or a tempering furnace regardless of the size of the units, with little or no difference in feed rates or resource consumption related to size.

The joint effect of these two observations is an understanding in the glass industry of the average relationship between unit size and unit profit that is depicted in Exhibit 1. Margin percentages for passenger car lites are somewhat higher than the industry average.

Recent changes in the competitive structure of the OE automotive glass industry have led to the possibility of "unbundling" sets of windows. Major customers are considering not only allowing different manufacturers to supply units for the same car model (for example, windshields from one supplier and rear windows from another) but also setting target prices based on the manufacturing costs of the units, a process already begun by General Motors. Under these circumstances, the costs reported by the accounting system for individual units of glass would now have far more strategic implications than in the past.

## Current Product Costing Process

Exhibit 2 shows the cost center groupings for the production process. The float and fabricating operations report to the same plant manager and have a common support staff. Raw glass is transferred from float to fab at standard variable plus standard fixed cost. (Profits are measured only at the point of sale of the finished product to the customer.) Direct labor and overhead costs are assigned to units of final product as follows:

1.  Direct labor costs are assigned to equipment centers (lines of machines in PC&E and furnaces in Tempering) on the basis of standard crew sizes. Thus, a labor cost per equipment hour is developed for each of the several machines and furnaces according to crew sizes and standard wage and fringe benefit rates.

2.  Overhead costs, both variable and fixed, that are directly traceable to a specific equipment center are pooled to develop a rate per equipment hour for that center.

3.  A standard feed rate is established for each lite for each applicable cutting machine and furnace, and costs are applied to product on the basis of costs per equipment hour per units fed per hour. (Feed rates to different tempering furnaces differ substantially.)

4.  General (indirect) plant overhead costs are allocated in two steps:
    a.  20% of the total is allocated to the float process, and 80% to fabricating, then
    b.  the 80% allocated to fabricating is assigned to units of product at a flat rate per square foot (approximately $1 per square foot in 1987, adjusted for differing yield rates).

The costs classified as general plant overhead amount to 30% of the total indirect costs of the plant. General plant includes approximately 100 salaried employees involved in plant management, engineering, accounting, materials control, pollution control, quality control, maintenance management, research and development, production management, and human resources. It also includes depreciation of equipment and buildings not assigned to operating departments, property taxes and insurance, general plant maintenance, and postretirement costs.

MacGuidwin decided to limit his initial analysis to the automotive glass fabricating facility at the Rossford Plant. He and Lackner were confident that the process of assigning costs to units of raw float glass was sufficiently accurate. They also believed that the direct costs of labor and overhead associated with the PC&E and Tempering Furnace equipment centers were being properly attached to units of product on the basis of the units' standard feed rates per hour. The rates had been set with downtime assumptions intended to cover mechanical and electrical problems, stockouts, and part changeovers.

"On the whole, Ed Lackner and I felt pretty good about what we were discovering," commented MacGuidwin, "Over two-thirds of the costs of the plant were being assigned to units of product on the basis of metered usage of our two constraining resources, machine time in the PCB center and furnace time in the Tempering center."

"On the other hand," Lackner pointed out, "we had a potential problem with our general plant costs. For years we had been assigning them to units produced on the basis of square footage. We knew that this allocation base didn't capture activities that were driving the overhead costs, but we didn't know whether the allocation process was substantially distorting the final product costs. Until recently it didn't matter how these costs were allocated because unit price and cost differentials did not enter into any strategic decisions."

## Alternative Allocation Method

The allocation of general plant overhead costs between float and fab seemed reasonable to the two controllers. They analyzed a number of factors that could have been driving the allocation, including the number of hourly employees, the space occupied, and the variable costs incurred. They also interviewed managers concerning where time was spent by employees in the overhead base. All indicators pointed to the appropriateness of assigning 20% of the general plant costs to float and 80% to fab.

"The principal outcome of our analysis was to propose and implement on a test basis an alternative method for reallocating the 80% allocated to fab," explained MacGuidwin. "Under the old method, we allocated a flat rate per square foot produced. This might be reasonable if each square foot of glass costs the same to make in the PC&E and Tempering departments. But we knew from our production engineers and from our own

tracking of direct costs in those cost centers that this was just not the case."

To test an alternative cost assignment method, MacGuidwin and Lackner chose four parts with the following characteristics:

1. A small, high-volume, low-profit-margin part (Truck Vent)
2. A small, high-volume, moderate-profit-margin part (Passenger Car Rear Quarter Window)
3. A large, high-volume, moderate-profit-margin part (Passenger Car Front Door)
4. A large, moderate-volume, high-profit-margin part (Passenger Car Back Lite, Heated)

As indicated in the following table, the direct costs of fabricating these parts differ substantially:

| PART | SQUARE FEET PER UNIT | COST PER SQUARE FOOT CUTTING | COST PER SQUARE FOOT FURNACE |
|---|---|---|---|
| Truck vent | 0.77 | $2.870 | $1.676 |
| Passenger car rear quarter | 0.73 | 1.494 | 3.312 |
| Passenger car front door | 5.03 | 0.340 | 0.634 |
| Passenger car back lite | 7.07 | 0.206 | 0.682 |

The input measure selected as the basis for allocating general plant overhead costs to units of product was the scarcest (bottleneck) resource in the facility: time spent in the tempering furnaces. The production plan indicated a furnace capacity of 48,500 hours per year. Dividing the portion of the costs assigned to fab by the furnace capacity resulted in a rate of $503 per furnace hour.

Using the feed rates of the individual pieces, MacGuidwin was able to compute a new standard cost for each of the four prod-

ucts. Table 1 shows the standard cost per square foot, the cost per lite, and the gross margin percentage of each product under both the old and new methods of allocating general plant overhead. The corporate controller seemed pleased with the results:

Although the results shown for the four products are not as dramatic as I've seen for some manufacturers, they do indicate a need to rethink and reanalyze our cost allocation system. Basically, the new method of allocating general plant overhead represents more closely what the engineering and

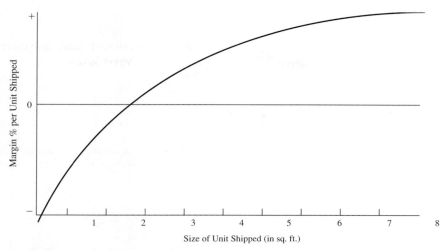

**EXHIBIT 1**  Unit Size/Unit Profit Relationship

manufacturing vice presidents were telling me about cost incurrence. The old system allocated a large pool of indirect costs equally to output, whereas the new system makes some attempt to associate those costs with the resource demands placed on our productive capacity by individual products. The old method clearly distorted our product costs. The new method should work better as long as we produce at plant capacity.

### Required

(1)   What is the cost object before the change in the product costing system? After the change? Why did MacGuidwin and Lackner change the focus of the system?

(2)   What are the characteristics of a good product costing system?

(3)   How do the process control and product costing functions of Rossford's cost accounting system interact? What conversion costs are treated as direct product costs in the system?

(4)   In your opinion, is the new cost assignment method for general plant costs better than the old method? Why or why not?

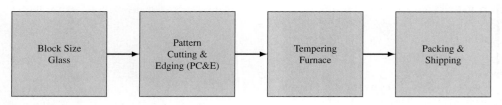

**EXHIBIT 2**  Production Cost Centers

**TABLE 1** Unit Data under Old and New Allocation Methods

| | TRUCK VENT | | | | PASSENGER CAR FRONT DOOR | | | |
| | OLD | | NEW | | OLD | | NEW | |
| | AMOUNT | PERCENT | AMOUNT | PERCENT | AMOUNT | PERCENT | AMOUNT | PERCENT |
|---|---|---|---|---|---|---|---|---|
| Cutting | $2.870 | 47 | $2.870 | 42 | $ 0.340 | 12 | $ 0.340 | 14 |
| Furnace | 1.676 | 27 | 1.676 | 24 | 0.634 | 23 | 0.634 | 25 |
| General plant | 1.020 | 17 | 1.740 | 25 | 1.036 | 38 | 0.800 | 32 |
| All other costs | 0.566 | 9 | 0.566 | 8 | 0.716 | 26 | 0.716 | 29 |
| Std. cost per sq. ft. | $6.132 | 100 | $6.852 | 100 | $ 2.726 | 100 | $ 2.490 | 100 |
| Sq. ft. per lite | 0.770 | | 0.770 | | 5.030 | | 5.030 | |
| Cost per lite | $4.722 | | $5.276 | | $13.712 | | $12.525 | |
| Selling price | $2.820 | | $2.820 | | $16.820 | | $16.820 | |
| Gross margin (percent) | (67) | | (87) | | 18 | | 26 | |

| | PASSENGER CAR REAR QUARTER | | | | PASSENGER CAR BACK LITE | | | |
| | OLD | | NEW | | OLD | | NEW | |
| | AMOUNT | PERCENT | AMOUNT | PERCENT | AMOUNT | PERCENT | AMOUNT | PERCENT |
|---|---|---|---|---|---|---|---|---|
| Cutting | $1.494 | 21 | $1.494 | 16 | $0.206 | 5 | $0.206 | 6 |
| Furnace | 3.312 | 47 | 3.312 | 36 | 0.682 | 18 | 0.682 | 20 |
| General plant | 1.022 | 14 | 3.020 | 33 | 1.064 | 28 | 0.674 | 20 |
| All other costs | 1.266 | 18 | 1.266 | 14 | 1.810 | 48 | 1.810 | 54 |
| Std. cost per sq. ft. | $7.094 | 100 | $9.094 | 100 | $2.726 | 100 | $2.490 | 100 |
| Sq. ft. per lite | 0.730 | | 0.730 | | 7.070 | | 7.070 | |
| Cost per lite | $5.179 | | $6.637 | | $26.597 | | $23.840 | |
| Selling price | $6.680 | | $6.680 | | $56.120 | | $56.120 | |
| Gross margin (percent) | 22 | | 1 | | 53 | | 58 | |

# THE PORTABLES GROUP*
## (John Jonez and Michael Wright)

Tektronix, Inc., headquartered in Portland, Oregon, is a world leader in the production of electronic test and measurement instruments. The company's principal product since its founding in 1946 has been the oscilloscope (scope), an instrument that measures and graphically displays electronic signals. The two divisions of the Portables Group produce and market high- and medium-performance portable scopes.

Through the 1970s, Tektronix experienced almost uninterrupted growth based on a successful strategy of providing technical excellence in the scope market and continually improving its products in terms of both functionality and performance for the dollar. In the early 1980s, however, the lower-priced end of the division's medium-performance line of scopes was challenged by an aggressive low-price strategy of several Japanese competitors. Moving in from the low-price, low-performance market segment in which Tektronix had decided not to compete, these companies set prices 25% below the U.S. firm's prevailing prices. Rather than moving up the scale to more highly differentiated products, the group management decided to block the move.

The first step was to reduce the prices of higher-performance, higher-cost scopes to the prices of the competitors' scopes of lower performance. This short-term strategy resulted in reported losses for those instruments. The second step was to put in place a new management team whose objective was to turn the business around. These managers concluded that, contrary to conventional wis-

dom, the Portables Group divisions could compete successfully with foreign competition on a cost basis. To do so, the divisions would have to reduce costs and increase customer value by increasing operational efficiency.

### Production Process Changes

The production process in the Portables Group divisions consisted of many functional islands, including etched circuit board (ECB), insertion, ECB assembly, ECB testing, ECB repair, final assembly, test, thermal cycle, test/QC, cabinet fitting, finishing, boxing for shipment, and shipment. The new management team consolidated these functionally oriented activities into integrated production lines in open work spaces that allowed visual control of the entire production area. Parts inventory areas were also placed parallel to production lines so that, at each workstation, operators would be able to pull their own parts. This arrangement in essence created an early warning system that nearly eliminated line stoppages due to stockouts.

Additional steps were taken in the early to mid 1980s to solve managerial and technical problems, including implementation of just-in-time (JIT) delivery and scheduling techniques, total quality control (TQC), movement of manufacturing support departments into the production area, and implementation of people involvement (PI) techniques to move responsibility for problem solving down to the operating level of the divisions. The results of these changes were impressive: substantial reductions in cycle times, direct labor hours per unit, and inventory and increases in output dollars per person per day

*Reprinted with permission from Volume 5 of *Cases from Management Accounting Practice*, from the IMA/AAA Management Accounting Symposium series.

and operating income. The cost accounting group had dutifully measured these improvements, but it had not effectively supported the strategic direction of the divisions.

### Cost Accounting System

**Direct Material and Direct Labor** Exhibit 1 shows the breakdown of the total manufacturing cost of the newest portable scopes produced with the latest technologies. In most cases, materials and labor are easily traced to specific products for costing purposes. Before the mid-1980s, however, the divisions' attempts to control direct labor had been a resource drain that actually *decreased* productivity.

There were approximately 25 production cost centers in the Portables Group plant. Very detailed labor efficiency reports were prepared monthly for each cost center and each major step in the *production* process. In addition, an efficiency rating for each individual employee was computed daily. Employees reported the quantity of units produced and the time required to produce them, often overestimating the quantity produced to show improved efficiency against continually updated standards. The poor quality of collected data resulted in semiannual inventory

write-downs when physical and book quantities were compared. Michael Wright, Financial Systems Application Manager, commented on the problems:

> The inadequacy of our efficiency reporting system became clear when we analyzed one of our new JIT production lines. On a JIT manufacturing line, once the excess inventory has been flushed out, it is essentially impossible for any person to work faster or slower than the line moves. However, if one person on the line is having a problem, it immediately becomes apparent because the product flow on the line stops. Corrective action is then taken, and the line is started up again.

> On that line, the system told us that the efficiency of each of the workers was decreasing. However, stepping back from the detail of the situation allowed us to look at the overall picture. We found that the costs incurred on the line were going down and its product output was going up. Obviously, it was becoming more, not less, efficient.

The quantity of direct labor data collected and processed also was a problem. Production employees often spent 20 minutes per day completing required reports when they could have been producing output. In addition, the accounting staff was processing 35,000 labor transactions per month to account for what amounted to 3% of total manufacturing cost. "Transactions cost money," observed John Jonez, Group Cost Accounting Manager, "and lots of transactions cost lots of money."

In response to these problems, the group accounting staff greatly simplified its procedures. It abandoned the measurement of labor performance for each operation and greatly reduced the number of variances reported. Labor transactions fell to less than 70 per month, allowing the staff to spend more time on overhead allocation and other pressing issues.

**Overhead** The product costing system allocated all manufacturing overhead costs to

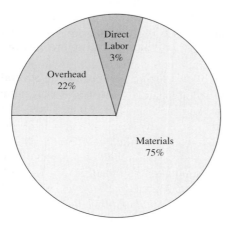

**EXHIBIT 1** Manufacturing Costs

products on the basis of standard direct labor hours. A separate rate was computed for each manufacturing cost center. This system led to rapidly increasing rates; the direct labor content of the group's products had been continually decreasing for years, while overhead costs were increasing in absolute terms. Jonez noted the problems:

> Because the costing system correlated overhead to labor, our engineers concluded that the way to reduce overhead costs was to reduce labor. The focus of cost reduction programs therefore had been the elimination of direct labor. However, most of this effort was misdirected, because there was almost no correlation between overhead cost incurrence and direct labor hours worked. Our system penalized products with proportionately higher direct labor, but it wasn't those products that caused overhead costs. We proved that. We attacked direct labor and it went down, but at the same time overhead went up.

> We knew that we needed a new way to allocate overhead. More fundamentally, we needed a way for the cost accounting system to support the manufacturing strategy of our group. The objective was clear—to provide management with accounting information that would be useful in identifying cost reduction opportunities in its operating decisions as well as provide a basis for effective reporting of accomplishments.

### Approach to Method Change

**Initial Steps**   The first step taken by Wright and Jonez in developing a new overhead allocation method was to establish a set of desirable characteristics for the method. They decided that it must accurately assign costs to products, thus providing better support for management decisions than the old method. It must support the JIT manufacturing strategy of the Portables Group. It also must be intuitively logical and easily understandable by management. And finally, it must provide information that is accessible by decision makers.

The next step was to interview the engineering and manufacturing managers who were the primary users of product cost information. These users were asked, "What is it that makes your job more difficult? What is it that makes certain products more difficult to manufacture? What causes the production line to slow down? What is it that causes overhead?" The answers to those questions were remarkably consistent; there were too many unique part numbers in the system. This finding revealed a major flaw in the ability of the direct labor–based costing method to communicate information critical for cost-related decisions. Manufacturing managers realized that there were substantial cost reduction opportunities through the standardization of component parts, but there was no direct method to communicate this idea to design and cost-reduction engineers who made part selection decisions.

Although difficult to quantify, some costs are associated with just carrying a part number in the data base. Each part number must be originally set up in the system, built into the structure of a bill of materials, and maintained until it is no longer used. Moreover, each part must be planned, scheduled, negotiated with vendors, purchased, received, stored, moved, and paid for. Having two parts similar enough that one could be used for two applications requires unnecessary duplication of these activities, and therefore unnecessary costs.

Standardizing parts results in several indirect benefits. Fewer unique part numbers usually means fewer vendors and greater quality of delivered parts. It also means smoother JIT production, fewer shutdowns of manufacturing lines, and greater field reliability. These observations led to a preliminary consensus on the need to develop a product costing method that would quantify and communicate the value of parts standardization.

**Cost Analysis**  Jonez described the next steps:

> To confirm our assessment, we segmented the total manufacturing overhead cost pool. The costs of all cost centers comprising the pool were categorized as either material-related or conversion-related based upon rules developed in conjunction with operating managers. [See Exhibit 2.]
>
> Material-related costs relate to procurement, scheduling, receiving, incoming inspection, stockroom personnel, cost-reduction engineering, and information systems. Conversion-related costs are associated with direct labor, manufacturing supervision and process-related engineering. Application of the rules resulted in an approximately 55/45 split between material overhead (MOH) and conversion overhead (COH). This finding further confirmed the inadequacy of the existing method, which applied all overhead based on direct labor.

The accounting analysts decided to focus their initial efforts on the MOH pool. To improve their understanding of the composition of the pool and thus assist them in developing a method for its allocation, Wright and Jonez consulted operating managers and further segmented it into:

1. Costs due to the value of parts
2. Costs due to the absolute number of parts used
3. Costs due to the maintenance and handling of each different part number
4. Costs due to each use of a different part number

The managers believed that the majority of MOH costs were of type 3. The costs due to the value of parts (type 1) and the frequency of the use of parts (types 2 and 4) were considered quite small by comparison.

The analysts therefore concluded that the material-related costs of the Portables Group would decrease if fewer different part numbers were used in its products. This cost reduction would result from two factors. First, greater volume discounts would be realized by purchasing larger volumes of fewer unique parts. Second, material overhead costs would be lower. "It was the latter point that we wanted our new allocation method to focus on," commented Wright. "Our goal," continued Jonez, "was to increase customer value by reducing overhead costs. Our strategy was parts standardization. We needed a tactic to operationalize the strategy."

*Required*

(1) Using assumed numbers, develop a cost allocation method for material overhead (MOH) to quantify and communicate the strategy of parts standardization.
(2) Explain how use of your method would support the strategy.

---

**EXHIBIT 2**  Rules for Overhead Segmentation by Cost Center Classification

---

1. **Production**  The overhead costs of any cost center containing direct labor employees are assigned 100% to the COH pool.
2. **Group/Division/Product Group Staff**  The total costs of any manufacturing staff cost center are assigned 50% to the COH pool and 50% to the MOH pool.
3. **Group/Division/Product Group Support**  The total costs of any manufacturing support cost center (e.g., Material Management or Information Systems) are assigned 100% of the MOH pool.
4. **Manufacturing Cost-Reduction Engineering**  The total costs of any cost-reduction engineering cost center are assigned 100% to the MOH pool.
5. **Manufacturing Process-Related Engineering**  The total costs of any process-related engineering cost center are assigned 100% to the COH pool.

(3)   Is any method that applies the entire MOH cost pool on the basis of one cost driver sufficiently accurate for product decisions in the highly competitive portable scope market? Explain.

(4)   Are MOH product costing rates developed for management reporting appropriate for inventory valuation for external reporting? Why or why not?

---

# John Deere Components Works (A) (Abridged)*

The phone rang in the office of Keith Williams, manager of Cost Accounting Services for Deere & Company. On the line was Bill Maxwell, accounting supervisor for the Gear and Special Products Division in Waterloo, Iowa. The division had recently bid to fabricate component parts for another Deere division. Maxwell summarized the situation:

> They're about to award the contracts, and almost all of the work is going to outside suppliers. We're only getting a handful of the parts we quoted, and most of it is low-volume stuff we really don't want. We think we should get some of the business on parts where our direct costs are lower than the outside bid, even if our full costs are not.

Williams asked, "How did your bids stack up against the competition?" Maxwell replied:

> Not too well. We're way high on lots of parts. Our machinists and our equipment are as efficient as any in the business, yet our costs on standard, high-volume products appear to be the highest in the industry. Not only are we not competitive with outside suppliers, but our prices are also higher than two other Deere divisions that quoted on the business.

## Deere & Company

The company was founded in 1837 by John Deere, a blacksmith who developed the first commercially successful steel plow. One

hundred years later, Deere & Company was one of seven full-line farm equipment manufacturers in the world and, in 1963, had displaced International Harvester as the number one producer. During the 1970s, Deere spent over a billion dollars on plant modernization, expansion, and tooling.

During the three-decade, post–World War II boom period, Deere expanded its product line, built new plants, ran plants at capacity, and still was unable to keep up with demand. Deere tractors and combines dotted the landscape throughout America.

During this same period, Deere had diversified into off-the-road industrial equipment for use in the construction, forestry, utility, and mining industries. In 1962, it also began building lawn and garden tractors and equipment. By the mid-1980s, Deere had the broadest lawn and garden product line in the world.

The collapse of farmland values and commodity prices in the 1980s, however, led to the worst and most sustained agricultural crisis since the Great Depression. Several factors exacerbated the crisis. The high dollar reduced U.S. exports and thus hurt both American farmers and American farm equipment producers. Farmers had been encouraged to go into heavy debt to expand and buy land, so when land values and farm prices plummeted, the number of farm foreclosures skyrocketed. Few farmers were in a position to buy new equipment, and resale of repossessed equipment further reduced the market for new equipment.

---

*This case was prepared by Research Associate Artemis March, under the supervision of Professor Robert S. Kaplan. Copyright © 1987 by the President and Fellows of Harvard College. Harvard Business School case 187–107.

In response, Deere adjusted its level of operations downward, cut costs where possible, increased emphasis on pushing decision making downward, and restructured manufacturing processes. Although outright plant closings were avoided, Deere took floor space out of production, encouraged early retirements, and did not replace most of those employees who left. Employment was reduced from 61,000 at the end of 1980 to about 37,500 at the end of 1986. It implemented new manufacturing approaches such as just-in-time production and manufacturing cells that grouped a number of operations for more efficient flow-through production and placed quality control directly at the point of manufacture. To add production volume, Deere wanted its captive component divisions to supply other companies and industries.

### John Deere Component Works

For many years, all the parts for tractors were made and assembled at the tractor works in Waterloo. To generate more production space in the 1970s, Deere successfully split off parts of tractor production. Engine machining and assembly, final tractor assembly, and product engineering each were moved into new plants in the Waterloo area. By the end of the decade, the old tractor works buildings were used only for component production, ranging from small parts to large, complex components such as axles and transmissions. The old tractor works buildings in Waterloo were renamed the John Deere Component Works (JDCW).

In 1983, JDCW was organized into three divisions. The Hydraulics Division, which was soon consolidated into a nearby, refurbished warehouse, fabricated pumps, valves, and pistons. The Drive Trains Division made axles, transmissions, and drive trains. The Gear and Special Products Division made a variety of gears, shafts, and screw machine

parts and performed heat treating, cast iron machining, and sheet metal work.

As part of a vertically integrated company, JDCW had been structured to be a captive producer of parts for Deere's equipment divisions, particularly tractors. Thus, it had to produce a great variety of parts whose volume, even in peak tractor production years, was relatively low. During the 1970s, operations and equipment had been arranged to support tractor production of approximately 150 units per day; by the mid-1980s, however, JDCW was producing parts for less than half as many tractors. The lower volume of activity had a particularly adverse effect on JDCW's screw machine and sheet metal businesses, because their machines were most efficient for high-volume production.

**Internal Sales and Transfer Pricing**  Virtually all of JDCW's sales were internal. Deere equipment-producing factories were required to buy internally major components, such as advanced design transmissions and axles, that gave Deere a competitive advantage. For smaller components, corporate purchasing policy placed JDCW in a favored, but not exclusive, position for securing internal business.

Corporate policy stated that transfers between divisions would take place at full cost (direct materials + direct labor + direct overhead + period overhead). Corporate also had a make-buy policy that when excess capacity was available, buying divisions should compare component divisions' direct costs, rather than full costs, with outside bids. (Direct costs equal full costs less period overhead.) Thus, for example, if JDCW full costs were $10, its direct costs $7, and an outside bid $9, the make-buy decision rule held that the buying division should buy from JDCW. But the transfer pricing policy required the buyer to pay $10 to the component division. Bill Maxwell described the conflict:

> The equipment divisions looked only at price and acted like profit centers rather than cost centers. They are starting to act in the interest of their factory rather than the corporation as a whole. The transfer pricing policy wasn't a problem until times got bad and capacity utilization went down. At Component Works, we said to our sister divisions, "You should look at our direct costs and buy from us." They replied, "We don't want to pay more than it would cost us from outside vendors."

In practice, equipment divisions did not always follow the corporate guidelines for internal sourcing, and JDCW lost a portion of the equipment factories' business to outside vendors.

### Turning Machine Business

Deere's effort to push decision making down into more manageable units encouraged divisions to view their product lines as stand-alone businesses that sold to external markets. By early 1984, JDCW operations were so far below capacity that managers realized they could not wait for the agricultural market to turn around. In the Gear and Special Products Division, several people thought that turning machine products offered a promising niche.

Turning machines transformed raw materials (primarily steel barstock) into finished components and were the most autonomous of the division's operations. As one manager put it, "We could shut down the turning machine area and not affect the rest of the plant—except that we would then have to buy machined parts from outside suppliers." Only the master schedule connected the area with the activities of the rest of the plant.

The turning machine operations were organized into three departments. These departments were distinguished by the diameter of the barstock its machines could handle and by the number of spindles on each machine. A six-spindle machine could handle six different orientations, for example, and thus make more-complex parts than a four-spindle machine.

**Turning Machine Capabilities and Operations** Turning machines automatically fabricated small metal parts. Raw barstock was brought to a staging area near the machines by an overhead crane, the amount depending on the lot size to be run. Barstock (in round, square, or hexagonal sections) was fed horizontally by the operator into the back of the machine. Multiple stations each performed different operations simultaneously on what would become parts; when the longest cycle time (they ranged from a few seconds to 6 minutes) was completed, a machine indexed to the next position. Small parts, such as pinions, collars, gears, bushings, and connectors continually emerged from the final station. Finished parts were transported in 50-pound baskets stacked in trailers that carried up to 1,500 pounds.

Once set up, automatic turning machines were very fast, had excellent repeatability, and were particularly good at drilling, threading, grooving, and boring out large holes. New, the machines could cost as much as $500,000 each; their replacement value was estimated at about half that amount.

Operators were assigned to a battery of two or three specific machines; they did their own setups and tool changes. Setups, like runs, were timed; operators punched in and out, creating a record of how long setups actually took. Operators were also responsible for quality, machine cleanup, and housekeeping in their areas. After a first-part inspection by an inspector, operators ran the lot. Roving inspectors also checked samples from each lot or basket for conformance to quality standards.

**Layout**  Component Works had 120 automatic turning machines lined up in four long rows in an 80,000-square-foot building (almost the size of two complete football fields). The chip and coolant recovery system was constructed under the floor, running the entire length of the building. It was connected up to each machine, much as houses are connected to a sewer system, to carry off the tremendous amount of chips generated by the machines as well as to cool and lubricate the machines. The layout of the cooling system made it infeasible to redesign the turning machine layout into cellular configurations that would group attendant secondary and finishing operations together.[1] Machines could be shifted around or dedicated to certain parts, but owing to the prohibitive expense of duplicating a chip coolant system, they were forced to remain in rows in S Building.

During the 1970s, secondary operations had been moved off the main floor in S Building to make room for more turning machines; this move increased materials handling distances for most parts. For example, the enormous heat treatment machines were located about one-quarter mile from the main turning machine area.

**Process Engineering**  To bring a new part into production required extensive process engineering activities. Operations had to be sequenced, and tooling requirements had to be specified for each spindle. If the appropriate specialized tooling did not exist, it had to

be either purchased or designed and built (usually outside). Both setups and runs had to be timed and standards established. Process engineers had to make sure that the process they had designed would in fact make the part correctly. Data bases then had to be set up for each machine.

All of these activities had to be conducted whether or not the part number ever ran. John Gordon, head of the process engineering group for turning machines, commented, "We have to do as much work for a part we run once a year—or one we never ever run—as for one we set up every month or that runs every day."

Recently, process engineering and production people had begun to make changes in how they ran turning machine parts. . . . As Andy Edberg, head of process engineering for the division, noted, "Turning machines are extremely high-volume machines, so you want to dedicate them if possible." Process engineers were starting to outsource some low-volume parts or to transfer them to more labor-intensive processes. Edberg pointed to the fundamental nature of the shift:

> We always made all the components for tractors, so we ran lots of part numbers but never really looked at the costs of individual parts. What was important was the efficiency of the whole rather than the efficiency of making the parts.

**Competition and Strategy**  By 1984, Gear and Special Products had roughed out a general strategic thrust toward marketing machine parts to the outside world such as automobile OEMs [original equipment manufacturers]. Initial efforts to gain outside business, however, soon made it obvious that competing in the external market was going to be harder than anticipated. Competition came in two forms: captive producers of other vertically integrated companies (about whom Deere found it difficult to obtain infor-

---

[1]Secondary operations included heat treating, cross-drilling, plating, grinding, and milling; most parts required one or more secondary operations.

mation) and independent machine shops. The latter had sprung up around geographical clusters of end users. On the East Coast, the independent shops fed the defense industry, particularly shipyards; on the West Coast, they supplied the aircraft industry; and in Michigan and Indiana, they sold to the automotive industry. Dick Sinclair, manufacturing superintendent, observed:

> The key to successful competition in the outside market is price. We found we have a geography problem. We are not in the midst of heavy users, and it is expensive to ship steel both in and out. We also found our range of services to be less useful than we thought they would be.

### Bid on 275 Turning Machine Parts

Both excess capacity and its new thrust toward developing stand-alone business moti-vated Gear and Special Products to bid on 275 of the 635 parts Deere & Company offered for bid in October 1984. All 635 parts had high potential for manufacture on automatic turning machines. Gear and Special Products bid on a subset for which it had the capability, and where the volume was large enough to exploit the efficiencies from its multiple-spindle machines. The buying group consisted of several equipment factories plus a corporate purchasing group; its aims were to consolidate turning machine purchasing by dealing with just a few good vendors and to gain improved service, quality, and price for these parts. Gear and Special Products had one month to prepare its bid.

Results of the bid are summarized below (dollars are in thousands and represent the annual cost for the quantity quoted):

Comparison—JDCW vs. Vendor

|  | PARTS WITH JDCW LOW TOTAL COST | PARTS WITH JDCW LOW DIRECT COST | TOTAL JDCW DIRECT COST HIGH | TOTAL ALL PARTS |
|---|---|---|---|---|
| Part numbers | 58 | 103 | 114 | 275 |
| JDCW direct cost | $191 | $403 | $1,103 | $1,697 |
| JDCW full cost | 272 | 610 | 1,711 | 2,593 |
| Low outside quote | 322 | 491 | 684 | 1,507 |
| Percent of $ value | 22% | 33% | 45% | 100% |
| % JDCW of low vendor: |  |  |  |  |
|    Direct cost | 58 | 82 | 161 | 113 |
|    Full cost | 82 | 124 | 250 | 172 |

The purchasing group awarded Gear and Special Products only the 58 parts for which it was the low bidder on a full-cost basis. Most of these were low-volume parts that the division did not especially want to make. Gear and Special Products could be the source for the 103 parts on which its direct costs were below the best outside bid only if it agreed to transfer the parts at the same price as the low outside bidder. The division passed on this "opportunity."

The bidding experience generated a good deal of ferment at Gear and Special Products and confirmed the feeling of many that "we didn't even know our costs." Sinclair recalled:

> Some of us were quite alarmed. We had been saying, "Let's go outside," but we couldn't even succeed inside. Deere manufacturing plants in Dubuque and Des Moines also quoted and came in with lower prices—not across the board, but for enough parts to cause concern. If we weren't even competitive relative to other Deere divisions, how could we think we could be successful externally? And when we looked at the results, we knew we were not costing things right. It was backwards to think we could do better in low-volume than high-volume parts, but that's what the cost system said.

## JDCW Standard Cost Accounting System

A standard cost accounting system was used throughout Component Works. . . . The standard or full cost of a part was computed by adding up the following:

- Direct labor (run time only)
- Direct material
- Overhead (direct + period) applied on direct labor
- Overhead (direct + period) applied on material dollars
- Overhead (direct + period) applied on ACTS [actual cycle time standard, see below] machine hours

**Establishing Overhead Rates** Once a year, the JDCW accounting department reestablished overhead rates on the basis of two studies, the normal study and the process study. The normal study determined the standard number of direct labor and machine hours and total overhead for the following year by establishing a "normal volume." In order to smooth out sharp swings, normal volume was defined as the long term "through the business cycle" volume. One of the measures for setting normal volume was the number of drive trains produced per day.

The process study broke down projected overhead at normal volume among JDCW's 100-plus processes, such as painting, sheet metal, grinding, turning machines, and heat treating. To determine the overhead rate for each process, accounting computed the rate from actual past charges, and then asked, "Do we expect any changes?" (Accumulated charges were collected by charging the specific process code as production took place.) Applying judgment to past rates, next year's normal volume, and any probable changes, accounting established a new overhead rate for each process for the coming year.

**Evolution of Bases for Overhead Rates** For many years, direct labor run time was the sole basis for establishing overhead rates at Component Works. Thus if $4,000,000 in overhead was generated by $800,000 of direct labor, the overhead rate was 500%. In the 1960s, a separate materials overhead rate had been established. This rate included the costs of purchasing, receiving, inspecting, and storing raw material. These costs were allocated to materials as a percentage markup over materials costs. Over time, separate rates had been established for steel, castings, and purchased parts to reflect the different demands these items placed on the materials handling resources.

Both labor- and materials-based overhead were subdivided into direct and period overhead. Direct (or variable) overhead, such as the costs of setups, scrap, and materials handling, varied with the volume of production activity. Period (or fixed) overhead included accounts, such as taxes, depreciation, interest, heat, light, and salaries, that did not vary with production activity.

In 1984, Component Works introduced machine hours as well as direct labor and materials to allocate overhead. With the increased usage of automated machines, direct labor run time no longer reflected the amount of processing being performed on parts, particularly when one operator was responsible for several machines. Every process was studied and assigned a machine hour or ACTS (actual cycle time standard) rate. Labor hours was retained for processes in which labor time equaled machine time; if these were different, ACTS hours were used to allocate overhead. Total overhead (other than materials overhead) was then split between direct labor overhead and ACTS overhead. As before, each overhead pool was subdivided between direct and period overhead.

### *Launching a Cost Study for Turning Machines*

Keith Williams had been aware that the existing standard cost system, although satisfactory at an aggregate level, was ineffective for costing and bidding individual parts. He was experimenting with other ways to apply overhead to products. When Maxwell called him in November 1984, Williams realized that the situation at Gear and Special Products provided an opportunity to demonstrate the weaknesses of the current system and to develop a new approach that would be more useful for decision making.

After his phone conversation with Maxwell, Williams quickly put together a proposal to management at Deere & Company, and to the Division Manager of Gear and Special Products. The study would focus on one cost center—the three turning machine departments—because turning machine ACTS hours were the highest chunk of costs in the bid; more than 60% of total machining for the parts occurred on the turning machines. To conduct the study, Williams chose Nick Vintila, who had begun his career at Deere as a manufacturing supervisor at Com-

ponent Works. During his second year, Vintila had worked in the turning machine area. Not only had he become very familiar with its operation, but he had worked with people such as Gordon, then in methods, and Edberg, then a manufacturing superintendent, who would now also be working on the cost study. Vintila had subsequently served as a liaison between systems development and manufacturing to implement a labor reporting system that tied into Manufacturing Resource Planning System, and then became an accounting supervisor at the Tractor Works.

As a first step, Williams and Vintila studied a sample of 44 of the 275 bid parts (see Exhibit 1). This examination showed: (a) an enormous range of variation among quotes for many parts; (b) a large dispersion between JDCW and vendor quotes, ranging from 50% to 60% on some parts and 200% to 300% on others; (c) that JDCW estimated standard costs exceeded vendor prices by 35%, on average; and (d) that JDCW appeared to be most cost-effective on low-volume and low-value parts. (See Exhibit 2 for summary measures of the characteristics of the 44 sample parts.) These findings raised numerous questions about the validity of the standard cost system for determining costs of individual parts and reaffirmed the need for an alternative costing method.

Vintila spent the first half of 1985 working full-time on what became known as the ABC—activity-based costing—study. After detailed study of the shop process flow, he and Williams learned that use of overhead resources could be explained by seven different types of support activities: direct labor support, machine operation, setup hours, production order activity, materials handling, parts administration, and general and administrative overhead. Vintila then went through each overhead account (e.g., engineering salaries, crib attendant costs), asking others

**EXHIBIT 1** Comparison of JDCW vs. Outside Vendor Bids for Sample of 44 Parts

| PART NUMBER | PART DESCRIPTION | QUOTE VOLUME | JDCW EST | | COMPETING VENDOR QUOTES | | | | | | | % TO JDCW to VDR. 2 | | DIRECT LABOR $ EACH |
|---|---|---|---|---|---|---|---|---|---|---|---|---|---|---|
| | | | DIR. COST | MFG. COST | 1 | 2 | 3 | 4 | 5 | 6 | 7 | DIR. COST | MFG. COST | |
| *Component Works Low on Full-Cost Basis:* | | | | | | | | | | | | | | |
| F382 | Fitting | 4,009 | $ 2,248 | $ 3,153 | $ 3,940 | 9,822 | $13,550 | | | | | 23% | 32% | $0.05 |
| S209 | Spacer | 950 | 183 | 291 | 399 | 522 | 551 | $ 1,244 | $ 1,244 | | | 35 | 56 | 0.03 |
| P594 | Pin | 692 | 297 | 430 | 692 | 796 | 817 | 1,012 | 1,509 | | | 37 | 54 | 0.03 |
| T815 | Stud | 3,150 | 719 | 1,162 | 1,712 | 1,859 | 2,158 | 2,300 | 3,131 | $ 9,356 | | 39 | 62 | 0.03 |
| P675 | Pin | 3,596 | 1,703 | 2,649 | 3,587 | 3,740 | 6,024 | 7,947 | | | | 46 | 55 | 0.07 |
| H622 | Hub | 4,450 | 3,207 | 4,365 | 5,687 | 6,324 | 6,743 | 7,518 | 8,463 | 12,875 | $12,875 | 51 | 69 | 0.05 |
| S245 | Spacer | 4,912 | 1,249 | 1,917 | 2,210 | 2,335 | 2,536 | 3,276 | 3,585 | 4,076 | | 53 | 82 | 0.03 |
| R647 | Sprocket | 5,167 | 6,792 | 9,196 | 11,907 | 12,142 | 12,400 | 13,124 | 16,116 | 16,674 | 17,516 | 56 | 76 | 0.10 |
| T501 | Stud | 4,879 | 902 | 1,492 | 1,537 | 1,610 | 1,625 | 1,820 | 2,196 | 2,976 | 6,294 | 56 | 93 | 0.03 |
| S071 | Spacer | 5,661 | 4,896 | 6,885 | 8,378 | 8,433 | 10,133 | | | | | 58 | 82 | 0.09 |
| C784 | Cap | 71,200 | 13,101 | 19,537 | 17,088 | 22,072 | 22,606 | 23,332 | 29,832 | 41,253 | | 59 | 89 | 0.04 |
| P583 | Pin | 3,402 | 2,775 | 4,285 | 4,380 | 4,467 | 4,826 | 5,233 | 5,391 | 17,200 | | 62 | 96 | 0.09 |
| R410 | Sprocket | 792 | 878 | 1,226 | 658 | 1,349 | 2,162 | 2,273 | 2,866 | 2,946 | 3,983 | 66 | 91 | 0.08 |
| Total or Average | | 112,860 | $ 38,949 | $ 56,590 | | $ 75,471 | | | | | | 52% | 75% | $0.05 |
| *Component Works Low on Direct-Cost Basis:* | | | | | | | | | | | | | | |
| R918 | Rocker | 1,091 | $ 663 | $ 1,063 | $ 905 | 1,036 | $12,655 | $14,642 | $18,711 | | | 64% | 103% | $0.05 |
| P220 | Pin | 3,204 | 6,685 | 11,754 | 9,048 | 10,413 | | | | | | 64 | 113 | 0.45 |
| P057 | Pin | 1,281 | 979 | 1,675 | 1,460 | 1,487 | 2,306 | 2,985 | | | | 66 | 113 | 0.09 |
| T566 | Stud | 2,452 | 7,925 | 12,037 | 9,563 | 11,843 | 12,628 | 13,461 | 18,568 | 22,983 | | 67 | 102 | 0.42 |
| P736 | Pin | 38,955 | 6,837 | 10,475 | 9,181 | 10,167 | 11,492 | 11,492 | 13,323 | | | 67 | 103 | 0.03 |
| P904 | Pin | 950 | 1,170 | 1,801 | 1,606 | 1,729 | 1,767 | 1,995 | 3,420 | | | 68 | 104 | 0.10 |

| Part | Desc. | | | | | | | | | | | | | |
|---|---|---:|---:|---:|---:|---:|---:|---:|---:|---:|---:|---:|---:|---:|
| H355 | Hub | 1,155 | 1,947 | 3,090 | 2,552 | 2,872 | 2,979 | 3,026 | 4,775 | 6,846 | | 68 | 108 | 0.13 |
| P423 | Pin | 3,402 | 2,661 | 4,157 | 2,994 | 3,912 | 5,137 | 5,477 | 11,805 | 4,718 | | 68 | 106 | 0.09 |
| B605 | Bolt | 10,561 | 2,239 | 3,373 | 2,893 | 3,273 | 3,485 | 3,707 | 3,970 | 4,034 | $ 4,718 | 68 | 103 | 0.03 |
| H346 | Hub | 1,088 | 2,223 | 3,570 | 3,007 | 3,122 | 3,151 | 3,242 | 3,438 | 2,459 | 4,128 | 71 | 114 | 0.15 |
| H554 | Hub | 1,490 | 1,551 | 2,214 | 1,967 | 1,997 | 2,077 | 2,216 | 2,298 | | 2,459 | 78 | 111 | 0.06 |
| P244 | Pin | 7,383 | 7,438 | 10,948 | 7,591 | 8,786 | 9,498 | 10,705 | 11,270 | 12,677 | 23,773 | 85 | 125 | 0.11 |
| L209 | Lever | 5,351 | 2,480 | 3,827 | 1,578 | 2,745 | 3,692 | 4,334 | 4,486 | 4,548 | 4,826 | 90 | 139 | 0.05 |
| R316 | Roller | 18,058 | 2,470 | 4,610 | 2,257 | 2,691 | 3,250 | 4,050 | 4,231 | 4,939 | 4,984 | 92 | 171 | 0.03 |
| S451 | Spacer | 2,785 | 645 | 1,226 | 390 | 697 | 852 | 1,104 | 1,253 | 1,276 | 1,306 | 93 | 176 | 0.04 |
| P333 | Pin | 4,258 | 6,818 | 12,088 | 6,898 | 7,324 | 9,197 | 11,113 | 12,008 | | | 93 | 165 | 0.32 |
| P379 | Pin | 6,807 | 6,984 | 10,249 | 5,037 | 7,352 | 7,760 | 9,394 | 9,421 | 21,919 | | 95 | 139 | 0.11 |
| P682 | Pin | 3,402 | 4,037 | 5,880 | 2,824 | 4,208 | 5,035 | 5,817 | 11,533 | | | 96 | 140 | 0.08 |
| Total or Average | | 113,673 | $ 65,753 | $104,038 | $ 85,654 | | | | | | | 77% | 121% | $0.08 |
| Cumulative | | 226,533 | $104,703 | $160,629 | $161,125 | | | | | | | 65% | 100% | $0.08 |

*Component Works Not Cost Competitive:*

| Part | Desc. | | | | | | | | | | | | | |
|---|---|---:|---:|---:|---:|---:|---:|---:|---:|---:|---:|---:|---:|---:|
| H265 | Hub | 4,464 | 15,311 | 24,341 | 13,570 | 15,236 | 17,275 | 17,454 | $20,489 | | $ 9,450 | 100% | 160% | $0.57 |
| A152 | Shaft | 2,972 | 7,749 | 12,841 | 6,685 | 7,667 | 8,470 | 10,877 | 7,887 | 8,868 | | 101 | 167 | 0.38 |
| R717 | Sprocket | 4,869 | 6,834 | 10,003 | 6,205 | 6,707 | 7,421 | 7,839 | 1,852 | 2,107 | 2,203 | 102 | 149 | 0.16 |
| S771 | Spacer | 11,092 | 971 | 1,689 | 909 | 942 | 1,053 | 1,275 | 4,624 | 4,709 | 5,599 | 103 | 179 | 0.02 |
| R428 | Sprocket | 3,180 | 4,374 | 6,888 | 3,637 | 4,226 | 4,285 | 4,293 | | | 19,837 | 103 | 163 | 0.18 |
| R946 | Roller | 5,904 | 6,254 | 10,727 | 4,815 | 6,022 | 6,199 | 6,494 | 9,269 | 9,269 | | 104 | 178 | 0.14 |
| R157 | Roller | 3,181 | 1,651 | 2,934 | 1,082 | 1,565 | 1,645 | 1,749 | 1,890 | 1,917 | 2,004 | 106 | 188 | 0.08 |
| B823 | Button | 18,200 | 3,296 | 5,622 | 2,347 | 3,094 | 3,257 | 3,276 | 3,314 | 3,516 | 6,042 | 107 | 182 | 0.03 |
| T863 | Stud | 7,120 | 11,136 | 17,790 | 8,231 | 8,590 | 9,185 | 13,243 | 24,706 | 16,606 | | 130 | 207 | 0.37 |
| T237 | Stop | 4,258 | 12,719 | 18,713 | 7,877 | 8,516 | 9,112 | 9,623 | 10,228 | 8,925 | | 149 | 220 | 0.35 |
| N281 | Nut | 8,500 | 6,350 | 11,322 | 3,392 | 3,789 | 4,114 | 6,375 | 7,548 | | 15,640 | 168 | 299 | 0.18 |
| T166 | Stud | 5,645 | 8,766 | 16,014 | 3,912 | 5,024 | 5,701 | 13,209 | | 26,700 | | 174 | 319 | 0.41 |
| T586 | Stud | 10,000 | 15,957 | 27,273 | 7,525 | 8,900 | 9,540 | 11,000 | 11,520 | | | 179 | 306 | 0.40 |
| Total or Average | | $ 89,385 | $101,367 | $166,157 | $ 80,278 | | | | | | | 126% | 207% | $0.21 |
| Total/Avg. all Parts | | 315,918 | $206,069 | $326,786 | $241,403 | | | | | | | 85% | 135% | $0.11 |

143

**EXHIBIT 2** Characteristics of Sample of 44 Parts

| CATEGORY | NUMBER | VOLUME | DIRECT LABOR $ | ACTS HOURS PER 100 PARTS | ANNUAL ACTS HOURS | DL $/ MATERIALS $ |
|---|---|---|---|---|---|---|
| Low on full-cost basis | 13 | 4,009* | 0.05 | 0.04 | 19 | 21% |
| | | [692; 71,200] | [0.03; 0.10] | [0.3; 1.5] | [2; 266] | [9; 51] |
| Low on direct-cost basis | 18 | 3,402 | 0.09 | 1.2 | 31 | 23% |
| | | [950; 38,955] | [0.03; 0.45] | [0.3; 2.8] | [10; 159] | [9; 224] |
| Not cost competitive | 13 | 5,645 | 0.18 | 1.5 | 70 | 57% |
| | | [2972; 18,200] | [0.02; 0.57] | [0.2; 3.4] | [18; 150] | [22; 480] |
| Total | 44 | | | | | |

*Top number is the median value in that category.
The range [minimum; maximum] appears beneath the median.

and himself, "Among the seven activities, which cause this account to occur? What creates work for this department?" He began to estimate the percentages of each overhead account that were driven by each of the seven activities. He conducted specific studies to estimate the total volume of each of the seven overhead driving activities (such as number of production orders, total machine hours). This work was circulated among people like Maxwell, Edberg, Gordon, and Sinclair, who, drawing on their experience and judgment, accepted the seven activities as the key overhead drivers and adjusted the final percentages for allocating budgeted items to each activity. (See Appendix A for a description of the seven overhead drivers and how Vintila arrived at the seven overhead rates.) When the ABC method was used to allocate overhead, 41% of the overhead shifted to activity bases 3–7 (see Exhibits 3 and 4). The data needed to estimate the cost of a particular part are shown in Exhibit 5.

The detailed work to design the ABC system had now been completed. The next step for Williams and Vintila was to test and gain acceptance for their new costing approach.

## Appendix A: John Deere Component Works Activity-Based Costing (A)

**ABC Activities for Applying Overhead to Turning Machine Parts** The ABC study used the accounting estimate of normal volume and total overhead costs as its starting point. Overhead costs were then allocated to seven rather than just two activities. A separate overhead rate was derived for each activity. (see Exhibits 3 and 4 for comparison of the two methods.) Vintila used the following approach to apportion overhead and to develop overhead rates:

1. *Direct Labor Support* overhead was generated by incentive employees working on parts. It included allowances for benefits, break periods, and a percentage of supervision, personnel, payroll, and industrial engineering salaries. All direct labor support overhead costs were summed ($1,898,000 in 1985) and divided by the total amount of direct labor dollars ($1,714,000) to derive an overhead rate for this activity (111%).

2. *Machine Operation* overhead was generated by operating the turning machines, plus an allocation of facility and capacity charges. This activity received most of the

**EXHIBIT 3**  1985 Turning Machine Overhead Allocation Using Standard Cost System

| | APPLIED BASED ON DIRECT LABOR (DL) | | APPLIED BASED ON MACHINE HOURS | | TOTAL $000s | % TOTAL |
|---|---|---|---|---|---|---|
| **Direct Overhead** | | | | | | |
| Maintenance | $    32 | 0.3% | $1,038 | 10.2% | $  1,070 | 10.5% |
| Labor allowances | 459 | 4.5 | 0 | 0.0 | 459 | 4.5 |
| Machine setups | 0 | 0.0 | 524 | 5.2 | 524 | 5.2 |
| Other OH lab | 130 | 1.3 | 164 | 1.6 | 294 | 2.9 |
| Scrap & misc. | 80 | 0.8 | 96 | 0.9 | 176 | 1.7 |
| Employee benefits | 1,296 | 12.7 | 556 | 5.5 | 1,852 | 18.2 |
|    Total direct OH | $1,997 | 19.6% | $2,378 | 23.4% | $  4,375 | 43.0% |
| **Period Overhead** | | | | | | |
| Maintenance | $  127 | 1.2% | $   527 | 5.2% | $    654 | 6.4% |
| Salaries | 796 | 7.8 | 826 | 8.1 | 1,622 | 15.9 |
| Depreciation | 0 | 0.0 | 1,790 | 17.6 | 1,790 | 17.6 |
| Gen. & misc. | 227 | 2.2 | 717 | 7.0 | 944 | 9.3 |
| Employee benefits | 354 | 3.5 | 432 | 4.2 | 786 | 7.7 |
|    Total period OH | $1,504 | 14.8% | $4,292 | 42.2% | $  5,796 | 57.0% |
| **Total overhead** | $3,501 | 34.4% | $6,670 | 65.6% | $10,171 | 100.0% |
| Overhead base | $1,714 DL$ | | 242,000 ACTS hrs | | | |
| Direct overhead rate | 117% | | $  9.83 per hr | | | |
| Period overhead rate | 88% | | 17.73 per hr | | | |
| **Total overhead rate** | 205% | | $27.56 per hr | | | |

costs of machine maintenance, small tools, jigs, and dies, as well as smaller proportions of inspection and defective work, engineering and supervision salaries. Allocations were also made for depreciation, taxes, interest, and utilities. The total dollars required to operate the machines ($4,045,000) were divided by the total number of machine hours (242,000) to develop the $16.70 per hour overhead rate for this activity.

Whereas the standard cost system used the same ACTS rate for all machines, Vintila examined the machines individually and ultimately developed separate rates for four different-sized machines. He gathered data on several factors to create machine-specific estimates of the costs of running them. For example, kilowatt-hours multiplied by the load factor was used to generate utilities cost; replacement costs to estimate the share of insurance, taxes, and depreciation; square footage to calculate a proportion of facilities costs; and the "spindle factor" to allocate tooling and maintenance costs. The spindle factor took into account the number of spindles on a machine; when multiplied by its annual load (or ACTS hours), it provided a basis for allocating tooling and maintenance costs according to size and use of the machine. For all of these factors, Vintila obtained percentages by dividing the total (e.g., replacement costs of all machines) by that for the particular machine. To obtain an overall direct overhead rate for a machine, he divided all its direct overhead by its ACTS hours.

Once this information had been generated

# EXHIBIT 4 1985 Turning Machine Overhead Allocation Using ABC Method

| | DIRECT LABOR (DL) SUPPORT OVERHEAD | | MACHINE OPERATION OVERHEAD | | MACHINE SETUP OVERHEAD | | PRODUCTION ORDER OVERHEAD | | MATERIAL-HANDLING OVERHEAD | | PART ADMIN. OVERHEAD | | GENERAL AND ADMINISTRATION OVERHEAD | | TOTAL | |
|---|---|---|---|---|---|---|---|---|---|---|---|---|---|---|---|---|
| | $000s | % TOTAL | $000s | % TOTAL | $000s | % TOTAL | $000s | % TOTAL | $000s | % TOTAL | $000s | % TOTAL | $000s | % TOTAL | $000s | % TOTAL |
| **Direct Overhead** | | | | | | | | | | | | | | | | |
| Maintenance | $ 0 | 0.0% | $ 899 | 8.8% | $ 45 | 0.4% | $ 62 | 0.6% | $ 63 | 0.6% | $ 0 | 0.0% | $ 0 | 0.0% | $ 1,069 | 10.5% |
| Labor allowances | 329 | 3.2% | 47 | 0.5% | 61 | 0.6% | 10 | 0.1% | 12 | 0.1% | 0 | 0.0% | 0 | 0.0% | 459 | 4.5% |
| Machine setups | 0 | 0.0% | 146 | 1.4% | 378 | 3.7% | 0 | 0.0% | 0 | 0.0% | 0 | 0.0% | 0 | 0.0% | 524 | 5.2% |
| Other OH lab | 0 | 0.0% | 67 | 0.7% | 0 | 0.0% | 106 | 1.0% | 122 | 1.2% | 0 | 0.0% | 0 | 0.0% | 295 | 2.9% |
| Scrap & Misc. | 0 | 0.0% | 141 | 1.4% | 0 | 0.0% | 30 | 0.3% | 6 | 0.1% | 0 | 0.0% | 0 | 0.0% | 177 | 1.7% |
| Employee benefits | 1,100 | 10.8% | 339 | 3.3% | 246 | 2.4% | 77 | 0.8% | 90 | 0.9% | 0 | 0.0% | 0 | 0.0% | 1,852 | 18.2% |
| Total direct OH | $1,429 | 14.0% | $1,639 | 16.1% | $ 730 | 7.2% | $285 | 2.8% | $293 | 2.9% | $ 0 | 0.0% | $ 0 | 0.0% | $ 4,376 | 43.0% |
| **Period Overhead** | | | | | | | | | | | | | | | | |
| Maintenance | $ 10 | 0.1% | $ 333 | 3.3% | $ 40 | 0.4% | $ 9 | 0.1% | $ 8 | 0.1% | $238 | 2.3% | $ 17 | 0.2% | $ 655 | 6.4% |
| Salaries | 270 | 2.7% | 179 | 1.8% | 62 | 0.6% | 243 | 2.4% | 0 | 0.0% | 421 | 4.1% | 448 | 4.4% | 1,623 | 16.0% |
| Depreciation | 27 | 0.3% | 1,424 | 14.0% | 226 | 2.2% | 25 | 0.2% | 0 | 0.0% | 43 | 0.4% | 45 | 0.4% | 1,790 | 17.6% |
| Gen. & Misc. | 59 | 0.6% | 323 | 3.2% | 19 | 0.2% | 152 | 1.5% | 0 | 0.0% | 90 | 0.9% | 298 | 2.9% | 941 | 9.3% |
| Employee benefits | 103 | 1.0% | 147 | 1.4% | 34 | 0.3% | 103 | 1.0% | 2 | 0.0% | 207 | 2.0% | 190 | 1.9% | 786 | 7.7% |
| Total period OH | 469 | 4.6% | $2,406 | 23.7% | $ 381 | 3.7% | $532 | 5.2% | $ 10 | 0.1% | $999 | 9.8% | $998 | 9.8% | $ 5,795 | 57.0% |
| Total overhead | $1,898 | 18.7% | $4,045 | 39.8% | $1,111 | 10.9% | $817 | 8.0% | $303 | 3.0% | $999 | 9.8% | $998 | 9.8% | $10,171 | 100.0% |
| Overhead base | $1,714 DL$ | | 242,000 annual ACTS hours | | 32,900 annual setup hours | | 7,150 annual orders | | 15,600 annual loads | | 2,050 part nos. | | $10,887 value added* | | | |
| Direct overhead rate | 83.4% | | $ 6.77 per hour* | | $22.18 per hour | | $ 39.86 per order | | $18.78 per load | | — | | — | | | |
| Period overhead rate | 27.4% | | $ 9.94 per hour | | $11.58 per hour | | $ 74.41 per order | | $ 0.64 per load | | $487 per part | | 9.1% | | | |
| Total overhead rate | 111.0% | | $16.71 per hour | | $33.76 per hour | | $114.27 per order | | $19.42 per load | | $487 per part | | 9.1% | | | |

9.1%

$ 1,714 DL$
1,898 DL$ OH
4,045 Mach. oper. OH
1,111 Setup OH
817 Prod. order OH
303 Mat. h. OH
999 Part. adm. OH
$10,887 Value added

*Rates shown are averages across all turning machines. In practice, separate machine overhead rates were calculated for each major class of machines.

**EXHIBIT 5** Elements for Costing Part A103 in 1985

$6.44 materials cost/100 parts
    Materials Overhead Rates:
      2.1%         Direct
      7.6%         Period
0.185            Direct labor hours/100 parts
0.310            ACTS hours/100 parts
$12.76         Labor rate for screw machine operation
4.2 hr         Machine setup time
0.176 lb       Part weight
8,000 quote volume (annual volume as specified by user)
    2 runs/year

6-spindle machine rates:      Direct: $8.99
(under ABC systems)        Period: $7.61

---

for each of the machines, similar-sized machines were grouped, and a single overhead rate was determined for each group. In this way, machines that happened to have a lower load would not be penalized by a higher rate.

3. *Setup Hours* overhead was generated by changing the job to be run. It included actual setup costs; a small share of machine and small tool maintenance, supervision, and engineering salaries; and a share of depreciation and other facility costs. These costs ($1,111,000) were divided by the estimated number of setup hours (32,900) to arrive at an hourly overhead rate ($33.80).

The number of setup hours was estimated through an examination of production control data that showed the average setup time to be 4 hours. This figure was multiplied by the average number (4) of annual runs per part number and by the 2,050 parts in the system.

4. *Production Order Activity* was generated by shop activity resulting from each production order. The largest cost was material control salaries. Percentages of crib attendant costs, inspection, defective work, and manufacturing costs were also applied. The sum was divided by the total number of annual production orders (7,150) to yield a cost of $114 per production order.

5. *Materials Handling* overhead arose from moving barstock to the machines and then moving the parts to the next operation. The major cost elements were materials handling labor and equipment maintenance. This activity also received a share of inspection and defective materials costs. An overhead rate ($19.42) was derived by dividing the total allocated costs ($303,000) by the number of loads (15,600).

The number of loads was estimated through a six-step process:

a. $\dfrac{\text{part weight} \times \text{annual volume}}{\text{runs/year for that part}} = \text{weight/run}$

b. $\dfrac{\text{weight/run}}{\text{pounds/load}} = \text{loads/run}$
(average of 2000 lb per transport container)

c. loads/run + 0.5, then round result to nearest full integer (a calculation to correct for incomplete loads)

d. multiply result in (c) by number of runs of that part/year = number of loads/year moved away from machines

e. loads/year × 2 (movement to and from machine) = total number of loads/year for that part

f. repeat process for all part numbers, and add number of loads/part to obtain total number of loads per year

6. *Parts Administration* overhead was incurred just by having a part number in the de-

partment's repertoire. It included the cost of establishing and maintaining records and systems documentation and a share of salaries in process engineering, industrial engineering, supervision, and materials control. The sum of $999,000 in overhead, when distributed among the 2,050 parts in the system, generated a head tax of $487 per part number.

7. *General and Administrative* overhead was attributed to the entire factory, not to a particular manufacturing process or activity.

It included a large share of taxes, utilities, and depreciation, as well as smaller shares of salaries such as accounting, reliability, and manufacturing engineering. The $998,000 of general and administrative (G&A) overhead was prorated to products on the basis of their value added: the sum of direct labor plus the other six overhead activity costs for each part. The value-added sum became the denominator for determining the G&A rate to be applied to the part.

# 5

# Activity-Based Management

In Chapter 4, we saw how activity-based costing enables managers to calculate the costs of their individual products. Typically, an ABC product costing application has its most dramatic impact for a diverse product line, one in which there are hundreds or even thousands of models and variants. Analytically, such a product line will have a graph of cumulative sales volume versus cumulative number of products as shown in Exhibit 5-1:

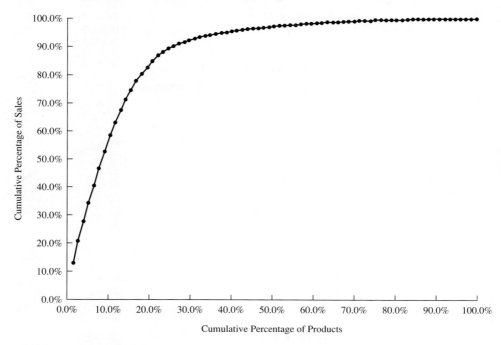

**EXHIBIT 5-1** Cumulative Sales Curve

Exhibit 5-1 shows the normal 20–80 rule associated with business activities; the highest-volume 20% products generate about 80% of sales. More revealing, however, is the 60–99 rule: The highest-volume 60% of products generate 99% of sales. Or, looking at the curve from the other direction, the lowest-volume 40% of products generate a cumulative total of 1% of sales. A company's traditional costing system (not a new ABC system) usually indicates, however, that all of the low-volume products are profitable because prices are set as a markup over fully (if inaccurately) allocated costs.

## THE PRODUCT PROFITABILITY WHALE CURVE

An activity-based cost analysis, in which the costs of indirect and support resources are applied on the basis of activities performed and the demand for the activities by individual products, can reveal a quite different story about the profitability of many of the company's products. After assigning the costs of setup, purchasing, quality assurance, inventory management, and product support activities, Exhibit 5-2 shows the cumulative profitability across the same product line shown as that in Exhibit 5-1, with products ranked on the horizontal axis from the most profitable to the least profitable. In this example, the most profitable 20% of products generate about 300% of profits. The remaining 80% of products are either break-even or loss items and collectively lose 200% of profits. The curve shown in Exhibit 5-2 is referred to by ABC analysts as the "whale curve." The height, or hump, of the whale indicates the profits earned by the business unit's most profitable products. The remaining products, either just break-even or lose money, bringing total profits back down to "sea level."

Companies encounter a whale curve of cumulative product and customer profitability (such as Exhibit 5-2) in activity-based cost systems built for business units that meet two rules:

1. Large expenses in indirect and support resources
2. Diversity in products, customers, and processes

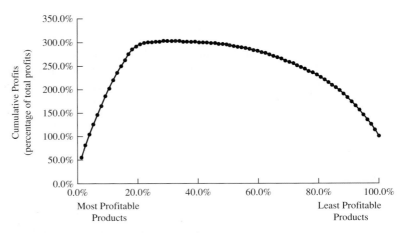

**EXHIBIT 5-2** Cumulative Profitability "Whale Curve"

Many companies, operating with signals from either their traditional standard cost system or a direct (marginal) costing system, overproliferate their product lines, overcustomize their product offerings, and overserve their customers. They fail to see how decisions on product variety, customization, and customer support inevitably lead to much higher expenses in the indirect and support resources required to implement a full-line product strategy.

Managers, once they understand their product costs after an ABC analysis, have a great array of actions available to them to increase the profitability of their product lines. The actions, some of which are identified below, are often called activity-based management, referring to managers' decision making using information about activities.

1. • Reprice products
2. • Substitute products
3. • Redesign products
4. • Improve processes and operations strategy
5. • Technology investment
6. • Eliminate products

## PRICING

Some companies have little discretion in product pricing. Their high-volume products are sold in highly competitive markets in which it is difficult to differentiate the product along quality or functionality dimensions and where customers find it easy to switch suppliers to obtain the lowest price. Or a company may be a small player in an industry dominated by much larger companies. Unless such a small company has strong customer loyalty (or its customers have high switching costs), the company must follow the pricing policies of the industry leaders. In such situations, companies may not be able to modify their pricing policies, even after conducting a careful cost analysis. These companies must look to actions other than pricing to improve the profitability of their products: for example, redesigning, substituting, or eliminating products or improving processes.

Many companies, however, have considerable discretion for adjusting prices, particularly on their highly customized products. In situations in which products are not sold in competitive markets, managers often set prices using standard markups over the products' standard costs or by extrapolating from prices charged for existing, physically similar products. When pricing policies are derived from a traditional (unit-level) standard costing system, with overhead applied using direct labor or machine hours, managers can make poor pricing decisions. For example, prices for high-volume blue and black pens get established from competitive market forces. Specialty products, such as fuchsia and lavender pens, which appear similar and follow a similar production process, will be priced perhaps a little higher than standard blue and black pens because of their unusual features. Missing from this analysis, however, are the much higher costs for product development, product enhancement, purchasing, receiving, inspection, setup, and maintenance resources required for these specialty colors. Often, for a customer, the item is a small fraction of its total costs (the cost of purchasing specialty pens for writing wedding invitations is less than 0.01% of the total cost of the wedding) and the customer may be willing to pay a considerable price premium for the high-quality, reliable supply and unique functionality of the specialty product.

Companies, after an initial ABC analysis, have frequently been able to sustain price increases of 50% or more for their specialty, customized, and—as they now see—much more costly products. Conversely, once the costs of the low-volume specialty products have been correctly assigned, the costs of high-volume standard products decrease. Costs of mature products may drop by 5% to 8%. Although such a cost reduction may appear minimal, the high-volume mature products are typically sold in competitive markets, where margin increases of even 3% to 5% are extremely hard to generate. In reality, these products may already be earning such higher margins, once the expenses of resources not being used for these products are not assigned to them. In this situation, companies can now bid more aggressively to increase the sales of these profitable products even further. Managers now see that increased production of these products involves only increases in unit-level expenses but no increases in batch and product-sustaining expenses.

Economists argue that pricing should be set with a recognition of demand considerations not just of costs. They show mathematically—after making appropriate assumptions—that firms in a somewhat monopolistic situation can maximize their profits at the price-output combination where marginal revenue equals marginal costs. In situations in which managers know the algebraic form of both the demand and the cost curves, it is a simple computation to calculate the price-output combination that maximizes company profits.

In practice, however, managers rarely follow the economists' prescriptions. Two big factors have limited the applicability of the economists' pricing model:

1. Difficulty in estimating the demand curve
2. Difficulty in estimating the cost curve

The development of activity-based costing since the mid-1980s has overcome the second of these problems and is the basis for the discussion in this chapter. But the explicit calculation of the demand curve for the company's products remains a major hurdle for following the economists' prescription explicitly.

## Demand Curve Estimation

Thinking about the demand curve for the company's products is a useful exercise because it focuses managers' attention on the external environment in which products must be sold. It forces managers to think about not just what it costs to manufacture a product but also about what customers may be willing to pay for it. In practice, however, actual demand curves for products are not readily available. Techniques for estimating demand curves have been developed and have been applied by skilled practitioners for standard products such as agricultural commodities, automobiles, housing, and alcoholic beverages. The techniques have been applied, however, mostly to aggregate demand at the industry level. They have rarely been applied to estimate the demand curves for the products of an individual company.

Certainly for major categories of products, say automobile sales for General Motors or beverage sales for Coca Cola and Pepsi Cola, it is possible to estimate demand relationships at an aggregate level (total number of cars sold, total gallons of carbonated soda). But even these firms have dozens or even thousands of individual products and varieties with complex complementarity and substitutability relationships so that estimating demand curves for individual products becomes an essentially impossible task.

Apart from the difficulty of estimating price-quantity tradeoffs, if the firm is not in a monopolistic situation, it must also recognize the potential reactions of competitors to price changes. Competitive reactions by producers of substitute products, if major price changes were implemented, could upset the calculations of forecasts embedded in a calculated demand curve.

And additional complications arise because price is only one input into a customer's purchasing decision. In fact, much of the entire discipline of marketing helps companies to bypass head-to-head pricing competition. Considerations such as product characteristics and functionality, product quality and innovativeness, advertising and promotion, distribution, service, delivery, credit terms, and postsales service all attempt to transform what appears initially to be a homogeneous, commodity-like product into a differentiated product with unique features, attributes, and services. Studies that look only at price will fail to capture all of the factors that contribute to a customer's purchasing decision. All of these reasons help to explain why many firms make pricing decisions without the "benefit" of a calculated demand curve for each of its products.

Nevertheless, as we stated at the outset, thinking conceptually about demand relationships remains a useful exercise. If managers can identify their price inelastic customers—those for whom demand is relatively insensitive to price—then they can set prices well above any cost-based reference point and can earn substantial profits from sales to these customers. Conversely, for price elastic customers—those for whom small changes in price can lead to large changes in the quantity demanded—managers will know to think a great deal about the consequences of raising or lowering prices. In this case, having an accurate knowledge of product (and customer) costs will be necessary to avoid discounting that attracts additional volume but that leads to net prices falling below the costs of producing products for and serving these customers.

## Short-Term Pricing

The discussion in this chapter focuses on setting prices on a long-term basis. Companies do encounter situations in which a customer comes in with a request for a special order and the company must decide whether to accept such a one-time order and at what price. In this situation, many of the longer-run costs embedded in an ABC analysis are not relevant to the decision about pricing or order acceptance. In effect, almost all the resources the organization needs to fulfill the order have already been acquired, and the costs associated with those resources will be incurred whether the order is taken or not. Such a situation moves us back to the discussion and analysis in Chapters 1 and 2 on short-term cost-volume-profit analysis.

When thinking about the relevant costs for short-term decision making, the company needs an estimate of the incremental costs associated with the order. Typically, for a manufacturing company, the incremental costs include:

- The extra materials that must be acquired to produce the order
- Any part-time or additional labor that must be paid to process the materials
- The extra energy and maintenance costs for the machines that will work on the order

In service companies, there may be hardly any incremental expenses associated with an extra order for a customer: For an airline, there's a trivial amount of extra fuel and some food expense (perhaps a bag of peanuts and a can of soda pop); for a health-care institution, perhaps some medicine and medical supplies, such as bandages.

Given how few costs will vary, in the short-run, decisions about one-time special orders have more to do with marketing and competitive issues than with incremental costs. Before agreeing to a low price for the special order, one that covers short-term incremental costs but offers little contribution to cover the expenses of resources already supplied and available, managers should consider the following guidelines:

- Available capacity exists for all resources required to fulfill the order.
- The order requires only a short-term commitment from available resources so that the resources will soon become available again to handle potentially more profitable opportunities in the future.
- The price offered to the customer for the one-time special order will affect neither the pricing to existing customers nor the price the same customer will expect the next time he or she places an order.
- The customer cannot resell the product or service to other customers.

If any of these conditions is violated, then accepting orders that just cover short-term incremental costs can lower company profits. In the remainder of the chapter, we will focus on using cost information for longer-term decision making.

## ABC Costing for a New Order

As a specific example of developing an activity-based cost analysis for a new order, consider the Glenn Company, a manufacturer of electromechanical components. It has identified the following principal activities and activity cost driver rates for its manufacturing operations:

| ACTIVITY | ACTIVITY COST DRIVER RATE |
|---|---|
| Direct labor processing | $50/ hour |
| Machine processing | $60/ hour |
| Purchase and receive components | $150/ purchase order |
| Schedule production orders and perform first item inspection | $200/ production run |
| Set up machines | $80/ setup hour |
| Process customer orders (negotiate, package, ship, invoice, collect) | $100/ customer order |
| Perform engineering design and support | $75/ engineering hour |

The Glenn Company has recently received a request from a customer for 100 units of a product with the following characteristics:

| | |
|---|---|
| Material cost per unit | $12.40 |
| Direct labor time per unit produced | 0.6 hours |
| Machine hours per unit produced | 0.8 hours |
| Number of component purchases | 10 |
| Number of production runs | 6[1] |
| Average setup time per production run | 3 hours |
| Number of shipments | 1 |
| Engineering design and process time | 20 hours |

The cost buildup for the product is:

| | |
|---|---:|
| Materials (12.40 * 100) | $1,240 |
| Direct labor (0.6 * 50 * 100) | 3,000 |
| Machining (0.8 * 60 * 100) | 4,800 |
| Unit-level expenses | $9,040 |
| Acquiring materials (10 * 150) | 1,500 |
| Production runs (6 * 200) | 1,200 |
| Set up machines (6 * 3 * 80) | 1,440 |
| Process customer order (1 * 100) | 100 |
| Batch-level expenses | $4,240 |
| Engineering support (20 * 75) | $1,500 |
| Product-sustaining expenses | $1,500 |
| Total product expenses | $14,780 |

In this example, the direct costs (materials and labor) are only about 30% of the total costs, and all unit-level expenses combined (materials, labor, and machine time) represent only 60% of total expenses. The relatively small order size and the high number of components that must be purchased and machined lead to high levels of batch expenses, which actually exceed the direct labor costs of the order. Also, the engineering time required to design the components and the associated manufacturing processes add more than 10% to the total costs.

Notice that many of the costs will be incurred regardless of the number of items produced. For example, if the customer wanted 1,000 units, rather than 100, and if the number of production runs and purchase orders remained the same (because the company orders 1,000 components rather than 100 on the purchase order, and each production run for a component processes 1,000 items rather than 100), the unit-level costs would increase by a factor of 10 (because 10 times as many units are produced), but the batch and product-sustaining costs would remain the same (as shown in the following calculation):

| | |
|---|---:|
| Materials (12.40 * 1,000) | $12,400 |
| Direct labor (0.6 * 50 * 1,000) | 30,000 |
| Machining (0.8 * 60 * 1,000) | 48,000 |
| Unit-level expenses | $90,400 |
| Acquiring materials (10 * 150) | 1,500 |
| Production runs (6 * 200) | 1,200 |
| Set up machines (6 * 3 * 80) | 1,440 |
| Process customer order (1 * 100) | 100 |
| Batch-level expenses | $4,240 |
| Engineering support (20 * 75) | $1,500 |
| Product-sustaining expenses | $1,500 |
| Total product expenses | $96,140 |

The cost, with the 1,000-unit order size, drops to about $96 per unit from the $148 per unit cost with the 100-unit order size. By seeing how order size, number of unique components, number of production runs, complexity of setups, number of shipments, and engineering time required affect total order costs, the company's sales representatives are in a much better position to discuss both the functionality of the product and the economics of the order with the customer.

## Determining Profit Margins

A cost buildup for a product or a new order just establishes a floor or reference level for pricing, not the actual price itself. Some firms use a standard markup over costs, such as 20%, to obtain a quoted or target price for a product. Few firms, however, follow such a uniform markup price for all their products or keep it constant over time. Most vary their profit markups for individual products, by type of product, and over time in response to economic and competitive conditions. As we will discuss in the next section, the markup, or the discount from a list price, can be adjusted on the basis of the cost to serve individual customers. A standard markup over a full cost calculation (such as from an ABC analysis) serves mainly as a reference point to simplify the hundreds or thousands of pricing decisions that the firm would otherwise have to make on an individual basis. Once calculated, the reference prices are adjusted up or down to reflect competitive and market conditions. For example, for orders that will require resources that currently have a great deal of unused capacity, managers may choose a much lower markup or even accept a price that does not cover all the resource costs required to fulfill the order. Conversely, managers may adjust target profit markups upward for orders that will require processing by resources whose capacity is already fully used.

### Target ROI Pricing

Over the long run, companies need to price their products so that they recover all of the resource costs and obtain an adequate return on invested capital. This goal suggests that the profit percentage markups over costs be a function of the invested capital required by individual products, services, and customers. Such invested capital would include long-term assets, such as property, plant, and equipment plus working capital, especially inventory and accounts receivable, used by products and customers.

Let us continue the example of the Glenn Company. Suppose, in addition to the facts already presented, the new order (for 100 units) will require 5% of the capacity of plant and equipment resources whose book value is $300,000. In addition, additional (annual equivalent) inventory levels of purchased components, work-in-process, and finished goods will be $30 per unit ordered, and the customer typically pays for the order 90 days after receiving it. Glenn's risk-adjusted weighted average pretax cost of capital is 16%. The target price, $P$, that incorporates all production costs and the 16% capital costs must satisfy the following equation:

$$P = \$14,780 + 0.16 * [0.05 * \$300,000 + 100 * \$30 + (90/365) * P]$$

$$P(1 - 0.04) = 14,780 + 0.16 * [15,000 + 3,000]$$

$$P = \frac{14,780 + 2,880}{0.96} = \$18,396$$

In this example, the cost of invested capital equals $3,616, the difference between the target price and the estimated manufacturing and development costs.

## Properties of ROI Pricing

Target return-on-investment (ROI) pricing is intuitively appealing because it relates price not only to the operating expenses of product development and manufacturing but also to the capital investment required for the production and distribution of the product. With pure cost-plus pricing, the percentage markup over costs can be arbitrary and will be unrelated to the use of the firm's assets (unless the assets employed are correlated with costs incurred). The target ROI approach generates a markup over costs that is proportional to the investment dedicated to the product and its customers. Also, as indicated in the above numerical example, the approach is very compatible and consistent with using economic value added (see discussion in Chapter 10) as a performance metric for a division. The cost of capital used for the economic value added calculation can be directly applied in the pricing formula.

Second, target ROI pricing provides some stability to a company's pricing policies. When activity cost driver rates and investment are based on practical capacity, prices will not fluctuate with short-term changes in actual sales. If prices were targeted on the basis of anticipated actual annual sales volumes, the company would find itself following a perverse pricing policy. In high-demand years, the activity cost driver rates and cost of invested capital would be calculated on a large number of production units, lowering the targeted selling price. Conversely, in low-demand years, target prices would have to be raised, because activity cost driver rates and invested capital would be spread over a smaller number of units. Such a policy (low prices in high-demand years; high prices in low-demand years) would be exactly opposite to what a manager would normally wish to do. With the proposed scheme, prices can be established on the basis of expected long-run utilization of capacity so that above-average ROIs will be earned in high-demand years and below-average ROIs in low-demand years.

The target ROI approach also provides a defensible price, permitting the company to cover its costs and earn a competitive return on its invested capital. It provides guidance to an industry price leader wishing to obtain a "fair" return—not so high that it attracts new entrants into the industry or the attention of entrepreneurial antitrust lawyers, but not so low that the company can be accused of predatory pricing by its less-efficient competitors.

Despite these attractive features, ROI pricing has some disadvantages as well. The ROI formula could automate a decision that should demand considerable judgment and evaluation. As one example, the ROI pricing formula usually uses the same cost of capital for all fixed assets (property, plant, and equipment). In practice, a few such resources will likely be used much more heavily than others. Considerable differences may exist among products in their demands for these scarce, or bottleneck, resources. One way to ration scarce capacity is to raise the target return for those products that make heavy demands on scarce resources and lower the target return for products produced on surplus (slack) resources.

As another example of rote use of the formula, in the 1960s and 1970s, managers of many industrial U.S. companies came to feel that they were entitled to the price derived from an ROI calculation. They did not look closely at competitive forces, particularly from companies in East Asia, such as Japan and South Korea. Rigid adherence to a target ROI price can make a company complacent and unresponsive to the actions of competitors, both domestic and foreign. A price based on an overly optimistic ROI percentage (well above the cost of capital) may encourage competitors to invest heavily in new capacity. Once installed, the new capacity in the industry can place heavy pressure on the profit margins of all companies in the industry. Target ROI pricing will be dysfunctional if it encourages an inward viewpoint by the company: Recover existing costs and get adequate returns on currently invested capital. Competitive and demand elasticity considerations may be suppressed when little consideration is given about whether targeted volumes can be achieved with the price calculated by the ROI pricing formula.

In practice, companies can ameliorate these potential disadvantages. First, managers use the ROI pricing formula iteratively. They determine the price on the basis of full costs and long-run utilization of capacity. Then marketing personnel evaluate whether the forecasted volume can be achieved at the calculated price, with the price adjusted up or down on the basis of their input. In this way, the target ROI price is viewed as a first approximation, with adjustments made about this price to exploit specific information about the nature of demand and competition for the product.

Alternatively, the target price could be established first, independent of costs, by marketing people, on the basis of their judgment as to what price would permit the company to achieve a desired sales volume. Then, after a standard or desired profit margin has been deducted, the pricing formula would be run in reverse to get to a targeted cost for the product. This figure, if below the current projected costs, would stimulate two forms of activity. First, product designers would determine, through a value engineering approach, whether the same functionality could be achieved at a lower cost, or which features should be eliminated to save costs. Second, process and manufacturing engineers would investigate methods and process changes that would improve manufacturing efficiencies so that the targeted cost could be achieved. For a product with an expected productive life of 3–5 years or more, managers may agree to launch the product even with an initial cost above the target cost, if they felt confident that continuous improvement and experience curve effects would enable the target cost to be achieved within, say, 18–24 months of launch. Japanese companies have been particularly successful in this target costing approach,[2] working back from a competitive market price to a targeted cost that must be achieved through collaborative and intensive efforts of marketing and finance people, product designers, and process engineers.

## USING ABC FOR ANALYZING CUSTOMER PROFITABILITY

In addition to helping managers understand manufacturing costs, activity-based costing also enables managers to identify the characteristics that cause some customers to be more expensive or less expensive to serve than others. Exhibit 5-3 shows the characteristics of hidden cost (high cost-to-serve) and hidden profit (low cost-to-serve) customers.

All companies can generally recognize customers that exhibit some or all of the high cost-to-serve characteristics. Occasionally companies are fortunate to enjoy low cost-to-serve customers as well. The only downside from having a low cost-to-serve customer arises when the customer itself realizes that its behavior reduces costs to its supplier and demands low prices (high discounts from list price) in exchange.

**EXHIBIT 5-3**  Characteristics of High and Low Cost-to-Serve Customers

| HIGH COST-TO-SERVE CUSTOMERS | LOW COST-TO-SERVE CUSTOMERS |
| --- | --- |
| Order custom products | Order standard products |
| Small order quantities | High order quantities |
| Unpredictable order arrivals | Predictable order arrivals |
| Customized delivery | Standard delivery |
| Change delivery requirements | No changes in delivery requirements |
| Manual processing | Electronic processing (EDI) |
| Large amounts of presales support (marketing, technical, and sales resources) | Little to no presales support (standard pricing and ordering) |
| Large amounts of postsales support (installation, training, warranty, field service) | No postsales support |
| Require company to hold inventory | Replenish as produced |
| Pay slowly (high accounts receivable) | Pay on time |

When companies apply activity-based costing to their customers, they can view them through the lens of a simple 2 × 2 diagram (see Exhibit 5-4). The vertical axis shows the net margin earned from sales to the customer. The net margin equals net price, after all sales discounts and allowances, less manufacturing cost (as measured by an ABC product costing model, of course). The horizontal axis shows the cost of serving the customer, including order-related costs plus the specific customer-sustaining marketing, technical, selling, and administrative expenses associated with serving each individual customer, as measured by an ABC customer costing model of these expenses.

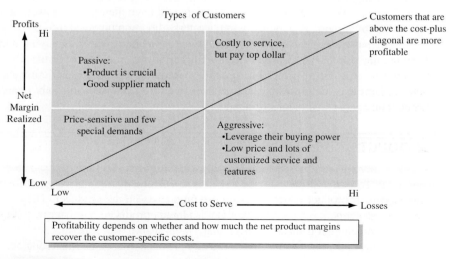

**EXHIBIT 5-4**  Options for Managing Customers

*Source:* B. Shapiro, K. Rangan, R. Moriarty, and E. Ross, "Manage Customers for Profits (Not Just Sales)", *Harvard Business Review*, (September–October 1987).

This diagram shows that companies can enjoy profitable customers in different ways. Some customers may be simple to serve but may also demand low prices. In this case, net margins are low, but by working closely with its suppliers, the customer reduces the costs to serve it. High cost-to-serve customers, exhibiting characteristics in the left-hand column of Exhibit 5-3, can also be profitable (these would be located in the upper right-hand corner of Exhibit 5-4), if the net margins earned on sales to these customers more than compensate the company for the cost of all the resources deployed for these customers. Companies can contemplate menu-based pricing where the price is determined not only by the product characteristics but also by the cost to serve calculated by the company's activity-based costing model.[3]

Customers in the upper left-hand quadrant generate high margins and have low cost to serve. These customers should be watched closely because they could be vulnerable to competitive inroads. Managers should be prepared to offer modest discounts and incentives or special services to retain the loyalty of these highly profitable customers if a competitor threatens.

The most interesting set of customers are those in the lower right-hand corner: low margins and high cost to serve. Companies can use the bill of activities in the net margin and cost-to-serve ABC calculations to modify relationships with such customers and move them in a northwest direction, toward break-even and profitability. For example, the bill of activities may reveal that some of the company's internal processes are quite costly and inefficient and are leading to high manufacturing costs or high costs to serve. The first action should be to improve the performance of the processes now revealed to be critical. The bill of activities may also show that high cost to serve is caused by customer ordering patterns: unpredictability, changes, excessive frequency, customized products, nonstandard logistics and delivery requirements, large demands on technical and sales personnel. The company can share this information with the customer, indicate the costs associated with such actions, and encourage the customer to work with the company in a less costly manner. Both improvement of internal activities and business processes and better coordination between the company and its customers will have the effect of lowering the cost to serve, thereby moving the company in a westerly direction on Exhibit 5-4.

Alternatively, if the customer is not able or willing to shift its buying and delivery patterns, the company can modify its pricing arrangements, lowering the discounts it is prepared to grant and pricing for special services and features. Many companies do not link the discounts and allowances they offer to actual performance by the customer or to the economics of the relationship with the customer.

## PRODUCT SUBSTITUTION

An alternative to raising prices on low-volume, customized products is to substitute existing, lower-cost alternatives. In many instances, customers are relatively indifferent to certain aspects of product variety that impose high costs on the producer. They may wish to have a lavender pen, but a purple pen that is already produced in moderate to high volume may be good enough if it can be offered at a significantly lower price.

Pricing and product substitution are complementary actions. Marketing and sales representatives can give the customer the choice between paying a higher price for exactly the functionality specified by the customer or obtaining a lower price by relaxing the specifications so that a lower-cost alternative can be substituted. Using the information from an ABC analysis, marketing and sales representatives can have intelligent, fact-based discussions with customers to learn their tradeoff among functionality, uniqueness, and price. So if a customer balks at paying a newly established 50% price premium for a particular product, the unit's marketing or sales representative can show how changes in specifications can allow essentially the same functionality to be delivered by an existing product for which a high price premium will not be charged. Some companies have given their sales representatives notebook computers, with ABC models installed, so that the representatives can conduct real-time discussions with customers about tradeoffs between product variety and price.

## 3 REDESIGN PRODUCTS

Many products are expensive because of poor product designs. Without an activity-based cost system to guide their product design and product development decisions, engineers ignore many of the costs of component and product variety and process complexity. They design products for functionality and do not consider the costs of adding new and unique components, new vendors, and complex production process requirements. The best opportunities for lowering product costs through excellent design occur when the products are first designed. The ABC analysis will reveal design aspects—a particularly expensive or complex component or a complex process specification that adds little to product performance and functionality—that can be eliminated or modified even for existing products. Redesigning products offers an attractive option because it will usually be invisible to customers. If the redesign is successfully done, the company does not have to reprice or substitute another product.

## 4 IMPROVE PROCESSES AND OPERATIONS STRATEGY

Opportunities for process improvement are also revealed from careful examination of ABC costs calculated at the product level. Traditional product costing of complex products relies on a *bill of materials* that identifies all the components and subassemblies that are brought together and assembled into the final product. A product cost calculated under an ABC analysis retains, of course, the bill of materials structure and adds a new dimension, a *bill of activities* (see Exhibit 5-5).

---

**EXHIBIT 5-5**  Bill of Activities

| | |
|---|---|
| Materials used | $1,240 |
| Direct labor processing | 3,000 |
| Machine components | 4,800 |
| Expenses of unit-level activities | $9,040 |
| Acquire materials | 1,500 |
| Schedule production runs | 1,200 |
| Set up machines | 1,440 |
| Process customer orders | 100 |
| Expenses of batch-level activities | $4,240 |
| Perform engineering support | $1,500 |
| Expenses of product-sustaining activities | $1,500 |
| Total product expenses | $14,780 |

The bill of activities in Exhibit 5-5 still shows costs associated with materials, labor, and machine hours. But the ABC analysis also reveals the costs of batch and product-sustaining activities performed for this product, in this case ordering components, scheduling and handling production orders, setting up machines, processing customer orders, and performing product and process engineering. Previously, we discussed how to use this information to price the product or discuss with the customer possibilities for substituting less-expensive products. The bill of activities suggests an additional set of actions that can lead to lowering the costs of resources required by this product. For example, the company could attempt to improve its operating processes for ordering materials, handling production orders, setting up machines, and processing orders, invoices, and payments from customers.

As improvements in operating processes are made, the same tasks can be accomplished with fewer organizational resources. Such efficiency gains will be quantified, in future ABC models, by having lower activity cost driver rates, which in turn will lead to lower assigned costs to products that use these activities.[4] Thus, the ABC analysis shows how improvements in operating activities and processes will result in quantifiably lower product costs.

Several companies, allured by Toyota's goal of "efficient lot sizes of one," made arbitrary reductions in their batch sizes and allowable inventory levels. This tactic led to many low-volume runs and more frequent shipments to customers. Subsequently, with the insight from an initial ABC model, the companies realized that their cost structure had increased substantially because of the increased number of batch-level activities. A little knowledge is a dangerous thing. In effect, these companies heard only part of the Toyota story. Efficient lot sizes of one are the *result* of success in reducing the cost of batch-level activities, not the driver of the cost reduction. Because no fundamental improvements had been made in performing batch-level activities, frequent changeovers not only raised batch-level expenses, they also consumed valuable equipment capacity. The ABC model pointed out that blind adherence to fashionable management slogans, without making fundamental improvements in the underlying business processes, will raise, not lower, costs.

In addition to its ability to set priorities and make visible the benefits from continuous improvement initiatives, the ABC bill of activities and associated classification by cost hierarchy also provides the understanding for the advocacy by operations management scholars for focused factories.[5] These recommendations can now be understood as advocating that the production of high-volume products (lots of unit-level activities, few batch and product-sustaining ones) be separated from the production of low-volume, customized products (low level of unit-level activities, lots of batch and product-sustaining activities). With focused factories, high-volume products are produced in facilities optimized to perform unit-level activities efficiently. Such facilities, however, may be extraordinarily inefficient for performing batch and product-sustaining activities. Therefore, low-volume, high-variety products are produced in facilities that perform batch and product-sustaining activities highly efficiently—such as a job shop, with skilled operators and general purpose equipment—but that may be quite inefficient for unit-level activities. The unit level activities are more expensive in the job shop because higher quantities and quality of direct labor are required to operate the general purpose machines, and the general purpose machines run more slowly than the specialized, highly automated production equipment. But for the small run sizes of new and customized products, the much lower batch and product-sustaining expenses in a job shop environment more than compensate for the somewhat higher unit-level labor costs and machine run times.

## TECHNOLOGY INVESTMENT

Recent work on flexible manufacturing systems (FMS)[6] articulates how advanced manufacturing technologies can break through tradeoffs between mass production efficiency and flexibility. The capabilities of FMS, and other information-intensive production technologies such as computer-aided design (CAD), computer-aided engineering (CAE), and computer-aided software engineering (CASE), can all be viewed as greatly reducing the cost of performing batch and product-sustaining activities (such as changing over production from one product to another, scheduling production runs, inspecting products, moving materials, and designing products) while retaining the efficiencies of high-speed automated production. Thus, the business case for investing in these advanced (and expensive) information-intensive manufacturing technologies can now be justified by appealing to the reduction in costs currently incurred for performing batch and product-sustaining activities with conventional manufacturing technology. These costs, however, are visible only if the organization has developed an ABC system for explicitly measuring the costs of batch and product-sustaining activities. These large and now visible batch and product-sustaining costs become the prime targets for elimination with new investments in computer-integrated manufacturing technology.[7]

## ELIMINATE PRODUCTS

We have now illustrated a wide variety of actions that managers can take to transform unprofitable products into profitable ones: reprice, substitute, redesign, process improve, focus factories, and invest in new technology. If none of these actions is feasible or economically justified, then managers may have to confront the final solution: kill unprofitable products.

Marketing and sales personnel may object to dropping unprofitable products, even when no other action is feasible to make them profitable. They argue that these products are complementary to other products that are profitable. Clearly, such an argument is based on the products' demand curves not on their cost curves. ABC, as a cost-estimating model, says nothing about products' demand curves so one cannot respond to such objections from the logic and evidence contained within an ABC model.

Rather than engage in an unproductive debate on the issue, it may suffice to assign the loss from unprofitable products to the appropriate responsibility—say a product manager or customer representative—and allow that person to manage the mix of profitable and unprofitable products to maximize total profitability. One can make small shifts in the incentive structure, by awarding commissions and incentive pay on the basis of profitability rather than sales. Or, even simpler, allow unprofitable products to continue to be produced, marketed, and sold but do not count sales from unprofitable products in salespersons' quotas and incentive pay. In this way, if the unprofitable products do increase total profitability, salespersons can continue to sell them; but if they do not contribute to total profitability, the incentive to continue selling them is dramatically reduced.

## SUMMARY

The product-related actions described above, if implemented successfully, will reduce the resources required to produce products and to service customers. Pricing and explicit product substitution will shift the product mix from difficult-to-produce products to simple-to-produce products. Redesign, process improvement, focused manufacturing facilities, and new technology will enable the same products to be produced with fewer organizational resources. And eliminating products entirely clearly implies that fewer resources are required for the remaining products. In order for the organization to capture the benefits from these actions, however, it must eliminate the spending associated with the resources no longer needed. Most if not all of the batch and product-sustaining expenses associated with unprofitable products are not variable costs, as conventionally defined. Performing one fewer setup, ordering one fewer batch of materials, moving one fewer load of materials, and performing one fewer engineering change notice will not result in any automatic reduction in spending. The totality of product and customer-related actions discussed in this chapter will create additional unused capacity. Benefits will accrue only when managers take action to eliminate the unused capacity created. Doing so requires either reducing spending on the resources no longer needed or deploying the unused capacity to alternative and more profitable applications. This is why activity-based management ultimately must be combined with capacity management if it is to deliver the promised benefits.

## ENDNOTES

1. The large number of production runs is required to machine several of the unique components before they can be assembled into the final product.

2. Target costing will be discussed in Chapter 6.

3. See, for example, the new price incentives established by Procter & Gamble in order to influence the retail and wholesale trade to adopt more-efficient practices in logistics and promotions: *Supermarket News* (September 4, 1995), p. 1; and *U.S. Distribution Journal* (October 15, 1995), p. 10.

4. This scenario assumes, of course, that activity cost driver rates are calculated on the basis of practical capacity, not actual utilization. The importance of calculating activity cost driver rates using practical capacity was stressed in R. Cooper and R. S. Kaplan, "Activity-Based Systems: Measuring the Costs of Resource Usage," *Accounting Horizons* (September 1992), pp. 1–13.

5. W. Skinner, "The Focused Factory," *Harvard Business Review* (May–June 1974), pp. 113–21; R. H. Hayes and S. C. Wheelwright, "Link Manufacturing Process and Product Life Cycles," *Harvard Business Review* (January–February 1979), pp. 133–40.

6. R. Jaikumar, "Postindustrial Manufacturing," *Harvard Business Review* (November–December 1986), pp. 69–76.

7. Additional discussion of investments in advanced manufacturing and information technology will appear in Chapter 12.

## ■ PROBLEMS

### 5-1    *Pricing in an Imperfect Market (CMA, Adapted)*

Stac Industries is a multiproduct company with several manufacturing plants. The Clinton Plant manufactures and distributes two household cleaning and polishing compounds—regular and heavy duty—under the Cleen-Brite label. The forecasted operating results for

Cleen-Brite Compounds—Clinton Plant Forecasted Results of Operations For the
Six-Month Period Ending June 30, 1998 ($000 omitted)

|  | REGULAR | HEAVY DUTY | TOTAL |
|---|---|---|---|
| Sales | $2,000 | $3,000 | $5,000 |
| Cost of sales | 1,600 | 1,900 | 3,500 |
| Gross profit | $ 400 | $1,100 | $1,500 |
| Selling and administrative expenses |  |  |  |
| Flexible | $ 400 | $ 700 | $1,100 |
| Committed* | 240 | 360 | 600 |
| Total selling and administrative expenses | $ 640 | $1,060 | $1,700 |
| Income (loss) before taxes | $ (240) | $ 40 | $ (200) |

*The fixed selling and administrative expenses are allocated between the two products on the basis of dollar sales volume on the internal reports.*

the first six months of 1998 when 100,000 cases of each compound are expected to be manufactured and sold are presented in the following table.

The regular compound sold for $20 a case and the heavy duty sold for $30 a case during the first six months of 1998. The manufacturing costs per case of product are presented in the following table. Each product is manufactured on a separate production line. Annual normal manufacturing capacity is 200,000 cases of each product. However, the plant is capable of producing 250,000 cases of regular compound and 350,000 cases of heavy duty compound annually.

|  | COST PER CASE | |
|---|---|---|
|  | REGULAR | HEAVY DUTY |
| Raw materials | $ 7.00 | $ 8.00 |
| Direct labor | 4.00 | 4.00 |
| Flexible manufacturing overhead | 1.00 | 2.00 |
| Committed manufacturing overhead* | 4.00 | 5.00 |
| Total manufacturing cost | $16.00 | $19.00 |
| Flexible selling and administrative costs | $ 4.00 | $ 7.00 |

*Depreciation charges are 50% of the fixed manufacturing overhead of each line.*

The following table reflects the consensus of top management regarding the price/volume alternatives for the Cleen-Brite products for the last six months of 1998.

These are essentially the same alternatives management had during the first six months of 1998.

| REGULAR COMPOUND | | HEAVY DUTY COMPOUND | |
| --- | --- | --- | --- |
| ALTERNATIVE PRICES (PER CASE) | SALES VOLUME (IN CASES) | ALTERNATIVE PRICES (PER CASE) | SALES VOLUME (IN CASES) |
| $18 | 120,000 | $25 | 175,000 |
| 20 | 100,000 | 27 | 140,000 |
| 21 | 90,000 | 30 | 100,000 |
| 22 | 80,000 | 32 | 55,000 |
| 23 | 50,000 | 35 | 35,000 |

Top management believes the loss for the first six months reflects a tight profit margin caused by intense competition. Management also believes that many companies will be forced out of this market by next year and profits should improve.

***Required***

***Each question should be considered independently.***

(1)   What unit selling price should Stac Industries select for each of the Cleen-Brite compounds (regular and heavy duty) for the remaining six months of 1998?
(2)   Assume the optimum price/volume alternatives for the last six months were a selling price of $23 and volume level of 50,000 cases for the regular compound and a selling price of $35 and volume of 35,000 cases for the heavy duty compound. Should Stac Industries consider closing down its operations until 1999 in order to minimize its losses?

## 5-2   *Seneca Foods*

Seneca Foods is a regional producer of low-priced private-label snack foods. Seneca contracts with local supermarkets to supply good-tasting packaged snack foods that the retailers sell at significantly lower prices to price-sensitive consumers. Because Seneca's production costs are low, and it spends no money on advertising and promotion, it can sell its products to retailers at much lower prices than can national-brand snack food companies, such as Frito-Lay. The low purchase prices often allow the retailer to mark this product up and earn a gross margin well above what it earns from brand products, while still keeping the selling price to the consumer well below the price of the brand products.

Seneca has recently been approached by several large discount food chains who wish to offer their consumers a high-quality but much lower-priced alternative to the heavily advertised and high-priced national brands. But each discount retailer wants the recipe for the snack foods to be customized to its own tastes. Also, each retailer wants its own name and label on the snack foods it sells. Thus, the retailer, not the manufacturer, would be providing the branding for the private-label product. In addition, the retail chains want their own retailer-branded product to offer a full snack product line, just as the national brands do.

Seneca's managers are intrigued with the potential for quantum growth by becoming the prime producer of retailer-brand snack foods to large, national discount chains. As they contemplated this new opportunity, Dale Williams, the senior marketing manager, proposed that if Seneca enters this business, it can think of even higher growth opportunities. Seneca does not have to sell just to the discount chains that have approached it. Local supermarket chains may also be attracted to the idea of having their own brand of high-quality but lower-priced snack products that could compete with the national brands, not just be a low-priced alternative for highly price-sensitive consumers. Perhaps Seneca could launch a marketing effort to regional supermarket chains around the country for a retail-brand snack food product line. Williams noted, however, that the local supermarket chains were not as sophisticated as the national discounters in promoting products under their own brand name. Each supermarket chain likely would need extensive assistance and support to learn how to advertise, merchandise, and promote the store-brand products to be competitive with the national-brand products.

John Thompson, director of logistics for Seneca Foods, noted another issue. The national-brand producers used their own salespeople to deliver their products directly to the retailer's store and even stocked their products on the retailer's shelves. Seneca, in contrast, delivered to the retailer's warehouse or distribution center, leaving the retailer to move the product to the shelves of its various retail outlets. The national producers were trying to dissuade the large discount chains from following their proposed private-label (retailer-brand) strategy by showing them studies that the apparently higher margins they would earn on the private label would be eaten away by much higher warehousing, distribution, and stocking costs for these products.

Heather Gerald, the controller of Seneca, was concerned with the new initiatives. She felt that Seneca's current success was due to its focus. It currently offered a relatively narrow range of products aimed at the high-volume snack food segments to supermarket chains in its local region. Seneca got good terms from its relatively few suppliers because of the high volume of business it did with each of them. Also, the existing production processes were efficient for the products and product range currently produced. She feared that customizing products for each discount or supermarket retailer, plus adding additional products so that they could offer a full product line, would cause problems with both suppliers and the production process. She also wondered about the cost of providing new services, such as consulting and promotions, to the supermarket chains and of developing some of the new items required for the proposed full product line strategy. Heather was attracted to the growth prospects offered by becoming the preferred supplier to major discount and supermarket chains. But she was not as optimistic as Dale Williams that these retailers truly believed that selling their own private-label foods would be more profitable than selling the national brands. Perhaps they were only using Seneca as a negotiating ploy, threatening to turn to private labels to increase their power in setting terms with the national manufacturers. Once production geared up, how much volume would these retailers provide to Seneca? How could Seneca convince the large retailers about the profitability associated with the new private-label strategy?

Gerald knew that Seneca's existing cost systems were adequate for their current strategy. Most expenses were related to materials and machine processing, and these costs were well assigned to products with their conventional standard costing system. But the new strategy would seem to involve a lot more spending in areas other than purchasing materials and running machines. She wished she knew how to provide input into the strategic deliberations now under way at Seneca, but she didn't know how to quantify all the effects of the proposed strategy.

### Required

How can activity-based costing help Heather Gerald assess the attractiveness of the proposed policy? Assuming that Seneca starts to supply new customers—large discounters and supermarkets outside its local region—what ABC systems would be helpful to guide the profitability of the strategy and assist Seneca managers in making decisions? Be sure to think about the totality of Seneca's operations, including its relationships with both suppliers and customers.

---

## ■ CASES

### PRICE LEADERSHIP IN AN OLIGOPOLY*

#### General Motors Corporation

In an article in the *NACA Bulletin*, January 1, 1927, Albert Bradley described the pricing policy of General Motors Corporation. At that time, Mr. Bradley was general assistant treasurer; subsequently, he became vice president, executive vice president, and chairman of the board. There is reason to believe that current policy is substantially the same as that described in the 1927 statement. The following description consists principally of excerpts from Mr. Bradley's article.

**General Policy**    Return on investment is the basis of the General Motors policy in regard to the pricing of product. The fundamental consideration is the average return over a protracted period of time, not the specific rate of return over any particular year or short period of time. This long-term rate of return on

investment represents the official viewpoint as to the highest average rate of return that can be expected consistent with a healthy growth of the business, and may be referred to as the economic return attainable. The adjudged necessary rate of return on capital will vary as between separate lines of industry as a result of differences in their economic situations; and within each industry there will be important differences in return on capital resulting primarily from the relatively greater efficiency of certain producers.

The fundamental policy in regard to pricing product and expansion of the business also necessitates an official viewpoint as to the normal average rate of plant operation. This relationship between assumed normal average rate of operation and practical annual capacity is known as standard volume.

The fundamental price policy is completely expressed in the conception of standard volume and economic return attainable. For example, if it is the accepted policy that standard volume represents 80% of practical annual capacity, and that an average of 20%

---

*This case was prepared from published material. Copyright © 1960 by the President and Fellows of Harvard College. Harvard Business School case 160-005.

per annum must be earned on the operating capital, it becomes possible to determine the standard price of a product—that is, that price which with plants operating at 80% of capacity will produce an annual return of 20% on the investment.

**Standard Volume**   Costs of production and distribution per unit of product vary with fluctuation in volume because of the fixed or nonvariable nature of some of the expense items. Productive materials and productive labor may be considered costs which are 100% variable, since within reasonable limits the aggregate varies directly with volume, and the cost per unit of product therefore remains uniform.

Among the items classified as manufacturing expense or burden there exist varying degrees of fluctuation with volume, owing to their greater or lesser degree of variability. Among the absolutely fixed items are such expenses as depreciation and taxes, which may be referred to as 100% fixed, since within the limits of plant capacity the aggregate will not change, but the amount per unit of product will vary in inverse ratio to the output.

Another group of items may be classified as 100% variable, such as inspection and material handling; the amount per unit of product is unaffected by volume. Between the classes of 100% fixed and 100% variable is a large group of expense items that are partially variable, such as light, heat, power, and salaries.

In General Motors Corporation, standard burden rates are developed for each burden center, so that there will be included in costs a reasonable average allowance for manufacturing expense. In order to establish this rate, it is first necessary to obtain an expression of the estimated normal average rate of plant operation.

Rate of plant operation is affected by such

factors as general business conditions, extent of seasonal fluctuation in sales likely within years of large volume, policy with respect to seasonal accumulation of finished and/or semifinished product for the purpose of leveling the production curve, necessity or desirability of maintaining excess plant capacity for emergency use, and many others. Each of these factors should be carefully considered by a manufacturer in the determination of size of a new plant to be constructed, and before making additions to existing plants, in order that there may be a logical relationship between assumed normal average rate of plant operation and practical annual capacity. The percentage accepted by General Motors Corporation as its policy in regard to the relationship between assumed normal rate of plant operation and practical annual capacity is referred to as standard volume.

Having determined the degree of variability of manufacturing expense, the established total expense at the standard volume rate of operations can be estimated. A *standard burden rate* is then developed which represents the proper absorption of burden in costs at standard volume. In periods of low volume, the unabsorbed manufacturing expense is charged directly against profits as unabsorbed burden, while in periods of high volume, the overabsorbed manufacturing expense is credited to profits, as overabsorbed burden.

**Return on Investment**   Factory costs and commercial expenses for the most part represent outlays by the manufacturer during the accounting period. An exception is depreciation of capital assets which have a greater length of life than the accounting period. To allow for this element of cost, there is included an allowance for depreciation in the burden rates used in compiling costs. Before an enterprise can be considered successful and worthy of continuation or expansion, however, still another element of cost must be reckoned with. This is the cost of capital, including an allowance for profit.

Thus, the calculation of standard prices of products necessitates the establishment of standards of capital requirement as well as expense factors, representative of the normal operating condition. The standard for capital employed in fixed assets is expressed as a percentage of factory cost, and the standards for working capital are expressed in part as a percentage of sales, and in part as a percentage of factory cost.

The calculation of the standard allowance for fixed investment is illustrated by the following example.

| | |
|---|---|
| Investment in plant and other fixed assets | $15,000,000 |
| Practical annual capacity | 50,000 units |
| Standard volume, percent of practical annual capacity | 80% |
| Standard volume equivalent (50,000 × 80%) | 40,000 units |
| Factory cost per unit at standard volume | $1,000 |
| Annual factory cost of production at standard volume (40,000 × $1,000) | $40,000,000 |
| Standard factor for fixed investment (ratio of investment to annual factory cost of production; $15,000,000/$40,000,000) | 0.375 |

The amount tied up in working capital items should be directly proportional to the volume of business. For example, raw materials on hand should be in direct proportion to the manufacturing requirements—so many days' supply of this material, so many days' supply of that material, and so on—depending on the condition and location of sources of supply, transportation conditions, etc. Work in process should be in direct proportion to the requirements of finished production, since it is dependent on the length of time required for the material to pass from the raw to the finished state, and the amount of labor and other charges to be absorbed in the process. Finished product should be in direct proportion to sales requirements. Accounts receivable should be in direct proportion to sales, being dependent on terms of payment and efficiency of collections.

**The Standard Price** These elements are combined to construct the standard price as shown in Table 1. Note that the economic return attainable (20% in the illustration) and the standard volume (80% in the illustration) are long-run figures and are rarely changed;[1] the other elements of the price are based on current estimates.

**Differences among Products** Responsibility for investment must be considered in calculating the standard price of each product as well as in calculating the overall price for all products, since products with identical accounting costs may be responsible for investments that vary greatly. In the illustration given below, a uniform standard selling price of $1,250 was determined. Let us now suppose that this organization makes and sells two products, A and B, with equal manufacturing costs of $1,000 per unit and equal working capital requirements, and that 20,000 units of each product are produced. However, an analysis of fixed investment indicates that $10 million is applicable to Product A, while only $5 million of fixed investment is applicable to Product B. Each product must earn 20% on its investment in order to satisfy the standard condition. Table 2 illus-

---

[1]A Brookings Institution Survey reported that the principal pricing goal of General Motors Corporation in the 1950s was 20% on investment after taxes.

**TABLE 1** Illustration of Method of Determination of Standard Price

| | IN RELATION TO | TURNOVER PER YEAR | RATIO TO SALES ANNUAL BASIS | RATIO TO FACTORY COST ANNUAL BASIS |
|---|---|---|---|---|
| Cash | Sales | 20 times | 0.050 | — |
| Drafts and accounts receivable | Sales | 10 times | 0.100 | — |
| Raw material and work in process | Factory cost | 6 times | — | $0.16\frac{2}{3}$ |
| Finished product | Factory cost | 12 times | — | $0.08\frac{1}{3}$ |
| Gross working capital | | | 0.150 | 0.250 |
| Fixed investment | | | — | 0.375 |
| Total investment | | | 0.150 | 0.625 |
| Economic return attainable, 20% | | | — | — |
| Multiplying the investment ratio by 20%, the necessary net profit margin is arrived at | | | 0.030 | 0.125 |
| Standard allowance for commercial expenses, 7% | | | 0.070 | — |
| Gross margin over factory cost | | | 0.100 | 0.125 |
| | | | $a$ | $b$ |

$$\text{Selling price, as a ratio to factory cost} = \frac{1 + b}{1 - a} = \frac{1 + 0.125}{1 - 0.100} = 1.250$$

$$\text{If standard cost} = \$1{,}000$$
$$\text{Then standard price} = \$1{,}000 \times 1.250 = \$1{,}250$$

trates the determination of the standard price for Product A and Product B.

From this analysis of investment, it becomes apparent that Product A, which has the heavier fixed investment, should sell for $1,278, while Product B should sell for only $1,222, in order to produce a return of 20% on the investment. Were both products sold for the composite average standard price of $1,250, then Product A would not be bearing its share of the investment burden, while Product B would be correspondingly overpriced.

Differences in working capital requirements as between different products may also be important due to differences in manufacturing methods, sales terms, merchandising policies, etc. The inventory turnover rate of one line of products sold by a division of

General Motors Corporation may be six times a year, while inventory applicable to another line of products is turned over 30 times a year. In the second case, the inventory investment required per dollar cost of sales is only one-fifth of that required in the case of the product with the slower turnover. Just as there are differences in capital requirements as between different classes of product, so may the standard requirements for the same class of product require modification from time to time due to permanent changes in manufacturing processes, in location of sources of supply, more efficient scheduling and handling of materials, etc.

The importance of this improvement to the buyer of General Motors products may be appreciated from the following example. The total inventory investment for the 12 months

**TABLE 2**  Variances in Standard Price Due to Variances in Rate of Capital Turnover

| | PRODUCT A | | PRODUCT B | | TOTAL PRODUCT (A PLUS B) | |
| --- | --- | --- | --- | --- | --- | --- |
| | RATIO TO SALES ANNUAL BASIS | RATIO TO FACTORY COST ANNUAL BASIS | RATIO TO SALES ANNUAL BASIS | RATIO TO FACTORY COST ANNUAL BASIS | RATIO TO SALES ANNUAL BASIS | RATIO TO FACTORY COST ANNUAL BASIS |
| Gross working capital | 0.150 | 0.250 | 0.150 | 0.250 | 0.150 | 0.250 |
| Fixed investment | — | 0.500 | — | 0.250 | — | 0.375 |
| Total investment | 0.150 | 0.750 | 0.150 | 0.500 | 0.150 | 0.625 |
| Economic return attainable, 20% | — | — | — | — | — | — |
| Multiplying the investment ratio by 20%, the necessary net profit margin is arrived at | 0.030 | 0.150 | 0.030 | 0.100 | 0.030 | 0.125 |
| Standard allowance for commercial expenses, 7% | $\dfrac{0.070}{0.100}$ | $\dfrac{—}{0.150}$ | $\dfrac{0.070}{0.100}$ | $\dfrac{—}{0.100}$ | $\dfrac{0.070}{0.100}$ | $\dfrac{—}{0.125}$ |
| Gross margin over factory cost | $a$ | $b$ | $a$ | $b$ | $a$ | $b$ |
| Selling price, as a ratio to Factory cost $\Big\} = \dfrac{1+b}{1-a}$ | $\dfrac{1. + 0.150}{1. - 0.100} = 1.278$ | | $\dfrac{1. + 0.100}{1. - 0.100} = 1.222$ | | $\dfrac{1. + 0.125}{1. - 0.100} = 1.250$ | |
| If standard cost equals | $1,000 | | $1,000 | | $1,000 | |
| Then standard price equals | $1,278 | | $1,222 | | $1,250 | |

ended September 30, 1926, would have averaged $182,490,000 if the turnover rate of 1923 (the best performance prior to 1925) had not been bettered, or an excess of $74,367,000 over the actual average investment. In other words, General Motors would have been compelled to charge $14,873,000 more for its products during this 12-month period than was actually charged if prices had been established to yield, say, 20% on the operating capital required.

**Conclusion** The analysis as to the degree of variability of manufacturing and commercial expenses with increases or decreases in volume of output, and the establishment of "standards" for the various investment items, makes it possible not only to develop "Standard Prices," but also to forecast, with much greater accuracy than otherwise would be possible, the capital requirements, profits, and return on capital at the different rates of operation, which may result from seasonal conditions or from changes in the general business situation. Moreover, whenever it is necessary to calculate in advance the final effect on net profits of proposed increases or decreases in price, with their resulting changes in volume of output, consideration of the real economics of the situation is facilitated by the availability of reliable basic data.

It should be emphasized that the basic pricing policy stated in terms of the economic return attainable is a policy, and it does not absolutely dictate the specific price. At times, the actual price may be above, and at other times below, the standard price. The standard price calculation affords a means not only of interpreting actual or proposed prices in relation to the established policy, but at the same time affords a practical demonstration as to whether the policy itself is sound. If the prevailing price of product is found to be at variance with the standard price other than to the extent due to temporary causes, it follows that prices should be adjusted; or else, in the event of conditions being such that prices cannot be brought into line with the standard price, the conclusion is necessarily drawn that the terms of the expressed policy must be modified.[2]

### Required

(1) An article in the *Wall Street Journal*, December 10, 1957, gave estimates of cost figures in "an imaginary car-making division in the Ford-Chevrolet-Plymouth field." Most of the data given below are derived from that article. Using these data, compute the standard price. Working capital ratios are not given; assume that they are the same as those in Table 1.

---

[2]This paragraph is taken from an article by Donaldson Brown, then vice president, finance, General Motors Corporation, in *Management and Administration*, March 1924.

| | |
|---|---|
| Investment in plant and other fixed assets | $600,000,000 |
| Required return on investment | 30% before income taxes |
| Practical annual capacity | 1,250,000 |
| Standard volume—assume | 80% |
| Factory cost per unit: | |
| Outside purchases of parts | $ 500* |
| Parts manufactured inside | 600* |
| Assembly labor | 75 |
| Burden | 125 |
| Total | $1,300 |

*Each of these items includes $50 of labor costs.*

"Commercial cost," corresponding to the 7% in Table 1, is added as a dollar amount and includes the following:

| | |
|---|---:|
| Inbound and outbound freight | $ 85 |
| Tooling and engineering | 50 |
| Sales and engineering | 50 |
| Administrative and miscellaneous | 50 |
| Warranty (repairs within guarantee) | 15 |
| Total | $250 |

Therefore, the 7% commercial allowance in Table 1 should be eliminated, and in its place $250 should be added to the price as computed from the formula.

(2) What would happen to profits and return on investment before taxes in a year in which volume was only 60% of capacity? What would happen in a year in which volume was 100% of capacity? Assume that nonvariable costs included in the

$1,550 unit cost above are $350 million; i.e., variable costs are $1,550 − $350 = $1,200. In both situations, assume that cars were sold at the standard price established in Requirement 1, since the standard price is not changed to reflect annual changes in volume.

(3) In the 1975 model year, General Motors gave cash rebates of as high as $300 per car off the list price. In 1972 and 1973, prices had been restricted by price control legislation, which required that selling prices could be increased only if costs had increased. Selling prices thereafter were not controlled, although there was always the possibility that price controls could be reimposed. In 1975, demand for automobiles was sharply lower than in 1974, partly because of a general recession and partly because of concerns about high gasoline prices. Does the cash rebate indicate that General Motors adopted a new pricing policy in 1975, or is it consistent with the policy described in the case?

# SIEMENS ELECTRIC MOTOR WORKS (A) (ABRIDGED)*

Ten years ago our electric motor business was in real trouble. Low labor rates allowed the Eastern Bloc countries to sell standard motors at prices we were unable to match. We had become the high cost producer in the industry. Consequently, we decided to change our strategy and become a specialty motor producer. Once we adopted our new strategy, we discovered that while our existing cost system was adequate for costing standard motors, it gave us inaccurate information when we used it to cost specialty motors.

*Mr. Karl-Heinz Lottes,* Director of Business Operations, EMW

---

*This case was prepared by Professor Robin Cooper and Professor Karen Hopper Wruck.

Copyright © 1990 by the President and Fellows of Harvard College. Harvard Business School case 191-006.

## *Siemens Corporation*

Headquartered in Munich, Siemens AG, a producer of electrical and electronic products, was one of the world's largest corporations. Revenues totaled 51 billion deutschmarks [DM] in 1987, with roughly half this amount representing sales outside the Federal Republic of Germany. The Siemens organization was split into seven major groups and five corporate divisions. The largest group, Energy and Automation accounted for 24% of total revenues. Low wattage alternating current (A/C) motors were produced at the Electric Motor Works (EMW), which was part of the Manufacturing Industries Division of the Energy and Automation Group. High wattage motors were produced at another facility.

### The Electric Motor Works

Located in the small town of Bad Neustadt, the original Siemens EMW plant was built in 1937 to manufacture refrigerator motors for "Volkskuhlschraenke" (people's refrigerators). Less than a year later, Mr. Siemens halted the production of refrigerator motors and began to produce electric motors for other applications. At the end of World War II, the Bad Neustadt plant was the only Siemens factory in West Germany capable of producing electric motors. All the other Siemens production facilities had been completely destroyed or seized by Eastern Bloc countries. After an aggressive rebuilding program, Bad Neustadt emerged as the firm's primary producer of electric motors.

Through the 1970s, EMW produced about 200 different types of standard motors, at a total annual volume around 230,000 motors. Standard motors accounted for 80% of sales volumes—the remaining 20% was customized motors. The production process was characterized by relatively long runs of a single type of motor. Because identical motors were used by a wide range of customers, standard motors were inventoried and shipped as orders were received. The market for standard A/C motors was extremely competitive. The firm was under constant pressure to reduce costs so that it could price aggressively and still make a profit. Despite a major expansion and automation program begun in 1974, by the early 1980s EMW found it could not lower its costs sufficiently to offset the lower labor rates of its Eastern Bloc competitors.

### Change in Strategy

An extensive study revealed that EMW could become a profitable producer of low volume, customized A/C motors. To help implement this strategy, the Bad Neustadt plant was enlarged and dedicated to the manufacture of A/C motors with power ratings ranging from 0.06 to 18.5 kilowatts. These motors supported a number of applications including automation engineering, machine tools, plastic processing, and paper and printing machines.

For the new strategy to succeed, EMW needed to be able to manufacture efficiently a large variety of motors in small production runs. Between 1985 and 1988 EMW spent DM50 million a year to replace almost every machine on the shop floor and thereby create a production environment that could support its new strategy.

By 1987 the production process was highly automated with numerically controlled machines, flexible machining centers and robotically fed production processes used throughout the factory. Large volume common components were manufactured using dedicated automated equipment, while very low volume components might be made in manual production processes. Where possible flexible manufacturing was used to produce small volume specialty components. While a normal annual production volume for common components might be 100,000 units, a single component could have up to 10,000 custom variations that might have to be produced one at a time.

To design a custom motor, modifications were made to a standard motor design. The process involved determining where standard components could not be used. These standard components were replaced by custom components that provided the functionality required by the customer.

By 1987, the EMW strategy seemed to be successful (see Exhibit 1). Of a total of 65,625 orders accepted, 90% were for custom motors; 48% for only one motor and 74% for fewer than five motors. But EMW high-volume standard motors still accounted for al-

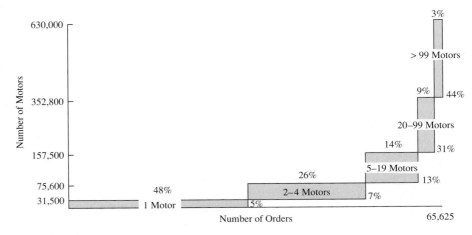

**EXHIBIT 1** Distribution of Orders Accepted for Production in 1987

most half the total annual output of 630,000 motors.

### Change in the Calculation of Product Costs

EMW's product cost system assigned materials and labor costs directly to the products. Overhead costs were divided into three categories: materials related, production related, and support related. Materials-related overhead, containing costs associated with material acquisition, was allocated to products based on their direct materials costs. Production-related overhead was directly traced to the 600 production cost centers. A production cost center had been created for each type of machine. Cost centers with high labor intensity used direct labor hours to allocate costs to products. For centers with automated machines whose operation required few direct labor hours, machine hours was used as the allocation base. Support-related overhead was allocated to products based on manufacturing costs to date: the sum of direct materials and direct labor costs, materials overhead, and production overhead. The breakdown of each cost category as a percent of total costs was as follows:

|  | PERCENT OF TOTAL COSTS | BURDEN RATE |
|---|---|---|
| Direct materials | 29% | |
| Direct labor | 10% | |
| Materials overhead | 2% | 6% of materials cost |
| Production overhead | 33% | DM/DLH or DM/MH (600 rates) |
| Support-related overhead | 26% | 35% of other manufacturing costs |
| Total | 100% | |

special components are processed in each case total # times scrap are processed is the appropriate driver

Two years after the change in strategy, problems with the traditional cost system became apparent. The traditional cost system seemed unable to capture the relation between the increased support costs and the change in product mix. Management felt that most support costs related more closely to the number of orders received or the number of customized components in a motor rather than to materials expense or to the quantity of labor and machine hours required to build the motor.

An extensive study was undertaken to identify the support costs that management believed were driven by the processing of orders and the processing of special components. The following departments' costs were most affected by the large increases in number of orders and number of special components.

---

**Costs Related to Order Processing** ① Batch
  Billing
  Order receiving
  Product costing and bidding
  Shipping and handling
**Costs Related to Special Components** ② # of special components processed
  Inventory handling
  Product costing and bidding
  Product development
  Purchasing
  Receiving
  Scheduling and production control
  Technical examination of incoming orders

---

An analysis of the Order Processing costs revealed that the same resources were required to process an order of one custom motor as for an order of 200 standard motors. A similar analysis indicated that the number of different types of special components in each motor design determined the work load for the departments affected by Special Components. The demand for work in these departments was not strongly affected by the total number of special components produced. For example, an order of five custom motors requiring ten special components per unit generated the same amount of work as an order of one custom motor with a design requiring ten special components. In 1987, the factory used 30,000 different special components to customize their motors. The special components were processed 325,000 different times for customized orders.

The costs in each support department associated with these two activities were removed from the support related cost pool and assigned to two new cost pools. Exhibit 2 illustrates, for 1987, the formation of the two new cost pools. The first column presents total costs grouped by traditional costing system definitions. The new cost system removes 6.3 million from engineering support costs, and 27.0 million from administrative support costs. These expenses are then assigned to the new cost pools, 13.8 million to order processing costs, and 19.5 million to special components costs.

Exhibit 3 shows the cost buildup for five typical motor orders. The Base Motor cost includes direct materials and labor costs, materials and production overhead, and the portion of support overhead not assigned to the two new cost pools. To this Base Motor cost must be added the cost of processing the order, and the materials, labor, production overhead and support overhead required for the special components.

### Effect of the New Cost System

In 1987 EMW received close to DM1 billion in orders, accepted only DM450 million, and ran the factory at 115% of rated capacity. Mr. Karl-Heinz Lottes, Director of Business Operations, EMW commented on the role of the redesigned cost system with the new strategy:

> Without the new cost system, our new strategy would have failed. The information it

---

**EXHIBIT 2**   1987 Reconciliation Transforming the Traditional Cost System (000 DM)

| | TRADITIONAL | TRANSFERRED | NEW |
|---|---|---|---|
| Materials | 105,000 | | 105,000 |
| Materials overhead | 6,000 | | 6,000 |
| Labor | 36,000 | | 36,000 |
| Labor or machine overhead | 120,000 | | 120,000 |
| Manufacturing cost | 267,000 (74%)* | | 267,000 (74%) |
| Engineering costs | 12,000 | 6,300 | 5,700 |
| Tooling costs | 22,500 | 0 | 22,500 |
| Administrative costs | 60,000 | 27,000 | 33,000 |
| Support-related cost | 94,500 (26%)† | 33,300 (9%) | 61,200 (17%) |
| Order processing cost | | 13,800 | 13,800 |
| Special components cost | | 19,500 | 19,500 |
| Total cost | 361,500 | 0 | 361,500 |

*Percent of total cost.
†This figure corresponds to the 26% of support-related overhead discussed in the text.

---

**EXHIBIT 3**   Manufacturing Costs for Five Motor Orders

| | A | B | C | D | E |
|---|---|---|---|---|---|
| Cost of base motor (without assignment from new cost pools) | 295.0 | 295.0 | 295.0 | 295.0 | 295.0 |
| Cost of all special components* (without assignment from new cost pools) | 29.5 | 59.0 | 88.5 | 147.5 | 295.0 |
| No. of different types of special components per motor | 1 | 2 | 3 | 5 | 10 |
| No. of motors ordered | 1 | 1 | 1 | 1 | 1 |

| | BASE MOTOR COST | SPECIAL COMPONENTS COST |
|---|---|---|
| Materials | 90 | 9.0 |
| Materials O/H | 5 | 0.5 |
| Direct labor | 35 | 3.5 |
| Manufacturing O/H | 110 | 11.0 |
| | 240 | 24.0 |
| Support-related overhead† | 55 | 5.5 |
| Unit manufacturing costs | 295 | 29.5 |

*For illustrative purposes, all different types of special components are assumed to cost 29.5 apiece.
†Support-related overhead excludes the expenses associated with processing individual customer orders and handling special components.

generated helped us to identify those orders we want to accept. While some orders we lose to competitors, most we turn down because they are not profitable. Anyone who wants to understand the importance of the system, can simply compare some typical orders costed with the traditional system with the costs produced by our new system.

## KANTHAL (A)*

Carl-Erik Ridderstråle, president of Kanthal, was describing his motivation for developing a system to measure customer profitability.

> Before, when we got an order from a big, important customer, we didn't ask questions. We were glad to get the business. But a small company, competing around the world, has to concentrate its sales and marketing resources. We needed an account management system if we were to achieve our strategy for higher growth and profitability. An account management system as part of the Kanthal 90 Strategy will enable us to get sales managers to accept responsibility for promoting high-margin products to high-profit customers.

### History

Kanthal, the largest of six divisions in the Kanthal-Hoganas group of Sweden, was headquartered in Hallstahammar a town of 17,000 persons about 150 km northwest of Stockholm. The company's history can be traced back to an ironworks founded in the seventeenth century to exploit the water power available from the stream running through the town. Kanthal specialized in the production and sales of electrical resistance heating elements. "We work for a warmer world," was its motto.

Kanthal had about 10,000 customers and 15,000 items that it produced. Sales during 1985 through 1987 had been level at about SEK 850 million.[1] Export sales, outside of Sweden, accounted for 95% of the total.

Summary statistics for the past two years appear in Exhibit 1.

Kanthal consisted of three divisions:

Kanthal Heating Technology supplied manufacturers of electrical appliances and heating systems with wire that generated heat through electrical resistance. Products included heating wire and ribbon, foil elements, machinery and precision wire. Kanthal's 25% market share made it a world leader in supplying heating alloys. Sales growth was sluggish in Europe and the United States but rapid growth was occurring in the Far East and Latin America.

Kanthal Furnace Products produced a wide range of heating elements for electric industrial furnaces. Its 40% market share gave it a dominant position in the large markets of the United States, Japan, West Germany, and the United Kingdom. A new product, Kanthal Super, was generating substantial growth because of its substantially improved performance over conventional materials, including longer service life, lower service costs, and higher operating temperatures.

Kanthal Bimetals was one of the few companies in the world with fully integrated manufacturing of thermo-bimetals for temperature control devices used in the manufacture of thermostats, circuit breakers, and household appliances.

**EXHIBIT 1**  Summary of Operations

|  | 1986 | 1987 |
| --- | --- | --- |
| Invoiced sales (MSEK)* | 839 | 849 |
| Profit after financial items | 87 | 107 |
| Return on capital | 20% | 21% |
| Number of employees | 1,606 | 1,591 |

*MSEK, million Swedish kroner.

---

*Professor Robert S. Kaplan prepared this case.
Copyright © 1989 by the President and Fellows of Harvard College. Harvard Business School Case 190-002.
[1]In 1988, the Swedish kroner (SEK) was worth about US$0.16.

Kanthal's manufacturing facilities were located in Hallstahammar, Brazil, the United Kingdom, West Germany, the United States, and Italy.

### Kanthal 90

Ridderstråle, upon becoming president in 1985, saw the need for a strategic plan for Kanthal.

> The company had been successful in the past. We needed to use this base of experience to influence the future. We had to have a consolidated view to ensure that we did not sub-optimize in narrow markets or with a narrow functional view. Resources were to be allocated so that we could increase profits while maintaining a return on employed capital in excess of 20%.

The Kanthal 90 plan specified overall profit objectives by division, by product line, and by market. Currently, however, salespersons were compensated mostly on gross sales volume. Higher commissions were being paid for selling obviously higher-margin products, such as Super, and higher bonuses were being awarded for achieving sales targets in the high-margin products. But Ridderstråle wanted to achieve the additional growth planned under Kanthal 90 without adding sales and administrative resources to handle the increased volume anticipated.

> We needed to know where in the organization the resources could be taken from and redeployed into more profitable uses. We did not want to eliminate resources in a steady-state environment. We wanted to reallocate people to generate future growth.

> With our historically good profitability, and lacking any current or imminent crisis, we could not realistically consider laying off people at the Hallstahammar plant. But we wanted to be able to redeploy people so that they could earn more profit for us; to move people from corporate staff to divisions, from the parent company to operating subsidiaries, and from staff functions into sales, R&D, and production. Ideally, if we could transform an accounting clerk at Hallstahammar into a

salesman of Kanthal-Super in Japan, we could generate a substantial profit increase.

Exhibit 2 shows the distribution of Kanthal's incurred costs. The existing cost system treated most sales, marketing, and administrative costs as a percentage of sales revenue. Therefore, customers whose selling price exceeded the standard full cost of manufacturing plus the percentage mark-up for general, selling, and administrative expenses appeared to be profitable, while a customer order whose selling price was below standard manufacturing cost plus the percentage mark-up appeared unprofitable. Ridderstråle knew, however, that individual customers made quite different demands on Kanthal's administrative and sales staff.

> Low profit customers place high demands on technical and commercial service. They buy low-margin products in small orders. Frequently they order nonstandard products that have to be specially produced for them. And we have to supply special selling discounts in order to get the business.

> High profit customers buy high-margin, standard products in large orders. They make no demands for technical or commercial service, and accurately forecast for us their annual demands.

He felt that a new system was needed to determine how much profit was earned each time a customer placed a particular order. The system should attempt to measure the costs that individual customer orders placed on the production, sales, and administrative resources of

---

**EXHIBIT 2** Cost Structure

| COST COMPONENT | PERCENTAGE |
| --- | --- |
| Materials | 23 |
| Production salaries and wages | 19 |
| Variable processing costs | 5 |
| Fixed processing costs | 16 |
| Subcontracted services | 3 |
| Selling and administrative | 34 |
| Total costs | 100 |

the company. The goal was to find both "hidden profit" orders, those whose demands on the company were quite low, and the "hidden loss" orders, those customer orders that under the existing system looked profitable but which in fact demanded a disproportionate share of the company's resources to fulfill.

Ridderstråle pointed out the weaknesses with the present method of profitability measurement.

> We distribute resources equally across all products and customers. We do not measure individual customer's profitability or the real costs of individual orders. In this environment, our sales and marketing efforts emphasize volume, more than profits. In the future, we want Kanthal to handle significantly increased sales volume without any corresponding increase in support resources, and to gain the share in our most profitable products.

> Our current method of calculating product costs may show two customers to be equally profitable on a gross margin basis. But there could be hidden profits and hidden costs associated with these customers that we are not seeing (see Exhibit 3). If we could get more accurate information about our own manufacturing cost structure, as well as the costs of supplying

individual customers and orders, we could direct our resources to customers with hidden profits, and reduce our efforts to customers with the hidden losses. We might end up with the same market share, so that our competitors would not even see this shift in our strategy, but our profitability would be much higher. To execute such a strategy, however, we need better information about the profitability of each order, each product, and each customer.

The biggest barrier we have to overcome is the notion that production overhead, selling, and administrative costs are "fixed." The definition of strategy is to recognize that all costs are variable. Our sales people must learn how to deploy resources to their most profitable use.

### The New Account Management System

Per O. Ehrling, Financial Manager of Kanthal, worked with SAM, a Swedish management advisory group, to develop a system to analyze production, sales, and administrative costs at the Hallstahammar facility. Over a period of several months, finance managers and the consultants conducted extensive interviews with all department heads and key personnel. The interviews were designed to elicit information about the nature of the activities being per-

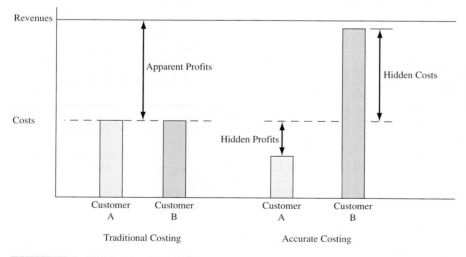

**EXHIBIT 3** Hidden Profit and Hidden Cost Customers

formed by support department personnel and the events that triggered the demands for these organizational activities. Ehrling described the philosophy of the new approach:

> In our previous system, indirect costs were either manufacturing costs that were allocated to products based on direct labor, or they were Selling & Administrative Costs, that were treated as period expenses and were unanalyzed. This treatment may have been correct 100 years ago when we had one bookkeeper for every 10 blacksmiths, but today we have eight bookkeepers for every three blacksmiths. This means that most of our costs today are indirect and our previous system didn't know how to allocate them.
>
> We wanted to move away from our traditional financial accounting categories. We found that most of our organizational costs could be classified either as Order-related or Volume Costs. Actually, we did investigate three

additional cost drivers—product range, technical support, and new products. But the total costs assigned to these three categories ended up being less than 5% of total costs so we eliminated them.

Using the interview information, the project team determined how much of the expenses of each support department related to the volume of sales and production and how much related to handling individual production and sales orders (see Exhibit 4). The manufacturing volume costs, in addition to material, direct labor, and variable overhead, also included the costs of production orders to replenish inventory stocks. Only 20% of Kanthal's products were stocked in inventory, but these products represented 80% of sales orders so the cost of continually replenishing these products was assumed to be related to the volume of production. Manufacturing order costs therefore included only the

**EXHIBIT 4** Order and Volume Costs

| TYPE OF PERSONNEL | ORDER-RELATED WORK | VOLUME-RELATED WORK |
|---|---|---|
| **Production** | | |
| Stock replenishment | None | All activities |
| Production planning | Order planning<br>Order follow-up | Inventory management |
| Operators | Set-up<br>Start-up expense | Direct hours |
| Foremen | Order planning<br>Order support | Machine problems |
| Stock | Order input<br>Order output | Order handling |
| Transportation | Order planning<br>Order handling | |
| **Selling and Administrative** | | |
| Management | Offer discussion<br>Offer negotiation | General management |
| Sales | Offer work<br>Order negotiation<br>Delivery follow-up | Sales unrelated to orders<br>General public relations<br>Sales management |
| Secretarial | Offer typing | |
| Administration | Order booking<br>Order adjustment<br>Invoice typing<br>Customer ledger<br>Supervision | Accounting |

cost of set-up and other activities that were triggered when a customer ordered a product not normally stocked. Manufacturing order costs were calculated separately for each major product group. The sales order costs represented the selling and administrative costs that could be traced to processing an individual customer's order. The S&A costs that remained after subtracting sales order costs were treated as sales volume costs and were allocated proportionately to the manufacturing volume costs.

For example, the Sales Department activities (see Exhibit 4) relating to preparing a bid for an order, negotiating with the customer about the order, and following-up with the customer after the order was delivered were classified as "order-related." All remaining activities, such as public relations and sales management, that could not be traced to individual orders were classified as "volume-related."

Follow-up interviews were conducted to corroborate the split of effort in each department between volume- and order-related activities. Sample calculations are shown in Exhibit 5.

---

**EXHIBIT 5**   Sample Calculation of Order and Volume Costs, by Product Group

**Step 1. Calculate Selling & Administrative (S&A) Order Costs**

| | | |
|---|---|---|
| Total selling & administrative order costs | | SEK2,000,000 |
| Total number of orders | 2,000 | |
| Stocked products | 1,500 | |
| Non-stocked products | 500 | |
| S&A order costs per order | | SEK  1,000 |

**Step 2. Calculate Manufacturing Order Cost for Non-stocked Products**

| | | |
|---|---|---|
| Total manufacturing order costs (for non-stocked products) | | SEK1,000,000 |
| Number of orders for non-stocked products | | 500 |
| Manufacturing order costs per non-stocked order | | SEK  2,000 |

**Step 3. Calculate Allocation Factor for S&A Volume Costs**

| | | |
|---|---|---|
| Compute total manufacturing and S&A costs | | SEK7,000,000 |
| Subtract order costs | | |
| Non-stocked products | 1,000,000 | |
| Selling & administrative order costs | 2,000,000 | 3,000,000 |
| Total volume costs | | SEK4,000,000 |
| Manufacturing volume costs of goods sold (CGS) | 3,200,000 | |
| Selling & administrative volume-related costs | 800,000 | |
| S&A volume allocation factor: S&A volume costs/mfg. volume CGS (800/3,200) | | 25% |

**Step 4. Calculate Operating Profit on Individual Orders for Non-stocked Products**

| | | |
|---|---|---|
| Sales value | | SEK  10,000 |
| Less: Volume costs: Manufacturing cost of goods sold (@ 40% of sales value) | | 4,000 |
| Volume costs: Selling & administrative (@ 25% of mfg. CGS) | | 1,000 |
| Margin on volume-related costs | | 5,000 |
| Less: Mfg. order cost for non-stocked product | | 2,000 |
| Selling & administrative order cost | | 1,000 |
| Operating profit for order | | SEK  2,000 |

*SEK, Swedish kroner.*

**EXHIBIT 6** Customer Order Analysis

Standard order cost: SEK 572
Manufacturing order cost for non-stocked products:    Foil Elements:    SEK1508
    Finished Wire:    SEK2340

| COUNTRY CUSTOMER | ORDER LINES | INVOICED VALUE (SEK) | VOLUME COST (SEK) | ORDER COST (SEK) | NON-STOCKED (SEK) | OPERATING PROFIT (SEK) | PROFIT MARGIN % |
|---|---|---|---|---|---|---|---|
| Sweden | | | | | | | |
| S001 | 1 | 1,210 | 543 | 572 | 0 | 95 | 8 |
| S002 | 3 | 46,184 | 10,080 | 1,716 | 4,524 | 29,864 | 65 |
| S003 | 8 | 51,102 | 50,567 | 4,576 | 12,064 | (16,105) | −32 |
| S004 | 9 | 98,880 | 60,785 | 5,148 | 13,572 | 19,375 | 20 |
| S005 | 1 | 3,150 | 1,557 | 572 | 2,340 | (1,319) | −42 |
| S006 | 5 | 24,104 | 14,889 | 2,860 | 4,680 | 1,675 | 7 |
| S007 | 2 | 4,860 | 2,657 | 1,144 | 4,680 | (3,621) | −75 |
| S008 | 1 | 2,705 | 1,194 | 572 | 0 | 939 | 35 |
| S009 | 1 | 518 | 233 | 572 | 0 | (287) | −55 |
| S010 | 8 | 67,958 | 51,953 | 4,576 | 12,064 | (635) | −1 |
| S011 | 2 | 4,105 | 1,471 | 1,144 | 0 | 1,490 | 36 |
| S012 | 8 | 87,865 | 57,581 | 4,576 | 12,064 | 13,644 | 16 |
| S013 | 1 | 1,274 | 641 | 572 | 2,340 | (2,279) | −179 |
| S014 | 2 | 1,813 | 784 | 1,144 | 0 | (115) | −6 |
| S015 | 2 | 37,060 | 15,974 | 1,144 | 3,016 | 16,926 | 46 |
| S016 | 2 | 6,500 | 6,432 | 1,144 | 3,016 | (4,092) | −63 |

*Note: All financial data reported in Swedish kroner (SEK).*

Bo Martin Tell, controller of the Furnace Products Division, recalled the amount of tedious work required to collect all the numbers.

> It took almost a year to develop a system to collect the data in the proper form. Even in production, we had problems identifying the costs that related to stocked and non-stocked orders.

### *Initial Output from the Account Management System*

Exhibit 6 shows a profitability report for a sample of individual orders from Swedish customers. Profit margins on these individual orders ranged from −179% to +65%. Previ-

ously, almost all of these orders would have appeared profitable. Similar reports were prepared to show total profitability by customer, by product group, or by all the orders received from customers in a country. For example, Exhibit 7 shows, for a given product group—Finished Wire N, the sales volume and profitability of a sample of Swedish customers.

Leif Rick, general manager of Heating Technology remembered the initial reactions to the account management reports:

> The study was a real eye-opener. We saw how the traditional cost accounting system had been unable to truly report costs and profits by market, product, and customer.

**EXHIBIT 7**   Finished Wire N Customer List

| CUSTOMER NO. | INVOICED SALES (SEK) | VOLUME COSTS (SEK) | ORDER COST (SEK) | NON-STOCKED COST (SEK) | OPERATING PROFIT (SEK) | PROFIT MARGIN (%) |
|---|---|---|---|---|---|---|
| 33507 | 3,969 | 1,440 | 750 | 0 | 1,779 | 45 |
| 33508 | 4,165 | 1,692 | 750 | 2,150 | (427) | −10 |
| 33509 | 601 | 139 | 750 | 2,150 | (2,438) | −406 |
| 33510 | 13,655 | 6,014 | 750 | 2,150 | 4,741 | 35 |
| 33511 | 2,088 | 350 | 750 | 2,150 | (1,162) | −56 |
| 33512 | 1,742 | 637 | 750 | 0 | 355 | 20 |
| 33513 | 4,177 | 932 | 750 | 2,150 | 345 | 8 |
| 33514 | 7,361 | 3,134 | 750 | 0 | 3,477 | 47 |
| 33515 | 1,045 | 318 | 750 | 0 | (23) | −2 |
| 33516 | 429,205 | 198,277 | 9,000 | 0 | 221,928 | 52 |
| 33517 | 31,696 | 13,128 | 3,750 | 0 | 14,818 | 47 |
| 33518 | 159,612 | 58,036 | 2,250 | 6,450 | 92,876 | 58 |
| 33519 | 48,648 | 17,872 | 9,750 | 12,900 | 8,126 | 17 |
| 33520 | 5,012 | 1,119 | 750 | 2,150 | 993 | 20 |
| 33521 | 4,933 | 2,170 | 1,500 | 4,300 | (3,037) | −62 |
| 33522 | 17,277 | 7,278 | 1,500 | 0 | 8,499 | 49 |
| 33523 | 134 | 120 | 1,500 | 4,300 | (5,786) | −4,318 |
| 33524 | 1,825 | 523 | 1,500 | 0 | (198) | −11 |
| 33525 | 13,874 | 4,914 | 3,750 | 6,450 | (1,240) | −9 |
| 33526 | 3,762 | 1,452 | 750 | 0 | 1,560 | 41 |
| 33527 | 64,875 | 18,559 | 3,750 | 8,600 | 33,966 | 52 |
| 33528 | 13,052 | 5,542 | 3,000 | 6,450 | (1,940) | −15 |
| 33529 | 39,175 | 12,683 | 3,750 | 8,600 | 14,142 | 36 |
| 33530 | 383 | 87 | 750 | 0 | (454) | −119 |
| 33531 | 6,962 | 1,865 | 750 | 2,150 | 2,197 | 32 |
| 33532 | 1,072 | 314 | 1,500 | 0 | (742) | −69 |
| 33533 | 14,050 | 6,333 | 1,500 | 2,150 | 4,067 | 29 |
| 33534 | 820 | 244 | 750 | 0 | (174) | −21 |
| 33535 | 809 | 181 | 750 | 2,150 | (2,272) | −281 |
| 33536 | 1,366 | 316 | 750 | 2,150 | (1,850) | −135 |
| 33537 | 155,793 | 65,718 | 21,750 | 49,450 | 18,875 | 12 |
| 33538 | 7,593 | 2,772 | 2,250 | 2,150 | 421 | 6 |
| Total | 1,060,731 | 434,159 | 84,000 | 131,150 | 411,422 | 39% |

*Note: All financial data reported in Swedish kroner (SEK).*

At first, the new approach seemed strange. We had to explain it three or four times before people started to understand and accept it. People did not want to believe that order costs could be so high; that order costs had to be treated as an explicit cost of selling. Most surprising was finding that customers thought to be very profitable were actually break-even or even loss customers. Salesmen initially thought the approach was part of a master

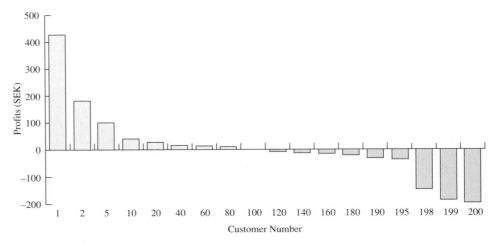

**EXHIBIT 8** Customer Profitability: Ranked from Most to Least Profitable Customers

plan to get rid of small customers. But people who have been working with the system now are convinced of its value and are beginning to take sensible actions based on the information.

Exhibit 8 shows the profits from Swedish customers, ranked by customer profitability. The results surprised even Ridderstråle. Only 40% of Kanthal's Swedish customers were profitable and these generated 250% of realized profits. In fact the most profitable 5% of the customers generated 150% of the country's profits. The least profitable 10% of customers lost 120% of the profits (see cumulative profitability chart in Exhibit 9).

Even more surprising, two of the most unprofitable customers turned out to be among the top three in total sales volume. These two

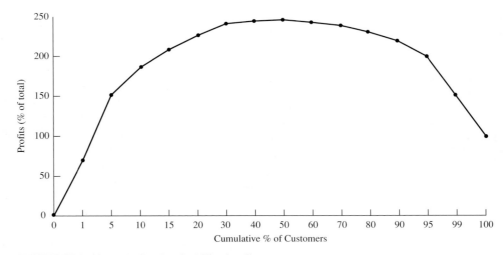

**EXHIBIT 9** Cumulative Profitability by Customers

customers had gone to just-in-time (JIT) delivery for its suppliers. They had pushed inventory back onto Kanthal which had not recognized the new demands being placed on its production and order-handling processes by the JIT approach. Moreover, further investigation revealed that one of these customers was using Kanthal as a backup supplier, to handle small special orders of a low-priced item when its main supplier could not deliver. Because of the size and prestige of the two customers, Kanthal people had always welcomed and encouraged their orders. Ridderstråle now realized how expensive it had become to satisfy them.

The immediate problem was to devise a strategy for the large number of nonprofitable customers, particularly the very high volume ones. Corporate management had started a series of meetings with the general and sales managers of the operating divisions in Sweden to discuss how to handle these customers.

Also, while the account management system had been developed for the Swedish operating divisions, some overseas divisions remained skeptical about the value of the exercise. The account management system was seen as yet another intrusion of the headquarters staff into their operations. Ridderstråle knew he faced an uphill battle gaining acceptance for the account management system around the world.

## INDIANAPOLIS: ACTIVITY-BASED COSTING OF CITY SERVICES (A)*

Introducing competition and privatization to government services requires real cost information. You can't compete if you are using fake money.

*Stephen Goldsmith, Mayor of the City of Indianapolis*

### The City

The City of Indianapolis is located in the center of Indiana, about 200 miles southeast of Chicago. For the past 25 years the city had enjoyed a healthy economy and steady population growth. When Stephen Goldsmith took office in 1992, Indianapolis had a population of 800,000 and was the 13th largest city in the country. Historically, the city was known mainly for one weekend a year when cars raced 500 miles around an oval track at speeds in excess of 200 miles per hour. The city was shedding its reputation as a sleepy midwestern town by building strength in a number of industries including health care (Eli Lilly), automotive (Cummins Engine) and professional and amateur sports (the city had major league football and basketball teams, and hosted more Olympic governing bodies than any other).

The 1992 city government employed about 5,600 people and the budget was approximately $480 million dollars. The city's budget was divided among six operating departments whose responsibilities ranged from sewage treatment and trash collection to police and fire protection. Prior to Stephen Goldsmith's election in November 1991, the budget had grown at a 6% compounded annual rate since the mid-1980s. In every year since 1987, budgeted expenses had exceeded revenues by between $8 and $14 million dollars and the projected annual deficit when

*This case was prepared by Professor Robert S. Kaplan, with assistance from Matt Ridenour, '95 MBA student.

Copyright © 1996 by the President and Fellows of Harvard College. Harvard Business School case 196-115.

Mayor Goldsmith first took office was a record $20 million dollars.

### Robomayor

"No more business as usual for many cities." Indianapolis' Goldsmith, a former Republican prosecutor dubbed "Robomayor" by the local press, pushed 60 city services into free-market competition in three years. City "business agencies" now bid against private firms on everything from filling potholes to handling welfare clients.

USA *Today* (*February* 16, 1995)

During the election campaign in 1991, Stephen Goldsmith, a former Republican prosecutor, had pledged to reduce the size of government, hold the line on taxes, and re-invest in the city's infrastructure. Unfortunately, during his first year the mayor would also have to deal with the prior leadership's largely unfunded commitments to two of the largest capital projects in the history of the city: the construction of a $250 million downtown shopping mall, and the opening of a new $500 million United Airlines maintenance terminal at the airport. Additionally, the local chamber of commerce had recently completed a report identifying over $1 billion dollars in badly needed infrastructure improvements. Not only was the city running in the red on an operating basis, but it had a $1.75 billion dollar gap in needed capital funds.

Aside from the financial challenges confronting him, Mayor Goldsmith was generally unhappy with the way government conducted business. After spending 12 years as a prosecutor within Indianapolis government the mayor had seen many problems:

> While the private sector attempts to improve services while reducing cost, the public sector generally spends more money each year while providing the same or lower quality service to the public. Traditional public management tools were clearly incapable of solving the problems our government faced. The staff organizations in the city were worthless; they impeded progress, and subtracted value. The multi-layered bureaucracy was out of control. Lots of unnecessary people were on the payroll because of the patronage process.

> Although on many measures Indianapolis was a good deal better off than other cities, we shouldn't be benchmarking ourselves against a failing industry, government. This seemed to be a particularly curious way to approach improving the system.

Mayor Goldsmith established several guiding principles for his administration:

- People governed least are governed best.
- Government should be a rudder, not an engine.
- People know better than government.
- Government should be measured the same way every other enterprise is measured: by its results.

The mayor wanted to make government smaller, to make it more responsive, and to make its managers think about value—the cost and quality of services delivered to its customers, the citizens. A senior manager in the new administration reinforced this philosophy:

> Smaller government is a core philosophy. We believe that individual choice, individual freedom and a lack of intrusiveness are important values; to the extent we can limit government's role or shrink the size of government, then in most cases we are probably doing good.

> Now at some point the core philosophy runs up against reality. If you were to eliminate, for example, all police officers, even if you return 100% of the tax dollars back to the citizens, would they be in a better position? Probably not. But there are hundreds of millions of dollars in opportunity before you ever begin to intrude on the essential missions of government.

**Pressure from the Mayor**   After the election but before entering office, the mayor called the current department leaders and asked them for management and financial reports about their departments' performance. He commented on the responses to this request:

> All people had were the income and expense numbers for this and last year's budget. Nothing was broken down by activity and they had no performance-based measurements, so it was impossible to measure anything. Although we were anxious to get in and make changes, we couldn't manage without data.

In the past few years the city had installed a "work management system." This system tracked how many people went out on particular street repair projects, how many hours they worked, and the equipment they used. But the data did not allow city managers to know how much, in total, they had spent to repair roads or to collect garbage.

Upon taking office, Mayor Goldsmith replaced many senior managers and requested that his new team install better systems to measure the performance and efficiency of government, "down to the unit." The mayor wanted to attack the problems of government from two directions. First, he demanded that departments describe and measure the services they provided as well as the cost of providing these services. Second, he established a new office, Enterprise Development, to create competition for the provision of city-supplied services.

Skip Stitt, the first director of the Enterprise Development office, articulated the new philosophy of city government:

> Competition was our core strategy—we defined service quality and price with private-sector marketplace measures. If there were rigorous competition for filling potholes, what would it cost? How would it be done? For some services, such as managing public golf courses, we would ask ourselves if taking a tax dollar out of John Public's pocket to subsidize golf was appropriate at all. If it's not, perhaps we should get out of that business and let the private sector fill the void.

Stitt's office would oversee initiatives to increase the competitiveness of the municipal departments, and to privatize services where these services could be delivered more efficiently by a private service company.

**The Department of Transportation**   Mitch Roob, a former management consultant, was appointed as the new head of the Department of Transportation. The department had a $50 million annual budget, most of it committed to two operating divisions: maintenance and construction. Roob was immediately struck by the lack of planning in the department:

> Programs were not linked to dollars. Management had no idea about the value of the city infrastructure. There was no balance sheet, no capital plan, no maintenance plans. The department simply did what they did the year before and requested a 10% higher budget. We went back through the archives and discovered that their current activities were descendants of priorities established in the mid 1970s. These were not necessarily bad plans, but they were no longer appropriate in the mid-1990s.

Roob faced some long-term issues. How should money be spent among road reconstruction and enhancement, repaving, resurfacing, or simply pot-hole filling? He began by asking the senior managers in the Department of Transportation for a list of their current activities and their cost.

> It seemed like these were simple questions. But we couldn't begin to answer them. We didn't have any relevant data and we had no costing system. No one had ever focused on what they did, on how much it cost to do whatever it was they did, and, certainly, on whether whatever they were doing was being done effectively and efficiently.

Roob also asked the managers what they believed the desired outcome should be from street repair work. The question seemed obvious, but it had not been asked before. Roob believed that the objective of the street maintenance division should be smooth streets, and that any activities that did not help to reach that objective were probably unnecessary.

Roob called a number of accounting firms to help him measure the costs of the Department's activities. One accounting firm said that it could start work on the project in six weeks. Another, KPMG Peat Marwick, said it could start the next day. Time was of the essence. The Mayor wanted rapid results to build momentum for the reforms. Thus, Roob chose KPMG Peat Marwick for a six-week pilot project. KPMG brought experience with implementing activity-based costing (ABC) in local manufacturing firms. Bridget Anderson, a Peat Marwick manager, was assigned to the project and began meeting with Roob and other DOT employees to determine where the costing study should begin.

**The Pothole Repair Contract** The newly formed team wanted to focus on a service that was highly visible and important to the average citizen. The cost study was scheduled for completion in early Spring, just when the maintenance division would be repairing streets damaged by the freezing and thawing cycle during the winter. The team quickly decided to study the cost of filling potholes. Roob set a tight deadline for completing the study and he announced publicly that pothole maintenance would be put out for open bid after the study's results had been received. On a certain date, private sector bids would be solicited and the cost system would provide the basis for the bid submitted by the city to keep doing the work. The department's cost team had the burden of both understanding the current cost of filling potholes and then working to lower its cost to

compete with the bids that would be forthcoming from the private sector.

Bridget Anderson described her introduction to municipal accounting.

> We started by asking people how much it cost them to provide services. People couldn't answer that question. Lots of data were available but none of it was useful for management decisions. No data could be traced to the cost of the activities that delivered services, like filling potholes or keeping streets clean for citizens.

Anderson formed a project team, that included several representatives from the unionized work force and the non-unionized management team, to perform the costing study. Peat Marwick developed a training program that every member of the street maintenance division attended. The goal was for each employee to understand why ABC was being used and how the cost estimates would be determined. Anderson described her working relationship with the city union:

> The mayor and Mitch Roob made it very clear that the union would have to be heavily involved in the process of costing the work activity. In essence, we would be working with the union to help them understand what it cost for them to do a certain job. Then, once they knew the cost, and made efforts to improve it, they would face a bid process. So, both the union and the private sector would have to believe ABC costing was legitimate because it would be the basis of the union's bid. The union's initial reaction to our presence, however, was very cautious, even hostile.

Anderson and her team applied a five-phase approach to implement activity-based costing at the city (see Exhibit 1).

> In Phase 1, we interviewed the people in street maintenance to find out what they did. This was an interesting process. Once they got over their surprise that we were asking them about what they did, they began by telling us they only did 5 or 6 major things for street maintenance—things like "fix a pothole, seal

---

**EXHIBIT 1**  Five-Phase Approach to Activity-Based Costing (ABC)

---

Phase 1:    **Define project objectives and establish department activities and outputs.**
            The first phase focuses on familiarizing the project team with department operations, personnel, and means of quantifying data. The most effective means of identifying activities and outputs, the foundation for the ABC model, are determined.

Phase 2:    **Collect and analyze appropriate costs and cost drivers.**
            Collect relevant cost information. Choose appropriate cost drivers for the activities defined in Phase I. Determine the most effective means of measuring departmental outputs.

Phase 3:    **Collect remaining direct and indirect cost information**
            Establish resource cost pools on PC-based spreadsheets. Resource cost pools include personnel, direct materials, vehicles and equipment, fixed asset and facility costs, and administrative overhead.

Phase 4:    **Develop an ABC Model**
            Develop an ABC model. First, assign resource costs to activities, and second, use cost drivers to assign activity costs to departmental outputs.

Phase 5:    **Summarize cost information; expand departments' capabilities to continue to use the ABC model.**
            Hold training session to assist departmental personnel to learn how to use the ABC model on an ongoing basis.

---

cracks on the street, or paint a curb." After much discussion and some process mapping we helped them to discover the literally hundreds of activities that go into providing these services. In the end, we were able to consolidate similar activities and ended up with a list of about 35 basic activities that we described in an Activity Dictionary (see Exhibit 2).

In Phase 2, Peat Marwick and the city team gathered data from the controller's office, from the work management system, and from interviews to determine the cost of performing each of the basic activities. Most of the effort was spent estimating how people spent their time among the 35 defined activities since, by far, the largest cost and resource in city government was people. Anderson recalled some of the difficulties at this stage:

> We quickly found out that the data in the work management system weren't all inclusive and had input errors as well. We went through some reconciliation procedures back to payroll registers to try and make the information as credible as it could be.

The team also had to identify the indirect and support costs associated with the 35 primary activities. Support costs included indirect labor, supplies, fixed assets (trucks and buildings), and the cost of services in city offices—human resources, payroll, legal, information systems, and controller. Much of the indirect cost assignments were available from an indirect cost recovery plan performed for reimbursement on federal grants. All the direct and indirect cost data were entered into a personal computer using ABC software.

In Phase 3, the team selected a cost driver, such as hours worked or pounds of material, for each of the 35 activities. The cost driver would be used to assign activity costs to the output of the activities. The team initially had difficulty defining outputs for some of the activities. For example, potholes, unlike standard manufactured products, are all different. They don't come in standard sizes and shapes. The team realized quickly that attempting to find out what it costs to fill potholes would be answering the wrong question. They decided to measure the cost of

---

**EXHIBIT 2** Activity Listing: City Services

---

| MAINTENANCE SECTION (9) | ASSET MANAGEMENT DIVISION (10) |
|---|---|
| Snow control | Bridge rehabilitation |
| Curb repair | Bridge replacement |
| Guardrail repair | Intersection improvements |
| Crack sealing | Road widening |
| Strip patching | Street reconstruction |
| Special maintenance | Street rehabilitation |
| Mowing and brush cutting | Signal interconnects |
| Alley repair | Signal upgrades |
| Drainage repair | Resurfacing |
| | Curbs and sidewalks |

| TRAFFIC MANAGEMENT (11) | PARKING MANAGEMENT DIVISION (5) |
|---|---|
| Pavement markings | Administration and planning |
| Sign installation | Parking lot and garage operations |
| Sign repair | Parking meter enforcement |
| Signal installation | Collections |
| Signal maintenance | Adjudications |
| Street cleaning | |
| Sidewalk repair | |
| Berm repair | |
| Pothole patching | |
| Street paving | |
| Sidewalk paving | |

---

putting a ton of asphalt in potholes, so the "cost object" of the study was the fully loaded cost of filling potholes with a ton of asphalt.

In Phases 4 and 5, the team reviewed the preliminary ABC cost reports and made refinements to the model and to the data after checking against the controller's records to assure that all costs were captured. Exhibits 3A and 3B show the total and unit costs for filling potholes in Indianapolis's five geographic sectors. The collection of costs for each of the five sectors allowed variations in terrain and work procedures in the five sectors to be reflected in the calculated cost of filling potholes.

Some people questioned the tracing of the fixed asset and indirect support costs to pothole filling. They acknowledged that the equipment and vehicles used directly for pothole filling were costs that should be included. But Anderson argued for including the cost of all assets that the city owned:

> What about all the desks, chairs, and computers being used by support people throughout the city? We found that the city did have a fixed asset accounting system that could produce reasonable depreciation figures. Even though the city did not calculate depreciation in its financial statements, we felt that in order to have a true cost to provide services, we needed to adjust out the current year capital purchases, and then add back the cost

**EXHIBIT 3A**  Pothole-Filling Costs: Five Districts, 1992 Actual (Jan.–March)

| ACTIVITY | NORTHWEST | NORTHEAST | CENTER | SOUTHWEST | SOUTHEAST | TOTAL |
|---|---|---|---|---|---|---|
| C Labor (laborers) | 27,455 | 27,927 | 83,482 | 41,954 | 25,162 | 205,980 |
| C Labor overtime | 462 | 2,658 | 1,558 | 1,210 | 908 | 6,797 |
| D Labor (truck drivers) | 175,608 | 181,869 | 354,628 | 188,468 | 163,748 | 1,064,322 |
| D Labor overtime | 5,225 | 10,183 | 16,133 | 6,192 | 6,057 | 43,790 |
| E Labor (equipment oprs.) | 43,604 | 90,373 | 27,038 | 20,089 | 35,844 | 216,949 |
| E Labor overtime | 2,693 | 6,162 | 1,067 | 7,201 | 3,579 | 20,702 |
| Supervisors | 41,893 | 47,085 | 60,008 | 55,790 | 38,267 | 243,044 |
| Transp. supervisors | 47,997 | 89,372 | 33,440 | 18,798 | 43,855 | 233,463 |
| Personnel costs | $344,939 | $455,629 | $577,354 | $339,703 | $317,421 | $2,035,046 |
| Binder | | 432 | | | 83 | 514 |
| Cold mix | 6,185 | 7,266 | 3,265 | 4,659 | 5,589 | 26,964 |
| Hot mix | 14,901 | 21,644 | 51,301 | 23,175 | 56,987 | 168,009 |
| Special mix | 11,028 | 11,271 | 7,320 | 21,864 | 17,289 | 68,772 |
| Tack | 2,578 | 1,070 | 1,601 | 484 | 3 | 5,735 |
| Direct materials costs | $34,692 | $41,683 | $63,487 | $50,183 | $79,950 | $269,994 |
| Central admin. expense | 99,774 | 134,680 | 160,199 | 89,172 | 91,152 | 574,977 |
| Central operations | 38,206 | 51,573 | 94,792 | 52,765 | 34,908 | 272,244 |
| Central maintenance | 34,588 | 46,688 | 55,548 | 28,480 | 31,604 | 196,908 |
| Facility expense | 14,554 | 42,218 | 29,129 | 8,007 | 12,278 | 106,187 |
| Fixed assets | 1,098 | 828 | 1,536 | 1,029 | 936 | 5,428 |
| Maintenance admin. | 17,375 | 23,456 | 27,891 | 14,280 | 15,885 | 98,888 |
| Operations admin. | 18,172 | 24,544 | 29,193 | 14,946 | 16,601 | 103,456 |
| Overhead costs | $223,767 | $323,987 | $398,290 | $208,679 | $203,364 | $1,358,080 |
| Cargo van | | | | 3,086 | | 3,086 |
| Crew cab | | 11,167 | | | | 11,167 |
| Crew: Cab pickup 86 | 12,369 | | | 11,699 | 14,150 | 38,218 |
| Grader | | 2,727 | | 4,236 | | 6,963 |
| Hotbox | 16,276 | 4,954 | 11,396 | 13,272 | 18,335 | 64,233 |
| Loader | 1,457 | 8,958 | 1,024 | 1,271 | 358 | 13,067 |
| Paver | | 207 | | | | 207 |
| Pickup mini | 1,815 | 11,478 | | 4,014 | | 17,307 |
| Roller | | 69 | | | | 69 |
| Roller VIB: 2 ton | 104 | | | 2,541 | 330 | 2,976 |
| SAD | 40,090 | 35,607 | 25,203 | 41,853 | 45,535 | 188,287 |
| SADA | 9,005 | 20,833 | 19,953 | 12,243 | 9,333 | 71,367 |
| Sedan | | 6,990 | | | | 6,990 |
| Tack wagon | | 777 | | | | 777 |
| TAD | 5,607 | 1,225 | 7,213 | 95 | 1,432 | 15,571 |
| TADA | 29,397 | 38,542 | 18,971 | 37,940 | 16,738 | 141,588 |
| Trailer | | | 5,314 | | | 5,314 |
| Truck: 1-ton dump | 4,647 | 11,909 | 11,054 | 13,716 | 10,847 | 52,173 |
| Truck: Patch 91 | 11,514 | | 3,713 | | | 15,227 |
| Unused equipment | 3,769 | 6,127 | | 7,402 | 20,537 | 37,836 |
| Rolling stock costs | $136,050 | $161,571 | $103,840 | $153,367 | $137,595 | $692,423 |
| Total cost | $739,447 | $982,871 | $1,142,971 | $751,932 | $738,330 | $4,355,549 |
| Tons filled | 1,156 | 1,726 | 2,134 | 2,017 | 2,753 | 9,786 |
| Cost per ton | $639.66 | $569.45 | $535.60 | $372.80 | $268.19 | $445.00 |

**EXHIBIT 3B** Pothole-Filling Costs per Ton: Five Districts, 1992 Actual (Jan.–March)

| ACTIVITY | NORTHWEST | NORTHEAST | CENTER | SOUTHWEST | SOUTHEAST |
|---|---|---|---|---|---|
| C Labor (laborers) | 23.75 | 16.18 | 39.12 | 20.80 | 9.14 |
| C Labor overtime | 0.40 | 1.54 | 0.73 | 0.60 | 0.33 |
| D Labor (truck drivers) | 151.91 | 105.37 | 166.18 | 93.44 | 59.48 |
| D Labor overtime | 4.52 | 5.90 | 7.56 | 3.07 | 2.20 |
| E Labor (equipment oprs.) | 37.72 | 52.36 | 12.67 | 9.96 | 13.02 |
| E Labor overtime | 2.33 | 3.57 | 0.50 | 3.57 | 1.30 |
| Supervisors | 36.24 | 27.28 | 28.12 | 27.66 | 13.90 |
| Transp. supervisors | 41.52 | 51.78 | 15.67 | 9.32 | 15.93 |
| Personnel costs | $298.39 | $263.98 | $270.55 | $168.42 | $115.30 |
| Binder | | 0.25 | | | 0.03 |
| Cold mix | 5.35 | 4.21 | 1.53 | 2.31 | 2.03 |
| Hot mix | 12.89 | 12.54 | 24.04 | 11.49 | 20.7 |
| Special mix | 9.54 | 6.53 | 3.43 | 10.84 | 6.28 |
| Tack | 2.23 | 0.62 | 0.75 | 0.24 | 0.00 |
| Direct materials costs | $ 30.01 | $ 24.15 | $ 29.75 | $ s24.88 | $ 29.04 |
| Central admin. expense | 86.31 | 78.03 | 75.07 | 44.21 | 33.11 |
| Central operations | 33.05 | 29.88 | 44.42 | 26.16 | 12.68 |
| Central maintenance | 29.92 | 27.05 | 26.03 | 14.12 | 11.48 |
| Facility expense | 12.59 | 24.46 | 13.65 | 3.97 | 4.46 |
| Fixed assets | 0.95 | 0.48 | 0.72 | 0.51 | 0.34 |
| Maintenance admin. | 15.03 | 13.59 | 13.07 | 7.08 | 5.77 |
| Operations admin. | 15.72 | 14.22 | 13.68 | 7.41 | 6.03 |
| Overhead costs | $193.57 | $187.71 | $186.64 | $103.46 | $ 73.87 |
| Cargo van | | | | 1.53 | |
| Crew cab | | 6.47 | | | |
| Crew: Cab pickup 86 | 10.70 | | | 5.80 | 5.14 |
| Grader | | 1.58 | | 2.10 | |
| Hotbox | 14.08 | 2.87 | 5.34 | 6.58 | 6.66 |
| Loader | 1.26 | 5.19 | 0.48 | 0.63 | 0.13 |
| Paver | | 0.12 | | | |
| Pickup mini | 1.57 | 6.65 | | 1.99 | |
| Roller | | 0.04 | | | |
| Roller VIB: 2 ton | 0.09 | | | 1.26 | 0.12 |
| SAD | 34.68 | 20.63 | 11.81 | 20.75 | 16.54 |
| SADA | 7.79 | 12.07 | 9.35 | 6.07 | 3.39 |
| Sedan | | 4.05 | | | |
| Tack wagon | | 0.45 | | | |
| TAD | 4.85 | 0.71 | 3.38 | 0.05 | 0.52 |
| TADA | 25.43 | 22.33 | 8.89 | 18.81 | 6.08 |
| Trailer | | | 2.49 | | |
| Truck: 1-ton dump | 4.02 | 6.90 | 5.18 | 6.80 | 3.94 |
| Truck: Patch 91 | 9.96 | | 1.74 | | |
| Unused equipment | 3.26 | 3.55 | | 3.67 | 7.46 |
| Rolling stock costs | $117.69 | $ 93.61 | $ 48.66 | $ 76.04 | $ 49.98 |
| Total cost per ton | $639.66 | $569.45 | $535.60 | $372.80 | $268.19 |

(depreciation) of having fixed assets like vehicles and equipment of all types, as well as the maintenance and repair of these fixed assets. The mayor wanted to have his departments compete against the private sector and these calculations would put city services on a more level playing field with private sector companies.

The team decided, however, not to assign the headquarters expenses to the costs for pothole filling. The rationale was that these expenses would remain in the city, whether the pothole filling was done by municipal workers or private contractors. So only the costs of resources expected to be directly affected by the decision were included in the contract costs.

The ABC team did decide to load the depreciation and maintenance costs of unused equipment into a line item, "unused equipment," in the pothole-filling cost calculation. The cost of unused equipment ranged up to 10% of total costs for some city services. Anderson described how this problem arose:

> The city workers all liked having vehicles available, just in case. We talked with them about only having equipment that they needed on a regular and routine basis; that for the couple of times each year they needed the back-up equipment, because the regular equipment had broken down, it would be cheaper to rent than to maintain the stand-by reserve capacity. Also, they might get better utilization by acquiring multiple-use equipment. Many of the crews may not need a different vehicle for each separate use. The departments could realize savings by sharing their equipment and vehicles with each other. At present, each department had a lot of excess equipment in their fleets.

After six weeks, the work team arrived at an average cost of $445 per ton of asphalt placed in potholes (see Total column in Exhibit 3A).

Skip Stitt recalled the surprise from seeing all the costs associated with performing city services:

> It was fascinating. Prior to activity-based costing, employees and their managers only thought about the number of hours that employees spent filling a pothole that day. Nobody ever thought about unproductive time, excess equipment, real estate, inventory, or about overhead, including management. When we began seeing the results from the early ABC studies, it was astonishing. You could look at a specific pothole-filling team and see how many take-home vehicles had been allocated to them, what their annual supplies budget was, and their costs for rent and maintenance of both their facilities and their vehicles. People weren't used to thinking of all the costs that get buried with the asphalt in a pothole. In many cases, employees' hourly wages were only 20% of the fully loaded cost. Before ABC, management might have placed that number at 80%–90% of the cost.

> Senior management and line employees suddenly came to the same question: how could they reduce or eliminate costs. As one example, they began to scrutinize the cost to maintain a vehicle, which was done in another division, because the inefficiencies in the equipment-maintenance group and their expensive oil changes were hitting the union employees' and DOT's bottom line cost of fixing potholes.

Bob Larson, a supervisor (and union member) in the Maintenance Department, recalled how the employees started to work to reduce costs:

> Both management and the union sat down and admitted that we had to do better. We shouldn't be going out with a five or six-man repair crew, plus a supervisor, if we could do the job, safely, with a three or four-man self-managed crew. When you had 75 hourly employees out on a street with 36 supervisors, that ratio was not right. A supervisor should be able to handle ten people. It's ridiculous to have that many supervisors. That's why the overhead got so high, paying salary and

benefits to all these people. The guy in the front line doesn't need 20 people to support him.

Steve Fantauzzo, the state executive director of AFSCME,[1] the municipal workers' union, commented on the results of the cost study:

> The ABC system really highlighted the amount of overhead, particularly managers, that existed on the city side. We urged city management to "get these guys off our backs." We didn't want to lose bids because the city made us carry managers who don't help us fill potholes.

Mitch Roob responded by dismissing half the supervisors, most of whom had been placed in those jobs by the local Republican party. The union was surprised by this action and Roob recalled its impact:

> They now realized that they had no choice. If we were willing to fire half of our guys, we would certainly be prepared to fire all of their guys.

In the following weeks every line item on the ABC report was closely examined and there was tremendous pressure on support groups to justify their expense. The union reconfigured its approach to filling potholes by reducing manpower on each team and changing the type and amount of equipment used. Larson explained how he worked with his union crews to get the cost down:

> I move around quite a bit. I just take my laptop loaded with the ABC model out to a work site and say, "OK, suppose we get rid of that single-axle dump, delete that extra mixer off there, take that truck driver off, now look what it would cost you to do a ton a day." The guys know that the next time they show up on a job they better have those improvements made or they'll lose a bid to the private sector and be out of a job.

We also got some benefits by doing multiple tasks with the same resources. While the patching crew was waiting for the asphalt to be picked up and delivered to the pothole, I had them doing other jobs, like sweeping a bridge or picking up limbs. Those were all activities in the ABC model so we could charge their time to those tasks. This way our people are kept busy doing useful tasks, and the pothole filling activity is not charged for unproductive time.

As the improvements in staffing, equipment utilization, and work processes were being made, management and the union recalculated the savings. Soon they would be submitting bids for pothole filling in competition with private sector contractors. Ray Wallace, Assistant to the Mayor, was the liaison for the activity-based costing initiative.

> Initially, I was viewed as a bad guy by the union people because I was "management" and a lot of the employees thought this was the mayor's way to break the union. There was a lot of uncertainty and animosity not only towards the process but to Mitch Roob, myself, the consultants, and anyone else from management involved in the process. But when we put together the bid with them, we were all working together, eating pizza at 10:00 in the evening, and staying until 3:00 in the morning. The last night, we worked from 6:00 A.M. through the next day without going home to sleep. So they saw us working just as hard as they were, committed to putting together a quality bid. Somewhere in the middle of that process, the barriers started to lift and we began to win the trust of the people.

By eliminating half the supervisors, changing the crew assignments for filling potholes, from eight down to four or six, and gaining efficiencies in the use and assignment of trucks and other equipment, the union team could realize significant cost reductions. The first test would come when they submitted bids for two pothole filling contracts that would be awarded; one in the Northwest sec-

---

[1]American Federation of State, County, and Municipal Employees.

**EXHIBIT 4**  Union Estimates of Resources Required for Two Pothole-Filling Contracts

|  | NORTHWEST | | NORTHEAST | |
|---|---|---|---|---|
|  | QUANTITY | RATE* | QUANTITY | RATE* |
| **Personnel Cost Pool** | | | | |
| C Labor (laborers) | 2.60 hours/ton | $23.25/hour | 2.60 hours/ton | $11.18/hour |
| D Labor (vehicle drivers) | 2.60 hours/ton | 20.00/hour | 2.60 hours/ton | 23.08/hour |
| E Labor (eqpmt. operators) | 0.35 hours/ton | 44.49/hour | 1.15 hours/ton | 28.01/hour |
| **Materials Cost Pool** | | | | |
| Hotmix for potholes | 1 ton | $22.00/ton | 1 ton | $22.00/ton |
| Tack | 2.5 gallons/ton | 1.54/gallon | 2.5 gallons/ton | 1.54/gallon |
| **Vehicle Cost Pool** | | | | |
| Crew cab | 1 hour/ton | $8.65/hour | 1 hour/ton | $8.60/hour |
| Hotbox | 1 hour/ton | 17.65/hour | 1 hour/ton | 11.26/hour |
| One-ton truck | .6 hours/ton | 15.20/hour | .6 hours/ton | 18.22/hour |
| Arrowboard | 1 hour/ton | 2.00/hour | 1 hour/ton | 2.00/hour |
| **Indirect Cost Pool** | 5.55 hours/ton | $17.06/hour | 6.35 hours/ton | $19.56/hour |

*Labor rates based on projections from union contract; material rates based on actual contractor price quotes.*

tor and one in the Northeast sector of the city. The union estimated the resources—people, materials, and equipment—they now felt they would need to fill potholes using the revised work procedures and submitted their estimates to Bridget Anderson for verification (see Exhibit 4). Anderson, who had been monitoring how the new work procedures were being implemented, concurred that the union's estimates of resources required to do the job were reasonable and consistent with current practice. The union workers submitted a bid based on their revised cost estimates and waited anxiously for the announcement of whether they had won the business against the several private contractors who had also submitted bids for the pothole filling business.

# THE CO-OPERATIVE BANK*

We were prepared to make bold, innovative decisions to enhance our profitability. But if you are going to be bold, you had better be sure your facts are correct.

*Terry Thomas, Managing Director, The Co-operative Bank*

*This case was prepared by Professors Srikant Datar and Robert S. Kaplan with extensive assistance from Robin Webster of The Cooperative Bank.

Copyright © 1995 by the President and Fellows of Harvard College. Harvard Business School case 195-196.

## History

In 1994, the co-operative movement celebrated the 150th anniversary of its founding. A small group of people, in 1844, had started a grocer's shop in Rochdale, England (near the city of Manchester):

> to provide the local community with a source of pure, unadulterated goods at fair prices; their guiding principle was that the co-operative should exist for the benefit of the people it served, sharing its profits among them in proportion to their purchases.

---

**EXHIBIT 1** Founding Statement of International Co-operative Alliance*

---

August 22, 1895

---

The time has come for gathering together the scattered parts of the great co-operative movement, one in aim and one in principle into a strong international alliance.

It is to carry this great idea into execution that the International Co-operative Alliance has been resolved upon. Without interfering in local or national matters or narrowing in any way the independence of each association or national union, the alliance will form a link uniting cooperators who are pursuing very various objects in different countries.

It will thus secure mutual support to each and all, produce a more powerful volume of co-operative opinion than can be created by separate action, help to carry cooperation more successfully foward to new developments, and create means by which cooperators will be enabled steadily to learn from one another by an interchange of opinions, or reports, and of publications.

In carrying out this program the alliance will be an added cause of peace through the inhabited world.

The objects of the alliance are[†]:

(1) To bring into relation of mutual helpfulness those who are seeking in different countries and in various ways to end the present deplorable warfare between Capital and Labor, and to organize industrial peace based on co-partnership of the worker.

(2) To promote the formation or aid the development in each country of a central institution for helping working people to establish and maintain self-governing workshops and for assisting employers and employed to establish just and harmonious profit-sharing arrangements.

(3) To form an international means of connection and communication between these central institutions through which they may render one another mutual assistance.

(4) Generally to promote the employment of the profits of productive industry.

---

*From draft outline of a plan for an International Alliance of the friends of cooperative production, to be considered at an inaugural meeting at the Crystal Palace on Monday, August 22, 1895 at 3:00 P.M.*
[†]*From ICA archives.*

---

The founders of the co-operative movement articulated a strong statement of mission and ethical standards (see Exhibit 1). The movement spread throughout the country and was an active force, even 150 years later. In 1994, U.K. co-operative societies generated a turnover of £6 billion, mostly in food retailing, farming, food production, milk sales, funeral supplies, general retailing, car sales and financial services.

### The Co-operative Bank

The Co-operative Bank (The Bank) was founded in Manchester in 1872 as a department of the Co-operative Wholesale Society (CWS), a central organization formed by co-operative societies across the country, who were, by then, the dominant retailing force in the U.K. Exhibit 2 summarizes recent financial statistics for the Co-operative Bank. During its first 75 years, The Bank functioned mainly to serve the treasury needs of CWS's operations. Personal accounts were not emphasized though The Bank did attract some personal customers from employees of co-operative societies and local authorities (municipalities).

From the late 1940s through 1971, The Bank began to expand its branch network to support the needs of the CWS and the increasing number of other co-operative societies and local authorities that were bringing their business to The Bank. During this time, the co-operative societies were generating large amounts of cash from their highly suc-

**EXHIBIT 2**  Selected Financial Statistics: 1990–1994 (£000,000)

|                                      | 1990    | 1991   | 1992  | 1993  |
|--------------------------------------|---------|--------|-------|-------|
| Deposits                             | 2,621   | 2,438  | 2,707 | 2,983 |
| Loans and advances                   | 2,597   | 2,408  | 2,637 | 2,740 |
| Profit (loss) before taxes           | (14.9)  | (6.0)  | 9.8   | 17.8  |
| Pre-tax return on shareholder funds  | (9.4%)  | (4.0%) | 6.7%  | 12.0% |

cessful trading operations and, by 1971, The Bank's deposits had grown to more than £300 million.[1] With this expansion of banking activities, CWS managers realized that they needed to separate the banking business from all their other activities. In 1971, an Act of Parliament established The Bank as a separate legal entity, with the CWS holding the entire issue of share capital. Previously, The Bank's results and financial position had been consolidated with those of the CWS.

Lewis Lee, the first Chief Executive of the newly structured bank, strengthened and broadened The Bank's management expertise by recruiting several senior and middle managers from the larger UK clearing banks. An immediate challenge emerged when The Bank's strong deposit base declined rapidly as the co-operative movement (which supplied 96% of deposits) was confronted with strong competitive pressure on its trading activities. The Bank's managers recognized the need for immediate and radical actions.

To replace the lost retail deposits, The Bank began to pursue, much more aggressively, deposits from personal customers. It became the first UK bank to introduce free banking for customers who maintained credit balances in their current accounts. Over the next ten years, the number and size of personal accounts increased sharply and, while deposits never regained their 1971 highs, the

reliance on deposits from the co-operative sector was sharply reduced to 4% of the total.

The Bank pursued a similarly aggressive policy for the asset side of the balance sheet. In 1971, loans to the co-operative movement represented 90% of assets. By the 1990s, this percentage had declined to about 10%–12%, with the remaining assets evenly split between the Personal and Corporate sectors. In 1975, The Bank's broadened customer base for both assets and deposits enabled it to obtain status as a settlement bank so that it could now perform clearing activities and settlements. It was the first new settlement bank in 39 years and the first ever to achieve this status from internal growth.

The Bank, during the 1970s and 80s, also broadened the range of products and services for personal and corporate customers. It introduced credit cards and launched several sophisticated savings products. This broadened mix of product and services, coupled to an increasingly stringent regulatory environment, created demands for more capital, demands that the CWS found difficult to supply given the heavy demands for investment from all its other operations. Therefore, The Bank had to devise a strategy to generate sustainable capital growth from its own operations.

Terry Thomas was appointed Managing Director in 1988, after a 15-year career at The Bank. Thomas had joined The Bank in 1973 as its first Marketing Manager, and had taken on increasing general management re-

---

[1]This amount was far greater in inflation-adjusted terms, than The Bank's deposits in 1994.

sponsibilities, including election to the Board in 1983. He took command of a bank that had successfully managed the transition from an almost total reliance on the cooperative movement to a viable, broad-based retail clearing bank. But new challenges had to be faced.

The UK financial services market had entered a period of radical change and restructuring. Government legislation to deregulate the financial sector was blurring traditional industry boundaries. Constraints on Building Societies' operations had been relaxed and they were now competing aggressively for products, such as current accounts, credit cards, and personal loans, that had historically been provided only by banking institutions. One of the UK's largest Building Soci-

eties, Abbey National, had even changed its status to become a bank in early 1989. New players with radically different cost structures were also entering the financial services market. First Direct was a postal/telephone/ATM service bank that had no branches. Several companies formed just to offer credit cards. And large retailers, like Marks and Spencer, were now marketing credit products to their considerable customer base.

Customer expectations and behavior were changing as well. Customers were more willing to switch banks, and to take products from several institutions. They were becoming more price sensitive and vocal in their demands for service, including expanded use of electronic banking through telephones and

---

**EXHIBIT 3**  Mission Statement—1988

We, the Co-operative Bank Group, will continue to develop a successful and innovative financial institution by providing our customers with high quality financial and related services whilst promoting the underlying principles of co-operation which are . . .

**1.  Quality and Excellence**

To offer all our customers consistent high quality and good value services and strive for excellence in all that we do.

**2.  Participation**

To introduce and promote the concept of full participation by welcoming the views and concerns of our customers and by encouraging our staff to take an active role within the local community.

**3.  Freedom of Association**

To be non-partisan in all social, political, racial and religious matters.

**4.  Education and Training**

To act as a caring and responsible employer encouraging the development and training of all our staff and encouraging commitment and pride in each other and the Group.

**5.  Co-operation**

To develop a close-affinity with organizations which promote fellowship between workers, customers, members and employers.

**6.  Quality of Life**

To be a responsible member of society by promoting an environment where the needs of local communities can be met now and in the future.

**7.  Retentions**

To manage the business effectively and efficiently, attracting investment and maintaining sufficient surplus funds within the business to ensure the continued development of the Group.

**8.  Integrity**

To act at all times with honesty and integrity and within legislative and regulatory requirements.

ATMs. The introduction and expansion of electronic technology was transforming all existing cost structures. Significant over-capacity began to appear and institutions were competing aggressively on price for business in all sectors.

While profitability had continued to grow for The Bank through the UK's economic boom of the early and mid-1980s, the UK's worst recession in more than 50 years hit the bank hard. The Bank recorded losses in 1990 and 1991, particularly in loans made to the small and medium-sized enterprises that were now a significant share of the asset base. Significant losses were also occurring with personal customers, who were under great financial pressure from record levels of unemployment in the country.

Thomas recognized that the Bank had to rethink its operating philosophy for the current and future competitive environment. Before undertaking any redirection, however, Thomas wanted to re-affirm the bank's fundamental values. The twenty most senior managers met to develop a Mission Statement (see Exhibit 3) that stressed the bank's responsibility to its customers, its employees, and its communities. The Mission Statement was enhanced by a research program culminating with a statement of Our Ethical Policy (see Exhibit 4). The Ethical Policy statement was informed by questionnaires sent to 30,000 current customers and a study of co-operative values over the past 150 years. The Mission and Ethical Policy statements created a far greater awareness of the bank's val-

---

**EXHIBIT 4**  Our Ethical Policy—1992

---

The Bank's position is that

1. It will not invest in or supply financial services to any regime or organization which oppresses the human spirit, takes away the rights of individuals, or manufactures any instrument of torture.
2. It will not finance or in any way facilitate the manufacture or sale of weapons to any country which has an oppressive regime.
3. It will encourage business customers to take a proactive stance on the environmental impact of their own activities.
4. It will actively seek out individuals, commercial enterprises and non-commercial organizations which have a complementary ethical stance.
5. It will not speculate against the pound using either its own money or that of its customers. It believes it is inappropriate for a British clearing bank to speculate against the British currency and the British economy using deposits provided by their British customers and at the expense of the British tax payer.
6. It will try to ensure its financial services are not exploited for the purposes of money laundering, drug trafficking or tax evasion by the continued application and development of its successful internal monitoring and control procedures.
7. It will not provide financial services to tobacco product manufacturers.
8. It will continue to extend and strengthen its Customer Charter, which has already established new standards of banking practice through adopting innovative procedures on status inquiries and customer confidentiality, ahead of any other British bank.
9. It will not invest in any business involved in animal experimentation for cosmetic purposes.
10. It will not support any person or company using exploitative factory farming methods.
11. It will not engage in business with any farm or other organization engaged in the production of animal fur.
12. It will not support any organization involved in blood sports, which it defines as sports which involve the training of animals or birds to catch and destroy, or to fight and kill, other animals or birds.

We will regularly re-appraise customers' views on these and other issues and develop our ethical stance accordingly.

---

ues and position in the marketplace. While some customers closed their accounts in protest, a much higher number of new personal and corporate accounts were opened after publicizing these statements.

Thomas's initial steps to restructure the Bank's operations were accomplished through consolidation of personal and corporate account processing tasks. Back office tasks of personal banking operations, previously processed in branches, were consolidated into a Personal Customer Service center. Customers could call this center for the most up-to-date information regarding their accounts and could perform a variety of transactions over the telephone. Similarly many corporate banking tasks were consolidated into Regional Processing Centers. These new centers created 200 new jobs, but they also required eliminating 1,000 jobs (out of a total employee base of nearly 4,300) principally in retail branches. Laying off workers was a sensitive issue for a bank with such close ties to the co-operative and trade union movements. The Bank offered attractive retirement packages and was able to achieve the 1,000 job reduction entirely through voluntary retirements. Most of the terminations, however, were junior, low-level employees and the bank was now operating with a disproportionate number of middle managers.

The Bank also increased its cross-selling activities to existing customers, and began to offer a much wider array of products for customers. Among its major new products were:

| | |
|---|---|
| VISA Gold Card | A "free for life" (no annual fee) credit card aimed at high net worth individuals |
| VISA Affinity Cards | Credit cards for specialized groups of customers (for example, The Royal Society for the Protection of Birds) |
| Pathfinder | A high interest-bearing current account for personal customers, based on a plastic card with no checkbook |
| Delta | A point of sale debit card/ATM card/check guarantee card hybrid |

Major new services introduced by the bank included:

| | |
|---|---|
| Telephone banking | Comprehensive remote banking through a centralized operation for personal and corporate customers |
| Independent financial advice | Investment advice for customers, selling products provided by other financial institutions |

Some of these products, particularly Visa Gold and Visa Affinity credit cards, were highly successful. In 1990, the Bank was not an issuer of Gold cards, but two years later, it had become the largest issuer of Visa Gold cards in the U.K., and by 1994 was the largest issuer in all of Europe.

Despite the new products and headcount reduction, the bank's cost-to-income ratio was high, especially when compared to building societies, with whom it was increasingly in direct competion.[2] Also, The Bank was still a small player in the U.K.'s corporate and personal markets.

### Project SABRE

Terry Thomas recalled the bank's situation in late 1992.

In 1988 we had identified the need to be much more focused, in terms of both market niches

---

[2]The cost-to-income ratio is defined in the U.K. as the ratio of all costs (which exclude the provision for bad debts) to net interest revenue earned plus commissions.

and our operations. We began to concentrate on those niches and segments where we had particular advantages, and we had taken a number of steps to re-structure our operations. However, these were first steps in a process of transforming our business, and in order to continue and accelerate this process, we needed better information to help us make some important decisions.

I felt we had too many products for our customer base. But none of us could agree on which were the profitable or unprofitable products and customers. Some thought the corporate sector was the most profitable by contributing a large number of profitable personal accounts. Others justified the full-line consumer product strategy by asserting that unless you offer a wide range of products the customers won't come to you in the first place. How should we balance the benefits of a wide product range against the costs? Should we promote these extra services or just have the capability to provide these extra services to the extent that certain customers want them? Or should we be out-sourcing many of these services if we cannot do them effectively internally?

I can remember many unproductive meetings when all we did was argue what the numbers were. Each player came to the table with his or her own set of numbers. Human nature being what it is, each of us believed my set of numbers was right and yours must be wrong, especially if yours say my products are losing more money than I think. We never actually got around to arguing or discussing, given any particular set of numbers, what are we going to do?

I wanted to run the bank on the facts and not on perceptions. Having a set of numbers derived by a systematic process to which everyone agrees cuts out the arguing and focuses attention on action plans. It is not very difficult, really, then to make innovative and bold decisions.

In early 1993, Thomas launched Project SABRE (Sales And Business REengineering), a project with several related streams aimed at improving the cost income ratio and the service to customers. A key element of the project was to develop information that would enable the bank to address five corporate needs:

1. Overhead reduction
2. Reengineering of business processes, particularly those that did not add value to customers
3. Product profitability
4. Customer profitability
5. Segment profitability

John Marper, Executive Director of Finance, recognized that the Bank's cost structure, particularly those costs traditionally considered "fixed"—such as in centralized services like technology, transmission, and finance—had to be attacked. "If you are going to attack the fixed cost base, you need to have a better cost system, especially one that can relate the fixed costs to products."

The Bank's existing cost system was a traditional responsibility accounting system that measured expenses for geographic and departmental cost centers. Central headquarters expenses, such as information systems and document transmission, were allocated to operating segments using high-level drivers related to the volume and size of the businesses. The bank measured product revenues using fee income and net interest (equal to gross interest minus funding costs). But the estimated costs of producing these revenues were not identified.

Following a pilot exercise in The Bank's check clearing center, managers became interested in activity-based costing (ABC) as a promising methodology for assigning the bank's operating expenses to its varied products and customers. An ABC team, consisting of Robin Webster, Senior Manager (and later Head of Project SABRE), Dennis Goodman, Head of MIS [Management Information Systems], Steve Kemp, Senior Business Analyst, and eight middle managers from different areas of the bank, began model building and process data gathering. The bank also brought in Gemini Consulting to assist in the model development and to advise on the reorganization and action implications from the study in conjunction with internal management.

The bank's project team had to make several choices as it began considering the implementation of activity-based costing. How should it define resource pools? What activities should it define? Should it analyze costs by product or by customer? The bank divided its fiscal year into 13 four-week periods. Over what period should it collect the data for an initial historical analysis?

The team concluded that three periods would be reasonably representative to understand the bank's cost structure. They chose to do the analysis for March–May, 1993, the most recent three periods for which data were available.

The ABC team scanned the general ledger and identified about 210 resource cost pools, divided into three broad resource categories:

| OPERATIONAL STAFF (85) | INFRASTRUCTURE (85) | MISCELLANEOUS (40) |
| --- | --- | --- |
| Personal network—Staff | Personal network | Outsourced processing fees |
| Processing centers—Staff | VISA administration | Stationery costs |
| Personal Accts. Opening | Processing centers | Personal checkbooks |
| | ATM network | VISA statements |

The numbers in parentheses indicate the number of resource pools in each broad resource category. The rows in Exhibit 5 identify the major resource cost pools that service the personal banking side of The Bank's business.

Once the resource cost pools were specified, the ABC team spent eight weeks out in the operational areas identifying activities and mapping them on brown paper pasted around the project work room. The team used their knowledge, supplemented with interviews, to identify 235 activities or tasks undertaken at the bank. Examples of activities were open customer accounts, maintain customer accounts, accept checks, process transactions, close accounts, handle customer queries, issue check books, market and sell products, money market transfers, Visa transactions, ATM transactions, encode, train, process loan applications, manage risk, recover money, and prepare financial state-

ments and management reports. The columns of Exhibit 5 identify the eighteen principal activities related to The Bank's personal banking business.

With the resource pools specified and activities selected and defined, the ABC team then asked each area of the bank to match resource costs to the activities (see the cell entries in Exhibit 5). For example, to trace staff costs to activities, all employees of the bank from senior management to the clerical staff filled out time sheets identifying the time they spent on various activities. The employees' compensation (salary and benefits) was then assigned to each activity in proportion to the time spent. Computer costs were assigned based on the amount of computer time required to perform various activities. By aggregating all of the resource pool costs assigned to each activity, the ABC team derived the total costs of each activity (see Total Activity Costs row in Exhibit 5).

# EXHIBIT 5  Personal Sector Products—Matrix of Costs by Resource and Activity*

| RESOURCE COST POOLS | TOTAL RESOURCE COSTS | PROVIDE ATM SERVICES | CLEAR DEBIT ITEMS | BRANCH OPERATIONS DEBIT ITEMS | ISSUE PERSONAL CHEQUE BOOK | CLEAR CREDIT ITEMS | BRANCH OPERATIONS CREDIT ITEMS | LENDING CONTROL & SECURITY | CUSTOMER INQUIRIES | CUSTOMER CORRESPONDENCE | MARKETING AND SALES ACTIVITY | COMPUTER PROCESSING |
|---|---|---|---|---|---|---|---|---|---|---|---|---|
| Account management center | £ 1,557,280 | £ 0 | £ 2,388 | £ 66,293 | £ 0 | £ 509 | £ 0 | £ 5,647 | £ 903,565 | £196,803 | £ 134 | £ 49,745 |
| Account opening teams | 368,355 | 0 | 0 | 0 | 0 | 0 | 0 | 0 | 0 | 0 | 0 | 0 |
| ATM network | 111,031 | 111,031 | 0 | 0 | 0 | 0 | 0 | 0 | 0 | 0 | 0 | 0 |
| Branch operations | 3,475,959 | 95,229 | 40,756 | 487,269 | 0 | 11,641 | 545,606 | 5,709 | 306,263 | 460,845 | 1,478,735 | 0 |
| Clearing operations | 833,575 | 20,099 | 650,287 | 1,291 | 0 | 135,744 | 1,394 | 4,791 | 0 | 2,109 | 25 | 2,339 |
| Collections | 968,256 | 0 | 0 | 36 | 0 | 0 | 1,168 | 912,190 | 41,378 | 10,578 | 0 | 0 |
| Collections fees | 329,205 | 0 | 0 | 0 | 0 | 0 | 0 | 329,205 | 0 | 0 | 0 | 0 |
| Outsourced fees | 2,120,071 | 104,151 | 0 | 0 | 0 | 0 | 0 | 41,611 | 37,796 | 3,109 | 0 | 22,061 |
| Financial advisors | 1,214,383 | 0 | 0 | 0 | 0 | 0 | 0 | 0 | 9,799 | 3,601 | 81,970 | 0 |
| Information technology | 1,669,453 | 0 | 0 | 65,293 | 0 | 0 | 0 | 67,261 | 0 | 0 | 1,765 | 1,535,134 |
| Marketing fees and staff | 884,380 | 16,236 | 0 | 0 | 0 | 0 | 0 | 0 | 0 | 279 | 867,865 | 0 |
| Postage | 713,474 | 92,397 | 0 | 0 | 107,706 | 0 | 0 | 0 | 0 | 48,019 | 0 | 0 |
| Regional processing centers | 485,102 | 25,023 | 328,709 | 61,263 | 0 | 70,107 | 0 | 0 | 0 | 0 | 0 | 0 |
| Stationery | 277,746 | 0 | 0 | 0 | 156,243 | 0 | 0 | 0 | 0 | 0 | 0 | 24,728 |
| Telesales | 129,235 | 0 | 0 | 0 | 0 | 0 | 0 | 0 | 0 | 0 | 129,235 | 0 |
| VISA stamps and statements | 433,491 | 0 | 0 | 0 | 0 | 0 | 0 | 0 | 0 | 0 | 0 | 0 |
| Other | 55,671 | 26,136 | 0 | 2,655 | 0 | 0 | 0 | 14,349 | 0 | 863 | 2,317 | 7,240 |
| Total activity costs | £15,626,667 | £490,302 | £1,022,140 | £684,100 | £263,949 | £218,001 | £548,168 | £1,380,763 | £1,298,801 | £726,206 | £2,562,046 | £1,641,247 |

**EXHIBIT 5** Personal Sector Products—Matrix of Costs by Resource and Activity* *continued*

| RESOURCE COST POOLS | STATEMENTING & POSTAGE | ADVISE ON INVESTMENTS & INSURANCE | PROCESS VISA TRANSACTIONS | ISSUE VISA STATEMENTS | OPEN AND MAINTAIN HANDYLOANS | OPEN AND CLOSE ACCOUNTS | ADMINISTER MORTGAGES |
|---|---|---|---|---|---|---|---|
| Account management center | £ 0 | £ 0 | £ 138,792 | £ 0 | £ 0 | £193,404 | £ 0 |
| Account opening teams | 0 | 0 | 0 | 0 | 0 | 294,181 | 74,174 |
| ATM network | 0 | 0 | 0 | 0 | 0 | 0 | 0 |
| Branch operations | 0 | 40,930 | 0 | 0 | 0 | 2,976 | 0 |
| Clearing operations | 15,364 | 0 | 0 | 0 | 0 | 132 | 0 |
| Collections | 0 | 0 | 0 | 0 | 0 | 2,906 | 0 |
| Collections fees | 0 | 0 | 0 | 0 | 0 | 0 | 0 |
| Outsourced fees | 0 | 0 | 942,629 | 0 | 846,806 | 0 | 121,908 |
| Financial advisors | 0 | 1,119,013 | 0 | 0 | 0 | 0 | 0 |
| Information technology | 0 | 0 | 0 | 0 | 0 | 0 | 0 |
| Marketing fees and staff | 0 | 0 | 0 | 0 | 0 | 0 | 0 |
| Postage | 455,736 | 0 | 0 | 9,616 | 0 | 0 | 0 |
| Regional processing centers | 0 | 0 | 0 | 0 | 0 | 0 | 0 |
| Stationery | 3,989 | 0 | 92,786 | 0 | 0 | 0 | 0 |
| Telesales | 0 | 0 | 0 | 0 | 0 | 0 | 0 |
| VISA stamps and statements | 0 | 0 | 0 | 433,491 | 0 | 0 | 0 |
| Other | 2,111 | 0 | 0 | 0 | 0 | 0 | 0 |
| Total activity costs | £477,200 | £1,159,943 | £1,174,207 | £443,107 | £846,806 | £493,599 | £196,082 |

*Numbers disguised to maintain confidentiality.

The next step traced the costs of each activity to the different bank products. The tracing was accomplished by defining activity cost drivers for each activity (see first two columns in Exhibit 6). The activity cost driver represented the event that triggered the performance of each activity, such as a deposit that was processed or an account that was opened. The team collected information about the quantities of each activity cost driver that occurred during the estimation period (March-May 1993). These data came from various sources: the bank's automated infor-mation system (for data such as the number of Visa transactions, checks processed, and cash deposited), manual records (for data like the number of personal accounts opened), and statistical sampling procedures (for data not recorded such as the number of customer queries and complaints handled).

Activity cost driver rates (see the last column in Exhibit 6) were calculated by dividing the cost of each activity by the quantity of the associated activity cost driver. The activity cost driver rate could now be used to trace activity costs to individual products and customers.

**EXHIBIT 6** Personal Sector Products: Activity Cost Driver Quantities and Rates*

| ACTIVITY DESCRIPTION | ACTIVITY COST DRIVER | TOTAL ACTIVITY COST | QUANTITY OF ACTIVITY COST DRIVER | COST PER UNIT OF ACTIVITY COST DRIVER |
|---|---|---|---|---|
| Provide ATM service | ATM transactions | £ 490,302 | 1,021,963 | £0.48 |
| Clear debit items | Number of debits processed | 1,022,140 | 5,110,299 | 0.20 |
| Branch operations for debit items | Number of branch counter debits | 684,100 | 762,111 | 0.90 |
| Issue personal cheque book | Number of books issued | 263,949 | 40,628 | 6.50 |
| Clear credit items | Number of credits processed | 218,001 | 871,004 | 0.25 |
| Branch operations for credit items | Number of branch counter credits | 548,168 | 512,986 | 1.07 |
| Lending control and security | Number of interventions | 1,380,763 | 765,591 | 1.80 |
| Customer inquiries | Number of telephone minutes | 1,298,801 | 7,205,560 | 0.18 |
| Customer correspondence | Number of customer letters | 726,206 | 221,204 | 3.28 |
| Marketing and sales activity | Number of accounts opened | 2,562,046 | 62,120 | 41.24 |
| Computer processing | Number of computer transactions (electronic impulses) | 1,641,247 | 16,112,471 | 0.10 |
| Statementing and postage | Number of statements issued | 477,200 | 1,724,285 | 0.28 |
| Advise on investments and insurance | Hours of advice given | 1,159,943 | 32,956 | 35.20 |
| Process VISA transactions | Number of VISA transactions | 1,174,207 | 5,125,248 | 0.23 |
| Issue VISA statements | Number of VISA statements issued | 443,107 | 1,714,258 | 0.26 |
| Open/maintain handyloans | Number of Handyloan accounts | 846,806 | 201,521 | 4.20 |
| Open and close accounts | Number of accounts opened/closed | 493,599 | 57,951 | 8.52 |
| Administer mortgages | Number of mortgages | 196,082 | 18,609 | 10.54 |
| | | £15,626,667 | | |

*Numbers disguised to maintain confidentiality.

The project team identified approximately 50 products or groups of closely related products. Corporate products included business loans, corporate current accounts, and leases. Personal banking products included personal loans and advances, current accounts and Visa accounts. Product costs were calculated by determining the quantity of each activity cost driver used by each of the products, multiplying these quantities by the associated activity cost driver rate, and summing across all the activities used by the individual products.

Exhibit 7 summarizes the distribution of activity costs, including funding charges, to various personal banking products (current accounts, ultra account, personal loans, Visa cards and other personal banking products. The last row of Exhibit 7 calculates the product cost as the sum of the activity costs used by individual products.

Not all operating expenses were assigned to banking products. The project team categorized the costs of 10 large activities as sustaining costs—costs of activities that were not directly related to any products, but rather that supported the organization as a whole. No activity cost drivers were defined for these activities, which included accounting, finance, strategy, planning, human resource management, and information technology development activities. These sustaining costs accounted for 15% of the bank's operating expenses.

Product profitability was calculated by subtracting the cost of all activities undertaken to support a particular product (bottom row of Exhibit 7) from the net interest revenue earned from each product plus the fees derived for performing various services for customers. For asset and liability products (such as loans, current accounts, and savings), the bank used a transfer interest rate to represent the rate at which excess funds could be invested or needed funds borrowed on the money markets.[3] The transfer rate used for most products was the LIBOR[4] rate + ¼% (which equaled 6¼% during the initial estimation period); however, where funds were invested or borrowed specifically for certain products ("matched"), the actual matched rate was used.

Robin Webster, the manager leading the ABC study, described the bank's motivation for calculating product profitability for both asset and liability products:

> In addition to fee income, the bank makes money from asset and liability products in two ways: (1) by accessing sources of funds from liability products; and (2) by lending at higher risk-adjusted rates for our asset products. Using transfer rates allows us to see how well we are doing on both sides of the balance sheet. Are we raising funds from liability accounts at a net cost below our LIBOR borrowing cost? If so, and even without good lending opportunities, we could profit by investing these funds at the LIBOR rate. Are our lending operations healthy? Could we borrow money from the markets at the base rate and still turn a profit from our lending and related fee-generating activities?

Exhibit 8 shows the profitability of the individual personal banking products.

### Product Decisions

The Bank had always regarded the provision of independent financial advice and the sale of associated investment products as a highly profitable business. The ABC analysis (see Exhibit 8), however, indicated that this business was only generating small profits on the basis of the activity costs that could be directly assigned to it, even with no allocation

---

[3]For example, the net interest revenue on business loans equaled the actual interest received minus the transfer rate. For liabilities, like corporate deposits and current accounts, net interest revenue equaled the transfer rate minus the interest actually paid.

[4]LIBOR is the London Inter Bank Offer Rate.

**EXHIBIT 7** Matrix of Activity Costs Used by Personal Sector Products*

| ACTIVITY | TOTAL | CURRENT ACCOUNT PLUS (1) | FREE-FLOW (2) | PERSONAL LOANS (3) | MORT-GAGES (4) | VISA CLASSIC (5) | VISA AFFINITIES (6) | VISA GOLD (7) | HANDY-LOAN/ FASTLINE (8) | INDEPENDENT FINANCIAL ADVICE AND INSURANCE (9) | PATH-FINDER (10) | DEPOSIT PRODUCTS (11) |
|---|---|---|---|---|---|---|---|---|---|---|---|---|
| Provide ATM services | £ 490,302 | £ 403,360 | £ 4,873 | £ 0 | £ 0 | £ 25,410 | £ 7,729 | £ 15,447 | £ 921 | £ 0 | £ 22,515 | £ 10,047 |
| Clear debit items | 1,022,140 | 921,643 | 31,915 | 0 | 0 | 33,792 | 10,397 | 14,296 | 0 | 0 | 10,071 | 26 |
| Branch operations for debit items | 684,100 | 487,796 | 9,774 | 1,770 | 0 | 90,131 | 35,775 | 44,617 | 6,151 | 0 | 5,985 | 2,101 |
| Issue personal checkbook | 263,949 | 252,663 | 11,286 | 0 | 0 | 0 | 0 | 0 | 0 | 0 | 0 | 0 |
| Clear credit items | 218,001 | 91,982 | 2,432 | 4 | 0 | 53,731 | 20,381 | 45,284 | 1,149 | 0 | 3,004 | 34 |
| Branch operations for credit items | 548,168 | 506,273 | 14,964 | 0 | 0 | 3,131 | 103 | 807 | 0 | 0 | 3,807 | 19,083 |
| Lending control and security | 1,380,763 | 532,918 | 26,288 | 91,501 | 20,825 | 540,563 | 6,809 | 143,906 | 5,387 | 4,798 | 4,528 | 3,240 |
| Customer inquiries | 1,298,801 | 850,569 | 26,974 | 97,014 | 324 | 107,052 | 14,749 | 57,630 | 5,959 | 21,053 | 84,287 | 33,190 |
| Customer correspondence | 726,206 | 462,178 | 15,510 | 64,409 | 970 | 56,701 | 2,439 | 23,598 | 6,332 | 13,277 | 58,797 | 21,995 |
| Marketing and sales activity | 2,562,046 | 673,641 | 4,189 | 815,211 | 0 | 202,552 | 54,000 | 197,334 | 41,210 | 398,548 | 85,366 | 89,995 |
| Computer processing | 1,641,247 | 1,215,933 | 54,979 | 113,403 | 0 | 31,292 | 11,317 | 19,256 | 38,131 | 0 | 49,563 | 107,373 |
| Statementing and postage | 477,200 | 336,094 | 18,687 | 19,179 | 66 | 15,241 | 1,433 | 49,277 | 4,430 | 4,088 | 22,740 | 5,965 |
| Advise on investments and insurance | 1,159,943 | 0 | 0 | 0 | 0 | 0 | 0 | 0 | 0 | 1,159,943 | 0 | 0 |
| Process VISA transactions | 1,174,207 | 223,320 | 0 | 18,672 | 0 | 468,257 | 177,895 | 270,904 | 15,159 | 0 | 0 | 0 |
| Issue VISA statements | 443,107 | 0 | 0 | 0 | 0 | 235,406 | 94,017 | 113,684 | 0 | 0 | 0 | 0 |
| Open/maintain handyloans | 846,806 | 0 | 0 | 0 | 0 | 0 | 0 | 0 | 846,805 | 0 | 0 | 0 |
| Open and close accounts | 493,599 | 188,373 | 2,786 | 104,346 | 0 | 51,505 | 1,078 | 35,397 | 11,934 | 0 | 63,062 | 35,118 |
| Administer mortgages | 196,082 | 10,596 | 815 | 17,117 | 121,907 | 0 | 1,631 | 0 | 0 | 0 | 13,042 | 30,974 |
| Total activity costs | £15,626,667 | £7,157,339 | £225,472 | £1,342,626 | £144,092 | £1,914,764 | £439,753 | £1,031,437 | £983,569 | £1,601,707 | £426,767 | £359,141 |

*Numbers disguised to maintain confidentiality.

209

# EXHIBIT 8 Profitability Analysis of Personal Sector Products*

| ACTIVITY | CURRENT ACCOUNT PLUS | FREEFLOW | PERSONAL LOANS | MORT-GAGES | VISA CLASSIC | VISA AFFINITIES | VISA GOLD | HANDY-LOAN/FASTLINE | INDEPENDENT FINANCIAL ADVICE AND INSURANCE | PATH-FINDER | DEPOSIT PRODUCTS | TOTAL |
|---|---|---|---|---|---|---|---|---|---|---|---|---|
| Net interest | £5,283,472 | £1,041,384 | £4,530,963 | £331,027 | £2,856,713 | £463,204 | £ 808,592 | £1,811,526 | £ 0 | £ 261,717 | £960,437 | £18,349,035 |
| Net commission | 3,593,898 | 358,867 | 780,608 | 147,909 | 2,101,002 | 686,117 | 1,562,720 | 65,987 | 1,549,634 | 4,284 | (1,141) | 10,849,885 |
| Bad debts | (782,000) | (130,000) | (1,192,000) | (274,000) | (882,000) | (182,000) | (508,000) | (274,000) | 0 | 0 | 0 | (4,224,000) |
| Gross profit | 8,095,370 | 1,270,251 | 4,119,571 | 204,936 | 4,075,715 | 967,321 | 1,863,312 | 1,603,513 | 1,549,634 | 266,001 | 959,296 | 24,974,920 |
| Activity costs (from Exhibit 7) | 7,157,339 | 225,472 | 1,342,626 | 144,092 | 1,914,764 | 439,753 | 1,031,437 | 983,569 | 1,601,707 | 426,767 | 359,141 | 15,626,667 |
| Direct profit | 938,031 | 1,044,779 | 2,776,945 | 60,844 | 2,160,951 | 527,568 | 831,875 | 619,944 | (52,073) | (160,766) | 600,155 | 9,348,253 |
| Allocated infrastructure costs | 1,014,145 | 36,845 | 204,822 | 4,213 | 156,768 | 22,086 | 81,053 | 20,864 | 263,078 | 65,066 | 59,685 | 1,928,625 |
| Net profit | £ (76,114) | £1,007,934 | £2,572,123 | £ 56,631 | £2,004,183 | £505,482 | £ 750,822 | £ 599,080 | £(315,151) | £(225,832) | £540,470 | £ 7,419,628 |

*Numbers disguised to maintain confidentiality.

of the 15% of expenses classified as "sustaining costs." This came as a particular surprise because the Bank had targeted financial advice and new investment products as a growth area in the deregulated environment.

The analysis showed that several other products were failing to generate adequate returns to pay for the sustaining costs and to support hoped-for improvements in the Bank's cost-income ratio aspirations. For example, The Bank's basic and core product, personal current accounts ("Current Account Plus"), was at best breaking even after considering sustaining costs. This finding was consistent with conventional wisdom at the Bank, and also in the U.K. banking market, where many banks were openly commenting in the press that current accounts were unprofitable. The Bank began contemplating several courses of action to improve the profitability of current accounts.

On a more positive note, all three Visa accounts were revealed to be highly profitable products. The Gold Card is a free for life card that carries a slightly lower interest rate than the Classic Card (which is an ordinary Visa Card) and the Affinity Card. The Affinity Card is attractive to some customers because a portion of the income earned on the Affinity Card is given to specified charities. The Bank saw a clear message to focus its limited marketing resources into growing its personal current accounts and Visa account businesses.

### Customer Profitability

The ABC team wanted to extend the analysis to individual customers, but the bank's information systems, many dating back to the 1960s, could not readily access customers' transactions data. The team performed a limited study of customer-specific expenses, based on a sample of current accounts. They did not need to study other products in detail,

since most savings accounts had fewer than two transactions per quarter, all loan products had a predictable 12 transactions per year, and credit card costs were found to be mostly constant per account.

The team determined that 55% of current account expenses were related to processing transactions, and 45% were related to maintaining accounts. The maintenance-related costs were divided by the number of accounts, and assigned equally to each account. For assigning transactions-related expenses, the team split customers into three segments—Low, Medium, and High—based on the annual turnover of funds in their accounts. From a month-long sample of customer transactions, they assigned transactions-related expenses to these three segments in the ratios of: 15%, 40% and 45%.

The revenue side was simpler. The team identified, for each product, the income earned from credit balances and fees by individual customers. By matching this income with the assigned cost, the team could now estimate the profitability of each customer.

Next, the Bank identified the entry product (the first product bought by a customer). The five main entry products were Current Accounts, VISA Gold, VISA Affinity cards, VISA Classic and the Pathfinder savings account. All subsequent sales of other products (cross sales) were assigned to the entry product. The results showed that the vast majority of cross sales originated from Current Accounts.

The customer profitability analysis revealed that up to half of all current accounts, particularly those with low balances, were unprofitable. Managers at the Bank began to debate several questions about current accounts. How can it make current accounts attractive to profitable customers? Should The Bank combine and enhance its current account products with features such as service level warranties and restructured charges? Should the Bank aggressively market these accounts using a special sales force backed by an advertising campaign in local newspapers and on television?

How should the Bank discourage unprofitable customers? Should the Bank alter its tariff to give a wide differential between customers taking credit within approved overdraft limits, and those overdrawing accounts outside approved limits where the greatest risk of loss existed, and which prompted high levels of intervention activity?

The Bank segmented Visa customers into profitable and unprofitable customers. The most profitable customers were customers with large unpaid balances that generated interest income, and customers who transacted frequently, thereby generating high processing fees. The Bank developed a profile of the profitable customers, and its marketing was being redirected to attract the customers with profitable behavior.

David Fawell, Marketing Manager, faced an interesting decision:

> Excluding sustaining costs, both current account and Visa customers are profitable, as I thought. But with pressure to reduce our operating expenses, I have only a limited amount of funds to market these products. I'm not sure whether these funds should be directed to prospective personal current account customers or to Visa account customers? Or should I spread the funds across both types of prospects?

## *Overhead Reduction and Business Process Reengineering*

In addition to decisions about products and customers, the initial information from Project SABRE helped to refocus The Bank from a functionally oriented organization to a process-oriented organization. Activity costs provided a metric to evaluate the effects of business process reengineering decisions.

Managers were now attempting to identify which processes were adding value to the customer and which were not, and how the efficiency of different processes could be improved. Improving efficiency would enable the bank to either take costs out of the system, or to use the extra capacity to generate more revenue.

Deeper analysis showed that much of the cost base had a high element of costs that were, in the short to medium term, fixed (for example, computer systems and bank branches) and that radical solutions were required to impact on these costs. In 1994, the Bank outsourced its computer development and ATM network, and began serious negotiations to outsource its London check clearing center with a view to eliminating excess capacity and replacing fixed with variable costs.

## *Next Steps*

While stimulated by the interesting findings of the first-pass ABC analysis, many bank managers were still unsure about the action implications. A newly introduced product like foreign currency exchange seemed to be unprofitable. Should it be discontinued or should it be retained as part of a full-service package for current account customers? Also, would department managers, accustomed to high autonomy and control over their operations, be willing to reengineer their organization to facilitate process flows, and eventually to down-size their operations to achieve a lower cost-to-income ratio. Some managers expressed concern that as profitability improved, from better selection of products and customers, the organization's commitment to reorganize and improve would start to diminish.

Robin Webster and Steve Kemp were disappointed that such a large amount of expenses (15% of costs) had been classified as sustaining costs, where they could not be driven down to products and customers. They felt that these sustaining expenses could be reduced but because they had been treated as "fixed," independent of products and customers, they would not be targets for cost reduction. Ken Lewis, Executive Director, Group Resources, concurred. He observed that the bank's people costs had been traced readily and easily to activities that related to products and customers, but that property and information technology resources had been largely classified as business-sustaining. Lewis believed that significant opportunities existed to downsize sustaining costs by making better decisions about the types of properties the bank owned and leased, and the level and extent of information technology the bank deployed. Decisions on information technology could be critical. Unmanned, totally automated kiosks were starting to perform activities formerly done by the bank's labor-intensive branch network.

# JOHN DEERE COMPONENT WORKS (B)*

Frank Stevenson had been appointed division manager of Gear and Special Products in September 1986 after spending 20 years in manufacturing and manufacturing engineering. He summarized his division's response to activity-based costing (ABC):[1]

> Few things have generated more excitement. Even though it's still an allocation, it's such an improvement. Parts we suspected we were undercosting have turned out to be even more expensive than we had thought. It's proven what we suspected about the costs of material handling and transport distances, and triggered our making layout changes. When it showed us the costs added by secondary operations, we brought them back onto the main floor.

## ABC Cost Estimating Model

In order to use ABC for costing individual parts, a model was developed that could be run using a Lotus 1-2-3 spreadsheet on an IBM personal computer (separate from the overall accounting and data processing systems). It provided considerably more information than the standard cost model, and some elements of the model were interactive. The ABC model, for example, calculated material costs on the basis of the type of steel, part length, and machine number (which affected tools used and waste). Also, materials that were delivered directly to the machines on the floor, bypassing receiving, inspection, and storage, were not charged for any materials overhead. Therefore, material costs depended on how the material was used, as well as its purchase price. (The standard cost system, by contrast, calculated an average cost for parts of a certain weight based entirely on the purchase price of the barstock.) Materials of different prices could be fed into the ABC system, and the model would make cost trade-offs among them. The model could calculate the number of annual runs that produced the lowest manufacturing costs on an annual basis for a part number; it included inventory holding costs as a factor in making this assessment. It could also compare setups on different machines for their differential cost effects.

Although the ABC method was developed on the basis of normal volume, the model could also calculate costs at a par (full capac-

---

*Research Associate Artemis March prepared this case under the supervision of Professor Robert S. Kaplan.

Copyright © 1987 by the President and Fellows of Harvard College. Harvard Business School case 187-108.

[1]See "John Deere Component Works (A)," HBS No. 9-187-107 in Chapter 4.

ity) level of utilization. Par volume was higher than current normal volume and represented what Gear and Special Products managers considered a more reasonable level of utilization than the currently existing very depressed normal volume. Par overhead rates spread period overhead across higher volumes of parts than did normal rates.

### Completing the ABC Study

Keith Williams and Nick Vintila, the authors of activity-based costing, were able to demonstrate the change in estimated costs, from standard to ABC, for the sample of 44 parts examined earlier (see Exhibit 1). They also experimented with changing the lot size from that currently being used in the division's MRP system. In particular, the ABC model recommended that the average lot size be doubled—thereby halving the number of annual runs per part—in order to optimize manufacturing costs (see Exhibit 2). The costs saved in reduced setups, materials handling, and production order processing more than offset the increased inventory holding costs.

A third study showed the impact of shifting the product mix to exploit the efficiencies from running longer jobs on the turning machines. Exhibit 3 shows the current workload on the turning machines based on the annual machine hours (ACTS) for each part. The overhead assignment (using the new ABC model) to each class of parts is shown at the bottom of the exhibit. Exhibit 4 shows a simulated overhead assignment assuming that the more than 1,000 parts with less than 100 annual ACTS hours run time were transferred from the machines, with the freed-up machine time used to produce 30 new parts that each required at least 500 annual ACTS hours. This change would reduce by 77% the number of part numbers being processed on the machines and reduce the number of setup

hours and orders processed by about 60%. Williams explained the rationale for this study:

> We wanted to estimate the impact from substituting a few high-volume parts for the large number of low-volume parts we are now running. Overhead is reduced by $2.2 million, or about 21%. The overhead rate declines from 593% to 467% of direct labor. The key question is whether actual overhead reductions of that scale would result from such a change.
>
> Our impression is that at least this amount of overhead reduction should occur. The reduced number of parts should directly reduce the expenses for machine setups and for material management scheduling and coordination. Process and tool and industrial engineering would be supporting only a fifth of the part numbers now being supported. Such a change should make it much easier to standardize raw material, which should reduce coordination in that area. Also, it should be much easier to implement other operational improvements such as sequencing jobs so as to minimize setups, using pick-offs or other attachments to eliminate secondary operations, or possible rearrangements to create a cell environment for the high-volume parts.

### Division Changes

Stevenson located activity-based costing in the context of a division trying to reorient itself to a new reality: "We must dramatically increase our competitive position in the worldwide market. That requires a quantum leap in manufacturing quality and in reducing our costs." To this end, the division had, during the 1985–1986 period, formally demarcated its product lines into five businesses: gears and shafts, machined parts, cast iron machining, heat treating, and sheet metal work. Wherever possible, departments were reorganized from processes to manufacturing cells and a just-in-time approach adopted to shorten lead times, improve quality, and thus lower costs. Stevenson stated, "We want 'visual management' to replace routing; we want

**EXHIBIT 1** Comparison of Machined Parts Overhead: Standard Costing versus Activity-Based Costing for the 44 Sample Items—Turning Machine Operations Only

| PART NUMBER | PART DESCRIPTION | QUOTE VOLUME | PART WEIGHT | ACTS HR ABC RUNS/YEAR | ACTS HR PER 100 | ACTS HR ANNUAL | DIRECT LABOR | JDCW OVERHEAD COST DIRECT OH | JDCW OVERHEAD COST PERIOD OH | JDCW OVERHEAD COST TOTAL OH | ABC OVERHEAD COST DIRECT OH | ABC OVERHEAD COST PERIOD OH | ABC OVERHEAD COST TOTAL OH | ABC OVERHEAD AS % JDCW DIRECT OH | ABC OVERHEAD AS % JDCW PERIOD OH | ABC OVERHEAD AS % JDCW TOTAL OH |
|---|---|---|---|---|---|---|---|---|---|---|---|---|---|---|---|---|
| **The 10 Parts Most Helped by ABC** | | | | | | | | | | | | | | | | |
| H265 | Hub | 4,464 | 3.703 | 4 | 3.4 | 150 | $1,127 | $3,750 | $4,905 | $8,654 | $3,347 | $3,104 | $6,451 | 89% | 63% | 75% |
| R946 | Roller | 5,904 | 0.600 | 3 | 2.4 | 139 | 695 | 2,621 | 3,700 | 6,321 | 2,064 | 2,726 | 4,792 | 79 | 74 | 76 |
| R428 | Sprocket | 3,180 | 1.556 | 2 | 2.2 | 70 | 527 | 1,672 | 2,187 | 3,859 | 1,575 | 1,744 | 3,319 | 94 | 80 | 86 |
| R717 | Sprocket | 4,869 | 1.956 | 2 | 2.0 | 95 | 713 | 2,035 | 2,661 | 4,696 | 2,181 | 2,087 | 4,266 | 107 | 78 | 91 |
| A152 | Shaft | 2,972 | 1.252 | 3 | 1.7 | 51 | 379 | 1,359 | 1,777 | 3,136 | 1,363 | 1,618 | 2,981 | 100 | 91 | 95 |
| P244 | Pin | 7,383 | 1.085 | 3 | 1.8 | 132 | 706 | 2,198 | 3,064 | 5,262 | 2,358 | 2,696 | 5,054 | 107 | 88 | 96 |
| H355 | Hub | 1,155 | 3.052 | 1 | 2.3 | 26 | 130 | 677 | 955 | 1,632 | 540 | 1,028 | 1,568 | 80 | 108 | 96 |
| R157 | Roller | 3,181 | 0.243 | 1 | 1.5 | 46 | 231 | 839 | 1,185 | 2,024 | 711 | 1,274 | 1,984 | 85 | 108 | 98 |
| C784 | Cap | 71,200 | 0.166 | 4 | 0.4 | 266 | 1,994 | 4,151 | 5,425 | 9,576 | 4,929 | 4,472 | 9,401 | 119 | 82 | 98 |
| P379 | Pin | 6,807 | 1.116 | 3 | 1.8 | 133 | 651 | 2,039 | 2,843 | 4,882 | 2,238 | 2,561 | 4,798 | 110 | 90 | 96 |
| | Total/Average | 11,112 | 1.473 | 2.6 | 1.9 | 110 | $7,152 | $21,341 | $28,702 | $50,043 | $21,306 | $23,310 | $44,614 | 100% | 81% | 89% |
| **The 10 Parts Most Penalized by ABC** | | | | | | | | | | | | | | | | |
| S771 | Spacer | 11,092 | 0.039 | 1 | 0.2 | 20 | $100 | $329 | $466 | $795 | $411 | $934 | $1,346 | 125% | 200% | 169% |
| P675 | Pin | 2,596 | 0.412 | 1 | 0.4 | 14 | 69 | 263 | 371 | 634 | 377 | 858 | 1,236 | 144 | 231 | 195 |
| P220 | Pin | 3,204 | 0.743 | 3 | 0.6 | 19 | 139 | 444 | 580 | 1,024 | 824 | 1,188 | 2,011 | 186 | 205 | 196 |
| T815 | Stud | 3,150 | 0.281 | 1 | 0.4 | 12 | 58 | 237 | 336 | 573 | 317 | 828 | 1,144 | 134 | 246 | 200 |
| N281 | Nut | 8,500 | 0.222 | 3 | 0.2 | 18 | 135 | 411 | 537 | 949 | 817 | 1,183 | 2,000 | 199 | 220 | 211 |
| T566 | Stud | 2,452 | 1.779 | 3 | 1.0 | 24 | 178 | 564 | 738 | 1,302 | 1,228 | 1,519 | 2,748 | 218 | 206 | 211 |
| R918 | Rocker | 1,091 | 0.703 | 1 | 0.9 | 10 | 40 | 193 | 281 | 473 | 262 | 783 | 1,047 | 136 | 279 | 221 |
| R410 | Sprocket | 792 | 2.786 | 1 | 0.7 | 6 | 42 | 172 | 225 | 397 | 339 | 766 | 1,105 | 197 | 341 | 278 |
| P594 | Pin | 692 | 0.722 | 1 | 0.3 | 2 | 11 | 61 | 87 | 148 | 207 | 702 | 910 | 338 | 811 | 615 |
| S209 | Spacer | 950 | 0.141 | 1 | 0.3 | 3 | 15 | 58 | 82 | 140 | 173 | 688 | 862 | 299 | 842 | 617 |
| | Total/Average | 3,229 | 0.712 | 1.5 | 0.5 | 12 | $788 | $2,732 | $3,702 | $6,434 | $4,955 | $9,449 | $14,409 | 181% | 255% | 224% |

**EXHIBIT 1** Comparison of Machined Parts Overhead: Standard Costing versus Activity-Based Costing for the 44 Sample Items—Turning Machine Operations Only *continued*

| PART NUMBER | PART DESCRIPTION | QUOTE VOLUME | PART WEIGHT | ABC RUNS/ YEAR | ACTS HR PER 100 | ACTS HR ANNUAL | DIRECT LABOR | JDCW OVERHEAD COST DIRECT OH | PERIOD OH | TOTAL OH | ABC OVERHEAD COST DIRECT OH | PERIOD OH | TOTAL OH | ABC OVERHEAD AS % JDCW DIRECT OH | PERIOD OH | TOTAL OH |
|---|---|---|---|---|---|---|---|---|---|---|---|---|---|---|---|---|
| **Remaining Parts** | | | | | | | | | | | | | | | | |
| H346 | Hub | 1,088 | 3.614 | 2 | 2.8 | 31 | $ 151 | $ 823 | $ 1,166 | $ 1,989 | $ 735 | $ 1,225 | $ 1,960 | 89% | 105% | 99% |
| B823 | Button | 18,200 | 0.069 | 2 | 0.5 | 84 | 417 | 1,305 | 1,844 | 3,149 | 1,317 | 1,898 | 3,215 | 101 | 103 | 102 |
| R316 | Roller | 18,058 | 0.042 | 2 | 0.4 | 80 | 401 | 1,266 | 1,784 | 3,050 | 1,278 | 1,854 | 3,132 | 101 | 104 | 103 |
| T237 | Stop | 4,258 | 1.818 | 5 | 2.7 | 116 | 706 | 2,072 | 2,924 | 4,996 | 2,413 | 2,753 | 5,176 | 116 | 94 | 104 |
| P682 | Pin | 3,402 | 1.347 | 2 | 1.8 | 61 | 325 | 1,131 | 1,577 | 2,708 | 1,253 | 1,618 | 2,872 | 111 | 103 | 106 |
| T586 | Stud | 10,000 | 0.602 | 4 | 0.7 | 77 | 573 | 1,595 | 2,086 | 3,681 | 1,888 | 2,061 | 3,947 | 118 | 99 | 107 |
| S071 | Spacer | 5,661 | 1.507 | 2 | 1.0 | 54 | 407 | 1,167 | 1,527 | 2,694 | 1,449 | 1,545 | 2,994 | 124 | 101 | 111 |
| P583 | Pin | 3,402 | 1.253 | 2 | 1.5 | 52 | 258 | 935 | 1,320 | 2,255 | 1,056 | 1,479 | 2,534 | 113 | 112 | 112 |
| P736 | Pin | 38,955 | 0.160 | 2 | 0.4 | 159 | 795 | 1,944 | 2,742 | 4,686 | 2,480 | 2,915 | 5,394 | 128 | 106 | 115 |
| P423 | Pin | 3,402 | 1.354 | 2 | 1.5 | 52 | 258 | 931 | 1,314 | 2,245 | 1,131 | 1,489 | 2,619 | 121 | 113 | 117 |
| P333 | Pin | 4,258 | 0.937 | 3 | 1.3 | 56 | 282 | 1,021 | 1,441 | 2,462 | 1,232 | 1,668 | 2,899 | 121 | 116 | 118 |
| L209 | Lever | 5,351 | 0.533 | 2 | 0.8 | 41 | 204 | 747 | 1,054 | 1,801 | 858 | 1,332 | 2,190 | 115 | 126 | 122 |
| P057 | Pin | 1,281 | 0.569 | 1 | 1.5 | 20 | 97 | 438 | 618 | 1,056 | 404 | 926 | 1,330 | 92 | 150 | 126 |
| T863 | Stud | 7,120 | 1.110 | 4 | 1.0 | 74 | 553 | 1,396 | 1,825 | 3,220 | 2,217 | 2,100 | 4,316 | 159 | 115 | 134 |
| T166 | Stud | 5,645 | 0.258 | 3 | 0.6 | 36 | 232 | 757 | 1,023 | 1,780 | 1,098 | 1,415 | 2,511 | 145 | 138 | 141 |
| B605 | Bolt | 10,561 | 0.286 | 2 | 0.3 | 32 | 242 | 659 | 864 | 1,523 | 911 | 1,250 | 2,161 | 138 | 145 | 142 |
| P904 | Pin | 950 | 2.179 | 1 | 1.8 | 17 | 86 | 384 | 542 | 925 | 430 | 894 | 1,325 | 112 | 165 | 143 |
| R647 | Sprocket | 5,167 | 3.522 | 3 | 1.4 | 74 | 372 | 1,254 | 1,769 | 3,023 | 2,329 | 2,054 | 4,383 | 186 | 116 | 145 |
| H622 | Hub | 4,450 | 1.913 | 2 | 0.6 | 26 | 130 | 548 | 773 | 1,320 | 756 | 1,171 | 1,927 | 138 | 152 | 146 |
| S451 | Spacer | 2,785 | 0.120 | 1 | 0.6 | 17 | 83 | 347 | 490 | 837 | 370 | 887 | 1,257 | 107 | 181 | 150 |
| H554 | Hub | 1,490 | 1.582 | 1 | 1.1 | 16 | 79 | 361 | 510 | 871 | 423 | 895 | 1,319 | 117 | 176 | 152 |
| T501 | Stud | 4,879 | 0.151 | 1 | 0.3 | 17 | 85 | 322 | 454 | 775 | 376 | 894 | 1,269 | 117 | 197 | 164 |
| F382 | Fitting | 4,009 | 0.711 | 2 | 0.5 | 20 | 153 | 488 | 636 | 1,124 | 738 | 1,103 | 1,840 | 151 | 173 | 164 |
| S245 | Spacer | 4,912 | 0.281 | 1 | 0.4 | 19 | 94 | 336 | 475 | 811 | 433 | 921 | 1,355 | 129 | 194 | 167 |
| Total/Average | | 7,054 | 1.080 | 2.2 | 1.1 | 51 | $ 6,983 | $22,226 | $30,757 | $ 52,982 | $27,575 | $36,357 | $ 63,925 | 124% | 118% | 121% |
| Total/Avg. All Parts | | 7,180 | 1.102 | 2.1 | 1.1 | 56 | $14,924 | $46,299 | $63,161 | $109,459 | $53,836 | $69,116 | $122,948 | 116% | 109% | 112% |

*Note: Dollar figures are annual totals for the quote quantity.*

**EXHIBIT 2** Comparison of Costs: Changing Lot Size

| PART DESCRIPTION | MACHINE SETUP TIME | ANNUAL REQUIREMENTS | ACTS HOURS/ C | ANNUAL ACTS | PRESENT OPERATION | | | | INDICATED BY ABC | | | | | | | COMPARISON | | |
|---|---|---|---|---|---|---|---|---|---|---|---|---|---|---|---|---|---|---|
| | | | | | OBSERVED RUN SIZE | ANNUAL RUNS | ANNUAL SETUP HOURS | % ANNUAL SETUP TO ANNUAL ACTS | ANNUAL RUNS PER YEAR | ANNUAL SETUP HOURS | % ANNUAL SETUP TO ANNUAL ACTS | ANNUAL ABC SETUP AND ORDER COST | | | % ABC SETUP HR IMPACT | ABC SAVINGS TO IDCW SETUP AND ORDER COST | | |
| | | | | | | | | | | | | DIRECT | PERIOD | TOTAL | | DIRECT | PERIOD | TOTAL |
| Valve | 2.80 | 6,566 | 5.63 | 370 | 1,112 | 6 | 16.8 | 5% | 3 | 8.4 | 2 | $ 326 | $ 300 | $ 626 | -50 | $ 326 | $ 300 | $ 626 |
| Pin | 5.61 | 9,330 | 3.16 | 295 | 1,034 | 10 | 56.1 | 19% | 4 | 22.4 | 8 | 709 | 505 | 1,214 | -60 | 1,064 | 757 | 1,821 |
| Bushing | 5.61 | 8,505 | 2.17 | 185 | 1,991 | 5 | 28.1 | 15% | 3 | 16.8 | 9 | 532 | 378 | 911 | -40 | 355 | 252 | 607 |
| Pin | 5.61 | 12,461 | 1.69 | 211 | 2,970 | 5 | 28.1 | 3% | 3 | 16.8 | 9 | 532 | 379 | 911 | -40 | 355 | 253 | 607 |
| Blocker | 5.61 | 2,350 | 3.02 | 71 | 518 | 5 | 28.1 | 40% | 2 | 11.2 | 16 | 355 | 252 | 607 | -60 | 532 | 379 | 911 |
| Sleeve | 4.20 | 16,568 | 1.02 | 169 | 6,904 | 3 | 12.6 | 7% | 3 | 12.6 | 7 | 429 | 340 | 769 | 0 | 0 | 0 | 0 |
| Swivel | 4.20 | 20,055 | 0.31 | 62 | 3,750 | 6 | 25.2 | 41% | 2 | 8.4 | 14 | 287 | 227 | 513 | -67 | 574 | 453 | 1,027 |
| Neck | 3.27 | 6,381 | 1.05 | 67 | 1,598 | 4 | 13.1 | 20% | 2 | 6.5 | 10 | 240 | 209 | 449 | -50 | 240 | 209 | 449 |
| Washer | 4.20 | 17,014 | 0.34 | 58 | 7,480 | 3 | 12.6 | 22% | 1 | 4.2 | 7 | 145 | 112 | 257 | -67 | 289 | 225 | 514 |
| Connector | 5.61 | 11,467 | 1.92 | 220 | 1,014 | 12 | 67.3 | 31% | 5 | 28.1 | 13 | 886 | 631 | 1,517 | -58 | 1,241 | 883 | 2,124 |
| Pinion | 5.61 | 642 | 5.80 | 37 | 371 | 2 | 11.2 | 20% | 2 | 11.2 | 30 | 355 | 252 | 607 | 0 | 0 | 0 | 0 |
| Pin | 2.34 | 91,629 | 0.19 | 174 | 19,440 | 5 | 11.7 | 7% | 3 | 7.0 | 4 | 293 | 284 | 577 | -40 | 195 | 189 | 385 |
| Plug | 4.91 | 20,825 | 0.48 | 100 | 4,279 | 5 | 24.6 | 25% | 4 | 19.6 | 20 | 641 | 479 | 1,120 | -20 | 160 | 120 | 280 |
| Connector | 4.20 | 11,892 | 0.32 | 38 | 3,370 | 4 | 16.8 | 44% | 2 | 8.4 | 22 | 285 | 226 | 511 | -50 | 285 | 226 | 511 |
| Spacer | 3.27 | 2,154 | 0.56 | 12 | 841 | 3 | 9.8 | 81% | 1 | 3.3 | 27 | 120 | 104 | 225 | -67 | 240 | 209 | 449 |
| Rod | 4.20 | 582 | 1.22 | 7 | 305 | 2 | 8.4 | 18% | 1 | 4.2 | 59 | 143 | 113 | 256 | -50 | 143 | 113 | 256 |
| Total/Average | | | | 2,075 | 56,977 | 80 | 370 | 18% | 41 | 189 | 9% | $6,279 | $4,791 | $11,070 | -49% | $6,000 | $4,567 | $10,567 |

217

**EXHIBIT 3** Assignment of Machine Overhead by Activity: Present Distribution of Parts

PART GROUPING BY ANNUAL ACTS HOURS

| ACTIVITY DATA | 0 | 1–50 | 50–100 | 100–500 | 500–1000 | OVER 1000 | TOTAL |
|---|---|---|---|---|---|---|---|
| Direct Labor ($000) | $0 | $ 251 | $ 207 | $ 783 | $ 236 | $236 | $ 1,713 |
| % of total | 0.0 | 14.7 | 12.1 | 45.7 | 13.8 | 13.8 | 100.0 |
| Machine (ACTS) Hours | 0 | 17,000 | 14,000 | 53,000 | 16,000 | 16,000 | 116,000 |
| % of total | 0.0 | 14.7 | 12.1 | 45.7 | 13.8 | 13.8 | 100.0 |
| Number of Part Numbers | | | | | | | |
| Parts with no requirements | 1,110 | | | | | | 1,110 |
| Parts with requirements | | 877 | 208 | 256 | 22 | 8 | 1,371 |
| % of total | | 64.0 | 15.2 | 18.5 | 1.6 | 0.6 | 100.0 |
| Annual Setup Hours (est.) | | | | | | | |
| Orders/part (est.) | 0 | 4 | 6 | 8 | 10 | 12 | |
| Hours/setup (est.) | 4 | 4 | 5 | 5 | 5 | 3 | |
| Total setup hours | 0 | 14,032 | 6,240 | 10,240 | 1,100 | 288 | 31,900 |
| % of total | 0.0 | 44.0 | 19.6 | 32.1 | 3.4 | 0.9 | 100.0 |
| Annual Production Orders | | | | | | | |
| Orders/part numbers (est.) | 0 | 4 | 6 | 8 | 10 | 12 | |
| Total production orders | 0 | 3,508 | 1,248 | 2,048 | 220 | 96 | 7,120 |
| % of total | 0.0 | 49.3 | 17.5 | 28.8 | 3.1 | 1.3 | 100.0 |
| Material Handling Data | | | | | | | |
| Loading factor (est.) | 0 | 0.67 | 0.8 | 1.0 | 1.0 | 0.8 | |
| Cost weighting | 0 | 25,373 | 17,500 | 53,000 | 16,000 | 20,000 | 131,873 |
| % of total | 0.0 | 19.2 | 13.3 | 40.2 | 12.1 | 15.2 | 100.0 |
| Overhead Assignments ($000) | | | | | | | |
| Direct labor support | $0 | $ 278 | $ 229 | $ 867 | $ 262 | $262 | $ 1,898 |
| Machine operation | 0 | 593 | 488 | 1,848 | 558 | 558 | 4,045 |
| Machine setup | 0 | 498 | 211 | 356 | 37 | 10 | 1,112 |
| Production orders | 0 | 401 | 143 | 237 | 25 | 11 | 817 |
| Material handling | 0 | 58 | 40 | 122 | 37 | 46 | 303 |
| Part administration | 5 | 636 | 151 | 186 | 16 | 6 | 1,000 |
| General administration | 1 | 268 | 137 | 393 | 102 | 97 | 998 |
| Total overhead | $6 | $2,732 | $1,399 | $4,009 | $1,037 | $990 | $10,173 |
| Total overhead/DL$ | NA | 1,088% | 676% | 512% | 439% | 419% | 594% |

to stand here at the beginning of the process and see parts being completed right within our view." In addition, a marketing department had been added at the factory level.

## Use of ABC

ABC was widely embraced for decision making in the machined parts business and for implementing other changes more effectively.

**Bidding** The ABC model was being used to cost machined parts and to prepare bids to both Deere and outside customers. Sinclair commented, "We are more confident now about our quote prices. And because ABC more properly penalizes low-volume products, we now know which business we don't want." Also, the ABC model could generate costs at either normal or par volume, making it easier to prepare par-based

**EXHIBIT 4**  Assignment of Machine Overhead by Activity: Assumed Distribution of Parts

| ACTIVITY DATA | 0 | 100–500 | 500–1,000 | OVER 1,000 | TOTAL | % | ($000) |
|---|---|---|---|---|---|---|---|
| | | PART GROUPING BY ANNUAL ACTS HOURS | | | | INDICATED CHANGE IN ACTIVITY/COST | |
| Direct Labor ($000) | $0 | $ 783 | $ 465 | $ 465 | $1,713 | 0 | |
| % of total | 0.0 | 45.7 | 27.1 | 27.1 | 100.0 | | |
| Machine (ACTS) Hours | 0 | 53,000 | 31,500 | 31,500 | 116,000 | 0 | |
| % of total | 0.0 | 45.7 | 27.2 | 27.2 | 100.0 | | |
| Number of Part Numbers | | | | | | | |
| Parts with no requirements | 1,110 | | | | 1,100 | 0 | |
| Parts with requirements | | 256 | 44 | 16 | 316 | −77 | |
| % of total | | 81.0 | 13.9 | 5.1 | 100.0 | | |
| Annual Setup Hours (est.) | | | | | | | |
| Orders/part (est.) | 0 | 8 | 10 | 12 | | | |
| Hours/setup (est.) | 4 | 5 | 5 | 3 | | | |
| Total setup hours | 0 | 10,240 | 2,200 | 576 | 13,016 | −59 | |
| % of total | 0.0 | 78.7 | 16.9 | 4.4 | 100.0 | | |
| Annual Production Orders | | | | | | | |
| Orders/part numbers (est.) | 0 | 8 | 10 | 12 | | | |
| Total production orders | 0 | 2,048 | 440 | 192 | 2,680 | −62 | |
| % of total | 0.0 | 76.4 | 16.4 | 7.2 | 100.0 | | |
| Material Handling Data | | | | | | | |
| Loading factor (est.) | 0 | 1.0 | 1.0 | 0.8 | | | |
| Cost weighing | 0 | 53,000 | 31,500 | 39,375 | 123,875 | −6 | |
| % of total | 0.0 | 42.8 | 25.4 | 31.8 | 100.0 | | |
| Overhead Assignments | | | | | | | |
| Direct labor support | $0 | $ 867 | $ 515 | $ 515 | $1,897 | 0 | $   0 |
| Machine operation | 0 | 1,848 | 1,098 | 1,098 | 4,044 | 0 | 0 |
| Machine setup | 0 | 356 | 74 | 19 | 449 | −60 | (663) |
| Production orders | 0 | 237 | 50 | 22 | 309 | −62 | (508) |
| Material handling | 0 | 122 | 72 | 90 | 284 | −6 | (19) |
| Part administration | 5 | 186 | 32 | 12 | 235 | −77 | (765) |
| General administration | 1 | 393 | 200 | 191 | 785 | −21 | (213) |
| Total overhead | $6 | $4,009 | $2,041 | $1,947 | $8,003 | −21 | $(2,170) |
| % Overhead/DL$ | na | 512% | 439% | 419% | 467% | −21% | |

*Note: Assumes transfer of parts with less than 100 ACTS and replacing available ACTS hours with parts having more than 500 ACTS.*

quotes for the machining portion of the parts.

The division had also changed its transfer pricing and bidding practices. Attempting to bid and transfer at full cost had lost Gear and Special Products much internal business. It began to negotiate "market-based prices," which could be below the full costs calcu-

lated by the existing cost accounting system. After a period of experimentation, the use of market pricing became official corporatewide policy in April 1986.

**Process Planning**  John Gordon, head of process engineering for the machining area, was using the model to compare relative machining efficiencies for different types of steel and part numbers in order to decide which parts should be run on which types of machines. Because ABC revealed much higher setup and production order costs than those used in the MRP ordering formula, larger lot sizes and fewer annual runs per part number were indicated. Process engineering was using ABC to cost parts on the basis of optimal runs per year and to negotiate with customers to accept fewer runs at lower prices.

**Low Value-Added Parts** Gear and Special Products was already accelerating the movement of low-volume, short-running parts off the turning machines. About one-third (31%) of parts required over 20 hours each of direct labor; collectively these accounted for 97% of all direct labor hours and were likely to all remain on the machines. But parts with less than eight hours of labor were being outsourced or would soon go to the low value-added (LVA) jobshop that was being set up adjacent to the machining area. The fate of the remaining parts was still undetermined, but decision making was now aided by the much more accurate costing under ABC. This would eventually allow the division to determine the breakeven point; Dick Sinclair, the manufacturing superintendent, commented, "We don't yet know where the point is that says, 'Put it on the turning machine.' We've eliminated the clearly LVA parts and are working our way up."

The combination of moving LVA parts off the turning machines and moving toward fewer runs for the remaining parts was expected to increase the average run time, reduce scheduling complexity, and eventually reduce the demands for staff support.

**Cell Arrangements** While physical manufacturing infrastructure constrained dramatic rearrangement from rows of machines to cells, certain machines could be clustered together and dedicated to a particular high-run part. For example, twelve adjacent machines were now dedicated to running just two parts for General Motors.

**Layout** ABC was helping division managers decide how to arrange the machining departments. Sinclair noted, "We did a lot of things in the 1970s that made a lot of sense then, but now we must undo them." The high cost of secondary operations caused management to move these operations not only back into the division (they had been part of Drive Trains for years), but into a corner of the main floor in S Building where they were now being requalified. To make room for these operations, less-efficient turning machines had been scrapped; relative efficiencies had been revealed by Vintila's detailed machine study. To reduce handling distances, barstock staging had been made more efficient, and packaging and shipping were being relocated closer to final operations.

These layout changes had not yet been tried out during production. They had been made during the August 1986 vacation shutdown, but the factory had been closed until January 1987 by a corporatewide UAW strike.

One layout change implemented in April 1985, however, already had made a considerable impact. Gordon's process engineering group, formerly one-half mile from the shop floor, was now located right in the middle of the machining area. According to Andy Edberg, division head of process engineering, "The effect has been tremendous. The output of our process engineers has tripled, and communication between them and the operators has improved enormously."

### Future of ABC

Useful as it was, ABC's impact was still limited. First, it was run on a personal computer and not integrated with the other division data bases; and second, it was being applied only to turning machine operations.

Extending ABC to secondary operations was Sinclair's top ABC priority: "If we are to price the whole business, we need to extend the model to secondary operations." While the model costed machine operations for parts that would eventually be assembled into major parts such as drive trains, the old standard cost system was still being used for inventory valuation and for costing major parts. Stevenson noted:

> We don't want parallel systems; their development and maintenance is too costly. We would like to get rid of the standard system and have just one system—ABC.

# 6

# Cost-Based Decision Making

There are three important managerial uses of cost information. To:

1. Understand costs so as to determine whether to make or abandon a product and to influence the nature of customer relationships
2. Develop a cost basis for a price (as in cost-based transfer pricing or for a contract that calls for a cost-based price)
3. Identify opportunities for, or the need to, improve product or process design and process operation

This chapter considers the last use of cost information.

Exhibit 6-1 provides a useful way to think of the opportunities and perspectives that costs provide for product and process design and improvement and provides an outline for the discussion in this chapter. Exhibit 6-1 describes a time line from the initial planning for the product to its eventual removal from the market. There are three broad phases in a product's life cycle: the planning phase, the manufacturing phase, and the service and abandonment phase. **Life cycle costing** is used predominately in the planning phase. It attempts to estimate the product's cost over its lifetime. **Target costing** is used during the planning cycle and drives the process of choosing product and process designs that will result in a product that can be produced at a cost that will allow an acceptable level of profit, given the product's estimated market price, selling volume, and target functionality.[1] **Kaizen costing** focuses on identifying opportunities for cost improvement during the manufacturing cycle. Each costing method has a distinctive perspective and unique use, which we will now discuss.

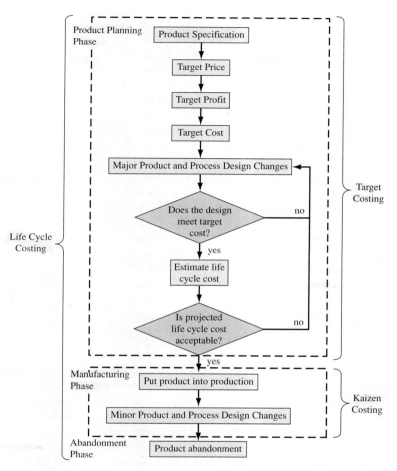

**EXHIBIT 6-1**  Costing Tools for Decision Making

## ⚡ TARGET COSTING

A widely accepted rule is that 80% of a product's costs are committed, or locked in, during the product design stage.[2] During this time, planners choose the product design and design the process that the organization will use to make the product. Although the pattern will vary among products, Exhibit 6-2 summarizes the typical pattern of cost commitment and cost incidence during a product's three phases.

    As Exhibit 6-2 implies, effective cost control is exercised during the product's planning and design phase not when the product and process have already been designed and the product is being made. During the product manufacturing phase, most of the product costs have been committed and the focus is cost containment. This understanding of the pattern of costs has led to interest in controlling costs during the product's planning phase.

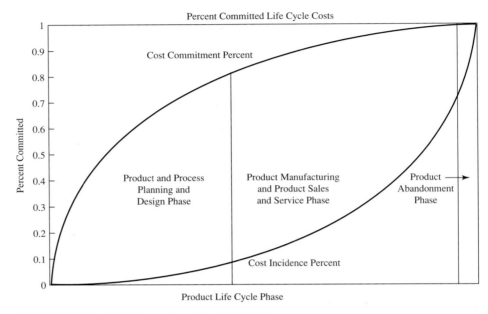

**EXHIBIT 6-2** Cost Commitment versus Incidence

Target costing is a cost management tool that planners use during product and process design to drive improvement efforts aimed at reducing the product's future manufacturing costs. Above all, target costing is a tool that promotes and facilitates communication among the members of the cross-functional team that is responsible for product design. Target costing is customer-oriented; it begins with price, quality, and functionality requirements defined by customers. For this reason, observers call target costing price-led costing in contrast to conventional cost plus approaches to pricing, which they call cost-led pricing.

## Customer Orientation

As suggested in Exhibit 6-1, target costing begins with an estimate of the product's price, which reflects the product's functions and attributes and competitive forces in the marketplace. One approach that planners have used to describe customer requirements is the notion of value, which is the ratio of functionality to the price paid by the customer. Organizations increase customer value by increasing the product's functionality while holding the price constant or by reducing the price while holding functionality constant.

Any given product may have many elements of functionality, with each function commanding an additional premium over the basic product price. The input to the target costing process is a market price-product functionality vector to which the product's planning process must conform. That is, the target price reflects a set of product functions that the product must deliver to the customer. There are two critical elements here. First, the customer, or more generally the market, defines the price that will be paid for the product and its designated functions. Second, to the extent that there is a market for the same product with different functions, for example an automobile with different options, the organization can choose which product functions to supply, but the market or consumer will choose a price that reflects the set of product functions supplied.

## The Target Costing Process

Once the product price-functionality-quality targets have been set, planners then subtract a target profit from the target selling price. This target profit is the contribution that the product is expected to make toward the organization's business-sustaining costs. The residual is the target cost, which is the focus of, and the driving force behind, the product and process design efforts. As shown in Exhibit 6-1, the target costing process is iterative and continues until the design team finds a product design with a projected cost that meets the target cost.

A major strength of target costing is that it is embedded in a team environment. The team members include representatives from design, process engineering, purchasing, manufacturing, and marketing—a cross-functional process called **concurrent design**. With concurrent design all the members of the design team are focused on the same objective: to deliver a product with the target functionality, quality, and price to a specific market segment. In this environment, there is no room for individual groups to specify product features that reflect a functional fixation. For example, design engineers are notorious for designing into products features that customers do not value but that increase cost.[3] Customers will not pay for functions they do not value. Therefore an important consideration during the product design process is to eliminate product functions or features that add cost but provide no market price increment because they provide no value to the customer.

Another strength is that target costing is deployed at a time, the product and process design phase, when design choices can have a maximum impact on a product's cost. For example, without the discipline of a team approach to product design, an engineering group might design a production process that uses the latest production technology without regard for its effects on cost or manufacturability—which is what happened to General Motors in the 1980s when it built its automated guided vehicle assembly plants. Operating on its own, a marketing group might specify many product features that customers would like to have but do not consider essential in the product and therefore would not be willing to pay to have included in the product design.

Some organizations, such as Chrysler, include representatives from their suppliers on the design team. Chrysler involves its suppliers through its **SCORE** (Supplier Cost Reduction Effort) program.[4] This program includes suppliers as active members of the product design teams to elicit their expertise. This approach requires a sharing of ideas and information—a relationship requiring trust that, in turn, takes time to develop.

The paybacks for suppliers are long-term contracts, a negotiated return on the investment they make in product design and manufacturing, and participation in the cost savings that they generate. The goal is to reduce product costs but not by squeezing the suppliers. Rather the approach is to use lower-cost commodity components rather than custom-designed components and to reduce production costs by implementing process improvements. For example, Magna, a Chrysler supplier, recommended an exterior molding that cost less while offering the same functionality as what Chrysler was using.[5] Owens Corning described one of the suggestions that it made to Ford Motor Company:

> In the award-winning Ford Taurus radiator support, Owens Corning glass fibers enabled a composite material to replace metal, yet support the weight of several radiator components. The design flexibility and structural integrity available with composites enabled Ford to consolidate what formerly required 23 separate parts into a two-piece modular assembly. (Owens Corning, 1996 Annual Report, p. 6)

This model of suppliers' reducing costs by designing components that provide the same functionality at lower cost or by improving existing processes is the model suggested by the Japanese *keiretsu* and South Korean *chaebols*, which are affiliations of companies interrelated by supplier-purchaser relationships. Although this approach seems promising and interesting, there is some evidence that it does not always work. Recently, several large and important Japanese keiretsu were disbanded because evidence suggested that the protected suppliers had become inefficient and noncompetitive. Chrysler is trying to avoid this situation through provisions that allow it to drop poorly performing suppliers when performance is based on cost savings resulting either from design proposals or from manufacturing process improvements, quality, and on-time delivery.

Suppliers often can offer suggestions, such as modest design changes, so that a product design will include a standard component or part, rather than a custom-designed part, that will reduce the product's target cost and increase its quality.[6] Alternatively, suppliers can offer their expertise when new components or parts are required so that, for a given level of functionality, the part can be supplied at the lowest cost.[7]

A major strength of involving different functional areas concurrently in the product and process design is that it reduces product development time and cost by reducing required design changes. A second, and related strength, is that each subgroup within the team (e.g., purchasing, design, engineering) is assigned cost reduction targets that it is expected to meet in order to achieve the team's overall target cost objective. This approach has the effect of assigning individual responsibilities but within an overall structure of group objectives relating to product quality, functionality, and price.

The concept of target costing is simple to state and hard to accomplish. The idea is that the team will continue its product and process design efforts until it finds designs that yield an expected cost that is equal to, or below, the target cost. Design teams are not allowed to reduce planned costs by eliminating desirable product functions or features. Design teams reduce costs by improving product or process design to deliver a product while still delivering a product that meets the target level of functionality.

Recall that the design team is working toward a target cost that reflects a product's set of functions. Occasionally design teams encounter situations in which the cost of adding a function exceeds the price increment that the customer is willing to pay for that function. At this point, the design team must decide whether each function must cover its incremental costs or whether the excess of customer value over cost for some functions will subsidize the excess of cost over customer value for other functions.[8] In general, this choice will reflect strategic and product evolution considerations.

The target costing idea reflects the reality that most product and process design decisions are not the lowest-cost designs but rather designs that the organization has decided it can live with. This is the notion of satisficing: We use solutions that are good enough, not necessarily the best solutions. Target costing takes the organization beyond the effort levels usually chosen in satisficing operations and drives the planning activity toward the target cost.

Target costing places huge pressures on the design team. The design team has a common objective: to meet target cost. There is no possibility of renegotiation in target costing; the product will not be launched unless the team meets the target cost, which ultimately reflects what the customer demands and what the suppliers of capital expect as a reasonable return on their investment. Therefore, there is pressure on design teams to develop and use tools that can help them reach their target cost objectives. The major tools planners use in target costing are tear-down analysis, value engineering, and reengineering.

## Target Costing in Action: Toyota Motors[9]

Toyota Motors seems to have invented the process of target costing during the 1960s. At Toyota, the target costing process begins when the marketing group specifies the target price. The market value of additional functions added to existing vehicles determines the increment of the price of the new model over the existing model. Planners then multiply this price by the estimated production volume over the product's life cycle to determine the total product revenue.

The next step is to estimate the costs of the new product. These costs are estimated by adding to the cost base of the existing product the incremental costs of the design changes associated with the new product. The design team then compares revenues and costs to compute an estimated margin. A margin that fails to achieve the target return on costs needed to provide an appropriate return on investment triggers a redesign process.

This redesign process begins by computing the required cost reduction. The leader of the design team then distributes this target cost reduction among the members of the design team.[10] For example, the assembly division may have estimated an increase in assembly costs on the basis of an increase in the number of parts in the new vehicle. The assembly division would be asked to identify ways that the assembly process could be redesigned so that the expected cost increment would be reduced. Another possibility would be for the assembly group to negotiate with the design engineers to reduce the number of parts by increasing the number of preassembled modules or components used in the vehicle. This is where the insights provided by people experienced in making the product, working with other members of the design team, can result in considerable cost savings.[11] This process of finding improvements in existing production practices or in altering the design of the product so as to deliver the same functionality at a lower cost continues until the design team achieves its target cost.

## Tear-Down Analysis

Tear-down analysis, or reverse engineering, is a process of evaluating a competitor's product to identify opportunities for product improvement. In tear-down analysis, the competitor's product is taken apart piece by piece to identify the product's functionality and design and to make inferences about the process that made the product. Tear-down analysis provides insights into the cost of the product and suggests the relative advantages or disadvantages of the competitor's approach to product design. The major element of tear-down analysis is **benchmarking**, which involves comparing the tentative product design with the designs of competitors.

## Quality Function Deployment

Quality function deployment (QFD) is a management tool originally developed during the 1970s in Japan's Kobe shipyards. Quality function deployment provides a structure to identify customer requirements, a key input into the target costing process. Organizations use QFD to identify what customers want from a product before the product design is undertaken. The process then compares what the customer wants with how the design team proposes to satisfy those requirements. As such, QFD supports the process of value engineering, a critical element in the target costing process.

## Value Engineering

**Value engineering**, also known as value analysis, is a systematic, usually team-based, approach to evaluating a product's design in order to identify alternatives that will improve the product's value—defined as the ratio of functionality to cost. Therefore, there are two ways to improve value: Hold functionality constant and reduce cost, or hold cost constant and increase functionality. Value engineering looks at all of the product's elements, including the raw materials, the manufacturing process, the type of labor and equipment used, and the balance between purchased and self-manufactured components.

Value engineering achieves its assigned target cost in two ways: (1) by identifying improved product designs (or even new products that may meet functionality in different ways) that reduce component and manufacturing cost while not sacrificing functionality[12] and (2) by eliminating unnecessary functions that increase the product's cost and complexity.[13]

The process of value engineering begins with a detailed specification of the product's functions, an activity often called **functional analysis**.[14] This is the heart of the value engineering approach and results in a detailed specification, usually in the form of a diagram called a function analysis systems technique (**FAST**) diagram, that specifies the product's major functions. By focusing on the product's functions, the design team will often consider components that perform the same function in other products, thereby increasing the possibility of using standard components, which often leads to increased quality and lower costs. At the same time, developing a specific statement of product functions allows the design team to compare the cost of the functions of the product it is building with what customers are willing to pay for each function.

The design team then considers how existing products achieve those functions and then evaluates new ways of achieving those functions and the cost of each of the alternatives. The alternatives are then rated, and, if possible, the best elements are taken from each of the alternatives to develop the proposed product design.

Some companies belonging to the Siemens group have carried functional analysis one level further. These companies use functional analysis to specify the functions of each of a product's components. Then, planners identify what customers are willing to pay for each function and what each function costs. Because this process is driven by values that customers place on functions, of particular interest are situations in which the cost of a component's function is higher than the value placed on that function by customers. This process often identifies component functions that are not wanted or valued by customers and are there solely to serve engineering objectives.

## Reengineering

The tear-down and value-engineering approaches focus mainly on the product design. Another critical element in determining the cost of a product is the process that the organization uses to make the product. In fact, the target costing team will consider both product and process design simultaneously since the product's cost and quality will be jointly affected by the product and process design. Reengineering is the activity of redesigning a planned or existing process, and it is driven by the desire to improve a product's cost and quality attributes.[15]

## ¥  KAIZEN COSTING

Once planners have fixed and implemented the product and process designs, interest turns to operating the process in the most efficient way—an activity driven by **kaizen costing**.[16] Kaizen costing focuses the organization's attention on things that managers or operators of an existing system can do to reduce costs. Therefore, unlike target costing, which planners use before the product is in production, operations personnel use kaizen costing when the product is in production. However, target and kaizen costing are similar in that targets drive them. Whereas target costing is driven by customer considerations, kaizen costing is driven by periodic profitability targets set internally by senior management.

The focus of the cost reduction efforts driven by kaizen costing is incremental improvements to the current production process or product design. These improvements take the form of developing improved setup processes, improving machine performance to reduce waste, and increasing employee training and motivation to encourage employees to identify and implement the incremental daily changes that can improve cost and quality performance. In short, the focus in kaizen costing is the process and not the product itself.

Organizations attack continuous improvement in different ways, and the kaizen costing system will reflect the cost reduction strategy. For example, Olympus Optical Company implemented a kaizen costing system with four components: production costs, costs of defects, capacity use costs, and overhead expenses. Each subsystem gathered and reported costs that directed attention to areas for improvement.[17]

Some observers have criticized both target and kaizen costing on the grounds that they often place huge stress on employees. Some organizations have responded to this charge and to the effect of using target and kaizen costing techniques by lowering their performance expectations. However, by their nature, which focuses on motivating intense effort at reducing costs, these measures are stressful.

Operational **activity-based management** drives the process of reengineering. Analysts map out the steps or activities in an existing or proposed process—an activity called **process mapping**, or **flowcharting**. Planners then look for opportunities to reduce cost by eliminating factors that cause delay or waste in the planned process design. Activities that consume resources without adding functionality to the product that the *customer* values are called nonvalue-added activities. Nonvalue-added activities reflect things that the organization does because of poor design or poor planning rather than what is inherently required to make the product. Moving, storing, and inspecting are all activities that cause delay or waste in the manufacturing process while consuming resources. A product or process redesign that eliminates the need for non-value-added activities will reduce costs and cycle time and often will increase product quality. The steps in operational activity-based management include:

1. Chart the process to identify each activity.
2. Identify the cost of each activity.
3. Identify opportunities for improvement (reengineering to eliminate the need for non-value-added activities and continuous improvement to improve the performance of value-added activities).
4. Set priorities for improvement. (Usually, improvement efforts are ordered by value added; that is, they attack the non-value-added activity with the greatest difference between cost added and cost to eliminate or the value-added activity that has the highest cost.)
5. Provide the financial justification (business plan) for the reengineering efforts.
6. Identify what needs to be done to eliminate or otherwise reduce the activity's cost.
7. Make the required changes.
8. Track the benefits to compare them with the costs.

## TARGET COSTING: A COMPREHENSIVE EXAMPLE

The Power Division supplies engines to the seven assembly divisions at Giant Motors, which, over its lifetime of 80 years, evolved from an automobile assembler that purchased all its components to a fully integrated automobile manufacturer. Reflecting its history of evolution through buying existing components manufacturers, Giant Motors had always been operated on a profit center basis in order to compute divisional profits that were intended to approximate what the individual divisions would report as independent operating units.

Recently, the assembly division managers had expressed dissatisfaction with the current arrangement. They argued that the internal component suppliers, who had a protected status, had become lazy and inefficient. The assembly division managers argued that they should be allowed to source their components externally.

After many years of disputes between management and the board of directors and the union, Giant Motors decided that, for any new engines, it would immediately allow the assembly division managers to source components from whatever supplier they preferred. External suppliers were given the blueprints for existing engines and told that they could compete to supply existing engines starting in two years. The managers of the component divisions were put on notice that any division not showing the potential for adequate profitability would be liquidated.

It was with this in mind that Roberta Ward, the manager of the engine division, ordered a review of Engine Division's operations. A study group, comprising division employees and a consultant, prepared a report that suggested that the Engine Division's costs were about 25% higher than the costs of organizations producing comparable engines. With this information, Ward immediately instructed her senior managers to implement a process of target costing that she believed would focus the division on cost reduction efforts. Ward's objective was to better any market price offered by any competitor.

A study and interviews with customers, including automobile assembly divisions inside and outside the company, concluded that there were four important engine requirements: power, fuel consumption, weight, and noise level. Costs increased with designs that increased engine power and quietness, and, in general, costs decreased as fuel consumption and weight increased. In addition, there were complex interactions between the four engine characteristics.

Based on a study of the existing cost structure, Ward and her staff decided that the division would reduce product line complexity and therefore costs by offering three new engines that were adaptations of existing engines. Each engine offered a unique mix of the power, fuel consumption, weight, and quietness features. These basic engines could be modified to meet the demands of individual customers. The following table provides the details for each of the three engines.[18]

|  | ENGINE 1 | ENGINE 2 | ENGINE 3 |
|---|---|---|---|
| Projected lifetime volume | 850,000 | 2,200,000 | 1,500,000 |
| Target average selling price | $7,500 | $4,500 | $6,000 |
| Target average margin | $1,100 | $ 800 | $1,000 |
| Target cost | $6,400 | $3,700 | $5,000 |
| Raw materials cost | $2,500 | $1,800 | $2,300 |
| Purchased components | 2,200 | 1,400 | 1,200 |
| Indirect costs | $3,317 | $1,649 | $2,699 |
| Projected cost | $8,017 | $4,849 | $6,199 |

The excess of projected cost over the target cost motivated an intense target costing exercise. The first step of this target costing exercise was to identify the nature of the indirect costs for each engine. An analysis provided the indirect cost details reported in the following tables.

## Unit-Related Indirect Costs

|  |  |  | DRIVER UNITS | | |
|---|---|---|---|---|---|
| COST ITEM | DRIVER | DRIVER COST | ENGINE 1 | ENGINE 2 | ENGINE 3 |
| Assembly | Assembly hours | $35 | 7 | 3 | 5 |
| Quality assurance | Inspection hours | $42 | 2 | 1 | 2 |
| Rework | Labor hours | $35 | 3 | 1 | 3 |
| Materials handling | Helper hours | $28 | 5 | 2 | 4 |

## Batch-Related Indirect Costs

|  |  |  | DRIVER UNITS | | |
|---|---|---|---|---|---|
| COST ITEM | DRIVER | DRIVER COST | ENGINE 1 | ENGINE 2 | ENGINE 3 |
| Moving | Number of moves | $ 50 | 7 | 5 | 4 |
| Setup | Setup hours | $250 | 8 | 4 | 7 |

### Product-Related Indirect Costs

|  | ENGINE 1 | | ENGINE 2 | | ENGINE 3 | |
|---|---|---|---|---|---|---|
| COST ITEM | TOTAL COST | COST/ UNIT | TOTAL COST | COST/ UNIT | TOTAL COST | COST/ UNIT |
| Engineering | $80 million | $94 | $45 million | $20 | $55 million | $37 |
| Supervisory | $ 8 million | $ 9 | $ 8 million | $ 4 | $ 8 million | $ 5 |

### Facility-Sustaining Indirect Costs

|  |  |  | DRIVER UNITS | | |
|---|---|---|---|---|---|
| COST ITEM | DRIVER | DRIVER COST | ENGINE 1 | ENGINE 2 | ENGINE 3 |
| General administrative | Labor hours | $  18 | 17 | 7 | 14 |
| General overhead | Materials costs | $0.02 | $2,500 | $1,800 | $2,300 |

The cost per unit for product-related costs was computed by dividing total budgeted costs by the projected volume of sales over the product's life. The driver cost for facility-sustaining costs was estimated by dividing Giant Motors' total cost deemed to be capacity by the estimated practical capacity, stated in cost driver units. The implication of this calculation was that as volume changes, in the long run, capacity, and therefore these facility-sustaining costs, will adjust accordingly.

The cost estimates produced the following unit budget calculations.[19]

|  | ENGINE 1 | ENGINE 2 | ENGINE 3 |
|---|---|---|---|
| Lifetime volume | 850,000 | 2,200,000 | 1,500,000 |
| Price | $7,500 | $4,500 | $6,000 |
| Materials Cost |  |  |  |
| Raw materials cost | 2,500 | 1,800 | 2,300 |
| Components cost | 2,200 | 1,400 | 1,200 |
| Unit-Related Costs |  |  |  |
| Assembly | 245 | 105 | 175 |
| Quality assurance | 84 | 42 | 84 |
| Rework | 105 | 35 | 105 |
| Materials handling | 140 | 56 | 112 |
| Batch-Related Costs |  |  |  |
| Moving | 350 | 250 | 200 |
| Setup | 2,000 | 1,000 | 1,750 |
| Product-Related Costs |  |  |  |
| Engineering | 94 | 20 | 37 |
| Supervisory | 9 | 4 | 5 |

*continued*

|  | ENGINE 1 | ENGINE 2 | ENGINE 3 |
|---|---|---|---|
| Facility-Sustaining Costs |  |  |  |
| General administrative | 306 | 126 | 252 |
| General overhead | 50 | 36 | 46 |
| Total projected costs | $8,017 | $4,849 | $6,199 |
| Projected profit | −517 | −349 | −199 |
| Target profit | 1,100 | 800 | 1,000 |
| Excess of projected profit over target | −$1,617 | −$1,149 | −$1,199 |

## Value Engineering

Suppose, in response to the need to reduce projected costs, that the Engine Division puts together a project team to undertake a target costing exercise relating to the three engines. As a first step, the team undertakes a value-engineering exercise. The team purchases engines from competitors and dismantles the engines to develop alternative engine design ideas. In addition, the team works with design engineers to identify new designs that will accomplish the same functions with a lower cost and to eliminate unneeded functions. The value-engineering activity results in the changes shown in the following table.

| CHANGED ITEM | ENGINE 1 | ENGINE 2 | ENGINE 3 |
|---|---|---|---|
| Raw materials costs | $2,400 | $1,600 | $2,200 |
| Purchased components costs | $2,100 | $1,300 | $1,000 |
| Assembly hours | 6 | 2 | 4 |
| Rework hours | 2 | No change | 2 |

These changes result in the following cost projections.

|  | ENGINE 1 | ENGINE 2 | ENGINE 3 |
|---|---|---|---|
| Lifetime volume | 850,000 | 2,200,000 | 1,500,000 |
| Price | $7,500 | $4,500 | $6,000 |
| Materials Cost |  |  |  |
| Raw materials cost | 2,400 | 1,600 | 2,200 |
| Components cost | 2,100 | 1,300 | 1,000 |
| Unit-Related Costs |  |  |  |
| Assembly | 210 | 70 | 140 |
| Quality assurance | 84 | 42 | 84 |
| Rework | 70 | 35 | 70 |
| Materials handling | 140 | 56 | 112 |

*continued*

|  | ENGINE 1 | ENGINE 2 | ENGINE 3 |
|---|---|---|---|
| Batch-Related Costs |  |  |  |
|   Moving | 350 | 250 | 200 |
|   Setup | 2,000 | 1,000 | 1,750 |
| Product-Related Costs |  |  |  |
|   Engineering | 94 | 20 | 37 |
|   Supervisory | 9 | 4 | 5 |
| Facility-Sustaining Costs |  |  |  |
|   General administrative | 270 | 108 | 216 |
|   General overhead | 48 | 32 | 44 |
| Total projected costs | $7,709 | $4,492 | $5,791 |
| Projected profit | −209 | 8 | 209 |
| Target profit | 1,100 | 800 | 1,000 |
| Excess of projected profit over target | −$1,309 | −$792 | −$791 |

## Functional Analysis

Next, the design team evaluates the power, fuel consumption, weight, and quietness levels for each of the three engines. The team interviews customers to identify situations in which a change in any of these elements, up or down, will increase (or decrease) costs less (or more) than the corresponding increase (decrease) in the price that the customer is willing to pay. Suppose that this process results in the following changes in each of these functions for the three engines.

Based on the function changes, the prices of engine 1, 2, and 3 become $7,200, $4,800, and $6,300, respectively; the raw materials costs become $2,200, $1,700, and $2,400; the assembly hours become 4, 3, and 5; the materials handling hours become 5, 3, and 4; and the engineering costs become $70,000,000, $50,000,000, and $62,000,000. These changes result in the following cost projections:

|  | ENGINE 1 | ENGINE 2 | ENGINE 3 |
|---|---|---|---|
| Lifetime volume | 850,000 | 2,200,000 | 1,500,000 |
| Price | $7,200 | $4,800 | $6,300 |
| Materials Cost |  |  |  |
|   Raw materials cost | 2,200 | 1,700 | 2,400 |
|   Components cost | 2,100 | 1,300 | 1,000 |
| Unit-Related Costs |  |  |  |
|   Assembly | 140 | 105 | 175 |
|   Quality assurance | 84 | 42 | 84 |
|   Rework | 70 | 35 | 70 |
|   Materials handling | 140 | 84 | 112 |
| Batch-Related Costs |  |  |  |
|   Moving | 350 | 250 | 200 |
|   Setup | 2,000 | 1,000 | 1,750 |
| Product-Related Costs |  |  |  |
|   Engineering | 82 | 23 | 41 |
|   Supervisory | 9 | 4 | 5 |

*continued*

|                                        | ENGINE 1 | ENGINE 2 | ENGINE 3 |
|----------------------------------------|----------|----------|----------|
| Facility-Sustaining Costs              |          |          |          |
| General administrative                 | 234      | 144      | 234      |
| General overhead                       | 44       | 34       | 48       |
| Total projected costs                  | $7,387   | $4,695   | $6,053   |
| Projected profit                       | −187     | 105      | 247      |
| Target profit                          | 1,100    | 800      | 1,000    |
| Excess of projected profit over target | −$1,287  | −$695    | −$753    |

## Reengineering

With these changes in mind, the design team proceeded to the process design, which involved considering changes to the current process the Engine Division was using to make motors. This process was the basis for the cost projections for the new motors. The design team focused specifically on the production process and on identifying new ways to design the sequencing and assembly of engines. In conjunction with suppliers, the team developed a just-in-time manufacturing process and reorganized the production lines from a batch-oriented system that involved moving assembly components in different parts of the plant to a continuous flow system that used manufacturing cells. These changes were directed particularly at eliminating non-value-added activities in the assembly process but also considered efficiencies in value-added activities. These process design changes resulted in the following activity changes. For engines 1, 2, and 3, respectively:

1. Assembly hours became 3, 2, and 4.
2. Inspection hours became 1, 1, and 2.
3. Rework hours became 1, 1, and 1.
4. Materials handling hours became 3, 2, and 2.
5. The number of moves became 4, 2, and 2.
6. Setup hours became 4, 2, and 5.
7. Engineering costs, which included the cost of process redesign, became $115,000,000, $80,000,000, and $95,000,000.

These changes resulted in the following cost projections:

|                     | ENGINE 1 | ENGINE 2  | ENGINE 3  |
|---------------------|----------|-----------|-----------|
| Lifetime volume     | 850,000  | 2,200,000 | 1,500,000 |
| Price               | $7,200   | $4,800    | $6,300    |
| Materials Cost      |          |           |           |
| Raw materials cost  | 2,200    | 1,700     | 2,400     |
| Components cost      | 2,100    | 1,300     | 1,000     |
| Unit-Related Costs  |          |           |           |
| Assembly            | 105      | 70        | 140       |
| Quality assurance   | 42       | 42        | 84        |
| Rework              | 35       | 35        | 35        |
| Materials handling  | 84       | 56        | 56        |

*continued*

|  | ENGINE 1 | ENGINE 2 | ENGINE 3 |
|---|---|---|---|
| Batch-Related Costs |  |  |  |
| Moving | 200 | 100 | 100 |
| Setup | 1,000 | 500 | 1,250 |
| Product-Related Costs |  |  |  |
| Engineering | 135 | 36 | 63 |
| Supervisory | 9 | 4 | 5 |
| Facility-Sustaining Costs |  |  |  |
| General administrative | 144 | 108 | 162 |
| General overhead | 44 | 34 | 48 |
| Total projected costs | $6,074 | $3,960 | $5,277 |
| Projected profit | 1,126 | 840 | 1,023 |
| Target profit | 1,100 | 800 | 1,000 |
| Excess of projected profit over target | $26 | $40 | $23 |

At this point, the process concluded because the projected cost was less than the target cost.

## LIFE CYCLE COSTING

Life cycle costing is the process of estimating and accumulating costs over a product's entire life. Life cycle costing is particularly important in environments in which there are large planning and development costs (for example, developing a new jetliner) or large product abandonment costs (for example, decommissioning a nuclear generating facility).

There are three broad purposes of life cycle costing. First, life cycle costing helps to develop a sense of the total costs associated with a product in order to identify whether the profits earned during the active, manufacturing, phase will cover the costs in the development and decommissioning phases. Life cycle costing often will identify products that are no longer profitable when their decommissioning costs are factored into the product evaluation process. Second, because of its comprehensive consideration of costs, life cycle costing will identify a product's environmental cost consequences and will spur action to reduce or eliminate those costs. Third, life cycle costing helps to identify the planning and decommissioning costs during the product and process design phase in order to control and manage costs in that phase. For example, several design or process alternatives may promise the same product cost for a given level of product quality and functionality. However, one of the product or process designs may offer clear advantages when the costs of development and decommissioning are considered. In general, life cycle costing provides a comprehensive accounting of a product's costs, both manufacturing and environmental, from cradle to grave to help decision makers understand the cost consequences of making that product and to identify areas in which cost reduction efforts are both desirable and effective.

## OTHER COSTING TOOLS

### Quality Cost

Over the years, organizations have developed many approaches to monitor and control the cost of quality. One of the most popular recognizes four types of quality costs:

1. The costs of *preventing* quality problems. Examples include the cost of designing improved processes that reduce quality failures, employee training, and supplier training.
2. The costs of *finding* quality problems. Examples include the cost of the equipment and personnel who perform quality checks on work in process.
3. The costs of *fixing* quality problems that are found when the product is still in the manufacturer's hands. Examples are the cost, both out of pocket and opportunity, of personnel, materials, and machine time that are used to rework the product into a saleable condition.
4. The costs of *fixing* quality problems that are found when the product is in the hands of the consumer. Examples are warranty-related costs, the profits on sales lost when the organization's image is damaged by quality problems, and the costs of lawsuits prompted by product failures.

The idea in quality costing is to manage the total cost of quality, which is usually expressed as a percentage of sales, in order to provide a shifting standard as sales levels rise or fall. The strategy is to invest in preventing and finding quality problems as long as the cost incurred is less than the costs of fixing quality problems that would otherwise occur.

### Taguchi Cost

A variation of quality costing is Taguchi cost, which was proposed by a Japanese academic. Conventional approaches to computing quality cost begin by classifying output as conforming or nonconforming. Conforming output is deemed to create no quality cost, whereas all nonconforming output is deemed to create equal quality cost.[20]

Taguchi's observation was that output failing to meet the target value of the characteristic creates quality losses and that quality losses increase quadratically with the deviation from the target characteristic. That is, if a machine is supposed to mill bolts to 2 centimeters, a machine that consistently mills bolts to 1.8 centimeters with virtually no variance will create fewer quality problems than a machine that produces bolts with an average of 2.0 centimeters but with a variance of 4 millimeters.

Taguchi proposed three types of quality loss functions:

1. When any deviations from the target are undesirable, the quality loss function can be written as

$$L(y) = k(y - T)^2$$

Where $k$ is a parameter that reflects customer and process characteristics, $y$ is the actual value of the output characteristic, and $T$ is the target value.

2. When the objective is to make the process characteristic as small as possible, as in the case of contaminants in a piece of steel, the loss function can be written as

$$L(y) = k(y)^2$$

3. When the objective is to make the process characteristic as large as possible, as in the case of the reliability of a safety device, the loss function can be written as

$$L(y) = k(1/y)^2$$

The basis for Taguchi's hypothesis was observations of manufacturing environments. Therefore, Taguchi costing aims at one of three possible goals:

1. Reduce the variability of a process by identifying the factors that create variability in the process
2. Adjust the process mean so that it moves closer to the desired target
3. Reduce the variability and adjust the process mean toward its target

## ENVIRONMENTAL, SALVAGE, AND DISPOSAL COSTS

Organizations have experienced a rapid rise in environmental costs. It is normal for organizations in the chemical industry to spend in excess of $1 billion annually on environmental costs. The sheer magnitude of these expenditures has forced organizations to think systematically about controlling these costs. Emphasis has changed from accepting environmental costs as an inevitable part of doing business to a business-related cost that, with appropriate management, can be reduced. As part of this process of managing environmental costs, organizations are beginning to develop detailed cost records that attribute environmental costs to activities and ultimately to products in order to identify the processes and products that create these environmental costs. Armed with this knowledge, organizations are taking steps to reduce or eliminate the drivers of environmental costs. Many organizations base part of incentive compensation on steps employees have taken to reduce environmental costs. For example, they may provide for bonuses based on measures of environmental performance that include elements such as the level of waste discharged.

Organizations face environmentally related costs during and after the product manufacturing phase. The cost of waste disposal is the most common environmental cost organizations incur during a product's manufacturing stage. Many organizations face significant costs in winding up projects or products. These costs are part of the product's life cycle, or cradle-to-grave, costs. There are two components of these winding-up costs: costs related to shutting down or decommissioning the manufacturing facility[21] (for example, shutting down a mine or a nuclear reactor) and the costs of disposing of products, which have come to be called take-back costs.[22] The effects of recognizing and accounting for environmental costs are to:

1. Provide an accurate picture of product profitability (currently most organizations simply charge these costs to corporate overhead thus obscuring both the nature and source of these costs)
2. Focus attention on developing products that have lower decommissioning and take-back costs (by identifying the magnitude of these costs)
3. Increase efforts to recycle or otherwise remanufacture existing product waste

## CONCLUSION

Costs play many roles in organizations, but the most important is to inform and guide product-related decision making. Life cycle costing is an approach to costing that attempts to determine a product's cost over its entire life cycle including the design stage (the domain of target costing), the manufacturing stage (the domain of kaizen costing), and the postmanufacturing stage (the domain of take-back costing and costing systems that compute the cost of decommissioning manufacturing systems).

Target costing is a tool that organizations use to focus attention on, and to manage the process of, product and process design. Because most of the opportunities to improve cost performance are at the design stage, target costing is a particularly important tool in the organization's attempt to improve its profitability. The objective of target costing is to achieve a product and process design that allows the company to meet a profit target at a price customers are willing to pay.

Kaizen costing focuses on improving an existing process. The role of kaizen costing is to direct the continuous improvement of process cost performance.

Finally, organizations are developing costing systems to identify the costs of decommissioning production systems and recovering their products from customers.

The importance of target costing is that it provides a management tool that coordinates and focuses attention on the process of cost reduction. The importance of kaizen costing is that it focuses attention on the activity of improving the efficiency of existing production systems. Finally, the importance of emerging systems designed to compute product abandonment costs are that the costs that are identified will spur management efforts to design products with lower abandonment costs and also to manage the abandonment process more efficiently.

## ENDNOTES

1. Although organizations have used target costing in some form since at least the early 1960s, the period since 1990 has seen an explosion in the articles and texts on target costing. Readers interested in a detailed treatment that includes design and implementation issues should consult S. L. Ansari, J. E. Bell, Irwin Professional Publishing, and CAM-I Target Cost Core Group, *Target Costing: The Next Frontier in Strategic Cost Management* (Burr Ridge, IL: Irwin Professional Publishing, 1997), Chapter 11 of the CAM-I book provides a detailed and interesting illustration of target costing in a hypothetical firm. Another useful reference is R. Cooper and R. Slagmulder, *Confrontational Cost Management, Volume 1: Target Costing and Value Engineering* (Portland, OR: Productivity Press, 1997).

2. See, for example, CAM-I/CMS, *Cost Management for Today's Advanced Manufacturing Systems* (Arlington, TX: CAM-I/CMS, 1991).

3. Historically, Hewlett-Packard frequently designed features into its printers that reflected engineering considerations that customers did not value. When Hewlett-Packard began to design printers that reflected customer requirements, printer costs declined dramatically as features the customers found irrelevant were designed out of the printers. Mercedes Benz automobiles are another example of a product that many automobile industry observers claim are overengineered. Organizations that can set a market price based on realized cost plus a markup, the antithesis of target costing, are becoming rare with the advent of global competition.

4. For a description of Chrysler's SCORE program see J. H. Dyer, "How Chrysler Created an American Keiretsu," *Harvard Business Review* (July–August 1996), p. 42.

5. This example reflects what happens when designers operate without knowledge of what customers value or what product functions cost. For example, the supplier of carpets that Ford uses in its car trucks pointed out that the proliferation of carpet types and colors was creating additional costs without providing a product funtionality that customers wanted or valued. By moving to a single carpet type and color, Ford was promised a savings on carpet materials of more than 5%. Because the cost of purchased components amounts to about 80% of the cost of the automobile, effective supplier relationships are critical for automobile assemblers. The

critical nature of supplier relationships may explain why competitive bids are not used for most parts sourcing in the automobile assembly industry.

6. This perspective is illustrated in the following observation. "Instead of having company engineers provide potential suppliers with detailed designs for a piece of equipment, most steelmakers today issue functional specifications. The functional specs define the equipment needs in terms of the steelmaker's business objectives. . . . Equipment suppliers can propose several ways to meet the goal. This reduces engineering costs and lets the steelmaker take full advantage of the suppliers' expertise." J. Schriefer, "Completing Mill-Construction Projects Faster and Smarter," *Iron Age New Steel* 12, no. 7 (July 1996), pp. 46–52. The idea is to make parts more manufacturable, with higher quality and lower costs, by involving the supplier in part design.

7. For an interesting and detailed description of this process at Komatsu, see R. Cooper and W. B. Chew, "Control Tomorrow's Cost through Today's Design," *Harvard Business Review* (January–February 1996), p. 88.

8. For example, in the early 1990s the General Electric jet engine division fell on hard times as the military and commercial airlines cut back on purchases. General Electric realized that it had to reduce its costs to become more competitive. The organization moved from cost-plus pricing to target costing based on market requirements. In this process, engine customers advised General Electric that an expensive valve used to reduce the fuel consumption of one of its engines was useful but its costs outweighed its benefits. Based on this customer feedback, General Electric eliminated this part from the engine, thereby reducing its costs and increasing its ability to meet the market price.

9. The summary provided in the section is based on T. Tanaka, "Target Costing at Toyota," *Journal of Cost Management* (Spring 1993), pp. 4–11. Readers interested in descriptions of the nature and evolution of target costing can consult Y. Kato, G. Boer, and C. W. Chow, "Target Costing: An Integrative Management Process," *Journal of Cost Management* (Spring 1995), pp. 39–51, or J. Fisher, "Implementing Target Costing," *Journal of Cost Management* (Summer 1995), pp. 50–59.

10. An alternative approach is to focus on product components and to assign the target cost to individual product components on the basis of functionality and the perceived opportunity for improvement. For example, in designing its brakes, ITT Automotive assigns the total target cost for a brake system first to assemblies, then to subassemblies, and ultimately to individual components. A cross-functional team undertakes the process of meeting the assigned target cost. For details on the ITT Automotive approach see G. Schmelze, R. Geier, and T. E. Buttross, "Target Costing at ITT Automotive," *Management Accounting (USA)* (December 1996), p. 26.

11. There are many examples of these types of cost savings. For example, a factory worker on a General Motors design team pointed out that a tiny change in the design of a body panel would reduce the number of stampings needed to shape that panel from seven to five, resulting in a significant cost savings. A factory worker on a Ford design team pointed out that increasing the size of the access opening in a door would significantly reduce the time to install the lock and window hardware and would improve the quality of the work.

12. For example, a manufacturer of food-processing equipment found that it could replace a steel drive shaft with a plastic composite to reduce costs. In turn, this substitution allowed the manufacturer to use a smaller motor in the equipment, further reducing costs. These changes increased functionality to the customer in three ways: the product was lighter, it was more durable, and it consumed less electricity. In this case, value engineering increased functionality while reducing costs.

13. For example, in 1996, after experimenting for several years with a higher grade of dual-coated steel, Toyota switched back to conventional galvanized steel. This was an example of an overengineered product. That is, the functionality was beyond what the customers wanted. Therefore, the customers were unwilling to pay for this feature—meaning that this feature represented a non-value-added cost that could be eliminated without affecting product sales. Earlier, reflecting similar considerations, Toyota announced that it was suspending the practice of painting car parts that were not visible to the customer.

14. Interestingly, the management literature seems to have borrowed this term from the sciences, both physical and behavioral, where it has long been used to describe the contributions of individual factors in multifaceted behavior.

15. The product's design determines its functionality.

16. Japanese manufacturers originally developed kaizen costing. *Kaizen* is the Japanese word for small, continuous, and incremental improvements. Therefore, kaizen costing refers to applying kaizen to cost reduction.

17. For an interesting and detailed description of Olympus Optical Company's approach to costing, see Olympus Optical Company, Ltd. (A), Case Number 9-195-072, Harvard Business School Publishing, Boston.

18. The interested reader can follow along this discussion using the Excel spreadsheet **ch6ex.xls**.

19. The details underlying these, and subsequent cancellations can be found in the Excel worksheet **amach6(a).xls** through **amach6(d).xls**. These have been made available to your instructor.

20. For example, the relevance of measures such as parts per million defects and percent conforming are based on the implicit assumptions that output can be classified as conforming or nonconforming and that every element in each set creates an equal amount of quality cost. Gen'ichi Taguchi (*Taguchi Methods, Research and Development*, American Supplier Institute, 1992, Dearborn, Michigan.)

21. For a discussion of some of the issues related to developing costing systems to compute shutdown costs, see J. G. Kreuze and G. E. Newell, "ABC and Life-Cycle Costing for Environmental Expenditures," *Management Accounting (USA)* (February 1994), p. 38.

22. For an interesting summary of some of the legislation that regulates product take-back see M. J. Epstein, "Accounting for Product Take-back: Accounting for Future Disposal Cost of Products," *Management Accounting (USA)* (August 1996), p. 29.

## ■ PROBLEMS

### 6-1   Cost Commitment

Using published sources, identify the process of cost commitment during various phases of some product's life cycle. Try to find several examples so that you can contrast the rate of cost commitment for different products.

### 6-2   Functional Analysis

Consider the task of designing an automobile. Identify what you think are the major functions of an automobile and the key components that supply those functions. How might this information be used in a target costing exercise? What is the role of management accounting in this process?

### 6-3   Reengineering

Using published sources find an example of reengineering. Identify, if you can, what motivated or promoted the reengineering process, the objectives of reengineering, and how the organization decided whether the process was successful. What was the role of management accounting in the example that you found?

### 6-4    Kaizen Costing

Many observers of contemporary management practice have criticized Kaizen costing because of the intense pressures that it places on organization members. Give an example that you have seen or read about that illustrates the type of continuous improvement activity sought by kaizen costing. Do you believe that there is any way of mediating this pressure, or is it an inevitable part of the kaizen costing process?

### 6-5    Activity Management

Consider the process of finding and purchasing a list of grocery items in a grocery store. What activities involve moving, storing, and inspecting? How might the process be changed so that the cycle time, that is the time you spend in the store, is reduced?

### 6-6    Activity Management

Is reducing cycle time always important? Why is reducing cycle time likely to be more important in a fast-food restaurant than in a five-star restaurant?

### 6-7    Quality Cost

By consulting published sources, see if you can develop evidence to support the hypothesis that money spent on preventing, finding, and fixing quality problems before the product reaches the customer outweighs the cost of fixing quality problems once the product is in the customer's hands.

### 6-8    Quality Cost

Can you think of products for which it would be less expensive to forgo prevention and inspection costs and to just fix a quality problem when the customer reports it? Can you think of a general rule for making such prevention/repair decisions?

### 6-9    Take-back Costs

Identify three products for which the take-back costs are high and three products for which the take-back costs are low. Why is it important to identify take-back costs? Find a published example of a situation in which an organization was motivated to change its behavior when it understood the magnitude of one of its product's take-back costs.

### 6-10    Life Cycle Costs

Construct a credible example in which an organization that, in considering a product's life cycle costs, might make a decision not to make the product but that, in the same circumstances, if considering only costs during the product's manufacturing stage it might produce the product. Can you find a published example of a product that would clearly not have been made if the organization had computed the product's life cycle costs?

## 6-11    Life Cycle Costs

Most organizations do not compute the life cycle costs of their products. Why do you think they do not?

## 6-12    Target Costing

The Smiths Falls Time Company (SFTC) assembles sports watches. The watches consist of three main components: the quartz mechanism, the case, and the strap. SFTC sources the components from suppliers and assembles the watches in its factory.

Extensive customer surveys have established that there are three functions for the watches in the niche that SFTC has chosen: time, water resistance, and style. Time is provided by the quartz mechanism; water resistance and style are provided by the case and strap. Replaceable batteries power all the watches. However, once the case is opened to replace the battery, the waterproof nature of the watch is usually lost.

Market surveys have established three price points for three new watches that SFTC now has in the design stage: (1) $30 for a basic watch, (2) $50 for a basic chronograph, and (3) $120 for a multifunction watch.

SFTC has determined, given its facility-sustaining costs and its cost of capital, that the three watches must provide a margin of $4, $8, and $15 to be acceptable.

Based on initial specifications, the supplier of the quartz mechanisms has quoted prices of $8, $15, and $40 for the three watches. Because these mechanisms use standard components and well-understood technology, planners at SFTC consider these costs to be about as low as they can be with very little variation due either to functionality or to cost efficiencies among suppliers. The implication is that any needed target cost reductions will not be wrung out of the quartz mechanism component of the watch.

There are many sources for the watch straps, and prices vary widely based on functionality, which includes appearance, composition, and wearability. Suppliers quoted price ranges for the three watches as follows: $2–$7, $6–$9, and $20–$30. For any given level of functionality chosen, there is very little price variation among suppliers because the watch straps are virtually commodity products and are produced very cost-effectively.

The case provides two critical functions—style and water resistance. And, given the commodity nature of the quartz mechanism, it is the distinguishing feature of the watch. All cases have to be guaranteed to a depth of 50 meters minimum, and customer focus groups indicate that customers find a guaranteed depth of 100 meters desirable. Depending on style and degree of water resistance, suppliers quoted the following price ranges for the watch cases: $5–$15, $10–$25, and $20–35. Both style and water resistance increased in the product price.

Conversations with factory personnel indicated that the estimated costs of assembling, packaging, and shipping each watch were about $5, $7, and $15.

Discussions with the primary supplier of the watch cases have yielded the following facts. For an investment estimated at about $5,000,000, SFTC could provide management advice to one of its case suppliers. This advice would be related to developing better manufacturing methods. These improved methods would likely reduce the cost of each case supplied by about 25%.

### Required

    (1)   Compute the cost ranges for the three watches.
    (2)   Identify how you would choose the specific strap and case for each watch.
    (3)   What role does management accounting have in the decisions you made in Part 2?
    (4)   How would you decide whether to make the investment to improve the efficiency of the case supplier?
    (5)   Factory personnel indicate that for an investment of about $10,000,000 the existing factory layout could be altered to accommodate more-efficient production. The result would be to reduce assembly, packaging, and shipping costs by about $2 per unit. How would you decide whether to make this investment?

## 6-13     *Reengineering*

Southhampton Fabricating makes steel storage boxes. The steel storage boxes have a standard design but are made in different sizes to accommodate customer requirements.

    The factory is laid out on a functional basis. Sheet steel is stored at one end of the factory near the loading dock where it is received. Production is triggered when inventory of a particular product reaches a reorder point. Production is in batches that vary from 40 to 200 boxes and depends on the individual product's demand, carrying costs, and setup costs.

    When a production order is issued, workers are directed to withdraw an indicated amount of sheet steel from inventory. The steel is moved to the area of the factory where it is cut into the required pieces. The pieces are then moved to the area of the factory where stamping and shaping machines are kept. The machines are then set up for the particular box being made.

    When the stamping and shaping work is completed, the work in process is moved to the assembly area, where the pieces are welded into the finished storage boxes and all the work is inspected. The storage boxes are then moved to a storage area where they are held until they are shipped to customers. Therefore, the existing production process requires one major setup for each batch and four moves.

    In response to falling profits, senior management undertook a costing analysis of the various factory activities. This costing analysis revealed that, on average, the cost of moving a batch of production was approximately $300, and the cost of setting up the stamping and shaping machines for each batch was $200. An activity analysis revealed that the company processed about 4000 batches of storage boxes each year.

    An engineering study suggested that the factory could be reorganized into a cell format with five cells that would specialize in making boxes of various sizes. This reorganization would cost about $20,000,000 and would reduce the number of moves per batch from five to two, and the average number of setups for every five batches would fall from three to one.

    Should this process reengineering be undertaken? Make any assumption you feel is necessary to answer this question, but make your assumptions clear in your solution.

## 6-14     *Target Costing and Functional Analysis*

Many people have complained that modern computer suites offer programs with many features that users find not only confusing but also useless. (For example, consider how many of the features of your word processor that you use, let alone understand.) How might target costing and functional analysis be applied to software design in order to provide customers with software that has both a target cost and target functionality?

## 6-15    Activity Management

The Paris Bank specializes in loans for automobiles. The automobile loan process is organized as follows. The bank has arrangements with more than 500 automobile dealers to be the preferred supplier of loans. The referring dealership receives a fee of 0.5% of every loan that is written by the Paris Bank.

The business manager of the dealership completes a form with the customer that is required by the bank. The form is then mailed to the bank's main office, where the information on the form is entered into a computer file. Cursory credit checks are then run to identify whether the customer is a potential credit risk. If nothing is found, an interview is scheduled with the customer at a branch that is convenient for the customer. During the interview, a bank representative verifies the information and obtains a signature. The completed form is then forwarded to the bank's main credit office for approval. This process usually takes three to five working days.

The Paris Bank is concerned that it is losing customers to other financial institutions. Evidence suggests that the fastest time for loan approval is two days. Estimates by bank personnel suggest that the cost of the delay in approving a loan *beyond two days* is

$$\text{Cost} = \$30,000,000^{(\sqrt{\text{days delay} - 2})}$$

Automobile dealers are also complaining that 10% of the customers balk; that is, they withdraw their offer of purchase during the time that they are waiting for approval. The present value of the lost profits from a lost customer amounts to about $3,000 to both the bank and the dealership.

What would you suggest in this case? Make any assumptions concerning the cost of making improvements, the number of customers, or any other relevant matter that you feel are necessary to answer this question.

## 6-16    Life Cycle Costing

St. Agatha Company manufactures laser printers. Government agencies have advised the company that for all new products it will have to provide for recycling of used toner cartridges.

A study has determined that St. Agatha Company has three options. It can design a printer with cartridges that the customer refills with toner, eliminating the need to recycle the cartridges. It can design cartridges that it will recover and refill with toner. Or it can design cartridges that it will recover, crush, and sell the resulting plastic as scrap.

Planners at St. Agatha are considering the design of a cartridge for a new printer. The company expects that customers will use about 600,000 cartridges a year during the five-year manufacturing life of the new printer. After that, the company expects that cartridge use will fall at the rate of 200,000 per year. The cost of making a cartridge is $60. Assume that the company's before tax cost of capital is 12%.

Marketing staff estimates that printer sales will suffer if it offers a cartridge that customers have to refill. Therefore they plan to cut the printer prices to maintain volume. The net effect on profits is expected to be about $6,000,000 per year during the five-year manufacturing life of the printer. Under this alternative, the company would price the replacement toner to break even and would make 250,000 cartridges in each of the five-year manufacturing life of the new printer with the balance of use in the first five years and the last two years accounted for by refills.

The marketing staff has estimated that for every 100 cartridges used, only 80 will be returned. Returns are made in the year that the cartridge is used. The company is expected to pay a $15.00 landfill fee at the end of the product's lifetime for every cartridge disposed of.

The cost to clean and refill a cartridge is $20. Under this alternative, the company would make 500,000 cartridges in each of the first two years and rely on recovered cartridges after that.

If the company chooses the crushing alternative, it must purchase a plastic recovery machine at the start of the project. The cost of the machine is $5,000,000 and it would be useless when the product is abandoned. The recycled plastics and other materials can be sold to yield $38.00.

Ignore the effects of taxes in answering this question.

If the company's objective is to minimize the take-back cost, which alternative should it pursue: (1) make a cartridge that customers can refill, (2) make a cartridge that is recycled, or (3) make a cartridge that is recovered, crushed, and remanufactured?

---

## ■ CASES

---

### PIEDMONT EXPRESS FORMS: PROCESS ANALYSIS FOR STRATEGIC DECISION MAKING[1]

#### Part A—Introduction

Henry faces a tough decision. Although the forms business is undergoing structural changes, his business is growing, so his organization needs to change and grow. However,

Paul E. Juras, Paul A. Dierks, and Henry Johns. Reprinted with permission from AICPA Case Development Program, Case No. 94-09. Copyright 1994 by the American Institute of Certified Public Accountants, Inc. (AICPA).

[1]This problem illustrates the use of process mapping to support reengineering. You should begin this exercise by reading M. Morrow and M. Hazell, "Activity Mapping for Business Process Redesign," *Management Accounting (U.K.)* (February 1992), pp. 36–38.

there is no space for expanding in the building rented by his company. He and his partner are planning to build a warehouse and office complex to house the company to meet its space needs well into the future, but they are not sure how big a facility to build. To address this issue, Henry needs to make an analysis of his firm's existing operations, and in light of the industry's change, make a decision on how much emphasis to put on the various aspects of his business.

**Company Profile**  Piedmont Express Forms, Inc. (PEF) was started in 1983 by Henry Johns and Larry Atkins. There are now nine employees generating revenues of approximately $2,000,000 per year. The company occupies about 1,500 square feet of office space and 3,500 square feet of warehouse space in Greensboro, North Carolina.

PEF is a distributor organization providing business forms in both national and local markets. The firm also provides other products and services to businesses, including printed products, plastic cards, data collection and bar coding devices for information transfer, consulting work in the form of systems analysis for work simplification, and advertising specialties (promotional products or "give aways"). The latter is expected to be at least 10% of the company's revenue in the current year.

For clients in its local market, consisting of the counties surrounding Greensboro, N.C. (referred to as the Piedmont Triad Area), PEF specializes in providing forms management and inventory control for clients with large forms budgets. Within this market PEF offers three levels of service:

*Level 1.* Clients with no warehousing needs for forms are serviced by having a sales representative go by on a regular basis to take orders, offer solutions to problems, etc. Any goods purchased are shipped directly to the client by the supplier and billed at the time of shipment. No warehouse or delivery service is provided.

*Level 2.* For clients using large volumes of forms, but with inadequate storage space, PEF performs the services outlined in level 1, plus receiving and storing goods in their warehouse for later distribution, usually on a just-in-time basis. The goods are billed in full when they arrive at PEF's warehouse.

This level of service requires much more activity. The warehouse must receive and store goods, generate picking tickets, pick the items, and deliver them, while accounting must process the release, adjust inventory, and process an invoice for a small amount of freight.

*Level 3.* Identical to level 2, except that a custom product is stored, and billings for the goods aren't made until the goods are delivered to a client.

PEF currently averages between 120 and 150 deliveries each month to Level 2 and Level 3 firms.

In their national market, PEF has formed strategic alliances with software vendors around the country to provide the necessary forms for purchasers of the software. PEF guarantees the compatibility of their forms with the software system. This market represents about 15% of PEF's business and serves 210 clients in 30 states. While the national market represents nearly 50% of the customer base and less than 20% of revenue, Henry believes that once such a client is obtained, only 10 to 15 minutes of staff time per order is needed and little, if any, warehouse support is required of these customers. PEF's average gross margin on it's national customers is 38%.

Although he takes pride in keeping up with the changes in the forms industry, Henry Johns feels that the main focus of his business is to help capture and manage the movement of information through an organization, whether or not it requires a paper form. The services that help meet customer needs include ordering, warehousing and distribution, the redesign of business forms to make them more useful, and gathering and distributing management information relating to the use of these products. Form usage information includes showing past usage and stock-outs by end users, past ordering behavior, the possibility of combining orders based on expected usage to save on order processing and delivery costs, and information on what has been shipped where and when. For example, an insurance client may want to know how many insurance application forms were used each month nationwide for a two year period. PEF could provide this information in seconds, whereas the client might take days to gather the same information.

Henry is aware that his firm must offer a variety of products and services, it must be service oriented, and be ready to adopt or adapt to the latest trend. His firm has responded to these pressures through diversification into such areas as bar coding services and a newly formed imaging division. However, Henry feels that forms, as his "base business," provide an entree to new clients who will use the variety of other products and services PEF offers. Thus, forms will always be a product line of PEF, and the only issue is how big the local segments of PEF's business will be—and how much warehouse space is needed.

PEF's managers understand that different activities are required to support each service or product offered, and a different markup is used for each service level. However, since management doesn't know the costs of providing the support required, they: (a) don't know how much net profit is generated from each level of service; and (b) have no way of knowing whether or not any given client is profitable.

More importantly, as PEF looks to the future, it becomes difficult to target any specific type of client (i.e., national or local) since they don't know which type is the most profitable to serve. At the local level, they prefer serving at Levels 2 and 3 because gross profits are higher and there are fewer competitors, but they think the support required at those levels absorbs much of the gross profit. Thus, they are unsure over how aggressively they should pursue this segment of the business, or, to focus their efforts on the national market. This decision impacts their long run plan to build an office and warehouse facility, and, if they build, what warehouse capacity to provide.

**Financial Information** Table 1 presents PEF's Sales, Cost of Sales, and Profits for 1993. Table 2 shows the sales and gross profits for the largest local customers not requiring warehousing and the largest local customers needing warehousing.

A quick computation of the costs and revenues involved in the delivery of goods, in-

## TABLE 1

| | | |
|---|---|---|
| Sales | | |
| Sales—Custom | | $1,519,433 |
| Sales—Stock | | 225,785 |
| Sales—Other | | 236,247 |
| Sales—Forms Design | | 13,333 |
| Freight Out | | 96,550 |
| Freight Out-Forms Express | | 7,271 |
| | Total Sales | $2,098,619 |
| Cost of Sales | | |
| Cost of Sales—Custom | | $ 947,158 |
| Cost of Sales—Stock | | 164,433 |
| Cost of Sales—Other | | 162,371 |
| Forms Design Cost | | 22,256 |
| Freight In | | 110,046 |
| | Total Cost of Sales | $1,406,264 |
| | Gross Profits | $ 692,355 |
| | Selling, General, and Administrative | 586,355 |
| | Pretax Profit | $ 106,000 |

## TABLE 2

| | LOCAL NO WAREHOUSING | | | LOCAL WITH WAREHOUSING | |
|---|---|---|---|---|---|
| CLIENT | TOTAL SALES | GROSS PROFITS | CLIENT | TOTAL SALES | GROSS PROFITS |
| 1 | $ 99,599 | $ 31,839 | 1 | $ 147,789 | $ 50,302 |
| 2 | 87,220 | 14,109 | 2 | 33,079 | 8,644 |
| 3 | 30,825 | 11,006 | 3 | 181,545 | 56,341 |
| 4 | 23,660 | 7,992 | 4 | 210,300 | 46,986 |
| 5 | 20,702 | 7,413 | 5 | 66,739 | 22,091 |
| 6 | 28,945 | 9,920 | 6 | 21,413 | 7,819 |
| 7 | 19,055 | 6,922 | 7 | 24,472 | 10,530 |
| 8 | 124,468 | 24,521 | 8 | 209,580 | 93,392 |
| | | | 9 | 71,679 | 28,147 |
| | | | 10 | 76,617 | 25,432 |
| | | | 11 | 22,437 | 5,919 |
| Totals | $434,474 | $113,722 | | $1,065,650 | $355,603 |

cluding running "Forms Express" is given in Table 3. Some clients will not accept separate billing for "Forms Express" or delivery services so the delivery charge is built into the selling price for these customers.

## TABLE 3

Expenses

| | |
|---|---|
| Local delivery expense | $ 215.23 |
| Gas expense | 1,200.00 |
| Van maintenance | 1,181.46 |
| General warehouse | 873.99 |
| Compensation warehouse | 20,679.00 |
| Insurance—medical warehouse | 1,375.23 |
| Insurance—disability warehouse | 388.08 |
| Insurance—van warehouse | 432.84 |
| Temporary help warehouse | 1,331.03 |
| Workman's compensation warehouse | 875.00 |
| FICA warehouse | 1,551.00 |
| Rent | $ 8,250.00 |
| Subtotal | $ 38,352.86 |
| Freight-in | 110,046.00 |
| Total delivery costs | $148,398.86 |

Revenues

| | |
|---|---|
| Freight-out revenue | $ 96,550.00 |
| Forms Express revenue | 7,271.00 |
| Subtotal | $103,821.00 |
| Reclassify sales as delivery revenue | $ 5,000.00 |
| Total delivery revenue | $108,821.00 |

### Part A—Questions

(1) Using only the information in Part A, prepare a brief report giving Henry Johns your assessment of the situation at PEF in light of the decision(s) they face (e.g., whether to build a warehouse) and the available data. Your report should address PEF's overall profitability, and the profitability of its various markets and customers. How would you advise Henry at this point concerning the two local markets and the construction of a warehouse? (Refer to this report as the Preliminary Analysis.)

(2) Read the Overview of the Forms Industry in the Appendix. In light of this overview and the preliminary analysis of PEF's financial data, how would you advise Henry Johns?

(3) Henry Johns heard about activity-based costing at a professional meeting and wonders if it could be used at PEF. Describe activity-based costing, explain "how it works," and point out how it might be useful to PEF in their current situation. How would you go about applying activity-based costing at PEF? What additional information would you want from PEF to apply it to their operations? How would you go about acquiring this information?

### Appendix to Part A: Overview of the Forms Industry

The forms industry is a mature, $8 billion industry, but it is declining even as new players enter. It's an industry that doesn't have to build a need for the products it provides, since the need for forms to operate a business already exists—and will probably continue to exist. But, the industry is facing a smaller market as technology and hardware make it possible for end users to design and print their own forms.

Customers are also reducing the number of vendors they buy from. Suppliers that cannot "do it all" are likely to lose out to those that can. Being a full service supplier (warehousing, distribution, consulting, information support) is becoming more important.

Profits have been reduced and competition has increased significantly. Clients have always wanted price, service and quality, but today they'll switch suppliers as soon as something goes wrong, or for the difference of "a few dollars." Also, the line between distributor and manufacturer has begun to blur. Many distributors now have print shops and manufacturers are selling directly to customers. Mergers and acquisitions have been, and will continue to be, a means of survival. But some owners, who are too close to retirement to start over, are likely to sell out. Others will stay in the business through mergers.

The key word for the industry is "change." In order to survive, distributors must add services, expand product lines or diversity to add value and maintain margins. However, diversification means that traditional forms products are a smaller percentage of sales.

The industry SIC code (2761) description of the industry is "Manifold Business Forms." In an earlier time this may have appropriately described the central focus of designing, printing and distributing continuous, multi-copy, fan-fold, and custom business forms. However, today it is far too succinct a label for an industry whose members refer to themselves as either distributors, manufacturers, "forms professionals," or "customer service professionals"—the strength of this trend is seen by the latter group's formation of a new association: Society for Service Professionals in Printing (SSPP).

The degree of industry diversification is found in the product and service ads regularly appearing in *FORM* magazine, the official publication of NBFA, the Association for Independent Marketers of Business Printing and Information Management Services. Segments of the industry include:

Forms—pre-printed, custom continuous, instantaneous (computer generated and forms composition software), tax forms, "smart cards" (contain microprocessors), stock mailers, guest checks

Printers—of forms, checks, stationery, announcements

Graphics services

Office stationery supplies, like "plain" envelopes, peel apart envelopes, paper stock (cutsheet), rubber stamps, cash register rolls

Labels and tags

Direct mail servicing

Bar coding scanners and supplies

Plastic cards (for credit cards, ATM cards, etc.)

Among the more popular products that firms in the forms industry have added are advertising specialties—promotional products or "give aways." Ad specialties have had a strong growth pattern for several years. In 1990, sales of ad specialty items were more than $5 billion, which was an 11.9% increase from the prior year. The following year saw a 2.9% increase.

Forms firms are also placing increased emphasis on security documents to reduce the chance of forgery by using specialty papers and adding foil stamping, embossing, diffractional holographic foils, and artificial watermarks.

Greater use of computers and laser printers in firms of all sizes provides new opportunities to the forms industry for supplying equipment, supplies and services. Laser printers and computer generated forms software make it possible to create electronic templates for data entry, and the completed form can be saved and printed on demand. Instead of stocking preprinted multilayer forms, low cost and high speed laser printers make it faster and cheaper to print multiple copies of the same form.

A natural extension of an industry built on printing and distribution forms, is document imaging. Bulky paper forms are converted to electronic format for storage and processing by an expanding service labeled as "document imaging."

Also, the simplicity of form creation often results in non-standard forms, which open opportunities for forms and work process consulting.

However, it is service that tends to set companies apart from their competition: "It's the little extras that count the most." The

most important service a distributor offers is information about new products and technologies: "Distributors must become more knowledgeable and help customers find new solutions to their problems."

The forms industry has matured and forms have become commodity items. To survive in a mature marketplace, firms must expand product lines, add services, offer new value-added products, and become full service vendors capable of providing just about any printed item or related service, including distribution. The survivors will be those who proactively exploit the changes in the industry, not those merely reacting to them. Some forms distributors and manufacturers may not survive the changes.

Despite the implications of the changes occurring in the forms industry, Henry Johns

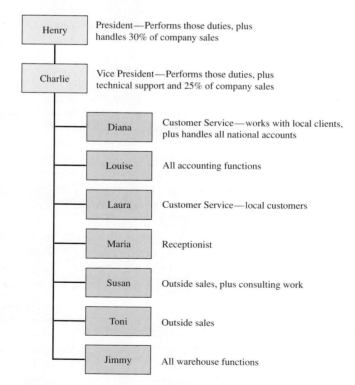

| | |
|---|---|
| Henry | President—Performs those duties, plus handles 30% of company sales |
| Charlie | Vice President—Performs those duties, plus technical support and 25% of company sales |
| Diana | Customer Service—works with local clients, plus handles all national accounts |
| Louise | All accounting functions |
| Laura | Customer Service—local customers |
| Maria | Receptionist |
| Susan | Outside sales, plus consulting work |
| Toni | Outside sales |
| Jimmy | All warehouse functions |

**EXHIBIT 1**  Organizational Chart

**EXHIBIT 2** Business Process Outline

| | IDENTIFY PERSON WHO PERFORMS THE ACTIVITY | | |
|---|---|---|---|
| DESCRIPTION OF ACTIVITY | NATIONAL MARKET | LOCAL— DIRECT SHIPMENT | LOCAL— VIA PEF WAREHOUSE |
| 1. Solicit new client(s) | Inside sales | Sales rep. | None |
| 2. Solicit business from a client | | Sales rep. | None |
| 3. Client requests a quote | Inside sales | Sales rep. | None |
| 4. Follow up quote with a client contact | Inside sales | Sales rep. | None |
| 5. Contact plants to determine cost (bid) | Inside sales | Customer service | None |
| 6. Wait for arrival of bids | Inside sales | Customer service | None |
| 7. Select quote to give to client | Inside sales | Sales rep. | None |
| 8. Give quote to client | Inside sales | Sales rep./cust. serv. | None |
| 9. Client places order | | | None |
| 10. Write up order | Inside sales | Sales rep./cust. serv. | None |
| 11. Do forms composition | Inside sales | Sales rep./cust. serv. | None |
| 12. Key order into computer | Inside sales | Sales rep./cust. serv. | None |
| 13. Proof obtained | Inside sales | Sales rep./cust. serv. | None |
| 14. Send proof to client | Inside sales | Sales rep./cust. serv. | None |
| 15. Wait for proof from client | Inside sales | Sales rep./cust. serv. | None |
| 16. Proof approved by client | Inside sales | Sales rep./cust. serv. | None |
| 17. Order printed out of computer | Inside sales | Customer service | None |
| 18. Order sent to plant | Inside sales | Customer service | None |
| 19. Wait for acknowledgment of order | | Customer service | None |
| 20. Verify acknowledgment | Customer service | Customer service | None |
| 21. Contact plant if problem exists | Inside sales | Sales rep./cust. serv. | None |
| 22. File acknowledgment | Customer service | Customer service | None |
| 23. Plant ships order and invoices IBP | Plant | Plant | None |
| 24. Key accounts payable into computer | Accounting | Accounting | None |
| 25. Invoice the client | Accounting | Accounting | None |
| 26. Assemble order and file it | Admin. assist | Admin. assist | None |
| 27. Pay invoice to plant | Accounting | Accounting | None |
| 28. Receive client's payment | Accounting | Accounting | None |
| 29. Shipment arrives at warehouse (re: 24) | Warehouse | None | None |
| 30. Check shipment for damage | Warehouse | None | None |
| 31. Mark quantities on shipping papers | Warehouse | None | None |
| 32. If not damaged, put stock away | Warehouse | None | None |
| 33. Send shipping papers to accounting | Warehouse | None | None |
| 34. Write up a release | Inside sales | None | Customer service |
| 35. Enter release into the computer | Inside sales | None | Customer service |
| 36. Picking ticket printed by computer | Inside sales | None | Customer service |
| 37. Picking ticket forwarded to warehouse | Inside sales | None | Warehouse |
| 38. Warehouse pulls product | Warehouse | None | Warehouse |
| 39. Warehouse ships or delivers order | Warehouse | None | Warehouse |

*continued*

| | IDENTIFY PERSON WHO PERFORMS THE ACTIVITY | | |
|---|---|---|---|
| DESCRIPTION OF ACTIVITY | NATIONAL MARKET | LOCAL— DIRECT SHIPMENT | LOCAL— VIA PEF WAREHOUSE |
| 40. Warehouse files papers and forwards to acct | Warehouse | None | Warehouse |
| 41. Accounting completes the release | Accounting | None | Accounting |
| 42. Paperwork is filed away | Admin. assist | None | Admin. assist. |
| 43. Invoice the client, if appropriate | Accounting | None | Warehouse |

is confident of the continued existence of the forms business, and its profitability. He once stated, "A forms professional could move to Los Angeles tomorrow, open a forms business, and survive."

## Part B

The Preliminary Analysis confirmed Henry's belief that forms firms must offer a variety of products and services, be service-oriented, and be ready to adopt, or adapt to, the latest "trend." Thus, he must closely manage his current range of activities, but he must also be vigilant in finding and evaluating other forms-related business lines that can "turn a profit." More specifically, the analysis didn't provide a great deal of insight into the fundamental problem he faced: how much emphasis to put on the local markets, especially those that use warehouse space, in order to decide whether or not to build a new warehouse facility.

The preliminary analysis provided mainly firmwide, general information. What is needed is detailed information, including work done to run the warehouse (picking, loading and delivering orders by market and client category), and a breakdown of administrative costs, especially those that relate to

sales and customer support for the local markets. To address this issue, Henry needs to analyze his firm's sales, administrative and support operations. A more sophisticated analysis is necessary, and process analysis is the logical step to take.

As the initial step in this analysis, Henry prepared the organizational chart in Exhibit 1 and the description of how PEF goes about doing its work, which appears in Exhibit 2.

## Part B—Questions

(1) Henry was unsure of what process analysis was and what kind of work it entailed. Describe process analysis, including the steps involved and its benefits to an organization.

(2) Using the Business Process Outline provided in Exhibit 2, draw a process flowchart.

(3) (a) Prepare a memo to PEF management evaluating the information added as the result of completing the process flowchart in Question B2. (b) Point out what additional steps would be needed to use activity-based costing to determine the cost of serving each of PEF's major markets or service levels and, ultimately, to calculate the profitability of a specific customer. Include the types of data needed and describe how they can be obtained.

# ACTIVITY-BASED MANAGEMENT
# AT STREAM INTERNATIONAL*

All these proposals for cost reduction seem worthwhile. But we don't have the managerial resources to do them all at the same time. How shall we choose among them?

*Michael Michalski, Division Director*

Stream International was a new company, created in April of 1995, when the Global Software Services group of RR Donnelley was merged with a previously independent company, Corporate Software. In July of 1995, the six senior managers of Stream's Crawfordsville, Indiana facility were about to meet with Division Director Mike Michalski. (See Exhibit 1 for the senior organization chart at Stream's Crawfordsville plant.) The plant had just completed the first three months of an activity-based management (ABM) project. The data collected to date revealed unexpectedly high costs for administrative and support processes such as materials management, quality, billing, and shipping. Michalski had asked the six managers to prepare recommendations for process changes at the plant based on the ABM data. The managers had spent two weeks poring over the activity cost data as they prepared their recommendations for the meeting (see summaries of the five proposals in the Appendix). During the meeting, the senior management team would listen to presentations about the proposals and make a decision about which to implement. The stakes were high for Crawfordsville. The business and operations at the plant had changed dramatically during the past ten years. In addition,

the Crawfordsville facility was one of the first in an RR Donnelley-owned company to perform an ABM study, and the results could be pivotal for the success of ABM in Stream and the larger world of RR Donnelley.

## Background

In the early 1970s, the Crawfordsville plant was part of RR Donnelley's Book Division. It was the leading printer of religious books, texts, encyclopedias, and other reference books. The huge web presses and extensive storage in the Crawfordsville plant were well suited to this market niche. In the mid-1970s, the Book Division installed several smaller "narrow web" presses in the Crawfordsville plant so that it could enter the trade book market. With the flexibility from the new machines, Donnelley soon became the largest trade book publisher in the United States.

Short response time and a flexible production environment enabled the Book Division to evolve in a new direction in the early 1980s when it became the leading supplier of manuals and documentation for IBM personal computers. In 1987, the division installed a diskette duplication facility in the Crawfordsville plant so that the Book Division could be a full-line supplier to IBM and also attract additional work from other personal computer companies. Two years later, the software documentation business had grown sufficiently that Donnelley created a new business unit called "Documentation Services." By 1993, the growing demand for diskette duplication services was helping to offset declines in traditional printing services. That year the name of the business unit was changed to Global Software Services (GSS). The name change reflected the division's

---

*Norman Klein and Professor Robert Kaplan prepared this case as the basis for class discussion rather than to illustrate either effective or ineffective handling of an administrative situation.

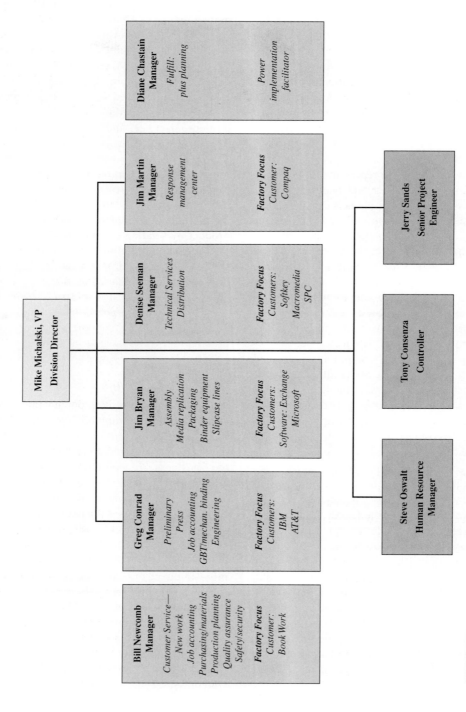

**EXHIBIT 1**  Organizational Chart for Crawfordsville Facilities

much broader mix of customers, which now included, in addition to personal computer manufacturers, many software companies that supplied operating systems and application programs, and companies developing computer-based games and educational programs. GSS also expanded its packaging capabilities and moved into the order fulfillment business. When consumers called to order software products, GSS was often at the other end of the "1-800" phone line. This business quickly grew to include phone representatives who received calls to register and license software products. In 1994, the phone licensing group celebrated its millionth call, and in 1995, it logged over 2 million calls.

Corporate Software, the other half of the newly formed Stream company, had been founded in Norwood, Massachusetts in 1983, with an initial focus on providing information and consulting services to software companies. First-year sales were $1.7 million. Internal growth and new services, such as reselling software to corporations, enabled sales to reach almost $60 million in 1987, when the company went public. Corporate Software launched a U.K. subsidiary in 1986, and in 1991 introduced consulting services to provide assistance to companies when they encountered problems with new software packages and hardware configurations, especially as companies migrated to Microsoft Windows. In 1993, the company expanded its support services to include call-in help desks and call-in technical support services for major business software products. With two acquisitions in 1994, Corporate Software had become the largest reseller of microcomputer software to businesses and institutions. Its approximately 1,000 worldwide technical support specialists handled nearly 3.5 million support calls annually on more than 1,000 products. In 1994, a group of investors, led by Bain Capital, took the company private again.

Stream was created in April 1995 by a merger between Donnelley's GSS division and Corporate Software. Each of the new partners had revenues of approximately $650 million in 1994, and thus Stream anticipated sales of more than $1.3 billion in 1995. Stream offered software companies a complete set of fulfillment services. It could produce, package, and distribute a product, license or register it, provide customer support to retail customers, and offer a broad range of support services to businesses and institutions. The range and power of Stream's business model was illustrated when Microsoft released its Windows 95 product by sending the product code to nine Stream locations around the world. Stream first translated the program into foreign languages and then manufactured and packaged the product. Stream also sold and distributed Windows 95 to corporations and provided consulting, call-in support services, and product registration.

### *Crawfordsville Plant*

In the mid-1980s, printing documentation for IBM personal computers at the Crawfordsville plant meant large orders for hefty manuals that required long press runs. But the business of printing documentation changed dramatically in the 1990s. More information was being provided within the software itself so that documentation manuals became shorter and less substantial. Also, as software makers shortened the time between versions and upgrades, they placed more frequent orders for smaller quantities. Because smaller press runs reduced the demand for printing services, Michalski had recently accepted printing work from the Donnelley book division that lived on the other side of the huge plant they shared. This work fully occupied three of Stream's six large web presses.

Fortunately, as income from printing diminished, the demand for diskette duplication, customized packaging of software and documentation, and distribution and licensing services increased. In 1994, the demand for diskette duplication peaked at 46 million. Technology for delivering software was continuing to evolve as software and personal computer companies began to use a single compact disc (CD-ROM) to replace multiple magnetic diskette packages for newly purchased software. To keep abreast of these developments, Stream arranged for a partnership with another company to replicate CD-ROMs.

Crawfordsville's commitment to the fulfillment business seemed to be working. Software companies increasingly wanted to focus on their core business of software design and marketing, and were willing to outsource to suppliers, like Crawfordsville, the production, distribution, and support services for their products. This trend, however, was leading Crawfordsville to serve many more customers, most of whom placed small, customized orders, and were expecting response times of less than two weeks, down from the 1980s expected turnaround of two months.

Stream was now doing short runs of several hundred items on expensive machines, specifically designed for customized runs, as well as runs of more than 10,000 items on efficient, high-volume machines. But even more than putting ink on paper, Stream was also involved in customer administration and technical support, diskette and CD-ROM replication, and customized packaging. As Michalski recalled: "The new opportunities forced us to confront what business were we in. Was our business putting ink on paper or content on media?"

Michalski loved the challenge of keeping Crawfordsville ahead of the curve of a rapidly evolving industry, and was well aware that getting in and out of technology at the right time was part of the game. But given the many variables that were so tough to manage,

and the rapidly evolving technology and customer base of the business, he needed knowledge and control of his cost structure. For example, administrative expenses had been rising steadily, from 2.9% of sales in 1992 to an estimated 3.4% of sales in 1995. Also, inventory, which in 1990 used just under 100,000 square feet of storage, was projected to require nearly 250,000 square feet in 1995. Some of this inventory was diskettes held on consignment for specific customers, and work-in-process more than one-year old.

### Implementing Activity-Based Management

Michalski's introduction to activity-based management came in early 1995, when RR Donnelley executives told him of an initial project undertaken in an Ohio plant with the help of consultants from KPMG Peat Marwick LLP (KPMG). When the ABM concept was explained, Michalski agreed that Crawfordsville was an ideal candidate to be the next ABM project at Donnelley.

Stream was using a traditional job cost accounting system. All machines were in a separate cost center. The cost of the 2- to 15-person crews to operate the machines, the traceable machine costs, plus an allocated share of period plant expense were added together and divided by budgeted machine hours to compute a machine burden rate per hour. All other expenses were applied to jobs based on a per-person crew burden rate per hour, which included direct wages, fringe benefit costs, shift and overtime premiums, plus an allocated share of plant salaried expense. A work ticket system assigned direct materials, direct labor, and crew and machine time burden rates to individual jobs.

Michalski expressed his frustration with the existing costing system:

> The system couldn't report on the costs of individual businesses. The dollars were spread out across everything. In addition to not

knowing the costs of doing business with external customers or with the Book Division next door, we were throwing resources at problems relying on our instincts to tell us what was worth doing. I needed to know what kinds of process changes mattered most, and how much should I be willing to spend.

Activity-based management promised a more accurate way of understanding and assigning costs to jobs and customers. With ABM, Stream could link the range and extent of services required by each customer, and then estimate how much it was costing to serve the customer. When the project was complete, Stream would also be able to do predictive costing and develop new pricing guidelines. Equally important, ABM would allow Stream to see early profit trends, or better predict the cost of new business activity.

Michalski knew that he had to balance the interests of Stream's various constituencies as he embarked on the ABM project. The new shareholders wanted cost reduction, higher return on net assets, and business growth. Customers valued faster time-to-market, lower prices, and better value for their money. Software companies, like Microsoft and Lotus, were now offering suites containing word processors, spreadsheets, database managers, and graphics presentation packages that had previously been sold separately. These companies received much lower prices from software sold within suites, causing them to place great pressure on suppliers to reduce the costs of documentation, media, and support services.

The employees were especially important. Michalski viewed the ABM effort as an alternative to the brute force approach to solving problems, asking employees to work harder and for extended hours. He brought workers into the picture by explaining the ABM project to worker committees, communicating to them through the biweekly newsletter, and asking for the help of supervisors. He under-

stood the delicate paradox of management wanting to solicit information from employees to learn what process changes should be made, but at the same time having to assure workers that they would not lose their jobs. Fortunately, Michalski knew that the Book Division, with whom he shared the facility, was growing its business through expanded production of trade books, especially those related to personal computers, such as Que's highly popular ". . . for Dummies" series written for the myriad newly released and continually updated software programs and operating systems. Michalski felt that the Book Division could likely absorb any employees that were no longer needed as a result of process improvements in Stream.

Michalski appointed a three-person team for the initial ABM project. Denise Seeman, a five-year veteran at Crawfordsville, was the project manager. Seeman, initially a supervisor on the floor was now manager of the information technology department, manager of distribution, and of two customer service teams. Kathy Reik, also in the information technology organization, supervised technical services and formerly supervised areas such as production scheduling and materials handling. Karen Session, an accounting supervisor from the controller's division, completed the team.

The project started with the team getting training and project planning from the KPMG consultants. The team, after talking to supervisors and managers, agreed to collect activity information for 12 basic business and support processes. Then, the team and consultants began to create an all-inclusive activity dictionary that listed every kind of work activity done in the plant (other than that performed by direct labor). Eventually, the team identified 161 different activities. (See Exhibit 2 for a summary of the activity dictionary, organized by the 12 basic processes.) Session and Reik then conducted surveys over the next two weeks, asking a sample of approximately

**EXHIBIT 2**  Summary of ABM Project Dictionary for Crawfordsville

1.  **Understand Markets and Customers**
    1.1  Determine customer needs and wants
    1.2  Measure customer satisfaction
    1.3  Monitor changes in market or customer expectations

2.  **Develop Vision and Strategy**
    2.1  Monitor the external environment
    2.2  Define the business concept and organizational strategy
    2.3  Design the structure, goals, incentives, and relationships between organizations

3.  **Design Products and Services**
    3.1  Develop new product/service concepts and plans
    3.2  Design, build, and evaluate prototype products/services
    3.3  Refine and test existing products/services
    3.4  Prepare for production

4.  **Market and Sell**
    4.1  Market products or services
    4.2  Sell products or services
    4.3  Accept and enter customer orders

5.  **Produce and Deliver**
    5.1  Plan for and acquire necessary resources or inputs
    5.2  Convert resources or inputs into products
    5.3  Make delivery of manufactured product (bulk shipment)
    5.4  Fulfill orders (variable quantity fulfilled shipments)
         Includes any fulfilled orders in all buildings
         Includes D.R.O.P.P.
    5.5  Deliver revenue-generating service to customer
    5.6  Manage production and delivery

6.  **Invoice and Service Customers**
    6.1  Bill the customer
    6.2  Provide after-sales support
    6.3  Respond to customer inquiries

7.  **Develop and Manage Human Resources**
    7.1  Create human resource strategy
    7.2  Hire employees
    7.3  Train and educate employees
    7.4  Recognize and reward employee performance
    7.5  Ensure employee well-being and morale
    7.6  Plan employee compensation and benefits

8.  **Manage Information (excludes prelim computer manufacturing equipment: Scitex, etc.—see 5.6.4)**
    8.1  Plan for information resources management
    8.2  Develop and deploy information systems
    8.3  Manage and maintain existing information systems
    8.4  Manage and maintain other communication systems

9.  **Manage Financial and Physical Resources**
    9.1  Manage financial resources
    9.2  Process finance and accounting transactions
    9.3  Report information
    9.4  Conduct internal audits
    9.5  Manage the tax function
    9.6  Manage physical resources (building, property, and nonmanufacturing equipment)

10. **Executive Environmental Management Program**
    10.1  Execute environmental management program

*continued*

---

**EXHIBIT 2** Summary of ABM Project Dictionary for Crawfordsville

---

**11. Manage External Relationships**
   11.1 Manage external relationships
**12. Manage Improvement and Change**
   12.1 Measure and monitor overall organizational performance
   12.2 Conduct quality assessments
   12.3 Benchmark performance
   12.4 Make process improvements
   12.5 Implement TQM and employee involvement

---

250 workers how much time they spent on the 161 activities. While the surveys were under way, Michalski spent extra time on the floor to make sure the workers understood and were comfortable with the process.

Session reflected on the complexity of this initial effort:

> Management really liked seeing costs grouped by activities. But maybe we went into too much detail when we created the dictionary. The activity dollars showed that some of these activities were pretty inconsequential and could have been combined into a higher-level definition.

During the next project phase, Session prepared data files for import. She had to format the general ledger files and personnel data into import files that were downloaded into the personal computer containing the ABC software. The ABC software processed the data into activity costs and provided a variety of reports and graphic presentations of the results.

### Early Results

By June 1995, the ABM team had calculated costs for the 161 activities, and the 12 aggregate business processes. (See Exhibit 3 for the expenses and personnel assignments to the 12 business processes, and Exhibit 4 for a list of the 20 activities with the highest personnel costs.) Bill Newcomb, manager of administrative and support activities, recalled the initial surprise from the numbers.

The costs of some of the activities seemed surprisingly high. But as people delved into the numbers, they came to agree that if that's what I said, it's probably true. The data forced people to think in a new way. The big insight was that we had lots of small volumes of cost involved with an activity, a little here, a little there, and all these little pockets added up to a big number.[1]

The team shared selected parts of the analysis with about 100 people to get their opinions on what to do with this information. Some of the results made a strong and immediate impression on Stream managers. For example, there were large lots of old product that was not turning. Many of the orders placed by IBM in 1992 and 1993 were still sitting in storage in the Crawfordsville facility. Additional storage space had been added to the plant in December 1993 to handle the growing supply of mostly IBM-specific inventory.

Newcomb explained that existing practices had led to a similar problem with work in progress (WIP):

> It's standard publishing practice to print 11,000 items to fill an order for 10,000. Then you will bind 10,500 and store the extra 500 believing it will be useful. But once you store that as WIP, its on your books as an asset, and you can't just throw it away.

The division had acquired additional warehouse space at the Elmore St. facility

---

[1]Newcomb was pointing to Exhibit 5, which showed the costs of the activity "Respond to Customer Requests" being incurred in seven departments.

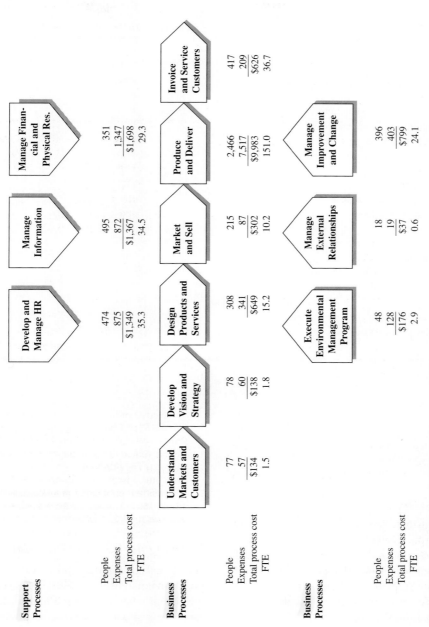

**Support Processes**

| | Develop and Manage HR | Manage Information | Manage Financial and Physical Res. |
|---|---|---|---|
| People | 474 | 495 | 351 |
| Expenses | 875 | 872 | 1,347 |
| Total process cost | $1,349 | $1,367 | $1,698 |
| FTE | 35.3 | 34.5 | 29.3 |

**Business Processes**

| | Understand Markets and Customers | Develop Vision and Strategy | Design Products and Services | Market and Sell | Produce and Deliver | Invoice and Service Customers |
|---|---|---|---|---|---|---|
| People | 77 | 78 | 308 | 215 | 2,466 | 417 |
| Expenses | 57 | 60 | 341 | 87 | 7,517 | 209 |
| Total process cost | $134 | $138 | $649 | $302 | $9,983 | $626 |
| FTE | 1.5 | 1.8 | 15.2 | 10.2 | 151.0 | 36.7 |

**Business Processes**

| | Execute Environmental Management Program | Manage External Relationships | Manage Improvement and Change |
|---|---|---|---|
| People | 48 | 18 | 396 |
| Expenses | 128 | 19 | 403 |
| Total process cost | $176 | $37 | $799 |
| FTE | 2.9 | 0.6 | 24.1 |

**EXHIBIT 3** Process Costs for Crawfordsville Facilities

---

**EXHIBIT 4**  Top 20 ABM Activities for Crawfordsville Facilities

| TOP 20 ACTIVITIES | SIX-MONTH SALARY AND WAGE DOLLARS (IN THOUSANDS) |
|---|---|
| Prepare and issue job specifications | $198 |
| Train and educate employees | 159 |
| Develop and deploy information systems | 156 |
| Make process improvements | 146 |
| Track job status and expedite jobs | 135 |
| Perform application maintenance | 132 |
| Prepare/make-ready equipment/process for production | 131 |
| Respond to customer information requests | 118 |
| Develop new product/service concepts and plans | 117 |
| Provide consulting and technical support | 117 |
| Evaluate employee performance | 109 |
| Find material to be moved | 106 |
| Schedule production lines/equipment and crewing | 100 |
| Ensure ISO 9000 compliance | 97 |
| Prepare for production | 94 |
| Compile and maintain billing information | 94 |
| Obtain customer intellectual property | 89 |
| Maintain job file and enter transactions for completed jobs | 86 |
| Plan for information resources/management | 83 |
| Monitor line performance | 82 |
| Total | $2,349,000,  or 44% of all people activities |

*Source: Stream ABM model; KPMG analysis.*
*Note:* Stream employee costs for period 7/1/95 to 12/31/95.

---

three miles away to provide storage for the manuals and documentation produced for newer customers like Microsoft, Intuit, and Macromedia. While large lots of IBM work-in-process and finished goods inventory sat inactive in the main (South St.) Crawfordsville facility, products finished for newer customers had to be shipped immediately to the Elmore St. warehouse, where it was stored, prior to shipment to customers. By December 1994, 80% of the output from the South St. plant was being trucked over to Elmore St. This output was often shipped one week later to the customer.

Diane Chastain, manager of planning and order fulfillment, commented on this practice:

Some costs of this arrangement were obvious, like the $150,000 spent annually on trucking. But lots of other costs were hidden until they were revealed through the ABM activity analysis. To address this problem, we had to overcome a major psychological hurdle. This business started with IBM in 1983, and it was a big deal to acknowledge how much our business model had changed in recent years.

### Selecting the Winning Proposal

As Michalski thumbed through the five proposals that had been presented, he stopped for a moment when he saw the half-million-dollar price tag accompanying Chastain's proposal. At Donnelley, a manager did not request that kind of money without compelling

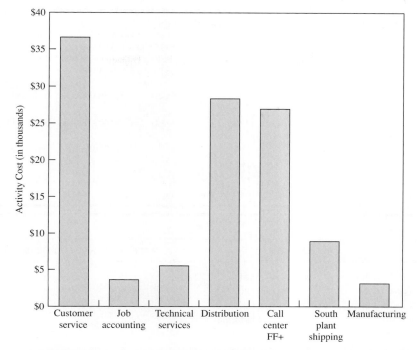

**EXHIBIT 5** Costs of the Activity "Respond to Customer Requests"—by Department

financials. He was curious to see just how his managers would respond to the ABM data as they helped him to select the winning proposal. He wondered what kind of criteria his management team would bring to the table to help them make their choice.

## Appendix: Five Proposals

**Presentation 1:** ABM Process Improvement Proposal: Responding to Customer Information Requests, Presented by Bill Newcomb    (Quality)

Problems:
1. Seven Stream departments respond to information requests from customers, with no policy or directives to guide the gathering or reporting of information.
2. Customers frequently request the same information from two different departments.

3. Customers refused a request for a special report by department A will go to department B and get a positive response.

Action Steps:
1. Standardize/reduce ad hoc reporting.
2. Eliminate redundant reporting.
3. Clarify roles/reduce redundant follow-up.
4. Adjust price levels and structure.
5. Generate revenue for select "information services."
6. Create process to share/consolidate client information.

**Presentation 2:** Price of Quality, Presented by Denise Seeman

Although Stream pays $838,586 annually in quality costs, most of this money is spent gathering information that is never analyzed and never used to drive process improvements.

## Cost Reduction Opportunities Could Provide Substantial Savings

| ACTIVITY | FTES | HEAD-COUNT | FRAGMEN-TATION | SIX-MONTH ABM COSTS | ANNUAL PEOPLE COSTS | TARGET SAVINGS (25%) |
|---|---|---|---|---|---|---|
| Respond to customer information requests | 8.2 | 66 | 12% | $118,000 | $236,000 | $ 59,000 |
| Manage customer complaints | 4.9 | 57 | 9% | $ 73,000 | $146,000 | $365,000 |
| Track/expedite jobs | 8.5 | 67 | 13% | $135,000 | $270,000 | $675,000 |
| Maintain job files | 4.5 | 34 | 13% | 86,000 | $172,000 | $ 43,000 |
| Total | | | | $412,000 | $824,000 | $206,000 |

A 25% cost reduction would yield approximately $200,000 in annual savings.

## Workplan and Resources

| TEN-WEEK SCHEDULE | RESOURCES | WEEKLY UPDATE AND FEEDBACK |
|---|---|---|
| 2–3 weeks—Where are we today? | 1 Director/sponsor | |
| 8–10 weeks—Redesign and implementation | 1 Project manager | |
| | 1 Systems analyst | |
| | 3 Managers (part time) | |
| | 3 Researchers (full time) | |
| | KPMG support/involvement | |

### Problems:
1. Line workers assigned to do quality assurance have never been trained.
2. Inspection methods and sampling protocols have never been reviewed.
3. ISO 9000 documentation is never analyzed. There is no assumption that data will be used for continuous improvement.

### Action Steps:
1. Redefine what the Division and our customers need from our Quality Services.
2. Provide the training and direction required.

The analysis will consider:

***Pull/Inspect Samples***
Improved methods to collect data
Definition of customer reporting requirements
***Ensure ISO 9000 Compliance***
Isolate and improve hard dollars associated with ISO

***Ensure Compliance with Other Requirements (Blue Book)***
Measurement definition—related to customer reports and process capabilities
Duplication of effort
What do we do with this information?

***Benchmark Performance***
Where should we focus?
Currently low dollars; potentially large savings

***Make Process Improvements—Fragmented***
What are we currently doing with quality information?
Who is doing this, and are they the right people?
What is the return on what we are doing, or have done?
Are we prioritizing by need or potential?
Identify potential

***Ensure Process Capabilities***
Established operation vs. start-ups

***Estimated Results of Project: $257,000***
(30% savings of wage dollars)
Plus additional saving from intangibles: benchmarking, process improvements, and best practices

## Employee Involvement and Cost

| | | FTE | HEADCOUNT | ANNUAL COST |
|---|---|---|---|---|
| 5.6.3.2.1 | Pull samples | 1.35 | 12 | $ 43,462 |
| 5.6.3.2.2 | Inspect samples | 4.0 | 16 | 155,735 |
| 5.6.3.3 | Ensure process capabilities | 1.95 | 20 | 70,307 |
| 12.2.1 | Ensure ISO 9000 compliance | 7.17 | 48 | 194,738 |
| 12.2.2 | Ensure compliance—other | 2.55 | 31.6 | 59,711 |
| 12.3 | Benchmark performance | 0.45 | 5.6 | 23,410 |
| 12.4 | Make process improvements | 7.19 | 56.3 | 291,223 |
| | + all direct labor employees | | | $838,586 |

## What Do We Know Today?

Load movement indirect expense   =   $1,412,048 annually
Managing inventory expense   =   $  447,660 annually
Physical facility expense   =   $  614,758 annually
(see below for breakdown by activity)

RELATED ANNUAL EXPENSE—MANAGING INVENTORY
LOAD MOVEMENT INDIRECT EXPENSE SUMMARY

| ITEM NO. | DESCRIPTION | PEOPLE | EXPENSE | TOTAL | FTES | HEAD-COUNT |
|---|---|---|---|---|---|---|
| 5.2.3.1 | Find material to be moved | $212,542 | $227,103 | $439,645 | 6.80 | 29 |
| 5.2.3.3 | Move WIP | 58,754 | 68,473 | 127,227 | 2.15 | 17 |
| 5.2.3.4 | Move FG within plant | 111,552 | 193,092 | 304,644 | 4.25 | 24 |
| | Move to/from Elmore Street | 81,174 | 77,077 | 158,251 | 2.70 | 13 |
| 5.2.3.5.4 | Move material to/from outside | 24,594 | 88,017 | 112,611 | 0.60 | 5 |
| 5.2.3.8 | Material equipment cost/(depreciation/rent) | | 269,670 | 269,670 | | |
| | Total | $488,616 | $923,432 | $1,412,048 | 16.50 | 88 |
| **Managing inventory expense** | | | | | | |
| 5.6.2.2 | Managing WIP | $110,621 | 65,023 | $  175,824 | 3.10 | 36 |
| 5.6.2.3 | Managing finished goods | 108,699 | 163,136 | 271,836 | 3.85 | 32 |
| | Total | $219,320 | $228,159 | $  447,660 | 6.95 | 68 |

**Physical facility expense**

| | | SQUARE FEET | $/SQUARE FOOT | TOTAL | | |
|---|---|---|---|---|---|---|
| | Elmore Street warehouse rent | 80,630 | $3.00 | $  241,890 | | |
| | Elmore Street energy, insurance, taxes | | | 76,400 | | |
| | WIP rent—all areas | 45,630 | 2.53 | 115,287 | | |
| | FG rent—rack aisles only | 50,512 | 2.54 | 128,381 | | |
| | Outside warehouse | | | 52,800 | | |
| | Total | | | $  614,758 | | |
| **Total Annualized Expense** | | | | $2,474,466 | 23.45 | |

---

POTENTIAL BENEFIT $—LOAD STORAGE

1. *Store all active loads in CSS*

| | |
|---|---|
| $318,290 | Annual savings in finished goods rent at Elmore Street |
| (115,000) | Rent 35,000 square feet for long-term storage |
| (75,000) | Moving expense admin./Mitrak/loads |
| $128,290 | |

2. *Load movement improvement*

| | |
|---|---|
| $158,251 | Load movement to Elmore |
| 112,611 | Move to/from outside storage |
| 91,393 | Move FG within plant—30% |
| 38,135 | Move WIP within plant—30% |
| 87,929 | Find material—20% |
| 26,967 | Equipment savings of 10% |
| $515,286 | |

3. *Manage WIP improvement*

| | |
|---|---|
| $ 43,956 | 25% improvement |
| ⋮ | |

4. *Manage FG improvement*

| | |
|---|---|
| $ 67,959 | |
| | 25% improvement |

5. *Eliminate outside warehouses*

$ 52,800

**Total Annualized Potential Benefit—$808,291**

---

**Presentation 3:** Manage Work in Progress and Finished Goods Inventory Space: ABM Project—July 13, 1995, Presented by Diane Chastain

Problems:

1. We currently have too much inactive inventory stored in the South Street plant, and too much active inventory being shipped to Elmore Street, stored for a week or two, and then shipped to the customer, or end user.

2. We haven't known true cost of storage.

3. The vast majority of WIP inventory is never shipped or used. Storage costs outweigh potential for use.

Action Steps:

1. Eliminate WIP inventory:
   - Define process to store inventory
   - Kill all parts with no known use
2. Exchange warehouses:
   - Install Mitrak-FG in South Street plant
   - Move active loads to South Plant
   - Keep all inactive loads at Elmore

Associated Costs of Implementation Provide Direct and Immediate Payback

| | |
|---|---|
| Demolition and rack erection | $ 25,000 |
| Build production office | 150,000 |
| Electric, air and data connections | 65,000 |
| Equipment for parcel and pick/pack | 230,900 |
| Consultant fees | 72,400 |
| System hardware (M.A.U., controller, and token rings) | 25,000 |
| Pallet flow racks for freight staging | 15,000 |
| Total | $583,300 |

### Resources/Timeline

- Define guidelines and process for keeping WIP material by KPMG and CSRs. Goal to complete by 8/15
- WIP inventory reconciliation by 8/31/95
- Analysis and detailed plan to switch active versus inactive inventory to South Plant as outlined by KPMG, Engineering, and fulfillment staff. Goal to move before heavy activity of fourth quarter.

---

- Press clients to remove inventory or pay higher storage costs
- Redesign South Street for minimum movement layout
- Eliminate outside warehouse (1,001 loads)

### Presentation 4: Billing Costs, Presented by Michael Michalski

Problems:
1. It costs Stream $492,000 annually to compile and maintain billing information, to bill the final invoice, and to respond to billing inquiries.
2. Eight different Stream departments are involved in compiling and maintaining billing information, and later responding to billing inquiries.

Action Steps:
1. We need to first understand the process better; to determine which departments are doing what and detect any obvious redundancies.

2. We then want to determine what kinds of information are worthwhile for the division— what data are tied to customer complaints, profitability analysis, etc.
3. We want to centralize the function, simplify the process, and reduce the number of people involved.

See following display for costs and required FTEs by activity.

### Presentation 5: Human Resource Management in FF+, Presented by Jim Martin and Molly Day

Problems:
1. HR activities are conducted by 34 different people in FF+* and amount to 10 FTEs.
2. Many activities are duplicated by HR department, payroll, and others in FF+.
3. Phone service reps work under three levels of supervision, at a ratio of less than five reps for every supervisor. (See diagram below for current reporting structure.)
4. Roles of the 14 team leaders, 5 team coordinators, 4 assistant account administrators, 10 account administrators, and 7 supervisors are not clear.

Action Steps:
1. Reduce number of supervisors and number of kinds of supervisory positions.

---

*FF+ is short for fulfillment plus all other phone activity, which includes product registration, licensing, password listing, and "upselling" related to these activities.

---

### Extended Billing Process—$246,000 per Six-Month Period and 20.6 Full-Time Equivalents

| | (8 depts. involved) | (5 depts. involved) | (8 depts. involved) |
|---|---|---|---|
| | 6.1.1.2 Compile and maintain other billing information | 6.1.2.2 Bill final invoice | 6.1.3 Respond to billing inquiries |
| People | $ 94,000 | $57,000 | $25,000 |
| Expenses | 42,000 | 14,000 | 14,000 |
| Total cost | $136,000 | $71,000 | $39,000 |
| FTEs | 10.8 | 7.7 | 2.1 |

**Total Net Sales = $108M**          **Net Sales per FTE = $5.3M**

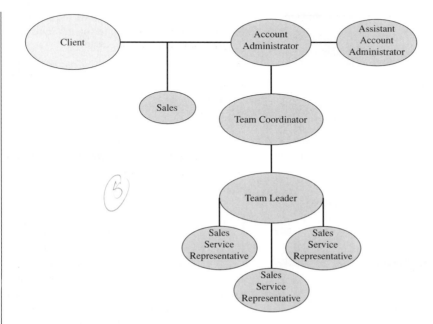

Current Information Flow

2. Clarify roles.
3. Reduce fragmentation of employee activities.
4. Realize cost savings in salary and wage.
5. Create a model that improves communication with clients as it eliminates redundant supervision.

# MosCo, Inc.: A Case Study*

The evening before the annual two-year budget review, Cosmos "Chip" Offtiol, MosCo's director of operations, was confident. While he waited for the latest financial estimates, he thought of the plan he and his staff had methodically prepared which successfully addressed all the crises this new business unit was facing: competitive transfer pricing on an aging product, developing and marketing new products to external customers against an established market leader, reducing manufacturing costs, improving manufacturing utilization, and improving its slim levels of profitability.

When Jonathan Janus, MosCo's controller, solemnly delivered the requested pro-forma income statements, Offtiol's mood dramatically changed. Instead of sustained profit, Chip was shocked to see significant projected operating losses. He wondered why his extensive planning had not improved MosCo's 1995 and 1996 financial results. With less than 24 hours before he was to

*Prepared by Richard J. Block, Digital Equipment Corporation, and Lawrence P. Carr, Babson College, as the basis for class discussion rather than to illustrate effective or ineffective handling of an operational situation. Material prepared with the cooperation of Digital Equipment Corporation and the Digital Semiconductor Business Unit.

Babson College case 195-007-1. Copyright © 1994, 1995 by Richard J. Block and Lawrence P. Carr.

offer senior management a viable business plan, he felt abandoned and hopeless.

## Background

MosCo, a semiconductor design and manufacturing company, is a wholly owned subsidiary of Computer Systems, Inc. (CSI), a leading manufacturer of client/servers, workstations, and personal computers. During 1993 and 1994, MosCo manufactured and sold to CSI a single product, the ×100, a 100 MHz, 10 nanosecond microprocessor. The ×100 is a .75 micron device packaged in a 339 pin-grid array (PGA) and is used in CSI's servers and workstations. MosCo has sold to CSI 150,000 units of the ×100 in each of the past two years.

Although MosCo sells entirely to its corporate parent, MosCo was required to establish competitive prices for its devices by Q394 [third quarter of 1994]. Previously, the ×100 had been sold to CSI at full cost. Establishing competitive prices was but one of many changes CSI required MosCo to make. In 1995, CSI planned on changing all of its major business units into profit centers. CSI management felt each business unit needed flexibility and independence to react to rapidly changing market conditions. As profit centers, CSI believed each of its business units would be more accountable for their own financial success. Their strategies and annual performance would, as well, be more visible and measurable. For MosCo, this meant the ability to sell their devices to external customers utilizing available manufacturing capacity. MosCo could also recover the large development costs for future products and control their destiny.

MosCo established the competitive market selling price of the ×100 at $850, based on industry price/performance comparisons. CSI approved of this market-based method of establishing transfer prices. It ensured CSI could purchase internally at a competitive price while placing the burden of cost management appropriately on MosCo. MosCo's controller, Jonathan Janus, prepared revised financial statements applying the $850 transfer price to MosCo's 1993 and 1994 shipments (Exhibit 1). Gordon Scott, MosCo's Vice President and General Manager, was pleased to see MosCo had generated profits of $4.9M and $1.9M for 1993 and 1994, respectively, on annual revenues of $127.5M after applying the newly established transfer price. The profit decline in

**EXHIBIT 1**  MosCo, Inc.—Income Statement

|  | 1993 | 1994 |
|---|---|---|
| Revenue | | |
| ×100: 150,000 @ $850 | $127,500,000 | $127,500,000 |
| Cost of Sales | | |
| Wafers: (16,595 @ $45) | $ 746,775 | $ 746,775 |
| Packages: (175,000 @ $50) | $ 8,750,000 | $ 8,750,000 |
| Mfg. spending | $ 91,112,000 | $ 91,112,000 |
| Total cost of sales | $100,608,775 | $100,608,775 |
| Gross margin | $ 26,891,225 | $ 26,891,225 |
| % | 21% | 21% |
| Process development | $ 14,000,000 | $ 14,000,000 |
| Product development | $ 5,000,000 | $ 5,000,000 |
| Marketing & administration | $ 3,000,000 | $ 6,000,000 |
| Operating profit | $ 4,891,225 | $ 1,891,225 |

1994 reflected the establishment and staffing of MosCo's new marketing department. This department was created to identify and open external market opportunities for new products currently under development.

As FY95 approaches, MosCo management is faced with a number of pressures and unknowns. CSI is under severe competitive pressures in their server and workstation product lines and is already demanding a price reduction on the ×100. They also insist MosCo remain profitable. Carlotta Price, head of MosCo's new marketing department, determined from industry studies the price/performance for microprocessors halves every 18 months (Moore's Law). To remain competitive, merchant semiconductor companies were consistently offering some combination of price reductions and/or performance improvements, such that their products' price/performance (price per unit of speed) halved every 1.5 years. Thus, for the ×100, and for every CPU MosCo developed and manufactured, Price believed the market would require similarly timed price/performance offerings. Price knew any price reductions would require offsetting cost reductions if MosCo was to remain profitable and wondered what the manufacturing organization was thinking.

As product development was no longer working on any ×100 performance improvements, Price computed required price reductions on the ×100 following the industry model. The ×100 would continue at the $850 price through Q195, then drop to $637.50 at the start of Q295, drop to $425.00 at the start of Q196, and to $318.75 at the start of Q496. Price was troubled by these prices as she knew CSI was requesting 150,000 units in FY95, but only 75,000 in FY96. CSI indicated it expected a customer shift away from workstations and into CSI's new personal computer line. (Appendix I presents an overview of the semiconductor manufacturing process typically found in a microprocessor supplier like MosCo. Appendix II presents an overview of the product costing process used by MosCo.)

Product cost for the ×100 had remained constant during FY93 and FY94 at approximately $665 (Exhibit 2). Price computed cost reductions of approximately $166.25 per year (to $498.75 in FY95 and $332.50 in 1996) would be necessary to maintain the ×100's current gross margin of −22%. She wondered if manufacturing could achieve a cost reduction that steep.

Concurrently with the ×100 pricing activities, P. J. Watt, head of product development,

**EXHIBIT 2** FY94 Product Cost Worksheet for the ×100

| DESCRIPTION | COST/WAFER | COST/DIE | CUM COST/DIE |
|---|---|---|---|
| Yielded raw wafer | $ 50.00 | $ 1.00 | $ 1.00 |
| Wafer production cost | $5,245.15 | $104.90 | $105.90 |
| Probe production cost | $ 785.71 | $ 15.71 | $121.62 |
| Probe yield | | 25% | $486.47 |
| 339 PGA package cost | | $ 50.00 | $536.47 |
| Assembly production cost | | $ 9.26 | $545.73 |
| Assembly yield | | 90% | $606.36 |
| Test production cost | | $ 32.14 | $638.51 |
| Test yield | | 96% | $665.11 |
| Total ×100 Product Cost | | | $665.11 |

*Note: Gross die/wafer: 50.*

sent an urgent request to Scott, Price, Janus, and Offtiol, requesting $3M in funding. This would accelerate the completion of an integer-only microprocessor, the ×50 and the follow-on CPU, the ×75. The ×50, a new product already under development, could be completed with $1M of the additional funding and made available for volume shipment by the beginning of FY95. The remaining $2M would be spent during FY95 and FY96 to complete development and ready the ×75 for volume shipment by the beginning of FY97.

The ×50 is a 50 MHz, 20 nanosecond CPU, which, like the ×100, is manufactured using the present .75 micron technology. But unlike the ×100, the ×50 does not have a floating-point processor. The elimination of the floating-point processor reduces the size and the power requirements of the CPU. The ×50 and ×75 can be packaged in a 168 pin-grid array (PGA), which costs $15, $35 less than the 339 PGA used by the ×100. However, the testing parameters of the ×50 and ×75 are significantly different than the ×100 and require a Bonn tester, which MosCo does not currently own. This $2M tester, if purchased, will add $1.2M in annual depreciation and other direct operating costs and $800,000 in incremental annual support costs to the present level of manufacturing spending.

The ×50 and ×75 are targeted as entree devices for CSI's personal computer business. NoTel is the market leader in .75 micron integer-only microprocessors. Their N50 CPU (also 50 MHz, 20 nanoseconds) sells for $500. The N50 has just been announced, with volume shipments to coincide with the beginning of MosCo's FY95. MosCo's new marketing department estimates the demand for the ×50 from CSI and potential new external customers could easily exceed 1M units per year. To break into this market, Price recommended heavy market promotion and a price/performance two times the competition. Estimates for unit sales po-

tential from advertising are 100,000 for the first $1M, up to 500,000 for the second $1M, and over 1M for a third million dollar advertising expenditure.

With the increased pricing pressures from both CSI and the external marketplace, product cost reduction became critical. This, coupled with the request from product development for additional funding, had Gordon Scott very concerned. He knew it was important to bring out the ×50 and ×75 quickly, but the pricing pressures for their market entrance and the pricing pressures from CSI on the ×100 seemed almost impossible to meet and still achieve a profit in FY95 and 96. He knew, however, if he didn't maintain a profitable operation, his tenure would be short.

Reduced production costs leading to competitive manufacturing appeared to be the critical factor necessary to sustain MosCo's slim profit levels. Scott asked Offtiol to formulate a series of recommendations to develop and manufacture an expanded CPU product line in FY95 and FY96, and to have them completed by the annual two-year budget review, scheduled to commence in a month. Scott knew soon after MosCo's budget review, he would have to present a credible business plan to CSI management. He worried how he could develop a viable plan in light of the obstacles.

### The Offtiol Plan

Offtiol started his preparation by reviewing the detailed ×100 product cost (Exhibits 2, 3, and 4). He immediately assembled a team, comprised of Janus, from Finance, T. Q. Marcel, from Quality, and Beeb Ruby, from Training. The team, led by Marcellus deStepper, the manager of wafer fabrication, conducted a cost review by activity. Chip, like Scott, believed to maintain profitability, significant cost reductions would be necessary. He had recently taken an executive development course in activity-based costing and

**EXHIBIT 3** FY94 Used Capacity and Process Costs Worksheet for the ×100

| OPERATION | PER YEAR | MFG. SPENDING | COST/UNIT |
|---|---|---|---|
| Planned wafer capacity | 16,595 | | |
| Engineering test wafers | 1,040 | | |
| Planned wafer starts | 15,555 | | |
| Wafer fabrication yield | 90% | | |
| Planned wafer production | 13999.50 | $73,429,500 | $5,245.15 |
| Planned probed wafer starts | 14,000 | $11,000,000 | $ 785.71 |
| Gross die/wafer for ×100 = 50 | 50 | | |
| Total gross die thru probe | 700,000 | | |
| Probe yield for ×100 | 25% | | |
| ×100 probed die output | 175,000 | | |
| Planned assembly starts | 175,000 | $ 1,620,000 | $     9.26 |
| ×100 assembly yield | 90% | | |
| Planned assembly completions | 157,500 | | |
| Planned test starts | 157,500 | $ 5,062,500 | $   32.14 |
| ×100 test yield | 96% | | |
| Planned test output | 151,200 | | |
| Total Manufacturing Spending | | $91,112,000 | |

knew it was a proven method for better understanding cost structures, cost drivers, and highlighting non-value-added work. Offtiol was excited, given the size of the assignment and his belief there were both cost reduction opportunities in manufacturing and necessary improvements in the current standard cost system. He felt the current standard cost system did not properly capture the complexity of MosCo's production process. He felt an ABC analysis could provide the needed insight necessary to reduce the ×100 product cost by the $166 marketing had requested.

The team mapped the processes of the entire operation and then reassigned costs to the newly defined activities (Exhibits 5a–c). The direct manufacturing operation was now better delineated by equipment use (Exhibit 5b). The manufacturing support organizations were also better understood. Their key activities were costed, then each was aligned to the manufacturing operation it supported (Exhibit 5c). MosCo's ABC team reset the ×100

product cost in line with the true practical capacity of the manufacturing process. The team saw capacity utilization as a major driver of product cost. The old product costing methodology was based on the planned utilization of each manufacturing process with underutilized manufacturing costs absorbed into product costs.

The revised ×100 product cost (Exhibits 6 and 7) was pleasing but not totally surprising to Offtiol. It confirmed his belief in the inaccuracies of the old costing method. The new ×100 product cost of $437.50 was $227.61 lower than the $665.11 original cost before the ABC study. It did not make sense to charge the ×100 for the costs of resources it did not consume. Chip felt he could immediately commit to Price's 1995 product cost reduction request of $166.

To achieve the 1996 product cost goal of $332.50, Chip and his team looked further into the activity-based costing results. The study clearly showed wafer fabrication was the largest area of manufacturing costs. Chip,

**EXHIBIT 4** FY94 Spending Summary by Organization

| ORGANIZATION | MANUFACTURING | | | | RESEARCH & DEVELOP | | SG&A | TOTAL |
| | FABRICATION | PROBE | ASSEMBLY | TEST | PROD DEVP | PROC DEVP | MKT & ADM | |
| --- | --- | --- | --- | --- | --- | --- | --- | --- |
| Direct mfg | $57,000,000 | $11,000,000 | $1,620,000 | $5,062,500 | | | | $ 74,682,500 |
| Res & devp | | | | | $2,000,0008 | $9,000,000 | | 11,000,000 |
| Mkt & adm | | | | | | | $5,000,000 | 5,000,000 |
| Support orgs | | | | | | | | |
| Facilities | 5,500,000 | | | | 1,000,000 | 3,000,000 | 500,000 | 10,000,000 |
| Yield eng | 2,000,000 | | | | | | | 2,000,000 |
| CIMT | 4,000,000 | | | | 2,000,000 | 2,000,000 | | 8,500,000 |
| Qual & rel | 3,537,500 | | | | | | 500,000 | 3,537,500 |
| Purchasing | 1,392,000 | | | | | | | 1,392,000 |
| Tot support | $16,429,500 | | | | 3,000,000 | $ 5,000,000 | $1,000,000 | $ 25,429,500 |
| Tot spending | $73,429,500 | $11,000,000 | $1,620,000 | $5,062,500 | $ 5,000,000 | $14,000,000 | $6,000,000 | $116,112,000 |
| Fabrication | $73,429,500 | | | | | | | |
| Probe | 11,000,000 | | | | | | | |
| Assembly | 1,620,000 | | | | | | | |
| Test | 5,062,500 | | | | | | | |
| Tot mfg spend | $91,112,000 | | | | | | | |

**EXHIBIT 5A** FY94 Activity-Based Spending Summary by Organization

| ACTIVITY | MANUFACTURING | | | | RESEARCH & DEVELOP | | SG&A | TOTAL |
|---|---|---|---|---|---|---|---|---|
| | FABRICATION | PROBE | ASSEMBLY | TEST | PROD DEVP | PROC DEVP | MKT & ADM | |
| Direct mfg (see Exhibit 5b) | $57,000,000 | $11,000,000 | $1,620,000 | $5,062,500 | | | | $74,682,500 (≈ 58) |
| RES & DEVP | | | | | $2,000,000 | $9,000,000 | | $11,000,000 |
| MKT & ADM | | | | | | | | |
| Marketing | | | | | | | $3,000,000 | $3,000,000 |
| Administration | | | | | | | $1,000,000 | $1,000,000 |
| Finance/hr | | | | | | | $1,000,000 | $1,000,000 |
| Total | | | | | | | $5,000,000 | $5,000,000 |
| Tot support (see Exhibit 5c) | $10,392,000 | $2,000,000 | | $3,037,500 | $3,000,000 | $6,000,000 | $1,000,000 | $25,429,500 (50) |
| Tot spending | $67,392,000 | $13,000,000 | $1,620,000 | $8,100,000 | $5,000,000 | $15,000,000 | $6,000,000 | $116,112,000 |
| Fabrication | $67,392,000 | | | | | | | |
| Probe | $13,000,000 | | | | | | | |
| Assembly | $1,620,000 | | | | | | | |
| Test | $8,100,000 | | | | | | | |
| Tot mfg spend | $90,112,000 | | | | | | | |

**EXHIBIT 5B** FY94 Direct Manufacturing Activity-Based Spending Summary

| ACTIVITY | MANUFACTURING | | | | RESEARCH & DEVELOP | | SG&A | TOTAL |
|---|---|---|---|---|---|---|---|---|
| | FABRICATION | PROBE | ASSEMBLY | TEST | PROD DEVP | PROC DEVP | MKT & ADM | |
| Equipment Capacity: driven by equipment installation | | | | | | | | |
| Depreciation | $30,000,000 | $ 3,500,000 | $ 520,000 | $1,400,000 | | | | $35,420,000 |
| Utility costs | $ 5,000,000 | $ 1,000,000 | $ 50,000 | $ 500,000 | | | | $ 6,550,000 |
| Property/site | $ 5,000,000 | $ 500,000 | $ 50,000 | $ 100,000 | | | | $ 5,650,000 |
| Total | $40,000,000 | $ 5,000,000 | $ 620,000 | $2,000,000 | | | | $47,620,000 |
| Equipment Capacity: driven by equipment uptime | | | | | | | | |
| Equip. engnrs | $ 8,000,000 | $ 2,000,000 | | $1,762,500 | | | | $11,762,500 |
| Monitor wafer | $ 1,000,000 | | | | | | | $ 1,000,000 |
| Opn supplies | $ 1,000,000 | $ 1,000,000 | $ 100,000 | $ 300,000 | | | | $ 2,400,000 |
| Total | $10,000,000 | $ 3,000,000 | $ 100,000 | $2,062,500 | | | | $15,162,500 |
| Equipment Capacity: driven by production | | | | | | | | |
| Direct labor | $ 5,000,000 | $ 2,000,000 | $ 800,000 | $ 700,000 | | | | $ 8,500,000 |
| Monitor wafer | $ 1,000,000 | | | | | | | $ 1,000,000 |
| Opn supplies | $ 1,000,000 | $ 1,000,000 | $ 100,000 | $ 300,000 | | | | $ 2,400,000 |
| Total | $ 7,000,000 | $ 3,000,000 | $ 900,000 | $1,000,000 | | | | $11,900,000 |
| Tot Dir Mfg | $57,000,000 | $11,000,000 | $1,620,000 | $5,062,500 | | | | $74,682,500 |
| Tot Dir Mfg (new Bonn tester) | | | | $1,215,000 | | | | |

**EXHIBIT 5C** FY94 Support Group Activity-Based Spending Summary

| ACTIVITY | FABRICATION | PROBE | ASSEMBLY | TEST | PROD DEVP | PROC DEVP | MKT & ADM | TOTAL |
|---|---|---|---|---|---|---|---|---|
| | MANUFACTURING | | | | RESEARCH & DEVELOP | | SG&A | |
| Facilities | | | | | | | | |
| D/i water | $ 1,000,000 | | | | | $ 500,000 | | $ 1,500,000 |
| site support | $ 500,000 | | | $ 100,000 | $ 500,000 | $ 500,000 | $500,000 | $ 2,100,000 |
| utilities | $ 3,000,000 | | | $ 400,000 | $ 500,000 | $ 2,000,000 | | $ 5,900,000 |
| chemicals | $ 500,000 | | | | | | | $ 500,000 |
| Total | $ 5,000,000 | | | $ 500,000 | $1,000,000 | $3,000,000 | $500,000 | $10,000,000 |
| Yield Eng: yield improvement: $2,000,000 | | | | | | | | $ 2,000,000 |
| CIMT | | | | | | | | |
| Shop floor sys | $ 1,000,000 | | | $1,000,000 | | | | $ 2,000,000 |
| Networks | $ 500,000 | | | $ 500,000 | $1,000,000 | $ 500,000 | $250,000 | $ 2,750,000 |
| Field svc | $ 500,000 | | | $ 500,000 | $ 500,000 | | $250,000 | $ 1,750,000 |
| System devp | | | | | $ 500,000 | $ 500,000 | | $ 1,000,000 |
| Equip connect | | | | | | $1,000,000 | | $ 1,000,000 |
| Total | $ 2,000,000 | | | $2,000,000 | $2,000,000 | $2,000,000 | $500,000 | $ 8,500,000 |
| Quality | | | | | | | | |
| Doc control | $ 1,000,000 | | | | | | | $ 1,000,000 |
| Fail analysis | $ 500,000 | | | $ 100,000 | | $ 250,000 | | $ 850,000 |
| Equip calibrate | $ 500,000 | | | $ 437,500 | | $ 750,000 | | $ 1,687,500 |
| Total | $ 2,000,000 | | | $ 537,500 | | $1,000,000 | | $ 3,537,500 |
| Purchasing | $ 1,392,000 | | | | | | | $ 1,392,000 |
| Tot Sup Spend | $10,392,000 | $2,000,000 | | $3,037,500 | $3,000,000 | $6,000,000 | $1,000,000 | $25,429,500 (5X) |
| Tot Sup Spend (new Bonn tester) | | | | $ 810,000 | | | | |

*ABC*

**EXHIBIT 6**  FY94 Revised Product Cost Worksheet for the ×100

| DESCRIPTION | COST/WAFER | COST/DIE | CUM COST/DIE |
|---|---|---|---|
| Yielded raw wafer | $   50.00 | $  1.00 | $    1.00 |
| Wafer production cost | $3,000.00 | $60.00 | $  61.00  *vs  20.33* |
| Probe production cost | $   500.00 | $10.00 | $  71.00 |
| Probe yield | | 25% | $284.00 |
| 339 PGA package cost | | $50.00 | $334.00 |
| Assembly production cost | | $  8.00 | $342.00 |
| Assembly yield | | 90% | $380.00 |
| Test production cost | | $40.00 | $420.00 |
| Test yield | | 96% | $437.50 |
| Total ×100 Product Cost | | | $437.50 |

*unit ( perdie)*
*die = unit*
*1 wafer = 50 dies*

*Note: Gross die/Wafer: 50.*

with the help of Janus, computed that if the ×100 wafer cost was reduced from the 1995 level of $3,000/wafer to $1866/wafer, the ×100 total product cost would be lowered by $105 achieving the desired $332.50. To obtain a wafer cost of $1,866, spending reductions of about $25.5M, or 38%, in wafer fabrication would have to be achieved

(Chart I). Chip again asked Marcellus deStepper to review the fabrication area for further cost reduction opportunities. Chip asked deStepper to formulate a plan which could reduce direct wafer fabrication spending by about $25.5 million (from $67.4 to $41.9 million).

**EXHIBIT 7**  FY94 Revised Capacity and Process Costs Worksheet for the ×100

| OPERATION | PER YEAR | MFG. SPENDING | COST/UNIT |
|---|---|---|---|
| Planned wafer capacity | 26,000 | | |
| Engineering test wafers | 1,040 | | |
| Planned wafer starts | 24,960 | | |
| Wafer fabrication yield | 90% | | |
| Planned wafer production | 22,464 | $67,392,000 | $3,000.00 |
| Planned probed wafer starts | 26,000 | $13,000,000 | $  500.00 |
| Gross Die/Wafer for ×100 = 50 | 50 | | |
| Total gross die thru probe | 1,300,000 | | |
| Probe yield for ×100 | 25% | | |
| ×100 probed die output | 325,000 | | |
| Planned assembly starts *— bottleneck* | 202,500 | $  1,620,000 | $      8.00 |
| ×100 assembly yield | 90% | | |
| Planned assembly completions | 182,250 | | |
| Planned test starts | 202,500 | $  8,100,000 | $     40.00 |
| ×100 test yield        96% | | | |
| Planned test output | 194,400 | | |
| Total Manufacturing Spending | | $90,112,000 | |

*bottleneck, still have to throw some*

**Chart I:** ×100 1996 Target Product Cost Analysis

| MANUFACTURING AREA | COST/ WAFER | COST/DIE | CUM COST/DIE |
|---|---|---|---|
| Desired wafer cost | $1,866.00 | $37.32 | $    37.32 |
| Yielded raw wafer cost | 50.00 | 1.00 | 38.32 |
| Probe cost/wafer | 500.00 | 10.00 | 48.32 |
| Probe yield | | 25.0% | 193.28 |
| 339 PGA package cost | | $50.00 | 243.28 |
| Assembly cost | | 8.00 | 251.28 |
| Assembly yield | | 90.0% | 279.20 |
| Test cost | | $40.00 | 319.20 |
| Test yield | | 96.0% | 332.50 |
| Current fabrication spending | | | $67,392,000 |
| Desired level of spending | | | |
| (22,464 annual wafer production @ $1,866) | | | $41,917,824 |
| Required spending reduction | | | $25,474,176 |
| | | | 38% |

*Note: ×100 gross die/wafer = 50.*

deStepper returned in two weeks with an alternative plan (Chart II). His team found nominal spending opportunities by (1) reducing monitor wafer usage, (2) redesigning wafer lot handling procedures, and (3) by the better placement of inspection stations. deStepper's most significant discovery was the 64% increase in capacity attained by increasing equipment uptime (the time equipment is not undergoing repair or preventive maintenance). Higher uptime, however, required an annual investment of about $1.8 million in additional equipment engineers. While this investment would increase wafer fabrication spending to about $69.2 million, wafer fabrication capacity would increase from 26,000 to about 42,700 in annual wafer starts. The increased capacity actually decreased the cost per wafer to $1,845, $21 lower than Offtiol had demanded.

**Chart II:** deStepper Alternative Capacity and Spending Plan

| | CURRENT LEVEL | PROPOSED LEVEL |
|---|---|---|
| Total wafer start capacity | 26,000 | 42,707 |
| Engineering wafer starts | 1,040 | 1,040 |
| Production wafer starts | 24,960 | 41,667 |
| Fabrication line yield | 90% | 90% |
| Annual wafer completions | 22,464 | 37,500 |
| Annual spending level | $67,392,000 | $67,392,000 |
| deStepper's added spending | | $ 1,797,120 |
| Proposed spending level | | $69,189,120 |
| Cost wafer | $      3,000 | $      1,845 |

Offtiol dismissed deStepper's alternative plan outright. "Spending needs to decrease, not *increase!*" he exclaimed, and reiterated his request to reduce fabrication spending by 38%.

Offtiol then focused his team's cost reduction efforts on packaging costs, another major cost component of the ×100. (MosCo had spent close to $8.8 million annually on chip packages.) He asked MosCo's purchasing manager, Polly Nomial, to pressure MosCo's 339 PGA supplier to lower their $50 price. Polly told Chip she had already made this request and was reminded by the vendor that the 339 PGA was a unique design, only used by MosCo for the ×100. With order volumes declining by 50% in a year, Polly said it would be difficult to keep the $50 package price from increasing.

The final area of review was the ×50 proposal. Chip and the team reviewed its product cost, necessary manufacturing process and spending requirements (Exhibits 8 and 9). Chip compared the ×50 product cost (computed assuming all production capacity was used to manufacture the ×50) with the ×100 and noted a few significant cost differences. The reduced size of the ×50 (no floating point processor) increased the number of die able to be placed on each wafer, thus reducing the fabrication cost per die 67% from the ×100 ($61.00 for the ×100; $20.33 for the ×50). The increase in the number of die on each wafer, however, increased the probe time and increased the probe cost per wafer by 25% ($500 for the ×100; $625 for the ×50). He was pleased with the doubling of assembly capacity resulting from the smaller package required by the ×50 (202,500 annual assembly starts for the ×100; 405,000 for the ×50). The increase in assembly throughput reduced the ×50 assembly costs by 50%. Chip was pleasantly surprised at the ×50's lower test costs. Even though the ×50 required a new tester, the lower annual operating costs versus the ×100 along with the reduced testing time (from the elimination of the floating point unit) resulted in a per unit test cost of only $5 versus $40 for the ×100.

With the ×50's cost structure now soundly understood, Chip could better appreciate the high, but achievable, profit margins of the ×50. The margins ranged from 75%, during Q1–Q395 to about 67% in Q495 when the marketing-required price reduction took effect (Chart III). If deStepper could

---

**EXHIBIT 8**  FY95 Product Cost Worksheet for the ×50

| DESCRIPTION | COST/WAFER | COST/DIE | CUM COST/DIE |
|---|---|---|---|
| Yielded raw wafer | $    50.00 | $  0.33 | $  0.33 |
| Wafer production cost | $3,000.00 | $20.00 | $20.33 |
| Probe production cost | $   625.00 | $  4.17 | $24.50 |
| Probe yield | | 70% | $35.00 |
| 168 PGA package cost | | $15.00 | $50.00 |
| Assembly production cost | | $  4.00 | $54.00 |
| Assembly yield | | 96% | $56.25 |
| Test production cost | | $  5.00 | $61.25 |
| Test yield | | 98% | $62.50 |
| Total ×50 Product Cost | | | $62.50 |

*Note: Gross die/Wafer: 150.*

**EXHIBIT 9** FY95 Projected Capacity and Process Costs Worksheet for the ×50

| OPERATION | PER YEAR | MFG. SPENDING | COST/UNIT |
|---|---|---|---|
| Planned wafer capacity | 26,000 | | |
| Engineering test wafers | 1,040 | | |
| Planned wafer starts | 24,960 | | |
| Wafer fabrication yield | 90% | | |
| Planned wafer production | 22,464 | $67,392,000 | $3,000.00 |
| Planned probed wafer starts | 20,800 | $13,000,000 | $ 625.00 |
| Gross die/wafer for ×50 = 150 | 150 | | |
| Total gross die thru probe | 3,120,000 | | |
| Probe yield for ×50 | 70% | | |
| ×50 probed die output | 2,184,000 | | |
| Planned assembly starts | 405,000 | $ 1,620,000 | $ 4.00 |
| ×50 assembly yield | 90% | | |
| Planned assembly completions | 364,500 | | |
| Planned test starts | 405,000 | $ 2,025,000 | $ 5.00 |
| ×50 test yield | 96% | | |
| Planned test output | 388,800 | | |
| Total Manufacturing Spending | | $84,037,000 | |

achieve the $1866 wafer cost by the start of 1996 (Exhibits 10 and 11), the ×50 could achieve a very respectable margin of about 59% in the second half of 1996 at the required price of $125. Using the capacity available in 1995 and 1996 to produce 50,000 and 215,000 units, respectively, eas-ily convinced Offtiol to fund the ×50 development effort and purchase the new tester. While the product specifications for the ×75 were not yet available, he also agreed to fund its development effort. He felt the ×75 would achieve the same product margins the ×50 demonstrated.

**EXHIBIT 10** FY96 Revised Product Cost Worksheet for the ×50 (Reflecting Requested Wafer Fabrication Spending Reduction)

| DESCRIPTION | COST/WAFER | COST/DIE | CUM COST/DIE |
|---|---|---|---|
| Yielded raw wafer | $ 50.00 | $ 0.33 | $ 0.33 |
| Wafer production cost | $1,866.00 | $12.44 | $12.77 |
| Probe production cost | $ 625.00 | $ 4.17 | $16.94 |
| Probe yield | | 70% | $24.20 |
| 168 PGA package cost | | $15.00 | $39.20 |
| Assembly production cost | | $ 4.00 | $43.20 |
| Assembly yield | | 96% | $45.00 |
| Test production cost | | $ 5.00 | $50.00 |
| Test yield | | 98% | $51.02 |
| Total ×50 Product Cost | | | $51.02 |

*Note: Gross die/wafer: 150.*

**EXHIBIT 11**  FY96 Projected Capacity and Process Costs Worksheet for the ×50 (Reflecting Requested Wafer Fabrication Spending Reduction)

| OPERATION | PER YEAR | MGF. SPENDING | COST/UNIT |
|---|---|---|---|
| Planned wafer capacity | 26,000 | | |
| Engineering test wafers | 1,040 | | |
| Planned wafer starts | 24,960 | | |
| Wafer fabrication yield | 90% | | |
| Planned wafer production | 22,464 | $41,917,824 | $1,866.00 |
| Planned probed wafer starts | 20,800 | $13,000,000 | $  625.00 |
| Gross Die/Wafer for ×50 = 150 | 150 | | |
| Total gross die thru probe | 3,120,000 | | |
| Probe yield for ×50 | 70% | | |
| ×50 probed die output | 2,184,000 | | |
| Planned assembly starts | 405,000 | $  1,620,000 | $    4.00 |
| ×50 assembly yield | 90% | | |
| Planned assembly completions | 364,500 | | |
| Planned test starts | 405,000 | $  2,025,000 | $    5.00 |
| ×50 test yield | 96% | | |
| Planned test output | 388,800 | | |
| Total Manufacturing Spending | | $58,562,824 | |

**Chart III**

| | Q195–Q395 | Q495–Q296 | Q396 & Q496 |
|---|---|---|---|
| Price | $250.00 | $187.50 | $125.00 |
| Cost | $62.50 | $62.50 | $51.02 |
| Margin | $187.50 | $125.00 | $73.98 |
| Margin 59.2% | 75.0% | 66.7% | 59.2% |

Just as Chip was completing his ×50 product development meeting, Polly called and suggested outsourcing and then disinvesting MosCo's assembly operations. Polly had found an assembly house who could assemble the ×50 in its required 168 PGA for $5 per device (in volume levels of 500,000) with equivalent yields to those MosCo projected. Chip thought this idea had merit until he compared the $5 external assembly cost per device with the internal cost estimate of $4. He quickly concluded outsourcing would only increase the overall product cost and therefore was not a viable option.

A week before the budget review, Chip asked Janus to prepare new proforma income statements for FY94, FY95, and FY96. He wanted to reflect all of his cost reduction targets and product funding levels. He was curious to see the levels of profit he would generate in 1995 and 96 from (1) the revised ×100 product cost, (2) the 1996 cost reduction targets in wafer fabrication and their effect on the ×100 and ×50, (3) the funding of the ×50 and ×75, (4) the purchase of the Bonn tester the ×50 required, (5) the utilization of 1995 and 96 capacity for manufacturing the ×50, (6) the additional advertising expense necessary to fully promote the ×50 in the marketplace and, (7) the selling of the ×100 and ×50 using the marketing department pricing model. Chip was confident his decisions would prove sound and keep MosCo profitable in 1995 and 96.

Now, after a second review of Janus's pro-

**EXHIBIT 12A** Janus's Proforma Income Statement

|  | 1994 REVISED | 1995 RECOM'D | 1996 RECOM'D |
|---|---|---|---|
| Revenue | $127,500,000% | $115,312,500% | $ 63,476,562% |
| Cost of Sales |  |  |  |
|   Raw material costs | $ 9,496,755 | $ 10,348,010 | $ 8,282,255 |
|   Production costs | $ 90,112,000 | 59,063,500 | $ 27,788,853 |
|   Total product cost | $ 99,608,775 | $ 69,411,510 | $ 36,071,108 |
| Product gross margin | $ 27,891,225 | $ 45,900,990 | $ 27,405,454 |
|   % | 21.9% | 39.8% | 43.2% |
| Underutilized costs | $ 0 | $ 33,073,500 | $ 38,873,971 |
| Total cost of sales | $ 99,608,775 | $102,485,010 | $ 74,945,079 |
| Gross Margin | $ 27,891,225 | $ 12,827,490 | ($11,468,516) |
|   % | 21.9% | 11.1% | −18.1% |
| Process development | $ 15,000,000 | $ 15,000,000 | $ 15,000,000 |
| Product development | $ 6,000,000 | $ 6,000,000 | $ 6,000,000 |
| Marketing & administration | $ 6,000,000 | $ 7,000,000 | $ 8,000,000 |
| Operating profit (loss) | $ 891,225 | ($15,172,510) | ($40,468,516) |

**EXHIBIT 12B** FY95 Janus's Proforma Income Statement Worksheet

|  | ×100 | ×50 | FY95 |
|---|---|---|---|
| Revenue |  |  |  |
|   Q1 (37,500 @ $850) | $ 31,875,000 |  |  |
|   Q2–Q4 (112,500 @ $637.50) | $ 71,718,750 |  |  |
|   Q1–Q3 (37,500 @ $250) |  | $ 9,375,000 |  |
|   Q4 (12,500 @ $187.50) |  | $ 2,343,750 |  |
|  | $103,593,750 | $11,718,750 | $115,312,500 |
| Raw Material Costs |  |  |  |
|   Wafers: (16,595 @ $45) | $ 746,775 |  |  |
|   (583 @ $45) |  | $ 26,235 |  |
|   Packages: (175,000 @ $50) | $ 8,750,000 |  |  |
|   (55,000 @ $15) |  | $ 825,000 |  |
|  | $ 9,496,775 | $ 851,235 | $ 10,348,010 |
| Production Costs |  |  |  |
|   Fabrication: (14,000 @ $3000) | $ 42,000,000 |  |  |
|   (524 @ $3000) |  | $ 1,572,000 |  |
|   Probe: (14,000 @ $500) | $ 7,000,000 |  |  |
|   (524 @ $625) |  | $ 327,500 |  |
|   Assembly: (175,000 @ $8) | $ 1,400,000 |  |  |
|   (55,000 @ $4) |  | $ 220,000 |  |
|   Test: (157,000 @ $40) | $ 6,280,000 |  |  |
|   (52,800 @ $5) |  | $ 264,000 |  |
|  | $ 56,680,000 | $ 2,383,500 | $ 59,063,500 |
| Underutilized Costs |  |  |  |
|   Fabrication ($67,392,000 − ($42,000,000 + $1,572,000)) |  |  | $ 23,820,000 |
|   Probe ($13,000,000 − ($7,000,000 + $327,500)) |  |  | $ 5,672,500 |
|   Assembly ($1,620,000 − ($1,400,000 + $220,000)) |  |  | $ 0 |
|   Test ($8,100,000 − $6,280,000 + $2,025,000 − $264,000) |  |  | $ 3,581,000 |
|  |  |  | $ 33,073,500 |

*(handwritten margin note, left side: "Budgets 7/s")*

*(handwritten notes in middle of table: "expected units", "standard cost when prod @ max capacity")*

**EXHIBIT 12C** FY96 Janus's Proforma Income Statement Worksheet

| | ×100 | ×50 | FY96 |
|---|---|---|---|
| Revenue | | | |
| Q1–Q3 (56,250 @ $425) | $23,906,250 | | |
| Q4 (18,750 @ $318.75) | $ 5,976,562 | | |
| Q1–Q2 (107,500 @ $187.50) | | $20,156,250 | |
| Q3–Q4 (107,500 @ $125) | | $13,437,500 | |
| | $29,882,812 | $33,593,750 | $63,476,562 |
| Raw Material Costs | | | |
| Wafers: (7,991 @ $45) | $ 359,595 | | |
| (2448 @ $45) | | $ 110,160 | |
| Packages: (86,875 @ $50) | $ 4,343,750 | | |
| (231,250 @ $15) | | $ 3,468,750 | |
| | $ 4,703,345 | $ 3,578,910 | $ 8,282,255 |
| Production Costs | | | |
| Fabrication: (6,950 @ $1,866) | $12,968,700 | | |
| (2,203 @ $1,866) | | $ 4,110,798 | |
| Probe: (6,950 @ $500) | $ 3,475,000 | | |
| (2,203 @ $625) | | $ 1,376,875 | |
| Assembly: (86,875 @ $8) | $ 695,000 | | |
| (231,250 @ $4) | | $ 925,000 | |
| Test: (78,187 @ $40) | $ 3,127,480 | | |
| (222,000 @ $5) | | $ 1,110,000 | |
| | $20,266,180 | $ 7,522,673 | $27,788,853 |
| Underutilized Costs | | | |
| Fabrication ($41,917,824 − ($12,968,700 + $4,110,798)) | | | $24,838,326 |
| Probe ($13,000,000 − ($3,475,000 + $1,376,875)) | | | $ 8,148,125 |
| Assembly ($1,620,000 − ($695,000 + $925,000)) | | | $ 0 |
| Test ($8,100,000 − $3,127,480 + $2,025,000 − $1,110,000) | | | $ 5,887,520 |
| | | | $38,873,971 |

forma income statements (Exhibits 12a–c), Offtiol had become very anxious. He had to present a viable set of recommendations to MosCo's senior management the following day. He thought he and his team had explored and included all viable options in Janus's statements. Finally, Chip concluded the cause of the projected FY95 and FY96 losses was the overly aggressive pricing model. He decided he would present Janus's projections, highlight the losses in spite of the cost reductions reflected, and suggest keeping the ×100 price at $850 for all of 1995, and $637.50 for all of 1996. The $23.9M increase in FY95 revenue would turn the approximately $15.2 million loss into an $8.7 million profit. But the $17.9M increase in FY96 revenue would only improve the loss of about $40.5 million to about $22.6 million. Chip was convinced Scott would also agree Price's pricing model was too aggressive. He was certain Scott would approve a revised ×100 price and be receptive to a higher price for the ×50, which could offset the remaining projected 1996 loss. Chip felt it would take a combination of his cost reduction efforts and higher prices to maintain MosCo's profitability and thus demonstrate to CSI MosCo's ability to transform itself into a competitive business unit.

---

**EXHIBIT 13** Product Specifications

|  | ×100 | ×50 | N50 |
|---|---|---|---|
| Function | CPU/CISC | CPU/CISC | CPU/CISC |
| Technology | CMOS .75u | CMOS .75u | CMOS .75u |
| Frequency | 100 MHZ | 50 MHZ | 50 MHZ |
| Selling Prices |  |  |  |
| Actual: 1994 Q1 |  |  |  |
| 1994 Q2 |  |  |  |
| 1994 Q3 | $850.00 |  |  |
| 1994 Q4 |  |  |  |
| Proposed: 1995 Q1 |  | $250.00 | $500.00 |
| 1995 Q2 | $637.50 |  |  |
| 1995 Q3 |  |  |  |
| 1995 Q4 |  | $187.50 | $375.00 |
| 1996 Q1 | $425.00 |  |  |
| 1996 Q2 |  |  |  |
| 1996 Q3 |  | $125.00 | $250.00 |
| 1996 Q4 | $318.75 |  |  |
| Raw wafer cost | $ 45 | $ 45 | $ 45 |
| Wafer production cost | $ 3000 | $ 3000 |  |
| Probe cost/wafer | $ 500 | $ 625 |  |
| Gross die/wafer | 50 | 150 | 200 |
| Good die thru test (eqs) | 10.8 | 98.8 | 141.0 |
| Probe yield | 25% | 70% | 75% |
| Package type | 339 PGA | 168 PGA | 168 PGA |
| Package cost | $ 50 | $ 15 | $ 15 |
| Assembly cost | $ 8 | $ 4 |  |
| Assembly yield | 90% | 96% |  |
| Test cost | $ 40 | $ 5 |  |
| Test yield | 96% | 98% |  |

### *Discussion Questions*

Review Offtiol's cost reduction assessments, pricing beliefs, and 1995 and 1996 recommendations to improve MosCo's profitability. Has he proposed appropriate or optimal actions? Specifically:

(1) What caused the 1995 ×100 product cost to drop by $227 after reflecting the results of the activity-based costing approach?

(2) What are the cost drivers of process manufacturing? What are the other cost drivers contributing to total product cost?

(3) Was it practical or plausible to reduce wafer fabrication spending by 38%, or about $25.5 million as Offtiol demanded deStepper do?

(4) Should Offtiol have explored cost reduction opportunities in other manufacturing or nonmanufacturing areas? If so, where?

(5) Was Offtiol's ABC team staffed appropriately?

(6) Is there still underutilized manufacturing capacity when the ×50 is manufactured?

(7) Is Price's pricing model too aggressive? If so, why?

(8) What pricing advantages does MosCo's competitor, NoTel, have, due to their N50's having 33% more die on each wafer than the ×50?

(9) What other manufacturing, development, and/or pricing actions could be taken to improve MosCo's financial performance in 1995 and 1996? Can Offtiol's recommendations be improved?

**EXHIBIT 14** FY95 & FY96 Capacity Availability [handwritten: Plan after figuring out Prod Mix]

| | TOTAL CAPACITY AVAILABLE | ×100 CAPACITY USED | | CAPACITY AVAILABLE FOR ×50 | | MAXIMUM USED BY ×50 | | AVAILABLE CAPACITY | |
|---|---|---|---|---|---|---|---|---|---|
| | | FY 95 (150,000) | FY 96 (75,000) | FY95 | FY96 | FY95 | FY96 | FY95 | FY96 |
| Fab starts | 26,000 (w) | 16,595 | 7,991 | | | | | | |
| Eng'r starts | 1,040 (w) | 1,040 | 1,040 | | | | | | |
| Prod'n starts | 24,960 (w) | 15,555 | 7,723 | 9,405 | 17,237 | 582 | 2,447 | 8,823 | 14,790 |
| Prod'n completes | 22,464 (w) | 14,000 | 6,950 | 8,464 | 15,514 | 524 | 2,202 | 7,940 | 13,312 |
| ×100 probe starts | 26,000 (w) | 14,000 | 6,950 | 12,000 | 19,050 | | | | |
| ×50 probe starts | 20,800 (w) | | | 9,600 | 15,240 | 524 | 2,202 | 9,076 | 13,038 |
| 339 PGA assy starts | 202,500 (d) | 175,000 | 86,875 | 27,500 | 115,625 | | | | |
| 339 PGA assy completes | 188,250 (d) | 157,500 | 78,187 | | | | | | |
| 168 PGA assy starts | 405,000 (d) | | | 55,000 | 231,250 | 55,000 | 231,250 | 0 | 0 |
| 168 PGA assy completes | 388,800 (d) | | | 52,800 | 222,000 | 52,800 | 222,000 | 0 | 0 |
| ×100 test starts | 202,500 (d) | 157,500 | 78,187 | | | | | 45,000 | 124,313 |
| ×100 test completes | 194,400 (d) | 151,200 | 75,060 | | | | | 43,200 | 119,340 |
| ×50 test starts | 405,000 (d) | | | 405,000 | 405,000 | 52,800 | 222,000 | 352,200 | 183,000 |
| ×50 test completes | 396,900 (d) | | | 396,900 | 396,900 | 51,744 | 217,560 | 345,156 | 179,340 |

[handwritten bracket beside the 0, 0 values: "limiting factor"]

*Note: w = wafers; d = die.*

### Appendix I: Overview of the Semiconductor Manufacturing Process[1]

Semiconductor devices are made from silicon, which is material refined from quartz. Silicon is used because it can be easily altered to promote or deter electrical signals. Electronic switches, or transistors, that control electrical signals can be formed on the surface of a silicon crystal. This is done by the precisely controlled addition of certain elements designed in microscopically small patterns.

Silicon is first melted to remove impurities and grown into long crystals (ingots), which vary in size from .5 inches to 16 inches in diameter (typical sizes in use today are 6 and 8 inches). The purified silicon is sliced into wafers on which integrated circuits will be patterned. As the size of an integrated circuit is extremely small, hundreds, even thousands, of circuits can be formed on a wafer at the same time.

Integrated circuits (typically referred to as "chips" or "die") are an array of transistors made up of various connected layers, designed to perform specific operations. Each layer is a specific circuit pattern (approximately 20 are used in present processes). A glass plate (called a reticle), is used to pattern each layer on the wafer during the fabrication process.

**Fabrication**  In the fabrication process, blank wafers are first insulated with a film of oxide, then coated with a soft light-sensitive plastic called photoresist. The wafers are masked by a reticle and flooded with ultraviolet light, exposing the reticle's specific circuit pattern on the unmasked portion of the wafer. Exposed photoresist hardens into the proper circuit layer outline. Acids and solvents are used to strip away unexposed photoresist and oxide, baring the circuit pattern to be etched by either chemicals or superhot gases. More photoresist is placed on the wafer, masked, and stripped, then implanted with chemical impurities, or dopants, that form negative and positive conducting zones. Repeating these steps builds the necessary layers which are required for the integrated circuit design to be completed on the wafer.

**Probe**  In the probe process, an electrical performance test of the functions of each of the completed integrated circuits is performed while each of the die is still on the wafer. The nonfunctioning die are marked with ink; the functioning die are left unmarked and moved to assembly.

**Assembly**  In the assembly process, each of the die is diced from the wafer with a diamond saw. The good die are placed in the cavity of a ceramic package. The bonding pads from the die are connected by very thin aluminum wires into the leads of the package. This creates the necessary electrical connection from the chip to the package. The ceramic package is then sealed with a metal lid placed over the exposed die in the package.

**Test**  Once the device is completely packaged, it is tested to ensure all electrical specifications of the integrated circuit are met.

The completed packaged semiconductor device is now ready to be soldered to a printed circuit board, which in turn will be installed into a computer system.

### Appendix II: Overview of the Product Costing Process

Semiconductor product costing is a multiple-step process, where manufacturing costs measure value added to raw material as it is produced. Value added is typically defined as

---

[1]Summarized from the *Semiconductor Manufacturing Mini-Process Overview Guide*, rev. C, U.S. Semiconductor Manufacturing Training and Development Group, Digital Semiconductor Business Unit, Digital Equipment Corporation, May 1992.

production or capacity throughput divided by spending. The cost system collects, accumulates, and yields material and manufacturing costs through each stage of production.

1. First, the costs of raw materials used and the unit costs of each stage of manufacturing are established.

2. Next, raw wafer and wafer production costs are converted to die costs. In wafer fabrication and probe, manufactured material is in wafer form. As such, the unit costs of the raw wafer and manufacturing in these stages are initially captured as cost/wafer. In assembly, where the wafer is cut into die, the unit of measure also changes to die. Thus, to complete the costing of the final product which is in die form, cost/wafer must be converted to cost/die.

3. Finally, the unit die costs are accumulated in the sequence of the manufacturing process and yielded at each stage. Yield refers to the production units successfully manufactured in each stage. The semiconductor manufacturing process typically loses much of its production due to misprocessing or nonfunctioning die. Yielding the accumulated unit cost at each manufacturing stage applies the cost of lost production units to the cost of good production units.

In MosCo, the unit production cost of each major manufacturing stage (wafer fabrication, probe, assembly, test) has been determined by applying that stage's annual spending to the annual volume of production (Exhibits 2 and 6) or capacity (Exhibits 3 and 7).

Exhibits 3 and 7 highlight the computation of unit cost at each stage of manufacturing. In wafer fabrication and probe, the production unit is a wafer. Unit cost through these two stages is computed as wafer cost. In assembly and test, the wafer has been diced to remove the die. The good die continue through assembly; the nonfunctioning die are discarded. Unit cost through these two manufacturing stages is computed as die cost.

At each stage of production, production loss (or yield) is experienced. Yield loss is typically greatest during probe, when each die on the wafer is first tested to determine if it is functioning as designed. At probe, the effectiveness and quality of the wafer fabrication process, through which the multiple circuit layers have been placed on the wafer, are revealed. In wafer fabrication, the wafers used solely for engineering testing (to ensure equipment is properly calibrated, and not used for production) are also eliminated (treated similar to production yield loss) in the calculation of wafer cost.

Exhibits 2 and 6 highlight the computation of product cost. The unit cost of each manufacturing stage is listed. For the raw wafer, wafer fabrication and probe, the unit cost (wafer) is converted to die cost. The material cost is reflected at the manufacturing stage where it is introduced. To determine a final or complete product cost, the cost per die is accumulated through each manufacturing stage and yielded for the production loss experienced in that stage. Yielding the accumulated die cost has the effect of placing the total cost of manufacturing on the good production units (or expected good production units if the total production capacity costing method is used).

Exhibit 2 highlights the accumulation of costs the ×100 incurs during manufacturing. The cost and application of raw material can be seen at the start of wafer fabrication and assembly. Wafer to die conversion, based on the ×100's specification of 50 die on each wafer, is used to compute the equivalent die cost from the raw wafer, and at wafer fabrication and probe. Finally, the treatment of production loss (yield) can be seen throughout the costing process, as the accumulated cost at each stage of production is increased by the planned or expected yield at that stage, resulting in an accumulated cost which reflects the total cost of production applied to the good die produced or expected after each stage.

# 7

## Decentralization

In large multiproduct, multilocation, hierarchical entities, typical of our modern business enterprises, managers must decide who in the organization will have the authority and responsibility for making particular decisions and how such a decision maker will be evaluated and rewarded. In this and the chapters that follow, we will introduce the notion of decentralized operations: the benefits, costs, and special problems that arise in the management and evaluation of decentralized organizational units.

A large corporation contains many diverse entities and departments. These units perform activities as varied as product design and development, operations and production, logistics, purchasing, financing, information systems, marketing, and sales activities. The units typically interact with each other but may still be operated separately. For production operations, the output products of one activity may be the inputs to another, making it important that the volume of these two activities (such as component production and assembly, or production and marketing) be balanced. Some commodities may have to be purchased from external vendors, stored at various sites, transported among and within plants, and assigned to the activities that use these commodities. Some activities produce finished goods that need to be transported, stored, and sold by the other activities. Coordination is needed not only at a single point in time but continually—over many time periods—as the diverse activities respond to changes in the marketplace.

In addition to the production and marketing activities, a whole range of support and service activities must be coordinated. Functions such as personnel, information systems, finance, legal, research and development, utilities, maintenance, and engineering must be made part of the firm's overall planning and control process.

One approach to managing the diverse and complex activities of a large organization has been to stress central control. With this view, organizations are characterized by vertical, hierarchical relations; control is exercised by orders from above and executed as specified by those below. Interacting activities are coordinated by plans set at higher levels. Accounting systems and periodic reports provide the central management with all the information needed to formulate plans and to detect any departures from centrally determined policies.

In practice, of course, no central management can possibly know everything about an organization's many activities. Therefore, central management cannot make all the decisions for lower-level managers. Many decisions must be made at the lower or local levels of any organization. The challenge in organizational and informational design is to balance the benefits and costs from decentralized decision making—benefits and costs that are a function of a firm's particular resources, constraints, and opportunities.

Alfred Chandler, in his landmark studies of the development of American industrial enterprises, clearly articulated the demand for decentralized organizations:

> The lack of time, of information, and of psychological commitment to an overall entrepreneurial viewpoint were not necessarily serious handicaps if the company's basic activities remained stable, that is, if its sources of raw materials and supplies, its manufacturing technology, its markets, and the nature of its products and product lines stayed relatively unchanged. But when further expansion into new functions, into new geographical areas, or into new product lines greatly increased all types of administrative decisions, then the executives in the central office became overworked and their administrative performance less efficient. These increasing pressures, in turn, created the need for the building or adoption of the multidivisional structure with its general office and autonomous operating divisions.[1]

That a certain amount of decentralized decision making is necessary within a firm should not be surprising. A modern corporation, after all, is an economy in miniature (some of our largest corporations actually produce more goods and services than many developing nations around the world). A large corporation has internal capital and labor markets—or at least mechanisms for allocating capital and labor within the firm. It has unemployment problems, suffers from cyclic fluctuations, and must be concerned with its supply of money. The firm employs planners, forecasters, and stabilizers. The actions of one organizational unit can affect many other organizational units, so that externalities among organizational units are abundant.

Socialist economies, with central direction and resource allocation, failed because they had ineffective production enterprises that lacked adequate incentives to respond to consumer preferences and the continually changing demands of the marketplace. If information and computational complexities make it desirable to have decentralized resource allocation and decision making in an economy, then a certain degree of decentralization must also be desirable within large organizational units that function within a market-based economy.

A major control problem that arises when decentralizing decision making within a company is that prices, which play such a vital role in a capitalist economy, are not as readily available within the firm to guide local decision making. There are not enough economic agents within a firm to simulate a full market system. Moreover, because of the external owners' lack of information or inability to audit behavior, managers may be motivated to act in a way that promotes their own self-interest at the expense of the owners of the firm. Therefore, a firm uses a collection of nonmarket mechanisms—such as internal communication, contracts, standards, budgeting, reporting, and reward and punishment systems—that facilitate resource allocation and decision making in the presence of information constraints that prevent markets from operating well. In this chapter and the remainder of the book, we consider these nonmarket institutional arrangements within the firm.

## WHY DECENTRALIZE?

The above introductory remarks provide some general motivation for the demand for decentralized decision making. Let us now look more closely at specific incentives for firms to decentralize.

### The Environment of the Firm

Successful managers must continually track the key variables in their external environment so that the firm can act before external events overwhelm it. The need to constantly scan the environment has important implications for the internal organization of the firm.

Contingency theory, a popular organizational model, predicts that the complexity of a firm's environment will determine the complexity of the internal structure of the firm. Paul R. Lawrence and Jay W. Lorsch, after an extensive study, concluded that firms whose internal processes were consistent with external demands were the most effective firms in dealing with their environment.[2] Complex and uncertain external environments demand that more resources be expended to monitor that environment and that more decision making will have to be decentralized within the firm to experts who can specialize in developing information about, and developing the expertise to deal with, the changes in the firm's environment. These local experts can then respond quickly and effectively to opportunities and changes.

In one of the most famous studies in the organization design literature, T. Burns and G. M. Stalker discovered a predictable relationship between the external environment and the management structure of the firms in their study.[3] R. L. Daft summarized their results as follows:

> When the external environment was stable, the internal organization was characterized by rules, procedures, and a clear hierarchy of authority. Organizations were formalized. They were also centralized, with most decisions made at the top. Burns and Stalker called this a "mechanistic" organization system.
>
> In rapidly changing environments, the internal organization was much looser, free-flowing, and adaptive. Rules and regulations often were not written down, or if written down were ignored. People had to find their own way through the system to figure out what to do. The hierarchy of authority was not clear. Decision-making authority was decentralized. Burns and Stalker used the term "organic" to characterize this type of management structure.[4]

The results reported by Burns and Stalker are summarized in the following list:

| MECHANISTIC FORM | ORGANISTIC FORM |
| --- | --- |
| Appropriate for stable conditions | Appropriate for changing conditions |
| Tasks are highly specialized and differentiated | Tasks are shared jointly and on a cooperative basis |
| Tasks and obligations are precisely defined | Tasks evolve and are defined by the nature of the problem faced |
| Control, authority, and the flow of information are hierarchical | A network structure of control, authority, and information is used |
| The many operating rules and procedures are rigidly enforced | The few rules that exist are commonly ignored |
| The hierarchical structure of the organization is reinforced by locating knowledge and the control of tasks exclusively at the top of the hierarchy | Knowledge and control are located where the decision is made in the network |
| Communications are downward and vertical and consist mainly of rules, instructions, and decisions to implement | Communications are lateral and consist primarily of sharing information and advice |

## Information Specialization

Perhaps the strongest factor leading to decentralization is the difficulty, if not impossibility, of sharing all local information with the central management. Local managers, through observation and experience, develop specific expertise on such matters as local market opportunities, production possibilities and constraints, morale and capabilities of their labor force, and quality and reliability of local suppliers. It would be extremely difficult, costly, and time-consuming for local managers to communicate all the relevant information they possess to a central management. Many of these observations would be difficult to quantify or even to verbalize. Language limits people's ability to articulate their knowledge and intuition, whether using words, numbers, or graphics, in ways that will be understood by others. Managers will find, despite their best efforts, that their information is not sufficiently well formulated to communicate their intuition and judgment about relevant local information. Thus, an extremely important force toward decentralization is the desire to place decision making where the relevant information is acquired, stored, accessed, and processed.

## Timeliness of Response

Decentralization also permits local managers to respond quickly when making and implementing decisions. By allowing some degree of local decision making, the decentralized unit can respond to unexpected conditions faster than if all actions had to be approved by a central management group. Centralized decision making introduces delays during (1) transmission of the decision-relevant information from the local to the central unit; (2) assembly of the relevant people in the central decision-making unit plus the time they require to assimilate information, deliberate, and reach a decision; and (3) transmission of the recommended decision from the central unit back to the local unit where it will be implemented. Ralph Cordiner, one of the prime forces for decentralization during his tenure as president of General Electric during the 1950s, expressed this view well:

> Unless we could put the responsibility and authority for decision making closer in each case to the scene of the problem, where complete understanding and prompt action are possible, the Company would not be able to compete with the hundreds of nimble competitors who were, as they say, able to turn on a dime.[5]

## Conservation of Central Management Time

Presumably, the time of the central management group is one of the firm's scarcest resources. The vast numbers of local decisions called for would overwhelm even the most talented, hard-working, and resourceful group of top executives. The law of comparative advantage operates within firms, as well as among firms. Even though, for any particular local decision, a top executive may make a somewhat better local decision (once all the relevant situation-specific factors are effectively communicated and explained) than the less-experienced or less-talented local manager, it is not necessarily optimal for the top executive to make all the local decisions. If the senior executives spend their scarce time making slightly superior day-to-day operating decisions, they may ignore the strategic decisions that in the intermediate to long run are more vital to the firm's success. Therefore, central management's attention should be committed to setting broad policy and strategic direction, leaving local managers with the authority and responsibility to make the appropriate day-to-day operating decisions, consistent with the high-level objectives established by top management.

## Computational Complexity

Even if it were decided to centralize all decision making, it may not be possible to compute globally optimal decisions. With exceedingly complex operations characterized by extensive interactions and discontinuities in scale, it may be virtually impossible to solve reasonably sized resource allocation problems centrally. Limits exist to the complexity of problems that can be solved by human decision makers (a situation referred to as bounded rationality), and even computer-based algorithms cannot optimize very large systems, especially systems with nonlinearities and discrete (integer) variables. When the environment is also characterized by uncertainty, the simplifications and heuristics required for centrally determined decisions could easily lead to decisions inferior to those that would be reached at decentralized levels. Again, the analogy between a centralized firm and a socialist economy is instructive. Socialist economies have found it impossible to make all major resource-allocation and production decisions centrally. Examples of these types of difficulties are the shortages and bottlenecks reflecting, perhaps among other things, the difficulty of coordination that must be faced in planned economies. In decentralized organizations, general directions and guidelines are provided to local plant managers, who still retain discretion for decisions on resource acquisition, product mix, and distribution. These decisions are guided by incentive plans and a limited use of the price system.

## Training for Local Managers

If all significant decision making were done centrally, local managers would mainly be implementing the centrally determined plans. The managers would acquire experience in motivating employees and meeting production or distribution schedules but would not receive training in decision making. How, then, would the next generation of central management acquire the requisite experience to become good resource allocators and strategic decision makers? And on what evidence could we determine who, among the many local managers, would be best qualified for advancement to the higher decision-making levels? Some degree of local decision making is desirable to (1) provide training for future general managers and (2) indicate which managers seem best qualified for advancement to higher levels of decision making.

## Motivation for Local Managers

Finally, good managers are ambitious and take pride in their work. If their role is restricted to carrying out instructions determined at higher levels, they may lose interest in their assignments and cease applying their talents to their assignment. The firm may also find it difficult to attract creative and energetic people to serve merely as decision implementors. Managers will become more motivated and interested in their assignments when they are permitted more discretion in performing their tasks. Allowing for decision making at a local level encourages managers to be more aggressive in their acquisition of local information and more entrepreneurial and strategic in their actions. The challenge, of course, is to design incentive systems so that such aggressive, entrepreneurial, and strategic activities at a local level are consistent with overall corporate goals and objectives.

## Summary

The arguments for decentralization seem compelling. The outcome, or payoff, of any reasonably sized organization depends on many interrelated decisions about decentralized, or local, activities. Different members in the organization have different bodies of knowledge and abilities to act. It is impossible for any individual or central group to possess all the relevant information, experience, time, and computational power to determine the detailed operating plans for the organization. Accepting this argument, however, still leaves us with the extremely difficult problem of how to decentralize decision making in practice. Present practice provides evidence on five types of decentralized organizational units. These units differ depending on the degree of authority and responsibility given to the local manager.

## ORGANIZATION OF DECENTRALIZED UNITS

All units in an organization acquire inputs and produce outputs, either goods or services. Units differ, however, in the ease with which the outputs can be measured and in the discretion given to the local manager for acquiring inputs and choosing the type and mix of outputs. These considerations make different types of decentralized units appropriate depending on the difficulty of measuring outputs and the discretion or responsibility given to the local manager.

We start the discussion by considering organizational types that are evaluated solely by financial measures. This has been the traditional method used to measure and monitor the performance of decentralized units. In Chapter 8, however, we will discuss the Balanced Scorecard, a recent innovation that allows the performance of decentralized units to be assessed using a comprehensive set of financial and nonfinancial measures.

Financial performance measures can be applied to five types of decentralized units:

1. Standard cost centers
2. Revenue centers
3. Discretionary expense centers
4. Profit centers
5. Investment centers

Here, we briefly review these types of organizational units. Profit centers and investment centers are treated in more depth in later chapters.

## Standard Cost Centers

**Standard cost centers** can be established whenever we can define and measure output well and can specify the amount of inputs required to produce each unit of output. Usually, we think of standard cost centers as arising in manufacturing operations in which, for each type of output product, a standard amount and standard price of input materials, labor, energy, and support services can be specified. Standard cost centers, however, can be used for any repetitive operation for which we can measure the physical amount of output and specify a production function relating inputs to outputs. Thus, even in service industries such as fast-food franchises, banking, or health care, we can establish standard cost centers based on the number of hamburgers and milk shakes sold, on the number of checks processed, or on the number of patient tests or radiological procedures performed.

In general, managers of standard cost centers are not held responsible for variations in activity levels in their centers. They are held responsible for the efficiency with which they meet externally determined demands as long as the demands are within the capacity of the cost center. Efficiency is measured by the amount of inputs consumed in producing the demanded level of outputs. The implication is that if a full-cost scheme is being used, the managers are not responsible for underabsorbed overhead due to volume variances. They are, however, responsible for controlling the overhead costs expected to vary with activity volumes and the level of discretionary fixed costs in the center.

Managers of standard cost centers do not determine the price of their outputs, so they are not responsible for revenue or profit. Nevertheless, if the output does not meet the specific quality standards or is not produced according to schedule, the actions of the cost center will adversely affect the performance of other units in the organization. Therefore, quality and timeliness standards must be specified for any standard cost center, and its manager must produce output according to those standards.

For a standard cost center, then, efficiency is evaluated by the measured relation between inputs and outputs, and effectiveness is evaluated by whether the center achieved the desired production schedule at specified levels of quality and timeliness.

Standard cost centers and the detailed analysis of variances from standards are discussed extensively in cost accounting textbooks, so further discussion is not required here. For our purposes, standard cost centers will be useful when we can objectively measure output, including quality and timeliness as well as the quantity of physical units, and when we have a well-specified relationship between outputs and inputs. The product (or output) must be standard enough that the manufacturing unit need not make decisions on price, output quantity, or product mix; these decisions can be made centrally or delegated to a marketing unit. Also, decisions on plant equipment and technology for the standard cost center will usually be made centrally, not by the cost center manager. Perhaps the only variation of this simple model would be those firms that impute a capital charge for raw material and work-in-process inventory to encourage cost center managers to achieve production goals while attempting to reduce inventory quantities.

## 2 Revenue Centers – for selling + distributing 3/4 from sales dept

Revenue centers exist in order to organize marketing activities. Typically, a revenue center acquires finished goods from a manufacturing division and is responsible for selling and distributing those goods. If the revenue center has discretion for setting the selling price, then it can be made responsible for the gross revenues it generates. If pricing policy is determined outside the revenue center (say, at the corporate level), then the manager of the revenue center is held responsible for the physical volume and mix of sales.

When a performance measure is chosen for a revenue center, some notion of the cost of each product should be included so that the center is motivated to maximize gross operating margins rather than just sales revenue. If evaluated solely on sales revenue, managers may be motivated to cut prices to increase total sales, spend excessive amounts on advertising and promotion, or promote low-profit products. Each of these actions could increase total sales revenue but decrease overall corporate profitability.

On the basis of recent developments in activity-based costing (see Chapters 4 and 5), sales units can now be assigned both the costs of items they sell and the costs of serving their individual customers. Consequently, companies can use activity-based costing to transform revenue centers that perform marketing and sales activities into profit centers. Before the development of ABC, companies did not have accurate measures either of the specific product costs purchased by customers or of the costs of serving individual customers. Lacking such specific information, companies could not evaluate the profit contributions from marketing and sales organizations. With the increased application of ABC concepts to distribution, marketing, and sales activities, the rationale for treating many units only as revenue centers is sharply diminished.

## 3 Discretionary Expense Centers

Discretionary expense centers are appropriate for units that produce outputs that are not measurable in financial terms or for units where no strong relation exists between resources expended (inputs) and results achieved (outputs). Examples of discretionary expense centers are general and administrative (G&A) departments (controller, industrial relations, human resources, accounting, legal), research and development (R&D) departments, and some marketing activities such as advertising, promotion, and warehousing. The output of G&A departments is difficult to measure. For departments such as R&D and marketing, often no strong relation exists between inputs and outputs. For the R&D and marketing functions, we can determine whether the responsible departments are being effective. That is, we can see whether they are meeting the company's goals in terms of new products and improved technologies (for R&D) and sales volume or market penetration (for marketing). Because of the weak relationship between inputs and outputs in these departments, however, we are unable to determine whether they are operating efficiently—that is, producing the actual amount of output with the minimally required inputs. For the G&A departments, it is even more difficult to measure output, so neither effectiveness nor efficiency can be determined. Instead, companies usually control such departments by monitoring the amount of resources provided to them—spending, people, and equipment—rather than by the outcomes they achieve. They use controls on the inputs used by the discretionary expense centers rather than using results control.[6]

Given the difficulty of measuring the efficiency of discretionary expense centers, a natural tendency may arise for their managers to desire a very high quality department even though a somewhat lower quality department would provide almost the same service at significantly lower costs. Accentuating this tendency, the white-collar professionals who typically staff these centers prefer to have the best people in their discipline associated with them so that they can take pride in the quality of their department. Thus, it becomes difficult for central management to determine appropriate budget, quality, and service levels for the firm's discretionary expense centers.

One solution is to look at industry practice to see whether the company's expenditures on a given function are in line with those of other companies. (A cynic could deride this guideline as the blind following the blind.) We frequently see a company's R&D budget, for example, expressed as a percentage of sales. Even though there is no plausible reason why a company's R&D expenditures should be causally related to its sales, such a percentage rule facilitates intercompany comparisons.

Basically, determining the budget for a discretionary expense center requires the judgment of informed professionals. The central management needs to trust and work closely with the managers of discretionary expense centers to determine the appropriate budget level. The managers of such centers are in the best position to predict the consequences of changing the budget by +10% or +20%. After finding out which activities would be augmented or reduced by changes, central management could then decide on the budget and hence on the quality or intensity of effort for the next period. Discretionary expense centers are an excellent example of cases in which great information asymmetry is most likely to exist between a local unit manager and central management.

Once the budget for a discretionary expense center has been determined, no great benefit can result from pressuring the local manager to bring actual costs in under budget. Having actual spending below budgeted levels is not necessarily favorable or a sign of efficiency, as would be the situation in a standard cost center. In a standard cost center, we have good measures of output quantity and quality, so producing a given amount of output for less-than-budgeted costs is a favorable indication. For a discretionary expense center, however, a favorable cost variance may only mean that the center has operated at a lower level of quality, service, or effectiveness than was intended when the budget was established. Typically, the control process for such expenses will involve ensuring that the quality and level of service of the center have been maintained. Similarly, cost overruns in a discretionary expense center may be caused by favorable circumstances, such as a new-product breakthrough that justifies higher development expenditures or an improved marketing climate in which increased advertising and distribution expenditures may yield great returns.

The existence of budgeted and actual expenses for discretionary expense centers may give an illusion of precision about their operations. But without good measures of the output from such centers, such data may yield little insight into whether the centers are operating effectively or efficiently. For some of these centers, the control of discretionary expense centers requires the informed judgment of knowledgeable professionals on the level and quality of service the centers are producing.

As with revenue centers, however, companies have begun to apply activity-based costing to their staff departments. ABC enables companies to treat their staff departments as standard cost centers, or even as profit centers if they are given the option of selling their outputs to external users. ABC facilitates the measurement of the quantitative output from corporate staff departments.[7] With such measures, executives can hold the staff departments responsible for the costs incurred in delivering their service output to operating units just as they do production departments that produce and deliver products to subsequent production stages. Thus, the ABC innovation permits many organizational units, previously treated as discretionary expense centers, to become standard cost or profit centers.

## Profit Centers   — operational dm + no investment rights

Standard cost centers, revenue centers, and discretionary expense centers have limited decentralization of decisions. Managers of standard cost centers may acquire and manage inputs at their discretion, but the outputs from these centers are determined and distributed by other units. Revenue centers distribute and sell products but have no control over their manufacture. Discretionary expense centers must produce a service or staff function demanded by the rest of the organization.

A significant increase in managerial discretion occurs when managers of local units are given responsibility for both production and sales. In this situation, they can make decisions about which products to manufacture, how to produce them, the quality level, the price, and the selling and distribution system. The managers must make product-mix decisions and determine how production resources are to be allocated among the various products. They are then in a position to optimize the performance of their centers by making tradeoffs among price, volume, quality, and costs.

If the managers do not have responsibility or authority for determining the level of investment in assets in their centers, then profit may be the single best performance measure for the center, although any profit figure may need to be supplemented with a variety of nonfinancial indicators of short-term performance. Profit, properly measured, can provide a short-run indicator of how well managers are creating value from the resources at their disposal and the input factors they acquire. Units in which the managers have almost complete operational decision-making responsibility and are evaluated by a profit measure are called **profit centers**. The importance of profit centers and the difficulties associated with measuring profit in them justify a separate discussion, which is presented in Chapter 9.

## Investment Centers   — Profit centre + right to invest

When local managers have all the responsibilities described above for profit centers and also have responsibility and authority for working capital and physical assets, then a performance measure based on the level of physical and financial assets employed in the center is preferred. Investment centers are generalizations of profit centers in which profitability is related to the assets used to generate the profit. Return on investment (ROI) and economic value added are typical investment center performance measures; these measures are discussed in Chapter 10.

## DEVELOPING A PERFORMANCE MEASURE FOR DECENTRALIZED OPERATING UNITS

Control rules, or principles, can be divided into two classes: operating rules and enforcement rules.[8] Operating rules tell people what to do, and enforcement rules specify the consequences to a decision maker of not following the operating rules.

In a simple firm, or for observable tasks, the operating rules tell people specifically what they must do. The enforcement rules can then be related directly to the accomplishment of the task. For example, a clerk can be told (the operating rule) to order 2,000 units of some part. Subsequently, it is easy to observe whether this instruction has been carried out. The consequence (the enforcement rule) of not carrying out the instruction may be dismissal.

With decentralization, however, local decision makers who have specialized in the assigned task and concentrated on gathering information relevant to the task can often judge better than their superiors the best course of action. Thus, in decentralized organizations, operating rules seldom take the form of telling people what they must do. Rather, the operating rules are stated in terms of the firm's objectives, and people are given decision rights that enable them to take actions that will best attain the goals of the firm. These types of operating rules require very different enforcement rules than those used when a specific directive is given. Enforcement rules must use an incentive scheme to provide the motivation for the decision maker to follow the operating rules. For example, the operating rule "Do whatever you need to do to maximize the profit of your division" may have associated with it an enforcement rule that provides the decision maker with a share in reported division profits.

In each of the five types of decentralized centers, the centers' managers have discretion in selecting and implementing actions. To guide the managers' decisions and evaluate the performance of the managers and their centers, we require a performance measure. Specification of the local performance measure is perhaps the most difficult problem in decentralizing decision making and responsibility. Through this measure, the organization communicates how it wishes the local manager to behave and how this behavior will be judged and evaluated. Central management needs to determine rules, measures, and rewards for local decision making that are compatible with overall corporate goals. These guidelines and incentives must facilitate the coordination of individual or divisional goals with those of the overall corporation goals and must attempt to minimize information gathering and processing costs as well as dysfunctional costs from local suboptimizing. Clearly, this is not an easy task. Perhaps the most thoughtful and best articulated views on the challenges in organizing a decentralized firm have come from Alfred P. Sloan, who provided the organizational archetype for the multidivisional firm during his long tenure as president of General Motors. Sloan, and his brilliant chief financial executive, Donaldson Brown, described their views as "decentralized responsibility with centralized control":

> Good management rests on a reconciliation of centralization and decentralization, or "decentralization with coordinated control."
>
> Each of the conflicting elements brought together in this concept has its unique results in the operation of a business. From decentralization we get initiative, responsibility, development of personnel, decisions close to the fact, flexibility—in short, all the qualities necessary for an organization to adapt to new conditions. From coordination we get efficiencies and economies. It must be apparent that coordinated decentralization is not an easy concept to apply. There is no hard and fast rule for sorting out the various responsibilities and the best way to assign them. The balance which is struck between corporate and divisional responsibility varies according to what is being decided, the circumstances of the time, past experience, and the temperaments and skills of the executives involved.[9]

In a centralized decision-making environment, the local managers follow detailed operating rules that instruct them how to act. The decisions are determined centrally and implemented locally. Any failure to perform in a centralized system is relatively obvious because job descriptions and tasks are well specified.

In decentralized operations, the operating rules (the "centralized control" that guides the "decentralized responsibilities" of local managers) are much less specific; hence performance evaluation is more difficult. We can think of the operating rules as consisting of two parts: constraints and objectives. First, the bounds of permissive or admissible behavior are specified, and the action alternatives of the managers are limited; for example, illegal behavior is proscribed, and managers may be instructed to use certain suppliers, meet certain quality standards, meet the demands of particular customers, and refrain from disposing of certain assets.[10]

Once their range of action alternatives has been specified, the local managers must also be given a well-specified reward or incentive function that they are expected to maximize. Thus, managers may be instructed to maximize divisional income, return on investment, or economic value added. Managers in a sales division may be instructed to maximize sales revenues, or managers in a production division to minimize costs when satisfying an externally derived demand for the product, including achieving stringent quality and timeliness goals. The specification of the local reward or incentive function is extremely important because this function will be used to motivate and evaluate the local managers' performance. Therefore, local managers could act to improve their measured performance, perhaps at the expense of the goals of the corporation or other divisions. For example, the sales manager of a revenue center may try to increase total revenue rather than total contribution margin. The expectation that managers will attempt to improve their local measure to the exclusion of all other goals or measures is what makes the appropriate specification of a single local reward measure so difficult.

Increasingly, executives are aware of the shortcomings of using only financial measures of performance as the local reward measure. Many people are now questioning the appropriateness of assessing performance using a highly aggregate number such as net income. Instead, these people advocate that a broad set of financial and nonfinancial measures, all derived from the mission and strategy, be used to motivate and evaluate the performance of the business unit. In this way, a broad set of objectives and measures can be identified and communicated through the organization. Such a balanced scorecard approach, described in Chapter 8, will allow the firm to be more responsive in identifying and responding to important changes in its environment.

To gain a better understanding of why managers are moving beyond single, financial performance measures for decentralized units, we analyze the dysfunctional aspects associated with developing a measure of performance for a decentralized operation.

## Problems of Goal Congruence

The measure of performance of a decentralized unit is a new piece of information that must be developed by the firm. As discussed at the beginning of this chapter, simple firms may not need internal measures of efficiency and performance. They can assess their performance by measuring the difference in prices between buying and selling transactions conducted with economic agents external to the firm. More complex, decentralized firms must expend resources to acquire relevant data and to compute the performance measures for decentralized units that conduct many transactions within the firm.

The consequences of developing the local performance measure, though, go far beyond the cost of data acquisition and computation. Ideally, the local performance measure should be consistent with overall corporate goals. But it is just about impossible in complex and uncertain environments for any single performance measure to achieve perfect goal congruence between a decentralized unit and the overall corporation. That is why companies are using a balanced set of measures to communicate company-level strategy to local divisions and departments. When only a single measure of performance is used, the measure tends to become an end in itself, more important than the economic performance that it attempts to represent. In a revenue center, for example, the sales force may be motivated to sell only high-priced items in an attempt to maximize revenues rather than contribution margin. Any single measure may be manipulated to benefit the decentralized unit at the expense of the corporation.

This fundamental problem arises because, unlike the situation in the physical sciences, the act of measurement in the social sciences and in management changes the event and the observer.[11] Measurement is neither neutral nor objective. The measure chosen for evaluating performance acquires value and importance by the fact of being selected for attention. People within the system change their behavior as a function of the measure chosen to summarize the economic performance of their organizational unit.

A second problem arises because most measures of performance are based on internal achievement rather than on external opportunities. A unit may be perceived as having performed well because it exceeded last year's measure of performance or the budgeted measure. But the current good performance may have been caused by an unexpected expansion of demand in the industry, in which all the companies in the industry participated. When viewed against overall industry performance, the decentralized unit may not have maintained its market share or relative profitability. In this case, the performance will not look as favorable against an external reference base as it does against the more typically measured internal criterion. Senior managers of highly diversified corporations (conglomerates), however, may not be able to use such relative performance evaluations effectively because they possess less information about the market conditions of individual divisions than do the managers of those divisions.

(3)   A third limitation on a single performance measure occurs when the future economic consequences from current activities are ignored. Typical performance measures focus on short-term operating results and ignore longer-term effects that are harder to measure. These longer-term effects usually arise from expenditures on intangibles—research and development, advertising and promotion, plant design, maintenance, human resource development, and quality control. Because the benefits from such expenditures on intangibles are subjective and difficult to measure, we tend to ignore them and concentrate on aspects of performance that we can measure more easily. Managers will then have an incentive to spend less on intangibles and maintenance than would be desirable for long-term corporate goals. Such expenditures on intangibles reduce the current performance measure, and the adverse effects of neglecting them do not show up until later, perhaps much later when the current managers are in entirely different positions in the organization.

Similarly, many transactions in a period have characteristics and longer-term consequences that are difficult to measure objectively. The quality of the product, the morale of the employees, and the output of professional services (legal, R&D, controller's office), for example, are important characteristics that affect the long-term performance of the organizational unit but are not easily captured in a short-term performance measure, particularly a financial one. Undesirable consequences will occur if too much reliance is placed on a single measure of performance that ignores longer-term, less objectively measured consequences of current-period decisions. Again, the inability of any single measure, particularly a financial measure, to incorporate value-creating and value-destroying activities during a period is a principal driver for developing a comprehensive, balanced-scorecard (see Chapter 8), set of measures for communicating and implementing an organization's long-term strategy.

## Problems of Externalities

Interactions among organizational units introduce a second set of problems when local units focus narrowly on their individual performance measures. When such interactions exist, the actions of an individual unit affect not only its own measure of performance but also the measures of other units. For example, when goods or services are transferred from one unit to another, these goods or services are frequently priced in order to recognize revenue for the supplying unit and an input-factor cost to the purchasing unit. This **transfer-pricing** process is one of the most contentious activities in decentralized firms. We will examine the relevant issues surrounding transfer pricing in Chapter 9.

Even assuming that the transfer-pricing problem can be solved in a satisfactory manner, many problematic nonprice aspects are associated with transactions among organizational units. The quality of a product or service and the timeliness of the transfer will affect the operation of the unit receiving the good or service, but the financial impact of varying quality or delivery times will be difficult to quantify. In principle, a price system could be established as a function of delivery delay (or product quality), but such a system would be extremely complex. It would be difficult to develop and to maintain. It would also introduce uncertainty to both units about the price of the transfer, since some delay might be caused by random, unexpected factors. Both units might then change their operations to minimize the effect of this inherent uncertainty. This change in operation could reduce overall output, thereby affecting the firm adversely.

The performance of other decentralized units may also affect the performance measure of an individual unit. For example, the efficiency of a manufacturing plant may be affected by the quantity and timing of output demanded from it, which are determined in part by the activities of a sales division. Solely under conditions of certainty, it can be argued that the performance measure of the manufacturing plant should not be affected by the activities of the selling division; effects due to variations in activity level should be the responsibility of the sales division, not the manufacturing unit. But once we recognize conditions of uncertainty and private information, it is no longer obvious that the manufacturing plant's performance measure should be made independent of sales activity. We argued earlier that there are nonprice characteristics of transactions from one unit to another, especially quality and timeliness. Therefore, the performance of the manufacturing division could affect the performance of the sales division in ways that are difficult to capture in a price system (because of uncertainty, lack of observability, and so on). One remedy would be for part of the performance measure of the manufacturing division to depend on the level of sales. Such a measure would provide strong incentives for manufacturing and sales managers to coordinate their decisions. More generally, the performance measure of individual local units could include a component reflecting the performance of other organizational units and, perhaps, the overall corporation. This measure would provide an incentive for managers of individual units to cooperate, avoid unnecessary frictions, and emphasize a corporate rather than a local viewpoint when managing their operations. For example, Jeremy Dent described a company in which product development managers were held responsible for the sales revenues of the products they developed, and sales managers were held responsible for the development costs of the products they sold.[12] We will return to the local versus corporate performance measurement debate when we discuss models of incentive contracts in Chapter 13.

In general, the performance of a decentralized unit, such as a manufacturing division, can be assessed by measures beyond financial ones. The balanced-scorecard approach retains financial performance measures for business units but supplements these with measures along customer (e.g., on-time delivery, defects of received items), internal business process (e.g., innovation, quality, cycle time), and learning and growth (e.g., employee and systems capabilities) dimensions.

## Overconsumption of Perquisites

A further problem arises in decentralization if a local manager with discretionary spending authority consumes an excessive amount of perquisites. For example, the manager may decide to improve his local working environment by acquiring a large, expensively decorated office space, by hiring an unnecessarily large number of administrative assistants and support personnel, and by purchasing the latest and most elaborate office equipment. These expenditures will reduce the manager's performance measure, but the manager may prefer the direct consumption of these perquisites to the perhaps small increase in pecuniary compensation that could be earned by foregoing these expenditures.

Also, some managers may engage in an activity called empire building, which attempts to increase the size of the organization they are managing. The nonpecuniary rewards from empire building include the increased power and prestige associated with managing a larger organization. These nonpecuniary factors can even become pecuniary if the managers' compensation or promotion probability is made an increasing function of the size of the units they are managing.

## SUMMARY

The complex environment in which business is conducted today makes it impossible for any but the smallest firm to be controlled centrally. Some degree of decentralization will be essential to capture the benefits from the specialized information and response flexibility of local managers. Decentralization also conserves the scarce time of top executives and frees them from making complex, interdependent resource-allocation decisions. Providing local managers with discretion in managing their operations has the additional benefits of developing their capabilities as general managers and making their daily job more interesting.

Decentralization can take many forms. Repetitive processes producing well-specified and easily measured outputs can be managed as standard cost centers, in which the manager must meet externally generated demands for products according to a cost-minimizing, efficient standard. Marketing departments can be organized as revenue centers with the objective of meeting targeted goals in sales revenue, market share, or contribution margin. Some functions for which the outputs are not easily measurable or are not causally and deterministically related to the inputs expended cannot be controlled by the use of traditional techniques such as standard costs or budgets. These functions are usually organized as discretionary expense centers in which the level of expenditures and the number of personnel are determined by negotiation with the central management to determine appropriate levels of quality and service. Much greater decentralization can occur when an operating unit is given responsibility both for acquiring inputs and for selling or distributing its outputs. Such units can be organized as profit or investment centers.

Although decentralization seems essential for organizing complex operations, it introduces many problems of its own. Local managers are evaluated with a performance measure that captures some but not all of the economic consequences of their decisions. Therefore, managers may engage in dysfunctional behavior, failing to internalize the effects of their decisions on other organizational units or on the future of the entire firm. Conflicts between decentralized units can arise over the transfer of goods.

All these problems are inherent costs of decentralization. We would prefer to have easy solutions to them, but we must settle for understanding the costs as well as the benefits of decentralization, keeping alert to situations in which narrow-minded local optimizing performance or misrepresentation of local information is significantly impairing the overall well-being of the firm. The challenge is to devise the right combination of delegation of effort and decision making, observation of effort, and reward or incentive schemes to balance the benefits and costs of decentralization. Such a balance requires the judgment and experience of the owners and senior managers of the organization. The Balanced Scorecard, a new approach for communicating strategy and empowering decision making at decentralized units, allows such judgment and experience to be reflected in operational decisions.

## ENDNOTES

1. A. D. Chandler Jr., *Strategy and Structure: Chapters in the History of the Industrial Enterprise* (Cambridge, MA: M.I.T. Press, 1962), p. 297.

2. P. R. Lawrence and J. W. Lorsch, *Organization and Environment* (Homewood, IL: Richard D. Irwin, 1969).

3. T. Burns and G. M. Stalker, *The Management of Innovation* (London: Tavistock Publications, 1961).

4. R. L. Daft, *Organization Theory and Design* (St. Paul, MN: West Publishing, 1983), p. 61.

5. R. J. Cordiner, *New Frontiers for Professional Managers* (New York: McGraw-Hill, 1956), pp. 45–46.

6. See K. Merchant, *Control in Business Organizations* (Marshfield, MA: Pittman Publishing, 1985).

7. See D. Loewe and H. T. Johnson, "How Weyerhaeuser Controls Corporate Overhead Costs," *Management Accounting* (August 1987).

8. K. J. Arrow, "Control in Large Organizations," *Management Science* (April 1964), pp. 397–408.

9. A. P. Sloan Jr., *My Years with General Motors* (New York: Doubleday, 1964), p. 429.

10. See the discussion of boundary systems, pp. 39–55 in R. Simons, *Levers of Control* (Boston: Harvard Business School Press, 1995).

11. Strictly speaking, the Heisenberg uncertainty principle establishes that even in the physical sciences the act of measurement affects the phenomenon being measured. But such effects show up at the subatomic level of observation and do not affect everyday measurement of speed, weight, and dimensions of physical objects.

12. See J. Dent, "Tension in the Design of Formal Control Systems: A Field Study in a Computer Company," in *Accounting & Management: Field Study Perspectives*, ed. R. S. Kaplan and W. J. Bruns Jr. (Boston: Harvard Business School Press, 1987), pp. 119–45.

## ■ *PROBLEMS*

### 7-1    *Emphasis on Short-Term Performance*

"A lot of what is preached at business schools today is absolute rot," claimed a New York financial consultant. "Business schools teach that business is nothing but the numbers—and the numbers only for the next quarter."

The overemphasis on short-term performance measures was echoed by other critics. "There has been too much emphasis on short-term profit, not enough on long-range planning; too much on financial maneuvering, not enough on the technology of producing goods; too much on readily available markets, not enough on international development."

One U.S. expert on productivity added, "Our managers still earn generally high marks for their skill in improving short-term efficiency, but their counterparts in Europe and Japan have started to question America's entrepreneurial imagination and willingness to make risky, long-term investments."

Finally, even foreign executives criticized the U.S. system. "The misguided emphasis on short-term profit seems to blind U.S. managers to the need for more research and development; moreover, they appear unable to develop strategies for dealing with long-range problems of chronic inflation and soaring energy costs. Also the quality of U.S. manufactured goods is declining because managers have cared less about what they produce than about selling it."

### Required

(1) Are business schools, in general, and cost accounting and management control courses, in particular, to blame for the alleged preoccupation of recent business school graduates with measurable short-term performance? What conditions provide the environment for short-term rather than long-term optimizing behavior?

(2) What forces provide explanations for the accusations that U.S. managers are more concerned with short-term "safe" strategies rather than longer-term risky, entrepreneurial strategies?

(3) What are the implications of these charges for the design of management control systems in decentralized organizations?

## 7-2   *Measuring the Output of Corporate Staff Departments*

Dennis Johns, manager of the financial services department of Hyde Papers, was complaining:

> The CEO is really on my case. He keeps asking why corporate staff departments, like finance and information technology, can't develop methods of cost control and cost assignment just like our production departments. I keep explaining, but he doesn't seem to understand, that you can't use the same techniques for white-collar departments, staffed by professionals, that you use for our production and production support departments that do repetitive, predictable work.

The financial services department at Hyde Papers is a staff unit in the corporate controller's department responsible for all central accounting activities, including consolidations, general accounting, salaried payroll, accounts payable, accounts receivable, and invoicing. Hyde Papers is a large diversified producer of paper and pulp products. Its product divisions range from timber growing and harvesting to paper and pulp production, to paper office supplies production and distribution. All the operating divisions are supported by corporate staff departments, such as the controller's department, at company headquarters.

The functions of the financial services department are:

> *Consolidations, General Accounting, and Database Administration*: Consolidation activities include report preparation, reconciliations, special projects or analyses, and report changes for business units and divisions. Database administration involves maintaining and updating the data and systems required for all corporate financial reports. Costs include personnel, computers, and supplies.
>
> *Payroll*: The payroll function provides the biweekly check and earnings statement for each employee, the annual W-2 statement for employee tax returns, and special payments such as bonus checks, commissions, special rewards, and deferred compensation.
>
> *Accounts Payable*: The accounts payable unit verifies, prepares, and mails invoice payments to suppliers, maintains records on all suppliers, and mails paychecks to employees.

*Accounts Receivable*: This unit processes all payments made by customers. It verifies the payment against the invoice and deposits the payment into a company's bank account. It also maintains the customer file (name and address of each customer) and conducts periodic credit checks on customers.

*Invoicing*: The invoicing process records the pricing and delivery terms for each shipment and sends an invoice to the customer for the appropriate amount.

### Required

(1) Do you agree with Dennis Johns's claim that white-collar, support department work cannot be controlled in the same manner as production processes?

(2) Could the financial services department be treated as a standard cost center rather than a discretionary expense center?

## ■ CASES

## PINNACLE MUTUAL LIFE INSURANCE COMPANY*

Grumbling is the only weapon we have as managers in these newly formed profit centers. When the Executive Committee decided to institute this new concept at Pinnacle, the members made it clear *what* they wanted, but not *how* it was to be accomplished. For example, as vice president, Individual Equity and Pension Products, I continue to manage that area and do the work I've always done in that function; with the creation of profit centers, I also have responsibility for the new Institutional Pension Products and Services: Nonparticipating profit center, but I have no additional staff! It's difficult to take advantage of the company's support systems, especially the accounting group, because none of these groups has ever had to think in terms of profit before. There's really a paucity of numbers to help us do our jobs.

All of us who were appointed as profit center managers (PCMs) to get this idea off the ground are very visible. The process of converting to profit centers and changing the attitudes of employees is turning out to be a lot more difficult than we thought.

These words were spoken by Elizabeth Duncan, vice president, Individual Equity and Pension Products, and profit center manager for Institutional Pension Products and Services: Nonparticipating. She and the other seven PCMs had been in their new positions for seven months and they were discovering that their uncharted road posed challenges at almost every turn. One of the biggest problems they faced was the lack of financial information to help them forecast and budget; they complained that when they finally did get financial reports, the numbers were often out of date and not useful. Pinnacle management looked ahead to addressing these and other problems, and to putting a great deal of time and effort into making the profit centers successful.

*This case was prepared by Associate for Case Development Karen E. Hansen, under the supervision of Professor William J. Bruns Jr. All of the data have been disguised.

### Rationale for Developing Profit Centers at Pinnacle

The profit center concept was introduced at Pinnacle in May 1985 and the first profit center managers were identified and appointed. By creating profit centers, the Management Committee (composed of the chairman, president, and heads of Marketing, Product Services, Law, Corporate Operations, and Investment Operations) hoped to provide greater focus to product development and marketing around the expanding set of financial service products offered by the company; in addition to life insurance, these included annuities, consumer banking, securities, real estate, equipment leasing, and home mortgage financing. Profit center managers would become the promoters of their products inside the company, thereby giving greater vitality to the competitiveness of the company.

The concept of profit centers seemed very new to many at Pinnacle. The mutual company form of organization emphasized the idea of service to customers who would benefit because they became part of the organization. (A mutual life insurance company is owned by its policy holders and differs from a stock insurance company, which is owned by anyone who buys stock in that company.) The mutual form and its regulated accounting procedures emphasizing reserves and safety had led to little concern or emphasis on profit. Volume of revenues and preservation and growth of assets were much more familiar performance criteria than profits. Only recently, as the company's range of financial services expanded, had efforts begun to convert accounting reports to a generally accepted accounting principles (GAAP) basis.

Most life insurance companies used Statutory Accounting Principles (SAP) rather than GAAP. SAP was a set of principles required by statute which had to be followed by an insurance company when submitting its financial statements to the state insurance department. Such principles differed from GAAP in some important aspects; one was that SAP required that expenses be recorded immediately and not be deferred to be matched with premiums as they were earned and taken into revenue. The adoption of GAAP was intended to produce financial results consistent with those of other industries and to assure consistency in financial reporting.

When Pinnacle decided to emphasize profit, it switched to GAAP for internal purposes, to gain the benefits of that reporting basis. GAAP helped match benefits and expenses to premium income, which resulted in earnings emerging as a more nearly level percent of the premiums collected. To accomplish this matching, natural reserves were developed based on actuarial assumptions appropriate at the date of issue. Natural reserves included benefit, acquisition, and maintenance expense reserves. The reserve assumptions included provisions for adverse deviation from that assumed for ratemaking. GAAP also allowed profits to emerge in proportion to the release from the risk for adverse deviation.

The profit center concept was also at odds with the way Pinnacle had always been organized. At various times, the company's organization had emphasized type of customer (individual vs. group, for example) or functions (sales, investments, or customer service). The creation of profit centers focused attention on how products and services could be developed and sold for the good of the company as a whole. Inevitably, some profit centers would compete with each other as they developed and sold products; this competition was a radical idea in a mutual company.

Despite both anticipated and unanticipated problems and resistance from corporate culture, top management was committed to the profit center form of organization. If Pinnacle was to be customer-driven, a stated management goal, then the company had to be able to respond quickly to customer demands and competitor threats. The industry was changing rapidly as more companies offered financial services outside their traditional businesses. A profit center organization seemed necessary for Pinnacle to maintain a leadership position in the areas of insurance and financial and administrative services for individuals and groups.

### The Pinnacle Companies

Pinnacle Mutual Life Insurance Company had been chartered in Connecticut and was nearly 100 years old. This strong, stable company had long been known for its product line of various types of life insurance. Through the years, Pinnacle had grown steadily to become an industry leader; among its competitors in the life insurance business were Connecticut Mutual, Prudential, John Hancock, Aetna, Hartford Life, Massachusetts Mutual, Metropolitan Life, Allstate, and New York Life. But Pinnacle's competition wasn't limited to insurance companies. Any company offering financial services or administrative services was really vying for the same customers as Pinnacle. This included companies which offered banking products, brokerage services, institutional investment, and management of data systems.

In the 1970s and 1980s, Pinnacle had expanded the number and type of financial services it offered to its customers in an attempt to satisfy consumers who were looking for more profitable ways to invest in times of higher inflation. Not only were new types of insurance and annuities added, such as a disability income insurance and single premium deferred annuities, new services were developed for individual, institutional, and corporate clients. As a result, the company found itself offering a broad range of products and services in real estate; home mortgage financing; data processing; farming; commercial development; equipment financing and leasing; medical and dental preferred provider organizations; and financial services in broker-

age, banking, and mutual funds. Management expected that much of the company's future growth would be in areas and activities outside its traditional insurance areas.

Until 1984, the company organization reflected its emphasis on the distinction between products and services sold to individuals and those sold to groups. In 1984, the company reorganized to emphasize functions. Under the new structure, products would be sold or serviced by one part of the organization, regardless of the nature of the customer, to minimize duplication of functional efforts across product or customer lines.

Pinnacle management felt that the reorganization contributed to stronger performance in 1984. The company's mission that year was to emphasize those products and services which would provide an attractive return on investment, competitive product value to their clients, and opportunities for growth by providing additional products and services for existing customers or attracting new customers to their expanded array of financial services. Pinnacle began to change its image, and to examine not only the range of investment opportunities it could offer its clients, but how the company could manage those investment areas most profitably.

Prior to the reorganization, Pinnacle management had not thought in terms of competitive stance or aggressively seeking new customers; the company had always been proud of its concern for existing customers and their life insurance needs. Elizabeth Duncan comented:

> A mutual life insurance company environment is about as uncompetitive as you can get. Because our participating policy holders are our owners and the company is run for their benefit, the best thing for them, financially speaking, is for Pinnacle to stop selling new life insurance! Every new policy sold actually diminishes the amount of funds that can be returned to current policy holders in dividends because the cost of both the agent's commission and issuing the new policy usually exceeds the first year premium.

But Pinnacle's aggressive plans for the future did not include the alternative of dropping out of the life insurance business. As Pinnacle continued to expand into noninsurance products and services, it competed directly with other financial service institutions. Managers focused on this new competition and began to develop ways to manage change while continuing to meet client needs.

## The Process of Creating Profit Centers

The Executive Committee favored profit centers organized around existing products and services as the way to focus managers on profit, cost, and competition. But its members were unsure how to make the transition to this new form of management. Therefore, the Committee appointed Stephen Cooper, vice president, Corporate Analysis, to coordinate the creation and staffing of profit centers.

In a memorandum to the Executive Committee on January 23, 1985 (Exhibit 1), Cooper summarized the beginning of this process and reviewed reasons to have profit centers. He was eager to ensure agreement on rationale and goals. The memo also established the agenda for a meeting two days later to discuss how many profit centers to create, how to select their managers, and how to measure their performance.

At that meeting, the Executive Committee decided to create eight profit centers to handle current products and services. However, no one was sure how to change the roles of the functional groups and then coordinate interaction between the two groups to maximize company earnings. The meeting emphasized the company's emerging needs, which members decided could be best served by creating "value centers" out of the existing functional groups (Marketing, Product Services, Financial Operations, Law and Corporate Secretary, and Corporate Operations). Value centers, for a fee or at least an allocation of cost, would

provide services including market research and data on competition, information on pricing products, accounting information and suggestions, and tax and legal advice. For example, if a PCM needed legal counseling from the Law and Corporate Secretary value center, that value center would charge the PCM for the lawyer's time to research and answer the PCM's questions. In the future, other services might be created as needed and offered to PCMs by Value Center managers (VCMs).

In order to give the new structures time to develop and a fair chance at success, profit centers would be required to use the services of the value centers for two to three years. During this start-up phase, PCMs and VCMs would work together to negotiate services and fees and establish quality measures which could be used by the PCMs to help them determine the value of the services for which they would be paying. The VCMs' Incentive Compensation would eventually be influenced by how well expense and quality measures were attained. At the end of this time, PCMs would be allowed to go outside the company to contract for these and other services if they discovered sources which would give them better service, reduce their costs of doing business, or improve their profit centers' performance.

Allowing PCMs to go to outside vendors for services which were offered internally was unusual; management hoped this competition from external sources would inspire each VCM to operate efficiently and to try to win the business of the profit centers by competing against other service providers. PCMs would be required to state their intentions to seek outside services and the reasons for doing so. This would give the value center a chance to respond and to try to meet the PCMs' needs, if possible, so that value centers would continue to provide necessary service. But if PCMs could prove that continuing to use the value center, rather than an external supplier, would result in failure to meet profit goals, then

**EXHIBIT 1** Pinnacle Mutual Life Insurance Company

M E M O R A N D U M

TO:     Executive Committee        DATE:  January 23, 1985

FROM:  Stephen Cooper           CC:     CMCP
        Vice President
        Corporate Analysis

    The purpose of this memorandum is to briefly review what transpired on January 4, describe what I hope we'll address and accomplish on January 25, and enumerate the tasks to be worked on over the next few months, and into the future.

I.  *Review of January 4 meeting*:
    I delineated what I felt were the two primary reasons for having profit centers:

    1.  To define *meaningful* units within the company whose results (e.g., profits) can be measured in a satisfactory manner. This will help the company determine which of its "parts" are doing well, and which need improvement (or should be discarded).
    2.  To more precisely define areas of responsibility for company managers; to measure how well those managers are performing and to provide a valid basis for determining incentive reward based on a manager's performance within his/her area of responsibility.

Clarification added to the above by Executive Committee members included the following:

1.  Changing attitudes of the business community, management, and the public dictate a greater emphasis on profitable operations.

* * *

The next area of discussion concerned what "units" should be defined as profit centers. I expressed a predilection for a primary profit center level based on our functional organization, with secondary and tertiary levels being product based. However, most discussion indicated an inclination for product-based profit centers. It was felt that the organization was susceptible to change or, alternatively, may be adjusted to support agreed-upon profit center structures. Product performance measures were felt to be the primary concern, and thus the driving force behind profit centers.

Final discussion involved appropriate measures for profit center results. ROSN (Return on Surplus Needs), GAAP (Generally Accepted Accounting Principles), net income (before and after dividends), and PSI (Product and Service Income) were all suggested, and the pros and cons of each were touched upon briefly.

*continued*

II.   *January 25 Agenda*

I'll commence with a review of the information obtained thus far on profit center techniques and problems of other companies. I'd then want to confirm what the basic profit center unit should be (opinions expressed favored product segments), explore the ramifications of that decision (organization coordination requirements, etc.), determine an *initial* number of profit centers to be measured, decide on *specific* profit centers as a result of the foregoing, and decide on the method to be used to select profit center managers (i.e., who will name them and when). Further discussion would consider whether the above structure is complete or whether it should be supplemented by any "cost centers" measured on fees for services less actual expenses.

I'd then like to continue our previous discussion on profit center measures. . . .

Finally, I'd be interested in the Executive Committee's opinion on the time period they envision to implement the various aspects of profit center measurement and organization. . . .

\* \* \*

I look forward to a fruitful session on the 25th.

PCMs could seek outside resources. While not wanting to limit PCMs' freedom, management wanted to avoid having them focus on short-term profit at the expense of long-term growth goals. Consequently, certain restrictions, in the areas of use of outside vendors, personnel policies, management development programs, and community relations programs would be placed on PCM actions.

The January 25 meeting also covered performance measures and incentive compensation for PCMs and VCMs. The Management Committee decided that PCMs would be measured on three criteria: GAAP profits, Return on Surplus Needs (ROSN), and Product and Service Income (PSI). "Surplus needs" was a calculation, for internal purposes only, of the appropriate amount of equity for a profit center, given its liabilities. In a mutual company, ROSN was similar to return on equity. Insur-

ance companies usually maintained a "policyholders' surplus," which was an amount in addition to liabilities, available to meet future obligations to its policyholders; for a mutual insurer, this was the whole equity section of the balance sheet. PSI was similar to gross operating revenue and was earned by selling new products and accruing revenue each year from those sales. In order to protect PCMs during the start-up phases in 1985, their compensation would not be tied to their profit center's performance. In 1986, however, they would be measured against their profit goals, but not on their profit center's growth.

During the first two weeks of February, the Committee for the Measurement of Corporate Performance (CMCP), chaired by Stephen Cooper, worked on the creation of profit centers. Even though the Executive Committee had decided that eight profit centers should be created, the CMCP felt that 10 or 12 would encourage better focus of sales efforts as well as allow for the creation of future products and services. The Management Committee approved the CMCP's list of 10 profit centers, but decided to appoint only eight PCMs; two of the eight PCMs would each manage two similar profit centers. They discussed which senior managers to appoint to these positions. Exhibit 2 shows a grid of the profit centers and value centers; the X's indicate the intended interactions between the two groups.

As Elizabeth Duncan had mentioned, management was clear about *what* they wanted the PCMs to do. Within six weeks of the approval of the 10 profit centers, the CMCP had developed a lengthy description of the PCMs' responsibilities and relationships (Exhibit 3). On April 1, 1985, Stephen Cooper sent a memo to the Chairman of the Board and to the president

**EXHIBIT 2**  Profit Center/Value Centers Grid

| VALUE CENTER | PROFIT CENTERS* | | | | | | | | | |
|---|---|---|---|---|---|---|---|---|---|---|
| | 1 IND LIFE TRAD | 2 IND LIFE NONT | 3 IND ANN | 4 IND HLTH | 5 INST INS | 6 INST PEN NONP | 7 INST PEN PAR | 8 INV PROD TRAD | 9 INV PROD SPEC | 10 INT NAT'L INS |
| Law & Corp secty | X | X | X | X | X | X | X | X | X | X |
| Corporate Ops | | | | | | | | | | |
|   Info Services | X | X | X | X | X | X | X | X | X | X |
|   Other Corp Ops | X | X | X | X | X | X | X | X | X | X |
| Product Services | | | | | | | | | | |
|   Group Servs | | | | | X | X | X | X | X | X |
|   Under & Pol Serv | X | X | X | X | | | | | | X |
|   International | | | | | X | X | X | X | X | X |
|   Other Prod Serv | X | X | X | X | X | | | | | X |
| Marketing | | | | | | | | | | |
|   Dist Agency | X | X | X | X | X | | | | | |
|   Gen Agency | X | X | X | X | X | | | | | |
|   Gr Pens Sales | | | | | | X | X | X | X | |
|   Group Ins. | | | | | X | | | | | |
|   Other Mktg | X | X | X | X | X | X | X | | | X |
| Investment Ops | | | | | | | | | | |
|   Bond & Corp Fin | X | X | X | X | X | X | X | X | X | X |
|   Mort & R E | X | X | X | X | X | X | X | X | X | X |
|   Inv Mktg | | | | | | | | | X | |
|   Other Inv Ops | X | X | X | X | X | X | X | X | X | X |
| Executive | X | X | X | X | X | X | X | X | X | X |

*Complete names of profit centers shown above:*
1. Individual Life Insurance Products and Services: Traditional
2. Individual Life Insurance Products and Services: Nontraditional
3. Individual Annuity Products and Services
4. Individual Health Products and Services
5. Institutional Insurance Products and Services
6. Institutional Annuity Products and Services: Nonparticipating
7. Institutional Annuity Products and Services: Participating
8. Investment Products and Related Services: Traditional
9. Investment Products and Related Services: Specialty
10. International Insurance Operations

**EXHIBIT 3**  Profit Center Managers' Responsibilities and Relationships

The primary responsibility of the profit center manager (PCM) is to achieve maximum profitability and growth as measured by the following:

- Return on Surplus Needs (ROSN)—definition and requirements established by the Surplus Committee.
- Profitability—bottom line as produced by Product Profitability Accounting and Reporting System (PPARS)—definitions established by the Committee for the Measurement of Corporate Performance (CMCP).
- Product and Service Income (PSI)—measures determined by the CMCP.

As straightforward as this definition of responsibilities appears to be, it raises a number of questions and poses a number of problems which must be addressed. One such problem arises from the fact that many PCMs will actually be responsible for a number of products rather than a single product.

\* \* \*

A second complication affecting the PCM's job results from the need to coordinate activities of people within different functional areas. Because the company is not organized by product lines, the PCM must work within a management team crossing several organizational lines.

\* \* \*

The PCM will negotiate with value center managers (VCMs) for services at certain expense and quality levels. It is important to note that this process of negotiation will not initially take place in a "free market" setting, in that the PCM wil be required, for the time being, to obtain services from sources available in the Pinnacle companies rather than immediately going outside for them. It is highly likely, of course, that PCMs will quickly become aware of competing sources which may provide the required services more inexpensively and will use this information in their negotiations. The availability of such data will no doubt place considerable pressure on each VCM to operate as efficiently as possible.

Since this kind of pressure may not suffice, however, we contemplate a policy under which the PCM will be able to give advance notice of his/her intention to use non-Pinnacle resources with reasons for doing so. If the Pinnacle department cannot provide the service at the stated cost within that time period (e.g., 2–3 years), the restrictions on utilizing outside resources will be eased, particularly if the PCM can demonstrate that failure to do so will prevent the attainment of his/her profitability goals which otherwise could be met.

\* \* \*

An important aspect of the negotiation process may prove to be the determination by the PCM, in conjunction with VCMs, of acceptable trade-offs between quality and cost. Inappropriate resolution of such questions could easily result in sacrificing long-term goals for short-term profits.

Relationships

In many cases, the PCM will have a dual reporting relationship. First, as a functional manager, he/she will continue to report, directly or indirectly, to an executive area head. As a PCM, however, he/she will report to the Management Committee as a whole. In addition, there will be a third relationship resulting from the need for teamwork referred to above. These third relationships will be rather extensive. Most PCMs will be negotiating and contracting for such services as:

Pricing—for both new and existing products
Marketing—including sales, training, etc.
Market research
Underwriting
Claims processing
Systems development, testing and maintenance
Data processing programming and production
Accounting services
Legal services
Personnel services, such as hiring, salary administration

---

**EXHIBIT 3** Profit Center Managers' Responsibilities and Relationships *continued*

---

As long as this list may at first appear to be, it is undoubtedly not complete; but it does serve to drive home the point that the PCM will have many relationships which he/she will have to manage (or at least coordinate) in order to operate profitably.

\* \* \*

PCM as Entrepreneur

While the PCM clearly has the responsibility for managing his/her product portfolio profitably, the nature of the PCM's responsibility to demonstrate a truly entrepreneurial approach to the job may be less evident. In addition to doing everything possible to see that he/she receives the best possible services from VCMs or others at the best possible price, the PCM should continually be on the watch for opportunities to introduce new products, expand existing products to meet new market needs, etc. A truly entrepreneurial PCM will not sit back and let others uncover opportunities to perform more efficiently or to develop new products and markets. He/she should therefore consider the identification and development of such opportunities as a major responsibility and should, through the compensation system, be rewarded accordingly.

---

of Pinnacle containing this description and the list of 10 recommended profit centers.

The announcement of the creation of profit centers was somewhat out of character for this stately, old mutual life insurance company. At an annual management meeting in May, attended by about 100 officers of Pinnacle, the eight senior managers who were appointed PCMs were introduced and given Captains' hats and megaphones as symbols of their new responsibilities and authority. Many of the PCMs were actuaries, some had experience in the areas they would now manage, and all had successful track records at Pinnacle. They were congratulated and told that they would be responsible for making the profit centers viable, for working out the bugs inherent in new systems, for establishing strategic plans, and for creating budgets. At the same time, they would continue to do their current jobs, and they would be given no additional staff to do their new jobs.

The new PCMs had many questions for top management about their new roles. To help answer initial and future questions, Stephen Cooper remained in his role as coordinator of the profit center project and served as organizer and advocate to address the needs and concerns of the PCMs.

In initial meetings with the PCMs, Cooper noted that their major complaints centered on two items: the PCMs had enormous goals but no staff, and they had difficulty getting accurate financial information about their products and services. To help address these problems, Cooper asked PCMs in November 1985 to submit "wish lists of tools" which would make their new jobs easier. Seven PCMs responded; Elizabeth Duncan's list (Exhibit 4) was representative of the kinds of tools many PCMs wanted. She went one step further and listed tools the Management Committee needed to help make profit centers work and sent these in a separate memo to Cooper (Exhibit 5).

Three items appeared consistently on the wish lists: (1) rules on the allocation of expenses to new products, (2) rules on deferring the expenses of Developmental Funds Programs (DFPs), and (3) earlier and more extensive involvement in the planning, evaluation, and approval of DFPs. DFPs were essentially R&D expenditures that were budgeted independently of regular operational budgets and were approved on a program by program basis. A decision on how DFPs would be treated was important because DFPs could be costly and out of proportion to the benefit received by some profit centers;

**EXHIBIT 4** Pinnacle Mutual Life Insurance Company

M E M O R A N D U M

TO:         Stephen Cooper              DATE:   November 15, 1985
            Vice President

FROM:       Elizabeth Duncan
            Vice President

SUBJECT:    Tools Necessary for My Profit Center to Work Right

1.  Clear definitions of which costs are fixed and which are variable, including
    as part of the exercise:

    a)  Expenses which are agreed upon in advance going into the year and
        change only with activity measures and/or a value center's failure to
        meet its budget with me—not with someone else's failure to meet an
        activity measure.

    b)  An understanding of how change in an activity measure, such as Sin-
        gle Premium Deferred Annuity (SPDA) sales, will affect expenses by
        value center.

    c)  A clear grasp of how expenses for a new product will be treated. (Allo-
        cations are not now made until more than 1 year after a new annuity
        product is introduced. Heaven knows who pays them in the mean-
        time.)

2.  A thorough analysis of how costs compare with the competition's, in areas
    such as distribution, overhead, marketing, etc. The competition includes
    other large insurance companies, companies selling through general agen-
    cies, brokers, direct response, etc.

3.  Detailed expense and revenue data by product for all my products with
    some understanding of why the numbers were derived that way.

4.  GAAP profit data for my profit center (if prospective sales look as though it
    can be cost-justified).

5.  An understanding of how Product and Service Income (PSI) is defined for
    each of my products and what a hurdle Return on Surplus Needs (ROSN)
    really means in terms of a profit margin for each. (This is undoubtedly
    available somewhere, once I make the effort to track it down.)

---

**EXHIBIT 5** Pinnacle Mutual Life Insurance Company

M E M O R A N D U M

TO:        Stephen Cooper          DATE:  November 15, 1985
              Vice President

FROM:    Elizabeth Duncan
              Vice President

SUBJECT:  Tools the *Management Committee* Needs to Make Profit Centers Work

1. A capital budget for the whole company (including subsidiaries) that would set limits for both true investment and development expenses affecting the corporation.

2. A list of potential capital and development projects which might surface over the next five years with associated price tag estimates and a probability of occurrence in each of the years.

3. A way to tie target Return on Surplus Needs (ROSN) hurdle rates to the capital budget on the theory that exceeding the capital budget will force up our cost of capital and should therefore drive up the hurdle rate.

4. A method to force every profit center manager and subsidiary CEO to implicitly pay back his/her cash flow each year and then to compete with everyone else for it. This will be necessary to free up resources for new projects and shifts in priorities.

---

other profit centers might not even be allocated a share of DFP projects under the current system. Cooper agreed that the CMCP would act on the first two items. For resolution of the third issue, he sent two memos (Exhibit 6) to George Steiner in his capacity as senior vice president and controller and as chairman of the DFP Steering Committee.

"Although I think we're making progress, it will be an on-going process for the PCMs to figure out what they need and how to get it," said Stephen Cooper. "I think it would be enlightening to talk to some of them. They are in the planning and budgeting cycle now and have some pretty strong feelings about the implementation of the profit center concept here at Pinnacle."

### Interviews with Profit Center Managers

**Elizabeth Duncan:** Vice President, Individual Equity and Pension Products; Profit Center Manager for Institutional Pension Products and Services–Nonparticipating

Creating profit centers has been a lot more difficult than any of us thought it would be. Our past culture of not thinking competi-

**EXHIBIT 6** Pinnacle Mutual Life Insurance Company

M E M O R A N D U M

TO:        George Steiner                              DATE:   January 9, 1986
           Senior Vice President
           and Controller
           Controller's Department

FROM:      Stephen Cooper            CC:      Profit Center
           Vice President                     Managers
           Corporate Analysis

SUBJECT:   Profit Center Data

The profit center managers recently enumerated a list of the "tools" (primarily data and information) they need to do their jobs. A compilation of these lists indicates some consensus on areas where controllers could help the profit centers acquire those tools. The following is a summary of their requests:

A. **Expenses**

All expense data are needed in the following configuration:

  c   three years historical and one year projected, on an annual basis
  c   one year historical and one year projected, on a quarterly basis
  c   direct and indirect expense components separated wherever possible

1.   GENERAL EXPENSE INFORMATION

  c   profit center expenses, broken down by cost center and grouped by value center
  c   cost center expenses and value center groupings, broken down by the Committee for the measurement of Corporate Performance (CMCP) product segment
  c   the function performed by each cost center should be indicated
  c   the present allocation assumptions and methods should be briefly explained

2.   INDIRECT EXPENSE ANALYSIS

  c   a definition of the various components of indirect expense is required
  c   indirect expense components, broken down by such items as: personnel, health clinic, food services, advertising, legislative activities, library, and institute
  c   the profit center allocation assumptions and methods should be briefly explained
  c   a comparison of competitors' indirect expenses (to help judge the reasonableness of such expenses)
  c   ratios of indirect expenses to direct expenses (to help judge the reasonableness of indirect expenses)

*continued*

3. DEVELOPMENTAL FUNDS PROGRAM (DFP) EXPENSE ANALYSIS

  c for each DFP project, budgeted expenses broken down by cost center

  c profit center allocation assumptions and methods for budgeted DFPs should be briefly explained

  c an analysis of actual DFP expenses and allocations compared with budgeted values is required

4. UNIT FUNCTIONAL EXPENSE ANALYSIS

  c profit center expenses, broken down by Life Office Management Association (LOMA) functional expense category such as: cost for underwriting, issue, maintenance, acquisition, and marketing

  c a comparison of competitors' functional expenses (to judge the reasonableness of such expenses)

5. FIELD EXPENSE ANALYSIS

  c profit center field expenses, broken down by such activities as: sales compensation, supervisory costs, training costs, and employee benefit costs

  c a comparison of competitors' field expenses (to judge the reasonableness of such expenses)

6. INVESTMENT EXPENSE ANALYSIS

  c profit center investment expenses, broken down by type of investment (e.g., bond, mortgage) and shown as a percentage of that investment's asset value

  c each of the above expense categories should be split into acquisition and maintenance components and shown as a percentage of the appropriate asset values

B. **Income Statement**

  1. income statements by CMCP product segment are needed on a Statutory Accounting Principles (SAP) and GAAP basis

  2. after-tax GAAP results require a deferred tax analysis by segment

  3. surplus reconciliations should be included with income statements

  4. provide three years historical and one year projected, on an annual basis

  5. provide one year historical and one year projected, on a quarterly basis

  6. resource personnel are needed for answering questions, performing active tax planning, and providing other analyses

*continued*

C.  **Balance Sheet**

1.  balance sheets by CMCP product segment are needed on a SAP and GAAP basis
2.  provide three years historical and one year projected, on an annual basis
3.  provide one year historical and one year projected, on a quarterly basis

D.  **Cash Flow Analysis**

1.  cash flow data, developed at the CMCP product segment level
2.  detailed data on sales and in-force premium income should be included
3.  provide three years historical and one year projected, on an annual basis
4.  provide one year historical and one year projected, on a quarterly basis

As all of this information would be useful to all profit centers, I assume your department would prepare it for each profit center, and forward it directly to them. What would be helpful at this time is a proposed timetable as to when each item would be available.

Corporate Analysis is available to coordinate this process, and provide any other help we can, so please feel free to call on us.

---

M E M O R A N D U M

TO:  George Steiner
Chairman, DFP Steering
Committee

DATE:  January 9, 1986

FROM:  Stephen Cooper
Vice President, Corporate
Analysis

CC:  Profit Center
Managers

SUBJECT:  Profit Center Manager Involvement in Developmental Funds Program (DFP) Process

Last month, I asked the profit center managers to provide me with lists of items which would allow them to more effectively do their jobs. One item that was generally agreed upon was an earlier and more extensive involvement in the planning, evaluation, and approval of DFP projects.

I realize your committee has stated its desire to involve the profit center managers in the DFP approval process, and you intend to invite PCMs to the 1986 meetings involving discussion of DFP project memorandums. Therefore, the purpose of this memo is simply to apprise you of the PCMs' concurrence with such involvement, and to suggest that when planning for the 1987 DFP cycle, you consider participation of the PCMs at the earliest stage possible.

tively has been hard to overcome; no one had ever asked which products were winners and which were losers.

Pinnacle needs a mechanism for deciding which profit centers will get resources. We've never had to pick and choose before. Right now, I'm having to fight for resources in the legal department and this takes a lot of my time. I can only spend about 25% or 35% of my time managing my profit center. My current job of managing Individual Equity and Pension Products keeps me pretty busy; in addition, I'm a director of two subsidiaries, and I serve on the Surplus Committee, the Demutualization Committee, and the Asset Allocation Committee.

As a profit center manager, I'm fairly unique. I have the least relationship naturally to my profit center in terms of other work I do. In the beginning, this compounded my difficulties because I wasn't already in the channels of distribution for information about my products and services. In some instances, it was a case of not even knowing what I didn't know!

All of the PCMs are still learning and discovering what they need. Upper management is grappling with understanding this process, too. It's like the story of the blind men and the elephant; the problems look different to the executive vice presidents and the PCMs because they are standing in different places. In some cases, no one is sure where the authority lies to make decisions when the viewpoints are so different.

**Benjamin Field:** Vice President and Group Actuary; Profit Center Manager for Individual Annuity Products and Services

The problem is that we all have different ideas of how things should be done and there are no tools in place to either direct our efforts or provide information. A big part of achieving our goals will be attributable to our ability to negotiate with the value centers to

get good information on which to base decisions. But in the fall of 1985, the Controllers didn't want to make the move to the profit center system because it would change the way they would have to compile reports.

Pinnacle has operated for nearly 100 years without worrying about profit; it's a slow process to change our orientation. We're experiencing problems with levels of authority on some decisions and with communicating. For example, the CEO occasionally disagrees with what PCMs think is the right thing to do to keep costs down. Who really makes the final decisions? It's also been hard to convince value centers that we need accurate information and we need it in a hurry, even when that information has never been compiled before.

The profit center managers don't have much time to devote to pressuring value centers for what we need. Some weeks I spend 40% of my time being a profit center manager, and other weeks I don't spend any time on it at all. I'm also a value center manager which puts me in an interesting situation; I was already in the information flow, unlike Elizabeth Duncan, which made my life easier. But the two hats I wear as PCM and VCM will probably create some conflicting situations in the future. What's good for the profit center may not be good for the value center.

**Peter Wright:** Vice President, Policyholder Services; Profit Center Manager for Individual Life Insurance Products and Services–Nontraditional

I see the role of the profit center manager more as a catalyst than a coordinator, more entrepreneurial in nature. But the corporate culture has often avoided change and confrontation. This makes it difficult to switch to profit-oriented thinking.

I have an advantage over some of the other PCMs in that I was already familiar with the products and services of my profit center. I also have value center departments which report to me, so I have established working relationships.

One problem we're all facing is that we wear too many hats to be able to get deeply immersed in some profit center issues. For example, the Controller sent a memo to some of the PCMs saying that they would be charged for a new accounting system, but the memo didn't mention a dollar amount. No one complained, partly because they couldn't find out the cost because the tools aren't in place to do that, and partly because they couldn't focus on this issue and do the 60 other things they were trying to do in their regular jobs. There's a lot of confusion now; the system is still evolving.

# WATTIE FROZEN FOODS LTD.: A NEW ZEALAND CASE STUDY IN MANAGEMENT ACCOUNTING AND EXTREME DECENTRALIZATION*

Businesses will not discover the pathway to competitiveness simply by reforming their existing management accounting systems. What they need is a new way of thinking about business, not improved management accounting information. Companies need information that triggers actions aimed at building strong customer relationships and at removing constraints that cause variation, delay, and excess in processes. No top-down accounting information—not even new activity-based cost management information—focuses on customers and processes. To stimulate competitiveness, management information must follow the "bottom-up empowerment cycle." It must come from customers and from processes and it must be gathered and used primarily by people in the work force who face the customers and who run the processes. Empowerment implies ownership of information—the key to learning. Constant learning by empowered workers is the key to change—the demand for unceasing change being caused by the power of choice that new information technologies give the customer.

H. *Thomas Johnson, Relevance Regained* (Free Press, 1992)

*William D.J. Cotton, Gerard La Rooy, AICPA case 96-06.
Reprinted with permission from AICPA Case Development Program, 1994. Copyright © 1994 by the American Institute of Certified Public Accountants, Inc.

Wattie Frozen Foods Ltd. (WFF) manufactures frozen and dehydrated foods and markets their products in New Zealand, Australia, and the Pacific rim, including Japan. The frozen foods business was originally part of J. Wattie Canneries Ltd., a food processing company formed in New Zealand in the 1930s. The Wattie organization passed through a number of different stages until in 1992 it was floated as a separate company by its then owner, Goodman Fielder Wattie Ltd. This current company, which comprises five New Zealand business units including WFF, was purchased by H.J. Heinz of the U.S.A. in late 1992. The WFF business unit consists of corporate headquarters and marketing staff located in Auckland, and four factories located respectively in Gisborne, Hastings, Fielding, and Christchurch.

Although the approach and systems are in use throughout WFF, this case focuses on the management control and performance evaluation system in the Christchurch Branch factory. This branch produces frozen and dehydrated vegetable products with the main products being peas, beans, and french fried potatoes. The production process is highly integrated from crop supply in the field through processing and distribution. The business is seasonal in nature.

Growers are contracted to WFF and are provided with a significant amount of technical assistance, including the availability of quality seed stock, and a wide variety of agricultural management assistance. Relevant crop supply data are maintained, including air temperature summaries, rainfall summaries, daily wind run summaries, and solar radiation summaries. Once crops are deemed ready they are harvested quickly and transported immediately to the branch factory, where the crop reception department tests the quality of the incoming produce. Unacceptable lots are rejected.

During the season processing occurs around the clock and involves a series of integrated steps. For example, potatoes for french fries are first washed, then sliced, deep fried, frozen, and packed. Peas for freezing are washed, graded, frozen for bulk storage, and then released throughout the year for packing in consumer packs. Beans for dehydration are washed, graded, dried, stored in bulk or immediately packed in consumer packs for distribution or storage.

The production process is supported by a number of service departments. These support departments include logistics, personnel, engineers, boilers, fork lifts, process bins, dry goods, weigh bridge, crop storage, effluent, yard, and quality assurance.

In 1986 WFF adopted the principle of "Work Center Management" (WCM). This involved the division of the organization into a set of semi-autonomous work centers, and the empowering of the supervisors and employees in each work center with the ability to make decisions critical to the manufacture of a quality product in a timely fashion. Since 1986 the company has worked hard to develop the work center culture and to provide the management and employees with the appropriate management tools and systems.

When describing the new system, Gerard La Rooy (then WFF's Corporate Support Manager) stated:

The introduction of the new culture and associated systems meant big changes for the company and staff and naturally we experienced some difficulties along the way. However, as we have made considerable gains in many areas, we feel that the changes have been most worthwhile. Because of the gains made to date and the scope for further improvements, we are confident that managing the work center way is the way for us.

## *Motivation for Work Center Management*

The company identified a number of principal needs which they felt had to be satisfied in their quest for a new and better approach to management, particularly in the four factories. These principal needs were:

1. The need to change the emphasis from reporting to managing.

   This involved shortening drastically the time between actions taken and the subsequent reporting on results. In particular, monthly costing reports, even if they were produced promptly at month end, were perceived as relatively useless for real control and improvement of the operations. Also, since the application of more technology produced an on-going shift in costs from direct to indirect, there was a need to focus on the *management* of overheads rather than their mere allocation. Finally there was a need to ensure focused accountability through clearly-defined responsibilities for costs and the power to act.

2. The need for staff involvement and operational improvement.

   The firm wished to inculcate in staff at the workface an increased awareness of cost and quality issues and to recognize that quality and costs can be managed effectively only at each stage of the process, not just at the end. This required ownership of information by supervisors and workers. If the information is provided primarily to assist the actual day-to-day operation at the workface, ownership of that information is much more likely. But information which is produced primarily to enable control to be exercised from the top will not provide the basis for performance improvement. In other words the management at WFF recognized the need for the "bottom-up empowerment" advocated by Johnson.

## Changing the Organizational Culture

The WCM system was designed and implemented following the adoption by the company of the philosophy of management by work centers. The issue of the prior adoption of the appropriate culture was regarded by WFF management as important since it was their strong conviction that such a system as WCM could not be overlaid on a traditional organization. Prior to the implementation of the system the firm carried out a comprehensive set of training sessions throughout all levels of the organization in an attempt to imbue all employees with the changed philosophy. These training sessions and meetings emphasized a number of aspects.

1. The culture required a special way of managing.

   It needed to be recognized that WCM was a consistent and all-encompassing approach that embraced all of the following: quality, budgeting, cost control, physical and financial reporting, waste and losses management, training, performance improvement, capital expenditure justification, purchasing, and asset management. The culture also required the adoption of the concept of internal customers who must be satisfied and who could refuse to accept substandard inputs. Since the new system would result in a flat organizational structure, it would require managers who were empowered, responsible, and above all, highly competent. Managers would be fully responsible for their outputs and their use of inputs and resources including labor, equipment, services, and inventories.

2. The culture required an understanding of a commitment to the concept of work centers.

   Each factory needed to be divided into units which were largely self-contained and small enough to ensure focused management and accountability. Each of these units, to be known as work centers, would become the smallest units of management and thus become the building blocks of the organization. It was important that managers subscribe to the work center concept, in that work centers must:

   - Reflect the logical flow of factory operations.
   - Have clear and agreed boundaries.
   - Be created so that there are no overlaps.
   - Cover the entire scope of the factory operations including production, service functions, and administrative functions. (There should not be any "no-man's-land").
   - Have only one manager. However one manager could supervise more than one work center.
   - Provide, as far as possible, for the measurement of all labor, materials and resources consumed by the work center.
   - Be mirrored in the general ledger.

   Work center managers would be encouraged to appreciate, and in time expected to understand, the full workings of the "mini-business" under their control.

3. The culture required a supportive site manager.

   The site manager (factory manager) should recognize that his/her role was to support work center managers, to coordinate work centers, and to solve any conflicts between work centers. This would require daily contact with work center management and staff and a recognition that problems between work centers as to quality, quantities, and services need to be resolved promptly.

4. The focus of the culture must be on continuous improvement.

   Staff should be encouraged to be proactive, and systems should be designed and implemented with improvement of performance in mind, rather than just control. There should be a deliberate shift in focus away from the result to the process. In discussing this point Gerard La Rooy stated: "Merely focusing on results month after month will be of little assistance in our drive to improve. Only by monitoring and understanding the underlying processes can we begin to improve our performance."

### The Work Center Management System

The work center management system outlined in this section was developed by WFF to fit in with the firm's managerial philosophy and practices. The system's conceptual and development work, including database design, was done in-house by WFF. The actual construction of the database and programming was carried out by an external consulting firm.

The work centers were constructed to reflect the logical flow of operations through the factory, and resulted in a flat organizational structure. The organization chart of the Christchurch factory is outlined in Exhibit 1. From this it may be observed that the WCM system covers the entire factory environment including all production activities from crop harvesting through to product distribution, and all service and support activities. The factories are divided into definable units which have measurable inputs and outputs, and there are virtually no general overheads since each service or support operation is itself defined as a work center.

### WCM System Features

The object of the system is to support decentralized management at the work center level with decisions regarding input, output and problems being addressed by work center staff rather than administrative staff. That is, all work centers are regarded as "mini businesses" which consume inputs and produce outputs. The system provides ready information at the factory floor to enable *daily* control to be exercised with proper accountability. Costs are assigned to processes at source based upon actual consumption to enable control at or shortly after the time of the event. The major features of the system are that it:

- Attempts to treat all costs as controllable so as to minimize general overheads. This even extends to the administrative and accounting function which is itself treated as a work center with inputs and outputs: see Appendix A.
- Translates the physical quantities into dollar values for automatic posting into the general ledger.
- Encourages production and optimum staffing levels, because all work center related costs stay within the work center. This discourages the recharging of work center staff to such a general administrative activity as cleaning.
- Encourages *quality* production. The output of one work center becomes the consumption of the next, and a consuming work center can refuse substandard input. *This is a key feature of the WCM system.*
- Values input to a work center (consumption) at the standard all-inclusive cost to that point. Any cost over-runs are the responsibility of the producing work center and are not passed on to the consuming work center.
- Treats all work center losses as a cost attributable to the work center where the loss occurs. Minimizing losses is a key element of managerial control in the frozen food industry so this is a critical feature of the WCM system. See Appendix B for an example of the concept.
- Provides for a service work center to consume its own output, as in the case of engineers performing work on their facilities.
- Requires all work centers to record as "production" all goods sent to or services performed for another work center.
- Requires the receiving work center to record all inputs as "consumption."
- Requires consumption to be recorded for each work center as a cost for that work center. In addition the consumption may be allotted to products or other cost objects within the consuming work center.

### Costing Without Dollars

The WFF system comprises two distinct parts, the physical and the financial. When designing and implementing the system, management realized that they were able to gradually implement physical measurements without initially having to impact the old managerial cost accounting system. Thus the first stage of the WCM project enabled the

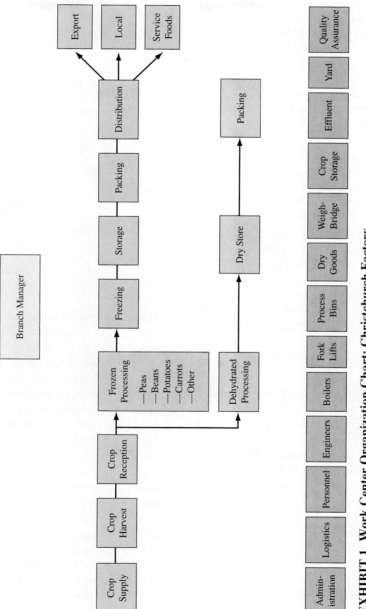

**EXHIBIT 1  Work Center Organization Chart: Christchurch Factory**

company to engage in "costing without dollars." Gerard La Rooy commented on this:

> In the event it proved a sound decision. It meant that by focusing on the physical side we were not required to implement the system on an all or nothing basis. On the contrary we were able to gain real progressive benefits as each work center was being implemented. It also meant that the learning could be much less traumatic. If mistakes were made we could alter the physical quantities without affecting our financial figures. We also reckoned that once the system was completely installed and operating in a physical sense, applying standard dollar values would not be unduly difficult. As an interim measure we were able to use the physical figures from the new system as input into the old costing system to provide the posting into the ledger.

The firm found that the initial lack of real financial integration did not prove to be too much of a problem. Indeed many of the benefits of WCM come not from financial reports but from improved daily control at the physical level. The experience of WFF suggests that "costing without dollars" can be very useful.

## Dynamic Activity-Based Costing Application

Once the physical measurement system was operating in a satisfactory fashion the firm was able to turn their attention to redesigning the financial system. This has been an ongoing process, but as of mid-1993 had been virtually completed at the four factories. An interesting feature of the financial system is that the design of the financial costings was driven by the physical measurement system. This has prompted Gerard La Rooy to refer to the WFF costing system as "a dynamic activity-based costing application." That is the system does not employ an ex post activity analysis to assign costs, but costs are assigned to processes or products *at source* on the basis of the actual consumption of physical resources.

Examples of service department work centers and associated activity-based cost drivers are:

| Service Work Center | Cost Driver |
| --- | --- |
| Quality assurance | Quality labor hours |
| | Number of Bacto tests |
| Engineering | Engineering labor hours |
| Storage bins | Packed weight tons |
| | Dry packed weight tons |
| Boiler | Kg steam used |
| Dry goods | Seed tons |
| | Packed weight tons |
| | Dry packed weight tons |
| Crop reception | Clean intake tons |
| Electrical | Electrical labor hours |
| | Megawatts of electricity used |

Annual budget estimates are calculated for each service center, and divided by the estimated number of cost driver units to compute a rate per cost driver unit. The managers of work centers consuming the services are then permitted to negotiate with the producing center in order to finalize a rate to be charged during the year. For example, the manager of the freezing work center may negotiate with the engineering work center over the rate for engineering services, and is even permitted to contract engineering services outside the company. This had rarely happened since users of outside engineering service must also pay a contribution towards the fixed cost of maintaining the in-house engineering facility. The branch manager may arbitrate disputes between work center managers.

Once the costing rates are established for the year they are used to cost *actual* activities as they occur. An example of the rates established for the 1995 financial year for the

**EXHIBIT 2**  Steam Budget Rates for 1995 Financial Year

| Total Service Center Cost | $759,000 | |
|---|---|---|
| Variable—fuel | 416,000 | |
| Fixed—wages, Repairs and Maintenance, depn | 343,000 | Variable fuel steam cost    $22.94/kg |

| | | | VARIABLE—FUEL COST | | | | | |
|---|---|---|---|---|---|---|---|---|
| FROZEN CROP | TOTAL BUDGET TONNES | PWT PER HOUR | KG CROP PER KG STEAM | TOTAL KG STEAM | TOTAL FUEL COST | FIXED COST (SPREAD ON TONNES) | TOTAL COST | COST PER KG STEAM F95 BUDGET |
| Peas | 22,000 | 18.0 | 7.0 | 3,143 | 72,082 | 202,310 | 274,392 | 87.31 |
| Green beans | 6,033 | 8.0 | 5.0 | 1,207 | 27,674 | 55,479 | 83,152 | 68.91 |
| Carrots | 1,101 | 1.5 | 3.0 | 367 | 8,417 | 10,125 | 18,542 | 50.52 |
| Potatoes | 6,485 | 2.0 | 0.5 | 12,970 | 297,469 | 59,635 | 357,105 | 27.53 |
| Broad beans | 527 | 1.5 | 4.5 | 117 | 2,686 | 4,846 | 7,532 | 64.38 |
| Whole beans | 900 | 3.0 | 4.5 | 200 | 4,587 | 8,276 | 12,863 | 64.32 |
| Other | 0 | 0.5 | 1.0 | 0 | 0 | 0 | 0 | |
| Brassica | 50 | 0.7 | 1.0 | 50 | 1,147 | 460 | 1,607 | 32.13 |
| Squash | 0 | 1.0 | 1.3 | 0 | 0 | 0 | 0 | |
| Baby carrots | 199 | 1.5 | 3.0 | 66 | 1,521 | 1,830 | 3,351 | 50.52 |
| Total | 37,295 | | | 18,120 | 415,583 | 342,961 | 758,544 | |

Boiler Service Work Center at the Christchurch factory is contained in Exhibit 2. The budgeted rates for 1995 are in every case less than the rates agreed for 1994 and it is evident that the WCM system is proving effective in motivating managers and supervisors to control costs. This is achieved not only by "sharp pencil" negotiating among work center managers, but also by encouraging work center staff to reduce costs by managing effectively the activities which drive them.

An illustration of a *daily* performance and cost report is shown in Exhibit 3. Note the physical measures of tonnage consumed and produced, units packed, packaging materials used, and labor hours used including overtime statistics. Also observe that the activity-based costing rates for the "overhead" costs relating to the services provided are based upon *actual* quantities of cost driver units consumed by the work center on that day.

In addition to the daily work center perfor-

mance and cost reports, the accounting department operates a direct costing system to cost inventories. This system traces the direct costs of the crop supply, production, and packaging to inventory accounts in the branch and head office (Auckland) ledgers. A diagrammatic example of this is shown in Exhibit 4.

## WCM Integration with Other Systems and Programs

The work center management system is integrated with other systems and programs at WFF. An important managerial reporting tool is the monthly branch report which is used by upper level management to evaluate the performance of operating units. This important monthly report covers six areas:

- Branch overview
- Cost and financial performance
- Work center performance
- Previous agreed action

**EXHIBIT 3** Daily Work Center Performance and Cost Report CPCKV Work Center, 8 June 1994

| Tonnes consumed | 65.085 | Units packaged: | 8434 |
|---|---|---|---|
| Tonnes produced: | 64.395 | Total packaging used: | 98045 Poly |
| | | | 7486 Cases |
| | 98.94% | | 80416 |
| | | Total Labor Hours Used: | 332.25 Ord |
| | | | 16.75 Time & Half |

| SERVICE | QTY | $ PER TONNE | ACTUAL OVERHEADS PER TONNE | BUDGET OVERHEADS |
|---|---|---|---|---|
| Packing eng labor | 9.00 | 145.35 | | |
| Engineering | 6.00 | 173.72 | 4.95 | 5.58 |
| Electricity | | 112.10 | 1.74 | 1.18 |
| Forklift | | 78.25 | 1.18 | 0.86 |
| GA | 17.50 | 318.93 | 4.95 | 5.36 |
| Dry store | 3.00 | 132.50 | 2.06 | 2.84 |
| Waste disposal | | 92.08 | 1.43 | 1.43 |
| Consumables | | 211.80 | 3.29 | 3.29 |
| Other | | 45.08 | 0.70 | 0.70 |
| Packing labor (indirect) | 16.75 | 228.82 | 3.55 | 3.28 |
| | | $1,538.63 | $23.85 | $24.52 |

- Information and new action topics
- Capital expenditure

The WCM system not only provides the basis for cost and financial performance measures, but also provides monthly summaries of a wide variety of physical measures used to evaluate the performance of work centers. For example, the Crop Supply Work Center at the Christchurch factory reports include:

1. Crop harvest details (for each type of vegetable), including planned tons, year to date tons, total crop estimate, and estimated harvest dates.
2. Overtime hours.
3. Seed stock summary for each type of vegetable.
4. Agricultural research activities.
5. Weather details, including air temperature summary charts, rainfall summary charts, daily wind run summary charts, and solar radiation summary charts.
6. Grower contract updates.

The monthly report for the Dehydration Work Center includes:

1. Narrative summary of drying achievements, tonnage statistics, and financial summary.
2. Narrative summary of packing achievements, detailed packing statistics including variance analysis by product types, analysis of overtime hours.
3. Summaries of research activities for new products and markets, particularly in Japan.
4. Outline of continuous improvement team meetings.

The work center management system also supports the firm's continuous improvement program. This program is known as IMPACS which is an acronym for "Improving Management Performance and Customer Satisfaction." The management of WFF is committed to the continuous improvement philosophy and each work center is required to report

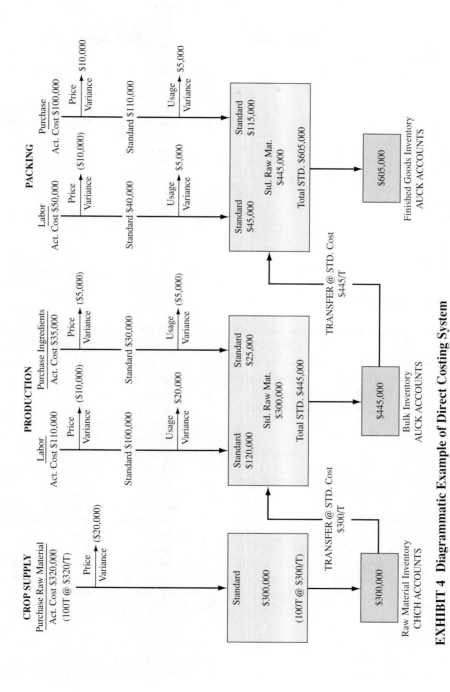

**EXHIBIT 4  Diagrammatic Example of Direct Costing System**

monthly on their IMPACS activities. An example of this is shown in Appendix C, and which exhibits the level of commitment to continuous improvement which exists in the firm. The WCM system facilitates improvement programs since it provides a variety of physical performance measures which are candidates for improvement. Before the advent of the WCM, system managers focused on identifying and "controlling" (manipulating?) costs, whereas now they can concentrate on identifying improvement opportunities and on the implementation of ideas.

### *Benefits of Work Center Management*

The firm has achieved significant benefits from the WCM system, but recognizes that obtaining full benefits is a long process which has not yet been fully realized. Gerard La Rooy states: "Generally speaking our expectations have been (or are in the process of being) realized in that we are gradually becoming a company with the right culture and the right systems."

Top management are convinced that managing by work centers and the use of the WCM system has resulted in improved control and very worthwhile cost reductions in such previously difficult to control areas as forklifts and engineering. Production work center managers have come to realize that there are no "free" resources since they have to pay for such services as forklifts and engineering. This has had some interesting outcomes: The firm no longer owns forklifts, but now leases some on a long-term basis and rents additional equipment during the busy season. Engineers have been forced to become competitive with outside suppliers of service and must give value for money to the users of engineering service. This cultural change has not necessarily come easily. Murray Norton, former manager of the Christchurch Branch commented:

> Some of our engineers have had difficulty embracing the work center philosophy. There are a few people who have been here a long time who are resisting the change. It may be that some would be more comfortable in a different organization and it is possible that we may give them that opportunity.

Among the additional benefits of the WCM system are:

- An improved focus on quality production

  There is a reluctance by work center staff to accept substandard inputs of either product or service. This extends back as far as the crop reception work center which has refused to accept out-of-spec. truckloads of incoming vegetables, since it is known that the processing work center will reject the batch. This has led to a good appreciation of the concept of internal customers.

- A focus on physical measurements

  Physical measures of performance have proved meaningful to work center staff. Monitoring and understanding physical measurements on a daily basis has resulted in significant performance improvements in many areas.

- Increased accuracy

  Costing and inventory information has become more reliable. Mistakes are generally picked up on the day they occur and fixed at the time rather than having to be traced later, or worse still, not at all.

- Value added thinking

  Staff have been encouraged to focus on value added activities, and one of the outcomes of this has been improved control of waste and losses.

- Improved staff morale

  A very valuable benefit has been improved staff morale in most work centers. The ability and freedom for staff to manage the work center as a "mini-business" and the "ownership" of information related to the work center has had a positive impact on productivity and quality.

- Increased focus on improvement

  The availability of detailed information on work center activities has enhanced the firm's quality improvement initiatives.

- Shift from results to processes

  The focus on processes on a real-time basis rather than results on an after-the-fact basis has been a most important step in improving employees' understanding at their segment of the business.

These benefits have not been easy to realize and it has taken years rather than months to reach the level of achievement currently attained. In addition, WFF is aware that their WCM system needs to be continuously developed and improved as the firm adapts to the needs of the 1990s and beyond.

## Questions

(1) Discuss the firm's competitive environment and product range.
(2) Outline the production process and discuss problems potentially created by the seasonality of the business.
(3) What is "work center management" (WCM) as practiced by Wattie? Why is there daily reporting?
(4) What was the motivation for WCM?
(5) Why was it necessary to change the organizational culture? How was this culture change achieved?
(6) How do the physical numbers tie into the financial accounting system?
(7) What are the benefits claimed for WCM?
(8) What problems can you see in operating the WCM system?
(9) What types of operations lend themselves to daily financial reporting?

## Appendix A: Wattie Frozen Foods Ltd., Christchurch Branch, Administration and Accounting Service Work Center, Excerpts from Financial Year 1994

### Mission Statement

To contribute to improving the operations of the branch through the provision of reliable and meaningful financial and administrative services.

### Function and Core Activities

- Oversee and assist in data accumulation.
- Ensure translation of data into meaningful information.
- Provide reliable and meaningful financial advice and analysis.

- Assist users to interpret information.
- Provide administration services.
- Provide a focus to effect branch financial control.
- Maintain and enhance computer systems and improve their use.

### Current Situation Analysis

- Recognition of our continuing role in organization from data gatherers to information interpreters.
- Improved quality of content and presentation of information.
- Increased awareness of Service Center nature by our customers.
- Increased team involvement.
- Increased project analysis.
- Improved recognition of responsibility for Branch Financial well-being through utilization of control systems, forecasting, etc.
- Improved ability to meet deadlines.
- Improving understanding by users of usefulness of financial information.

### Key Actions 1993 Financial Year

- Improve R & M control system to provide forecasting control.
- Initiate project analysis to investigate:
  Cafeteria Operation
  Non W.F.F. Site Users
- Review all information and accounting systems to ensure economy, efficiency and compliance.
- Branch review of all management reports to ascertain, advise and fulfill users' needs.
- Drive to effect physical recovery of service centers.
- Provide variable cost center reports with flex budgets and include direct and variable costs by crop reports in monthly reports.
- Provide basic accounting course to improve users' understanding and ability to use accounting information.
- Analyze administration staff current skill level and commence cross skilling.

### Strategic Thrust 1994 Financial Year

- To be providers of relevant and timely information and analysis.
- Increase control systems to allow for more effective branch financial control.
- To continually improve the value of financial information systems and propose improvements as applicable.

- To continue to improve users' ability to utilize information.
- To ensure staff ability to strive for and achieve ongoing improvement, through relevant training, team building and identifying objectives.
- To ensure ongoing availability of service through staff cross skilling.

---

### S.W.O.T Analysis: The Branch

| STRENGTHS | WEAKNESSES |
|---|---|
| Enthusiasm and willingness to learn | Lack of training |
| Work center nature of responsibility accounting | Continuing day-to-day pressure limiting longer term focus ability |
| Understanding of branch operations | |
| Increasing awareness of value of using financial information as a control tool | Availability of accurate measuring systems |
| Increasing understanding of financial information and financial systems | |
| Sophisticated E.D.P. systems | |

| OPPORTUNITIES | THREATS |
|---|---|
| To continue training and increase use of information as manufacturing tool | Allowing day-to-day pressure to prevent planning and forward focus |
| Maximum use of E.D.P. systems | Nonutilization of control systems |
| Increase accuracy of data input | |

---

### S.W.O.T. Analysis: The Service Center

| STRENGTHS | WEAKNESSES |
|---|---|
| Enthusiastic staff willingness to participate and learn | Understanding of manufacturing process |
| Sophisticated E.D.P. tools available | Time management to ensure adequate planning |
| Stable and experienced staff | Full understanding of work center requirements |
| Diverse skill base | Full understanding of capability of E.D.P. systems |
| Availability of Auckland support systems | Lack of structure for E.D.P. support services |
| | Inadequately documented systems |

| OPPORTUNITIES | THREATS |
|---|---|
| Maximize service continuity through cross skilling | Allowing day-to-day pressure to prevent planning and forward focus |
| Improve systems and use of them with further training | |

## Key Strategies, Actions

| KEY STRATEGY | KEY ACTION | CHAMPION |
|---|---|---|
| Control branch E.D.P. systems | Set up system expert group | S.S. |
| | Implement training programs | S.S. |
| | Set up TPM for EDP hardware | S.S. |
| Improve quality of reception function | Oversee implementation of new telephone system | C.M./B.W. |
| | Set up system to know people's whereabouts | C.M./T.F. |
| | Set up message distribution system | C.M./T.F. |
| Improve service from crop supply | Gain full understanding of growers' system | S.G./R.E./T.F. |
| Improve accounts payable: User interface | Implement formal end of month timetable and train users | J.A./T.F. |
| | Investigate use of order entry system | J.A./B.W. |
| Improve value and use of financial information to assist manufacturing operations | Review specific management reports to improve their usefulness | D.K./S.S./R.S. |
| | Continue appraisal of service centers to recover by units through W.C.M. | D.K./B.W. |
| | Trend direct and variable costs by crop by year | R.S. |
| | Improve summarization and regularity of direct and variable overhead reporting to ensure no month-end "surprises" | D.K./B.W. |
| Effect financial control of branch operations | Continue user training to improve understanding and use of financial information and accounting systems | B.W. |
| | Improve R&M control and forecasting systems | B.W. |
| | Commence conversion of fixed asset register to recognize tagged identifiable assets | D.K./B.W. |
| | Investigate absorption of unattributed fixed costs | B.W. |
| | Ensure orderly implementation of user defined payroll system | B.W. |
| | Implement fixed cost (other than R&M) forecasting system and trend analysis | B.W. |
| | Commence internal audit and system review | D.K./B.W. |
| Ensure department staff are able to provide high level of service | Implement structured cross-skilling program based on preference | All |
| | Increase staff knowledge of manufacturing process through greater contact during processing | All |

## Capital Plan 1994 Financial Year

| PROJECT | COST | MONTH (1993) | CHAMPION |
|---|---|---|---|
| PABX System | $ 50,000 | June | B.W./C.M. |
| P.C.s | $ 45,000 | June | S.S. |
| File server upgrade | $ 10,000 | July | S.S. |
| Laser printer | $  9,000 | July | S.S. |
| Branch manager's car | $ 22,000 | June | M.N. |
| General | $ 50,000 | | |
| IMPACS | $ 30,000 | | |
| | $216,000 | | |

---

## Cost of Administration Services

**Administration Services Provided**
- Accounting
- Administration
- Systems support
- Communication
- Training

---

|  | F94 | F93 |
|---|---|---|
| Budget | $530,000 | $625,000 |
| Staff level | 8 | 9 |
| Total hours | 16,000 | 18,000 |
| Cost per hour* | $  33.13 | $  34.72 |

---

*This "cost per hour" is the charge-out rate used to charge administration and accounting services to other support and production work centers.*

## *Appendix B: Example of Treatment of Waste and Losses*

### Objectives

- Knowledge of the true "value-added" cost of waste and losses at each stage of production
- Treating the cost of waste (or at least the avoidable part) as a work center cost

### Example of Traditional Treatment of Waste and Losses

- Buy in 100 tonnes at $400/t to produce 80 tonnes finished product.
- Cost of purchase = 100t × $400/t = $40,000
- Production costs direct and indirect are $80,000
- Recovery = $\frac{80t}{100t} \times 100\% = 80\%$
- Loss = 20t @ $400/t = $8,000
- Cost per tonne = $\frac{\$40,000 + \$80,000}{80t}$ = $1,500/t

**Waste and Losses Employing Work Centers**  Using the same detail but in addition assuming there are four work centers and that the production cost is evenly spread over the work centers.

We can draw the situation like this:

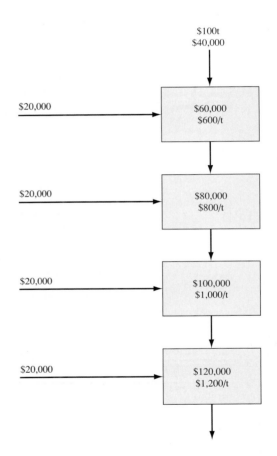

**Waste and Losses at Added Value**  Assume that the 20 tonnes unrecovered are lost at the rate of 5t per work center. The situation now becomes:

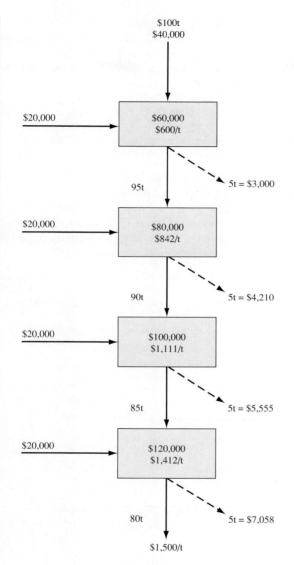

| Sum of Losses | |
|---|---|
| Tonnes | $ |
| 5 | 3,000 |
| 10 | 7,210 |
| 15 | 12,765 |
| 20 | 19,823 |

Note that in our example the added value of the sum of the losses is *$19,823* whereas the conventional approach shows the losses to be *$8,000*. There is no doubt that the added value figure approximates the true situation much more closely than the figure obtained using the conventional approach.

## Appendix C: IMPACS Dehydration Work Center— March: Ways to Build a Team

We have three different types of team meetings.

1.  Where = The team build process started.
    Who = Linda, Craig, Bill, Dawn, Robert.

Place = Linda's place once a month in our own time.

Why = To find our goals and to learn to work together.

NOTE: This is where the team building started as I believe if you haven't a team at the supervisor, manager, chargehand level there is no way that you can hope to achieve the team process anywhere else.

2. Involves all staff including Dehy Packing—David, Sarah, where available Craig.

Time = Once a fortnight in the cafe over a cup of tea.

Duration = ½ hour—Morning shift = 1:30 P.M.–2:00 P.M. Afternoon shift = 9:30 P.M.–10 P.M. Night shift = 5:30 A.M.–6 A.M.

Why = Because unless everyone is kept informed and involved then no matter what a few want to achieve it will never be possible.

From the first meeting came the AIMS's of what we want to achieve.

- To mold the team spirit.
- To air everyone's problems in an open manner.
- Everyone's progress on the line.
- To learn each others' skills so we can be a multiskilled team.
- To help each other achieve a top quality product at a maximum throughput.
- To improve the line to make the work easier and reduce overall costs.

These team talks have increased costs to our work center on a fortnightly basis but the savings overall have more than compensated for the monetary outlay of 3 hours overtime each fortnight, by increased productivity (e.g., last year's carrot production up by 50%).

3. Wattie Frozen Foods team brief. Usually incorporated with our own team talk. This I feel is a strong facet in bonding good staff into a great team.

- Below are some of the items brought up.

| Morning Shift | | Action by |
|---|---|---|
| White board & pin up board | —Packing | L. Watson |
| Hugger dangerous | —Packing | C. Agnew |
| Hook for air hose | —Dehy | B. Frost |
| Any overtime after peas | —Dehy | C. Agnew |
| Lids on make-up tank | —Dehy | L. Watson/C. Agnew |
| Scarifier taken apart too much | —D.T. of 2 hours | Chargehands |

| Afternoon Shift | |
|---|---|
| Clean downs disgusting; afternoon shift having to redo night shift work | D. Roper & L. Watson talk to night shift people |
| Ladder for cleaning tanks. Save time on cleaning | B. Hopkinson |
| Portawas have interchangeable connection on them. Save costs due to being able to move them around. | D. Roper |
| Lighting over slicer and dryer bad, makes cleaning difficult and can be dangerous at night. | C. Agnew |

| Night Shift | |
|---|---|
| Asahi corn—how do we mix chemicals to put into shaker; a heavy job, at moment. | The Whole Team |
| Nail brushes in toilets. | Talk to S. Williams |
| Pallets not blown down. | Dehy Packing staff plus Dryer staff |

# INDUSTRIAL CHEMICALS COMPANY*

## Background

In 1995, events that had been thought about and planned for the past several years in the Industrial Chemicals Company culminated in the most significant change in the company's 80-plus-year history. A major corporate restructuring was announced, including the purchase of a large U.S.-based pharmaceutical company, for $2.8 billion.

In February of 1996, the chairman of the board and chief executive officer told a reporter for a major financial magazine, "We felt that if we were to build a strong technology base of biology and biotechnology that would simultaneously serve agriculture, animal nutrition, and health care, we could build a unique powerhouse backing it up in a way that the companies in these individual businesses couldn't do, and we've built it." The changes initiated were thus not merely pruning and trimming, but changing the very direction of the company by getting out of commodity chemicals and into more innovative areas.

The magazine made a key observation in its February 10 issue:

> A major problem looms: Can the remaining product lines support the level of research needed to make a major impact in biotechnology? Earnings for the first three quarters of 1995 dropped and the company expects to show a loss for the fourth quarter, even before write-offs on closed chemical plants.
>
> The company suffered further losses in the silicon wafer business, in which it invested close to $500 million since 1991. And it was hurt by the sharp downturn in the farm economy. For 1996, however, analysts estimate earnings of $4.50 per share vs. $3 last year before special charges.

The chairman of the board was well aware of the major concern as to the remaining product lines' capability to support the level of research needed to make a major impact in biotechnology. In fact, as 1995 drew to a close, he commissioned a special subgroup of the Executive Management Committee (the EMC is the senior management group dealing with major strategic and operational issues) to review the company's overall R&D spending, its affordability and priorities, and bring back recommendations to the EMC in time for inclusion in the 1996 budgeting process.

In addition to wrestling with the affordability and priority of research programs controlled within the operating units of the company, the EMC subcommittee also focused on the corporately managed R&D effort as to both affordability and organizational placement in terms of operations and control. Views among the subcommittee on this latter issue were varied. The most significant differences in viewpoint are characterized as follows:

> One perspective was to disassemble the corporate R&D effort and place it directly with the businesses being supported wherever possible with, of course, all costs moving directly to those units. The operating unit manager would then be held accountable for the "bottom line" results and would have direct control over all R&D. R&D would thus be moored to managers with a future obligation to commercialize successfully.
>
> Another perspective reasoned that if biotechnology was in fact to be the cornerstone of the transformation of the company, there must be a minimum threshold below which discovery efforts must not go. This viewpoint further reasoned that such effort must be

---

*Reprinted with permission from Volume 4 of *Cases from Management Accounting Practice*, from the IMA/AAA Management Accounting Symposium series.

managed corporately and not turned over to operations. Retention of control at the corporate level would ensure a long-term profit pressure.

A major part of the 1995 restructuring was a thrust to study and decentralize all corporate staff units to the fullest extent possible into the operating units that are held accountable for overall financial results. The corporate R&D group was to undergo perhaps one of the most substantial reviews of all corporate staff groups.

## Research and Development

From a total corporate perspective, the R&D effort falls into three classifications:

Class I: Maintain existing businesses. This effort is associated with managing existing business assets, maintaining competitiveness of products in existing businesses, and supplying technical service.

Class II: Expand existing businesses. R&D associated with expanding existing business assets, expanding markets of existing products, or substantially lowering costs of existing processes.

Class III: Create new businesses. R&D associated with creating new business assets.

Table 1 is a summary of total R&D costs from 1990 through 1994 within these three categories. Table 2 provides comparative data on overall R&D spending for the company and its new acquisition against competitors.

Organizationally, each of the operating units administers its own R&D efforts, which cut across all three categories above. In very simple terms, the operating unit is relatively self-sufficient across all three categories where technology *already exists*. They "purchase" some support services from the corporate R&D group as described later. In terms of performance assessment for incentive compensation, the operating unit R&D groups are tied to the "bottom-line" results achieved by their respective units.

## Corporate R&D

The corporate R&D group, in addition to providing support services to the operating unit's R&D efforts, is primarily responsible

**TABLE 1** R&D Costs by Major Category

|  | 1994 | | 1993 | | 1992 | | 1991 | | 1990 | |
|---|---|---|---|---|---|---|---|---|---|---|
|  | AMOUNT | PERCENT | AMOUNT | PERCENT | AMOUNT | PERCENT | AMOUNT | PERCENT | AMOUNT | PERCENT |
| Class I: Maintain existing businesses | $107 | 29% | $ 92 | 32% | $ 84 | 32% | $ 80 | 34% | $76 | 37% |
| Class II: Expand existing businesses | 81 | 22% | 68 | 23% | 65 | 24% | 62 | 27% | 65 | 31% |
| Class III: Create new businesses | 150 | 40% | 102 | 35% | 78 | 30% | 55 | 24% | 44 | 21% |
| Other: Unclassified | 32 | 9% | 28 | 10% | 37 | 14% | 36 | 15% | 23 | 11% |
| Total | $370 | 100% | $290 | 100% | $264 | 100% | $233 | 100% | $208 | 100% |

**TABLE 2**  R&D Spending Comparative Data

| 1994 R&D Expenditures for the Chemical Industry | | | |
|---|---|---|---|
| | SALES ($M) | R&D AS % OF SALES | NET INCOME |
| Industrial chemicals (preacquisition) | $ 6,691 | 5.5% | $   439 |
| Competitors | | | |
| 1 | 1,340 | 4.7 | (21) |
| 2 | 9,508 | 2.8 | 380 |
| 3 | 3,857 | 6.1 | 216 |
| 4 | 3,328 | 2.8 | 161 |
| 5 | 11,418 | 4.4 | 549 |
| 6 | 35,915 | 11.0 | 1,431 |
| 7 | 10,734 | 4.0 | 623 |
| 1995 R&D for the Drug Industry | | | |
| | SALES ($M) | R&D AS % OF SALES | |
| Pharmaceutical (preacquisition) | $1,246 | 9.6% | |
| Competitors | | | |
| 1 | 4,700 | 4.2 | |
| 2 | 4,500 | 5.1 | |
| 3 | 40 | 12.6 | |
| 4 | 60 | 5.7 | |
| 5 | 160 | 6.3 | |
| 6 | 3,295 | 11.0 | |
| 7 | 296 | 14.4 | |
| 8 | 3,600 | 11.0 | |
| 9 | 4,000 | 6.5 | |
| 10 | 1,224 | 3.1 | |
| 11 | 700 | 6.9 | |
| 12 | 560 | 5.4 | |
| 13 | 1,910 | 8.7 | |
| 14 | 3,190 | 9.5 | |
| 15 | 2,300 | 8.0 | |
| 16 | 1,835 | 4.8 | |
| 17 | 949 | 13.5 | |
| 18 | 2,000 | 10.5 | |
| 19 | 3,280 | 6.2 | |

for required *new technology* in creating new businesses. At the point in the product invention time line when new-technology-based products reach a level of commercial viability, these programs are "handed off" to an operating unit R&D group for eventual movement to commercialization. In the past several years, this corporate R&D group has been successful in "inventing" and "handing off" commercial product leads to operating units and keeping the new product discovery pipeline filled with potential products with a high probability of commercial success. A more detailed description of the corporate R&D group follows:

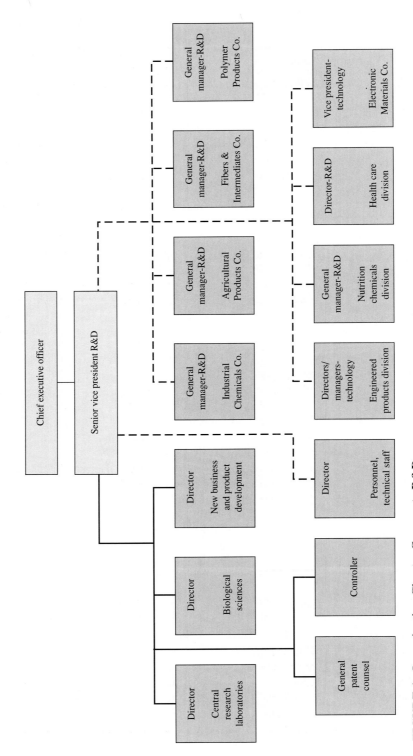

**FIGURE 1  Organization Chart—Corporate R&D**

The corporate research and development group is headed by a senior vice president reporting to the chairman of the board and CEO. The organization, before the 1995 restructuring, is depicted in Figure 1.

The central research laboratory group consists of an information center (20% of its costs are charged to operating units on a fee-for-service basis), an MIS facility, bioprocess development and cell culture groups (which are essentially involved in devising production processes for biotechnology-based products), a physical sciences center (a central analytical chemistry group providing very specialized and highly skilled support to many users across the company—65% of this group's costs are charged out directly on a fee-for-service basis), a group called controlled delivery (which develops vehicles for the transfer of pharmaceutical and animal science products into the living systems within which they must act), and a chemistry group providing very specialized skills for both conventional and biotechnology process chemistry (about 25% of this group's costs are charged directly on a fee-for-service basis). In addition to the direct fee-for-service chargeouts described above, a portion of the costs of this central research laboratory group (primarily the bioprocess development and cell culture groups) is assigned to the biological sciences segment. The remaining costs, along with overall corporate R&D administrative costs, are allocated as a part of corporate charges.

The biological sciences group has been the major focal point for new technology in the pharmaceutical and animal sciences area. It supports plant sciences for the agricultural unit as well. The costs for the biological sciences group are reported as new direction basic research. Also controlled within corporate R&D and reported in this segment are the costs of key university relationships supporting basic and applied biomedical, crop chemicals, and animal sciences research efforts.

The patent group has always been decentralized with a patent counsel and staff assigned to each operating unit reporting on a "dotted line" basis to the operating unit and administratively to the general patent council. Thus, about 80% of patent cost is already directly borne by operating units, with the remainder allocated as a part of corporate charges.

The "bottom line" of the above operating unit/corporate R&D cost picture was as follows when 1995 ended:

|  |  | PERCENTAGE |
|---|---|---|
| Directly controlled and administered by operating units |  | 80% |
| Controlled and administered by corporate research and development |  |  |
| Charged to operating units on fee-for-service basis | 4% |  |
| Allocated to operating units as "corporate charge" based upon net investment | 3% |  |
| Reported as part of biological sciences segment (new direction basic research) | 13% | 20% |
| Total research and development cost |  | 100% |

### Required

As the controller reflected on the information obtained and the important issues being addressed by the EMC subcommittee, the following thoughts and questions surfaced in his mind:

(1) Would operating unit control of our key R&D growth programs enhance or mitigate our chances of meeting our goals?

(2) I know there'll be pressure to level off R&D spending across the company, including corporate R&D. We've got to make sure we get more "bang for our R&D buck" in terms of prioritizing those efforts to go after the most promising commercial opportunities if we're going to achieve our goals in biotechnology! How can we be sure we're prioritizing these efforts toward increased commercial success?

## BP AMERICA: COST CENTERS AND PROFIT CENTERS*

John Bishop, Corporate Controller of BP America, gazed out his office window on the thirty-seventh floor of the BP America building, admiring the activities of the ice breakers that were clearing the shipping lanes on Lake Erie. He was contemplating this year's upcoming negotiations between the "businesses" and the "staff departments" to determine the costs of, and responsibility for, centrally provided services. (See Tables 1 and 2 for lists of businesses and staff departments.) His thoughts faded to last year, which saw the beginning of the end of the old cost allocation system and the dawning of a new, more imaginative and innovative process for managing corporate charges. He was trying to imagine how this year's procedure would differ from last year's, what guidelines to use to judge its success, and what new problems possibly could arise.

### Background

BP America was formed from the combination of Standard Oil and BP North America. The original link between BP and Standard

---

**TABLE 1** BP America Business

| | |
|---|---|
| BP Exploration | BP Nutrition |
| BP Oil | Carborundum Division |
| BP Chemicals | BP America Ventures |
| BP Advanced Minerals | Research and Development |
| BP Titanium Minerals | Chase Brass |
| BP Minerals | Kaldair |
| BP Coal | |

---

**TABLE 2** BP America Staff Departments

| | |
|---|---|
| Audit | Information Management |
| Control | Other Administrative and Information Services |
| Finance | Human Resources |
| Planning | External Affairs–Cleveland |
| Tax | Federal Government Affairs |
| Law | State Government Affairs |
| Executives | Public Affairs |
| Administrative Services | Patent and License |
| Health, Safety, and Environmental Quality | |

---

*Reprinted with permission from Volume 6 of *Cases from Management Accounting Practice*, from the IMA/AAA Management Accounting Symposium series.

Oil was forged in 1970 when, in exchange for an increased shareholding in Standard Oil, BP transferred to the company its crude oil leases at Prudhoe Bay on the North Slope of Alaska, along with some other upstream and downstream assets. That arrangement brought together BP's large oil reserves in Alaska and the marketing expertise of the long-established American company. In 1987, a total merger of the two companies occurred when BP purchased the minority shareholding in Standard Oil, and BP America was formed. Along with the physical exchange of assets, Standard Oil, in becoming BP America, also had to wrestle with the cultural and philosophical attitudes of a new global parent.

The 1970s and 1980s saw significant changes in the oil industry. By the 1980s, a higher degree of concentration and more intensive competition was evident, which forced BP America to reconsider both its internal and external business methodologies. One of the outcomes was greater responsibility passing out from the center of the organization to the individual businesses, creating a more decentralized company. Sir Peter Walters, chairman of BP described this as "central control over strategy and delegation of business operating decisions." The result was more day-to-day decision making at lower levels in the organization. The change also affected accountability for costs at both the corporate and business levels.

Historically, central costs were divided by the corporate staff into (1) costs directly applicable to the businesses and (2) corporate costs. The business-related costs were allocated from internal cost centers to the businesses using several allocation bases, including headcount, billable hours, and space occupied. Corporate costs were defined as all costs controlled by the CEO that benefited the corporation as a whole,

not individual businesses per se. These included items solely related to the CEO's activities, such as Planning, Control, and Executives.

## New Procedures

Although the old allocation process was not considered "broken," top management believed that a change was necessary to adhere to the new philosophy of increased profit responsibility of the businesses. A new procedure was initiated to encourage a buyer-seller relationship between the central staff departments and their primary "customers," the businesses. The BP America CEO also was considered to be one of the customers of the staff departments because of his stewardship role over corporate costs, which were renamed "stewardship costs." The staff departments and their customers were required to negotiate both the level of services to be provided and the amounts to be charged for services. Under this scheme, each staff department was required to:

1. Demonstrate value for dollars spent to convince its customers to use its services
2. Be competitive with respect to alternatives: for example, services from third parties
3. Ensure the satisfaction of its customers

Conversely, the businesses had the option to:

1. Continue to use the BP America corporate staff at negotiated charges
2. Purchase services from external sources
3. Perform services themselves
4. Do without services, if expected costs were greater than expected benefits

From a corporate viewpoint, this procedure:

1. Decreased corporate overhead by dispersing more costs to users
2. Made the businesses aware of the value of corporate services

3. Helped eliminate inefficient or unnecessary services

John Bishop mentally reviewed the mechanics of the process. About a year ago, Robert "Bob" Horton, then CEO of BP America, had created the Business Forum. This group, comprising the BP America business heads and senior corporate staff, introduced the new buyer-seller procedure. Bishop considered this procedure a masterstroke, because it focused the business heads on the need to more accurately distribute central costs between stewardship and the businesses. Effectively, the process took business-related activities out of stewardship and placed them in the businesses. It also ensured the businesses' total involvement from the start.

At a meeting of the Business Forum, each staff department presented its operating plan for the year. Items presented were as follows:

1. Role and mission of the staff department
2. Input expected from businesses for the staff department to be able to fulfill its responsibilities
3. Expected headcount and budgeted costs of the staff department
4. A review of services provided to businesses, billing procedures for these services, and expected annual charges

The Business Forum then provided a recommendation to the CEO of BP America on the appropriate distribution of costs between stewardship and the businesses. The chairman of the Forum, Bill Johnson, insisted on an agreement; silence was considered to be consent. The Business Forum also made recommendations to eliminate activities that the group no longer considered to be needed. However, at no point did the Business Forum attempt to carry out the role of negotiator or mediator between individual buyers and sellers. James Ross (who replaced Robert Horton as CEO in April 1988) immediately endorsed this entire process.

### The Discussion

Bishop's thoughts were interrupted by David Sourwine, Controller, Headquarters and Treasury, who was arriving for a meeting on this very subject. After exchanging pleasantries, they got down to business:

JB: Let's look at where we've been and where we're going this year with the annual review of corporate charges.

DS: As I recall, the overall process worked pretty well last year, although there is no doubt that it was a dramatic change for some people. Of the $141 million of budgeted costs, only $11 million was in disagreement after the first cut, and we managed to whittle that down to $1.1 million. One of the problems was that some of the staff departments were uncomfortable with being challenged, both on what they do and their associated costs. They felt they were being put in an adversarial position, which wasn't necessary.

JB: Yes, and some of the business heads believed that staff departments didn't attack their costs vigorously enough. I have a feeling it may be very different this time around. And it's our responsibility to get the job done with as little residual ill will as possible. I know that James Ross wants us to develop an atmosphere in which constructive challenge is healthy and expected.

DS: When is the Business Forum meeting this year?

JB: In April, when it will review the process and remind everyone that they should prepare in advance for the staff/business discussions. And this time we'll make sure that everyone understands the costs which have to be borne by the businesses and can't be hidden in stewardship any longer.

DS: A couple of the businesses seemed to be "playing games" last year—deliberately negotiating low charges and then not reducing the amounts of services they used.

JB: There are no free lunches. We'll have to make sure that everyone knows this. We'll also have to stress that the businesses must think longer-term. They must realize that if they decide not to use corporate services this year or if they underestimate their expected usage, these services may not be available when they want them. BP America cannot reduce its corporate headcount and costs one year and then go back into the market to rehire the next. And of course, Mr. Ross and the CEO Committee have the power to oversee the process for the overall good of BP America. Ross has to be satisfied that any changes made are in the corporation's best interests.

DS: I've heard rumors that some of the people in corporate staff are worried the businesses will try to unreasonably reduce billing rates.

JB: One purpose of this process is to satisfy the businesses that they're getting value for the dollars they spend on services. If they really don't want what the corporate departments are providing, that will certainly come out in the wash.

DS: Do you believe Mr. Ross is expecting the stewardship costs to be reduced again this year?

JB: If you are referring to the $16 million shifted last year from stewardship to the businesses, I don't think he will expect the same to happen again. However, I believe the potential exists for some further transfers of business-related costs from stewardship. Also, recall that James Ross said this year he will not pick up any discrepancies, like the $1.1 million of unbilled service he absorbed into stewardship last year.

### Required

(1) Should BP America's corporate staff departments be designated as profit centers? If so, should they be allowed to solicit business outside the corporation?

(2) What measures should be used to evaluate the performance of staff departments?

(3) BP America recently sold BP Minerals, a business that accounted for over 10% of the corporation's assets. What effect would you expect this sale to have on corporate staffing requirements under the new chargeout procedures?

(4) What effect would you expect the new procedures to have on total corporate costs?

# EMPIRE GLASS COMPANY (A)*

In fall 1963 Peter Small of the Harvard Business School began to write case material on the budgetary control system of the Empire Glass Company, a manufacturing company with a number of plants located throughout Canada. In particular, Peter Small was interested in how James Walker, the corporate controller, saw the company's budgetary control system. Therefore, Small focused his research on the budgetary control system in relationship to the company's Glass Products Division. This division was responsible for manufacturing and selling glass food-and-beverage bottles.

## Organization

Empire Glass company was a diversified company organized into several major product divisions, one of which was the Glass Products Division. Each division was headed by a vice president who reported directly to the company's executive vice president, Landon McGregor. (Exhibit A shows an organization chart of the company's top management group.) All of the corporate and divisional management groups were located in British City, Canada.

---

*This case was prepared by Assistant Professor David F. Hawkins.

Copyright © 1964 by the President and Fellows of Harvard College. Harvard Business School case 109-043.

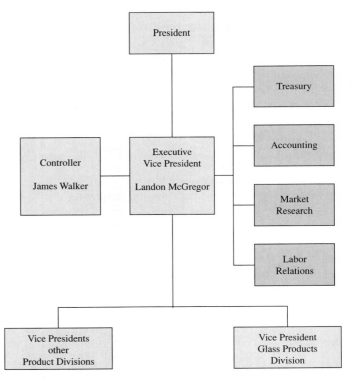

**EXHIBIT A  Top Management Group**

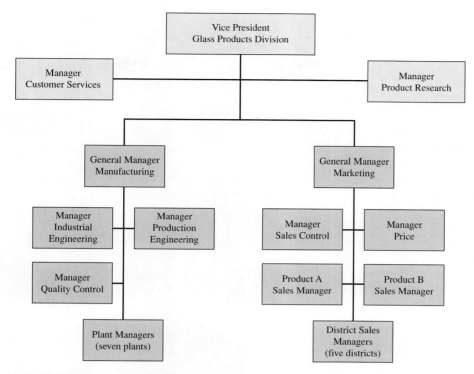

**EXHIBIT B  Glass Products Division—Top Management and Staff**

McGregor's corporate staff included three people in the financial area—the controller, the chief accountant, and the treasurer. The controller's department consisted of only two people—Walker and the assistant controller, Allen Newell. The market research and labor relations departments also reported in a staff capacity to McGregor.

All of the product divisions were organized along similar lines. Reporting to each product division vice president were several staff members in the customer service and product research areas. Reporting in a line capacity to each divisional vice president were also a general manager of manufacturing (responsible for all of the division's manufacturing activities) and a general manager of marketing (responsible for all of the division's marketing activities). Both of these execu-

tives were assisted by a small staff of specialists. Exhibit B presents an organization chart of the Glass Products Division's top management group. Exhibit C shows the typical organization structure of a plant within the Glass Products Division.

## Products and Technology

The Glass Products Division operated a number of plants in Canada, producing glass food-and-beverage bottles. Of these products, food jars constituted the largest group. Milk bottles, as well as beer and soft drink bottles were also produced in large quantities. A great variety of shapes and sizes of containers for wines, liquors, drugs, cosmetics, and chemicals were produced in smaller quantities.

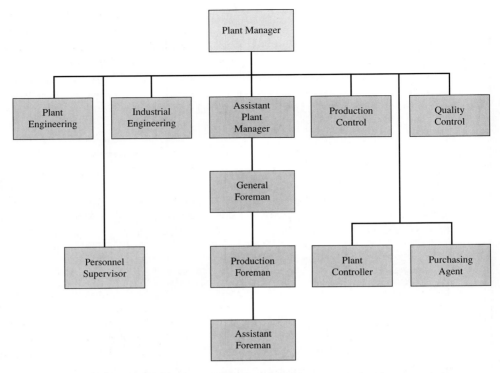

**EXHIBIT C  Glass Products Division—Typical Plant Organization**

Most of the thousands of different products, varying in size, shape, color, and decoration, were produced to order. According to British City executives, the typical lead time between the customer's order and shipment from the plant was between two and three weeks during 1963.

The principal raw materials for container glass were sand, soda ash, and lime. The first step in the manufacturing process was to melt batches of these materials in furnaces or tanks. The molten mass was then passed into automatic or semiautomatic machines that filled molds with the molten glass and blew the glass into the desired shape. The "ware" then went through an automatic annealing oven or lehr, where it was cooled slowly under carefully controlled conditions. If the glass was to be coated on the exterior to increase its resistance to abrasion and scratches, this coating—often a silicone film—was applied in the lehr. Any decorating (such as a trademark or other design) was then added, the product was inspected again, and the finished goods were packed in corrugated containers (or wooden cases for some bottles).

Quality inspection was critical in the manufacturing process. If the melt in the furnace was not completely free from bubbles and stones (unmelted ingredients or pieces of refractory material), or if the fabricating machinery was slightly out of adjustment, or molds were worn, the rejection rate was very high. Although a number of machines, including electric eyes, were used in the inspection process, much of the inspection was still done visually.

Glass making was one of the oldest arts, and bottles and jars had been machine-molded at relatively high speeds for over half a century, but the Glass Products Division had spent substantial sums each year modernizing its equipment. These improvements had greatly increased the speed of operations and had reduced substantially the visual inspection and manual handling of glassware.

No hand blowing was done in the division's plants; in contrast to the methods used in the early days of the industry, most of the jobs were relatively unskilled, highly repetitive, and gave the worker little control over work methods or pace. The mold makers, who made and repaired the molds, the machine repairers, and those who made the equipment setup changes between different products were considered to be the highest skilled classes of workers.

Wages were relatively high in the glass industry. The rumble of the machinery and the hiss of compressed air in the molding operation, however, plus the roar of fuel in the furnaces, made the plants extremely noisy. The great amount of heat given off by the furnaces and molten glass also made working conditions unpleasant. Production employees belonged to two national unions, and for many years bargaining had been conducted on a national basis. Output standards were established for all jobs, but no bonus was paid to hourly plant workers for exceeding standard.

## Marketing

Over the years, the sales of the Glass Products Division had grown at a slightly faster rate than had the total market for glass containers. Until the late 1950s, the division had charged a premium for most of its products, primarily because they were of better quality than competitive products. In later years, however, the quality of the competitive products had improved to the point at which they matched the division's quality level. In the meantime, the division's competitors had retained their former price structure. Consequently, the Glass Products Division had been forced to lower its prices to meet its competitors' lower market prices. According to one division executive: "Currently, price competition is not severe, particularly among the two or three larger companies that dominate the glass bottle industry. Most of our competition is with respect to product quality and customer service. In fact, our biggest competitive threat is from containers other than glass."

Each of the division's various plants to some extent shipped its products throughout Canada, although transportation costs limited each plant's market primarily to its immediate vicinity. Although some of the customers were large and bought in huge quantities, many were relatively small.

## Budgetary Control System

In fall 1963 Peter Small interviewed James Walker, who had been the Empire Glass Company's controller for some 15 years. Excerpts from that interview are reproduced in the following sections.

SMALL: Mr. Walker, what is the overall function of your budgetary control system?

WALKER: Well, Peter, to understand the role of the budgetary control systems you must first understand our management philosophy. Fundamentally, we have a divisional organization based on broad product categories. These divisional activities are coordinated by the company's executive vice president, with the head office group providing a policy and review function for the company's executive vice president.

Within the broad policy limits, we operate on a decentralized basis, with each of the decentralized divisions performing the full management job that normally would be inherent in any independent company. The only exception to this philosophy is that the head office group is solely responsible for the sources of funds and the labor relations with those bargaining units that cross division lines. Given this form of organization, the budget is the principal management tool used by the head office to coordinate the efforts of the various segments of the company toward a common goal. Certainly, in our case, the budget is much more than a narrow statistical accounting device.

### Sales Budget

Walker and Small discussed the preparation of the sales budget. This was the first step in the budget preparation procedure.

WALKER: As early as May 15 of the year preceding the budget year, the top management of the company asks the various product division vice presidents to submit preliminary reports stating what they think their division's capital requirements and outlook in terms of sales and income will be during the next budget year. In addition, corporate top management also wants an expression of the division vice president's general feelings toward the trends in the particular items over the two years following the upcoming budget year. At this stage, the head office is not interested in too much detail.

SMALL: Does the market research group get involved in these forecasts?

WALKER: No. What we want is an interpretive statement about sales and income based on the operating executives' practical feel for the market. All divisions plan their capital requirements five years in advance and have made predictions of the forthcoming budget year's market when the budget estimates were prepared last year, so these rough estimates of next year's conditions and requirements are far from wild guesses.

After the opinions of the divisional vice presidents are in, the market research staff goes to work. They develop a formal statement for the marketing climate in detail for the forthcoming budget year and in general terms for the subsequent two years.

SMALL:    Putting together the sales forecast, then, is the first step in developing the budget?

WALKER:   Yes. This is an important first step because practically all of the forecasts or estimates used in planning either start with or depend in some way on a sales forecast.

The market research group begins by projecting such factors as the general economic condition, growth of our various markets, weather conditions related to the end uses of our products, competitive effort, and labor disturbances.

Once these general factors have been assessed, a sales forecast for the company and each division is developed. Consideration is given to the relationship of the general economic climate to our customers' needs and Empire's share of each market. Also, basic assumptions as to price, weather conditions, and so forth, are developed and stated explicitly.

In sales forecasting, consideration is given also to the introduction of new products, gains or losses in particular accounts, forward buying, new manufacturing plants, and any changes in our definition of, say, gross sales.

The probable impact of information such as the fol-lowing is also taken into account: industry growth trends, packaging trends, inventory carry-overs, and the development of alternative packages to or from glass.

This review of all the relevant factors is followed for each of our product lines, regardless of its size and importance. The completed forecasts of the market research group are then forwarded to the appropriate divisions for review, criticism, and adjustments.

SMALL:    How would you summarize the role of the head office group in developing these sales forecasts?

WALKER:   Well, I suppose our primary goal is to assure uniformity between the divisions with respect to the basic assumptions on business conditions, pricing, and the treatment of possible emergencies. Also, we provide a yardstick so as to assure us that the company's overall sales forecast will be reasonable and obtainable.

Next, the product division top management goes back to its district sales managers. Each district sales manager is asked to tell his top management what he expects to do in the way of sales during the budget year. The head office and the divisional staffs will give the district sales managers as much guidance as they request, but it is the sole responsibility of each district sales manager to come up with his particular forecast.

After the district sales manager's forecasts are received by the divisional top management, the forecasts are consolidated and reviewed by the division's general manager of marketing. At this time the general manager of marketing may go back to the district sales managers and suggest they revise their budgets. For instance, a situation such as this might arise: We enjoy a very large share of the liquor market. In one year, however, it may be predicted on the basis of the consolidated district sales manager's estimates that we can look forward to a 20%–25% increase in sales.

Obviously, this prediction is unreasonable. What has happened is this: Each district sales manager has been told by each of his liquor customers that they expect an increase in sales. When all these anticipated individual sales increases are summed, it looks as if the market is going to grow considerably. However, this is not going to happen. What is going to occur is that company A will take sales from company B and company C will take sales from company D, and so forth.

Individually, the district sales managers know little of what's happening outside their territory. However, from the headquarters' point of view, we can ascertain the size of the whole market and the customer's probable relative market share. That's where the market research group's studies come in handy.

Let me emphasize, however, even in this case nothing is changed in the district sales manager's budget, unless the district manager agrees. Then, once the budget is approved, nobody is relieved of his responsibility without top management approval. Also, no arbitrary changes are made in the approved budgets without the concurrence of all the people responsible for the budget.

SMALL: At this point, have the plant managers—or the divisional general managers of manufacturing—been involved in the preparation of the sales budget?

WALKER: Not in a formal way. Informally, of course, the plant managers know what's going on. For example, when a plant manager prepares his capital equipment investment program he is sure to talk to the district sales manager closest to his plant about the district's sales plans.

Next, we go through the same process at the division and headquarters levels. We keep on repeating the process until everybody agrees that the sales budgets are sound. Then, each level of management takes responsibility for its particular portion of the budget. These sales budgets then become fixed objectives.

SMALL:   Besides coming up with a realistic sales budget, what other objectives do the divisions have in mind when they review the sales forecasts?

WALKER:   I would say they have four general objectives in mind: First, a review of the division's competitive position, including plans for improving that position. Second, an evaluation of its efforts to gain either a larger share of the market or offset competitors' activities. Third, a consideration of the need to expand facilities to improve the division's products or introduce new products. Finally, a review and development of plans to improve product quality, delivery methods, and service.

## Manufacturing Budgets

Walker and Small then turned their conversation to the preparation of the manufacturing budgets. According to Walker, each plant had a profit responsibility.

SMALL:   When are the plant budgets prepared?

WALKER:   Once the vice presidents, executive vice president, and company president have given final approval to the sales budgets, we make a sales budget for each plant by breaking the division sales budget down according to the plants from which the finished goods will be shipped. These plant sales budgets are then further broken down on a monthly basis by price, volume, and end use. With this information available, the plants then budget their gross profit, fixed expenses, and income before taxes.

SMALL:   How do you define gross profit and income?

WALKER:   Gross profit is the difference between gross sales, less discounts, and variable manufacturing costs—such as direct labor, direct material, and variable manufacturing overheads. Income is the difference between the gross profit and the fixed costs.

SMALL:   Is the principal constraint within which the plants work the sales budget?

WALKER:   That's right. Given his sales budget, it is up to the plant manager to determine the fixed overhead and variable costs—at standard—that he will need to incur so as to meet the demands of the sales budget.

In some companies I know of, the head office gives each plant manager sales and income figures that the plant has to meet. We don't operate that way, however. We believe that type of directive misses the benefit of all the field experience of those at the district sales and plant levels. If we gave a profit figure to our plant managers to meet, how could we say it was their responsibility to meet it?

What we say to the plant managers is this: Assuming that you have to produce this much sales volume, how much do you expect to spend producing this volume? And what do you expect to spend for your programs allied to obtaining these current and future sales?

SMALL: Then the plant managers make their own plans?

WALKER: Yes. In my opinion requiring the plant managers to make their own plans is one of the most valuable things associated with the budget system. Each plant manager divides the preparation of the overall plant budget among his plant's various departments. First, the departments spell out the programs in terms of the physical requirements—such as tons of raw material—and then the plans are priced at standard cost.

SMALL: What items might some of these departmental budgets include?

WALKER: Let me tell you about the phase of the budget preparation our industrial engineering people are responsible for. The plant industrial engineering department is assigned the responsibility for developing engineered cost standards and reduced costs. Consequently, the phase of budget preparation covered by the industrial engineers includes budget standards of performance for each operation, cost center, and department within the plant. This phase of the budget also includes budget cost reductions, budgeted unfavorable variances from standards, and certain budgeted programmed fixed costs in the manufacturing area such as service labor. The industrial engineer prepares this phase of the budget in conjunction with departmental line supervision.

SMALL: Once the plant budgets are completed, are they sent directly to the divisional top management?

WALKER: No. Before each plant sends its budget into British City, a group of us from head office goes out and visits each plant. For example, in the case of the Glass Products Division, Allen [Newell, assistant controller] and I, along with representatives of the Glass Products division manufacturing staffs visit each of the division's plants.

Let me stress this point: We do not go on these trips to pass judgment on the plant's proposed budget. Rather, we go with three purposes in mind. First, we wish to acquaint ourselves with the thinking behind the figures that each plant manager will send in to British City. This is helpful because when we come to review these budgets with the top management—that is, the management above our level—we will have to answer questions about the budget, and we will know the answers. Second, the review is a way of giving guidance to the plant managers as to whether or not they are in line with what the company needs to make in the way of profits.

Of course, when we make our field reviews we do not know what each of the other plants is doing. Therefore, we explain to the plant managers that, although their budget may look good now, when we put all the plants together in a consolidated budget, the plant managers may have to make some changes because the projected profit is not high enough. When this happens we have to tell the plant managers that it is not their programs that are unsound. The problem is that the company cannot afford the programs.

I think it is very important that each plant manager has a chance to tell his story. Also, it gives them the feeling that we at headquarters are not living in an ivory tower.

SMALL: How long do these plant visits take?

WALKER: They are spread over a three-week period, and we spend an average of half a day at each plant.

SMALL: I gather the role of the head office and divisional staff is to recommend, not decide. That's the plant manager's right.

WALKER: Correct.

SMALL: Who on the plant staff attends these meetings?

WALKER: The plant manager is free to bring in any of his supervisors he wishes. We ask him not to bring in anybody below the supervisory level. Then, of course, you get into organized labor.

SMALL: What do you do on these plant visits?

WALKER: During the half-day we spend at each plant we discuss the budget primarily. However, if I have time, I like to wander through the plant and see how things are going. Also, I go over in great detail the property replacement and maintenance budget with the plant engineer.

SMALL: After you have completed the plant tours, do the plant budgets go to the respective division top management?

WALKER: That's right. About September 1, the plant budgets come into British City, and the accounting department consolidates them. Then the product division vice presidents review their respective divisional budgets to see if the division budget is reasonable in terms of what the vice president thinks the corporate top management wants. If he is not satisfied with the consolidated plant budgets, he will ask the various plants within the division to trim their budget figures.

When the division vice presidents and the executive vice president are happy, they will send their budgets to the company president. He may accept the division budgets at this point. If he doesn't, he will specify the areas to be reexamined by division and, if necessary, plant management. The final budget is approved at our December board of directors' meeting.

SMALL: As I understand it, the district sales managers have a responsibility for sales.

WALKER: Specifically volume, price, and sales mix.

SMALL: And the plant manager is responsible for manufacturing costs?

WALKER: His primary responsibility extends to profits. The budgeted plant profit is the difference between the fixed sales dollar budget and the budgeted variable costs at standard and the fixed overhead budget. It is the plant manager's responsibility to meet this budgeted profit figure.

SMALL: Even if actual dollar sales drop below the budgeted level?

WALKER: Yes.

## Comparison of Actual and Standard Performance

The discussion turned to the procedures and management philosophy related to the periodic comparison by the head office group of the actual and standard performance of the field organization. In particular, the two men discussed the manufacturing area.

SMALL: What do you do with the actual results that come into the head office?

WALKER: We go over them on the basis of exception: that is, we only look at those figures that are in excess of the budgeted amounts. We believe this has a good effect on morale. The plant managers don't have to explain everything they do. They only have to explain where they go off base.

SMALL: What cost and revenue items are of greatest interest to you?

WALKER: In particular, we pay close attention to the net sales, gross margin, and the plant's ability to meet its standard manufacturing cost. Incidentally, when analyzing the gross sales, we look closely at the price and mix changes. All this information is summarized on a form known as the Profit Planning and Control Report #1 [see Exhibit 1]. This document is backed up by a number of supporting documents [see Exhibit 2].

SMALL: When you look at the fixed costs, what are you interested in?

# EXHIBIT 1  Profit Planning and Control Report (PPCR) #1

| MONTH | | | REF. | | YEAR TO DATE | | |
|---|---|---|---|---|---|---|---|
| GAIN(+) OR LOSS (–) FROM | | ACTUAL | | | ACTUAL | INCOME GAIN(+) OR LOSS (–) FROM | |
| PREV. YEAR | BUDGET | | | | | BUDGET | PREV. YEAR |
| | | | 1 | GROSS SALES TO CUSTOMERS | | | |
| | | | 2 | DISCOUNTS & ALLOWANCES | | | |
| | | | 3 | NET SALES TO CUSTOMERS | | | |
| % | % | | 4 | % GAIN (+)/LOSS (–) | | % | % |
| | | *DOLLAR VOLUME GAIN (+)/LOSS (–) DUE TO:* | | | | | |
| | | | 5 | SALES PRICE | | | |
| | | | 6 | SALES VOLUME | | | |
| | | | 6(a) | TRADE MIX | | | |
| | | | 7 | VARIABLE COST OF SALES | | | |
| | | | 8 | PROFIT MARGIN | | | |
| | | *PROFIT MARGIN GAIN (+)/LOSS (–) DUE TO:* | | | | | |
| | | | 9 | PROFIT/VOLUME RATIO (P/V) | | | |
| | | | 10 | DOLLAR VOLUME | | | |
| % | % | % | 11 | PROFIT/VOLUME RATIO (P/V) | | % | % | % |
| INCOME ADDITION (+) | | | | | INCOME ADDITION (+) | | |
| | | | 12 | TOTAL FIXED MANUFACTURING COST | | | |
| | | | 13 | FIXED MANUFACTURING COST – TRANSFERS | | | |
| | | | 14 | PLANT INCOME (STANDARD) | | | |
| % | % | % | 15 | % OF NET SALES | | % | % | % |
| INCOME ADDITION (+) INCOME REDUCTION (–) | | | | | INCOME ADDITION (+) INCOME REDUCTION (–) | | |
| % | % | % | 16 | % PERFORMANCE | | % | % | % |
| | | | 17 | MANUFACTURING EFFICIENCY | | | |
| INCOME ADDITION (+) | | | | | INCOME ADDITION (+) | | |
| | | | 18 | METHODS IMPROVEMENTS | | | |
| | | | 19 | OTHER REVISIONS OF STANDARDS | | | |
| | | | 20 | MATERIAL PRICE CHANGES | | | |
| | | | 21 | DIVISION SPECIAL PROJECTS | | | |
| | | | 22 | COMPANY SPECIAL PROJECTS | | | |
| | | | 23 | NEW PLANT EXPENSE | | | |
| | | | 24 | OTHER PLANT EXPENSES | | | |
| | | | 25 | INCOME ON SECONDS | | | |
| | | | 26 | | | | |
| | | | 27 | | | | |
| | | | 28 | PLANT INCOME (ACTUAL) | | | |
| % | % | | 29 | % GAIN (+)/LOSS (–) | | % | % |
| % | % | % | 30 | % OF NET SALES | | % | % | % |

| INCREASE (+) OR DECREASE (–) | | | | EMPLOYED CAPITAL | | INCREASE (+) OR DECREASE (–) | |
|---|---|---|---|---|---|---|---|
| | | | 37 | TOTAL EMPLOYED CAPITAL | | | |
| % | % | % | 38 | % RETURN | | % | % | % |
| | | | 39 | TURNOVER RATE | | | |

19

PLANT            DIVISION            MONTH

---

**EXHIBIT 2** Brief Descriptions of PPCR #2 through PPCR #11

---

| REPORT | DESCRIPTION |
|--------|-------------|

**Individual Plant Reports**

PPCR #2    *Manufacturing Expense:* Plant materials, labor and variable overhead consumed. Details of actual figures compared with budget and previous years' figures for year-to-date and current month.

PPCR #3    *Plant Expense:* Plant expenses incurred. Details of actual figures compared with budget and previous years' figures for year-to-date and current month.

PPCR #4    *Analysis of Sales and Income:* Plant operating gains and losses due to changes in sales revenue, profit margins, and other sources of income. Details of actual figures compared with budget and previous years' figures for year-to-date and current month.

PPCR #5    *Plant Control Statement:* Analysis of plant raw material gains and losses, spoilage costs, and cost reductions programs. Actual figures compared with budget figures for current month and year-to-date.

PPCR #6    *Comparison of Sales by Principal and Product Groups:* Plant sales dollars, profit margin and P/V ratios broken down by end-product use (e.g., soft drinks, beer). Compares actual figures with budgeted figures for year-to-date and current month.

**Division Summary Reports**

PPCR #7    *Comparative Plant Performance, Sales, and Income:* Gross sales and income figures by plants. Actual figures compared with budget figures for year-to-date and current month.

PPCR #8    *Comparative Plant Performance, Total Plant Expenses:* Profit margin, total fixed costs, manufacturing efficiency, other plant expenses and P/V ratios by plants. Actual figures compared with budgeted and previous years' figures for current month and year-to-date.

PPCR #9    *Manufacturing Efficiency:* Analysis of gains and losses by plant in areas of materials, spoilage, supplies, and labor. Current month and year-to-date actuals reported in total dollars and as a percentage of budget.

PPCR #10    *Inventory:* Comparison of actual and budget inventory figures by major inventory accounts and plants.

PPCR #11    *Status of Capital Expenditures:* Analysis of the status of capital expenditures by plants, months and relative to budget.

---

WALKER:    We want to know whether the plants carried out the programs that they said they would carry out. If they have not, we want to know why they have not. Here we are looking for sound reasons. Also, we want to know if they have carried out their projected programs at the cost they said they would.

SMALL:    Do you have to wait until you receive the monthly PPCR #1 [Profit Planning and Control Report #1] before you know how well the various plants performed during the month?

WALKER:    No. At the end of the sixth business day after the close of the month, each plant wires to the head office certain operating variances, which we put together on what we call the variance analysis sheet [see Exhibit 3]. Within a half-hour after the last plant report comes through, variance analysis

**EXHIBIT 3**　Variance Analysis Sheet for Various Divisions and Plants

| Line No. | Division or Plant | Budget Income | Gross Sales | Sales Price | Manufacturing Cost | Labor | Overtime | Employee Benefits | Outside Warehouse | Utilities | Overhaul and Repair | Depreciation, Rent, Insurance and Taxes | Controllable Plant Fixed Cost | Other Fixed Cost | Manufacturing Efficiency | Cost Reduction | Other Operating Gains and Losses | Income from Seconds | Wage Changes | Price Changes | Division Expenses | Actual Income | Income Adjusted by Volume |
|---|---|---|---|---|---|---|---|---|---|---|---|---|---|---|---|---|---|---|---|---|---|---|---|
| 1 | | | | | | | | | | | | | | | | | | | | | | | |
| 2 | | | | | | | | | | | | | | | | | | | | | | | |
| 3 | | | | | | | | | | | | | | | | | | | | | | | |
| 4 | | | | | | | | | | | | | | | | | | | | | | | |
| 5 | | | | | | | | | | | | | | | | | | | | | | | |
| 6 | | | | | | | | | | | | | | | | | | | | | | | |
| 7 | | | | | | | | | | | | | | | | | | | | | | | |
| 8 | | | | | | | | | | | | | | | | | | | | | | | |
| 9 | | | | | | | | | | | | | | | | | | | | | | | |
| 10 | | | | | | | | | | | | | | | | | | | | | | | |
| 11 | | | | | | | | | | | | | | | | | | | | | | | |
| 12 | | | | | | | | | | | | | | | | | | | | | | | |
| 13 | | | | | | | | | | | | | | | | | | | | | | | |
| 14 | | | | | | | | | | | | | | | | | | | | | | | |
| 15 | | | | | | | | | | | | | | | | | | | | | | | |
| 16 | | | | | | | | | | | | | | | | | | | | | | | |
| 17 | | | | | | | | | | | | | | | | | | | | | | | |
| 18 | | | | | | | | | | | | | | | | | | | | | | | |
| 19 | | | | | | | | | | | | | | | | | | | | | | | |
| 20 | | | | | | | | | | | | | | | | | | | | | | | |
| 21 | | | | | | | | | | | | | | | | | | | | | | | |
| 22 | | | | | | | | | | | | | | | | | | | | | | | |
| 23 | | | | | | | | | | | | | | | | | | | | | | | |
| 24 | | | | | | | | | | | | | | | | | | | | | | | |
| 25 | | | | | | | | | | | | | | | | | | | | | | | |
| 26 | | | | | | | | | | | | | | | | | | | | | | | |
| 27 | | | | | | | | | | | | | | | | | | | | | | | |
| 28 | | | | | | | | | | | | | | | | | | | | | | | |
| 29 | | | | | | | | | | | | | | | | | | | | | | | |
| 30 | | | | | | | | | | | | | | | | | | | | | | | |
| 31 | | | | | | | | | | | | | | | | | | | | | | | |
| 32 | | | | | | | | | | | | | | | | | | | | | | | |
| 33 | | | | | | | | | | | | | | | | | | | | | | | |
| 34 | | | | | | | | | | | | | | | | | | | | | | | |
| 35 | | | | | | | | | | | | | | | | | | | | | | | |

sheets for the divisions and plants are compiled. On the morning of the seventh business day after the end of the month, these reports are usually on the desks of the interested top management.

The variance analysis sheet highlights the variances in what we consider to be critical areas. Receiving this report as soon as we do helps us at head office to take timely action. Let me emphasize, however, we do not accept the excuse that the plant manager has to go to the end of the month to know what happened during the month. He has to be on top of these particular items daily.

SMALL: Is there any way the head office can detect an adverse trend in operations before you receive the monthly variance analysis sheet?

WALKER: Yes. At the beginning of each month, the plant managers prepare current estimates for the upcoming month and quarter on forms similar to the variance analysis sheets.

Because our budget is based on known programs, the value of this current estimate is that it gets the plant people to look at their programs. Hopefully, they will realize that they cannot run their plants just on a day-to-day basis.

If we see a sore spot coming up, or if the plant manager draws our attention to a potential trouble area, we may ask for daily reports concerning this item to be sent to the particular division top management involved. In addition, the division top management may send a division staff specialist—say, a quality control expert if it is a quality problem—to the plant concerned. The division staff members can make recommendations, but it is up to the plant manager to accept or reject these recommendations. Of course, it is well known throughout the company that we expect the plant managers to accept gracefully the help of the head office and division staffs.

SMALL: When is the monthly PPCR #1 received at British City?

WALKER: The plant PPCR #1 and the month-end trial balance showing both actual and budget figures are received in British City at the close of the eighth business day after the end of the month. These two very important reports, along with the supporting reports [PPCR #2 through PPCR #11, described in Exhibit 2] are then consolidated by the accounting department on PPCR-type forms to show the results of operations by division and company. The consolidated reports are distributed the next day.

### *Sales-Manufacturing Relations*

Small was curious about the relationship between the sales and manufacturing groups, particularly at the plant level.

SMALL: If during the year, the actual sales volume is less than the budgeted sales volume, what changes do you make in the plant budget?

WALKER: This is one of the biggest risks we run with our budget system. If the sales decline occurs during the early part of the year, and if the plant managers can convince us that the change is permanent, we may revise the plant budgets to reflect these new circumstances. However, if toward the end of the year the actual sales volume suddenly drops below the predicted sales volume, we don't have much time to change the budget plans. What we do is ask the plant managers to go back over their budget with their staffs and see where reduction of expense programs will do the least harm. Specifically, we ask them to consider what they may be able to eliminate this year or delay until next year.

I believe it was Confucius who said "we make plans so we have plans to discard." Nevertheless, I believe it is wise to make plans, even if you have to discard them. Having plans makes it a lot easier to figure out what to do when sales fall off from the budgeted level. The understanding of operations that comes from preparing the budget removes a lot of the potential chaos and confusion that might arise if we were under pressure to meet a stated profit goal and sales decline quickly and unexpectedly at year-end—just as they did this year.

Under these circumstances, we don't try to ram anything down the plant managers' throats. We ask them to tell us where they can reasonably expect to cut costs below the budgeted level.

SMALL: What happens when a plant manager's costs are adversely affected by the sales group's insisting that a production schedule be changed so as to get out an unexpected rush order?

WALKER: As far as we are concerned, the customer's wants are primary—our company is a case where sales wags the rest of the dog.

Whenever a problem arises at a plant between sales and production, the local people are supposed to solve the problem themselves. Let's take your example: A customer's purchasing agent insists that he wants an immediate delivery, and this delivery will disrupt the production department's plans. The production group can make recommendations as to alternative ways to take care of the problem, but it's the sales manager's responsibility to get the product to the customer. The salesmen are supposed to know their customers well enough to judge whether or not the customer really needs the product. If the sales manager says the customer needs the product, that ends the matter.

Of course, if the change in the sales program involves a major expense at the plant that is out of line with the budget, then the matter is passed up to division for decision.

As I said earlier, the sales department has the sole responsibility for the product price, sales mix, and delivery schedules. They do not have direct responsibility for plant operations or profit. That's the plant management's responsibility. However, it is understood that the sales group will cooperate with the plant people wherever possible.

SMALL: I guess cooperation is very important to the success of your system.

WALKER: Definitely. We believe the whole budgetary control system works best if we can get cooperation. But, within the framework of cooperation the sales and production groups have very clear responsibilities.

## Motivation

SMALL: How do you motivate the plant managers to meet their profit goals?

WALKER: Well, first of all, we only promote capable people. Also, a monetary incentive program has been established that stimulates their efforts to achieve their profit goal.

SMALL: What other incentive devices do you use?

WALKER: Each month we put together a bar chart that shows, by division and plant, the ranking of the various manufacturing units with respect to manufacturing efficiency.[1]

We feel that the plant managers are one hundred percent responsible for variable manufacturing costs. I believe this is true since all manufacturing standards have to be approved by plant managers. Most of the plant managers give wide publicity to these bar charts. The efficiency bar chart and efficiency measure itself is perhaps a little unfair in some respects when you are comparing one plant with another. Different kinds of products are run through different plants. These require different setups, etc., which have an important impact on a position of the plant. However, in general the efficiency

---

[1]Manufacturing efficiency = (total actual variable manufacturing costs ÷ total standard variable manufacturing costs) × 100%.

rating is a good indication of the quality of the plant manager and his supervisory staff.

Also, a number of plants run competitions within the plants which reward department heads, or foremen, based on their relative standing with respect to a certain cost item. The plant managers, their staffs and employees have great pride in their plants.

SMALL: While I waited to see you this morning, I read some of the company publications for employees. They all seemed to stress profits and product quality.

WALKER: That's true. In my opinion, the number one item now stressed at the plant level is quality. The market situation is such that in order to make sales you have to meet the market price and exceed the market quality. By quality I mean not only the physical characteristics of the product but also such things as delivery schedules.

As I read the company employee publications, their message is that if the company is to be profitable it must produce high-quality items at a reasonable cost. This is necessary so that the plants can meet their obligation to produce the maximum profits for the company under the circumstances prevailing.

SMALL: Do you analyze the sales reports?

WALKER: No. It is the sales group's responsibility to comment on the sales activity. They prepare their own reports. They also control their selling costs against budgets prepared by the sales managers.

Initial sales statistics are developed from plant billings summarized by end use and are available on the third business day after month-end. Detailed sales statistics by end use and customer indicating actual and variance to both budget and prior year are prepared by data processing at British City and available on the eighth business day after month-end. Sales and price and mix variances by plant and end use can be obtained from PPCR #1, PPCR #4, and PPCR #6.

### The Future

SMALL: Mr. Walker, do you intend to make any changes in your budgetary control system?

WALKER: An essential part of the budgetary control system is planning. We have developed a philosophy that we must begin our plans where the work is done—in the line organization and out in the field. Perhaps, in the future, we can avoid or cut back some of the budget preparation steps and start putting our sales budget together later on in the year than May 15. However, I doubt if we will change the basic philosophy. Frankly, I doubt if the line operators would want any major change in the system—they are very jealous of the management prerogatives the system gives to them.

It is very important that we manage the budget. We have to be continually on guard against its managing us. Sometimes, the plants lose sight of this fact. They have to be made conscious daily of the necessity of having the sales volume to make a profit. And, when sales fall off and their plant programs are reduced they do not always appear to see the justification for budget cuts. Although, I do suspect that they see more of the justification for these cuts than they will admit. It is this human side of the budget to which we will have to pay more attention in the future.

## Notes

During his conversation with James Walker, Small asked him to describe the various items listed on PPCR #1.

WALKER: Let's start with reference 3, net sales to customers. This is the difference between the gross sales to customers [ref. 1] and any discounts or allowances [ref. 2].

The next line, % gain (+)/loss (−) [ref. 4], is the increase or decrease in net sales dollars expressed as a percentage of the budget and previous year's actual figures.

Next, we break the cause of the dollar volume gain or loss into its component parts: namely, changes due to sales price, volume, and mix. Variable cost of sales [ref. 7] includes such items as direct materials, operating labor, and that part of indirect labor that varies in monthly dollar amounts directly with changes in unit production volume. These costs are constant per unit of production. The amount listed in the budget column is the standard cost of the actual production. Reference 8, profit margin, is the difference between the total net dollar sales and the total variable manufacturing costs of products sold. Next, we identify further the causes of the change in profit margin. The item reference 9, profit margin gain (+)/loss (−) due to profit/volume ratio (P/V), is that portion of the profit margin gain or loss resulting from changes in the relationship between the net selling price and the standard variable manufacturing costs of the products sold to customers. This relationship, expressed as a percentage, is known as the P/V ratio [see ref. 11].

The profit margin gain (+)/loss (−) due to dollar volume [ref. 10] is that portion of the profit margin or loss resulting from the changes in dollar volume of net sales to customers, exclusive of changes in P/V. It is the algebraic difference between the total profit margin variance and reference 9.

We keep a close check on the P/V ratio because it shows us how much we are making over our variable costs. Of course, volume changes alone never affect the P/V ratio.

Total fixed manufacturing costs [ref. 12] are the costs that should remain unchanged irrespective of fluctuation in volume during the year. Included in this category are depreciation, rent, general insurance, general taxes, and most supervision costs. Fixed costs are calculated on an annual basis, and each monthly figure is shown as one-twelfth of the annual total.

The next item, fixed manufacturing cost—transfers [ref. 13], doesn't apply to the Glass Products Division as they have very little intra- or interdivision transfers. Therefore, in the case of the Glass Products Division plant income (standard) [ref. 14] is the difference between profit margin dollars [ref. 8] and total fixed manufacturing cost [ref. 12].

In the actual column of reference 16, % performance, we enter the ratio of

the standard to the actual manufacturing cost expressed as a percentage.

In the gain/loss column for this same item, we enter the difference in percentage points between current performance and budget, and between the current performance and previous year.

In the actual column of reference 17, manufacturing efficiency, we put the difference between standard and actual manufacturing efficiency dollar costs.

In the gain/loss columns of reference 17, we enter the increase or decrease in income resulting from changes in manufacturing dollar savings or excesses.

References 18 through 25 are self-explanatory. In addition to cost savings or excesses resulting from efficiency, special conditions may arise to cause other departures from standard cost. These additional differences are classified according to cause, and the more significant ones are shown individually on separate lines in this portion of PPCR #1. Reference 28, plant income (actual), is the income remaining after adjusting reference 14 for all the departures from standard manufacturing listed on references 18 through 25, inclusive.

Total employed capital [ref. 37] is the value of employed capital at the end of the month, and average for the year to date. At the plant level employed capital consists of inventories [mostly work-in-process and finished goods] valued at their standard direct costs plus the replacement value of fixed assets. At the division level, accounts receivable are included in employed capital.

SMALL: How do you calculate the replacement value of fixed assets?

WALKER: We have formulas that give us the current cost of equipment capable of doing the same job as the installed equipment.

SMALL: Why do you use replacement costs?

WALKER: We have two basic reasons. First, within a single division it places all plants on an equal footing from the standpoint of measuring return, since it eliminates distortions arising from the use of widely disparate acquisition costs for similar equipment. Second, it eliminates distortions arising from the use of unrecovered costs, which, even though based on comparable replacement values, are heavily influenced by cumulative depre-ciation charges that vary widely depending upon the length of time a given facility has been in use.

SMALL: What about the rest of the items on PPCR #1?

WALKER: Reference 38 is plant income (actual) dollars expressed as a percentage of employed capital. Reference 39 is the net sales dollars divided by employed capital and expressed as a multiple of employed capital.

SMALL: What are the three most important items on PPCR #1?

WALKER: The P/V ratio, plant income (actual), and % return (employed capital).

SMALL: Are the budgets prepared on forms similar to the PPCR series?

WALKER: Yes. The only major difference is that the budget forms include columns for recording the current year's budget figures and previous year's actual figures. In addition, variances are shown between the proposed budget figures and the current year's estimated actuals[2] and the previous year's actual figures.

---

[2]Actual-to-date plus estimated costs for the remainder of the year.

# 8

# The Balanced Scorecard: Measuring Total Business Unit Performance

Companies are now shifting from industrial age competition to information age competition. During the industrial age, financial control systems were developed in companies, such as General Motors, DuPont, Matsushita, and General Electric, to facilitate and monitor efficient allocations of financial and physical capital.[1] Summary financial measures, such as operating profits and return-on-capital-employed, could evaluate the effectiveness and efficiency by which operating divisions used financial and physical capital to create value for shareholders. We will discuss such financial control measures in Chapters 9 and 10.

The emergence of the information era, however, has made obsolete many of the fundamental assumptions of industrial age competition. No longer can companies gain sustainable competitive advantage just by rapidly deploying new technology into physical assets or by excellent management of financial assets and liabilities. The information age environment for both manufacturing and service organizations requires new capabilities for competitive success. The ability of a company to mobilize and exploit its intangible or invisible assets has become far more decisive than investing in and managing physical, tangible assets.[2] Intangible assets enable an organization to:

- Develop customer relationships that retain the loyalty of existing customers and enable new customer segments and market areas to be served effectively and efficiently
- Introduce innovative products and services desired by targeted customer segments
- Produce customized high-quality products and services at low cost and with short lead times
- Mobilize employee skills and motivation for continuous improvements in process capabilities, quality, and response times
- Deploy information technology, data bases, and systems

As companies invested in programs and initiatives to build their capabilities, however, the primary evaluation system consisted of monitoring progress by means of monthly, quarterly, and annual financial reports. Ideally, the financial accounting model should have expanded to incorporate the valuation of the company's intangible and intellectual assets, such as high-quality products and services, motivated and skilled employees, responsive and predictable internal processes, and satisfied and loyal customers. If intangible assets and company capabilities could be valued within the financial accounting model, organizations that enhanced those assets and capabilities could communicate this improvement to employees, shareholders, creditors, and communities. Conversely, when companies depleted their stock of intangible assets and capabilities, the negative effects could be reflected immediately in the income statement. Realistically, however, difficulties in placing a reliable financial value on assets—such as a new product pipeline, process capabilities, employee skills, motivation, flexibility, customer loyalties, data bases, and systems—precluded them from ever being recognized in organizational balance sheets. Yet these are just the assets and capabilities that are critical for success in today's and tomorrow's competitive environment.

## THE BALANCED SCORECARD

The Balanced Scorecard (BSC) was developed to communicate the multiple, linked objectives that companies must achieve to compete on the basis of capabilities and innovation, not just tangible physical assets. The Balanced Scorecard translates mission and strategy into objectives and measures, organized into four perspectives: financial, customer, internal business process, and learning and growth (see Exhibit 8-1).

### Financial Perspective

The Balanced Scorecard retains the financial perspective since financial measures are valuable in summarizing the readily measurable economic consequences of actions already taken. Financial performance measures indicate whether the company's strategy, implementation, and execution are contributing to bottom-line improvement. Financial objectives typically are related to profitability—measured, for example, by operating income, return-on-capital-employed, or, more recently, economic value added. Alternative financial objectives can be rapid sales growth or generation of cash flow.

### Customer Perspective

In the customer perspective of the Balanced Scorecard, managers identify the customer and market segments in which the business unit will compete and the measures of the business unit's performance in these targeted segments. The customer perspective typically includes several core or generic measures of the successful outcomes from a well-formulated and implemented strategy. The core outcome measures include customer satisfaction, customer retention, new customer acquisition, customer profitability, and market and account share in targeted segments (see Exhibit 8-2).

These measures may appear to be generic among all types of organizations. For translating a particular strategy, however, they should be customized to the targeted customer groups from whom the business unit expects its greatest growth and profitability to be derived. We provide more-detailed descriptions of these core customer outcome measures in Chapter 11.

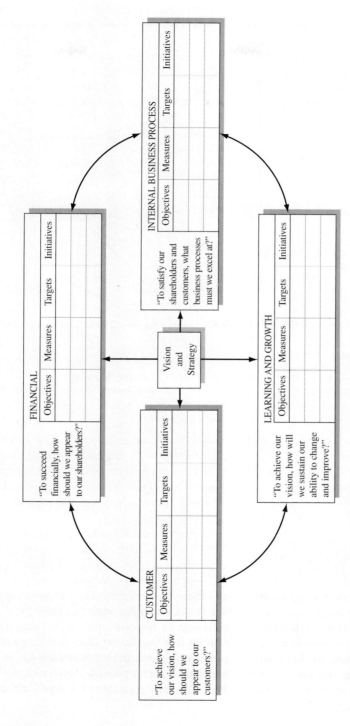

**EXHIBIT 8-1  Translating Vision and Strategy: Four Perspectives**

*Source:* R. S. Kaplan and D. P. Norton, *The Balanced Scorecard: Translating Strategy into Action* (Boston: Harvard Business School Press, 1996), p. 9.

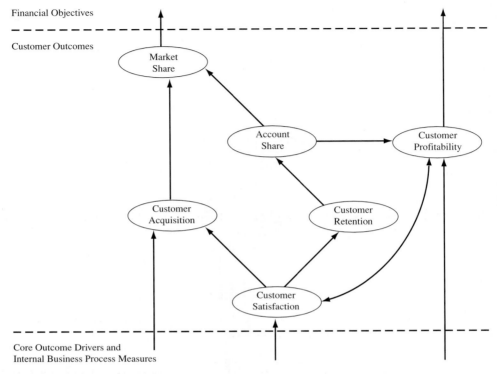

**EXHIBIT 8-2  Customer Perspective: Core Outcome Measures**
*Source:* R. S. Kaplan and D. P. Norton, "Linking the Balanced Scorecard to Strategy," *California Management Review* (Fall 1996), p. 59.

What truly makes a strategy unique is the value proposition the business unit decides to deliver to attract and retain customers in its targeted segments. Although value propositions vary among industries, and among market segments within industries, we have observed a common set of attributes that organizes the value propositions in many manufacturing and service industries. These attributes are organized into three categories (see Exhibit 8-3):

- Product and service attributes
- Customer relationship
- Image and reputation

**Product and service attributes** encompass the functionality of the product or service, its price, and its quality. The **customer relationship** dimension includes the delivery of the product or service to the customer, including the response and delivery time dimension and how the customer feels about the experience of purchasing from the company. The **image and reputation** dimension enables a company to proactively define itself for its customers.

In summary, the customer perspective enables business unit managers to articulate their unique customer and market-based strategy for producing superior future financial returns.

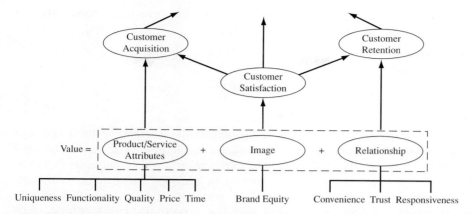

**EXHIBIT 8-3  Customer Perspective: Linking Unique Value Propositions to Core Outcome Measures**

*Source:* R. S. Kaplan and D. P. Norton, "Linking the Balanced Scorecard to Strategy," *California Management Review* (Fall 1996), p. 62.

## Internal Business Process Perspective

In the internal business process perspective, executives identify the critical internal processes in which the organization must excel (see Exhibit 8-4).

The critical internal business processes enable the business unit to:

- Deliver the value propositions that will attract and retain customers in targeted market segments
- Satisfy shareholder expectations of excellent financial returns

The internal business process measures are focused on the internal processes that will have the greatest impact on customer satisfaction and achieving the organization's financial objectives.

Each business has its unique set of processes for creating value for customers and producing financial results. A generic value chain model, however, provides a template that companies can customize for their own objectives and measures in their internal busi-

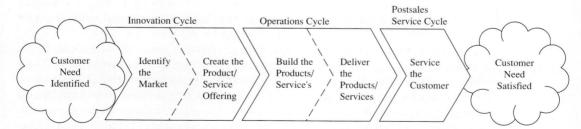

**EXHIBIT 8-4  The Internal Value Chain**

*Source:* R. S. Kaplan and D. P. Norton, "Linking the Balanced Scorecard to Strategy," *California Management Review* (Fall 1996), p. 63.

ness process perspective. The generic value chain model encompasses three principal business processes:

1. Innovation
2. Operations
3. Postsales service

### Innovation

In the innovation process, the business unit researches the emerging or latent needs of customers and then creates the products or services that will meet those needs. The innovation process represents the "long wave" of value creation in which companies first identify and nurture new markets, new customers, and the emerging and latent needs of existing customers. Then, continuing in this long wave of value creation and growth, companies design and develop the new products and services that enable them to reach the new markets and customers and to satisfy customers' newly identified needs. The operations process, in contrast, represents the short wave of value creation, in which companies deliver existing products and services to existing customers.

The innovation process consists of two components. In the first component, managers perform market research to identify the size of the market and the nature of customers' preferences and the price points for the targeted product or service. As organizations deploy their internal processes to meet specific customer needs, accurate, valid information on market size and customer preferences becomes vital. In addition to surveying existing and potential customers, this segment could also include imagining entirely new opportunities and markets for products and services that the organization could supply.

### Operations

The operations process, the second major step in the generic internal value chain, is where existing products and services are produced and delivered to customers. The operations process represents the short wave of value creation in organizations. The operations process can start with receipt of a customer order and finish with delivery of the product or service to the customer. This process stresses efficient, consistent, and timely delivery of existing products and services to existing customers.

The operations process has historically been the focus of most organizations' performance measurement systems. Operational excellence and cost reduction in manufacturing and service delivery processes remain important goals. The internal value chain in Exhibit 8-4 shows, however, that such operational excellence may be only one component, and perhaps not the most decisive component, in an entire internal value chain for achieving financial and customer objectives.

Existing operations tend to be repetitive, so scientific management techniques can be readily applied to control and to improve customer order receipt and processing and vendor, production, and delivery processes. Traditionally, these operating processes have been monitored and controlled by financial measures such as standard costs, budgets, and variances. Over time, however, excessive focus on narrow financial measures such as labor efficiency, machine efficiency, and purchase price variances led to highly dysfunctional actions: keeping labor and machines busy building inventory, usually not related to current customer orders, and switching from supplier to supplier to chase cheaper purchase prices (but ignoring the costs of large-volume orders, poor quality, uncertain delivery times, and disconnected ordering, receiving, invoicing, and collection processes between lower-priced suppliers and the customer). By now, the defects associated with using traditional cost accounting measures in today's short-cycle-time, high-quality, customer-focused environment have been amply documented.[3]

The influence, in recent years, of the total quality management and time-based competition practices of leading Japanese manufacturers has led many companies to supplement their traditional cost and financial measurements with measurements of quality and cycle time.[4] Measurements of operating processes' quality, cycle time, and cost have been developed extensively during the past 15 years. Some aspects of these quality, time, and cost measurements will likely be included as critical performance measures in any organization's internal business process perspective. These will be discussed in Chapter 11.

In addition to these time, quality, and cost measurements, managers may wish to measure additional characteristics of their processes and product and service offerings. Such additional measures could include measurement of flexibility and of the specific characteristics of products or services that create value for customers. For example, companies may offer unique product or service performance, which could be measured by accuracy, size, speed, clarity, or energy consumption, that enables them to earn high margins on sales to targeted market segments. Companies that can identify the differentiating characteristics of their products and services will want the focus and attention that measurement on the Balanced Scorecard can command. Such critical product and service performance attributes (beyond response time, quality, and cost) are incorporated into the operating process component of the Balanced Scorecard's internal business process perspective.

### Postsales Service

The third and final stage in the internal value chain is service to the customer after the original sale or delivery of service. Postsales service includes warranty and repair activities, treatment of defects and returns, and the processing and administration of payments, such as credit card administration. Some companies have explicit strategies to offer superior postsales service. For example, companies that sell sophisticated equipment or systems may offer training programs for customers' employees to help them use the equipment or system more effectively and efficiently. They may also offer rapid response to actual or potential failures and downtime. Newly established automobile dealerships, such as Acura and Saturn, have deservedly earned superb reputations by offering dramatically improved customer service for warranty work, periodic car maintenance, and car repairs. A major element in the value proposition these car companies deliver to their customers is responsive, friendly, and reliable warranty and service work. Another aspect of postsales service is the invoicing and collection process. Companies with extensive sales on credit or on company-specific credit cards will likely need to apply cost, quality, and cycle-time measurements to their billings, collection, and dispute resolution processes. Several department stores offer generous terms under which customers can exchange or return merchandise.

And companies that deal with hazardous or environmentally sensitive chemicals and materials may introduce critical performance measures associated with the safe disposal of waste and byproducts from the production process. For example, one distributor of industrial chemicals developed a capability to maintain detailed documentation and disposal services for used chemicals, freeing its customers from an expensive task, fraught with liability and subject to intense governmental scrutiny by agencies such as the Environmental Protection Agency and the Occupational Safety and Health Administration. Recognizing that excellent community relations may be a strategic objective for continuing to enjoy a franchise to operate production and service facilities, other companies set objectives, under postsales service, for excellent environmental performance. Measures such as waste and scrap produced during production processes may be more significant for their impact on the environment than for their slight increase in production costs. All of these activities add value to the customers' use of the company's product and service offerings.

The internal business process perspective reveals two fundamental differences between the traditional and the Balanced Scorecard approaches to performance measurement. Traditional approaches attempt to monitor and improve existing business processes. They may go beyond mere financial measures of performance by incorporating quality and time-based metrics, but they still focus on improving existing processes. The Balanced Scorecard approach, however, will usually identify entirely new processes at which the organization must excel to meet customer and financial objectives. For example, the organization may realize that it must develop a process to anticipate customer needs or one to deliver new services that targeted customers value. The BSC internal business process objectives highlight the processes, several of which the company may not be currently performing at all, that are most critical for the organization's strategy to succeed.

The second departure of the Balanced Scorecard approach is to incorporate innovation processes into the internal business process perspective. Traditional performance measurement systems focus on the processes of delivering today's products and services to today's customers. But the drivers of long-term financial success may require the organization to create entirely new products and services that will meet the emerging needs of current and future customers. The innovation process is, for many companies, a more powerful driver of future financial performance than the short-term operating cycle. For many companies, their ability to manage successfully a multiyear product development process or to develop a capability to reach entirely new categories of customers may be more critical for future economic performance than managing existing operations efficiently, consistently, and responsively. The internal business process perspective of the Balanced Scorecard incorporates objectives and measures for both the long-wave innovation cycle and the short-wave operations cycle.

## Learning and Growth Perspective

The fourth Balanced Scorecard perspective, learning and growth, identifies the infrastructure that the organization must build to create long-term growth and improvement. The customer and internal business process perspectives identify the factors most critical for current and future success. Businesses are unlikely to be able to meet their long-term targets for customers and internal processes using today's technologies and capabilities. Also, intense global competition requires that companies continually improve their capabilities for delivering value to customers and shareholders.

Organizational learning and growth come from three principal sources: people, systems, and organizational procedures. The financial, customer, and internal business process objectives on the Balanced Scorecard will typically reveal large gaps between existing capabilities of people, systems, and procedures and what will be required to achieve targets for breakthrough performance. To close these gaps, businesses must invest in reskilling employees, enhancing information technology and systems, and aligning organizational procedures and routines. These objectives are articulated in the learning and growth perspective of the Balanced Scorecard. As in the customer perspective, employee-based measures include several generic outcome measures: employee satisfaction, employee retention, employee training, and employee skills. In addition, the learning and growth perspective includes specific drivers of these generic measures, such as detailed, business-specific indexes of specific skills required for the new competitive environment. Information systems capabilities can be measured by real-time availability of accurate, critical customer and internal process information to employees on the front lines of decision making and actions. Organizational procedures can examine alignment of employee incentives with overall organizational success factors and measured rates of improvement in critical customer-based and internal processes.

## Summary of Balanced Scorecard Perspectives

The Balanced Scorecard retains traditional financial measures. Financial measures alone, however, are inadequate for guiding and evaluating how information age companies create future value through investment in customers, suppliers, employees, processes, technology, and innovation. Financial measures tell the story of events already completed, an adequate story for industrial age companies for whom investments in long-term capabilities and customer relationships were not critical for success.

With the Balanced Scorecard, company executives can measure how their business units create value for current and future customers, how they must build and enhance internal capabilities, and the investment in people, systems, and procedures necessary to improve future performance. The Balanced Scorecard captures the critical value-creation activities performed by skilled, motivated organizational participants. While retaining, via the financial perspective, an interest in short-term performance, the Balanced Scorecard clearly reveals the value drivers for superior long-term financial and competitive performance.

In addition, the Balanced Scorecard enables financial and nonfinancial measures to be part of the information system for employees at all levels of the organization. Front-line employees can understand the financial consequences from their decisions and actions, and senior executives can understand the drivers of long-term financial success. The Balanced Scorecard represents a translation of a business unit's mission and strategy into tangible objectives and measures. The four perspectives of the scorecard permit a balance (1) between short- and long-term objectives, (2) between external measures—for shareholders and customers—and internal measures of critical business processes, innovation, and learning and growth, (3) between outcomes desired and the performance drivers of those outcomes, and (4) between hard objective measures and softer, more-subjective measures.

Many people think of measurement as a tool to control behavior and to evaluate past performance. The measures on a Balanced Scorecard should be used in a different way: to articulate the strategy of the business, to communicate the strategy of the business, and to help align individual, organizational, and cross-departmental initiatives to achieve a common goal. Used in this way, the scorecard does not strive to keep individuals and organizational units in compliance with a preestablished plan, the traditional control system objective. The Balanced Scorecard should be used as a communication, informing, and learning system, *not* as a controlling system.

The multiplicity of measures on a Balanced Scorecard may seem confusing. However, properly constructed scorecards, as we will see, contain a unity of purpose because all the measures are directed toward achieving an integrated strategy.

## LINKING MULTIPLE SCORECARD MEASURES TO A SINGLE STRATEGY

Typically, each of the four perspectives in the Balanced Scorecard has between four and seven separate measures, thus creating a scorecard with up to 25 measures. Is it possible for any organization to focus on 25 separate things? If a scorecard is viewed as 25 (or even 10) independent measures, will it be too complicated for an organization to absorb?

The multiple measures on a properly constructed Balanced Scorecard should consist of a linked series of objectives and measures that are both consistent and mutually reinforcing. The Balanced Scorecard should be viewed as the instrumentation for a *single* strategy. When the scorecard is viewed as the manifestation of a single strategy, then the number of measures on the scorecard becomes irrelevant. Companies can indeed formulate and communicate their strategy with an integrated system of approximately two dozen measurements. The integrated system of scorecard measures should incorporate the complex set of cause-and-effect relationships among the critical variables—including leads, lags, and feedback loops—that describe the trajectory, the flight plan, of the strategy. The linkages should incorporate both cause-and-effect relationships and mixtures of outcome measures and performance drivers.

### Cause-and-Effect Relationships

A strategy is a set of hypotheses about cause and effect. The measurement system should make the relationships (hypotheses) among objectives (and measures) in the various perspectives explicit so that they can be managed and validated. The chain of cause and effect should pervade all four perspectives of a Balanced Scorecard. For example, return on capital employed (ROCE) may be a scorecard measure in the financial perspective. The driver of this financial measure could be repeat and expanded sales from existing customers, the result of a high degree of loyalty among existing customers. So, customer loyalty is included on the scorecard (in the customer perspective) because it is expected to have a strong influence on ROCE. But how will the organization achieve customer loyalty? Analysis of customer preferences may reveal that on-time delivery (OTD) of orders is highly valued by customers. Thus, improved OTD is expected to lead to higher customer loyalty, which, in turn, is expected to lead to higher financial performance. So both customer loyalty and OTD are incorporated into the customer perspective of the scorecard.

The process continues by asking at what internal processes must the company excel to achieve exceptional on-time delivery. To achieve improved OTD, the business may need to achieve short cycle times in operating processes and high-quality internal processes, both factors that could be scorecard measures in the internal perspective. And how do organizations improve the quality and reduce the cycle times of their internal processes? By training operating employees and improving their skills, an objective that would be a candidate for the learning and growth perspective. We can now see how an entire chain of cause-and-effect relationships can be established as a vertical vector through the four Balanced Scorecard perspectives:

Financial                    Return on capital employed/Economic Value Added*
                                              ⇑

Customer                              Customer loyalty
                                              ⇑

                                        On-time delivery
                                      ⇑              ⇑

Internal business process      Process quality Process cycle time
                                      ⇑              ⇑

Learning and growth                 Employee skills

*See Chapter 10 for a discussion of EVA.

Thus, a properly constructed Balanced Scorecard should tell the story of the business unit's strategy. It should identify and make explicit the sequence of hypotheses about the cause-and-effect relationships between outcome measures and the performance drivers of those outcomes.

## Performance Drivers

A good Balanced Scorecard should also have a mix of outcome measures and performance drivers. Outcome measures without performance drivers do not communicate how the outcomes are to be achieved. They also do not provide an early indication about whether the strategy is being implemented successfully. Conversely, performance drivers alone, such as cycle times and part-per-million defect rates, without outcome measures may enable the business unit to achieve short-term operational improvements. But they will fail to reveal whether the operational improvements have been translated into expanded business with existing and new customers and, eventually, into enhanced financial performance. A good Balanced Scorecard should have an appropriate mix of outcomes and performance drivers of the business unit's strategy. In this way, the scorecard translates the business unit's strategy into a linked set of measures that define both the long-term strategic objectives and the mechanisms for achieving those objectives.

## DIAGNOSTIC VERSUS STRATEGIC MEASURES

Most organizations today already have many more than 16 to 25 measures to keep themselves functioning. Some managers are incredulous that a Balanced Scorecard of no more than two dozen measures can be sufficient for measuring their operations. They are, of course, correct in a narrow sense but are failing to distinguish between *diagnostic measures* (which monitor whether the business remains "in control" and are able to signal when unusual events are occurring that require immediate attention) and *strategic measures* (which define a strategy designed for competitive excellence and future success).

A simple example clarifies this point. Many of our bodily functions require narrow operating parameters. If our body temperature rises or falls five degrees or more or our blood pressure drops too low or escalates too high, our survival is endangered. In such circumstances, all of our energies (and those of skilled professionals) are mobilized to restore our bodies to their normal levels. But we do not devote enormous energy to optimizing our body temperature and blood pressure. Being able to control our body temperature to within 0.01° of the optimum will not be one of the strategic success factors that will determine whether we become a chief executive of a company, a senior partner in an international consulting firm, or a tenured full professor at a major university. Other factors are much more decisive in determining whether we achieve our unique personal and professional objectives. Are body temperature and blood pressure important? Absolutely. Maintaining them within a normal range is *necessary*; it is not, however, *sufficient* for the achievement of our long-run goals.

Similarly, corporations should have hundreds, perhaps thousands, of measures that they can monitor to ensure that they are functioning as expected and to signal when corrective action must be taken. But these are not the drivers of businesses' competitive success. Such measures capture the necessary vital signs that enable the company to operate. Vital signs that must meet standards are not the basis for competitive breakthroughs. But if the vital signs do not meet the standards, they can prevent the organization from meeting even modest objectives, much less its strategic aspirations. Vital signs should be monitored diagnostically. A diagnostic control system measures performance against a preset standard, and management need not take action as long as actual performance meets the standard; this process is management by exception. Diagnostic measures, however, are not the basis for competitive breakthroughs.[5]

The Balanced Scorecard is not a replacement for an organization's day-to-day performance measurement system. The measures on the Balanced Scorecard are chosen to direct the attention of managers and employees to those factors for which superb performance can be expected to lead to competitive breakthroughs for the organization. The outcome and performance-driver measures on the Balanced Scorecard should be the subjects of intensive and extensive interactions among senior and middle-level managers as they evaluate strategies based on new information about competitors, customers, markets, technologies, and suppliers.

For example, in the 1980s, the product and process quality of many Western companies were so poor compared with their Japanese competitors that the companies had to put quality improvements at the top of their priorities. After years of diligent work, many companies have now achieved excellent quality and are now at parity with their competitors. At this point, quality may have been neutralized as a competitive factor. Companies may need to maintain existing quality and continue to make incremental improvements, but quality may no longer be the most important factor for determining future strategic success. In such a situation, quality is monitored diagnostically, and the company needs to find other dimensions in the value proposition it delivers to customers to distinguish itself from competitors. These other dimensions become elevated to the Balanced Scorecard.

## FOUR PERSPECTIVES: ARE THEY SUFFICIENT?

The four perspectives of the Balanced Scorecard should be considered a template, not a straitjacket. No mathematical theorem exists that four perspectives are both necessary and sufficient. Companies rarely use fewer than four perspectives, but depending on industry circumstances and a business unit's strategy, one or more additional perspectives may be needed. For example, some people have expressed concern that, although the Balanced Scorecard recognizes explicitly the interests of shareholders and customers, it does not explicitly incorporate the interests of other important stakeholders, such as employees, suppliers, and the community.

The interests of shareholders—the owners and capital contributors to the organization—appear on the scorecard through objectives and measures in the financial perspective. Customer measures also appear on every scorecard (in the customer perspective) since customers are essential for meeting the financial objectives. And objectives and measures for employees, suppliers, and the community appear on the Balanced Scorecard when outstanding performance along those objectives and measures will lead to breakthrough performance for customers and shareholders.

When relationships with key stakeholders, such as suppliers or the community, however, are required only to be "in control" and consistent with implicit or explicit contracts between the company and the stakeholder, then performance for those contracts can be monitored by the company's diagnostic performance measurement system. In effect, such relationships become vital signs; they are necessary but not decisive for strategic success.

The employee perspective has been incorporated in virtually all scorecards through the learning and growth perspective. That is, improvements in employee capabilities in critical jobs and in employee motivation are essential components for the learning and growth perspective. Employee objectives and measures appear with other learning and growth enablers, such as information technology deployment. These objectives appear because they are necessary to drive improved performance in the internal business process, customer, and financial perspectives. Similarly, when strong supplier relationships are part of the strategy leading to breakthrough customer or financial performance, then outcome and performance driver measures for supplier relationships should be incorporated within the organization's internal business process perspective. And, when outstanding environmental and community performance is a central part of a company's strategy, then objectives and measures for that perspective also become an integral part of a company's scorecard.[6]

---

## SUMMARY

Information age companies succeed by investing in and managing their intellectual assets. Functional specialization must be integrated into customer-based business processes. Mass production and service delivery of standard products and services are being replaced by flexible, responsive, and high-quality delivery of innovative products and services that can be individualized to targeted customer segments. Innovation and improvement of products, services, and processes will be generated by reskilled employees, superior information technology, and aligned organizational procedures.

As organizations invest in acquiring these new capabilities, their success (or failure) cannot be motivated or measured in the short run solely by the traditional financial accounting model. This financial model, developed for trading companies and industrial age corporations, measures events of the past not the investments in the capabilities that provide value for the future.

The Balanced Scorecard integrates measures derived from strategy. While retaining financial measures of past performance, the Balanced Scorecard introduces the drivers of future financial performance. The drivers—encompassing customer, internal business process, and learning and growth perspectives—are derived from an explicit and rigorous translation of the organization's strategy into tangible objectives and measures.

## ENDNOTES

1. See A. D. Chandler, *The Visible Hand: The Managerial Revolution in American Business* (Cambridge: Harvard University Press, 1977); and H. T. Johnson and R. S. Kaplan, *Relevance Lost: The Rise and Fall of Management Accounting* (Boston: Harvard Business School Press, 1987).

2. H. Itami, *Mobilizing Invisible Assets* (Cambridge: Harvard University Press, 1987).

3. See J. Lessner, "Performance Measurement in a Just-in-Time Environment: Can Traditional Performance Measurements Still Be Used?" *Journal of Cost Management* (Fall 1989), pp. 22–28; R. Kaplan, "Limitation of Cost Accounting in Advanced Manufacturing Environments," in *Measures for Manufacturing Excellence*, ed. R. S. Kaplan (Boston: Harvard Business School Press, 1990), chap. 1; and E. M. Goldratt and J. Cox, *The Goal: A Process of Ongoing Improvement* (Croton-on-Hudson, NY: North River Press, 1986).

4. Many references could be cited here. A representative sample includes C. Berliner and J. Brimson, "CMS Performance Measurement," in *Cost Management for Today's Advanced Manufacturing* (Boston: Harvard Business School Press, 1988), chap. 6; C. J. McNair, W. Mosconi, and T. Norris, *Meeting the Technology Challenge: Cost Accounting in a JIT Environment* (Montvale, NJ: Institute of Management Accountants, 1988); and R. Lynch and K. Cross, *Measure Up! Yardsticks for Continuous Improvement* (Cambridge, MA: Basil Blackwell, 1991).

5. The important distinction between the measures monitored in the organization's diagnostic control systems and those that are part of the continual interactions among managers has been articulated in R. L. Simons, *Levers of Control: How Managers Use Innovative Control Systems to Drive Strategic Renewal* (Boston: Harvard Business School Press, 1995).

6. See comments of D. W. Boivin, President and COO of Novacor Chemicals, "Using the Balanced Scorecard," letter to the editor, *Harvard Business Review* (March–April 1996), p. 170.

## ■ *CASES*

### CHADWICK, INC.: THE BALANCED SCORECARD (ABRIDGED)*

The "Balanced Scorecard"[1] article seemed to address the concerns of several division managers who felt that the company was over-emphasizing short-term financial results. But the process of getting agreement on what measures should be used proved a lot more difficult than I anticipated.

*Bill Baron, Comptroller of Chadwick, Inc.*

### *Company Background*

Chadwick, Inc. was a diversified producer of personal consumer products and pharmaceuticals. The Norwalk Division of Chadwick developed, manufactured and sold ethical drugs

---

*Professor Robert S. Kaplan prepared this case.

Copyright © 1996 by the President and Fellows of Harvard College. Harvard Business School case 196-124.

[1] R. S. Kaplan and D. P. Norton, "The Balanced Scorecard: Measures That Drive Performance," *Harvard Business Review* (January–February 1992).

for human and animal use. It was one of five or six sizable companies competing in these markets and, while it did not dominate the industry, the company was considered well-managed and was respected for the high quality of its products. Norwalk did not compete by supplying a full range of products. It specialized in several niches and attempted to leverage its product line by continually searching for new applications for existing compounds.

Norwalk sold its products through several key distributors who supplied local markets, such as retail stores, hospitals and health service organizations, and veterinary practices. Norwalk depended on its excellent relations with the distributors who served to promote Norwalk's products to end users and also received feedback from the end users about new products desired by their customers.

Chadwick knew that its long-term success depended on how much money distributors could make by promoting and selling Norwalk's products. If the profit from selling Norwalk products was high, then these products were promoted heavily by the distributors and Norwalk received extensive communication back about future customer needs. Norwalk had historically provided many highly profitable products to the marketplace, but recent inroads by generic manufacturers had been eroding distributors' sales and profit margins. Norwalk had been successful in the past because of its track record of generating a steady stream of attractive, popular products. During the second half of the 1980s, however, the approval process for new products had lengthened and fewer big winners had emerged from Norwalk's R&D laboratories.

### Research and Development

The development of ethical drugs was a lengthy, costly, and unpredictable process. Development cycles now averaged about 12 years. The process started by screening a large number of compounds for potential benefits and use. For every drug that finally emerged as approved for use, up to 30,000 compounds had to be tested at the beginning of a new product development cycle. The development and testing processes had many stages. The development cycle started with the discovery of compounds that possessed the desirable properties and ended many years later with extensive and tedious testing and documentation to demonstrate that the new drug could meet government regulations for promised benefits, reliability in production, and absence of deleterious side effects.

Approved and patented drugs could generate enormous revenues for Norwalk and its distributors. Norwalk's profitability during the 1980s was sustained by one key drug that had been discovered in the late 1960s. No blockbuster drug had emerged during the 1980s, however, and the existing pipeline of compounds going through development, evaluation and test was not as healthy as Norwalk management desired. Management was placing pressure on scientists in the R&D lab to increase the yield of promising new products and to reduce the time and costs of the product development cycle. Scientists were currently exploring new bio-engineering techniques to create compounds that had the specific active properties desired rather than depending on an almost random search through thousands of possible compounds. The new techniques started with a detailed specification of the chemical properties that a new drug should have and then attempted to synthesize candidate compounds that could be tested for these properties. The bio-engineering procedures were costly, requiring extensive investment in new equipment and computer-based analysis.

A less expensive approach to increase the financial yield from R&D investments was to identify new applications for existing compounds that had already been approved for use. While some validation still had to be submitted for government approval to demonstrate the effectiveness of the drug in the new applications, the cost of extending an existing product to a new application was much, much less expensive than developing and creating an entirely new compound. Several valuable suggestions for possible new applications from existing products had come from Norwalk salesmen in the field. The salesmen were now being trained not only to sell existing products for approved applications, but also to listen to end users who frequently had novel and interesting ideas about how Norwalk's products could be used for new applications.

## Manufacturing

Norwalk's manufacturing processes were considered among the best in the industry. Management took pride in the ability of the manufacturing operation to quickly and efficiently ramp up to produce drugs once they had cleared governmental regulatory processes. Norwalk's manufacturing capabilities also had to produce the small batches of new products that were required during testing and evaluation stages.

## Performance Measurement

Chadwick allowed its several divisions to operate in a decentralized fashion. Division managers had almost complete discretion in managing all the critical processes: R&D, Production, Marketing and Sales, and administrative functions such as finance, human resources, and legal. Chadwick set challenging financial targets for divisions to meet. The targets were usually expressed as Return on Capital Employed (ROCE). As a diversified company, Chadwick wanted to be able to deploy the returns from the most profitable divisions to those divisions that held out the highest promise for profitable growth. Monthly financial summaries were submitted by each

division to corporate headquarters. The Chadwick executive committee, consisting of the chief executive officer, the chief operating officer, two executive vice presidents, and the chief financial officer met monthly with each division manager to review ROCE performance and backup financial information for the preceding month.

## The Balanced Scorecard Project

Bill Baron, Comptroller of Chadwick, had been searching for improved methods for evaluating the performance of the various divisions. Division managers complained about the continual pressure to meet short-term financial objectives in businesses that required extensive investments in risky projects to yield long-term returns. The idea of a Balanced Scorecard appealed to him as a constructive way to balance short-run financial objectives with the long-term performance of the company.

Baron brought the article and concept to Dan Daniels, the President and Chief Operating officer of Chadwick. Daniels shared Baron's enthusiasm for the concept, feeling that a Balanced Scorecard would allow Chadwick divisional managers more flexibility in how they measured and presented their results of operations to corporate management. He also liked the idea of holding managers accountable for improving the long-term performance of their division.

After several days of reflection, Daniels issued a memorandum to all Chadwick division managers. The memo had a simple and direct message: Read the Balanced Scorecard article, develop a scorecard for your division, and be prepared to come to corporate headquarters in 90 days to present and defend the divisional scorecard to Chadwick's Executive Committee.

John Greenfield, the Division Manager at Norwalk, received Daniel's memorandum with some concern and apprehension. In principle, Greenfield liked the idea of developing a scorecard that would be more responsive to his operations, but he was distrustful of how much freedom he had to develop and use such a scorecard. Greenfield recalled: This seemed like just another way for corporate to claim that they have decentralized decision making and authority while still retaining ultimate control at headquarters.

Greenfield knew that he would have to develop a plan of action to meet corporate's request but lacking a clear sense of how committed Chadwick was to the concept, he was not prepared to take much time from his or his subordinates' existing responsibilities for the project.

The next day, at the weekly meeting of the Divisional Operating Committee, Greenfield distributed the Daniels memo and appointed a three man committee, headed by Divisional Controller, Wil Wagner, to facilitate the process for creating the Norwalk Balanced Scorecard.

Wagner approached Greenfield later that day:

> I read the Balanced Scorecard article. Based on my understanding of the concept, we must start with a clearly defined business vision. I'm not sure I have a clear understanding of the vision and business strategy for Norwalk. How can I start to build the scorecard without this understanding?

Greenfield admitted: "That's a valid point. Let me see what I can do to get you started."

Greenfield picked up a pad of paper and started to write. Several minutes later he had produced a short business strategy statement for Norwalk (see Exhibit 1). Wagner and his group took Greenfield's strategy statement and started to formulate scorecard measures for the division.

---

**EXHIBIT 1**   Norwalk Pharmaceutical
Division—Business Strategy

---

1.  Manage Norwalk portfolio of investments
    Minimize cost to executing our existing
       business base
    Maximize return/yield on all development
       spending
    Invest in discovery of new compounds
2.  Satisfy customer needs
3.  Drive responsibility to the lowest level
    Minimize centralized staff overhead
4.  People development
    Industry training

    Unique mix of technical and commercial skills

---

## CHEMICAL BANK: IMPLEMENTING THE BALANCED SCORECARD*

In early 1995, Michael Hegarty, Head of the Retail Bank of Chemical Banking Corporation, was overseeing a transformation in his organization. The process had begun with the merger of Chemical and the Manufacturers Hanover Corporation at year-end 1991. The new, larger banking company was better positioned to compete in a marketplace characterized by intense pricing competition, an outflow of deposits to mutual funds, rapidly evolving technology, and increased customer demand for value. Hegarty commented on just one indicator of the future competitive environment for retail banking:

> At the time of the merger, the old Chemical Banking Corporation with assets of $75

*This case was prepared by Norman Klein and Professor Robert S. Kaplan.

billion, had a market capitalization of $2 billion. Less than four years later, Microsoft has offered to buy Intuit, a personal financial software company with $223 million in sales for $1.5 billion. What do you think Bill Gates is buying for all that money?

Historically, retail banking had emphasized efficient collection and processing of deposits. Hegarty wanted to transform the bank into a market-focused organization that would be the financial service provider of choice to targeted customer groups. To implement this strategy, Hegarty knew that the bank had to make major investments to understand customer needs and to identify attractive customer segments. The bank also had to develop and tailor new products such as annuities, investment products, and technology-based payment services to meet customer needs in the targeted segments. With a broader product and service line, and excellent knowledge of its customer base, the bank would then be able to find ways to develop new relationships with its most desirable customers, and expand the bank's business with them—increasing its share of its customers' financial transactions (or "share of wallet" as it was described in the bank).

When asked how he expected to implement such dramatic and extensive strategic change, Hegarty said:

> My biggest problem is communicating and reinforcing strategy. The Balanced Scorecard is one of a set of tools we are using—along with Mission and Vision Statements, Gap Analysis, Strategy Consensus, and Brand Positioning—for strategy formulation and communication. The Balanced Scorecard can't win without a good mission statement and vision, an excellent strategy, and good execution. But it is certainly part of the architecture of success. It is an element in a major communications program to 15,000 individuals.
>
> No one owns a process end-to-end (most do just a small snippet). But every individual

should understand how they fit in; what their role is for helping the company achieve its strategy. The scorecard gives us the measures we need to stay focused on performance, while at the same time enabling us to clarify and communicate our vision, and focus our energies for change. The measurement allows learning, and the learning renews the vision and refuels our energy for change.

## Retail Banking in the 1990s

Experts predicted that the 1990s would prove to be an intensely competitive decade in retail banking. In the past 10 years, the approximately 14,000 banks in the United States had shrunk to 10,000, and there were predictions of as few as 4,000 to 5,000 banks by early in the next century.

Customers were demanding new investment and insurance products, and far more convenient ways to do their banking. They were asking banks for new telephone options, and for improved access to ATMs with enhanced functionality. These changes meant that branch personnel would be doing fewer deposit, withdrawal, and check-cashing transactions and would have to become more involved with higher-value interactions with customers, including sales of new products. But even with the move to higher-value services, banks anticipated operating fewer branches at the turn of the decade.

Research indicated that 61% of retail banking customers between the ages of 18 and 24 actively used ATMs, while only 27% of customers 55 to 64 did so. The trend lines were clear. The banks that would survive and prosper would be deploying superior technology, offering new products, and delivering service through new channels. Further, technology would be the key to new partnerships, especially with insurance companies and brokerage firms, and new strategies to identify, attract, and retain more profitable customers.

Ted Francavilla, Managing Director of Strategic Planning and Finance, noted that the traditional retail deposit business had become very tough. Revenue growth was slow due to lower interest rates and outflows of deposits to nonbanking service providers, such as mutual funds. Growth in core operating expenses and the need to invest in new delivery systems added to the challenge.

> Currently we have over $800 million in operating expenses and 8,000 employees in our New York Markets division. Landlords expect rental increases on their properties and employees expect raises. These factors, coupled with low revenue growth, produce a real profitability squeeze for retail banking. We need to demonstrate to our corporate parent that we can earn good returns on the $800 million we spend each year and free up funds for investment in the future.

### Chemical Bank's Strategy

After the merger had been completed in 1992, the Retail Bank's New York Markets division had identified the following six critical success factors:

1. Commit to business processes driven by service quality.
2. Implement a continuous process for understanding markets, segments, and individual customers.
3. Develop a rapid, customer-focused product management and development process.
4. Ensure flexible and market-responsive delivery channels.
5. Develop information management processes and platforms driven by business needs.
6. Implement expense management process to streamline the cost base.

In 1994, New York Markets was responsible for managing $27 billion in consumer and small business deposits, as well as over 300 branches, over 800 proprietary ATMs, a state-of-the-art telephone service center, and other related distribution channels. The division also acted as a distributor and referral source for Chemical's mortgages, credit

**EXHIBIT 1**  New York Markets
(Dollars in Millions)

| INCOME STATEMENT ITEM | ACTUAL 1993 | PLAN 1994 |
|---|---|---|
| Net interest income | $693.3 | $666.8 |
| Total noninterest income | 209.8 | 245.1 |
| Total revenue | $903.1 | $911.9 |
| Noninterest Expense | | |
| Total salaries and benefits | $345.7 | $354.7 |
| Occupancy and equipment | 171.3 | 175.0 |
| FDIC | 73.0 | 61.0 |
| Other | 105.4 | 108.6 |
| Total direct expense | $695.4 | $699.3 |
| Total indirect | 177.5 | 159.1 |
| Total noninterest expense | $872.9 | $858.4 |
| Operating margin | $30.2 | $53.5 |
| Provision for loan loss | 2.9 | 2.4 |
| Income before taxes | $27.3 | $51.1 |
| Income taxes | 12.0 | 22.5 |
| Net income | $15.3 | $28.6 |
| Average Gross Deposits ($billions) | | |
| Consumer | $24.3 | $23.4 |
| Commercial | 4.1 | 4.0 |
| Total NY markets | $28.4 | $27.4 |

cards, home equity loans and other consumer credit products, which were managed by Hegarty as national business lines. Mutual funds were also sold through a branch-based brokerage operation.

The New York Markets division had the number one market share among small commercial companies (under $1 million in sales) with a total of roughly 150,000 accounts. This represented a 24% market share in the metropolitan area. New York Markets also claimed a 16%–17% share of the consumer market, with 1.5 million customers holding approximately 3 million accounts. Net income of $15.3 million for 1993 was planned to improve to $28.6 million in 1994. Exhibit 1 shows summary financial information for New York Markets division, and Exhibit 2 shows the organization chart of the Retail Bank.

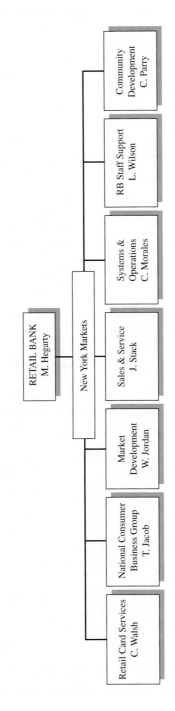

**EXHIBIT 2  Organization Chart of the Retail Bank, August 1994**

### Developing the Balanced Scorecard

Francavilla had been introduced to the BSC concept in mid-1992 while attending a one-week business school executive program. He had immediately sensed that the BSC insistence on clear specification of strategic objectives and appropriate measures in four areas—financial, customer, internal business, and learning and growth—would be a useful way to create change at Chemical Bank.

Francavilla asked Tony LoFrumento, Vice President–Retail Bank Strategic Planning and Finance, to chair a middle-management task force to build a Balanced Scorecard for the New York Markets division. LoFrumento recalled the task force experience:

> The group worked hard and generated good ideas and analysis. But we soon realized that a mid-level group would find it difficult to push performance measures up to senior management. If the BSC was going to have an impact, Mike Hegarty had to be committed to the concept.

In May 1993, Hegarty attended a presentation introducing the BSC and was convinced that this approach could help create the cultural change he desired at the Retail Bank. Other senior managers at the bank, however, remained skeptical. David Norton, one of the co-authors of the initial BSC article, was brought in for a presentation to the senior management group. After the presentation, the group became committed to moving ahead with a scorecard project.

### The Retail Bank's Balanced Scorecard

Francavilla, as head of Strategic Planning and Finance, functioned as the internal champion for the BSC. LoFrumento led the day-to-day functioning of BSC activities, and Norton was retained for consulting support. They divided the senior management group into four subgroups, each one responsible for developing objectives for one of the BSC perspectives. By October 1993, strategic objectives had been identified for each of the four BSC perspectives (see Exhibits 3A–3D).

---

**EXHIBIT 3A**   Strategic Financial (Shareholder) Objectives for BSC

I.   Financial (Shareholder)
Improve Return on Spending
  Return on spending reflects our ability to create wealth with the corporation's funds. ROS is the appropriate objective because the business is assigned a low level of capital by the corporation due to its low credit risk. ROS will align our expense outlays with the revenue generated. By aligning our spending with high value and high return activities, we will increase the return we achieve on dollars spent.
Reduce Costs
  By becoming more streamlined and efficient, we will focus resources and help to achieve acceptable profitability over the 3–5 year span. We will accomplish this by eliminating expenses that do not lead to revenue generation, by improving productivity, and by streamlining and redesigning key business processes
Increase Revenues
  To achieve our financial vision, we need to grow our revenue streams. We need to redefine our core businesses and increase the number of valuable customers. We will achieve this by retaining and acquiring valuable customers, and broadening valuable customer relationships through the cross-sell of existing products and the sale of new products.
Reduce Risk
  We plan to move away from a dependence on net interest income by broadening and selling our portfolio of fee-based products to cover a greater portion of our expense base. Changing our mix toward more fee-based business will cushion Chemical from the risks of the interest rate cycle.

---

**EXHIBIT 3B** Strategic Customer Objectives for BSC

II. Customer

Differentiators

Offer customized value propositions to targeted customer segments:

  i. Define propositions that different customers value.

  ii. Understand the economics of fulfilling various propositions.

  iii. Target those customers whose value propositions can be fulfilled profitably.

Differentiate ourselves through employees capable of recognizing customer needs and possessing the knowledge to proactively satisfy them:

  A greater knowledge of Chemical's product and service offerings will help our customers better fulfill their banking needs. This knowledge, along with cross-selling, consultative skills, and a supporting operating structure will satisfy a greater proportion of our customer's financial needs.

  Give customers access to banking services or information 24 hours a day, consistent with the appropriate value proposition for the segment they represent.

Essentials

  Perform consistently and seamlessly in the eyes of the customer.

  Service customers expediently: the timeliness of the response should meet or exceed the customer's perceived sense of urgency.

  Eliminate mistakes in all customer service encounters.

**EXHIBIT 3C** Strategic Internal Objectives for BSC

III. Internal

A.  Innovation

  Make the Market

    Identify the needs of customer segments who represent high current profitability and their underlying economic potential. Understand the risk of each and how Chemical Bank can sustain differentiation with these target customers in the market by exploiting its key competencies.

  Create the Product

    Create profitable, innovative financial service products which are among the first to market, easy to use, and convenient to our targeted customers, yielding perceived superior value by the customer, and cost effective for Chemical Bank.

B.  Delivery

  Market and Sell

    Cross-sell our products and services through organized, knowledgeable, consultative and proactive employees. We must listen to our customers, proactively educate them about our products and communicate to them how our products can meet their financial needs. To perform these activities, our salespeople must have a high level of systematic and regular contact with our customers and employ professional sales management practices.

  Distribute and Service

    Achieve service excellence based on our people and systems providing customers with the best reliability/availability, responsiveness, and no defects/errors. Quality delivery of our products and services is not an area of differentiation, but it is critical to our survival. Service excellence is the key to maintaining existing relationships and prerequisite to entering the battle for new customers. Without excellent performance on the "hygiene factors," we cannot move off square one.

---

**EXHIBIT 3D**  Strategic Learning and Growth Objectives for BSC

---

IV. Learning and Growth

Strategic Information Assets

The ability to extract, manipulate, and use information holds the key to competitive advantage in our industry. First, we must recognize, harvest, and disseminate the considerable amount of information we have today. Second, business units and decision makers need to understand what and how much data are required to make a decision with a reasonably high degree of confidence. Third, we must improve the utility, access, ease of use and timeliness of information.

Reskilling: Strategic Jobs and Competencies

Build our marketing, sales, and customer services competencies to accomplish our aggressive revenue generation targets. First, our people need the competency to cross-sell our products and services. This demands a customer-focused orientation, the ability to recognize customer needs, the initiative to proactively solicit business, and superior consultative selling skills. Second, our people need a broader knowledge of our product portfolio and financial markets to support their cross-selling activities.

Accountability and Reward Linkage

Performance management systems are the pivotal points used to communicate, motivate, and reward employees for behavior that supports the Balanced Scorecard business objectives. We will align incentive plans to BSC business objectives to encourage behavior toward our business vision.

Focus Our Resources

We will focus our resources to align our capital, expense, and personnel decisions with strategic priorities. Allocating resources where the return is the highest, setting priorities on competing expenditures based on that criterion, and remaining focused will enable us to operate more predictably and profitably.

---

The subgroups, with assistance from lower-level managers, then developed measures for the objectives in their assigned BSC perspective. By the end of 1993, the entire group had reached consensus on a complete scorecard for the New York Markets division (see Exhibit 4).

Francavilla noted that an immediate impact of the BSC project was to simplify the bank's strategy statements:

Formerly, we communicated our strategy to the 8,000 people in the organization using the five dimensions on the left [see below]. We found we could boil it down to three core strategic themes which aligned well with three of the perspectives of the BSC. The scorecard focused our thinking in this way, and Mike [Hegarty] now communicates these three themes continually to all 8,000 people. It's been branded into their minds so that they know that if they're doing something that doesn't fit into one of these three themes, they probably shouldn't be doing it. And as we were building the scorecard, we found that we could relate each measure to one of those three themes.

| ORIGINAL STATEMENTS | CORE STRATEGIC THEMES | BALANCED SCORECARD PERSPECTIVE |
|---|---|---|
| Focus on attractive markets  Increase fee revenue | Shift the Customer/  profit mix | Customer |
| Improve service quality  Improve operating efficiency | Improve productivity | Internal |
| Promote continuous learning  and improvement | Create an enabled organization | Learning and growth |

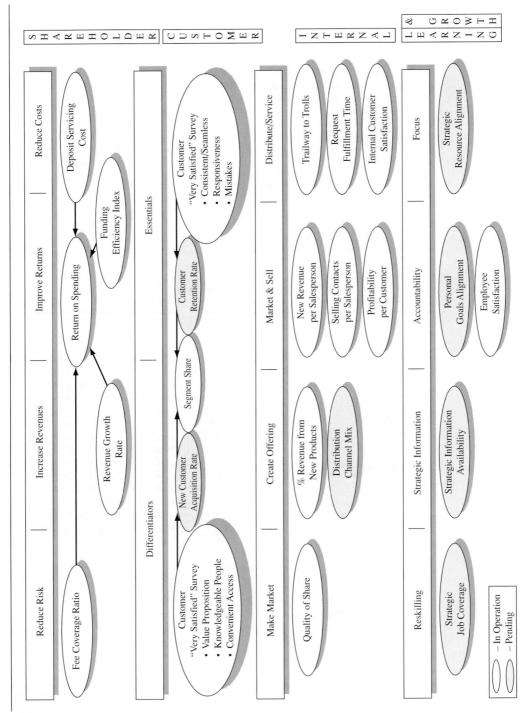

**EXHIBIT 4  Retail Bank's Balanced Scorecard—Overview**

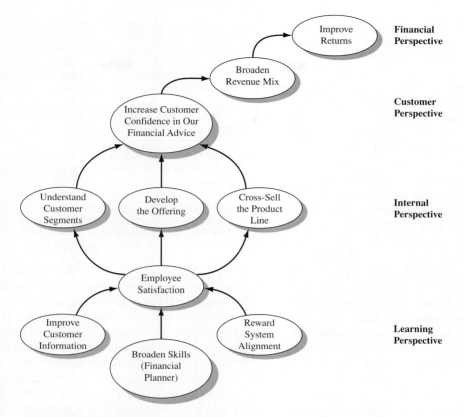

**EXHIBIT 5   Strategic Objectives for Revenue Growth Strategy**

In addition to aligning the scorecard measures to the three strategic themes, the team developed causal links across the objectives and measures. For example, two of the financial objectives—Revenue Growth and Reduce Risk—were expected to be outcomes from the theme Shift the Customer/Profit Mix. The BSC group linked the Revenue Growth and Reduce Risk outcome objectives back to objectives in, respectively, the customer, internal, and learning and growth perspectives that were the performance drivers of these outcomes (see Exhibit 5). This chain of cause-and-effect relationships illustrated that if the bank was to broaden and increase the set of financial products that retail customers transacted with the bank, then it must

shift its image from a provider of a narrow set of banking services to becoming a financial adviser and service provider for targeted customer groups—an objective to *Increase customer confidence in our financial advice*.

Having specified the link from financial objectives to customer objectives for the Broaden Revenue Mix objectives, the BSC team then linked to three of the internal objectives that its people must excel at if the bank were to create its new image as a broad provider of financial services:

Understand customer segments
Develop new products
Cross-sell the product line

These internal processes were now identified as vital to implementing the bank's Broaden Revenue Mix strategy. Previously, performance measurement had focused on continuous improvement of existing processes like check processing and teller transactions. Thus the BSC process, starting from identifying financial and customer objectives, had highlighted several new internal processes for the organization to develop best-in-class delivery capabilities.

The three internal perspective objectives led naturally to objectives in the learning & growth perspective. The bank's customer representatives would have to expand their skills, so that they could serve as a customer's financial counselor, and communicate credibly and knowledgeably about an expanded set of financial products. The customer representatives also would need ready access to information on all the bank's relationships with each customer. The incentive system for the bank's employees would also have to be changed to encourage the new behavior and skill acquisition. These three enablers—new skills, access to strategic information, and aligned incentives—would contribute to more capable and skilled employees who, in turn, would drive the internal process objectives. Each objective in the Retail Bank's BSC was similarly linked in a series of cause-and-effect relationships that told the story of how the bank's strategy would be accomplished.

Francavilla commented on the benefits from establishing the linkages in BSC objectives and measures:

> In the past, we found it hard to get and maintain focus on our infrastructure—things like MIS and employee training and skills. We talked about their importance, but when financial pressure was applied, these were among the first spending programs to go. Now with measures of Strategic Information Availability and Strategic Job Coverage on the BSC, people can see the linkages between improving these capabilities and achieving our long-term financial goals. The BSC kept these issues front and center for the senior management group, so that a focus on these infrastructure investments could be sustained even in a highly constrained environment for corporate spending.

Lee Wilson, Chief of Staff for the Retail Bank, concurred with this view:

> The process has increased learning in the organization. Everybody agrees on the overall objectives, but it takes time to align 8,000 people and make appropriate infrastructure investments and commitments. If we stay the course, the BSC's learning perspective will enable Chemical Bank to really deliver superior service sooner than other banks.

By the end of 1993, measures for each of the objectives had been selected and a senior manager had been designated for collecting the information and reporting on each measure. For example, the owner of the three measures, under "Market & Sell" was Dave Mooney, manager of the Manhattan branch network, who reported to Jack Stack, the Managing Director of Sales and Service (see Exhibit 2). Mooney met frequently with branch marketing and selling managers and with Jack Stack to discuss progress along these three measures.

### Impact of the Balanced Scorecard

Lee Wilson had not come to the bank until April 1994. While he had missed the 1993 process that led to the BSC, he could offer observations from his somewhat independent perspective:

> I see the BSC as a very valuable tool for the management team, but one that needs to keep evolving. To begin to appreciate the value of BSC at Chemical, you have to understand that its primary benefit was to pull together the two management teams. At Manufacturers Hanover, company-wide policies had been handed down by a strong central staff. Chemical, on the other hand, relied on a more decentralized approach. Given the two

cultures, there were inevitable tugs-of-war between them after the merger.

In early and mid-1993, the BSC meetings provided a mechanism for the senior people to focus on a common objective: devise a new strategy for the Retail Bank. Those meetings allowed people to come together and overcome their differences in assumptions and styles. A powerful shared sense emerged in these meetings about how the combined bank could capitalize on the potential from its new scale of operation. The BSC gave the senior executive group a positive perspective, focused on serving customers in a learning environment.

Francavilla concurred, recalling the frustration of attempting to develop a consensus on strategy in 1992, shortly after the merger:

Everyone had agreed to the strategy—"Provide superior service to targeted customers." But we couldn't agree on how to implement this strategy since everyone had a different opinion about what superior service really meant, and who our targeted customers should be. The BSC process gave us specific and operational definitions of superior service and targeted customers.

But the glow of consensus-building gave way to frustration in late 1993 as work teams began to struggle with implementation. Several of the measures were difficult to obtain. People debated whether to use substitute measures or leave the measures blank until improved data systems could be developed.

Senior managers also noted that the BSC was quite visible only in the lives of 27 top-level managers in the Retail Bank. It was not yet being used to drive change throughout the organization. Some of the BSC themes had been communicated to employees through the monthly newsletter, *News & Views* (see Exhibit 6), and at the annual Branch Managers meeting. But the BSC had not been communicated to rank and file employees as a new management tool. LoFrumento explained:

We got delayed by gaps in our measurement system. We had most of the information on customer satisfaction and customer profitability, but we didn't have the requisite data on customer share and retention by segment. The data for some of the new measures, like Strategic Job Coverage and Strategic Resource Alignment, did not exist at all and had to be created and developed by the responsible department. Even when we had some data, such as the mix of transactions in different channels, we had problems bringing together the information from diverse systems. As a result, we haven't built a credible base yet. The measures are just now on board. The tracking has just begun.

Wilson felt that some of the BSC measures were not critical for customer satisfaction goals, nor actionable. He explained:

We have an internal measure called "Trailway to Trolls" [Trolls are unhappy customers]. This index aggregates over a hundred different measures of customer complaints and degrees of dissatisfaction, but it isn't actionable. If the Trailway to Troll Index starts to deteriorate, I don't know if it's been caused by performance that valued customers consider critical, or whether it's a minor matter. When it was first developed, it was quite valuable in focusing management's attention on service quality. But we can't do quality for quality's sake. We need to focus on those dimensions most critical for meeting or exceeding customer expectations of service quality. And to do that we need measures that are actionable.

### *Measuring Customer Profitability*

William Jordan, Managing Director, had market management responsibility for the consumer and small business activities in New York Markets. When asked for his perspective on the BSC, he immediately voiced his support, and expressed, in strategic terms, the fundamental importance of BSC:

We tend to focus on the short term and the month-by-month financials. This makes us excellent at tactics, but sometimes we find it difficult to think strategically about where we should be three to five years out. The Balanced Scorecard provided a forum for

---

**EXHIBIT 6** Retail Bank *News & Views* (Fall 1994): "Customer Focus" (page 3, excerpts)

---

### Segmentation: A Way to Get to Know Our Customers Better

Consumer Market Management recently completed analysis of the files of all 1.2 million deposit households of the Retail Bank and has assigned each household two scores: one indicating current relationship profitability and the second indicating the customer's Financial Personality segment—a strong indicator of potential profitability. The availability of this information is critical progress towards putting segmentation data into action.

Shifting the Customer/Profit Mix in New York Markets

One of our strategic goals is to increase the number of profitable customers. There are two related ways to develop and maintain a more profitable customer base. One is to provide exceptional service with targeted offerings to those customers who are currently highly profitable in order to strengthen the relationship and retain them longer. The other is to encourage customers who are most likely to become profitable to do more business with Chemical. The profit scores and segment codes can help us achieve these ends by helping us identify those customers.

The Segment Coding Process

The data-gathering process began with a comprehensive study involving 2,000 customers and noncustomers who were asked over 200 questions about how they handled money, their attitudes toward banks, and many other subjects. This initial study resulted in the identification of five financial segments. After establishing the Financial Segmentation framework, Consumer Market Management administered a much shorter questionnaire to more than 25,000 customers.

Measuring Customer Profitability

In addition to the segment codes which have been assigned to all retail deposit customers, actual profitability scores were assigned to customers of record as of December 1993. The profit score incorporates both the revenues and expenses associated with deposits, consumer and shelter loans, and revolving products for each individual household. There are four profitability levels:

**Premier** The most profitable customers.

**High** Profitable because the revenues from fees and spreads more than cover the costs of the products and services we provide them.

**Medium** The bulk of our customers yield a small profit on the products and services we provide them.

**Low** Generate little or no profit for the Retail Bank. In many cases, the revenues generated by their accounts do not cover the costs of providing the services.

How We Will Utilize This Information

During the first quarter of 1995, a profitability and segment information will be available on-line. With information provided in a workbook, a video, and an interactive training disk, branch staff will be able to improve their sales efforts by customer segment and profit score. The ability to identify the most profitable customers for superior service will be made possible with this information. This should ultimately result in more business from our most profitable customers and more profitability for the Bank.

---

senior management to have active discussions about both the present performance and future targets we must achieve. I like the way it forced us to think about revenue opportunity and potential, and how we should measure our progress down the path that will insure our future.

The BSC reinforces the need for a new focus on the customer, especially the need to get to a more profitable mix of customers, and to retain and deepen our relationship with our best customers.

Jordan for years had believed that most of the Retail Bank's small business accounts were profitable. Recently an activity-based cost study had matched "costs to serve" with "revenues earned" down to individual customers. The study showed that only 55% of small business accounts were profitable on a fully loaded basis. This information prompted Jordan to launch several new initiatives to enhance small-business customer profitability. He wanted to know the defining characteristics of profitable and unprofitable customers so that he could begin thinking about how unprofitable accounts could be made profitable by changing earnings credit, or minimum balance, or perhaps introducing fees and better control over fee waivers.

Jordan, however, emphasized:

> Although we have raised our consciousness about strategic measures, the measures are not yet integrated. For 1995, I would like the BSC teams to identify a number of top-of-mind measures, perhaps as few as two or three, that reflect our strategic themes and priorities. I want to see a graphical presentation of the BSC that gives us a five-year view of the journey, and to be able to view short-term performance in terms of progress towards our five-year targets.

### Taking Sales Measures to the Branches

Dave Mooney was implementing one of the first BSC measures—"Selling Contacts per Salesperson"—in the Manhattan branches. He recalled his first impressions of the BSC:

> I remember thinking, as we were going through it, how valuable the process was. It forced us to specify and understand the simple causal linkages from high-level financial objectives to operational measures. The BSC was well accepted because it was very consistent with our management philosophy to focus on activities, process, and components that, according to our theory of linkages, must be accomplished to produce the outcomes we desire.
>
> But as simple as that sounds, we weren't working the fundamental processes. Like most other banks, we had been managing by hammering on outcomes. We kept telling people, "Get more deposits!"
>
> In the summer of 1993, we started to focus on a measure at the beginning of the causal chain—how to make more sales contacts with customers. We now realized that a necessary condition to produce new sales was for our

sales people to have more customer contacts. So my first step was to ask for 10 *completed* contacts per sales person every week. The sales people responded, "We can't do that. We're too busy." But we dug in and told them that we were serious about this objective. Selling was no longer to be an optional or discretionary activity, to be done if time allowed. Selling must become something that you find time to do.

Mooney emphasized the importance of taking hold and managing the problem at that point. "There is an important lesson here," he said. "Measures don't manage. The BSC gave us an engine, but it was management that had to put the vehicle in motion." Mooney was asked why the Balanced Scorecard was required to encourage sales people to do more selling. He replied:

> A lot of ideas were converging at the same time. We were just putting into place a more formal, highly structured customer calling process that produced the customer-contact measure. But then this measure had to survive a highly competitive debate that the senior management team put all prospective measures through to create the BSC. My confidence increased about the importance of that measure and of the selling activity. The great value of the BSC was that it articulated the key levers of performance and reduced these to a few important drivers.

He recalled that implementation became easier when the first results of increasing sales contacts with customers were known:

> We started to see phenomenal results, two and a half to three product sales for every 10 contacts. That helped. But there was something else going on as well. People learned that the senior executives at the bank were not going to stop caring about this measure. The four or five people who ran the branch districts knew I was going to have to report out on the measure to Jack Stack and Mike Hegarty. That's one of the powerful features of the BSC: it's both motivating and obligating. The BSC forced us to stay on track and to follow up.

## *Looking Ahead*

When asked to assess the current status of the BSC, Francavilla stressed that the work was well under way but nowhere near complete.

> The scorecard has been very useful in helping us better understand the key drivers of our business. Our monthly financial review meetings have now become strategic review sessions with some excellent learning and idea generation.
>
> But the BSC is still a senior- and middle-management tool, a work in progress that we are not yet ready to introduce to the entire organization. If you were to walk into any branch in Manhattan today and ask how things are going with the BSC, they wouldn't know what you're talking about.

He and LoFrumento were intent on refining the BSC for 1995, hoping to identify fewer and better measures. They continued to live with the frustration of finding that certain measures were harder to get than they had anticipated. In 1994, they had contracted with an outside vendor to track customer retention data. After months of reported "progress," the vendor finally admitted that it could not deliver the data. The implementation team had therefore assigned this task to an in-house expert.

At the same time, LoFrumento felt that they had come a long way:

> There's a lot we know we have to do, things like being able to track customer acquisition and retention. But we're probably ahead of the competition. Most banks are working with aggregate bottom-line information. They may know that 20% of their customers are generating most of their profits, but they don't know who those customers are. They are still living in a world where a marketing program would be hailed as a success for bringing 10,000 checking accounts into a bank—and the bank would never know that 9,000 of those accounts were going to lose money.
>
> We are well beyond that point. We now have three million accounts in our data base, and we can do any number of cross cuts on those accounts. We can look at deposits, credit cards, and very soon loans, and know just how profitable each account and each customer is.

Francavilla added that knowledge of customer segments and customer profitability was already driving the pricing of some products, and was allowing the bank to be far more sophisticated in designing new products and marketing programs.

In summing up, Francavilla said that there was more to be done on the infrastructure. "We've just scratched the surface on the power of Lotus Notes, for instance. Not just for E-mail but the database side," he said. "And, of course, BSC itself is a tool that we will apply increasingly more rigorously as it improves." Then he went on to describe a future that would find performance goals, and performance reviews, aligned to the BSC. And once that happened he and LoFrumento expected that results would follow.

Lee Wilson concurred that for the BSC to truly drive behavior, it would have to be linked to compensation of senior executives:

> In 1994, the size of the compensation pool was tied to financial measures and BSC measures, such as customer satisfaction and customer retention. In 1995, we are making linkages much more explicit between BSC measures and the compensation to Top-20 executives. In future years, we will drive this process down through the organization.

Mike Hegarty summarized his views on the BSC:

> I like the BSC because it is both a forward-thinking tool and one that will supply the measures that will drive improved performance in our branches. And while BSC is not promoted in the branches under the name "BSC," it is visible in the branches. For example, if an ATM at a given branch isn't serviced, a computerized monitoring system will make a phone call to a branch manager and tell her that ATM number 3 will go down

in 10 minutes. And if a branch manager should, say, decide to let three ATMs go down, the computer will call Dave Mooney and give him a status report.

The team that made that kind of monitoring possible understands how that all fits with BSC, but the branch manager probably doesn't think of it that way. The 2,000 tellers in our branches will be able to tell you the dozens of things we are tracking—from customer satisfaction data to cleanliness in the ATM areas—but they won't know it by the name BSC.

By the end of the year, branch managers will not only tell you what we are tracking but also tell you how they are performing on key measures. They will know, because they will be evaluated on how they perform on designated measures. We will even have bonuses determined by multiple measures that are weighted by revenue contribution to the bank.

I'm not saying we have done it all. One major problem right now is that I have no idea how good my salesforce is. That evaluation is not

happening. We're also just beginning to rethink training, and we will have to find new measures to evaluate that training. But again, that's the virtue of the BSC. It is a tool that can get us to new goals and measures, and then to a process that will take us beyond those measures.

We always had communication. That part isn't new. But the communication was by anecdotes, and not a basis for setting priorities for programs or for resource allocation. The BSC came along in the resource-constrained environment of the 1990s, where excellence in revenue, expense, and investment management would be decisive. The BSC will help us to take the "noise" out of the anecdotes, it will tell us whether we have the right priorities for our activities and whether our activities are in synch with our strategy.

And finally, it provides us with feedback on our strategies, whether they are working and whether we have set our targets high enough. The scorecard is helping us all to learn and to enable change.

---

# UNITED WAY OF SOUTHEASTERN NEW ENGLAND (UWSENE)*

The Balanced Scorecard is really a managerial tool, not a policy tool. A CEO needs to keep the Board fully informed but not overwhelm the members with details and operational decision making. There is a delicate balance about how much information and detail you provide. I certainly report to the board and seek their approval of where I want to take the organization. But the vision is mine. Having said this, I would be comfortable sharing the BSC in depth with the board and reporting how we are doing on the measures.

*Doug Ashby, President,* UWSENE

## History

United Way of Southeastern New England (UWSENE) is a not-for-profit corporation operating in the state of Rhode Island and adjacent communities in Connecticut and Massachusetts. United Way organizations provide services to donors, communities, and social service agencies. They enable individual donors to contribute, in an annual consolidated campaign at their workplace, to a wide range of human service programs in their communities. UWSENE conducts workplace campaigns at over 900 work establishments. A separate mail campaign solicits thousands of individual givers not associated with a workplace. United Way organizations provide community services by giving local

*Professor Robert S. Kaplan and Research Associate Ellen L. Kaplan prepared this case.

human service agencies access to the fundraising capabilities of United Way. UWSENE directly funds more than 100 agencies through its Community Care Fund and Critical Issues Funds allocation processes. In addition, a donor choice option enables individuals to reach directly many additional agencies (more than 1,300 in 1995). UWSENE also provides agencies and other funders with information and technical assistance to assist in program planning, service coordination, and service improvement. Its community building initiatives support community development, children and families, welfare reform, and jobs.

Consolidated fund raising in Rhode Island originated in 1926 to eliminate the inefficiency and disorganization caused by having each individual social service agency conduct its own annual fund-raising drive. The first Providence Community Chest drive raised its goal of $442,000. The organization subsequently was known as The Providence–Cranston Community Chest, the Red Feather, and the United War Fund. Over time, the federation of separate drives throughout towns and cities in Rhode Island, and nearby communities in Massachusetts and Connecticut, coalesced into the United Way of Southeastern New England. In 1995, UWSENE raised more than $17.4 million from about 68,000 donors; 63% from workplace campaigns, 21% from corporate gifts, and 16% from individual and foundation contributions.

UWSENE has an endowment of $50 million, the largest endowment of any United Way in the country. The income from this endowment, of about $2.5 million per year, and other income of about $400,000, covers all of UWSENE's fund-raising and management expenses. The endowment enables the organization to offer a guarantee that 100% of all funds collected from donor contributions will flow to community services.

Competition had emerged even in UWSENE's charitable and volunteer-based industry. Since the 1970s, the number of not-for-profit agencies seeking funding had tripled, and several of them had formed new federations to seek access to workplace campaigns. In addition, many organizations, such as hospitals, colleges, and the arts, had greatly expanded their fund-raising capabilities. Nationally, United Way's share of total philanthropy dollars was shrinking. Locally, UWSENE's share of agency budgets had fallen from the 40% level in 1975 to an average of about 10% in the mid-1990s.

UWSENE faced particular local challenges with declines in regional employment, downsizing and relocation of large corporate divisions, and shifts in employment to small, entrepreneurial enterprises. At the same time, increases in substance abuse, homelessness, single-parent households, and unemployment were increasing in the urban areas and old industrial communities served by UWSENE-funded agencies throughout Rhode Island.

### Organization

Doug Ashby was president of UWSENE from 1987 to 1996, a period in which the organization had enjoyed fund-raising increases that were among the highest in New England.[1] Six vice presidents reported directly to Ashby: five executive vice presidents responsible for finance, donor services, community services, management information systems, and organizational development and marketing and a senior vice president of communications. Of the seven senior staff, three held MBAs, two had Bachelor's degrees, and two had Master's degrees—in social planning and communications. There were 40 additional staff providing profes-

---

[1] In late 1995, Ashby announced his intentions to resign on June 30, 1996.

sional and support services: 25 salaried and 15 hourly employees. UWSENE's president reported to a 21-member board of directors. The board consisted of representatives of UWSENE's constituent groups, primarily corporations, agencies, unions, and local government. The volunteer board of directors met monthly and was responsible for setting policy. In addition, UWSENE had an extensive volunteer committee system to make recommendations to the board on specific policy issues. For example, the finance committee, with staff assistance, made recommendations on all major financial matters. An extensive volunteer system, involving hundreds of individuals each year, assisted in donor and agency services.

In 1990, Ashby, with the support of senior managers and key volunteers, had developed and gained acceptance of mission and vision statements for UWSENE (see Exhibit 1). In

1991, the board began work on a five-year strategic plan based on the vision. Also, in 1991, Ashby and senior staff initiated a major effort to instill a total quality management (TQM) culture in the organization. By December 1991, the president and senior staff had developed the Eight Elements of Continuous Improvement (See Exhibit 2) and received approval from the board of directors and all the staff. Senior management would, through their actions and practices, set the leadership for improving customer satisfaction. They would involve all employees in activities and behaviors that would make UWSENE a more successful organization. During 1992, Ashby distributed copies of Stephen Covey's *Seven Habits of Highly Effective People* and developed a full-day workshop to encourage employees to translate the message into a framework for individual and organizational growth.

---

**EXHIBIT 1**  Mission and Vision Statement

---

**Mission: Increase the Organized Capacity of People to Care for One Another.**

**Vision Statement**

We see a future in which every person can have adequate food and shelter. Every individual can be safe from abuse and violence. Every individual in our community can learn to read. Everyone in our community can be healthier in significant, measurable ways. Every individual can have a drug-free future. Every child can succeed in becoming a happy, productive adult. Every elderly person can have a dignified life. Every individual can live in a clean and healthy environment. Every disabled person can live up to his/her full potential. And family life can be enhanced for everyone.

Our vision rests on the values inherent in private philanthropy and our belief that community needs, donor needs, and agency needs are one and the same. To bring about our vision, United Way will be an organization of the best volunteers and staff working together to:

- Increase private philanthropy for health services through a communitywide campaign
- Increase understanding of urgent community problems through year-round communications with donors, agencies, and other public and private institutions
- Increase value to donors through an inclusive system of donor choice
- Increase support to quality not-for-profit agencies that accomplish specific, measurable results
- Increase cooperation and develop alliances with public and private groups
- Increase our influence on public policy related to health and human service issues

To successfully implement these long-term community problem-solving strategies:

- We must ensure that our strategic direction, goals, and activities are aligned with our vision.
- We must ensure efficient and effective internal services to support the achievement of United Way's vision.
- We must constantly strive for the highest level of volunteer and staff excellence.

---

**EXHIBIT 2** Eight Elements of Continuous Improvement

---

1. **Integrated Planning for Results** —All of the components of our planning effort—mission, vision, strategic plan, annual plan, and plans for departments and individuals—will be consistent with each other and will form a continuous, smooth cycle of operations. We will develop measurable objectives at each step in the process and regularly measure our progress. The end result of integrated planning is a cohesive, customer-focused, results-focused plan that drives our United Way forward as it is executed.

2. **Customer Focus** —United Way's customer groups include donors, agencies, recipients, volunteers, and staff. The needs of each customer group will be understood and satisfied to the utmost of our ability. Satisfied customers will be the most important measure of our success.

3. **Benchmarking** —To achieve excellence, we will seek out those businesses, United Ways, and other organizations who "do it best," find out how they do it, and import those ideas and programs as standards for our organization. Then we will improve our efforts until we meet or exceed those standards.

4. **Employee Involvement** —All employees will be encouraged to participate through multiple opportunities to make suggestions and in planning, decision making, and problem solving. Supervisors and department heads will set an example by seeking out and being open to diverse ideas and opinions, by responding to every idea with respect and appreciation, and by coaching employees to take risks and try new ideas.

5. **Teamwork** —Everyone in the organization will be an active, contributing member of various teams. Everyone will be able to see how his or her role is an integral part of achieving our goals. Participation on teams—one's own department, cross-functional project teams, and continuous improvement teams—will be the vehicle to achieving success. Teamwork will be facilitated through strong, ongoing employee communication efforts.

6. **Training—Training—Training** —Learning is never over. At every level of the organization, new knowledge will be systematically and purposefully acquired and deployed. We will develop a training program that involves the whole organization on topics of major importance and will provide targeted training for departments and individuals to expand their capacity to do their jobs and achieve their goals, such as workshops, readings, and conferences, lectures, skills development.

7. **Research-Based Decision Making** —Decision making will be based on facts, not best guesses or assumptions based on limited information. Ongoing market research, community needs analysis, special studies, and staying close to the customer are our most reliable tools for finding out what is going on and responding effectively.

8. **Performance- and Skill-Based Compensation** —We will reward the accomplishment of what we set out to achieve, not just what happens. We will develop performance standards and skill level standards that, when attained, will be rewarded with employee growth and advancement and incentives for results achieved. Programs will be designed to celebrate individual, team, department, and organization success.

---

As part of the continuous improvement commitment, UWSENE collected and reported extensive information about operations. Financial summaries of cash flow, payables, and receivables were reviewed daily by the controller. Each month, management and the board reviewed financial statements that tracked collections, other revenues, investments, disbursements, and the balance sheet. Statistics on individual, company, and division giving were scrutinized daily during the annual campaign. Trends in donor designation and satisfaction were also monitored. As part of the employee empow-

erment initiative, UWSENE began an annual employee satisfaction survey and also started to track dollars spent on training and number of courses taken. Ashby commented on the importance of TQM for the organization:

> In the past, the United Way customers were told to give, and they gave. They felt good about it, but they didn't have an alternative since we were almost a monopoly. But with increased competition, we woke up one day and noticed our customers were going away. TQM has been a savior, focusing us on listening to the customer. If the customer doesn't agree with what you're doing, even if you've been around for 100 years, you won't

be successful. So we picked up the ball and shaped TQM to fit a not-for-profit. We worked on providing consistent quality and reducing our cycle time. Customers want answers right now, today. That's what we're working on.

UWSENE submitted an application in 1994 to the United Way national competition for the Excellence in Service Quality Award, modeled after the private-sector Malcolm Baldrige National Quality Award. The agency received the Bronze Award, signifying "a formal prevention-based system deployed and used in many major areas, with evidence of positive trends caused by the approach."

### Launching the Balanced Scorecard

In late 1995, Doug Ashby received a phone call from United Way of America (UWA) to determine whether he would be interested in a pilot project. Faculty from the Social Enterprises (SE) interest group at the Harvard Business School (HBS) had contacted UWA asking it to participate in a joint research program to investigate the applicability of a new performance measurement approach, called the Balanced Scorecard (BSC), developed for the corporate private sector. The BSC retained *financial measures* but supplemented these with the drivers of future performance: *customers, internal business processes*, and *learning and growth*. The BSC's emphasis on non-financial dimensions of performance seemed quite applicable to not-for-profit organizations. The request came at a propitious time for UWSENE. Ashby knew that the five-year strategic plan adopted in 1991 was nearing the end of its cycle. He felt that the current planning process was not sufficiently integrated with the organization's quality initiative and envisioned that the BSC might provide the missing linkages. He consulted with his senior staff, and they agreed to learn more about the proposed project.

An HBS team conducted a morning briefing session for the seven senior managers in January 1996 at the Providence offices of UWSENE. The session introduced the BSC, gave examples of how it was working in private-sector companies, and what the benefits might be in a not-for-profit setting. After the meeting, the management team concurred that this approach might help them achieve even greater alignment of employees to UWSENE's vision and mission. Before proceeding, however, they wanted to expose all of their professional employees to the concept and gain their approval and commitment to the project. One month later, the HBS team gave an afternoon briefing to all the staff. After a lively discussion, the organization agreed to go forward with developing a Balanced Scorecard for UWSENE.

### Developing the Scorecard

Eileen Moser, Executive Vice President of Organizational Development and Marketing, was selected to be the senior manager responsible for spearheading the BSC project. Moser had directed the implementation of the TQM effort at UWSENE. Under Moser's direction, Kelly Nevins, Director of Donor Services, assumed the role of on-site facilitator. An outside consultant, Ellen Lasher, volunteered to facilitate the scorecard-building process.

Moser launched the project with a series of brainstorming meetings and senior-level interviews, facilitated by Lasher and Nevins. During these initial meetings and interviews, managers were challenged to translate the mission of UWSENE—*increase the organized capacity of people to care for one another*—into meaningful, measurable objectives. They attempted to identify the critical drivers for strategic success and to reach a consensus on the highest priorities for achievement and improvement at UWSENE.

The senior staff found it relatively easy to agree on objectives for the financial and the learning and growth perspectives. For example, the financial objectives stressed the cost-effective generation of funds. The learning and growth perspective emphasized employee development and alignment with organizational goals. Much more debate occurred about who were the customers of UWSENE, what were the drivers of customer satisfaction, and which were the internal business processes that would deliver the products and services valued by customers.

Several constituencies could have been represented in the customer perspective: donors, volunteers, employees, agencies, and the individuals who were the ultimate recipients or consumers of agency services. Ashby framed the choice:

> United Ways have three primary choices. They can be donor-focused, agency-focused, or community-focused.
>
> With a donor-focused organization, you let the donors have free rein about their funding decisions. A significant proportion of donors will allocate their money outside traditional United Way member agencies, and these agencies will get less money. Funds will be more widely and differently dispersed.
>
> An agency-focused organization would identify and collect the best agencies in the community, ensure that they are well operated, and monitor that they do the best job and provide the best results. The agencies become the power behind the United Way, but agencies outside the system will feel unfairly treated by United Way, will want to access corporate payroll deduction campaigns, and may join with rivals of United Way for this access.
>
> A community focus would identify the most pressing needs of individuals in the community and aim United Way efforts at solving those problems. Success by Six[2] is a good example. The downside of this approach is that many

agencies get left out, and you may not meet the interests and needs of many of your donors.

> Each of the three strategies is good, with the potential to yield positive end results. But each entails considerable downside risk. Many United Ways switch strategies, say, to meet specific community needs, for very good reasons but then are surprised when their agencies and donors get upset. UWSENE has definitely become a donor-focused organization, believing that if the donors are satisfied, then agencies will be provided for. That is why we chose the donor as the primary customer on the scorecard.

With this choice, the objectives for donors on the customer perspective became relatively straightforward to articulate. And the team formulated initial internal business process objectives that would deliver the financial and customer objectives. The team also discussed whether the four perspectives of a for-profit BSC were adequate and appropriate for its scorecard. Lasher suggested adding additional perspectives, say for agencies and for volunteers. Agencies, using United Way funds, supplied needed services to communities. Volunteers, through their board service and extensive participation in the annual campaign, provided substantial personnel resources to UWSENE. Ashby, however, felt that the four basic perspectives had sufficient flexibility to include objectives that would address the organization's relationship with agencies and volunteers.

The decision to exclude agencies remained a concern through the remainder of the project. Moser admitted that by excluding agencies from the BSC a gap existed:

> We could not sort through the issues of whether agencies are suppliers or customers. They are definitely a constituency, but where do we put them? We've been arguing about this for years, and this process has brought it home one more time, big-time. This issue is hanging out there like a red flag because we've got to figure out the meaningful relationships that we should have with our agencies.

---

[2]This initiative was a strategy to improve the education and well-being of children under six years old.

Lasher also suggested that the BSC might include a perspective to represent the overriding vision of the organization. Unlike for-profit organizations, where excellent financial performance is the ultimate objective, not-for profit organizations use their financial resources to fulfill humanitarian missions. Keeping the mission visible in the BSC would serve as a constant reminder that the ultimate goal of UW was to contribute to the betterment of the community. But the senior staff wanted a BSC that resembled those produced in the private sector and decided to work within the existing four-perspective framework.

### *Employee Involvement*

Ashby, Moser, and other senior managers presented the tentative objectives for the four scorecard perspectives to the entire staff. They assigned employees to the four teams that would refine and define the objectives for each perspective, establish the linkages between perspectives, and determine drivers and measures for the objectives on the scorecard. Employees were assigned based on individual preferences while still trying to achieve a mix of gender, department, level, ethnicity, age and personality type (measured by Myers-Briggs scores).

Initially, employees were both skeptical and concerned about the process. Many saw the BSC as just another "flavor of the month," an effort that would take a substantial amount of time and then fall by the wayside. Others did not want senior managers to get too involved with the process, such as by editing or rejecting the drivers and measures they had selected. These employees saw the BSC as an opportunity for increasing employee empowerment, and they wanted ownership rights without senior management veto rights over their contributions.

Ashby felt that employees had lost sight about the primary purpose of the BSC. It was not a mechanism for employees to make decisions about strategy and objectives. Senior management wanted active staff involvement in contributing to the scorecard, but employees had to realize that senior managers retained the right to edit and eliminate measures. Also, the implementation plan for the scorecard would be the prerogative of senior managers. At the request of senior management, Lasher addressed the ownership issue with the employee teams, discussing with them how they could develop the drivers and measures for the objectives identified by senior management. Ideally, she explained, the final BSC would reflect how staff roles and responsibilities would link to achieving the strategy and vision formulated by senior management.

The internal business process team had the most active debates. One related to how the BSC was linked to the total quality culture at UWSENE. Initially, the team proposed to have dozens of quality measures, one for each major process, on the scorecard. Eventually, they decided to use a few aggregated quality indices, such as *timeliness of processes compared to customer expectations* and *reduction of errors and rework,* to summarize individual process quality performance. The detailed measures of individual process quality would be presented on the relevant departmental scorecard.

The internal business process team also recognized the need to evaluate UWSENE products and services. Several new products and services were added each year, and rarely was an existing product or service eliminated. No methodology existed to review the contribution of new or existing products to the organization. The team struggled with developing an evaluation program, and this became a central focus of the group. The team started to get side-tracked on an issue that, while important, was quite complex and not central to the development of the scorecard. The team agreed to a suggestion made by Lasher to include as a scorecard objective *a timely review of effectiveness of all products and services.* The organization, over time, could establish an initiative to develop a comprehensive evaluation procedure. The BSC identified this objective as critical and strategic; how it would be accomplished was not a BSC issue.

When the teams presented the scorecard to management and management made their final modifications, several staff members were disappointed that changes and cuts had been made to their document. Ashby brought the document back to the teams for a discussion of why the changes had been made. This step succeeded in restoring some goodwill; the staff now felt that management cared about what the teams thought. Not everything was put back in the scorecard, but the teams felt that they had been consulted. Employees remarked, however, that, had Kelly Nevins been involved in the final senior management decisions, their views would have been better represented and fewer alterations would have been made. The staff felt that Nevins, as a midlevel manager and facilitator, was more objective about the scorecard and did not have as much vested interest in the project as Moser and Lasher.

UWSENE reached closure on its initial BSC by the end of June 1996. The objectives and measures in the four perspectives are shown in Exhibit 3. The process had taken about four calendar months and the active involvement of all levels of management. An immediate task was to obtain the data for the BSC. Moser noted:

> Even with all the focus on data gathering and measurement from our TQM program, we still needed new data for some of the scorecard measures. About half the measures will require repackaging existing data or gathering entirely new data.

The BSC was handed over to departments and teams to develop stretch targets and initiatives for each measure and to assign responsibility for each measure. The responsibility included specified dates for reporting on results: monthly, quarterly, or annually.

## Balanced Scorecard and Total Quality Management

Some employees wondered about how the BSC related to the organization's TQM program. The senior managers believed that the BSC provided a valuable complement to UWSENE's TQM efforts. Moser noted an important connection:

> In many not-for-profits, the strategic plan can be very much board driven, while quality is a staff initiative. This leads to a large disconnect between strategy and operations. Even in our organization, where senior staff are heavily involved in both planning and quality, the two efforts were far apart. We tried, with our strategic planning structure, to bring the two pieces together, but it was too complex. With the BSC, we now see what we have to do to accomplish our mission and fulfill our vision. The BSC gave us a structure that linked our quality initiatives to the strategic plan. For example, by building a new system to measure the success of a new product, we're building quality into our business processes.

Ashby concurred:

> The BSC gave us a way to pull all the pieces together with some specific measures. Rather than have each department come up with its own goals, the BSC demonstrated how the organizational efforts fit together and how departments coordinated with one another. We could now look at UWSENE as a single interconnected system.

Bill Allen, Executive Vice President of Community Services, also agreed with the connection:

> The BSC provided a unity and focus to our TQM efforts, and also to our annual and long-

**EXHIBIT 3**  Strategic Objectives and Measures in Four Perspectives—Balanced Scorecard

| PERSPECTIVE | OUTCOMES | STRATEGIC OBJECTIVES | MEASURES |
|---|---|---|---|
| Financial | External growth | Increase net amount of funds raised. | Achieve targeted annual giving in all categories (employee, corporate leadership, etc.). |
| | | | Broaden mix of sources of funds (special events, grants, endowment, new products, etc.). |
| | | | Achieve targeted number of donors in each category. |
| | Internal stability | Balance internal income and expenses to maintain our 100% guarantee to donors. | Achieve a balanced internal budget. |
| | | | Reserve funds as a targeted percentage of operating budget. |
| | | | Achieve targeted internal income. |
| | | | Achieve targeted internal expense |
| | Community building | Increase amount of funds that go to services. | Achieve targeted dollar amount of funds sent to agencies. |
| | | Increase amount of funds that go to proprietary products. | Achieve targeted dollar amounts of funds sent to proprietary products (CCF, CI, Phil Fund). |
| Customer | Customer satisfaction | Recognition | Customer feedback on current recognition programs |
| | | | Strong recognition programs for donors and volunteers |
| | | | Customer wants and needs regarding recognition |
| | | Ease of giving | Low level of error or rework |
| | | | Donor satisfaction survey |
| | Market growth | Products that customers care about and that will improve the community | Identify products that customers want and will invest in. |
| | | | Assess results achieved by products. |
| | Customer retention | Information on results | Increase frequency of testing donor perception of and satisfaction with results through surveys and other feedback mechanisms. |
| | | | Track the number of information vehicles and success stories providing results, and assess their effectiveness. |
| | | Quality, timely service | Reduce errors and cycle time in customer service. |
| | | | Identify customer expectations for "timely" service regarding products, inquiries, information, complaints. |
| | | | Track number of opportunities we give customers to give us feedback on our service. |
| | | | Improve customer retention rate. |
| Internal business process | Key internal business processes based on quality | Improve key internal processes in the following areas: Fund raising Fund distribution Community building | Timeliness of process vis-à-vis customer requirements |

**EXHIBIT 3** Strategic Objectives and Measures in Four Perspectives—Balanced Scorecard
*continued*

| PERSPECTIVE | OUTCOMES | STRATEGIC OBJECTIVES | MEASURES |
|---|---|---|---|
| | | Information processing/ communications | Steps in process have a value-add to customer |
| | | Pledge processing | Reduce error rate and rework |
| | | Product development | Timeliness of information/feedback per customer requirement |
| | | Volunteer/staff develop--ment | |
| | | Customer service | |
| | | Interdepartmental communications | |
| | Develop innovative products | Develop a research and development process to come up with new, innovative products. | A process to generate and evaluate new products/services will be in place within one year. |
| | | | Number of products or services the new system generates and evaluates. |
| | | | Number of new products or services that do not go through the process. |
| | Maintain viable product line | Develop a consistent process for evaluating existing products and services. | Process for product/service evaluation will be in place within one year. |
| | | | Number of products/services evaluated by new process. |
| | | | Number of products/services changed, improved, or discontinued due to evaluation. |
| | | | Level of customer satisfaction with products/services after improvement. |
| Learning and growth | Employee productivity | Training and development | Percentage of employees with a training plan developed in conjunction with supervisor |
| | | | Number of opportunities for training |
| | | | Number of training hours |
| | | Technology | Extent of technology deployment |
| | | | Degree of skill/advancement in use of technology |
| | | Teamwork | Number of active teams that exist |
| | | | Number of successful teams that have "produced" something in the past year |
| | Employee satisfaction | Open and effective communication | Number of communications opportunities |
| | | | Employee satisfaction survey |
| | | Employee ownership and involvement | Percentage of employees with a BSC for his/her position |
| | | | Number of opportunities for employee empowerment/involvement |
| | | Agency assistance | Training and development resources that improve agencies |

range planning. We had a lot of teams doing a lot of things, but the efforts were ad hoc. Our TQM experience gave us a strong emphasis on teamwork and on good data gathering and measurement. The BSC brought this all together into a unified systematic approach. Now when we develop teams or assign responsibilities to departments, we do it within a framework. That's why we have been so excited about it.

### Reactions to the BSC

Nevins had played a critical role in facilitating the employee teams that worked on the scorecard. She commented on how it should be used on an ongoing basis:

> When each department formulates objectives each year, we should make sure that everything we do is on the BSC. If not, we should question whether we should do it. Or if we're doing something because we think it is important, then why isn't it on the BSC. For the BSC to be effective, it must be a living document. Each year, as the organization reviews our annual objectives and formulates next year's objectives, it must modify the BSC to reflect the new priorities.

Moser concurred:

> The BSC needs to be driven by senior management. Any roadblock will come from us, since the staff want the senior managers to keep them involved, to hold everyone's feet to the fire. They worked very hard on the BSC, and they want to see it happen.

> The president and the senior managers have the responsibility to revisit the BSC with their staff and update it on a regular basis. This document can really direct our energies and help us eliminate a lot of the busy work and things we shouldn't be doing.

For example, the organization had been sponsoring a partnership with a local elementary school. Developing the BSC had raised the issue of whether to continue this initiative since it didn't seem to relate to any objective or measure on the BSC. Nevins noted the enthusiasm among the staff for the BSC.

> Everyone was involved in it. People could speak up. We had different teams providing input. We used to have strategic plans handed down from on high, and there wasn't the buy-in we now have from the BSC. It should start to change behavior.

> In the past, if you raised more money than the previous year, you felt that you had done a good job. But those departments not involved with fund raising didn't get any recognition for the success of the organization. Now we will look to all the BSC measures to assess our success in reaching our goals. Each employee can be seen as making an important contribution. Even someone who just writes letters sees that this task is critical for our fund-raising objective. Recognition will be spread around the table.

One manager, however, was disappointed in the lack of an overriding mission on the scorecard:

> The final document seemed like a much colder document than I would have imagined for an organization that is so mission-driven. Our scorecard doesn't have a feeling component to it. It seems so dry. Maybe it's only because of where I am in the organization, in community services, where the work that the few of us do here is so mission-driven, it carries a passionate meaning to us. The only way that seems to be captured is half of a phrase, "improve the community." And product, it's hard for us to think what we do is a product. I'm surprised at what the BSC looks like, though it is technically accurate.

But most expressed enthusiasm for the scorecard; as one middle manager said:

> You can relate to the BSC. It shows where you fit in the organization. You can see how you contribute to the customer or financial needs of the organization and to staff advancement. It's nice to feel that what you're doing is worthwhile, that it relates to the big picture. I learned things I never knew, even after working here five years. I heard a lot of people say "I never knew that!"

Scott Famigletti, chief financial officer, related a conversation with United Way's custodian about the BSC:

> Initially he felt that the BSC was only for senior management, not him. His job was to plow snow, paint walls, and remove trash, and these didn't have anything to do with strategy or mission. I explained that his efforts were very important to us. We generate considerable rental income from tenants in our building. By maintaining the property well, tenants and United Way employees will be pleased to work in the facility. That will help us generate more rental income that helps us fulfill our 100% guarantee to donors and also to attract, retain, and motivate our employees. In addition, donors and volunteers who visit our building will value a clean building, attractive landscaping, and streets from which the snow has been removed. I could see the light of recognition cross his face. He said, "You're right; I can see now how what I do is important." The BSC lets every employee see how he or she fits into the organization.

Another employee reacted similarly to the BSC:

> From the secretaries' point of view, we never felt like we fit in the picture. But we really do; we just didn't know it. The scorecard made me think of the little things I do every day that I never thought mattered, but I now see are important.

> I created my own individual BSC. You don't take as much ownership in a departmental scorecard as you do in an individual one. I can now see how to do things differently to help balance the internal budget. For example, someone tells me to subscribe to magazines. But we never determine if anyone actually reads these magazines. Are we just spending money on magazines to put at the front desk? Also, do we have duplicate subscriptions? I plan to start a project to determine which magazines are really useful to us. We get lots of magazines, and we could certainly cut costs by eliminating many of them.

Moser commented, however, that not everyone embraced the concept:

> Some people in the organization just don't do well with change. They are unwilling to participate and resist any new initiative.

## The Board and the Balanced Scorecard

During his tenure as president of UWSENE, Ashby had worked closely with the chairman of his board of directors, Richard Plotkin, a CPA and managing partner of a regional accounting firm. Ashby and Plotkin had been in close contact, sometimes speaking three times a day. Ashby planned to present the completed scorecard to the board as a working document that could be modified based on board reactions. Plotkin noted: "The board has been informed about the Balanced Scorecard and is very supportive of it. At this time, however, the board is not as knowledgeable as it should be. More board involvement with the BSC would be desirable."

Bill Allen, who would be acting president after Ashby retired from UWSENE, believed that the scorecard would improve communication with the board:

> We will be able to provide organized, regular reports to the board on our progress on the strategic plan. Here is the plan, here's what we want to do, here's how we will measure it, here's when the data will be available, and this is when we'll have a report based on the measurements that we define. It should enable the board to play a more active role in the management of the organization.

Ashby agreed that the BSC would prove a more effective communication device:

> Many not-for-profit boards get too focused on organizational finances. Money is something that everyone can relate to and is interested in. Every month, the board sees a financial report, and often that is the first item on the agenda. I've participated in meetings where 75% of the time was taken up by the financials and only 25% by what is being done with the money. The Balanced Scorecard should provide an opportunity to broaden the discussions at board meetings.

Plotkin indicated how the BSC could improve board deliberations:

Board members are willing to work hard if they feel they are actually contributing to the organization. I am always searching for ways to increase participation at our meetings. The BSC can facilitate interaction by defining a more intense dialogue. Right now, the board advises, and that's the limit of our involvement.

Building the scorecard, however, while a search process for a new president was being conducted, had raised concerns. Ashby reported:

Everyone on the staff wonders whether the new president will buy into the BSC. We've made such an investment in the document that it would be very hard for a new person to come in and just dump it. People would just not have the energy to start work on another model. So a lot depends on the style and mindset of the new person who walks in this door. That is the enormous question mark. The staff wants to go forward, and somebody will have to pay a high price to discard the scorecard.

Moser, however, felt that an opportunity may have been missed:

Several presentations were made to the board about the BSC, but the members did not have any involvement. Our board is a brain trust of people with great understanding, and we missed an opportunity to use that resource and get a perspective that was not available from a purely staff-driven project.

Ashby commented on the impact of the BSC on the current search process:

The board's search committee is reluctant to say to an incoming executive, "You must use this document." They want to give the next executive the opportunity to shape his or her own systems, initiatives, and management processes. Had the scorecard been in place at the time of the search process, I believe it would have been quite helpful to the board. But these two events were happening concurrently.

Plotkin, who was chairing the search committee for Ashby's replacement, wondered how the scorecard project should influence the search for the new chief executive:

I think the new CEO should welcome the BSC with open arms and not feel threatened by it. We certainly want leadership that values quality and new ideas. Then again, the new CEO might not like to have his or her hands tied in this way. This could become an issue because of the commitment that senior and middle management now have to the BSC.

Ultimately, the BSC should improve UWSENE and help it to push out the envelope of performance. Board involvement with the BSC is the key to its long-term success. The board must be part of the process, because the BSC defines the strategy of the organization.

## MOBIL USM&R (A1)*

From what I can see, we had a good quarter even though financial results were disappointing. The poor results were caused by unusually warm winter weather that depressed sales of natural gas and home

*Professor Robert S. Kaplan prepared this case. Mr. Ed Lewis of Mobil's Business and Performance Analysis group provided invaluable assistance.

Copyright © 1996 by the President and Fellows of Harvard College. Harvard Business School case 197-120.

heating oil. But market shares in our key customer segments were up. Refinery operating expenses were down. And the results from our employee-satisfaction survey were high. In all the areas we could control, we moved the needle in the right direction.

Bob McCool, executive vice president of Mobil Corporation's U.S. Marketing and Refining (USM&R) Division, had just commented on first quarter 1995 results. One executive thought to himself: "This is a total departure from the past. Here was a senior Mobil executive publicly saying, 'Hey, we didn't make any money this quarter but I feel good about where the business is going.'"

## Mobil U.S. Marketing & Refining

Mobil Corporation, headquartered in Fairfax, Virginia, and with operations in more than 100 countries is, with Exxon and Shell, among the world's top three integrated oil, gas, and petrochemicals companies. Mobil's 1995 return-on-capital-employed of 12.8% ranked it fourth among the 14 major integrated oil companies; its 19.1% average annual return to shareholders from 1991 to 1995 was the highest among the 14 major oil companies and exceeded the average annual return on the S&P 500 by more than 2 percentage points. Summary sales and earnings information are shown in Exhibit 1.

The corporation consists of five major divisions: Exploration & Producing (the "upstream" business), Marketing & Refining (the "downstream" business), Chemical, Mining & Minerals, and Real Estate. The Marketing & Refining (M&R) Division processes crude oil into fuels, lubricants, petrochemical feed-

stocks and other products at 20 refineries in twelve countries. M&R also distributes Mobil products to 19,000 service stations and other outlets in more than 100 countries. Total product sales had grown more than 5% per year over the past five years.

The United States Marketing & Refining (USM&R) Division was the fifth-largest U.S. refiner. It operated five state-of-the-art refineries, and its more than 7,700 Mobil-branded service stations sold about 23 million gallons per day of gasoline. This represented a 7% national share (number four in the United States). Mobil's retail network was highly concentrated. In the eighteen states where it sold nearly 95% of its gasoline, Mobil had a 12% market share. Mobil was also the largest marketer of finished lubricants in the United States, with a 12% market share and recent growth rates of about 3%, especially in premium quality blends.

In 1992, USM&R had reported an operating loss from its refining and marketing operations, and ranked 12 out of 13 oil companies in profitability from U.S. marketing and refining operations.[1] A profit tunaround started

---

[1] "Benchmarking the Integrated Oils, 1995," U.S. Research (Goldman Sachs, July 15, 1996), pp. 83, 85.

---

**EXHIBIT 1** Mobil Summary Financial Information, 1991–1995 (000,000)

| REVENUES, JUNE 19, 1997 | 1991 | 1992 | 1993 | 1994 | 1995 |
|---|---|---|---|---|---|
| Revenues | $63,311 | $64,456 | $63,975 | $67,383 | $75,370 |
| Operating earnings | 1,894 | 1,488 | 2,224 | 2,231 | 2,846 |
| Capital and exploration expenditures | 5,053 | 4,470 | 3,656 | 3,825 | 4,268 |
| Capital employed at year-end | 25,804 | 25,088 | 25,333 | 24,946 | 24,802 |
| Debt-to-capital ratio | 32% | 34% | 32% | 31% | 27% |
| Rates of return based on: | | | | | |
|   Average S/H equity | 10.9% | 8.8% | 13.2% | 13.2% | 16.2% |
|   Industry average | | | | 10.0% | 14.0% |
|   Average capital employed | 9.4% | 7.5% | 10.2% | 10.3% | 12.8% |
|   Industry average | | | | 8.1% | 10.0% |

**EXHIBIT 2**  U.S. Marketing and Refining: Financial Summary, 1991–1995 (000,000)

|  | 1991 | 1992 | 1993 | 1994 | 1995 |
|---|---|---|---|---|---|
| Sales and services |  |  |  |  |  |
| Refined petroleum products | $10,134 | $10,504 | $10,560 | $10,920 | $ 2,403 |
| Other sales and services | 3,879 | 3,702 | 3,481 | 3,522 | 3,698 |
| Total sales and services | $14,013 | $14,206 | $14,041 | $14,442 | $16,101 |
| Excise and state gasoline taxes | 2,421 | 2,606 | 2,957 | 3,663 | 3,965 |
| Other revenues | 80 | 118 | 90 | 88 | 108 |
| Total revenues | $16,514 | $16,930 | $17,088 | $18,193 | $20,174 |
| Operating costs and expenses | 16,304 | 17,125 | 16,822 | 17,792 | 19,796 |
| Pretax operating profit | 210 | $ (195) | $ 266 | $ 401 | $ 378 |
| Income taxes | 94 | (50) | 115 | 160 | 152 |
| Total USM&R earnings | $ 116 | $ (145) | $ 151 | $ 241 | $ 226 |
| Special items | (96) | (128) | (145) | (32) | (104) |
| USM&R operating earnings | $ 212 | $ (17) | $ 296 | $ 273 | $ 330 |
| Assets at year-end | $ 6,653 | $ 7,281 | $ 7,248 | $ 7,460 | $ 7,492 |
| Capital employed at year-end | 4,705 | 5,286 | 5,071 | 5,155 | 5,128 |
| Earnings: gasoline and distillate |  |  |  |  |  |
| (cents/gallon) | 3.6 | 0.2 | 3.7 | 4.1 | 4.6 |
| (Industry average) | 3.5 | 2.2 | 4.0 | 3.6 | 2.6 |
| Return on assets | 4.2% | (0.2%) | 5.2% | 4.8% | 5.9% |
| (Industry average) | 7.0 | 4.5 | 7.6 | 6.8 | 4.9 |
| Gasoline market share (top 18 states) |  |  | 11.4% | 11.6% | 11.9% |

in 1993, and earnings and return-on-assets, which had been depressed in 1991 and 1992, soon exceeded industry averages. Summary financial data of the USM&R Division are presented in Exhibit 2.

Until 1994, USM&R was organized functionally. The supply group obtained crude oil and transported it to one of Mobil's refineries. The manufacturing function operated refineries that processed crude oil into products like gasoline, kerosene, heating oil, diesel fuel, jet fuel, lubricants, and petrochemical feedstocks. The product supply organization transported refined petroleum products, through pipelines, barges, and trucks, to regional terminals around the country. The terminal managers received, stored, and managed the extensive inventories of petroleum products and distributed the products to retailers and distributors. The marketing function determined how

USM&R would package, distribute, and sell Mobil products through wholesalers and retailers to end-use consumers.

### Reorganization: 1994

In the early 1990s, USM&R faced an environment with flat demand for gasoline and other petroleum products, increased competition, and limited capital to invest in a highly capital-intense business. McCool recalled:

In 1990 we weren't making any money; in fact there was a half-billion-dollar cash drain. Expenses had doubled, capital had doubled, margins had flattened, and volumes were heading down. You didn't need an MBA to know we were in trouble.

McCool spent the next couple of years attempting to stabilize the business to stop the bleeding: "We succeeded, but then we had to

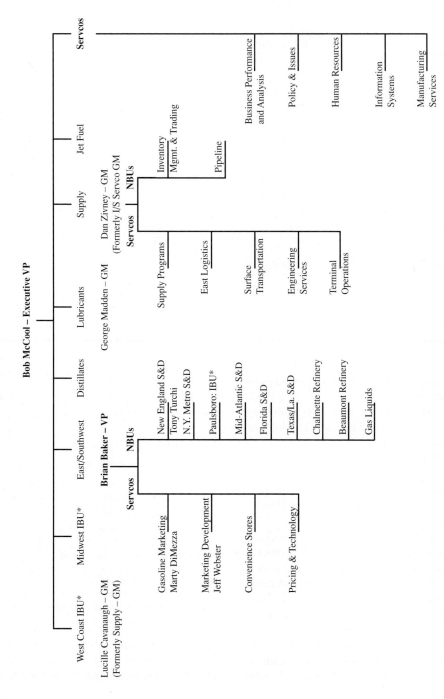

**EXHIBIT 3 USM&R Natural Business (NBUs) and Service Companies (SERVCOs)**

*IBU: Integrated Business Units (Refinery, Sales, Distribution)

412

confront how we could generate future growth."

A climate survey in 1993 revealed that employees felt internal reporting require-ments, administrative processes, and top-down policies were stifling creativity and in-novation. Relationships with customers were adversarial, and people were working nar-rowly to enhance the reported results of their individual, functional units. McCool, with the assistance of external consultants, initiated major studies of business processes and orga-nizational effectiveness. Based on the studies, McCool concluded that if USM&R were to grow, it had to make the most of its existing assets and to focus more intensively on cus-tomers, giving motorists what *they* want, not what the functional specialists in the organi-zation thought motorists should want.

In 1994, McCool decided to decentralize decision making to managers and employees who would be closer to customers. He reor-ganized USM&R into 17 Natural Business Units (NBUs) and 14 Service Companies (see Exhibit 3). The NBUs included (1) sales and distribution units, (2) integrated refining, sales and distribution units, and (3) special-ized product (e.g., distillates, lubricants, gas liquids) and process (stand-alone refinery) units. McCool commented on the need for the reorganization:

> We had grown up as a highly functional organization. We had a huge staff, and they ran the business. We needed to get our staff costs under control. But more important, we had to learn to focus on the customer. We had to get everyone in the organization thinking not how to do their individual job a little bit better, but how to focus all of their energies to enhancing Mobil products and services for customers.

Brian Baker, vice president of USM&R, concurred:

> We were a big central organization that had become a bit cumbersome and perhaps had lost

touch with the customer. We didn't have the ability to move quickly with new marketing programs in various parts of the country.

USM&R's reorganization occurred simul-taneously with a newly developed strategy on customer segmentation. Historically, Mobil, like other oil companies, attempted to main-tain volume and growth by marketing a full range of products and services to all con-sumer segments. The gasoline marketing group had conducted a recent study that re-vealed five distinct consumer segments among the gasoline-buying public (see Ex-hibit 4 for descriptions of the five segments):

- Road Warriors (16%)
- True Blues (16%)
- Generation F3 (27%)
- Homebodies (21%)
- Price (20%)

USM&R decided that its efforts should be focused on the first three of these segments (59% of gasoline buyers), and not attempt to attract the price-sensitive but low-loyalty Price Shopper segment that accounted for only 20% of consumers. The new strategy re-quired a commitment to upgrade all service stations so that they could offer fast, friendly, safe service to the three targeted customer segments. It also required a major shift in the role for Mobil's on-site convenience stores (C-stores). Currently, C-stores were snack shops that catered to gasoline purchasers' im-pulse buying. USM&R wanted to redesign and reorient its C-stores so that they would become a destination stop, offering con-sumers one-stop, convenient shopping for frequently purchased food and snack items.

### USM&R Balanced Scorecard

The newly appointed business unit managers had all grown up within a structured, top-down, functional organization. Some had been district sales managers, others had man-

**EXHIBIT 4** Five Gasoline Buyer Segments

| | |
|---|---|
| Road Warriors (16%) | Generally higher-income middle-aged men who drive 25,000 to 50,000 miles a year, buy premium gasoline with a credit card, purchase sandwiches and drinks from the convenience store, will sometimes wash their cars at the car wash. |
| True Blues (16%) | Usually men and women with moderate to high incomes who are loyal to a brand and sometimes to a particular station; frequently buy premium gasoline and pay in cash. |
| Generation F3 (27%) | (F3—fuel, food, and fast) Upwardly mobile men and women—half under 25 years of age—who are constantly on the go; drive a lot and snack heavily from the convenience store. |
| Homebodies (21%) | Usually housewives who shuttle their children around during the day and use whatever gasoline station is based in town or along their route of travel. |
| Price Shoppers (20%) | Generally aren't loyal to either a brand or a particular station, and rarely buy the premium line; frequently on tight budgets; the focus of attention of marketing efforts of gasoline companies for years. |

aged a pipeline or a regional distribution network. McCool anticipated problems with the transition:

> We were taking people who had spent their whole professional life as managers in a big functional organization, and we were asking them to become the leaders of more entrepreneurial profit-making businesses, some with up to a $1 billion in assets. How were we going to get them out of their historic area of functional expertise to think strategically, as general managers of profit-oriented businesses?

McCool realized that the new organization and strategy required a new measurement system. Historically, USM&R relied on local functional measures: low cost for manufacturing and distribution operations, availability for dealer-based operations, margins and volume for marketing operations, and environmental and safety indicators for the staff group in charge of environment, health, and safety. McCool was unhappy with these metrics:

> We were still in a controller's mentality, reviewing the past, not guiding the future. The functional metrics didn't communicate what we were about. I didn't want metrics that reinforced our historic control mentality. I

wanted them to be part of a communication process by which everyone in the organization could understand and implement our strategy. We needed better metrics so that our planning process could be linked to actions, to encourage people to do the things that the organization was now committed to.

Baker also noted the need for new metrics:

> Our people were fixated on volume and margins at the dealer level. Marketing didn't want to lose gasoline dealers. But we didn't have any focus or measurement on dealer quality so we often franchised dealers who didn't sustain our brand image. Also, we drove so hard for short-term profits that when volumes declined, our marketing people attempted to achieve their profit figure by raising prices. You can do that for a while if you have a strong brand, which we have, but you can't sustain this type of action for the long term.

In mid-1993, Ed Lewis, formerly the financial manager for U.S. marketing, was on a special assignment with Dan Riordan, deputy controller of USM&R, to examine the effectiveness of financial analysis for the entire division. They concluded that a lot of excellent financial analysis was being done—plenty of measures, plenty of analysis—but none of it was linked to the division's strategy. In late

1993, Lewis saw an article on the Balanced Scorecard[2] and thought,

> This could be what we are looking for. We were viewed as a flavor-of-the-month operation. Our focus shifted frequently so that if you didn't like what we were doing today, just wait; next month we will be doing something different. Nothing we did tied to any mission. The Balanced Scorecard seemed different. It was a process that tied measurement to the organization's mission and strategy. It could start us on the journey to implement USM&R's new organization and strategy by keeping us focused on where we were heading.

Lewis and Riordan recommended to McCool that USM&R develop a Balanced Scorecard [BSC]. McCool was receptive since he had heard of the concept in a briefing he had received earlier that year. USM&R's senior management team launched a BSC project in early 1994. They hired Renaissance Solutions, the consulting company founded by David Norton, a co-author of the Balanced Scorecard article, to assist in the process.

A senior-level executive leadership team (ELT), consisting of McCool, Baker, the vice presidents of all staff functions, the division controller, and the manager of financial analysis of downstream operations, provided oversight and guidance for the BSC project. The actual project team was led by Lewis and Riordan, assisted by Renaissance consultants.

Starting in January 1994, Lewis and his project team conducted two-hour individual interviews with all members of the ELT to understand each person's thoughts on the new strategy. The team synthesized the information received from the interviews and, with David Norton facilitating, led several workshops to develop specific objectives and measures for the four Balanced Scorecard perspectives: financial, customer, internal business process, and learning and growth. The workshops always involved active dialogues and debates about the implications of the new strategy. Lewis noted:

> Forcing the managers, during the workshops, to narrow the strategy statements into strategic objectives in the four perspectives really developed alignment to the new strategy. You could just see a consensus develop during the three-month period.

Among the new aspects of the USM&R scorecard was a recognition that the division had two types of customers. The immediate customer was, of course, the extensive network of franchised dealers who purchased gasoline and petroleum products from Mobil. The other customer was the millions of consumers who purchased Mobil products from independent dealers and retailers. The project team wanted the customer perspective on the scorecard to incorporate strategic objectives and measures for both types of customers.

By May 1994, the project team had developed a tentative formulation of the USM&R scorecard. At that point, they brought in more managers and split into eight subteams to enhance and refine the strategic objectives and measures: a Financial team (headed by the VP of Strategic Planning); two Customer teams—one focused on dealers, the other on consumers; a Manufacturing team, focused on measures for refineries and manufacturing cost; a Supply team, focused on inventory management and laid-down delivered cost; an Environmental, Health and Safety team; a Human Resources team; and an Information Technology team. Each sub-team identified objectives, measures, and targets for its assigned area.

The financial perspective subteam had extensive discussions to fine-tune the financial objectives developed as a strawmodel by the executive leadership team (ELT). They even-

---

[2]R. S. Kaplan and D. P. Norton, "The Balanced Scorecard: Measures That Drive Performance," *Harvard Business Review* (January–February 1992).

---

**EXHIBIT 5** USM&R Strategic Objectives: Financial

| | |
|---|---|
| Return on capital employed | Earn a sustained rate of return on capital employed (ROCE) that is consistently among the best performers in the U.S. downstream industry, but no less than the agreed corporate target ROCE of 12%. |
| Cash flow | Manage operations to generate sufficient cash to cover at least USM&R's capital spending, net financing cost, and pro rata share of the Corporate shareholder dividend. |
| Profitability | Continually improve profitability by generating an integrated net margin (cents per gallon) that consistently places us as one of the top two performers among the U.S. downstream industry. |
| Lowest cost | Achieve sustainable competitive advantage by integrating the various portions of the value chain to achieve the lowest fully allocated total cost consistent with the value proposition delivered. |
| Meet profitable growth targets | Grow the business by increasing volume faster than the industry average and by identifying and aggressively pursuing profitable fuels and lubes revenue opportunities that are consistent with the overall division strategy. |

---

tually chose objectives that retained the historic focus on cost reduction, and also highlighted profitability and growth objectives (see Exhibit 5). The subteam then found it relatively easy to gain consensus on an appropriate set of measures:

- Return on capital employed
- Cash flow
- Profitability (cents per gallon before tax, relative ranking among competitors)
- Total operating expense (cents per gallon)
- Volume growth for gasoline retail sales, distillate sales, lubricants

The learning and growth subteams worked hard to refine the high-level objectives already established by the ELT. The teams eventually proposed that USM&R should strive to increase:

- Organizational involvement
- Core competencies and skills
- Access to strategic information

(See Exhibit 6 for definitions of these three objectives.)

The two subteams then required many more meetings to decide how to measure these new strategic objectives. McCool main-

tained special interest in these deliberations since he believed that USM&R's new strategy required a significant upgrading of leadership skills and an enhancement of critical employee capabilities. The teams eventually suggested three measures for human resources and information technology capabilities:

- Climate survey index
- Strategic competency availability %
- Strategic systems availability

The measures were somewhat generic and several participants remained unsure whether there weren't better measures to drive behavior and describe success. Much of the data for these measures already existed in the organization, but none of the proposed measures was currently being used by senior managers.

The remaining subteams, responsible for determining the objectives and measures for the customer and internal perspectives (for consumers, dealers, manufacturing, supply, and environmental, health and safety), were also working to devise objectives and measures that would reflect the new customer-based strategy, and also satisfy the high-level financial objectives. For example, the con-

---

**EXHIBIT 6**  USM&R Strategic Objectives: Learning and Growth

---

| | |
|---|---|
| Organizational involvement | Enable the achievement of our vision by promoting an understanding of our organizational strategy and by creating a climate in which our employees are motivated and empowered to strive toward that vision. |
| Core competencies and skills | |
|    Integrated view | Encourage and facilitate our people to gain a broader understanding of the marketing and refining business from end to end. |
|    Functional excellence | Build the level of skills and competencies necessary to execute our vision. |
|    Leadership | Develop the leadership skills required to articulate the vision, promote integrated business thinking, and develop our people. |
| Access to strategic information | Develop the strategic information support required to execute our strategies. |

---

sumer subteam knew that the strategy to delight consumers in the three targeted market segments required that all Mobil gasoline stations deliver a speedy purchase, have friendly, helpful employees, and recognize consumer loyalty. At the time, however, several businesses had no measures for evaluating dealer performance on these now critical processes.

In parallel with the consumer subteam, the dealer subteam was working to choose objectives and measures that would communicate the importance of creating win-win channel partnerships with its dealers.

# MOBIL USM&R (A2)*

By August 1994, the Balanced Scorecard development process at Mobil U.S. Marketing & Refining (see Mobil USM&R [A1] case) had made considerable progress. Managers had formulated the strategic objectives for the four Balanced Scorecard perspectives and selected the initial set of measures for these objectives. Building the initial scorecard had consumed two to three full-time equivalent weeks from all members of the Executive Leadership Team (McCool and all his direct reports, including the managers of the business units). . . .

Between June and August 1994, while the subteams had been refining the strategic objectives and measures, the Steering Committee went through each perspective to identify one or two critical themes. The project team produced a brochure to communicate these strategic themes to USM&R's several thousand employees.

## *Linking the Balanced Scorecard to NBUs and Servcos*

While the USM&R scorecard was still being developed in April 1994, the project team launched pilots to develop business unit scorecards (in the West Coast and Midwest NBUs [natural business units]). Senior management wanted the NBUs to work from the strategic themes established at the USM&R Division level and to translate the division strategy into local, NBU objectives and measures that would reflect the particular oppor-

---

*Professor Robert S. Kaplan prepared this case. Mr. Ed Lewis of Mobil's Business and Performance Analysis group provided invaluable assistance.

tunities and competitive environment encountered by each NBU. This was part of McCool's belief that NBU managers had to learn to take responsibility for the strategy of their business units.

Ed Lewis, with consultant support, went to the NBUs and replicated the scorecard development process with their personnel:

> We did the interviews, conducted the workshops, and, over a six week period, developed a local scorecard. We used the USM&R scorecard as a guiding light, but that's all it was, a light. When an NBU developed a scorecard, it was their scorecard and they would live by it.

McCool concurred:

> Mobil in the Midwest is not the same as Mobil in New England, or on the West Coast. In each market, the consumer looks at us differently, our competition in each region is different, and the economics of operating in each market are different. I don't want to dictate a solution from Fairfax. We have a basic strategy and set of support programs that we can roll out to each NBU. We do have a few constraints: we want our dealers to operate under a sign that says "Mobil," there's a basic design for the station and for the C-store that we want to share across regions, and we think we have a winning segmentation strategy with fast and friendly service. But if an NBU thinks it has a better driver for success, I'm willing to hear it. I want the NBU head to tell me, here's my business, this is my vision and strategy, and this is how I am going get there from here. Our job in Fairfax is to approve (or disapprove) the strategy and ask what additional resources they might need to get the job done.

The NBU scorecards, in general, mirrored the USM&R scorecard, though with slightly fewer measures, particularly in the internal perspective since the NBUs were focused on particular functions—such as regional marketing and sales, refining, and distribution—so the full range of internal measures were not relevant to each NBU.

Several of the NBUs devoted a section of their monthly newsletters to Balanced Scorecard information. In the first few issues, the section reviewed a single scorecard perspective, explaining the importance of the perspective, articulating the reasoning behind the specific objectives that had been selected, and describing the measures that would be used to motivate and monitor performance for that perspective. After communicating the purpose and content of the scorecard in the first few issues, the content of the newsletter section shifted from education to feedback. Each issue reported recent results on the measures for one of the perspectives. Raw numbers and trends were supplemented with the human stories on how a department or an individual was contributing to the reported performance. The vignettes communicated to the workforce how individuals and teams were taking local initiatives to help the organization implement its strategy. The stories created role models of individual employees contributing to strategy implementation through their day-to-day activities.

### Servco Service Agreements

The Steering Committee also wanted the servcos to be accountable for their performance. Previously, each staff function operated from the Fairfax headquarters, providing strategy, direction, and services to the field organization. After the reorganization, staff functions were now free-standing service units that had to sell services to the NBUs and get agreement from them on prices and level of service provided. USM&R established buyers' committees, consisting of three to five representatives from the NBUs, to work with each servco. In this way the offerings from every servco would be linked to the mission and strategy of NBUs and to USM&R. Eventually, each servco and its buyers' committee agreed on the priorities and prices for the offerings it would provide.

Dan Zivny, manager of Finance and Information Services, endorsed the new process:

> Discussions with the buyers committee helped us to communicate to the NBUs about what we do and what our deliverables will be. Previously, the NBUs would complain about the costs and charges for information services. Now the NBUs are part of the process that specifies the outputs we will produce and the prices we will charge.

Several of the servcos began to develop their own Balanced Scorecards. Marty Di Mezza, manager of the Gasoline Marketing servco, noted:

> The service agreement with the buyers committee and our Balanced Scorecard have enabled my organization to become more customer focused. People now realize they have to sell their services and that we have to fit into the entire picture of USM&R.

In addition to developing their own BSC's, key servco people were assigned to collect the data and report on each measure on the USM&R scorecard. Each measure was assigned to a "metric owner." The metric owners verified that the measures appropriately reflected the strategic objectives, and could, based on feedback from the field, make recommendations to the Executive Leadership Team for modified or new measures. People within the metric owner's servco collected the actual data from operations and reported current values of the measures to the metric owner.

### Linking the Balanced Scorecard to Compensation

All salaried employees of USM&R were tied to the Mobil corporate award program. This program was based on performance relative to Mobil's top seven competitors on two financial measures: return-on-capital employed and earnings-per-share growth [EPS] (see Exhibit 1). This program awarded up to a 10% bonus if Mobil ranked number 1 on ROCE and EPS growth.

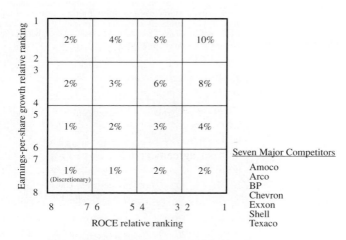

**EXHIBIT 1   Corporate Performance Share (CPS)— Salary Groups 13–19 Metrics and Award % (of Reference Salary)**

McCool initiated an additional program within USM&R that awarded bonuses up to 20% to managers in each business unit. NBU employees got 30% of the award based on USM&R performance, and 70% based on their NBU performance. Servco employees also got 30% on USM&R performance, 20% on the linkages to other business units, and 50% on their servco BSC. The linkage measures for servcos represented the objectives and results they could influence either in the NBUs or at USM&R.

The bonus plan was part of a new variable pay compensation program. Employees' base pay reference point had been set at 90% of competitive market wages. The remaining 10% of compensation could be achieved with average performance on three factors:

- A component based on the two corporate financial performance competitive rankings
- A division component based on the USM&R Balanced Scorecard metrics
- A business unit component based on key performance indicators, from the NBU or servco Balanced Scorecard metrics

An additional 20% of compensation could be received for exceptional performance along these three components. The theory for the variable pay plan was simple: award below average compensation for below average performance, average pay for average performance, and above average pay for above average performance.[1]

McCool wanted each business unit to work with the metric owners to develop its own targets for the scorecard measures. In addition, the BUs assigned a percentage weight associated with achieving this target. This percentage, which summed to 100 across all the targeted measures, would determine the relative contribution of each scorecard measure to the bonus pool. Most business units chose to weight all measures on their scorecards; the remaining ones still weighted most of their scorecard measures. Only one business unit put more than a 50% weight on its financial measures.

The business units, beyond establishing targets for each scorecard measure, also assigned a performance factor that represented the perceived degree of difficulty of target achievement (see Exhibit 2). The perfor-

---

[1]In addition, the plan included individual awards, administered within a narrow range, to adjust for performance not captured by the metrics. Business unit managers were awarded a fixed "pot of money" for such individual awards, but this allowance could not be overspent.

| Performance Factor | Qualitative |
|---|---|
| 1.25 | Best in class |
| 1.20 | |
| 1.15 | Well above above |
| 1.12 | |
| 1.09 | |
| 1.06 | Above average |
| 1.03 | |
| 1.00 | Average |
| 0.90 | |
| 0.80 | Below average |
| 0.70 | |
| 0.60 | |
| 0.50 | Needs improvement |
| 0.40 | |

How to think about performance factors:

1. Objective:
   External Benchmark
   1.00 means target equals the average of competition
   1.25 means target equals the top of the competitive group

2. Subjective:
   Internal Benchmark
   1.00 means the difficulty of the target is average

**EXHIBIT 2  Metrics—Performance Factor**

mance factor would be multiplied by the weight assigned to the measure to arrive at a total performance amount, much the way a diving competition is scored (absolute performance on a dive gets weighted by the dive's degree of difficulty). The maximum index score of 1.25 occurred when the target would put the Mobil unit as best in class. An average target received a performance factor of 1.00, and a factor score as low as 0.7 would be applied when the target represented poor performance, or was deemed very easy to achieve. The individual business units proposed the performance factors for each measure, but these had to be explained and defended in a review with the Executive Leadership Team and metric owners. Business unit managers also were able to see (and comment on) the targets, weights, and performance factors proposed by the other BUs.

Brian Baker was a strong advocate for the indexed targets:

> Historically, people were rewarded for meeting targets and penalized when they missed a target. So sandbagging targets became an art form around here. I prefer the current system where I can give a better rating to a manager who stretches for a target and falls a little short than to someone who sandbags with an easy target and then beats it.

## *Managing with the Balanced Scorecard*

McCool reflected on the experience to date with the Balanced Scorecard:

> It's enabled us to teach the NBU managers about strategy; about lead and lag indicators; and to think across the organization, not just in functional silos. It's exposed the managers to issues outside their expertise and to understand the linkages they have with other parts of the organization. People now talk about things that are outside their immediate responsibility, like safety, environment, and C-stores. The scorecard has provided a common language, a good basis for communication.

We were also fortunate that when Mobil asked us to go to a pay-for-performance plan we could use our scorecard measures. Variable pay plans only work if you have a good set of metrics. Managers accepted the compensation plan based on the scorecard since they believed the measures represented well what they were trying to achieve.

> The learning and growth perspective has been the biggest problem. Ultimately, that perspective will be the differentiator for the company, our people's ability to learn and to apply that learning. The good news is at least we now talk about learning, as much as we talk about gross margin. But we are struggling to get good output measures for the learning objective.

McCool commented on the changes in the meetings he conducts with NBU managers:

> For a meeting with an NBU manager, like West Coast, I have the manager plus representatives from various servcos, like supply, marketing, and C-stores. And we have a conversation. In the past we had a bunch of controllers sitting around talking about variances. Now we discuss what's gone right, what's gone wrong. What should we keep doing, what should we stop doing? What resources do we need to get back on track, not explaining a negative variance due to some volume mix.

> The process enables me to see how the NBU managers think, plan, and execute. I can see the gaps, and by understanding the manager's culture and mentality, I can develop customized programs to make him or her a better manager.

Baker commented on the reviews he recently conducted with the managers of nine NBUs and four servcos that reported to him:

> I went into these reviews thinking they would be long and arduous. I was pleasantly surprised how simple they were. Managers came in prepared. They were paying attention to their scorecards and using them in a very productive way—to drive their organization hard to achieve the targets. How they weighted their measures spoke clearly about their priorities of relative importance up and down the four perspectives.

Basically, there's no way I can understand and supervise all the activities that report to me. I need a device like the scorecard where the business unit managers are measuring their own performance. My job is to keep adjusting the light I shine on their strategy and implementation, to monitor and guide their journeys, and see whether there are any potential storms on the horizon that we should address.

Baker felt that relying on only a single financial measure, like earnings or return-on-capital-employed, was dangerous.

A big shareholder may not care about local business conditions or competitive environments. Just achieve a 12% ROCE, produce the money, and don't tell me about your problems. That's his right as the shareholder, and some people would say, "Those are the rules, and let's set strict earnings objectives for each of our business units and that's it."

But there's another side of me that says to motivate people there are things managers can influence and things they cannot. In a strong market, you can do a bloody bad job and have a great year. And you can do a superb job and fall way short of earnings because the market was so weak. The scorecard has several elements that help me understand how well a manager performs against the market. Without the understanding we now have from the scorecard, we would force people to do some pretty bizarre things to make short-term earnings targets, and they could be gone before the problems fall in.

Managers do seem to be using the scorecard for their management processes. They're not just doing it because McCool and I have imposed it on them. It's a system they know that everyone is using; all the other business units are living by the same set of rules. That's incredibly important. Also, the degree of difficulty index allowed them to be more ambitious and aggressive in setting their targets.

McCool concluded:

In three to four years, we have come from an operation that was worst in its peer group, draining a half billion dollars a year, to a company that ranks number 1 in its peer group and generates hundreds of millions of dollars of positive cash flow.[2]

The Balanced Scorecard has been a major contributor. It's helped us to focus our initiatives and to keep them aligned with our strategic objectives. It's been a great communication tool for telling the story of the business and a great learning tool as well. People now see how their daily job contributes to USM&R performance. Our challenge is how can we sustain this performance. We have just seen the tip of the iceberg. I want people to use the scorecard to focus attention on the great opportunities for growth.

---

[2]USM&R's 1995 income per barrel of $1.02 greatly exceeded the industry average of $0.65. Global operating return from refining, marketing and transportation operations of 10.1% per dollar of assets was the highest in the industry (up from 8.6% and fifth place in 1994) ("Benchmarking the Integrated Oils, 1995," U.S. Research [Goldman Sachs, July 15, 1996], pp.7, 9).

---

# MOBIL USM&R (B): NEW ENGLAND SALES AND DISTRIBUTION*

The New England Sales & Distribution (NES&D) was one of seven regional sales and distribution business units within Mobil's

---

*Robert S. Kaplan prepared this case. Mr. Ed Lewis of Mobil's Business and Performance Analysis group provided invaluable assistance.

U.S. Marketing and Refining (USM&R) operations. NES&D's responsibilities included:

- The 1,400 branded Mobil stations in the six New England states—Maine, New Hampshire, Vermont, Massachusetts, Connecticut, and Rhode Island

- Terminal operations in New England that received and stored gasoline and home heating oil brought in by ship from Canada, Europe, and Venezuela

- Three pipelines that transported petroleum products to regional terminals, such as at Boston's Logan Airport
- A fleet of delivery trucks, including the unionized truck drivers, that transported gasoline and heating oil to dealers and wholesalers

Tony Turchi, general manager of NES&D, had held a series of assignments in finance and planning before becoming marketing manager for New England region. He was appointed general manager in the 1994 reorganization (see USM&R [A1] case). Turchi recalled the rules under the old regime: "It was pretty simple. Our goals were to increase sales volume and reduce controllable costs. We had lots of measures, and they all related to these two goals."

In early 1994, shortly after NES&D had been established as an independent business unit, its senior management team conducted a strategic planning exercise. The exercise started with a traditional SWOT analysis [strengths, weaknesses, opportunities, threats]. The team then developed a high-priority list of strategic opportunities that blended national strategies, such as fast-friendly-serve and On-the-Run convenience stores, with regional strategies, for example dealer development, felt to be critically important for the future success of New England. Turchi recognized, however, that the strategic planning exercise had two gaps.

We now had a vision, we had clearly identified strategic opportunities, and we had developed some strategic initiatives. But we didn't have a good measurement tool. We were still just measuring, in fact overmeasuring, volume and costs. Second, a climate survey of our employees revealed a real hunger for a reward and recognition system. It didn't have to be big money, but our people wanted to understand where we were taking the business and to be more actively involved with that direction.

Turchi had not participated in the development of the USM&R Balanced Scorecard.

In retrospect, I wish that could have been involved in the process to understand better why some of the measures were placed on the scorecard. On the positive side, however, it was great to be able to see the thought process spelled out: how McCool and the ELT [Executive Leadership Team] were going to be measuring the performance of the overall business, how a regional sales and distribution business unit fit into the overall picture, what measures were important to the ELT, and what strategies they were recommending. Even more important, the USM&R scorecard gave us a great template to follow. It took a lot of the guess work out of what the ELT meant by a Balanced Scorecard.

A NES&D team worked in the second half of 1994 to develop a New England Balanced Scorecard. The project team talked to employees in the terminals, the truck drivers, and to NES&D's channel partners, the independent gasoline dealers and wholesalers. The team also coordinated with USM&R servcos[1] to get their input for the New England strategic objectives and measures.

By the end of 1994, the effort produced NES&D's first Balanced Scorecard (see Exhibit 1). The group also linked the strategic issues and opportunities it had identified from its SWOT exercise to the Balanced Scorecard measures (see list in Exhibit 2). Turchi felt it was important for people to see how the Balanced Scorecard could measure progress along the strategic issues they had identified.

Our first opportunity [see Exhibit 2] was to integrate the best client experience with our franchise offerings, like fast-friendly-serve,

---

[1]Servcos are the service organizations within USM&R, such as gasoline marketing, communications, finance, and information systems that provided support services to the operating business units. The operating business units, such as NES&D, had very little internal staff support.

**EXHIBIT 1** The New England Scorecard

| | | OBJECTIVE | MEASURES |
|---|---|---|---|
| **Financial** | | | |
| | F1 | Return on capital employed | ROCE |
| | F2 | Cash flow | Cash flow |
| | F3 | Profitability | Net margin |
| | | | Net profit after tax |
| | F4 | Lowest cost | Full cost per gallon |
| | F5 | Meet profitable growth targets | Gasoline volume growth rate |
| | | | Existing oil, gas, and lubricant growth rate |
| | | | Premium product growth rate |
| **Customer** | | | |
| | C1 | Delight the customer | Mystery Shopper rating |
| | | | Customer complaints |
| | | | Customer compliments |
| | C2 | Dealer/wholesaler marketer profitability | Dealer/distributor gross margins |
| **Internal** | | | |
| | I1 | Marketing and product development | Alternative Profit Centers (APC) gross profit/store |
| | I2 | Salesforce focus | Number of oil, gas, and lubricant units meeting upgrade standards |
| | | | Number of "our commitment" stations |
| | I3 | Manage the business | Gasoline runouts |
| | | | Distillate runouts |
| | | | Station runouts |
| | I4 | Improve Health, Safety, and Environment | Environmental incidents |
| | | | Days away from work due to injuries |
| | | | Accidents |
| | I5 | Quality | Percentage of stations scoring 100% in quality assessment program |
| **Learning and Growth** | | | |
| | L1 | Organization involvement | Climate surveys |
| | L2 | Core competencies and skills | Progress on developmental plans—focus on leadership |
| | L3 | Access to strategic information | Availability of profit and loss data, BSC, cash flow, field marketing tools |

destination C-store, and our car care and maintenance services. If we succeeded in this opportunity with our dealer-partners, we would hit our targets for F5 (profitable growth), C1 (delight the customer), I1 (marketing and product development) and I2 (focus salesforce). Number 3 on our hit parade was one of our most important objectives—to provide awesome new training and development for our people and partners. This was one of our most critical leading indicators. It would show up in two of our learning and growth measures (L1, L2), but it would also impact C1, the Mystery Shopper rating.

Turchi worked with his leadership team, consisting of the top managers in NES&D plus three representatives from key USM&R servcos, to set targets and weights for linking the scorecard measures to the bonus plan for the entire New England team (see Exhibit 3). The linkage included the performance factor [degree of difficulty] for each measure to reflect how close the target was to best-in-class capabilities. Turchi recalled:

I had to estimate many of these factors midway through the year, because the process wasn't

**EXHIBIT 2**   Linking Strategic Opportunities and Initiatives to Balanced Scorecard Measures

| STRATEGIC OPPORTUNITY | BALANCED SCORECARD MEASURES |
|---|---|
| 1.   Integrate the best buying opportunity with our franchise offerings<br>        Target our C-stores, service bays, gasoline offering service to<br>            Road Warriors, Generation F3, True Blues | F5, C1, I1, I2 |
| 2.   Address the deadly gap (against key competitor)<br>        Aggressive marketing tactics<br>        Managing distributor consolidation of "Have-Nots" into "Haves"<br>        Partnering in product supply and logistics—improve asset<br>            utilization | <br>F3, F5<br>F5<br><br>F4 |
| 3.   Provide comprehensive training and development for our people | C1, I2, L1, L2 |
| 4.   Improve the climate: Open communication, feedback, rewards,<br>        and recognition | <br>L1 |
| 5.   Improve health, safety, and environmental performance | I4 |
| 6.   Premium products | F5 |
| 7.   Legislation/regulation—potential threat to volume and profit | F3, F5 |
| 8.   Improve cost structure | F4, L2 |

**EXHIBIT 3**   New England S&D—1995 Compensation Linkage

| | 1995<br>WEIGHT | "NET"<br>WEIGHT | 1995<br>PERFORMANCE<br>FACTOR | 1995<br>GOAL* |
|---|---|---|---|---|
| *Financial* (30%) | | | | |
| Net profit after tax | 15% | 5% | 1.00 | 22 |
| Full cost per gallon | 30% | 9% | 1.00 | 6.8 |
| Gasoline volume growth | 15% | 5% | 1.06 | 103% |
| Existing oil, gas, and lubricant growth rate | 30% | 9% | 1.06 | 101.5% |
| Premium product | 10% | 3% | 0.96 | 100% |
| *Customer* (15%) | | | | |
| Mystery Shopper rating | 60% | 9% | 1.10 | 82 |
| Customer complaints | 40% | 6% | 1.00 | 824 |
| *Internal* (35%) | | | | |
| APC gross profit/store | 20% | 7% | 0.96 | 12,500 |
| No. of "Our Commitment" stations | 20% | 7% | 1.00 | 527 |
| Environmental incidents | 20% | 7% | 1.06 | 19 |
| Days away from work due to injuries | 20% | 7% | 1.06 | 16 |
| Accidents | 20% | 7% | 1.06 | 20 |
| *Learning and Growth* (20%) | | | | |
| Climate survey | 50% | 10% | 1.03 | 4 |
| Developmental plans | 50% | 10% | 1.00 | 2 |
| Total index | | 100% | | |
| Performance factor | | | 1.03 | |

*Numbers disguised to maintain confidentiality.*

set up at the beginning of 1995. But I tried to be honest; I gave a 0.96 on several measures. Overall I came out with a performance factor of 1.03. I worked this through with Brian Baker, who's my ELT coach, and defended the weights at a meeting with a whole bunch of servco representatives.

Turchi felt, however, that the scorecard was too complicated to communicate to his 300 employees in the field.

In 1995, we were doing Balanced Scorecard 101. We had to learn to walk before we could run. We needed to make it simple and understandable to all our people. We also wanted to create some fun and excitement.

In late January, the weekend after the Super Bowl, the NES&D leadership team organized a major meeting in Waterville Valley, New Hampshire. They decorated a meeting hall like a football field, gave everyone football sweatshirts, showed video-tapes of the great teams like the Green Bay Packers and Pittsburgh Steelers, and had an announcer from NFL films describe how the great football teams had all the elements—offense, defense, coaches, the support groups—working together. The leadership team then announced the New England region's Super Bowl for 1995. The team had selected five critical measures from NES&D's Balanced Scorecard:

- Gasoline volume
- Return on capital employed
- Customer complaints
- Mystery Shopper rating
- Our commitment to dealers

These five measures would serve as the scorecard for the New England Super Bowl. The Super Bowl metaphor became clearer when the team stretched the targets on these five measures beyond the levels communicated to USM&R's Fairfax headquarters. For example, the official ROCE target for the New England region required a net income

after tax of $22 million.[2] The Super Bowl target, however, was set at $27 million in net income, an additional $5 million stretch. The team set similar stretch goals for sales volume, mystery shopper ratings, customer complaints, and dealer commitment. For the NES&D organization to win the Super Bowl, it would have to hit the stretch targets on all five measures. If it hit all five, everyone would get a cash bonus of $250 and a great weekend next winter at a resort hotel in Vermont. If it failed in any one, no reward.

The leadership team then rolled the Super Bowl program out to all the people in the field. Dan Quinn, NES&D field logistics manager, described the process:

We talked to the drivers, the union people and took them through the strategy, the Super Bowl concept, and asked for their support to help us achieve our goals, how they could impact the measures. The truck drivers didn't believe us. They said, "the marketing guys get all the good rewards and go out and have a good time; they never include the terminal guys." We had to convince them that we were serious. They were going to get the same reward as the marketing people.

Then they started to ask us about the threats and the weaknesses, and told us how they had tried to make improvements over the years. They wanted to know how they could continue to help. How do you explain ROCE to a truck driver? We talked about the components of ROCE they could impact, like how their safe driving could affect expenses and productivity. If they could deliver when there's snow on the ground, while other drivers had an accident with their trucks lying on the side of the road, that would mean a lot to our customers in terms of product availability and satisfaction. We explained the Mystery Shopper program and how we would rate stations that were doing great and how we would deal with stations that could be a problem.

By the end of the first quarter 1995, all 300 employees in NES&D understood the vi-

---

[2]Numbers have been disguised for confidentiality.

sion, the strategy, and the main business threats as well as the stretch targets for the five Super Bowl elements. The employees began to use this information to set priorities for their work, and to stop doing work that didn't directly relate to these issues. The NES&D project team maintained communication through the year in meetings, e-mail, voice mail, and newsletters. The information included up-to-date reports on the five Super Bowl measures. In every meeting that Turchi and his senior leadership people had with people in the field, they discussed performance against the Super Bowl targets. Turchi saw the impact:

> We had drivers calling in with concerns about a dealer they had just visited somewhere in New Hampshire that would flunk if a mystery shopper showed up. Half the lights were out at night and the Mobil sign was down. The drivers also were generating volume opportunities. They would ask us why we didn't have a station in a certain middle- to high-traffic area.

During 1995, Turchi had three strategic reviews with Brian Baker, the USM&R representative on the Executive Leadership Team who oversaw NES&D. Baker included, in these meetings, key people from servcos that were supporting programs in the region. Turchi recalled:

> The headquarters people were completely focused on our Balanced Scorecard. That sent a strong signal. The discussions also helped the servco people understand from our leadership team how their national programs were working or not working in the region.

By the end of the year, NES&D had greatly exceeded the stretch targets on four of the five Super Bowl measures. Only on the mystery shopper rating was performance short of the target. People acknowledged that the Super Bowl targets and the associated individual goals and objectives had driven this

outstanding performance. But Turchi faced a dilemma:

> I had set our Mystery Shopper Super Bowl target at 85% even though my commitment to the ELT at Fairfax was to hit 82%. The actual score came in at 83.3%. We had started the year at about 75% so we had made an 8 percentage point increase in our 1,400 stations, and exceeded our commitment to the ELT. But we didn't hit our stretch goal. We had lots of discussion about what to do. Some said that the rules we established at the beginning required us to hit all five, or get nothing. But others argued that we exceeded four of the five, and came close on the fifth. This issue was a concern to me because we were about to enter 1996 with another set of very stretched targets, and I wanted people to feel good about these targets, and be motivated to achieve them.

The NES&D leadership team was also updating the Balanced Scorecard for 1996. The five Super Bowl measures were retained but other measures got modified. Turchi explained:

> The scorecard objectives and about 80% of the measures remained the same. We deleted some measures and added 20% new measures. We found that if something was not measured on the Balanced Scorecard, it wasn't perceived as being important and we lost focus on it. For example, our 1995 volume measure related to total gasoline sales volume and we hit the target. But we did not sell enough of the higher grades that are critical for our regional and national strategy. So we added a measure of the percentage sold of special and super unleaded, the premium higher octane products.

> We are, in 1996, going to drive the variable pay bonus plan based on scorecard percentages and weights down to individual and teams. We will have to explain this to all the people. I think we'll use a baseball analogy; have them think about what sets the salary for a star player: a weighted average of various statistics, like home runs, batting average, runs batted in, reducing number of strike-outs, etc.

> The only exception will be the union people, since the new contract, covering about 100 people, doesn't allow this type of variable pay

compensation plan. So we will probably have another Super Bowl program for them, using a subset of the measures that everyone else is being paid on.

Turchi concluded:

You can see the difference in our people. Pre-BSC, the scorecard for an area manager was pretty simple: sales, sales, and sales. For the manager of a terminal, it was cost, cost, cost, and perhaps a little safety. Now we are trying to have the people in both positions be mini–general managers, to have them think broadly about our entire business. People in these positions are the ones that are absolutely critical for the success of our organization.

---

# MOBIL USM&R (C): LUBRICANTS BUSINESS UNIT*

In an ideal world, you pick up a scorecard and it tells you the five or ten things you need to do every day. That's what we're working towards.

*George Madden, General Manager, Mobil Lubricants Business Unit*

The Lubricants Business Unit was an operating division within Mobil's U.S. Marketing and Refining Group (USM&R). The Lubes unit had about $1 billion in sales and 900 employees of whom 350 were unionized. Mobil's Lubes Division was the largest marketer of finished lubricants in the United States with a 12% market share and strong growth, especially in the premium quality blends, Mobil 1 and Delvac 1300 Super. New products included an Environment Awareness Lubricant product line that was used with ozone-safe refrigerants in industrial refrigerant compressors. This product had a more than 50% US market share.

Since 1991, the Lubes Division had been integrating and consolidating operations that were formerly scattered among Mobil's functional organization. The division received input product from the Beaumont and Pauls-boro refineries. It then processed the product through blending and packaging plants. Lubes also had its own operations for sales, order fulfillment, product development, and product management.

George Madden, the General Manager of the Lubes Division, was on the USM&R Executive Leadership Team that developed the division scorecard during the first half of 1995. Madden recognized that the Balanced Scorecard could provide focus and direction to his complex business.

We have four very different businesses: industrial, automotive, base stock, and specialty products such as wax, asphalt, and petroleum coke. Each business has its own strategy. We sell through distributors, through retail, and direct to customers. Cutting across these diverse businesses and selling arrangements are our business processes like order management, base stock manufacturing, finished product manufacturing, and logistics/distribution.

We had been working on initiatives to help get a handle on our cost drivers: activity-based costing, process management, process reengineering, complexity cost, you name it. As I came to understand the Balanced Scorecard, I saw the opportunity to tie all of our business operations together, to have focus and to run the business on an integrated basis.

In mid-1995, Madden launched a Balanced Scorecard project for the Lubes busi-

---

*Robert S. Kaplan prepared this case. Ed Lewis and Todd d'Attoma of Mobil USM&R provided invaluable assistance.

ness to be completed by December 1995. The scorecard process would affect the first three levels of the organization, about 50–60 people. In mid-October 1995, however, Madden called in Todd D'Attoma, one of his business analysts, and gave him a challenging assignment:

> If the scorecard project is really going to have an impact, everyone has to be on board. I want you to put together a team to have all of our 550 non-unionized employees understand and be part of the Balanced Scorecard process.

D'Attoma formed a seven person cross-functional/cross-level team. It included a blend plant manager, a blend plant shift supervisor, representatives from industrial and automotive marketing, the customer response center, and headquarters people like himself. The team developed a mission and a small set of simple and focused deliverables:

| | |
|---|---|
| Mission | Deliver a Balanced Scorecard process that challenges each individual and team to link their goals to the Lube Business vision and strategies, and drive their skill development. |
| Deliverables | Cause and effect tree Criteria Build team scorecard Create link to performance appraisal Implementation tool kit |

The team started by constructing its own Balanced Scorecard for the project (see Exhibit 1). The team spent two weeks in Fairfax launching the project. Ryan England, a consultant from Renaissance Solutions, encouraged the team to develop and validate a cause-and-effect tree that linked high-level business unit objectives down to positions or tasks for every individual in the organization. The team

created a comprehensive cause-and-effect tree that filled a large wall (a simplified version is shown in Exhibit 2). The internal perspective contained nearly 100 individual processes.

The team then took to the field. During the next 12 working days, the team held about 40 meetings in 20 different locations to help individuals and teams implement their own scorecards.

D'Attoma described a typical meeting:

> Most of the people had never heard of the Balanced Scorecard. We started off telling them what it was, our objectives in using the scorecard, and the role of the scorecard in the organization. Then we walked them through the tree, we talked about the alignment of objectives and strategies and about cross-functional relationships, which the tree allows you to do. And then we asked them, "where do you fit on the tree?" They were generally excited to find how their job fit into our overall strategies and objectives. They went up to the tree, pointed to their box, saw what they affected, and traced how their job or position affected everything, eventually impacting ROCE. It was powerful for individuals to see that. Once we found their location on the tree, we broke that task down further, and helped them develop some objectives and measures.

The team developed specific criteria for individuals to follow in building their scorecards:

- Personal scorecard must support supervisor/manager's scorecard
- Scorecard must include an objective and measure that supports another part of the business
- Every supervisor/manager must have an objective and measure related to coaching, counseling, or employee development
- Scorecard must include a mix of lead and lag indicators
- Minimum of one objective/measure per quadrant [perspective]
- Do not exceed 15 measures
- Any change must be agreed to by both supervisor and employee

# EXHIBIT 1 Lubes Team Balanced Scorecard

| STRATEGIC THEME | OBJECTIVE | MEASURE | MINIMUM 1995 | 1996 ACTUAL RESULTS | | | TARGET | % OF TARGET | × WEIGHT | = SCORE |
|---|---|---|---|---|---|---|---|---|---|---|
| | | | | CURRENT | YTD | AS OF | | | | |
| **Financial** Reward our shareholders by providing a long-term return which exceeds our peers' | Control team cost | Dollar savings | | 6,590 | 6,590 | Dec. 19 | N/A | 0% | | |
| **Customer** Become easy to do business with Deliver on our promises | Deliver the BSC process | Percent employees with BSC | 85% | 86% | 86% | Jan. 1 | 100% | 86% | 45% | 0.39 |
| **Internal** Develop market-focused strategies | Effective presentations | Survey feedback | 3.5 | 3.8 | 4.2 | Dec. 19 | 4.0 | 105% | 25% | 0.26 |
| | Deliver on process | Deliverables by Jan 1 '96 | Yes | Yes | Yes | Dec. 19 | Yes | 100% | 10% | 0.10 |
| Support cost-effective P&D | Educate Lubes organization | Presentations made per plan | 90% | 100% | 100% | Dec. 19 | 100% | 100% | 10% | 0.10 |
| **Learning and Growth** Create a high-performance organization by equipping our people to succeed | Start GAP analysis process | Develop template for GAP | Yes | Yes | Yes | Dec. 19 | Yes | 100% | 10% | 0.10 |
| | | | | | | | | Total | 100% | 0.95 |

Performance factor 1.12 × unfactored score 0.95 = adjusted score 1.06

*The Performance Factor indicates how difficult it will be to achieve the stated objectives/measures and associated plan or outcome. Performance factors may range as follows: 0.7 for plan which is easy to obtain; 1.0 for average plans; 1.12 for plans which are difficult to achieve; and 1.25 for plans that are exceptionally hard to achieve.*

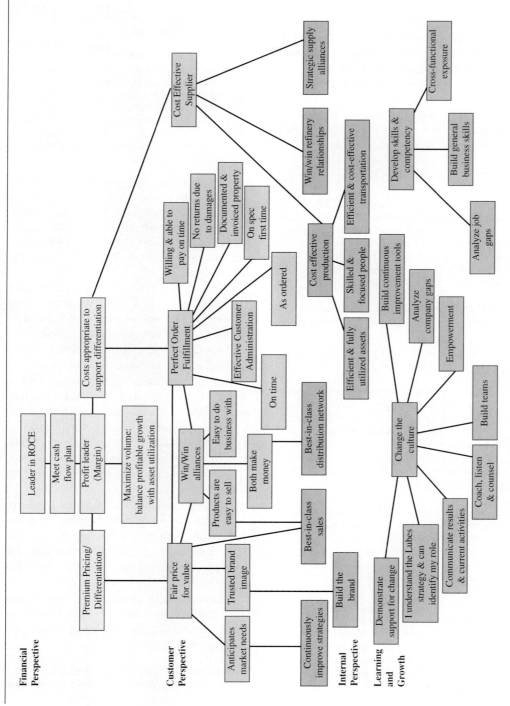

**EXHIBIT 2  Mobil Lubes Balanced Scorecard Cause-and-Effect Tree: Summary**

By the end of 1995, 86% of the 550 non-unionized employees had developed scorecard templates, with objectives and measures. In early 1996, the employees would work with their supervisors to develop goals and targets for the measures. People reported that they appreciated having no more than 15 measures; also that they could see their supervisor's scorecard and understand what he or she was focused on accomplishing.

D'Attoma recalled:

> People really liked the focus on the drivers of the Lubes business, the leading measures. They also liked the idea that, going forward, their compensation would be determined, in part, by the same measures used for George Madden, Bob McCool, and Lucio Noto's [Mobil Corporation CEO] compensation.

Madden, pointing to Exhibit 3, gave an example of the linkages that now existed:

> I've been talking for four years about the need to fulfill the perfect order. I guarantee that every person in Lubes has heard that from me personally, probably several times. But what did it mean? No one knew, outside of the order fulfillment people. Now the vast majority of the people in this organization own a piece of that measure.

D'Attoma used Exhibit 3 to give another example of the linkages:

> A measure in Madden's financial perspective was integrated [total] cost. When we went to the Beaumont plant, we asked the next six levels of people, down to the truck driver, how can you affect Madden's integrated cost measure? You can see the drill down through the seven levels in this exhibit.
>
> It was neat how the truck drivers developed ownership of their scorecards. For example, even though the legal speed limit had been raised to 65 mph in most states, Mobil had retained a 55 mph limit for its drivers. The drivers told us, "put safety and energy conservation on our scorecards, and let us

decide how fast we can legally drive." They wanted to decide by themselves how to achieve the outcomes. For their cross-functional objective, they noted that they drive 200,000 miles a year and basically live in truck stops. They offered to support the Mobil truck stop business by working with commercial engine oil people to develop a survey they could administer to determine other drivers' perceptions of engine oils. So they will be providing feedback to people in the marketing and distribution side of Mobil's business.

As additional examples of the linkages, Exhibit 4 presents a condensed version of the personal scorecards for B.W. Schwieters, manager of an automotive region (Level 3), and Lisa Giacometti, a marketing representative (Level 4) who reports to Schwieters.

In addition, to the scorecard itself, each individual developed an action plan for the learning and growth objective: What will be done during the next period to maximize the likelihood of achieving scorecard targets and enhancing personal development? Exhibit 5 is Schwieters's Competency Development Summary and Personal Development Plan. A competency checked in the Leverage column of Exhibit 5 indicates that enhancement will produce a higher likelihood of achieving or exceeding the individual's BSC objectives in the next period. A competency checked as Growth has a payoff over a longer period. The Personal Development Plan (lower half of Exhibit 5) shows the action plans for achieving the individual's competencies and key measures for identifying whether the action has been accomplished.

Madden, while pleased with the impact from drilling the Lubes scorecard down to teams and individuals, still noted some shortcomings with the effort to date:

> We've now identified what we need to measure to run the business. But we don't have

**EXHIBIT 3** Lubes Balanced Scorecard Implementation—An Example of Linkage and Taking Ownership

| STRATEGIC THEME | LEVEL 1 | LEVEL 2 | LEVEL 3 | LEVEL 4 | LEVEL 5 | LEVEL 6 | LEVEL 7 |
|---|---|---|---|---|---|---|---|
| | G. D. Madden, Lubes | M. L. Mullins, Order Fulfillment | A. J. Giaquinto, Manager of Plant Operations | K. F. Goode, Facility Manager | C. W. Slimp, Delivery Supervisor | J. G. Lege, Terminal Coordinator | G. W. Stewart, MV Driver |
| **Financial**<br>Reward our shareholders by providing a long-term return which exceeds our peers'. | ROCE (%)<br>Cash flow ($MM)<br>Integrated cost ($MM)<br>Integrated income | LOB integrated cost<br>Net integrated income | FA&Inv value ($MM)<br>Transformation cost | Inventory carrying cost<br>Line 44/CPG Formulation giveaway | Line 25 CPG<br>Backhaul $ | Line 2 CPG<br>Unavailable hours<br>Backhauls savings | Line 24 CPG<br>Idle time<br>Out of route miles<br>GPM |
| **Customer**<br>Provide value-added business solutions to our customers and channel partners.<br><br>Market Share: Finished | Percent perfect orders<br>Distributor survey<br>Develop/implement customer survey | Percent perfect orders<br>Distributor survey<br>Develop/implement customer survey | Percent perfect orders | Percent perfect orders<br>Service failures of strategic product lines | % On-time delivery<br>Develop CEO market info survey | % On-time delivery<br>Empty drums returned | % On-time delivery<br>Returns<br>Drums<br>Lube |
| **Internal**<br>Develop market-focused strategies and become operationally excellent. | Safety index<br>Environmental index<br>Continuous improvement cost reduction ($MM)<br>Develop/implement capital plan | Safety index<br>Environmental index<br>Develop/implement standard offering<br>Asset utilization /refinery/capacity (%), network vs optimum (5)<br>Inventory accuracy | Safety index<br>Environmental index<br>Complexity index<br>Inventory accuracy | DAFW<br>No. of NOV<br>No. of hits<br>No. of off-spec receipts<br>No. of transfers to move excess base stock | No. of motor vehicle accidents DAFW<br>No. of NOV | Complete environmental self-audit<br>No. of safety meetings complete<br>% attendance safety meeting | Accurate reporting rept. 731, 601, 727<br>No. of log book violations<br>No. of completed CEO market surveys<br>Customer assessment |
| **Learning and Growth**<br>Create a high-performance organization by equipping our people to succeed. | Employee development plans completed (%)<br>Develop inclusiveness metrics (3/31)<br>Develop/implement/measure progress of change programs | Employee development plans completed (%)<br>Develop/implement marketing comp. plan, product mgt. comp. plan, distr/logistics comp. plan | Employee development plans completed (%)<br>Attendance | Employee development plans completed (%)<br>Develop plant climate survey | Employee development plans completed (%)<br>No. of employees trained ISO 9000 certification | Vacation relief for shift coordinator<br>Training on CCE | Develop personal improvement plan<br>Vacation relief: term. coordinator |

**EXHIBIT 4** Personal Balanced Scorecard, Automotive Lubes*

| STRATEGIC THEME | OBJECTIVE | B. W. SCHWIETERS, AUTO REGION MANAGER MEASURE | LISA GIACOMETTI, MARKETING REPRESENTATIVE MEASURE |
|---|---|---|---|
| **Financial** Reward our shareholders by providing a long-term return which exceeds our peers. | Improve profit results | Sales volume: Branded motor oil Net profit: Branded motor oil | Region 2 sales volume: Branded motor oil Region 2 net profit: Branded motor oil Expenses: Line 5 Line 13 |
| | Product differentiation | Sales volume: Premium motor oil | Region 2 sales volume: Premium motor oil |
| **Customer** Become easy to do business with. Deliver on our promises. | Grow target market | Market share: Branded motor oil | Region 2 market share: Branded motor oil Targeted customers sales volume |
| | Maintain/grow existing market | Develop/implement customer satisfaction plan | |
| **Internal** Develop market focused strategies. Support cost effective P&D. | Strategy implementation Optimize distribution network | Investment $ in distribution network Distribution strategy: % implemented Implement basic offering | Investment $ in distribution network Distribution strategy: % implemented |
| | Perfect order fulfillment | Perfect order % Demand forecast accuracy | Perfect order % |
| **Learning and Growth** Create a high-performance organization by equipping our people to succeed. | Strategic reskilling | Personal improvement plan: % implemented | Attend AMA course |
| | Cross-functional exposure | % workforce with experience outside line of business | Spend time learning other aspects of lubes business |
| | Empowerment/innovation | Develop something that doesn't exist today | Participate on the Installed Strategy Workteam |

*Data omitted for confidentiality.*

434

---

**EXHIBIT 5**  1996 Key Performance and Growth Areas

---

COMPETENCY DEVELOPMENT SUMMARY

| Competency | Leverage | Growth | Comments |
|---|---|---|---|
| Effective communication | X | X | Critical to gain consensus/alignment of organizations strategies, tactics and deliverables. |
| Develops and coaches | X | X | Help people work more efficiently and effectively. |

PERSONAL DEVELOPMENT PLAN SUMMARY

| Development action | Plan/BSC measure | Practice | Critique |
|---|---|---|---|
| Develop and coach | Attend "coaching" seminar and develop appraisal/survey template<br>Milestone dates:<br>Attend seminar by June 30<br>Develop survey template by July 30 | Preparation of 1996 SOR and profit plan | Survey assessment |

---

all the information systems available to generate these measures, and that's a huge concern to me. We have had unstructured management information. We've had too much in some area, and too little in others. I have this dream of a streamlined information capability designed around what we really need to run the business. The Balanced Scorecard has given us a blueprint for designing such a streamlined information system.

# MOBIL USM&R (D): GASOLINE MARKETING*

Gasoline Marketing (formerly known as Resale Services) was responsible for developing strategies for the sale of Mobil-branded gasoline in the US. Mobil conducted such sales through three channels. Lessee dealers operated stations for which Mobil owned or leased the underlying real estate. Non-lessee dealers were individuals who owned the real estate and operated the service stations under a contractual supply agreement. The third channel were distributors who sold Mobil products through their own network of dealers. In December 1995, Gasoline Marketing contained 165 people and an annual budget of $34 million.

Prior to 1994, operational relationships with dealers and distributors had been determined by senior executives operating from USM&R's Fairfax headquarters. The executives determined strategy and direction for all channels and drove their policies down through the sales organization. In June 1994, Mobil's US Marketing and Refining Division was reorganized to shift decision-making and profit responsibility from headquarters down to 17 natural busi-

---

*Professor Robert S. Kaplan prepared this case. Mr. Ed Lewis of Mobil's Business and Performance Analysis group provided invaluable assistance.

Copyright © 1996 by the President and Fellows of Harvard College. Harvard Business School case 197-028.

ness units (NBUs), responsible for refining, sales, and distribution of Mobil products. The previous top-down staff functions would now be performed in 14 free-standing service companies (referred to as servcos). In the short run, the NBUs would have to "purchase" services from the servcos. But by 1997, USM&R's Executive Leadership Team planned to allow NBUs to acquire services from an outside vendor if such an arrangement would be more cost effective for Mobil.

Marty DiMezza, a 30-year veteran at Mobil and former head of the Resale Services department, was appointed head of the new Gasoline Marketing servco. In the new decentralized organization, each servco had to develop and negotiate a service agreement, specifying service offerings and associated costs, with a buyers' committee consisting of four or five representatives from the 17 NBUs. DiMezza described the new challenge for his organization.

> We had to go through a major mental change: from a direction-giving organization to a service provider. Our people would have to learn how to partner with the NBUs [natural business units] to assist them in accomplishing their strategies.

---

**EXHIBIT 1** Gasoline Marketing and Strategic Role

---

**Mission**

**To build the best fuels franchise in the industry**

Provide value-added, cost-effective consulting services, programs, functional expertise, and marketing strategies with the goal of providing the best buying experience for the consumer and assisting the NBUs and our channel partners in achieving their profitable growth objectives

**Strategic Role**

**The role Gasoline Marketing plays in contributing to the achievement of the USM&R challenge is to:**

Partner with the NBUs to develop and help implement national and regional strategies
- Offer effective tools to improve execution of new and existing programs
- Implement real estate acquisition, disposal, and lease management strategies
- Provide profitability analysis for potential N deals
- Evaluate, endorse, provide economics, and develop proposals for all new distributor opportunities
- Provide training to develop the skill sets and knowledge of sales associates, channel partners, and NBU personnel on delivery of front-line service, c-store expertise, and retail excellence

Serve a leadership role to provide channel management expertise within USM&R
Foster functional alignment across USM&R
- Ensure consistency of national wholesale and retail gasoline marketing programs
- Maintain brand and image standards

Provide administrative support that allows NBU personnel and channel partners to focus their energy on the delivery of the best buying experience by:
- Accurate and timely contract/lease administration
- Maintaining fiduciary responsiblity for accounts receivable
- Ensuring legal integrity of contracts and leases
- Servicing dealers and distributors needs for POS maintenance and inquiry resolution
- Managing the Trammell Crow outsource relationship for real estate services
- Provide financial analysis to ensure credit worthiness and security requirement for new and existing assets

Provide NBU/SERVCO learning interventions and associated follow-up to develop a core business leadership competence
Create a value-added working relationship. We will work with our clients in a way that reflects the following values:
- Customer driven
- Client oriented
- Cost-effective
- Trusted
- Expertise
- Innovative
- Value added
- Responsive

Forging a service agreement with the buyers' committee created a lot of anxiety within our organization. For the first time in Mobil's history, we had to put together a bundle of services that someone else had to agree to buy. We had never before asked people whether they were willing buyers.

Gasoline Marketing set a mission to develop "the best fuel franchise within the oil industry" enabling it to increase the profitability of both franchisees and Mobil. The unit wished to shift away from its traditional arm's-length contractual arrangement with dealers to a more proactive alliance relationship. DiMezza's unit conducted benchmarking studies that examined the practices of 15 leading franchising companies, including McDonald's, Boston Markets, Goodyear, and Midas. The studies revealed the opportunity to forge innovative relationships that would attract the best entrepreneurs to become Mobil franchisees. The relationships included assistance in the training and development of dealers' front-line employees, customer-focused marketing programs, and new leasing and rental agreements. By December 1994, Gasoline Marketing had developed its first draft of a mission statement, and strategic role (see Exhibit 1) to support the NBUs. Shortly thereafter, it completed its first service agreement with its buyers' committee.

The effort by servcos to develop service agreements coincided with the USM&R's Balanced Scorecard project. DiMezza volunteered to have Gasoline Marketing be the pilot case study for developing a servco Balanced Scorecard: "I saw the scorecard as helping us achieve our mission to provide services to the field that would be competitive with those of any outside service organization."

Gasoline Marketing translated its overall mission into a set of strategic objectives organized around the four scorecard objectives: financial, client (the unit believed that the NBUs were more like clients than customers), internal, and learning and growth. The financial perspective focused on the cost of operating the unit and of the value created for the NBUs. The client perspective focused on services to the NBUs, as expressed through the service agreement negotiated with the buyers' committee, and also services provided to the executive leadership team (ELT) of USM&R. The internal perspective was geared to understanding the clients' needs, and the learning and growth perspective identified the needed commitments and strategies for developing Gasoline Marketing people to perform its new roles.

DiMezza noted the linkage between the service agreement and the scorecard:

> Several items we had identified in our menu of services were not perceived as valuable enough by the buyers' committee for them to purchase. If the buyers' committee didn't think the services were worth the price tag, we had to negotiate about whether to drop the service entirely or to reduce some of the bells and whistles we had incorporated. Conversely, we had not understood some of the areas that were high priority to them, and for which they wanted us to have more active programs. So it was an iterative process, revising our menu of services and reallocating our manpower and expense resources to the objectives that the field organization wanted to accomplish. But it was a learning and bonding process as we went through each iteration of the scorecard and service agreement.

Translating scorecard objectives to measures also proved challenging. Consultants from Renaissance Solutions facilitated the process of developing strategies and metrics for how servcos could help NBUs and USM&R attain their short and long-term strategic objectives. By the end of March 1995, the effort produced a Balanced Scorecard of objectives and measures for Gasoline Marketing (see Exhibit 2). The upper half (topside) of the scorecard, labeled "Link-

| MISSION |
| --- |

To Build the Best Fuels Franchise in the Industry

↓

| | Strategic Objective | Measurement |
| --- | --- | --- |
| Financial | Support USM&R market share and profitable growth<br><br>Support USM&R cost reduction | ❏ Market share<br>❏ NPBRE<br>❏ Rent income<br>❏ Retail P&L<br>❏ Wholesale P&L<br>❏ COT sales results<br>❏ Class of trade expenses (cpg) |
| Customer | Continually focus on delivery of the best buying experience | ❏ Customer satisfaction<br>❏ Mystery Shopper rating<br>❏ Dealer/distributor satisfaction |

↑ USM&R/NBU Linkages →

| | Strategic Objective | Measurement |
| --- | --- | --- |
| Financial | F1. Servco Operating Efficiency | ❏ Budget variance<br>❏ Indirect/direct ratio<br>❏ Cost per hour |
| Client | C1. Develop and maintain resale vision and strategies<br>C2. Develop and support programs that enhance franchise value<br>C3. Assist NBUs with strategy implementation<br>C4. Provide relevant information and facilitate communication<br>C5. Value-added working relationship | ❏ Client satisfaction (Service Agreement feedback)<br>• NBU<br>• ELT<br><br>❏ Tracking vs. program/tool KPIs |
| Internal | 11. Understand client needs<br>12. Reengineer the franchise offering<br>13. Excel in channel management<br><br>14. Enhance Servco operating efficiency<br>15. Support implementation of marketing plan<br>16. Optimize salesforce effectiveness | ❏ Key initiative tracking vs. milestones<br>❏ Tracking vs. channel strategy KPIs<br>❏ Competitive assessment (best practices)<br>❏ $ of cost reduction initiatives originated within the Servco or jointly<br>❏ Area manager feedback |
| Learning & Growth | L1. Core competencies and skills<br><br>L2. Organizational involvement<br>L3. Access to strategic information | ❏ Strategic competency availability —% coverage by competency<br>❏ Climate survey<br>❏ I/T reliability |

← Gasoline Marketing Scorecard →

**EXHIBIT 2  Gasoline Marketing Balanced Scorecard: 1995**

ages," identified the NBU/USM&R financial and customer objectives that Gasoline Marketing could impact. In general, the topside of a servco scorecard focused it on areas where it had the greatest impact on the business. The bottom half of the scorecard identified the strategies and measures for the servco to achieve its mission. The financial objective focused on operating efficiencies. Data were readily available for measures in this perspective. For the other three perspectives, however, almost no data were available for the desired measures. Plans were put in place to develop preliminary data for the remaining measures during the next few months. A high priority, the client perspective, would draw upon a new semi-annual survey of field operations to assess how the unit was performing against its service agreement (see sample form for the unit's support of retail dealer operations, one of eight major subunits run by Gasoline Marketing in Exhibit 3).

DiMezza observed:

> The topside linkages have added a lot of clarity to our people in the unit about how what they do day-to-day links to overall USM&R scorecard objectives. Reporting quarterly on the client satisfaction metrics on the unit's scorecard communicates and adds clarity to the individual service agreements and commitments we had made to the field organization.

In 1995, the variable compensation of senior managers in Gasoline Marketing was tied 50% to achievement of USM&R's scorecard targets, and 50% to individual performance.

Not everyone in USM&R believed that servcos needed their own Balanced Scorecards. Lucille Cavanaugh the new general manager of the Western Region business unit had formerly served as head of two NBUs and four servcos. Cavanaugh questioned the role of the Balanced Scorecard for servcos.

She felt that the buyers' committees were extremely useful and powerful in aligning servcos to business unit strategies. But having forged a service agreement, she had found the effort to translate the agreement to a servco Balanced Scorecard to be time-consuming and with little incremental payoff.

> Servcos should be focused on fulfilling their service agreement: did they deliver the service they committed to, and did they meet their cost target for the service? Either they did or they didn't so they don't require a Balanced Scorecard to communicate that information.

Dan Zivney, general manager (during 1995) of the Information Services servco felt, however, that the client satisfaction metrics provided better focus for his organization:

> The servco scorecard helps all our employees understand the importance of satisfying the customers who are the consumers of our projects. At the end of the day, did our project really do what the business unit wanted, in accordance with the efficiency, quality and responsiveness they expected? Were our people friendly, did we make errors, were we on time, within budget? All these attributes can be measured and incorporated into a servco scorecard. If I am held accountable to customer satisfaction, I will put in a greater effort, particularly at the front end, to understand what the customer is asking for in the first place, before I even start the project or activity.

Most servco scorecards had relatively light weight on the financial objectives, recognizing that once head count had been determined in the budgetary process linked to the service agreement, the financials during the year were largely determined. Much more weight was placed on measures in the client or customer perspective. But this introduced a new problem, identified by Jeff Webster, general manager of the Marketing Development servco: It's a little more difficult for servcos to develop Balanced Scorecards than the NBUs. The business units can use hard fi-

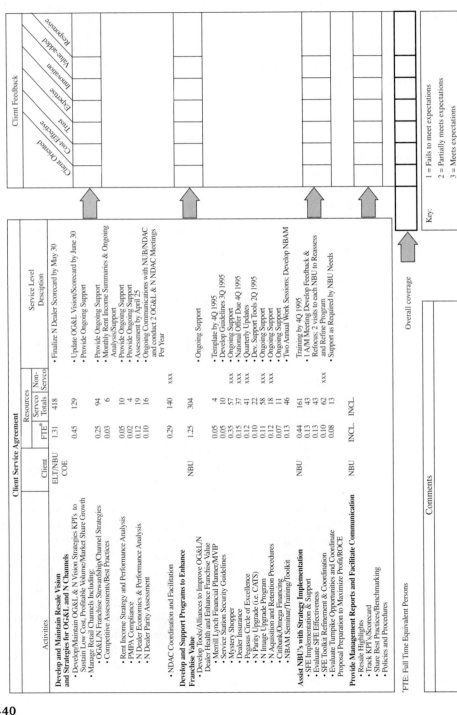

**Client Service Agreement**

| Activities | Client (ELT/NBU, COE, NBU) | Resources FTE* | Servco Totals | Non-Servco | Service Level Description |
|---|---|---|---|---|---|
| **Develop and Maintain Resale Vision and Strategies for OG&L and N Channels** | ELT/NBU COE | 1.31 | 418 | | |
| • Develop/Maintain OG&L & N Vision Strategies KPI's to Sustain Low Cost, Profitable Volume/Market Share Growth | | 0.45 | 129 | | • Finalize N Dealer Scorecard by May 30<br>• Update OG&L Vision/Scorecard by June 30<br>• Provide Ongoing Support |
| • Manage Retail Channels Including: | | | | | |
|   • OG&L/N Franchise Stewardship/Channel Strategies | | 0.25 | 94 | | • Provide Ongoing Support |
|   • Competitive Assessments/Best Practices | | 0.03 | 6 | | • Monthly Rent Income Summaries & Ongoing Analysis/Support |
|   • Rent Income Strategy and Performance Analysis | | 0.05 | 10 | | • Provide Ongoing Support |
|   • PMPA Compliance | | 0.02 | 4 | | • Provide Ongoing Support |
|   • N Dealer Economics & Performance Analysis | | 0.12 | 19 | | • Assessment by April 25 |
|   • N Dealer Parity Assessment | | 0.10 | 16 | | • Ongoing Communications with NUB/NDAC and conduct 2 OG&L & N NDAC Meetings Per Year |
| • NDAC Coordination and Facilitation | | 0.29 | 140 | xxx | |
| **Develop and Support Programs to Enhance Franchise Value** | NBU | 1.25 | 304 | | |
| • Develop Tools/Alliances to Improve OG&L/N Dealer Health and Enhance Franchise Value | | | | | • Ongoing Support |
|   • Merrill Lynch Financial Planner/MVIP | | 0.05 | 4 | | • Template by 4Q 1995 |
|   • Service Station Security Guidelines | | 0.05 | 10 | | • Develop Guidelines 3Q 1995 |
|   • Mystery Shopper | | 0.35 | 57 | | • Ongoing Support |
|   • Dealer Insurance | | 0.15 | 37 | xxx | • National Offer Due 4Q 1995 |
|   • Pegasus Circle of Excellence | | 0.12 | 41 | xxx | • Quarterly Updates |
|   • N Parity Upgrade (i.e. CATS) | | 0.10 | 22 | xxx | • Dev. Support Tools 2Q 1995 |
|   • N Image Upgrade Program | | 0.11 | 58 | xxx | • Ongoing Support |
|   • N Aquisition and Retention Procedures | | 0.09 | 18 | xxx | • Ongoing Support |
|   • Citibank/Omega Financing | | 0.07 | 11 | | • Ongoing Support |
|   • NBAM Seminar/Training/Toolkit | | 0.13 | 46 | | • Two Annual Work Sessions; Develop NBAM |
| **Assist NBU's with Strategy Implementation** | NBU | 0.44 | 161 | | |
| • SFE Implementation & Support | | 0.13 | 43 | | • Training by 4Q 1995 |
| • Evaluate SFE Effectiveness | | 0.13 | 43 | | • 1 A/M Meeting Develop Feedback & Refocus; 2 visits to each NBU to Reassess and Refine Program |
| • SFE Toolkit Refinement & Coordination | | 0.10 | 62 | | • Support as Required by NBU Needs |
| • Evaluate Turnpike Opportunities and Coordinate Proposal Preparation to Maximize Profit/ROCE | | 0.08 | 13 | xxx | |
| **Provide Management Reports and Facilitate Communication** | NBU | INCL. | INCL. | | |
| • Resale Highlights | | | | | |
| • Track KPI's/Scorecard | | | | | |
| • Share Best Practices/Benchmarking | | | | | |
| • Policies and Procedures | | | | | |

Client Feedback column headers: Client Oriented, Cost-Effective, Trust, Expertise, Innovation, Value-added, Response

Overall coverage

Comments

*FTE: Full Time Equivalent Persons

Key:
1 = Fails to meet expectations
2 = Partially meets expectations
3 = Meets expectations
4 = Exceeds expectations
5 = Greatly exceeds expectations

**EXHIBIT 3 Client Feedback—Retail Dealer Operations**

nancial measures; servcos must use more subjective, softer measures.

Tony Turchi, general manager of the New England Sales and Distribution business unit (see Mobil USM&R [B] case) and a member of the Gasoline Marketing buyers' committee, raised an additional concern with the servco scorecards.

> The issue comes down to whether the people from the servco are focused on supporting the business unit or the parent organization. The greatest success stories have occurred when the servco people are completely focused on the service agreements we have established, especially with the individual business units. Some servco people, however, appear to be focused only on how well the NBUs are performing on the topside measures, such as volume and profit. That's my responsibility. I don't need them on my case on these measures. When some of the servco general managers visited NES&D, most of the discussion was on how the business unit was performing and not a lot on how their servcos were supporting my business unit. They should stay focused on the deliverables in the service agreement.

Cavanaugh supported Turchi's argument: "Servco people out in the field should be thinking about how well they are linked to the business units they directly support, and how that linkage supports overall divisional goals."

The Gasoline Marketing group used the feedback from NBU managers when they revised their scorecard for 1996. The 1996 scorecard also incorporated explicit weights and targets for the topside and servco components.

The 1996 variable compensation of senior managers in Gasoline Marketing would be based on four components:

- USM&R BSC performance
- Topside (NBU linkage) performance
- Gasoline Marketing BSC performance
- Individual performance

with the USM&R and Topside performance representing slightly more than 50% of the weight.

DiMezza commented on the experiences during 1995.

> It's been a learning process to understand what involvement Fairfax should have in the individual business units. Initially there was some ambiguity about all the linkages between the servcos, the business unit, and the entire division. The difficulties were probably inevitable as we shifted from an organization that had been top-down driven to one that must clearly be field-business-unit driven, with support from Fairfax. I think that the 1996 scorecards will more clearly emphasize client satisfaction along our service agreements.

DiMezza concluded by reaffirming his support for a servco Balanced Scorecard:

> The scorecard and service agreement played a critical role for our leadership team to implement the servco concept and become a strategic partner with the USM&R business units. My challenge for 1996 is to communicate even better through the Gasoline Marketing organization about our strategic direction and to keep everyone focused on satisfying clients' needs. Starting in 1996, all individuals in the unit, from secretaries through general managers, will have their variable compensation linked to achieving USM&R and Gasoline Marketing scorecard targets.

# 9

## Financial Measures of Performance

## THE NATURE OF FINANCIAL CONTROL

Control refers to the tools and methods that organizations use to keep on track toward achieving their objectives. The process of control usually involves setting a performance target, measuring performance, comparing performance against that target, computing the difference (variance) between measured performance and the target, and taking action, if necessary, in response to the variance.

In this chapter, we will discuss some of the principal tools in financial control, including profit variance analysis, profit centers, transfer pricing, and productivity measures.

Central to the process of control is a target level of performance. Performance measures can be financial or nonfinancial. However, financial measures of performance have traditionally been, and continue to be, the most widely used. This chapter discusses the most common approaches to financial control.

## CONTROL IN THE AGGREGATE USING FINANCIAL MEASURES

There are two main reasons for the widespread use of financial performance measures. First, financial performance measures, such as profit, articulate directly with the organization's long-run objectives, which are almost always purely financial. Second, properly chosen financial performance measures provide an aggregate view of an organization's performance.

An aggregate financial performance measure, such as corporate or division profitability, is a summary measure of the success of the organization's strategies and operating tactics. Profit results that are below expectations provide a signal that the organization's strategies or tactics are not achieving their intended results and may be inappropriate. Such a signal will trigger a study that will uncover the reason for the unfavorable profit variance. Historically, these studies investigate whether the sales group achieved its sales volume and revenue targets and whether the manufacturing group achieved its cost targets. Now the focus has changed. In the 1980s, interest centered on discovering the drivers of organization costs—a process that came to be called activity-based costing. As we saw in Chapter 4, the role of activity-based costing is to uncover the organization's cost behavior so that the organization can manage and predict its costs. In the 1990s, managers also wished to discover the drivers of revenue (such as customer satisfaction and employee innovation)—a process widely called strategic performance measurement or the Balanced Scorecard discussed in chapters 5–8 and 10. When an organization understands what drives its revenue levels, it can take steps to manage the factors that create sales.

## CONTROL IN THE SMALL USING NONFINANCIAL MEASURES

Although organizations traditionally practiced control in the large, that is overall organization performance, using financial measures, they practiced control in the small, that is control of processes, using nonfinancial measures to supplement financial measures. For example, the performance of a manufacturing unit might be measured in terms of both cost per unit produced and number of defects. In general, interest in nonfinancial measures of performance reflected an understanding that financial measures of performance are, by their nature,

1. Short-run measures of results
2. Neither familiar nor intuitive ways for people to manage operations

Nonfinancial measures, such as quality, not only provide an explanation of current sales levels but also are potentially a predictor of future sales levels. Unfortunately, few organizations have undertaken a systematic consideration of how nonfinancial measures such as quality or productivity rates affect profitability levels[1]. Therefore, nonfinancial measures have mostly been used as relative measures of performance—the invocation to workers being to increase quality or productivity with the expectation that, somehow, doing so would result in higher profits. The key, as we saw in the discussion of the Balanced Scorecard, is to develop a systematic performance measurement system that allows the organization to identify the drivers of its long-run financial performance.

Despite the important and exciting insights offered by strategic performance measurement systems such as the Balanced Scorecard, financial control—that is, organization control driven by the use of financial measures—will continue to be an important management tool because of its aggregate nature and its direct relationship to the primary objectives of profit-seeking organizations.

## OPERATIONS CONTROL AND MANAGEMENT BY EXCEPTION USING VARIANCE ANALYSIS

A longstanding and widely used financial control tool is variance analysis. Variance analysis is the process of comparing a target level of revenues or costs with the realized level to compute a variance. The variance is a signal that the assumptions underlying the financial plan were not realized. Analysts investigate variances (typically unfavorable variances) deemed to be material to understand why expectations were not met and what course of action should be taken in light of the variance.

## An Example: Jersey River Book Publishing Company

The process of variance analysis is best illustrated by an example. The following example provides the basis for understanding the scope and nature of conventional variance analysis in financial control.

Jersey River Book Publishing Company publishes academic books. Emma Barker, the editor in chief, is studying the financials for an existing textbook. The analysis will help decide whether to offer a new edition. Jersey River not only publishes books but also prints the books, a practice that is unusual in the publishing industry, which usually contracts with outsiders for printing and distribution services.

Marketing and development people expected the textbook to sell 160,000 copies over its three-year life at an average price of $55. The book actually sold 180,625 copies at an average price of $52 (because of the unexpected release by a competitor of a new book). To manage total inventory-related costs, which include both setup costs and inventory carrying costs, Jersey River produces books in batches. The batch size planned for this text was 4,000 units per batch. The actual batch size realized was 5,000 books per batch because the production people believed that larger batch sizes would reduce salesforce complaints that there were too few books in the warehouse. Batch-related costs include equipment setup costs, which were planned to be $1,200 per batch but were actually $1,225 per batch because of chronic problems with the printing machines; work-in-process moving costs, which were planned to be $400 per batch but were actually $390 per batch because of improvements in the printing plant layout; and inventory holding costs, which were planned to be $32 per average unit held (average unit held equals one-half average batch size since demand is expected to be uniform during the life of the book) but were $34 per average unit held because of increases in insurance for inventory and water damage to some of the books.

Jersey River recognized seven types of unit-related costs per book. These costs were: paper—planned was $9.80 but actual was $10.20 reflecting the use of a higher grade of paper when complaints were received about the quality of paper in early batches; ink—planned was $0.95 but actual was $0.80 when the purchasing group found a new supplier; printing plant supplies—planned was $1.35 but actual was $1.30 because of unexpected price decreases in items such as electricity; sales commissions—5% of selling price and fixed by contract; royalties—15% of selling price and fixed by contract; binding costs—planned was $1.50 but costs increased to $1.63 when a new binding machine was purchased to deal with problems in applying glue and in early batches; and shipping costs—planned was $0.50 but actual was $0.44 with reductions in carton costs and a new agreement with the courier.

Product-related costs for the book were related to: the cost of the editorial staff—budgeted costs were $875,000 but were actually $825,000 because a staff vacancy occurred that was not immediately filled; the cost of preproduction—budgeted at $750,000 but actually $950,000 because of unanticipated graphics and demonstration software development costs; and promotion costs—budgeted at $475,000 but actually $540,000 (along with the price cut, in response to the competitor's new book).

Jersey River allocates its printing plant (factory) sustaining costs to each book using a complicated formula involving book size and production complexity. The rate used for this text was $8.00 per unit. Jersey River allocated its general and administrative (capacity-sustaining) costs to each product. The rate is based on the wages paid to editorial staff on the grounds that this figure reflects the long-term cost driver for these costs. The rate used is 75% of the salaries paid to editorial staff working on the book.

Exhibit 9-1 summarizes these events.[2] Note that the planned (master budget) profit was $619,750 for this book and that actual profit was $394,914, a difference of −$224,836. Emma Barker was very unhappy with the results. She wanted to know why profits were lower than planned given that unit sales were 20,625 more than expected.

## The Role of Variance Analysis

As illustrated in Exhibit 9-1, the variance analysis focuses exclusively on financial numbers that may suggest, but do not explicitly state, the cause of the variance. The variance analysis triggers a search to determine the underlying cause of the variance. The narrative for this problem suggested why costs differed from plan. These causes most likely would have been discovered in an investigation triggered by the variance.

## The Planning Variance

Conventional variance analysis decomposes the total variance between the budgeted and actual profit into the underlying components of the variance. In this case, the variance to be explained, the difference between master budget profit of $619,750 and actual profit of $394,914, is −$224,836. By convention, planners compute variances by subtracting the plan from the actual. Therefore, a positive variance for revenues is favorable—that is, revenue was more than planned—and a positive variance for costs is unfavorable—that is, cost was more than planned.

The first step in the reconciliation is to remove the effects of volume from the variance by recasting the master budget to targets that reflect the level of volume actually achieved. This step is done in the flexible budget. As shown in Exhibit 9-1, when the plan is recast to reflect the achieved level of sales of 180,625, the profit expectation rises from the master budget level of $619,750 to the flexible budget level of $1,062,638. Therefore, if the organization kept prices constant and achieved all its planned unit revenue and cost levels, with only volume changing, profits should have increased by $442,888 to reflect the increase in volume. Planners call this variance the **planning variance**, and it reflects the financial consequence of operating at an actual activity level different from that assumed in the master budget. Note that Exhibit 9-1 shows the planning variance for all revenue and cost items.

## The Flexible Budget Variance

Accounting for the volume effect has not explained the −$224,836 difference between planned and actual profits. In fact, the volume effect predicts further a profit increase of $442,888, whereas actual profits fell below the profit target in the original plan. The question is: What happened to the $667,724 of lost profits? This variance, called the **flexible budget variance** is explained by reconciling the flexible budget targets with actual results. Recall that the volume effect has been removed. Therefore, the remaining differences reflect variances that are due to the price or use of the budgeted items.

# EXHIBIT 9-1  Jersey River Book Publishing Company

① Planning Variance — due to vol (Revenue variance)

② Flexible Budget Variance — due to price or usage of budgeted items

| | Target Values | Master Budget (PLANNED) | Planning Variance | Flexible Budget (ACTUAL VOLUME) | Flexible Budget Variance | Actual Results |
|---|---|---|---|---|---|---|
| **Target Values** | | | | | | |
| Unit sales | 160,000 | 160,000 | 20,625 | 180,625 | 0 | 180,625 |
| Selling price | $55 | $55 | | $55 | | $52 |
| Units per batch | 4,000 | 4,000 | | 4,250 | | 5,000 |
| Revenue | | $8,800,000 | $1,134,375 | $9,934,375 | (541,875) | $9,392,500 |
| **Unit-Related Costs** | | | | | | |
| Paper | 9.80 | 1,568,000 | 202,125 | 1,770,125 | 72,250 | 1,842,375 |
| Ink | 0.95 | 152,000 | 19,594 | 171,594 | (27,094) | 144,500 |
| Supplies | 1.35 | 216,000 | 27,844 | 243,844 | (9,031) | 234,813 |
| Sales commissions | 2.75 | 440,000 | 56,719 | 496,719 | (27,094) | 469,625 |
| Royalties | 8.25 | 1,320,000 | 170,156 | 1,490,158 | (81,281) | 1,408,875 |
| Binding | 1.50 | 240,000 | 30,938 | 270,938 | 23,481 | 294,419 |
| Shipping | 0.50 | 80,000 | 10,313 | 90,313 | (10,838) | 79,475 |
| Unit carrying cost | 32.00 | | | | | |
| Total unit-related costs | | $4,016,000 | $517,688 | $4,533,688 | ($559,606) | $4,474,081 |
| **Batch-Related Costs** | | | | | | |
| Setup | 1,200.00 | 48,000 | 3,600 | 51,600 | (6,275) | 45,325 |
| Moving | 400.00 | 16,000 | 1,200 | 17,200 | (2,770) | 14,430 |
| Inventory holding costs | | 64,000 | 4,000 | 68,000 | 17,000 | 85,000 |
| Total batch-related costs | | $128,000 | $8,800 | $136,800 | $7,955 | $144,755 |
| **Product-Related Costs** | | | | | | |
| Editorial staff | 875,000 | 875,000 | 0 | 875,000 | (50,000) | 825,000 |
| Book development | 750,000 | 750,000 | 0 | 750,000 | 200,000 | 950,000 |
| Promotion | 475,000 | 475,000 | 0 | 475,000 | 65,000 | 540,000 |
| Total product-related costs | | $2,100,000 | $0 | $2,100,000 | $215,000 | $2,315,000 |
| **Facility-Sustaining Costs** | | | | | | |
| Factory-related costs | 8.00 | 1,280,000 | 165,000 | 1,445,000 | 0 | 1,445,000 |
| General and administrative | 75% | 656,250 | 0 | 656,250 | (37,500) | 618,750 |
| Total facility-sustaining costs | | $1,936,250 | $165,000 | $2,101,250 | ($37,500) | $2,063,750 |
| Total Costs | | 8,180,250 | 691,488 | 8,871,738 | 125,849 | 8,997,586 |
| Master Budget Profit | | $619,750 | | | | |
| Planning Variance | | | + 442,888 = | | | |
| Flexible Budget Profit | | | | $1,062,638 | | |
| Total Profit Variance | | | | ($224,836) | | |
| Flexible Budget Variance | | | | | (667,724) | |
| Actual Profit | | | | | | $394,914 |

## Flexible Budget Variances for Unit-Related Costs—Price and Quantity Effects

Recall that the numbers reported in the budget are the product of price and quantity elements. Therefore, in general, a variance, whether it is a cost or revenue variance, will have two components: a cost component and a quantity component.

One explanation for the revenue variance at Jersey River Book Publishing Company is the lower-than-planned revenue per book. The revenue variance was $3 per unit on 180,625 units: a total of $541,875 unfavorable. Note that the price variance identifies the effect of a price change but not the cause of the price change. This is the common feature of financial control tools; they identify the financial effect of a change but not its cause. This variance would trigger an investigation into the cause of the price decrease: marketing's response to competitive pressures or perhaps discounting to achieve the higher sales volume.

Note also the variances for the individual unit-related costs. These variances would trigger investigations that would result in the explanations mentioned in the narrative. Small variances, favorable or unfavorable, would not trigger an investigation. Most plans are subject to small variances because of uncertainties in estimating costs. An organization should investigate a variance only when the variance is large enough to suggest that something significantly different from what was planned happened and that something needs to be reconsidered to improve future planning.[3] For example, setup costs will vary because of the random nature of machines and the people who set them up. However, a large variance will signal more than a random event; there was something that systematically differed from plan.

To understand the meaning of a flexible budget variance, consider the variance for paper. The standard allowance for paper is $9.80 per book. The allowance will include both a price and a quantity component. Suppose that each book requires 20 units of paper at $0.49 per unit. Therefore, the target allowance of $1,770,125 in the master budget could be written either as

$$\text{Target allowance} = 180,625 \text{ books} * \$9.80 \text{ per book} = \$1,770,125$$

or as

180,625 × 20 units

$$\text{Target allowance} = 3,612,500 \text{ units of paper} * \$0.49 \text{ per unit of paper} = \$1,770,125$$

The actual results show that $1,842,375 was spent on paper. Suppose that further investigation reveals the following price and quantity components of total cost: 3,500,000 units of paper used at an average cost of $0.526 per unit. The excess use of paper reflects the problem that arose with the original paper and the decision to switch to a higher grade of paper—which is reflected in the higher average unit cost of the paper purchased. This example illustrates the standard elements of variance analysis; part of the variance is attributable to excess use (the quantity component), and part of the variance is attributable to the cost of the raw material (the price component).

Note that flexible budget variances are controllable by two groups of people in the organization. The price variance is related to the activities of the purchasing group, whereas the quantity variances are related to efficiencies in the production operations group. Variances may not be easily assignable to a responsibility center. For example, a purchasing group might purchase materials of a lower grade than planned in order to generate favorable price variances. However, the lower-grade materials might cause excess use in production because of defects. Therefore, the price variance must be conditioned on the quality of input (material, labor, supplies) envisioned in the plan, and the investigation should ensure that the variances were not caused by unplanned shifts in input quality.

## Flexible Budget Variances for Batch-Related Costs— Batch Size and Batch Cost Effects

The flexible budget called for production of 180,625 units in batches of 4,250, or 43 batches. The actual production took place in batches of 5,000 units, or 37 batches. Therefore, batch setup costs will fall by $7,200 (6 batches * $1,200 per batch) to $44,400 because production took place in larger-than-planned batches. However, batch setup costs were $45,325, meaning that the cost per batch was about $1,225 ($45,325/37) instead of the planned $1,200. Therefore, the setup cost per batch was $25 higher per batch than planned. Again, note the approach of decomposing the total flexible budget variance into a quantity and a price component. The same type of analysis would be applied to decomposing and investigating the flexible budget variance related to materials moving costs.

## Flexible Budget Variances for Product-Related Costs

Whereas flexible budget variances for unit-related costs and batch-related costs are deemed controllable in the short run by either purchasing (materials prices) or production (quantity) personnel, flexible budget variances for product-related costs have a very different nature. Unit-related costs are often called **engineered costs** because they have an engineered, or designed, relationship with the number of units made. For example, each automobile will have one steering wheel, one motor, one alternator, and so on. Engineered costs have a specified relationship with the number of units made. The role of the production personnel is to manage production so that the expected relationship between units produced and inputs consumed is achieved.

Product-related costs are quite different. Product-related costs arise from periodic decisions and are not directly tied to the number of units made. For example, the cost of editorial staff and the cost of preproduction development reflect the amount of work done getting the book ready and are not based on the number of units sold. For this reason, these costs are usually called **discretionary costs** to distinguish them from engineered costs. Discretionary costs are controlled by ensuring that the required amount of work was done and comparing the actual cost with the planned cost.[4] Therefore, actual discretionary costs that are higher or lower than planned amounts do not necessarily reflect either poor or good management; they may simply reflect the fact that less than the planned amount of discretionary work (that is, work that is not driven by the number of units made) was done.

## Facility-Sustaining Costs

The facility-sustaining costs in this example are assignments of the organization's facility-sustaining costs to products. They are intended to be an estimate of the increments to long-run costs caused by the production of the book. Therefore, these are not costs that production personnel can control or manage in the short run. Improved production methods can, in the long run, lead to decreases in these costs, but the lower costs of the improved production methods may not be reflected in the cost allocations.

## Summary

Exhibit 9-1 summarizes the elements of the flexible budget variance that provide insights into why the target level of profit in the flexible budget was not achieved. In general, these flexible budget variances reflect price or quantity variances in the use of the components of unit-related and batch-related costs and discretionary spending variances underlying product-related and facility-sustaining costs. For batch-related costs, in this example, the variances reflect the difference between the standard (flexible budget) and actual use of the deemed cost driver of the costs.

The variance analysis[5] is a classic example of financial control. It involves comparing an actual financial value with a target financial value to compute a variance. A variance deemed to be material indicates that some planning element (a price or a quantity) has not been realized. The variance is a warning signal that triggers an investigation to determine why the planned result was not realized.

---

# ORGANIZATION CONTROL USING PROFIT MEASURES

## Using Profits to Assess Organization Unit Performance

Profit is the most widely used measure of performance for a business firm. By evaluating the performance of decentralized units with a profit measure, senior managers hope to promote goal congruence between decentralized units and the firm by focusing attention on profitability.

Many definitions of a profit center have been proposed. At a purely descriptive level, one could define a profit center as any organizational unit for which some measure of profit is determined periodically.[6] But this definition fails to capture one of the major purposes behind the use of profit centers: to encourage local decision making and initiative. Merely measuring the profit generated by some organization unit does not make that unit autonomous or independent.

For our purposes, then, a **profit center** is a unit for which the manager has the authority to make decisions on sources of supply and choice of markets. In general, a profit center should sell most of its output to outside customers and should be free to choose the sources of supply for most of its materials, goods, and services. With this definition, it is unlikely that manufacturing or marketing divisions will be profit centers, even though many firms attempt to simulate local authority by assigning transfer prices to products transferred between manufacturing and sales divisions. This practice creates pseudo–profit centers since the company can now report a profit figure for these divisions even though they have limited authority for sourcing and pricing decisions.

Many managers of profit centers are evaluated not just on profit but also on the level of profit related to the fixed investment for their units. In this case, we refer to the unit as an **investment center**. Return on investment and residual income (also known as economic value added) are the most common performance measures used for investment centers. In this chapter, we will restrict our attention to profit measurement, deferring discussion of investment centers and their performance measures to Chapter 10. A profit center (as opposed to an investment center) is an appropriate structure for evaluating the performance of a unit manager if the quantity of plant and equipment is stable from year to year or is not controllable by the profit center manager. For example, if all major capital expenditure decisions are made at the top management level, then the local profit center manager is not controlling the level of investment and should not be held accountable for the past decisions on plant and equipment. Thus, the performance of the manager must be differentiated from the performance of the organization unit, especially when the best managers are assigned to problem or failing units in an attempt to revive those units.

Problems encountered in measuring profit include (1) choosing a profit index, including the allocation of jointly incurred costs and jointly earned revenues to the center, and (2) pricing the transfer of goods between profit centers.

## Choosing a Profit Index

Consider the following data from a division of the Easler Corporation:

| | |
|---|---|
| Revenue from division sales | $15,000 |
| Costs that vary with capacity use | 10,000 |
| Costs that vary with the level of capacity that are avoidable in the short run | 800 |
| Costs that vary with the level of capacity that are avoidable in the long run | 1,200 |
| Allocated G&A expense of corporation | 1,000 |

We can construct a structured divisional income statement as follows:

| | |
|---|---|
| Revenues | $15,000 |
| Costs that vary with capacity use | 10,000 |
| 1. Short-run operating margin | $ 5,000 |
| Other costs controllable in the short run | 800 |
| 2. Controllable contribution | $ 4,200 |
| Other costs controllable in the long run | 1,200 |
| 3. Divisional segment margin | $ 3,000 |
| Allocated corporate expenses | 1,000 |
| 4. Divisional profit before taxes | $ 2,000 |

We have a choice of at least the four indicated measures to evaluate the division's performance.

## Short-Run Operating Margin

The division short-run operating margin of $5,000 may be important for understanding the ability to control revenues and cost that vary with capacity use within the division, but it is not useful for performance evaluation. The division manager has control over other costs not included in this performance measure and has the option of trading off costs that vary in proportion to capacity use (for example, labor hours) for costs that are proportional to capacity acquired (for example, machine time). Therefore, the performance evaluation of the division manager should include, as a minimum, controllable costs that vary in proportion to capacity acquired.

## Controllable Contribution

The controllable contribution of $4,200 is the total division revenues less all costs that are (1) directly traceable to the division and (2) controllable by the division manager. This measure includes costs of providing capacity such as indirect labor, indirect materials, and utilities. The division manager can reduce these costs by streamlining operations or reduce complexity and diversity in product lines and marketing channels.

Controllable contribution is perhaps the best performance measure of division managers' performance because it measures managers' ability to use effectively the resources under their control and authority. An important limitation of this measure is the difficulty of distinguishing between controllable and noncontrollable capacity-related costs. For example, depreciation, insurance, and property taxes on fixed assets would be controllable if division managers had the authority to dispose of these assets but would not be controllable if they did not have that discretion. Also, salary levels of employees and supervisors may be set centrally, but division managers may choose how many workers and supervisors to employ at the division. In any event, controllable contribution ignores the capacity-related costs that can legitimately be attributed to a division and, therefore, some of the costs that a division imposes on the organization.

A tradeoff exists between the need to evaluate managerial performance and the need to measure the economic contribution of the segment to the overall organization. Segment performance can be affected by market conditions beyond the manager's control. For example, a good segment performance can result from excellent market opportunities but weak managerial performance. On the other hand, a weak segment performance can result from terrible market conditions but excellent managerial performance. Any profit performance reported by a segment must be evaluated relative to the potential of that segment, perhaps as expressed in the annual budget for the segment. But the manager usually participates in the budget-setting process and may be motivated to misrepresent potential opportunities in order to avoid the imposition of high performance standards. Kenneth Merchant described how several companies resolved the conflict between controllability and responsibility in their decentralized units.[7]

Controllable contribution measures, to some extent, the performance of the division manager, unencumbered by costs that may have been committed by other managers. On the other hand, controllable contribution, by ignoring attributable but noncontrollable (in the short run) capacity-related costs, provides an incomplete picture of the division's economic contribution to the organization.

## Divisional Segment Margin

The divisional segment margin of $3,000 represents the assessed contribution that the division is making to corporate profit and capacity-related costs that provide general purpose capacity, such as administrative and office resources. For the reasons mentioned above, it evaluates the performance of the division more than it does the performance of the division manager. Some of the division's capacity-related costs, such as the costs of factory space, warehouses, administrative personnel, and machinery, may result from past investment decisions made by top management. Also, the salaries of the divisional executives may be set by central management. The divisional contribution is clearly an important figure for evaluating the division's profitability, but unless the division manager is given the authority to restructure the investments or key personnel of the division, these costs are not controllable and hence may not be relevant in evaluating the manager's performance.

## Divisional Profit before Taxes

Many companies allocate all capacity-related costs incurred at the corporate level to their divisions. The motivation, apparently, is to alert division managers to the level of these common costs and indicate that the company as a whole is not profitable unless the revenue-producing divisions generate enough contribution margin to cover a fair share of these costs. Because the profits generated by divisions must exceed centrally incurred costs before the company is profitable, there is considerable interest in allocating these costs in order to identify each division's contribution to the company.

There are two broad complaints raised when centrally incurred capacity-related costs are allocated to divisions. The first complaint is that these allocations are often arbitrary. This complaint can be partially resolved by partitioning centrally incurred capacity-related costs into two groups: those that provide the primitive level of capacity that is required to be in business and those that reflect increments required to service the needs of the divisions. The argument is that organizations can use the cost driver for the second group of costs—those that reflect increments required to service the needs of divisions—to allocate those costs to divisions. However, the allocation of the costs of the primitive capacity is invariably arbitrary and clouds the interpretation of the results and often creates confusion and complaints within the organization.

The second complaint is that these centrally incurred capacity-related costs are usually not controllable at the divisional level since they reflect capacity choices made by other people. This complaint is partly addressed by basing cost allocations on centrally used capacity and requiring the central authority to absorb the costs of unused capacity.[8] Therefore, an unfavorable profit variance caused by an unexpectedly large corporate expense allocation cannot be attributed to division managers, who may have no control over expenditures on corporate staff functions.

If central management wishes to have divisions be profitable enough to cover not only their own operations but corporate expenses as well, it is probably better to establish a divisional contribution standard that will allow the recovery of centrally incurred capacity-related costs. The division managers can then concentrate on increasing revenues and reducing costs that are under their control and not be concerned with costs that they cannot control and that are allocated arbitrarily. Otherwise, division managers may attempt to increase their reported profits by negotiating allocation percentages rather than by spending time creating real economic value within their operations.

## Common Revenues

Occasionally, a conflict may arise on the allocation of revenues among profit centers. Such a conflict can occur if the salesforce for one division promotes the sale of products made by other divisions when calling on customers or when the organization is a complex value chain wherein each division adds a unique piece to the final product that the organization sells.

If a division receives no credit for selling the products of other divisions, little motivation exists for attempting to make such sales. A similar problem arises when branch banks are evaluated as profit centers. A customer may establish an account near her residence but conduct the majority of banking transactions with a branch near her place of work. Conflict between the branches could occur if all the revenues from the time and savings deposits were credited to the home branch and the costs of supplying banking services were charged to the branch near the business location. In this instance, it seems reasonable to construct a fee schedule that will provide some compensation (such as a finder's fee) from the product division to a salesperson from another division who makes a sale and from the home bank to the service bank for providing services. Such arrangements are complicated, and they illustrate the problems that arise from decentralized profit-directed operations.

## Transfer Pricing

We have already noted some of the difficulties that arise when decentralized organizational units have to interact with each other. Nowhere is there greater potential for conflict in such interactions than when goods produced in one unit are transferred to a second unit. If both units are organized as profit centers, a price must be placed on such transfers; this price represents a revenue to the producing division and a cost to the buying division. Therefore, the transfer price affects the profitability of both divisions, so the managers of both divisions have a keen interest in how this price is determined.

Early applications of transfer pricing were designed to facilitate the evaluation of unit performance. General Motors was one of the first and most energetic proponents of using transfer pricing to evaluate unit performance. This attitude reflected the history of General Motors, a company built by acquiring independent companies. The objective of evaluating unit profitability and using transfer pricing was to allow these formerly independent companies to maintain their identities and their competitive edge—to allow them to operate and to be evaluated as if they were independent organizations.

Alfred Sloan and Donaldson Brown, the senior managers of General Motors in the 1920s, understood well the importance of transfer pricing in this role:

> The question of pricing product from one division to another is of great importance. Unless a true competitive situation is preserved, as to prices, there is no basis upon which the performance of the divisions can be measured. No division is required absolutely to purchase product from another division. In their interrelation they are encouraged to deal just as they would with outsiders. The independent purchaser buying products from any of our divisions is assured that prices to it are exactly in line with prices charged our own car divisions. Where there are no substantial sales outside, such as would establish a competitive basis, the buying division determines the competitive picture—at times partial requirements are actually purchased from outside sources so as to perfect the competitive situation.[9]

In a survey of transfer pricing practice in large firms in Canada,[10] 85% of the responding firms reported that they used transfer pricing. In the responding firms, the transfer price was determined by:

| | |
|---|---|
| cost | 57% |
| market | 30% |
| negotiated | 7% |
| other | 6% |

The rationales for using transfer pricing included:

| | |
|---|---|
| for profit evaluation | 47% |
| for cost determination | 21% |
| for control and accountability | 23% |
| other | 9% |

Transfer prices serve two roles, which, unfortunately, usually conflict. First, as prices, they guide local decision making; they help the producing division decide how much of the product to supply and the purchasing division decide how much to acquire. Second, the prices and subsequent profit measurement help senior management evaluate the profit centers as separate entities.

There is a potential for conflict whenever a number, such as divisional profit, that can be manipulated or otherwise affected by managerial behavior is used to evaluate performance. The problem is that when managers take actions to manipulate the performance measure, decision making often suffers. If division managers are encouraged to maximize their individual divisional profits, they may take actions with respect to other division managers that cause overall corporate profits to decline. For example, a purchaser may want to source outside the company from a supplier that is offering distress prices that cannot be sustained over the long term.

The conflict between decision making and evaluation of performance is the essence of the transfer pricing conundrum. A further conflict occurs if managers emphasize short-term performance in their transfer price negotiations at the expense of long-run profitability of their division and the firm.

## Market Prices

Under a restrictive set of conditions, which are rarely realized in practice, the choice of a transfer price is clear. If a highly competitive market for the intermediate product exists, then the market price (less certain adjustments) is the proper transfer price. The conditions of a highly competitive market imply that the producing division can sell as much of the product as it wishes to outside customers, and the purchasing division can acquire as much as it wishes from outside suppliers without affecting the price. In this case, the market provides an objective valuation of the intermediate product, and that price should be used to price transfers and guide decisions within the firm.

If the purchasing division cannot make a long-run profit at the outside market price (assuming that the market price is a reasonable approximation of the long-run price and not simply a short-run distress price), then the company is better off to not produce the product internally and to go to the external market for its supply. Similarly, if the purchasing division cannot make a long-run profit when it must acquire the product at the external price, the division should cease acquiring and processing this product and should allow the producing division to sell all its output to the external market. With a competitive market for the intermediate product, the market price provides an excellent basis for allowing the decisions of the producing and purchasing divisions to be independent of each other.[11]

Some modifications to the pure market price rule facilitate its use in practice. The company will usually benefit if the transaction occurs internally rather than having a producing division sell a certain amount externally while the purchasing division is acquiring the same amount from its own outside suppliers. Internal rather than external transfers are encouraged by means of a discount from market price that is offered to reflect savings on selling and collection expenses and the delivery, service, or warranty terms associated with external sales. This discount will encourage an internal transfer, all other factors being held equal.

Offsetting the desire to coordinate transactions within the firm is the frequent difficulty that division managers have in negotiating the terms of transfers with other divisions in the company. Hidden costs can arise if the buying division makes unreasonable delivery demands (which may not be imposed on external suppliers) on the selling division or when the selling division manager has concerns that any foul-up in product quality or delivery will become publicized throughout the organization, as expressed by the following complaint from the manager of a supplying division:

> It is more difficult to work inside than externally. In the smallest impasse, a person can go up the line. Nobody wants to have the boss coming and making accusations of not cooperating. It is always difficult, so you need a financial incentive or something else, such as recognition for being a good corporate citizen.

Sometimes the transaction must occur internally, rather than externally, to maintain product quality or product confidentiality requirements. In this case, the market price may be adjusted to reflect the extra cost required to meet a more stringent quality standard or special features available only from internal manufacture. The challenge is to keep an accumulation of such special charges from driving the price far above the prices of comparable products available externally. A profit-conscious manager of the purchasing division will usually provide the necessary discipline.

Additional problems arise from the conflict between short-run and long-run considerations. An external supplier may quote a low price in an attempt to buy into the business, with the expectation of raising prices later. The company ordinarily should not switch its source of supply from an internal division to an outside company unless it is confident that the outside company has the potential to maintain the quoted price for a substantial period. A similar conflict arises when the price for the intermediate product or service is quoted on both a long-term-contract and a spot-market basis. As more of these complicating factors intrude into the price-setting process, they begin to violate our basic assumption of a perfectly competitive market for the intermediate product. When the market is not perfectly competitive, as it usually is not for most manufactured goods, the transfer price problem becomes much more complicated.

As more of these complications intrude into the transfer pricing mechanism, we get additional evidence of the difficulty of using market prices to coordinate transactions within the firm. If market prices existed that allowed optimal resource allocation and managerial evaluation decisions to be made within the firm, little reason would exist to keep the different divisions within a single corporate entity. The units could function as independent market entities, since no gain apparently would arise from centralized control. Thus, an ability to uncouple divisional operations through an extensive array of market-based transfer prices is inconsistent with any gains accruing from operating these divisions within a single corporate organization.[12]

## Using Marginal-Cost Transfer Prices

It is a trivial mathematical exercise to show that the optimal level of production, and therefore the optimal transfer level of an intermediate product, takes place when price equals marginal cost. Unfortunately, economic theory is vague about the meaning of marginal cost. However, classical economic theory makes the assumption, which can never be met in practice, that capacity can be adjusted continuously without adjustment costs. Not only does this mean that, in classical microeconomic theory, the firm is always operating at the level of capacity that minimizes average cost, but it also means that any incremental change in costs will cause capacity to adjust and therefore cause capacity-related costs to change. Therefore, in classical microeconomic theory, marginal cost includes capacity-related costs.

Unfortunately, accountants have been careless in applying this pricing prescription from microeconomic theory to practice. They attempted to use the economic reasoning that suggests that the optimal transfer price should be the price that equates supply and demand. Using this rule means that the transfer price will equal the short-run short-term variable cost to supply the intermediate product plus an increment to ration existing capacity. Whenever capacity is not constraining production, this rule suggests that the transfer price should equal marginal costs, which accountants have interpreted as the short-term variable costs.

A widely used variation of this rule, which produces the same result, is to set the transfer price equal to short-term variable cost plus the opportunity cost of the capacity used to make the product. So, for example, if the product has an outside market, the transfer price will be market price since the opportunity cost of using the product internally will be the profits foregone by not selling the product in the external market.

Despite being promoted in the academic literature for many years, this rule of using a transfer price that equals short-term variable cost plus an increment to equate supply and demand for capacity has been consistently rejected by practitioners. The reasons are that product-related decisions are long-run decisions that must reflect long-run pricing considerations and that this rule would be impractical to implement in practice anyway.

The point is that organizations must consider all the consequences of pricing rules. Recall that organizations are a value chain that requires complex interactions among the links or components of the value chain. A transfer price is intended to help manage and moderate the level of coordination required. A transfer price that varies up or down as capacity changes provides mixed signals to the other links in the value chain about the economic value of the transferred commodity and creates chaos in the value chain as the various downstream links adjust to the varying transfer price. Long-run planning, which is necessary in most product situations, requires some stability in pricing and a good estimate of the long-run costs, which include the costs of all the resources required to sustain and produce the product.

Therefore, short-term variable cost transfer pricing is rejected for most situations for two reasons. First, short-term variable cost transfer pricing will not provide an economic signal about the long-run cost of supplying the commodity, which is required for long-term planning and stability in a complex value chain. Second, modifying short-term variable cost transfer pricing by adding an arbitrary markup to reflect capacity costs does not deal with the problem identified in the first objective. Not only does the transfer price not reflect the long-run cost of making the product, but, through continuous variation, it causes confusion and disorder in the value chain.

## Using Activity-Based Costs for Transfer Pricing

The reconciliation between the economists' plea for using long-run marginal cost for transfer pricing and how costs are measured in practice can now be accomplished by using activity-based cost estimates as the transfer pricing mechanism.[13] In this approach, the purchasing unit is charged for the unit- and batch-related costs associated with any products transferred to it, plus an annual fixed fee, calculated from the product-related and facility-sustaining costs, for the privilege of obtaining these transfers. Under this scheme, the purchasing division sees the marginal long-run costs of the transfers and can use this information to choose an output level to maximize profits by equating long-run marginal cost to marginal revenue. The producing division has the opportunity to recover all its costs, including its capacity-related costs. If the transfer price also includes a component related to the assets employed (as discussed in Chapter 5 and revisited in Chapter 10, with the discussion of economic value added), it can earn a profit through the fixed fee charged each period. The assignment of product and facility-sustaining costs represents a reservation price that the purchasing division pays for the privilege of acquiring the intermediate product during that year at short-run marginal cost—defined as the unit and batch costs associated with the production of incremental units.

Assigning product and facility-sustaining costs as a fixed annual fee raises some interesting motivational and control issues. Suppose that the fixed fee assigned to each user is based on that user's planned (or long-run average) use of the product and facility. For example, if a division uses 20% of the average capacity, the division is assigned 20% of the fixed costs of the facility. The prepaid capacity would be reserved for the user paying for that capacity. This scheme has two desirable economic traits. First, in the short run, transfers will take place at short-run marginal (unit plus batch) cost, as economic theory dictates. Second, people will tend to be more honest in the capacity acquisition stage. If they overstate their expected requirements, perhaps to ensure adequate capacity for their own use, they will pay a higher fixed fee in later years. If they understate their expected requirements, to avoid the fixed fee for capacity, they may not have sufficient capacity for their needs as capacity either is not acquired or is reserved for others who have expressed a willingness to pay the fixed fee for that capacity.[14]

Suppose, however, that expectations are not realized. Then the approach will not be best for the firm overall unless some reallocations of capacity take place. When expectations are not realized, capacity allocations based on expectations may no longer be assigned to the most profitable current uses. This problem can be overcome by allowing divisions to subcontract with each other so that a division, facing better opportunities, could rent the capacity previously reserved by another division.

This flexible transfer pricing, which incorporates both marginal and capacity-related costs, is perfectly generalizable. For example, suppose an automobile dealership, after negotiations with the managers of the new- and used-car departments, chooses a level of capacity for its service operations. The negotiations end up with the new-car operations reserving 20% of capacity, the used-car department reserving 30% of capacity, and the service department's expecting to use (for outside customers) 50% of capacity. Now suppose that the used-car operation falls upon hard times. It must still pay its share of the capacity-related costs of the service department. This is proper: Its estimates were used in the capacity acquisition decision. If these capacity-related costs were not assigned to the used-car department, they would be reallocated to the other two departments—in effect, causing them to bear the costs of the used-car department's failure to use the capacity that it reserved. Therefore, this scheme is consistent with responsibility accounting.

In the limit, the fixed-fee plus short-term variable scheme yields either a pure market or a pure cost-plus operation. For example, suppose the service department did no outside work. In this case, it would be responsible for none of its capacity costs and would become a pure cost center. Jobs would be priced at standard costs, which include the cost of capacity used, and the only goal of the service department would be to provide quality service, on time, and at below-standard cost. On the other hand, suppose the service department did no internal work. Then it would be a pure profit center, and all transfers would be at market prices. Therefore, this scheme blurs the distinction between pure cost and pure profit centers by operating over a continuum. Also, the scheme provides a justification for retaining both production and acquisition activities within the firm. Such a dual-price scheme for internal transfers would be difficult to implement and enforce if the divisions did not operate under centralized control.

The approach of a budgeted fixed fee to cover capacity-related costs and to provide a return to capital, plus an incremental cost based on short-term variable cost per unit for each unit transferred leads to efficient resource allocation among divisions while still letting purchasing divisions see the full cost of obtaining goods or services from other divisions. One is motivated to ask: If this is such a great scheme, why is it not widely used? We can only speculate that the need to account for usage and to acquire capacity on a planned and systematic basis may have prevented a more widespread use of this approach to transfer pricing.

## Full Costs

Recent surveys of transfer pricing practice indicate that the most popular method of determining transfer price in practice is a full-cost pricing scheme, but one that uses the company's traditional standard costing system, not an ABC system, to calculate manufacturing costs.[15]

Serious problems arise when accountants estimate full cost using traditional accounting methods that assign capacity-related costs to products in arbitrary ways. One popular method is to divide capacity-related costs by the number of units produced to get a capacity-related cost per unit. That unit rate is then used to allocate capacity-related costs to current production. This approach to transfer pricing has three very unfortunate characteristics.

First, it provides a varying transfer price since the cost per unit is constantly changing as capacity use varies. Second, by mixing the short-run and long-run components of cost, it obscures the underlying cost structure from decision makers in the organization and therefore fails to suggest how cost savings can be obtained by using capacity more efficiently. What is worse, however, is that the full-cost approach is often implemented by using a formula approach that takes variable cost and adds an arbitrary markup to cover capacity-related costs and perhaps a targeted profit margin. In other words, many full-cost schemes are not *costing systems* at all but *cost recovery systems* that make no attempt to reflect underlying cost behavior.

As a simple illustration of the perverse effects of an inappropriately designed full-cost transfer pricing scheme, consider the practice of a large industrial company that allocates all corporate G&A (general and administrative) expenses to its operating divisions and imposes a transfer price based on cost plus profit markup for all internal transfers. Assume that it is manufacturing a product that must be processed through three divisions before final sale. The company allocates $12,000 of G&A administrative expenses to the three divisions manufacturing this product. Transfers between divisions are done at full cost plus 20% markup, which is also the procedure used to price the final product.

Suppose the G&A expenses are allocated equally to each division: $4,000 each. The first division takes the $4,000 allocation, marks it up by 20%, and transfers these costs to the second division (along with all other product-related costs). The second division now has not just its own $4,000 G&A expense allocation for the product but also the $4,800 from the first division ($4,000 + 20% markup). Division 2 takes the $8,800 G&A allocation, marks it up by 20%, and transfers a total of $10,560 to Division 3. The third division accumulates its own $4,000 allocation with the $10,560, adds the 20% markup to this sum of $14,560, and obtains a total of $17,472 of corporate G&A that must be added to the final price of the product. Thus, the $12,000 of G&A has been increased not by a standard 20% markup but by a 46% markup ([17,472 − 12,000]/12,000) because of the escalating effect as the product passes from one division to the next. When last heard from, the company was calling in a consultant to determine how competitors were able to price their products so much lower and why the company was steadily losing market share in its product lines. Poorly conceived transfer pricing policies can be highly dysfunctional.

With all these problems, we must ask why the full-cost approach to transfer pricing is so widely practiced. We must distinguish between two situations.

Where an external market price exists, there appears to be little justification for the use of a cost-based approach to pricing. Where there is no external market price, a full-cost price may be used as a surrogate for the long-run marginal cost to the firm of manufacturing the product if costs are appropriately modeled. As we saw in Chapter 4, activity-based costing does make this attempt by identifying the cost drivers for capacity-related costs. So why is not short-run cost used to price transfers, as economic theory dictates? One executive observed:

> When we add a product to our product line, we expect to continue to offer it on a full-time basis. It is not practical to offer products only in the short run when conditions seem right and then, in the longer run, or periodically, say to our customers that we cannot produce this product this period because our costs are now too high.

This executive believes that irrespective of the short-run cost, product decisions reflect long-run commitments and should therefore be based on long-run cost that includes a component related to capacity costs. Product decisions imply commitments to product continuity and the integrity of the product line and therefore provide a justification for full-cost pricing. The discussion in Chapter 4 on activity-based costing suggests how this method measures long-run variable cost and therefore aims to provide a transfer price that reflects the costs of the long-run commitments made in capacity and product introduction decisions.

## ✗Dual-Rate Transfer Prices

In a dual-rate transfer pricing scheme, the supplier receives the net realizable value (the market price less finishing costs) for the commodity that is transferred while the buyer pays the sum of out-of-pocket and opportunity costs of producing the product. In this way, both the buyer and the seller are motivated to demand and supply the optimal amount of the quantity. This scheme raises the issue of estimating opportunity costs, and, in an environment in which managers are rewarded based in divisional profits, it can motivate suppliers to misrepresent their opportunity costs. Possibly because of these problems, the dual-pricing scheme is implemented in practice by substituting an allocation of capacity-related cost as an estimate of the opportunity cost; that is, the selling division receives its full cost in the transfer, but the buying division is charged only for the marginal cost.

At first glance, the dual-pricing scheme seems very attractive, but several companies that have tried it eventually abandoned the practice.[16] Senior management objected to having the sum of divisional profits exceed overall corporate profits. In an extreme situation, buying and selling divisions could all show profits while the corporation as a whole is losing money. Thus, divisions would report profits at or above budget, only for large write-downs to occur, to eliminate the double counting of profits among divisions, when the books were closed at the corporate level. One company president noted:

> Dual pricing sort of died of its own complexity and conflict. There were situations in which divisions could get something internally that didn't exactly fit their needs but went ahead and got it because actual full cost was so much less than market price.

The dual-price system encouraged divisions to shift more of their mix to internal sales and purchases at the highly favorable terms. Internal sales increased well beyond expected levels. When business was poor and the selling units could not meet their budget for external sales, they generated excessive internal sales. Similarly, because buying units received internal product at cost, they had little incentive to negotiate for more-favorable prices from external or even internal suppliers. In general, neither division in a dual-pricing scheme has a high incentive to monitor the performance of the other division. Thus, the dual-pricing scheme, by lowering the incentives for buying and selling divisions to deal in the external market, could lower overall corporate profitability.

## Negotiated Market-Based Price

Given the lack of a perfectly competitive market for the intermediate product and the limitations of cost-based pricing rules, perhaps the most practical method for establishing a transfer price is through negotiation between the managers of the two divisions. The negotiating process typically begins when the producing division provides a price quotation plus all relevant delivery conditions (timeliness, quality, and so on). The purchasing division may

1. Accept the deal
2. Bargain to obtain a lower price or better conditions
3. Obtain outside bids and negotiate with external suppliers
4. Reject the bid and either purchase outside or not purchase at all

In a different sequence, the purchasing division may make an offer to the producing division for a portion of its current output or an increment to current output. The producing division can then bargain with the purchasing division over terms, talk to its existing customers, or decide not to accept the purchasing division's offer.

In either case, a negotiated transfer price requires that the managers of both divisions be free to accept or reject a price at any stage of the negotiation. Otherwise we would have a dictated price rather than a negotiated price.

The conditions under which a negotiated transfer price will be successful include

1. Some form of outside market for the intermediate product. This avoids a bilateral monopoly situation in which the final price could vary over too large a range, depending on the strength and skill of each negotiator.
2. Sharing of all market information among the negotiators. This should enable the negotiated price to be close to the opportunity cost of one or preferably both divisions.
3. Freedom to buy or sell outside. This provides the necessary discipline to the bargaining process.
4. Support and occasional involvement of top management. The parties must be urged to settle most disputes by themselves, otherwise the benefits of decentralization will be lost. Top management must be available to mediate the occasional unresolvable dispute or to intervene when it sees that the bargaining process is clearly leading to suboptimal decisions. But such involvement must be done with restraint and tact if it is not to undermine the negotiating process.

A negotiated-price system has the following limitations:

1. It is time-consuming for the managers involved.
2. It leads to conflict between divisions.
3. It makes the measurement of divisional profitability sensitive to the negotiating skills of managers.
4. It requires the time of top management to oversee the negotiating process and to mediate disputes.
5. It may lead to a suboptimal level of output if the negotiated price is above the opportunity cost of supplying the transferred goods.

The negotiated-price system depends also on the willingness of external suppliers or purchasers to supply legitimate bids to the company. If, each time these external bids are solicited, the transfer price is determined so that all transfers are eventually made internally, the external bidders will soon tire of participating in this exercise. Therefore, some amount of external purchase or sale should be a realistic expectation in order to keep the faith of these outside participants and thereby ensure a continuing source of legitimate external prices. Despite these limitations, however, a negotiated-transfer-price system seems to offer desirable mechanisms for permitting local managers to exploit the specialized information they possess about local opportunities.

## Transfer Pricing—A Summary of Practice

Transfer pricing is a tool that organizations use to coordinate the activities of organizational units. The objective of using this financial measure of performance is to drive the division units, acting in their individual self-interest and reacting to local signals (their own costs, prices, and market opportunities), toward behavior that is best for the organization.

But, as we have seen, transfer pricing practice can be quite complex since it is often implemented in difficult situations. As Ronald Coase[17] observed, economies of scale, synergies, and saving transactions costs motivate organizations to conduct transactions within the firm rather than using market-based transactions with external suppliers and customers. If successful, such vertical integration should lower costs as transactions occur among related parties. But the corporation cannot expect a pure transfer price solution to be able to treat buying and selling divisions as independent entities.

It is true that no one transfer pricing system will work best in all organizations. Rather, the transfer pricing practice chosen in a particular firm must reflect the requirements and characteristics of that firm and must ultimately be judged by the decision-making behavior that it motivates.

We have covered a lot of ground in our discussion of transfer pricing. We have obtained some results under fairly restrictive conditions, and we have discussed some pitfalls from using transfer prices inappropriately. We can summarize our current recommendations as follows:

1. Where a competitive market exists for the intermediate product, the market price, less selling, distribution, and collection expenses for outside customers, represents an excellent transfer price.

2. Where an outside market exists for the intermediate product but is not perfectly competitive and where a small number of different products are transferred, a negotiated-transfer-price system will probably work best, since the outside market price can serve as an approximation of the opportunity cost. At least occasional transactions with outside suppliers and customers must occur if both divisions are to have credibility in the negotiating process and if reliable quotes from external firms are to be obtained.

3. When no external market exists for the intermediate product, transfers should occur at the long-run marginal cost of production. This cost will facilitate the decision making of the purchasing division by providing the stability needed for long-run planning but at the same time exposing the cost structure so that short-run improvements and adjustments can be made. A periodic fixed fee based on capacity reserved for the buying division is incorporated in the marginal cost calculation. The fixed fee, ideally based on product and facility-sustaining costs from an ABC model, should allocate the capacity-related costs of the facility in proportion to each user's planned use of the facility's resources. The fixed fee forces the purchasing division to recognize the full cost of the resources required to produce the intermediate product internally, and it provides a motivation for the producing divisions to cooperate in choosing the proper level of productive capacity to acquire.

4. A transfer price based on fully allocated costs per unit (using present, that is, non-ABC, methods of allocation) or full cost plus markup has no discernible desirable properties. Although the full-cost transfer price, as presently computed, has limited economic validity, it remains widely used. The marginal cost calculated from an ABC model does provide the capability for managers to use a full-cost approach that is consistent with economic theory.

Robert Eccles, after an extensive field study of transfer pricing practices, found it useful to link the transfer pricing policy to two types of strategic decisions: sourcing decisions and pricing decisions.[18]

### Sourcing Decision

Some companies follow a deliberate strategy of vertical integration that mandates internal transfers between divisions. The vertical integration creates interdependencies among production, selling, and distribution profit centers, but the prices of the internal transfers are not factors in determining the sources of intermediate goods. When the firm has no explicit strategy of vertical integration, transfers are not mandatory and the price of the intermediate good determines whether a transfer is made internally or sold and sourced externally.

### Pricing Decision

The pricing decision determines whether the intermediate good contains a margin for profit (or loss). A margin for profit (or loss) is included in the transfer price when the selling division is regarded as a profit center for the transferred product. Alternatively, the selling division could be viewed as a cost center for internal transfers and a profit center only for products sold externally. In this case, the internal transfer could be made at some cost-based price, and all profits or losses for this product would be realized by the division making final sales to external customers.

With this classification scheme, Eccles found that companies without an explicit vertical integration strategy relied on negotiated transfer prices between buying and selling divisions. In general, the resulting transfer price included a margin for profit (or loss) for the selling division.

For firms following a vertical integration strategy, with mandated internal transfers of certain products between divisions, two possible transfer prices could occur. Market-based prices would be used when the selling division was to be viewed as a profit center for all its transactions. Full-cost, or occasionally dual-price, systems would be used when the selling division was treated as a cost center for internal transfers.

## Domestic versus International Transfer Pricing

Whereas internal transfer pricing issues that provide for motivational effects have been the focus of interest for management accountants, the rise of the multinational organization has generated a very different interest and perspective on transfer pricing. The international transfer price is the price that an organization uses to transfer products between a unit in one country and a unit in another country. Note two important issues. First, such transfers are not arm's-length transactions. Second, absent tax considerations, this transaction would reflect the same considerations that we have discussed so far.

Taxes introduce another layer of complexity into transfer pricing. Consider an organization that manufactures products in Country A, which has a marginal tax rate of 20%, and sells those products in Country B, which has a marginal tax rate of 30%. Obviously, this organization would like to locate most of its profits in Country A, where the tax rate is lowest. Therefore, it will want to use the highest possible transfer price for the commodity. For many organizations, these tax considerations outweigh the behavioral considerations in setting a transfer price, and transfer pricing policy is driven by the objective of minimizing global taxes.[19]

Needless to say, tax authorities understand this incentive and have taken steps to moderate corporate behavior. The tax authority in each country scrutinizes the international transfer pricing policies of companies doing business in that country to ensure that these companies are not using arbitrary transfer prices to avoid paying local taxes. The most important document relating to international transfer pricing is the 1995 Organization for Economic Co-Operation and Development (OECD) guidelines statement.[20] This document is important because it provides the foundation that many nations use to develop their individual tax laws that regulate transfer pricing behavior for organizations that do business in their respective countries.

With regard to transfer pricing, the OECD guidelines are very similar to discussions that surround domestic transfer pricing. The OECD guidelines clearly imply that, whenever possible, the transfer price should reflect economic circumstances.

The OECD guidelines divide transfer pricing practices into two main groups. The **transaction group** includes the comparable uncontrolled price (CUP), cost-plus, and resale price methods. The **other methods** include profit splits, transactional net margin methods, and other approaches that are related to partitioning the profits from trading. The OECD guidelines state that, whenever possible, the CUP method, which uses either the market price or an imputed market price, should be used. If there is no market price, preference falls to cost-plus.

Studies of practice suggest that the cost-plus method of transfer pricing is the most widely used for internal (domestic) transfer pricing but that the market price method is the most widely used for international transfer pricing. Apparently, if given free choice, firms that use market prices to meet international transfer pricing requirements would switch to cost-plus methods. In other words, there is a group of organizations that swing from using cost-based transfer prices to market-based transfer prices in the presence of a tax authority. Alternatively, the results of these studies may mean that firms use market-based transfer prices to meet the requirements of tax authorities because they are to the firms' advantage. But the firms do not really believe that the profit signals provided by these market prices are meaningful, so they prefer to use cost-based methods for internal decision making.

Other than this interesting anomaly, it is instructive to observe how tax authorities interpret the cost component of a cost-based transfer price. It appears that most tax authorities allow organizations to use whatever costing systems their external auditors have certified as conforming to GAAP. For example, the Canadian tax regulation states

> When using the "cost-plus method," cost must be computed in accordance with
> generally accepted accounting principles or normal commercial accounting practices
> in the industry in Canada, even though some other computation of cost may be
> acceptable in the foreign country.

Because GAAP was designed for external reporting purposes, and not for making sound economic operating decisions, it permits a huge variation in costing practice. Such flexibility creates an opening for opportunistic behavior by the taxpayer to select tax-minimizing methods when computing a cost-based transfer price.

## Other Measures of Performance

Apart from transfer pricing policies, two additional problems remain with using profit as a measure of divisional or firm performance:

1. Profit provides only an aggregate indication of the firm's ability to achieve the goals that are crucial to its success. It provides no direct indication to the organization members of what they can do individually to improve the performance of the firm.
2. Profit has a short-run orientation and therefore can be manipulated. The manager can take steps to improve short-run performance at the expense of long-run profit considerations.

We have identified a number of problems with profit measurement, but probably the most serious concern with a narrow focus on periodic profit reports is that managers will sacrifice long-term profitability to improve short-term reported profits, for example by lowering quality controls and maintenance standards and providing insufficient funding for R&D and employee training and insufficient attention to customer relations and employee morale.

To balance an exclusive concentration on reported accounting profits, some companies have developed performance appraisal systems in which profitability is only one component. For example, a division manager may be given objectives to meet in human resources, distribution, technology, product quality, or new products, depending on which of those key areas are most crucial to the long-run success of the division and which are susceptible to the greatest improvement. The manager would then be evaluated on whether targeted objectives were achieved in the key areas. This of course is the domain of strategic performance measurement and the Balanced Scorecard, discussed in Chapters 8 and 10.

At first glance, a multidimensional performance measurement system may seem like an intrusion into the decision-making authority of a division manager in a profit center, but it is not. Rather it represents a more accurate definition of the organization's goals and the factoring of those goals into the responsibilities of the individual decision makers in the firm. Discussing with each manager the specific goals that the manager is intended to achieve and the level of performance expected allows the performance metric to be much more clearly defined. Moreover, the intrusion may be necessary because of inadequate measurement of the long-term consequences of the manager's current actions. Because of limited observability of the division manager's actions and the cost of measuring the present value of all the relevant assets in a division (including customer goodwill, equipment availability and condition, quality of work force, product quality), it is likely that the best contract between the division manager and the corporation is a function of variables other than reported accounting profit. The focus on key areas with long-term benefit to the corporation may be seen as a means of ensuring that short-term profit maximizing is not the only objective of the division manager.

## PRODUCTIVITY MEASURES

Productivity measures that use financial measures are perhaps the oldest and most widely used measures of financial control. Productivity measures all have the same format.

$$\text{Productivity} = \frac{\text{output}}{\text{input}}$$

Organizations increase productivity either by increasing output while holding input constant or by decreasing input while holding output constant. Analysts can compute productivity ratios for any input factor of production. The objective is to evaluate the organization's efficient use of some factor of production (the input) to create results (the output) that the organization deems valuable.

One of the main problems with profit-related measures of performance is that profit is not a natural way for most people to think about an organization. It is more natural for people to think of physical units—such as units of production per shift—when describing operations. Many productivity measures are not financially based. For example, quality yield, the ratio of good units to total units is a productivity measure that has no financial component. However, many productivity measures will include a financial number in either the numerator or the denominator and then become financial control measures. We will now consider some of the important financial productivity measures that assess the efficiency with which the organization uses various factors of production.[21]

## Return on Investment

The most widely used and known financial control ratio is return on investment, which is a productivity ratio that assesses the organization's use of capital. Return on investment is the ratio of net income to investment.

$$\text{Return on investment} = \frac{\text{net income}}{\text{investment}}$$

Return on investment measures the ability to generate return (the output) from a given level of investment (the input). Chapter 10 discusses the insights and limitations of the return-on-investment measure.

## Material Yield

Material yield is the ratio of the weight of raw material in the final product to the total weight of raw material input. Expressed this way, material yield is not a financial measure. However, it is common to express the numerator and denominator of this expression in dollar terms, and then the ratio becomes a financial measure that assesses the organization's material productivity.

$$\text{Material yield} = \frac{\text{cost of material allowed for output produced}}{\text{actual cost of material used}}$$

In this ratio, the cost of material allowed reflects the standard use of material (standard quantity times standard cost) for the amount of output produced.

Material yield is a very important measure of performance in the natural resource industries such as oil and gas, meatpacking, forest products, fishing products, and food packaging. The material yield measures the underlying efficiency of the manufacturing process. The higher the material yield, the lower the material cost for a given level of output. For this reason this ratio is monitored closely in any organization that processes raw material and in which raw material is a large component of total cost.

## Labor Yield

Like material yield, the labor productivity measure, or labor yield, can be expressed in financial or nonfinancial terms. The financial expression is

$$\text{Labor yield} = \frac{\text{cost of labor allowed for output produced}}{\text{actual cost of labor used}}$$

Labor yield would be monitored closely in assembly or craft industries in which labor is a significant and controllable short-run cost.

## Equipment Yield

Following the pattern developed above for the other factors of production, we could compute an equipment yield as follows:

$$\text{Equipment yield} = \frac{\text{cost of machine hours allowed for production achieve}}{\text{actual cost of machine hours used}}$$

Since most equipment levels are fixed by capacity decisions for the long run, capital, unlike materials, and some labor, cannot be varied in the short run. Therefore, costs in the equipment yield ratio will reflect capacity-related costs that are committed and, therefore, not variable in the short run. For equipment, a more useful way to convert hours of machine time allowed and used is to assess the opportunity cost of the excess use of machine hours.

A widely used, and inappropriate, measure of equipment use is the ratio of machine hours allowed for production achieved and machine hours available—a use measure. This ratio encourages managers to use available machine time to create inventory, a practice that creates the huge inventory-related costs that just-in-time manufacturing systems try to avoid.

---

## SUMMARY

This chapter focused on financial control, perhaps the oldest and most widely practiced management accounting tool. Financial control is popular because it focuses on what matters most in most organizations: profitability. The idea in financial control is to identify a measure that can serve as an indicator of performance and provide a warning signal when performance varies from expected results. The warning triggers an investigation to correct the cause of the deviation. The second use of financial control measures is to focus attention on what matters—that is, to get organization members thinking about what success means in the organization.

The tools in organization control are many and varied and are customized to the specific needs of the individual organization. Variance analysis focuses on identifying situations in which actual results have deviated from planned results. Variance analysis provides an overall evaluation or summary of results. Most organizations would find it ineffectual to wait for a variance analysis to identify operational problems; they sense and deal with problems before the financial control results are developed and published. However, the variance analysis provides a summary that can serve as a talking point in retrospective analyses of operations. During this process, managers can discuss what created the variances and how they dealt with those disturbances. The variances provide an estimate of the financial consequences of the unexpected events.

We saw that organizations use transfer pricing to decompose an integrated organization into individual components that work together to achieve overall organization success. Transfer pricing does three things. First, it provides the means of decomposing profits that are jointly earned by all the organization's operating units into profits earned by individual units. Second, it provides an estimate of what each unit is contributing to the organization. Third, it provides a coordinating mechanism in the firm.

Market prices, when they exist, provide an objective and verifiable measure of the value of the commodity being transferred and should be used. Absent a market price, organizations use transfer prices that are based on cost, are negotiated, or are imposed. Cost-based transfer prices should be based on the full long-run costs, as calculated by the ABC model, in order to provide for long-run planning. Costs that are negotiated or imposed administratively may not reflect the economic attributes of the transferred product and therefore have unpredictable effects on profitability.

Like all financial control measures, productivity measures provide a signal that gives an overview of the financial effects of operations. Productivity is a measure of the organization's ability to create something desired—the output—from something that is controlled and managed by operations personnel—the input.

## ENDNOTES

1. For a notable exception see R. D. Buzzell, *The PIMS Principles: Linking Strategy to Performance* (New York: Free Press, 1987). This study investigated the link between, among other things, quality and sales.

2. We developed this exhibit using the Excel file AMACH9.XLS which is available to your instructor. Numbers in the exhibit may differ in the last digit from the spreadsheet number because of rounding effects.

3. Organization planners will often set a control limit (for example, a variance that is greater than two or three times the standard deviation of the variable under control) that will trigger an investigation of a reported variance.

4. Absent controlling for the amount of work done, managers can manipulate this variance. For example, a maintenance budget might be set on the basis of the amount of maintenance work required, which, by definition, is independent of the number of units made and sold. A manager could show a favorable variance by cutting back maintenance below the target level.

5. For a statistical approach to variance analysis see R. S. Kaplan, "Investigation and the Significance of Cost Variances: Survey and Extensions," *Journal of Accounting Research* (Fall 1975), pp. 278–96.

6. See R. F. Vancil, *Decentralization: Managerial Ambiguity by Design* (Homewood, IL: Dow Jones-Irwin, 1978).

7. K. A. Merchant, "How and Why Firms Disregard the Controllability Principle," in *Accounting & Management: Field Study Perspectives*, ed. R. S. Kaplan and W. J. Bruns Jr. (Boston: Harvard Business School Press, 1987), pp. 316–38.

8. This is done by choosing an allocation basis (cost driver rate) by dividing the cost of capacity by the total capacity acquired. This has the additional and desirable property of making the cost allocation independent of use of the capacity by other divisions. For example, consider the result of a cost allocation where the allocation rate is chosen by dividing the capacity cost by the total use of the capacity.

9. D. Brown, "Centralized Control with Decentralized Responsibilities," Annual Convention Series No. 57 (New York: American Management Association, 1927), p. 8. It is interesting to observe the erosin over the years of the original intention of not requiring divisions at General Motors to buy internally—in effect the assembly divisions became captive customers of the supplying divisions. General Motors endured strikes and labor discontent in the 1990s as it sought to return to the policy of allowing the assembly divisions to source parts wherever they wished.

10. A. A. Atkinson, *Intra-Firm Cost and Resource Allocation: Theory and Practice*, Studies in Canadian Accounting Research (Toronto: Canadian Academic Accounting Association, 1987).

11. More formal arguments exist to establish the validity of the market price as an optimal transfer price under competitive conditions. See J. Hirshleifer, "On the Economics of Transfer Pricing," *Journal of Business* (January 1956), pp. 172–84; and "Economics of the Divisionalized Firm," *Journal of Business* (April 1957), pp. 96–108; also D. Solomons, *Divisional Performance: Measurement and Control* (Homewood, IL: Dow Jones-Irwin, 1965), pp. 167–71.

12.  See R. H. Coase, "The Nature of the Firm," *Economica* (November 1937).

13.  For a discussion of using activity-based costing to provide a cost base for transfer pricing see R. S. Kaplan, D. Weiss, and E. Desheh, "Transfer Pricing with ABC," *Management Accounting* (May 1987), p. 28.

14.  For a discussion of the economic and behavioral properties of this approach to transfer pricing see Atkinson, *Intra-Firm Cost and Resource Allocations.*

15.  Variations can arise in practice. For example, many organizations that use cost-based transfer prices like to use standard costs for those costs that are based on use—what accountants call variable costs. This practice provides an incentive to the supply division to become more efficient and provides a stable cost around which the buying division can plan. On the other hand, as a division becomes more efficient, if it does not pass at least some of the resulting savings along to the buying division, the buying division's demand for product will remain unchanged if its cost structure and selling prices remain unchanged. Therefore, the organization as a whole will capture only the cost savings of increased efficiency and not the volume effects that would result from selling more at a lower price.

16.  See R. G. Eccles, "Control with Fairness in Transfer Pricing," *Harvard Business Review* (November–December 1983), pp. 153–54.

17.  See Coase, "Nature of the Firm."

18.  See Eccles, "Control with Fairness in Transfer Pricing"; R. G. Eccles, "Analyzing Your Company's Transfer Pricing Practices," *Journal of Cost Management for the Manufacturing Industry* (Summer 1987), pp. 21–83; and Eccles, *The Transfer Pricing Problem: A Theory for Practice* (Lexington, MA: Lexington Books, 1985).

19.  We anticipate the comments of the reader who is thinking: Why not have two transfer pricing systems—one to support the domestic (behavioral) issues that we have discussed so far and the other to support the international transfer pricing issues? As we will see shortly, international transfer pricing conventions argue that, whenever possible, the transfer price should reflect market or economic circumstances. Therefore, on the surface, if an organization chooses an internal transfer pricing system based on economic arguments, such as those discussed earlier, it should use the same system for international transfer pricing. Evidence of two transfer pricing systems has, in the past, attracted the attention of taxing authorities and called for revision in transfer prices that reflect the internal system.

20.  Organization for Economic Co-Operation and Development, *Transfer Pricing Guidelines for Multinational Enterprises and Tax Administrations* (Paris: OECD, 1995).

21.  For an extensive discussion of how organizations use productivity and other measures as indicators of the performance of an underlying process see H. M. Armitage and A. A. Atkinson, *The Choice of Productivity Measures in Organizations: A Field Study of Practice in Seven Canadian Firms.* The Society of Management Accountants of Canada Research Monograph Series (Hamilton, ON: Society of Management Accountants of Canada, 1990).

---

## ■ *PROBLEMS*

---

### *9-1     Comprehensive Variance Analysis*

Bayfield Chemical Company manufactures chemicals 1, 2, 3, and 4 using five ingredients: chemicals A, B, C, D, and E. The planned amount of input used to make 100 liters of each of the four products, the standard cost of the input chemicals, the amount of each of the input chemicals that is available for purchase, and the expected price received for each 100 liters of each product are shown in the following table.

| | | | PLANNED INGREDIENT USE | | | | | |
|---|---|---|---|---|---|---|---|---|
| CHEMICAL | A | B | C | D | E | PRICE | COST | MARGIN |
| 1 | 23 | 45 | 0 | 32 | 0 | $8,500 | $5,567 | $2,933 |
| 2 | 12 | 29 | 33 | 18 | 14 | $9,300 | $7,047 | $2,253 |
| 3 | 12 | 19 | 34 | 14 | 43 | $9,000 | $7,169 | $1,831 |
| 4 | 23 | 57 | 10 | 0 | 10 | $7,200 | $4,779 | $2,421 |
| Cost | $67 | $34 | $107 | $78 | $23 | | | |
| Available | 120,000 | 240,000 | 320,000 | 190,000 | 280,000 | | | |

Chemicals 1, 2, 3, and 4 are made in batches of either 2,000 or 5,000 liters. There are costs of setting up the blending tanks before a batch and cleaning them after a batch. These costs, along with the planned number of batches, are shown in the following table.

| | PLANNED BATCHES MADE | | |
|---|---|---|---|
| CHEMICAL | 2,000 | 5,000 | COST |
| 1 | 12 | 0 | $ 14,400 |
| 2 | 240 | 0 | $288,000 |
| 3 | 237 | 0 | $284,400 |
| 4 | 0 | 0 | $     0 |
| Cost | $1,200 | $1,900 | |

This planned production results in the following pattern of planned input chemical use.

| | | | PLANNED TOTAL CHEMICAL USE | | |
|---|---|---|---|---|---|
| CHEMICAL | A | B | C | D | E |
| 1 | 5,520 | 10,800 | 0 | 7,680 | 0 |
| 2 | 57,600 | 139,200 | 158,400 | 86,400 | 67,200 |
| 3 | 56,880 | 90,060 | 161,160 | 66,360 | 203,820 |
| 4 | 0 | 0 | 0 | 0 | 0 |
| Used | 120,000 | 240,060 | 319,560 | 160,440 | 271,020 |

With the exception of short-term variable inventory carrying costs, all the costs relating to the chemical-making operation are committed capacity-related costs that Bayfield Company feels are not avoidable in the short run. Therefore, they are ignored for short-run planning purposes. The inventory carrying costs are related to cost of carrying inventory including storage costs, the opportunity cost of capital tied up in inventory, obsolescence cost, loss, and waste. Input chemicals are purchased and arrive as needed, therefore they inflict no carrying cost in Bayfield Chemical. The inventory-related costs for chemicals 1, 2, 3, and 4 are estimated using the following steps.

1. For each of the four products, compute the weighted average number of units per batch by multiplying the number of units in each batch by the number of times that batch size is made, summing all the results, and dividing by the number of batches.
2. Since the sales of all four chemicals occur fairly uniformly during the planning period, for each of the four products, estimate the average inventory held by dividing the weighted average number of units per batch by two.
3. For each of the four products, compute the inventory carrying cost by multiplying the average inventory held by $400, $800, $300, $500 for each of chemical 1, 2, 3, and 4, respectively.

Therefore, the inventory carrying costs for the planned pattern of production are estimated as follows.

| PLANNED CARRYING COST | | |
|---|---|---|
| CHEMICAL | AVERAGE | COST |
| 1 | 1,000 | $400,000 |
| 2 | 1,000 | $800,000 |
| 3 | 1,000 | $300,000 |
| 4 | 0 | $0 |

This planned production results in the following planned revenues, cost, and margin from this operation.

| PLANNED TOTAL MARGINS | | | | |
|---|---|---|---|---|
| CHEMICAL | MARGIN | BATCH | CARRYING | NET |
| 1 | $703,920 | $14,400 | $400,000 | $    289,520 |
| 2 | 10,814,400 | 288,000 | 800,000 | 9,726,400 |
| 3 | 8,678,940 | 284,400 | 300,000 | 8,094,540 |
| 4 | 0 | 0 | 0 | 0 |
| Total | | | | $18,110,460 |

The following table shows the actual production during the period.

| ACTUAL BATCHES MADE | | | |
|---|---|---|---|
| CHEMICAL | 2000 | 5000 | COST |
| 1 | 52 | 18 | $100,000 |
| 2 | 36 | 15 | 73,800 |
| 3 | 42 | 53 | 150,000 |
| 4 | 22 | 9 | 44,800 |
| Cost | $1,300 | $1,800 | |

The following table shows the actual amount of input chemicals used, the price received for each product, and the cost of the input chemicals.

| | | | | ACTUAL INGREDIENT USE | | | | |
|---|---|---|---|---|---|---|---|---|
| CHEMICAL | A | B | C | D | E | PRICE | COST | MARGIN |
| 1 | 22 | 48 | 0 | 30 | 0 | $8,200 | $5,402 | $2,798 |
| 2 | 11 | 31 | 30 | 21 | 12 | 9,600 | 6,793 | 2,807 |
| 3 | 11 | 18 | 32 | 12 | 46 | 9,100 | 6,607 | 2,493 |
| 4 | 23 | 54 | 9 | 0 | 11 | 7,300 | 4,429 | 2,871 |
| Cost | $71 | $30 | $105 | $80 | $21 | | | |
| Available | 130,000 | 250,000 | 300,000 | 180,000 | 300,000 | | | |

The following table shows the actual total input chemical use.

| | | ACTUAL TOTAL CHEMICAL USE | | | |
|---|---|---|---|---|---|
| CHEMICAL | A | B | C | D | E |
| 1 | 42,680 | 93,120 | 0 | 58,200 | 0 |
| 2 | 16,170 | 45,570 | 44,100 | 30,870 | 17,640 |
| 3 | 38,390 | 62,820 | 111,680 | 41,880 | 160,540 |
| 4 | 20,470 | 48,060 | 8,010 | 0 | 9,790 |
| Used | 117,710 | 249,570 | 163,790 | 130,950 | 187,970 |

The following table shows the actual carrying costs.

| | ACTUAL CARRYING COST | |
|---|---|---|
| CHEMICAL | AVERAGE | COST |
| 1 | 1,386 | $582,000 |
| 2 | 1,441 | 1,124,118 |
| 3 | 1,837 | 587,789 |
| 4 | 1,435 | 645,968 |

The following table shows the actual total margin generated by the operations in this period.

| CHEMICAL | MARGIN | BATCH | CARRYING | NET |
|---|---|---|---|---|
| 1 | $5,428,120 | $100,000 | $582,000 | $4,746,120 |
| 2 | $4,126,290 | 73,800 | 1,124,118 | $2,928,372 |
| 3 | $8,700,570 | 150,000 | 587,789 | $7,962,781 |
| 4 | 2,555,190 | 44,800 | 645,968 | $1,864,422 |
| Total | | | | $17,501,695 |

*Required*

Prepare a variance analysis of the operations in this period.

## 9-2

The chapter describes a variance as a warning that signals that actual results differ from planned results. The variance would signal the need to undertake an investigation that would uncover the reason for the variance. Because variances are usually computed long after the fact, operating personnel seldom rely on variances to signal process problems. Rather they can usually predict variances on the basis of their direct observation of the process. Given this fact, does variance analysis really play any useful role in organizations?

## 9-3    Cost Allocations and Measurement of Division Profitability*

Paris Company has three operating divisions. The managers of these divisions are evaluated on their divisional net income before taxes, a figure that includes an allocation of corporate overhead proportional to the sales of each division. The operating statement for the first quarter of 1998 appears below:

|  | DIVISION (IN 000s) | | | |
| --- | --- | --- | --- | --- |
|  | A | B | C | TOTAL |
| Net sales | $2,000 | $1,200 | $1,600 | $4,800 |
| Unit and batch-related costs | 1,050 | 540 | 640 | 2,230 |
| Division capacity-related costs | 250 | 125 | 160 | 535 |
| Division margin | 700 | 535 | 800 | 2,035 |
| Allocated corporate expenses | 400 | 240 | 320 | 960 |
| Net income before taxes | $300 | $295 | $480 | $1,075 |

The manager of Division A is unhappy that his profitability is about the same as Division B's and much less than Division C's, even though his sales are much higher than either of these other two divisions. The manager knows that he is carrying one line of products with very low profitability. He was going to replace this line of business as soon as more-profitable product opportunities became available but has retained it until now, because the line was still marginally profitable and used facilities that would otherwise be idle. The manager now realizes, however, that the sales from this product line are attracting a fair amount of corporate overhead, which is allocated at the rate of 20% of net sales, and maybe the line is already unprofitable for him.

---

*Adapted from C. Horngren, *Cost Accounting*, 5th ed. (Englewood Cliffs, NJ: Prentice Hall, 1982).

This low-margin line of products had the following characteristics for the quarter:

| | |
|---|---:|
| Net sales (000) | $800 |
| Unit and batch-related costs | 600 |
| Division capacity-related costs | 100 |
| Division margin | $100 |

Thus, the product line accounted for 40% of divisional sales but less than 15% of divisional profit.

***Required***

(1) Prepare the operating statement for the Paris Company for the second quarter of 1998 assuming that sales and operating results are identical to the first quarter except that the manager of Division A drops the low-margin product line entirely from his product group. Is the Division A manager better off from this action? Is the Paris Company better off from this action?

(2) Suggest changes in the Paris Company's divisional reporting and evaluation system that will improve local incentives for decision making that is in the best interests of the firm.

## 9-4   *Interpreting Segment Margins*

The Plevna Hotel is a full-service hotel that provides rooms, extensive restaurant and banquet facilities, and convention meeting rooms and facilities. The hotel is organized into five responsibility units: rooms, meal services, other hotel services, maintenance, and administration. Rooms, meal services, and other hotel services are operated as profit centers. The hotel's accounting system accumulates revenues and costs by organization unit. The costs of maintenance and administration are charged to the three profit centers. Maintenance is charged on the basis of hours worked. Administration charges are divided into two groups: hotel-related costs such as depreciation and electricity are assigned to the three profit centers on the basis of space occupied; other costs, primarily administrative personnel costs, are charged to the profit centers on the basis of the direct cost of each unit. The rationale for administrative cost allocation is that the allocation base is regarded as the cost driver for the allocated costs.

Under this system, the accounting reports indicate that the rooms profit center is always very profitable, the other hotel services profit center breaks even, and the meal services profit center always operates with quite large losses.

This situation has continued for several years and, because bonuses and promotions are based on realized profit center profit, has caused concern and discouragement among the staff in the hotel services division and meal services division.

Recently, there have been suggestions that the extensive meal and convention facilities be closed down and the freed space be used to put in luxury suites and rooms. A profit analysis of the hotel several years ago suggested that the ratio of profit reported by the hotel to square feet occupied was about average for this type of hotel and higher than accommodation-only hotels.

*Required*

You have been hired to evaluate the current system and suggest improvements. Prepare a report.

## 9-5    Transfer Pricing Dispute

A transportation equipment manufacturer is heavily decentralized. Each division head has full authority on all decisions regarding sales to internal or external customers. Division P has always acquired a certain equipment component from Division S. However, when informed that Division S was increasing its unit price to $220, Division P's management decided to purchase the component from outside suppliers at a price of $200.

   Division S had recently acquired some specialized equipment that was used primarily to make this component. The manager cited the resulting high depreciation charges as the justification for the price boost. He asked the president of the company to instruct Division P to buy from S at the $220 price. He supplied the following information:

| | |
|---|---|
| P's annual purchases of component | 2,000 units |
| S's unit and batch-related costs per unit | $190 |
| S's capacity related costs per unit | $ 20 |
| S's required return on investment | $ 10 |

Suppose there are no alternative uses of the S facilities.

*Required*

   (1) Will the company as a whole benefit if P buys from the outside suppliers for $200 per unit?
   (2) Suppose the selling price of outsiders drops another $15 to $185. Should P purchase from outsiders?
   (3) Suppose (disregarding Requirement 2) that S could modify the component at an additional variable cost of $10 per unit and sell the 2,000 units to other customers for $225. Would the entire company then benefit if P purchased the 2,000 components from outsiders at $200 per unit?
   (4) Suppose the internal facilities could be assigned to other production operations that would otherwise require additional annual outlays of $29,000. Should P purchase from outsiders at $200 per unit?

## 9-6    Short- and Long-Run
## Transfer Pricing Considerations

Elora Manufacturing makes autoparts that it sells to automobile assemblers. Elora Manufacturing also makes its own branded autoparts that it sells in the automotive aftermarket. Each autopart is manufactured to the customer's specification.

   The price that Elora Manufacturing charges customers is based on the cost of the autopart. These costs include the unit and batch-related costs of filling the order and a share of capacity-related costs.

   At the moment Elora Manufacturing has four major customers: Giant Motors, Far East Motors, Tiger Motors, and Fargo Motors. The four customers, who are long-term, use, respectively, on average 10%, 20%, 15%, and 15% of available capacity. Elora Manufacturing uses 30% of available capacity to make its own autoparts. On rare occasions, Elora Manufacturing receives an order from another source, and those are treated on a one-off basis.

Elora Manufacturing is organized into three divisions: manufacturing, assembler sales, and aftermarket sales.

The automobile parts aftermarket is very competitive and margins there are slim.

The price paid by the assembler to the assembler sales division is invariably a contract price. This contract price is negotiated between the assembler sales division and the assembler and is done with a full exchange of information. That is, the assembler has full access to all Elora Manufacturing's cost records. The assembler usually demands efficiency improvements and therefore, price reductions, during the life of the contract. Three of the four assemblers have consultants who regularly visit their suppliers' manufacturing facilities to suggest process improvements that will lower costs. Usually, the contract specifies a price that equals full manufacturing cost plus a markup to cover corporate-level capacity-related costs and a return on invested capital. The manufacturing cost base of the contract usually falls by 5% to 10% per year during the life of the contract.

Senior management is determined to provide the highest possible level of motivation to its three divisions. Therefore, the three divisions are treated as profit centers, and the company uses transfer prices to price transfers between the divisions. Problems have arisen relating to determining transfer prices under the different circumstances faced by the two sales divisions.

### Required

You have been hired by Elora Manufacturing to evaluate this situation. Senior management will evaluate your proposal on the basis of its practicality and specificity.

## 9-7 Activity-Based Costing in Transfer Pricing

St. Jacob's Electronics manufactures electrical components. The company is divided into four divisions: manufacturing, residential products, commercial products, and industrial products. The manufacturing division supplies the other three divisions with all their product requirements. Because the manufacturing division has no control over product price or sales, it is treated as a cost center and transfers its products to the other divisions at full cost plus a profit margin that is intended to provide a return on capital invested in the manufacturing division.

In late 1995, St. Jacob's Electronics implemented an activity costing system to develop more-accurate product costs for planning purposes. A central part of the implementation plan was to use the new costing system as the foundation for computing transfer prices.

The costing system uses the four-level activity costing hierarchy: unit costs, batch costs, product-related costs, and facility-sustaining costs. The detailed analysis of the company's cost structure revealed the following information.

Most of the product-related costs were lodged in the three profit centers. The exceptions were the costs of specialized equipment housed in the manufacturing division that was used uniquely by each of the three profit centers for their products. These product-related costs in the manufacturing division were $1,500,000, $500,000, and $600,000 for the residential, commercial, and industrial divisions, respectively. The balance of the capacity-related costs in the manufacturing division, which amounted to $2,400,000 and included a charge for capital invested, were allocated to the three divisions in proportion to their long-run expected use of the facility. This amounted to 50% for the residential division, 30% for the commercial division, and 20% for the industrial division. The amount of capacity-related cost allocated to each division was the larger of amount of capacity used or amount of capacity reserved. Each division had the right to use its reserved level of capacity. If some capacity went unused by the division for which it was reserved and was used by another division, the division not using its capacity quota was given credit for its capacity that was used by other divisions.

In addition to the capacity-related costs, the manufacturing division incurred unit and batch-related costs when processing orders. All costs were charged to an order number. In this way, the cost sheet for each order accumulated the unit and batch-related costs for that order.

Some products were sold by more than one division. For example, connectors were sold by all three divisions. All the connectors used the same plastic formulation but different copper or brass components. Therefore, the manufacturing division accumulated orders for connectors, and when there were sufficient orders to make a batch of plastic, the plastic was made and then used to make the connectors for the different products. The cost of a batch of plastic included the raw materials cost and machine setup costs.

Once the plastic was made, it was used to complete the various batches of connectors for the different divisions. The only common component in these connectors was the plastic. Therefore the costs of other raw materials for each connector were accumulated separately and charged directly to the product. Recently, the manufacturing division completed an order of connectors that were sold to the residential division and the industrial division. The cost of the batch of plastic was $105,000, and it was used to make 50,000 connectors of two types—each connector using the same amount of plastic. The connectors are fed into a machine that inserts the brass fittings into the connector. It costs about $2000 to set up the machine for each batch of connectors; there were 30,000 connectors made for the residential division and 20,000 connectors made for the industrial division. The cost of the brass fittings were $0.56 for each residential connector and $1.78 for each industrial connector.

### Required

(1) For each of the following use levels by the residential, commercial, and industrial divisions respectively, determine the resulting allocation of capacity-related costs:
   (a)   45%, 35%, 15%
   (b)   45%, 25%, 10%
   (c)   45%, 30%, 25%
(2) What is the cost per unit for each of the residential connectors described above? Make any required assumptions to answer this question.

### 9-8 *Productivity Measures in Practice*

By consulting business periodicals, find an example of a yield type of productivity measure. Document exactly how the productivity measure is computed and how it is used. What insights does this productivity measure offer? What might be some of its limitations?

### 9-9 *Using a Productivity Measure*

Gogan Forest Products maintains its own woodlots from which it harvests trees. It keeps the trees that it can use in its sawmills to make lumber and sells the remaining trees to a nearby pulp mill.

Ronnie Gogan, the president and chief operating officer, is concerned about the profitability of the sawmill. In particular, he is concerned about the profits generated by his mill. From talking to other owners of small sawmills, Ronnie is convinced that his profit levels are lower than theirs even though he processes more logs.

A sawmill uses all the tree that arrives in its yard. The bark is stripped, packaged, and large basic pieces are sold to nurseries. Some bark pieces are packaged as forest mulch and sold to nurseries. Wood chips are used along with sawdust to make particle board. Any sawdust remaining from the particle board operation is used in the kilns used to dry the lumber.

Ronnie observed, "Based on the market price for sawlogs, the raw material component of our lumber is about 65%. We need to control material use to be profitable. I was thinking about using material yield but our material yield is 1 since we use all the log."

#### *Required*

Can you devise a financial productivity ratio that might provide Ronnie with an overview of his operations?

### 9-10 *Computing a Cost-Plus International Transfer Price*

Absent market prices, organizations compute cost-plus transfer prices that are intended to estimate a reasonable market price. As suggested by the title, the cost-plus transfer price has two components, a cost component and a markup component.

Most tax authorities allow organizations to use the cost basis that is generated by their conventional financial accounting systems—that is, the systems that provide the numbers for external reporting.

The markup component is usually undertaken by identifying the functions that the supplying organization undertakes. For example, suppose that Global Company manufactures a product in country A and then distributes that product to other countries, where it is sold. If Global Company does all the research and development and market analysis in country A, the number of functions and therefore the markup will be different than if country A simply acts like a contract manufacturer to manufacture products that were designed in other countries.

*Required*

Suppose that you are employed by the tax authority in one of the countries in which Global Company operates. What problems, if any, do you see in applying the cost-plus transfer pricing rule in practice? How would you propose to resolve these problems?

### 9-11   Computing an International Transfer Price with Joint Costs

Return to Gogan Forest Products in Problem 9-9. Suppose that logs are processed in batches. Batch-related costs amount to $35,000 for the logs, $600 for batch-related costs including moving and setting up, and $11,000 for capacity-related costs, which are allocated to each batch on the basis of the machine time the batch uses.

On average each batch produces

> 40,000 units of lumber
> 75,000 units of wood chips
> 65,000 units of sawdust

Ronnie is considering establishing a particle board facility in a foreign country. Ronnie would ship wood chips and sawdust, approximately 45,000 units of woodchips and 15,000 units of sawdust, from each batch to the foreign facility.

*Required*

There is no market for wood chips or sawdust. Ronnie feels that the transfer price for wood chips and sawdust will have to be computed on a cost-plus basis. How would you compute the cost base for wood chips and sawdust? Make any assumptions you feel are necessary to answer this question.

---

## ■ CASES

### TRANSFER PRICING IN AN AUTOMOBILE DEALERSHIP— SHUMAN AUTOMOBILES INC.*

Clark Shuman, the part owner and manager of an automobile dealership, was nearing retirement and wanted to begin relinquishing his personal control over the business's operations. (See Exhibit 1 for current financial statements.) The reputation he had established in the community led him to believe that the recent growth in his business would continue. His longstanding policy of emphasizing new car sales as the principal business of the dealership had paid off, in Shuman's opinion. This, combined with close attention to customer relations so that a substantial amount of repeat business was available, had increased the company's sales to a new high level. Therefore, he wanted

---

*This case was prepared by James S. Reece.
Copyright © 1976 by the President and Fellows of Harvard College. Harvard Business School case 177-033.

**EXHIBIT 1** Shuman Automobiles Inc. Income Statement for the Year Ended December 31

| | | | |
|---|---|---|---|
| Sales of new cars | | | $7,643,746 |
| Cost of new car sales* | | $6,312,802 | |
| Sales remuneration | | 324,744 | 6,637,546 |
| | | | $1,006,200 |
| Allowances on trade[†] | | | 232,224 |
| New cars gross profit | | | $ 773,976 |
| Sales of used cars | | $4,791,392 | |
| Cost of used car sales* | $3,814,554 | | |
| Sales remuneration | 183,308 | | |
| | | 3,997,862 | |
| | | $ 793,530 | |
| Allowances on trade* | | 122,236 | |
| Used cars gross profit | | | 671,294 |
| | | | $1,445,270 |
| Service sales to customers | | $ 695,022 | |
| Cost of work* | | 513,968 | |
| | | $ 181,054 | |
| Service work on reconditioning | | | |
| Charge | $ 473,160 | | |
| Cost* | 488,624 | (15,464) | |
| Service work gross profit | | | 165,590 |
| | | | $1,610,860 |
| General and administrative expenses | | | 983,420 |
| Income before taxes | | | $ 627,440 |

*These amounts include all costs that are attributable to the department and exclude allocated capacity related dealership costs.
†Allowances on trade represent the excess of amounts allowed on cars taken in trade over their appraised value.

to make organizational changes to cope with the new situation, especially given his desire to withdraw from any day-to-day managerial responsibilities. Shuman's three "silent partners" agreed to this decision.

Accordingly, Shuman divided up the business into three departments: new car sales, used car sales, and the service department (which was also responsible for selling parts and accessories). He then appointed three of his most trusted employees managers of the new departments: Jean Moyer, new car sales; Paul Fiedler, used car sales; and Nate Bianci, service department. All of these people had been with the dealership for several years.

Each of the managers was told to run his department as if it were an independent business. In order to give the new managers an incentive, their remuneration was to be calculated as a straight percentage of their department's gross profit.

Soon after taking over as manager of new car sales, Jean Moyer had to settle upon the amount to offer a particular customer who wanted to trade his old car as a part of the purchase price of a new one with a list price of $12,800. Before closing the sale, Moyer had to decide the amount he would offer the customer for the trade-in value of the old car. He knew that if no trade-in were involved, he would deduct about 15% from the list price of this model new car to be competitive with several other dealers in the area. However, he also wanted to make sure that he did not lose out on the sale by offering too low a trade-in allowance.

During his conversation with the customer, it had become apparent that the customer had an inflated view of the worth of his old car, a far from uncommon event. In this case, it probably meant that Moyer had to be prepared to make some sacrifices to close the sale. The new car had been in stock for some time, and the model was not selling very well, so he was rather anxious to make the sale if this could be done profitably.

In order to establish the trade-in value of the car, the used-car manager, Fiedler, accompanied Moyer and the customer out to the parking lot to examine the car. In the course of his appraisal, Fiedler estimated the car would require reconditioning work costing about $700, after which the car would retail for about $3,700. On a wholesale basis, he could either buy or sell such a car, after reconditioning, for about $3,200. The wholesale price of a car was subject to much greater fluctuation than the retail price, depending on color, trim, model, etc. Fortunately, the car being traded in was a very popular shade. The retail automobile dealer's handbook of used car prices, the "Blue Book," gave a cash buying price range of $2,750 to $2,930 for the trade-in model in good condition. This range represented the distribution of cash prices paid by automobile dealers for that model of car in the area in the past week. Fiedler estimated that he could get about $2,200 for the car 'as-is" (that is, without any work being done to it) at next week's auction.

The new car department manager had the right to buy any trade-in at any price he thought appropriate, but then it was his responsibility to dispose of the car. He had the alternative of either trying to persuade the used-car manager to take over the car and accepting the used-car manager's appraisal price, or he himself could sell the car through wholesale channels or at auction. Whatever course Moyer adopted, it

was his primary responsibility to make a profit for the dealership on the new cars he sold, without affecting his performance through excessive allowances on trade-ins. This primary goal, Moyer said, had to be "balanced against the need to satisfy the customers and move the new cars out of inventory—and there was only a narrow line between allowing enough on a used car and allowing too much."

After weighing all these factors, with particular emphasis on the personality of the customer, Moyer decided he would allow $4,270 for the used car, provided the customer agreed to pay the list price for the new car. After a certain amount of haggling, during which the customer came down from a higher figure and Moyer came up from a lower one, the $4,270 allowance was agreed upon. The necessary papers were signed, and the customer drove off.

Moyer returned to the office and explained the situation to Joanne Brunner, who had recently joined the dealership as accountant. After listening with interest to Moyer's explanation of the sale, Brunner set about recording the sale in the accounting records of the business. As soon as she saw the new car had been purchased from the manufacturer for $8,890, she was uncertain as to the value she should place on the trade-in vehicle. Since the new car's list price was $12,800 and it had cost $8,890, Brunner reasoned the gross margin on the new car sale was $3,910. Yet Moyer had allowed $4,270 for the old car, which needed $700 repairs and could be sold retail for $3,700 or wholesale for $3,200. Did this mean that the new car sale involved a loss? Brunner was not at all sure she knew the answer to this question. Also, she was uncertain about the value she should place on the used car for inventory valuation purposes. Brunner decided that she would put down a valuation of $4,270 and then await instructions from her superiors.

When Fiedler, manager of the used-car department, found out what Brunner had done, he went to the office and stated forcefully that he would not accept $4,270 as the valuation of the used car. His comment went as follows:

> My used-car department has to get rid of that used car, unless Jean (Moyer) agrees to take it over himself. I would certainly never have allowed the customer $4,270 for that old tub. I would never have given any more than $2,500, which is the wholesale price less the cost of repairs. My department has to make a profit too, you know. My own income is dependent on the gross profit I show on the sale of used cars, and I will not stand for having my income hurt because Jean is too generous toward his customers.

Brunner replied that she had not meant to cause trouble but had simply recorded the car at what seemed to be its cost of acquisition, because she had been taught that this was the best accounting practice. Whatever response Fiedler was about to make to this comment was cut off by the arrival of Clark Shuman, the general manager, and Nate Bianci, the service department manager. Shuman picked up the phone and called Jean Moyer, asking him to come over right away.

"All right, Nate," said Shuman, "now that we are all here, would you tell them what you just told me?" Bianci, who was obviously very worried, said, "Thanks Clark; the trouble is with this trade-in. Jean and Paul were right in thinking that the repairs they thought necessary would cost about $700. Unfortunately, they failed to notice that the rear axle is cracked, which will have to be replaced before we can sell the car. This will probably use up parts and labor costing about $530."

"Besides this," Bianci continued, "there is another thing which is bothering me a good deal more. Under the accounting system we've been using, I can't charge as much on an internal job as I would for the same job performed for an outside customer. As you can see from my department statement [Exhibit 2], I lost almost eight thousand bucks on internal work last year. On a reconditioning job like this, which costs out at $1,230, I don't even break even. If I did work costing $1,230 for an outside customer, I would be able to charge him about $1,660 for the job. The Blue Book[1] gives a range of $1,620 to $1,700 for the work this car needs, and I have

---

[1] In addition to the Blue Book for used car prices, there was a Blue Book which gave the range of charges for various classes of repair work. Like the used car book, it was issued weekly, and was based on the actual charges made and reported by vehicle repair shops in the area.

**EXHIBIT 2**   Shuman Automobiles Inc. Analysis of Service Department Expenses for the Year Ended December 31

|  | CUSTOMER JOBS | RECONDITIONING JOBS | TOTAL |
|---|---|---|---|
| Number of jobs | 2,780 | 1,051 | 3,831 |
| Direct labor | $213,860 | $197,640 | $ 411,500 |
| Supplies | 74,124 | 65,510 | 139,634 |
| Department capacity-related costs | 63,116 | 52,134 | 115,250 |
|  | $351,100 | $315,284 | $ 666,384 |
| Parts | 162,868 | 173,340 | $ 336,208 |
|  | $513,968 | $488,624 | $1,002,592 |
| Charges made for all jobs | 695,022 | $473,160 | 1,168,182 |
| Gross profit (loss) | $181,054 | $(15,464) | $ 165,590 |
| Allocated corporate capacity costs |  |  | $ 114,160 |
| Departmental profit for the year |  |  | $ 51,430 |

always aimed for about the middle of the Blue Book range. That would give my department a gross profit of $430, and my own income is based on that gross profit. Since it looks as if a high proportion of the work of my department is going to be the reconditioning of trade-ins for resale, I figure that I should be able to make the same charge for repairing a trade-in as I would get for an outside repair job."

Fiedler and Moyer both started to talk at once at this point. Fiedler, the more forceful of the two, managed to edge out Moyer: "This axle business is unfortunate, all right; but it is very hard to spot a cracked axle. Nate is likely to be just as lucky the other way next time. He has to take the rough with the smooth. It is up to him to get the cars ready for me to sell."

Moyer, after agreeing that the failure to spot the axle was unfortunate, added: "This error is hardly my fault, however. Anyway, it is ridiculous that the service department should make a profit out of jobs it does for the rest of the dealership. The company can't make money when its left hand sells to its right."

At this point, Clark Shuman was getting a little confused about the situation. He thought there was a little truth in everything that had been said, but he was not sure how much. It was evident to him that some action was called for, both to sort out the present problem and to prevent its recurrence. He instructed Brunner, the accountant, to "work out how much we are really going to make on this whole deal," and then retired to his office to consider how best to get his managers to make a profit for the company.

A week after the events described above, Clark Shuman was still far from sure what action to take to motivate his managers to make a profit for the business. During the week, Bianci, the service manager, had reported to him that the repairs to the used car had cost $1,376, of which $640 represented

the cost of those repairs which had been spotted at the time of purchase, and the remaining $736 was the cost of supplying and fitting a replacement for the cracked axle. To support his own case for a higher allowance on reconditioning jobs, Bianci had looked through the duplicate invoices over the last few months and had found examples of similar (but not identical) work to that which had been done on the trade-in car. The amounts of these invoices averaged $1,610, which the customers had paid without question, and the average of the costs assigned to these jobs was $1,192. (General overhead was not assigned to individual jobs.) In addition, Bianci had obtained from Brunner, the accountant, the cost analysis shown in Exhibit 2. Bianci told Shuman that this was a fairly typical distribution of the service department expense.

### Required

(1) Suppose the new car deal is consummated, with the repaired used car being retailed for $3,700, the repairs costing Shuman $1,376. Assume that all sales personnel are on salary (no commissions) and that departmental overheads are fixed. What is the dealership contribution on the total transaction (i.e., new and repaired-used cars sold)?

(2) Assume each department (new, used, service) is treated as a profit center, as described in the case. Also assume in a-c it is known with certainty *beforehand* that the repairs will cost $1,376.

   (a) In *your* opinion, at what value should this trade-in (*unrepaired*) be transferred from the new car department to the used car department? Why?

   (b) In *your* opinion, how much should the service department be able to charge the used-car department for the repairs on this trade-in car? Why?

   (c) Given your responses to a and b, what will be each of the three departments' contributions on this deal?

(3) Is there a strategy in this instance that would give the dealership more contribution than the one assumed above (i.e., re-

pairing and retailing this trade-in used car)? Explain. In answering *this* question, assume that the service department operates at capacity.

(4) Do you feel the three profit center approach is appropriate for Shuman? If so, explain why, including an explanation of how this is better than other specific alternatives. If not, propose a better alternative and explain why it is better than three profit centers and any other alternatives you have considered.

# TRANSFER PRICING AMONG RELATED BUSINESSES—KIRKPATRICK ASSOCIATES, INCORPORATED*

Richard (Rick) Kirkpatrick Sr. started Columbus Realty, Inc., a real estate firm, about 40 years ago. His personality and honesty made this undertaking a success. When his eldest son, John Kirkpatrick, graduated with an engineering degree. Kirkpatrick Sr. incorporated K & S Construction Company and put John in charge. Forty percent of the stock was given to John, and 60% was deposited with Kirkpatrick Associates, Incorporated, which Kirkpatrick Sr. controlled 100%. Having intimate knowledge of the housing market, Kirkpatrick Sr. suggested, and John agreed, that the construction company should concentrate on custom designed and built houses in the price range of $100,000 to $200,000. John Kirkpatrick's technical knowledge and imagination made the construction company a success.

Kirkpatrick Sr.'s second son, Court, received a degree in architecture but upon graduation was not ready to enter employment. Upon the suggestion of several friends and the family, Court Kirkpatrick continued with his education and pursued an MBA degree. During this study, and because of a special project he was assigned, he became interested in the development of living complexes around shopping centers. In this project, both the living complex and the shopping center were designed with a continental motif. Fur-

ther research convinced him that this project would not only be feasible but also very profitable. He discussed his idea and all the information he had gathered with his father, who agreed that this kind of design seemed to be the upcoming style. Upon Court's graduation, the Columbus Rental Company was incorporated with the same stock arrangement as with the K & S Construction Company.

Court bought land and proceeded with the design and building of a shopping center and several apartment buildings around this shopping center. This undertaking was an instant success, too. The shopping center has an extraordinary 100% lease commitment and some prospects on a waiting list. The apartments have an 85% occupancy rate. This complex has been and still is the "in thing" in this community. Mostly young upper-middle-class people are living there.

Until several years ago, Court had to maintain a large maintenance crew whose task was to keep up both the shopping center and the apartment buildings. However, when the youngest of the children, Richard Kirkpatrick Jr., graduated, this function was separated from his brother's company, and the Columbus Remodeling Company was incorporated. Stock arrangements were the same as for the other companies. Rick Jr. was put in charge of this company. Over the years, the various family members have retired from active participation in the day-to-day activities of the companies. Each still sets

---

*Copyright © 1976 by Professor Felix P. Kollaritsch. Reproduced with permission.

overall policies and objectives for the entities but leaves the daily operations to the general managers. Each general manager shares in the profit of his company. Although there still exists very close cooperation among these companies, they have grown to be rather independent of each other. If one inside company wants any service from the other, these services are priced the same as to outsiders. Managers of each feel they are competitive and offer the best service for the lowest cost. For instance, the Columbus Remodeling Company does all the maintenance for the Columbus Rental Company. However, to keep this contract, Columbus Remodeling must be competitive with other maintenance companies.

These arrangements have generally been successful, although occasional complaints have been raised. Recently, however, the complaints have become more vocal. To some degree they were due to poor general economic conditions. Last year was a depression year, and, although the Kirkpatrick complex fared better than the average real estate company, the general managers experienced a considerable cut in their profit participation and are now very conscious of any dealing that would reduce their profits.

During the last year, the Kirkpatrick family came up with another innovation in the real estate business—the "house trade-in." The Construction Company will construct a house for a buyer with the understanding that his old residence be taken in as a trade, providing it is located in Columbus. In many instances, this practice would avoid down payments for the buyer, as well as the inconveniences of selling the house.

The value of the trade-in is established by the real estate company and the Remodeling Company. The Remodeling Company will determine what should be done to the house and give an estimate for necessary repair work. The real estate company will make suggestions as to certain remodeling needs which make a house more valuable and sellable. The Remodeling Company will also give firm estimates on these suggestions. The real estate company will then give the construction company a realistic market value of the house.

The value of the renovated house, less the renovation costs, is used internally by the construction company to determine its profit on a sale and trade-in. Externally, the construction company will quote the buyer the renovated house value as the trade-in value but also will increase its normal price for a given house for the costs of the remodeling. The reason for this valuation is that the buyer may see the asking price for his old house in a sales advertisement and may feel cheated if the price is more than he received. Very likely, he may not be aware of the total renovation costs.

Until the house is sold, the construction company has title to the house. It is responsible for any house repairs and remodeling and for any interest, taxes, insurance, or other costs. The real estate company will list and sell the house, collecting a 6% commission from the buyer. This plan has been successful and has made the name of Kirkpatrick a household word in the real estate business throughout the state. However, the plan is not without drawbacks. The following transaction is an example, and your advice is solicited.

The K & S Construction Company sold a newly constructed house to Mr. Baxter as follows:

| | |
|---|---:|
| Price of new house | $200,000 |
| Trade-in from old house | 50,000 |
| Cash (from mortgage) | $150,000 |
| Value received | |
|   Cash | $150,000 |
|   Trade-in | 40,000 |
|   Total | $190,000 |
| Cost of building new house | 160,000 |
| Profit | $ 30,000 |

The trade-in value was established as follows: the fair market value of the house, if fixed up, was determined as $50,000 by the real estate company. The renovation needs were jointly determined by the manager of the real estate company and by the manager of the remodeling company. These needs were costed by the manager of the remodeling company as $10,000.

Two days after the deal was closed, a heavy rain occurred, and it was discovered that the roof must be replaced and the basement water-sealed. The costs for these repairs were established at $4,000 and $2,000.

The managers of the real estate and construction companies think that these repairs should be priced at $3,000 only, since the remodeling company has a 50% variable cost factor. The remodeling company's manager says that under no condition will he make the repairs for a price other than that quoted. He claims to have enough outside business to keep him occupied during the present high season. He might consider doing it for a somewhat lesser price during the off-season, which will begin in seven months. But his delay would mean not selling the house for at least a full year. Also, predictions for next year's prices for houses are impossible to make.

To complicate matters further, the manager of the rental company stated that he would like to acquire the house, since it is located within the general territorial boundaries which he would like, eventually, to incorporate. Furthermore, some of the people in the continental complex would prefer houses to apartments, if they were available. He is unwilling to pay more than $50,000 and the commission. He estimates rental income to be $500 per month, with an estimated 80% occupancy. Real estate taxes are $951 per year, maintenance is estimated to be about $500 per year, and allocated management expenses, $500 per year. Management expenses are fixed and would not change with the acquisition of this house. Income tax rate is 50%. Land value is estimated at $8,000. Life of the building is 30 years.

### Required

(1) Determine the profit of the K & S Construction Company for this sale.
(2) What should the charge be for fixing up the house?
(3) Who should be charged with the fixing-up costs? Why? Are there any changes in procedures you would suggest?
(4) If the house is to be sold to outsiders, what alternatives are open to the company?
(5) If the house is sold to the rental company, what is its price?
(6) Should the house be rented or sold?

## TRANSFER PRICING IN A MULTINATIONAL CORPORATION—DEL NORTE PAPER COMPANY (A)*

"If I had purchased the kraft linerboard for the African box sale from one of our mills, I would have paid $360 per ton, $140 per ton higher than the price I actually paid by purchasing the linerboard in the spot market," said Frank Duffy, Managing Director of Del Norte Paper's Italian subsidiary (DNP–Italia). "I can't possibly make a profit for Del Norte if I have to pay so much for my principal raw material."

Del Norte Paper Company was a large, fully integrated paper manufacturer. 1974

*This case was prepared by William Sahlman under the supervision of M. Edgar Barrett.

Copyright © 1976 by the President and Fellows of Harvard College. Harvard Business School case 177-034.

sales were about $2.8 billion, making Del Norte Paper one of the 75 largest industrial companies in the United States. The company's product line ranged from raw pulp to a large variety of converted paper products, including corrugated boxes.

DNP–Italia purchased kraft linerboard from outside suppliers and converted it into corrugated boxes. These boxes were sold primarily within Italy, though occasional sales were made outside of Italy. DNP–Italia had six plants, each of which represented a separate profit center.

### The African Bid

In mid-1975, an African firm asked a number of paper companies to submit bids on a large quantity of corrugated boxes. In total, 22 companies submitted bids, including DNP–Italia and another Del Norte subsidiary, DNP–Deutschland. The bids were said to have ranged from approximately $340 per ton to over $550 per ton, with most of them within 5% of $400 per ton. Del Norte–Italia won the contract by submitting the lowest bid from a firm viewed as being capable of meeting the customer's desired delivery and quality standards.

The price quoted by DNP–Italia had been substantially below that quoted by DNP–Deutschland. The primary difference between the two bids was the raw material (kraft linerboard) cost calculation embedded in each. DNP–Deutschland had formed its estimate using a per ton price for kraft linerboard of $360; DNP–Italia had used $220. The $360/ton figure was the price (inclusive of freight) quoted for export by a Del Norte Paper mill located in the eastern United States. The $220 figure was the price for kraft linerboard of comparable quality in the European "spot" market.

There were basically two reasons why the Del Norte Paper mill price was so much higher than the European spot price. First, Del Norte Paper was a member of the Kraft Export Association (KEA), a group of kraft linerboard manufacturers which was responsible for setting and stabilizing linerboard prices for the export market. The Del Norte Paper Company mill could not, as a member of the KEA, offer a lower price to its own converting plant than to any other external customer.

The second reason for the large price differential was the extremely weak economic conditions present in mid-1975. The paper and container industries were suffering from a worldwide slump. As a result of this slump, many non-KEA producers of kraft linerboard were selling their product at very low prices. This was the exact opposite situation as had existed in 1973, a year in which there was a worldwide paper and container economic boom, when the spot price for kraft linerboard had actually exceeded by a small amount the KEA set price.

### Del Norte's Transfer Pricing System

Prices on domestic (U.S.) intracompany sales of linerboard at Del Norte Paper were set at the "market" level. That is, the transfer price was the price at which the linerboard could be bought or sold in the marketplace. However, on international intracompany sales, the product price was set at a level determined by the Kraft Export Association. The KEA price could vary according to market conditions but tended to fluctuate less than the so-called spot price. Officials of Del Norte Paper in San Francisco estimated that, even if all foreign subsidiary managers agreed to take all of the KEA-priced, Del Norte Paper linerboard available, some 60% to 65% of their linerboard would have to come from other sources.[1]

---

[1]This 60% to 65% was basically in grade lines not produced by DNP mills in the United States. In addition, it generally consisted of lower-quality material than was normally found in the American market.

When a Del Norte Paper converting plant located in the United States purchased its linerboard from a company mill, the profit made by the mill on the transaction was included as part of one of the reported profit figures of the converting plant. The method employed for allocating the profit was rather complex. At the time of preparing the annual budget, the converting plant made a commitment to purchase a specific amount of kraft linerboard from a specific mill. The income statement of the converting plant was then credited with the actual mill profit resulting from delivery of actual orders placed against the commitment.

The figure used for the "mill profit" was determined by taking the mill profit applicable to the specific shipment after a full allocation of both fixed and variable costs and amending it for two specific items. First, any manufacturing variances were added to or subtracted from the mill profit. Second, in the event that the converting plant did not take as much of the mill's production as expected, the proportional cost of the resulting mill downtime was charged to the converting plant.

In Del Norte's international operations, the profit allocation process was similar. The foreign converting plant entered into a commitment for its U.S.-produced requirements. The "mill profit," as defined above, was credited to the converting plant and its manager. However, in contrast to domestic operations, the set of financial statements in which this amount was credited was not made freely available to the foreign subsidiary's managing director and other management personnel. The reason was to maintain a legal, arms-length business relationship. Such statements of "integrated profit" were, however, available upon request to the managing director of each foreign subsidiary.

## The African Sale

The bid submitted by DNP–Italia to the African customer was $400 per ton of corru-

gated boxes. DNP–Italia's direct costs (variable costs) were approximately $325 per ton, of which 72%, or $235,[2] represented the cost of kraft linerboard.

The bid submitted by DNP–Deutschland was $550 per ton of corrugated boxes. DNP–Deutschland's direct costs on the transaction were approximately $460, of which $385 represented the cost of kraft linerboard.

The average Del Norte Paper mill had a direct cost per ton of linerboard of $190.[3] Thus, the contribution per ton at the mill was approximately $170, given the KEA selling prices of $360 per ton. The $170 contribution figure minus the actual freight costs from the United States to Germany (approximately $45 per ton) and the allocated overhead at the mill level would have been credited to the DNP–Deutschland converting mill had Germany won the contract.

## *An Informal Discussion*

Late one afternoon in July 1975, Frank Duffy, Managing Director of DNP–Italia held a discussion with John Powell, General Manager–International Operations of Del Norte Paper's Container Division. The specific topic of the discussion was the African container sale, but the conversation also touched on the transfer pricing system used by Del Norte Paper.

DUFFY:  John, you know I would prefer to buy all my linerboard from a Del Norte Paper mill, but I just cannot compete if I have to pay $360 per ton. The price competition in the box

---

[2]*Editor's note:* This figure represents the linerboard cost per ton of corrugated box sold. The actual cost per ton of linerboard used was $220.

[3]The direct cost figure of $190 per ton at the linerboard mill included the cost of raw wood going into the mill. Approximately 30% to 40% of the raw wood used by the mill was purchased from the Del Norte Paper Company Woodlands Division at a market-determined transfer price.

market has been absolutely fierce this year. If I paid that much for linerboard, I would have to price my corrugated boxes below cost in order to win any contracts. If I am supposed to be a profit center, you can't expect me to report a loss on every sale I make, which is exactly what I would do using $360 per ton linerboard.

POWELL: But you would get credited with the mill profit in the transaction. You wouldn't have to report a loss.

DUFFY: Maybe on your books I wouldn't show a loss, but on my books I sure would. We never see that profit here in Italy. The transaction is noted in some secret little book back in San Francisco. How am I supposed to convince my plant managers and salespeople they are being credited with the mill profit when they never see it? Furthermore, from a financial point of view, the transfer pricing system doesn't make sense. Even if the mill profit were put directly into our profit and loss statement, our cash flow would not benefit. As you know, John, this is a completely self-financed operation in Italy. If I have to borrow more money than I need to, then I incur extra interest costs. There is no offsetting credit for these expenses.

POWELL: I sympathize with you, Frank, but we also have a re-

sponsibility to keep our mills operating. Further, by not purchasing Del Norte Paper linerboard when times are bad, you run the risk of not being able to buy linerboard from our U.S. mills when there is a shortage like there was two years ago. As you know, we're moving increasingly toward long-term commitments for delivery by our kraft linerboard mills. You also don't help maintain the pricing stability we've been working so hard to establish through the KEA.

DUFFY: I appreciate the problem, but I also have the responsibility to keep my plants running. Unlike in the United States, I can't fire any of my laborers in Italy; the unions just won't allow it. Any orders I can get to keep those laborers busy is pure contribution to me.

POWELL: I still think you're making a mistake by not purchasing Del Norte Paper linerboard. However, we're not going to resolve the issue today. If it were not for this damn recession, the problem probably wouldn't even exist. If it's O.K. with you, Frank, I'd like to have a chance to give the problem some more thought.

### Required

Analyze the Del Norte transfer pricing situation.

# MANAGING PROFIT CENTER PERFORMANCE—
# WILKINSON TRANSPORT (B)*

In December 1979, the managing director of Wilkinson Transport was considering a change in the organization. Wilkinson Transport was a wholly owned subsidiary of the Lex Service Group Limited. Lex was a diversified service company with 1979 sales of £500 million and profits of £22.8 million before taxes and £19.7 million after taxes. It was organized into seven business groups. Wilkinson Transport was one of the five subsidiaries included in the Transportation Business Group.

In general, Lex Service was highly decentralized. The top management of the business group participated in strategic planning; it reviewed and approved the annual budget. It reviewed accounting and budget performance reports each month. As long as Wilkinson was performing within expectations, top management did not involve itself in the day-to-day operations.

## *Operations*

**Collection and Delivery Operations**
Wilkinson Transport was an express parcel company that collected and delivered parcels weighing between 10 kilograms and one metric ton. It operated throughout the United Kingdom and in Ireland through an arrangement with an associated company located there. Wilkinson typically collected 58,000 parcels a day from 2,300 customers and delivered these parcels to 10,000 addresses, ranging from retail outlets to industrial users. The average consignment was 5.3 parcels weighing 80 kilograms.

Wilkinson operated 16 depots throughout the United Kingdom. Each depot was respon-

sible for a geographic area. Daily, it collected parcels from the customers in its area and delivered parcels for the entire network to the consignees within its area.

Each morning vans from each depot delivered parcels to the consignees within its area and then collected the consignments from its customers. The vans returned to the depot, were off-loaded, and the parcels consolidated for the depot located in the area to which the parcels were to be delivered. Thus, each day a depot would have 15 different consolidations for delivery to other depots, plus the retention of its own delivery traffic.

**Trunking** Each consolidation was loaded into vans and, during the night, the vans delivered the parcels to the appropriate depot and collected the parcels for consignees within its area. This operation was known as "trunking." There were a variety of trunking configurations. For example, Depot A and Depot B vans would meet at an intermediate point and exchange loads. Or Depot A would do the entire trunking for Depot B by delivering to Depot B and picking up its own parcels. In some instances, a depot would not have enough activity to warrant direct shipments from all depots. In this case, Depot A might deliver to Depot B parcels for delivery by Depot C. The next day Depot B delivered the parcels to Depot C. This was called transshipment. About 80% of the trunking was made directly to the depot that was to deliver the parcels, and about 20% were transshipped. The trunking configurations were determined periodically by a computer model that simulated the optimum trunking configuration based on the past six months' collections and delivery patterns.

---

*This case was prepared by John Deardon.
Copyright © 1980 by the President and Fellows of Harvard College. Harvard Business School case 181-056.

The delivery schedule for a typical parcel was as follows:

Monday: The parcel was collected from the customer.

Monday night: The parcel was trunked to the depot that was to deliver it.

Tuesday: The parcel was unloaded and assigned to the appropriate route.

Tuesday night: The parcel was loaded onto a delivery van.

Wednesday: The parcel was delivered.

About 10% of deliveries were overnight shipments. In this case, parcels are placed onto the back of the appropriate van that evening, removed immediately upon arrival at the delivery depot, and loaded onto delivery vehicles.

## Marketing

The volume and quality of sales depended on three factors: service, price, and personal sales effort. Each is discussed below.

**Service**   The most important factor in retaining present customers was the reliability of the service provided. Also, to a considerable extent, the ability to obtain new customers was affected by the company's reputation for service. Service was measured by the speed and reliability of delivery, although other factors, for example the ability to inform the customer quickly as to the status of a consignment or the prompt settlement of claims for lost or damaged goods, were also important.

Speed and reliability depended on:

1. The proper marking of the parcel and the correct information on the waybill
2. The correct classification of the destination at the collection depot
3. The correct classification of the route at the delivery depot
4. The handling of parcels so as to minimize damage
5. The control of theft

**Price**   The transport business was extremely competitive, and price was an important factor in obtaining new customers and retaining present customers. Wilkinson published a price card that provided the prices for all of the usual types of deliveries. Prices were based on the weight of the consignment and the distance traveled. Discounts from the price card were made for special circumstances. For example, large customers were sometimes quoted a fixed price per kilogram delivered. Or salespersons discounted the list price to take account of competition.

**Salespersons**   A third factor in selling the service was the personal contacts made by individual salespersons. Salespersons also handled complaints or contacted present customers to ascertain that the service was satisfactory.

By July of 1980 Wilkinson Transport had largely completed a program of computerization and mechanization started two years previously. This part of the case describes these programs.

## Wilkontrol

WILKONTROL was the name of the computer system that had been designed to:

1. Keep track of consignments during the collection and delivery process
2. Provide current operating data to management

The WILKONTROL system was installed in 1979.

**The Consignment Note**   The consignment note was the main source of information in the WILKONTROL system. The consignment note was initially prepared at the collection point and contained all of the relevant information about the consignment; for example, the shipper's name and address, the consignee's name and address, and the number and weight of the packages in the consignment. The consignment note was prepared in duplicate and was numbered for identification. One copy of the consignment note remained with the consignment; the other copy was retained by the depot.

**Keeping Track of Consignments** The information from the consignment notes was recorded in a central computer by clerks in the depot. From this information, the computer calculated additional data such as the revenue from the consignment.

When the consignment moved from the collecting depot to the delivery depot, this information was recorded into the computer. The information was continually updated as the consignment was moved through the system. Finally, after the consignment was delivered, the driver returned the receipted copy of the delivery manifest to the depot and the final delivery was recorded.

Throughout the system there were computer terminals with visual display devices that gave access to the information stored in the central computer. Thus, the status of any consignment could be ascertained within four seconds from any point within the system. The WILKONTROL system allowed management to identify quickly shipments that deviated from the standard pattern and to take appropriate corrective action.

Wilkinson was the only transport company in the United Kingdom that employed such a computer control system in 1980.

**Operating Statistics** The WILKONTROL system made it possible to provide detailed operating statistics on a daily and weekly basis. For example, at 10 A.M. every morning, the following information about the previous day's operation was available by depot and, if desired, by route:

- Number of consignments
- Number of waybills
- Total weight
- Number of packages
- Total revenue

In short, it was possible on a daily basis to observe the "profile" of the business being done on the preceding day down to the smallest organization unit. This information was then summarized by week and month.

In addition to the profile information, the depot managers were provided daily or weekly with all information relevant to the effective operation of the system. Statistics on any deviations from standard were available. This information was also required by regional and headquarter executives.

### Depot Mechanization

It was Wilkinson's plan to mechanize most depots by 1983. It was expected that mechanization would increase both the efficiency and the capacity of the depots. Also, since much of the labor would be machine-paced, better standards and performance measures against these standards would be possible.

**The Hub** *The Hub*, a highly mechanized central depot, was built in Nuneaton, a town near Birmingham. It was designed to be fully operational in the latter part of 1980. The Hub would completely transform the trunking patterns. When operational, *all* depots would send their collection to the Hub. There, the parcels would be sorted mechanically and trunked to the delivery depots. This had several important advantages.

First, the collecting depots would not be required to sort and consolidate the collected parcels except those that were to be delivered within their area. This increased the effective capacity of the depots.

Second, vans from both the depots and the Hub would move fully loaded because all collections and deliveries were made to the same location. Under the present system, each depot sent vans to 15 other locations, many of them with less than a full load.

Third, it would be possible for all drivers to reach the Hub in eight hours. EEC regulations by 1981 would require that a driver work a maximum of eight hours. Under the present system, some locations required more than eight hours driving time to reach their destination.

Fourth, the Hub was designed to provide a highly mechanized, efficient method for handling parcels. It would be possible to exercise greater control over all of the aspects of parcel handling.

## The Organization

Exhibit 1 is an organization chart of Wilkinson Transport as of July 1, 1980. There were five staff officers and three regional managers

reporting to the managing director. The commercial manager was responsible for the rate structure, the settlement of claims, public relations, and advertising. Other staff offices are self-explanatory.

**The Region**   Each region was a profit center. Four staff officers and the general managers of the depots reported to the regional manager.

**The Depot**   Each depot was also a profit center. The depot manager was responsible for operations, sales, accounting, and the repair shop. Although depot managers came from a variety of backgrounds, many had worked their way up from hourly employ-

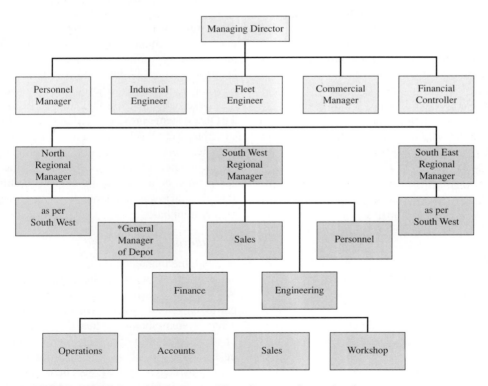

**EXHIBIT 1  Wilkinson Transport (B)—Current Organization**
*N.B. Typical profit center consolidation at region.

ment. Each depot had its own accounting system, which collected from customers and paid suppliers. Throughout the system, costs were recorded in the area where they were incurred and revenues were recorded in the area where they were received. Each month, the depot accounts were consolidated by the regional accounting staff, and the regions were consolidated by the headquarters staff.

Purchasing was also done locally, although some items were controlled through companywide contracts.

**The Financial Control System**  The Lex organization exercised short-term control through an annual profit budget. Each year a budget was presented by Wilkinson's management to the management of the Transportation Business Group. The proposed budget was reviewed and either accepted or adjusted. The final version became the basis for the monthly reports that provided a comparison of the actual results with the budget on both a monthly and year-to-date basis. The report included the analyses of variances and explanations of the causes of the variances and the action being taken.

Within Wilkinson a similar type of control was used for each region and for each depot within the region. Each depot prepared a profit plan which was approved by the regional manager, and each region prepared a regional profit plan that was approved by the managing director. Comparisons of actual performance to plan were made monthly by depot and consolidated by region. These reports included a great deal of operating statistics in addition to the financial comparisons.

In addition, there was a weekly information system that provided network profit contribution and efficiency indicators.

**Transfer Pricing**  Each depot typically performed two services for other depots and used similar services from other depots. The most important was to deliver parcels collected by other depots. Since the entire revenue was paid to the collecting depot, under a profit center system, part of this revenue must be reassigned to the delivering depot. Several methods of transfer pricing had been used. Currently, the intracompany charge made by the delivering depot to the collecting depot was a flat charge of £2.50 for each delivered consignment plus a variable charge of £10 per metric ton. This charge, on average, would compensate the delivery depot for its costs plus providing an allowance for profits.

The second service performed by one depot for the other was trunking, or delivering consignments between depots. This charge was £0.40 a mile, which also was sufficient to cover costs plus providing a profit.

**Operating Control**  Although the profit plan was an important tool for measuring managerial performance, management at all levels had access to detailed operating statistics daily and weekly. (These operating statistics were developed through the WILKONTROL system previously described.) For example, each week four pages of operating statistics were developed for each depot. One of the unique features of Wilkinson's measurement system was the amount of operating statistics that was available to management on a current basis.

## Consideration of Change

In 1980, the managing director began to consider seriously whether the organization of Wilkinson Transport should be changed. In particular, he wondered whether the profit center system should be abandoned in favor of some other form of organization. Although he had always had some reservations about the profit center system, recent events had made it desirable to consider a change at this time. It seemed logical to him that if the organization were to be changed, it should be done in 1980.

**The Strategic Plan**    In 1979, Wilkinson Transport, together with the management of Lex, developed a new strategic plan. Among other things, the plan called for sales volume to be increased by 1985 to two and a half times the 1979 volume at 1979 prices. The managing director wondered whether volume increases of this magnitude could be accomplished with the present organization. Of principal concern was whether such a large increase in sales could be realized with a sales force that was decentralized into 16 separate depot organizations.

**The Hub and Depot Mechanization**    It is expected that the Hub would change significantly network operations and would result in a greater central control. In the same way, the mechanization of the depots would change the way that parcels were handled and, to some extent, would make central control easier. Although neither the Hub nor the depot mechanization would have an important direct impact on the profit center system, the managing director believed that these developments would have an impact on the timing of any organizational change. The operations of the depots would be changed considerably by these developments. It seemed to him that a change in organization, if one was to be made, would be more acceptable to those executives affected if it were done coincidentally with the operating changes.

**Concerns about the Profit Center System**    Although the adoption of the 1979 strategic plan was the immediate cause for reconsidering the profit center form of organization, the top management of Wilkinson had experienced some concerns about the profit center system for some time. These concerns are described in this part of the case.

First, there was a question as to whether the depot manager controlled the critical elements of profit generation. For example, most of the delivery business was generated by other depots and most of the business generated by a depot was completed by other depots.

Second, there were questions as to whether excessive demands were being made on the depot manager. Was it not enough for the depot manager to be responsible only for operating the depot? Should not responsibility for sales, finance, and purchasing be assigned to functional experts? In fact, did the depot manager even have enough expertise in these areas?

Third, the profit center system tended to encourage depot managers to optimize depot profits at the expense of company profits. There was simply no incentive to sacrifice depot profits for the benefit of the company. For example, a depot manager could turn down (or, at least, not pursue aggressively) business that might benefit the company. If a depot was very busy, additional business might not be profitable to the collecting depot even though it might benefit the company. On the other hand, business that might be profitable to collect but marginal to deliver might be pursued aggressively. The problem was that the depot manager evaluated the desirability of business from the collection point of view only.

Finally, there was a question as to whether the transfer price system divided the revenue among contributing depots fairly. A related concern was whether the paperwork required to implement the transfer price system was not only a waste of money but might even be producing misleading information.

**Advantages of Profit Centers**    In deciding upon any organizational changes, the managing director was well aware of the benefits that had accrued to the company because the profit center system *had* worked very well in the past. The depot general managers viewed themselves as managing their own business. Parcel collection and delivery was a geographic function, and the depot general manager controlled all aspects within his area.

Three considerations were of particular importance in any change from the profit center system.

First, what would be the effect if responsibility for sales was taken from the depot manager? How would the tradeoff between simply increasing the level of sales volume and increasing the quality of the sales be resolved? For example, additional business obtained from customers on established routes required almost no additional cost to collect; however, business in other locations might require considerable additional cost. If salespersons did not report to the depot manager, would they not be motivated to increase the level of sales regardless of location?

Second, the level of costs were to some extent a function of volume. The volume of activity, particularly of deliveries, was largely outside the control of the depot manager. Without the profit center system, how could the performance of a depot manager be measured?

Finally, the depot manager controlled the most important element of sales volume—service. Without profit centers, how would this be taken into consideration in the measurement system?

### Required

(1) Should Wilkinson Transport change its organization? If so, how? If not, explain why the present system should not be changed.

(2) How would you change the performance measurement system to accompany your revised organization? In particular, how would you evaluate depot managers to ensure goal congruence?

(3) In order of potential severity, list the problems that you anticipate would occur in implementing your revised organization and measurement system. How would you handle these problems?

---

## INTERNAL TRANSFER PRICING WITH AN OUTSIDE MARKET—THE NEW BRUNSWICK COMPANY*

### Background

The New Brunswick Company is a midsized subsidiary of the Sun Corporation, which manufacturers various textile and similar material composites. Sales are made to affiliate companies within the Sun Corporation, as well as to external companies. Approximately one-half of New Brunswick's sales are to affiliated companies.

New Brunswick's formal mission statement reads as follows:

New Brunswick's mission is to develop and supply unique, cost effective fabrics and related nonconventional structures to proactively support the Sun Corporation's worldwide consumer and professional markets.

An extension of New Brunswick's mission is to capitalize on the resultant unique product and fabric capabilities by developing profitable franchises in selective growth-oriented consumer and industrial markets.

This will be accomplished while satisfying the expectations of the company and fostering commitment, challenge, and reward for our employees.

This statement has received wide approval from the corporate level and from the affiliate

*From *Management Accounting Practice*, vol. 3, of IMA/AAA Management Accounting Symposium series. Reprinted with permission.

management boards. It serves as the driving force for New Brunswick's management and sets clear objectives.

### The Product

Fifteen years ago, New Brunswick research began evaluating a fabric formation technology (originally developed by the Smith Company, a competitor) called Super Weave. In this technology, fibers are entangled mechanically using water sprayed under high pressure. The resulting fabric is very clothlike in appearance, feel, and comfort. The Smith Company realized early on that this fabric would make an ideal barrier in the operating room. The new fabric would provide an effective disposable replacement for operating room drapes and gowns, providing a greater degree of sterility than had been attainable in the past.

Within the Sun Corporation's family of companies, Sanitech is responsible for asepsis within the operating room. To this end, Sanitech markets operating room apparel, gloves, and disinfectants.

Ten years ago, Sanitech began marketing operating room packs and gowns using the Smith fabric. Although the franchise was successful, the relationship between supplier and customer did have drawbacks, which the Sun Corporation, Sanitech, and New Brunswick fully understood:

1. Product improvements made by Smith might not be exclusive to Sanitech in the future, because Smith could sell to Sanitech's competitors.
2. Smith's capacity versus Sanitech's demand.
3. Lack of a second source.
4. Fear of monopolistic pricing practices.

### New Brunswick's Entry into the Market

Six years ago, New Brunswick developed a material equivalent to the Super Weave fabric for sale to Sanitech. Entering this business

required New Brunswick to make a significant capital investment in plant and equipment. The total investment would approach $30 million, the largest single investment in the company's long history. Given the Sun Corporation's policy of decentralized operating companies and New Brunswick's mission, New Brunswick's resources alone were used to fund the project. In addition, Sanitech as the marketing company was at liberty to select the fabric that, from its perspective, would best meet its customers' requirements at the lowest cost to Sanitech.

New Brunswick's proposal was presented to the executive committee of the Sun Corporation, who gave final approval for New Brunswick to proceed.

### Smith's Response

Three years ago, New Brunswick began making fabric of a quality comparable to Smith's. However, New Brunswick found itself in a significantly changed market environment:

1. Concurrent with New Brunswick's entry, Smith's prices to Sanitech immediately dropped.
2. Smith introduced pricing strategies that rewarded Sanitech for high volume and provided multiyear incentives.
3. With the exception of price escalation, Sanitech and Smith had developed an effective partnership since 1975.
4. After several years of manufacturing, Smith had been able to maximize manufacturing efficiencies and achieve lower cost. New Brunswick realized it was at a cost disadvantage and could not price on the basis of intercompany transfer formulas (normally, full cost plus a percent return on invested capital and working capital).

New Brunswick understood very quickly and clearly that, in order to be successful, it must beat Smith's pricing and in the long run minimize manufacturing costs or New Brunswick would have to be content as a secondary source of supply.

## New Brunswick's Problem

The vice president of affiliate marketing at New Brunswick requested the assistance of the chief financial officer in developing a plan that would enable New Brunswick to sell its product to Sanitech while achieving the following objectives:

1. Establish a price that is competitive while recovering the capital investment in a reasonable number of years.
2. Establish the longer-term profitability for New Brunswick.
3. Provide the corporation with the lowest-cost product over the long run.

## Required

(1) How should New Brunswick develop its pricing strategy?
(2) How should the benefit to the Sun Corporation be measured?
(3) What might Smith's reaction be to your strategy?
(4) Should vertically integrated corporations be forced to procure raw materials from other divisions?
(5) Should intercompany pricing policy be inflexible?

# Financial Measures of Performance: Return on Investment (ROI) and Economic Value Added (EVA™)[1]

## RELATING PROFITS TO ASSETS EMPLOYED

In most decentralized profit centers (or strategic business units, as they are often called), the general manager has authority to not only make operating decisions on product mix, pricing, customer relationships, and production methods but also to determine the level and type of assets used in the unit. For such units, the financial measure used to evaluate managerial and business unit performance should relate the amount of profit earned to the level of assets employed. By measuring a unit's profits relative to the assets employed, corporate managers can assess whether the profits are generating an adequate return on the capital invested in the unit.

Capital always has alternative uses, so corporate managers must be concerned about whether the returns being earned on invested capital in a business unit exceed the cost of this capital, as measured by the returns available from alternative uses. A second reason for measuring the returns on capital is to promote discipline in the organization's capital-budgeting process. Most companies have elaborate systems for authorizing capital expenditures (see discussion in Chapter 12). Without some form of measurement of the ex post returns to capital, little incentive may exist, during the capital-budgeting process, for business unit managers to estimate accurately the future cash flows. Measuring returns relative to invested capital also focuses managers' attention on how to reduce the levels of working capital—particularly accounts receivable and inventory—used by the decentralized unit.

## A HISTORICAL PERSPECTIVE

Despite the intuitive appeal of a measure that relates profits to employed assets, it was not until the early part of the twentieth century that the return-on-investment criterion was developed. Although business firms used net earnings to measure performance long before 1900, earnings were measured relative to either sales revenue or the costs of operations. They were not measured relative to the organization's investment in productive assets.[2] The typical nineteenth-century owner-entrepreneur—whether of a textile mill, a railroad, a steel company, or a retail organization—had to concentrate on performing only a single type of economic activity efficiently. In the short run, the owner attempted to manage operating costs in this single activity. He did not have to choose among alternative types of activities in which to make investments. He only had to determine the appropriate scale of activity in his principal line of business. For this purpose, the operating ratio of costs to revenues or the return on sales apparently provided an adequate guide for investment profitability.

The DuPont Powder Company, formed in 1903 when several previously separate and independently managed enterprises were combined, had a new organizational challenge not faced by nineteenth-century organizations: to coordinate and allocate resources to the manufacturing, purchasing, and selling activities of units performing quite different activities. In making decisions on the allocation of investment funds, the founders of the DuPont Company declared that there "be no expenditures for additions to the earning equipment if the same amount of money could be applied to some better purpose in another branch of the company's business."

The founders understood that

> a commodity requiring an inexpensive plant might, when sold only 10% above its cost, show a higher rate of return on the investment than another commodity sold at double its cost, but manufactured in an expensive plant. The true test of whether the profit is too great or too small is the rate of return on the money invested in the business and not the percent of profit on the cost.[3]

To guide their investment decisions, the DuPont Company developed the return-on-investment (ROI) criterion, measured by net earnings (after depreciation but before deduction of interest on long-term debt) divided by net assets (total assets minus goodwill and other intangibles, current liabilities, and reserves for depreciation).

Donaldson Brown, the chief financial officer of DuPont (and subsequently at General Motors starting in the 1920s), greatly extended the value of the ROI measure by showing how it could be written as the product of two ratios commonly used in nineteenth-century organizations: the profit ($P$), or return-on-sales, measure and the turnover ($T$) ratio of sales to assets:

$$\text{ROI} = \frac{\text{profit}}{\text{sales}} * \frac{\text{sales}}{\text{assets}} = PT$$

The $P$ and $T$ ratios could be decomposed, in turn, into their component parts, representing accounts from the income and expense statement or the balance sheet so that senior managers could understand how performance of individual activities contributed to the overall measure of organizational effectiveness. A copy of an actual chart describing operations for the year 1923 is shown in Exhibit 10-1.

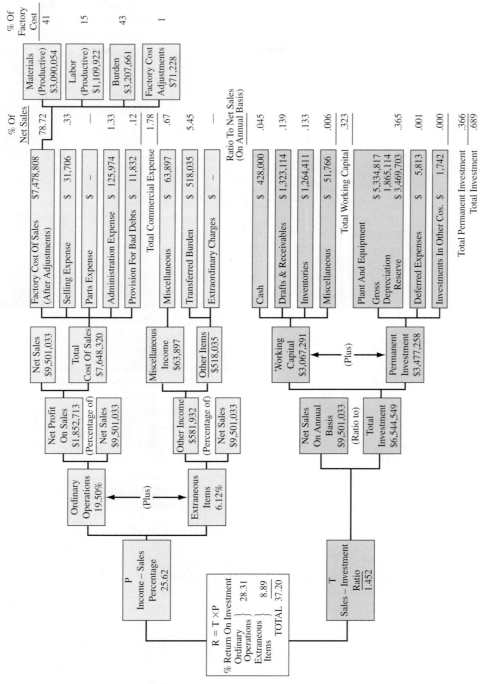

**EXHIBIT 10-1**  Analysis of Return on Investment, 12 Mos. Ended Dec. 31, 1923

Exhibit 10-1 shows how the overall ROI of 37.2% was earned by a return-on-sales profitability ($P$) percentage of 25.62% multiplied by a sales-to-investment turnover ($T$) ratio of 1.452. The $P$ percentage is decomposed into its component income and expense accounts, and the $T$ ratio is decomposed into the major balance sheet accounts as they relate to sales.

## THE MATSUSHITA INTERNAL CAPITAL SYSTEM

Interestingly, a parallel and apparently independent development of the investment-center organizational form occurred during the 1930s in the Matsushita Corporation of Japan. The founder, Kohnosuke Matsushita, believed in "optimally scaled businesses." Concerned by health-imposed restrictions on his own ability to travel among all the new businesses of Matsushita, the founder understood that he could not manage a dynamic, growing company by himself. His management strategy was to select a suitable person for each business field and to delegate production and sales authority to that manager. The role of the president was to control division managers so that their actions would contribute to achieving organizational goals.[4]

Matsushita believed that each business must have independent, autonomous power in terms of funds and R&D ability. (Matsushita, unlike almost all other Japanese corporations, did not rely on debt to finance its operations.) Each business was to have a buffer of funds (and other corporate resources—including facilities, human resources, and technology) to adapt to change and continue to grow even under adverse economic conditions. Therefore, each division had to manage and rely on its own capital. Division managers were responsible for two principal tasks: *profit* management and *funds* management.

The company developed its own internal capital system for implementing decentralized funds management. A division's internal capital was the sum of its fixed assets and its working capital. Working capital was measured relative to a standard based on budgeted sales and production (see Exhibit 10-2). For example, the standard allowance for accounts receivable was computed from an estimated collection period, say 30 days, so that the allowance would be one month's worth of sales. Accounts payable was measured by assuming that the ratio of materials to total manufacturing costs was 50% and the turnover period was 35 days.

The rules for the internal capital system were as follows:

1. Internal capital = standard working capital + fixed assets − reserves.
2. Interest charged for internal capital = 1% per month, paid to central office each month.
3. Central office tax (to cover headquarter's expenses) = 3% of divisional sales, paid to central office each month. After this payment was deducted, divisional *net profit* should equal 10% of sales (the target goal for *profit management*).
4. Dividends and tax equal to 60% of divisional profit were remitted to the central office in the following month. The remaining 40% of divisional profit was retained to support additional working capital and fixed investment.
5. If divisional funds fell short of required amounts, the division could borrow temporarily from the central office. Any excess cash could be deposited in the Matsushita Bank, where it earned a competitive rate of interest.
6. When a division required large funds for a major new investment, the proposal was submitted to the central office for approval and funding.

**EXHIBIT 10-2**  Structure of Standard Working Capital

| ACCOUNT TITLE | COMPUTATION BASIS FOR STANDARDS | | STANDARD AMOUNT (YEN) | RATIO TO MONTHLY SALES |
| --- | --- | --- | --- | --- |
| | BASIS | COMPUTATIONS | | |
| **Current Assets** | | | | |
| Notes receivable | Ratio of notes: 30% | (Sales) | | Months |
| | Term of notes: 90 days | $100 \times 30\% \times \dfrac{90 \text{ days}}{30 \text{ days}}$ | 90 | 0.90 |
| Accounts receivable | Turnover period: 30 days | (Sales) | | |
| | | $100 \times 70\% \times \dfrac{30 \text{ days}}{30 \text{ days}}$ | 100 | 1.00 |
| Finished products | Ratio of cost of sales: 70% | (Sales) | | |
| | Turnover period: 30 days | $100 \times 70\% \times \dfrac{30 \text{ days}}{30 \text{ days}}$ | 70 | 0.70 |
| Work-in-process | Ratio of manual cost: 70% | (Production) | | |
| | Turnover period: 3 days | $100 \times 70\% \times \dfrac{3 \text{ days}}{30 \text{ days}}$ | 7 | 0.07 |
| Materials | Ratio of materials: 50% | (Production) | | |
| | Turnover period: 15 days | $100 \times 50\% \times \dfrac{15}{30}$ | 25 | 0.25 |
| Other current assets | Sales amount: 3% | (Sales) $100 \times 3\%$ | 3 | 0.03 |
| Total A | | | 295 | 2.95 |
| **Current Liabilities** | | | | |
| Notes payable (materials) | Ratio of materials: 50% | (Production) | | |
| | Ratio of notes: 10% | $100 \times 50\% \times 10\% \times \dfrac{90}{30}$ | 15 | 0.15 |
| | Term of notes: 90 days | | | |
| Accounts payable | Ratio of materials: 50% | (Production) | | |
| | Turnover period: 35 days | $100 \times 50\% \times \dfrac{35 \text{ days}}{30 \text{ days}}$ | 60 | 0.60 |
| Other current liabilities | Sales amount: 35% | (Production) $100 \times 35\%$ | 35 | 0.35 |
| Total B | | | 110 | 1.10 |
| Balance: A − B = Working Capital | | | 185 | 1.85 |

Profit management performance was evaluated by assigning its return on sales to one of four ranks:

Rank A:   Greater than 9%

Rank B:   Between 6% and 9%

Rank C:   Between 4% and 6%

Rank D:   Less than 4%

Any division manager receiving rank D for two consecutive years was transferred. Interest revenues were excluded from the return-on-sales calculation. Matsushita believed that profits should be earned from manufacturing high-quality goods at low cost, not from financial transactions.

## THE DANGER OF ROI CONTROL

In the original uses of ROI at the DuPont Company and subsequently at General Motors, the measure was used to supplement the intuition and insight of managers who were quite familiar with the technology and competitive conditions of the operating divisions. Even in its use to encourage decentralized decision making at Matsushita, the operating divisions were working with products, processes, and customer markets that were well understood by senior corporate executives. In the post–World War II era, however, companies began to diversify their scope of operations, especially by acquiring companies in other industries. This massive increase in diversification meant that top managers often had little specific knowledge of, or experience with, the technology and markets of many of the businesses they had acquired. Also, the large number of different businesses acquired created huge demands for decision making that could no longer be performed by the corporate office. As noted by a leading business historian:

> Statistical ROI data about performance, profit, and long-term plans were no longer the basis for discussion between corporate and operating management. Instead, ROI became a reality in itself—a target sent down from the corporate office for division managers to meet. Since managers' compensation and promotion prospects depended on the ability to meet targets, these middle managers had a strong incentive to adjust their data accordingly.[5]

### A Simple Example

The opportunity to manipulate the ROI measure can be illustrated with the following numerical example. Consider the performance of a division during a consecutive three-quarter period:

| QUARTER | ROI | PROFITABILITY | TURNOVER |
|---------|-------|---------------|----------|
| 1 | 12.6% | 17.1% | 0.736 |
| 2 | 13.4 | 20.2 | 0.664 |
| 3 | 15.4 | 22.7 | 0.679 |

At first glance, the operating performance seems excellent, with a nice increase in ROI each quarter. The decomposition, however, reveals a sharp increase in profitability (return on sales) that overcomes a drop in asset turnover. Upon investigating the reasons for the increase in profitability and decrease in turnover, central management learned that the division manager had greatly increased production in quarters 2 and 3, with excess production accumulating as finished goods inventory. The much higher rates of production enabled period costs to be absorbed into inventory, allowing for a higher return on sales percentage on the goods actually sold. The buildup of inventory relative to sales was signaled by the decrease in the asset turnover ratio. Thus, by analyzing the contrary trends in profitability and turnover, central management was able to discover how the division manager had attempted to manipulate his performance evaluation.

In many diversified corporations, the ROI measure gave the illusion of insight and control, when, in fact, managers were taking actions that increased ROI but decreased the long-run value of their business units. Many of these problems have already been discussed in earlier chapters, in which we pointed out that excessive focus on any single short-run measure, such as profits, can motivate undesirable actions by decentralized managers. These shortcomings led to development of the Balanced Scorecard (see Chapter 8), in which short-term financial measures could be supplemented with measures that drive future financial performance.

## TECHNICAL SHORTCOMINGS OF THE ROI MEASURE

In addition to the problems introduced by the inadequacy of the profit measure to assess the creation of long-term economic value, problems arise even when using ROI for evaluating short-term profit performance. Actions that increase the divisional ROI can make the corporation worse off and, conversely, actions that decrease divisional ROI may increase the economic wealth of the corporation.[6] These perverse effects can occur whenever performance is measured by a percentage or a ratio, such as with ROI, in which operating income is normalized by a measure of investment. Consider a division with assets of $90,000 and net income before taxes (NIBT) of $20,000. Its ROI will be measured at 22.2%:

$$\text{ROI} = \frac{\text{NIBT}}{\text{assets}} = \frac{20{,}000}{90{,}000} = 0.222$$

Suppose the cost of capital for the division is 15% and a new opportunity appears that requires an investment of $15,000, yielding an annual profit improvement of $3,000 per year. The return from this new investment opportunity is 20%, which is well above the division's cost of capital. But the new ROI for the division, should the project be funded, would be

$$\text{ROI} = \frac{20{,}000 + 3{,}000}{90{,}000 + 15{,}000}$$
$$= \frac{23{,}000}{105{,}000}$$
$$= 0.219$$

a decrease from the previous level of 22.2%. The ROI measure causes the division manager to be motivated to refuse this investment, since, even though it returns in excess of the cost of capital (it generates $750 per year in additional profits after paying the investment financing cost of 15%), the project lowers the divisional ROI. If left uncorrected, this defect alone may cause ROI to be an inappropriate measure of divisional performance.

Problems arise when contemplating asset disposal as well. If the division has an asset carried at a $20,000 cost that earns $3,600 per year (an 18% return), the division can increase its ROI by disposing of the asset even though it is earning above the division's cost of capital. The division manager can perform the following calculation of the postdisposal ROI:

$$\text{ROI} = \frac{20{,}000 - 3{,}600}{90{,}000 - 20{,}000}$$

$$= \frac{16{,}400}{70{,}000}$$

$$= 0.234$$

A similar problem arises when two divisions with different investment bases are compared. For example, a second division with assets of $50,000 and net income of $12,500 will show an ROI of 25%. It might appear that the second division is more profitable, since its ROI of 25% exceeds the 22.2% ROI of the first division. But, on closer inspection, we see that the first division has $40,000 more in assets, on which its incremental earnings are $7,500 (from $20,000 − $12,500). Therefore, its incremental ROI is 7,500/40,000, or 18.75%, well above the cost of capital of 15%. Hence, the first division is more profitable, after subtracting capital costs, than the second division.

The above problems are caused by evaluating divisional performance by a ratio (ROI). Managers who wish to maximize a ratio can either increase the numerator (by earning more profits with existing assets) or decrease the denominator (by shrinking the investment base). The investment base is shrunk when managers decline profitable new investment opportunities that can earn in excess of the divisional cost of capital but whose returns are below the current average ROI of the division. In general, any project or asset whose return is below the average ROI of the division will be a candidate for disposal or will not be recommended for funding, because its inclusion in the investment base would lower the divisional ROI measure. Carrying this process to its logical but absurd limit, the division manager shrinks the investment base to the single project that earns the highest ROI but on an extremely low capital base.

## ECONOMIC VALUE ADDED (RESIDUAL INCOME)

The limitations and dysfunctional actions associated with using a ratio to evaluate the performance of a manager or division have been known and discussed for decades. Businesses, such as General Electric in the 1950s, and academics[7] have shown how to overcome these limitations by using an alternative performance measure, originally called residual income. To implement the residual income approach, corporate managers must specify an additional parameter, the risk-adjusted cost of capital for the division, which is then multiplied by division's net investment base to obtain a capital charge for the division. Careful readers will note that the residual income computation is identical to the calculation developed at the Matsushita Company. The capital charge is subtracted from net income before taxes, and the remainder is called the residual income: the income remaining after charging for the cost of capital. The residual income also corresponds closely to the economist's (but not the accountant's) measure of income.

For the examples of the two divisions described above, the residual income (RI) calculation is presented in Exhibit 10-3.

**EXHIBIT 10-3**  Residual Income Calculation

|                          | DIVISION 1 | DIVISION 2 |
|--------------------------|-----------|-----------|
| Invested capital         | $90,000   | $50,000   |
| Net income before taxes  | $20,000   | $12,500   |
| Capital charge (@15%)    | 13,500    | 7,500     |
| Residual income          | $ 6,500   | $ 5,000   |

The residual income calculation in Exhibit 10-3 shows that Division 1 is indeed more profitable than Division 2, since its residual income is higher. The RI difference of $1,500 is precisely due to the return in excess of the cost of capital of 0.0375 (obtained from 0.1875 − 0.15) applied to the incremental investment of $40,000 [since 0.0375 * 40,000 = 1,500] in Division 1.

Also, if Division 1 takes its 20% project opportunity ($15,000 investment, $3,000 annual return), its RI will increase, whereas if it disposes of the $20,000 asset earning $3,600 per year, its RI will decrease (see Exhibit 10-4).

The RI measure will always increase when we add investments earning above the cost of capital or eliminate investments earning below the cost of capital. Therefore, it produces goal congruence between the evaluation of the division and the actions that maximize the economic wealth of the division and the firm. The firm will always prefer the division to have a higher rather than a lower residual income. In this regard, RI offers significant advantages over the ROI measure; we have already found examples in which actions that increased divisional ROI made the firm worse off. The RI measure is also more flexible, because a different percentage can be applied to investments of different risks. The cost of capital for divisions in different lines of business may differ, and even assets within the same division may be in different risk classes (contrast the risk of cash or accounts receivable with the risk of long-lived highly specialized fixed assets). The RI evaluation allows managers to recognize different risk-adjusted capital costs that the ROI measure cannot.

Despite the appeal of the residual income calculation and its apparent theoretical superiority over the ROI measure, virtually no company used it extensively for measure-

**EXHIBIT 10-4**  Options for Division 1

|                          | NOW      | OPTION 1 (NEW $15,000 INVESTMENT) | OPTION 2 (DISPOSE OF $20,000 ASSET) |
|--------------------------|----------|-----------------------------------|-------------------------------------|
| Invested capital         | $90,000  | $105,000                          | $70,000                             |
| Net income before taxes  | $20,000  | $ 23,000                          | $16,400                             |
| Capital charge (@15%)    | 13,500   | 15,750                            | 10,500                              |
| Residual income          | $ 6,500  | $ 7,250                           | $ 5,900                             |

ment of business unit performance. But a revolution in thinking occurred starting in the late 1980s, when several financial consulting firms published studies that showed a high correlation between the changes in companies' residual incomes and changes in their stock market valuation. These correlations were significantly higher that the correlations between changes in ROI and stock price changes. The move toward the RI measure received even greater publicity when it was renamed into a far more accessible and acceptable term—Economic Value Added—by the Stern Stewart consulting organization, a prime advocate for the Economic Value Added concept. Their ideas were publicized in the *Journal of Applied Corporate Finance*[8] and culminated in a cover story in the September 20, 1993, issue of *Fortune* magazine, entitled "EVA—The Real Key to Creating Wealth." The article described the apparent success that many companies had enjoyed by using economic value added to motivate and evaluate corporate and divisional managers.

The economic value added concept extended the classic residual income measure in several ways. First, it built upon recent developments in financial economics, particularly the capital asset pricing model (CAPM), to derive a cost of capital based on the industry and risk characteristics of individual divisions. Therefore, rather than using an average corporatewide rate, perhaps based on the traditional weighted average cost of capital (WACC), the CAPM could be used to derive a specific, market-based evaluation of risk for an individual business unit. Second, EVA is calculated after adjusting for distortions introduced by generally accepted accounting principles (GAAP) required for financial reporting. Several of these will be discussed in this chapter.

It is interesting to speculate about why it took companies so long to see the benefits from a relatively simple change that is able to overcome well-documented difficulties with the ROI calculation introduced at the DuPont Corporation almost a century ago.

1. The types of dysfunctional behavior from concentration on either accounting income or ROI were not perceived for many years as a real problem in practice. This perception changed, probably under the influence of the leveraged-buy-out (LBO) and management-buy-out (MBO) activities in the 1980s. These activities were directed at companies that were not exploiting effectively their capital base for shareholders. The LBO and MBO activities provided an external, market-based visibility and discipline to corporate decisions on retention and investment of capital. This visibility and discipline helped to encourage corporate managers in the 1990s to pay much more attention to maximizing returns to shareholders, not maximizing purely accounting-based measures.

2. Economic value added requires that companies specify a cost of capital either overall for themselves or for their individual divisions and business units. Senior managers were for many years unwilling to specify the company's or divisions' cost of capital, especially if they must make explicit calculations about appropriate risk adjustments for divisions and classes of assets. Until the widespread knowledge and acceptance of the CAPM approach, which was developed in academic finance departments in the mid-1960s, corporate managers had only arbitrary, somewhat ad hoc techniques for estimating a risk-adjusted cost of capital.

3. In an EVA calculation, the cost of equity capital is explicitly recognized. As this capital cost is subtracted from divisions' net incomes, the combined total of divisional net income falls far short of the corporation's financial accounting net income, as reported under GAAP to shareholders, because the cost of equity capital is not considered an expense (or profit reduction) under GAAP. Most companies want complete consistency be-

tween internal and external accounting numbers and hence rejected for many years a procedure for internal purposes that they could not employ in their published financial statements.

**4.** Perhaps managers preferred a percentage measure of profitability, such as that obtained with ROI, rather than the absolute EVA measure. A percentage profitability measure could be more convenient when comparing a division's profitability with other financial measures, such as inflation rates, interest rates, and the profit rates of other divisions in the company or outside.

Interestingly, however, despite the long-time lack of acceptance of residual income or EVA for divisional evaluation, we will see in Chapter 13 that the bonus plans for senior executives were often based on an EVA-type measure. In these plans, the bonus pool is defined as a percentage (say 10%) of net income in excess of a prespecified rate of return on invested capital.

The discussion so far has focused on properties that distinguish EVA from the ROI measure. Both measures, however, have additional significant problems that should be addressed to improve their usefulness as measures of divisional and business-unit performance.

## EXPENSE VERSUS CAPITALIZE

For certain expenditures, especially on intangibles, discretion exists as to whether the expenditures should be expensed in the period in which they are incurred or should be capitalized and amortized over the future periods when their benefits are expected to be realized. The Financial Accounting Standards Board (FASB) discourages the capitalization of most intangible expenditures (see, for example, Statement 2 on Accounting for Research and Development Costs[9]), but internal performance evaluation need not be bound by regulations established for external reporting. In a steady-state situation, in which roughly equal expenditures on intangibles are made each year, net income is not affected, because the sum of amortization expenses of current and past expenditures will equal the current year's expenditures. But the failure to capitalize expenditures with expected future benefits will penalize earnings in the short run until the steady state is reached and will overstate the ROI and EVA in the steady state, because the expenditures on intangibles will not be included in the measured investment base.

We can illustrate these distortions by considering a division with five identical assets of different ages. Each asset costs $30,000 and generates a net cash flow (revenues less variable costs and traceable fixed cash costs) of $10,000 per year for five years. After five years of operation, the asset is worthless and is scrapped for zero salvage value. The division has reached a steady state; each year a five-year-old asset is scrapped and a new one is purchased. To keep the analysis simple, we will ignore tax effects, and we will assume that all cash flows and investment occur at a single point in time, on the last day of the year.[10] Also, we assume that the division uses straight-line depreciation (of $6,000 per year per asset) for financial reporting purposes.

With five assets, each generating a depreciation charge of $6,000 per year (computed as $30,000 divided by five years), the total depreciation charge equals $30,000 per year. Subtracting depreciation from the net cash flow of $50,000 per year (from the five assets) yields a net income of $20,000. The net book value of the division can easily be derived, as shown below:

| AGE OF ASSET (YEARS) | BOOK VALUE |
|:---:|:---:|
| 0 | $30,000 |
| 1 | 24,000 |
| 2 | 18,000 |
| 3 | 12,000 |
| 4 | 6,000 |
| Total book value | $90,000 |

Therefore, the ROI of this division equals 20,000/90,000, or 22.2%.[11]

Assume that our five-asset division also engages in research each year. This research costs $3,000 but produces incremental cash flows of $1,000 for each of the next five years. (Note that this research is analogous to purchasing an additional 10% of one of our basic assets.) If this expenditure is expensed, we will observe the following sequence of net income measures:

| | YEAR | | | | | |
|---|:---:|:---:|:---:|:---:|:---:|:---:|
| | 0 | 1 | 2 | 3 | 4 | 5 |
| Cash flows | $47,000 | $48,000 | $49,000 | $50,000 | $51,000 | $52,000 |
| Depreciation | 30,000 | 30,000 | 30,000 | 30,000 | 30,000 | 30,000 |
| Net income | $17,000 | $18,000 | $19,000 | $20,000 | $21,000 | $22,000 |

Initially, the $3,000 expenditure reduces net income with no compensating benefit. By year 5, the annual $3,000 expenditure is more than offset by the five $1,000 increments in cash flows from the research expenditures in the previous five years, and overall the net income has increased by $2,000 from these cumulative investments in new products and processes.

If the annual $3,000 expenditure had been capitalized and amortized over five years, the sequence of net income figures would be:

| | YEAR | | | | | |
|---|:---:|:---:|:---:|:---:|:---:|:---:|
| | 0 | 1 | 2 | 3 | 4 | 5 |
| Cash flows | $50,000 | $51,000 | $52,000 | $53,000 | $54,000 | $55,000 |
| Depreciation/ amortization | 30,000 | 30,600 | 31,200 | 31,800 | 32,400 | 33,000 |
| Net income | $20,000 | $20,400 | $20,800 | $21,200 | $21,600 | $22,000 |

Thus, the two methods eventually reach the same net income figure in the steady state, but the capitalization/amortization alternative has a more gradual transition.

When used to evaluate investment-center performance, however, the two methods yield quite different measures, as shown below for each of the first five years:

| GAAP TREATMENT: EXPENSE R&D EXPENSE AS INCURRED | | | | |
| --- | --- | --- | --- | --- |
| Year | 1 | 2 | 3 | 4 | 5 |
| ROI | 18.9% | 20.0% | 21.1% | 22.2% | 24.4% |
| EVA | $3,500 | $4,500 | $5,500 | $6,500 | $8,500 |

| CAPITALIZE AND AMORTIZE R&D SPENDING | | | | |
| --- | --- | --- | --- | --- |
| Year | 1 | 2 | 3 | 4 | 5 |
| ROI | 21.5% | 21.4% | 21.5% | 21.8% | 22.2% |
| EVA | $6,090 | $6,220 | $6,440 | $6,750 | $7,150 |

We conclude from this exercise that divisions that treat expenditures with future-period benefits as current-period expenses will:

1. Show depressed profits either until a steady-state level of such expenditures is reached or at any time an unusually large expenditure is made in a year
2. Report a higher ROI and EVA than are actually being earned in the steady state because of the failure to properly classify such expenditures as investments

Divisions with a high proportion of expenditures on intangibles such as research and development, customer and market development, and employee skill enhancement will tend to show higher EVA and ROI in the steady-state than, say, divisions in which most expenditures with future-period benefits tend to be tangible; that is, one can see and touch what the division acquired for these expenditures. This is why marketing divisions with heavy advertising and promotional expenditures, or divisions with large numbers of professional employees (whose human capital is not recorded on the balance sheet), will show unusually high ROI and EVA performance measures. These divisions are not as profitable as they appear. Their currently high profitability (as measured by either EVA or ROI) occurs because profitability in earlier years was understated, as all expenditures on intangibles were expensed as incurred. In the current years, the firms are enjoying the benefits from these previous investments in intangibles, but the current benefits are not being related to the intangible investment base developed in previous years. Thus, these divisions' EVA and ROI appear to be higher because they have many assets that are not being counted as part of their investment base.

## Leased Assets

Another version of the expense versus capitalize option occurs when clever managers, knowing that they will be evaluated by an ROI or EVA measure, lease assets instead of purchasing them. We have already noted the pervasive tendency for divisional accounting procedures to be driven by the procedures for external reporting. The limited capitalization of leases that existed before FAS 13[12] provided an incentive for managers to acquire assets through leases because the leases would not appear in the division's investment base. The flexible conditions in FAS 13 (plus all subsequent modifications and interpretations) still enable managers to structure many leases so that the assets need not be capitalized for financial reporting purposes and hence will probably be excluded from the divisional investment base.

The incentive for leasing instead of purchasing assets can easily be illustrated in the context of our five-asset division. Suppose that, at the end of the year, instead of purchasing a new asset to replace the one just retired, the division manager finds a supplier willing to provide the asset on a five-year lease. The supplier has the same 15% cost of capital as the division and computes the equivalent annual lease payment using the five-year 15% annuity factor, 3.3522, as

$$\text{Annual lease payment} = \frac{\$30,000}{3.3522} = \$8,950$$

After one year with the leased asset, the division has the same physical assets and revenues but an extra cash expense of $8,950, a decrease in recorded investment of $30,000, and a decrease in (straight-line) depreciation expense of $6,000. The ROI and EVA for the first several years is shown in Exhibit 10-5.

The ROI of the division increases dramatically as leased assets are substituted for purchased assets. Eventually, when all the assets are leased, the division will show an infinite ROI because it will be earning net income of $5,250 with no recorded assets. The EVA of the division also increases initially but eventually declines as the higher lease payments from the leased assets more than offset the lower capital charges on owned assets. These fluctuations in ROI and EVA are purely an artifact of excluding leased assets from the investment base. The size of the division and its profitability are identical to the situation in which all five assets were purchased and owned by the division. Regardless of what the company does for financial reporting purposes, there seems to be no reason for it to exclude leased assets from the divisional investment base. The exclusion provides an incentive for a division to substitute leased assets for

**EXHIBIT 10-5** Effect of Substituting Leased Assets for Owned Assets

|  | YEAR | | | |
| --- | --- | --- | --- | --- |
|  | 0 | 1 | 2 | 3 |
| Investment | $90,000 | $60,000 | $36,000 | $18,000 |
| Net cash flows | $50,000 | $41,050 | $32,100 | $23,150 |
| Depreciation | 30,000 | 24,000 | 18,000 | 12,000 |
| Net income | $20,000 | $17,050 | $14,100 | $11,150 |
| Capital charge | 13,500 | 9,000 | 5,400 | 2,700 |
| EVA | $ 6,500 | $ 8,050 | $ 8,700 | $ 8,450 |
| ROI | 22.2% | 28.4% | 39.2% | 61.9% |

purchased assets even when no apparent economic advantage exists for such a substitution; that is, the division faces equivalent purchase price and cost of capital whether the assets are owned or leased.

This condition can be remedied by including leased assets in the investment base at their fair market value. If an independent estimate of the cost of the asset is not available, then the leased asset can be valued at the discounted present value of the lease payments, although this calculation sounds simpler than it actually is. Considerable controversy still exists as to the appropriate discount rate for evaluating the leasing option. Tax effects that we are ignoring here become important.

Once the annual lease payment is on the books, the firm has two options on how to treat it. It would be incorrect to charge the full $8,950 lease payment as an expense of the period, because much of this payment represents a financing cost and financing costs are not charged to specific assets in an ROI or EVA computation. We would be double counting interest expense: once as a subtraction from operating cash flows and a second time as the capital charge in computing EVA. This is the same reason why interest costs are not subtracted when performing a discounted cash flow analysis for evaluating a proposed capital acquisition. The preferable method would be to have the depreciation schedule follow the amortization of the debt as represented by the capitalized lease payments. The amortization and depreciation schedule appears below:

| YEAR | DEBT—START OF YEAR | LEASE PAYMENT | EFFECTIVE INTEREST EXPENSE | DEBT AMORTIZATION (DEPRECIATION EXPENSE) |
|---|---|---|---|---|
| 1 | $30,000 | $8,950 | $4,500 | $4,450 |
| 2 | 25,550 | 8,950 | 3,833 | 5,117 |
| 3 | 20,443 | 8,950 | 3,065 | 5,885 |
| 4 | 14,548 | 8,950 | 2,182 | 6,768 |
| 5 | 7,780 | 8,950 | 1,167 | 7,783* |

*Rounding error caused by using annual lease payment of $8,950 instead of $8,949.50.*

Only the depreciation expense, shown in the last column, would be charged as an expense to the division.

Most companies, however, will depreciate capitalized leased assets using the traditional straight-line method. In this case, the depreciation expense will be $6,000 per year (just as for owned assets), and the annual depreciation charge will have no particular relationship with the annual $8,950 lease payment. As we subsequently show, straight-line depreciation distorts both the ROI and EVA calculations, but at least the firm will be consistent in distorting owned and leased assets in the same manner.

In summary, companies will need to modify the practices they use for external financial reporting to obtain more economically meaningful ROI and EVA measures of divisional performance. Adjusting for investments in intangibles (such as R&D) that yield multiperiod benefits and for leased versus owned assets are just two examples of the types of adjustments that corporate managers should be making when evaluating divisional performance.

## PRICE-LEVEL ADJUSTMENTS

A third source of distortion arises from assuming a stable price level over time. During and after inflationary periods, both ROI and EVA measures will be highly overstated unless special care is taken to compensate for known changes in the price level. The principal distortion arises because revenues and cash costs are measured in current-year currency values (e.g., current dollars or cruzeiros), whereas the investment base and depreciation charges are measured in the currency units of the year in which the asset was acquired (e.g., 1985 dollars or cruzeiros). Depreciation based on historical costs considerably underestimates what the depreciation charge would be on the basis of either restated or current-dollar costs. This understatement of depreciation expense causes the net income of the firm to be overstated. At the same time, the investment of the firm is understated because most of the firm's assets were acquired in previous years at lower price levels than those currently prevailing. The combination of overstated net income and understated investment causes both the ROI ratio and the EVA measure to be much higher than if inflation had not occurred. The increase in ROI and EVA measure is not a signal of higher profitability; it is due solely to a failure to adjust for the money illusion caused by inflation. We add together 1985 dollars and 1995 dollars as if they were the same units, when in fact they are more different than dollars and deutsche marks.

During the high inflation of the 1970s, some steel companies claimed that their operations were finally yielding a good return to shareholders (i.e., ROI had increased) but that conditions still did not support new investment. This apparent contradiction (deciding not to invest when returns exceeded the cost of capital) clearly arose from the companies' failure to adjust both their income and their investment base for inflationary effects. The distortions from not adjusting for inflation are easy to demonstrate with our simple five-asset division. Recall that we calculated the ROI of this division as 22.2%. The calculation of the 22.2% ROI, however, assumed that the price level remained constant over a five-year period. Suppose, however, that a 10% per year inflation exists in the economy and that the price of the division's asset also increases at this 10% per year inflation rate. During this inflationary period, the division is not able to raise prices fast enough to keep pace with either its asset costs or its variable input costs. Its net cash flow increases by only 6% per year during the four-year inflationary period. After four years, the net cash flow of the division will be

$$\$50,000 \times (1.06)^4 = \$63,124$$

The investment and associated depreciation charges for the assets acquired in each of the past years are shown in Exhibit 10-6.

The ROI and EVA of the division are now calculated as follows:

| | |
|---|---:|
| Investment | $116,847 |
| Net cash flows | $ 63,124 |
| Depreciation | 36,631 |
| Net income | $ 26,493 |
| Capital charge (15%) | 17,527 |
| EVA | $ 8,966 |

$$\text{ROI} = \frac{26,493}{116,847} = 22.7\%$$

**EXHIBIT 10-6**  Investment and Depreciation: 10% Annual Inflation

| AGE OF ASSET (YEARS) (1) | ASSET COST (2) = 30,000 × (1.1)$^{4-(1)}$ | ANNUAL DEPRECIATION (3) = (2)/5 | NET BOOK VALUE, END OF YEAR 4 (4) = (2) − (1)(3) |
|---|---|---|---|
| 0 | 30,000 (1.1)$^4$  = $ 43,923 | $ 8,785 | $ 43,923 |
| 1 | 30,000 (1.1)$^3$  =   39,930 | 7,986 | 31,944 |
| 2 | 30,000 (1.1)$^2$  =   36,300 | 7,260 | 21,780 |
| 3 | 30,000 (1.1)$^1$  =   33,000 | 6,600 | 13,200 |
| 4 | 30,000         =   30,000 | 6,000 | 6,000 |
|   | $183,153 | $36,631 | $116,847 |

After four years of a general 10% yearly inflation, during which the division was able to increase its net cash flows by only 6% per year, the division shows an ROI of 22.7%, a figure that exceeds its preinflationary ROI. Its most recent EVA of $8,966 also exceeds its preinflationary figure of $6,500. Finally, the net income of $26,493 also exceeds the preinflationary figure of $20,000. Thus, the financial results seem to have improved significantly over this four-year period. Clearly, however, these reported numbers make no economic sense. Apart from misrepresenting the underlying economics of the business, the distorted signals might delude corporate and division management into thinking that, despite an inability to pass on cost increases to the marketplace, the division seems to be coping rather well during a difficult inflationary period.

The apparent increases in net income, ROI, and EVA are all caused by the failure to restate the assets' historical acquisition cost into units of current costs or current purchasing power. Were the inflation rate to cease suddenly at the end of year 4 (a situation analogous to the precipitous drop in inflation rates in the United States and other countries in the early 1980s), the division would maintain its then-current net operating cash flows, replace its older assets—one per year—at the most recent price ($43,923), and eventually see the consequences from its failure to keep net cash flows in line with the past inflation:

| | |
|---|---|
| Investment* | $131,769 |
| Net cash flows | $ 63,124 |
| Depreciation† | 43,923 |
| Net income | $ 19,201 |
| Capital charge (15%) | 19,765 |
| EVA | $    (564) |

*Investment, at (price-level adjusted) net book value, equals $43,923 * (1 + 4/5 + 3/5 + 2/5 + 1/5) = $131,769.
†From $8,784.60 * 5.

$$ROI = \frac{19,201}{131,769} = 14.6\%$$

Net income has declined, economic value added is now negative, and the postinflation ROI of 14.6% is well below the preinflationary figure. The postinflation figures of both ROI and EVA are now below the misleading high figures reported at the end of the inflation cycle when the firm had yet to replace its older assets. The effect is dramatic when inflation suddenly stops as in the above example. Were inflation to continue at its previous high rates, with the division's cash flows continuing to trail the inflation rate, the division might continue to show satisfactory profits for a while but it would find itself running out of cash to purchase new assets to replace the ones being retired.

The message from this example is simple and direct. During inflationary periods, the use of historical cost to compute depreciation expense and to measure the investment base causes net income, ROI, and EVA to be deceptively high. During inflationary periods, divisions and companies find it easy to look highly profitable with these unadjusted measures. Worse, managers may be misled into thinking that asset returns are much better than they actually are. Reality sets in when the inflationary cycle is broken and assets have to be replaced at the now higher price level but price increases can no longer be sustained in the marketplace.

The failure to adjust for price-level changes affects not only the measurement of a single division over time but also the comparison among different divisions at the same point in time. Divisions with newer assets will tend to show lower ROI and EVA measures than equally (or even less) profitable divisions whose assets were acquired at lower price levels. Unless some provision is made to neutralize such inflationary biases, managers will be reluctant to make new investments because of the negative impact on their ROI and EVA. Conversely, managers will tend to delay the replacement of their low (historical) cost assets because of the misleading high ROI and EVA apparently being earned on these assets.

Adjusting financial statements for the effects of inflation has been a contentious accounting issue. Hundreds of books and articles have been written on the subject; mandatory external disclosure was implemented for several years and then rescinded in the United States; and many authoritative people still show confusion about the difference between movements in the general price level and changes in relative prices. Therefore, one can safely conclude that a consensus hardly exists on the subject. Even during the period when inflation adjustments had to be disclosed for external reporting purposes (so the information was already being produced in virtually all large U.S. firms), only a handful— literally one handful—of companies opted to use inflation-adjusted statements for internal evaluation of divisions and their managers.[13]

One final issue on this subject is the effect of inflation on the cost of capital. During a period of anticipated inflation, investors and creditors will demand a higher rate of return from their invested capital to compensate them for the lower purchasing power of the dollars or cruzeiros they will receive in the future. The nominal cost of capital, therefore, which is derived from data on market interest rates and expected rates of return on equity capital, is a function of anticipated inflation. Understanding the economics of adjusting assets for the effects of inflation and the cost of capital for changes in nominal interest rates and equity returns is not a trivial exercise. We present (without proof) the following advice to guide managers, students, and their teachers on this subject.[14]

We assumed a 15% cost of capital in our initial example when no inflation or price-level changes existed.[15] Then we assumed an environment with 10% annual inflation. Investors and creditors are not dummies. They are not going to leave their capital with companies during periods of inflation unless they are compensated, with higher expected returns, when they receive cash in future years. The exact relation between expected inflation and the cost of capital is not known precisely, but an excellent approximation is to assume that today's cost of capital equals the cost of capital in the absence of inflation (15% in our example) plus the expected inflation rate (10%), for a total of 25%. Many managers believe that the 25% rate they would currently be observing in the marketplace provides the benchmark to evaluate their operations. But if inflation adjustments have already been made to asset values, it would be double counting to use the nominal 25% cost of capital. One should use the real rate of 15% as a benchmark in an ROI calculation or for calculating a capital charge in a residual income calculation after the assets' costs have been adjusted for the effects of inflation.

For example, suppose the nominal cash flows projected from a three-year project are:

| YEAR | CASH FLOW |
| --- | --- |
| 1 | 10,600 |
| 2 | 11,236 |
| 3 | 11,910 |

These cash flows reflect an anticipated annual rate of inflation of 6%. The deflated cash flows (measured in current-year dollars) are:

| YEAR | CASH FLOW |
| --- | --- |
| 1 | 10,000 |
| 2 | 10,000 |
| 3 | 10,000 |

and the present value of this three-year project, using a real interest rate of 10% per year, is $24,869.

Alternatively, we could use a nominal interest rate of

$$[(1 + 0.10) * (1 + 0.06)] - 1 = 16.6\%$$

to discount the nominal annual cash flows we first forecast

| YEAR | CASH FLOW | PRESENT VALUE @ 16.6% |
| --- | --- | --- |
| 1 | 10,600 | 9,091 |
| 2 | 11,236 | 8,265 |
| 3 | 11,910 | 7,513 |
| Total | | 24,869 |

to get exactly the same answer.

## DEPRECIATION METHOD

The accounting rate of return obtained from an ROI calculation is frequently assumed to be an estimate of the division's economic rate of return on invested capital. Unfortunately, except in very special circumstances, the accounting ROI will not equal the underlying yield of the assets in the division. The difference between the asset's yield and its accounting ROI is easily illustrated by returning to our division with $90,000 in assets and annual net income of $20,000. Although the accounting ROI equals 22.2%, each asset actually generates a return of about 20%. Exhibit 10-7 shows that the discounted present value, using an interest rate of 20%, of five annual cash flows of $10,000, is just short of the $30,000 initial investment.[16]

Even in this simple example, the accounting ROI of 22.2% does not equal the actual rate of return of slightly less than 20%. Therefore, we cannot infer the actual yield of assets in a division or company from the accounting ROI. The difference between these two measures arises from using a financial depreciation method—straight-line, in this case—that bears no relation to the periodic loss in present value of the asset. In order for the accounting ROI to equal the actual yield, a depreciation method derived from the decline in present value of the asset must be used.

The perverse incentives that are created by inappropriately using financial accounting depreciation methods for a managerial ROI calculation are also easy to demonstrate. Observe how the manager of our division can increase his ROI measure by working less hard—that is, by deciding to stop investing in a new asset each year to replace the five-year-old asset just scrapped (see Exhibit 10-8). The ROI steadily increases each year as the asset base shrinks, because the book value of the assets decreases faster than the net income falls. Note, however, that the manager of this division should hope for a promotion or transfer some time before the end of the fourth year after adopting this ROI-increasing policy. After that time, the division will be rather short of operating assets.

We would not expect that many managers would manipulate their ROI measures so transparently; nevertheless, the example serves to demonstrate how, on the margin, managers can improve their ROI measure by postponing new investment and continuing to operate with fully or nearly fully depreciated assets.[17] Conversely, we see that managers who invest in new equipment will show a lower ROI than their counterparts who operate with older equipment. The penalty arises not just from acquiring assets at the higher price

**EXHIBIT 10-7**  Discounted Present Value of Cash Flows

| YEAR | CASH INFLOW | PRESENT VALUE FACTOR AT 20% | DISCOUNTED CASH FLOW |
|------|------------|------------------------------|----------------------|
| 1 | $10,000 | 0.8333 | $ 8,333.33 |
| 2 | 10,000 | 0.6944 | 6,944.44 |
| 3 | 10,000 | 0.5787 | 5,787.04 |
| 4 | 10,000 | 0.4823 | 4,822.53 |
| 5 | 10,000 | 0.4019 | 4,018.78 |
|   | $50,000 | 2.9906 | $29,906.12 |

**EXHIBIT 10-8**  ROI by Year, No Asset Replacement, Straight-Line Depreciation

| | YEAR | | | | |
|---|---|---|---|---|---|
| | 0 | 1 | 2 | 3 | 4 |
| Net cash flow | 50,000 | 40,000 | 30,000 | 20,000 | 10,000 |
| Depreciation | 30,000 | 24,000 | 18,000 | 12,000 | 6,000 |
| Net income | 20,000 | 16,000 | 12,000 | 8,000 | 4,000 |
| Investment | 90,000 | 60,000 | 36,000 | 18,000 | 6,000 |
| ROI | 22.2% | 26.7% | 33.3% | 44.4% | 66.7% |

level, as we discussed in the preceding section, but also because financial accounting depreciation methods artificially produce lower accounting ROIs in the initial years that an asset is placed into service.

Because of the bias against new investment when using straight-line depreciation and an ROI performance measure, several companies measure assets at their gross book value rather than net book value, a practice followed by the DuPont Corporation for many decades starting in the 1920s. When assets are measured at gross book value, the incentive to avoid investing in new assets is eliminated. In fact, a new incentive—to replace existing assets with new assets—is created, since the measured increase in investment is only the difference between the historical cost of the existing asset and the purchase cost of the new asset. This difference is well below the actual net outlay for the new asset, as measured by the purchase cost less trade-in or salvage value of the existing asset.

It is certainly possible to devise a depreciation schedule, based on the decline in present value of the asset each year, so that the accounting ROI will equal the economic rate of return of the asset. The economic or present value depreciation method can be derived directly from the cash flow schedule used to justify the acquisition of the asset.[18] But using the present value depreciation method would require that companies use a depreciation method for managerial accounting purposes completely different from the methods used for financial and tax accounting purposes. During the 1970s when inflation rates exceeded 10%, fewer than 1% of U.S. companies adjusted their accounting statements for inflation for internal purposes—even though data already existed from mandated supplementary disclosure. Therefore, we are not optimistic about managers' receptivity to implement an entirely new depreciation method for internal motivation and evaluation. Consequently, we will not burden readers with the derivation of economic depreciation methods.

The lack of interest in economic or present value depreciation methods for assets is curious, since the technology for performing such calculations is well known and, in fact, is already being used in financial statements, but to amortize liabilities, not to depreciate assets. The amortization of principal in a mortgage calculation, or the amortization of bond discounts and premiums, generates a nonlinear amortization schedule in order to maintain a constant yield-to-maturity of the liability. We are unsure why such a constant yield-to-maturity approach is easily accepted for liabilities but is considered unacceptable when one moves from the right to the left side of the balance sheet to amortize the cost of asset acquisitions. Lacking such insight, we can only alert readers to the pitfalls lurking when using financial accounting depreciation methods for managerial accounting calculations but without offering much hope that the pitfalls will be eliminated by using more cash flow-based depreciation methods.

## SUMMARY OF TECHNICAL ADJUSTMENTS TO ROI AND EVA℠ CALCULATIONS

Clearly, to obtain improved measures of return on investment and economic value added, financial managers may have to make numerous adjustments to expenses that have been recorded in their general ledger. The information for financial reporting or even for short-run operational control may not be the most useful for assessing the economic performance of business units. We have discussed adjustments that could be made for

- cost of capital on assets employed - *to incorporate risk?*
- investments in intangible assets (e.g., R&D, advertising, training)
- leased assets
- changes in general and specific price levels
- depreciation method

And these are just a few of the many adjustments that could be made to GAAP-prepared financial statements. Stern, Stewart has a list of 164 different issues that could be used, depending on circumstances and the materiality of the adjustment, to modify reported accounting results in order to improve the accuracy with which EVA measures real economic income.[19]

The message is clearly that effective management accounting requires that financial managers understand the assumptions behind the numbers they report. They should not mechanically make a calculation which could lead to a distorted and misleading signal to managers who are not familiar with the assumptions and limitations behind practices adopted for financial accounting purposes.

## LINKING ABC TO ECONOMIC VALUE ADDED: ASSIGNING ASSETS

The greatest leverage for improving ROI or EVA may come from making decisions not at the business unit (SBU) or corporate level but at the level of activities, products, and customers—activity-based management—as we discussed in Chapter 5. It is simple to extend activity-based costing (ABC) to the assignment of assets as well as to operating expenses. After all, many expenditures, such as for plant and equipment and to acquire materials, are temporarily classified as assets before they flow through the income statement as expenses. Many assets represent expenditures on their way to becoming expenses.

We can illustrate the integration of ABC and EVA with a simple example. Take an SBU with the income statement shown below in Exhibit 10-9.

This statement reveals a marginally profitable business unit, with a net operating margin of 9% of sales. After assigning a cost of capital of 12% to the net assets employed, this business unit has destroyed economic value during the year; that is, its earnings are below the cost of capital employed to generate the earnings.

Executives' initial reaction to a negative EVA business unit, as shown in Exhibit 10-9, may be to search for ways to raise margins (through price increases and cost cutting)

**EXHIBIT 10-9**  Business Unit Income
Statement

| | INCOME STATEMENT | (%) |
|---|---|---|
| Sales | $1,000,000 | 100% |
| Cost of Goods sold | 480,000 | 48 |
| Gross margin | 520,000 | 52 |
| Selling expense | 210,000 | 21 |
| Disn. expense | 116,000 | 12 |
| Admin. expense | 108,000 | 11 |
| Operating profit | 86,000 | 9 |
| Capital employed | 840,000 | 84 |
| Capital charge (@12%) | 100,800 | 10 |
| Economic Value Added | $($14,800) | −1% |

or to increase asset intensity. They may instruct the business unit managers to cut selling expenses or administrative expenses as a percentage of sales, or they may raise prices across the board, cut production support expenses, and demand lower inventory levels and accounts receivable in their attempt to increase reported EVA. But such across-the-board actions, designed to cut away fat and waste, may end up also cutting into muscle and bone. Consider a situation in which the business unit consists of two distinct product lines. One product line is well established, runs on efficient, focused production processes, and is sold to customers with whom the business unit has long-standing relationships. The other product line was developed to enter into new customer markets, is a highly customized business with many product variants and short production runs, and has heavy marketing and selling expenses to service existing customers and to reach new ones. An activity-based cost analysis permits the product line income statements shown in Exhibit 10-10.

The ABC financial report in Exhibit 10-10 shows the danger of using a meat cleaver to cut costs. No problem exists for product line 1. Its efficient processes and loyal customer base enables it to earn high gross and operating margins. Any attempt to cut costs further or to raise prices may seriously compromise this highly attractive segment. The business unit's profitability and EVA problems arise from product line 2. Managers' attention should not be focused on across-the-board spending reductions; it needs to be focused on specific actions to make product line 2 profitable.

The connection of ABC to EVA appears in the bottom section of Exhibit 10-10. The EVA analysis reinforces the message beyond the profitability analysis alone. It points managers to a range of opportunities to improve both margins *and* asset intensity for product line 2. The ABC analysis of assets employed reveals that product line 1 requires only $0.70 of assets per dollar of sales, whereas product line 2 requires $1.05 per dollar of sales. This differential arises because product line 1's managers have established close relationships with a few suppliers, so raw materials shipments are generally made on a just-in-time basis; its predictable demand pattern enables machines to operate near capacity levels (so it has little to no unused capacity); and its dedicated efficient and JIT production processes enable it to operate with low work-in-process and finished goods inventory lev-

**EXHIBIT 10-10** Applying ABC to EVA Analysis

|  | TRADITIONAL | | PRODUCT GROUP 1 | | PRODUCT GROUP 2 | |
|---|---|---|---|---|---|---|
|  | INCOME STATEMENT | (%) | INCOME STATEMENT | (%) | INCOME STATEMENT | (%) |
| Sales | 1,000,000 | 100 | 600,000 | 100 | 400,000 | 100 |
| Cost of Goods sold | 480,000 | 48 | 240,000 | 40 | 240,000 | 60 |
| Gross margin | 520,000 | 52 | 360,000 | 60 | 160,000 | 40 |
| Selling expense | 210,000 | 21 | 90,000 | 15 | 120,000 | 30 |
| Disn. expense | 116,000 | 12 | 36,000 | 6 | 80,000 | 20 |
| Admin. expense. | 108,000 | 11 | 48,000 | 8 | 60,000 | 15 |
| Operating profit | 86,000 | 9 | 186,000 | 31 | −100,000 | −25 |
| Capital employed | 840,000 | 84 | 420,000 | 70 | 420,000 | 105 |
| Capital charge (@12%) | 100,800 | 10 | 50,400 | 8 | 50,400 | 13 |
| Economic Value Added | ($14,800) | −1% | 135,600 | 23% | ($15,400) | −38% |

els. Further, its excellent customer relationships keep accounts receivable to a minimum. Product line 2, in contrast, requires $1.05 of assets per dollar of sales because it uses high inventory levels at all production processes, it has extensive setups and idle time on machines, and its customers pay slowly. Thus, there is a large differential—13% of sales versus 8% for product line 1—in the EVA capital charges applied to the two product lines.

Driving EVA from a divisional or business unit level down to activities and calculating individual product and customer EVA gives managers far more leverage to increase total EVA for the unit. Instead of using a meat-cleaver—cutting all expenses, assets, products, and customers—managers can apply a surgical scalpel to the particular activities and to individual products or customers that exhibit negative EVAs.

The assignment of many assets to individual products should be straightforward. Some assets, such as inventory, are already directly attributable to individual products. Dedicated assets, such as specialized production equipment, tooling, and test equipment, can be assigned to the narrow range of products that use those resources. Other assets, such as general purpose equipment, may be used by a wide range of products. In this case, the asset assignment can be done with the same cost drivers—machine hours—used to drive the operating expenses (depreciation, maintenance, power) of the equipment to individual products. The Stern Stewart methodology for EVA also encourages companies to capitalize many expenditures—such as research and development, marketing, and promotion—and amortize them over a specified useful life.[20] The assignment of such intangible assets to individual products should be obvious.

As with operating expenses, not all asset assignments should be made to individual products. Some assets can be causally attributed to individual customer behavior. The easiest example of a customer-specific asset is accounts receivable. As another example, some customers may cause their suppliers to hold specific inventory for them. In such cases, the asset (inventory) may be better attributed to the customer, not to the product. Also, the company may have purchased specific equipment, done specific research and product and process development, or developed specific software for an individual customer or identifiable segment of customers. The capitalized value of these intangible assets can then be attributed to specific customers or segments.

The integration between ABC and EVA is natural. Both ABC and EVA were developed to solve a distortion in the financial reporting of company economics. ABC corrected the arbitrary allocations of factory overhead to products and the failure to assign other indirect expenses to products and customers. EVA corrected the failure of financial accounting statements to recognize the cost of capital as an economic expense before arriving at a profitability figure (see example in Exhibit 10-9, in which a division shows an accounting profit while failing to earn a return sufficient to repay its use of capital employed). When ABC and EVA are used together, managers obtain a clearer map of economic profitability and losses and can direct their attention and specific actions—through operational and strategic activity-based management—to operations where economic losses are incurred, and they can retain, protect, and expand economically profitable operations.

## SUMMARY

Investment centers are decentralized units or divisions for which the manager has maximum discretion in determining not only the short-term operating decisions on product mix, pricing, and production methods but also the level and type of investment in the center. The accounting return on investment (ROI) is the most common measure used to evaluate investment-center performance, but this measure suffers from many defects. Managers, in attempting to maximize their ROI measure, have an incentive to reject investments that will earn below the division's average ROI but are still above the divisional cost of capital. This particular problem can be avoided by using the economic value added (EVA) measure (formerly, or alternatively, known as residual income), which is obtained by subtracting a capital charge for the average investment in the division from divisional net income. Both measures, ROI and EVA, can be greatly distorted by failing to adjust financial accounting practices. Financial managers should attempt to adjust financial accounting practices to obtain managerial information that is closer to economic reality.

## ENDNOTES

1.  EVA™ is a trademark of Stern Stewart & Co., New York.
2.  See the discussion in H. T. Johnson and R. S. Kaplan, *Relevance Lost: The Rise and Fall of Management Accounting* (Boston: Harvard Business School Press, 1987), chap. 2.
3.  Quotations taken from original records at the DuPont Corporation as referenced in H. T. Johnson, "Management Accounting in an Early Integrated Industrial E I. duPont de Nemours Powder Company, 1903–1912," *Business History Review* (Summer 1975), pp. 187–88.
4.  This discussion of the Matsushita history and control system was derived from Y. Monden, "Japanese Management Control Systems," in *Innovations in Management: The Japanese Corporation*, ed. Y. Monden et al., (Institute of Industrial Engineers, Industrial Engineering and Management Press, 1985), pp. 41–58.
5.  A. D. Chandler Jr., "The Competitive Performance of U.S. Industrial Enterprises Since the Second World War," *Business History Review* (Spring 1994), p. 19.
6.  Technical limitations to the ROI measure have been pointed out in D. Solomons, *Divisional Performance: Measurement and Control* (Homewood, IL: Richard D. Irwin, 1968), chap. 5; J. Dearden, "The Case against ROI Control," *Harvard Business Review* (May–June 1969); and J. Dearden, "Measuring Profit Center Managers," *Harvard Business Review* (September–October 1987).

7. See Solomons, *Divisional Performance*, chap. 5.

8. See, for example, G. B. Stewart, "EVA™: Fact and Fantasy," *Journal of Applied Corporate Finance* (Summer 1994), pp. 71–84.

9. Financial Accounting Standards Board, *FASB Statement No. 2*, Accounting for Research and Development Costs (Issue Date 10/74), Stamford, CT.

10. This last assumption is made to eliminate the need to use continuous discounting procedures and does not reduce the generality of the analysis that follows.

11. This division could have been the one used to illustrate the difference between ROI and residual income earlier in this chapter.

12. Financial Accounting Standards Board, *FASB Statement No. 13*, Accounting for Leases (Issue Date: 11/76).

13. See J. Hertenstein, "Management Control System Change: The Adoption of Inflation Accounting," in *Accounting & Management: Field Study Perspectives*, ed. W. J. Bruns Jr., and R. S. Kaplan (Boston: Harvard Business School Press, 1987); also J. Hertenstein, *FMC Corporation's Use of Current Cost Accounting* (Montvale, NJ: National Association of Accountants, 1988).

14. The arguments can be found in F. Modigliani and R. Cohn, "Inflation, Rational Valuation and the Market," *Financial Analysts Journal* (March–April 1979), pp. 24–44.

15. Fifteen percent was used for illustrative purposes only. As will be discussed in Chapter 12, the weighted-average real cost of capital for most organizations will be well under 10%.

16. The discounted present value would have been exactly $30,000 had we used an interest rate of 19.86% in the calculations.

17. German companies commonly charge depreciation, based on their replacement value, for assets still in use even if the assets have been fully depreciated for financial and tax purposes.

18. Present value depreciation is discussed in Dearden, "Case against ROI Control," and Solomons, *Divisional Performance*.

19. Stewart "EVA™: Fact and Fantasy," p. 73.

20. Stewart, "EVA™: Fact and Fantasy," p. 77.

## ■ PROBLEMS

### 10-1    *ROI and Divisional Performance*

The Solomons Company uses ROI to measure the performance of its operating divisions. A summary of the annual reports from two divisions is shown below. The company's cost of capital is 12%.

|  | DIVISION A | DIVISION B |
| --- | --- | --- |
| Capital invested | $2400 | $4000 |
| Net income | $ 480 | $ 720 |
| ROI | 20% | 18% |

### Required

(1) Which division is more profitable?

(2) At what cost of capital would the two divisions be considered equally profitable?

(3)   What performance measurement procedure would more clearly show the relative profitability of the two divisions?

(4)   Suppose the manager of Division A were offered a one-year project that would increase his investment base (for that year) by $1,000 and show a profit of $150. Would the manager accept this project if he were evaluated on his divisional ROI? Should he accept this project?

## 10-2   *Evaluating Divisional Performance (CMA, Adapted)*

Darmen Corporation is one of the major producers of prefabricated houses in the home building industry. The corporation consists of two divisions:

1. Bell Division, which acquires the raw materials to manufacture the basic house components and assembles them into kits

2. The Cornish Division, which takes the kits and constructs the homes for final home buyers. The corporation is decentralized, and the management of each division is measured by its income and return on investment.

Bell Division assembles seven separate house kits using raw materials purchased at the prevailing market prices. The seven kits are sold to Cornish for prices ranging from $45,000 to $98,000. The prices are set by corporate management of Darmen using prices paid by Cornish when it buys comparable units from outside sources. The smaller kits with the lower prices have become a larger portion of the units sold because the final house buyer is faced with prices that are increasing more rapidly than personal income. The kits are manufactured and assembled in a new plant purchased by Bell this year. The division had been located in a leased plant for the past four years.

All kits are assembled upon receipt of an order from the Cornish Division. When the kit is completely assembled, it is loaded immediately on a Cornish truck. Thus, Bell Division has no finished goods inventory.

The Bell Division's accounts and reports are prepared on an actual-cost basis. There is no budget, and standards have not been developed for any product. A factory overhead rate is calculated at the beginning of each year. The rate is designed to charge all overhead to the product each year. Any under- or overapplied overhead is allocated to the cost of goods sold account and work-in-process inventories.

Bell Division's annual report is presented below. This report forms the basis of the evaluation of the division and its management by the corporation management.

Additional information regarding corporate and division practices is as follows:

- The corporation office does all the personnel and accounting work for each division.
- The corporate personnel costs are allocated on the basis of number of employees in the division.
- The accounting costs are allocated to the division on the basis of total costs excluding corporate charges.
- The division administration costs are included in factory overhead.
- The financing charges include a corporate-imputed interest charge on division assets and any divisional lease payments.
- The division investment for the return-on-investment calculation includes division inventory and plant and equipment at gross book value.

## Bell Division Performance Report for the Year Ended December 31, 1997

| | 1997 | 1996 | INCREASE (OR DECREASE) FROM 1996 | |
| --- | --- | --- | --- | --- |
| | | | AMOUNT | PERCENT CHANGE |
| Summary Data | | | | |
| Net income ($000 omitted) | $ 34,222 | $ 31,573% | $ 2,649 | 8.4 |
| Return on investment | 37% | 43% | (6)% | (14.0) |
| Kits shipped (units) | 2,000 | 2,100 | (100) | (4.8) |
| Production Data (in units) | | | | |
| Kits started | 2,400 | 1,600 | 800 | 50.0) |
| Kits shipped | 2,000 | 2,100 | (100) | (4.8) |
| Kits in process at year-end | 700 | 300 | 400 | 133.3 |
| Increase (decrease) in kits in | | | | |
| process at year end | 400 | (500) | — | — |
| Financial Data ($000) | | | | |
| Sales | $138,000 | $162,800 | $(24,800) | (15.2) |
| Production costs of units sold | | | | |
| Raw material | $ 32,000 | $ 40,000 | $ (8,000) | (20.0) |
| Labor | 41,700 | 53,000 | (11,300) | (21.3) |
| Factory overhead | 29,000 | 37,000 | 8,000) | (21.6) |
| Cost of units sold | $102,700 | $130,000 | $(27,300) | (21.0) |
| Other Costs: Corporate Charges for | | | | |
| Personnel services | $228 | $ 210 | $ 18 | 8.6 |
| Accounting services | 425 | 440 | (15) | (3.4) |
| Financing costs | 300 | 525 | (225) | 42.9 |
| Total other costs | $953 | $1,175 | $(222) | (18.9) |
| Adjustments to Income | | | | |
| Unreimbursed fire loss | — | $52 | $(52) | (100.0) |
| Raw material losses due | | | | |
| to improper storage | $125 | — | 125 | — |
| Total adjustments | $125 | $52 | $73 | (140.0) |
| Total deductions | $103,778 | $131,227 | (27,449) | (20.9) |
| Division income | $ 34,222 | $ 31,573 | $ 2,649 | 8.4 |
| Division investment | $ 92,000 | $ 73,000 | $ 19,000 | 26.0 |
| Return on investment | 37% | 43% | (6)% | (14.0)% |

### Required

(1) Discuss the value of the annual report presented for the Bell Division in evaluating the division and its management in terms of
    (a) The accounting techniques employed in the measurement of division activities
    (b) The manner of presentation

       (c)  The effectiveness with which it discloses differences and similarities between years
          Use the information in the problem to illustrate your discussion.
    (2)  Make specific recommendations to the management of Darmen Corporation that would improve its accounting and financial reporting system.

## 10-3    *Effect of Depreciation on ROI Computations*

The Streetorn Corporation is contemplating the purchase of a new piece of equipment. The equipment has an expected life of five years and is expected to produce the following after-tax cash flow savings for the following five years:

| YEAR | AFTER-TAX CASH FLOW SAVINGS |
|------|------------------------------|
| 1 | $50,000 |
| 2 | 46,000 |
| 3 | 42,000 |
| 4 | 36,000 |
| 5 | 30,000 |

    The asset will cost $138,300 and thus has an after-tax yield of 16%, which is above the company's after-tax cost of capital of 15%. The declining pattern of annual cash flow savings is caused by higher maintenance costs as the equipment ages, as well as the reduction in tax benefits from use of the sum-of-years-digits (SYD) method for depreciation. For example, the gross cash flow savings in year 3 (before depreciation and before taxes) is $51,560. The net after-tax cash flow savings is obtained by the following computation:

| | |
|---|---|
| Gross cash flow savings | $51,560 |
| Depreciation (138,300)(3/15) | 27,660 |
| Taxable income | 23,900 |
| Taxes (@ 40%) | 9,560 |
| Net income after taxes | 14,340 |
| + Depreciation | 27,660 |
| After-tax cash flow savings | $42,000 |

(Optional Assignment: Compute the gross cash flow savings for years 1–5.)
    The president's bonus is based on the company's return-on-investment (net income after taxes/investment at start of year). The company prides itself on its conservative accounting policies and therefore uses the same depreciation method for financial reporting

as it does for its tax return. The controller of Streetorn has prepared the following table to show the president the annual ROI from the new piece of equipment:

| YEAR | BOOK VALUE START OF YEAR (1) | NET CASH FLOW AFTER TAXES (2) | SYD DEPRECIATION (3) | NET INCOME AFTER TAXES (4) = (2) − (3) | ROI (5) = (4)/(1) |
|---|---|---|---|---|---|
| 1 | $138,300 | $50,000 | $46,100 | $ 3,900 | 2.8% |
| 2 | 92,200 | 46,000 | 36,880 | 9,120 | 9.9% |
| 3 | 55,320 | 42,000 | 27,660 | 14,340 | 25.9% |
| 4 | 27,660 | 36,000 | 18,440 | 17,560 | 63.5% |
| 5 | 9,220 | 30,000 | 9,220 | 20,780 | 225.4% |
| Average (5 years) | $ 64,540 | $40,800 | $27,660 | $13,140 | 20.4% |

The president is astonished by this table. He says, "Something's very wrong here. According to your cash-flow analysis, this piece of equipment has a 16% after-tax yield. Yet our financial statements show a different yield each year, and the low ROI in the first two years is going to keep me out of bonus money. Sure the equipment shows a fantastic ROI in its last two years, but I may not be with the company by then. I need results right away, not four years from now!"

The controller decides that the trouble may be with the firm's conservative accounting practices. Perhaps if the firm used straight-line depreciation for financial reporting, as do most of the other firms in the industry, the numbers would look better. He proceeds to produce the following table:

| YEAR | BOOK VALUE START-OF-YEAR | NET CASH FLOW AFTER TAXES | STRAIGHT-LINE DEPRECIATION | NET INCOME AFTER TAXES | ROI |
|---|---|---|---|---|---|
| 1 | $138,300 | $50,000 | $27,660 | $22,340 | 16.2% |
| 2 | 110,640 | 46,000 | 27,660 | 18,340 | 16.6% |
| 3 | 82,980 | 42,000 | 27,660 | 14,340 | 17.3% |
| 4 | 55,320 | 36,000 | 27,660 | 8,340 | 15.1% |
| 5 | 27,660 | 30,000 | 27,660 | 2,340 | 8.5% |
| Average | $ 82,980 | $40,800 | $27,660 | $13,140 | 15.8% |

The president is much happier with this presentation, especially since now the asset shows good returns in the earlier years. But he is still puzzled as to why an asset with a yield of 16% does not show a 16% ROI each year.

### Required

(1) Verify that this piece of equipment does have a 16% yield.
(2) Show, using the present-value depreciation method, how the equipment can have a 16% ROI for each of the five years of the asset's life.

(3)    Why did the ROI using the straight-line depreciation method approximate the actual yield reasonably well (for at least the first four years of the asset's life)?

## 10-4    *Effects of Inflation on ROI*

The Carter Company uses the ROI criterion to evaluate the performance of its divisions. The company prides itself on the formal capital-budgeting procedures it uses for approving new investments and the subsequent control procedures it has implemented to measure the performance of those new investments. Recently, however, the ROI measure has been producing performance statistics quite at variance with the criterion used to screen the investments. The company believes that recent high inflation rates may be contributing to the erratic performance evaluation measures. The problem is well illustrated by comparing the performance of two divisions.

Division Y made a major investment 10 years ago. This investment cost $3,000,000 and had an expected life of 15 years and annual after-tax cash flows of $525,000. The rate of return of slightly more than 15% was above the Carter Company's cost of capital. During the past 10 years, the price level had risen by 67%, and the after-tax cash flows from the investment had increased to an annual level of $800,000. The ROI for Division Y for the most recent year was computed as:

| | |
|---|---:|
| Investment book value (start-of-year) | $1,200,000 |
| Investment book value (end-of-year) | 1,000,000 |
| Average investment | $1,100,000 |
| Net cash flow | $ 800,000 |
| Depreciation | 200,000 |
| Net income | $ 600,000 |
| ROI—Division Y | 54.5% |

Division Z, in a different region than Division Y, made a major investment of a very similar type just two years ago. Because of the increase in construction and equipment costs, the investment now had cost $4,500,000. The expected life of this investment was 10 years, and the annual after-tax cash flow was $900,000. This investment also had a yield slightly in excess of 15%, so the performance measure of Division Z was expected to be similar to that of Division Y. In fact, Division Z's investment appeared to be much less profitable than Division Y's and did not even reach the expected 15% ROI cutoff figure. The most recent year's data show:

| | |
|---|---:|
| Investment book value (start-of-year) | $4,050,000 |
| Investment book value (end-of-year) | 3,600,000 |
| Average investment | $3,825,000 |
| Net cash flow | $1,000,000 |
| Depreciation | 450,000 |
| Net income | $ 550,000 |
| ROI—Division Z | 14.4% |

The price index was 120 10 years ago when Division Y's investment was made. Two years ago, when Division Z made its investment, the index was 180, and in the most recent year, for which the above data were prepared, the index averaged 200.

### Required

Analyze this situation explaining why two divisions with such similar investments (15% after-tax returns from the discounted cash flow analysis) are showing such disparate ROIs.

## 10-5 ROI and Leasing

The Malone Division of the Stoudt Corporation is organized as an investment center. Because of excellent operating results, the division manager, Terry Trocano, has been given considerable freedom in investment decisions. Terry knows that the top management of the Stoudt Corporation measures the performance of the operating divisions using an ROI criterion and that it is important for her to maintain a divisional ROI of 20% before taxes and 14% after taxes. Her annual bonus depends on achieving these targeted levels, and her compensation can increase considerably if she is able to obtain even higher ROIs.

Trocano has just completed a five-year forecast of annual operating performance for the Malone Division. The best estimate is that the current net investment level of $20,000,000 will be maintained over this period (that is, new investment will about equal the depreciation charge each year) and that the net income before taxes will be $4,000,000 and net income after taxes will be $2,800,000 each year.

Although Trocano is pleased that her forecasted results indicate that she will achieve both the before- and after-tax ROI targets, she is actively looking for projects that will enable her to exceed the targeted rates. A new investment proposal has recently emerged that seems particularly promising. The project requires an initial investment of $15,000,000 and will generate annual before-tax cash flows of $6,000,000 for five years. The discounted cash flow analysis indicates that the project has a before-tax yield in excess of 28% and an after-tax yield of more than 19%. (The Stoudt Corporation has a marginal tax rate of 40% and uses sum-of-years-digits depreciation for computing taxable income.) Both of these yields are well in excess of the company's targeted ROI, so the proposed project seems like an excellent investment.

Before making a final decision on the $15,000,000 investment, Trocano has asked the division controller to forecast the first year's operating results for the Malone Division, including the income generated by the new project. She is surprised when she receives the following proforma results:

| Before-Tax Analysis (000) | |
|---|---|
| Net income from existing projects | $ 4,000 |
| Cash flow—new project | 6,000 |
| Less: Depreciation (straight-line, 5-year life) | (3,000) |
| Net income | $ 7,000 |
| Investment: Existing projects | $20,000 |

*continued*

| | |
|---|---:|
| New project | 15,000 |
| Total investment | $35,000 |
| ROI | 20% |
| After-Tax Analysis (000) | |
| Net income after taxes—existing projects | $ 2,800 |
| Net income before tax—new project | 3,000 |
| Taxes on new project* | |
| (sum-of-years-digits depreciation) | (400) |
| Net income after taxes | $ 5,400 |
| Total investment | 35,000 |
| ROI | 15.4% |

*The company uses actual tax expense, based on the accelerated depreciation schedule, in allocating tax expense to divisions.*

The project does not hurt the measured performance of the Malone Division, but it certainly does not show the large increase in divisional ROI that Trocano had hoped for.

The controller proposes an alternative scheme for undertaking the investment. He has learned that another company is willing to acquire the buildings and equipment for the new project and lease them to the Malone Division at an annual rental payment of $5,200,000 for five years. The terms of the lease can be structured so that it is considered an operating lease and hence will not be capitalized on the Stoudt Corporation's financial statements. The controller has prepared the following proforma analysis of the lease option.

| | |
|---|---:|
| Before-Tax Analysis (000) | |
| Net income from existing projects | $ 4,000 |
| Cash flow—new project | 6,000 |
| Less: Lease payment | (5,200) |
| Net income | $ 4,800 |
| Investment—existing projects | 20,000 |
| ROI | 24% |
| After-Tax Analysis (000) | |
| Net income after taxes—existing projects | $ 2,800 |
| Income from new project—net of lease payment | 800 |
| Taxes—new project | (320) |
| Net income after taxes | $ 3,280 |
| Investment | 20,000 |
| ROI | 16.4% |

The lease option seems much more attractive to Trocano, since it generates a significant increase in both before- and after-tax ROI for her division. She submits the proposed new project, with a recommendation to lease the new facilities, to the central administration staff. She expects a routine approval for this attractive investment opportunity.

*Required*

Assume that you are the newly hired assistant to the head of the corporate finance division and have been asked to review the project proposed from the Malone Division.

(1) Verify that the proposed project will yield the forecasted returns (more than 28% before tax and more than 19% after tax).

(2) Compute the before- and after-tax ROI for the Malone Division for each of the next five years for both the purchase and the lease options. The investment base for each year is the book value (using straight-line depreciation) of investment at the start of the year.

(3) At the company's after-tax cost of capital of 14%, is it better to purchase or lease the asset?

(4) Why does the leasing option generate higher ROI measures than the purchase option?

(5) Suggest an alternative scheme that will reduce the incentive to lease rather than to purchase assets. Demonstrate how your scheme would work were the Malone Division to enter into the five-year lease with annual payments of $5,200,000.

## ■ CASES

### USING EVA AND MVA AT OUTSOURCE, INC.*

"I've been hearing a lot lately about something called MVA, which stands for Market Value Added, and I was curious whether it is something we can use at OSI." This was Keith Martin's comment as he finished eating his lunch. Keith is president and CEO of OutSource, Inc. His guest for lunch that day was a computer-industry analyst from a local brokerage firm. Keith invited him to lunch to get more information on MVA and its uses.

"Yes," replied the analyst, "I've heard a great deal about MVA. It's based on Economic Value Added, or EVA, which is a residual income approach where a firm's net operating profit after taxes—called NOPAT—is compared with a minimum level of return a firm must earn on the total amount of capital placed at its disposal."

"Have you seen the most recent issue of *Fortune*?" he continued, as he handed a copy of the

publication to Keith. "It has an article[1] in it updating Stern Stewart's list of the top 1,000 firms ranked by MVA. You will also be interested in an earlier *Fortune* article[2] on EVA; however, don't be misled by the simplicity of the EVA calculations in that article. The after-tax operating profit—NOPAT—and the amount used for capital don't come directly off the financial statements. You have to analyze the footnotes to determine the adjustments that have to be made to come up with those amounts; Bennett Stewart calls them equity equivalents."

"Those articles sound like very interesting reading for me at the point I'm at on this topic," said Keith. "Can you send me a copy of the earlier article too?"

"Yes, I will," said the analyst. "But tell me, what is it about MVA and EVA that piqued your interest in trying them at OSI?"

---

*This case was prepared by Professor Paul A. Dierks of the Babcock School of Management, Wake Forest University, and appeared in *Management Accounting* (January 1997), pp. 56–59.

[1]"Who Are the Real Wealth Creators?" R. B. Lieber, *Fortune* (December 9, 1996), pp. 107–08, 110, 112, 114.
[2]"The Real Key to Creating Wealth," S. Tully, *Fortune* (September 20, 1993), pp. 38–40, 44–48, 50.

"In tracking our industry," Keith replied, "I see the stock prices of some of our key competitors, like Equifax, increasing. Yet, when I compare OSI's recent growth in sales and earnings, our return on equity and earnings per share compare well, but our stock price doesn't achieve nearly the same rate of increase, and I don't understand why."

The analyst offered that "some of those firms might be benefiting from using EVA already, and the market value of their stock probably reflects the results of their efforts. It's been shown that a higher level of correlation exists between EVA and a stock's market value than has been found with the traditional accounting performance measures, like ROE or EPS."

"But the MVA 1,000 ranking probably includes only large firms," Keith observed after looking over the article the analyst had given him. "Will EVA work in a small service firm like OSI?"

"Most of the largest U.S. firms are in the Stern Stewart MVA ranking," said the analyst, "but I've read about EVA being used at smaller firms. And some firms in the ranking are service firms, such as AT&T, McDonald's, Marriott International, and Dun & Bradstreet. I'm not an expert on MVA or EVA, but I don't see any reason why it wouldn't work at OSI."

"I'd like to find out more in detail about MVA and EVA and how we can use it at OSI. For example, we've talked about a new incentive plan; will it work in that area? And, if so, will it help us in deciding how we should organize and manage our operations as we expand and grow in the future? What can you do to get more information on these things to me fairly soon?"

"An application EVA is touted for is its use in incentive plans," replied the analyst. "I have a team of MBA students from Wake Forest assigned to me this fall to do an industry-related project and I was looking for something 'meaty' for them to do. This looks like just the ticket. I'll brief them on it and

have them come over to get the necessary information and interview you."

"Great! I look forward to meeting them," said Keith. "And, in that case, lunch is on me," as he reached for the check.

## Company Information

OutSource, Inc. (OSI) is a computer service bureau that provides basic data processing and general business support services to a number of business firms, including several large firms in their immediate local area. Its offices are in a large city in the mid-Atlantic region, and it serves client firms in several mid-Atlantic states. OSI's revenues have grown fairly rapidly in recent years as businesses have downsized and outsourced many of their basic support services.

The CorpInfo Data Service (CIDS) classifies OSI as an information services firm (SIC 7374). This group is composed, in large part, of smaller, independent entrepreneurs that provide a variety of often disparate services to both corporate and government clients. Market analysts feel a continuously healthy economy translates into strong potential for higher earnings by members of this group. A factor sustaining an extended period of growth is the increased attention of firms to control costs and to outsource their noncore functions, such as personnel placement, payroll, human resources, insurance, and data processing. This trend is expected to continue, probably at an increasing rate, through to the end of the decade. Several firms in this industry have capitalized on their growth and geographic expansion to win lucrative contracts with large clients that previously had been awarded on a market-by-market basis.

Although OSI operates out of its own facilities, which include some computing equipment and furniture, the bulk of its computer processing power is obtained from excess computer capacity in the local area, primarily rented time during third-shift operations at a large local bank. However, to be successful in the long-term, OSI management knows it must expand its business considerably, and, to ensure it has full control over its operations, it must set up its own large-scale computing facility in-house. These items are included in OSI's long-range strategic plan.

As OSI's reputation for accurate, reliable, quick response service has spread, the firm has found new business coming its way in a variety of data processing and support services. The issue has been deciding which services to take on or to stay out of in light of the current limitations on OSI's computing resources and to ensure that they can continue to provide high-quality service to customers. Things are definitely looking up for OSI, and industry market analysts have recently begun to look more favorably on their stock.

In 1993, OSI's board decided to pursue additional opportunities in payroll processing and tax filing services, and OSI purchased a medium-sized firm that had an established market providing payroll calculating, processing, and reporting services for several Fortune 500 firms on the East Coast. OSI is now in the midst of developing a new payroll processing system, called PayNet, to replace the outmoded system that was originally created by the firm it acquired.

Once PayNet is developed, it will give users an integrated payroll solution with a simple, familiar graphical user interface. From an administrative perspective, it will allow OSI to reduce its manual data entry personnel, speed data compilation and analysis, and simplify administrative tasks and the updating of customer files for adds, moves, and changes. PayNet will serve as the backbone for OSI's service bureau payroll processing operations in the future; however, developmental and programming costs are proving to be higher than expected and will delay the roll-out of the final ver-

sion of the new payroll engine. Beta testing of the production version of PayNet is being delayed from the second to the third quarter.

### Additional Accounting Information

OSI's financial statements for 1995 appear in Exhibit 1. The following is a list of information pertinent to calculating a firm's EVA extracted from the footnotes to OSI's financial statements for 1995.

A. Inventories are stated principally at cost (last-in, first-out), which is not in excess of market. Replacement cost would be $2,796 greater than in 1994 and $3,613 greater than in 1995.

B. Deferred tax expense results from timing differences in recognizing revenue and expense for tax and reporting purposes.

C. On July 1, 1993, the Company acquired CompuPay, a payroll processing and reporting service firm. The acquisition was accounted for as a purchase, and the excess of cost over the fair value of net assets acquired was $109,200, which is being amortized on a straight-line basis over 12 years. One-half year of goodwill amortization was recorded in 1993.

D. Research and development costs related to software development are expensed as incurred. Software development costs are capitalized from the point in time when the technological feasibility of a piece of software has been determined until it is ready to be put on line to process customer data. The cost of purchased software, which is ready for service, is capitalized on acquisition. Software development costs and purchased software costs are amortized using the straight-line method over periods ranging from three to seven years. A history of the accounting treatment of software development costs and purchased software costs follows:

|      | EXPENSED  | CAPITALIZED | AMORTIZED |
|------|-----------|-------------|-----------|
| 1993 | $166,430  | $9,585      | 0         |
| 1994 | 211,852   | 5,362       | $4,511    |
| 1995 | 89,089    | 18,813      | 5,111     |
|      | $467,371  | $33,760     | $9,622    |

**EXHIBIT 1**  OSI 1995 Financial Statements

OUTSOURCE, INC. BALANCE SHEET (DECEMBER 31)

| ASSETS | 1995 | 1994 |
|---|---|---|
| Current Assets | | |
| Cash | $144,724 | $169,838 |
| Trade and other receivables (net) | 217,085 | 192,645 |
| Inventories | 15,829 | 23,750 |
| Other | 61,047 | 49,239 |
| Total current assets | $438,685 | $435,472 |
| Noncurrent Assets | | |
| Property, plant, and equipment | $123,135 | $109,600 |
| Software and development costs | 33,760 | 14,947 |
| Data processing equipment and furniture | 151,357 | 141,892 |
| Other noncurrent assets | 3,650 | 8,844 |
| | $311,902 | $275,283 |
| Less: Accumulated depreciation | 85,018 | 57,929 |
| Total noncurrent assets | $226,884 | $217,354 |
| Goodwill | 88,200 | 96,600 |
| Total assets | $753,769 | $749,426 |
| Liabilities and Shareholders' Equity | | |
| Current Liabilities | | |
| Short-term debt + current portion of long-term note | $ 27,300 | $ 31,438 |
| Accounts payable | 67,085 | 57,483 |
| Deferred income | 45,050 | 32,250 |
| Income taxes payable | 19,936 | 12,100 |
| Employee compensation and benefits payable | 30,155 | 28,950 |
| Other accrued expenses | 28,458 | 27,553 |
| Other current liabilities | 17,192 | 29,769 |
| Total current liabilities | $235,176 | $219,543 |
| Long-term debt less current portion | 98,744 | 117,155 |
| Deferred income taxes | 6,784 | 4,850 |
| Shareholders' Equity | | |
| Cumulative nonconvertible preferred stock, $100 par value, authorized 5,000 shares, issued and outstanding 1,000 shares | 100,000 | 100,000 |
| Common stock, $1 par value; 300,000 shares authorized; 219,884 shares issued and outstanding | 219,884 | 219,884 |
| Additional paid-in capital | 32,056 | 32,056 |
| Retained earnings | 61,125 | 55,938 |
| Total shareholders' equity | 413,065 | $407,878 |
| Total liabilities and shareholders equity | $753,769 | $749,426 |

*continued*

|  | 1995 |
|---|---|
| **Statement of Income for Year Ended December 31, 1995** | |
| Operating revenue | $2,604,530 |
| Less: Costs of services | 1,466,350 |
| Gross profit | $1,138,180 |
| Less: Operating expenses | |
| Selling, general and administrative | 902,388 |
| Research and development | 89,089 |
| Other expense (income) | 59,288 |
| Write-off of goodwill and other intangibles | 13,511 |
| Earnings (loss) before interest and taxes | $73,904 |
| Interest income | 1,009 |
| Interest expense | 12,427 |
| Earnings (loss) before income taxes | $62,486 |
| Income tax provision | 21,870 |
| Earnings (loss) | $40,616 |

| **Statement of Cash Flows for Year Ended December 31, 1995** | |
|---|---|
| Cash Flows from Operating Activities | |
| Net Earnings (Loss) | $40,616 |
| Depreciation | 21,978 |
| Amortization of software & development costs | 5,111 |
| Decrease (Increase) in accounts receivables | (24,440) |
| Decrease (Increase) in inventories | 7,921 |
| Decrease (Increase) in other current assets | (11,808) |
| Increase (Decrease) in deferred income | 9,602 |
| Increase (Decrease) in accounts payable | 12,800 |
| Increase (Decrease) in income taxes payable | 7,836 |
| Increase (Decrease) in employee compensation | 1,205 |
| Increase (Decrease) in other accrued expenses | 905 |
| Increase (Decrease) in other current liabilities | (12,577) |
| Increase (Decrease) in deferred income taxes | 1,934 |
| Net cash provided by operating activities | $61,083 |
| Cash Flows from Investing Activities | |
| Expended for capital assets | ($36,619) |
| Goodwill amortized | 8,400 |
| Net cash used for investing activities | ($28,219) |
| Cash Flows from Financing Activities | |
| Payment of long-term note | ($4,138) |
| Payment of short-term note | (18,411) |
| Preferred dividends | (11,000) |
| Common stock dividends | (24,429) |
| Net cash used for financing activities | ($57,978) |
| Net cash flows used ($25,114) | |
| Cash at beginning of year | $169,838 |
| Cash at end of year | $144,724 |

## Additional Financial Information

OSI's common stock is currently trading at $2.00 per share. A preferred dividend of $11 per share was paid in 1995, and the current price of the preferred stock is approximately at its par value. Other information pertaining to OSI's debt and stock follows:

|  |  | RATE |
| --- | --- | --- |
| Short-term debt: | $8,889 | 8.0% |
| Long-term debt: |  |  |
|  Current portion | $18,411 | 10.0% |
|  Long-term portion | $98,744 | 10.0% |
| Total long-term debt | $117,155 |  |
| Stock market risk-free rate (90-day T-bills) |  | 5.0% |
| Expected return on the market |  | 12.5% |
| Beta value of OSI's common stock |  | 1.20 |
| Growth rate of dividends |  | 8.00% |
| Income tax |  | 35.0% |

## Requirements

The management of OutSource, Inc., has asked you to prepare a report explaining EVA (economic value added) and MVA (market value added), how they are calculated, and how they compare with traditional measures of a firm's financial performance. OSI's management would also like to know the advantages and disadvantages of using EVA to evaluate the firm's performance on an ongoing basis as well as in assessing the performance of individual managers throughout its organization. As part of your report, calculate EVA and MVA from OutSource, Inc.'s, financial statements for 1995. Finally, OSI's management would like to know if EVA can be used as part of an incentive system for its employees and how they should proceed to implement such an incentive system at OutSource, Inc.

---

# PURITY STEEL CORPORATION, 1995*

"I'm no expert in high finance," said Larry Hoffman, manager of the Denver branch for the Warehouse Sales Division of Purity Steel Corporation, to Harold Higgins, general manager of the division, "so it didn't occur to me that I might be better off by leasing my new warehouse instead of owning it. But I was talking to Jack Dorenbush over in Omaha the other day and he said that he's getting a lot better return on the investment in his district because he's in a leased building. I'm sure that the incentive compensation plan you put in last year

*Doctoral Candidate Antonio Dávila and Professor Robert Simons prepared this updated case based on an earlier version.

Harvard Business School case 9-197-082. Copyright © 1997 by the President and Fellows of Harvard College.

is fair, but I didn't know whether it adjusted automatically for the difference between owning and leasing and I just thought I'd raise the question. There's still time to try to find someone to take over my construction contract and then lease the building to me when it's finished, if you think that's what I ought to do."

Purity Steel Corporation was an integrated steel producer with annual sales of about $4.5 billion in 1995. The Warehouse Sales Division was an autonomous unit that operated 21 field warehouses throughout the United States. Total sales of the division were approximately $225 million in 1995, of which roughly half represented steel products (rod, bar, wire, tube, sheet, and plate) purchased from Purity's Mill

Products Division. The balance of the Warehouse Sales Division volume was copper, brass, and aluminum products purchased from large producers of those metals. The Warehouse Sales Division competed with other producer-affiliated and independent steel warehousing companies and purchased its steel requirements from the Mill Products Division at the same prices paid by outside purchasers.

Harold Higgins was appointed general manager of the Warehouse Sales Division in mid-1994, after spending 12 years in the sales function with the Mill Products Division. Subject only to the approval of his annual profit plan and proposed capital expenditures by corporate headquarters, Higgins was given full authority for his division's operations, and was charged with the responsibility to "make the division grow, both in sales volume and in the rate of return on its investment." Prior to his arrival at division headquarters in St. Louis, the Warehouse Sales Division had been operated in a centralized manner; all purchase orders had been issued by division headquarters, and most other operating decisions at any particular warehouse had required prior divisional approval. Higgins decided to decentralize the management of his division by making each branch (warehouse) manager responsible for the division's activities in his or her geographic area.

In Higgins's opinion, one of the key features of his decentralization policy was an incentive compensation plan announced in late 1994 to become effective January 1, 1995. The description of the plan, as presented to the branch managers, is reproduced in Exhibits 1, 2, and 3. Monthly operating statements had been prepared for each warehouse for many years; implementing the new plan required only the preparation of balance sheets for each warehouse. Two major asset categories, inventories and fixed assets (buildings and equipment), were easy to attribute to specific locations. Accounts receivable were collected directly at Purity's central accounting department, but an investment in receivables equal to 35 days' sales (the average for the Warehouse Sales Division) was charged to each warehouse. Finally, a small cash fund deposited in a local bank was recorded as an asset of each branch. No current or long-term liabilities were recognized in the balance sheets at the division or branch level.

At the meeting in December 1994, when the new incentive compensation plan was presented to the branch managers, Higgins had said:

Howard Percy [division sales manager] and I have spent a lot of time during the last few months working out the details of this plan. Our objective was to devise a fair way to compensate those branch managers who do a superior job of improving the performance in their areas. First, we reviewed our salary structure and made a few adjustments so that branch managers do not have to apologize to their families for the regular pay check they bring home. Next, we worked out a simple growth incentive to recognize that one part of our job is simply to sell steel, although we didn't restrict it to steel alone. But more importantly, we've got to improve the profit performance of this division. We established 5% as the return-on-investment floor representing minimum performance eligible for a bonus. As you know, we don't even do that well for 1994, but our budget for next year anticipates 5% before taxes. Thus, in 1995 we expect about a third of the branches to be below 5%—and earn no ROI bonus—while the other two-thirds will be the ones who really carry the weight. This plan will pay a bonus to all managers who help the division increase its average rate of return. We also decided on a sliding scale arrangement for those above 5%, trying to recognize that the manager who makes a 5% return on a $10 million investment is doing as good a job as one who makes a 10% return on only a half million dollars. Finally, we put a $50,000 limit on the ROI bonus because we felt that the bonus shouldn't exceed 50% of salary, but we can always make salary adjustments in those cases where the bonus plan doesn't seem to adequately compensate a branch manager for his or her performance.

**EXHIBIT 1**  Branch Managers' Compensation Plan, Warehouse Sales Division

I.    Objectives

The Warehouse Sales Division has three major objectives:

A. To operate the Division and its branches at a profit.

B. To utilize efficiently the assets of the Division.

C. To grow.

This compensation plan is a combination of base salary and incentive earnings. Incentive earnings will be paid to those managers who contribute to the achievement of these objectives and in proportion to their individual performance.

II.    Compensation Plan Components

There are three components to this plan:

A. Base Salary

Base salary ranges are determined for the most part on dollar sales volume of the district(s) in the prior year. The higher the sales volume, the higher the range to which the manager becomes eligible. The profitability of dollar sales or increases in dollar sales is an important consideration. Actual salaries will be established by the General Manager, Warehouse Sales Division, and the salary ranges will be reviewed periodically in order to keep this Division competitive with companies similar to ours.

B. Growth Incentive

If the district earns a net profit before federal income tax for the calendar year, the manager will earn $1,750 for every $500,000 of increased sales over the prior year. Proportionate amounts will be paid for greater or lesser growth.

C. Return-on-Investment Incentive

In this feature of the plan, incentive will be paid in relation to the size of investment and the return-on-investment. The manager will be paid in direct proportion to his effective use of assets placed at his disposal.

The main emphasis of this portion of the plan is on increasing the return at any level of investment, high or low.

III.    Limitations on Return-on-Investment Incentive

A. No incentive will be paid to a manager whose branch earns less than 5% return on investment before federal taxes.

B. No increase in incentive payment will be made for performance in excess of 20% return on investment before federal taxes.

C. No payment will be made in excess of $50,000 regardless of performance.

IV.    Calculations on Return-on-Investment Incentive

Exhibit 2 is a graphic presentation of this portion of the incentive. Since all possible levels of investment and return on investment cannot be detailed on the chart, exact incentive figures cannot be determined. However, a rough estimate can be made by:

A. Finding the approximate level of investment on the horizontal scale.

B. Drawing a line vertically from that point to the approximate return-on-investment percent.

C. Drawing a line horizontally from that point to the vertical scale which indicates the approximate incentive payment.

The exact amount of incentive can be determined from Exhibit 3 by the following procedure and example.

**Example:**

|  |  |
|---|---|
| Investment: | $8,263,750 |
| ROI: | 7.3% |

Step 1.   Subtract 500,000 from the last six digits of investment figures if they are above 500,000.
EXAMPLE: 263,750 is below 500,000; nothing is subtracted.

Step 2.   Divide the number from Step 1 by 500,000. The result is a percentage.
EXAMPLE: 263,750/500,000 = 0.5275

*continued*

Step 3. In the 1% column in Exhibit 3, take the difference between the next highest investment and next lowest investment.

EXAMPLE:

| Investment | 1% | Difference |
|---|---|---|
| $8,000,000 | $2,100 | |
| | | $50 |
| $8,500,000 | $2,150 | |

Step 4. Multiply the result of Step 3 by the result of Step 2 and add to the 1% column figure for the next lowest investment.
EXAMPLE: $50 × 0.5275 = $26.37 + $2,100 = $2,126.37

Step 5. Multiply the result of Step 4 by the actual ROI%.
EXAMPLE: $2,126.37 × 7.3 = $15,522.54 Incentive Payment

---

After the telephone call from Larry Hoffman in May 1996, quoted in the opening paragraph, Harold Higgins called Howard Percy into his office and told him the question that Hoffman had raised. "We knew that we probably had some bugs to iron out of this system," Percy responded. "Let me review the Denver situation and we'll discuss it this afternoon."

At a meeting later that day, Percy summarized the problem for Higgins:

As you know, Larry Hoffman is planning a big expansion at Denver. He's been limping along in an old multistory building with an inadequate variety of inventory, and his sales actually declined last year. About a year ago he worked up an RFE [request for expenditure]

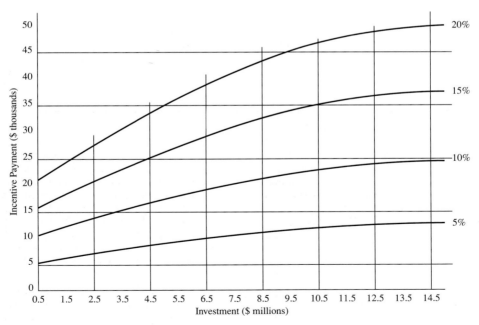

**EXHIBIT 2** Incentive Payments at Various ROI Percentages

**EXHIBIT 3**  Incentive Payments at Various Investments and ROI Percentages

| | ROI PERCENTAGE | | | | |
|---|---|---|---|---|---|
| INVESTMENT | 1%* | 5% | 10% | 15% | 20% |
| $   500,000 | 1,045 | 5,225 | 10,450 | 15,675 | 20,900 |
| 1,000,000 | 1,125 | 5,625 | 11,250 | 16,875 | 22,500 |
| 1,500,000 | 1,205 | 6,025 | 12,050 | 18,075 | 24,100 |
| 2,000,000 | 1,285 | 6,425 | 12,850 | 19,275 | 25,700 |
| 2,500,000 | 1,365 | 6,825 | 13,650 | 20,475 | 27,300 |
| 3,000,000 | 1,445 | 7,225 | 14,450 | 21,675 | 28,900 |
| 3,500,000 | 1,525 | 7,625 | 15,250 | 22,875 | 30,500 |
| 4,000,000 | 1,605 | 8,025 | 16,050 | 24,075 | 32,100 |
| 4,500,000 | 1,685 | 8,425 | 16,850 | 25,275 | 33,700 |
| 5,000,000 | 1,750 | 8,750 | 17,500 | 26,250 | 35,000 |
| 5,500,000 | 1,810 | 9,050 | 18,100 | 27,150 | 36,200 |
| 6,000,000 | 1,875 | 9,375 | 18,750 | 28,125 | 37,500 |
| 6,500,000 | 1,935 | 9,675 | 19,350 | 29,025 | 38,700 |
| 7,000,000 | 2,000 | 10,000 | 20,000 | 30,000 | 40,000 |
| 7,500,000 | 2,050 | 10,250 | 20,500 | 30,750 | 41,000 |
| 8,000,000 | 2,100 | 10,500 | 21,000 | 31,500 | 42,000 |
| 8,500,000 | 2,150 | 10,750 | 21,500 | 32,250 | 43,000 |
| 9,000,000 | 2,200 | 11,000 | 22,000 | 33,000 | 44,000 |
| 9,500,000 | 2,250 | 11,250 | 22,500 | 33,750 | 45,000 |
| 10,000,000 | 2,300 | 11,500 | 23,000 | 34,500 | 46,000 |
| 10,500,000 | 2,325 | 11,625 | 23,250 | 34,875 | 46,500 |
| 11,000,000 | 2,350 | 11,750 | 23,500 | 35,250 | 47,000 |
| 11,500,000 | 2,375 | 11,875 | 23,750 | 35,625 | 47,500 |
| 12,000,000 | 2,400 | 12,000 | 24,000 | 36,000 | 48,000 |
| 12,500,000 | 2,425 | 12,125 | 24,250 | 36,375 | 48,500 |
| 13,000,000 | 2,450 | 12,250 | 24,500 | 36,750 | 49,000 |
| 13,500,000 | 2,475 | 12,375 | 24,750 | 37,125 | 49,500 |
| 14,000,000 | 2,500 | 12,500 | 25,000 | 37,500 | 50,000 |
| 14,500,000 | 2,500 | 12,500 | 25,000 | 37,500 | 50,000 |
| 15,000,000 | 2,500 | 12,500 | 25,000 | 37,500 | 50,000 |

*This column is for calculation purposes only. No incentive will be paid for less than 5% ROI.*

for a new warehouse which we approved here and sent forward. It was approved at corporate headquarters last fall, the contract was let, and it's to be completed by the end of this year. I pulled out one page of the RFE which summarizes the financial story [Exhibit 4]. Larry forecasts nearly a triple in his sales volume over the next eight years, and the project will pay out in about seven and a half years.

Here [Exhibit 5] is a summary of the incentive compensation calculations for Denver that I worked up after I talked to you this morning.

Larry had a very high ROI last year, and received one of the biggest bonuses we paid. Against that background, I next worked up a projection of what his bonus will be in 1997 assuming that he moves into his new facility at the end of the year. As you can see, his ROI will drop from 17.3% to only 7.2%, and even on the bigger investment his bonus in 1997 will go down substantially.

Finally, I dug out the file on New Orleans where we're leasing the new warehouse that was completed a few months ago. Our lease there is a so-called operating lease, which

**EXHIBIT 4** Warehouse Sales Division—Denver Branch: Forecast Additional Sales, Expenses, and After-Tax Profits Due to New Facility (Dollars in Thousands)

| | ESTIMATED TO 12/31/95 | 1ST YEAR | 2ND YEAR | 3RD YEAR | 4TH YEAR | 5TH YEAR | 6TH YEAR | 7TH YEAR | 8TH YEAR |
|---|---|---|---|---|---|---|---|---|---|
| Sales dollars | $ 12,300 | 1,565 | 2,620 | 5,125 | 7,870 | 11,020 | 15,250 | 18,635 | 22,670 |
| Gross profit dollars | 2,385 | 245 | 400 | 801 | 1,259 | 1,732 | 2,346 | 2,851 | 3,489 |
| Service income | 255 | (125) | (120) | (110) | (100) | (90) | (80) | (80) | (80) |
| Total income | 2,640 | 120 | 280 | 691 | 1,159 | 1,642 | 2,266 | 2,771 | 3,409 |
| Less expenses excluding depreciation | (1,645) | (305) | (585) | (785) | (1,000) | (1,175) | (1,455) | (1,610) | (1,655) |
| Pretax net profit excluding depreciation | 995 | (185) | (305) | (94) | 159 | 467 | 811 | 1,161 | 1,754 |
| Additional mill profit | | 65 | 120 | 290 | 495 | 625 | 785 | 920 | 1,165 |
| | | (120) | (185) | 196 | 654 | 1,092 | 1,596 | 2,081 | 2,919 |
| Less relocation | | (100) | | | | | | | |
| | | (220) | (185) | 196 | 654 | 1,092 | 1,596 | 2,081 | 2,919 |
| Less depreciation | | (53) | (53) | (53) | (53) | (53) | (53) | (53) | (53) |
| | | (273) | (238) | 143 | 601 | 1,039 | 1,543 | 2,028 | 2,866 |
| Less 35% tax | | 96 | 83 | (50) | (210) | (364) | (540) | (710) | (1,003) |
| Net income | | (177) | (155) | 93 | 391 | 675 | 1,003 | 1,318 | 1,863 |
| Add back depreciation and relocation | | 153 | 53 | 53 | 53 | 53 | 53 | 53 | 53 |
| Annual return of funds | | (24) | (102) | 146 | 444 | 728 | 1,056 | 1,371 | 1,916 |

Total return over 8 years (in dollars) $5,534,549

Capital expenditures required (in dollars):

| | |
|---|---|
| Land | $ 300,000 |
| Building | 2,612,500 |
| Equipment | 1,059,650 |
| Relocation expense | 100,000 |
| Total | $4,072,150 |
| Payback period | 7.3 years |

**EXHIBIT 5**  Return-on-Investment and Incentive Compensation (in Dollars)

| | TOTAL WAREHOUSE SALES DIVISION 1995 ACTUAL | DENVER BRANCH 1995 ACTUAL | 1997 PROJECTED OWNED BUILDING | 1997 PROJECTED LEASED BUILDING |
|---|---|---|---|---|
| **Investment at Year-end** | | | | |
| Land | $  5,144,500 | $  124,500 | $  300,000 | $ — |
| Buildings (net of depreciation) | 13,950,500 | 324,500 | 2,568,960 | — |
| Equipment (net of depreciation) | 2,722,000 | 32,000 | 1,010,425 | $1,010,425 |
| Subtotal | 21,817,000 | 481,000 | 3,879,385 | 1,010,425 |
| Cash fund | 1,382,500 | 50,000 | 50,000 | 50,000 |
| Accounts receivable | 22,517,500 | 1,241,500 | 1,386,500 | 1,386,500 |
| Inventories | 55,295,500 | 3,132,000 | 3,466,250 | 3,466,250 |
| Total year-end investment | 101,012,500 | 4,904,500 | 8,782,135 | 5,913,175 |
| Investment at start of year | 99,795,500 | 5,263,500 | 8,395,650 | 5,483,150 |
| Average investment during year | 100,404,000 | 5,084,000 | 8,588,895 | 5,698,150 |
| Profit before depreciation & taxes | 4,147,310 | 917,870 | 710,000 | 710,000 |
| Less: depreciation | (648,705) | (40,000) | (92,765) | (49,225) |
| Less: lease payments | (420,565) | — | — | $ (243,200) |
| Net pretax profit | $  3,078,040 | $  877,870 | $  617,235 | $  417,575 |
| Return on investment | 3.07% | 17.27% | 7.19% | 7.33% |
| **Incentive Compensation** | | | | |
| Sales volume increase (decrease) | | $ (870,000) | $1,565,000 | $1,565,000 |
| Bonus @ $1,750 per $500,000 | — | — | 5,478 | 5,478 |
| ROI bonus: | | | | |
| Base investment | | 5,000,000 | 8,500,000 | 5,500,000 |
| Value for 1% column, Exhibit 3 | | 1,750 | 2,150 | 1,810 |
| Difference to next base | | 60 | 50 | 65 |
| Interpolated portion | | 10.08 | 8.89 | 25.76 |
| Total value per percentage point | | 1,760 | 2,159 | 1,836 |
| ROI bonus | | 30,392 | 15,515 | 13,453 |
| Total incentive compensation | | $  30,392 | $  20,993 | $  18,931 |

Assumptions used for 1997 projections at Denver:
1. Old facility and equipment sold at the end of 1996, proceeds remitted to corporate headquarters.
2. Depreciation on new facilities in 1997 is $43,540 (60 years, straight line) and $49,225 on equipment (various lives, straight line).
3. Year-end investment in receivables and inventory will approximate 1995 relationship: receivables at 10% of annual sales, inventories at 25% of annual sales.
4. Average total investment assumes that new fixed assets are acquired on December 31, 1996, and that other assets at that date are the same as at the end of 1995.
5. Profit taken from RFE (Exhibit 4) as $995,000 less $185,000 first-year decline, less $100,000 relocation expense. Additional mill profit of $65,000 does not reflect on divisional books and was used only at corporate headquarters for capital expenditures evaluation purposes.

means that we pay the insurance, taxes, and maintenance just as if we owned it. The lease runs for 20 years with renewal options at reduced rates for two additional 10-year periods. Assuming that we could get a similar deal for Denver, and adjusting for the difference in the cost of the land and building at the two locations, our lease payments at Denver during the first 20 years would be just under $250,000 per year. Pushing that through the bonus formula for Denver's projected 1997 operations shows an ROI of 7.3%, but Larry's bonus would be about 15% less than if he was in an owned building.

"On balance, therefore," Percy concluded, "there's not a very big difference in the bonus payment as between owning and leasing, but in either event Larry will be taking a substantial cut in his incentive compensation."

As the discussion continued, Larry Hoffman and Howard Percy revisited the formula for ROI:

$$\text{Return-on-investment} = \frac{\text{net income}}{\text{investment in operating assets}}$$

$$= \frac{\text{net income}}{\text{sales}} \times \frac{\text{sales}}{\text{investment in operating assets}}$$

$$= (\text{return on sales}) \times (\text{asset turnover})$$

Both wondered whether the proposed bonus plan needed further revision or clarification.

## WESTERN CHEMICAL CORPORATION: DIVISIONAL PERFORMANCE MEASUREMENT*

The fact is that we really have not yet figured out the best way to measure and report on the performance of some of our foreign operations. Because of different ownership arrangements and the use of local financing, when we use conventional accounting principles and standards, we often get financial reports that seem to contradict what we believe to be the true results of operations. This creates problems within the company because people who are not familiar with particular operations see the reports and draw erroneous conclusions about how this one or that one is performing relative to others.

Now that you are beginning to get questions from shareholders and analysts about how some of these investments are performing, I realized that Cynthia and I had better brief you on what some of the problems are that we have with division performance measurement.

Stan Rogers, president of Western Chemical Corporation (WCC), was meeting with Samantha Chu, recently appointed director of Investor Relations, and Cynthia Sheldon, who had recently been appointed vice president and controller. Chu had that morning received an inquiry from a well-known chemical industry analyst who had some fairly specific questions about some of the company's investments in Europe and the Far East. When she questioned Sheldon, Cynthia suggested that they meet with Rogers to examine some of the issues that Rogers and Sheldon had been discussing, so that Chu could answer the analyst's requests more accurately.

The information on the financial performance of WCC's foreign operations was prepared by the same accountants who maintained the company's accounts and who prepared its quarterly and annual reports. A

*Professor William J. Bruns and Professor Roger Atherton of Northeastern University prepared this case.

Copyright © 1995 by the President and Fellows of Harvard College. Harvard Business School case 196-079.

single database for all accounting had been established some years earlier in the belief that it could serve all accounting needs of both managers and those external to the company. A common chart of accounts and accounting policies was used throughout the company and in all of its subsidiaries.

A variety of new alliances and ownership arrangements had been used in recent international ventures to speed entry to new international markets and to minimize investment and risk. Because of these, Rogers had become convinced that some of the reports the accountants were preparing about some of the ventures could be quite misleading. It was for that reason that he and Sheldon were already discussing alternative ways to measure divisional performance, and that Sheldon thought Chu should be brought into their discussion before trying to answer the analyst's queries.

## *The Company and International Ventures*

In 1995, WCC was a 75-year-old, Fortune 300 chemical company. Its largest business marketed chemicals and chemical programs for water and waste treatment. Additional products and chemical services targeted manufacturing processes where the quality of a customer's product could be enhanced. The company was proud of its industry reputation for quality of its solutions to customer problems and exceptional service to customers. WCC had 4,900 employees and operated more than 35 plants in 19 countries. Financial information by geographic area is shown in Exhibit 1.

WCC manufactured in many different countries using a variety of ownership arrangements. Some plants were wholly owned manufacturing sites, and others were operated as joint ventures with local affiliates. Three of these plants were useful illustrations as background for discussing the

problems the company faced in measuring the performance of its international ventures. All had been constructed and had come on-stream in the 1991–1993 period.

A chemical plant on the outskirts of Prague in the Czech Republic was operated as a joint venture with a local partner. Total investment in the plant was between $35 and $40 million, including working capital. WCC retained a controlling interest in the joint venture and operated the plant. The company had invested about $5 million in the venture, and the balance of the investment had come from the venture partner and local borrowing.

A similar plant in Poland was 100% owned, and the total capital investment of $40 to $45 million including working capital had been funded by WCC. The venture itself had no external debt.

A third plant in Malaysia was also 100% owned. The plant was built to add capacity in the Pacific region, but the plant was considered part of the company's production capacity serving the global market. WCC had invested approximately $35 million in this Malaysian plant.

## *Measuring the Performance of Three International Ventures*

Cynthia Sheldon had prepared some exhibits using representative numbers, and she began by explaining the income statement for the venture in the Czech Republic to Samantha Chu.

The first case is Prague. It is pretty much a classic situation. What I have put together here is a basic income statement for the facility for the first three quarters of 1995 (Exhibit 2). What this helps to show is how the difference between the ownership structures in Prague and Poland lead to apparent differences in reported income.

This is a nine-month year-to-date income statement for the joint venture. Earnings before interest and taxes of $869,000 is what we

---

## EXHIBIT 1  Financial Information by Geographic Area

Western Chemical Corporation (WCC) is engaged in the worldwide manufacture and sale of highly specialized service chemical programs. This includes production and service related to the sale and application of chemicals and technology used in water treatment, pollution control, energy conservation, and other industrial processes as well as a super-absorbent product for the disposable diaper market.

Within WCC, sales between geographic areas are made at prevailing market prices to customers minus an amount intended to compensate the sister WCC company for providing quality customer service.

Identifiable assets are those directly associated with operations of the geographic area. Corporate assets consist mainly of cash and cash equivalents; marketable securities; investments in unconsolidated partnerships, affiliates, and leveraged leases; and capital assets used for corporate purposes.

GEOGRAPHIC AREA DATA (IN MILLIONS)

|  | 1994 | 1993 | 1992 |
|---|---|---|---|
| Sales |  |  |  |
| North America | $ 886.9 | $ 915.1 | $ 883.7 |
| Europe | 288.9 | 315.6 | 346.5 |
| Latin America | 72.2 | 66.4 | 60.7 |
| Pacific | 127.7 | 116.7 | 108.2 |
| Sales between areas | (30.1) | (24.4) | (24.6) |
|  | $1,345.6 | $1,389.4 | $1,374.5 |
| Operating Earnings |  |  |  |
| North America | $ 181.6 | $ 216.9 | $ 211.3 |
| Europe | (10.2) | 41.8 | 48.9 |
| Latin America | 9.3 | 11.4 | 10.0 |
| Pacific | 14.3 | 14.4 | 14.4 |
| Expenses not allocated to areas | (20.3) | (21.6) | (24.3) |
|  | $ 174.7 | $ 262.9 | $ 260.3 |
| Identifiable Assets |  |  |  |
| North America | $ 485.2 | $ 566.6 | $ 562.2 |
| Europe | 245.2 | 227.4 | 225.5 |
| Latin America | 66.9 | 45.4 | 42.7 |
| Pacific | 147.9 | 126.3 | 124.7 |
| Corporate | 337.0 | 246.7 | 395.5 |
|  | $1,282.2 | $1,212.4 | $1,350.6 |

---

Amounts for North America sales in the tabulation above include exports to the following areas:

| | | | |
|---|---|---|---|
| Latin America | $21.9 | $19.2 | $16.0 |
| All other | 7.3 | 13.0 | 12.0 |

The decrease in operating earnings in 1994 was mainly attributable to the pretax provision of $68 million for consolidation expenses. Of that amount, approximately $34 million was included in European operations.

---

would normally report internally for a wholly owned subsidiary, and that is what would be consolidated. As you proceed down the income statement, there is a charge for interest because we have the ability to leverage these joint ventures fairly highly, anywhere from 60% to 80%. This is interest on external debt—cash going out. We account for it this way because

**EXHIBIT 2**  9/95 Year-to-Date Income from Czech Republic Joint Venture (in Thousands)

| | |
|---|---:|
| Revenues | $11,510 |
| Cost of sales | (9,541) |
| Selling, technical expenses, and administrative expenses | (891) |
| Other income/other charges | (209) |
| Income before interest and taxes | $    869 |
| Interest | (1,120) |
| Fees | (867) |
| Foreign exchange | (60) |
| Income (loss) | $(1,178) |
| Minority interest | 532) |
| Taxes | — |
| Net income (loss) | $    (646) |

the venture has its own Board of Directors, even though we have management control and retain much of the ability to influence operations, which is not always the case. The fees of $867,000 are coming to WCC under a technical agreement that we have with the joint venture, as a percentage of revenues. In this case, we have put a minority interest line to get down to a net income for WCC. That is the actual income that we would report to the outside world.

We are reporting externally a loss of $646,000 on this business, when in truth, relative to our other businesses which are reported before interest charges and before fees, it is contributing to our corporate income. This report makes it appear that we are operating at a loss of just under $1.2 million, $532,000 of which is the share of our joint venture partner, and our share is the $646,000.

### Stan Rogers described the investment:

In this business WCC has invested, in addition to its technical knowledge and technology, $5 million of its money. In addition, we do not guarantee the debt, which is off balance sheet so far as WCC is concerned. One other way that we can look at these businesses is to look at cash flows to WCC, and cash return on investment to WCC. When we do that, because

of the $867,000 in fees which are paid to WCC, there is some return. Although the return is small, it is reasonable at this stage of development of a new business. This business, because of the fees, has been in a loss position, but because of the fees it has shown a positive cash return on investment to WCC.

### Sheldon continued:

Our actual return consists of the fees paid to WCC, or $867,000, and our share of the reported operating losses, for a net income of $221,000. That is the return on our approximately $5 million investment. If the subsidiary were wholly owned with a total investment of approximately $40 million, we would be looking at the $869,000 income before interest and taxes, to which we might decide to apply a tax, on the investment of $40 million. That is how we measure the performance of wholly owned divisions.

One of the reasons that this report appears as it does was that, a few years ago, then current management decided to work from a single data base and to have one group prepare both the external financial reports and the management reports for internal use. It was a fine decision, except for the fact that the external reporters did not have the interest or ability to report what was actually going on in the affiliates.

Now, let's look at the report for our subsidiary in Poland (Exhibit 3). This plant is 100%

**EXHIBIT 3**  9/95 Year-to-Date Income from Poland Plan (in Thousands)

| | |
|---|---:|
| Revenues | $32,536 |
| Cost of sales | (28,458) |
| Selling, technical expenses, and administrative expenses | (2,529) |
| Other income/other charges | (121) |
| Income before interest and taxes | $  1,428 |
| Interest | — |
| Fees | — |
| Foreign exchange | 34 |
| Income | $  1,462 |
| Minority interest | — |
| Taxes | — |
| Net income | $  1,462 |

owned, so we do not report any interest or fees. The total capital investment was funded by the company and totaled about $40 or $45 million including working capital. There is no external debt or minority interest and no fees. The other charges include the amortization of interest that was capitalized during the construction of the plant. The cost of sales includes some profit from materials that are purchased from other plants, but the prices paid are reasonable if you compare them with competitors' prices. This is another interesting problem that we struggle with, since we are probably reporting $2 or $3 million in profits elsewhere because of these plant purchases. But consider how this would look if we were deducting interest on $30 million of debt, and fees of 8% of revenues as we do in the case of the Prague affiliate. We would then be showing a loss from the business of about $3 million. The accountants do not consider this, and their report makes it appear that the business was doing just fine.

Samantha Chu spoke up:

Your explanation implies that there must be some other measures of performance that tell you how these plants are performing. What are those?

Sheldon:

We use budgets and the original business plans. We look at the performance against those expectations.

Rogers:

Also, although we do not monitor cash flows to the degree that we ought to, we have in our head the cash contribution compared to the amounts that we have invested. In the Czech Republic we can look ahead and see that in the future we will have a 35% to 45% cash on cash return. Poland is draining cash out of us at a remarkable rate, and we have not yet figured out a way to stop it. There are still a lot of unresolved business problems. Compared to the original business plan we have not been able to generate the revenues that were forecasted and the costs have been higher. We do not present cash flow reports to our managers, so these analyses all have to be done

in our heads. The information we would need to bring this about formally is all available, but we just have not asked anyone to do it.

What we have are three new plants built at about the same time, each having very complex and different financial reporting issues that lead you to have completely different views of the business. Cynthia, show Samantha the report on the plant in Malaysia and what happens when we introduce an economic value added (EVA) approach. . . .

Sheldon:

The third plant was built to supply a high margin part of our business. That part of our business is truly a global business in that we can actually ship our product from any of several plants to anywhere in the world. When the decision to build a plant in Malaysia was made we were running out of capacity. We made a strategic decision that we wanted to be located in Malaysia, but this was to be part of our production facilities to serve the global market. We do not usually build a separate plant to supply only the high margin products. The volumes sold and shipped tend to be small, and adding the technostructure of technical service and laboratories to a plant makes the economics somewhat unfavorable unless there are several other units in the same plant producing higher volume products to help carry the costs of these necessary add-ons.

Looking at the column labeled "Region of Manufacture," you can see the sales and profitability of the manufacturing facility in Malaysia [Exhibit 4]. It sells $12 million worth of product, and you can see that with the costs being what they are, the plant is losing a lot of money. The capital charge that we show is an attempt to get a measure of the economic value added by the plant. As was the case with Poland, this report does not include any interest on the total investment of almost $35 million, or any fees.

The EVA approach uses a 12% capital charge based on the assets employed such as working capital, including accounts payable, and fixed capital. Depreciation is included in cost of sales. I think the way we use EVA is very simple, exactly the way it is employed by other folks, but some get much more sophisticated about allocations, capitalized

**EXHIBIT 4**  9/95 Year-to-Date Income from Malaysia and Southeast Asia (in Thousands)

|  | REGION OF MANUFACTURE | REGION OF SALE |
|---|---|---|
| Revenues | $  12,020 | $ 36,052 |
| Cost of sales | (12,392) | (26,648) |
| Selling, technical expenses, and administrative expenses | (3,775) | (4,845) |
| Other income/other charges | (685) | (285) |
| Income before interest and taxes | $ (4,832) | $  4,274 |
| Taxes (40%) | — | (1,710) |
| Net income | $ (4,832) | $  2,564 |
| Capital charges | (3,600)* | (6,686)[†] |
| Economic value added | $ (8,432) | $ (4,122) |

*$30,000 @ 12% = $3,600.*
[†]*($110,000 @ 12%) $\times$ [(36,052 − 12,020)/102,800] + (30,000 @ 12%) = $6,686.*

research and development, and the like. We do not do that.

In addition we have recently started to look not just at "region of manufacture" but also at "region of sale," primarily to get an understanding of whether or not a market is attractive. The second column labeled "Region of Sale" is all product being sold in Southeast Asia even if it is being manufactured outside, so it includes the cost of manufacturing product, shipping it, and delivering it to customers in the region. On that basis the earnings before interest and taxes are about $4 million. If we wanted to get down to economic value added we would need to deduct taxes and a capital charge and the economic value added would still be negative but not so much so that we could not develop some reasonable strategies to fix it compared to the region of manufacture measure which is pretty daunting.

Stan Rogers interjected:

There is an incremental layer of complexity here in that this plant is starting to produce for the rest of the world because we are running out of capacity and are using this plant as the swing plant. Those shipments will show up in the region of manufacture numbers, but they will not show up in the region of sale numbers. We have not yet sorted this out, but

my suspicion is that you cannot look at it this way and get an intriguing view—a solid view—of the business. We probably have to look at the whole system and analyze the incremental revenues and costs of the whole business.

The reason why I see this as another iteration of the same or complexity of the same problem, is that in Prague and Poland we had the different corporate structures that led to different accounting treatments of interest and fees, which gave us completely warped views on what was going on in the business. This presents the same challenge but adds the dimensions of region of manufacture and region of sale accounting and the need for total system analysis.

Samantha Chu broke the silence of the pause which followed: "Have you found a solution to the problem yet?" Rogers answered:

We understand it. We have not institutionalized a management reporting system that would lead someone who is intelligent but does not understand the background to understand what is really going on. We do not have a management reporting system in place that shows the relative performance of the three plants in a clear manner. On this basis the system does not work.

## Some Possible Solutions to the Performance Measurement Problem

Cynthia Sheldon began a discussion of some possible solutions to the division performance measurement problem:

> We are scratching away at a solution, perhaps using the concept of economic value added. We probably will also separate the people who are preparing the managerial reports from those who are concerned with external reporting, even though both groups will be working from the same databases. Until now, when we report to external public relations and to the Chairman about the performance of the business, we have used external reporting standards and bases. I have concluded that to get away from that we have to have a separate group engaged with the businesses.

Stan Rogers chimed in:

> From a business standpoint we understand this, we think. When we want to do a presentation we will do a one time analysis, pulling the numbers together that we think best reflect the situation. But we do not have a disciplined, repetitive reporting system that produces an analysis of how these businesses are doing in any other way than the way the external reporting system does it. That is an issue of priorities. We just do not have the time or resources to fix the system now. It is not that we do not understand the problem, or that we could not do it. I think we understand the problem, and we understand the intellectual underpinnings of a solution.
>
> I know that does not help you in responding to the analyst's questions today, so you will just have to respond very carefully.

Cynthia Sheldon continued:

> We are really just beginning to use EVA as a tool to get people to understand the issues. There is nothing wrong with using cash flow, return on net assets, and other familiar financial measures. There are always problems with any single financial measure, but right now in order to get people to focus it is easier to have one number and EVA is the most effective single number. We know that in order to make the business viable in our Southeast Asia region we have to go down a path of expanding the business. When you expand, EVA goes down, so if you focus on only that measure you risk saying that I do not want to do that. That is not the right answer. We are already seeing that kind of problem. But at least EVA gets people to focus on the cost of the capital associated with the income that they earn, and it gets more of a sense of cash flow, but we do not rely solely on it.

Stan Rogers summed up his feelings on the division performance measurement problems, echoing some of the conclusions of Sheldon:

> You know, I would say the same thing. There is not a planning department here that thinks about EVA and all that kind of stuff. We probably could use better numbers, but driving the business off any single number probably would not work.

### Required

(1) What is causing the problems in measuring division performance at Western Chemical Corporation?

(2) Are there alternative methods for measuring division performance that would avoid the problems that WCC management is having with the methods that they have been using?

(3) Evaluate the approach to using economic value added (EVA) that WCC management is discussing and using experimentally. What are the strengths and weaknesses of this approach?

(4) How should the performance of divisions of WCC be measured?

(5) What should Samantha Chu tell the analyst if he asks specifically about the investments in the Czech Republic, Poland, and Malaysia?

# 11

# Measuring Customer, Internal Business Process, and Employee Performance

In Chapter 8, we introduced the Balanced Scorecard, a system of measuring performance across four integrated and linked perspectives: financial, customer, internal business processes, and learning and growth. In Chapters 9 and 10, we discussed financial performance measurement, including return on investment and economic value added. In this chapter, we explore measurements in the other three Balanced Scorecard perspectives.

## CUSTOMER PERSPECTIVE

As noted in Chapter 8, the customer perspective encompasses several generic measures of the successful outcomes of a well-formulated, well-targeted strategy. These generic customer measures typically include:

- Market share
- Account share
- Retention and loyalty
- Acquisition
- Satisfaction
- Profitability

We discuss each in turn.

## Market and Account Share

Market share reflects the proportion of business in a given market that a business unit sells. Market share can be measured in terms of number of customers, dollars spent, or unit volume sold. This measure, especially for targeted customer segments, reveals how well a company is penetrating a desired market. For example, a company may temporarily be meeting sales growth objectives by retaining customers in nontargeted segments but not increasing its share in targeted segments. The measure of market share with targeted customers would balance a pure financial signal (sales) to indicate whether an intended strategy is yielding expected results.

When companies have targeted particular customers or market segments, they can also use a second market share–type measure: the account share of those customers' business (some analysts refer to this as the share of the "customers' wallet"). The overall market share measure, calculated as the volume of business done with targeted customers, could be affected by the total amount of business those customers are offering in a given period. That is, the share of business with the targeted customers could be decreasing because the customers are offering less business to all their suppliers. Companies can measure for each customer and for each segment how much of the customer's and market segment's business they are receiving. Such a measure provides a strong focus to the company when trying to dominate its targeted customers' purchases of products or services in categories that it offers.

## Customer Retention

Customer retention and loyalty can be measured by the rate at which a business unit retains or maintains ongoing relationships with its customers. Clearly, a desirable way for maintaining or increasing market share in targeted customer segments is to retain existing customers in those segments. The insights from research on customer loyalty and the service profit chain[1] have demonstrated the importance of **customer retention.** Many companies can readily identify all of their customers; such companies include, for example, industrial companies, distributors and wholesalers, newspaper and magazine publishers, computer on-line service companies, banks, credit card companies, and long-distance telephone suppliers. These companies can readily measure customer retention from period to period. Beyond just retaining customers, many companies will wish to measure customer loyalty by the percentage growth of business with existing customers.

## Customer Acquisition

Customer acquisition can be measured by the rate at which a business unit attracts or wins new customers and business. Companies seeking to grow their business will generally have an objective to increase their customer base in targeted segments. Customer acquisition could be measured by either the number of new customers or the total sales to new customers in the targeted segments. Many companies solicit new customers through broad, often expensive, marketing efforts. Examples include companies in the credit and charge card business, magazine subscriptions, cellular telephone service, cable television, and banking and other financial services. These companies can examine the number of customer responses to solicitations and the conversion rate—number of actual new customers divided by number of prospective inquiries. They can measure solicitation cost per new customer acquired and the ratio of new customer revenues per sales call or per dollar of solicitation expense.

## Customer Satisfaction

Both customer retention and customer acquisition are measures of outcomes; they indicate whether the company has been successful in meeting customers' needs. A measure of customer satisfaction provides a *leading* indicator of these outcomes; it is a feedback measure on how well the company is doing, at least with existing customers. Recent research has indicated that just scoring adequately on customer satisfaction is not sufficient for achieving high degrees of loyalty, retention, and profitability. Only when customers rate their buying experience as *completely* or *extremely* satisfied can the company count on their repeat purchasing behavior.[2]

Customer satisfaction measures do have some limitations. They assess attitudes, not actual behavior. Therefore satisfaction measures should not be the only customer-based measure used by an organization. Satisfaction measures will work best when they are used to indicate the critical factors necessary to generate repeat and new business. Customer satisfaction measures should be coupled with more-objective outcome measures of behavior such as customer retention and new customer acquisition.

## Customer Profitability

Success in the core customer measures of share, retention, acquisition, and satisfaction, however, does not guarantee strategic success. Obviously, one way to have extremely satisfied customers (and angry competitors) is to sell products with many features and services at very low prices. Because customer satisfaction and high market share are themselves only a means of achieving higher financial returns, companies will probably wish to measure not just the extent of business they do with customers but also the profitability of that business, particularly in targeted customer segments. This measure couples the Balanced Scorecard perspective with the activity-based cost approach described in Chapters 4 and 5, which permits companies to measure individual and aggregate **customer profitability.** Companies should want more than satisfied and happy customers; they should want profitable customers. A financial measure, such as customer profitability, helps to keep customer-focused organizations from becoming customer-obsessed.[3]

The customer profitability measure may reveal that certain targeted customers are unprofitable. Newly acquired customers are particularly likely to be unprofitable because the considerable sales effort to acquire a new customer has yet to be offset from the margins earned by selling multiple products and services. In these cases, lifetime profitability becomes the basis for deciding whether to retain or discourage currently unprofitable customers.[4] Newly acquired but unprofitable customers can still be valued because of their growth potential. But unprofitable customers who have been with the company for many years will likely require explicit action to cope with their incurred losses.

## Beyond the Core: Meeting Customer's Expectations

Once a company identifies its targeted customers, managers must determine what will cause these customers to purchase a product or service from the company. These factors will drive success with the core customer outcome measurements of satisfaction, acquisition, retention, and market and account share. For example, customers could value short lead times and on-time delivery. Or they could value a constant stream of innovative products and services. Or they could value a supplier able to anticipate their needs and capable of developing new products and approaches to satisfy those emerging needs. As noted in Chapter 8, these attributes are organized into three categories:

- Product/service attributes
- Customer relationship
- Image and reputation

Individual companies have developed their own ways of measuring attributes along these three dimensions, as a function of their strategy and their targeted customer segments.[5] In virtually all Balanced Scorecards, however, three dimensions stand out as particularly important: time, quality, and price. We discuss here representative measures that companies can use to develop time, quality, and price metrics for enhancing performance for targeted customers.

### Time

Time has become a major competitive weapon in today's competition. Being able to respond rapidly and reliably to a customer's request often is the critical skill for obtaining and retaining valuable customers' business. For example, Hertz's #1 Card enables busy travelers to walk off their arriving flight and go directly to their rented car, where the completed paper work has previously been placed, the trunk opened for luggage, and the car already air-conditioned in summer or heated in winter. Banks accelerate approval of mortgage and loan applications, reducing waiting times from weeks to minutes. Japanese auto manufacturers can deliver a newly ordered customized car to a consumer's driveway in less time (one week) than it takes the purchaser to obtain a valid parking sticker from government authorities for the vehicle. Companies competing on the time dimension can measure customer lead times, the time from when the customer initiates a request for a product or service until the time when the product or service has been delivered. Such a measure signals the importance of achieving and continually reducing lead times for meeting targeted customers' expectations.

Other customers may be more concerned with the reliability of lead times than with just obtaining the shortest lead times. For example, many shippers still prefer to use trucks rather than rail but not because trucks are cheaper or even faster for long-distance moves. Most railroads still cannot deliver reliably within the specified one day (or less) receiving window demanded by the customer, so many shippers (and their customers) would rather take a more expensive, even longer, transport medium that can guarantee arrival within a desired time interval. Such reliability is especially important for manufacturers who operate without inventories under a just-in-time discipline. Those companies want deliveries to their assembly plants to arrive within a one-hour time window. A late delivery will shut down an entire production facility that operates with zero inventories of raw materials and purchased parts. For service companies, think about the frustration of a consumer who has taken time off from work to be at home but then has to wait for hours because a promised delivery or installation is not made at the scheduled time or is not made at all. If reliable delivery is vital for important customer segments, then a measure of on-time delivery (OTD) will be a useful performance driver for customer satisfaction and retention.

The OTD measure should be based on the customer's expectations. Telling Honda or Toyota that your definition of "on-time" is ±1 day, when their production process can tolerate a delivery window no wider than $\pm 1$ hour, will not likely win you much business from these demanding companies.

Lead time is important not only for existing products and services. Some customers value suppliers who can offer a continual stream of new products and services. For such market segments, a short lead time for introducing new products and services could be a valued performance driver for customer satisfaction. This objective could be measured as the elapsed time from when a new customer demand has been identified to the time when the new product or service has been delivered to the customer. We will talk more about this time-to-market measure when discussing metrics for the innovation process.

## Quality

Quality was a critical competitive dimension during the 1980s and remains important to this day. By the mid-1990s, however, quality had shifted from a strategic advantage to a competitive necessity. Many organizations that could not reliably deliver defect-free products or services ceased to be serious competitors. Because of all the attention devoted to improving quality during the past 15 years, it may now offer limited opportunities for competitive advantage. It has become a hygiene factor; customers take for granted that their suppliers will execute according to product and service specifications. Nevertheless, for certain industries, regions, or market segments, excellent quality may still offer opportunities for companies to distinguish themselves from their competitors. In this case, customer-perceived quality measures would be highly appropriate to include in the Balanced Scorecard's customer perspective.

Quality measures for manufactured goods could be measured by incidence of defects, say parts-per-million (PPM) defect rates, as measured by customers. Motorola's famed $6\sigma$ program strives to reduce defects to fewer than 10 PPM. Frequently, third-party evaluations provide feedback on quality. The J.D. Power organization provides information and rankings on defects and perceived quality in automobiles and airlines. The Department of Transportation provides information on each airline's frequency of late arrivals and lost baggage incidents.

Other readily available quality measures include returns by customers, warranty claims, and field service requests. Service companies have a particular problem not faced by manufacturers. When a manufacturer's product or piece of equipment fails to work or satisfy the customer, the customer will usually return the product or call the company asking for repairs to be made. In contrast, when a quality failure occurs from a service company, the customer has nothing to return and usually no one responsive to complain to. The customer's response is to cease patronizing the service organization. The service organization may eventually note a decline in business and market share, but such a signal is delayed and, by that time, almost impossible to reverse. The organization will typically not even know the identity of customers who tried the service, were poorly treated, and then decided never to use that organization's services again. For this reason, several service organizations offer service guarantees.[6] This offer, to immediately refund not only the purchase price but generally a premium above the purchase price, provides several valuable benefits to the company. First, it allows them to retain a customer who otherwise might be lost forever. Second, it receives a signal about the incidence of defective service, enabling them to initiate a program of corrective action. And, finally, knowledge of the existence of the service guarantee provides strong motivation and incentives for the people delivering customer service to avoid defects that would trigger a request for the service guarantee. Companies with service guarantee programs can use the incidence and cost of service guarantees as a customer-based quality measure.

Quality can also refer to performance along the time dimension. The on-time delivery (OTD) measure, previously discussed, is actually a measure of the quality of the company's performance in achieving its promised delivery date.

### Price

With all the emphasis on time responsiveness and quality, one might wonder whether customers still care about price. One can be assured that whether a business unit is following a low-cost or a differentiated strategy, customers will always be concerned with the price they are paying for the product or service. In market segments in which price is a major influence on the purchasing decision, units can track their net selling price (after discounts and allowances) with those of competitors. If the product or service is sold after a competitive bidding process, the percentage of bids won, especially in targeted segments, will provide an indication of the unit's price competitiveness.

Even price-sensitive customers, however, may favor suppliers who offer not low prices but low costs to acquire and use the product or service. At first glance, one may think we are playing with semantics by distinguishing between low price and low cost, but real and important differences exist between them. Take a manufacturing company that is sourcing a key purchased part from a supplier. The low-price supplier may turn out to be an extremely high-cost supplier. The low-price supplier may deliver only in large quantities, thereby requiring extensive storage space and receiving and handling resources plus the cost of capital associated with buying and paying for the parts well in advance of when they are used. The low-price supplier may also not be a certified supplier; that is, the quality of the parts received may not be guaranteed to conform to the buyer's specifications. Therefore, the buying company has to inspect the incoming items, return those found to be defective, and arrange for replacement parts to arrive (which themselves have to be inspected). The low-price supplier may also not have a stellar on-time delivery capability. In that case, its failure to deliver reliably at scheduled times would make it necessary for the buying company to order well in advance of need and to hold protective stock in case delivery was not as expected. Late deliveries cause higher costs for expediting orders and rescheduling the plant around the missing items. And low-price suppliers may not be electronically connected to their customers, thereby imposing higher costs on customers when they order and pay for the purchased parts.

In contrast, a low-cost supplier may have a slightly higher purchase price but also the ability to deliver defect-free products, directly to the workstation, just in time, as they are needed. The low-cost supplier also enables customers to order and pay electronically. The buying company incurs virtually no costs for ordering, receiving, inspecting, storing, handling, expediting, rescheduling, reworking, and paying for parts purchased from this low-cost supplier. Some companies allow certain suppliers to replace their purchasing function, not taking ownership of parts until they are released, just-in-time, directly to a workstation. Suppliers should strive to organize their production and business processes so that they can be their customers' lowest-cost supplier. They may choose to compete along the cost (to the customer) dimension, not just by offering low prices and discounts.

Such a measure requires that the suppliers set an objective to minimize their customers' total costs for acquiring parts from them.

Companies in several industries have the opportunity to do even better than to become their customers' lowest-cost supplier. If the customer is an organization that resells purchased items to its own customers and consumers—such as a distributor, wholesaler, or retailer—the supplier can strive to become its customers' **most profitable** supplier. Using activity-based costing techniques, the supplier can work with its customers to build an ABC model that enables the customer to calculate the profitability by supplier. For example, Maplehurst, a frozen bakery goods company, works directly with its customers—in-store bakeries in supermarkets—to calculate profitability by different classes of products: purchased bread, cakes, and muffins, in-store prepared goods, and in-store-heated frozen bakery products (Maplehurst's product line). Maplehurst has been able to demonstrate to customers that the frozen (and subsequently in-store-heated) goods are among the most profitable in the product line, a discovery that invariably leads to increased business for Maplehurst.

The current battle between national-brand beverages, such as Coca-Cola and Pepsi-Cola, versus retail-brand private labels, such as Presidents' Choice and Safeway Select, is being fought on both sides by calculations for the retail grocery store to determine which products are more profitable for the store to stock and sell. The calculation is more complex than the traditional gross margin (net selling price less purchase price) used by most distributors, wholesalers, and retailers to calculate their profitability by product line or supplier. For example, the national-brand beverage companies deliver their product directly to the store and use their delivery people to stock the product on the shelves. The retail-brand beverage companies deliver their product to warehouses and require the store resources for receiving, handling, storing, delivery, and merchandising. But the national brands also tend to occupy some of the most visible and valuable space in the stores, whereas the retail-brand products occupy normal shelf space. So care must be taken to correctly and fully account for all costs when comparing the profitability of alternative suppliers.

The benefits, to the excellent supplier, from a customer's profitability calculation are enormous. What more powerful message can a company deliver to its customers than a demonstration that it is the most profitable supplier the customer has? Thus, companies supplying customers who stock and resell their products or services can drive customer satisfaction, loyalty, and retention by measuring the customers' profitability and striving to become a highly profitable supplier. Of course, the supplier must also balance this measure by calculating its own profitability of supplying each of its customers. Decreasing its own profitability to increase its customers' may lead to satisfied and loyal customers but not happy shareholders and bankers.

## INTERNAL BUSINESS PERSPECTIVE: OPERATIONS AND INNOVATION PROCESSES

Once a company has identified the critical factors required to attract, retain, and satisfy targeted customers, it can specify measures for the critical internal processes at which it must excel to deliver performance along the identified factors. As discussed in Chapter 8, companies typically have to be excellent at both the "long-wave" of value creation in their innovation process and the "short-wave" operating process. We start by focusing on operational excellence, characterized by performance measures of time, quality, and cost of internal operating processes.

## Operational Excellence: Time, Quality, and Cost Measurements

### Process Time Measurement

The value proposition being delivered to targeted customers often includes short response times as a critical performance attribute. Many customers strongly value short lead times, measured as the time elapsed from when they place an order until the time when they receive the desired product or service. They also value reliable lead times, as measured by on-time delivery. Manufacturing companies generally have two ways of offering short and reliable lead times to customers. One way is to have efficient, reliable, defect-free, short-cycle order fulfillment and production processes that can respond rapidly to customer orders. The other way is to produce and hold large stocks of inventory of all products so that any customer request can be met by shipments from existing finished goods inventory. The first way enables the company to be a low-cost and timely supplier. The second way usually leads to very high production, inventory carrying, and obsolescence costs, as well as to an inability to respond quickly to orders for nonstocked items (because the manufacturing processes are typically busy building inventories for normally stocked items). Because many manufacturing companies are attempting to shift from the second way of satisfying customer orders (producing large batches for just-in-case inventory) to the first way (producing small orders, just in time), reducing cycle or throughput times of internal processes becomes a critical internal process objective.

Cycle, or throughput, times can be measured many different ways. The start of the cycle can correspond to the time the:

1. Customer order is received
2. Customer order, or production batch, is scheduled
3. Raw materials are ordered for the order or production batch
4. Raw materials are received
5. Production on the order or batch is initiated

Similarly, the end of the cycle can correspond to the time the:

1. Production of the order or the batch has been completed
2. Order or batch is in finished goods inventory, available to be shipped
3. Order is shipped
4. Order is received by the customer

The choice of starting and ending points is determined by the scope of the operating process for which cycle time reductions are being sought. The broadest definition, corresponding to an order fulfillment cycle, would start the cycle with receipt of a customer order and would stop when the customer has received the order. A much narrower definition, aimed at improving the flow of physical material within a factory, could correspond to the time between when a batch is started into production and when the batch has been fully processed. Whatever definition is used, the organization would continually measure cycle times and set targets for employees to reduce total cycle times.

In many factories, processing time is less than 5 or 10% of throughput (or cycle) time; that is, for a total throughput time of one month (22 working days), less than eight hours of actual processing time may actually be required. During the remaining time, the part is waiting, either in storage or on the factory floor, or just before or just after a processing operation, until the next operation can be scheduled and the part fixtured into place. In an ideal JIT system, the throughput time for a part exactly equals its processing time. While this goal, just like zero defects, may be unattainable, it sets a target by which progress can be measured.

To motivate employees to achieve JIT operating processes, several organizations use a metric, manufacturing cycle effectiveness (MCE), defined as:

$$\text{MCE} = \frac{\text{processing time}}{\text{throughput time}}$$

This ratio is less than 1 because:

$$\text{Throughput time} = \text{processing time} + \text{inspection time} + \text{movement time} + \text{waiting/storage time}$$

The Japanese manufacturers who had led the way in devising and implementing JIT systems emphasize the importance of reducing throughput time by rewriting the above equation as

$$\text{Throughput time} = \text{value-added time} + \text{non-value-added time}$$

where *value-added time* equals processing time (the times during which work is actually being performed on the product); and *non-value-added time* represents the time the part is waiting, being moved, or being inspected. Many Japanese manufacturers also refer to the non-value-added time as *waste time* to highlight that no value is being created for the customer when the product is not being processed. The time has been wasted by inefficiencies in the manufacturing process.

Poor and uncertain quality are prime sources of delays. Time required to inspect parts, rework parts, replace a scrapped part by starting a new item into production, or wait for a machine breakdown to be repaired all contribute to lengthening throughput times. Thus, as a firm reduces its incidence of in-process failures, it can also reduce its production throughput time.

Perhaps the major source of delays in conventional manufacturing processes is producing quantities of products in excess of current demand. The traditional rationale for such excess production is the need to economize on setup and ordering costs. In effect, the existence of large setup and ordering costs makes small lot sizes uneconomical. Conventional wisdom in U.S. businesses and universities led managers to attempt to optimize lot sizes through the use of mathematical models. Engineers and operations analysts computed economic order quantities (EOQs) that seemingly provided an optimal balance among setup or ordering costs, storage and holding costs, and stockout costs. Needless to say, this treatment understated considerably the cost of creating inventory. Also, the large EOQ lot sizes led to substantial throughput delays—first to complete the batch production run and then to move it into storage until the subsequent processing operation could be freed up to handle the large batch of work.

The approach of attempting to optimize lot sizes was similar in philosophy to the erroneous search for the optimal number of defects in order to minimize manufacturing costs. Leading manufacturers no longer believe that a tradeoff exists between total manufacturing costs and defect rates, so they are now striving to continually reduce PPM (parts-per-million) defect rates. Analogously, many of these same companies are attempting to drive their setup times to zero.

Reliance on the EOQ formula had a further and more subtle insidious effect on production processes. Because people believed that the economics of lot sizes and setups had been well handled by the EOQ formula, little attention was paid to the time spent on setups or whether production orders were being completed on time. Toward the end of the month, when productions and sales quotas had to be met, or when an important customer complained bitterly about a delayed shipment, production specialists—called expediters—were empowered to "hot wire" a production order through completion, overriding the "scientifically" computed production plan.

The just-in-time philosophy takes a more dynamic view of how to optimize production. The EOQ formula accepted existing setup or ordering costs as given, and it attempted to choose lot sizes that were optimal with respect to those parameters. With the JIT approach, lot size is not optimized; it is minimized by attempting to drive setup times to zero. In JIT, inventory is viewed as a form of waste, a cause of delays, and a signal of production inefficiencies (in that mounds of inventory are created to buffer production stages from one another).

### Applying Process Time Measurements in Service Industries

Just-in-time production processes and the manufacturing cycle effectiveness (MCE) ratio were developed for manufacturing operations, but they are just as applicable to service companies. If anything, eliminating waste time in a service delivery process is even more important than in manufacturing companies, because consumers are increasingly intolerant of being forced to wait in line for service delivery.

Take an example from the banking industry. Many of us are familiar with the process of gaining approval for a mortgage application on a house that we wish to purchase. The process starts by showing up at a local bank branch and filling out an extensive application form that includes employment history, salary, assets and liabilities, as well as a description of the house. After we have completed the application, the bank employee thanks us for choosing her bank and then tells us that we can expect to hear in three to four weeks whether the mortgage application has been approved.

One bank vice president, well familiar with the normal cycle time of 26 days to process such requests, asked employees to keep track of how much time was spent actually processing the application during the 26 days. The answer turned out to be about 15 minutes of work, spread over 26 days: an MCE ratio of 0.0004 (0.25 hours/[26 days * 24 hours per day]) . The vice president set a target to reengineer the approval process so that it would take only 15 minutes from completion of the application to a decision. This target corresponded to an MCE of 1.0. Bank personnel could continue to do all of the value-added processing work but had to eliminate all the non-value-added waiting times. At first, all of the employees involved in the mortgage approval process claimed that this was an impossible target. Among other tasks, credit references had to be requested and confirmed, a process that took at least a week or two. Further study revealed that credit references could be accessed on-line for almost all possible customers. Much of the analytic work and approval routines could also be automated. A reengineered mortgage approval process, supported by enhanced information technology, was designed that yielded a decision within 15 minutes. After customers filled out the mortgage request, they were directed to a cafeteria for a cup of coffee, and by the time they returned, a decision was available.[7] A 15-minute one-stop mortgage approval process turned out to be highly attractive to a broad market segment of customers.

Similar studies in other service industries yielded similar conclusions: long cycle times for customer service during which actual processing time was remarkably low. Automobile rental companies and a few hotel chains have now automated, for targeted customer segments, all aspects of check-in and check-out, enabling valued customers to bypass all waiting in line when initially accessing the service and upon completion of the service delivery process. Thus, companies attempting to deliver products and services on demand to targeted customers can set objectives to have MCE ratios approach 1, thereby producing dramatically shortened lead times to customer orders.

## Process Quality Measurement

Almost all organizations today have quality initiatives and quality programs in place. Measurement is a central part of any quality program, so organizations are already familiar with a variety of process quality measurements:

- Process parts-per-million (PPM) defect rates
- Yields (ratio of good items produced to good items entering the process)
- First-pass yields
- Waste
- Scrap
- Rework
- Returns
- Percentage of processes under statistical process control

Service organizations, especially, should identify the defects in their internal processes that could adversely affect costs, responsiveness, or customer satisfaction. They can then develop customized measures of quality shortfalls. Chemical Bank, profiled in a case study in Chapter 8, as one of its measures of service quality, developed an index called Trailway to Trolls (trolls are unhappy customers) to indicate the defects in its internal processes that lead to customer dissatisfaction. The index included items such as:

- Long waiting times
- Inaccurate information
- Access denied or delayed
- Request or transaction not fulfilled
- Financial loss for customer
- Customer not treated as valued
- Ineffective communication

## Process Cost Measurement

Amidst all the attention to process time and process quality measurements, one might lose sight of the cost dimension of processes. Traditional cost accounting systems measure the expenses and efficiencies of individual tasks, operations, or departments. But these systems fail to measure costs at the process level. Typically, processes such as order fulfillment, purchasing, and production planning and control use resources and activities from several responsibility centers. Not until the advent of activity-based cost systems could managers obtain cost measurement of their business processes.

In general, ABC analysis will enable organizations to obtain process cost measurements that, along with quality and cycle time measurement, will provide three important parameters to characterize important internal business processes. As companies use either continuous improvement (such as total quality management) or discontinuous improvement (such as reengineering or business process redesign) of important internal business processes, the three sets of measurements—on cost, quality, and time—will provide data on whether the goals of these improvement programs are being achieved.

## Cost of Quality

Companies, during the 1980s, developed a measure, *cost of quality*, that integrated quality with cost considerations. Before 1980, quality advocates found it difficult to get senior management attention and commitment to a total quality control program. Although agreeing in principle that better quality was preferable to lesser quality, the executives still devoted their efforts to actions that promised immediate impact on short-term financial performance as measured by earnings per share and return on investment. Relative to these financial measures, improvements in quality represented an abstract, somewhat intangible, target.

To overcome this indifference to quality improvement, quality advocates devised a financial approach to quality that they hoped would capture the attention of senior, financially oriented managers. The cost of quality (COQ) approach collects all costs currently being spent on preventing defects and fixing them after they have occurred. The cost of quality, also called the cost of nonconformance, attempts to compute a single aggregate measure of all the explicit costs attributable to producing a product that is not within specifications. It is a comprehensive, plant- or companywide financial measure of quality performance.

The costs of nonconformance can be classified into four categories:[8]

1. Prevention: The costs of designing, implementing, and maintaining an active quality assurance and control system; includes the costs of design and process engineering, quality control systems, quality planning, and quality training

2. Appraisal: The costs of ensuring that materials and products meet quality conformance standards; includes the costs of inspecting raw materials and purchased parts, inspecting in-process and finished products, lab tests, quality audits, and field tests

3. Internal failure: The costs of manufacturing losses from materials and products that do not meet quality standards; includes the costs of scrap, repair, rework, upgrade, downtime, and discounts on sales of substandard parts and materials

4. External failure: The costs of shipping inferior-quality products to customers; includes the costs of handling customer complaints and claims, warranty and replacement costs, and freight and repairs of returned merchandise

The cost of quality metric typically includes only costs already being recorded somewhere in the company's cost system; not included are unrecorded or opportunity costs (such as lost future sales) or the difficult-to-measure costs of disruption caused by out-of-conformance purchased materials and produced goods. The goal of a cost of quality measurement exercise is simply to identify how much the organization is currently spending on quality. Most companies are surprised to learn that they are currently spending between 15% and 20% of sales revenue on quality-related costs. This figure can then be used as the lever to get top management's attention that perhaps this large amount can be reduced significantly by a wiser allocation among the four quality categories.

In particular, companies that have been paying little attention to quality, choosing implicitly to inspect quality in rather than to design it in, incur large costs in the internal and external failure categories (fixing bad items after they have been built). They also spend heavily in the appraisal category. One semiconductor company adopted a total quality control program after it estimated that it would need more inspectors than workers to achieve, under current operating procedures, the quality levels demanded by its customers. An electronics instrument company learned that it was far cheaper to detect and replace a faulty two-cent resistor at the start of the production process than to repair and perhaps replace the $5,000 piece of equipment containing this part, after the instrument had been installed at the customer's site.

Such companies discovered that by spending more in the prevention category, they could greatly reduce the amount spent in the internal and external failure categories. As product design, vendor relations, and process control improved (again by increasing investments in prevention), the companies could also substantially reduce the costs they incurred in the appraisal category. Far less inspection was required once quality was designed into products and processes. Thus, by monitoring total costs of quality and their distribution among the four categories, a company could assess the decline in total quality costs as it shifted efforts from inspection and repair back into prevention.

Although cost of quality measurement is attractive when used in the above fashion, it cannot be the sole basis for measuring the success of a total quality management program. First, as are most financial measures, it is a lagging indicator of quality efforts. Employees need continual feedback to guide their experiments to improve quality and eliminate waste. They cannot wait until the end of a reporting period to learn how successful they have been in their learning and improvement activities. Second, there is no long-run target for the "optimal" level of quality costs. Spending 15% to 20% of sales dollars on quality-related costs is clearly excessive, but the optimal level for cost of quality spending is unknown and undoubtedly varies from company to company. Companies have found that they can drive quality costs down to about 5% of sales, but further reductions may be counterproductive. Also, although there are high payoffs from initially shifting quality costs from the appraisal, internal failure, and external failure categories to the prevention category, the most desirable distribution among these four categories is unknown. Often, companies can, just by being more effective and efficient with their prevention programs, lower internal and external failure costs without having to increase spending on prevention and appraisal.[9] Furthermore, the allocation of quality costs in and among the four categories is a subjective exercise that requires reasonable but still arguable judgments. Thus, the data provide a useful managerial summary of quality efforts and progress, but they probably do not provide a good basis for performance evaluations.

Also, however the existing costs are aggregated among the four cost of quality categories, the total cost of producing bad-quality items will still be underestimated. Omitted from the calculation are the costs of disruption in operations caused by out-of-conformance purchases and production and the loss of sales caused by actual external failures and associated reputational effects. Although some of the cost of production scheduling, setups, and engineering change orders can be assigned to one or more of the categories, the implicit cost of factory confusion and excessive inventory levels may be difficult to track down.

In summary, the cost of quality measurement appears to be valuable to gain the attention of senior management: to make them aware of, first, how much the company is currently spending to produce out-of-conformance items and, second, how, by reallocating effort from detection and repair categories to prevention, it can realize substantial benefits. But nonfinancial quality measures (e.g., yield, PPM defect rates—both internal and external, and measures of scrap, rework, and unscheduled machine downtime) provide more timely, objective feedback to employees and serve as better targets for their quality improvement efforts.

### Supplier Relationships

For many companies, especially those in manufacturing assembly operations (such as electronics, optical equipment and instruments, automobile, aerospace, and agricultural equipment industries) and in retailing, success is driven by having superb suppliers and supplier relationships. These companies depend critically on their suppliers to achieve their price, quality, and lead time goals with customers. When excellent supplier relationships are critical for strategic success, companies develop supplier rating systems. The systems identify which vendors have been certified—for direct, on-floor delivery without inspection—and which vendors require inspection for incoming items. Quality measures, both the frequency of defects and the percentage of dollars defective, are computed and tracked for each vendor. In addition to such incoming quality measures, the company can track on-time performance and price trends.[10]

## Innovation Measures

For many companies, particularly those in pharmaceutical, semiconductor, computer, telecommunications, and chemicals industries, the value created during the innovation process may be even more important than the value created by operational excellence. For these companies, measures of excellence for the design and development processes for new products and services are particularly important.

During the product or service design and development processes, the organization's research and development group:

- Performs basic research to develop radically new products and services for delivering value to customers
- Performs applied research to exploit existing technology for the next generation of products and services
- Conducts focused development efforts to bring new products and services to market

Historically, little attention has been devoted to developing performance measures for product design and development processes. Such inattention could have been caused by several factors. Decades ago, when most organizations' performance measurement systems were designed, the focus was on manufacturing and operational processes, not on research and development. This was a rational focus since far more money was being spent in production processes than in R&D processes, and the key to success was efficient manufacture of high-volume products. Today, however, many organizations gain competitive advantage from a continued stream of innovative products and services, so the R&D process has become a much more important element of a business' value chain. The success of this process should be motivated and evaluated by specific objectives and measures.

The increased importance of the research and development process has also led to organizations' spending much more money in their R&D processes. In fact, some businesses spend more in their research, design, and development processes than they do to support their production and operating processes. Many companies' performance measurement systems, however, remain anchored to operational efficiencies rather than to the effectiveness and efficiency of their research and development processes.

Of course, the relationship between inputs expended (on salaries, equipment, and materials) during R&D processes and the outputs achieved (innovative products and services) is much weaker and less certain than in manufacturing processes, in which standards can relatively easily be established for the conversion of labor, materials, and equipment resources into finished goods. A typical product development process in the electronics industry could have two years of product development followed by five years of sales. So the first success indicator of a product's development process may not appear for three years (the first year after the initial year of sales). Manufacturing processes with cycle times measured in time intervals ranging from minutes to several days are much more amenable to the use of standards, yields, and a variety of productivity measures for evaluation and control. But difficulty in measuring the conversion of inputs to outputs in R&D should not prevent organizations from specifying objectives and measures for such a critical organizational process. Companies should not fall into the trap of "if you can't measure what you want then want what you can measure."

## Measures for Product Development

Despite the inherent uncertainty in many product development activities, consistent patterns can still be found that can be exploited in a measurement process. For example, pharmaceutical product development goes through a systematic, sequential process that starts with screening large numbers of compounds, then investigating promising ones in more detail, moving from laboratory to animal testing, shifting from animal testing to human testing, and then traversing through complex governmental review and certification processes. Each stage can be characterized by measures such as yields (number of compounds that successfully pass to the next stage divided by number of compounds that entered from the prior stage), cycle time (how long do compounds stay in a stage), and cost (how much was spent processing compounds in a stage). Managers can establish objectives to increase yields and reduce both cycle times and cost at each stage of the development process.

An electronics company did a root cause analysis of the high time and cost of its new product development process. The analysis revealed that the number one cause for long-time-to-market of new devices was products that failed to function properly the first time they were designed and hence had to be redesigned and retested, often several times. Therefore, the company retained time-to-market as a critical outcome measure for the product development process, but it added a performance driver measure: the percentage of products for which the first design of a device fully met the customer's functional specification. Another performance driver was the number of times the design needed to be modified, even slightly, before it was released for production. The company estimated that each design error cost $185,000. With an average of two errors per product introduced, and with 110 new products introduced each year, the total amount spent on design errors was about $40,000,000, an amount that represented more than 5% of revenue. Added to this calculation must be the value of sales lost from late market introduction of new products caused by the time delays of redesigning the products to eliminate the errors.

Hewlett-Packard engineers developed a metric called break-even time (BET) to measure the effectiveness of its product development cycle.[11] BET measures the time from the beginning of product development work until the product has been introduced and has generated enough profit to pay back the investment originally made in its development (see Exhibit 11-1). BET brings together in a single measure three critical elements in an effective and efficient product development process. First, for the company to break even on its R&D process, it must recover its investment in the product development process. So BET incorporates not only the outcome from the product development process but also the cost of the design and development process. It provides incentives to make the product development process more efficient. Second, BET stresses profitability. Marketing managers, manufacturing personnel, and design engineers are encouraged to work together to develop a product that meets real customer needs, including offering the product in an effective sales channel at an attractive price, at a cost that enables the company to earn profits that will repay the product development investment cost. And third, BET is denominated in time: It encourages the launch of new products faster than the competition so that higher sales can be earned faster to repay the product development investment.

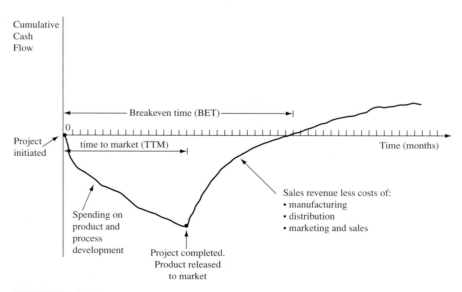

**EXHIBIT 11-1** Breakeven Time

## EMPLOYEE CAPABILITIES

The fourth perspective on a company's Balanced Scorecard focuses on employee capabilities. Investing to enhance the capabilities and performance of employees provides the platform for ongoing learning and improvement, a precondition for real future growth.

One of the most dramatic changes in management thinking during the past 15 years has been the shift in the role of organizational employees. In fact, nothing better exemplifies the revolutionary transformation from industrial age thinking to information age thinking than the new management philosophy of how employees contribute to the organization. The emergence of giant industrial enterprises a century ago and the influence of the scientific management movement left a legacy in which companies hired employees to perform well-specified and narrowly defined work. Organizational elites—the industrial engineers and managers—specified in detail the routine and repetitive tasks expected of individual workers and established standards and monitoring systems to ensure that workers performed them just as designed. Workers were hired to do physical work, not to think.

Today, almost all routine work has been automated: Computer-controlled manufacturing operations have replaced workers for routine machining, processing, and assembly operations, and service companies are, increasingly, giving their customers direct access to transactions processing through advanced information systems and communications. In addition, doing the same job over and over, at the same level of efficiency and productivity, is no longer sufficient for organizational success. For an organization just to maintain its existing relative performance, it must continually improve. And, if it wants to grow beyond today's financial and customer performance, adhering to standard operating procedures established by organizational elites is not sufficient. Ideas for improving processes and performance for customers must increasingly come from front-line employees who are closest to internal processes and the organization's customers. Standards for how internal processes and customer responses were performed in the past provide a baseline from which improvements must continually be made. They cannot be a standard for current and future performance. This shift requires major reskilling of employees so that their minds and creative abilities can be mobilized for achieving organizational objectives.

## Core Employee Measurement Group

We have found that most companies use employee objectives drawn from a common core of three outcome measurements. These core outcome measurements are then supplemented with situation-specific drivers of the outcomes. The three core employee measurements are:

- Employee satisfaction
- Employee retention
- Employee productivity

Within this core, the employee satisfaction objective is generally considered to be the driver of the other two measures, employee retention and employee productivity.

### Measuring Employee Satisfaction

The employee satisfaction objective recognizes that employee morale and overall job satisfaction are now considered highly important for most organizations. Satisfied employees are a precondition for increasing productivity, responsiveness, quality, and customer service. One company noticed early in its Balanced Scorecard implementation process that employees who scored highest in the satisfaction surveys tended to have the most satisfied customers. So companies that want to achieve a high level of customer satisfaction may need to have the customers served by satisfied employees.

Employee morale is especially important for many service businesses, in which, frequently, the lowest paid and lowest skilled employees interact directly with customers. Companies typically measure employee satisfaction with an annual survey or a rolling survey, in which a specified percentage of randomly chosen employees is surveyed each month. Elements in an employee satisfaction survey could include:

- Involvement with decisions
- Recognition for doing a good job
- Access to sufficient information to do the job well
- Active encouragement to be creative and to use initiative
- Support level from staff functions
- Overall satisfaction with company

Employees would be asked to score their feelings on a scale of 1 to 3 or 1 to 5, anchored at the low end with "Discontented" and at the high end with "Very (or Extremely) Satisfied." An aggregate index of employee satisfaction could then be calculated, with executives' having a drill-down capability to determine satisfaction by division, department, location, and supervisor.

### Measuring Employee Retention

Employee retention captures an objective to retain those employees in which the organization has a long-term interest. The theory underlying this measure is that the organization is making long-term investments in its employees, so any unwanted departure represents a loss in the intellectual capital of the business. Long-term, loyal employees carry the values of the organization, knowledge of organizational processes, and, we hope, sensitivity to the needs of customers. Employee retention is generally measured by percentage of key staff turnover.

### Measuring Employee Productivity

Employee productivity is an aggregate outcome measure of the impacts of employee skills and morale, innovation, internal process improvement, and customer satisfaction. The goal is to relate the output produced by employees to the number of employees used to produce that output. There are many ways in which employee productivity has been measured.

The simplest productivity measure is revenue per employee. This measure represents how much output can be generated by each employee. As employees and the organization become more effective in selling a higher volume and a higher value-added set of products and services, then revenue per employee should increase.

## Strategic Job Coverage

Several organizations, in different industries, have developed a new employee-based measure, the strategic job coverage ratio, for its reskilling objective. To calculate this ratio, managers must first define the set of skills that employees in critical front-line and managerial jobs must possess if they are to do that job effectively and deliver the organization's strategy from that organizational position. Then the managers must measure the knowledge and skills currently possessed by the employees in those positions and whether, with these skills and knowledge, they can deliver the key capabilities for achieving particular financial, customer and internal business process objectives. The strategic job coverage ratio is then calculated as the percentage of strategically critical jobs filled with qualified employees.

Usually, the strategic job coverage ratio reveals a significant gap between present competencies—as measured along dimensions of skills, knowledge, and attitudes—and future needs. This human resource staffing gap provides the motivation for strategic initiatives designed to close it. For organizations requiring massive reskilling, another measure could be the length of time required to take existing employees to the new, required levels of competency. If the massive reskilling objective is to be met, the organization itself must be skillful in reducing the cycle time required for each employee to achieve the reskilling.

## SUMMARY

Measures on customers, internal business processes—both operations and innovation—and employees provide companies with the leading indicators of creation of long-term economic value. Financial measures provide adequate indicators of past performance but fail to signal contemporary improvement or decrement in organizational capabilities. In this chapter, we identified how managers can select measures to help them communicate, motivate, and evaluate the drivers of future financial performance. Having a balanced set of financial and nonfinancial measures, explicitly derived from and linked to the business unit's strategy, will enable companies to manage both short- and long-term value creation.

## ENDNOTES

1.  F. F. Reichheld, *The Loyalty Effect* (Boston: Harvard Business School Press, 1996); F. F. Reichheld, "Learning from Customer Defections," *Harvard Business Review* (March–April 1996); and J. L. Heskett, W. E. Sasser, and L. A. Schlesinger, *The Service Profit Chain* (New York: Free Press, 1997).

2.  T. O. Jones and W. E. Sasser, "Why Satisfied Customers Defect," *Harvard Business Review* (November–December 1995), pp. 88–99.

3.  R. S. Kaplan, "In Defense of Activity-Based Cost Management," *Management Accounting* (November 1992), pp. 62–63.

4.  The interplay among customer acquisition, retention, and lifetime profitability is at the heart of the comprehensive measurement system proposed in Reichheld, *Loyalty Effect*, chapter 8. The approach advocated by Reichheld, including explicit incorporation of the value drivers to and from the customer, is highly compatible with the approach we have articulated for the customer perspective of the Balanced Scorecard.

5.  See examples in R. S. Kaplan and D. P. Norton, *The Balanced Scorecard: Translating Strategy into Action* (Boston: Harvard Business School Press, 1996), pp. 73–84.

6.  C. Hart, "The Power of Unconditional Service Guarantees," *Harvard Business Review* (July–August 1988), pp. 54–62; J. Heskett, E. Sasser, and C. Hart, *Service Breakthroughs: Changing the Rules of the Game* (New York: Free Press, 1990).

7. Some aspects of the application could not be verified within 15 minutes. An approval decision was made contingent on the information supplied on the application being valid, including employment history, salary, and market value of purchased house. This information would be confirmed during the next several days. But the analytic work and the credit record check could be accomplished within the 15-minute processing window.

8. See W. Morse and H. P. Roth, "Let's Help Measure and Report Quality Costs," *Management Accounting* (August 1983), pp. 50–53; J. Clark, "Costing for Quality at Celanese," *Management Accounting* (March 1985), pp. 42–46; and W. Morse and H. P. Roth, *Quality Costs* (Montvale, NJ: National Association of Accountants, 1987).

9. C. D. Ittner, "Exploratory Evidence on the Behavior of Quality Costs," *Operations Research* (January–February 1996), pp. 114–30.

10. See C. D. Ittner and L. P. Carr, "Measuring the Cost of Ownership," *Journal of Cost Management* (Fall 1992), pp. 42–51.

11. C. H. House and R. L. Price, "The Return Map: Tracking Product Teams," *Harvard Business Review* (January–February 1991), pp. 92–100; also M. L. Patterson, "Designing Metrics," in *Accelerating Innovation: Improving the Process of Product Development* (New York: Van Nostrand Reinhold, 1993).

## ■ *PROBLEMS*

### *11-1*

The Stoneland Company was in the construction business. In building its Balanced Scorecard, managers interviewed many of its current and potential customers. They found that some customers were highly price-sensitive and wanted to continue business as usual. These customers developed internally all the specifications for their bids, put the detailed bidding document out to tender, and chose, from among all qualified suppliers, the one submitting the lowest bid. As one price-sensitive customer said during an interview:

> We don't have the resources of time for doing anything fancy with our suppliers. Our business has become ruthlessly competitive, with price and margin reductions in recent years, and the need for us to cut costs wherever we can. We can't afford to choose anyone but the lowest-price supplier.

Historically, Stoneland competed by attempting to be the selected low-price bidder for price-sensitive customers.

But the interviews also revealed that several large and important customers were looking for more than low price from their most valued supplier of construction services. They said:

> We have to cut costs wherever we can. But we are looking to our suppliers to help us in this goal. If it's cheaper and more effective for them to take over some of our engineering functions, we should let them do that, and reduce our internal engineering staffs accordingly. We don't have any special capabilities in construction. We want suppliers that can suggest new ways of doing business, and who can develop improved technologies for this task. Our best suppliers of engineering and construction services will anticipate our needs and suggest creative ways to meet these needs through new technologies, new project management approaches, and new financing methods.

These companies acknowledged that rapidly changing technology and an increasingly competitive marketplace for their final products had motivated them to look to their suppliers for innovative ways to lower their costs. Although price would still be a factor, a supplier's ability to offer innovative and more cost-effective approaches would be a strong influence on supplier selection. Stoneland referred to these companies as those wanting *differentiated services*.

### Required

(1) How would the customer and internal business process perspectives of Stoneland's Balanced Scorecard differ, depending on whether it selected the price-sensitive or differentiated services customer types as the target for its future strategy? Be specific about how the measures would differ depending upon which strategy Stoneland followed.

(2) What new internal business processes would Stoneland have to perform very well if it wanted to meet the expectations of its customers wanting differentiated services?

## 11-2

Kenyon Stores, a large clothing retailer, developed an image of who its targeted customers were.

- Range: 20- to 40-year-old female (target: 29 years)
- College-educated
- Works full-time in professional executive position
- Innovatively fashionable
- Self-confident, great sense of humor

It then communicated this targeted customer image externally, through a variety of advertising and in-store promotional materials.

By communicating a clear image to potential customers, the store enabled its existing and future customers to imagine themselves as fitting an image associated with purchasing clothes at Kenyon Stores. The company creates for its customers an image of who they can be, in addition to selling them fashionable clothing of high quality at reasonable prices.

Kenyon Stores started the development of its customer objective by defining a customer strategy:

1. Kenyon must increase its customer share of wardrobe
2. Increased share of wardrobe will be achieved by *customer loyalty*: "We want the customer to visit us throughout the year and come to Kenyon for the complete range of her lifestyle needs."
3. To create this loyalty:
   - Our *Merchandise* must define our customer, her needs, and her aspirational image
   - Our *Brand* must satisfy the customer's aspirational and lifestyle goals
   - Our *Shopping Experience* must promote customer loyalty
4. We must do a superb job of defining who our customers are and their buying behavior.

Kenyon identified three objectives as key product attributes for its consumers' value proposition: price, fashion, and quality. The price objective was stated as: "Provide fashion and quality that the customers perceive as high-value and consider to be fairly priced." The fashion objective was to: "Provide fashionable merchandise that satisfies our customer's aspirational and wardrobe needs within the Kenyon brand." The quality objective was to: "Ensure the highest quality and consistency of fit both within a style and across all product categories."

The shopping experience dimension was considered extremely important. Key attributes were availability of merchandise and the in-store shopping experience. The instore shopping experience dimension was captured by an explicit vision of the six elements of the "perfect shopping experience":

1. Great looking stores with fashion impact
2. Customer welcomed by attractive associates, fashionably dressed, with a smile on their faces
3. Clear communication of special sales
4. Associates with good product knowledge
5. Personal name recognition by attending associate
6. A sincere thanks and an invitation to return soon

The goal was to deliver the six elements every time the customer enters a store.

Kenyon had constructed a very specific definition of its "ideal shopper." The ideal shopper image communicated to all employees the fashion expectations of their customers. The brand image objective for Kenyon was stated as: "We will build Kenyon into a dominant national brand by clearly understanding our target customer and differentiating ourselves in meeting her needs."

### Required

Select appropriate measures for Kenyon's customer and internal business process perspectives.

## 11-3

Consider a semiconductor manufacturer, competing in an industry with extremely rapid technological change. What measures might be appropriate for such a company's innovation process?

## 11-4

In the chapter, we discussed the use of several measures of the innovation process, including *percentage of sales from new products* and the *breakeven time* (BET) metric. Although both measures are attractive for communicating the economics and benefits from successful product development processes, each also has some limitations and dysfunctional consequences if managers focus too narrowly on them as a performance measure. Identify the potential limitations and weaknesses of both these outcome measures of the new product development process.

## 11-5    *The Way Things Were*

"Hi, John. How are things going out on the line?"

"Hi, Fred. Not bad, not bad at all, though I had to be careful the last couple of days. Someone from IE standards was following me around and I had to go back and work the way we used to do it. I didn't want to get him all upset by seeing the new way we go about our jobs."

"What do you mean? Have you found a new way to sandbag without them noticing?"

"Not at all. We're working smarter, thanks to our department manager, Monty. It all started several months ago when our output went way down even though all the efficiency measures said we were on target."

"How can that occur?"

"Basically, Monty discovered that most of our time was not spent working on producing good items. Let me give you an example. For one of our products we have to perform four welds to attach some metal parts together. We have detailed standards telling us how long it should take to do each step.

"One day, Monty watched Mike do these welds. Everything was done by the numbers. Mike walked over to the WIP storage area, picked out enough parts to prepare 10 products, put them on a dolly, and wheeled them over to his workstation. Then he read the job card telling what he had to do and which tools were needed. He grabbed the right tools from his tool crib, set his jig to fixture the parts into place, and proceeded to weld the parts together into the 10 units. After finishing the 10 units, Mike inspected them all, rejecting one because the hole in one of the parts had been drilled incorrectly in a previous operation, put the nine good parts on the dolly, wheeled them to the next storage area, and then put the one rejected part into the rework area.

"The whole process took about 100 minutes from start to finish—100 minutes to produce nine good subassemblies. But then Monty watched what happened to the nine items Mike had just finished. An inspector in a white coat was testing the welds in some kind of new X-ray device we had bought and ended up rejecting two more subassemblies. Then another guy came around to put tags on the two rejected items with a brief description of the problem and then took them to the rework area. And that wasn't all. Monty noticed someone counting inventory to make sure it corresponded to the job card attached to the batch and other people doing tests on tools and fixtures. There were more people checking work and moving parts than there were actually doing the work.

"Monty went bananas. He called over one of the IEs who (unfortunately for him) happened to be walking by at the time. Monty yelled at him, 'I just watched one of my workers spend 100 minutes to weld parts for 10 subassemblies, and three of them were rejected after finishing, 100 minutes to get seven good parts, 28 good welds. Near as I can tell, each weld takes about one minute to do. Is this normal—to spend 100 minutes to get 28 good welds?'

"The IE attempted to explain to Monty about scientific management and how standards for work and productivity were computed. First the IE confirmed Monty's observation. The standard time to do one weld is 1 minute and 7 seconds. But there were standards for getting the parts and fixturing them into place, standards for assembling and preparing tools, standards for inspection and small repairs, and standards for moving the parts to the next storage area. They even had an allowance for break time and idle time due to line imbalances. Everything had been measured and accounted for. In fact, the total standard time for the 10 units that Mike had done came to 108 minutes, so Mike's 100 minutes was considered good performance—about an 8% productivity improvement.

"This really got Monty riled up. Monty figured that he got 28 good welds from Mike which, according to the IE's standards, should have taken a little over 30 minutes. So right away, Monty figures that productivity was only around 30% of what's possible, not the 108% the IE was attempting to explain to him. Then he started thinking about all the other people who were standing around inspecting and moving things but who never did any work on the parts themselves. By the time he finished estimating the number of people he had in quality control, maintenance, and storing and handling things, he figured that there was at least one indirect worker for each guy like Mike who actually worked on products. Therefore actual productivity was only about half the 30% he computed initially."

"I can imagine he was upset. But what did he do about it?"

"Monty had the QC people analyze what caused the problems with the two parts that had been rejected after Mike had welded them. It turned out the materials were not exactly within specification and therefore didn't take the welds the way they were supposed to. So Monty took off down to the purchasing department to see why substandard materials had gotten through the system. He found out that this particular batch of materials had been bought from a new supplier. The purchasing guy was spending all his time trying to lower costs, and he had just uncovered this new vendor who agreed to supply parts 4% cheaper than the standard purchase price. I wish I had been there when the head of purchasing attempted to explain to Monty why it was cheaper to buy from this new supplier, when 20% of the subassemblies eventually had to be reworked or scrapped."

"All that running around and screaming couldn't have made Monty very popular."

"Wait—he wasn't finished. A few days later, a rush job that was already several weeks late got delayed further when a machine broke down in the middle of the run. It took maintenance people several days to get replacement parts and another couple of days to install them and get the machine running properly again. During this time, when everyone was waiting for the repairs so that we could finish the job, Monty dispatched a couple of workers to find out when the machine had last been serviced. Apparently there is a schedule for preventive maintenance, but the shop had been so busy that no one wanted to interrupt work to do maintenance; so it had gotten delayed and eventually the maintenance department had apparently forgotten to reschedule it. This didn't bother the maintenance foreman too much because his people were so busy responding to emergencies, like the one we had, that they didn't have much time to do regularly scheduled maintenance.

"Many of the foremen don't like to have maintenance done on their shift either. They get evaluated by labor and machine efficiency; some kind of ratio of earned hours to hours actually paid. A sure way to get the plant accountants sending nasty letters to you is to stop producing items in order to grease the machines and replace some parts that haven't worn out yet. The accountants claim this kind of work lowers efficiency, since nothing is getting produced and the workers are idle."

"I bet Monty had his hands full doing battle with the purchasing and maintenance departments."

"Not quite. He's a scrappy fellow who doesn't let a few disagreements stop him from doing what he thinks is right. Last month he took off after his monthly performance report. I don't understand all the details of what's in these reports or how they're calculated, but he started muttering about space charges. I think that lots of overhead costs get charged to departments on the basis of the space they take up in the factory. Monty wanted to know why the department occupied so much space. He dragged in one of the IEs and had him do a quick study on how much room was needed for the machines and the people who actually worked on the product. Less than 25% of the space was taken up for machines and workers. What really set him off again was learning that the testing and rework area took up about as much space as the productive workers and machines. Monty thought it dumb that as much space was used to test for and store bad items as to produce good items."

"Sounds like you've had an interesting few months here."

"You better believe it. I've seen more changes in the last few months than we've had in the past 20 years."

### Required

What operating changes do you think Monty instituted? What changes in the accounting and measurement system would be necessary to support the operating changes?

## 11-6   *General United*

Brad Lawrence, CEO of General United, a conglomerate consisting of a dozen companies in different industries, was wondering whether cycle time should be included in the Balanced Scorecards of his operating companies. Currently, the senior managers of each company were building Balanced Scorecards that would be used to assess their strategies and to measure their performance.

One company, GND Machinery, manufactured machinery for packaging companies. GND's customers, the packaging companies, often had difficulty in estimating the demand from their customers, so they greatly valued suppliers who could provide equipment with short lead times. Lawrence felt that if GND Machinery could reduce the time it took to produce machinery to fulfill customer orders, then sales and market share would increase, perhaps dramatically.

At the other extreme, General's defense company, Bradley Aerospace, produced long-lead-time products and systems for government contracts. According to the contract terms, Bradley got no benefit from early delivery, and the contracts allowed for reimbursement of Bradley's inventory holding costs.

A third General United company, Harvest Unlimited, produced agricultural machinery. Harvest's customers generally placed orders only at the beginning of the planting season, a two-month period during the spring. Currently, the lead time to produce Harvest's products was well in excess of two months, so virtually all production was based on sales forecasts, attempting to anticipate the volume and mix of customer orders. Often the forecasts were inaccurate, leading to high inventory and obsolescence of unordered machines, as well as shortages when demand for particular machines greatly exceeded the forecast. If the production cycle time could be reduced below the two-month ordering window,

Harvest could shift some of its production schedule from producing based on forecasts to producing based on actual customer orders.

***Required***

What role should lead time play in the Balanced Scorecards of the three operating companies?

## 11-7

Some companies use revenue per employee as a simple and easy-to-understand productivity measure of its employees.

(1) Why would revenue per employee represent a useful measure of employee productivity and capabilities?

(2) What limitations or dysfunctional consequences could arise from using revenue per employee as an employee productivity measure? How could these be overcome?

## 11-8    *National Aerospace Group—Measuring Vendor Performance (C. Ittner)*

National Aerospace Group (NAG) is a leading manufacturer of military and commercial aircraft and components. With the recent consolidation in the defense industry, National Aerospace faces increasing pressure to reduce costs and improve quality. One of the largest opportunities for cost reduction and quality improvement is in materials costs, which make up 70% of the firm's cost structure. A recent study revealed that 50% of the more than 100,000 receipts from suppliers during the previous year had paperwork or hardware discrepancies or did not meet delivery schedules. These problems were conservatively estimated to cost National Aerospace $20 million annually.

The obvious need for better quality and on-time delivery from suppliers led to the development of the Supplier Performance Rating System. The system measures the added administrative costs that NAG incurs to resolve suppliers' hardware, paperwork, and delivery deficiencies. Each type of nonconformance "event" is assigned a standard cost based on a study of the hours required to resolve the problem. The number of events over the previous year is multiplied by the associated standard cost to obtain the total cost of nonconformance. A supplier performance index (SPI) is then calculated as follows:

$$\text{SPI} = \frac{\text{nonconformance costs } + \text{ purchases}}{\text{purchases}}$$

The SPI is used to determine the total "cost of ownership" when selecting suppliers. For example, if the quoted price is $100 per unit and the supplier's SPI is 1.2, a value of $120 per unit is used in the supplier selection process. The 20% markup reflects the additional quality-related costs that NAG expects to incur if this supplier is selected. In addition to the SPI system, NAG conducts annual supplier audits to assess their technical and manufacturing capabilities and their assistance in cost reduction and new product development efforts. Audit scores range from a low of 0 to a high of 100.

NAG's purchasing department has just received four bids for a critical component needed for the firm's new commercial aircraft. Three of the bids are from existing suppliers; the fourth is from a highly recommended new supplier. The information in Table 1 is available on the four suppliers:

Nancy Gilbert, the head of purchasing, has called a meeting with the managers of engineering and manufacturing to review the bids. One issue is the lack of performance history on Delta Products. Discussions with other companies that have used all four suppliers indicate that Delta had the highest quality and best on-time delivery. NAG's purchasing procedures, however, require new suppliers to either be the low bidder or to have the lowest cost of ownership using the average SPI for all the bidders with performance history.

A second issue is Alpha's low audit score. Robert Bilsland, the manager of engineering, is adamant that audit scores should be considered in the decision. "Beta may have bid 15% higher than Alpha, but Beta has given us a lot more assistance in cost reduction efforts and product development. This is reflected in Beta's audit score, which is 40 points better than Alpha's audit score. We should weight audit scores at least 50% when selecting the supplier."

Given the importance of this component and the large number of units that need to be purchased, the managers realize that the contract should go to the supplier offering the best overall value to NAG, rather than the lowest quoted price.

### Required

(1) Calculate the adjusted bids from Alpha, Beta, and Gamma after taking into account the SPI. On the basis of the cost of ownership, which supplier is the lowest cost?

(2) Calculate the adjusted bid from Delta using the average SPI for Alpha, Beta, and Gamma. How does this adjusted bid change the supplier selection decision? Should this method be used for evaluating bids from new suppliers?

(3) Assume that NAG decides to place a 50% weight on audit scores and a 50% weight on the SPI-adjusted bids. Also assume that Delta would receive the average audit score from the other three bidders. Would these conditions change the supplier selection decision? Should the supplier audit be considered in the selection process?

## TABLE 1

| | STANDARD COST PER EVENT | ALPHA | BETA | GAMMA | DELTA |
|---|---|---|---|---|---|
| Quoted price/unit | | $100 | $115 | $130 | $105 |
| Purchasing History | | | | | |
| Total purchases | | $250,000 | $200,000 | $750,000 | $0 |
| Number of events | | | | | |
| Documentation errors | $ 79 | 5 | 0 | 2 | N/A |
| Return to supplier | 300 | 2 | 0 | 0 | N/A |
| Rework | 837 | 8 | 5 | 0 | N/A |
| Undershipment | 350 | 1 | 2 | 0 | N/A |
| Overshipment | 112 | 0 | 1 | 1 | N/A |
| Late delivery (weeks) | 500 | 8 | 2 | 0 | N/A |
| Audit score | | 60 | 100 | 80 | N/A |

## ■ *CASES*

# Draper Instruments*

At exactly two o'clock on the afternoon of February 8, 1992, Bill Wilcox, Manufacturing Manager of Draper Instruments, stepped into the conference room, motioned for quiet, and began to speak.

> As you know, we're here to discuss the possibility of introducing a new system of production control, Toyota's Just-in-Time system. All of you, I hope, have reviewed the materials that I sent around last week, outlining the project and providing a brief description of how the system works in Japan. Since this is our first meeting, I'd like to spend the next few hours reviewing the major elements of Just-in-Time and considering how it might be applied in Draper.
>
> To help answer your questions, I've invited Mark Kraft to join us at today's meeting. Mark is the president and founder of a consulting firm specializing in operations planning and control, as well as a leading expert on inventory management.
>
> I suppose some introductions are in order now. Working clockwise around the table, we have Sam Magnuson, manager of production control; David Petty, manager of planning; Bob Colson, a production control supervisor; Eric Samuels, first-line supervisor; and Henry Nelson, manager of shop operations.
>
> One final comment before I give Mark a chance to speak. You all know that inventory has been a perennial problem for us and that something must be done to bring inventory levels down. That's the whole purpose of this project. My personal view, after visiting a number of Japanese factories, is that our goals are relatively modest. We're shooting for a reduction in inventory from the present level of $6.2 million to $2.1 million after three years,

with a further reduction to $1.4 million or less after five years. Some of the Japanese companies we visited carried only six to eight days worth of inventory; many didn't even have stockrooms. I don't see why we can't do as well.

## *Plant Issues*

Most of Draper's hourly workers were paid on an incentive wage system, based on piece rates that had not been reviewed for several years. Standards were tighter for some parts than for others. Because workers normally had considerable autonomy in the parts they chose to make, they often focused on those with the loosest standards rather than on those that were in the greatest demand. The result was excess supplies of some parts and shortages of others. One product, for example, which an experienced worker could make at 150% of standard, had an inventory level estimated at six weeks' usage under normal demand conditions. One plant employee, commenting on the problem, observed: "How can anyone keep them [the workers] from making whatever they want? All of the materials they need are right there on the floor. The supervisor would have to watch every move those guys made to keep them making the right parts. And the union certainly won't stand for such intervention all of a sudden." In fact, several managers had noted a strong correlation between the tightness of standards and the percentage of time that parts appeared on the critical list (indicating a parts shortage).

Sheet metal welders, who were the most highly paid and most senior group of hourly workers, presented an additional problem.

---

*Adapted from General Electric—Thermocouple Manufacturing (A), Harvard Business School case 9-684-040, and (B), Harvard Business School case 9-685-002.

Several managers suspected that they were using the incentive system to their own advantage. Because the rate for reworking defective parts was higher than the rate for welding them in the first place, welders benefited from building in their own defects. As one manager noted: "Although the welding equipment that the welders have to work with isn't the greatest, I don't see how there could be a 22% defect rate without some help from them. But what can we do? No one has supervised those guys for years."

Managers believed that the emphasis placed on efficiency ratings had even encouraged foremen to bypass the production control system. For example, raw materials for resistors were left unmonitored on the shop floor. Because the foreman in charge of resistor assembly had ready access to these materials, and because he wished to maintain a high efficiency rating, he had instructed his people to make resistors every time they were without other work. Only when the inventory numbers rose steadily for two months in a row did Wilcox discover the problem. By then, $55,000 worth of resistors had been built (out of a total inventory on hand of $160,000). Moreover, demand for this type of resistor was expected to cease in December 1993, leaving $38,000 worth of obsolete parts

In addition to internal workforce issues, Draper's most important supplier, whose quality and reliability had historically been high, was currently in decline. Rumors were circulating that the plant was soon to be closed. Draper's management, however, did not feel that replacement suppliers should be approached until there was some official announcement about the supplier's future.

### Inventory Management

Draper used a production control system, called the Inventory Control Package (ICP), to manage inventories. ICP was a variant of material requirements planning (MRP), in that it exploded backward to determine raw materials needs. The system had been ordered from an outside consulting firm, which had not fully integrated it into Draper's operations. In-house systems people had therefore found it necessary to introduce modifications. Many of these changes were undocumented, and the people who had introduced them were no longer at Draper.

Production was planned on a monthly basis. Therefore, workers could theoretically be building product up to four weeks ahead, adding that much more work-in-process inventory. If production were planned on a weekly basis, the problem would be greatly reduced. However, the production planning department was not optimistic about this approach. One manager commented: "Those guys can't even level a monthly schedule! How do they expect to level a weekly one?"

One of Draper's most important customers contributed to the volatility in scheduling. In the past, this customer had been unwilling to commit in advance to a preset schedule. It wanted to preserve its ability to respond to last-minute orders. It was primarily these orders that caused the production schedule for finished instruments to be difficult to predict.

Materials control was relatively loose once materials left the stockroom (Draper's staff had nicknamed the shop floor "no man's land" because goods seemed to disappear there without a trace), so it was difficult to know the accuracy of the inventory balances reported by the ICP. The system was reinitialized every two months to clear old information from the computer, but this process did not reflect goods already on the shop floor. Once these goods left the stockroom, there was no further accounting of them until the yearly physical inventory. For one instrument, inventory on the production floor was estimated at between $300,000 and $315,000, approximately 80% to 85% of the total inventory on hand for that particular product line.

Loss factors, representing the percentage of raw materials expected to end up as scrap, had not been reviewed for several years. These normally reflected either yield losses on the production floor or rejects from incoming inspection. In 1991, these losses totaled 6.3% of sales. However, certain items were being purchased in as much as double the actual quantity needed because the yield on their processes had been only 50% when loss factors were initially established. Over the years, many of these processes had been streamlined; yields had often improved dramatically, although loss factors had not been similarly adjusted.

### The Meeting

Mark Kraft glanced around the room as he waited for a response to his comment. In the brief silence that followed, he added, "I'd like to walk out of this room with two things: a first cut at the problems that we're going to encounter when this program is implemented and a reasonable action plan, with responsibilities assigned to specific people. I'd also appreciate comments about what you perceive as being *good* about the plan."

David Petty jumped in. "I feel that the biggest problem will be with our vendors. It just doesn't make sense to talk about improving quality when our vendors are so unreliable. They neither produce good pieces nor deliver them on time.

"Our best vendor is having problems with a microcontroller, one of the most important parts we purchase. Just imagine what would happen if we were on a just-in-time system and the microcontroller or some other vendor quality problem came up. With the inventory reductions that you're describing, we would have to shut down the line. Are we really willing to take such risks? Our customers wouldn't be very happy with us if our delinquency rate went any higher.

"Talking about the Japanese and their great quality with so little inventory—do they have as much pressure to meet output goals as we do? Working in the shop, production comes first, with quality way behind. We would like quality to be better, but right now, output is the driver. Hell, even you Bill, as excited as you are about inventory levels and as much as you want to improve quality, know that when it comes to the bottom line, you've got to meet the shipment schedule. In other words, our next promotion has a lot more to do with meeting shipments than with improving quality or reducing inventory."

Magnuson interrupted: "Don't we share some of the blame? Don't we keep changing the schedule? We should establish and then stick to a six- to eight-month schedule, but we're willing to change at the drop of a hat."

Wilcox nodded, then added: "Let me give an example. An important customer has just submitted a request that would make us delinquent for the month of January. Originally, we were supposed to build 30 instruments. On January 7, they came in and told us to build 65 in January and 50 a month in February, March, and April, rather than the 30 originally planned. They don't want anything in August, September, or October, but a lot more in November, then none in December because they don't want a high year-end inventory. That's the kind of schedule changes we deal with regularly. What's important is not that we get these occasionally but that we get them on the average of one a week."

Mark Kraft rejoined the discussion at this point: "We should probably spend some time discussing your production process. How much will the current process have to change to adapt to just-in-time?"

"In the future, people will have to be more versatile," said Nelson. "Believe it or not, we've already started in that direction. We're now doing a lot more cross-training."

Wilcox observed: "In Japan, the most we saw were six labor grades, and they didn't even use the first one. We have 250–300 grades in this plant alone. In the assembly area alone, we have 12–18 grades, with hourly wages ranging from $8.60 to $10.62."

"We need to reduce setup costs," said Nelson. "That's the only way that we will be able to reduce our lot sizes. For example, one of our insertion machines requires three hours of setup time for a typical run of eight hours. We'll have to completely change our thinking in this area. Until now, we've always assumed that large lot sizes were the key to profitability." ⮑ high cost

"What kind of gains could be achieved if setup times were reduced from 3 hours to 10 minutes?" asked Kraft.

"It's impossible," said Nelson.

Kraft went on: "Let's take an example to see if that's true. How long does it take you to change a flat tire on your car?"

"More than an hour," Samuels laughed.

"How long does it take to change the tire of a racing car competing in the Indianapolis 500?"

"That's different. They have trained crews. It takes them only about 15 seconds," said Nelson.

"Then," continued Kraft, "why couldn't you make similar improvements in manufacturing? Couldn't you set up a special team to do setups? Or break down the tasks and have some performed in advance?"

"It could be done in stamping," replied Samuels. "We would have to set up a special rate for the setup team, but I guess that's not impossible."

Magnuson added, "I hear that the workers in Japan do a lot of the thinking about reducing setup times. Perhaps there's some way for us to get more input from our workers."

Wilcox noted: "In one plant we visited in Japan, there were 88 suggestions from each employee each year, even though workers received only token payments for their contri-

butions. Management tried to respond to all suggestions within a month. Those inputs from the workers can make a big difference."

"Let me introduce a new subject," suggested Kraft. "Tell me about your reject rates."

Nelson replied: "As you might expect, they vary by stage in the production process. In-process rejections, between subassembly and final assembly, run about 15%. At final inspection, the reject rate is 5%. In the field, the rate is less than 1%. That's not strictly accurate because we rework a lot before parts get to the in-process stage. At some early fabrication steps, our yield is only 60%. The major cause of this low yield is environmental contamination."

Samuels disagreed: "No, the problem is in the printed circuit boards. If you take 10 boards, no two are the same. That's why we have inconsistent quality. It's a vendor problem."

"What if," asked Kraft, "we could get the yield losses at that operation down to 25%, at final inspection to 2%, and in the field to less than 0.5%? What would that mean?"

"Great savings! Productivity increases, better product, lower inventories," enthused Samuels. "I think that we should set some goals that will get us moving in that direction."

Kraft stood up to terminate the meeting. "We've asked some very tough questions today, and you've been honest and open in your responses. If this project is going to work, that honesty will have to continue. Part of your job will be to lower the walls that now exist between the various functions represented here. You'll need to encourage a lot more cooperation for the common good. Somehow, Bill will have to figure out a way to reward you for your performance. He'll do that. But if you continue to develop cooperation and trust, you have a great opportunity. You're trying to discover a new way to manage the business. It will no longer be an inventory problem, a quality problem, a shipment problem, but *our* problem. I'm very excited about the possibilities."

### Required

(1) How did the previous performance measurement system influence the production process?

(2) What new measures should Draper introduce that will motivate employees to achieve the JIT objectives and track how well they are implementing the JIT concept?

# TEXAS INSTRUMENTS: MATERIALS & CONTROLS GROUP*

Although you can find a technical fault with every number, the Cost of Quality system has been successful in meeting its intended objectives. But the Cost of Quality figure probably includes only half of all the costs associated with quality and may no longer provide sufficient incentives to drive further improvements. Cost of Quality numbers should be as high as possible to aid in identifying areas for improvement. During the past five years, we have reduced the biggest boulders. Now we have a conflict between comparability and the need to redefine our measurements so that the smaller rocks become visible. Today's opportunities are mostly in indirect areas, but it would take a dramatic shift in attitude to focus on measuring indirect quality costs.

*Werner Schuele, Vice President, People and Asset Effectiveness*

The Materials & Controls Group was the third largest of seven major businesses within Texas Instruments. The M&C Group's activities centered on two primary technologies:

- Metallurgical Materials: M&C was currently the world's leading designer and manufacturer of industrial and thermostatic clad metals. Clad metals consisted of two or more wrought metal layers that were metallurgically bonded to offer properties not available in conventional metals. Examples of this technology included copper-clad aluminum wire, which combined the electrical conductivity of copper with lighter and lower-cost aluminum; stainless

steel–clad aluminum, offering the luster of stainless and the corrosion protection of aluminum; and thermostatic metals, which enabled the controlled movement of thermostat components through the bonding of two metals with different coefficients of expansion. M&C had pioneered the application of these layered materials in uses as diverse as cookware, coinage, cable and wire shielding, integrated circuits, and corrosion-inhibiting trim for automobiles.

- Control Products: The Control Products business manufactured a wide range of products combining electronic and electromechanical technologies with TI's semiconductor and clad-metals expertise. The business operated plants worldwide in support of a strategy based on strong, long-term customer relationships, primarily at the OEM [original equipment manufacturer] level. Principal markets included the automotive, appliance, heating/ventilating/air-conditioning, general industrial, and aerospace/defense industries. The business's products offered control, regulation, signaling, and protection functions in applications such as motor protectors, relays, automotive engine controls, pressure switches, circuit breakers, thermostats, and electronic sensors.

The last decade had brought increased competition as companies from Japan, Italy, and Brazil had improved their products while lowering costs. M&C had responded by improving quality and service so that it could compete on factors other than price alone.

### Organization

The Product Customer Center (PCC) served as the organizational building block within TI. PCCs had profit and loss responsibility for products and customers. M&C had 11 PCCs and two Fabrication Customer Centers (FCCs) located within four operating divisions (two domestic and two international). Three additional PCCs were located in a Latin American division. Each PCC had its own marketing, engineering, finance, and manufacturing functions. FCCs manufactured components and subassemblies that were common to PCCs in order to capitalize on economies of scale and specialized expertise.

Four staff support activities existed at the group level: Research and Development, Finance, People and Asset Effectiveness (responsible for quality assurance, training, purchasing, and materials management), and Personnel/Group Services (responsible for facilities, tool making, automation, and human resources).

### Quality at TI

Productivity, teamwork, and problem solving had always been important at TI. During the 1950s, work-simplification programs, the forerunner of what are now called quality circles, had been established. In the 1960s and 1970s, TI's productivity programs were expanded to include asset management as well as people effectiveness. As international competition intensified in the late 1970s, TI's People and Asset Effectiveness activities began to focus more specifically on quality improvement. Despite these trends, however, TI continued to emphasize financial controls and a quality philosophy which, while never formally stated, expected a certain amount of defective product to be returned by the customer.

In 1980, the short-run economic tradeoff approach to quality was abandoned when the company decided to commit to a "Total Quality Thrust." The new thrust was triggered when Hewlett-Packard, an important TI customer, publicized a study that had found the products of its best American sup-

pliers to be inferior to those of its worst Japanese suppliers. TI management understood well the message from this study: Its long-run competitive success required a greatly expanded commitment to quality control.

The TI Total Quality Thrust was based on the following principles:

1. Quality and Reliability (Q&R) is management's responsibility.
2. Q&R is a responsibility of all organizations.
3. Managers' performance on Q&R will be a key criterion in performance evaluation.
4. Managers' commitments to Q&R will not be measured—only the outcomes will be.
5. The only acceptable goal for Q&R is a level that surpasses TI's best worldwide competitors at any time.

In order to emphasize that quality was not just a program but had to become TI's normal way of doing business, a vice president of People and Asset Effectiveness was appointed at the corporate level. A written policy statement, signed by the CEO, was developed and communicated. It stated:

> For every product or service we offer, we will understand the requirements that meet the customers' needs, and we will conform to those requirements without exception. For every job each TIer performs, the performance standard is: Do it right the first time.

A massive training program for all operating personnel on the fundamentals of quality improvement was undertaken. During the first phase, 450 top managers, including 22 from M&C, were sent to quality training courses conducted by Philip Crosby, a leading quality expert. Subsequently, a series of 16 tapes on the quality improvement philosophy and techniques of Joseph Juran, another leading quality expert, was shown to all exempt employees within M&C, with classes taught by senior and operating management. Managers and operating personnel were also trained in quality tools such as control charts and statistical process control. The classes helped to instill awareness and to communicate the corporate commitment to quality improvement.

A quality reporting system was implemented to supplement TI's extensive system of financial indicators. For years, TI had evaluated the profit-and-loss performance of each business with a series of financial indices published each month in the "Blue Book." In 1981, TI began a "Quality Blue Book," with indices such as product reliability, customer feedback regarding TI quality, and data on the cost of quality. The Blue Book format was deliberately chosen to communicate to TI managers that quality performance was now to be judged on the same level as financial performance.

### Quality Blue Book

Like its financial counterpart, the Quality Blue Book contained three pages of indices presenting actuals versus goals, previous period comparisons, and three-month forecasts. Unlike the highly structured financial Blue Book, however, the Quality Blue Book performance indices were generally determined by the responsible PCC manager. This assignment allowed managers to tailor the report to reflect the key quality indicators in each business. Performance indicators for Motor Controls, a typical PCC, are defined in Exhibit 1.

### Cost of Quality

Cost of quality (COQ) was one of the performance measures that had to be included in every business unit's Quality Blue Book. COQ represented expenditures that arose because poor quality had occurred or to prevent poor quality from occurring. The COQ measure was designed to highlight the cost of poor quality, the cost of doing things wrong. Explained J. Fred Bucy, TI's president and chief operating officer, in a statement to the company's employees:

Some people think that quality costs money, because they see the costs of quality in terms of new testing equipment, added inspectors, and so on. But those are the costs of doing it wrong the first time. If we design a product right the first time, and build it right the first time, we save all the costs of redesign, rework, scrap, retesting, maintenance, repair, warranty work, etc.

Consider how much of your time is spent in doing something over again. How much of your assets are tied up in rework, retesting, repair, and making scrap? How much material is wasted at TI? If we could eliminate these costs by doing things right the first time, we would have true People and Asset Effectiveness, and improved profitability, without having to add a dollar to billings.

The cost of quality system was a key component of the Total Quality Thrust. By measuring quality in financial terms, the COQ system allowed M&C management to create a major cultural change by using a term familiar to everyone—the bottom line. Tom Haggar, Controller of the Metallurgical Materials Division, observed:

COQ ties quality progress into what we're here for—to be a profitable world-class manufacturer constantly improving quality. COQ numbers shocked PCC managers. We initially showed them COQ figures of 10%: 10% of sales value, and an even greater percentage of profits, down the hole. It is now down to a less shocking 4–5%. Managers are saying that they haven't found all of the costs but that the trend is right. Even today's lower percentage is not making them comfortable. A cultural change was needed from the old to the new. For example, we used to budget for 5% scrap, but no longer. We now recognize that budgeting for bad-quality production is ridiculous.

Implementation of the COQ system began in the fourth quarter of 1981 when the Quality Department undertook a quick top-down exercise to determine quality costs. By the following quarter, an ongoing system based on accounting data was in place. At present, Control and Finance provided the PCC's Quality Department with data from the ac-

---

**EXHIBIT 1** Quality Blue Book Performance Indicators—Motor Controls PCC

Concurrent Indicators

| | |
|---|---|
| Lot acceptance (%) | Percentage of lots accepted by Outgoing Quality Control. Tracked by product line. |
| Average outgoing quality level | Defective parts per million. Tracked by product line. |
| RMR% quality | Returned Merchandise Report percentage. Percentage of shipments returned from customers because of poor quality. |
| RMR% total | RMR% quality + percentage of shipments returned for reasons other than poor quality. These include incorrect quantity shipped, wrong parts, incorrect packaging, etc. |
| Customer report card | Customer lot acceptance level. A sample of customers is interviewed to get feedback on M&C quality. Lack of recordkeeping by customers limits the availability of quantified data on this indicator. |
| Competitive rank | Subjective self-ranking of competitiveness. Ranking is done by marketing and field sales personnel. The fraction presented in the report represents M&C's competitive ranking relative to the number of competitors in that product line. |
| On-time delivery | Shipment of at least 90% of the order on or before the acknowledgment date (indicator added in 1984).* |

Leading Indicators

| | |
|---|---|
| First-pass calibration yields | Most products produced by this PCC are calibrated to open at a specified temperature. After processing, 100% of the units are tested either manually or automatically to determine that the units were calibrated correctly. This indicator reflects the percentage of units that pass this inspection. |
| Cost of quality | Calculated as the percentage of quality costs to net sales billed. Quality costs are defined as costs that incurred due to poor quality or to prevent poor quality from occurring. |

---

*Some debate existed as to whether "on-time delivery" represented a quality indicator to be put in the Blue Book. Only in the last quarter of 1987 did most divisions in the group incorporate this measure. The on-time delivery percentage was calculated on events rather than dollars to ensure that shipments to smaller customers received equal weighting. The previous measure of delivery performance was whether a customer was ever forced to shut down, ignoring instances in which customers were forced to reschedule production due to late delivery. In 1981, on-time delivery was less than 50%. By 1987, 97% of the 2,000 shipments per week were delivered on time.*

---

counting system on the sixth working day following the close of the month. The Quality Department then processed this information into the Quality Blue Book.

The initial list of COQ variables included 77 items, a number that had since been reduced to 19 through the elimination of semantic overlaps between divisions and the merger of nonsignificant categories into other cost elements. The variables were grouped into four broad categories:

1. Prevention costs: Costs incurred to prevent nonconforming units from being produced

2. Appraisal costs: Costs incurred to ensure that materials and products that failed to meet quality standards were identified prior to shipment

3. Internal failure costs: Scrap costs and costs incurred in correcting errors caught at appraisal, before delivery of the product to the customer

4. External failure costs: Costs incurred in correcting errors after delivery of the product to the customer

The variables included in each category differed somewhat among PCCs, depending upon the nature of the business. The cost elements utilized by the Motor Controls PCC are shown in Exhibit 2.

**EXHIBIT 2** Cost of Quality Variables—Motor Controls PCC

| Prevention Costs | |
|---|---|
| Quality engineering | Total quality engineering expense from the monthly actuals report. |
| Receiving inspection | Total receiving inspection expense from the monthly actuals report. |
| Equipment repair/maintenance | Estimated percentage of actual repair and maintenance expenses spent on preventive maintenance. (An estimate of 15% of total R&M expenses was developed by PCC management in 1981. This percentage had not been revised since the original estimate was made.) |
| Manufacturing engineering | Estimated percentage of actual manufacturing engineering expenses spent on prevention. The estimated percentage is revised every six months by the manager of manufacturing engineering. |
| Design engineering | Estimated percentage of actual design engineering expenses spent on prevention. The estimated percentage is revised every six months by the manager of design engineering. |
| Quality training | Actual cost of quality training from the labor reporting system. Quality training time is charged to a special labor link (charge) number. |
| **Appraisal Costs** | |
| TSL laboratory | Total technical services laboratory expense from the monthly actual report. The Technical Services Laboratory is responsible for sophisticated quality-related testing. |
| Design analysis | Estimated percentage of actual design analysis expenses spent on appraisal. The percentage is revised every six months by the manager of design analysis. |
| Product acceptance | Total inspection (quality control) expenses from the monthly actuals report. |
| Manufacturing inspection | Actual cost of manufacturing inspection from the labor reporting system. Manufacturing inspection is charged to a special link (charge) number. |
| **Internal Failure Costs*** | |
| Quality scrap | Calculated as [(material issued at standard) − (material scheduled for production at standard)] multiplied by a labor and overhead factor. The labor and overhead factor represents the amount of labor and overhead costs incurred in the assembly prior to its scrapping.[†] Obsolete parts scrapped out of inventory are not included in this measure. |
| Rework | Actual cost of rework from the labor reporting system. Rework is charged to a special link (charge) number. |
| Manufacturing/process engineering | Estimated percentage of actual manufacturing/process engineering expenses spent on internal failure. The estimated percentage is revised every six months by the manager of manufacturing engineering. |
| **External Failure Costs** | |
| Net RMR* cost marketing | Cost of returns less good material to inventory.[‡] Estimated percentage of actual marketing expenses spent on external failure. The estimated percentage is revised every six months by the marketing manager. |
| Manufacturing/process engineering | Estimated percentage of actual manufacturing/process engineering expenses spent on external failure. The estimated percentage is revised every six months by the manager of manufacturing engineering. |
| Repair | Actual cost of repair from the labor reporting system. Repair time is charged to a special link (charge) number. |
| Travel | Actual travel costs related to quality problems. Computed from the monthly actual report. |

*continued*

| | |
|---|---|
| Liability claims | Infrequent claims. Liability claims are included when incurred or when a reserve is taken. Legal fees, which are not on the Group profit-and-loss statement, are not included. |

*\*Internal failure and net RMR costs are available at the product line level. All other elements are captured at the product (PCC) department level.*

*†In 1981, a study was conducted to determine at which point in the assembly process products were being scrapped. As a result of this study, a factor of 88% above scrapped material costs was calculated to account for labor and overhead. This factor had not been changed since the original study.*

*‡If a $5 product was returned due to defects, it could either be scrapped or reworked and returned to inventory. If the item were scrapped, the net RMR cost would be $5. If, on the other hand, the item were reworked at a cost of $1, rework costs of $1 would be reported and no costs would be included in net RMR.*

Several categories of quality costs, such as indirect costs and losses considered inherent to the manufacturing process, were not captured in the COQ system. Indirect quality costs arose when support department personnel repeated tasks because of problems with shipments (defective or incorrect parts, over- or undershipments, late deliveries, etc.) or because the tasks were not done correctly the first time. Examples included the cost of retyping orders, rebuilding tools, and rebilling customers as well as correcting paperwork errors and incorrect journal entries. Efforts were under way to determine the level of indirect quality costs through "Hidden Factory" reviews.

When originally implemented, the COQ system excluded costs that were considered to be a standard part of the manufacturing process. For example, a calibration process in production may have been imperfect, requiring parts to be manually checked on the line. The costs of the manual checking were not included in COQ, leading to an understatement of quality costs. Scrap costs were also underreported by a number of PCCs. The PCC managers argued that "engineered scrap," such as the material left when a round part was punched out of a square piece of metal, was inherent to the process.

The COQ system had been easy to implement since it used data that already existed in the accounting system. Now, however, the desire to maintain consistency over time, so that trends would be visible, had made it difficult to add new measures such as indirect quality or engineered scrap costs. In effect, attempts to update the COQ system to make it more accurate and relevant were in conflict with the need to maintain comparability across periods.

### Uses of COQ Data

Initially, the COQ system was resented as just another number to be judged against. Carl Sheffer, General Manager of the Motor Controls PCC, recalled his concern: "I resented the system, feeling that quality was a virtue in its own right. Attempting to assign costs to quality diminished its value. Value is not in the numbers but in the areas they represent."

By 1987, however, the quality indicators and the COQ data in the Blue Book had become widely utilized management tools at M&C. Two factors had contributed to the system's widespread acceptance. First, quarterly financial forecast reviews were supplemented by quality reviews. PCC managers were now allowed to present the results of operations in a less structured format with emphasis on the areas of importance to each business.

Second, the Quality Blue Book was not used to "hammer" the PCC managers. Performance was not measured exclusively on the achievement of quality goals, nor were quality measures compared across businesses. Rather, the quality measures were used to focus on long-term trends of quality improvement and to highlight potential sources of quality problems.

The Quality Blue Book was distributed to the group president, controller, vice president of People and Asset Effectiveness, and to the responsible division and PCC managers on a monthly basis. Although not formally distributed to operating personnel, the information was widely available to them. Jim Meehan, PCC Quality Manager, noted:

> I don't distribute Quality Blue books to anyone below the level of the PCC manager. The PCC manager must take responsibility for getting copies to all the operating functions. Everybody probably sees them, and anyone who asks me can have a copy. Different people use different measures—the PCCs use Cost of Quality, manufacturing uses internal failures, operations is interested in on-time delivery, and marketing wants to know about external failures.

Carl Sheffer discussed his use of the data:

> The reports go to all of my managers and team members. I take personal interest in Cost of Quality and ask for the numbers. At monthly meetings, the COQ numbers are discussed with the nonexempt employees. I highlight product

lines that have improved and lines that have deteriorated. We primarily focus on Internal Failure and RMR [Returned Merchandise Report] because they are "hard" numbers. The others are more helpful for trends.

This year, the Cost of Quality numbers provided the single best indicator that problems had arisen in production, problems that had caused a bad P&L performance. The Cost of Quality showed deterioration in internal failure when the department claimed that scrap rates were down. The discrepancy arose from the department's not realizing that it had not reduced the amount of overage (material in excess of the minimum required) issued from the stockroom. Eventually, a physical inventory check found unused material all around the shop. So, the Cost of Quality report signaled a problem that may have gone undiscovered for a while.

In addition to Quality Blue Book reports, Sheffer had developed special COQ reports for his area (see Exhibits 3–5). Problems reflected in the COQ reports were not always indicative of actual quality shortcomings, however. Continued Sheffer:

> A couple of years ago, we saw continually worsening trends in the Cost of Quality. After investigating, we found that the selling price had been reduced 10%. The same scrap rate led to the Cost of Quality, measured as a percent of net sales billed, to go way up. This is a profitability problem but not one caused by a quality problem.

**EXHIBIT 3** Product Line Failure Costs—Motor Controls PCC

| PRODUCT A | SEP | OCT | NOV | YTD 1987 |
|---|---|---|---|---|
| Activity $ | $522,833 | $467,380 | $424,051 | $5,398,635 |
| Internal Failure COQ $ | 14,637 | 28,597 | 2,170 | 232,221 |
| External Failure COQ $ | 425 | 0 | 85 | 4,420 |
| Total Failure COQ $ | 15,062 | 28,597 | 2,255 | 236,641 |
| Non-Conformance COQ % | 2.88% | 6.12% | 0.53% | 4.38% |
| Variance Prior Year % | 0.38% | −2.86% | 2.73% | −1.12% |
| Variance Prior Year $ | $1,982 | ($13,361) | $11,569 | ($60,645) |
| Cumulative $ | ($58,853) | ($72,214) | ($60,645) | |

**EXHIBIT 4** Failure Rates by Product—Motor Controls PCC

| | JAN | FEB | MAR | APR | MAY | JUNE | JULY | AUG | SEP | OCT | NOV | DEC | YEAR |
|---|---|---|---|---|---|---|---|---|---|---|---|---|---|
| **Product A** | | | | | | | | | | | | | |
| Overage % | 7.1% | 8.7% | 10.6% | 11.5% | 8.9% | 1.7% | 7.1% | −2.1% | 15.8% | 3.7% | 4.4% | — | 7.1% |
| Internal failure | 7031 | 8973 | 13548 | 11278 | 8310 | 2474 | 7031 | −1595 | 15341 | 3995 | 5914 | — | 82300 |
| External failure | 2805 | 3740 | 1020 | 0 | 340 | 0 | 85 | 8670 | 0 | 0 | 0 | — | 16660 |
| COQ % | 5.6% | 5.3% | 5.6% | 4.4% | 3.5% | 0.9% | 5.1% | 3.6% | 7.3% | 1.8% | 2.8% | — | 4.1% |
| **Product B** | | | | | | | | | | | | | |
| Overage % | 3.6% | 4.0% | 5.7% | 4.2% | 2.9% | 3.7% | 7.6% | 1.2% | 2.6% | 3.7% | −8.5% | — | 2.3% |
| Internal failure | 932 | 874 | 1506 | 1393 | 1107 | 1045 | 1523 | 600 | 1255 | 1543 | −2894 | — | 8884 |
| External failure | 0 | 0 | 0 | 0 | 0 | 0 | 0 | 0 | 0 | 0 | 0 | — | 0 |
| COQ% | 2.8% | 4.1% | 4.6% | 3.7% | 2.3% | 3.0% | 14.2% | 1.0% | 2.0% | 4.0% | 6.6% | — | 2.1% |

**EXHIBIT 5** Motor Controls PCC Departmental Non-Conformance Costs—YTD through November

| NC SAVINGS VS. 1986* | | YTD NC COQ % NSB | |
|---|---|---|---|
| Product A | $89K | Product A | 1.6% |
| Product B | 61K | Product B | 2.1% |
| Product C | 52K | Product C | 3.1% |
| Product D | 20K | Product D | 3.3% |
| Product E | 16K | Product E | 3.4% |
| Product F | 8K | Product F | 3.5% |
| | | Dept avg. | 3.1% |

*Represents the difference between actual 1987 quality costs and the quality costs that would have been incurred at the 1986 COQ percentage. Includes internal and external failure costs only.*

## COQ Projects

Quality improvements were aided by management's willingness to expend funds on projects that produced intangible benefits, such as quality and service, without rigorous financial justification. Concurrent with the financial planning cycle, quality improvement teams, consisting of department managers, their staff, and representatives of support organizations such as marketing, engineering, manufacturing, production control, quality, finance, and purchasing, met to establish Cost of Quality improvement projects, using COQ system numbers as priority-setting mechanisms. Anticipated savings from the COQ improvement projects were estimated and incorporated into the product line's profit forecast. COQ savings by project were subsequently tracked by the manufacturing engineering department (see Exhibit 6). Bob Porter, Vice President of Quality Assurance and Reliability, felt that the identification and implementation of COQ projects were the keys to instilling quality awareness and improving quality performance within the group:

> The critical issue is the "process." By that I mean getting management involved in identifying opportunities for quality improvement, establishing priorities, helping ensure that resources are available, and monitoring progress. We need to speak the right language on each of these issues, and COQ is the language of management.

> Two of the organizational mechanisms that support the process are the quality improvement teams (QIT) and the People and Asset Effectiveness (P&AE) reviews. The QITs, which are in place at the group, division, and department levels of the business, consist of natural work groups of managers and professionals who meet regularly to steer the quality excellence process. The quality (P&AE) reviews, which are held quarterly, are

**EXHIBIT 6** Motor Controls PCC Cost of Quality Project Savings—1987 Cost Reductions ($K)

| COQ PROJECTS | 1Q | 2Q | 3Q | 4Q | YR87 | VARIANCE FROM ANNUAL PLAN |
|---|---|---|---|---|---|---|
| Yield improvement | 26 | 61 | 55 | 54 | 196 | 150 |
| Upgrade assy machine | 20 | 24 | 32 | 44 | 120 | 53 |
| Redesign molded part | 16 | 20 | 24 | 53 | 113 | (55) |
| Non-destruct testing | 10 | 11 | 14 | 17 | 52 | 13 |
| Laser coding | 9 | 10 | 9 | 10 | 38 | 30 |
| Flash reduction | 8 | 9 | 11 | 10 | 38 | 22 |
| Stat. process contl. | 93 | 119 | 128 | 127 | 467 | (90) |
| Total | 182 | 254 | 273 | 315 | 1024 | 123 |

high-level management reviews in which business managers review progress against their short- and long-term quality goals.

Early in the year, the lowest-level QITs identify quality improvement opportunities. Frequently, senior management attends these department QITs, where the champions of these projects discuss the opportunities. These projects are dollarized, time-phased, assigned champions, and summarized at the division level. The forecasted COQ savings are recognized in the annual plan. Key COQ projects are summarized at the group level. The COQ trend is tracked and reviewed at every group and division QIT meeting.

At the P&AE reviews, the operating departments discuss their short- and long-term goals. Much of this is focused on the progress of key COQ projects—how the QITs are using quality tools such as statistical process control to drive continuous improvement in COQ. This process is not treated as an exact science. It is not preoccupied with testing the validity of the numbers or comparison of one entity versus another. It is focused on who, what, and when, and closing the loop on results.

In summary, the operating businesses have ownership. They establish priorities and wrestle with the resource tradeoffs. The quality organization provides lots of support, but quality improvement is clearly not a program of the quality organization. Operations managers work to achieve goals they helped to establish. Progress is monitored against milestones throughout the year at the QITs and P&AE reviews.

If this process works well, the COQ numbers will take care of themselves. Without the COQ numbers, however, this process wouldn't work.

### System Results

Between the formal inception of the COQ system in 1982 and the end of 1987, Cost of Quality as a percent of net sales billed had fallen from 10.7% to 7.8%. Reductions had occurred in each category of quality costs (see Exhibit 7). The system had also focused increased attention on the impact of improved quality on costs and profitability. Carl Sheffer, though, still had mixed feelings about the current COQ system:

> Motivating senior management wasn't a problem. They already knew that quality was critical. COQ was most helpful for middle managers to see the consequences of poor quality on overall income. COQ gives one number that focuses several things together. If we focused just on scrap, we would get lower scrap costs but would go out of business as we passed scrap on to the customer. On the other hand, if we tried to focus on reducing external failures through inspection alone, without actually reducing manufactured defects, we would become uncompetitive cost-wise. COQ forces us to think about an optimum relationship among the various factors. You have to improve the whole, not pieces at a time.

> The COQ system has proven to be a good attention getter, has forced priority setting, and has stimulated quality improvement activities. It also ends up being a good scorecard. It does much less well as a diagnostic tool, partially because it uses accounting techniques. It is sometimes difficult to find out what the problem is without supplementary diagnostic tools.

**EXHIBIT 7**   Cost of Quality, % of Net Sales Billed—Materials & Controls Group

|                  | 1982 | 1983 | 1984 | 1985 | 1986 | 1987 |
|------------------|------|------|------|------|------|------|
| Prevention       | 2.3  | 2.0  | 2.0  | 2.1  | 2.3  | 2.3  |
| Appraisal        | 2.2  | 1.9  | 1.7  | 1.9  | 1.9  | 1.8  |
| Internal failure | 5.3  | 4.8  | 4.5  | 4.2  | 3.6  | 3.3  |
| External failure | 0.9  | 0.7  | 0.6  | 0.4  | 0.4  | 0.4  |
| Total COQ        | 10.7 | 9.4  | 8.8  | 8.6  | 8.2  | 7.8  |

Maybe the things we track well, such as internal failure, should be reported more often, while COQ in general could be done less frequently. Indirect cost of quality tracking probably doesn't need to be continuous. We should look at each function and ask "Why does it exist?" If the function only exists to correct errors, we can probably eliminate it. Getting rid of the function will be more appropriate than tracking secretary time, paper processing, cost of calling customers, etc. We need to focus on the big items.

## *The Future*

As 1987 came to a close, Werner Schuele, Vice President of People and Asset Effectiveness, was evaluating potential changes to the Cost of Quality system as part of an overall company review of its cost systems. Although the COQ system remained a valuable tool to highlight quality trends, allocate resources, and instill quality awareness, Schuele was not sure that COQ could continue to drive improvements in quality unless improvements were made. He felt strongly that the costs tracked by the system were only 50% of actual quality costs, resulting in inadequate attention being focused on major sources of quality costs. But he also knew that changes to the system might distort trends in the data, perhaps the most valuable use of the information. Schuele felt some reticence in implementing an indirect quality cost tracking system:

> I would love to track it if I knew how. We could avoid the trend distortion issue just by having just two categories: direct and total (i.e., direct and indirect). My major concern is that determining the real cost of "indirect scrap" is not precise and has no foundation in our accounting system. For example, nowhere is the cost of retyping a letter with a misspelled word tracked. My dilemma is that I'm not sure that the cost of developing the tracking system is worth it. Also, there is no organizational mandate to develop a precise indirect system.

Finally, Schuele was not convinced that monthly COQ reporting was necessary. Over the next six months these questions would need to be addressed and recommendations presented.

# 12

# Investing to Develop Future Capabilities Technology

We have described how companies today are striving to (1) enhance their capabilities for delivering outstanding products and performance to customers in targeted segments, (2) develop new products and services, (3) enhance existing processes, and (4) provide their employees with advanced information technology. Few of these capabilities, however, come for free. Companies must invest today to obtain products, services, and capabilities for the future. How should such investments be guided? Should they be made on the basis of faith, by appealing to the organization's commitment to its mission and strategy? Or is there still a role for careful financial analysis? Can financial analyses, developed for capital investments in industrial age companies, be made relevant for investments in an era that stresses organizational capabilities?

Linking to other topics covered earlier in the book, the chapters on cost behavior made a strong distinction between committed and flexible costs. Activity-based costing concepts demonstrated how to measure and assign the costs of using both committed and flexible resources to cost objects, such as products, services, and customers. We noted that the supply of many organizational resources gets committed well in advance of realizing the demands for the resources.

In this chapter, we examine the decision making for acquiring resources, especially resources that are expected to produce benefits for several periods in the future. At the most familiar level, such multiyear resources include machinery and information systems for which the spending occurs first and then the resource provides a stream of benefits for several years in the future. But the initial spending could also be in new products and processes (such as in research and development), in which case the investment is expected to be repaid in the future with sales from the new products and cost, quality, and cycle time efficiencies from improved processes.

Whenever spending to acquire a resource or capability is expected to yield benefits in future periods, the problem arises of how to compare the cash inflows in future periods with the cash outflows occurring at the start of the project. Anyone who puts money in a savings or money market account, or who is paying off a mortgage or loan, understands that cash flows received or paid in the future are worth less than the same cash flows being received or paid today. Discounting future cash flows provides the logic by which cash paid out and cash received in many different years can be made commensurate so that all the cash flows can be summed together to provide an overall measure of investment worth.

Discounting procedures for evaluating investments in long-lived assets became widely adopted in corporations during the mid-1950s. Students today are trained extensively in these procedures in introductory finance and management accounting courses. Therefore, the mechanics of discounting techniques, especially net present value and internal rate of return calculations, should by now be familiar to all readers of this book. With the increased availability of spreadsheets on personal computers, no technical barrier exists to the widespread use of discounting procedures for evaluating proposed investments.

But, despite the extensive experience of many companies with the techniques and the theoretical training students receive in accounting and business programs, many people still believe the technique is too limited. They note that, in practice, discounted cash flow (DCF) techniques have usually been applied only to investments in plant and equipment and to new products. DCF techniques have rarely been applied to R&D, advertising, or employee training, because such investments did not provide simple, quantifiable cash flow benefit streams.

We believe that concerns with the applicability of financial analysis to investments in future capabilities arise from two principal sources:

1. Whether discounted cash flow techniques are consistent with today's technological investments for improvements created not only for efficiency and cost reduction but also for improved quality, reduced cycle times, and enhanced flexibility
2. Whether the analytic discounted cash flow approach can capture all the learning, growth options, and organizational capabilities that can be created from certain product and process investments

In this chapter, we will address both of these extensions to traditional capital budgeting and net present value analysis.

## IS A NEW THEORY NEEDED?

Our study of the actual practices used by firms in applying discounting procedures to proposed capital investments reveals many flaws; but these are flaws in application, not in the underlying theory. Therefore, if students wish to apply DCF procedures in practice, they need to understand these flaws and how to overcome them. The flaws occur when managers

1. Require payback over arbitrarily short time periods
2. Use excessively high discount rates
3. Adjust inappropriately for risk
4. Compare new investments with unrealistic status quo alternatives
5. Emphasize incremental rather than global opportunities

6.  Fail to recognize all the costs of the new investment
7.  Ignore important benefits from the new investment

We will address each of these problems in turn.

## Short Time Horizon

Many companies demand that investments, particularly new investments in untested process technologies, be paid back within a short time period, say two or three years. Various reasons have been offered to justify the use of short payback periods, including managerial distrust of the estimates of future cash flow savings and the need to stay liquid and self-financing in order to reduce the financial risk of the company. All of these are ad hoc explanations; none of them arises from the economics of discounted cash flow analysis. Certainly, if companies in the mining or timber industries demanded three-year payback periods, there would be little opportunity for such companies to grow or even survive.

Nothing in the theory of discounted cash flow analysis justifies the use of arbitrarily short evaluation periods. In fact, quite the contrary. DCF analysis permits cash flows received many years in the future to be made comparable with cash flows received now or one year from now. Thus, the critics' complaints of short time horizons must be about the decision horizons of their senior managers, not of the analytic technique itself.

## Excessively High Discount Rates

Perhaps the major pitfall to the successful application of DCF occurs when companies use discount rates in excess of 20% and 25% to evaluate proposed new investments. Use of an excessively high discount rate penalizes a long-lived investment just as much as the use of an arbitrarily short evaluation horizon. Because the discount rate compounds geometrically each time period, cash flows received five or more years in the future will be penalized severely in the analysis. For example, compare the difference in discount factors between a 12% rate and a 25% rate for years 5 and 10:

| YEAR | DISCOUNT FACTOR AT 12% | DISCOUNT FACTOR AT 25% |
|:---:|:---:|:---:|
| 5 | 0.567 | 0.328 |
| 10 | 0.322 | 0.107 |

Clearly, investments in long-lived technologies will be severely penalized by excessively high interest rates.

Discounting future cash flows serves to repay investors for the lost opportunity to invest their cash while waiting for the returns from the investment project. Therefore, the discount rate should reflect the opportunity cost of capital for such investors: what they could otherwise be earning from investments of comparable risk. Extensive empirical and theoretical research in finance and economics during the past three decades have established useful guidelines for determining the opportunity cost of invested funds.

One can estimate the cost of equity capital in either of two ways: Use the historical nominal return on corporate stocks of between 12% and 13% per year, or use the real return (net of inflation) of about 8% to 9% and add the expected future inflation rate over the life of the project. Either method is reasonable and would be a dramatic improvement over the practice of some firms of using rates in excess of 20%.

The erroneous use of interest rates in excess of 20% for discounting future cash flows probably arises from several sources. Some firms derive their cost-of-equity capital from their accounting statements. It would not be unusual for organizations to have accounting returns on shareholder equity that exceeded 20%. But the accounting return-on-equity figure has many defects that make it a poor estimate of the rate of return the firm has been earning on its capital investments. Apart from leverage effects (we will discuss debt financing shortly), the return-on-equity figure is distorted by financial accounting depreciation conventions, by decisions on capitalization and expensing, and by use of leased assets (among other explanations). We have already discussed the impact of accounting conventions on the periodic return-on-investment figure in Chapter 10. We noted there that it would be rare for a firm's return-on-equity ratio to be a good estimate of its rate of return from past investment.

A second error arises when managers use the discount rate to adjust for risk. With estimates of investment cost and future cash benefits already provided in the analysis, the discount rate becomes the only "free" parameter in the net present value analysis. Thus, it frequently serves not only to make future cash flows commensurate with present cash flows (its only real purpose) but also as a crude mechanism to adjust for risk. It is a crude mechanism because the geometric compounding of the interest rate over time implies that project risk must also be compounding geometrically, an assumption that is almost always wrong.

Much of the risk from new investment will probably be resolved early in the project's life. If there is uncertainty as to whether a new piece of equipment or a new technology will work, we will learn about this outcome in the first year or two. If there is uncertainty about demand for a new product, this too will undoubtedly become known relatively early. For example, for a new shopping center or office complex with a 20- to 30-year lease, the major uncertainty will be resolved when the project is built and occupancy and rental rates become established. There might be great risk about both occupancy and rental rates, but this is not a risk that is appropriately quantified by discounting 30-year rentals at an interest rate that has been grossed up by 10 or more percentage points.

As an extreme example, consider visiting a race track, where you make lots of risky investments. The risk is real, but there is no interest rate for the time interval between when you place your bet and when the outcome from that action is revealed several minutes later that will help you decide whether or how much you should invest in each race. Except for a narrow definition of risk (to be discussed shortly), raising discount rates arbitrarily as an ad hoc adjustment for risk is a crude instrument and one that will systematically penalize long-lived investments.

A third error occurs when firms use nominal interest rates (such as the 12%–13% long-term return to equity holders) to discount future cash flows but make no adjustment for inflation in the cash flows themselves. Many firms project future cash flows using today's prices, wage rates, material costs, and energy prices. But if inflation is embedded in the cost of capital estimates, such as by using the historical 13% return that reflects historical inflation experience of between 4% and 5%, then unit prices for output products and input resources should also incorporate expected future price increases. It is inconsistent to reflect expected inflation in the cost of capital used for the discount rate but to ignore price increases when projecting the future benefits from the proposed investment. An alternative possibility would retain the assumption of unchanging future unit prices but then use a real (not nominal) cost of equity capital of between 8% and 9%.

The analysis to this point has focused on the cost of capital for an all-equity-financed firm. Most companies finance some of their assets with long-term debt. The historical evidence from publicly traded high-grade corporate debt reveals that the cost of debt financing is well below the cost of equity capital. Long-term investment-grade corporate debt generally returns between 1% and 3% above the inflation rate. The return from smaller, riskier companies would have to be somewhat higher to compensate creditors for the higher risk that they were bearing.

The nominal interest paid on corporate debt is a tax-deductible expense for the corporation. Therefore, if the nominal cost of long-term debt is $I$% per year, the after-tax cost of debt capital to the company is $I * (1 - t)$, where $t$ is the marginal corporate tax rate.

The simplest way to incorporate a mixture of equity and debt capital is to calculate a weighted average cost of equity debt capital.[1] The weights should be the fraction of total market value represented by equity and debt capital, respectively. Many companies estimate their debt-equity ratios using book values from their accounting balance sheet; this basis is less desirable than the weights implied by the market values of equity and debt but produces an acceptable approximation if market values, particularly of privately held or off-balance sheet debt, are difficult to estimate.

When the 13% cost of equity capital is averaged with nominal after-tax debt costs in the 5% range, it is clear that the overall cost of capital for many firms will be in the single-digit range. This result makes the use of discount rates in the 20+% range even more indefensible. Thus, many of the concerns with DCF techniques may reflect nothing more than the frustration of attempting to push innovative projects through a corporate financial process that is systematically biased against investments in long-lived assets.

When a company has some debt in its capital structure, still another opportunity for error arises. Interest payments will appear as an expense in a company's income statement. When projecting the cash flows from an investment, companies frequently subtract a pro rata share of corporate interest expense from the cash flows of a project. This calculation is erroneous because the payment of interest (as well as dividends and capital gains to shareholders) is already included in the interest rate used to discount future cash flows. The cost of capital includes the ability to repay both interest and principal on any debt incurred for the project. Subtracting interest expense from a project's future cash flows will cause these payments to be counted twice (once in the numerator and once in the denominator) and will therefore cause the project to appear less attractive than it actually is.

## 3 Risk Adjustments

We have already expressed our skepticism about arbitrary escalation of interest rates in a misguided attempt to compensate for project risk. Both theory and evidence provide support for embedding some adjustment for risk into the discount rate. But this risk adjustment arises from risk that is not diversifiable by investors. Pure uncertainty in outcomes does not require a risk adjustment if the uncertainty is not correlated with the uncertainties faced by other companies. The only risk for which investors, holding diversified portfolios, demand compensation is systematic risk—risk that is not diversifiable across firms.

The systematic risk probably arises more from the nature of the firm's product markets than from uncertainties in its production processes. Therefore, this risk would be the same for both existing and proposed investments in process technology. The subject of measuring a company or division's systematic risk is complex and is discussed intensively in finance courses.[2] For our purposes, the contemporary conventional finance thinking leads us to use the division's "beta," as estimated from the capital asset pricing model, to adjust for risk. In practice, the beta adjustment could move the cost of equity capital up or down by several percentage points, depending on the typical business and financial risk of the division.

Adjusting for the systematic risk of shareholders through the use of the CAPM beta controls for one type of risk and avoids the distortions created by arbitrary escalations of the cost of capital. Nevertheless, managers still face risk that is specific to the project, and to their careers, any time they undertake a major capital investment project. We have argued that increasing the discount rate is a poor method for controlling for this type of risk. Much better would be for managers to formulate different scenarios to represent the possible outcomes from a major investment.[3] These simulations can now be performed with standard and widely available spreadsheet languages. Alternatively, managers could formulate most likely, optimistic, and pessimistic scenarios for the investment project. Returning to our example of constructing a shopping center or office complex, the three scenarios could correspond to normal occupancy and rental rates, full occupancy, and low occupancy. Under each alternative, the managers would estimate the investment cost and future cash flows that are consistent with the assumed scenario. The cost of capital would then be used to discount all future cash flows to the present—its intended and defensible purpose—with risk evaluation left to the manager after contemplating the distribution of net present values across the different scenarios.

## Alternatives to New Investment

Any new investment is evaluated, either explicitly or implicitly, against an alternative of not undertaking the new investment. The desirability of the new investment depends critically on how this alternative is evaluated. Many companies use the present conditions, the status quo, as the baseline alternative. That is, they assume that present cash flows can be maintained with no investment in new technology. Thus, the proposed investment must be justified by improvements in future cash flows—lower labor, material, or energy costs for example—relative to the present situation. This situation is captured by the diagram in Exhibit 12-1, in which the horizontal line represents the maintenance of present net cash flows into the future, and the small wedge above the line represents the cash flow improvements from undertaking the new investment. With this assumption, the area in the cash flow savings "wedge" may not be large enough to repay the initial investment in the new technology.

But the experience of many industries in Western countries has clearly shown that it is erroneous to assume that a firm could maintain level cash flows after rejecting new technology investment opportunities. For when a new process technology becomes available to one company, it will probably also be available to competitors. Even if existing competitors decide not to adopt the new process technology, a company overseas, such as

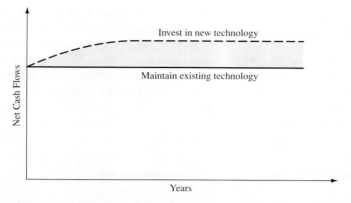

**EXHIBIT 12-1   Comparing New with Existing Technology:
Extrapolating the Status Quo**

in a newly industrializing country, could adopt the new technology when it built a new plant to produce competitive products. Therefore, the most likely alternative to adopting new process technology is to assume a declining cost or quality position relative to a leading-edge competitor. Once a firm has lost technological leadership, it will find it difficult to maintain present market share and gross margins. This difficulty will lead to declining cash flows in future years. It is this pattern of declining cash flows (see Exhibit 12-2) that represents the most likely cash flow pattern for maintaining the status quo in rejecting the new technology option.

   Once the process innovation "genie" is out of the bottle, it cannot be captured and corked up; it will flow to current or future competitors who will upset the existing market structure. Thus, the difference in cash flows between the new process investment and the status quo is the much larger area shown in Exhibit 12-2. Unfortunately, unlike our present cash flow position that we can estimate to considerable precision, we may not be sure

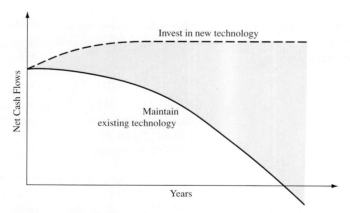

**EXHIBIT 12-2   Comparing New with Existing Technology:
Recognizing Loss of Technology Leadership**

how fast the curve in Exhibit 12-2 will decline in future years. Perhaps the experience of companies in U.S. industries such as consumer electronics, steel, and machine tools can be studied to determine the rate of decline once technological leadership is lost to overseas competitors. It may be 5% per year; it may be 12% per year. Sensitivity analysis can be usefully applied to test how conclusions may vary with different decay rates. But we can be quite sure that assuming a zero rate of decay is precisely wrong.

## Incremental versus Global Analysis

An additional problem with current practice is its bias toward incremental rather than revolutionary projects. The capital approval process for many companies specifies different levels of authorization as a function of the size of the request.[4] Small investments, under $100,000 say, may need only the approval of the plant manager, whereas expenditures in excess of several million dollars may require board of directors' approval. This apparently sensible procedure, however, creates an incentive for managers to propose a sequence of small projects that fall just below the cutoff point at which higher-level approval would be needed. Over time, a division may undertake lots of little investments, implementing minor changes in its basic facility, each one of which promises adequate savings in labor, material, or overhead costs or higher revenues by relieving an existing production bottleneck. But, collectively, the factory will become less efficient because of a less-than-optimal pattern of material flow. The factory may even become obsolete because of the outdated technology embedded in its core production equipment.

Each year, a division manager may propose and undertake a series of small improvements in the production process—to alleviate bottlenecks, to add capacity where needed, or to introduce islands of automation based on immediate and easily quantified benefits. Each of these projects, taken by itself, may have a positive net present value. By investing on a piecemeal basis, however, the division never gets the full benefit from a completely redesigned and reequipped plant that can exploit the latest organization and technology of manufacturing operations. At any point in time, there may be many of these annual, incremental projects scattered about from which the investment has yet to be recovered. Were the plant to be scrapped, the incremental investments made during the past several years would be proved incorrect.

One alternative to this piecemeal approach is to forecast the remaining technological life of the plant and then to enforce a policy of accepting no process improvements that will not be repaid within that period. At the end of the specified period, the old facility would be scrapped and replaced with a new one that incorporated the latest technology. Although none of the business-as-usual incremental investments might have been incorrect, the collection of incremental decisions could have a lower net present value than the alternative of deferring most investment during a terminal period, earning interest on the unexpended funds, and then replacing the plant. Again the failure to evaluate such a global investment is not a limitation of discounted cash flow analysis. It is a failure of not applying the analysis to all the relevant alternatives.

## Front-End Investment Costs

Most investment proposals seriously underestimate the initial costs associated with installing new equipment, particularly equipment that embodies dramatically new technological features. In general, the hardware costs will be estimated well after obtaining quotes from vendors. But much new equipment requires considerable software development as well. Companies relatively unfamiliar with digital processing technology may overlook the extensive software investment required to make their new equipment operational and effective. Aggravating this tendency is the financial accounting requirement that in-house expenditures on software be expensed as incurred. Numerous instances could be cited in which expensive new machines were never used to their capabilities because the projects were starved for software.

In addition to presenting a more realistic picture about the investment cost in the new technology, a behavioral reason exists for explicitly recognizing front-end software and programming costs. Many companies budget capital funds separately from operating expenditures. If front-end software and programming costs are not provided for in the capital budget, they will eventually have to be supplied from operating funds. As managers are pressed to meet short-term profit goals and budgets, it becomes seductive to reduce funding for "intangibles" such as software for new machines. The temptation exists to force the machines on-line prematurely, without sufficient software support, an action that will virtually guarantee the eventual failure of the new process technology thrust.

A similar mistake is often made when organizations fail to budget funds to retrain and educate workers, supervisors, and managers in the new process technology. We observed one automobile assembly plant where workers had been furloughed for the several months required to install electronically controlled welding, paint spray, and conveyor equipment. After all the hardware had been installed, the workers were called back and were instructed to start production on the new car line. This plant subsequently demonstrated the slowest ramp-up to capacity production in the company's history as workers struggled to learn, under severe production pressure, how to keep the radically new production equipment operating and how to troubleshoot and repair it when it broke down (which was often). As the TV commercial reminds us, "You can pay now (in training and education); or you can pay later (in low production, frequent downtime, low morale, high turnover, and expensive repair costs)." Roger Smith, chairman of General Motors during the 1980s, learned that "spending money on new technology without adequate investment in training and educating our workers merely enables us to produce scrap faster." As with software and programming, the financial accounting requirement that training and education costs be expensed as incurred has prevented many companies from recognizing that such costs are investments, just as much as hardware costs, in the new technology process.

Also, many investments in flexible production technology require complementary investments to create capacity for new product development. Instead of producing a standard mix of products, an organization, with flexible production technology, can now customize its products and services. But to exploit this capability, companies have to transform their salesforce. Previously, salespeople served mainly to take and negotiate orders for existing products. For the new technology, the salesforce must be capable of new market development, of understanding and anticipating customer needs, and of performing customized applications engineering. The salesforce must not only uncover new opportunities, it must translate such opportunities into specifications for new products. If a company does not make complementary investments to enhance salesforce skills, the capabilities of the new, flexible facilities will go untapped. The costs of such skill enhancement must also be considered part of the "investment" in new manufacturing technologies if the full promised benefits from these technologies are to be realized.

## Benefits Invisible Using Traditional Cost Systems

Investments in new technology, particularly information-intensive technologies such as flexible manufacturing systems (FMS), computer-aided design (CAD), and computer-aided engineering (CAE) provide companies with the capability for efficient design and production of small volumes of customized products. But these technologies provide little savings in direct labor, actual machining times, or direct materials usage. Before the advent of activity-based costing, the benefits case for investment in new machinery typically came from quantified savings in direct labor and machine times. Such labor and machine time savings could be directly tied to the company's traditional, volume-based costing system, in which operating expenses were allocated to products via direct labor and machine hour burden rates. Flexible design and manufacturing technologies (such as FMS, CAD, and CAE) typically do not provide labor and machine time savings relative to what could be achieved with much less expensive "hard-wired" special-purpose machines that do not contain sophisticated microprocessors, microcontrollers, and extensive automatically controlled materials and tool handling equipment. Therefore, it is difficult to justify the added expense to obtain these flexibility capabilities. In effect, the benefits from rapid introduction of new products and rapid changeover from one product to another are invisible in direct labor and machine hour costing systems.

Activity-based systems make visible the costs of batch and product development and product-sustaining activities (see Chapter 4). ABC systems reveal the high cost of the batch activities required by conventional manufacturing processes to:

- Change over (setup) from one product to another
- Move materials from one special-purpose machine to another
- Inspect items after each production run
- Schedule production runs, prepare materials and tools for production runs

ABC systems also reveal the high cost of producing a broad product line, with extensive customization, including the product-sustaining costs to:

- Design new models and variants for meeting individual customer needs
- Sustain the capabilities to produce a large number of products (such as maintaining engineering drawings, an updated bill of materials, labor and machine routings, and standard cost information)

And applying ABC to a company's entire supply chain reveals the high costs to:

- Order and schedule materials in small lots from many different suppliers
- Process customer orders for small lots of specialized products

Thus, many of the benefits—in real and quantifiable cost reductions and cost avoidance—associated with introducing flexible manufacturing and design technologies and electronic data interchange (EDI) between customers and suppliers were invisible because companies buried the costs of their support activities in overhead pools that were allocated on the basis of labor and machine hours. The advent of activity-based cost systems provides a much more visible basis for understanding the operating cost savings that can be realized from investments in advanced electronic manufacturing, design, and information technology.

## MEASURING ALL THE BENEFITS FROM THE NEW PROCESS

Traditional project evaluation procedures estimate future savings in material, labor, and energy because these inputs are generally measured and tracked well by the company's cost accounting system. Innovative process technologies, however, also provide benefits that are not measured by traditional cost accounting and project appraisal systems. These benefits include inventory reductions, reduced floor space requirements, and improved quality.

### Reduced Inventory Levels

The process flexibility, more orderly product flow, higher quality, and better scheduling that successful adopters of flexible automation technology have enjoyed will drastically cut both work-in-process (WIP) and finished goods inventory levels. Inventory reductions of 75% to 90% have been reported by many companies.

Reductions in inventory levels represent a large cash inflow at the time when the new equipment becomes operational and the inventory can be reduced. Because the reduction usually occurs early in the project's life, and thus is not discounted heavily, the cash flows from reduced inventory are especially valuable.

Consider a product line for which the anticipated monthly cost of sales is $500,000. Using existing equipment and technology, the producing division carries about three months' of sales in inventory. After investing in flexible automation, the division heads find that reduced waste, scrap, and rework, greater predictability, and faster throughput permit a two-thirds reduction in average inventory levels. Pruning inventory from three months to one month of sales produces a cash inflow of $1 million. If sales increase 10% per year, the company will also enjoy increased cash flows from the inventory reductions in future years; if the cost of sales rises to $550,000 in the next year, a two-month reduction in inventory saves an additional $100,000 that year, $110,000 the year after, and $121,000 the year after that. Furthermore, there will be less obsolescence when new variants and models of products are introduced.

In addition to the obvious reduction in cash demands from holding less inventory, many overhead costs that are largely driven by holding, moving, scheduling, and inspecting inventory can also be reduced when inventory reductions are accomplished. Studies that documented the decrease in productivity when new capital equipment is introduced have found strong increases in productivity as inventory levels are reduced.[5] Thus, the initial productivity decline from introducing new equipment can be offset by the higher productivity arising from operating with much lower inventory levels. Also, with less inventory and with continual flow production of small lots rather than batch production of large lots, the need for forklift trucks and drivers will be reduced, perhaps eliminated.

### Less Floor Space

New process technologies frequently enable the same job to be accomplished with far less floor space. Just eliminating inventory, which is stored on or about the floor in most factories, will free up large amounts of productive space. More-efficient grouping of machines through better scheduling and coordination will produce significant floor space reductions. Companies have reported space savings of 50% to 70% after installing flexible manufacturing systems. Such space savings are real but are rarely measured by traditional financial and cost accounting systems. Most organizations have a continually increasing demand for space, if not for production then for engineering, support, and administrative personnel, so any realized space saving represents a real cash benefit to the firm. The savings from reduced space requirements can be estimated either on an annual basis—using the square-foot rental cost for new space—or on a one-time basis, analogous to the computation of inventory reduction savings, based on new space construction cost.

## Quality Improvements

Greatly improved quality represents a major source of tangible benefits from new technology investments. Automated process equipment, properly installed and operated, leads directly to more uniform production and, frequently, to an order-of-magnitude decline in scrap, rework, and waste. As production uniformity is increased, fewer inspection stations are required and the number of inspectors is reduced. Automatic gauging can eliminate virtually all manual inspection of parts; out-of-tolerance parts can also be detected immediately rather than waiting for an entire batch of products to be produced before the production problem is detected.

The opportunities for savings in quality can be estimated by first collecting information on how much the organization is currently spending on producing, repairing, and discarding poor-quality items. Some of these costs will appear in categories such as inspection, scrap, waste allowance, and rework cost. These categories will fail to capture all the cost of substandard quality production. Storing substandard items in the factory, moving them around, and rescheduling the production line to accommodate rework of faulty items all impose high costs on the organization. Typically, these costs are buried in overhead accounts and allocated to all production, both good and bad. The analysis should attempt to identify all the costs incurred to produce poor-quality items, including inspection, expediting, and rescheduling costs.

All these expenses provide the pool of current expenses that improved production processes can reduce. Once the size of this pool is known, we can estimate the benefits from new process technologies that offer the potential for 50% or higher reductions in the incidence of substandard-quality production.

## More-Accurate, Less-Precise Estimates

Projected savings in inventory, floor space, and quality are frequently estimated from the experience of similar companies or divisions. These savings cannot be estimated to the four or five significant digits that are the customary precision from the firm's financial and cost accounting system. But many analysts err when they conservatively assume that difficult-to-estimate benefits must be zero. For purposes of financial justification, it will be sufficient to get the first and perhaps the second digit about right and to know how many zeros follow the first digit or two. It is better to be vaguely right than precisely wrong.

## The Difficult-to-Quantify Benefits

In Joseph Bower's classic study of capital budgeting procedures,[6] managers of a specialty plastics division wanted to build a flexible facility that would facilitate rapid changeovers in response to shifting demand and that could also efficiently produce small batches of new compounds conceived in the R&D laboratory. When corporate financial staff insisted on understanding the base case—what would happen if the flexible facility were not built— the managers had to concede that the products intended for the proposed facility could be built using spare capacity in existing facilities. The managers insisted that the existing facilities did not offer the quality and cost advantages of the proposed facility, but they could not translate their claims into tangible cash benefits. The corporate staff therefore assumed that the current incremental cost of producing the proposed products was essentially zero.

Nor could the managers articulate the flexibility advantages from the proposed facility, which would allow them to produce efficiently a changing volume and mix of products. The company's capital budgeting format insisted on estimating the cash flows for a particular mix of products. The managers were forced to assume a standard mix of products. This constraint prevented the analysis from capturing the benefits of flexibility for difficult-to-predict product mixes and for products not yet formulated. Eventually, the difficulty of communicating the savings and the benefits from the flexible facility caused the project to be abandoned.

New process technologies, especially those that are information-intensive, offer opportunities for radical changes in the way operations are performed. Some of these changes will be reflected in the substantial savings of inventory, space, and quality costs previously described. But even beyond those tangible reductions in costs that are currently being incurred, the new process technologies can provide dramatic improvements in flexibility, faster responses to market shifts, significant reductions in throughput and lead times, and opportunities to learn from and grow with technology advances.

## INVESTING IN ORGANIZATIONAL CAPABILITIES[7]

A recent analysis of several field studies identified investments leading to five different types of organizational capabilities:

1. External integration, leading to *quality*
2. Internal integration, leading to *speed* and *efficiency*
3. Flexibility, leading to *responsiveness* and *variety*
4. Experimentation, leading to *continuous improvement*
5. Cannibalization, leading to *radical innovation*

We briefly summarize each of these capabilities.

### External Integration: Linking Design to the Customer

Japanese manufacturers create high-quality products by investing in information systems that link customers, engineering teams, suppliers, and manufacturing operations. External integration is the ability to link knowledge of customers with the details of engineering design to create and improve products. The external integration must:

1. Build systems to gather, collate, and analyze information about customers and the ways they use the product. This process can include training the salesforce and service organization to gather in-depth knowledge of customer needs.
2. Link customers' needs to engineering design.

These two aspects of external integration are complementary. The organization must both understand how customers use their products and also communicate this knowledge to the engineers who are designing or redesigning the products that customers will use. If these costly investments are not made, the company is unlikely to be producing products that will work in ways that customers expect.

## 2  Internal Integration: Connecting Functions within the Organization

Internal integration exists when problem solving is tightly connected across departmental and functional boundaries. Decisions in one function, such as engineering design, should take into account the knowledge, skills, and concerns of other functions, such as manufacturing, sales, and finance. High degrees of internal integration enable a company to accelerate the time-to-market of new products and greatly reduce the cost of the product development process.

Internal integration in the order fulfillment process—booking and receiving customer orders, scheduling production, producing the order, and distributing the order to the customer—should provide the business unit with a just-in-time capability to meet customer demands with short lead times. Companies offering one- to two-week lead times when competitors are promising 60- to 90-day deliveries should be able to capture premium prices and higher market share. Greatly shortened lead times will also permit companies to respond quickly to changes in market demand. If the marketing department detects a shift in customer preferences, the factory can respond quickly to product mix and design modifications. The company will beat technologically inferior companies to the market and will avoid the obsolescence of in-process and finished goods inventory that its competitors with two- and three-month lead times must absorb.

Internal integration requires the specialists from different parts of the organization to have common vocabularies, concepts, and objectives. The specialists must also have specialized information systems to facilitate interaction, such as shared data bases, computer simulation and testing capabilities, rapid prototyping, and integrated systems from customers through production and distribution. The extensive communication and collaboration across organizational functions require investments in education, training, and career progression and explicit incentives to produce the desired payoffs in efficiency and speed for delivering existing products and launching new ones.

## 3  Flexibility: Responsiveness to Change

Flexibility allows a company to change product or process characteristics rapidly and at low cost. It enables a company to respond quickly to changes in customer demands and tastes, market conditions, and competitor initiatives. Flexibility can be measured along several dimensions:

- **Variety:** Capability to turn out a wide range of goods and change the mix quickly as demand shifts
- **Volume:** Capability to vary the rate of output, especially in continuous flow processes
- **Innovation:** Capability to introduce new products into manufacturing rapidly and efficiently

For example, companies with computer-integrated manufacturing (CIM) technologies can change product specifications easily, process engineering change orders rapidly, implement process improvements continually, accommodate schedule changes, both volume and mix, at low cost, and introduce entirely new products and variants on existing equipment with little disruption. Adoption of computer-based production processes has permitted some companies to produce efficiently in batch sizes of one.[8]

In the short run, CIM equipment may be performing the same functions as less-expensive, dedicated automation. In this case, the flexibility of CIM equipment is not being exploited, and it becomes difficult to justify the added expense of linkage to the computer workstations of product designers and engineers, the programmable controls and the flexible materials handling equipment. It is only over time, with CIM's ability to easily accommodate engineering changes, product redesigns, and major product changes and innovations, that the payoffs from CIM flexibility will be realized.

As another example, to achieve product flexibility, companies need to invest in modular designs, whereby common components and subassemblies can be combined in unique ways to meet a wide variety of end applications. Modularity raises the initial cost of design but enables a company to offer a more varied product line, without paying the normal high cost of small-lot customization. Process flexibility requires investments in operating procedures and software that permit rapid changeovers and ability to meet unexpected contingencies. Embedding such contingencies in routine operating procedures requires heavy front-end investments in training and simulation and in designing and testing software. The payoff comes from the capability to alter outputs within minutes rather than the hours or days required in conventional, nonflexible processes.

## 4   Experimentation: Achieving Continuous Improvement

Continuous improvement (*kaizen*) requires that organizational participants be constantly involved in experimentation and learning. This process requires skilled operators to conduct systematic investigation on processes, using the scientific method and statistical analysis.

The capacity to experiment requires two complementary types of investments. First, the firm must have research capacity, including extra manufacturing capacity, to allow experimentation in the plant. This capacity includes sensors and tools for collecting data as well as people and systems to organize, analyze, and report the data. Second, the firm must have systems for communicating between scientific and operating personnel and the human and organizational skills to implement rapidly and effectively the insights from the systematic data analysis. These capabilities will allow the organization to modify and improve existing practices by exploiting the knowledge gained through constant experimentation.

## 5   Cannibalization: Achieving Radical Improvement

Many companies are reluctant to replace an existing process with a new process whose cost improvements cannot be demonstrated. For example, U.S. steel manufacturers delayed for decades the introduction of continuous casting process technology, despite its cost and quality benefits relative to the companies' traditional batch production process. Missing from the capital budgeting analysis of these companies who wish to preserve the status quo is the recognition that a decision to acquire the new technology also gives the organization the opportunity to participate in future enhancements. Companies that invested in electronically controlled machine tools in the 1970s acquired a technology option, analogous to a stock option, in microprocessor and microcontroller technology advances. As the capabilities of integrated circuit chips improved by several orders of magnitude, these companies increased the machines' productivity by retrofitting the more-advanced electronic products. Companies that stayed with mechanical, manually operated machine tools failed to obtain an option in technology advances and hence could not benefit from the enormous performance-price improvements in electronic chips. Investing in new process technologies also permits the entire organization to learn about the capabilities of leading-edge production processes. Thus, many of the startup costs could ultimately be shared by other projects that use similar technologies. Assigning all the front-end costs to the specific project being authorized will fail to recognize the eventual benefits to future projects.

Despite these benefits, some managers, in the face of rapid technology changes, feel that it is safer to defer investment and wait until the rate of change and technological advance have slowed down. These companies fail to realize how important the learning process is when shifting to an entirely new production technology. By waiting, they delay their learning process and eventually find themselves organizationally and technologically so far behind their competitors that they can never catch up. In effect, they have not acquired an option in technological advances.

Even more common, companies resist or delay the introduction of a new product that will severely cut into the sales of their existing products. The slow reactions of IBM and Digital Equipment to personal computers and powerful workstations can, in part, be attributed to their managers' concerns about cannibalizing the far more profitable sales from their mainframe systems and minicomputers. As these examples show, the introduction of cannibalistic new processes or products have implications well beyond a simple financial comparison between the status quo and the proposed innovation. Sometimes, what appears to be a destructive innovation to existing processes and products will actually provide new organizational capabilities that will yield substantial future returns. But these future returns will be earned only if the introduction of the cannibalistic new product or process is accompanied with investments in procedures, information systems, and new employee skills, in addition to the investment in physical assets.

One type of investment will provide the organization with the capability to experiment with radical new opportunities at low cost and to test them in selected markets without disrupting existing efforts to support and improve existing products, customers, and processes. Another type of capability will be required to follow the new direction, if it proves successful in experiments and market tests. This second type involves excellent capabilities in new product design and process engineering. A complementary capability is to manage the ramp-up of the new product or process while simultaneously managing an orderly and profitable phase-out of the old product or process technology.

## SUMMARY ON BUILDING ORGANIZATIONAL CAPABILITIES

Investments in organizational capabilities may be among the most important that business units can make. For example, external integration reduces product risk; internal integration increases the frequency with which opportunities are generated and the speed with which the business unit can respond to customer requests; flexibility increases the range of options associated with a given investment; the capacity to experiment allows systematic improvement and value creation over time; and cannibalization deters entry and increases the value of a business unit's market position.

The benefits from these organizational capabilities are just as important, if not more so, than the cost, inventory, space, and quality savings measured by traditional capital budgeting systems, but they are much harder to quantify. We may not be sure how many zeros should be in our benefits estimates (are they to be measured in thousands or millions?), much less which digit would be first. The difficulty arises in large part because many of the benefits represent revenue enhancements rather than cost savings. It is fairly easy to get a ballpark estimate for percentage reduction in costs already being incurred. For revenue enhancements from features not yet in place, it may be difficult to know which city you are in, much less the size of the ballpark in which you are playing. But, although the benefits may be difficult to quantify, there is no reason to value them at zero when conducting a financial analysis. Zero is no less arbitrary than any other number, and we must avoid the trap of assigning zero value to benefits that we know exist but are difficult to quantify.

Because of the difficulty of quantifying the benefits, investments in organizational capabilities are often neglected. All organizational investments must be justified in an environment in which formal capital budgeting systems demand quantified benefits. Spending on some "intangibles"—such as R&D, advertising, and training—does coexist with formal capital budgeting systems, since such spending can be approved on the basis of the educated judgment of senior executives, or on faith, or perhaps on both. These expenditures can be formally budgeted and the outcomes reviewed periodically to assess whether results are in line with expectations. Investments in organizational skills, systems, and procedures, however, are difficult to segregate, and they affect value indirectly and in nonlinear combinations with each other. One source of nonlinearity, or nonadditivity, arises from threshold effects in which a capability might fail to be achieved because one small but critical element was omitted. Also, the capabilities usually complement each other: The value of two capabilities working together typically exceeds the sum of the values of either working alone.

## The Bottom Line

New organizational and accounting systems will need to track, in addition to financial flows, measures of quality, speed, flexibility, innovation, and rates of improvement.[9] New planning and capital budgeting systems must be developed that can measure a project's impact on these critical drivers of a business unit's performance. A capabilities view of investment will, over time, likely evolve to become integrated with the formal, financially based, capital budgeting systems that have been in use since World War II.

But lacking such new approaches for measuring and eventually valuing increments in organizational capabilities, we still need mechanisms for evaluating such investments today. One way to combine difficult-to-measure benefits with those more easily quantified is, first, to estimate the annual cash flows about which we have the greatest confidence. First we should estimate the relatively easily quantified annual cash flows: the cash outflows for new equipment and systems and to introduce the new equipment and processes into the organization. These enabling processes include data bases, systems, software, training, and education. In addition, for computer-based process technologies, we should estimate the tangible benefits from labor, inventory, floor space, and quality savings. We can then perform a discounted cash flow analysis, using a sensible and defensible discount rate, considering relevant and realistic alternatives, and examining possible scenarios. Should the new technology investment show a positive net present value at this point, we can be comfortable with the acquisition decision, since the financial hurdle has been passed even without adding in some of the difficult-to-quantify benefits.

If the net present value, however, is negative, then it becomes necessary to estimate how much the annual cash flows must increase before the investment begins to look favorable. Suppose, for example, that an extra $1,000,000 per year over the life of the investment is sufficient for the project to have the desired return. Then management can decide whether it expects heightened organizational capabilities in external and internal integration, flexibility, and organizational learning and the technology options including spillover effects to future projects to make the investment worth at least $1,000,000 per year. Would the company be willing to pay $1,000,000 annually to enjoy these benefits? If so, the project can be accepted with confidence. If, however, the additional cash flows needed to justify the investment turn out to be quite large—say, $10,000,000 per year—management, while still valuing improvements in organizational capabilities, can decide that they are not worth purchasing at $10,000,000 per year. In this case, it is perfectly sensible to turn a proposed investment down.

Rather than attempt to put a value on benefits that by their very nature are difficult to quantify, managers should reverse the process and estimate first how large these benefits must be in order to justify the proposed investment. Senior executives can be expected to judge that improved flexibility, rapid customer service, market adaptability, and options on new process technology may be worth $1 to $2 million per year but not, say, $10 to $15 million. In this final stage, we may be proceeding on faith, but at least our formal analysis has reduced the price that faith must pay.

## ENDNOTES

1. If this were a finance, not a managerial accounting course, we would have to spend much more time on choosing the appropriate cost of capital. Modern financial economics uses an adjusted present value calculation that separately values an asset's real cash flows and the cash flow impacts from financing, including tax shields, bankruptcy risk, options, and hedges; see T. A. Luehrman, "What's It Worth? A General Manager's Guide to Valuation," and Luehrman, "Using APV: A Better Tool for Valuing Operations," *Harvard Business Review* (May–June 1997) pp. 132–54.

2. Good treatments are available in R. Brealey and S. Myers, *Principles of Corporate Finance*, 5th ed. (New York: McGraw-Hill, 1996); and J. Van Horne, *Financial Management and Policy*, 10th ed. (Englewood Cliffs, NJ: Prentice Hall, 1995).

3. See, for example, D. B. Hertz, "Risk Analysis in Capital Budgeting," *Harvard Business Review* (January–February 1964), pp. 95–106; and D. B. Hertz, "Investment Policies That Pay Off," *Harvard Business Review* (January–February 1968), pp. 96–108.

4. Organizational and behavioral issues in the capital budgeting process are documented and discussed in J. L. Bower, *Managing the Resource Allocation Process: A Study of Corporate Planning and Investment* (Boston: Division of Research, Harvard Business School, 1970).

5. R. H. Hayes and K. B. Clark, "Why Some Factories Are More Productive Than Others," *Harvard Business Review* (September–October 1986), pp. 68–69; and "Exploring the Sources of

Productivity at the Factory Level," in *The Uneasy Alliance: Managing the Productivity-Technology Dilemma*, ed. K. B. Clark, R. H. Hayes, and C. Lorenz (Boston: Harvard Business School Press, 1985), pp. 183–84.

**6.** J. L. Bower, *Managing the Resource Allocation Process* (Boston: Harvard Business School Press, 1986).

**7.** This section is based on C. Y. Baldwin and K. B. Clark, "Capital-Budgeting Systems and Capabilities Investments in U.S. Companies after the Second World War," *Business History Review* (Spring 1994), 73–109.

**8.** Economies of scope from computer-integrated manufacturing are discussed in J. D. Goldhar and M. Jelinek, "Plan for Economies of Scope," *Harvard Business Review* (November–December 1983), pp. 141–48; and M. Jelinek and J. D. Goldhar, "The Strategic Implications of the Factory of the Future," *Sloan Management Review* (Summer 1984), pp. 29–37.

**9.** Recall the linkage of strategy to a combination of financial and nonfinancial measures in the Balanced Scorecard, discussed in Chapter 8.

## ■ *PROBLEMS*

### *12-1  Portsmouth Pottery Company*

The Portsmouth Pottery Company (PPC) manufactures a line of pottery that is primarily related to the commemorative and tourist industries. Sam Franklin, the production manager, is considering the possibility of purchasing a new kiln for the number 5 line. This line produces commemorative plaques. The kiln costs $700,000 and has a life of five years. PPC has a marginal tax rate of 35%. The tax depreciation schedule allows the following percentages of the cost of the kiln to be claimed during the kiln's life: year 1, 16%; year 2, 21%; year 3, 21%; year 4, 21%; and year 5, 21%.

The new kiln would be used to replace an existing kiln, which has a useful life of five years. The existing kiln has been fully depreciated and has a salvage value of $25,000.

The new kiln promises annual cost savings of $100,000 in the production of the existing plaques. In addition, the size and operating attributes of the new kiln will allow PPC to begin producing a new line of mugs that could be printed with the customer's promotional message. The net income before taxes expected from this new line of business is $120,000 per year.

The salvage value of the new kiln would be $50,000 in five years. PPC is required to take any salvage value, in excess of the undepreciated historical cost of an asset, into income to be taxed at the normal rate.

PPC's required after-tax return on this type of investment is 14%.

### *Required*

    (1)   Should the new kiln be purchased?
    (2)   What is the rate of return on this investment?
    (3)   What is the minimum level of total annual savings and new net income at which the new kiln is desirable?
    (4)   What is the maximum purchase price of the new kiln at which this project is desirable?

## 12-2    *Acme Telephone Company (William Cotton)*

The Acme Telephone company is a supplier of telephone service to a medium-sized community in the Northeastern United States. Scott White, the chief executive of Acme Telephone company, has just attended a trade exhibition entitled "Automate, Emigrate, or Evaporate." As a result of what he learned at this exhibition, and also from scuttlebutt he has picked up from his peers in other companies, Scott is concerned about Acme's ability to maintain its competitive position in the telecommunications market. Owing to deregulation in the telecommunications industry and the aggressive actions of new competitors in the local area, a significant number of Acme's customers have switched to other suppliers of telephone and related telecommunications service.

White feels that if Acme were to invest fully in new state-of-the-art fiber-optics technology as well as upgrade to the latest computer equipment, the loss of market share may be arrested, and operating efficiency may be improved. He contacted a leading vendor of fiber-optics systems and associated computer equipment to obtain information on operating characteristics and costs. This vendor would provide the necessary fiber-optics equipment, all associated installation costs, computer hardware, and initial software support for a total cost of $30,000,000.

Although powerful and flexible, the new equipment is also compact, requiring much less space than the existing equipment. In addition, the equipment will require fewer people to operate and support it. Thus, additional benefits are realized by savings in occupancy and personnel support costs. The new equipment promises to be highly reliable and easy to maintain, and these attributes will lead to substantial savings in maintenance and repair costs. After White had consulted with his engineering and managerial accounting staff, the staff developed the following estimated annual cost of savings from implementing the new system:

1. Reduction in occupancy costs due to reduced floor space requirements    $2.0 million
2. Lower maintenance and repair costs                                       $4.0 million
3. Reduced labor costs, fringe benefits, and associated overheads           $7.0 million

The new equipment should also lead to reduced levels of working capital. Because of the vastly improved reliability of the new equipment, inventories of spares and repair equipment will be minimized. And the high-quality customer service will result in far fewer disputed customer accounts, so more customers will pay their bills on time. White expects a $5,000,000 reduction in inventory and accounts receivable, which, for simplicity of analysis, he assumes will occur about the time the new equipment is put into operation.

In addition to the outlay costs for hardware and software, White is aware that there are likely to be substantial in-house expenses related to the installation of the new technology. The engineering and accounting staffs estimated $10,000,000 of one-time internal costs for implementing the new technology. These costs include the retraining of operating and maintenance personnel. For internal reporting purposes, the $10,000,000 internal costs will be capitalized along with the $30,000,000 purchase price when determining the investment required for the new proposal. In addition, the $10,000,000 internal costs will be amortized over the life of the project. For simplicity, it may be assumed that the

$10,000,000 implementation cost is required at the same time as the $30,000,000 equipment purchase is made.

The vendor of the equipment requires an annual maintenance contract of $1,500,000 for the computer equipment, and the annual costs of maintaining and upgrading the software programs are assumed to average about $2,000,000. The vendor is adamant that all the equipment will have at least a 10-year useful life if it is properly maintained. The estimated disposal price of the equipment and software programs is $5,000,000 at the end of five years and $2,000,000 at the end of 10 years. In evaluating capital expenditures, Acme normally uses a discount rate of 16% and a maximum time horizon of five years. Acme does its investment evaluation on a pretax basis.

Scott White has marshaled all these data and wishes to evaluate the proposed investment in the new technology. In addition to the quantifiable data, White knows that some difficult-to-quantify benefits from the new technology are not included in the analysis, and he is unsure how they should be handled.

### Required

(1)    What is the payback period for the proposal?

(2)    Calculate the net present value of the proposal assuming Acme's normal assumptions of a 16% cost of capital and five-year life. Should Acme adopt the new equipment given its existing investment criteria?

(3)    Scott White has read an article that argues that many companies are rejecting proposals because either the discount rate is too high or the time period over which the benefits are considered is too short. He believes that Acme should use a 10% discount rate and evaluate benefits over a 10-year period. Prepare some comments for White on the effect of making these changes in the net present value calculations.

(4)    What other issues would you recommend that Acme consider in deciding whether to accept the proposal, and how would you factor these into your analysis?

---

### ■ CASES

---

## OTHELLO CORPORATION (A): CAPITAL EQUIPMENT PLANNING AND CONTROL*

Our future as a business may well depend upon how well we invest in technology today," said Dan Krause, Vice Chairman of Othello Corporation, during a planning review meeting in April 1986. Joining him were Mike Sullivan, Director of Planning and Information Systems, and Mike Anderson, a newly hired MBA. "More than ever before," continued Krause,

> we are experiencing rapid changes in technology. These changes not only shrink our products' life cycles but also impact the methods we use to design and manufacture our products. To add to the challenge, our major customers, aircraft manufacturers and the federal government, are forcing our margins

*This case was prepared by Steve Young, under the direction of Professor Kavasseri V. Ramanathan, University of Washington, Seattle. Copyright © 1997 by Kavasseri V. Ramanathan.

down while demanding higher levels of quality and service. To survive and grow profitably in this business we need to invest aggressively. Developing new products and marketing, protecting, and enhancing our current market positions, keeping our design and operating costs down, and assuring quality and service— all these require substantial and judicious commitment of new capital expenditures. Are we making the right investments? Is our capital expenditure planning and control process helping us to identify and decide on the relevant projects and monitor actual payoffs from such investments?

Continuing the review, Sullivan provided a historical perspective and said, "Our capital equipment process may have been adequate in the past, but we are a much larger business now and are shortly going public. This may be a good time to review the general approach and policies that guide our investment planning and decisions and how well they integrate with our strategic plan."

After some further discussion, it was agreed that Anderson would study the Othello capital expenditure decision process and report his findings and recommendations to Krause and Sullivan before their May meeting.

### Background

Othello Corporation was founded in 1957 by a group of engineers from Boeing. At first, the corporation manufactured power conversion devices, such as transformers and power supplies, for military and aerospace applications. Since then it has grown in both size and scope to a corporation with 1,500 employees and fixed assets of $27 million. Its three revenue-producing divisions are expected to produce sales approaching $100 million in 1987.

The Power Conversion Division (PCD) retains Othello's original business and is the technology leader for the markets it serves. The Monitor and Control Division (MCD)

manufactures instruments for measuring fuel flow in jet engines, while the Aircraft Systems Division (ASD) produces proximity switches and systems and aircraft power conversion equipment for commercial and military aircraft. ASD currently has 95% of the one-piece proximity switch market.

### Capital Equipment Planning and Control

Prior to the annual operations planning meeting of Othello executive management in March, department managers are asked to identify items to be considered for the next fiscal year (April 1–March 31) capital budget. Department managers solicit ideas from their staff and then accept items they deem appropriate to support the production, sales, etc., forecast for their department. Ideas for new equipment may be based on the need for increased capacity, capability, productivity, or modernization required to operate effectively in the next year.

A Capital Facilities Plan FY is prepared listing the proposed items and is submitted to the division or support organization officer. One division requires a brief explanation of the reason for each equipment item to accompany the lists. The equipment lists of the various departments are reviewed by the officer, who may reject equipment items he deems as low priority or not appropriate. The equipment lists are then incorporated into the organization's fiscal year operations plan, which is submitted to the president/COO for review, approval, or modification.

At the annual operations planning meeting, the CEO reviews all division and support organization operations plans. The sales and profit plans are approved or directed to be modified. The CEO reviews each unit's capital equipment list and may question the need or reason for specific items. Subsequent to the reviews, capital equipment budgets for

**EXHIBIT 1**  Othello Capital Equipment Requests, Budgets, and Actual Expenditures ($000)

| FISCAL YEAR | | MCD | PCD | ASD | ALL OTHER* | TOTAL | ACTUAL EXPENDITURE |
|---|---|---|---|---|---|---|---|
| 1987 | Request | $556 | $1,981 | $1,719 | $3,198 | $7,454 | |
|      | Budget  | 500  | 1,200  | 900    | 1,800  | 4,400  | $4,319 |
| 1986 | Request | 138  | 1,385  | 1,418  | 1,707  | 4,648  | |
|      | Budget  | 150  | 100    | 100    | 1,475  | 3,625  | 3,307 |
| 1985 | Request | 465  | 950    | 800    | 890    | 3,105  | |
|      | Budget  | 350  | 700    | 600    | 650    | 2,300  | 2,251 |
| 1984 | Request | 218  | 719    | 1190   | 1,818  | 4,017  | |
|      | Budget  | 220  | 635    | 750    | 1,395  | 3,000  | 1,838 |
| 1983 | Request | 334  | 774    | 1038   | 1,646  | 3,792  | |
|      | Budget  | 330  | 700    | 800    | 1,400  | 3,230  | 2,217 |

*Central Technology, Central Operations, Finance, Central Services, Human Resources.*

each division and support unit are established by the CEO. These budgets are based on a percent of sales for divisions and perceived need for support units. Subsequent to the meeting, a representative list of capital equipment items and the capital equipment budgets are submitted by the CEO to the Othello board of directors. The board approves the annual capital equipment budget and must also approve any individual capital item over $200,000.

The equipment lists are then communicated back down through the layers of management. The rejected items from the planning process are summarized and returned to the department managers. These are reviewed, and a decision is made on each item to either resubmit it for reconsideration, hold it for the next period, or reject it entirely. Exhibit 1 shows the budget requests, approved budgets, and the amount actually spent for each Othello division for the 1983 through 1987 fiscal years.

Before approved items can be purchased, each must go through a justification process. The requester fills out a Capital Asset Request and Analysis, which specifies the costs and potential savings associated with the ac-

quisition. Bart Stein, CEO, has indicated that capital acquisitions are expected to provide an after-tax return of 15%.

The Capital Asset Request and Analysis form, along with a material requisition, and any supporting written justification, is then sent through an approval cycle. The approval cycle consists of successive levels of management review and approval, starting with the requester's supervision and ending with whichever management level retains final approval authority. Final approval authority is dependent on the asset cost and whether or not the item was part of the operations plan. Exhibit 2 shows the decision tree for final approval.

Having studied Othello policies and procedures concerning capital acquisition, Anderson considered his next step. Although specific information regarding past investments was not available, he concluded that the majority of purchases were under $15,000. To get a better feel for the process, he decided to talk with those involved—the managers responsible for purchasing equipment. He had already heard of some interesting acquisitions, so he knew just who to talk to.

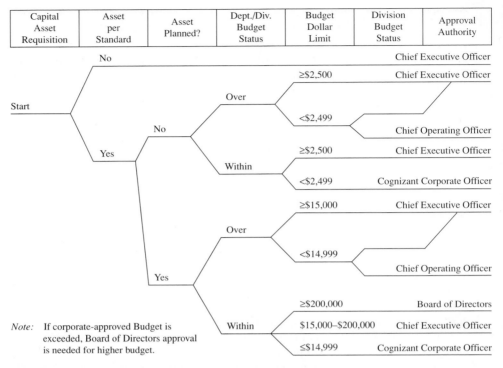

**EXHIBIT 2 Capital Asset Acquisition Approval Decision Tree**

### PCD Data Acquisition System

Early in 1982, Bob Runner, Production Test Engineering Supervisor, began to recognize the need for more comprehensive monitoring of the inputs and outputs of PCD's power supply products during burn-in. Since burn-in forces failures, monitoring the supplies' inputs and outputs would provide valuable information that could lead to better designs and lower failure rates in the future. As Runner said:

> Right now a major piece of the manufacturing process is invisible. All we know when we remove a supply from the oven is that it did or didn't fail. We don't know exactly when or why it failed. Our present setup just doesn't give us the visibility we need. Also, several of our customers have requested continuous monitoring of the inputs and outputs of the supplies during burn-in. A better test facility

would help us meet those requirements and give us the visibility into the process we need.

At that time, PCD was using several different methods of failure detection, ranging from simple periodic visual inspection by a technician for some products to a system employing rented data loggers for the products that require more extensive testing. All of the methods suffered from lack of consistency and an inability to document failure information. All methods proved to be cumbersome and time-consuming to perform.

After researching the problem, Runner concluded that the solution was to acquire a computer-controlled data acquisition system. Such a system would not only sample and store information during burn-in but also control the process itself. That is, it would control cycle times and temperatures as well as digitally program the burn-in loads.

Three data acquisition systems were included in PCD's operations plan for fiscal 1984. But, before the final purchase could take place, the systems had to be justified. Runner assigned Bob Smith, a test engineer, to prepare the formal justification.

Smith, like Runner, believed in the necessity of the data acquisition system and stated:

> We need the data acquisition system for more than just meeting customers' requests for continuous monitoring. At present, no one knows when a supply fails. Heck, no one is even here at night. How are we supposed to know when or under what conditions one failed if it goes overnight? If we can accurately determine the causes of failures we should be able to cut down on the failure rates of our products. But there is no way we can do that with the jerry-rigged setup we have now.

After preparing a material requisition (MR) for the three data acquisition systems, costing $25,000, Smith completed the Capital Assets Request and Analysis form.

> I didn't see any savings at first, so I gave the proposal to Justin [Justin Pearce, Division Controller] justifying the purchase solely on the basis of customer requests for continuous monitoring during burn-in.

The proposal was not approved. The request was returned to Smith with instructions to try and quantify the cost savings to justify the purchase. This instruction forced Smith to rethink the reasons behind the purchase. He came up with four alternatives against which to compare the cost of the data acquisition system:

1. Continue to rent the data loggers
2. Buy the data loggers
3. Hire additional personnel to run the tests
4. Negotiate out of the extra requirements

Alternative number four was ruled out because Smith believed that Othello had a need for the information. Smith resubmitted the request, basing his analysis on what it cost to

continue running the tests on the rented data loggers. Discounting the future cash savings at 20%, Smith found that the proposed system would pay back in about five years.

Again, the request was sent back to Smith, unapproved. Justin Pearce explained:

> A five-year payback tells me that this project shows more risk than it should. Something we need as much as this should pay back in around two years. If it does take five years to pay back, maybe we should reevaluate the idea.

Smith gave it one more try. This time, basing his analysis on PCD having to hire six additional personnel (three shifts per day, two people per shift) to perform the tests manually, he achieved a payback in two years. (See Exhibit 3 for the analysis). To ensure a better chance of having the proposal approved, Smith included with the analysis a thorough justification including all the specifications for the equipment. The resulting document was over an inch thick.

The request was approved by both Justin Pearce and PCD's general manager, Mark Price, and sent on for final approval to Stein. Stein sent the request back asking for an analysis of one system instead of three, preferring to let the system prove itself before purchasing the final two. The request was changed (see Exhibit 4 for the cover memo that accompanied the revised request), and the single system was purchased. But, as Bob Runner noted, "By the time we evaluate the first system we will have spent the cost of the other two renting the data loggers for handling what one system can't." Smith added, "We bought our system, but that little notebook [pointing to the data acquisition proposal] probably cost us more than the equipment."

### ASD—Automated Circuit Board Stuffing Machine

Art Campbell had just started his summer internship at ASD when Ewing Kendell, Direc-

# EXHIBIT 3  Capital Asset Request & Analysis

DESCRIPTION: Data Acquisition and Central System    [ ] JUSTIFIABLE AS COST SAVING (SEE BELOW)

ASSET COST (LINE 5) $ 35,000    [ ] NEEDED FOR _____

| PART NUMBER OR ACTIVITIES | | UNIT LABOR COSTS HRS | UNIT LABOR COSTS $ | UNIT $/ OH COSTS HRS | UNIT $/ OH COSTS $ | UNIT MATERIALS $ * 20% | TOTAL UNIT COST | | YEAR 1 '83 | YEAR 2 '84 | YEAR 3 '85 | YEAR 4 | YEAR 5 |
|---|---|---|---|---|---|---|---|---|---|---|---|---|---|
| 1. SAVINGS FROM ASSET USE | NEW | 4,160 | $10 | | | | 41,600 | | 41,600 | 41,600 | 41,600 | | |
| A _48 hrs/day_ | OLD | | | | | | | QTY | | | | | |
| | DIFF $ | | | | | | | SAVINGS/YR | | | | | |
| | NEW | | | | | | | | | | | | |
| B | OLD | | | | | | | QTY | | | | | |
| | DIFF $ | | | | | | | SAVINGS/YR | | | | | |
| | NEW | | | | | | | | | | | | |
| C | OLD | | | | | | | QTY | | | | | |
| | DIFF $ | | | | | | | SAVINGS/YR | | | | | |
| | NEW | | | | | | | | | | | | |
| D | OLD | | | | | | | QTY | | | | | |
| | DIFF $ | | | | | | | SAVINGS/YR | | | | | |
| | NEW | | | | | | | | | | | | |
| E | OLD | | | | | | | QTY | | | | | |
| | DIFF $ | | | | | | | SAVINGS/YR | | | | | |
| 1. TOTAL SAVINGS APPLICABLE TO PARTS COST (SUM OF 1A THRU 1E) | | | | | | | | | 41,600 | 41,600 | 41,600 | | |
| 2. OTHER COSTS (OR SAVINGS) | | | | | | | | | | | | | |
| A. MAINTENANCE | | | | | | | | | 2,500 | 2,500 | 2,500 | | |
| B. SUPPLIES | | | | | | | | | 900 | 900 | 900 | | |
| C. TOOLING | | | | | | | | | | | | | |
| D. SPOILAGE | | | | | | | | | | | | | |
| E. FLOOR SPACE $ 3 / SQ FT (FIGURE ON CHANGE FROM OLD TO NEW, USE ( ) IF LESS) | | | | | | | | | n/a | n/a | n/a | | |
| F. TAXES & INSURANCE OTHER THAN INCOME TAXES (.025 OF ORIGINAL COST PER YEAR) | | | | | | | | | 570 | 570 | 570 | | |
| G. INSTALLATION COSTS (ZERO AFTER YR1 UNLESS MOVE IS PLANNED) | | | | | | | | | 6000 | | | | |
| 3. SUBTOTAL ADDED COSTS (SUM OF 2A THRU 2G) | | | | | | | | | 9,970 | 3,970 | 3,970 | | |
| 4. CASH SAVINGS (LOSS) (1.) – (3.) | | | | | | | | | 31,630 | 37,630 | 37,630 | | |
| 5. ASSET COST (ENTER IN COL YR1 THRU YR5) (PRICE + SALES TAX + FREIGHT) | | | | | | | | | 25,000 | 25,000 | 25,000 | | |
| 6. DEPRECIATION FACTOR (DEPENDS ON TYPE OF ASSET) | | | | | | | | | 0.15 | 0.22 | 0.21 | | |
| 7. DEPRECIATION EXPENSE (5.) × (6.) | | | | | | | | | 3,750 | 5,500 | 5,250 | | |
| 8. TAXABLE SAVINGS (4.) – (8.) | | | | | | | | | 27,880 | 32,130 | 32,380 | | |
| 9. INCOME TAXES (8.) × 0.48 (CORP. TAX RATE = 48%) | | | | | | | | | 13,382 | 15,422 | 15,542 | | |
| 10. NET CASH SAVINGS (AFTER TAXES) (4.) – (9.) | | | | | | | | | 18,248 | 22,208 | 22,088 | | |
| 11. TAX CREDIT (10% OF ASSET VALUE, LINE 5.) (ENTER COL 1 ONLY) | | | | | | | | | 2,500 | | | | |
| 12. TRADE IN OR SALE OF REPLACED ASSET (ENTER COL 1 ONLY) | | | | | | | | | | — | — | | |
| 13. SALVAGE VALUE (ENTER COL 3 ONLY) | | | | | | | | | | — | — | | |
| 14. TOTAL CONTRIBUTION (10.) + (11.) + (12.) + (13.) | | | | | | | | | 20,748 | 22,208 | 22,088 | | |
| 15. PRESENT VALUE FACTOR 20% = DISCOUNT RATE | | | | | | | | | 0.833 | 0.694 | 0.578 | | |
| 16. PRESENT VALUE (14.) × (15.) | | | | | | | | | 17,283 | 15,412 | 12,767 | | |
| 17. CUMULATIVE PV (COLUMN TO COLUMN) | | | | | | | | | 17,283 | 32,695 | 45,461 | | |

Exhibit 4

M E M O R A N D U M

November 6, 1985

JMH85-81

TO:              B. Stein   30
FROM:        J. Pearce   20

SUBJECT:     Data Acquisition and Control System

REFERENCE:   Our Prior MR and Justification Submittal

The prior submittal was difficult, if not impossible to follow.

Rather than completely rewrite that document I have abstracted and extracted from that document to create a new one.

The problem that we are attempting to solve is to continuously monitor the output of power supplies during burn-in. Making the task more complex is the requirement to program the temperature setting and cycle the power on and off at certain points during the temperature cycle.

We attempted to solve this problem with an internally designed system based on Fluke 2280 data loggers. This system could not provide the interactive control required, the data logger has proven to be too noise-sensitive and not very reliable, and the nature of recorded data is not very suitable for analysis or customer presentation.

Using the data logger approach, however, did demonstrate that this concept works but more versatile equipment is needed.

Continuous monitoring would be a benefit for the burn-in of all of our products; however, today, on only a few do we have a contractual requirement. Table 1 [not shown] shows the products which have the continuous monitoring requirement which is either contractually imposed or self-imposed because of the complexity of the supply (i.e., potential of intermittent problems during temperature cycling).

We will be needing three systems during the next year; however, this request is for only one system to prove out the specific systems approach.

The cost savings and justification are based on this system's performing the work equivalent to two man-years per year.

This is an abstract concept. The data acquisition system can manage, control, and record data from two ovens at once, with each oven loaded with ten power supplies and each supply with seven outputs. The primary controlling and recording activity occurs on a cyclic basis, therefore the workload may be equivalent to six man-hour per hour loads per day plus one continuous man-day per day.

tor of Manufacturing, approached him with a project:

> Art, I've got a job that I'd like you to do. I've come to the conclusion that our circuit board stuffing could be improved. I know that a fully automated insertion machine is probably more than we can use, but a light-guided insertion machine may be just about right. I would like you to do a study and determine if it is cost-effective for us to purchase one.

Campbell began by researching the current process. He found that most boards were stuffed manually while the rest were stuffed on the slide line. Manual insertion rates ranged from 100 to 300 components per hour. The slide line boosted rates about 21%. The rates varied according to the complexity of the board (see Exhibit 5).

Consolidating data on ASD's product line, such as the number of boards per order, number of components per board, and time currently required to stuff each board, it was possi-

ble to define a "typical" board in terms of labor hours required for stuffing, rework, inspection, and test. The results are shown in Exhibit 6.

Given that historical data showed that 62,358 labor hours were required to complete 11,070 boards, a typical board required 5.6 hours to produce. Using the percentage figures from Exhibit 6, the labor hours involved in this typical board as 0.56 hours to stuff, 0.39 hours to rework, 0.08 hours to reinspect, and 0.29 hours to troubleshoot in the first test after stuffing (see Exhibit 7).

The next step was to find out what kind of performance the light-guided stuffing machine could provide. Light-guided insertion machines improve stuffing rates because they present the operator with the component and show the proper location and orientation for the insertion. With this assistance, operators can achieve rates of 300 to 600 components per hour. The vendor's literature also claimed possible reductions in error rates over unaided assembly of 50% to

**EXHIBIT 5**  Component Insertion Rates for Selected Boards

| PART NUMBER | SAMPLE SIZE (BOARDS) | COM-PONENTS BOARDS | STUFFING RATE (HR/BOARD) | INSERTION RATE (COMPONENTS/HR) | NOTES |
|---|---|---|---|---|---|
| 8-317003-01 | 138 | 48 | 0.30 | 160 | |
| 8-060-02 | 2,064 | 56 | 0.18 | 311 | Slide line |
| 8-341105-01 | 29 | 101 | 0.48 | 210 | |
| 8-336401-01 | 22 | 138 | 0.76 | 182 | |
| 8-355303-01 | 26 | 160 | 0.81 | 198 | |
| 8-336103-01 | 26 | 181 | 0.65 | 278 | |
| 8-336205-01 | 27 | 250 | 0.99 | 253 | |
| 8-336311-01 | 66 | 299 | 0.77 | 388 | |
| 8-356-01 | 315 | 413 | 1.20 | 344 | Unaided |
| | 626 | | 0.99 | 417 | Slide line |
| | 13 | | 0.81 | 510 | Guided (2 boards allowed for training) |
| 8-351-07 | 249 | 462 | 1.68 | 275 | Unaided |
| | 23 | | 1.47 | 314 | Slide line |
| | 14 | | 1.09 | 426 | Guided (2 boards allowed for training) |

**EXHIBIT 6**  Stuffing, Rework, Inspection, and Test for Selected Boards

| PART NUMBER | PERCENTAGE OF TOTAL HOURS | | | |
| | STUFFING* | REWORK† | INSPECTION‡ | TEST§ |
| --- | --- | --- | --- | --- |
| 8-317003-01 | 6.3 | 12.3 | 0.8 | 2.3 |
| 8-060-02 | 11.5 | 5.8 | 2.2 | 1.3 |
| 8-341105-01 | 8.6 | 8.5 | 1.1 | 16.4 |
| 8-336401-01 | 9.5 | 6.0 | 3.0 | 9.4 |
| 8-355303-01 | 9.9 | 6.4 | 1.1 | 5.2 |
| 8-336103-01 | 12.0 | 8.3 | 2.0 | 5.0 |
| 8-336205-01 | 15.2 | 4.9 | 0.5 | 5.2 |
| 8-336311-01 | 5.2 | 6.3 | 0.8 | 1.0 |
| 8-356-01 | 8.1 | 4.9 | 1.1 | 2.3 |
| 8-351-07 | 14.2 | 5.8 | 1.5 | 3.6 |
| $\overline{X} \pm S$ | 10.0 ± 3.2% | 6.9 ± 2.2% | 1.4 ± 0.8% | 5.2 ± 4.7% |

*Stuffing includes only actual run hours in the "stuff" step of the process flow.
†Rework includes only CBA "manufacturing originated" rework hours.
‡Inspection includes only "reinspection" hours in the first inspection after stuffing.
§Test includes only "trouble-shooting" hours in the first test after stuffing.

95%. But the extra costs associated with the machine included programming time for each type of board that Campbell estimated would require almost 200 hours per year. He also expected maintenance costs of $500 per year.

As he was analyzing the data he had collected, Campbell discovered that PCD had recently purchased its own light-guided machine. Recognizing a chance to obtain some actual data on machine performance, Campbell called PCD.

PCD personnel were enthusiastic about

**EXHIBIT 7**  Estimated Stuffing, Rework, Inspection, and Test Labor Hours for a Typical Board

| | MANUAL | LIGHT-GUIDED | DIFFERENCE |
| --- | --- | --- | --- |
| Stuffing | 0.56 | 0.37 | 0.19 |
| Rework | 0.39 | 0.16 | 0.23 |
| Inspection | 0.08 | 0.05 | 0.03 |
| Test | 0.29 | 0.18 | 0.11 |
| | 1.32 | 0.76 | 0.56 |

Assumptions:
1. Likely order size = 10 boards
2. Guided insertion requires 0.25 hour setup per order
3. Average insertion rates: manual = 280 components
   guided = 450 components
4. 50% of board failures are due to stuffing errors
5. 75% reduction in unaided error rates with guided insertion

# EXHIBIT 8 Capital Asset Request & Analysis

DESCRIPTION: Guided Component Insertion    [ ] JUSTIFIABLE AS COST SAVING (SEE BELOW)

ASSET COST (LINE 5) $ _____    [ ] NEEDED FOR _____

| PART NUMBER OR ACTIVITIES | | UNIT LABOR COSTS HRS | $ | UNIT $/ OH COSTS HRS | $ | UNIT MATERIALS $ * 20% | TOTAL UNIT COST | | YEAR 1 80% | YEAR 2 90% | YEAR 3 100% | YEAR 4 100% | YEAR 5 100% |
|---|---|---|---|---|---|---|---|---|---|---|---|---|---|
| I. SAVINGS FROM ASSET USE | NEW | | | | | | | QTY | 3,200 | 3,600 | 4,000 | 4,000 | 4,000 |
| A CBA STUFFING | OLD | | | | | | | | | | | | |
| | DIFF $ | | 0.19 | | 6.46 | | 1.23 | SAVINGS/YR | 3,928 | 4,419 | 4,910 | 4,910 | 4,910 |
| B CBA REWORK | NEW | | | | | | | QTY | | | | | |
| | OLD | | | | | | | | | | | | |
| | DIFF $ | | 0.23 | | 6.46 | | 1.49 | SAVINGS/YR | 4,755 | 5,349 | 5,943 | 5,943 | 5,943 |
| C INSPECTION | NEW | | | | | | | QTY | | | | | |
| | OLD | | | | | | | | | | | | |
| | DIFF $ | | 0.03 | | 7.34 | | 0.22 | SAVINGS/YR | 705 | 793 | 881 | 881 | 881 |
| D TEST | NEW | | | | | | | QTY | | | | | |
| | OLD | | | | | | | | | | | | |
| | DIFF $ | | 0.11 | | 8.86 | | 0.97 | SAVINGS/YR | 3,119 | 3,509 | 3,898 | 3,898 | 3,898 |
| E TOTAL | DIFF $ | | 0.56 | | | | 3.91 | | | | | | |
| 1. TOTAL SAVINGS APPLICABLE TO PARTS COST (SUM OF 1A THRU 1E) | | | | | | | | | 12,506 | 14,069 | 15,632 | 15,632 | 15,632 |
| 2. OTHER COSTS (OR SAVINGS) | | | | | | | | | | | | | |
| A. MAINTENANCE | | | | | | | | | 500 | 500 | 500 | 500 | 500 |
| B. SUPPLIES | | | | | | | | | 1,292 | 1,292 | 1,292 | 1,292 | 1,292 |
| C. TOOLING | | | | | | | | | | | | | |
| D. SPOILAGE | | | | | | | | | | | | | |
| E. FLOOR SPACE $ 3 / SQ FT (FIGURE ON CHANGE FROM OLD TO NEW. USE ( ) IF LESS) | | | | | | | | | | | | | |
| F. TAXES & INSURANCE OTHER THAN INCOME TAXES (.025 OF ORIGINAL COST PER YEAR) | | | | | | | | | 625 | 625 | 625 | 625 | 625 |
| G. INSTALLATION COSTS (ZERO AFTER YR1 UNLESS MOVE IS PLANNED) | | | | | | | | | | | | | |
| 3. SUBTOTAL ADDED COSTS (SUM OF 2A THRU 2G) | | | | | | | | | 2,417 | 2,417 | 2,417 | 2,417 | 2,417 |
| 4. CASH SAVINGS (LOSS) (1.) – (3.) | | | | | | | | | 10,089 | 11,652 | 13,215 | 13,215 | 13,215 |
| 5. ASSET COST (ENTER IN COL YR1 THRU YR5) (PRICE + SALES TAX + FREIGHT) | | | | | | | | | 25,000 | 25,000 | 25,000 | 25,000 | 25,000 |
| 6. DEPRECIATION FACTOR (DEPENDS ON TYPE OF ASSET) | | | | | | | | | 0.2500 | 0.1875 | 0.1406 | 0.1055 | 0.0791 |
| 7. DEPRECIATION EXPENSE (5.) × (6.) | | | | | | | | | 6,250 | 4,688 | 3,515 | 2,638 | 1,978 |
| 8. TAXABLE SAVINGS (4.) – (9.) | | | | | | | | | 3,839 | 6,964 | 9,700 | 10,578 | 11,238 |
| 9. INCOME TAXES (8.) × 0.48 (CORP. TAX RATE = 48%) | | | | | | | | | 1,843 | 3,343 | 4,656 | 5,077 | 5,394 |
| 10. NET CASH SAVINGS (AFTER TAXES) (4.) – (8.) | | | | | | | | | 8,246 | 8,309 | 8,559 | 8,138 | 7,821 |
| 11. TAX CREDIT (10% OF ASSET VALUE, LINE 5) (ENTER COL 1 ONLY) | | | | | | | | | 2,500 | — | — | — | — |
| 12. TRADE IN OR SALE OF REPLACED ASSET (ENTER COL 1 ONLY) | | | | | | | | | — | — | — | — | — |
| 13. SALVAGE VALUE (ENTER COL 3 ONLY) | | | | | | | | | — | — | — | — | — |
| 14. TOTAL CONTRIBUTION (10.) + (11.) + (12.) + (13.) | | | | | | | | | 10,746 | 8,309 | 8,559 | 8,138 | 7,821 |
| 15. PRESENT VALUE FACTOR 15% = DISCOUNT RATE | | | | | | | | | 0.928 | 0.807 | 0.702 | 0.610 | 0.531 |
| 16. PRESENT VALUE (14.) × (15.) | | | | | | | | | 9,972 | 6,705 | 6,006 | 4,965 | 4,150 |
| 17. CUMULATIVE PV (COLUMN TO COLUMN) | | | | | | | | | 9,972 | 16,677 | 22,683 | 27,648 | 31,798 |

their machine. Operators were said to "fight over" the chance to use the machine. Insertion rates had jumped to between 400 and 500 components per hour, while stuffing error rates had been reduced 90%. Also, the department could use lower skill level operators and still increase the level of reliability of the stuffing operation.

Campbell felt that he now had enough data to begin his analysis. Based on the data he had collected, he developed a comparison of labor hours between the current stuffing process and the proposed light-guided insertion machine. Exhibit 7 shows the results of Campbell's comparison.

Assuming the machine would be used at 80% capacity the first year, 90% the second, and finally reaching 100% in the third, payback on the $25,000 insertion machine was 3.5 years. Exhibit 8 is the completed Capital Asset Request and Analysis form.

The investment looked like a good opportunity, and it was approved by senior management, but Campbell was still concerned about his analysis:

> I really don't know how representative my analysis was of the investment. To be safe, I was conservative with my estimates, so if anything, the project is better than my justification shows. But I don't know if I used the correct discount rate for this type of investment. All I used was what was printed on the Capital Asset Request and Analysis form. Also, I had no way to quantify other benefits the machine provides. For example, because it can be operated by less-skilled workers, the more experienced people are freed up to do other things. How can you quantify the flexibility it gives us because of something like that? I'm glad it could be justified on cost savings alone.

## TCO—Computer-Aided Design System

Early in 1981, Joe Heefer, Director of Engineering for Technology and Central Opera-

tions, was looking for ways to improve the productivity of the Othello printed circuit board (PCB) designers. In researching how other firms were performing the same task, he discovered that many were using computer-aided design (CAD) systems as tools to speed the process and, at the same time, improve the quality of designs. Further research on the concept convinced Heefer that CAD was an important step that Othello should take.

## CAD

A CAD system is an integrated package of computers, graphics terminals, plotters, and specialized software aimed at helping the engineer with the design process. Within the CAD system, extensive data bases are developed that allow engineers to try many different designs and test the performance of those designs. This can greatly reduce the time for a product to reach production.

Ultimately, CAD can be extended to engineering analysis, manufacturing, and document control. The data base linking the various areas serves to improve both the speed and accuracy of the product development cycle. CAD software is available to do circuit simulation, thermal analysis, and mechanical design and to track engineering changes and even to program automatic manufacturing equipment.

### Feasibility Study

A study that took almost a year was conducted to assess the possibility of implementing an Othello CAD system. PCB design was anticipated to be the major use for the system initially. The analysis focused on determining possible cost savings with a CAD system. Both the historical and projected number of circuit boards designed by each division were determined to gauge potential savings.

A series of meetings with a Corporate Engineering User Committee were held to dis-

**EXHIBIT 9** Benchmark Results

| | TIME TO COMPLETE | |
|---|---|---|
| FUNCTION | SYSTEM X | SYSTEM Y |
| PCB Design | | |
| (130-hr manual job) | | |
| Schematic entry | 5.0 hr | 5.5 hr |
| Reference designation | 2.0 | 1.5 |
| Auto Placement | 1.0 | 0.3 |
| Interactive placement | 1.5 | 0.5 |
| Auto routing | 2.0 | 3.0 |
| Interactive routing | 8.0 | 20.0 |
| Run prints | 1.0 | 1.0 |
| Total | 20.5 hr | 31.8 hr |
| Net savings | 109.5 hr | 98.2 hr |
| Mechanical Part Design | | |
| (4- to 6-hr manual job) | | |
| Design part | 3+ hr | 2 hr |
| Run plots | 5 min | 5 min |
| Total | 3+ hr | 2+ hr |
| Net savings | 3 hr | 4 hr |

cuss CAD's role in the long-term growth of Othello. Discussions centered on whether CAD was the appropriate step for Othello to take and, if it was, how much capability was required. The committee reached a consensus that Othello needed a full-capability system and identified two possible vendors.

A benchmark design of a representative board was done using each of the two systems (X and Y) under consideration (see Exhibit 9). Exhibits 10 and 12 show the projected costs and savings from the proposed system. From the results of the benchmark design, an estimate of the number of hours saved using CAD was produced (see Exhibit 11).

The initial proposal called for two identical systems (Y) to meet the projected usage levels. Senior management was skeptical at first, preferring either to wait on moving to CAD or to purchase only one system and let it prove itself before expanding to a larger system. They felt that the savings might not be entirely realizable due to the risks involved with implementing such a system. After much discussion, they finally decided to purchase two systems. In approving the systems, Bart Stein required that adequate records be maintained to keep track of the output of the systems and the savings gener-

**EXHIBIT 10** Cost and Savings ($000)

| Nonrecurring Costs | | | |
|---|---|---|---|
| Equipment purchase | $568 | | |
| Facilities | 63 | | |
| Startup labor | 39 | | |
| Training | 25 | | |
| Initial lower efficiency | 70 | | |
| Total | $765 | | |

| Recurring Savings and Costs | FY83 | FY84 | FY85 |
|---|---|---|---|
| PCB & mechanical part design | $491 | $550 | $615 |
| Maintenance contracts | (71) | (71) | (71) |
| Photo plotting | (48) | (61) | (71) |
| Training | (5) | (6) | (7) |
| System overhead labor and materials | (69) | (76) | (83) |
| Total | $298 | $336 | $383 |

---

**EXHIBIT 11**  CAD Presentation Made to Executive Management on
December 14, 1981

| | CAD HOURS | | | |
|---|---|---|---|---|
| | MCD | PCD | SSD | TOTAL |
| FY 1983 | | | | |
| Manual | 8623 | 33049 | 20800 | 62472 |
| Caddable | 4623 | 29049 | 18800 | 52472 |
| CAD | 1934 | 9982 | 5800 | 17716 |
| FY 1984 | | | | |
| Manual | 9485 | 43841 | 26500 | 79826 |
| Caddable | 5485 | 39841 | 24500 | 69826 |
| CAD | 2294 | 13691 | 7500 | 23485 |
| FY 1985 | | | | |
| Manual | 10396 | 49313 | 35000 | 94709 |
| Caddable | 6396 | 43213 | 33000 | 82609 |
| CAD | 2676 | 14849 | 10100 | 27625 |
| CAD factor | | | | |
| (caddable/CAD) | 2.39 | 2.91 | 3.26 | |

**Calculation of Savings Possible**

1. CAD factor = CF = Weighted average of division cost improvement

$$CF = \frac{2.91\,(25) \,+\, 3.26\,(12.6) \,+\, 2.39\,(4.3)}{25 \,+\, 12.6 \,+\, 4.3*}$$

CF = 2.95

2. Capacity of system in hours
   A. Gross capacity @ 2 shifts
      4 stations $\times$ 2080 $\times$ 2 = 16640

   B. Factored:      20% for downtime and usage factor
                     10% for training

      16640 $\times$ 0.7 = 11,648 net hours available

   C. Hour savings = 11648 (CF $-$ 1) = 11,648 (1.95) = 22,713

3. Cost savings:
   Saving = manual hours (1 $-$ 1/CF) $\times$ rate =
   CF (CAD hours) (1 $-$ 1/CF) $\times$ rate = CAD hours (CF $-$ 1) $\times$ rate
   Calculation of FY83 weighted mechanical design rate

   $$Rate = \frac{25(12.04^{\dagger})(1.92^{\dagger}) \,+\, 12.6(11.95)(1.68) \,+\, 4.3(9.86)(1.73)}{25 \,+\, 12.6 \,+\, 4.3}$$

   Rate = \$21.60

   Savings = (CAD hours) (CF $-$ 1) (rate)

   FY 1983: Savings = (11,648)(1.95)(21.6) = 490,613
   FY 1984: Savings = (490,613)(1.12$^{\dagger}$) = 549,487
   FY 1985: Savings = (549,487)(1.12$^{\dagger}$) = 615,425

---

*Total hours of caddable labor = SSD 25,000; PCD 12,600; MCD 4,300.

†Inflation factor: 12.04 = hourly wage rate; 1.92 = overhead rate.

# EXHIBIT 12  Capital Asset Request & Analysis

DESCRIPTION: Computer Aided Design System  [ ] JUSTIFIABLE AS COST SAVING (SEE BELOW)
[ ] NEEDED FOR

ASSET COST (LINE 5) $ 765.00

| PART NUMBER OR ACTIVITIES | UNIT LABOR COSTS HRS | UNIT LABOR COSTS $ | UNIT $/ OH COSTS HRS | UNIT $/ OH COSTS $ | UNIT MATERIALS $*20% | TOTAL UNIT COST | | YEAR 1 '83 | YEAR 2 '84 | YEAR 3 '85 | YEAR 4 | YEAR 5 |
|---|---|---|---|---|---|---|---|---|---|---|---|---|
| 1. SAVINGS FROM ASSET USE  NEW | | | | | | | | | | | | |
| A  OLD | | | | | | | QTY | | | | | |
| DIFF $ | | | | | | | SAVINGS/YR | | | | | |
| NEW | | | | | | | | | | | | |
| B  OLD | | | | | | | QTY | | | | | |
| DIFF $ | | | | | | | SAVINGS/YR | | | | | |
| NEW | | | | | | | | | | | | |
| C  OLD | | | | | | | QTY | | | | | |
| DIFF $ | | | | | | | SAVINGS/YR | | | | | |
| NEW | | | | | | | | | | | | |
| D  OLD | | | | | | | QTY | | | | | |
| DIFF $ | | | | | | | SAVINGS/YR | | | | | |
| NEW | | | | | | | | | | | | |
| E  OLD | | | | | | | QTY | | | | | |
| DIFF $ | | | | | | | SAVINGS/YR | | | | | |
| 1. TOTAL SAVINGS APPLICABLE TO PARTS COST (SUM OF 1A THRU 1E) | | | | | | | | 298,000 | 336,000 | 383,000 | | |
| 2. OTHER COSTS (OR SAVINGS) | | | | | | | | | | | | |
| A. MAINTENANCE | | | | | | | | | | | | |
| B. SUPPLIES | | | | | | | | | | | | |
| C. TOOLING | | | | | | | | | | | | |
| D. SPOILAGE | | | | | | | | | | | | |
| E. FLOOR SPACE $ 3 / SQ FT (FIGURE ON CHANGE FROM OLD TO NEW, USE ( ) IF LESS) | | | | | | | | | | | | |
| F. TAXES & INSURANCE OTHER THAN INCOME TAXES (.025 OF ORIGINAL COST PER YEAR) | | | | | | | | | | | | |
| G. INSTALLATION COSTS (ZERO AFTER YR1 UNLESS MOVE IS PLANNED) | | | | | | | | | | | | |
| 3. SUBTOTAL ADDED COSTS (SUM OF 2A THRU 2G) | | | | | | | | | | | | |
| 4. CASH SAVINGS (LOSS) (1.) − (3.) | | | | | | | | 298,000 | 336,000 | 383,000 | | |
| 5. ASSET COST (ENTER IN COL YR1 THRU YR5) (PRICE + SALES TAX + FREIGHT) | | | | | | | | 765,000 | 765,000 | 765,000 | | |
| 6. DEPRECIATION FACTOR (DEPENDS ON TYPE OF ASSET) | | | | | | | | .25 | .1875 | .1406 | | |
| 7. DEPRECIATION EXPENSE (5.) × (6.) | | | | | | | | 191,250 | 143,438 | 107,559 | | |
| 8. TAXABLE SAVINGS (4.) − (8.) | | | | | | | | 106,750 | 192,560 | 275,441 | | |
| 9. INCOME TAXES (8.) × 0.48 (CORP. TAX RATE = 48%) | | | | | | | | 51,240 | 92,428 | 132,212 | | |
| 10. NET CASH SAVINGS (AFTER TAXES) (4.) − (8.) | | | | | | | | 246,760 | 243,570 | 250,788 | | |
| 11. TAX CREDIT (10% OF ASSET VALUE, LINE 5.) (ENTER COL 1 ONLY) | | | | | | | | | | | | |
| 12. TRADE IN OR SALE OF REPLACED ASSET  (ENTER COL 1 ONLY) | | | | | | | | — | — | — | — | — |
| 13. SALVAGE VALUE  (ENTER COL 3 ONLY) | | | | | | | | — | — | — | — | — |
| 14. TOTAL CONTRIBUTION (10.) + (11.) + (12.) + (13.) | | | | | | | | 246,760 | 243,570 | 250,788 | 250,788 | 250,788 |
| 15. PRESENT VALUE FACTOR 15% = DISCOUNT RATE | | | | | | | | .870 | .756 | .658 | .572 | .497 |
| 16. PRESENT VALUE (14.) × (15.) | | | | | | | | 214,680 | 184,139 | 165,019 | 143,451 | 124,642 |
| 17. CUMULATIVE PV (COLUMN TO COLUMN) | | | | | | | | 214,680 | 398,819 | 563,838 | 707,288 | 831,930 |

626

ated. The time spent designing PCBs on the CAD equipment was monitored and compared against historical figures.

Within a few months after installation, it became apparent that the systems would not generate the savings predicted. They were not able to reduce the time required to design circuit cards. Further analysis showed that the CAD software did not have the capability to handle the complex, tightly packaged PCBs Othello used.

Joe Heefer, however, remained convinced of the necessity of the project:

It's a shame the only thing we can measure on the CAD system is the one thing it failed

at. It does the job expected on mechanical design. Plus, I'm convinced our quality has gone up, but how can you quantify that? Maybe we should have presented a clearer picture of the extent we were justifying the equipment for immediate savings and the extent it was intended to serve long-term strategic goals.

### Conclusion

Having reviewed his notes, Mike Anderson considered in what ways Othello's capital equipment acquisition could be improved. Gathering all the information he had collected, he settled down to write his recommendation.

---

# WILMINGTON TAP AND DIE (ABRIDGED)*

Len Green pulled on his coat and walked out the door of the administration building toward the loading dock of the adjacent factory. Four new automated Icahn thread grinding machines used in the production of taps had just been delivered, and Len knew many of the managers would be gathering to see them. As he strolled toward the dock he couldn't help but remember taking this same walk seven months before in May 1978 when the first two Icahns had arrived. It had been his first day as plant manager of Wilmington Tap and Die (WTD).

WTD now had a total of seven Icahns (including this delivery and one prototype purchased in 1974). They had all been ordered by Len's predecessor as part of a manufacturing modernization program. The program called for the purchase of an additional 10 Icahns over a three-year period, but Len had

halted further purchases based on a September performance audit of the first three machines. The audit showed that the productivity and expenses associated with the Icahns had been much worse than expected. In addition, sales of WTD taps for the first half of 1978 had been 20% below forecast. Len had to decide whether he should proceed with the purchase of the four Icahns planned for 1979.

### Background of Wilmington Tap and Die

Wilmington Tap and Die was incorporated in 1912 after the merger of three machining firms. The three companies were located in the small industrial town of Wilmington and had started up based on an 1871 screw-cutting invention used to produce taps and dies. The company grew through a series of mergers and acquisitions in the 1920s, 1930s, and 1950s and added drill bits to the tools that it produced. Following a 1963 merger with the American Tool Corporation, WTD became one of the world's largest producers of

---

*This case was prepared by Research Associate Glenn Bingham under the supervision of Professor Robert S. Kaplan.

Copyright © 1988 by the President and Fellows of Harvard College. Harvard Business School case 189-032.

threading and cutting tools. In 1971, the company was acquired by United Industries, a diversified manufacturer of electronic, aerospace, and industrial products.

### United and WTD

WTD was a division in United's Industrial Products Group. WTD had sales of $18.5 million ($6 million from tap sales) in 1977 on total assets of $8.1 million. The division had been profitable even though sales had been stagnant for the past four years (see Exhibit 1). WTD had been acquired as part of United's strategy to purchase and rationalize high-quality manufacturing businesses with high engineering content. The merger with United had not caused many apparent changes in the management of WTD other than modifications made in the budgeting and accounting systems to conform with United's

practices. The plant manager prior to Len Green had been with WTD for over 26 years. WTD operated autonomously except that the plant manager could not make any unbudgeted capital expenditures over $10,000 without approval from United superiors. Under United's capital budgeting process, expenditures over $1,000,000 required CEO approval, expenditures above $500,000 required sector approval, and expenditures over $250,000 had to receive group-level approval. United normally applied a 20% ROI hurdle rate when evaluating capital expenditure requests.

### Tap Production and Marketing

Taps are used to cut threads into a drilled hole. WTD, with a 9% share of market, was one of the largest producers of taps in the country (see Exhibit 2). It produced a full line

**EXHIBIT 1** Income Statement Summary ($ Millions)

|  | 1974 | 1975 | 1976 | 1977 |
|---|---|---|---|---|
| Sales | 18.3 | 17.6 | 17.6 | 18.5 |
| Cost of sales—standard | 10.2 | 9.7 | 10.0 | 10.2 |
| Gross margin | 8.0 | 7.9 | 7.6 | 8.3 |
| Variances | 1.0 | 1.5 | 1.5 | 0.7 |
| Actual margin | 7.0 | 6.4 | 6.1 | 7.6 |
| SG&A | 3.7 | 3.2 | 4.8 | 4.6 |
| Profit before tax | 3.4 | 3.3 | 1.3 | 3.0 |
| Tax | 1.6 | 1.5 | 0.6 | 1.4 |
| Profit after tax | 1.8 | 1.7 | 0.7 | 1.6 |

Balance Sheet Summary ($ Millions)

|  | 1974 | 1975 | 1976 | 1977 |
|---|---|---|---|---|
| Receivables | 2.1 | 1.8 | 1.6 | 2.1 |
| Inventories | 4.8 | 3.7 | 3.6 | 4.3 |
| Current liabilities | −1.8 | −1.2 | −1.5 | −1.4 |
| PP&E | 1.9 | 1.9 | 2.2 | 3.1 |
| Total | 7.0 | 6.2 | 5.9 | 8.1 |
| ROI |  |  |  |  |
| (Net income/net assets) | 25.6% | 27.9% | 11.9% | 19.6% |

**EXHIBIT 2**   Market Share of Tap Market

| | |
|---|---|
| Greenfield | 12% |
| Winter Brothers | 10 |
| Wilmington | 9 |
| Bendix | 8 |
| Cleveland | 6 |
| Brubaker | 6 |
| Regal Beloit | 5 |
| Vermont | 4 |
| Jarvis | 4 |
| Hanson-Whitney | 4 |
| Morse | 4 |
| Sossner | 3 |
| Reiff & Nestor | 3 |
| Bath | 2 |
| Hypro | 1 |
| Wood & Spencer | 1 |
| Detroit Tap | 1 |
| New England Tap | 1 |
| New York Twist | New |
| Other | 16% |

of taps used in the automotive, hydraulic, construction, and machinery manufacturing industries. The company was known for its high-quality products and its sales support for distributors. WTD considered its strong distribution base as one of its principal strengths. WTD was especially strong among distributors that supplied the smaller end users.

WTD was considered one of the "traditional" manufacturers in the industry along with Greenfield, Winter Brothers, Besley, Cleveland, Union Twist, and some smaller operations. The "traditionals" generally represented the older companies (in business 50 years or more). Most were located in the Northeast (many near the Wilmington area), were unionized, and offered a full product line through a network of tool distributors.

The newer tap manufacturers ("independents") were mostly located in the South and generally had lower labor costs than the traditional firms. The independents had carved out part of the tap market by utilizing specialized marketing strategies. Low price was a key factor, and quality was also important because long and consistent tool life expectancy enabled end users to reduce the expense and disruption caused by frequent tap changes. Companies such as Regal Beloit and Vermont competed by providing 24-hour (or less) delivery of taps that had to be custom-produced. They were adept at producing small volumes that required frequent machine setups.

WTD anticipated that lower unit manufacturing costs when using the automated Icahn grinders would allow it to begin competing for the business of the large-volume, price-sensitive end users.

### Thread Grinding Machines

Grinding the threads onto a tap blank was the last major step in the production process. It was also the most critical step from a cost and quality standpoint. Thread grinding was the most labor-intensive part of production and required the use of expensive machining equipment and skilled machinists. The quality of the tap was almost exclusively a function of how accurately the threads were ground. WTD used two types of grinding machines prior to purchasing the Icahns.

There were 16 Wilmington Automatic Mechanical Thread Grinders that produced sizes #6 MS to ¼″ inclusive. These machines had been designed and built by Wilmington engineers as hand machines in the 1930s and had been automated in the late 1950s. They operated by a single-rib (grinds one thread at a time), multipass grinding method that had remained essentially the same for 20 years. The age of these machines made it increasingly difficult to ensure quality output. Much of WTD's historical success was due to the high productivity of these machines when first developed and especially after their automation in the 1950s. Now, however, they were no longer as productive as the machines used by competitors.

The company also had eight Jones & Lamson Hydraulic Automatic Thread Grinders that manufactured tap sizes 5/16″ through 3/8″. These machines were purchased in the late 1960s, when it became economically impractical to develop entirely new grinding equipment internally. The J&L grinders also operate using the single-rib, multipass grinding method. WTD had made several proprietary improvements to help increase the production efficiency of the J&Ls.

### Icahn Grinding Machines

Shortly after the 1971 acquisition, United made a strategic commitment to maintain WTD's quality and leadership position in the industry. Most other tap producers were also using modified J&L grinders, and any perceived quality gap was narrowing. Investment in the most modern equipment to improve manufacturing efficiency was considered an important part of WTD's future success. As a result, WTD formed a manufacturing engineering team in early 1973 to rationalize the manufacturing process and investigate the latest alternative equipment available. The company discovered that no new thread grinding technology had been developed, so WTD began work with Icahn, a Swedish company, to design a fully automated multirib thread grinder. A prototype, known as the "yellow bird" (because it was yellow), was purchased in 1975 and installed on an experimental basis in the Wilmington plant. The production experi-

ence with the yellow bird was encouraging. The machine was not only more efficient than other grinders but it produced a much higher quality tap. The principal quality advantage of the taps produced on the Icahn was a much longer life expectancy. This was apparently due to lower grinding temperatures, which produced less metallurgical damage to the hardened steel used for the taps. WTD engineers felt that over time several modifications could be made in-house to the Icahn machines to increase their efficiency and output quality beyond what had been achieved on the yellow bird prototype.

In January 1976, WTD prepared a capital budget request to purchase two Icahns as the initial phase of an overall plan to buy 16 of the machines. The Icahns would enable WTD to phase out the eight J&L grinders by 1979 and would meet the needs for additional capacity based on the sales forecast through 1980. The request called for the expenditure of approximately $217,000 per machine (a total of nearly $3,500,000) and represented the largest equipment expenditure in WTD's history. The original request was sent back to WTD by the group executives, who wanted a more thorough evaluation of the financial return that the investment would provide and a complete examination of alternatives open to WTD. A revised capital expenditure authorization request (known as a CEA) was submitted to United in 1977. Its principal justification was to maintain WTD's market share (see Exhibit 3) through the purchase of additional production equipment. The CEA explored several equipment alternatives. Two of these were:

1. Rebuild 16 WTD and 8 J&L Auto thread grinders. Total cost—$880,000.
2. Retire all thread grinders and purchase 16 Icahn Auto thread grinders. Total cost—$3,472,000.

## EXHIBIT 3

| | TAP MARKET OUTLOOK WITHOUT INVESTMENT ($000) | | | | |
|---|---|---|---|---|---|
| | 1976 | 1977 | 1978 | 1979 | 1980 |
| Total market in units | 27,761 | 29,146 | 30,553 | 32,015 | 33,565 |
| WTD market share | 9.00% | 9.00% | 8.65% | 8.31% | 7.98% |
| WTD sales (units) | 2,498 | 2,623 | 2,643 | 2,660 | 2,678 |
| WTD price (average) | $2.51 | $2.44 | $2.42 | $2.41 | $2.39 |
| WTD sales | $6,280 | $6,404 | $6,404 | $6,404 | $6,404 |
| Major Competitors' Market Shares* (units) | | | | | |
| Greenfield | 3,609 | 3,789 | 3,972 | 4,162 | 4,363 |
| Winter Brothers | 2,776 | 2,769 | 2,750 | 2,561 | 2,350 |
| Bendix | 2,221 | 2,405 | 2,597 | 2,881 | 3,189 |
| Cleveland | 1,943 | 2,113 | 2,291 | 2,561 | 3,021 |
| All other | 14,714 | 15,447 | 16,300 | 17,190 | 17,963 |

| | TAP MARKET OUTLOOK WITH INVESTMENT ($000) | | | | |
|---|---|---|---|---|---|
| | 1976 | 1977 | 1978 | 1979 | 1980 |
| Total market in units | 27,761 | 29,146 | 30,553 | 32,015 | 33,565 |
| WTD market share | 9.00% | 9.00% | 9.09% | 9.15% | 9.24% |
| WTD sales (units) | 2,498 | 2,623 | 2,779 | 2,929 | 3,102 |
| WTD price (average) | $2.51 | $2.44 | $2.42 | $2.41 | $2.39 |
| WTD sales | $6,280 | $6,404 | $6,724 | $7,060 | $7,413 |
| Major Competitors' Market Share* (units) | | | | | |
| Greenfield | 3,609 | 3,789 | 3,972 | 4,162 | 4,363 |
| Winter Brothers | 2,776 | 2,769 | 2,750 | 2,561 | 2,350 |
| Bendix | 2,221 | 2,405 | 2,597 | 2,881 | 3,189 |
| Cleveland | 1,943 | 2,113 | 2,291 | 2,561 | 3,021 |
| All other | 14,714 | 15,447 | 16,165 | 16,921 | 17,540 |

*Assumes that competitors will not have similar new quality machinery.

The rebuilding or purchase of the various thread grinders would be spread over a five-year period (see Exhibit 4).

WTD estimated the costs under each alternative to determine the net cash flow of the projects (see Appendix A for detailed pro-forma financial projections for the two alternatives). The capital expenditure request evaluated each alternative on the basis of incremental cash flow as shown below:

| | ALTERNATIVE 1 | ALTERNATIVE 2 |
|---|---|---|
| Cumulative net cash flow ($000) | 12,760 | 15,736 |
| Present value @ 20% ($000) | 5,198 | 5,656 |
| ROI | 42.0% | 43.6% |

**EXHIBIT 4** Production Machinery Schedule

|  | 1977 | 1978 | 1979 | 1980 | 1981 |
|---|---|---|---|---|---|
| Alternative 1 |  |  |  |  |  |
| WTD grinders | 14 | 14 | 14 | 14 | 16 |
| J&L grinders | 7 | 7 | 7 | 7 | 8 |
| Total | 21 | 21 | 21 | 21 | 24 |
| Alternative 2 |  |  |  |  |  |
| WTD grinders | 12 | 12 | 4 | — | — |
| J&L grinders | 8 | 8 | 8 | 4 | — |
| Icahn |  | 6 | 10 | 14 | 16 |
| Total | 20 | 26 | 22 | 18 | 16 |

The CEA recommended that WTD pursue alternative 2 and replace all existing equipment with the Icahn equipment. In late 1977, United approved the program to purchase 16 Icahns and authorized WTD to purchase six machines: two to be delivered immediately and four for delivery in 1978. It was also planned that four Icahns would be purchased each year in 1979 and 1980 and two machines would be added in 1981 to complete the program. Purchase of the final 10 machines would require final approval in each year conditional on the experience with the Icahns previously purchased.

### *Postaudit of the Icahns*

In September 1978, an analyst from the group-level financial staff was sent to the Wilmington plant to audit the initial operating statistics for the Icahn equipment. At the time of the audit, the first two nonprototype Icahns had been operational for three months. The audit was conducted on the three Icahns at Wilmington in anticipation of the request to proceed with the planned purchase of four additional machines to be delivered in 1979 (the four machines to be delivered in December 1978 had already been ordered). The audit revealed three areas in which the actual results differed substantially from the CEA projections as outlined below:

1.  The strength of the Swedish kronor in foreign exchange markets had caused the price of an Icahn to rise more than 15% to approximately $250,000.

2.  Sales and production of WTD taps were about 20% below the CEA projections in 1977. Unit sales were projected to be about 13% below in 1978 as noted below:

| 1977 | | 1978 | |
|---|---|---|---|
| CEA | ACTUAL | CEA | ACTUAL* |
| 2,623 | 2,107 | 2,779 | 2,415 |

*6 months actual, 6 months forecast.*

While sales were below the CEA projections in both years, the increase in sales from 1977 to 1978 was expected to be over 13%. This compared favorably with the 5% annual real growth forecast in the CEA.

The higher annual sales growth for alternative 2 (5% versus 2%) for WTD taps in the CEA was based on expected quality improvement in taps produced using the Icahn thread grinders. The postaudit revealed that, although the quality had improved (initial tests showed a 20% increase in tap life), the

WTD marketing group had not been able to capitalize on the improved quality. No effort had been made to publicize the improved Icahn taps because only a fraction of the WTD's total production was produced on the new equipment. This situation would continue for two or three more years until more of the Icahns were put into production.

3. The actual pieces produced per hour on the Icahns averaged about 10% below CEA projections, and the operating costs associated with the machines were significantly higher than planned.

The reduced output of the machine was caused by several problems:

1. The time required to change the grinding wheel had been omitted from the calculations of cycle times used in the CEA.

2. It was necessary to have the Icahn company build new work drivers (a mechanism that loads and aligns the tap into the machine) and install them for the machines to operate properly.

3. Maintenance technicians had difficulty in troubleshooting the machines' programmable controls. The older thread grinders were operated strictly with mechanical controls. The yellow bird prototype incorporated hydraulic controls that were manually adjusted. But the two recently purchased Icahns had been improved with electronic computerized controls, and the skills developed on the old thread grinders were not applicable to the new machines. WTD had decided to retrain its machinists rather than to hire new personnel. A substantial training program using Icahn factory personnel was undertaken to train the operators and maintenance support. Video equipment had been ordered to help develop better training tools.

4. Variations in the flute length of the tap blanks caused machine malfunctions. Unlike the other grinding machines, the Icahn's grinding stroke was a function of flute length as determined by a sensor on the machine.

5. The CEA production figures were based on the production of regulars. In actual practice, the Icahns were being used to produce some specials (custom-sized taps).

6. CEA labor costs were based on the use of one operator per four machines. Because, at the time of the audit, WTD had only three machines, there could be only three machines per operator.

The postaudit report was first sent to the auditor's superior at the group level. The group controller contacted Len Green and recommended that further Icahn purchases be stopped until a new CEA could be prepared using the actual data from the Icahns already in place. Len Green had already decided to halt further purchases of the Icahns when he received the memo from the group controller. He was concerned with the poor operating results of the Icahns, but he was also worried that thread grinding equipment might soon be available from other manufacturers that would be even more efficient than the Icahn machines.

### Postaudit Follow-Up

After the audit had been conducted, WTD recalculated the discounted cash flow rate of return of alternative 2 using the actual performance at the time of the audit rather than the projections contained in the CEA. Just the effect of the external factors (lower sales and higher cost of the machines) reduced the return to 9%. The reduced productivity of the Icahns would have lowered the return even further, but the exact level was not calculated because the accounting system was not structured to provide cost data on the Icahn machines alone.

There was considerable concern at WTD with these lower projections. The division had been averaging returns in excess of 20% in normal years, and the compensation plan for the senior managers of WTD included bonuses, based on divisional ROI, which could amount to up to 30% of total compensation. Len Green asked his financial group to look closely at the figures to see whether the return from the Icahn investment could reasonably be expected to exceed the 20% hurdle rate.

Further tests were conducted to determine the actual piecerate output of the Icahns. The

## Appendix A: Wilmington Tap and Die (Abridged)

**Financial Outlook without Investment—Alternative 1:** Rebuild present machines, no increase in production

($000)

|  | 1977 | 1978 | 1979 | 1980 | 1981 | 1982 | 1983 | 1984 | 1985 | 1986 |
|---|---|---|---|---|---|---|---|---|---|---|
| Sales | $6,404 | $6,404 | $6,404 | $6,404 | $6,404 | $6,404 | $6,404 | $6,404 | $6,404 | $6,404 |
| Cost of Sales |  |  |  |  |  |  |  |  |  |  |
| Labor | $ 168 | $ 168 | $ 168 | $ 168 | $ 168 | $ 168 | $ 168 | $ 168 | $ 168 | $ 168 |
| Material | 312 | 312 | 312 | 312 | 312 | 312 | 312 | 312 | 312 | 312 |
| Overhead (excl. depreciation) | 1,557 | 1,557 | 1,557 | 1,557 | 1,557 | 1,557 | 1,557 | 1,557 | 1,557 | 1,557 |
| Interest | 0 | 0 | 0 | 0 | 0 | 0 | 0 | 0 | 0 | 0 |
| Depreciation | 112 | 153 | 175 | 204 | 207 | 96 | 77 | 60 | 43 | 0 |
| Division operating expense | 1,473 | 1,473 | 1,473 | 1,473 | 1,473 | 1,473 | 1,473 | 1,473 | 1,473 | 1,473 |
| Staff allocations | 218 | 218 | 218 | 218 | 218 | 218 | 218 | 218 | 218 | 218 |
| Allocated finance charge | 96 | 96 | 96 | 96 | 96 | 96 | 96 | 96 | 96 | 96 |
| Tax rate | 50% | 50% | 50% | 50% | 50% | 50% | 50% | 50% | 50% | 50% |
| Assets & Liabilities |  |  |  |  |  |  |  |  |  |  |
| Inventory/sales | 20% | 20% | 20% | 20% | 20% | 20% | 20% | 20% | 20% | 20% |
| Other working capital/sales | 17% | 17% | 17% | 17% | 17% | 17% | 17% | 17% | 17% | 17% |
| Gross prop., plant, & eqpmt. | $2,225 | — | — | — | — | — | — | — | — | — |
| Net prop., plant, & eqpmt. | 544 | — | — | — | — | — | — | — | — | — |
| Capital expenditures | 220 | 220 | 220 | 220 | 0 | 0 | 0 | 0 | 0 | 0 |
| Investment tax credit | 22 | 22 | 22 | 22 | 0 | 0 | 0 | 0 | 0 | 0 |

# Financial Outlook with Investment—Alternative 2:  Retire present machines, purchase 16 Icahns

($000)

| | 1977 | 1978 | 1979 | 1980 | 1981 | 1982 | 1983 | 1984 | 1985 | 1986 |
|---|---|---|---|---|---|---|---|---|---|---|
| Sales | $6,404 | $6,724 | $7,060 | $7,413 | $7,784 | $7,784 | $7,784 | $7,784 | $7,784 | $7,784 |
| Cost of Sales | | | | | | | | | | |
| Labor | $ 167 | $ 154 | $ 148 | $ 148 | $ 152 | $ 152 | $ 152 | $ 152 | $ 152 | $ 152 |
| Material | 312 | 328 | 344 | 361 | 380 | 380 | 380 | 380 | 380 | 380 |
| Overhead (excl. depreciation) | 1,557 | 1,440 | 1,390 | 1,390 | 1,423 | 1,423 | 1,423 | 1,423 | 1,423 | 1,423 |
| Interest | 0 | 0 | 0 | 0 | 0 | 0 | 0 | 0 | 0 | 0 |
| Depreciation | 134 | 261 | 399 | 518 | 566 | 513 | 409 | 341 | 273 | 204 |
| Division operating expense | 1,473 | 1,547 | 1,624 | 1,705 | 1,790 | 1,790 | 1,790 | 1,790 | 1,790 | 1,790 |
| Staff allocations | 218 | 229 | 240 | 252 | 265 | 265 | 265 | 265 | 265 | 265 |
| Allocated finance charge | 96 | 101 | 106 | 111 | 117 | 117 | 117 | 117 | 117 | 117 |
| Tax rate | 50% | 50% | 50% | 50% | 50% | 50% | 50% | 50% | 50% | 50% |
| Assets & Liabilities | | | | | | | | | | |
| Inventory/sales | 20% | 20% | 20% | 20% | 20% | 20% | 20% | 20% | 20% | 20% |
| Other working capital/sales | 17% | 17% | 17% | 17% | 17% | 17% | 17% | 17% | 17% | 17% |
| Gross prop., plant, & eqpmt. | $2,439 | | | | | | | | | |
| Net prop., plant, & eqpmt. | 824 | | | | | | | | | |
| Capital expenditures | 434 | 868 | 868 | 868 | 434 | 0 | 0 | 0 | 0 | 0 |
| Investment tax credit | 43 | 87 | 87 | 87 | 43 | 0 | 0 | 0 | 0 | 0 |

original CEA projected an average output of approximately 85 pieces per hour per machine. The actual output of the Icahns averaged 69 pieces per hour. Len Green felt that this would improve over time as WTD went further down the learning curve with the Icahn equipment, but about half of the reduced output rate was due to wheel changing time that had been inadvertently left out of the original projections. Much of the lowered productivity was a result of the difficulty that had been experienced with the programmable controls.

In addition to the operating problems with the Icahns, Len Green had learned that his competitors Bay State and Bendix had ordered new Junker thread grinders and Greenfield was considering new Lindner grinders. He asked his manufacturing engineering manager to review the equipment from these German vendors. Preliminary indications were that the German equipment offered at best only marginal advantages over the Icahns, so the startup costs associated with the alternative machines would not alone justify switching to them in the future. Len, however, was concerned that WTD would be known in the industry for its Icahn equipment because it was the only tap manufacturer that had purchased Icahns. This could be an advantage if the Icahns were acknowledged as *the* thread grinding technology. However, if the Icahn became outmoded, it would be hard to overcome the stigma of being the only firm using Icahns when competitors were purchasing the newer Junker and Lindner grinders.

On a positive note, Len had just received a memorandum from the manager of product engineering, who had been performing extensive tests on a random sample of taps produced by the three types of grinding machines now in use at Wilmington. The conclusions showed the taps produced on the Icahn grinders had longer life and higher resistance to breakage than taps produced on the older grinding equipment.

The most recent sales figures indicated that 1978 sales would be within 2% of original projections, and sales were increasing at a faster rate than previously forecast. Len knew that he would have to proceed with the purchase of additional thread grinding equipment very soon if WTD were to have sufficient capacity to maintain or increase its share of market. He knew that it would be extremely difficult to gain approval for a new Icahn capital budget request based on recent operating data, but he was convinced that the productivity of the Icahns would improve with experience. United's group management, however, had asked that any additional requests to purchase Icahns be based on actual production data of the Icahns already in use.

## Required

(1) Evaluate the capital expenditure authorization request for the new machines.
(2) How should Len Green evaluate the post-audit report?
(3) What should Len Green do?

**Basis of Study** The financial study was based upon the comparison of the production of high-speed ground threaded taps, sizes #6-32 through ⅜″-24, under five different machine combinations involving three sales forecasts. Sales, production costs, and all other sales and production-oriented costs were determined on the basis of their relationship to production and sales levels for high-speed ground threaded taps as specified in the Wilmington marketing study.

## Sales

Sales dollars (at net less returns and allowances, cash discounts, and freight-out) and sales/production in units are per the Wilmington Tap & Die (WTD) Marketing Department marketing study.

## Material

Material dollar costs were developed using 1977 WTD standard material costs per 100 pieces and applying those costs against production levels as specified in the WTD marketing study.

## Labor

Labor costs encompass all direct labor operations for the 12 sizes specified in the range of #6-32 through ⅜″-24 at 1977 standard piece rates, adjusted for production levels per the WTD marketing study.

For direct labor operations other than thread grinding, a direct labor standard piecerate cost per 100 pieces for each of the 12 sizes of taps was applied against production for each size per the WTD marketing study to obtain piecerate direct labor for each size and for total production.

For the thread grinding operation, piecerate direct labor dollars per 100 pieces and direct labor man-hours per 100 pieces were obtained for each of the 12 sizes of taps from George Penrose, WTD standards department. Dollars per 100 pieces were divided by man-hours per 100 pieces to obtain direct labor piecerate dollars per hour for each of the 12 tap sizes. These 12 direct labor piecerate dollars per hour were then weighted by the percentage of units produced per each tap size to total units produced. A weighted average cost of $2.69 per man-hour was derived. This cost was then applied against direct labor hours for each alternative per the engineering hours loading schedule (see engineering summary) to obtain piecerate direct labor dollars for the thread grinding operation for each alternative.

## Overhead

Overhead was developed as a function of overhead rates and direct labor dollars. Overhead rates were developed on a plantwide basis taking into effect those changes in the overhead base caused by increased production of the 12 sizes of high-speed ground threaded taps. The overhead rates were then applied against direct labor piecerate dollars (see III. Labor) to derive the overhead applicable to the production of these taps. Overhead was computed *net* of depreciation (see Property, Plant, & Equipment—Depreciation).

## Property, Plant, & Equipment

Gross and net property, plant, and equipment are composed of the cost of new or rebuilt machinery, depending upon the production alternative, and a portion of other WTD plant, property, and equipment applicable to the production of the 12 tap sizes.

1.  The cost of sales applicable to the production of the 12 tap sizes represents 19.9% of total WTD cost of sales. This percentage was applied against the gross and net property, plant, and equipment (GPPE and NPPE, respectively) balances of WTD at December 31, 1977, to obtain property balances applicable to the specified 12 tap sizes. The cost of capital additions (rebuilding and/or purchase costs) was added to this other WTD plant GPPE and NPPE to obtain the total balances of GPPE and NPPE for each of the two alternatives.

2.  Depreciation for the other WTD plant, property, and equipment was obtained by applying the 19.9% rate against depreciation for 1977. The portion of depreciation obtained was applied on a straight-line basis until net book value for the related other property, plant, and equipment reached zero. Depreciation for the cost of rebuilding or purchasing equipment was calculated on a double-declining balance–sum-of-the-year digits method over 9.5 years, as specified in Tax Bulletin No. 15, dated November 11, 1974.

*Capital Expenditures*

Capital expenditures were obtained for the two alternatives from the engineering study. Alternative 2, the purchase of 16 Icahns, makes an allowance for the disposal of the Model Fs in the form of offsetting the net book value of the Model Fs against the cost of the Icahns in the year of disposal, obtaining a "net" capital expenditure.

*Investment Tax Credit*

Represents 10% of gross capital expenditures.

*Other*

The following expense ratios are based on historical data and were obtained from K. W. Stinger, controller, WTD.

| Percentage of Sales | |
| --- | --- |
| Division operating expense | 23.0% |
| Staff allocations | 3.4 |
| Allocated finance charge | 1.5 |
| Tax Rate | 50.0% |
| Other Ratios | |
| Inventory/sales | 20.0% |
| Other working capital/sales | 17.0 |

## STERMON MILLS INCORPORATED[*][1]

As he sat at his desk, waiting for the improvement team to arrive, Stan Kiefner, President and CEO of Stermon Mills stared blankly at the letter in front of him. The letter was from Pete Cushing of the Renfield Consulting Group:

10/1/92

Dear Stan:

I have given a lot of thought to our conversation of last Friday. Having looked at the latest price figures and the projections for the next five years, I would say that I have to agree with you: Stermon is unlikely to be competitive on the basis of cost without an investment in a new, state-of-the-art paper machine. Given the over-capacity projected for the industry, and the $500M cost—I'd say you have to find an alternative! Stermon just can't keep chiselling on price. In my opinion, the only way to maintain and grow your customer base is to offer something the bigger companies can't—you have to become more flexible than the competition.

The letter confirmed what Kiefner already knew. It was no longer possible for Stermon to match the price being offered by the large mills for commodity grade paper (see Exhibit 1). With the huge economic rewards available to large-scale technology in papermaking, Stermon's small machines simply cost too much to run for the output they produced. Since he left Boise Cascade in 1990, Kiefner had known Stermon was headed for trouble without some dramatic changes. But it was only recently, as the real price of Xerox grade paper hit a 20-year low, that the urgency of the situation had become clear.

If it was to continue to be viable, in both the short-term and the long-term, Stermon had to become more flexible. Kiefner had put together a team of his best managers to look at the problem. He had asked the head of the team, Bill Saugoe, to put together a two-year flexibility improvement plan, which would specifically address the competitive problems facing Stermon, and detail the steps which

*This case was prepared by Professor David Upton.

Copyright © 1992 The President and Fellows of Harvard College. Harvard Business School case 693-053.

[1]Names and data have been disguised.

**EXHIBIT 1** Monthly Statement of Income for Machine 4: September 1992

| ITEM | $ PER TON |
|---|---|
| Gross sales: paper | 769 |
|   Freight and other | (79) |
| Net sales: paper | 690 |
| Variable Costs | |
|   Wood | 58 |
|   Purchased pulp | 125 |
|   Chemicals and additives | 94 |
|   Electricity | 28 |
|   Fuel | 54 |
|   Other materials | 29 |
| Total Variable Cost | 390 |
|   Variable contribution | 300 |
| Fixed Costs | |
|   Mill operating labor | 99 |
|   Mill maintenance labor | 36 |
|   Contractor maintenance | 22 |
|   Maintenance materials | 27 |
|   Operating supplies | 19 |
|   Mill supervision | 17 |
|   Mill G&A: Salaries | 6 |
|   Mill G&A: Other | 16 |
|   Depreciation/amortization | 78 |
|   Insurance and taxes | 12 |
| Total Fixed Cost | 332 |
| Total cost of goods sold | 722 |
|   Income: Paper operations | (32) |
|   Nonoperating income (expense) | (2) |
| Net Income | (34) |

needed to be taken in order to make Stermon flexible.

Kiefner was unsure about the whole business. It was a lot easier to work on costs, he thought. You could count dollars after all. But flexibility was a different matter. How could they improve something if they weren't really clear what it was? How could they measure their competitors' performance? How would they even know if they had improved? This was not going to be easy.

Kiefner sat back and waited for Saugoe's knock at the door.

## The Stermon Story

Stermon Mills Incorporated was a small, independent fine-paper producer. It was founded by Tom Brasker, a second-generation Scot, in 1910. Located in the town of Fond du Lac, in Northern Minnesota, Stermon's (single) paper mill was a collection of some 20 buildings, housing one pulping plant and four paper machines of varying vintages. The oldest (no. 1) was the original machine installed when the company was founded. Though a giant in its time, it was now the smallest machine in the plant and was affectionately known as "Little Jack."

Stermon had added two additional machines in the 1950s—no. 2 and no. 3 machines were also the giants of their day. The no. 4 machine had been added in 1976 and was the largest machine on site: 186 inches wide, it ran at a speed of 1,700 feet per minute (about 20 miles per hour). Total output from the site was 570 tons of paper a day, with 280 tons of that being produced on machine 4.

The company's major products had always been uncoated wood-free papers (see Exhibit 2). This market was dominated by the demand for xerographic paper, although many other papers were produced in the general category of uncoated fine paper. For example, Stermon also made book paper and paper for writing tablets. Coated papers required extensive additional coating equipment, while mechanical papers could not be produced in Stermon's pulping plant. For this reason, Stermon restricted itself to the production of uncoated fine papers.

Uncoated fine paper was differentiated from other types of papers by both its end uses and its manufacturing process. The primary end uses were printing and writing, and included, for example, the paper on which this case was printed. The end uses could be categorized into four segments: publishing

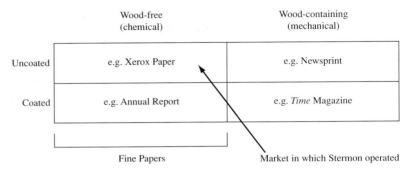

**EXHIBIT 2  Types of Paper and Pulping Processes**

(books), commercial printing, office/business (computer printers and copiers), and writing. Such papers varied from each other in a number of ways. First, and most important, was the basis weight of the paper. Paper could vary in area density from 15 pounds per unit area to 100 pounds per unit area in Stermon's plant. Xerox paper weighed 20 pounds per unit area. Second, paper could include different proportions of chemicals in the pulp that was used. This was called the furnish. Third, paper could be dyed in order to produce different colors of paper. Colored paper was made only on the smaller machines. The machines required a lengthy washdown after each run of paper, and few companies could afford to keep their larger machines idle for this task—Stermon was no exception.

### Making Paper

The first step in making paper and paperboard, after the wood was cut, involved "pulping." This process refined the wood so that only the cellulose, the substance required in paper, remained. Wood consisted of approximately 50% fiber, 30% lignin, a tough, resinous adhesive that gave structural support to the tree, and 20% extractable oils and carbohydrates. During pulping, the cellulose fiber was separated from the other components so it could be processed further; pulping

could be done either mechanically, by grinding the wood, or chemically, by boiling the wood with chemicals. Although newsprint manufacturers relied on mechanical pulping, the grinding process broke the cellulose into shorter fibers when tearing them apart and left some lignin in the resulting pulp. This created a weaker paper that turned yellow more quickly. Only products with less rigid quality requirements—newspapers and telephone books, for example—used mechanical pulp. Unlike mechanical pulping, which used 90%–95% of the wood harvested, chemical pulping used 45%–50%. Chemical pulp yielded 1.25 tons of paper per ton of pulp because inert "fillers" were added in the process.

When transformed into fine paper—the bright white type used in business and printing—chemical pulp went through an intermediate step: bleaching. Bleached pulp allowed producers to make a strong, bright paper that did not discolor during storage or when exposed to sunlight. It thereby satisfied the needs of paper products with high demands for purity, brightness, and permanence. Once the pulp was bleached, it was processed into "stock": a suspension of fibers and additives in water. Individual fibers of pulp were suspended in water and then "beaten" and refined to produce fibers with the proper characteristics of length, flexibility, surface area, and density. Chemicals could then be added to the stock: rosin, aluminum sulphate, or synthetics to reduce absorbency for writing papers; starch to add strength; dyes for colored paper. At the end of this process, stock could be made into a sheet of paper.

To produce a finished sheet of paper, a paper machine had to remove water from the stock—between 100 and 500 tons of water for every ton of pulp. Water was removed by three methods in sequence: first by gravity, second by squeezing, and finally by heating. In the "wet" end of the paper machine, the stock was deposited on a "wire"—a continuous belt of mesh material—with inclined blades of metal or plastic ("foils") underneath it, the wire drained the water from the stock. From the end of the wire, what was now a fragile paper web moved into the presses. Protected from above and below by continuous belts of felt, the paper moved through rollers, which pressed the sheet and drained water into catch basins (so the water could be used again). The paper web then travelled to the "dry" end of the paper machine. There the paper crossed double rows of steam-heated, cast-iron cylinders, again held by felt belts.

In the calender section, the paper was pressed further, as a set of hardened cast-iron rollers improved the surface-finish of the paper. From there the paper was wound onto a steel spool. In the final step of making paper, broadly called "finishing," large reels of paper were rewound into smaller reels, some were made into stacks of sheets (reams), and the paper was inspected. Fine paper, once inspected and packaged, was sold to merchants, who supplied end-users, or directly to the users themselves.

### The North American Fine Paper Industry

**Land of the Giants**   The North American market was the world's largest consumer and producer of uncoated fine paper. In 1989, the North American market accounted for an estimated 45% of the world's uncoated fine paper capacity, and 44% of the world's consumption. Almost all of the demand for uncoated fine paper in North America was met by domestic (United States and Canada) production. Exports and imports were not significant (around 5%) but had been growing spasmodically in recent years in top-end (high quality coated) and bottom-end (commodity uncoated) fine papers.

Despite industry fears to the contrary in the late 1970s, growth in demand for uncoated fine paper increased (rather than abated) because of information processing in the office/business segment. Since 1982, U.S. uncoated fine paper shipments had increased at 4.7% per year compared with 3.8% per year for the other three paper classifications. However, the strong growth in demand for uncoated fine paper during the 1980s had contributed to the industry's reduced profitability in the early 1990s. Significant capacity expansions to meet projected long-term demand, combined with the softening of demand during the 1989–1992 recession, had led to excess capacity and depressed prices. It was generally agreed that real prices for fine paper were currently the worst the industry had seen for many years.

International Paper was the world's largest paper company with sales totalling $12.96 billion in 1990. Uncoated fine paper accounted for about 18% of International Paper's total sales. The company was a full line producer of uncoated fine paper, possessing well known brands such as Hammermill and Springhill reprographic, printing, envelope and tablet papers. A survey among users of laser paper showed that Hammermill had a 30% brand preference compared to 12% for the next leading competitive brand. Georgia-Pacific was the world's second largest paper company after its acquisition of Great Northern Nekoosa (GNN) for $3.7 billion in

March, 1990. In 1990, Georgia-Pacific had sales totalling $12.67 billion. The GNN acquisition not only strengthened Georgia-Pacific's full line of uncoated fine papers, but also added paper distribution and envelope converting businesses. With the mid-1991 start up of a new 290,000 metric tons per year machine at Ashdown, Arkansas, Georgia-Pacific matched International Paper's uncoated fine paper capacity of 1,905,000 metric tons per year.

For the other top 10 producers of uncoated fine paper, the production and distribution of printing and writing papers (including uncoated fine paper) accounted for a significant percentage of their total sales. For example, the proportions for Champion International and Boise Cascade in 1990 were 40% and 53% respectively. The other producers competed primarily on the basis of having focused product lines, providing product and service flexibility, and/or owning channels of distribution. For example, Domtar, Canada's leading producer of fine papers, had its own distribution company and was developing a niche in the recycling and brokerage of waste paper. Paper companies that had a distribution company often needed to complement their limited product lines by carrying products made by other paper manufacturers.

**Recycling**   The most important change in the market for fine papers had been the growing emphasis on recycling. The very visible problem of the disposal of solid waste, of which, in the United States, 41% is paper and paperboard, had spurred businesses and governments to demand fine papers that contained significant amounts of recycled fiber. Unfortunately, the demand for recycled fine papers was not being adequately met because of a limited supply of suitable waste paper. The traditional sources of suitable, or high grade de-inking waste paper, such as printing and converting waste, were already being

heavily exploited. The current North American recovery rate for these preconsumer waste sources was about 85%. The largest untapped source of high grade de-inking waste paper was office/business waste. However, this source was limited due to logistical and technical difficulties. The logistical challenge involved the setting up of efficient and low cost collection programs for offices and businesses. The technical challenge was twofold. The first was controlling the variety of contaminants in the office waste. The second difficulty was the inability of current de-inking technology to remove key contaminants such as xerox and laser print.

These challenges had major implications for both consumers and paper companies. Consumers would assume a critical role in shaping not only the demand, but also the supply for recycled fine papers, since they would be generating and sorting the raw material to be used in the manufacture of the product. For paper companies, it was clear that the distribution of fine papers to businesses might become increasingly tied to the collection of high-grade de-inking waste from those businesses.

### Stermon's Integrated Mill

Plants in the industry were either "integrated" or "paper only." Integrated mills, like the one in Fond du Lac, had a pulp plant on site, while "paper only" mills had to ship in dried pulp from outside. Because of the cost of drying and transporting pulp, modern mills tended to be integrated, and only a few specialty mills now ran without pulping capacity on site. Larger pulp facilities were very much more efficient than smaller ones and the output of even a modest modern pulping plant exceeded the requirements of the world's largest machines. Because of the disparity in minimum efficient scale between pulp plants and paper machines, integrated mills usually included a central pulp plant feeding three to six paper machines on the same site. Plants were almost always located near a plentiful supply of both water and trees. Two types of tree were used to make fine paper. Pine trees supplied long-fiber pulp for strength, while deciduous trees supplied short fiber pulp for smoothness and consistency. For this reason, there were paper plants in both the North and South of the United States. Plants in the North shipped in short fiber pulp, while southern plants shipped in the faster-growing long-fiber. The ideal recipe for paper was around 50% of each type of pulp.

**Plants within Plants**   The four paper machines at Fond du Lac were like factories within factories. Each was housed in its own building, and was supplied with pulp through pipelines from the pulping plant. The huge buildings were old and splattered with dried pulp, particularly those housing the older machines. Each machine operated three shifts a day, seven days a week, with a two-week shutdown in the summer for maintenance. About 30% of the hourly workers in the plant worked in maintenance. The remaining direct operators worked in the pulping, papermaking, reeling/winding, and shipping areas.

Each machine required between four and six operators to run. Operators' tasks were ranked: from machine tender (the highest rank) to spare hand (the lowest). Movement through the ranks was strictly by seniority, and a bright young addition to the shop floor staff at Stermon could look forward to being a machine tender after about 15 years of service. The average length of service of the machine tenders in the plant was 24 years. While there were often disagreements within a shift on any machine, a shift formed a tight cluster of people who knew each other well, and had to solve problems arising on their machine, day and night. In keeping with the tradition of the paper industry, the key measure by which operators were judged was the utilization of the machines. Lew Frowe was a backtender on machine 4:

> There has been a big push recently on improving safety in the plant. A few weeks ago, a guy got caught in a storage tank when it filled with pulp: he died. We have far too many accidents. We've also had management pushing us on quality. Seems like whatever we do it isn't good enough. When all's said and done though, there's only one thing that really counts: "Tons is King" is what everyone knows in the paper industry. You try to get lots of other things right, but if you don't make your tons, your neck is on the block.

Stermon's hourly workers belonged to the United Papermakers Union (UPU). Disputes were frequent (274 recorded in 1991 alone), and two-thirds of cases centered around overtime allocation. Senior union members were supposed to take precedence for being allocated overtime, though management would often try to circumvent this rule. However, the most troubling disagreement for the plant's management concerned the demarcation of functions. Dave Yarrow, the pulp plant manager commented:

> Let's take unloading as an example. Pumping chemicals off a tanker coming into the rail yard is a pretty straightforward job. Here, it needs two people. You need a pipefitter to connect up the coupling, but you need a material's handler to actually turn the valve! It sounds ridiculous and it is, but it's true! The two of them have to sit there like twenty buck an hour hatstands while they watch the tanker empty.

Employee turnover was low in the plant—Stermon was by far the highest-paying employer in the area, and the union protected its employees well. There was a long waiting list for jobs at the plant. "You've got to wait till someone dies!" commented Frowe.

Machine operations had been dramatically altered in the 1980s when digital control was added. Rather than running around the plant altering the speed of drives manually, the operator of the machine used computer control, operated from a central cab midway down its length. A graphical display showed the condition of almost any motor or valve on the equipment. Stermon had found that computer control greatly improved utilization as the computer was able to adapt quickly to slight changes in input materials without production problems. While the computer system on machines 3 and 4 allowed grade changes to be carried out automatically, operators on machine 3 claimed that the computer was far too slow and changed grades manually by altering valves and drive speeds. The most common type of grade change was a simple change in basis weight—the most important way in which one type of fine paper differed from another.

> The computer never quite does it right—but it never messes up too bad either. We just let it take the reins in the middle of a run. For grade changes though, we prefer to do it on our own. (Back-tender, machine 3)

The smaller machines carried out four or five grade changes within a day, but machine 4 averaged one grade change a day, because of the high cost of having it not producing paper. Each machine ran on a two week cycle, and progressed up and then down the basis weight range for the machine, changing furnishes as it went. The order was important, since gradual grade changes kept the papermaking process more stable than large shifts. The machines stayed on each grade for a varying length of time depending on the orders for that particular grade.

### Selling the Sheet

Sylvia Tannar had worked in the sales department at Stermon for almost 15 years. "We've seen slumps before," said Tannar, "but never one as bad as this. We've got guys in this plant who say their fathers don't even remember it being this tough. Paper prices are through the floor. 20-lb Xerox paper has been selling as low as 650 bucks a ton. We can't even get close to that!"

In 1991, three new uncoated fine paper machines came on line in the United States. Georgia Pacific, Union Camp, and Boise Cascade all introduced state-of-the-art machines running at 4000 fpm, producing 850 tons per machine each day. All three were focused on 20-lb Xerox paper, with occasional runs of 18 lb or 24 lb. These gargantuan new machines took advantage of the tremendous economies of scale in the technology. Paper machines had consistently grown in size and speed since the early twenties. With each new machine introduced into the industry, its owner hoped to grab greater economies than competitors, and win out on price or margins. Each of the 1991 machines cost $500m. Historically, the big companies had often invested in new capacity at about the same time, each seeing the same window of opportunity. This magnified the already cyclical nature of the paper industry and 1991 saw the biggest capacity glut the world had ever seen. Fine paper prices fell from $950 per ton in 1988 to $650 per ton for comparable grades of paper in October 1992.

While such prices were hurting Georgia-Pacific, Boise Cascade, and Union Camp, they were devastating to a small company like Stermon, that lacked the scale economies of the bigger machines. "We've had to find new ways to win orders," noted Tannar. One way Stermon had kept machine 4 busy was to begin making grades which were lighter and heavier than were usually made on the machine. "We might not be able to run flat out on one grade," said Tannar "but we can try to keep busy by selling some cats and dogs at the ends of the range. People can come to us for stuff they can't buy elsewhere."

Forty-two percent of Stermon's paper went to paper merchants, who sold their paper to converters. Converters turned the paper into envelopes and forms. In the last two years, merchants and other customers alike had shown an increasing reluctance to carry inventory, pushing the inventory back into the struggling paper plants. "They want it Just-in-Time or not at all," complained Tannar. "I never thought I'd see the day when this JIT business would hit a process industry, but it's here. If we don't deliver in bits and pieces, we lose the business. It either ends up with us carrying the inventory, or pushing really short runs onto the machines. The manufacturing guys hate it—but what can we do?"

### Are We a Cessna or a 747?

Together with the other five members of his crew, Charley Jonn was responsible for keeping machine 4 running. John had worked the night shift tending machine 4 for 21 years.

> There's been a lot of pressure around here lately. I usually get in around 10ish, and deal with whatever problems the late shift has left me with. I set the machine back in trim: Hank on the last shift never does set it on its sweet-spot. Then, I start to take a look at any changes coming up in the schedule.

The paper machine operator's job was essentially one of monitoring the machine, keeping an eye open for equipment problems and making changes in paper grade from the control booth at the center of the machine. Operators generally liked to keep a machine stable, running on one grade. This gave the process stability and avoided a common but catastrophic source of failure—a paper break. As the name suggested, a paper break occurred when an instability in the process or some impurity in the web caused the paper running in the machine to tear. Paper tangled everywhere and the machine would shut down while the web was rethreaded. This meant having the whole crew clamber over the machine, tearing out paper. One intrepid member would throw the leading edge of a new web into the machine while precariously balanced between two rollers. It took anything from 10 minutes to 8 hours to repair a break, during which time production was at a standstill. Breaks were much more likely with thin papers and unfamiliar grades. Curiously, they seemed to occur much more often at the beginning of a shift than at any other time.

Jonn threw his hands up in despair at the increasing frequency of grade changes the crew was being asked to make.

> A big paper machine is like an airliner. It takes time to get up in the air and time to come down. If you want to do small hops, you go in a Cessna not in a 747. This paper machine was made to stay in one spot. We lose 30 minutes of production time every time we change grades. That might be OK on machines 1, 2, and 3 but this is a high-output machine and we lose a lot of output in 30 minutes. I know that times are hard, but if you're always changing over, you never have time to make paper.

> We're all measured on output. The bottom line is and always has been tons per day. You don't make your tons—you've got problems, so we're really careful when we change grade. We're careful and we try to get it right.

Even so, time lost due to grade changes had almost doubled, from 6% in the early 1970s to 10% in 1992. On average, machine 4 was making twice as many changes as it had in 1990, and productivity was suffering. "It's bad enough as it is, without losing all this time and making all this broke[1] changing grades."

**Quality**   "We've always prided ourselves on making a real quality product," noted Lars Robikoff, superintendent of machine 4,

---

[1]*Broke* was the term used for off-standard paper. Between runs, the off-specification paper made was repulped and cycled back through the plant.

"but some of the problems we've been having recently have really taken us by surprise." A large piece of holed paper pinned to the wall was testament to this. "This hole cost us $5,981.28" said the felt-penned inscription.

> It's only in the newer grades—we're so used to making 20 lb, that we make a mistake here and there on the heavy stuff and the light stuff. Customers are coming back screaming at us—you can't blame a printer for crying out when he's got a web with holes the size of lumberjack's thumbs breaking in his press.

Stermon relied heavily on sampling inspection to ensure the quality of the product shipped. Inspectors would check for moisture content, ash content, color, and a host of other features. Any discrepancies would be reported back to machine operators, who would take the appropriate action. Product quality was also monitored continuously by computer on machine 4—even so, the occasional problem slipped through the net.

Robikoff attributed the quality problems to the instability in the papermaking process, due to the higher frequency of changes and the "odd" papers that were becoming more common. He was nevertheless optimistic.

"All of these changes have to end soon. Once business picks up again we'll be back making one or two grades, I'm sure. It'll be the same as it was before."

### *No Paper Tiger*

"I don't think it's ever going to be the same as it was before," said Kiefner. "No matter what happens, we can't compete with the likes of Boise Cascade and Union Camp. We just can't hit those kind of costs in this plant. We'll always be marginal. But you know we're small—and we can do one thing those guys can't—we can be flexible." It was the only way to continue to compete. "Even if things pick up," he said "we'll still need

something we can be really good at; we need to become excellent at being flexible."

Kiefner had charged Saugoe with the job of developing an improvement program to set Stermon on a path that would make it once again, a world-class plant. But now it would be world-class in terms of its flexibility rather than its cost. The improvement scheme would begin on November 10, 1992, and was to set clear goals and milestones. The initial focus of the plan would be machine 4, the largest machine in the plant, and the one considered the most important and the least flexible.

Saugoe had been included in a number of improvement schemes in the past. In August, 1977, he had set up a real-time cost analysis system in the plant. In March 1983, he had led the Total Quality Initiative (TQI), with the specific aim of reducing defects in the paper. Saugoe had looked at a number of Quality Improvement Programs in the process industry before the team finally agreed on a scheme developed by Manzax Chemical in the UK, based on Philip Crosby's methods. Both schemes had been considered a success by management. But flexibility seemed different. What did it mean to "get flexible?" Saugoe didn't know, so he pulled together a team to find out.

**Flexibility in Manufacturing**   On September 12, Saugoe's team of manufacturing specialists discussed the flexibility improvement scheme. A handful of worried people crowded into his office. He had asked each of them to come up with ideas on how to improve flexibility.

Davie Pemthrall was superintendent on machine 3.

> We should figure out how to push this machine a little more. If we improved some of the process control systems, and put in higher powered dryers on machine 4, we'd really be flexible. We'd be able to dry real heavy papers,

but still be able to control the process well enough to make light papers. We'd be able to make almost anything if we did that, then we'd really be flexible.

Peter Lohresich (machine 2 superintendent) differed:

> I don't know Pem, I saw it a little differently. I think we need to improve the changeover times so we can switch between the grades a little more easily. Grade change time and paper breaks are really starting to eat into the efficiency on machine 4. Some of the guys on 3 have got together a fire-brigade. They figured out a way to beat the computer every time on grade changes. They run around like crazy when it comes to changing the machine. The computer does it in ten minutes. These guys are incredible! They do it in two or three.

> "Yes Pete, but number 3 is a little machine, you can play around with that kind of thing there. Machine 4 is making almost 300 tons a day. You need to be safe when you change grades."

> "I still think we should work on speeding up grade changes on 4. I don't see any reason why it can't start getting really flexible, just like number 3."

Lars Robikoff (Superintendent, machine 4) disagreed:

> No, I don't think either of these things really makes us flexible. It's all very well saying we should work on getting machine 4 to make a large range of weights or to changeover quickly, but you'll never be really flexible until you fix the fundamental problem: the machine was built for 20-lb Xerox paper. It likes to run there—that's where it's most efficient. You should forget about getting it to do real heavy, light and all those other weird papers. Let's get it to be efficient across the range of papers we make *now*—on 15-lb, 18-lb, and 24-lb—get the yields up there. Then we won't care which we produce—we'll really start to be flexible.

Pemthrall agreed:

> We have really patchy quality across the grades we make now on 4. Customers

shouldn't have to put up with holes in the web just because we're making stuff our machine doesn't like. As well as that, there are folks out there who've got machines that *are* set up specifically for 15-lb or 24-lb. We better learn to be as good as them, or they'll win every time.

**Flexibility in Sales**    "It means doing what the customer wants," said Elly Ryesham in the sales department. "Flexibility means being all things to all people—of course, you can never do it; but you do your best. It means giving the customer exactly what they want, when they want it, I suppose."

Saugoe wasn't sure that helped. What kinds of things did the customers want, and what exactly did they mean by flexibility? Saugoe set Ryesham a task. "Go back to your salespeople, and see if you can put together a list of things we need to do to be what our customers call "being flexible." Break them into categories, and see which kind of request comes up the most."

Two days later, Ryesham returned.

> Well, it wasn't real clear, but I guess we came up with three things. The first need is for customized paper—one-offs and specials—that kind of thing. Some of our customers would really like us to be able to make paper tailored to their specific needs, even real lights and heavies. Second, customers want us to deliver just-in-time frequently rather than pushing a whole run onto them. Finally, I guess they like the fact they can do one stop shopping here; we've got a lot of product lines. I have my own opinions about which of these is most important, but I also asked the salespeople.

Ryesham had taken a straw poll of the sales force, asking which of these were most important. "They all are!" replied one saleswoman. Eventually the committee ended up with a list, grading each type of flexibility from A (important) to E (unimportant) (see Exhibit 3). Unfortunately, some salespeople had added more "flexibility" items to the list.

**EXHIBIT 3**   Survey of Sales Force

| REQUIREMENT | ANDY NEWLAND | LIZ FOXELL | JIMMY MELLOR | TRACY SHAW | NICK WALKER |
|---|---|---|---|---|---|
| Customization | A− | A− | B− | D | B− |
| Responsiveness in delivery/JIT | A | A+ | A+ | B+ | A |
| Having a broad product line | B | A | B | B | B− |
| Having flexible, helpful salespeople | B | A | C | C | B |
| Bring in new products frequently | D | E | B | E | C |

*Note: A, important, to E, unimportant.*

"There are all types of flexibility," said Saugoe, "but now we have a better idea of what's really important to the customer." Saugoe still wasn't sure how this translated into a flexibility plan for the plant. One complicating problem was that there was already a flexibility improvement program in operation. For the past two years, HRM people had been negotiating a flexibility scheme with the union. Union officials had agreed to begin to relax the traditional constraints on workers taking each others' jobs. Aidan Waine, UPU representative in the pulp plant commented on the rumors he had heard: "We've been negotiating this deal for three years and now they're saying we've got to be even more flexible! Sounds to me like another way of getting something for nothing."

### Flexing the Factory

Saugoe sat in his office putting together his presentation on overhead foils for Kiefner. He felt that Kiefner had been losing some patience with the team recently. It took them two weeks just to work out what a flexibility improvement program meant! Kiefner was a man with cold, steely heart for warm, fuzzy ideas. Two weeks ago, the team had come up with some comparatively vague suggestions for an improvement program. Kiefner had in-

sisted that nothing would ever happen if the results could not be measured. Besides, he was concerned that Saugoe had no idea how to rank the various schemes in terms of their importance. Saugoe had remade a list of the flexibility improvement options, and was now working on which of these should be carried out.

First, Stermon could upgrade machine 4 with computer control, extra dryer capacity, and better training, so that it could make a much broader range of basic weights. With better control, the number of "recipes" the machine could make would also be increased. This would clearly improve the flexibility of the machine. If the machine were able to make heavier weights as well as slightly lighter weights than it could now, Stermon could make money by tailoring paper to customers' specific requirementsboth within the existing range of the machine, and outside it. Marketing estimated that a 7% premium (before freight) could be charged for such a service on these grades, though the machine would only produce such specialty jobs for 30% of the time. The capital cost of improving the flexibility of the machine in this way was $3.1 million.

The second option relied much more on the people in the plant being able to adopt new ways of working. It would mean completely breaking with paper industry tradition. Machine 4 could be taken to a one week cycle, and run through the existing grades every week instead of every two weeks. This would certainly save on inventory costs—but even if inventory stayed the same, marketing estimated that Stermon could charge a 3% prefreight premium for the ability to make weekly "JIT" production runs. This was not at all straightforward though. If changeover times remained the same, it would mean a lot more time lost due to grade changes on machine 4. Ten percent of available machine time was currently lost due to changeovers. Would the machine operators be able to learn to change over faster? Perhaps some of the machine tenders from machine 3 could help the crew on 4 to become more flexible among the grades.

The third option was to improve the yield

on machine 4 on the less frequently produced grades. In general, paper produced on the machine split into four categories, as shown in Exhibit 4. Machine 4 was strongly focused on 20-lb Xerox paper. Over the past year however, demand had been very soft for this paper because of the new capacity in the industry. For 28% of the past year's two-week machine cycles, there had been no demand for 20-lb paper (see Exhibit 5), and the capacity of the machine was shared among the other grades in their "normal" proportions to each other. This situation was expected to continue for at least two more years. These abnormal weeks were very unpopular on the floor, since it meant spending two weeks without running the machine on its sweet spot. The machine was not sufficiently flexible to produce all grades well.

**EXHIBIT 4**   Yields and Proportions of Output on Machine 4

| GRADE | <15-LB | 18-LB | 20-LB | 24-LB+ |
|---|---|---|---|---|
| Yield* | 78% | 86% | 95% | 89% |
| Usual proportion of production | 14% | 16% | 62% | 8% |
| Proportion when no 20-lb demand | 37% | 42% | — | 21% |

*Yield figures are net of grade changes. These are the yields once the machine is running the grade.*

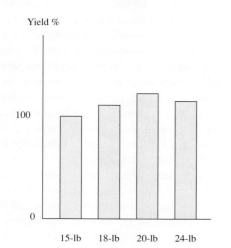

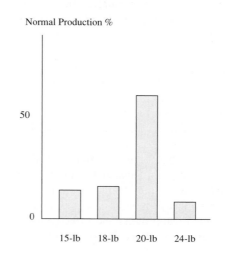

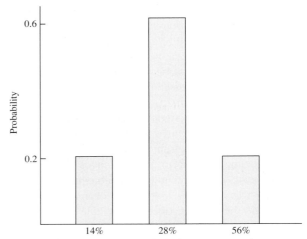

Proportion of two-week cycles in the next two years in which there will be no 20-lb. paper produced.

**EXHIBIT 5 Marketing Projections—
Best/Worst/Expected for 20-lb Xerox**

To improve this flexibility among the grades, a new expert system for process control could be installed. This system promised to raise the yields for 15-lb to 24-lb paper made on the machine so that they would be comparable to that for 20-lb, providing the machine with much more flexibility across its grade range. The machine would then be much more tolerant of a lack of demand for its "favorite" grade. In addition, quality would become more consistent across the grade range. The cost of this system and the associated actuator network was $5.05 million.

Finally, Saugoe could recommend accelerating the flexibility program that was being worked out with the union. There had been other fires to fight in recent months, and a lot of the original impetus in the program had drained away. This program had the advantage that it was already underway, and was important in improving the effectiveness of the labor in the plant. Seeing people sitting

around waiting for the "right" job to show up was getting to be really demoralizing for everyone in the plant.

While Stermon could go ahead with all four plans, Saugoe knew from his experiences with other improvement schemes that it would be much better to focus attention on one or two. In addition, he was concerned that some combinations of the flexibility improvement plans would conflict. He sketched out some notes to himself on how the plans might interact (see Exhibit 6). Saugoe wondered if there might be another way out. "Maybe we should work on having enough flexibility to get out of this business altogether!" thought Saugoe, half-cynically, half-seriously, as he put together the slides for his presentation to Kiefner.

As he checked his recommendation in indelible pen on the slide, Saugoe thought, "No changing my mind now I guess." With no flexibility left, he knocked on Kiefner's door.

**EXHIBIT 6**  Combinations of Improvement Plans

|  | INCREASE RANGE | ONE-WEEK CYCLE | UNIFORM YIELDS |
|---|---|---|---|
| One week-cycle | Might be difficult just to make new grades *without* trying to change between them quickly. Combination of unfamiliar grades and process instability might cause paper breaks and/or quality problems. |  |  |
| Uniform yields | Would be too difficult to improve yields at the same time as stretching the machine. With the new grades being anticipated, would not expect any yield improvement on existing grades. | In order to improve yields, would probably need to stay on grades for at least as long as current run lengths. Unlikely to get process stable enough to improve yields if more changes. Could do it—but results would be to raise non-20-lb yields only about 3%. |  |
| Labor multiskilling | Could use existing skill base and use this as an opportunity to cut across functional lines. People generally enthusiastic about "difficult" papers. Would need to relax "output" pressure. | Might cause a lot of discontent if people were being asked to change over faster/more often, as well as performing multiple functions. Not likely to work well. | This would already be seen as a way of improving output rather than improving flexibility. Hard to combine with a push on multitasking. |

# BURLINGTON NORTHERN: THE ARES DECISION (A)*

ARES will give Operations better control over its assets. We will schedule locomotives and cars more precisely, and get more efficiency and utilization of locomotives and tracks. ARES will also enable us to service our customers better by offering more reliable and predictable deliveries.

*Joe Galassi, Executive Vice President, Operations*

*Professors Julie H. Hertenstein and Robert S. Kaplan prepared this case as the basis for class discussion.
Copyright © 1991 by the President and Fellows of Harvard College. Harvard Business School case 191-122.

In July 1990, Burlington Northern's senior executives were deciding whether to invest in ARES (Advanced Railroad Electronics System), an automated railroad control system. ARES, expected to cost $350 million, would radically change how railroad operations were planned and controlled. The potential implications of this investment were so extensive that they affected virtually all parts of the BN organization. Nine years had passed since BN managers had begun to consider whether automated control technology could

**EXHIBIT 1** Recent Financial Data

| | YEAR ENDED DECEMBER 31 | |
|---|---|---|
| INCOME STATEMENTS ($000) | 1989 | 1988 RESTATED |
| Revenues | | |
| Railroad | $4,606,286 | $4,541,001 |
| Corporate and nonrail operations | | 158,516 |
| Total revenues | $4,606,286 | $4,699,517 |
| Costs and Expenses | | |
| Compensation and benefits | 1,701,146 | 1,630,283 |
| Fuel | 327,606 | 288,477 |
| Material | 319,497 | 341,126 |
| Equipment rents | 343,436 | 320,900 |
| Purchased services | 524,845 | 531,555 |
| Depreciation | 309,206 | 350,948 |
| Other | 410,266 | 406,459 |
| Corporate and nonrail operations | 13,748 | 150,869 |
| Total costs and expenses | $3,949,750 | $4,020,617 |
| Operating income | 656,536 | 678,900 |
| Interest expense on long-term debt | 270,272 | 292,050 |
| Litigation settlement | | (175,000) |
| Other income (expense)—net | 4,397 | (32,655) |
| Income from continuing operations before income taxes | 390,661 | 179,195 |
| Provision for income taxes | 147,670 | 80,493 |
| Income from continuing operations | $ 242,991 | $ 98,702 |
| Income from discontinued operations Net of income taxes | | 57,048 |
| Net income | $ 242,991 | $ 155,750 |

| | YEAR ENDED DECEMBER 31 | |
|---|---|---|
| BALANCE SHEETS ($000) | 1989 | 1988 RESTATED |
| Assets | | |
| Current Assets | | |
| Cash and cash equivalents | $ 82,627 | $ 83,620 |
| Accounts receivable—net | 430,355 | 685,018 |
| Material and supplies | 133,286 | 157,954 |
| Current portion of deferred income taxes | 119,589 | 98,339 |
| Other current assets | 31,137 | 39,740 |
| Total current assets | $ 796,994 | $1,064,671 |
| Property and equipment—net | 5,154,532 | 5,078,262 |
| Other assets | 196,254 | 187,401 |
| Total assets | $6,147,780 | $6,330,334 |
| Liabilities and Stockholders' Equity | | |
| Total current liabilities | $1,287,966 | $1,218,757 |
| Long-term debt | 2,219,619 | 2,722,625 |

*continued*

|  | YEAR ENDED DECEMBER 31 | |
| BALANCE SHEETS ($000) | 1989 | 1988 RESTATED |
| --- | --- | --- |
| Other liabilities | 268,721 | 270,702 |
| Deferred income taxes | 1,277,715 | 1,186,124 |
| Total liabilities | $5,054,021 | $4,398,208 |
| Preferred stock—redeemable | 13,512 | 14,101 |
| Common Stockholders' Equity | | |
| Common stock | 967,528 | 992,405 |
| Retained earnings (deficit) | 131,544 | (20,624) |
| Subtotal Equity | $1,009,072 | $ 971,781 |
| Cost of Treasury stock | (18,825) | (53,756) |
| Total common stockholders' equity | $1,080,247 | $ 918,025 |
| Total liabilities and stockholders' equity | $6,147,780 | $6,330,334 |

|  | YEAR ENDED DECEMBER 31 | |
| CAPITAL EXPENDITURES ($000,000) | 1989 | 1988 RESTATED |
| --- | --- | --- |
| Roadway | $297 | $305 |
| Equipment | 154 | 155 |
| Other | 14 | 14 |
| Total | $465 | $474 |

*Source: 1989 Annual Report.*

be applied to the railroad. Yet managers were still divided about whether the ARES project should be continued.

## Company Background

Burlington Northern Railroad was formed in 1970, by the merger of four different railroads. In addition to a vast rail system, the merged company owned substantial natural resources including extensive land grant holdings containing minerals, timber, and oil and gas. In 1989, up to 800 trains per day ran on BN routes generating revenues of $4,606 million and net income of $242 million (see Exhibit 1 for financial data).

BN's diverse operations and staffs were headquartered in three cities. The firm's CEO, COO, and corporate functions such as finance, strategic planning, marketing, and labor relations were located in Fort Worth, Texas. The Operations Department, headquartered in Overland Park, Kansas, was the largest department in BN. It oversaw operating divisions comprising train dispatchers, operators, and their supervisors, and it managed support functions such as research and development, engineering, and maintenance. Additional corporate staff functions, such as Information System Services, were located in St. Paul, Minnesota.

## Products, Markets, Competitors, and the Effects of Deregulation

BN's revenues came from seven primary segments: coal, agricultural commodities, industrial products, intermodal, forest products, food and consumer products, and automotive products.

Coal was BN's largest source of revenue, representing about one-third of total revenue. Over 90% of the coal carried by BN originated in the Powder River Basin of Montana and Wyoming. BN had invested heavily in the 1970s to build lines to serve the Powder River Basin. If the U.S. government enacted the anticipated acid rain legislation, demand for the Powder River Basin's low-sulphur coal was expected to increase substantially. Managers also believed that Powder River coal had promising export potential to Japan and other Pacific Rim nations from the west coast ports served by BN.

Coal was carried in unit trains or "sets" (108 cars, each holding 102 tons of coal, powered by three to six engines). Virtually all of the unit coal traffic was under long-term contract with fewer than two dozen customers. To insure good asset utilization, cycle time was important. A reduction in the average cycle time reduced the number of sets required to carry a given amount of coal, and hence, reduced the capital investment in coal cars, most of which were owned by customers. Thus, unit coal trains never stopped, and the coal business was almost totally predictable. Although sensitive to cycle time, the coal business was not sensitive to arrival time precision as coal could be dumped on the ground without waiting for special unloading facilities or warehouse space. Even electric utilities, however, were becoming aware of just-in-time delivery benefits.

BN's major competition in coal were other railroads, especially the Union Pacific (UP). UP had made substantial investments in heavy duty double track and in new technology, fuel efficient engines for carrying coal. BN management believed UP had excess capacity, whereas BN, with its single track lines, was running close to capacity on its coal lines.

Agricultural commodities, primarily grain, was BN's second largest segment. Strategically located to serve the Midwest and Great Plains grain-producing regions, BN was the number one hauler of spring wheat, and the number two hauler of corn. Although grain and coal were both bulk commodity businesses with little competition from trucks, the grain business differed substantially from coal. Demand for grain deliveries was more random since the time of harvest varied from year to year, and export demand for grain also fluctuated with the highly variable market price of grain. Grain traders dealt for the best prices, and long-term arrangements were uncommon. BN managers expected that with the change in economic policies in Eastern Europe (and possibly the Soviet Union), the standard of living in these countries would rise, leading to an increased demand for grain. With its ability to serve both the grain producing regions and west coast and Gulf ports, BN expected this segment of its business to grow significantly in future years.

During the late 1980s, BN changed the marketing of grain transportation through its Certificates of Transportation (COT) program. Under this program, BN sold contracts containing commitments to move carloads of grain within a three-day interval, six months in the future. The COT was helping to eliminate some of the randomness in grain shipments and pricing. BN, though, now had to have cars available reliably for the contracted shipment, or else incur a large penalty for failure to perform. The COT program had been a successful innovation but it put a premium on BN to coordinate and plan its grain operations.

John Anderson, Executive Vice President for Marketing and Sales, believed that BN's five other commodity businesses had many similarities:

Although the customers differ, these five businesses all have significant flat or boxcar movements. They have random movement and demand, and are strongly service sensitive. Customers make tradeoffs between price and quality and these businesses all put us into severe competition with trucks.

Think of a continuum of commodities. At one end of the continuum are commodities that should go by train such as coal or grain. These commodities are heavy and low cost, have low time sensitivity, and come in large lots. At the other end are commodities that should go by truck, such as strawberries, electronics, and garments. These are light and high cost, have extremely high time sensitivity, and come in small lots. In between these two extremes are many commodities where trucks and trains compete vigorously on price and service.

Historically, trucks had taken over the transportation of more and more of the contested commodities. At the end of World War II, about 70% of intercity freight had been shipped by rail. In the post–WW II era, rail's share of intercity shipments was lost, primarily to trucking, and especially in the service sensitive segments. Ed Butt, ARES project director, highlighted the reasons for trucking's inroads: "Trucks charge as much as two to three times what it would cost for rail service. But trucks go door-to-door, and people will pay for that level of service."

Recent trends in manufacturing, such as just-in-time production systems and cycle time reduction were making trucking's service time advantages even more valuable. Railroads were using their intermodal trailer/container-on-flatcar service to offer door-to-door delivery but still could not offer the reliability of delivery that trucks could obtain on a highway system where drivers could often make up for unexpected delays. As Butt explained:

We may have peaked at 75% on-time delivery for our general merchandise, and 80% for intermodal. But 75%–80% is not good enough for just-in-time service. Trucks are 90%–95% and we need to get into that range to attract the just-in-time customers, who are enormously sensitive to consistent reliable deliveries.

**Effects of Deregulation**   The deregulation of both the trucking and railroad industries in 1980 had changed both the railroads' and the truckers' competitive environment. The Motor Carrier Act of 1980 gave truckers much greater freedom in setting rates and entering markets. The Staggers Rail Act of 1980 gave railroads similar freedom in setting their own rates; it also included provisions allowing railroads to own other forms of transportation.

Following deregulation, BN modernized its railroad operations. Richard Bressler, the chairman in 1980, established a research and development department in Operations and hired Steve Ditmeyer to head the group. Numerous new technologies and innovations were considered and, where appropriate, were applied to railroad operations. During the 1980s, railroad productivity increased dramatically: the number of employees declined by 50% while revenue ton miles increased by over two-thirds.

But trucking rates fell significantly after deregulation, putting pressure on the railroads' chief advantage: the low-cost transportation of freight. In 1990, additional regulatory changes permitting trucks to be longer and heavier were under consideration. These changes would enable trucks to further reduce their costs. Dick Lewis, Vice President of Strategic Planning, however, recognized:

In our recent analysis we've been surprised to find that railroads and not trucks are some of our major competition. Since deregulation, intrarailroad competition is increasing and driving down prices at a fearsome rate. Trucks have carved off their own segments fairly solidly. Railroads want to compete in these segments, but they don't, and trucks are pretty secure in them.

### Existing Operations

In 1990 each day up to 800 trains traveled approximately 200,000 train-miles on the 23,356 miles of track on BN routes. The

5,000 junctions created 25 million possible distinct routings, or origin-destination pairs, for the cars that comprised BN trains. Meets and passes—two trains "meeting" on a single track with one of them directed off to a siding so that the other can "pass"—were carefully managed by the railroad's dispatchers. BN managers believed that thousands of meets and passes occurred each day but were unsure about the precise number; some believed the actual number was as high as 10,000 per day.

A train running off schedule could potentially affect many other trains due to the limited number of tracks—often only one—and sidings in any area. Thus, controlling train operations meant controlling an extensive, complex network of dynamic, interdependent train and car movements.

Trains were controlled by dispatchers, each responsible for a distinct territory. Dispatchers still utilized technology developed around 1920 and little changed since then. A dispatcher was responsible for the 20 or 30 trains operating on his shift in his territory. Operations personnel, however, estimated that a good dispatcher could really only focus on and expedite five to seven trains. The remainder were inevitably treated with less attention and lower priority. At present, dispatcher priority went to scheduling competitive segments like intermodal and merchandise traffic; unit trains carrying coal and grain were not scheduled. Dispatchers had little basis for trading off delaying an intermodal train versus reducing the cycle time for a coal train.

Dispatchers saw information only about their own territories, and not others. Thus, if a delayed train entered a dispatcher's territory, he would be unaware that enough slack existed farther down the line to make up all the lost time, and that he should not jeopardize the schedules of his other trains by trying to catch the delayed train up to its schedule. Typically, trains were directed to run as fast as they could and then halted to wait at sidings.

Dispatchers also scheduled maintenance-of-way (MOW) crews. MOW crews would travel to a section of track that needed maintenance and repair. But the crews were not allowed to initiate work on the track until the dispatcher was confident that no train would run down the track during the crew's work period. At present, train arrivals at MOW work sites could be predicted within a 30- to 45-minute window, but for safety reasons, the work crews were cleared off the track much sooner than the beginning of this window.

Dispatchers spent considerable time establishing communications with trains and MOW vehicles. Dispatchers had to search various radio frequencies to establish contact with trains; MOW vehicles often reported long waits until they were able to get through to the dispatcher for permission to get onto the track. In fact, on some occasions, the MOW crew traveled to the maintenance site but were unable to get through to the dispatcher before the maintenance window closed and another train was scheduled to arrive, hence wasting the trip.

Current information about railroad operations was difficult to obtain. For example, to know how much fuel was available, an engineer had to stop the train, get out, and look at the gauge on the tank at the back of the locomotive. Trains refueled nearly every time they passed a fueling station, even if the added fuel was not necessary for the next part of the trip. Further, despite daily maintenance checks of critical components such as brakes, lights, and bells, and scheduled periodic maintenance every 92 days, the only evidence of a locomotive performing poorly came from reports filed by the crew about observable failures or breakdowns. Except for the newest locomotives, no gauges or recording systems monitored conditions that could foreshadow failures such as oil pressure or temperature changes.

Information about the location of cars and trains was also subject to delay and error. Conductors were given instructions about which cars to set out and pick up at each location. Following completion of a set-out or pick-up, the conductor made a written notation. When the train arrived at the next terminal (conceivably hours later), the paper was given to a clerk who entered the data via keyboard to update management data files. Arrivals of trains at stations were recorded by clerks who, if busy, might not observe the actual arrival, thus recording a 12:00 train as 12:15, and then entering this fact at 1:00 to the management data files.

Some executives were exploring the application of modern management science philosophy to improve railroad scheduling. According to Mark Cane, Vice President, Service Design:

> There are many potentially useful operations research and artificial intelligence techniques that are not yet being used by the railroad. Decision support technology has made a quantum leap forward, and we are trying to take advantage of it.

Dick Lewis illustrated the contrast between the BN and another highly scheduled transportation company:

> A benchmark company in this area is UPS. UPS has 1200 industrial engineers working for them; BN has only half a dozen.

One view, integrated network management, was being discussed among BN's senior managers. Under this approach, scientifically designed schedules would be generated, broken down into "standards" for each task, plus the appropriate education and incentives would be provided for local operations personnel to cause them to run the railroad to schedule. One operating manager voiced the concerns of many about this approach to railroad train scheduling:

> BN has talked a lot about running a scheduled railroad. However, the real challenge is how to manage the unscheduled, for example, a broken air hose or a broken rail. The problem is that problems do not happen on schedule.

By mid-1990, BN's service design organization had begun to institute a reporting system called the service measurement system. Bands of acceptable performance were established for scheduled trains and compared with actual results. On-time scheduled performance measures became part of the bonus incentive system for nonunion operating personnel. Following the institution of the reporting scheme, service showed definite and steady improvement. The percentage of scheduled cars arriving within targeted performance bands jumped from 25% in January 1990 to 58% in June. This suggested to BN managers that service performance could be improved simply by better collection and reporting of performance measures.

### Strategic View of Operations

In late 1989, BN executives undertook a major strategic review to help shape the future. Gerald Grinstein, the chief executive officer of BN, focused the review on answering questions like, "What kind of railroad should we be?" Executives formed eight teams to examine in depth the following areas: operating strategies, customer behavior, information technology, labor, business economics, organizational performance, industry restructuring, and competitive analysis.

Dick Lewis explained the conclusions reached by this strategic directions project:

> This company, and the railroad industry, face two major challenges: service and capital intensity. We must improve our ability to deliver service. We must reform and reconstitute our service

offerings, especially in highly service-sensitive segments. Since World War II, railroads have retrenched from service sensitive segments. For example, they have stopped carrying passengers and less-than-carload shipments.

If we improve service, the first opportunity created is to increase volume, at the expense of other rail carriers. The second opportunity is to raise prices, but this is more questionable. To be able to raise price requires a *radical* service change, not a marginal one. The change must be radical enough to be perceived by a customer who says, "Wow! That's different!" For example, in our chemical business we recently made such a change. We reduced the average delivery time by more than half, and we also reduced the variability of the delivery time. The shipper found he could get rid of 100 rail cars. That had a measurable value significant enough for the customer to perceive the service improvement. We have subsequently been able to structure an agreement with the shipper to provide financial incentives to BN to further improve the service.

The other side of this equation is that BN must improve utilization of assets. We have high capital intensity, poor utilization of rolling stock, and low asset turnover ratios. Actually, BN is good for the industry, but the industry itself has very poor ratios. Not only are the ratios poor, but the capital requirements for the 1990s are daunting. Just the traditional investments in locomotives, freight cars, and track replacements are daunting. If we can improve utilization of these assets, then we can reduce the capital investment required during the 1990s.

### The ARES Project: The Origins

Steve Ditmeyer, Chief Engineer–Research, Communications and Control Systems, reached deep into his desk and withdrew a slip of paper with a handwritten note: "Any application to locomotives?" BN's chairman Bressler had written that note in 1981 shortly after Ditmeyer had joined the company and attached the note to an article on new aircraft instrumentation that promised lowered costs by improving fuel and other operating efficiencies. The note and article eventually filtered down to numerous railroad staffs.

In 1982, BN's R&D department contacted the Collins Air Transport Division of Rockwell International to learn whether aircraft technology could be applied to the rail industry. The two companies agreed to work together to identify workable solutions. By the end of 1983 they discovered that the technology existed to integrate control, communications, and information. An electronics unit, placed in each locomotive, could receive signals from the Department of Defense's Global Positioning System (GPS) satellites, and calculate the train's position to within $\pm$ 100 feet, a significant improvement over the existing $\pm$10–15 mile resolution from existing systems. By calculating its location every second, the train's speed could also be estimated accurately. A communications network could then be developed to carry information back and forth between the train and a control center.

The R&D department managed the early stages of the ARES project, with oversight by the R&D Steering Committee comprised of senior officers of Transportation, Engineering, Mechanical, Operations Services, Marketing and Information Systems. The Board of Directors in July 1985 viewed a demonstration of the proposed technology installed on two locomotives. In August 1985 BN's senior executives agreed to fund a prototype system: equipping 17 locomotives on BN's Minnesota Iron Range, putting the data segment in place in the Iron Range, and building those elements of the control segment that would permit BN to communicate with and control the locomotives from the Minneapolis control center. The Iron Range was chosen because it was a closed-loop segment of BN's network, with a variety of train control systems, and was served only by a limited set of equipment.

By 1986 the ARES project had grown too large to be carried out by the small R&D staff, and Don Henderson was chosen to oversee the formation of a separate ARES team to manage the project's development. Henderson ensured that team members represented various Operations departments that would potentially be affected by ARES: dispatching, mechanical, maintenance-of-way, control systems and communications, freight car management and information system services. The team members worked with their respective departments and with others such as general managers and operating vice presidents to ensure a system that met operational needs and worked in the railroad environment. Operations managers saw ARES as a means to accomplish key goals of service improvements, operating efficiencies, and improved capital utilization. Operations incorporated ARES into the strategic plans it prepared and presented to corporate.

The ARES prototype was installed on the Iron Range in 1987. The ARES team, BN field personnel, and system developer Rockwell spent the next several years testing, evaluating, and improving the ARES system.

Under Henderson's guidance, the ARES concept evolved to a full command, control, communications and information system that would enable BN to gain additional control over its operations. ARES, using high-speed computing, digital communications, and state-of-the-art electronics, could generate efficient traffic plans, convert those plans into movement instructions for individual trains and MOW units and display those instructions to engine crews. By knowing the position and speed of trains and other equipment on the tracks, ARES could automatically detect deviations from plan or potential problems and communicate these exceptions to control center dispatchers. Dispatchers could determine the corrective action required and use ARES to send and confirm new movement instructions to trains. In many ways, ARES could be considered analogous to the Air Traffic Control system that controlled the aviation industry. ARES eventually came to consist of three segments: Control, Data, and Vehicle.

The Control segment received information on train position and speed to produce schedules and to check that vehicles followed proper operating procedures. It warned dispatchers of violations to limits of authority and speed and produced authorities and checked them for conflict. The Control segment also helped to schedule the MOW crews to get much higher utilization of MOW equipment and labor time. The Control segment displayed for dispatchers the activity in their territories and supplied information about consists, crews, and work orders for any train.

The Data segment communicated data back and forth between the Control segment and locomotives, MOW vehicles, and track monitoring and control equipment. It made use of BN's existing microwave and VHF radio network.

The Vehicle segment on board each locomotive or MOW vehicle included a display (CRT) to provide information from the Control segment, a keypad to communicate back to the dispatcher, an on-board computer to monitor various aspects of locomotive performance, and a throttle-brake interface that the dispatcher or the on-board computer could activate to stop the train if the crew became disabled, if the train violated its movement authorities, or communication was lost with the ARES system. This segment included a receiver for satellite signals to calculate train position and speed, which were then communicated to the Control segment.

The Vehicle segment incorporated an Energy Management System that received information on track profile and conditions, speed limits, power, and car weight to determine a recommended train speed that met service requirements, while minimizing fuel consumption and providing good train-handling characteristics.

The Vehicle segment also included the Locomotive Analysis and Reporting System (LARS). LARS used a number of sensors and discrete signals to monitor the health and efficiency of locomotives and provide early warning signals about potential failures. LARS was expected to permit problematic locomotives to be pulled out of service for maintenance before they failed unexpectedly in a remote region and to provide a data base that maintenance people could analyze to prevent future malfunctions.

### The ARES Project: Current Status

By 1989, BN had spent approximately $15 million, cumulatively, on the ARES project. BN managers estimated that Rockwell had spent three times this amount. "Concept validation" had been accomplished through the Iron Range test, which had proved that the technology could locate trains under real operating conditions and could communicate back and forth between the control center and the locomotive. Rolling stock hardware had been tested for robustness and reliability. The Iron Range prototype system was demonstrated not only to numerous groups of BN executives and operating personnel but also to customers, representatives of other railroads, and numerous industry and governmental groups. By late 1989, testing of the prototype was completed.

The ARES team had seen enough from the Iron Range testing to believe that it would enable BN to provide better service, improve asset utilization, and reduce costs. The ARES project that senior executives were evaluating and deciding whether to authorize in 1990 was an integrated command, control, communication and information ($C^3$-I) system for controlling train movements with, according to the ARES staff, "unprecedented safety, precision, and efficiency." According to a document prepared by R&D and project staff members:

> ARES will allow BN to run a scheduled railroad with smaller staffs and more modest [capital] investments than current signaling systems. It will maintain accurate, timely information about train consists and locations. The results will be improved service, with higher revenue potential, and cost reductions. Another important benefit

will be the elimination of train accidents caused by violations of movement authority.

The ARES team now requested authorization for the expenditures needed to complete the development of the full operational system and to roll out implementation through the railroad. The ARES team, and its sponsors Don Henderson, Vice President–Technology, Engineering and Maintenance, and Joe Galassi, Executive Vice President–Operations, faced several important considerations as they prepared to present this investment for authorization.

First, corporate management was significantly changed from the management that had authorized earlier phases. Four CEOs, including the current executive, Gerald Grinstein, had held office since the 1981 inception of the project. None of the vice presidents who were on the R&D steering committee in 1982 and 1983 was still with the railroad. Of the board members who saw the ARES demonstration in July 1985, only one, the current chairman, remained. Thus, although ARES had undergone a lengthy development process within BN, many who must now support and authorize it were unfamiliar with the choices that had guided its development.

Second, there was a question of whether to propose a full-blown implementation of the ARES project or just an initial phase or two. Presenting the full-blown project would inform top management of the potential range of ARES features and would give them the bottom line for fully installing ARES for the entire railroad: about $350 million (see Exhibit 2 for cost breakdown). Even for a company of the size of BN, this investment was a large amount. And ARES was a complex project, different from typical railroad investments in modern locomotives, cars, track and ties. According to Henderson:

> We may not do the entire railroad; early implementation at least would inevitably be limited to specific geographic areas. Further, we may or may not implement all of the ARES

**EXHIBIT 2**   ARES Cost Breakdown

| MAJOR COST CATEGORIES | COST | COMMENTS |
|---|---|---|
| Control Center | ≅$80 million | Software development is a major component of this cost. |
| Data Link (Wayside Communications) | ≅$80 million | BN planned to replace much of its existing pole line communication network with an ARES-compatible data link regardless of the decision on ARES. However, this conversion had barely begun. |
| On-Board Equipment | ≅$200 million | Roughly $100,000 per road locomotive; less for switch locomotives and MOW vehicles. Of this, LARS = $16,000/ locomotive with total costs (including software development) expected to be less than $35 million. Although not expected to exceed LARS, Energy Management System costs had not been estimated in detail. |

LARS and the Energy Management System were generally considered modules separable from the rest of ARES. Beyond these two, however, it was difficult to identify ARES modules that could be implemented independently. For example, sending a movement authority to a train required the control segment to check conflicts with other vehicles' authorities, the data link to communicate the authority to the train, and the on-board equipment to enable the engineer to receive and confirm the authority. Thus, each of these three segments had to be implemented for ARES to operate in any given region. Although not every locomotive had to be equipped, as fewer locomotives in a region were equipped the overall system became less effective since ARES could no longer confirm the location of—and spacing between—all trains. Limiting ARES to a geographic region within BN reduced Data Link and On-Board equipment costs commensurate with track and vehicle reductions, and reduced Control costs somewhat.

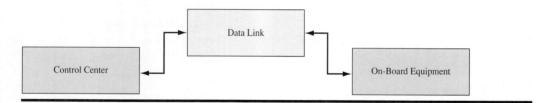

features; the LARS system and the energy management system are clearly very separable pieces.

Galassi explained the rationale for proposing the entire project:

> We figured that top management would want to have a picture of the total project, rather than being fed a piece at a time for incremental decisions and wondering where the end of the line was.

Finally, there was the issue of how to communicate the ARES benefits and credibly measure their value. Some of the benefits that the ARES team had identified were either difficult to measure because the values were unknown—how much more would a customer be willing to pay for a 1% improvement in service?—or because the railroad did not record and track certain data—how much time was lost by trains waiting for meets and passes? The team firmly believed that if they implemented this innovative technology, they would experience benefits they had not yet even anticipated.

**EXHIBIT 3** Consultants' Studies of ARES Benefits

| CONSULTANT | PURPOSE | APPROACH | RESULTS |
|---|---|---|---|
| A & L Associates | Measure effect of ARES improvements in terminal and line-haul performance on carload service. | Service improvements were modeled for a representative BN section using the Service Planning Model with inputs on existing conditions and expected changes in performance supplied by C.D. Martland, Wharton, and Zeta-Tech. | Reductions in line-haul times and increased terminal performance will decrease total trip times by 7–8% even if scheduled connections and blocking strategies are unchanged. |
| John Morton Company | Measure the increase in traffic expected with an increase in the level of service offered customers in given market/commodity areas. | Questionnaires were distributed to decisionmakers who routinely select modes/carriers for shipping commodities in or across BN territories. A demand elasticity model was constructed using conjoint analysis. The model was calibrated, tested, and sensitivity analyses were conducted to generate demand elasticities for each service attribute. | Perceived performance differences between truck and rail are most dramatic with respect to transit time, reliability, equipment usability, and level of effort. Improving reliability offers greatest leverage for increasing BN's revenues. A 1% improvement in reliabilty, if, and only if, fully implemented and perceived in the market place could yield a 5% increase in revenues; a 5% improvement in reliability could yield a 20% increase in prices. |
| Bongarten Associates | Evaluate the Locomotive Analysis and Reporting System (LARS). | A simulation using actual BN data on train information, trouble reports and repairs tested LARS in four modes: 1) inspection of units committed to shops; 2) examining component status during on-road failures; 3) using prospective diagnostics to schedule additional repairs when locomotive is already committed to the shop; 4) using prospective diagnostics to bring the unit into the shop before a failure occurs. | The two LARS modes which offer the greatest promise are modes 2 and 3; mode 3 offers higher savings but requires development of a prospective diagnostics system. Savings of 3% to 5% were calculated in five areas: departure delay, on-line delay, time off-line, maintenance manhours, and reduced severity of repair due to early detection. |
| Charles Stark Draper Laboratory | Analyze how safe ARES would be, compared to BN's existing train control systems. | Modeling using Markov analysis. | The probability of a train control system-related accident would be reduced by a factor of 100 when ARES is in place. The primary reason for this improvement is that ARES' integrated system architecture provides highly reliable checks and balances that limit the impact and propagation of human errors. |

| Zeta-Tech Associates | Measure gains in line-haul efficiency from Energy Management System (EMS) module and Meet/Pass Planning module. | Recorded actual operating data on 846 trains (55 were selected for detailed analysis) from 16 "lanes" chosen to represent BN's full range of operating conditions, control systems, traffic volumes and mixes. Modeled actual operation to establish baseline fuel consumption and running time; then modeled fuel consumption and running time using (1) EMS module and (2) Meet/Pass Planner. | EMS module produced only 2% net fuel savings and large increases in running times for some trains. Z-T argued this was due to software flaws in algorithm and priorities. Meet/Pass Planner reduced running time for all 846 trains by an average of 21%. For the 55 selected trains, travel time decreased 17% and fuel consumption decreased 2.5%. Reliability increased; the travel time standard deviation also decreased. |
| --- | --- | --- | --- |
| Wharton | Measure Meet/Pass efficiency and feasibility. | Modeled fuel consumption and running time using various Meet/Pass dispatching algorithms on selected study trains in the 16 lanes evaluated. | ARES can produce meet/pass plans consistent with operating policies which yield travel time and fuel savings in 30 seconds or less; a pacing algorithm produces further fuel savings. |
| C.D. Martland (MIT) | Measure of yard productivity. | Collected detailed data from several BN yards. Modeled effect of improved reliability of train operations on (1) yard efficiency through improved interface between line-haul, terminal operations, and crew assignments and enhanced capabilities for communications with and supervision of crews; (2) on yard processing times; and (3) on train connection reliability. | Train performance was variable enough to allow considerable room for increased reliability, reducing average yard times about one hour. Modest improvements in terminal efficiency and train connection performance could be achieved through better utilization of terminal crews. Overall ARES could reduce average yard time .5 to 2 hours at major terminals and reduce missed connections by 15 to 17%. |

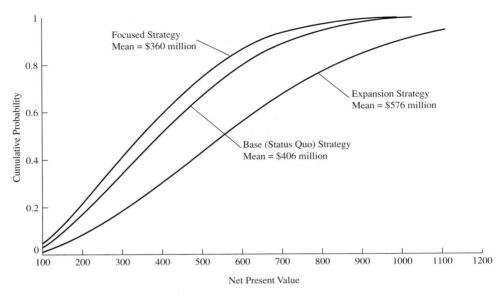

**EXHIBIT 4  Cumulative Probability Distribution of ARES Benefits under Three Scenarios**

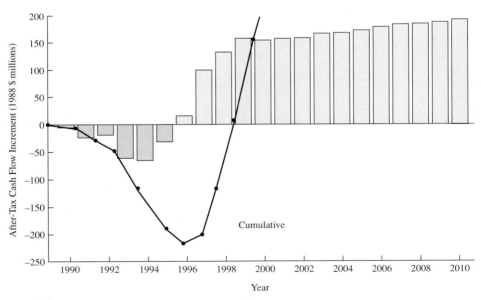

**EXHIBIT 5  ARES Projected Annual and Cumulative After-Tax Cash Flow**

---

**EXHIBIT 6**  Primary ARES Benefits

---

ARES offer many benefits that enable BN to reach its goals of safe and profitable rail operations. Following is a summary of those benefits.

- Increased rail operations safety results from constant monitoring of wayside signal and detector equipment, train movement, and locomotive health.
- Greater operating efficiency and improved customer service come from operating trains to schedule and handling trains that deviate from schedule, the results of improved traffic planning.
- Improved safety and increased customer service come from real-time position, speed and ETAs for all trains computed continuously and automatically provided to MOW crews and other BN users through existing BN computer systems.
- Improved dispatcher productivity results from automating routine dispatching activities such as threat monitoring, warrant generation, traffic planning, and train sheet documentation.
- Higher effective line capacity is provided by accurate vehicle position information and automatic train movement authorization.
- Improved MOW productivity results from improved traffic planning.
- Improved business management is possible with accurate, current information about the status and performance of operations and equipment.

**KEY POINTS**

- The study examined benefits in the following areas and estimates the present value of those benefits:

  - Fuel                                               $ 52 million
  - Equipment                                          $ 81 million
  - Labor                                              $190 million
  - Trackside equipment and damage prevention          $ 96 million
  - Enhanced revenues                                  $199 million
  
    Total                                              $618 million

- To account for uncertainty in these estimates, the study calculated ranges of values for them and probabilities of achieving values within the ranges.
- The factors with the largest potential for delivering benefits are also the most uncertain:
  - ARES' ability to improve transit time
  - The amount customers are willing to pay for better service
- Accounting for ranges and probabilities, ARES will make the following mean contribution to net present value for each corporate strategy:
  - Focused strategy                                   $360 million
  - Base strategy                                      $406 million
  - Expansion strategy                                 $576 million
- The probability of ARES' earning less than 9% real after-tax rate of return is extremely small.

---

To help measure the variety of benefits from a full-blown implementation of ARES, the team economist, Michael Smith, contracted with a half-dozen outside consultants, each of whom focused on a specific area such as measurement of market elasticity, measurement of LARS effects, measurement of meet/pass efficiency, and improved safety (see Exhibit 3 for a summary of each benefit study). Some benefits could be measured only partially in financial terms; for example, improved safety would reduce damaged equipment and freight by perhaps $20 million per year, although its value in human and political terms was even more significant. According to Steve Ditmeyer:

> ARES reduces the probability of a collision by two orders of magnitude because, in contrast with our existing railroad control system where

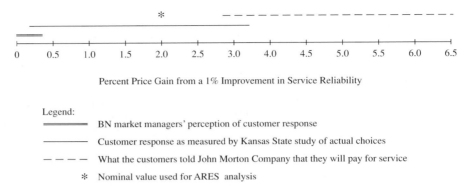

Percent Price Gain from a 1% Improvement in Service Reliability

Legend:

═══════ BN market managers' perception of customer response

───────── Customer response as measured by Kansas State study of actual choices

─ ─ ─ ─ What the customers told John Morton Company that they will pay for service

\* Nominal value used for ARES analysis

**EXHIBIT 7  Price Gain versus Increased Service Reliability**

one failure or a mistake by one person can cause an accident, with ARES no single person or piece of equipment can cause an accident; two must fail simultaneously.

The Strategic Decisions Group (SDG) was hired to help the ARES team integrate the results of the individual consulting studies with other BN data into a single, coherent analysis of benefits. The analysis was conducted using three strategic scenarios supplied by BN's planning and evaluation department: base, focused, and expansion. Using probability distributions of key uncertainties supplied by BN managers, a set of computer models were built to calculate the probability distributions of the net present value of ARES under each of the strategic scenarios. (The cumulative probability distributions of the net present value of ARES benefits under each of the strategic scenarios are shown in Exhibit 4.) Exhibit 5 illustrates a representative annual and cumulative after-tax cash flow for the ARES project. The SDG report concluded:

The potential benefit of ARES is large but highly uncertain. Using the best information currently available, we estimated the gross benefit in the range of $400 million to $900 million, with an expected present value of about $600 million. This benefit should be weighed against a cost of approximately $220 million (present value). . . . The benefits depend greatly on implementation success: The system design must be sound, a strong implementation plan must be developed, and functional groups across the BN system must be committed to using it to full advantage.

The ARES team concluded that the primary known benefits of ARES (see Exhibit 6) were to be measured in reduced expenditures on fuel, equipment, labor, and trackside equipment; damage prevention; and enhanced revenues. The largest component, revenue enhancements, however, had the most uncertain estimates (see Exhibit 7).

# BURLINGTON NORTHERN: THE ARES DECISION (B)*

ARES seems to be a technology in search of a problem. The projected benefits from ARES have been derived from a bottom-up approach, not from a top level strategic planning process.

*Dick Lewis, Vice President of Strategic Planning*

ARES has the aura of an R&D-driven project. It was never subjected to the company's long-term resource allocation financing process or to a ranking among strategic priorities.

*Jack Bell, Chief Financial Officer*

Ed Butt, ARES project director, and Don Henderson, Vice President–Technology, Engineering and Maintenance, had presented ARES benefits to senior executives. While the executives found the benefits "fairly convincing," according to CEO Grinstein, they still had questions: "Do we need those benefits? Will there be a return on the $350 million? Is there a cheaper way to get them?" Senior executives had a nagging feeling that BN might be able to obtain 80% of the benefits for only 20% of the costs. Jack Bell articulated these concerns:

> ARES is a very large, complex project. It has many bells and whistles. We need to figure out what is the most important aspect of the project. If it is meet and pass planning, then we should assess the most cost effective way of doing meet and pass planning. "Unbundling," however, is not the favorite activity of project teams, especially late in the development process.

Managers were also worried that the ARES team had become overcommitted to

their project and had lost their objectivity for analysis. Some referred to ARES team members as "zealots." It seemed that whenever senior managers identified a problem, ARES was offered as the solution; this confused some executives about exactly what ARES benefits were.

Executives also did not fully believe all aspects of the ARES benefits analysis, particularly the service-price elasticities. The marketing department considered the estimates overstated (see Exhibit 7 of (A) case), and wondered why its people had not been more involved in developing this analysis beyond providing suggestions on market research firms, research sites, and questionnaire content.

Others worried about the magnitude of the investment itself. A $350 million investment was not the largest BN had made, especially considering that the investment would be made over a several-year period. However, some were concerned that the actual investment would turn out to be much larger. According to Bill Greenwood, chief operating officer:

> Many things may be incomplete in the ARES system. Therefore, I don't know if the $350 million represents a bottom line price tag, or if the actual cost to design, program, implement and debug ARES will be a considerably larger number. The technology—vehicle identification, radio and satellite communication, and locomotive monitoring— is almost the least of our concerns. The technology alone does not deliver the benefits. We need to change our underlying business processes which are not only large in number, but intensely interrelated. And the roles and responsibilities of many of our operating positions must be redesigned in order to achieve the objectives and benefits of ARES. This kind of planning process was not

---

*Professors Julie H. Hertenstein and Robert S. Kaplan prepared this case.

Copyright © 1991 by the President and Fellows of Harvard College. Harvard Business School case 191-123.

undertaken in the piloting of ARES, but it will be vital to successful, widespread adoption.

The significance of the required organizational changes concerned other managers as well. Observers noted that this investment would catapult the organization from the Iron Age into the Electronic Age. According to Dick Lewis:

> We wanted to increase our confidence in how the railroad's traditional, hierarchical organization with its deeply rooted, hundred-year-old history would handle the major organization changes that would be necessary.

### Financial Operations and Restructuring

Even if ARES were justified, did BN have adequate funds to undertake it? During the late 1970s railroad industry financial performance had been generally poor. The industry was capital intensive, return on assets was low, and some railroads had been forced into bankruptcy.

Concurrently, concerns developed among some of BN's most senior managers that the firm was not doing enough to exploit its extensive land grant and natural resource holdings. They also believed that BN's stock price did not adequately reflect the value of its railroad operations and its natural resource holdings. This belief was made more tangible when T. Boone Pickens started to purchase Burlington Northern shares in 1987. BN management decided to restructure the company. Burlington Resources Inc. (BR) was created in May 1988 as a holding company for BN's natural resource operations. In July 1988, BR completed an initial public offering of its stock and in December, BN distributed its shares of BR common stock to BN's common stock holders thus spinning BR off from BN, and leaving BN with one principal subsidiary: Burlington Northern Railroad Company. To effect this spin-off, BN issued large amounts of debt, leaving the firm with a debt-to-total-capital ratio of 76%, a level considered high for the industry.

In his 1988 letter to shareholders, CEO Gerald Grinstein stated:

> We must manage the substantial debt load remaining after the spin-off of Burlington Resources Inc. This will require a clear strategic focus so that we can maximize the cash flows available for capital improvements while reducing the outstanding debt.

Jack Bell soon noticed the investment community's enthusiasm for debt repayment.

> Following the recapitalization, the investment community estimated BN's earnings per share at $3.20 and its share price at $22, a $7 \times$ P/E multiple. We queried analysts about why the multiple was so low and they told us about their concern with the level of debt for a company in a cyclical industry. To convince the investment community that BN had a viable program to pay down the debt and still invest in the railroad, we announced an accelerated debt repayment program that would repay more than the amount required in the debt covenants. Subsequently, we supported this program with progress reports of BN's cash flows and debt paydown in 1989 ($500 million as of year end) and a projection of 1990 cash flows (excluding net income). [See Exhibit 1.] BN's stock price rose significantly in the months following this report.

BN planned to continue to accelerate paydown. Grinstein's 1989 letter to shareholders said:

> One of our top priorities has been to improve our financial structure. We have undertaken a major improvement program and made significant first-year progress, retiring over $500 million in debt [debt-to-total-capital ratio: 68%]. . . . Our goal is to achieve a total debt level of 50% of total capitalization by 1994, paying down debt at an average rate of $200 million per year.

To emphasize the urgency of debt repayment, BN instituted a bonus plan in 1989 for all 3,000 of its salaried employees. The average percent bonus in any year depended on

## EXHIBIT 1

|  | ($ MILLIONS) | |
|---|---|---|
| **1989 Cashflow** | | |
| Sources of Cash | | |
| Net income | | $ 243 |
| Depreciation | | 310 |
| Deferred taxes | | 69 |
| Lease financing | | 100 |
| Cash balance drawdown | | 1 |
| Accounts receivable sale | | 250 |
| Working capital change | | 124 |
| Asset sales net | | 19 |
| Total | | $1,116 |
| Uses of Cash | | |
| Capital expenditures | | $ 473 |
| Dividends | | 109 |
| Debt service | | 505 |
| Required | 112 | |
| Optional | 393 | |
| ETSI | | 25 |
| Other | | 4 |
| Total | | $1,116 |
| **1990 Cash Flow Planning Assumptions** | | |
| Sources of Cash | | |
| Net income | | $    ? |
| Depreciation | | 350 |
| Deferred taxes | | 30 |
| Lease financing | | 100 |
| Cash balance drawdown | | 40 |
| Other | | 50 |
| Total | | $ 570   + Net income |
| Uses of Cash | | |
| Capital expenditures | | $ 537 |
| Dividends | | 92 |
| Required debt service | | 115 |
| ETSI | | 25 |
| Other | | 1 |
| Total | | $ 770   + Discretionary debt paydown |

the company's earnings per share, net income, and debt paid down. Individual performance could make individual bonuses somewhat higher or lower than average. Salaried employees below the level of vice president were divided into three groups whose bonuses could range up to 10%, 20%, or 40% of their annual salary respectively. Bonuses for employees at or above vice president level were administered separately.

In a era of accelerated debt paydown, funds for investment were tight, and there were many competing demands for available funds. Normal aging of equipment would require heavy expenditures to replace locomotives, freight cars and track. Recently acquired concrete ties had already demonstrated benefits beyond those originally projected, leading to proposals to make further investments in them as well. The growth in export potential caused some BN managers to consider whether additional railroad acquisitions with good access to west coast ports should be sought. Brock Strom, Vice President–Information System Services, believed that the new strategies resulting from the firm's strategic review would require additional MIS investments to support them. The strategies were still emerging so no specific demands were defined, though his "unsubstantiated guess" was that $100–200 million would be required. Jim Dagnon, Senior Vice President–Labor Relations, suggested that if the current round of labor negotiations produced an agreement that train crew sizes could be reduced, an investment of $100–200 million to "buy out" the excess crew would have an 18-month payback.

### Technology Concerns

Apart from financial considerations, some managers were concerned that BN was considering adopting an automated train control technology that differed from the Advanced Train Control System (ATCS) being developed by members of the Association of American Railroads (AAR). ATCS controlled trains; ARES controlled the entire railroad operation. By 1990, when BN had already tested the ARES prototype, the AAR was still developing specifications for ATCS. Some believed that the ARES system was as many as five years ahead of ATCS in development. Other comparisons between the two systems are shown in Exhibit 2.

Other managers pondered whether BN should be first in the industry with an automated train control technology. According to Joe Galassi:

> If the investment is unique for some period and represents a competitive advantage, then BN should be the first mover and get the additional business. However, if the technology does not offer a big marketplace advantage, then it is not best to be first. If other competitors implement it first, BN has the advantage of watching them and avoiding their mistakes.

**EXHIBIT 2** ATCS and ARES Comparisons

| FEATURE | ATCS | ARES |
|---|---|---|
| Accuracy (feet) | +100 | +100 |
| On-board equipment (per unit) | $20,000–$80,000 | $20,000–$80,000 |
| Wayside communications | UHF radio $146 million | VHF radio $78 million |
| Equipment maintenance | 5%* | 5% |
| On-board signaling | Yes | Yes |
| Train control | Yes | Yes |
| On-line locomotive condition | Yes | Yes |
| Set-out and pick-up instructions to train crews and confirmation from them | Yes | Yes |
| Full safety benefits | No[†] | Yes |
| Positioning system | Transponders between rails; plus dead-reckoning on locomotives | GPS satellites; plus dead-reckoning on locomotives |

*Add $0–$2,000/locomotive/year.
[†]ATCS cannot effectively monitor the location of maintenance-of-way vehicles due to the substantial time they spend between widely spaced transponders.

Many believed that the development of the control center represented another notable risk. Software development was a key element of the $80 million control center cost. Much of the complex set of control center software had yet to be developed and integrated although some algorithms had already been tested. Forecasts of development costs, or of development time, might be exceeded. Brock Strom suggested that some prior computer applications had not always gone exactly as planned. For example, the computerized track warrant system that one division got from the Canadian Pacific Railroad was supposed to take one year to implement; it actually took four. However, the remaining ARES software resembled existing software applications such as the FAA's air traffic control system. According to Brock Strom:

> The technology risks are not that significant. The hardware technologies have been used in other industries; therefore the issue is not developing a brand new technology but transitioning an existing technology to the railroad. ARES is a major software development effort with all the normal problems, but the programming effort is quite feasible and should be able to be implemented.

Gerald Grinstein believed:

> For the industry to succeed, it will inevitably have to get into some kind of new technology. I don't want BN to be the sole ARES advocate. I've invited other railroads to come and observe the prototype system in the Iron Range. If BN goes with ARES, it will probably drive the rest of the industry this way. The others have to stay competitive, and ATCS is not realistically available now, so ARES is the only operating solution at the current time.
>
> The ARES decision is caught up in another process, shaping BN's future. Major questions to be answered are, "What kind of railroad should we be?" If we deliver a much greater, more reliable level of service, can we profit from that?

Joe Galassi stated:

> There are really two reasons to do ARES. The first is better service. The second is that we will be better able to control assets by scheduling locomotives and cars more precisely and getting better productivity out of the assets. However, the real heart of the matter is service to the customer.

Mark Cane, Vice President–Service Design, concurred:

> ARES could bring higher reliability to the railroad. It could improve the mechanical quality of the railroad, through fewer engine breakdowns. It could improve reliability in terms of consistent arrival time through dispatching and schedule discipline. It could also increase the capacity of the physical plant by tightening the spacing between trains thus allowing more trains to travel on the existing track. If ARES cost $50 million, we might have already begun it, but $350 million is a problem in light of competing demands for capital.

Jim Dagnon also found that ARES offered significant advantages from his perspective:

> The union leadership had toured the ARES prototype facilities. They loved it. The work force is as ready to adopt ARES as any workforce I've ever seen. A significant aspect of ARES for all labor is safety; safety is extremely important, and they see ARES as increasing safety. They see ARES as making their job easier and more important, especially the engineers. Conductors are a little less enthusiastic; it may reduce their job responsibilities. Ultimately, ARES has the potential to schedule the crews' work; this would lead to a higher quality of life compared with today's unscheduled, on-call environment in which crews don't know whether or when they will be called to work.

As BN's executives pondered whether to proceed with ARES, they still were not fully comfortable with whether the assessment of ARES benefits was realistic or optimistic. They also struggled with whether the benefits, or many of them, could be attained at a lower cost: Were technologies cheaper than the one prototyped with Rockwell available to support the ARES project? Could the benefits be unbundled? For example, the recent experience with the service measurement system suggested to some executives that improved discipline and reporting could enhance service without the large capital investment required by ARES. Yet, in contrast to JIT experiences, which had taught manufacturing firms to fix their manufacturing processes before automating them, at BN, without automation—that is, ARES—managers lacked information on operations needed to fix the process. Could BN have the cake without the icing?

Before proceeding with a decision, BN's senior executives decided to conduct an outside audit of the ARES proposal. SRI International (formerly Stanford Research Institute) was engaged to audit the benefits analysis, to investigate the possibility of unbundling the benefits, and to study whether alternative, less-expensive technologies were feasible.

# 13

## Incentive and Compensation Systems

There is no topic that commands as much fervor in the management literature as incentive compensation. Many people consider pay for performance systems, along with private ownership, as the hallmarks of capitalism. To these people, modern organizations simply will not function effectively without good pay for performance systems.

Indeed, pay for performance seems to have appeared when owners first hired managers to manage their capital. Sharing in the profits of the trading voyages to the Far East and the New World in the early and late middle ages, piecerate pay used since at least the industrial revolution, and profit sharing in the modern corporation are all examples of pay for performance. Sharecropping, in which the worker shares in the output created on the landowner's property, may be the most ancient form of pay for performance. Pay for performance is an artifact of the widely held belief that if you want to motivate people to pursue organization objectives then you have to reward them based on the performance level they achieve.

## THE EXPECTANCY VIEW OF BEHAVIOR

In this book we adopt the so-called expectancy approach to motivation, which argues that people act in ways that they expect will create the rewards they desire. Given this view, the role of compensation is to provide individuals with rewards they value when their behavior promotes the organization's objectives.

Exhibit 13-1 describes the expectancy view of motivation. Organizations develop compensation systems that reward specified individual results or behavior that advance organization objectives. Individuals exert effort to develop skills and knowledge to make decisions that create results that provide the rewards they value and seek. Measured results, the domain of management accounting, provide the critical linkage in this motiva-

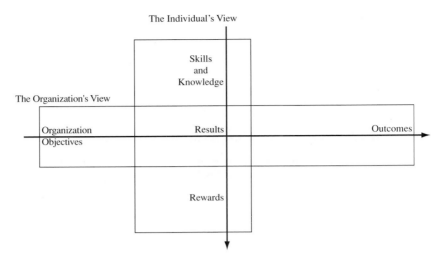

**EXHIBIT 13-1 Expectancy View of Motivation**

tion process. Results must have two critical properties. First, they must reflect organization objectives. That is, creating these results must create outcomes that lead the organization toward accomplishing its objectives. Second, the decision makers must clearly understand the linkage between results and rewards that they value.

## INTRINSIC AND EXTRINSIC REWARDS

There are two broad types of rewards that people value: intrinsic and extrinsic. Intrinsic rewards are those that come from within the individual, such as satisfaction from a job well done or taking satisfaction from acting in a way that is consistent with inner values or beliefs. No intervention by another person is required for someone to experience an intrinsic reward. Organizations can create the potential for people to experience intrinsic rewards through job design, organization culture, and management style, but individuals feel or experience intrinsic rewards on their own.

Extrinsic rewards are rewards that one person gives to another. Extrinsic rewards include recognition, plaques, prizes, awards, and, of course, pay based on performance, also known as incentive pay or pay for performance. Most of the interest and attention in management journals focus on extrinsic rewards in general and incentive pay in particular. However, there are some people who believe that this attention is misplaced. They believe that the motivational effect of intrinsic rewards is far more powerful than that of extrinsic rewards.[1] We will focus on pay for performance, which is an extrinsic reward, not because we believe that intrinsic rewards and extrinsic rewards other than performance pay are unimportant but because the conventional role of the management accountant is to develop the systems that identify the organization's desired results and tie results to managers' and employees' compensation.

## TYING REWARDS TO PERFORMANCE

The management accountant's role of identifying the organization's desired long-term outcomes (such as profitability) and corresponding short-term results (such as product quality and employee satisfaction) falls out of the strategic planning process. That role is the focus of the Balanced Scorecard discussed in Chapter 8. The idea in incentive compensation is to tie individual rewards to the organization's target outcomes and results.

### Rewards Based on Financial Performance

Traditionally, organizations have used measures from the financial control system, such as corporate or divisional profits, as the results to which individual rewards are tied. Alfred Sloan was one of the most enthusiastic advocates of incentive compensation plans for top management. He instituted the General Motors bonus plan in 1918 to increase the commonality of interests between the senior managers and the stockholders of the firm.[2] Annual bonuses were awarded on the basis of each manager's contribution to the overall success of the corporation. General Motors had decentralized its operating decisions, and before the bonus plan, which focused attention and rewards on *corporate* performance was instituted, the key executives had little incentive to think of the overall welfare of the organization. Rather, they tended to focus narrowly on their own division's profitability, occasionally at the expense of the corporation's welfare. After the bonus plan was installed, the senior executives were more sensitive to how their individual efforts affected the welfare of the entire organization. Sloan noted that the plan was successful in molding top-level executives into a cooperative constructive group but without destroying individual ambition and initiative.

The General Motors bonus plan was structured so that rewards were increased more than proportionately to salary as executives were promoted to higher positions. Therefore, managers had a major incentive to become eligible for bonus awards and then to continue to perform in an outstanding fashion so that they could be promoted to even higher ranks. Apart from the direct financial reward, the plan seemed to provide an intangible incentive just by the recognition that the executive had made a significant personal contribution to the success of General Motors. One executive claimed that the ego satisfaction from receiving the award was prized just as much as the actual monetary compensation.

### Rewards Based on Group or Individual Performance

The General Motors plan raises an important issue that must be considered by the designers of incentive plans. Should rewards be based on individual or on group performance? On the one hand, rewards that focus on rewarding individual behavior obviously do not promote group-oriented behavior. On the other hand, critics of rewards based on group behavior argue that many individuals fail to see how their individual behavior affects group rewards and ultimately their individual reward. The failure to see this link is thought to dilute the motivational effect of the reward. Critics also believe that group rewards can encourage shirking and free-riding on the efforts of others.

Many companies are asking employees to work in teams to achieve organization objectives. One way to combine individual and group rewards is to base the total group reward on group performance, such as corporate profit, but to base the individual shares of the group reward on performance points that reflect the individual's ability to achieve individual performance objectives. This approach avoids objections to performance shares that are based on salary or rank rather than on the individual's realized performance.

## Rewards Based on Nonfinancial Measures of Performance

Organizations have been using formal profit sharing and bonus systems based on profits for many years, and this practice has been criticized almost since these systems were first used. The criticism focuses on the short-run orientation of profits and the belief that individuals can, and will, sacrifice long-run performance to do well on a short-run measure to maximize their bonus. For example, a manager rewarded on the basis of the ability to control costs might reduce maintenance in the current period even though he knows that this reduction will increase breakdowns and failures in future years.

The short-run orientation of profit-based performance measures motivated the development of performance measures that combine short-run and long-run incentives. These measures have been developed in three ways: (1) by using stock options to reward managers and assuming that markets assess future consequences of current actions; (2) by forcing managers to bank bonuses and pay out those bonuses over several years; and (3) by rewarding current performance using a mix of performance measures including both short-run financial measures that focus on profits and nonfinancial measures, such as product quality, customer satisfaction, and innovation, thought to be the drivers of future financial performance.

The practice of rewarding managerial performance on a mix of short-term and long-term performance measures is still developing. In one study of practice,[3] less than 2% of the organizations in the sample used nonfinancial performance measures designed to assess the short-run drivers of long-run financial performance. The study did find that the short-run performance measures seemed to be chosen strategically in the sense that organizations that were competing using innovation were more likely to use nonfinancial measures to reward performance than were organizations that were competing based on cost.

More generally, firms that have implemented the Balanced Scorecard develop a performance measure that is a weighting of performance on both financial and nonfinancial measures. Because these performance measurement systems are just now being implemented, it is too early to draw conclusions about their effectiveness and value in organizations.

## Executive Compensation

Compensation contracts, particularly incentive and bonus plans, provide important direction and motivation for corporate executives. One cannot talk about decentralization without an explicit treatment of how the top-division managers are rewarded (or penalized). Almost all highly decentralized firms have incentive compensation contracts for their top-management group (usually less than 1% of all employees) to encourage profit-maximizing decisions at the divisional and corporate levels and to stimulate individuals to higher levels of performance.

Executive compensation plans should

1. Be competitive to attract and retain high-quality managers
2. Communicate and reinforce the key priorities of the firm by tying bonuses to key indices of performance

**3.** Foster the development of a performance-oriented climate within the firm by rewarding good performance relative to potential[4]

The enthusiasm of Alfred Sloan and the General Motors Corporation for executive incentive plans is now widespread. More than 90% of the top managers of decentralized profit centers in large corporations are eligible for an annual bonus. Reports in various periodicals indicate that the median bonus of senior executives that is based on short-term profit measures is now about one-quarter of annual compensation. The form of the bonus plan varies among corporations. Payments can be made in cash, in stock of the company, in stock options, and, more recently, in performance shares, stock appreciation rights, or participating units. The bonus can be made contingent on corporate results (as in General Motors) or on divisional profits. It can be based on annual performance or on performance over a four- to six-year period. It can be paid out immediately, deferred, or spread over a three- to five-year period.

No single bonus incentive plan dominates all other plans for all companies. Incentive plans will depend upon the degree of decentralization, the time horizon for critical decisions of the firms, the degree of interaction among divisions, the amount of uncertainty faced by the firm, the nature of its business activities, and the structure of the industry. In addition, many plans, alleged to provide incentives to managers, have as their greatest benefit the reduction of taxes of the manager and the firm. For example, stock options have become the most popular incentive form for three reasons. First, stock options that are out of the money when issued appear to minimize the joint tax burden of the organization and the manager. Second, stock options provide a means of coordinating the incentives of managers and owners. Third, for a long time many shareholders incorrectly believed that stock options were a costless way of motivating managers and were therefore not concerned about the amount and nature of stock options issued to executives.

In this chapter, we will survey existing practice and will comment on the properties, strengths, and weaknesses of different incentive schemes. In the next chapter, we will introduce the emerging literature in optimal contracting and describe some preliminary results for constructing optimal incentive contracts between owners and chief executives and between a central management group and its division executives.

## Incentive Compensation and the Principal-Agent Relationship

We begin our survey of incentive compensation arrangements by introducing the principal-agent paradigm.[5] The perspective provided by the theory of agency relationships gives us a systematic way to think about incentive compensation plans.

An agency relationship exists whenever one party (the principal) hires another party (the agent) to perform a service that requires the principal to delegate some decision-making authority to the agent. For our purposes, two types of principal-agent relationships arise in management control systems. First, the firm's owners or shareholders, acting as the principal (perhaps through the board of directors), hire the chief executive officer (or, more broadly, the top-management group) to act as their agent in managing the firm in their best interests. In the second principal-agent arrangement, the firm's top-management group acts as the principal and hires division managers as agents to manage the decentralized units of the organization.

Managers work to maximize the compensation they earn for their participation in the organization. But they incur personal costs as they devote their time, knowledge, and effort to the firm. Therefore, agency theory assumes that agents seek to balance the return from, and cost of, their efforts. Moreover, agency theory assumes that agents bear no moral burdens. Therefore, they are perfectly willing, given the opportunity, to renege on pledges that they make during contract negotiations about the level of effort, skill, and knowledge that they will provide the firm. This characteristic, combined with the principal's inability to monitor exactly what the agent is putting into the firm, creates what the agency literature calls the **moral hazard problem** and the need to monitor the agent's actions.

For example, the agency model argues that if only a straight salary compensates the top executives of the company, they may not be motivated to take actions that maximize the value of the firm to the shareholders. They may overconsume nonpecuniary items such as leisure, attractive working conditions, and company perquisites or will not invest sufficient time and effort to increase shareholder wealth. If the ownership group knew what actions were optimal for the firm and could costlessly observe the actions of the top managers, they could direct the managers to implement these optimal actions with the threat of withholding compensation if these actions were not carried out effectively and efficiently. But because a dispersed ownership group will probably have inadequate information and will find monitoring costly, the owners are unlikely to either know what the optimal decisions should be or whether the agent has acted in the principal's best interests.

Therefore, to encourage the top executives to take actions that are in the firm's best interests, the owners introduce an incentive compensation plan that enables the top executives to share in the firm's increased wealth or, more generally, to receive rewards designed to align the agent's interests with the principal's. These plans can take the form of stock options or bonuses based on reported performance.

Incentive compensation plans are designed to create a commonality of interest between the principal (owners) and the agents (managers). But because of differences in risk attitudes, the existence of private information (managers' knowing more than the owners about the environment and their actions), and limited or costly observability, some divergence of interest will always exist between the principal and the agents, creating a phenomenon called **agency cost**. The principal attempts to limit agency cost by establishing appropriate incentives for the agents and by incurring monitoring costs designed to limit actions that increase the agents' welfare at the expense of the principal.

Audited financial statements are an excellent example of a costly monitor of managerial behavior. They generate an accountability report from the agent (managers) to the principal (shareholders and creditors). Even with costly incentive and monitoring arrangements, however, the agents' decisions will still diverge from those that would maximize the principal's welfare. For example, audited financial statements provide a less-than-complete summary of the manager's decisions and actions. Thus, agency costs in the owner-manager relationship are the sum of the costs of the incentive compensation plan, the costs of monitoring the managers' actions, and the remaining costs of actions taken by managers that diverge from the preferences of the owners.

To see how agency costs affect the compensation management of top executives, let us informally trace through a simple scenario. We have already noted that because of the private information of managers and costly observation of managers' actions, owners may provide an incentive compensation scheme for the top executives. One obvious incentive scheme is to provide managers with a stock option or stock bonus plan, since actions that the managers take to increase stock prices should benefit the owners in a direct and obvious manner. Although certainly popular, this incentive scheme is not used by all companies with publicly traded stock.

What factors limit the desirability of stock ownership plans for top executives? First, risk aversion problems arise. The highly paid top executives of the firm already have most of their wealth, in the form of human capital (measured by the discounted present value of their expected compensation), directly tied to the firm's well-being. If the firm were to do poorly, their managerial reputations would suffer, limiting their outside job offers and slowing the rate of compensation increases within the firm. If a significant part of managers' compensation were invested in shares of the firm's stock, the managers could suffer a significant decline in their financial wealth at the same time that bad outcomes were affecting their human-capital wealth.

To avoid this situation, the executives would tend to avoid risky investments and risky decisions, even those with high expected returns, because risk aversion causes them to demand a risk premium and consequently value the potential gains far less than they fear the penalties from possible losses.[6] Therefore, stock ownership by top executives reinforces risk-avoiding behavior: avoidance of risks that the owners would prefer the executives take. The owners are less risk-averse because (1) their human capital may be independent of the firm's outcomes, and (2) they can diversify their wealth through ownership of many different firms and have only a small portion of their wealth at risk in any given investment. Therefore, owners may be risk-neutral in the small but, like the manager, risk-averse when faced with large gambles. Firm managers already have more of their wealth (in the form of nondiversifiable and nontradeable human capital) tied up in the firm than they would probably prefer. Additional stock ownership in the same firm increases their firm-specific risk even further. Michael Jensen summarized this problem: "The problem we are stuck with is one of achieving the proper balance between linking managements' interests with stockholder interests by making them bear a lot of market risk, and at the same time, insulating them from some of that risk."[7]

A second problem with executive stock ownership arises from the lack of a direct causal relationship between executive actions and stock market performance. Noncontrollable random events, such as general business conditions, competitors' actions, government actions, unexpected material, energy, or labor shortages, and international developments, may overwhelm the best (or worst) efforts of management. If the stock price unexpectedly rises because of these noncontrollable events, creating a general bull market, the executives obtain a windfall gain at the expense of the original set of owners. Conversely, if the stock price plunges, the executives suffer a significant loss in expected income or wealth. The uncertainty of the stock market introduces an additional component of noncontrollable risk into the executives' compensation schedule and does not provide reliable feedback on the quality of decisions and extent of effort exerted by these executives.[8]

In an attempt to obtain a performance measure more sensitive than stock prices to executive actions, owners may develop a measure based on an internal evaluation of the economic well-being of the firm. The stock market provides one estimate of the economic value of the firm's assets, but it has the problems described above. Appraising the value of the firm's assets provides another estimate, but this measure may be very costly to obtain each year and can be a source of controversy because of its subjectivity. An incentive contract could, however, be based on data that are already prepared and audited for external parties, namely, the historical-cost-based financial statements. Performance goals can be set on the basis of earnings per share or return on shareholders' investment. These figures are more under management's control than are stock prices and, at least in the long run, should be correlated with the economic welfare of the firm. In fact, many incentive compensation plans do depend directly on earnings per share (EPS) and accounting return on equity (ROE).

The accounting-based measures for executive compensation, however, introduce problems of their own because of the imperfect association between accounting income and the long-run economic well-being of the firm. Executives can take many actions that increase reported income—and hence increase their income from incentive compensation plans—but decrease the firm's value. For example, managers of U.S. corporations may choose to remain on FIFO (first in–first out) for inventory valuation rather than switch to LIFO (last in–first out). For most companies, LIFO decreases the present value of cash paid in taxes (and therefore increases the present value of the cash flows to the firm) but reports lower income in the short run and hence lower earnings-based performance measures.

Executives have many other opportunities to increase reported earnings by means of actions that do not benefit the firm and that may, in some cases, actually decrease the value of the firm. These actions include

1. Producing goods in excess of demand in order to absorb fixed costs into inventory and thereby increase reported income in the current period
2. Repurchasing debt or preferred stock selling at a discount
3. Switching to straight-line depreciation or the flow-through method for the investment credit for financial reporting
4. Purchasing other companies under terms that permit use of the pooling-of-interests method
5. Selling off assets whose market value is well in excess of book value
6. Increasing the leverage of the firm by issuing debt and acquiring assets whose returns exceed the after-tax debt cost but are below the risk-adjusted cost of capital

Conversely, executives could decline investments that would increase the long-run value of the firm but penalize short-run earnings. For example, profitable capital investments with heavy initial startup costs might not be undertaken, and research and development expenditures could be underfunded because of the longer-term risky nature of the rewards from such expenditures. Also factors such as new mandated accounting procedures that affect reported income will be viewed skeptically by executives rewarded under an earnings-based incentive scheme.

Thus, accounting-based performance measures may be preferable to stock incentives because they are related to activities that are more under the control of top executives. On the downside, however, such plans may be too controllable by executives who can manipulate the measures in ways that are detrimental to the owners. The board of directors must approve virtually all the actions that could increase an accounting-based performance measure without increasing the economic value of the firm, and the board can, in principle, play an important role in reducing the agency cost of the contractual relationship between owners and managers. For example, the board could define earnings for computation of executive bonuses to exclude expenditures on long-term intangibles (R&D, maintenance, quality control, personnel development) so that executives would not be motivated to underinvest in these important areas. Similarly, the board could undo accounting policies that increase reported income but do not benefit the company directly (holding gains reported under FIFO, flow-through of the investment tax credit, unadjusted historical cost, straight-line depreciation). In this way, more of the managers' reward would be related to actions that increase the long-run profitability of the firm. Such practices, although theoretically possible, do not seem common.[9] Apparently, directors are not comfortable rewarding managers on one income figure while reporting quite a different number to shareholders and creditors. Moreover, there is widespread evidence that the compensation committees of some, or even many, organizations are not independent and often act in the best interests of management at the expense of shareholders.

## IMPORTANT ATTRIBUTES OF COMPENSATION SYSTEMS

At their root, incentive compensation systems are designed to align the interest of owners and managers. To be effective, managers must have a clear understanding of:

1. The measured performance variables for their job
2. How their behavior affects the measured performance variables
3. How the measured performance variables translate into individual rewards

If managers do not have a clear image of this causal process, the incentive compensation system will lose its ability to motivate or influence decision-making behavior. Clearly, the management accountant is at the center of the process in terms of choosing the measured performance variable, designing the system that will measure performance, analyzing the results, and reporting results. The results then become the input into the mechanism that relates measured performance to the reward given to the employee. This sequence describes the causal chain shown in Exhibit 13-1, which relates individual performance to rewards and therefore provides the motivating potential of rewards.

Note the pivotal role played by the results, or performance measurement; this provides the link between individual motivation and the organization's goals. These results, or performance measures, must be chosen so that when individual decision makers pursue these results they move the organization toward achieving its objectives. Therefore, these performance measures must be rich enough to capture how the individual job contributes to the organization's objectives. Attributes of the job that are ignored by the performance measure will either be ignored or deemed unimportant by the individual.

For example, if an employee is told that getting the work done on time is all that matters and conformance to schedule is the only performance measurement, then other job attributes such as cost control and quality will be either ignored or sacrificed to achieve the measured objective. This example reflects the old performance measurement adage "What gets measured is what gets done." The performance measurement system sends powerful signals to the employee about what is important in the job. Therefore, the management accountant, who is usually a central figure in designing these performance measurement systems must have a clear understanding of both the organization's objectives and strategies and the individual's role in the organization when designing these systems.

Although clarity and understanding reflect the important technical characteristics of the performance measurement system required to ensure that decision makers understand the casual chain between performance and rewards, there are important behavioral considerations that the performance measurement system must reflect. First, and above all, the individual must believe that the system is fair. For example measuring and rewarding performance that the individual does not believe she controls will reduce or eliminate the motivational potential of a performance measurement system. Developing standards of performance that the individual feels are extremely difficult or impossible to meet will similarly inhibit the motivational potential of incentive compensation. The bottom line is that the employee must believe that she can legitimately influence the performance measures that are linked to her rewards. Absent this belief, the motivational potential of incentive compensation will be lost.

Second, the individual must believe that the organization's compensation policies are equitable. For example, rewarding senior executives with multimillion dollar bonuses while rewarding assembly-line workers with bonuses with a maximum potential of several hundred dollars will create an environment or culture in the organization that only senior organization members are valued by the organization. In such an environment, motivational systems that might otherwise do well become ineffectual.

Third, the incentive system should provide rewards on a timely basis to reinforce the relationship between decision making, measured performance, and the rewards. As time passes, the link in the decision maker's mind between activities and rewards fades, but prompt rewards can reinforce the decision maker's understanding about activities and rewards.

## Role for Bonus and Incentive Contracts

Arch Patton argues that the following conditions are ideal for the use of an incentive system:[10]

1. Profits are affected by numerous short-term decisions.
2. The managers have the authority to make the decisions (this is most characteristic of decentralized firms organized on a product-line basis).
3. The control system is well defined, and performance is evaluated on a systematic basis, either by comparison with a plan or by comparison with the performance of similar firms.
4. The managers are expected to be entrepreneurial and ambitious.

On the other hand, Patton argues that firms with the following characteristics are poor candidates for the application of executive incentive plans:

1. Profits are most affected by a few long-term decisions.
2. The company is organized on a functional basis (say by marketing, production, accounting, and finance).
3. Budgets are difficult to develop, or data do not exist about competitors, to judge the adequacy of managerial performance.
4. Decision making need not be rapid or responsive.

In the organization behavior literature, a line of research called **equity theory** appears to support the notion that individual performance-based compensation is both widely accepted and promoted in Western cultures.[11] G. S. Leventhal, J. W. Michaels, and C. Sanford summarized the results of this theory, as of 1972:

> Equity theory . . . suggests that individuals are motivated to allocate rewards in accordance with recipients' inputs or work contributions. This assumption is supported by results from studies on reward allocation in task-oriented groups. When members [provide] equal inputs, an individual member usually attempts to bring about an equal division of reward between himself and his co-worker. . . . And when members of a group have unequal inputs, an individual member allocates rewards in accordance with perceived work contributions. . . . It has also been shown that allocators distribute rewards in accordance with work inputs when they themselves are not members of the group of recipients among whom the rewards are distributed.[12]

The tendency to allocate rewards based on performance is mitigated by many factors, including whether the person allocating the rewards must make the allocation decision public. In general, equity theory supports the contention that an individual's reward should reflect that person's contribution to the organization. On the other hand, Paul Lawrence and Jay Lorsch argue that people who play an integrative role in organizations should be rewarded based on overall performance.[13] Lawrence and Lorsch conclude that

> rewards systems . . . can help induce either the "you do your job, and I'll do mine" attitude or the "let's pull together" attitude. Each can be suitable under certain conditions. Reward systems should be designed with these conditions more clearly in mind.

This line of reasoning would imply that people at senior levels of the organization who perform integrative tasks should be rewarded on the basis of corporate performance, whereas people who are not engaged in integrative tasks should be rewarded on the basis of individual performance.

For example, a survey of compensation practice[14] reported the following average distribution of the total compensation of chief executive officers in large corporations:

| | |
|---|---|
| Salary | 21% |
| Short-term incentives | 27% |
| Long-term incentives | 16% |
| Stock-based pay | 36% |

Thus, 79% of the total compensation of the executives was performance-related and, therefore, at risk, and 52% of this performance-related compensation was in the form of long-term incentives. The article also pointed out that the fraction of executive compensation at risk declined for lower-level executives. For example, the average percent of fixed pay for other senior executives was

| | |
|---|---|
| Chief operating officer | 23% |
| Chief financial officer | 26% |
| Chief counsel | 31% |
| Head MIS area | 41% |
| Head auditing area | 49% |

Such plans put more of a person's compensation at risk and tie long-term compensation to the achievement of strategic goals. The bonus percentage in total compensation was highest in the energy and wholesale retail trade industries and lowest in the public utility and construction industries. This pattern is consistent with our prediction that the more volatile the industry, the greater the motivation potential for performance-based compensation schemes.

## Types of Incentives

Executive compensation schemes can be characterized along several dimensions:

1. **Immediate versus long term:** Awards can be immediate (usually in the form of cash or equity awards based on current performance) or long-term (usually in the form of stock options whose value is tied to the long-run performance of the company's common equity or shares that must be held for an extended number of years before redemption).

2. **Cash versus equity:** Awards can be in the form of cash or in the form of equity (shares, stock options, phantom shares, and performance shares). Although both cash and equity rewards can be tied to short-term or long-term performance, cash awards are usually tied to short-term profit performance, and equity awards are usually tied to long-term price performance of the firm's common equity.

3. **Monetary versus nonmonetary:** Awards can be either cash or near-cash (equity) or perquisites and other nonmonetary entitlements. Perquisites take many forms. As reported by surveys of practice, the most common perquisites include vacation trips, executive parking privileges, use of a company car, life insurance, corporate loans at preferred rates of interest, club memberships, and specialized health care insurance packages. In some cases, the perquisite is provided because of the position held. In other cases, the perquisite is awarded based on an informal performance assessment. The granting of some perquisites, particularly vacation trips, may be tied directly to formal performance measurements, often in the form of a contest. The other nonmonetary awards include formal recognition in the form of a citation or a trophy, informal recognition in the form of social invitations from more-senior executives, and participation in personnel development programs that are reserved for executives being groomed for senior management. Superiors often base these awards on informal performance assessments.

In this chapter, we concentrate on the cash and equity types of incentives. This emphasis does not imply that the perquisite and other nonmonetary forms are unimportant. It merely reflects the greater availability of information on cash and equity incentive plans.

## Specific Forms Assumed by Monetary Compensation Plans

We consider the following forms of monetary compensation plans:[15]

1. Cash bonus or profit sharing and the stock bonus
2. Deferred compensation
3. Stock options
4. Performance shares or units
5. Stock appreciation rights
6. Participating units

### Cash or Stock Awards

Current bonuses, in either cash or stock, are awarded at the end of an accounting period. Corporate profit and individual performance are the most common bases used to determine the amounts of the bonuses. These awards reward executives for performance during the bonus period, which usually is one year. Therefore, these awards for short-run performance do not avoid the danger of promoting a preoccupation with short-run results that often is detrimental to the long-run interests of the firm. The short-run performance measure is usually a financial measure, such as profit or cost, but it could be a nonfinancial measure such as quality or on-time delivery. When the performance measure is nonfinancial it is usually chosen because it is felt to be a driver of long-term financial performance that is controllable by the person being rewarded.

Typical formulas (to be discussed later in more detail) are a fixed percentage of corporate profits or a percentage of profits in excess of a specified return on stockholders' equity. A hybrid type of reward is profit sharing, in which the rewards are used to purchase stock, which is then held in the recipient's name.

Current bonuses are equivalent to salaries in their tax consequences to the firm and its executives. But bonuses may be cut or eliminated during a year of poor economic performance, whereas salaries are rarely cut. A stock award creates a close affinity of interests between the top-management group and the shareholders. A disadvantage is that the executive will need to find cash or financing to pay taxes on the stock award if the shares are not sold immediately. Also, significant stock ownership by managers may lead to risk-averse behavior, as mentioned in our principal-agent discussion.

Profit-sharing plans are widely regarded as poor motivators for two reasons. First, beneficiaries of the plans almost never see a clear relationship between their effort and group performance and their effort and their individual rewards. Second, because there is no attempt to measure individual performance, there is an incentive for group members to free-ride on the efforts of others.

Another form of cash bonus is a system that provides awards based on of the organization's computed economic value added—an accounting-based evaluation tool discussed in Chapter 10. In fact, Stern and Stewart, the developers of economic value added, stress, above all, the motivational effects of tying executive rewards to economic value added.

On the surface, rewarding executives based on reported economic value added would seem like another scheme that rewards short-run performance. However, studies have found that economic value added is more highly correlated with stock prices than is accounting income—suggesting that the adjustments made to accounting income to correct its conservative bias may help in turning a short-run profit measure (GAAP profit) into a longer-run measure of performance (economic value added).

## Deferred Bonus and Compensation

Deferred compensation refers to any type of award, cash or stock, that is deferred until a future period. Deferred stock-compensation plans are often supplemented by restrictions that prevent the manager from selling the stock or that specify that the firm's contributions to the purchase price of the stock will not vest for some specified period of time, thus attempting to tie the manager to the firm.

In some companies, bonuses are not paid until the executive retires so that the executive will receive the income when in a lower tax bracket. As long as the deferred compensation is unfunded and based solely on the unsecured credit of the employer, current taxes can be avoided. The overall tax benefit of deferred compensation to the company and the executive combined is worthwhile only if the executive's original tax bracket on interest income exceeds the corporate tax rate.

Some plans defer the bonus over a period of three to five years after it is earned. Receipt is contingent on the employee's continuing to work for the company and continued strong organization performance. Referred to as **golden handcuffs,** these plans make it expensive for key executives to leave a company. These plans are especially useful in high-technology companies that attempt to minimize the loss of key executives to rivals.

## Stock Options

A stock option gives executives the right to purchase company stock at a future date, at a price established when the option was granted. Stock options are intended to motivate the executive to work hard to do things that investors value so that they will bid up the price of the stock, enhancing the value of the stock option. For incentive and tax reasons, the option price should be higher than the current price. However, there is evidence[16] that most stock options are issued in the money; that is, with an option price less than the existing market price. Moreover, reports of practice published in various business periodicals and reports filed by companies with the Securities and Exchange Commission suggest that many organizations will adjust the option price downward if the company's share price falls after the option was issued.[17] This behavior, along with the value and dilutive effect of the stock options, has created a storm of controversy about executive compensation.

With stock options, executives are presumed to attempt to influence long-term stock price performance rather than short-term profits. Of perhaps greater importance is that an option has no downside loss (since the executive does not actually own the stock) and unlimited upside potential. Therefore, executives may be encouraged to reduce the risk-averse behavior that would otherwise accompany their ownership of stock and to undertake riskier projects with higher payoffs.

Although most compensation experts believe that stock options are an effective motivational tool, stock options have a disadvantage in that events not directly under managerial control may strongly influence share prices. During the mid-1990s critics of executive compensation, in general, and stock options, in particular, complained that a strong bull market, wherein the prices of all securities were rising because of general economic conditions, provided lavish rewards to executives in many companies whose performance was mediocre or even poor relative to similar organizations. This view suggests an important role for management accountants: namely, to develop indices or perhaps even contribute insight to the development of derivative securities so that executives can be rewarded relative to the performance of comparable organizations, thereby eliminating the effect of general market movements on the value of compensation through stock options. Moreover, stock options can be very expensive. Estimates are that stock options, if fully exercised, would, for the average company, dilute profits by 5%, or about $70 million per year.

## Performance Shares

A performance share awards company stock (the share) for achieving a specified, usually long-term, performance target. The most common target is to achieve a growth in earnings per share over a three- to five-year period. A typical range for cumulative earnings per share (EPS) growth is between 9% and 15% per year. Executives generally receive no additional reward for exceeding the EPS growth and may receive a fraction of the rewarded shares if the objectives are partially met. Performance share awards suffer from the same limitations as stock options: the imposition of risk on the manager and the influence of factors beyond the manager's control on the amount of the award. Performance shares also are subject to the problems of basing awards on accounting measures that may promote decisions that improve the measured accounting performance rather than necessarily improving the economic worth of the firm.

Performance share plans can be quite complex and reflect the strategic and long-run considerations of strategic performance measurement schemes such as the Balanced Scorecard. For example, in one company that manufactured components used in the electronics industry:

1. Performance on six attributes of performance was measured. These attributes were (a) quality (measured by reported product failures), (b) timeliness of production (measured by comparing scheduled completion times with actual completion times), (c) cost control (measured by flexible budget variances), (d) sales growth, (e) profitability (measured by reported corporate profits), and (f) employee morale (measured by absenteeism).

2. Rewards were based on (a) the ability to meet annual targets and (b) the relative improvement of performance over a three-year period. Targets were set based on discussions between subordinates and their superiors. These discussions were related not only to the choice of the standards but also to the appropriateness and controllability of the attributes being measured.

3. Rewards were made annually and based on performance over the previous three-year period.

## Stock Appreciation Rights and Phantom Stock

Stock appreciation rights (SAR) are deferred cash payments based on the increase of the stock price from the time of award to the time of payment. SARs are frequently used in conjunction with stock option plans to provide a means for executives to purchase stock earned under stock option plans. Phantom stock plans are awards in units of number of shares of stock. After qualifying for receipt of the vested units, the executive receives in cash the number of units multiplied by the current market price of the stock. Both SARs and phantom stock are essentially deferred cash bonuses but with the value of the bonus a function of the future stock price. Thus, they have both the strengths and the weaknesses that result when compensation is a function of share price.

## Participating Units

Participating unit plans are similar to SARs except that payment is keyed to operating results rather than to stock price. Commonly used operating measures include pretax income, return on investment, sales and backlog, or a combination of these. The units awarded can vary continuously with the measure of operating results. Participating units are most useful for an organization with little or no publicly traded stock or for a specialized division whose fortunes are not closely linked to overall company results. Participating units permit the greatest flexibility in relating executive incentives to long-term performance measures internal to the organization. The measures are not affected by stock market fluctuations and therefore reduce some noncontrollable uncertainty in the executive's compensation function. The measures, however, suffer from a disadvantage because of the divergence of interests created between executives and shareholders. Participating unit plans require a careful and operational specification of the long-term operating results desired for the firm and the way in which incentive compensation will vary with partial or complete attainment of those operating results.

## Evaluating Accounting-Based Incentive Compensation Schemes

Within the broad framework of incentive schemes, ranging from the annual cash bonus to more recent and sophisticated schemes such as performance shares, many crucial design issues can determine whether the incentive plan provides the appropriate motivation at minimum cost to the firm's owners. The two most crucial questions are (1) how the total size of the bonus pool is determined each year and (2) how the bonus pool is allocated to the corporate and divisional executives.

### Establishing the Size of the Bonus Pool

In choosing the magnitude of the bonus pool, compensation specialists must decide what items to exclude and what items to include in defining the pool. The ideal would be to have a performance measure defined for each individual that reflects that individual's personal contribution to the organization and makes allowances for the positive or negative factors in the environment that were beyond the executive's control and might affect the performance measure. Unfortunately, it is generally impossible to measure the contribution each individual makes to the organization, and it is equally difficult to make the performance measure totally independent of the factors over which the executive has no control. For example, how can one evaluate the contribution of an individual violinist to the overall sound and performance of a symphony orchestra? As a compromise, some organizations assess individual performance by comparing actual results against targeted or budgeted results. For example, a production manager might be evaluated using a weighted performance rating or score based on her ability to meet production deadlines, quality goals, and cost control. Then rewards from the pool would be distributed using the individual performance scores.

We must often use less than perfect motivational devices that sometimes reward or penalize managers for factors that were beyond their control and that reflect joint, rather than individual, contributions to the organization. The simplest rule for determining the magnitude of executive bonuses is to compute the bonus pool as a fixed percentage of the profit earned by the organization. Some firms, however, determine the amount of the available bonus pool by performance relative to plan, irrespective of the absolute level of profits. The rationale for making awards, even at low or negative levels of corporate profits, is to retain executives in a severely depressed firm.

Profits, as a measure of performance, are closely related to the goals of the owners of the organization, are verified by an independent third party, and are well understood by the organization members. The most basic system defines the bonus pool as a percentage of reported profits, such as 15%. This rule, however, will award bonuses even with very low profits when the firm is earning a low return on invested capital. Variations on this basic system include a residual income concept wherein the bonus pool is activated only when the owners have received some predetermined return on investment (which raises the problem of defining the amount of the investment). In addition, maximum dollar limits, based on dividend payments, are often placed on the size of the bonus pool.

A fairly common procedure is to compute the bonus pool as a percentage of profits after a prespecified return on invested capital or shareholders' equity has been earned. For example, one firm described how the amount in its profit-sharing plan for officers and key personnel was determined each year:

> Under the present formula of the Plan, the company's consolidated net income after tax (adjusted) for any year must exceed 5% of the average amount of the consolidated book value of its capital stock before any amount becomes available for distribution to participants. Ten percent of the excess of adjusted net income [is distributed, subject to the approval and discretion of outside members of the board of directors in cash and stock].

Another company's incentive plan for its key employees indicated:

> There shall be credited to the incentive fund an amount not to exceed 5% of the company's total income before any provision for incentive payments, interest, income taxes and extraordinary items, after deducting 13% of invested capital.

And Alfred Sloan's favorite, the General Motors bonus plan:

> The Corporation maintains a reserve for purpose of the Bonus Plan to which may be credited each year an amount which the independent public accountants of the corporation determine to be 8% of the net earnings which exceed 7% but not 15% of net capital, plus 5% of the net earnings which exceed 15% of net income, but not in excess of the amount paid out as dividends on the common stock during the year.

A variety of issues arise in these formulas. First is the definition of the investment base: shareholders' equity or invested capital (generally computed as shareholders' equity plus long-term debt). The use of shareholders' equity provides an incentive to increase leverage as long as the net cash flows from the asset acquired exceed the after-tax borrowing cost plus straight-line depreciation. By including long-term debt in the investment base, we eliminate the bias to increase debt. A more comprehensive approach might include all interest-bearing debt, short and long term, in invested capital.

A second problem arises if only shareholders' equity is used for computing bonus payments. Several years of losses may reduce the shareholders' equity to a low level and make future bonuses very easy to earn, even though total return on assets is still not at highly profitable levels.

As an aside, it is interesting to speculate whether one of the forces giving rise to occasional big baths in earnings is related to incentive compensation schemes. Under the big-bath approach, disappointing (or even negative) earnings cause the company managers to write off a variety of dubious assets on the balance sheet so that bad news in a single year can be concentrated (who cares how negative a price-earnings ratio gets?) to clean up the books for future profitability. Such an action becomes easy to explain if the managers reason as follows:

1. With earnings this low, we're not going to earn a bonus this year anyway. Let's clean off these accruals so that we won't have to keep amortizing them against earnings in future years.
2. A good healthy loss reduces shareholders' equity and will make future bonuses a little easier to earn and a little larger.

A third and more serious problem with the use of shareholders' equity, either by itself or as part of total invested capital, is the failure to adjust for price-level changes. Shareholders' equity represents the capital contributed each year in the firm's history through retained earnings and sales of stock. This capital has been contributed at dramatically different price levels, yet it is added together as if it had all been contributed in the most recent year. For many companies, a simple price-level adjustment on shareholders' equity would probably completely eliminate what had been a lucrative bonus and incentive payment. The failure to restate shareholders' equity for price-level changes makes the bonus pool larger than it should be, if the goal is to reward the earning of income in excess of a specified return on invested capital.

A third method for establishing the bonus pool (in addition to a fixed percentage of profits or a percentage of income in excess of a specified return on invested capital) would base performance on profit improvement. With this procedure, bonuses would be awarded for annual increases in profits. Apart from increases in profits caused by accounting manipulations, as we discussed earlier in considering the principal-agent relationship, this procedure may reward or penalize executives for events beyond their control. General business conditions or specific industry factors could cause earnings to expand or contract for reasons not controllable by company executives. The result might be windfall gains or losses for these executives in their incentive plans.

The impact of uncontrollable factors could be reduced by comparing a company's performance with that of other firms in the same industry.[18] In this way, the executives of a company whose earnings increased 15% while the industry average earnings increased 25% would not be rewarded for a good absolute but weak relative performance. The following excerpt from a *Wall Street Journal* article raises this point:

> All for one and one for all. That theme has traditionally determined how many
> executives receive incentive rewards. When the whole company does well, the
> executive does well; when the company flops, so does the incentive pay. But many
> companies are starting to break from that tradition. They are now tailoring incentive
> plans to the performance of an executive's division or business unit over a three- to
> five-year period. The goal is to motivate executives and to reward them more fairly
> when their unit performs well—regardless of corporate results.[19]

The article provides two quotations from directors of corporate compensation plans to reinforce the need to assess individual contributions as well as to identify the specific contributions expected from each business unit:

> "If you want incentive pay to change behavior, a manager has got to believe he has
> some control over what is being measured." John Hillers, Director of Corporate
> Compensation, Honeywell Inc.

> "[The divisional compensation plan] ties our compensation in with the business unit
> strategy and helps focus the executive on what is important for that unit." Wallace
> Nichols, Director of Compensation, Premark International Inc.

The article recognizes the problems created by basing rewards on local measures of performance, which include the following:

1. In firms with highly interrelated business units, many problems will arise from attempting to allocate joint revenues (the transfer-pricing problem) and joint costs. Moreover, in

highly interrelated firms, a fiction may be created that the business units are separate economic units that can operate independently of each other. Measuring individual performance may create interdivisional competition and conflict that may discourage these business units from coordinating their activities.

2.  Goal setting will be difficult because of the specialized nature of the tasks of each business unit as well as the need to understand the potential of each unit.

3.  The use of long-term measures of performance would effectively end the practice of rotating managers among the various business units.

Awards based on overall corporate, rather than divisional, performance would seem to work best for dominant-product firms: that is, vertically integrated firms producing a single major product (such as automobiles, tires, or steel) and in which a high degree of interaction or coordination among divisions is required for the firm to function effectively. Awards based on divisional performance seem most appropriate when the firm is highly decentralized with little interaction among its divisions, which are organized as profit or investment centers. For example, firms that can be characterized as conglomerates, venture capitalists, or holding companies for diverse operating units can use incentive plans based primarily on divisional performance. For firms somewhere in the middle of the continuum between dominant-product and highly diversified firms, a combination of corporate and divisional performance may provide the right mixture of incentives for optimizing local performance while still looking out for overall corporate goals.

Finally, one can always attempt to evaluate managerial performance against a profit plan or budget and avoid all the problems that arise when using mechanical formulas for profitability. If the board of directors could obtain forecasts that truly represented what profits were achievable, given (1) anticipated business conditions, (2) high-quality managerial decision making, and (3) the best administrative efforts of the managers, then achievement of the profit plan would provide an excellent basis for incentive compensation. The problem, of course, with any incentive plan based on budgeted performance is to obtain information that is not biased or distorted in order to influence the ease of achieving the targeted plan.

## Allocating the Bonus Pool to Managers

Once the size of the bonus pool is defined, the next issue is to determine how to distribute the bonus pool to the members of the organization who are entitled to share in the bonus pool. The most basic distribution rule makes the share proportional to salary. In this system, a person's share equals the ratio of that person's salary to the total salaries of all the people entitled to share in the pool. Although this system is easy to implement, it is very crude. First, it assumes that a person's merit is proportional to that person's salary. This assumption is tenuous at best. Second, the scheme introduces a **free-rider** problem by providing bonuses for everyone who is entitled to share in the bonus pool, irrespective of whether that person did a good job or not. Some people may free-ride (relax, or shirk responsibility) and rely on the hard work of others to provide a big bonus pool. The people who have relaxed then participate in the division of the pool along with the diligent workers. Carried to an extreme, the system falls apart as everyone shirks, waiting for someone else to do the work, and nothing gets done. That is why many companies base bonuses on individual performance, such as the performance of the manager's division. But recall Sloan's admonition that basing rewards on individual performance inevitably causes managers to focus on local responsibility unit initiatives in ways that are detrimental to the overall organization. Also, many Japanese companies reward group performance so that everyone takes responsibility for the successes and failures of the entire organization. These group reward systems must include some formal or informal monitoring mechanisms to mitigate the free-rider problem.[20]

An alternative to basing the bonus pool distribution on salary is to award bonuses as a function of (1) the importance of the job that the person does and (2) the success that the person has in carrying out assigned tasks. This type of system requires that each individual's role in the organization be clearly defined and understood:

1. The content of a person's job is agreed to by both the person and the supervisor.
2. The individual develops performance targets for the job.
3. The individual and the superior discuss the performance targets, and a target is agreed upon.
4. A control system is established to monitor progress toward achieving the target.
5. The superior and the subordinate meet at the end of the period to discuss the results and the relationship of the results to the target.

For example, the performance review system used by Lee Iacocca at Ford and Chrysler required that, each quarter, superiors ask subordinates to specify their goals, priorities, and the manner in which they will seek their goals.

With this scheme, step 1 would be the point at which the importance of the job would be defined, and this would determine the potential bonus points that the individual could earn. Step 5 would determine whether all, some, or none of the potential bonus points defined in step 1 would be awarded. Although the approach seems sound, it appears to be seldom used. Perhaps the considerable effort required to operate and maintain the system makes it impractical.

In general, the bonus system will be more effective as an incentive and reward if top management and the board of directors review the bonus allocation. This review enables the bonus award to also be a function of longer-range, less-quantifiable performance criteria and thereby relieves the pressure on exclusive use of a short-term accounting-based measure of performance. The board of directors is in the best position to tie incentive payments to the establishment and implementation of plans for long-term profitability. Review by the board also permits an evaluation of relative performance, comparing results with industry performance, when awarding incentive payments.

## Short-Term versus Long-Term Performance Measures

A preoccupation with short-run performance may seriously damage the future potential of the firm. Classical examples of short-run suboptimization include curtailing discretionary cost expenditures, such as research and development, maintenance, and personnel development. Alfred Rappaport pointed out the myopia of most compensation plans.[21] Rappaport argued that incentive plans should be linked to the achievement of the long-run goals of the organization. Incentives should be paid for performance over several years rather than for just one year. Whether it is practical to devise incentive schemes that are tied to longer-run strategic factors, rather than shorter-run performance factors, is an open issue. Moreover, it may be difficult to measure an executive's performance over several years if the executive is constantly changing jobs within the company.

McDonald's evaluates its store managers based on performance in the following areas:

- Product quality
- Service
- Cleanliness
- Sales volume
- Personnel training
- Cost control

The manager's performance on each of these factors is measured and is then evaluated relative to targets that have been set by the manager and the manager's supervisor. Obviously, each of these factors will affect long-run profits. Evidently, the senior management at McDonald's feels it important to evaluate these key success variables in the short run. Moreover, focusing on these key success factors, rather than on short-run profits, identifies these factors as the key influences on long-run profitability.

## Are Chief Executives Overpaid?

The late spring of each year, after companies have released details of executive compensation in their annual reports and 10-K filings, sees a torrent of editorial comments and articles about the level and nature of executive pay. These editorials and discussions have promoted numerous debates about whether senior executives, particularly chief executive officers, are overpaid.

There are two broad complaints about the pay of chief executive officers (CEOs). First, people complain that CEO rewards should be more closely tied to organization performance. Second, people complain that CEOs are overpaid both in absolute terms and relative to other organization members.

On average, 79% of CEO compensation is variable with some measure of organization performance. The most common measures of performance for short-term rewards are GAAP income or some adjustment of GAAP income, earnings per share, return on assets or net assets, and economic value added. The most common measure of performance for long-term rewards is share price.

People who complain that CEO compensation is not variable enough argue that the correlation between executive pay and organization performance should be higher. That is, CEOs should get more when their organization does well and suffer more when their organization does poorly. The cause of the low correlation between executive rewards and organization performance seems to result from two factors: (1) Executives rarely are paid negative bonuses when performance is below standard, and (2) there are often caps on how much the executive can share in rewards when performance is above standard.

It would appear that the management accountants, who are invariably involved in designing incentive plans that are based on measured performance, must address this issue and must solve the problem of how to make the executive's pay more related to performance without allowing for the potential of huge losses if performance is bad (which the executive could not pay from personal funds) or for the potential of huge gains if performance is good (which invariably attracts criticism and may affect the motivation of other organization members). Perhaps one solution is for short-term performance rewards to be put into a fund that would be increased in good years and decreased in bad years and to allow an executive to withdraw only a portion of the accumulated amount in any given year.

The second broad issue relating to CEO pay is the matter of how CEO pay affects the motivation of other organization members. This issue is relevant to the management accountant who is involved in designing and implementing incentive systems for other organization members. There is widespread evidence that huge payouts to CEOs affect the morale and motivation of lower-level management and nonmanagement employees. Surveys suggest that people feel that the pay of the CEO is unfair when compared with the pay of other organization members. These notions of distributional fairness have existed for many years. The Greek philosopher Plato argued that for moral and ethical reasons, in any organization, the highest paid worker should earn no more than five times the pay of the lowest paid worker.[22] A study by Pearl Meyer & Partners Inc. reported that CEOs in 1965 earned 44 times the average production worker's wage. In 1996, the ratio was 212 times.

This phenomenon seems to be most pronounced in the United States. Exhibit 13-2 shows the Canadian Centre for Policy Alternatives report of the ratios of the pay (including salary, bonuses, stock option, etc.) of a typical CEO to that of a typical worker in 1995.

The approach to executive pay in which the CEO earns a huge salary relative to other organization members, including other senior executives, has been called the winner-take-all or **tournament** approach to paying senior executives. Whether this sports-event approach to executive pay has the effect of motivating executives to work hard to aspire to the top job is a question that remains unanswered. But one result is unequivocal; this approach has the potential to alienate workers who have no chance of winning the top job. The potential result of perceived inequity is for these workers to withdraw efforts and to put less effort and dedication into the organization.

Dealing with these issues is the domain of compensation experts, but the management accountant involved in designing compensation plans must be aware of the culture

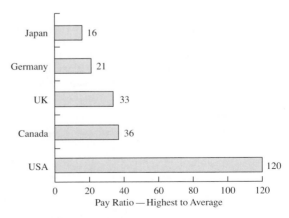

**EXHIBIT 13-2  The Wage Gap**

*Source:* Canadian Centre for Policy Alternatives

or climate in the organization that can affect motivation. Because there appears to be little doubt that relative pay can affect the organization's culture or climate, management accountants should be sensitive to the potential motivational effect of relative pay when designing performance measurement systems.

## REWARDING OTHER ORGANIZATION MEMBERS

Compensation experts seem to agree that, for organization harmony and motivation reasons, all organization members should participate in incentive compensation plans, although they might not all participate in the same plan. Unfortunately, this seemingly important objective is not widely met in practice. A recent survey[23] suggests that only 13% of employees in mid- to large-sized companies participate in profit-sharing plans, 3% participate in stock ownership plans, and only one-half of one percent participate in stock option plans.

We observed earlier that the scope and focus of an incentive plan should be tailored to the individual's responsibilities in the organization. Therefore, senior executives are usually rewarded on the basis of broad measures of organization performance. Other organization members may be rewarded on the basis of the identified contribution that they make to the organization.

### Gainsharing

Among the types of plans for rewarding production line workers is the gainsharing plan. The most common and widely known gainsharing program is the Scanlon plan, developed and first implemented in 1935, which provides for a sharing between the company and employees of labor cost savings associated with productivity improvements over a baseline level.[24] Over the years, the Scanlon plan has prompted variations:

> The Scanlon plan bases bonus payments on changes in the ratio of total payroll costs to the sales value of production. The Rucker plan, a variant of Scanlon, also uses total payroll in its rewards formula, but value added in production is adopted in place of sales value in an effort to discount the effects of changes in material cost and bought-in service and/or the ratios of materials employed in production. Improshare, the most recent of the gainsharing plans, dispenses entirely with economic productivity ratios; instead it bases rewards on changes in the ratio of actual labor hours expended per unit of production standard hours, where the latter reflects the labor hours content of a unit of output in the base period.[25]

More generally, gainsharing involves the sharing of the increased profits resulting from any targeted-level performance. For example, believing that improved quality leads to higher sales and increased profits, some organizations provide for payments to employees based on the estimated effect on profits of increased quality levels.

Gainsharing plans, focusing on labor costs, were widely adopted in the 1930s and 1940s but gradually fell into disfavor during the 1960s.[26] However, when a 1981 U.S. General Accounting Office study[27] estimated that gainsharing plans, on average, resulted in 17% labor cost savings, interest in gainsharing programs revived, and interest continues in using this approach to reduce labor costs. For example, gainsharing was a negotiated solution to a threat by workers at Canadian National Railways to go on strike.

## Piecerate Systems

In a piecerate system, a person is paid according to that person's measured production. Piecerate systems were common during the period of the industrial revolution and gradually, during the 1800s and 1900s, were replaced by wage systems. Managers felt that an hourly wage represented a more humane approach to pay, and workers in integrated, process-focused, operations lost their ability to control the pace of their individual output.

Piecerate systems are now infrequent enough to attract attention when they are used. For example, in 1995 Safelite Glass Corporation, an installer of autoglass, changed from a wage to a piecerate system. The workers were guaranteed a minimum wage of $11 per hour but were also offered a piecerate wage that paid them $20 for each unit they installed. The cost of repairing faulty installations was charged back to the location that originally did the work. Because the name of the original installer was known provided a basis for peer pressure on employees who were creating losses. The result was that productivity rose by 20%. The productivity gains were shared equally by the company and the employees.[28]

The best-known user of the piecerate system is Lincoln Electric, a manufacturer of arc-welding equipment and electric motors.[29] Almost all Lincoln Electric's production workers are paid using a piecerate system. The piecerate system is designed so that a worker producing at a reasonable rate will earn a wage equal to comparable jobs in the local job market. Rework is charged back to the originating worker so that there is no incentive to sacrifice quality for speed. The result is worker productivity that is higher than average and pay rates that are two to three times the national average of compensation paid to production workers. In addition, all workers share in a bonus pool, which varies in total from about 50% to 100% of the total wage bill. An individual worker's share in the pool is determined by ratings on four factors of performance: dependability (meaning not missing work), quality, output, and improvement suggestions.

## Labor-Related Plans

First widely implemented in the 1930s, labor-related incentive plans focus on labor cost savings. In labor-intensive settings where the workers can control the rate of production and where they have the authority and training to implement changes, labor-related plans share productivity gains between the organization and the worker. These plans have many forms, but the basic idea is the same in all of them. The amount of labor in a given piece of work is identified for a benchmark period. That labor amount becomes the standard against which subsequent work is compared. When the amount of labor for a given level of output is less than the budget based on the target, part of the labor savings (usually between 25% and 50%) goes into a bonus pool. When the amount of labor for a given level of output is more than the budget based on the target, part of the excess cost of labor is deducted from the pool. Each year, part of the pool is paid out to employees. Usually, the total is distributed equally among the employees. Critical attributes of these plans are:

1. How the benchmark standard is determined
2. How and how often the standard is revised
3. The sharing rules—both between the organization and the workers and among the workers
4. The payout rules

These plans continue to be popular because they provide a straightforward and manageable approach to motivation.

## Bonus Systems

Bonus systems are the simplest of the incentive plans. In these systems, the employee is paid a bonus, usually a percent of salary but often a fixed amount, for meeting or exceeding a performance target. For example, an employee might be rewarded with a day holiday or a day's wages for completing 500 days of work without an injury. Bonus systems are very targeted and reward specific behavior. Bonus systems focus on short-run and manageable behavior.

## SUMMARY

The use of executive incentive plans is widespread. Participation in these plans is usually limited to those employees whose activities have a significant effect on the performance of the firm.

The rewards provided by incentive plans are diverse and include cash, equity in the firm, perquisites, and intangible rewards. Of these rewards, cash, stock options, perquisites, and public recognition of outstanding performance appear to be the most commonly used.

Some people believe that individual performance should be evaluated relative to that person's tasks and assigned goals in the organization. In this approach, performance awards should be based on the individual's performance relative to a plan, with due consideration of the factors over which the individual had no control and that may have affected performance.

Others recommend that rewards should be based on group performance. The disadvantage of group rewards is that distinctive (good or bad) individual performance is not formally recognized, and, if no effective group sanctions exist, group rewards can lead to individual shirking.

Many contemporary incentive schemes also focus exclusively on short-run financial performance. To offset the pursuit of short-run goals, a company should construct incentives so that executives are motivated to pursue long-run objectives or, alternatively, evaluate performance relative to the firm's key success variable.

Incentive plans provide strong motivation for the top corporate executives to perform well along specified measures of performance. Formula-based plans reduce uncertainty and ambiguity about how performance will be evaluated, but devising mechanistic formulas that do not encourage dysfunctional behavior can be difficult. Limitations of accounting-based formulas, such as the failure to control for changes in price levels, can lead to the awarding of large bonuses even when the firm is earning less than a competitive return on capital.

The board of directors, particularly an independent compensation committee consisting solely of outside directors, can play a vital role in offsetting these potential limitations. Such a committee could control for

1. Increases or decreases in profits caused by accounting conventions rather than operating performance
2. Increases in profits caused by the failure to adjust for price-level changes

3. Increases in profits not commensurate with performance of similar companies in the same industry

4. Increases in profits caused by concentration on short-term rather than long-term performance measures

5. Actions that maximize divisional performance measures at the expense of overall corporate welfare

## ENDNOTES

1. For a critique of incentive pay see A. Kohn, "Why Incentive Plans Cannot Work," *Harvard Business Review* (September–October 1993). For a discussion of Kohn's views and his response to criticisms, see "Rethinking Rewards; What Role—If Any—Should Incentives lay in the Workplace. *Harvard Business Review* (November–December 1993), pp. 37–45.

2. The General Motors bonus plan is described in A. Sloan, *My Years with General Motors* (New York: Doubleday, 1964), chap. 22.

3. C. D. Ittner, D. F. Larcker, and M. V. Rajan, "The Choice of Performance Measures in Annual Bonus Contracts," *The Accounting Review* (April 1997), pp. 231–55.

4. D. Swinford, "Unbundling Divisional Management Incentives," *Management Review* (July 1987), pp. 35–37.

5. For an excellent summary of the agency literature see J. S. Demski, *Managerial Uses of Accounting Information* (Boston: Kluwer, 1994).

6. The value, or certainty equivalent, of the return is the expected, or acturial value of the gamble less the premium for taking the risk. The risk premium is often approximated in analytical work using the decision maker's personal risk aversion index and the variance of the gamble.

7. M. Jensen, "A Roundtable Discussion of Management Compensation," *Midland Corporate Finance Journal* (Winter, 1985).

8. One approach to mediating the effects of these uncontinuable events is to base rewards on the performance of share price relative to an index of the share prices of competitors.

9. See the evidence in P. Healy, S.-H. Kang, and K. Palepu, "The Effect of Accounting Procedure Changes on CEOs' Cash Salary and Bonus Compensation," *Journal of Accounting and Economics* (April 1987), pp. 7–34.

10. A. Patton, "Why Incentive Plans Fail," *Harvard Business Review* (May–June 1972).

11. A formal statement of this theory and some empirical evidence of its descriptive validity can be found in J. Stacy Adams, "Toward an Understanding of Inequity," *Journal of Abnormal and Social Psychology* (November, Volume 67, No. 5, 1963), pp. 422–36; and J. S. Adams, "Inequity in Social Exchange," in *Advances in Experimental Psychology*, ed. L. Berkowitz (New York: Academic Press, 1965).

12. Gerald S. Leventhal, James W. Michaels, and Charles Sanford, "Inequity and Interpersonal Conflict: Reward Allocation and Secrecy about Reward as Methods of Preventing Conflict," *Journal of Personality and Social Psychology* (July, Volume 23, Number 1, 1972), pp. 88–102.

13. P. L. Lawrence and J. W. Lorsch, *Organization and Environment* (Homewood, IL: Richard D. Irwin, 1969).

14. *Fortune*, March 31, 1997, p. 119.

15. For an extended discussion of these alternative forms of compensation and a collection of field studies illustrating the use of these plans see S. A. Butler and M. W. Maher, *Management Incentive Compensation Plans* (Montvale, NJ: National Association of Accountants, 1986).

16. "Executive Pay," *Business Week* (April 21, 1997).

17. For example, Apple Computer altered the option price for its executives eight times in 12 years in response to a falling stock price that the executives could not improve.

18. See M. W. Maher, "The Use of Relative Performance Evaluation in Organizations," in *Accounting & Management: Field Study Perspectives*, ed. W. J. Bruns Jr., and R. S. Kaplan (Boston: Harvard Business School Press, 1987), pp. 295–315.

19.  "Firms Trim Annual Pay Increases and Focus on Long Term," *Wall Street Journal* (April 10, 1987), p. 25.

20.  For example, a survey of practice found that 40.5% of respondents used bonuses based on team performance but used individual incentives to determine individual rewards. See J. Sheridan, *Industry Week* (March 4, 1996), p. 63.

21.  Alfred Rappaport, "Executive Incentives vs. Corporate Growth," *Harvard Business Review* (July–August 1978), pp. 81–89.

22.  For a discussion, see "Inequality," *The Economist* (November 5, 1994), p. 29.

23.  S. S. Roach, "The Hollow Ring of the Productivity Revival," *Harvard Business Review* (November–December 1996), pp. 81–90.

24.  Well-known and enthusiastic users of the Scanlon plan include Dana Corporation, Donnelly Corporation, and the Herman Miller Company.

25.  H. Y. Park, "A Comparative Analysis of Work Incentives in U.S. and Japanese Firms," *Multinational Business Review* (Fall 1996), pp. 59–70.

26.  For an interesting discussion of gainsharing plans see W. Imberman, "Is Gainsharing the Wave of the Future?" *Management Accounting (USA)* (November 1995), p. 35.

27.  *Productivity Sharing Programs: Can They Contribute Productivity Improvements?* (Washington, D.C.: Government Printing Office, 1981).

28.  *Business Week* (February 17, 1997), p. 25.

29.  For an interesting description of Lincoln Electric's approach to compensation see K. Chilton, "Lincoln Electric's Incentive System: Can It Be Transferred Overseas?" *Compensation and Benefits Review* (November 1993), p. 21.

## ■ PROBLEMS

### 13-1     Executive Compensation Plan

The formula at Federal Signal provides bonuses to executives based on the company's pretax profits as a percent of average shareholders' equity plus the average long-term debt.

#### Required

(1)   What is the motivation for basing rewards on this measure?
(2)   What are the strengths and weaknesses of this plan?

### 13-2     Changing the Incentive Plan

In 1996 the CEO at ICF Kaiser faced a bonus plan that required earnings per share of $0.10 or better. After losing a large contract, this target seemed out of reach. However, on the last day of 1996, the company sold its interest in a coal mine, allowing it to meet the performance target and providing a bonus payment of $175,000 to the CEO. The compensation committee of the company's board of directors considered this sale legitimate because the proceeds from the disposition were needed to make a debt repayment and because the company routinely sells off minority investments.

Many compensation experts believe that compensation committees regularly adjust the parameters of incentive plans, or even change compensation plans completely, to allow senior management to earn incentive compensation when committee members believe that the executive compensation is too low. Although there is considerable evidence that compensation committees are willing to boost pay in bad times, there is relatively little evidence that they are prepared to scale back pay when the compensation seems excessive.

### Required

What do you think of the practice of a compensation committee's managing the parameters of an incentive compensation plan after the fact in order to provide an executive with a target level of compensation?

## 13-3    *Incentives and Decision Making*

HS Custom Woodshop (HSCW) specializes in custom cabinet work. HSCW uses many different types of machines, which are repaired and replaced at regular intervals in order to ensure low-cost, high-quality operations.

The factory manager, Nero Oakie, recently authorized the purchase of an $85,000 automated lathe that will be used to make spindles for stairways. This machine has just been installed. At the projected level of operations, this machine is expected to last for 10 years and have annual operating costs of $40,000. The machine is assumed to be worthless at the end of its life.

Nero is concerned about a recent development. Susie Company has just announced the availability of a new machine that performs the same tasks as the machine just installed at HSCW. The Susie machine would cost $130,000, last for 10 years, and have annual operating costs of $35,000. This Susie machine will provide for improved quality that Nero expects will increase operating margins by $10,000 a year over and above the operating cost savings. The machine just installed has a value, net of salvage, of $50,000. The new machine would have no salvage value in 10 years.

Nero is currently paid a salary of $60,000 and receives a bonus of one-half of one percent of corporate net income. Nero estimates that he will remain with HSCW for "about two more years." At that time he expects to achieve a promotion and raise by moving to another company.

In the questions that follow, ignore income taxes and assume that HSCW's pre-tax required return is 12%. The company uses the straight-line method to compute depreciation.

### Required

(1)   Should the company keep the newly installed machine on buy the Susie machine?
(2)   Which machine would Nero prefer?
(3)   What motivation problems are caused by using short-run financial measures of performance as reward devices?
(4)   How might the inconsistencies raised in Requirements 1 and 2 and the problems raised in 3 be mitigated?

## *13-4*   *Designing an Incentive Compensation System*

[What follows is an excerpt from the Definitive Proxy Statement, SEC Form 14A, filed April 28, 1997 by Lincoln Electric.]

The executive compensation policy of the Company is based on the Company's longstanding commitment to incentive-based compensation generally for all employees, including officers. This commitment is exemplified by the cash bonus program. For many years the Company has administered a discretionary employee bonus program featuring a cash distribution determined on the basis of a formula that takes into account individual earnings and the results of a merit review process. Virtually all domestic employees participate in the program, and efforts have been made to include employees of foreign subsidiaries, when appropriate. The costs of this program, net of hospitalization costs but inclusive of payroll taxes, were $66.7 million in 1996, $66.4 million in 1995, and $59.6 million in 1994.

In 1996 the Committee directed, and management completed, a comprehensive review of the Incentive Management System that has served the Company so well for many years. The study reaffirmed the Company's commitment across the board to premium pay for premium performance and recognized the continuing importance of the piecework system to the Company's production employees. The study also acknowledged, however, the need for more vigorous performance management review and productivity gains among salaried employees and certain hourly employees; it also sought to define more clearly the connection between Company performance on the one hand and the size and equitable distribution of the cash bonus payments on the other hand.

Concurrent with the reconfiguration of the Company's Incentive Management System (which has been renamed the Incentive Performance System), the Committee recommended a reevaluation of the Company's executive compensation policy. The Committee had begun to refine the theory of its incentive-oriented executive compensation in 1995, when it first introduced a Management Incentive Plan (MIP) for officers. One purpose of the MIP as introduced was to benchmark base salary and cash bonus opportunities against comparable opportunities at comparable companies. As first introduced, the MIP focused on establishing individual base salaries at the median of comparable companies, with a maximum incentive target, assuming achievement of predetermined financial targets, placing individuals at approximately the 75th percentile for comparable companies. The MIP was also segmented to reflect the responsibilities of individual officers, with weighing on corporate or regional results accordingly. In early 1996, the Committee set the financial performance and individual award targets for the MIP participants, including those applicable to the executive officers named in the Summary Compensation Table, on that basis. The Committee recognized later in 1996, however, as the Incentive Management System review was completed, the need for additional improvements in the MIP and in executive compensation strategy generally.

Consistent with the overall philosophy of the Company's compensation system, the Committee decided that the base salaries of MIP participants should as a norm be set at the 40th percentile, rather than the median (i.e., base salaries will be somewhat below average). The Committee has reaffirmed, however, that cash bonus opportunities should be above average, with the 75th percentile retained as the maximum target for total cash compensation. The Committee also recognized, however, that individual circumstances and performance should be factors in incentive awards, both positively and negatively—notwithstanding the performance of the Company against financial targets. The financial targets for 1997 are based on earnings before interest, taxes, and the cash bonus referred to above. Financial targets were set on the same basis in 1996. An individual performance element, based upon the achievement of personal objectives, has been added to the MIP. These improvements to the MIP are effective in 1997.

The Committee also noted in its review of executive compensation that the Company had not emphasized long-term equity incentive compensation as an element of total compensation, notwithstanding the existence of the 1988 Incentive Equity Plan (the IEP), which the Committee administers. Awards under the IEP, which are made only to officers and other key employees responsible for or contributing to the management, growth, and/or profitability of the Company, may be of four types: (1) stock options, (2) stock appreciation rights attached to stock options, (3) restricted stock, and (4) deferred stock. In early 1996 the Committee approved, on a one-time basis, option grants for a total of 167,590 shares to 31 individuals in settlement of litigation arising from earlier awards under the IEP. The options were premium priced at the time of grant, with exercise prices of $30 and $34 per share. The Committee also approved in September 1996 nonqualified option grants at market for a total of 278,000 shares to 21 individuals in order to address the longer-term incentive compensation program. The Committee expects that equity compensation will be an important part of incentive compensation going forward. As of December 1996, 1,454,362 shares remained available for grant under the IEP.

### Required

Based on the information provided, evaluate the changes that Lincoln Electric made in its plans, including both the nature and the components of the plans.

## 13-5 Choosing the Bases for a CEO's Bonus Award

[The following is an except from the Definitive Proxy Statement, SEC Form 14A, filed by General Electric on March 12, 1997.]

The Committee's decisions concerning the specific 1996 compensation elements for individual executive officers, including the Chief Executive Officer, were made within this broad framework and in light of each executive officer's level of responsibility, performance, current salary, prior-year bonus and other compensation awards. As noted above, in all cases the Committee's specific decisions involving 1996 executive officer compensation were ultimately based upon the Committee's judgment about the individual executive officer's performance and potential future contributions, and about whether each particular payment or award would provide an appropriate reward and incentive for the executive to sustain and enhance the Company's long-term superior performance.

For 1996, Mr. Welch received total cash payments of $6,300,000 in salary and bonus. The Committee continued to consider this level of payment appropriate in view of Mr. Welch's leadership of one of the world's top companies in terms of earnings, balance sheet strength, creation of share owner value, and management processes.

In 1996, the Committee also granted Mr. Welch 320,000 stock options, half of which will become exercisable in 1999, and half in 2000. The primary basis for the Committee's determination to grant such stock options to Mr. Welch in 1996 was to provide a strong incentive for him to increase the value of the Company during the remainder of his employment.

The bases for the Committee's determinations regarding Mr. Welch's compensation in 1996 included his aggressive leadership, which drove the Company's outstanding financial results and improved its overall global competitive position; his vision and determination to achieve preeminent quality in all of the Company's products and services; and his drive to reinforce a culture of integrity, stretch targets, boundaryless behavior, and employee involvement throughout the Company. As in prior years, the key judgment the Committee made in determining Mr. Welch's 1996 compensation was its assessment of his ability and dedication to continue increasing the long-term value of the Company for the share owners, by continuing to provide the leadership and vision that he has provided throughout his tenure as Chairman and Chief Executive Officer.

### *Required*

(1)  What do you think about the scope of the bases used by the compensation committee to determine the bonus paid to Mr. Welch in 1996? Note that these are the particulars of the short-term bonus plan. Mr. Welch is also provided incentives by the long-run plan that relies on stock options to motivate behavior.

(2)  Suppose that as a management accountant you were asked to help the committee develop performance measures for the bases used by the committee to evaluate performance for the purpose of awarding the bonus. How would you measure each of the identified performance bases?

(3)  What performance measures, if any, would you add to the committee's group? Why?

(4)  What performance measures, if any, would you drop from the committee's group? Why?

## *13-6    Measuring the Awards Bases of the Annual Bonus Plan*

[The following is an excerpt from Rockwell International, Definitive Proxy Statement, SEC Form 14A, filed by Rockwell International, in 1996.]

Annual Incentives. Near the beginning of each fiscal year, the Committee reviews with the Chief Executive Officer and the President the Corporate Goals and Objectives for that year, including measurable financial return and shareowner value creation objectives as well as long-term leadership goals that in part require more-subjective assessments. Principal 1995 financial goals included increasing earnings per share well above fiscal 1994, achieving a return on equity of 20% and generating sufficient cash flow to provide at least $400 million for dividends, acquisitions, debt reduction, and share repurchases. In 1995, the Corporation achieved a primary earnings per share increase of 19%, return on equity of 20.8%, and met its cash flow goal. Shareowner value goals for 1995 included achieving a total return (stock price appreciation and dividends) exceeding a composite of the peer companies selected by the Corporation and utilizing interbusiness sharing of competencies, technology, product development, and facilities to achieve added leverage for competitive advantage. The Corporation's long-term goals included developing new products, investing in new technologies, and taking the management actions—focused on promoting teamwork, organizational effectiveness, streamlining, and empowerment—essential to assuring quality, reduced product cycle times, and enhanced customer responsiveness.

After the end of the year, performance against the Corporate Goals and Objectives is evaluated and the results are considered by the Committee in awarding annual incentive compensation to corporate executives who were not directly responsible for the management of a business unit. Individual awards to members of the senior management group, including the Named Officers other than the Chief Executive Officer and the President, are determined by the Committee after reviewing with the Chief Executive Officer and the President the recommended awards, taking into account the contributions made and the levels of responsibility of each of the participants. While the Committee believes achievement of the financial, shareowner value, and long-term leadership goals are each important, it accords greater significance to the first two in determining the total amount available for annual incentive payments.

The amount available for annual incentives is determined for the Corporation's senior executives and other key management under the Corporation's Incentive Compensation Plan. Under the Corporation's Plan, the addition to the incentive fund for a fiscal year cannot exceed either the aggregate amount of dividends declared on the Corporation's outstanding stock during the year or an aggregate amount computed by adding 2% of the first $100 million of the applicable net earnings (defined as net income, before provision for domestic and foreign taxes based on income, of the Corporation and its consolidated subsidiaries) for the year, and 3% of the next $50 million of such earnings, and 4% of the next $25 million of such earnings, and 5% of the balance of such earnings. Generally, the Committee makes awards under the Corporation's Plan in an aggregate amount well below the amount available thereunder.

### Required

Evaluate the positive and negative elements of Rockwell's bonus plan for senior executives. Note that this focuses only on the annual incentive plan. All senior Rockwell executives also participate in a long-run incentive plan.

## 13-7    Management Bonuses and Economic Value Added

[The following is an excerpt from the Definitive Proxy Statement, SEC Form 14A, filed on March 18, 1997, by Armstrong World Industries Inc.]

Economic Value Added (EVA®) serves as the Company's principal financial measure and is the basis for determining awards under the Management Achievement Plan. EVA equals the dollar amount arrived at by taking net operating profit after taxes and subtracting a charge for the use of the capital needed to generate that profit. For the corporate and business unit achievement segments, there are threshold levels of EVA performance below which no incentive awards are paid. For the corporate and major business unit segments, there are no caps or maximum award limits, so there will be incremental awards for higher levels of EVA achievement. The incentive awards for the Chairman and CEO, the Executive Vice President and the Senior Vice President, Finance, and Chief Financial Officer are based entirely on corporate EVA achievement. The incentive awards for all other executive officers are based solely on corporate and/or business unit EVA goal achievement.

The Management Achievement Plan has been structured so that the level of cash compensation (base salary plus annual bonus) will exceed the median level of cash compensation for the selected group of companies when high levels of corporate, business unit, and individual performance are achieved. Conversely, when the Company and business units fall short of established targets, the level of cash compensation will fall below the median level of cash compensation for the selected group.

### *Required*

The Management Achievement Plan is one unit in a set of incentive compensation plans used to motivate senior executives. Another important component of the incentive compensation set is a stock option plan. Evaluate the Management Achievement Plan.

## *13-8    Senior Executive Incentive Plan Components*

[The following is an excerpt from the Definitive Proxy Statement, SEC Form 14A, filed on March 18, 1997, by FMC Corp.]

The program comprises three different compensation components—base salary, variable cash and stock incentive awards, and long-term incentive awards (stock options). Base Salary. FMC uses external surveys to set competitive compensation levels (salary ranges) for its executives. In order to obtain the most comprehensive survey data for review, the group of companies in the surveys is broader than the Dow Jones Diversified Industrial Index and includes a majority of comparable companies at the Fortune 500 level. Performance graph companies are well represented.

Salary ranges for FMC executives are established that relate to similar positions in other companies of comparable size and complexity. Generally, the Company sets its competitive salary midpoint for an executive officer at the median level compared with the companies surveyed. Performance levels within the ranges are delineated to recognize different levels of performance ranging from "learner" or "needs improvement" to "exceptional." Thus, although compensation is nominally targeted to fall at or near the 50th percentile of such comparable organizations, it may range anywhere within the salary bracket based on performance.

Starting placement in a salary range is a function of an employee's skills, experience, expertise, and anticipated job performance. Each year, performance is evaluated against mutually agreed-upon objectives and performance standards that may, in large part, be highly subjective; a performance rating is established; and a salary increase may be granted. Performance factors used may include timely responses to downturns in major markets; setting strategic direction; making key management changes; divesting businesses and acquiring new businesses; continuing to improve operating efficiency; and developing people and management capabilities. The relative importance of each of these factors varies based on the strategic thrust and operating requirements of each of the businesses.

Variable Incentive Award (Annual Bonus). In 1995, the Committee and the Board recommended a revised Management Incentive Plan, which shareholders approved. This revised plan includes annual bonuses for achievement of both individual performance targets and multiyear targets for the improvement of Net Contribution (operating profit after tax less the product of an 11.5% capital charge and capital employed). All executives participate in this incentive plan. Achievement of high standards of business and individual performance are rewarded financially with both stock and cash, and significant compensation is at risk if these high standards are not met. At the executive level, target incentives approximate 50% to 65% of base salary, while actual payments can range from zero to almost three times target incentive.

The multiyear incentive period uses a three-year net contribution target and began in 1995. In 1997, participants, including all executives, received a draw against the second three-year award period, which will end on December 31, 1998. The draw is equal in percentage terms to their business performance incentive target (BPF) under the prior plan. Participants' three-year incentive awards, if any, shall be reduced (but not below zero) by the amount of their 1996 and 1997 draws. In the case of Mr. Burt, the draw is equal to 25% of his base salary.

At the executive levels, the annual individual performance incentive comprises 40% to 50% of the total target incentive. This incentive is less quantitative than the three-year net contribution incentive. It varies with individual performance and can range from zero to twice the target percentage. It is awarded based on achievement of annual objectives set for the individual's most important business responsibilities. In 1996, these included such disparate objectives as implementation of profit and growth strategies; improvements in operating efficiencies and market positions; acquisitions such as Frigoscandia; divestiture of FMC Gold Company and the Automotive Service Equipment Division; and demonstrated leadership in enhancing the teamwork, diversity, and management climate necessary to improve shareholder value.

Long-Term Incentive Awards. This plan is designed to link closely the long-term reward of executives with increases in shareholder value. The 1995 approval by the shareholders of an updated stock option plan continues to give the Committee broad discretion to select the appropriate types of rewards. 1996 awards consisted of nonqualified stock options. The award vesting period is three years, with an option term of 10 years.

To determine the number of options to be granted to an executive, the Committee first multiplies the midpoint of the salary range for an executive's salary grade by a percentage applicable to that grade and consistent with competitive industry practice as provided by an independent, outside consultant and divides that product by the then current market price of FMC's shares. The Committee then applies a percentage (ranging from 80% to 120%) based on the individual's contributions and potential. In approving grants under the plan, the number of options previously awarded to and held by executive officers is considered but is not regarded as a significant factor in determining the size of the current option grants.

Stock Retention Policy. The Company has established guidelines setting expectations for the ownership of FMC stock by officers and management. The guidelines for stock retention are based on a multiple of the employee's total compensation midpoint. The revisions to the 1995 Management Incentive and Stock Option Plans included incentives and enhancements to help executives meet these guidelines.

### Required

Evaluate the structure and nature of the incentive compensation systems used at FMC Corp. for senior executives.

## 13-9    *Determining and Distributing the Bonus Pool*

[The following is an excerpt from the Report of Compensation Committee in the Definitive Proxy Statement, SEC Form 14A, filed April 3, 1997, by Amgen Inc.]

The MIP (management incentive plan) has been established to reward participants for their contributions to the achievement of Company-wide performance goals. All executive officers of the Company and certain other key employees, as determined by the Compensation Committee, participate in the MIP. MIP payouts are established at a level designed to ensure that when such payouts are added to a participant's Base Salary, the resultant compensation for above average performance will exceed the average cash compensation level of comparable companies.

The structure of the MIP provides for the development of a compensation pool (the "Pool"). Amounts attributable to the Pool are based upon the achievement of certain specified performance goals and milestones established by members of management and approved by the Compensation Committee at the beginning of each MIP period. As implemented by the Compensation Committee, at least 50% of the Pool determination will be based upon Return on Capital Employed (ROCE) and Growth in Revenue, with the remainder based upon two or three major goals selected by the Committee from the goals established by management in connection with the planning process. Target awards for participants are established pursuant to a percentage formula relating to Base Salary. The MIP provides for a range of payouts based on actual achievements, with both the size of the Pool and the individual awards subject to an upside potential of 150% of applicable targets for the achievement of performance that is significantly above the target levels. No awards are made to the participants, regardless of the performance achieved on the other goals or by individual participants, unless either the ROCE or the Growth in Revenue goal is achieved.

At the beginning of each MIP period, participants in the MIP are required to work with upper management to define individual performance objectives that will contribute to the success of the Company. Each participant's payout from the MIP Pool is based upon the respective supervisor's and the Compensation Committee's assessment of achievement of the participant's goals. Performance objectives are stated as a range of possible measured achievements. In order to be eligible to receive a payout from the MIP, each individual participant must have achieved his or her individual performance objectives at least at the minimum threshold. The minimum threshold represents significant, but less than planned, performance. The payout at the minimum threshold is usually 50% of the target payout, assuming Pool goals are achieved at target. The maximum amount payable under the MIP to any participant may not exceed $900,000.

The Pool goals for the MIP period ended December 31, 1996, included goals related to ROCE, growth in revenue, specific product development objectives, and profit after taxes. The relative weightings of these four factors in determining the total Pool were 30%, 20%, 25% and 25%, respectively. Based upon evaluations by management and approved by the Compensation Committee, the Company achieved 142.2% of the target Pool goals established under the MIP for the period ended December 31, 1996. For 1996, in order to stimulate increased effort toward the development of potential products, the Pool included an incentive equal to 5% of the maximum payable under the Pool goals for the development and/or acquisition of two novel molecules. The achievement of these objectives resulted in the inclusion of this incentive in the MIP payout.

### Required

(1) What do you think of the management incentive plan at Amgen Inc.? Note that this plan is part of a wider incentive package that includes a base salary and stock options.
(2) Suppose that you were part of a group developing the relevant performance measures for employees in this plan. What performance measures would you use for each of the following executives: (a) a production supervisor, (b) a regional sales manager, and (c) the director of product research. Explain your choices.

## ■ CASES

### McDonald's Corporation: Designing an Incentive System*

Designing an equitable compensation system is not an easy task for the top management of any company, as the attention the subject has received in these pages and elsewhere makes clear. But the difficulties of designing a compensation program for managers in a service business are particularly severe. When a company's product—be it flying lessons, cleaner offices, waffles, or Caribbean cruises—is manufactured and consumed almost simultaneously, there is no second chance to sell or perform.

Although bank tellers, chambermaids, and short-order cooks may have little in common, they are all at the forefront of their employers' public images. How they perceive and perform their jobs can promote or undermine the success of their organizations, and their proper and effective management keeps many a banker, innkeeper, and restaurateur on his toes.

The problems of motivation and reward in service-oriented companies are increasingly important as the provision of service assumes an ever-growing role in our economy. In this article, we show how one such company—perhaps the world's largest and most successful food-service organization—is grappling with these problems and how other executives concerned with similar compensation issues view the plans the company has devised.

---

*Case originally prepared for classroom use by Charles Horngren, based on W. E. Sasser and S. H. Pettway, "Case of Big Mac's Pay Plans," *Harvard Business Review* (July–August 1974). Reproduced with permission of *Harvard Business Review* and Charles Horngren.

"We consider our first-line management to be the managers of our company-owned units," a senior executive of McDonald's Corporation told us. "And they do a tremendous job for us. Somehow we have to design a compensation system that will reward them for the hard work they do and still motivate them to continue putting in the extra effort that has made McDonald's a household name. We've tried various compensation programs, but none has proved to be totally successful."

The company's concern was not academic. At the time of the 1972 compensation system evaluation—the take-off point for this case—McDonald's and its subsidiaries operated, licensed, and serviced 2,127 fast-service restaurants throughout the United States and Canada and a few in other countries. About 25% of the units were company owned and operated. (The ratio has now risen to about 30%.) By 1977, the company has estimated, the system will have some 4,000 units, and company-owned outlets will number more than 1,000.

The average volume of a company-owned unit in 1971 was $540,000. The company expected sales to rise to about $600,000 by the end of 1972.

Pervasive throughout McDonald's operations has been a success formula often stated by the founder, Chairman Ray Kroc: quality, service, and cleanliness ("QSC" in the corporate shorthand). Accordingly, McDonald's maintains a year-round training program at all levels of operations, such as at the world's only Hamburger University, at Elk Grove, Illinois. At this $2 million facility licensees as well as managers of company-owned restaurants must take an intensive course on McDonald's operational policies; refresher courses are also available. In 1973 some 1,200 persons were graduated from Hamburger U.

Below the managerial level, most jobs are quite simple and can be easily taught to new employees within hours, with the aid of operating manuals and in-store visual material supplied by the corporate training staff.

### Initial Efforts

Between 1963 and 1972 McDonald's tried several compensation systems in an effort to encourage superior performance by managers of its company-owned outlets. But, as noted, none of the plans left front-line or top management entirely satisfied.

In 1963 a restaurant manager's bonus was merely a function of his sales increase over the previous year. The managers complained that volume frequently varied independently of their control, so they jockeyed for assignments to units with the most potential for revenue growth. Equally detrimental to corporate health was the lack of recognition offered the cost-conscious manager. In 1964 the plan was abandoned.

For the next three years the company had no formal incentive system in effect and awarded bonuses purely on the basis of subjective evaluations. Many managers felt that their regional superiors were not adequately recognizing and rewarding their performance. In 1967 this informal plan was abandoned.

McDonald's then made its first attempt to provide a comprehensive and equitable compensation program. The company tied the base salaries of each unit's manager and first assistant manager to their ability to meet the QSC standards. It made the quarterly bonus payments depend on a profit contribution defined as "the difference between sales volume and those costs over which unit management normally exercises direct or indirect control through managerial judgment, decision, and action." The list of controllable costs on which unit management was being judged appeared to be reasonable and complete.

But the plan proved unpopular with those on the front line because it mainly rewarded high volume. Since a restaurant's profit contribution depended considerably more on increased revenues than on cost control, superior management and cost control did not always gain a commensurate bonus. The result was a wide disparity in bonuses; the median was $2,000, but bonuses ranged from $700 to $8,000. In 1971 this plan was also abandoned.

### The 1972 Plan

In the 1972 compensation package for line managers, McDonald's tried to satisfy the complaints and at the same time to maintain harmony between managerial incentives and corporate goals. The unit manager's annual compensation consisted of his base salary and a quarterly bonus that rewarded his ability to meet predetermined objectives in the areas of labor costs, food and paper costs, QSC, and volume projections.

1. *The fixed salary.* After surveying each market in which it owned restaurants, McDonald's established three salary ranges according to prevailing labor rates and other economic factors. Range I, the highest, usually applied to very large metropolitan areas; Range II applied to somewhat smaller areas where industrial and rural influences on the labor market were about equal; and Range III applied to small metropolitan markets with little industrial influence. In addition, annual merit increases were awarded within each range according to whether an employee was judged superior, satisfactory, or still in the new employee bracket. In 1972, the base salary schedule began at $6,800 for a trainee in Range III and rose to $15,000 for a consistently outstanding manager in Range I.

2. *The bonus.* Meeting the optimum labor crew expenses—figured according to projected sales volume and labor crew needs for each month of the quarter—entitled the manager to a bonus of 5% of his base salary.

Together, the area supervisor and the unit manager determined the food and paper cost objective based on current wholesale prices, product mix, and other operating factors peculiar to the unit. By meeting the objective to which he had agreed previously, the manager earned another 5% bonus.

An excerpt from the monthly management visitation report (see attached sample) by which each store's QSC was—and still is—rated. Based on the average score for the quarter, units were designated A, B, or C. Managers of A stores received a bonus of 10% of base salary; B store managers 5%, and C store managers no bonus.

In addition, the manager received a bonus of 2.5% of the increase over the previous year's sales, up to 10% of his base salary. If unit volume was significantly affected by operating circumstances beyond his control, the regional manager could grant him a semiannual payout of 5% of his base salary.

Therefore, the maximum annual incentive bonus to an A store manager who met all his objectives was 20% of his base salary plus an additional 10% of his salary because of the volume gain at his restaurant. (His first assistant was entitled to a bonus of approximately 60% as much.)

Bonuses for meeting cost objectives were paid quarterly; those for meeting QSC standards and volume increases were paid semiannually.

### Still Another Try

While the 1972 compensation system eliminated many shortcomings of previous programs, unit managers now protested that it was much too complicated. Moreover, complaints about undue subjectivity and dependence on volume patterns were heard anew. McDonald's top management went back to the chalkboards and calculators and came up with four alternative plans.

## Management Visitation Report

Store Address:

_____

| NUMBER | STREET | CITY | STATE |

This store is in the _____ TV market. This report was completed by _____ at ___
A.M./P.M. on _____ 197___ and the day of the week was _____. There were
           MONTH    DATE
_____ cars on the lot, and _____ customers in line waiting to be served and _____
persons seated in the dining area. The person totally in charge of the store during this visit is _____
and his title is _____. The manager of this store is _____;
the supervisor is _____; and the operator is _____.
When completed this report was reviewed with _____ on _____.
                                                                                                DATE

_____

SCORE: Outside (Sec. I) _____ out of 30. Inside (Sec. II) _____ out of 35.
Food (Sec. IV) _____ out of 35. Overall _____ out of 100

(MAXIMUM SCORE PER QUESTION IS 5.)

| QUESTION NO. | SECTION I (OUTSIDE) | ITEM SCORE |
| --- | --- | --- |
| 1. | Is area within one block of the store free of all litter? | |
| 2. | Are flags being displayed properly and are they in good condition? Are entrance and exit and road signs in excellent condition? | |
| 3. | Are waste receptacles in an excellent state of repair and clean? Is trash being emptied as necessary? | |
| 4. | Is the parking lot and landscaping as clean, litter-free, and well picked up as you could reasonably expect for this business period? Do these areas reflect an excellent maintenance program? Is traffic pattern well controlled? | |
| 5. | Do the sidewalks surrounding the building and the exterior of the building reflect an excellent maintenance program? Were these areas being maintained properly during this visit? | |
| 6. | Were all inside and outside lights which should have been on, on, and were windows clean? | |

SECTION TOTAL

| QUESTION NO. | SECTION II (INSIDE STORE PREPURCHASE OF FOOD) | ITEM SCORE |
| --- | --- | --- |
| 7. | Was the restroom properly maintained? Was the inside lobby and dining area properly maintained? | |
| 8. | Does P. O. P. in the store present a unified theme? | |
| 9. | Is menu board in excellent repair and clean? Are napkins and straws available near all registers? | |
| 10. | Is the general appearance of all stations good? Is all stainless steel properly maintained? | |
| 11. | Is there an adequate number of crew and management people working for this business period and are they positioned properly? | |

*continued*

| | | |
|---|---|---|
| 12. | Are all crew members: wearing proper McDonald's uniforms, properly groomed, and does their general conduct present a good image? | |
| 13. | Are all counter persons using the Six Step Method and does their serving time per customer meet McDonald's standards? | |
| | SECTION TOTAL | |

| QUESTION NO. | SECTION IV (AFTER FOOD ORDER) | ITEM SCORE |
|---|---|---|
| 14. | Was the sub total, tax, and total charged to you exactly correct and did you receive the correct change? | |
| 15. | Was your order placed properly in the proper size bag, on the correct tray, and did the total packaging appear neat? Was the bag double folded? | |
| 16. | Was the Production Caller controlling production properly? | |
| 17. | Did sandwiches appear neat and do they reflect that the prescribed operational procedures were used when preparing the food? | |
| 18. | Were all sandwiches hot and tasty? | |
| 19. | Were your fries a full portion, hot, and did they meet finish fry standards? | |
| 20. | Did all soft drinks, shakes, or coffee meet McDonald's standards? | |
| | SECTION TOTAL | |

**Plan A**   The unit manager's base salary would be determined initially according to the range system described earlier. Thereafter he would be rated monthly by the regional operations staff on six factors: quality, service, cleanliness, training ability, volume, and profit. Each factor would be rated 0 for unsatisfactory, 1 for satisfactory, and 2 for outstanding. A manager whose semiannual total was 12 would earn a bonus of 40% of his base salary for half a year, a score of 11 would warrant a 35% bonus, and so on. At the end of the year his two semiannual scores would be averaged, and he would receive a salary increase of 12% for a score of 12, 11% for a score of 11, and so on, down to a point where the manager presumably would be encouraged to seek his fortune with a competitor.

**Plan B**   After receiving the base salary suggested by the range system in his first year as manager, the person would be placed on a draw against commission. The draw would be his salary as before; the commission would be a bonus of 10% of any sales gain plus 20% of the profit (provided that gross profit amounted to at least 10% of the gross take). For example, if sales increased by $50,000 this year to $550,000 and profits were 12% (or $66,000), the manager's total compensation package would be 10% × $50,000 plus 20% × $66,000 = $18,200.

A variation of this plan being considered

would incorporate a sliding scale—that is, 10% of the sales increase at units with sales up to $500,000, plus 20% of the profit; 7% of the sales increase at units with sales up to $700,000, plus 17% of the profit; and 7% of the sales gain at units with sales exceeding $700,000, plus 15% of the profit.

**Plan C**   Similar to Plan B in its draw against commission, the so-called supermanager program would base total compensation solely on sales volume. For units having volumes of $500,000 and less, salaries were set at different levels—for example, $10,500 for unit sales of $300,000, $11,500 for sales of $400,000, and $12,500 for $500,000.

Any volume exceeding $500,000 would be multiplied by 2% and added to the base of $12,500. For example, the manager of a $750,000 unit would earn $12,500 plus $5,000. Managers of new stores and of stores considered to be in inferior locations would be paid at the $12,500 base rate for the first 12 months of their stay.

**Plan D**   A predetermined lump sum based on the size of the management team and the volume of the store would be allocated for management salaries. Individual performance as evaluated by the regional operations staff would determine the percentage of the total

allocation to be received by each team member. The total amounts that would be available are shown in Table 1.

As this article was being written, McDonald's was still wrestling with these alternatives. A senior officer of the company summarized his feelings about the compensation dilemma in this way:

> When this company began, it was a fight for survival. Just meeting the payroll was an accomplishment. Later, as we became better known and began to grow, we could concentrate on perfecting our operations. We started the first comprehensive training program for fast-food service in the industry.
>
> Now is the first time we've been able to look carefully at an area that we really should have considered years ago—our compensation programs and how they affect our people. We know we have a real opportunity here, but quite frankly we're not sure how to proceed. When you're growing internally at a 30% annual rate plus acquiring licenses, the issue of management training in the company stores becomes acute, particularly when so much training must be on the job.
>
> In short, we're faced with a situation where our unit managers are putting great pressure on us to simplify and improve their compensation system. At the same time, we have to design a system somehow that's equitable across the board and encourages the manager to give close attention to training his subordinates.

**TABLE 1**   Total Compensation Availability by Unit According to Size of Management Team

| SALES | 2 PERSONS | 3 PERSONS | 4 PERSONS | 5 PERSONS |
|---|---|---|---|---|
| $      0–  300,000 | $19,500 | $28,500 | | |
| 301,000–  400,000 | 20,000 | 30,000 | | |
| 401,000–  500,000 | 22,500 | 32,500 | $45,000 | |
| 501,000–  600,000 | | 33,000 | 48,000 | $60,000 |
| 601,000–  700,000 | | 35,000 | 49,000 | 63,000 |
| 701,000–  800,000 | | | 52,000 | 64,000 |
| 801,000–  900,000 | | | 54,000 | 67,500 |
| 901,000–1,000,000 | | | 55,000 | 70,000 |

### Required

(1) What factors should McDonald's consider when designing a compensation plan for its first-line managers?

(2) Assume that you are a first-line manager. Outline your views on the 1972 plan and Plans A–D. Which plan would you prefer that McDonald's adopt and why?

(3) Assume that you are the senior officer charged with making recommendations on a compensation plan. Which plan would you recommend that McDonald's adopt and why?

## ANALOG DEVICES, INC. (A)*

In reference to Analog Devices, Inc. (ADI) bonus plans—one for management and one for technical personnel—Graham Sterling, Vice President, Strategic Planning, stated the following:

> The purposes of the Bonus Plans are first to communicate to the people that the company places a high value on concurrent growth and profitability and is willing to accept some tradeoff between the two, undertaking at the Corporate level to balance the portfolio so that the total corporation enjoys self-funded growth. The second purpose is to carry out our objective of paying above-average compensation, some substantial fraction of which is conditional on company or group performance.

> I do not like to refer to the plans as incentive plans. I visualize them as plans for communicating some important facts of life. The concept of rapid, self-funded growth has always been central to the corporate culture, because without rapid growth we could lose control of our markets, while without self-funding we might not long be viable as an independent owner–managed company. The bonus plans help us deliver this message and enable us to share the fruits of whatever success we accomplish as a total organization.

### The Company

ADI was a medium-sized semiconductor manufacturer with headquarters in Norwood, Massachusetts. Founded in 1965 with an initial capitalization of $100,000, the company had grown rapidly to a sales level of just over $100 million in fiscal year 1979 (ended November 3). Average annual growth from 1975 to 1979 was 35% (compared with an electronics industry growth rate over the prior decade of about 13%), and 1979 company sales were up nearly 50%.

ADI was primarily engaged in the design, manufacture and sales of precision electronic components and subsystems employed mostly in measurement and control applications. More than 90% of company sales were of components designed to acquire, condition, and convert electrical analogs (voltage or current) or real-world phenomena (temperature, pressure, flow, light, etc.). These components facilitate the recording, processing, and display of the information content of these signals, which is vital for managing a broad range of real-world processes. These components are designed for incorporation in measurement and control instruments for markets such as avionics, industrial automation, and medical and scientific testing. ADI was the leading producer in this market segment.

---

*Prepared by Kenneth A. Merchant.
Copyright © 1980 by the President and Fellows of Harvard College. Harvard Business School case 181-001.

ADI was able to compete with the giant semiconductor companies, such as Texas Instruments and National Semiconductor, which were able to generate high volume (and lower cost) because, in this market segment, product design was more important than price. Customers were generally willing to pay premiums for components that would best solve their particular problems. The market was highly fragmented: ADI served over 6,000 active accounts. The company's strategy was to capitalize on and expand its market leadership positions and gradually to integrate vertically by combining its data acquisition components into higher-level building blocks (subassemblies) and user-oriented, computer-based measurement systems.

ADI had two primary financial objectives: (1) growth of Sales at an average compound rate of 25% per year and (2) Pretax Return on average invested Capital of 19% per year. For internal control purposes, the 19% Return on Capital goal was translated to an equivalent 23% Operating Pretax Return on Assets (OPROA). Company financial models had shown that the 23% Operating Pretax Return would generate enough cash internally to support 25% annual growth and a modest cash dividend with a Debt/Equity ratio of not greater than 75%. The growth objective was considered to be a minimum goal, rather than a ceiling, so there was considerable emphasis on overachieving this goal, although it was realized that to be self-funding a higher growth rate would require some combination of higher Return on Capital, higher Debt/Equity ratio, and lower cash dividend payout.

The company's growth was primarily internally generated. From time to time, ADI would acquire a small company as an entree to a new product line, a new location or a new market, but these acquisitions were always small in proportion to the prior year's consolidated sales, so they served as bases for subsequent internal growth rather than as purchased expansions.

The rapid growth created the need for a substantial, continuous flow of innovative new products. Typically, 80% of the company's sales had come from products introduced in the prior five years. This created a strong demand for capital and personnel. ADI, like all companies in the electronics industry, faced a critical shortage of technical personnel, both for professional functions such as engineering, marketing, and manufacturing and paraprofessional areas such as technicians and draftspeople.

The company's operations were organized into two main product groups—Instruments and Systems, and Semiconductors. Each of these groups was divided into product divisions which were organized functionally. A sales group sold the products of all divisions.

Financial plans were prepared quarterly with a four-quarter planning horizon. The intent of planning was bottom-up, although if the corporate consolidation of plans revealed inconsistencies or failed to meet the corporate objectives, the groups were asked to revise their plans. The November rolling plan, prepared in September and October, set the target for the following fiscal year (November–October).

### The Parallel Ladder

To help conserve and develop the critical technical skills within the organization, ADI operated a Parallel Ladder organization structure that enabled technical employees to continue their career growth without the necessity of assuming line management responsibilities. The Parallel Ladder program provided technically oriented individuals the opportunity for long-term career growth within their technical discipline and the rewards that are commensurate with those available to managers—increased compensa-

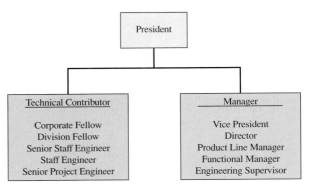

**FIGURE 1 Parallel Ladder**

tion, status, and recognition. By providing these rewards, the company hoped that technically competent personnel would not be tempted to leave their technical specialties for managerial positions when that choice was made for nothing more than a lack of alternatives for personal career growth.

The structure of ADI's Parallel Ladder is shown in Figure 1. It indicates the relationship between sample technical positions and those in the management hierarchy.

At the lower levels in the technical hierarchy, the emphasis was on individual contributions, perhaps as part of a technical team. At the Division Fellow level the emphasis was increasingly helping others, perhaps as a mentor helping develop younger employees or as a consultant helping solve difficult technical problems. Corporate Fellows had demonstrated an ability to influence broad corporate objectives, strategies, and policies and to help determine the future direction of corporate development.

### Bonus Plans

ADI operated two bonus plans, both providing supplementary awards for specific performance in the form of a cash payment. The Management Bonus Plan was designed to reward all personnel with significant management responsibilities. The New Product Bonus Plan was designed for people on the technical ladder involved in developing new products and introducing them to the market.

The bonus awards were based on collective (corporate and/or group) achievement, not on individual performance. The bonuses of top-level managers, corporate fellows, and corporate staff were based solely on corporate performance. Low-level managers and technical personnel were rewarded for the performance of their group (Instruments and Systems or Semiconductor). Upper-level managers and technical personnel in the groups received 50% of their bonus based on group performance and 50% on corporate performance, on the expectation that individually they could have a significant impact on corporate performance.

ADI established bonus plans to provide ADI employees with above-average compensation within an environment that encouraged concurrent achievement of personal and company goals. Graham Sterling explained:

> What we wanted was a wealth-sharing system which would make an objective determination of the incremental wealth available to be shared and would then share it among the people in an easily explainable and predictable manner. We felt that if we paid people well but

made some of the pay conditional on company performance, they would better understand and have more concern for what we defined as "performance" and would cause the performance to stabilize at a higher level than would otherwise be the case. The plans were expected to promote a sense of teamwork rather than competition and encourage acceptance of tradeoffs, where necessary, in the interests of the total corporation.

Also, the company puts a high value on stability of operating margins. When a recession causes a drop in returns because fixed expenses and capacity are temporarily out of phase with demand, the compensation plan automatically cushions the operating margin, giving us the benefits of compensation cuts without the effort of negotiation and with minimum withdrawal pains. The opposite is true during boom periods, when the bonus plan triggers high rewards and moderates what would otherwise be unsustainably high margins.

A strict bonus formula was used to assure objectivity in the bonus allocation process. This was explained by a middle-manager bonus plan participant:

> We used to have individually calibrated bonuses here, and the reason we're not doing that now, according to the general manager, is that it always ended up in a war. They only had so much money to divvy up, and individual managers had preferences for their people. For an outstanding performance it wasn't so bad, but as soon as you got away from there and started awarding to people who had done just a good job, not a terribly great job, then it got into a real shoving match. Given an ideal management committee where you didn't have some of the personalities involved (which is sort of an impossibility in this industry), I would recommend a more personalized plan based on your performance in that quarter and how you have met your objectives. But given the management here, we may be better off with our formula.

Despite use of the bonus formula, ADI management had the capability to recognize differences between people and to reward special accomplishments both within the rules of the bonus plans (e.g., assignment of level of participation) and outside the bonus plans (e.g., promotions, salary adjustments), so it was not seen as necessary or desirable to permit subjectivity in the calculation of the bonuses.

### The General Bonus Formula

The general formula for both bonus plans was as follows:

$$B = S \times I \times F$$

where:

$B$ = Amount of cash bonus (paid quarterly)

$S$ = Individual's base pay (quarterly)

$(I)$ = Individual Bonus Factor (described below)—varied with level in organization from 25% for top management to 10% for lower-level participants

$F$ = Bonus Payout Factor (described below)—derived from different performance-based functions, one for the Management Bonus Plan and one for the New Products Bonus Plan. Both were equal to 1.0 if plans were just achieved, and both were subject to a Maximum Personal Payout, an upper constraint, that varied by organization level.

### Individual Bonus Factors (I) and Maximum Personal Payout

The plans were designed to offer rewards commensurate with risk. Since risk was higher for individuals in more-responsible positions, the potential rewards were greater at higher organizational levels. This distinction was accomplished by assigning Individual Bonus Factors and Maximum Personal Payouts, upper limits on the Bonus Payout Factor, that varied with level. These are shown in Exhibit 1. The maximum bonus for top executives was 100% of salary (4 times 25%) for outstanding performance in both ROA and growth; the maximum for lower-level participants was 20% (2 times 10%).

**EXHIBIT 1** Plan Differences at Different Organizational Levels

| ORGANIZATIONAL POSITION | BONUS PLAN ASSIGNMENT | INDIVIDUAL BONUS FACTOR (% OF SALARY) | MAXIMUM PERSONAL PAYOUT |
|---|---|---|---|
| Officers, corporate staff | 100% Corporate | 10%–25% (varies) | 2.0–4.0x (varies) |
| General managers, senior operations managers, fellows | 50% Corporate 50% Group | 20% | 3.0x |
| Division-level functional managers | 50% Corporate 50% Group | 15% | 3.0x |
| Senior staff engineers | 100% Group | 15% | 3.0x |
| Senior functional managers, senior project engineers | 100% Group | 15% | 2.0x |
| Other designated line and staff managers and key engineers | 100% Group | 10% | 2.0x |

### Bonus Payout Factor (F)— Management Bonus Plan

When the Management Bonus Plan was first instituted in 1975, the Bonus Payoff Factor was defined as a matrix function of the Average Rate of Growth of Sales and the Average Rate of Return on Assets (shown in Exhibit 2). This operationalized the growth/profitability tradeoff mentioned by Graham Sterling in the comment at the beginning of the case. Larry Sullivan, Senior Vice President, Corporate Development and Finance, explained the rationale behind this two-dimensional performance measure:

> We at Analog Devices recognized several years ago the shortcomings of measuring corporate and divisional performance on short-term profit results such as net earnings and return on investment. In 1975, we developed an incentive bonus program for corporate and divisional management that is based on a tradeoff between Return on Assets and long-term growth management. The concept behind this incentive program is that management must both do a good job of utilizing operating assets in the short term and make sound strategic investments for future growth and profitability.

Graham Sterling further explained the choice of two dimensions:

> Although in principle a Bonus formula could take any number of performance measures and compress them to a single Payoff Factor, it is neither necessary nor desirable to employ more than two measures. In the first place, over the long term, Rate of Growth and Rate of Return characterize the activity so thoroughly that very little if any new information can be brought in by adding a measure such as market penetration or customer service level. In the second place, having more than one or two performance measures might interfere with the desired concentration and encourage suboptimization.

A measure of return on assets was included in the summary performance measure to motivate managers to consider profitability and asset productivity in their decision making and to encourage them to adjust expenses and production rates promptly as market conditions change. Return on assets was selected as an easily visualized internal measure that, unlike return on equity or capital, was independent of financing decisions. Return was defined as Operating Pretax Return so that managers were not held responsible for such corporate con-

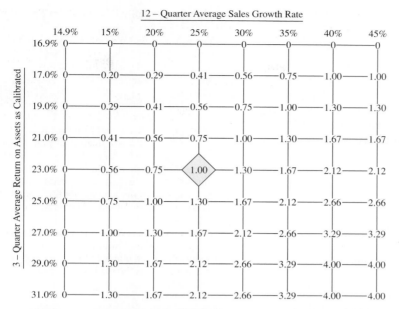

12 – Quarter Average Sales Growth Rate

| 3 – Quarter Average Return on Assets as Calibrated | 14.9% | 15% | 20% | 25% | 30% | 35% | 40% | 45% |
|---|---|---|---|---|---|---|---|---|
| 16.9% | 0 | 0 | 0 | 0 | 0 | 0 | 0 | 0 |
| 17.0% | 0 | 0.20 | 0.29 | 0.41 | 0.56 | 0.75 | 1.00 | 1.00 |
| 19.0% | 0 | 0.29 | 0.41 | 0.56 | 0.75 | 1.00 | 1.30 | 1.30 |
| 21.0% | 0 | 0.41 | 0.56 | 0.75 | 1.00 | 1.30 | 1.67 | 1.67 |
| 23.0% | 0 | 0.56 | 0.75 | 1.00 | 1.30 | 1.67 | 2.12 | 2.12 |
| 25.0% | 0 | 0.75 | 1.00 | 1.30 | 1.67 | 2.12 | 2.66 | 2.66 |
| 27.0% | 0 | 1.00 | 1.30 | 1.67 | 2.12 | 2.66 | 3.29 | 3.29 |
| 29.0% | 0 | 1.30 | 1.67 | 2.12 | 2.66 | 3.29 | 4.00 | 4.00 |
| 31.0% | 0 | 1.30 | 1.67 | 2.12 | 2.66 | 3.29 | 4.00 | 4.00 |

**EXHIBIT 2   Corporate Bonus Matrix (Payout Factor as a Function of ROA and Sales Growth)**

cerns as interest expenses and taxes. Operating Pretax Return on Assets (OPROA) was averaged over three quarters in the belief that, for ADI, it took about one quarter to detect a change in conditions, another quarter to implement corrective actions, and another quarter to see meaningful changes in results.

The sales growth dimension of the Summary performance measure was included because it was primarily a consequence of longer-term strategic decisions. Management was encouraged to maintain expenditures intended to produce future growth rather than to compromise to accomplish short-term profit objectives, and this suggested that sales growth (in dollars) should be averaged over a long period. ADI defined this averaging period as 12 quarters (3 years) because the delay between initiation of new product development and significant contribution to sales from most investments was about three

years. Although some investments might not have yielded returns in this period, longer horizons did not have much appeal as incentives for management performance because the career perspective of many executives in a single assignment did not extend beyond this time.

The Payoff Matrix was constructed so that the Bonus Payout Factor is equal to 1.0 when the corporate objectives of 23% ROA and 25% Growth were being achieved but not overachieved. The maximum Payout Factor possible was 4.0, at 29% ROA and 40% Growth, a level of performance considered outstanding, as established by assessing company capabilities and the performance of other companies in the industry. Lower limits were set so that no award was made if OPROA fell below 17% or Growth fell below 15%, performance levels considered poor.

The two performance elements, OPROA and sales growth, were weighted so that a 2% increase in OPROA performance was equivalent in payoff to a 5% increase in sales growth rate. This represented the feelings of management about the relative importance of these two areas to the future health of ADI. This weighting was held constant but could have been set differently to emphasize different business strategies.

The Matrix was constructed so that an improvement along either axis was rewarded, but the rewards increased most rapidly with progress along both axes simultaneously: that is, along the diagonal of the Payoff Matrix. This was consistent with the corporate goals of rapid growth concurrently with Return on Assets high enough to assure self-funding. Corporate financial models showed that at the center point of the Matrix, defined as the intersection of 23% ROA and 25% Growth, the Company was self-funding with a 10% cash dividend payout rate and a Debt/Equity Ratio of 75% and that movement in either direction along the diagonal connecting 23% ROA/25% Growth with 29% ROA/40% Growth preserved this self-fundability. Obviously, movement outward along this diagonal was very much desired. Progress horizontally through the matrix reduced or reversed the cash dividend payment ability and/or raised the Debt/Equity ratio, and, since this was less desirable from the company standpoint, through the bonus plan it was made less rewarding to the participants. The cutoff limits at 29% ROA and 40% Growth reinforced the desire that improvement generally be along a diagonal.

A bonus plan *calibration factor* was used to adjust the center point of the bonus payout matrices to the performance level of the annual plan if planned performance, as accepted by top management, was below the timeless standard.

## This was explained by Graham Sterling

The justification for a Calibration Factor arose when the company's performance had not reached but was clearly trending toward the objectives established. At that time, we considered direction and velocity of progress as well as absolute performance in determining what Bonus Payoff Factor should result from attainment of the annual plan for the following year. In effect we said that if last year's results compared favorably to the prior year and to plan and if this year's plan showed significant improvement over last year's results, we might give these facts the weight of a few points of Return on Assets and incorporate this as a Calibration Factor in the numerator of the Payoff Function. At the outset of the year, a separate constant Calibration Factor was assigned to each quarter of the annual plan, so that the Planned Payoff Factor was at the desired level, contingent on accomplishment of the plan.

Because the standards for corporate consolidated performance were considered "timeless," the concept of a "calibration factor" at the Corporate level was something of a contradiction and was being phased out. At the *Group* level, however, a Calibration Factor was always used to make the Planned Payoff Factor for each Group commensurate with the Planned Payoff Factor for the corporate consolidation, taking into account that Group's relative contribution to the corporate plan. The philosophy was that after a Group plan had been reviewed, iterated, and finally accepted into the corporate consolidation, the managers responsible for executing the plan deserved essentially the same Planned Bonus Payoff Factors as the managers of the corporate consolidation and the other Groups. Thus, if a Group achieved its plan (without overachieving), the Group Bonus Payout Factor would be 1.0, regardless of how the actual performance compared with the corporation's long-term objectives.

A year or so after the start of the plan, the

---

**EXHIBIT 3**   Illustration of Quarterly Bonus Calculation—Corporate Management Bonus Plan

---

Assume the following facts for a hypothetical corporate staff manager:

*a.*   he/she assigned 100% to corporate bonus plan
*b.*   salary = $3,000 per month
*c.*   personal bonus factor = 15%
*d.*   maximum personal payout = 3.0x
*e.*   summary performance standard = 33%
*f.*   3-quarter average OPROA = 26%
*g.*   12-quarter average sales growth = 28%
*h.*   calibration factor is zero

Bonus calculated as follows:

$$B = S \times I \times F$$

$$B = [3{,}000/\text{month} \times 3 \text{ months}] \times 0.15 \times \left[ \frac{26 + 0.4 \times 28}{33} \right]^{4.5}$$

$$B = 9000 \times 0.15 \times 1.714 = \$2{,}315 \text{ cash bonus this quarter}$$

Because of the maximum personal payout of 3.0x, the maximum quarterly bonus this manager could receive is (9000 × 0.15 × 3) = $4,050.

---

matrix function was replaced by an essentially equivalent algebraic formula. This simplification was desirable because use of the matrix required tedious double interpolation to determine the Bonus Payoff Factor for combinations of Growth and OPROA not explicitly defined on the matrix. The formula that most closely approximated the matrix for the Corporate Management Bonus Payout Factor was:

$$F_m = \left[ \frac{\text{OPROA} + C + 0.4G}{P_s} \right]^{4.5}$$

where:

$F_m$ = Management Bonus Payout Factor
OPROA = Operating Pretax Return on Average Assets (3-quarter average)
$C$ = Calibration Factor
$G$ = Sales growth (12-quarter average)
$P_s$ = Performance standard

The performance standard ($P_s$) was timeless, fixed by the corporate long-range objectives. For the corporate plan, the performance standard was 33, calculated as the ROA goal (23%) plus 40% of the sales growth goal (25%). The effect of the exponent (4.5) was to impart the nonlinearity present in the Matrix.

Exhibit 3 provides an illustration of a bonus calculation for a hypothetical manager, on the corporate staff, using the formula, with the assumption that the Calibration Factor was not used.

### Bonus Payout Factor (F)—New Products Plan

The New Product Bonus Plan was designed in 1978 and patterned after the Management Bonus Plan, with analogous performance dimensions—growth in new product bookings and return on new product investment, weighted equally. The assumption was that a successful technical contributor innovated and would have to keep inventing more and more products.

Larry Sullivan explained:

> Since the development of the bonus program for managers and executives, we have come to

realize that it is very important to plan and measure the results of investments in new products and reward the individuals that are involved in new product performance based on those results. With new product activities in virtually any industry, there are three issues that are involved in success: (1) establishing objectives for new product efforts such that they directly support corporate growth and return on investment objectives, (2) selecting the right areas in which to invest in new products such that these investments generate high return on engineering, marketing, and manufacturing startup expenses, and (3) executing the investment decision rapidly. This is important as in a dynamic market; the company that gets the right product to the market first usually ends up with the largest market share and hence long-term profits.

To reflect these realities, we have established objectives for new product bookings as a percent of total bookings, the growth in new product bookings, and the return we need to generate on new product investments. We have also devised the new product bonus system that pays off on the growth in new product orders from year to year and the return on investments made in new products.

In the New Products Plan, *Growth* was considered the short-term (i.e., highly responsive) performance measure. Growth was defined as a four-quarter average of the percent increase in total (corporate or group) new product bookings ($) in the quarter being measured over the same quarter a year ago. *New products* ranged from major strategic developments to minor modifications of existing products, anything for which a new product number was assigned. A product remained a new product for 15 months following the quarter in which it was introduced.

*Return* was conceptualized as a longer-term performance measure which put a high value on the volume and profitability of products released in the past three years. It was defined as the annualized value of the current quarter's marginal contribution from all new products (introduced in the past three years) divided by the development expense investment—engineering and marketing expense—needed to get the products to market (incurred in preceding four quarters). Marginal contribution was defined as revenue less manufacturing and selling costs, including variances (which could be significant during startup).

---

**EXHIBIT 4** Illustration of Quarterly Bonus Calculation—New Products Bonus Plan

Assume the following facts for a hypothetical project engineer:

*a.* he/she assigned 100% to group bonus plan
*b.* salary = $2,000 per month
*c.* personal bonus factor = 10%
*d.* maximum personal payout = 2.0x
*e.* actual group new product growth = 50%
*f.* standard group new product growth = 40%
*g.* actual group new product ROI = 12%
*h.* standard group new product ROI = 15%

Bonus calculated as follows:

$$B = S \times I \times F$$

$$B = (\$2000 \times 3) \times 0.10 \times \left[\frac{50 + 12}{40 + 15}\right]^2$$

$$B = \$6000 \times 0.10 \times 1.27 = \$762 \text{ cash bonus this quarter}$$

Because of the maximum personal payout of 2.0x, the maximum quarterly bonus this engineer could receive is $1,200.

The New Product Bonus Payout Factor formula was as follows:

$$F_{np} = \left[\frac{G_a + R_a}{G_s + R_s}\right]^2$$

where:

$F_{np}$ = New Products Bonus Payout Factor
$G_a$ = Growth in New Product Bookings (4-quarter average)
$R_a$ = Return on Investment
$G_s$ = Growth standard
$R_s$ = ROI standard

The performance standards were chosen as that level of performance necessary for the group to achieve the long-term corporate financial objectives. They were a function of such variables as asset intensity, growth rate, length of product life cycle, and profitability.

Payoff constraints were again selected at both upper and lower levels. At the upper level neither $G_a$ nor $R_a$ was allowed to exceed twice its respective standard. At the lower level, no payoff was allowed if either performance measure fell below 50% of standard.

The exponent (2) was chosen so that the payoff factor equaled 4.0 when both growth and ROI performance were at or above 200% of standard.

Exhibit 4 provides an illustration of a bonus calculation for a hypothetical project engineer.

### Required

Evaluate the ADI bonus plans. How, if at all, would you modify the plans?

---

## THE CHARLES RIVER COMPANY*

In a meeting to prepare for their upcoming management conference, Steve, Tom, and Bill Turner surveyed the view from the Dedham, Massachussetts, offices of the Charles River Company (CRC) and contemplated the success of the diversified holding company. The brothers recognized that one of the major factors in CRC's success was their philosophy of management, which rewarded managers based on the performance of their operating companies. CRC based its management control system on a unique concept called professional entrepreneurship. The company trained its managers to be professional managers while encouraging the risk-taking activity of entrepreneurs. As Tom Turner noted, "This training allows the managers to look for opportunities, but to manage the risks professionally."

As CRC entered its eighth year of operations, however, the Turners realized that CRC's operating philosophy and control system would need to conform to the changing corporate structure. Recently, CRC had hired Jack O'Meara as a *group* president and member of the executive committee. Unlike a CRC *company* president, O'Meara did not run an individual operating company but rather was responsible for coordinating, supervising, and advising four operating company presidents. One challenge for the Turners was to provide O'Meara with a bonus plan that was tied directly to the success of

*This case was prepared by Brian Jaffe, MBA '88, under the supervision of Assistant Professor George Baker. It is prepared as a basis for class discussion rather than to illustrate either an effective or ineffective handling of an administrative situation. All names have been disguised.

the operating companies for which he was responsible.

To encourage professional entrepreneurship, CRC provided company presidents with incentives tied directly to the performance of their operating companies. In addition to a base salary, the managers received a bonus if they exceeded a budget determined at the beginning of the year by the operating company management and by CRC headquarters. A bonus ceiling limited the amount that some managers could receive in compensation each year. However, Steve Turner was unsure of the effect the bonus cap had on incentives and was considering removing it from the system.

As the Turners prepared for CRC's annual management conference in Napa Valley, California, they were concerned with two major challenges to the CRC compensation system. First, they needed to develop a compensation system for Jack O'Meara, based on the principles of professional entrepreneurship. Second, the bonus cap would have to be reevaluated.

### History

The Charles River Company was founded one Sunday afternoon in January, 1976, when the Turner family was watching the Super Bowl. Bill Turner recalled, "We were bored, so someone said, "What do you want to do?' and someone else said, 'Well I don't know, why don't we start a company?" '

In June 1976, the Turners placed an ad in the *Wall Street Journal* reading,

> Principals looking to acquire businesses any size range, any profitability, anything goes, send us what you have on a first-come, first-served basis.

They received 980 replies, of which 979 were from business brokers.

After several false starts, they acquired the Capitol Plastics Corporation, a subsidiary of the Capitol Corporation, a $200 million producer of industrial products. At the time of the acquisition, the Capitol Plastics Company was losing $600,000 on sales of $5 million. CRC purchased the company for $1.8 million, investing only $100,000 in cash and financing the remainder with debt, much of which was bought back by the seller.

The Turners took over the company and took control of several key management tasks. In his capacity as treasurer, Steve found four inappropriate sales representative organizations, along with a number of unprofitable arrangements with suppliers. As Steve recalled,

> By signing the correct checks and not signing the incorrect checks, we were able to make a half a million dollar profit the following year. The seller could not believe that we were able to accomplish this. We were then able to use our profits as a springboard into other things.

The acquisition history of the Charles River Company is shown in Table A.

### Acquisition Strategy and Operating Philosophy

CRC organized and managed leveraged buyouts (LBOs) of small- to medium-sized companies and divisions. The company purchased the target firm by putting up a small amount of equity in the deal, and financing the rest of the purchase with debt. This debt was often secured with the assets of the acquired company or division. In leveraged buyouts, debt/equity ratios as high as 10 to 1 were not uncommon. Because of the financial structure of these deals, CRC was able to buy all of the equity in the companies that it bought without investing large amounts of capital. CRC put up the equity, and the debt was carried on the books of the acquired company or division.

CRC'S acquisition strategy changed as it achieved growth in capital. In its early years, CRC pursued turnaround opportunities, since they could be purchased for less cash. As the

**TABLE A**  Acquisition and Divestiture History

| COMPANY | BUSINESS | DATE ACQUIRED | COMMENTS |
|---|---|---|---|
| Capital Plastics Corp. | Plastic products | Oct 1978 | Sold 7/81 |
| Harris Paint Co. | Traffic paint | Nov 1979 | Sold 2/85 |
| Northern Paint Co. | Interior/exterior paint | Sept 1980 | Sold 3/84 |
| Benson Bakeries | Baked goods and cold storage | Dec 1980 | Sold 10/82 |
| Carter Steel Corp. | Steel minimill | Sept 1981 | |
| Business Furnishings | Office design and furniture distribution | June 1983 | |
| Forced-Air Manufacturing Co. | Heating and air-conditioning products | July 1983 | |
| ADC Corp. | Office design and furniture distribution | Aug 1984 | |
| J.T. Massie Co. | Automotive parts and metal products | Jan 1985 | |
| Holland Mills Inc. | Wood furniture manufacturing | May 1985 | |
| Cliftwood Ltd. | Wood furniture manufacturing | May 1985 | |
| General Technology Inc. | Static control products | May 1985 | Sold 12/86 |
| Carter Steel Corp., Bloomington, IN | Steel bars and shapes | Aug 1986 | |

company became more successful, it could afford to be more selective. The acquisition criteria that CRC used in 1987 are shown in Exhibit 1. CRC pursued midtechnology companies that had the potential to dominate their markets. As Bill Turner noted,

> The best industries to buy into are the ones that are changing dramatically, that are in the midst of some kind of transition, because if you

understand the industry, what the nature of the transition is, and where you think it is heading, you can then buy in at the right place, or maybe be a catalyst for change. It's tough to get rich by buying a cardboard box manufacturing company at the peak of its performance and just riding out their investment. There are higher returns in buying industries and companies in transition. That is our acquisition strategy.

Several of CRC's earlier acquisitions are detailed in Exhibit 2.

CRC's stated objective was to pursue a growth strategy through acquisition. Gross sales, as shown in Exhibit 3, had grown from approximately $80 million in 1982 to $380 million in 1987. Moreover, CRC's management philosophy set it apart from other LBO firms. As Bill Turner stated, "We have differentiated ourselves from the others by focusing on the management of the companies we buy, rather that just being financial players. That is the one thing that isn't cyclical. There is always going to be the need for good management."

CRC's operating philosophy was ex-

**EXHIBIT 1**  Acquisition Criteria

Sales: $20+ million

Turnaround situations: $40+ million

Manufacturer or value-added distributor

Break-even or better profitability on an operating basis

Modest technology content

Industries of specific interest:
  Commercial office–related (furniture, carpet, etc.)
  Steel
  Specialty window
  HVAC

| SIC Codes: | 3312 | 3433 | 3585 | 5021 |
|---|---|---|---|---|
| | 2514 | 2272 | 3743 | 2512 |

**EXHIBIT 2** Selected Acquisition Histories

### Carter Steel

CRC's purchase of Carter Steel Corp., made up of two divisions of United Steel located in Tulsa and St. Louis, made the front page of the *Wall Street Journal* as one of the biggest deals of 1981.

Carter's profits had been squeezed by foreign competition. Prior to 1981, United had gone into a strategic planning binge, moving away from steel and into insurance. United wanted to sell the 10 plants and the sales office of the steel company for the book value of $62 million. Included in the package were two minimills; the Tulsa mill, a continuous caster and merchant mill producing rebar for reinforced concrete, and the Marysville, Ohio, mill, which was old and had no continuous caster. CRC, unwilling to purchase the Marysville mill, offered to accept the package at the same price without the plant.

The divestiture was extremely traumatic for the United employees. The employees in the plant were distraught, believing that United had violated their trust. The steel men of the plant and fabrication shops resented the salespeople, and there was only limited cooperation with CRC. The company was in desperate need of new management.

CRC sent in a manager, John Haskins, centralized operations in Tulsa, and created overhead functions such as payables, receivables, and accounting systems. CRC renegotiated the note that they had given to United and Carter soon returned to profitability. As Steve Turner recalls, "There is a lot more involvement from everyone now, even the union. The people's spirits are high, and the management is committed." Carter Steel today is a profitable company, with revenues of over $100 million.

### Forced-Air Manufacturing

In 1983, Forced-Air Manufacturing was a small manufacturing subsidiary of the large propane gas distributor Yankee Propane. The company manufactured an array of product lines, holding a 30% share of the recreational vehicle heating unit market.

In 1980, Forced-Air had an impressive year. Capitalizing on the popularity of wood-burning stoves, the company achieved profits of $5 million on sales of $30 million. The following year, however, witnessed a lowered enthusiasm for wood-burning stoves, and sales for these items plummeted from $7 million to $3 million. Forced-Air also developed a revolutionary line of unvented heaters that burned propane or liquid natural gas. Forced-Air manufactured $1 million of these heaters and sold very few owing to regulations requiring the storage of propane outside the home.

Yankee Propane wanted book value, or $11 million for Forced-Air, which had annual sales of $25 million. The agreed upon price was $9 million, of which $6.5 million was for cash and $2.5 million was for a note with a two-year moratorium on principal and interest.

Prior to CRC's involvement in the subsidiary, Forced-Air was managed in an authoritarian manner. The company president was afforded much respect and had minimal contact with the shop employees. Subsequent to the sale, however, Tom Turner visited with the plant employees, smiled, and shook hands. Turner made some immediate changes and determined that the company president was ineffective. The president was moved upstairs as chairman, but not as chief executive officer.

The new company president, Jack Carter, significantly improved asset management as well as employee cooperation throughout the organization.

### Northern Paint

When CRC purchased Northern Paint from Dakota Corp., a diversified conglomerate, in September 1980, Northern was reporting zero profits on $20 million in sales. Prior to the sale, Dakota brought in a turnaround specialist, who had Northern focus on private-label paints, instead of pursuing their own national brands. CRC paid $6 million for Northern, of which $3 million was in cash and $3 million in a note. Another bidder offered $4 million in cash plus a $2 million note for Northern. Both the presidents of Dakota and Northern Paint preferred CRC's management to this bidder, and CRC was awarded the bid.

CRC employed incentives based on professional entrepreneurship and experienced substantial sales growth. In 1980, profits reached $1 million after interest expense. By 1984, profits were $3 million on sales of $33 million. During this period, while the paint industry was shrinking, Northern's market share increased and profitability improved dramatically. CRC sold Northern in 1984 for more than $20 million.

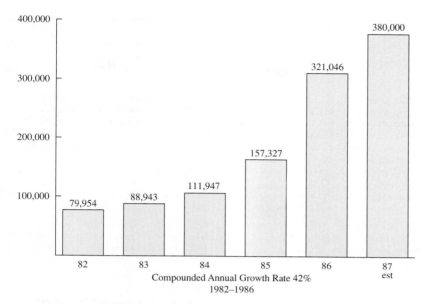

**EXHIBIT 3   Charles River Company Growth–Sales ($ Thousands)**

pressed in their Fundamental Beliefs, shown in Exhibit 4. The CRC operating companies were highly decentralized, with the managers of each of the subsidiaries responsible for its product development, manufacturing, and marketing strategies. The companies were treated as separate entities, each with individual banking, legal, and accounting relationships. This separation served to limit corporate liability and ensured that a bank did not lend money to an entity based on the viability of the corporation as a whole. The operating companies also maintained their own auditing and legal relationships. As Bill Peterson, Director of Financial Planning stated,

> We feel strongly that each one of those companies should operate as a stand-alone entity. We insist only that they send out their internal monthly reporting package to us. They also establish big eight accounting relationships and legal relationships in the city that they are in. If they need consultants, they bring in consultants; whatever it takes to run the company.

However, as the company grew the Turners recognized that they would need more management structure in Dedham to coordinate the growing number of operating companies. The hiring of Jack O'Meara reflected what was likely to be an ongoing company trend toward "Group Presidents." CRC's Principles for Successful Group Presidents is shown in Exhibit 5. The organization structure as of the spring of 1987 is shown in Exhibit 6.

### Professional Entrepreneurship

Steve Turner believed that managers could be characterized along a spectrum ranging from entrepreneurial to managerial. Entrepreneurial managers were free-wheeling risk takers, while professional managers were more analytical, utilizing skills developed in formal training. Professional entrepreneurship was a system of management training and control that encouraged professional management while promoting more risk taking. Ken Duf-

**EXHIBIT 4** Our Fundamental Beliefs

The company has developed a formalized belief system which governs our policies and guides our actions. These beliefs include:

Professional Entrepreneurship

We believe that individuals are the center of our company. Outstanding individuals create outstanding performance. We believe that entrepreneurial endeavors managed in a professional way are the key to realizing our goals and objectives.

Decentralization

We believe that an environment that promotes decentralized, entrepreneurial, professional management in self-reliant operating companies is the most effective structure for CRC.

Growth

We believe that our growth should be largely through acquisition of companies that meet our criteria in terms of sales, profits, market segment leadership, and management quality.

Communications

We believe that by communicating often and clearly, both verbally and in writing, we will improve our ability to excel in the markets in which we compete and we will create a positive internal environment which will enhance our team-effectiveness.

Education

We believe that continued personal growth is a key to creating better managers. We believe in being students.

Incentives/goals

We believe in incentive management with a modicum of controls. We will do this through our five principles of incentive management and our systems of planning and reporting.

Quality

We believe that quality is vital to achieving our growth and profitability objectives. By providing our customers with the highest level of quality in the products we produce and the services we provide, we will assure that we will repeat sales at attractive margins.

Decision Making

We believe that decision making is best achieved through consensus-style discussion where several individuals with different perspectives participate.

Integrity

We believe that trust and teamwork with ourselves, our supplies, our customers and others, is founded on absolute integrity in all interactions.

Leadership

We believe that it is essential to be a leader in the markets we serve. We also believe in being leaders in the communities in which we live and work.

Innovation

We believe that market leadership, growth and profitability result from creative, forward-looking, and responsive solutions to the product and service needs of the markets we serve.

fey, CEO and President of Business Furnishings, a distributor of office furniture, cited the benefits of professional entrepreneurship:

> CRC doesn't know the business as well as us (the operating company) so we are expected to think about the business long term, strategizing, recognizing opportunity. CRC is available for training and for consulting if we wish. I think it's a hell of a lot better than a company saying, "Well, we own you, and we'll tell you what to do and when to take risk and when not to take risk."

The Turners believed that professional entrepreneurship worked most effectively in ex-

**EXHIBIT 5**  CRC's Five Principles for Successful Group Presidents

| HIRE SMART | MOTIVATION | CONTROL | SUPPORT | STRATEGIC PLANNING |
|---|---|---|---|---|
| CEO of subsidiary or division | Self-fulfillment Responsibility Autonomy Decisions Planning Accountability | System vs. people Need respect for system (enforce it) Enforce system (issues) not people | Central issues Insurance Banking | Planning: help focus Strategy and analysis |
| Assure all "10s" for all Executive Committee positions | Short-term incentives CRC's five principles | Maximize their autonomy with maximum CRC's info. | Communicate Challenge Set high standards | Challenge them to be strategic thinkers |
| Organization is proper for company and industry | Long-term incentives CRC's equity sharing program | Ask good questions

Communication | Let them know you're there, but keep out of their way | Challenge them to manage change |

tremely competitive industries. Steve Turner stated,

> If you put the classic professional manager, who is more of a take-it-slow type, into an extremely competitive environment, the competition is going to chew him up.

Professional entrepreneurship was not something that all managers of acquired companies were comfortable with, and the Turners admitted that CRC had experienced some turnover in operating company management. This turnover, however, usually occurred long after the acquisition had taken place. As Steve Turner professed,

> One of the basic premises of this system is that all people have the basic capabilities to do the job, and if they don't they can be trained. Professional entrepreneurship is a system whereby anybody can succeed if they are open-minded. Only those people who have a negative attitude toward change can't make it.

> We do have to let people go, and it is not easy, but as a rule nobody ever fires anybody too early. When you have the feeling in your stomach that the person isn't right, that is the best time to move. That is difficult to do in our business, but our system depends on it.

According to Turner, company presidents who were used to entrepreneurial environments or private ownership initially had some difficulty with professional entrepreneurship. The strategy formulation and budgeting process at CRC was a bottom-up process, and the former owners had the greatest difficulty soliciting input from subordinates. Regarding the entrepreneurial company president, Turner stated,

> Not only does he not want to ask his managers about what to do, he doesn't want to show them the numbers. He doesn't know how to share information or how to get others involved. Often that is why he sold the company in the first place.

> Our view is that it is possible to train and encourage managers to use the right mix of professional management techniques and entrepreneurial judgement. That is a large part of our job.

### Control and Incentive Compensation System

CRC had few corporate rules and did not tamper with the authority structure of its operating companies after it bought them. However, CRC did implement its own planning

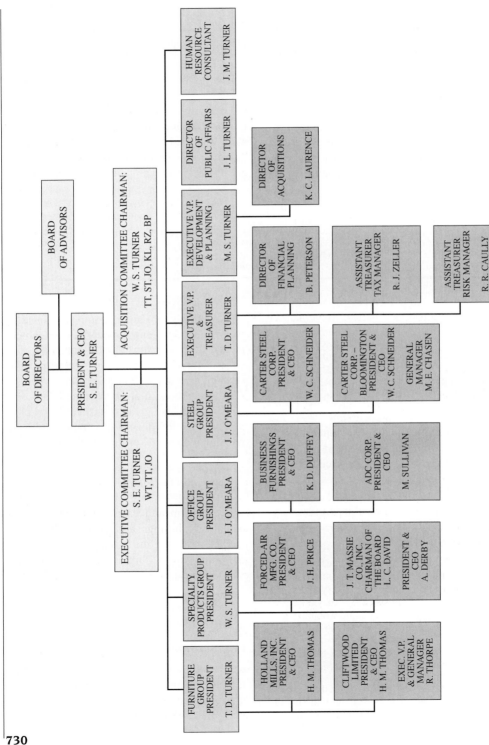

**EXHIBIT 6  Charles River Company—General Management and Staff Organization Chart, Spring 1987**

and budgeting system in all its companies. This system was the foundation on which the incentive compensation system was built.

CRC's planning and budgeting system consisted of several formal and informal devices. The two formal planning devices, a five-year strategic plan and an annual business plan, served to establish strategy for the operating companies. In October of each year, the president of each operating company presented a five-year strategic plan to CRC's executive committee. The strategic plan outlined the company's marketing plan, including projections of market share and expenditures. The purpose of this plan was not to commit the unit to a specific long-term plan but simply to force the operating presidents to think strategically about their businesses and to set direction. Because of market dynamics, CRC believed that managers should not be held strictly accountable to five-year plans. So, although the plan had to be submitted and approved by the executive committee, the operating presidents were not restricted to the targets outlined in these plans. As Bill Turner stated, "We just want to make sure that in doing the process of developing the thinking, people have agreement on where they are going, and that all members of the team are heading in the same direction."

The annual business plan, which the operating presidents presented to headquarters in March each year, was a comprehensive document that detailed marketing and production strategy, manpower planning, and R&D and capital expenditures. Initially, a company's business plan was acceptable if it "worked"; i.e., if the operating unit produced sufficient cash flow to pay the interest and debt repayments on the loan that were required to purchase the operating unit. In later years, CRC added measurements against competitors, such as market share and comparative industry profitability.

In addition to repaying the sinking fund re-

quirements and interest payments on the loan to fund the LBO, the unit had to maintain working capital requirements determined by the bank. The annual budget had to include capital expenditures that at least met the company's depreciation on fixed assets. Any significant variation in expenses as a percent of sales required explanation to headquarters. The operating unit also had to remain within a comfortable operating range with its bank in terms of bank loan availability. On the subject of bank relationships, Tom Turner stated,

> If the banker doesn't like the plan, he will call us up an say, 'I have been dealing with the local managers, and their plan doesn't seem to work for us. They are in trouble and you have to help us.' Then we will meet with the company presidents and with the bank to bail them out. Usually that requires a greater degree of communication, and some major changes in plans. It has happened a few times, and in one case the bank lived with us for two years before we made a management change.

In addition to submitting a five-year strategic plan and the annual budget, each operating company submitted monthly performance reports which outlined the performance on a monthly and year-to-date basis. The company presidents also submitted a Daily Flash Report that detailed daily cash flows and other key indicators. Included in this report were actual cash in and cash out numbers, bank availability, billings, and daily backlogs.

CRC provided the managers of its operating units with a "highly levered" incentive compensation program. If the operating unit reached the target defined in its annual budget, the company's management received bonuses equal to 25% of their base salaries. In addition, the operating company management received 25 cents for every dollar by which the budget was exceeded. The remaining 75% was reinvested in the company to fund growth. Exhibit 7 outlines the principles of CRC's incentive system.

---

**EXHIBIT 7** Five Principles for Incentive Management

---

People will have an incentive program for extra compensation. The plan may vary by profit center but should take into consideration CRC's principles for incentive management, which are:

1. Each team member knows his or her job; what's expected; and how the job is related to the rest of the company.

2. Each team member is involved in formulating job-specific goals and the company's objectives and strategies and, therefore, there is good communication of the company's strategic focus and business plan. Everybody should be comfortable with the game plan.

3. All team members receive timely and accurate measurements of how they and the company are progressing toward their objectives.

4. The incentives are based on realizing the agreed-upon goals and objectives and are agreed upon and understood in advance.

4. Participants receive timely realization of their incentives.


1/17/85
pma
Rev: 11/10/86

---

Under this compensation system, managers had an incentive to sandbag: that is, to submit plans that barely exceeded the requirement to make the plan "work." Steve Turner said of this, "We don't mind sandbagging. So long as they are making their plans, we want them to share in the upside. When they don't make their plans, then we have problems." The Turners felt that the bonus plan had been successful.

It was true, however, that a company president could take advantage of the bonus structure. Steve Turner cited an example of an entrepreneur who sold his business to CRC in 1982. He remained as president after the sale, and in the first year of CRC ownership, he presented a plan with a negative sales growth and a loss of $50,000. After lengthy negotiations, a compromise was struck on a budgeted income figure of $150,000, which the Turners suspected was still sandbagged by $400,000. When income came in at over $500,000, the management team was rewarded $100,000 in bonuses. CRC dealt with this manager by keeping his base salary and the salaries of those below him unchanged for four years. As Steve Turner stated, "Do I like that? You bet! Someday they are going to have a recession and we

are going to be damn lucky we have the lowest salaries in town. We don't mind carrying the extra compensation if they do well."

Bonuses were typically paid to the upper management team of the companies (3 to 10 people), in proportion to their base salaries. However, companies had experimented with other schemes. For example, the top management of Business Furnishings had relinquished roughly one-third of the bonus pool to the next level of management in its company. Recently, Business Furnishings went even further and introduced a plan that provides *all* of its employees with a bonus. Ken Duffy described the benefits of this system:

> I recognize that the way to provide incentives for a truck driver is really not by giving him something based on the profit of the company because he does not see immediately how his job relates to the bottom line. However, we have had this (bonus system) through three quarters, and they've earned this bonus every quarter. They're delirious about it.

As an additional incentive, CRC made stock or stock equivalents available to the management of each operating company over a period of years after the buyout. Up to 18%

of the company's stock could be awarded to the management team, with the president eligible for 8%–10% maximum. CRC awarded stock for good performance and vested it over a period of five years. The stock was highly restricted, however; there were no outside equity investors, and although the managers could cash out with CRC at book value, they could only redeem their stock back at the rate of 10% per year after a five-year holding period and up to a maximum of 50% of their original issue. If CRC sold the operating company, they would allow a manager to cash out 100%, and CRC would then buy back the managers' shares at a rate that reflected the selling price of the company. When managers retired or quit, they could also sell their stock back, but it was redeemed with junior debt from the company which matured at a rate of 20% per year.

### The Debate Over Incentives

As the Turners prepared for the annual management conference in California, they evaluated the challenges to CRC's compensation system. In particular, they contemplated how to effectively compensate Jack O'Meara, the

first nonfamily member to be appointed to the executive committee, as well as the company's first group president. The Turners hoped to design an incentive system that would provide O'Meara with incentives tied to his management of his four operating companies and that would be consistent with their existing incentive system for the company presidents.

The Turners were also unsure about whether the incentive compensation system should include a bonus cap. Initiated in 1984, the cap placed a ceiling on the bonuses of certain company managers. In recent months the cap had been removed, resulting in wide swings in operating profits. As Tom Turner recalled, "We had one company earning a fortune one year and zero the next. Since they knew that they were going to have a tough year the next year, they pushed everything into the prior year so they could maximize their bonuses." The Turners wanted their managers to share in unlimited upside potential but were unwilling to accept the wide profit variations that seemed to accompany the removal of the bonus caps.

---

## RKO WARNER VIDEO, INC.: INCENTIVE COMPENSATION PLAN*

On a cold morning in mid-January 1989, Steve Berns and Ken Molnar sat in a conference room at RKO Warner Video headquarters in Manhattan analyzing fourth quarter 1988 results and evaluating the company's

*Samuel L. Shimer, MBA '89 prepared this case under the supervision of Professor George P. Baker. It is intended for class discussion rather than to demonstrate either effective or ineffective handling of an administrative situation.

Copyright © 1989 by the President and Fellows of Harvard College. Harvard Business School case 190-067.

incentive compensation plan, which had been in effect for the past two quarters. Berns, RKO's president, and Molnar, the company's vice president of operations, were scheduled to meet with Michael Landes, the chairman and owner of RKO, at the end of the week to review the video chain's expansion plans for 1989 (see Exhibit 1).

Berns had been with the company, previously known as Video Shack, since its inception in 1979 when he joined as a salesperson.

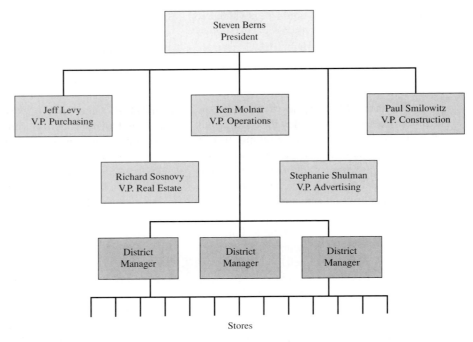

**EXHIBIT 1 Organization Chart of RKO Headquarters and Stores**

When Landes acquired the company in November 1986, Berns had risen to the position of president. Molnar had worked for Landes for six years at RKO Century Warner Theaters, which Landes had sold in 1986. While both men were pleased with the 1988 results and confident of their plans for the chain's future expansion, they were uneasy about the costs and the results of the incentive program that had been initiated on Landes's suggestion six months previously.

RKO's 24 stores were concentrated in the New York City area and sold or rented prerecorded videocassettes (PRCs) to consumers. The Broadway store, the first and largest RKO store, and the largest PRC retail outlet in the world, epitomized the chain's strategy. It had an enormous inventory of PRCs representing a broad range of titles, presented in an attractive and carefully designed environment. After a brief period of consolidation

following the acquisition, computer equipment was installed, the stores were redecorated to Landes's high standards, and RKO embarked on a store-opening spree designed to consolidate its dominant position in the New York market. Seventeen new stores had been opened in less than two years, with 15 additional stores projected to open in 1989. Berns reflected on the past, present, and future of RKO:

> Right now, we are positioned to dominate the video specialty retailing market in New York. We have already realized significant advantages over our competitors in both purchasing and advertising. In addition, our stores have greater tape selection and better appearance. One key to our future success will be our ability to attract and keep qualified help. You have to remember that we are drawing from the retail labor pool, the same pool as Macy's and Crazy Eddie's. But people have to work harder in video—everyone else is playing

when we're at work. A major goal of the incentive compensation program, in addition to recruiting, is to make all of our managers conscientious, to motivate them to build a future with RKO, and to take pride in their work.

As Berns and Molnar planned for their upcoming meeting with Landes they wondered if the incentive program was working, or if it was an unnecessary waste of time and money, which was not helping to achieve the goals they had for RKO. Berns concluded, "We want our stores to be well run, organized, and clean. The Bloomingdales of the video industry."

## The ALMI Group

The ALMI Group was formed in 1978 as a partnership between Michael Landes and Albert Schwartz. Schwartz, educated as a lawyer, had done real estate investment and development before creating a foreign film distribution company in 1976. In August 1978, Schwartz hired Michael Landes, also an attorney, to represent him in litigation over theatrical exhibition rights. Schwartz and Landes created ALMI in November 1978.

In 1980, ALMI began acquiring movie theaters in the New York area, beginning with five United Artists theaters. In March 1981, Landes and Schwartz acquired the Century Theaters chain for $8 million. In November of that year ALMI bought the RKO Stanley Warner Theaters chain for $40 million, forming the RKO Century Warner Theaters chain. ALMI's strategy was to renovate and rejuvenate the theaters, while selling off substantial theater assets for attractive prices. As a result of the successful implementation of this strategy, RKO Century Warner was able to build a reputation for quality and develop brand name recognition for the theater chain. This strategy resulted in higher market share and profitability. In September 1986

ALMI sold certain RKO Century Warner assets for $179 million to the Cineplex Odeon Theaters chain.

By early 1987, ALMI was active in a number of other entertainment businesses including film and video production and film distribution. Other investments included real estate and oil production ventures, a video game operation, an ice cream store, and a shirt manufacturer. In addition, Landes and Schwartz each continued to make investments as individuals. The Video Shack purchase was one such investment by Landes.

## The Videocassette Retailing Industry

Most PRCs were originally released as theatrical films. Movie studios traditionally produced these films themselves or bought complete rights from independent producers. The studios generally controlled all rights for a film, distributing to domestic movie theaters and to such "ancillary" markets as home video, commercial and pay television, and foreign theaters. The studios had historically received most of their revenues from their share of the box office receipts. However, by the mid-1980s, video sales were a substantial source of revenue for the studios.

Under the First Sale Doctrine, once a video store purchased a PRC it could rent it indefinitely without further reimbursing the distributor. By 1986, movie studio executives were concerned that studios were not sharing in the growth of rental revenues. One response by the studios was to dramatically lower the release price on selected hit titles, from the traditional $79.95 paid by rental stores, to below $30, in order to encourage consumers to buy rather than rent the films. This "sell-through" demand was far greater than the demand from rental outlets would have been, and thus resulted in higher total revenues for the studios. For example, the

1982 hit *E.T. The Extraterrestrial*, priced at $24.95 *sold* 10 million copies within two months of its release on PRC in November 1988. RKO management estimated that the average suggested retail price of a newly released PRC had declined from $45 in 1985 to $32 by the end of 1988. Consequently, many nonvideo retailers began to offer PRCs, primarily for sell-through but also for rental. Mass merchants, toy store chains, grocery and convenience stores, bookstores, major drugstore chains, and even dry cleaners and gas stations began to carry tapes.

The variety of retailers offering PRCs confused the typical video customer. One market survey indicated that 87% of rental customers had a specific title in mind on 60% of rental store visits, but 88% expected to browse for the title on 64% of visits. This seeming overlap between planned and impulse selections was ascribed to the frequent unavailability of desired titles. Indeed, if all titles were available, the average rental customer would rent an additional 6.9 titles per month. Customers buying PRCs selected roughly 45% of their purchases in the store. Another survey indicated that, on rental visits, 52% of customers choose the most convenient location.

### Video Shack History

In 1979, Arthur Morowitz concluded an experiment selling PRCs in the lobbies of certain movie theaters that he owned. Impressed with the success of that venture, Morowitz opened a store on Broadway and 49th Street to sell PRCs. Less than 3% of households owned videocassette recorders (VCRs) in 1979. Because these initial owners were primarily upper-middle class, Morowitz furnished the store with expensive jewelry-store-style display cases. Salespeople wore ties, and helped customers select tapes from locked cases.

Encouraged by the success of the first Video Shack store, Morowitz opened a second store on Long Island, feeling that the suburban market could serve as a barometer of the potential for the video retailing industry. That store was managed by Steve Berns, who had joined Video Shack in 1979 as a salesperson in the Broadway store. The new store was an immediate success, and within days Morowitz began to hire staff and plan for more outlets. Ten more stores were opened in the New York metropolitan area over the next three years. Growth slowed during 1983 as Morowitz devoted his time and money to developing other businesses. But, by the end of 1984, five more stores had been added to the chain. When Michael Landes purchased Video Shack in November 1986, the chain operated 17 stores.

### Postacquisition Moves

In the year following the Video Shack acquisition, Landes and his management team moved quickly to bring the chain up to Landes's appearance and performance standards. After conducting a name recognition survey, the chain was renamed RKO Warner Video. Five of the older, unprofitable Video Shack stores were closed. Then, as he had done with the theaters that he had acquired earlier in the decade, Landes renovated and remodeled the other Video Shack stores to be first-class in appearance. Joe Murphy, manager of the flagship 49th Street store remarked, "For appearance sake, RKO goes full out. No chain anywhere can compete with the look of RKO."

On the operations side of the business, management undertook a number of dramatic shifts from prior company practices. First, the membership fees of $24.95 and renewal fees of $14.95 were dropped.[1] Next, rental fees of

---

[1] In the early 1980s, most video chains offered memberships to rental customers for an annual fee. The membership usually entitled a customer to a number of "free" rentals and discounts on subsequent rentals. Nonmembers were charged a higher rental rate.

$2.99 to $3.99 were reduced to $1.99 per night. As a result of these actions rental volume surged 40%. In addition, all remaining lock and key displays were removed from the stores and all of the stores were computerized, including a standardized transaction system.

## RKO Strategy and Store Management

Steve Berns stated RKO's goals clearly: "We want to dominate the metropolitan New York video retailing market." Even as older Video Shacks were being closed, new RKO Warner Video stores were being opened. By the end of 1988, there were 24 open stores, of which only seven were original Video Shack stores. Due to the chain's tremendous size and sell-through tape volume, significant purchasing economies were realized. In addition, the chain's size made advertising much more economical for RKO than for its competitors.

Management believed that RKO's major sources of competitive advantage were quality appearance and the breadth and depth of the store's PRC inventory. Breadth of titles refers to the number of different titles in a store; depth of titles refers to the number of copies of an individual title in a store. The typical new, suburban RKO store was at least 4,200 square feet and contained a minimum of 7,500 tapes and 5,000 titles for rental and 2,500 tapes and 1,000 titles for sell-through. Manhattan stores were somewhat smaller. However, the capital requirements to build and stock a new store were significant barriers to the chain's historical competitors, "Mom and Pop" stand-alone stores. In addition, mass merchants offered a limited number of sell-through at significant discounts to list price in order to build traffic and encourage VCR purchases, but RKO management felt they could outdraw these competitors while selling at list prices. "People know to come to us for selection," said Joe Murphy. Steve Berns agreed, "Our 'discount' is in the selection and service we provide, not in the price."

Store locations, staffing, and inventory levels for all stores were determined centrally by Berns and Molnar. Each store required 10 to 20 clerks and two to four salaried managers, depending on that store's hours and its daily pattern of demand peaks. The company preferred to employ people over 18 years old, and paid entry-level clerks $5.00 per hour, which management considered competitive with other specialty retailers in New York. The store management task was divided among several people, since a typical store might be open 70 to 80 hours per week. All employees in a store reported to the store manager (see Exhibit 2). To assist in manage-

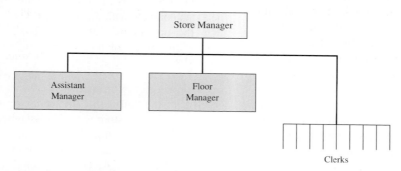

**EXHIBIT 2  Store Organization**

ment tasks during busy periods and to cover the store when the store manager wasn't present, there was an assistant manager and usually one (but sometimes none or two) floor managers.

Turnover among salaried and hourly workers was considered unacceptably high by RKO management. In addition, the quality and consistency of performance by store managers varied considerably across the chain. According to Ken Molnar, "The day-to-day responsibilities in this business are very important for store performance. Seemingly small things like alphabetizing the racks, keeping the store clean, opening on time, getting returned tapes onto the racks quickly, ordering product from the warehouse, and keeping checkout times short during busy times all make a difference." Given the rapid growth of RKO, management was very concerned about both the turnover and inconsistent quality across the chain.

### The Incentive Compensation Plan

Michael Landes had RKO's management issues in the back of his mind when he attended a series of executive education classes early in 1988. While at the meetings, he attended discussions on management compensation and developed a relationship with a consultant who specialized in the field. Landes returned to New York convinced that a properly designed incentive compensation plan would address many of management's concerns about store operations and would help RKO recruit managers for their stores. He asked Berns and Molnar, with the assistance of the consultant, to develop an incentive compensation plan.

Berns's staff originally designed a bonus plan that would be driven by performance reviews, based on a variety of subjective measures. These measures would include "day-to-day" objectives such as store cleanliness and organization, general measures of store manager effectiveness, and store performance. Berns and Molnar were very concerned about the so-called compliance issue: making sure the store managers were doing a good job on the details that were considered essential to the success of an RKO Video retail outlet.

The consultant, on the other hand, favored a totally objective bonus plan driven by store revenues. He believed this would maximize the effect of the plan on incentives by making it clear to store managers what they had to do to maximize their bonuses. It would also eliminate the need for RKO headquarters' people to regularly inspect the stores to monitor compliance. As the consultant said to Berns:

> The bonus plan will give the store managers an incentive to increase store revenue, which in turn will give them an incentive to do the little things. If keeping the store clean and keeping the tapes organized are as important to store revenues as you say that they are, then the managers will do these things to maximize their bonus, without the need for a team of inspectors to check on compliance.

A number of spirited debates ensued. Finally, Berns agreed to implement the revenue-based plan on a two-quarter trial basis.

### Details of the Plan

In early 1988, RKO store management personnel received annual salaries ranging from $21,000 to $28,500. Historically, annual raises ranged from 6% to 9%. Under the proposed plan, each store would be classified as an "A," "B," or "C" store based upon store size, volume, hours of operation, and an assessment of the "difficulty" of managing the store. Each class of store would be assigned a "base bonus" to be split by store management, on a quarterly basis, if revenue targets were achieved. The base bonuses were set as given in Table A.

## TABLE A

|  | ANNUAL STORE MANAGER BASE BONUS | ANNUAL ASSISTANT MANAGER BASE BONUS | ANNUAL FLOOR MANAGER BASE BONUS | TOTAL ANNUAL BASE BONUS |
|---|---|---|---|---|
| A store | $5,000 | $3,000 | $2,000 | $10,000 |
| B store | 3,000 | 1,800 | 1,200 | 6,000 |
| C store | 2,000 | 1,200 | 800 | 4,000 |

If a store achieved exactly its sales and rental target in a quarter, then the store management team would receive one-quarter of their annual base bonus.

Any revenue gained above the quarterly target would increase the bonus earned by the management team. Six percent of all rental revenue above target and 2% of all sales revenue above target would be distributed among the store management team in the same percentages as the base bonus. If stores achieved between 95% and 100% of their targets, then the base bonus would be reduced by 6% of rental shortfall and 2% of sales shortfall. If either sales or rental revenue failed to reach 95% of the target, no bonus would be paid. The bonus plan was thus described by the following formula:

If Actual quarterly sales > 95% of the quarterly sales target and

Actual quarterly rentals > 95% of the quarterly rental target then:

Total quarterly bonus = 0.25 × total annual base bonus + 0.06 × (actual rentals − target rentals) + 0.02 × (actual sales − target sales)

The base bonuses and targets were to remain essentially fixed from quarter to quarter, allowing the store management team to share in any revenue growth that occurred. According to Berns, the goal of the plan was to provide an objectively determined bonus plan driven by the economics of retail sales. He believed that the bonus plan would motivate all managers to run their stores efficiently, and in a way consistent with the chain's image and key success factors. He hoped that the revenue-based bonus plan would encourage store managers to monitor service-related performance such as the courteousness of the staff, cleanliness of the store and organization of the stock, all of which management felt directly affected store performance but could not be objectively measured. In addition, Berns had some other objectives in mind for the bonus plan. He hoped that the differences in the base bonuses would provide an incentive for store managers to move up through the chain, from suburban B and C stores to the more difficult to manage Manhattan stores. Finally, he felt that the plan would make it easier to attract and retain high-quality retail salespeople to run the ever-expanding network of stores in the chain. The program was announced to the stores, on a two-quarter trial basis, via a memo from Molnar dated May 19, 1988. [See Exhibit 3 for a copy of the memo.] A meeting was held on June 16

---

**EXHIBIT 3** Interoffice Correspondence

---

TO: Store Managers
FROM: Kenneth Molnar
DATE: May 19, 1988
SUBJECT: Managerial Incentive Plan

In recognition of the fact that it is store management who provides the direction and motivation so essential for a profitable and well-run store, we are rolling out a Managerial Incentive Plan effective July 1, 1988.

We want our stores to generate as much revenue and profit as possible. To accomplish this we will share increased revenue with store management upon attaining or exceeding reasonable revenue goals.

A meeting explaining this program in detail, assigning goals, and answering any questions you have will be held during the second or third week of June. In preparation for this meeting and to enable you to digest most of the technicalities in advance of this meeting, here is an outline of the program.

Stores have been configured into three strata predicated upon such factors as degree of business, size of store, hours of operation, and operational difficulty.
The structuring is as follows:

| A STORES | B STORES | C STORES |
|---|---|---|
| Paramus 260 | Toms River | Westwood |
| Hackensack | Little Falls | Coney |
| Amsterdam Ave. | 34th Street | Island |
| East Meadow | Lexington Ave. | Scarsdale |
| Greenwich | Union | |
| Morris Plains | | |
| Carle Place | | |
| Edison | | |

Each store will be given quarterly goals for both rentals and sales. The base bonus is determined by the class of the store as follows:

A stores $10,000 per year
B stores 6,000 per year
C stores 4,000 per year

Both sale and rental goals must be met each quarter. If store revenue is exactly on goal, the yearly bonus would be as indicated above.

If store revenue exceeds goal, the base bonus in addition to 2% of incremental sale revenue plus 6% of incremental rental revenue, would be distributed among management.

If store revenue falls short of goal but is within 5% of goal, management would receive base bonus minus 2% of missed sales revenue and 6% of missed rental revenue.

If a store falls short of either rental or sales goal by more than 5% no bonus would be given.

The outcome of one quarter would have no effect on subsequent quarters. Bonus for exceeding goal would be included in that quarter and falling short of goal would adversely affect only that quarter.

Bonus money would be qualified for quarterly and paid out in one additional check the following quarter.

Bonus money would be split in each store with

Store Manager receiving 50%
Assistant Manager receiving 30
Floor Manager receiving 20

| STORE TYPE (BASE BONUS) | 50% MANAGER | 30% ASST. MANAGER | 20% FLOOR MANAGER |
|---|---|---|---|
| A ($10,000) | $5,000 | $3,000 | $2,000 |
| B ( 6,000) | 3,000 | 1,800 | 1,200 |
| C ( 4,000) | 2,000 | 1,200 | 800 |

*continued*

In stores designated as four-manager stores, the floor manager bonus would be doubled then divided and applied to the third and fourth manager.

There are certain measurable areas of profit drain that can be directly or indirectly controlled by management. These measurable areas would be deducted from bonus.

    a. Net register shortages—all clerk overages and shortages will be netted out. If a shortage exists it will be deducted.

    b. Any missing safe funds and short deposits.

    c. Losses resulting from not following proper check procedures.

    d. Losses resulting from not following proper charge procedures.

This Incentive Plan has taken a considerable investment in time to develop. While we think most areas have been addressed and problems anticipated, "bugs" may exist and unanticipated problems may arise. Because of this, we are committing to the program in its present form for a period of two quarters. Evaluation of this plan will be ongoing and adjustments will be made accordingly.

We are looking forward to both seeing you in June and initiating this long-deserved Incentive Plan.

cc:   S. Berns
      J. Levy
      C. Meier
      M. Berlin
      R. Erdmann
      R. Stoneman

---

to answer questions and assign targets for the quarter beginning July 1.

## *Reactions and Results*

Store managers reacted to the announcement of the plan enthusiastically. According to Berns they were "ecstatic." Comments by store managers to the casewriter included:

"The plan was welcome, any chance to make more money is great."

"It's a great program. . . . It really generates a competitive feeling."

"I like it; this company had always been on the cheap side."

During the first quarter of the program, "easy" targets were set for the stores. As a result, 12 out of 17 stores received bonuses in the third quarter of 1988. Total bonus payments were $45,755. Two store managers individually received bonuses of over $3,000, well in excess of their base bonus of $1,250. (See Exhibit 4 for third and fourth quarter results.)

Fourth quarter targets were raised by Berns and Molnar to reflect three factors: third quarter performance, a rental price increase effective November 13 to $2.49 a tape, and generally greater sell-through demand for the Christmas season. However, rental targets were lowered mid-quarter to reflect lower than anticipated demand. For the fourth quarter, 11 out of 21 stores received bonuses totaling $29,448.

Manager reactions to the implementation of the program were mixed. Janet Harris, manager of the 34th Street store commented, "The targets used to be better. The new targets are too high." Jack Hilgartner, manager of the chain's second largest store agreed: "The Christmas targets were unrealistic. I ignored them." He actually stapled them shut to his bulletin board. He added, "I want to know how they come up with these targets. They can zap you so easily with targets that are impossible to hit."

Meanwhile, Berns and Molnar were unhappy with the results of the program. They

**EXHIBIT 4** Store Goals and Revenues for Third and Fourth Quarters, 1988

| STORE TYPE | STORE NAME | 3Q88 RENTAL GOAL | 3Q88 RENTAL ACTUAL | 3Q88 SALES GOAL | 3Q88 SALES ACTUAL | 3Q88 TOTAL BONUS |
|---|---|---|---|---|---|---|
| A | Carle Place | $126,100 | $ 168,014 | $ 59,800 | $ 64,022 | $ 5,099 |
| A | Edison | 97,500 | 123,603 | 148,200 | 172,319 | 4,549 |
| A | Greenwich | 93,600 | 125,429 | 104,325 | 94,071 | 0 |
| A | Hackensack | 143,000 | 203,314 | 78,000 | 84,229 | 6,243 |
| A | Little Falls | 202,800 | 229,565 | 130,000 | 111,434 | 0 |
| A | Morris Plains | 63,960 | 54,823 | 43,973 | 43,588 | 0 |
| A | Paramus | 72,800 | 97,696 | 89,700 | 93,037 | 4,061 |
| A | Lexington | 141,700 | 198,299 | 66,300 | 71,894 | 6,008 |
| A | East Meadow | 75,400 | 119,730 | 75,400 | 126,260 | 6,177 |
| B | Toms River | 72,800 | 88,547 | 32,500 | 35,444 | 2,504 |
| B | 34th Street | 89,700 | 127,348 | 36,400 | 49,806 | 4,027 |
| C | Neptune | 46,800 | 54,511 | 44,200 | 58,065 | 1,740 |
| C | Westwood | 54,600 | 71,249 | 52,000 | 49,327 | 0 |
| C | Union | 55,900 | 74,524 | 19,500 | 25,521 | 2,238 |
| C | Scarsdale | 88,400 | 90,108 | 18,200 | 19,489 | 1,128 |
| C | Amsterdam | 88,400 | 102,366 | 19,500 | 26,706 | 1,982 |
| | Total | | $1,929,126 | | $1,125,212 | $45,756 |

| STORE TYPE | STORE NAME | 4Q88 RENTAL GOAL | 4Q88 RENTAL ACTUAL | 4Q88 SALES GOAL | 4Q88 SALES ACTUAL | 4Q88 TOTAL BONUS |
|---|---|---|---|---|---|---|
| A | Bay Plaza | $103,950 | $ 59,437 | $ 52,500 | $ 104,803 | $ 2,811* |
| A | Carle Place | 166,768 | 190,348 | 100,400 | 92,756 | 0 |
| A | Oceanside | 94,511 | 106,468 | 45,000 | 81,757 | 3,953 |
| A | Edison | 120,109 | 116,326 | 237,600 | 260,513 | 2,731 |
| A | Greenwich | 123,658 | 122,881 | 146,400 | 154,583 | 2,617 |
| A | Hackensack | 204,992 | 186,189 | 111,600 | 133,663 | 0 |
| A | Little Falls | 227,142 | 247,753 | 187,400 | 200,520 | 3,999 |
| A | Morris Plains | 85,179 | 111,314 | 94,000 | 113,864 | 4,465 |
| A | Paramus | 97,332 | 97,982 | 118,800 | 152,875 | 3,221 |
| A | Lexington | 209,465 | 173,044 | 94,200 | 107,143 | 0 |
| A | East Meadow | 129,729 | 120,595 | 164,000 | 221,188 | 0 |
| B | Toms River | 89,716 | 103,779 | 59,400 | 59,440 | 2,345 |
| B | 68th Street | 69,300 | 40,885 | 35,000 | 78,490 | 2,103* |
| B | 34th Street | 134,167 | 110,075 | 55,200 | 83,523 | 0 |
| C | Neptune | 98,046 | 69,905 | 38,800 | 29,371 | 0 |
| C | Westwood | 70,200 | 71,045 | 36,800 | 44,405 | 1,203 |
| C | Union | 100,016 | 97,793 | 51,200 | 32,807 | 0 |
| C | Scarsdale | 71,952 | 71,523 | 77,800 | 64,934 | 0 |
| C | Amsterdam | 54,379 | 48,719 | 94,200 | 78,687 | 0 |
| C | Jersey City | 77,552 | 67,674 | 38,800 | 44,644 | 0 |
| | Total | | $2,213,735 | | $2,139,966 | $29,448 |

*Note: All figures are disguised. The 49th Street store figures are omitted.*
*These two stores were granted bonuses even though they failed to reach 95% of their rental goals.

acknowledged that the plan had helped re-cruiting efforts and that some managers were very attentive. However, in general they did not feel that the performance of the store managers had changed. Berns stated, "Plan or not, good managers are good and bad man-agers are bad. Performance related to prof-itability was not raised by an appreciable degree." He did acknowledge that the perfor-mance of some stores had improved. How-ever, he did not credit the plan, "Some stores were dramatically up, but I'm not sure that the incentive plan had anything to do with the increase in volume. Rental rates went up and we increased our advertising."

Berns felt that the program was expensive, "We're giving away far more incentive dol-lars than we're getting in incremental rev-enue dollars. The cost goes straight to the bottom line." In addition, according to Berns, service-related measures had not changed, "The performance level of the people out there has not been raised. Day-to-day compli-ance on things like ordering product has not improved." Molnar agreed with Berns's com-ments adding, "I can find the same things that bothered me six months ago going on today. Sitting here is frustrating because compliance is not getting better."

The store managers agreed that their be-havior had not changed dramatically. How-ever, numerous subtle indications were evi-dent in their comments. Joe Murphy said, "I've always done the little things well. I'm doing nothing better now. It's not like the plan would get me to beat my employees." Later, however, Murphy added, "Now I'm tracking weekly sales when I didn't do it be-fore. . . . Well, I do care more. The plan might get me to jump on people a little more." He did agree with Berns and Molnar that the plan would not effect bad managers,

"It would not change them. They did not have the tools in the first place." Jack Hilgart-ner also indicated that his performance had not changed. However, he and Murphy had both gone to the warehouse on an off day to pick up tapes so that their stores would be fully stocked. In addition, Hilgartner was also tracking his results and admitted that, "With six weeks to go in the first quarter, when we knew we could make our numbers, we really got into it."

### Conclusion

In summing up the results of the program Berns wondered, "How can an incentive program bring compliance into the picture without having to create a 20-page 'War and Peace' manual for the stores? Where do you draw the line on objectivity?" Berns and Molnar felt that RKO's rapid growth and the difficult labor market in the area prevented them from replacing the chain's "bad" man-agers. In any event, they both came back to the "Good managers are good. Bad man-agers are bad" observation to indict the rev-enue-based bonus plan. But Berns did wryly observe that, "Once giveth the plan, it is hard to taketh away." The store managers knew that the two-quarter test period had ended and they, too, were concerned about the fate of the plan. "We would all be angry if they took the program out," said Mike Batt.

Was the plan effective? Should it be modi-fied? What changes could be incorporated in the plan? Should the plan be dropped as a waste of money? Did the volatile nature of this evolving industry and changing company policies mask the true results? Berns and Molnar examined their information again from the beginning.

# DUCKWORTH INDUSTRIES, INC.—INCENTIVE COMPENSATION PROGRAMS*

In early 1992, Mr. John Duckworth, president and controlling shareholder of Duckworth Industries was considering a change in Duckworth Industries' management incentive compensation systems. If implemented the new plan for Duckworth management would, it was hoped, align more closely the interests of management and shareholders. Several industrial firms which were pioneers in value-based management had recently adopted similar management compensation systems. Adopting the new system would keep Duckworth in the vanguard of management incentive compensation planning

## Background

Mr. Duckworth was a strong believer in the power of incentives to guide management action. When he was first promoted to a plant management job in the 1950s, Mr. Duckworth took over a plant which had an operating loss of $2.7 million on sales of $9.0 million. He implemented what was then a "state-of-the-art" plan for factory incentives. The plan applied to all supervisors. Achievement of specified goals earned a 15% premium over an individual's base rate of pay. As noted by Mr. Duckworth:

> The more sobering side of the plan consisted of docking supervisors 12% of their base rate when goals were not achieved. Paychecks having a 12% deduction for failure were distributed in bright red envelopes. At that time I was plant manager of the operation, and I got several red pay envelopes. Some 15–18

months after the "12% Club" was profitably and smoothly functioning, the National Labor Relations Board issued a cease and desist order predicated on the fact you cannot tamper with an individual's base pay. Naturally, I complied, but the results were already in—the division was profitable.

Mr. Duckworth founded his own business in 1971. Sales grew from $400,000 in that year to almost $125 million in 1992 (**Exhibit 1**). In 1986, a holding company (Duckworth Industries) was established. It included the original business, Worth Corp., which was a highly profitable producer of proprietary fasteners and adhesives. In 1986, Hospitality Equipment Service was acquired at a purchase price of $5.5 million. In 1988, Hotel Telecom Services was acquired for about $15.0 million. The two newer acquisitions were service businesses rather than manufacturers, and to date had not yet generated satisfactory levels of profitability. In 1992, Duckworth Industries employed 755 people. The structure of the organization is shown in **Exhibit 2**.

## The Six Duckworth Incentive Plans

Pay for performance was firmly embedded in the corporate culture at Duckworth Industries. In the words of one senior executive, "we put incentives, within reason, behind everything we can."

For plant-level employees, Duckworth had an *attendance* bonus. A 60 cents per hour pay incentive was earned for each pay period during which an employee was never more than 2 minutes late for work.

For plant-level employees up to the shift supervisory level, there was also a *quality* in-

---

*This case was prepared by William E. Frahan, Jr. as the basis for class discussion rather than to illustrate either effective or ineffective handling of an administrative situation.

Copyright © 1993 by the President and Fellows of Harvard College. Harvard Business School case 293-091.

**EXHIBIT 1**  Consolidated Financial Statements 1975–1992, Fiscal Years Ended 5/31 ($000)

|  | 1975 | 1980 | 1985 | 1990 | 1991 | 1992 |
|---|---|---|---|---|---|---|
| Net sales | 5,811 | 15,109 | 40,793 | 116,220 | 123,545 | 122,570 |
| Cost of goods sold | 4,294 | 11,164 | 30,142 | 85,875 | 89,865 | 86,720 |
| Selling, gen'l & admin. | 1,231 | 3,199 | 8,638 | 24,610 | 25,080 | 28,800 |
| Operating income | 287 | 746 | 2,013 | 5,735 | 8,595 | 7,050 |
| Investment income | 68 | 177 | 479 | 1,365 | 1,375 | 1,545 |
| Interest expense | 129 | 334 | 902 | 2,570 | 2,390 | 1,635 |
| Profit sharing expense | 55 | 142 | 383 | 1,090 | 1,595 | 1,850 |
| Income before taxes | 172 | 447 | 1,207 | 3,440 | 5,985 | 5,105 |
| Taxes | 50 | 130 | 351 | 1,000 | 1,850 | 1,565 |
| Net income | 122 | 317 | 856 | 2,440 | 4,135 | 3,540 |
| Cash & marketable securities[a] | 1,067 | 2,775 | 7,492 | 21,345 | 24,790 | 26,085 |
| Accounts receivable | 578 | 1,502 | 4,056 | 11,555 | 12,760 | 13,210 |
| Inventory | 572 | 1,487 | 4,014 | 11,435 | 11,380 | 12,995 |
| Less: Lifo reserves | 51 | 131 | 355 | 1,010 | 1,111 | 1,125 |
| Net inventories | 522 | 1,356 | 3,661 | 10,430 | 10,270 | 11,870 |
| Other current assets | 46 | 119 | 321 | 915 | 960 | 990 |
| Total current assets | 2,212 | 5,752 | 15,530 | 44,245 | 48,780 | 52,155 |
| Construction in progress | 25 | 65 | 176 | 500 | 485 | 3,105 |
| Other net PP&E | 799 | 2,076 | 5,605 | 15,970 | 15,450 | 14,330 |
| Other assets[b] | 290 | 753 | 2,032 | 5,790 | 5,735 | 5,685 |
| Total assets | 3,325 | 8,646 | 23,343 | 66,505 | 70,450 | 75,275 |
| Short term debt | 734 | 1,909 | 5,154 | 14,685 | 17,390 | 15,910 |
| Other current liabilities | 1,048 | 2,724 | 7,355 | 20,955 | 19,790 | 23,700 |
| Total current liabilities | 1,782 | 4,633 | 12,510 | 35,640 | 37,180 | 39,610 |
| Long term borrowings | 496 | 1,290 | 3,482 | 9,920 | 8,355 | 7,175 |
| Other liabilities | 63 | 164 | 444 | 1,265 | 1,105 | 1,140 |
| Net worth | 984 | 2,558 | 6,908 | 19,680 | 23,810 | 27,350 |
| Total liab. & net worth | 3,325 | 8,646 | 23,343 | 66,505 | 70,450 | 75,275 |

[a]*Marketable securities were carried at the lower of cost or market. Market exceeded cost by $4,090 in 1990, $7,870 in 1991, and $10,940 in 1992.*
[b]*Other assets included goodwill of $5,130 in 1990, $4,995 in 1991, and $4,855 in 1992.*

centive plan (**Exhibits 3** and **4**). Quality measures included many variables such as meeting promised shipment dates and reducing customer complaints of any nature. The quality incentive payment target equaled $100 per employee per month. Performance was often a team effort, and the average employee working under this incentive plan received about $600 per year from it. Employees received a separate check each month for the quality bonus to highlight the importance of quality in the company culture.

All Duckworth employees were participants in a *profit-sharing* plan. At the level of each business unit a profit-sharing pool was created. The pool was equal in size to 15% of pretax profits after a deduction equal to 10% of the beginning-of-year net worth allocated to the business unit. At the end of each year the profit-sharing pool was allocated to employ-

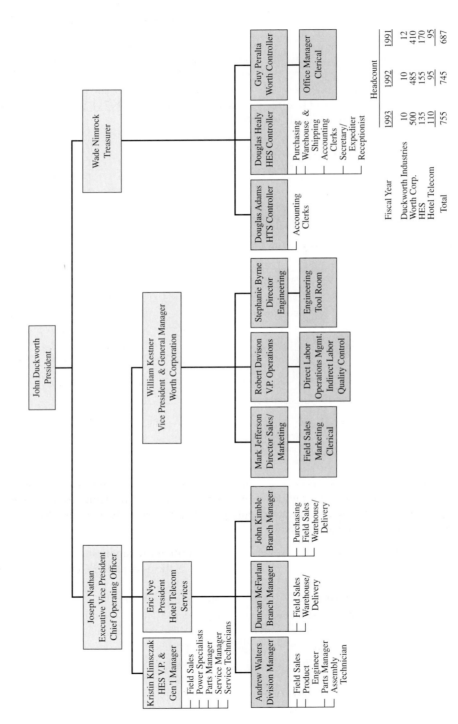

**EXHIBIT 2 Organization Chart, Duckworth Industries, Inc., June 1, 1992**

| Fiscal Year | 1993 | 1992 | 1991 |
|---|---|---|---|
| | | Headcount | |
| Duckworth Industries | 10 | 10 | 12 |
| Worth Corp. | 500 | 485 | 410 |
| HES | 135 | 155 | 170 |
| Hotel Telecom | 110 | 95 | 95 |
| Total | 755 | 745 | 687 |

**EXHIBIT 3   Duckworth Corporation, Quality Incentive Bonus Plan, Fiscal Year 1993**

The Quality Incentive bonus plan has been in its current form since FY90 (June of 1989).

As we have improved as a company it is important that our plan be modified to reflect these changes and more accurately represent what the "real world" reflects in terms of total quality performance. After a thorough review of this years' quality performance the following changes are being made to the Quality Incentive bonus plan effective June 1, 1992 (FY93). The monthly complaint ratio and bonus payout levels will be:

| COMPLAINT RATIO | MONTHLY BONUS PAYOUT |
| --- | --- |
| .6% | $100.00 |
| More than .6%, less than 2.0% | 75.00 |
| More than 2.0, less than 3.5% | $ 50.00 |

As you can see, the lower limits have been changed and the bottom payout of $25 eliminated, but we have increased the top level payout by 25% to $100.00. The total potential maximum yearly payout is now $1,200 compared to $900 with the old plan. This year through the first 11 months we have paid $800 in incentives to each participant. As you can see from the above, superior performance will be rewarded with high-level bonus payouts.

Duckworth quality performance in FY91 improved dramatically to an average 2.7% complaint ratio with the **last 6 months** of the year averaging 2%. The revised plan is designed to build on this success and increase our performance to "world class" levels.

The procedure for analyzing, charging responsibility, and tallying total number of complaints by Richard Sterling all remain the same as in the past. The only additional reporting will be a new category recording invoicing errors, such as billing errors or wrong prices on orders. Complete quality is a total system—from the first customer inquiry to billing of parts and all processes in between.

With constant dedication to teamwork, continuous quality improvement and satisfying our **customers requirements**, we are confident that our new goals will be achieved and even surpassed. You are doing it now and we are counting on you to make Duckworth—**Your Company**—The best quality company possible!

William Kestner
Vice President and General Manager

cc:   John Duckworth
Joseph Nathan

**EXHIBIT 4** **Worth Corporation, Quality Incentive Program, FY93 October Results**

| | |
|---|---|
| No. of Shipments | 207 |
| No. of Chargeable Complaints | 4 |
| Complaint Ratio | 1.9% |
| Quality Bonus—October | $ 75 |
| Quality Bonus—YTD | $300 |

With a record number of shipments, this month had the potential of being a **great quality month**, but we fell short because preventable errors were not caught. Without the large shipment level, the monthly payout would not have been $75.00.

If you look at the customer complaints listed below, you will see that these problems could have been detected by our systems. The key to continued improvement is your using the systems and informing others when the system does not work.

The XXX and YYY complaints are good examples of where the system in place was not followed and resulted in a complaint. The AAA and BBB complaints are examples of where people could have come forth to say the system doesn't adequately detect these kinds of defects.

The task of improvement needs to be continually addressed by all. We cannot just let things go on and expect good results. Good results are achieved by good people doing the right things at the right time.

| TYPE OF COMPLAINT | CUSTOMER | COMPLAINT |
|---|---|---|
| Manufacturing Process | AAA | Cracked AX47 parts and inventory not rotated. |
| Manufacturing Process | BBB | Cracked AX47 parts and inventory not rotated. |
| Color | YYY | Color significantly off standard (yellow). |
| Label | XXX | Label had wrong code printed. |

| | |
|---|---|
| Joy Meadow | Thomas Spencer |
| Quality Assurance Manager | Production Manager |

ees, pro rata, based on their individual share of total wages and salaries in the business unit. At the Worth business unit profit sharing had grown from about 2% of pay to about 15% of pay in recent years. A plant worker earning $15,000 per year would get $2,250. Information sharing with plant personnel as to profit and margin levels was common at Duckworth, so an estimate of the size of their individual profit sharing allocation could be made by employees as the year progressed.

For all sales and supervisory personnel the company had *individual* incentive plans. These typically afforded an employee the opportunity to earn incentives ranging from 10% to 40% of base pay. The incentive plan targets for a typical customer service representative are included as **Exhibit 5**.

### The Existing Senior Management Incentive Plans

The more senior managers at Duckworth (a group comprised of up to 40 people) all participated in an *annual* incentive compensation

**EXHIBIT 5**  Worth Corporation, FY93 Incentive Plan for Customer Service Representative— Maximum Award = 10% of Average Base Salary.

|  | ITEM RESULTS | % OF BONUS | % OF SALARY |
|---|---|---|---|
| I.  Order Accuracy: 4% maximum potential Accuracy equals percentage of acceptance of orders that have correct pricing and other critical information. This accuracy is tracked by Director of Sales with bonus being paid based on overall FY93 results. | 98.0% or higher 96.5% 95.0% <95.0% | 40.00% 30.00% 20.00% 0.00% | 4.00% 3.00% 2.00% 0.00% |
| II.  Order Acknowledgement/Turnaround: 3% maximum potential (effective 9/1/92—9 month period) Average number of days (excluding holidays & weekends) from order placement until printing of order acknowledgement for all orders received (except those requiring new part numbers). Results to be tracked weekly on late shipments report. | 2 days or less 3 days 4 days >4 days | 30.00% 15.00% 5.00% 0.00% | 3.00% 1.50% 0.50% 0.00% |
| III.  Sales Growth: 3% maximum potential Total net company sales growth over FY92 net sales of $63.5 million | $7,000M $6,000M $3,000M <$3,000M | 30.00% 15.00% 5.00% 0.00 | 3.00% 1.50% 0.50% 0.00% |

plan. A smaller subset of this group also participated in a *long-term* incentive program.

The incentive plans (both annual and long-term) for the senior managers had undergone considerable change in the 1983–1992 decade. Prior to 1990, the *annual* incentive plan would target for each manager a bonus of 20% to 50% of base salary if certain target levels of performance at the business unit level were reached during the year. Typical measures of performance (depending on the manager's area of responsibility) included at least three of the following:

1. Cash flow
2. Sales growth of proprietary products
3. Direct labor variances
4. Inventory turns
5. Accounts receivable (days sales outstanding)
6. Gross margins (less purchase price variances)
7. Special individual projects

In 1990 Duckworth abandoned the narrowly defined annual targets and opted to tie the annual bonus to a matrix built around sales growth and profitability goals. Annually goals for each business unit were set for both sales growth and profitability (**Exhibit 6**). These were determined with reference to the performance levels achieved by various peer group companies (**Exhibit 7**). Individual managers were assigned bonus targets (generally ranging from 25% to 50% of base compensation). Depending on the level of sales growth and prof-

Worth Corporation,
Annual Sales Growth %

| Return on Gross Assets % | | | 4.90 | 5.00 | 7.50 | 10.00 | 12.50 | 15.00 |
|---|---|---|---|---|---|---|---|---|
| | | | | | | GOAL | | |
| | 25.0 | | 0 | 1.74 | 1.81 | 1.88 | 1.95 | 2.03 |
| | 24.0 | | 0 | 1.55 | 1.61 | 1.67 | 1.74 | 1.81 |
| | 23.0 | | 0 | 1.37 | 1.42 | 1.48 | 1.55 | 1.61 |
| | 22.0 | | 0 | 1.20 | 1.25 | 1.31 | 1.37 | 1.42 |
| | 21.0 | | 0 | 1.05 | 1.10 | 1.15 | 1.20 | 1.25 |
| | 20.0 | GOAL | 0 | 0.91 | 0.95 | 1.00 | 1.05 | 1.10 |
| | 19.0 | | 0 | 0.78 | 0.82 | 0.87 | 0.91 | 0.95 |
| | 18.0 | | 0 | 0.67 | 0.71 | 0.74 | 0.78 | 0.82 |
| | 17.0 | | 0 | 0.57 | 0.60 | 0.63 | 0.67 | 0.71 |
| | 16.0 | | 0 | 0.48 | 0.51 | 0.54 | 0.57 | 0.60 |
| | 15.0 | | 0 | 0.40 | 0.42 | 0.45 | 0.48 | 0.51 |
| | 14.9 | | 0 | 0 | 0 | 0 | 0 | 0 |

Return on Gross Performing Assets will be determined by dividing Operational Cash Flow Earnings (OCFE) into Average Gross Performing Assets (AGPA).

OCFE is net profit adjusted to add depreciation and to eliminate (a) interest expense, (b) acquisition expenses, (c) net investment income, (d) expense or profit relating to LIFO, and (e) gains or loses from the disposition of depreciable assets. All adjustments will be made on an after-tax basis, using Worth Corporation's effective tax rate.

AGPA is a 13-month average of the company's gross book assets, with cumulative depreciation and the LIFO reserve added back, but investment securities and intercompany receivables eliminated.

The Board of Directors reserves the right to adjust the formula and its components, even after the fact, in any way it determines to be appropriate in order to better effectuate the plan and its purposes.

**EXHIBIT 6  Duckworth Industries, Inc., Fiscal 1992 Incentive Compensation**

itability achieved, a manager could read directly from the matrix the factor by which his/her target bonus would be multiplied to determine the actual bonus he/she would receive. The incentive compensation matrix for the Worth business unit (**Exhibit 6**) indicated the following: If, in fiscal 1992, a manager working at the Worth business unit had a target bonus of 40%, and the business unit provided a 20% return on assets and 10% sales growth, the manager would receive 1.00 times his/her 40% target bonus. In fact, in 1991 and 1992, business unit managers at Duckworth received the following percentages of their target bonuses from the annual incentive plan.

|  | 1991 | 1992 |
|---|---|---|
| Worth Corp. | 170% | 0% |
| Hotel Telecom | 0 | 24 |
| Hospitality Equipment | 0 | 0 |
| Duckworth Industries | 90 | 0 |

While Duckworth's annual incentive plan for senior managers covered several dozen employees by 1992, the long-term incentive

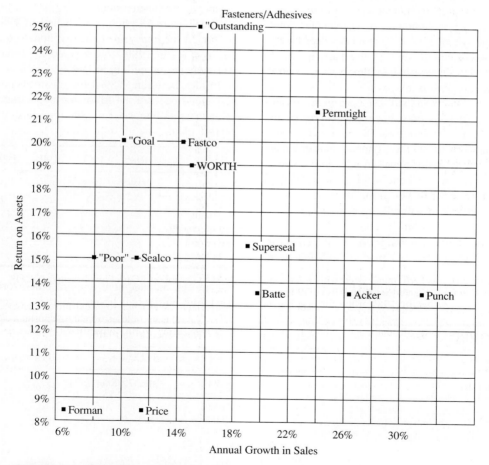

**EXHIBIT 7   ROA/Growth Matrix for Worth Peer Group**

plan covered fewer participants, particularly in the early part of the decade 1983–1992. In 1983 Duckworth implemented a five-year, long-term management incentive plan. The plan covered only two employees, the then vice president and general manager at Worth (now retired) and the then vice president, sales and marketing at Worth (now president of the Hotel Telecom Services operation). The plan made one payment at the end of five years. It was a phantom stock plan tied to the increase in book value per share multiplied by a performance factor (**Exhibit 8**). The performance factor was determined by several measures including a) the spread separating annual ROE from the sum of the bank prime rate plus two percentage points, b) the annual growth in net book value/share.

According to one of the participants the plan was a horror in complexity, but an attractive feature was that you could have one or two bad years and still get a payment. Because the plan paid only once at the end of five years, it was somewhat like a forced savings plan. "The size of the payment at the end made a meaningful difference in what you could do 'lifestyle'-wise. A check for $150,000 is quite significant when you bring it home. You are willing to make significant personal sacrifices along the way to make it happen."

In 1986 a new long-term management incentive plan was put in place at Duckworth. This plan was broadened to include more managers (15 by 1989) and was designed to begin payments in 1989 after the expiration of the previously described five-year plan. At the start of each year, beginning in 1986, new targets would be established so that incentive payments could be received annually. The business unit management participants in this plan would be awarded a specified percentage of base salary (generally from 25% to 40%) if a Challenge Earnings level of cumulative earnings before interest and taxes (approved by Duckworth's board of directors) was achieved by their business unit during the period. Lesser levels of earnings achievement would produce a proportionately reduced level of award (as shown in **Exhibit 9** for the Worth business unit).

The incentive system established in 1986 continued for four years. The last update was put in place in 1989, and covered the three-year time period ending in 1992.

In fact, between 1989–1992, business unit managers received the following percentages of their target bonuses from the long-term incentive plan.

|  | 1989 | 1990 | 1991 | 1992 |
|---|---|---|---|---|
| Worth Corp. | 112% | 97% | 92% | 91% |
| Hotel Telecom | — | 40 | 20 | 0 |
| Hospitality Equipment | — | — | 40 | 45 |
| Duckworth Industries | 85 | 80 | 75 | 73 |

For the top management team at Duckworth the target and actual bonus payments (mea-

**EXHIBIT 8** Worth Corporation, Inc., Executive Long Term Incentive Plan

| SUMMARY | 31-MAY-83 | 31-MAY-88 | 5-YR CHANGE |
|---|---|---|---|
| Total shareholder's equity at year end | $8,616,500 | $16,379,000 | |
| Per share, using standard of 500,000 shares | $   17.23 | $   32.76 | |
| Value weighting "Leverage Factor" | 0.50 | 1.70 | |
| Weighted share price (= Equity per share × leverage factor) | $    8.62 | $   55.69 | $47.07 |
| Per participant | $47.07 × 3000 shares | = $141,210 | |
| In total | × 2 participants | = $282,420 | |

**EXHIBIT 9**   Worth Division of Duckworth Industries—Management Long-Term Plan *Targets Established* for Successive Three Year Plans versus *Results Achieved*

| PLAN YEARS | CHALLENGE EARNINGS LEVELS (3 YR CUMULATIVE EBIT) | % OF TARGET AWARD EARNED | ACTUAL RESULTS DURING PERIOD |
|---|---|---|---|
| 1986–1989 | $12.0 million | 100% | $13.4 million and 112% |
|  | 10.0 | 50% |  |
|  | 7.5 | 10% |  |
|  | <7.5 | 0% |  |
| 1987–1990 | $20.0 | 100% | $19.3 million and 97% |
|  | 12.5 | 10% |  |
|  | <12.5 | 0% |  |
| 1988–1991 | 28.75 | 100% | $26.1 million and 92% |
|  | 20.0 | 10% |  |
|  | <20.0 | 0% |  |
| 1989–1992 | 33.0 | 100% | $30.1 million and 91% |
|  | 25.0 | 10% |  |
|  | <25.0 | 0% |  |

*Award Determination*

Each participant will, at the start of a Performance Period, be assigned a Target Award expressed as a percentage of the Participant's average annual base salary to be paid during the Performance Period. The percent of the Target Award earned by each Participant will be based upon the relationship of Performance Period Earnings to various Challenge Earnings Levels specified by the Board for such Performance Period.

The percent of Target Award earned will be awarded on a pro rata basis if the actual results fall between specified Challenge Earnings Levels. If a Participant significantly changes responsibility or positions during the Performance Period, the Board will consider the propriety of an equitable adjustment in the Target Award assigned.

A Participant's award is subject to organizational and environmental constraints affecting Performance Period Earnings. Unforeseen problems (other than those referred to in the next paragraph) or opportunities, as well as peer group performance, will be taken into account during the evaluation process. As soon as practicable after the end of a Performance Period, the Board will determine how successfully objectives were met. The Board will evaluate how unforeseen difficulties, as well as unexpected opportunities, were addressed. To allow recognition for quality of results and level of effort, award amounts may be adjusted (to a maximum of plus or minus 25% of the award) by the Board.

The Plan also recognizes that actions of Participants may be negated or overstated due to the occurrence of certain extraordinary events. Examples of extraordinary events include, but are not limited to, "Acts of God," financial difficulty of a major supplier or customer, unexpected tax law changes and acquisitions, divestitures, mergers or significant structural changes. Should such extraordinary occurrences take place, the Board may adjust the incentive awards (or the various formula components thereof) in any manner reasonably intended to reflect the impact of the extraordinary occurrence.

sured as a percentage of base salary) are presented as **Exhibit 10**.

### A Proposed New EVA Incentive System

As fiscal 1992 unfolded, both management and Mr. Duckworth (the controlling share-

holder) were looking for ways to more closely align the interests of management and shareholders through the incentive plan for senior management. A number of factors had contributed to dissatisfaction with the existing plans. One major factor had to do with

**EXHIBIT 10**   Target and Actual Payments (as a % of Base Salary) for Annual and Long-term Incentive Compensation Plans

|  |  |  | 1990 | | 1991 | | 1992 | |
|---|---|---|---|---|---|---|---|---|
|  |  |  | TARGET | ACTUAL | TARGET | ACTUAL | TARGET | ACTUAL |
| Manager | A | Annual bonus | — | — | 40[a] | 68 | 40[a] | 0 |
|  |  | L.T. Incentives | — | — | 35[a] | 32 | 35[a] | 32 |
| Manager | B | Annual bonus | — | — | 25[a] | 35 | 25[a] | 0 |
|  |  | L.T. Incentive | — | — | 25[a] | 23 | 25[a] | 23 |
| Manager | C | Annual bonus | 50[a] | 50 | 50[a] | 85 | 50[b] | 0 |
|  |  | L.T. Incentive | 40[a] | 39 | 40[a] | 37 | 40[b] | 0 |
| Manager | D | Annual bonus | 25[a] | 25 | 40[a] | 35 | 25[a] | 0 |
|  |  | L.T. Incentive | 25[a] | 24 | 40[a] | 37 | 40[a] | 36 |
| Manager | E | Annual bonus | 40[a] | 40 | 40[a] | 68 | 40[a] | 0 |
|  |  | L.T. Incentive | 40[a] | 39 | 35[a] | 32 | 35[a] | 32 |
| Manager | F | Annual bonus | — | — | 25[b] | 0 | 25[b] | 6 |
|  |  | L.T. Incentive | — | — | 25[b] | 5 | 25[b] | 0 |
| Manager | G | Annual bonus | 40[a] | 40 | 50[b] | 0 | 50[b] | 12 |
|  |  | L.T. Incentive | 40[a] | 39 | 40[b] | 8 | 40[b] | 0 |
| Manager | H | Annual bonus | — | — | 25[b] | 0 | 25[b] | 6 |
|  |  | L.T. Incentive | — | — | 25[b] | 5 | 25[b] | 0 |
| Manager | I | Annual bonus | 25[a] | 25 | 50[d] | 46 | 50[d] | 0 |
|  |  | L.T. Incentive | 25[a] | 25 | 25[c] | 10 | 60[d] | 44 |
| Manager | J | Annual bonus | — | — | — | — | 25[c] | 0 |
|  |  | L.T. Incentive | — | — | — | — | — | — |
| Manager | K | Annual bonus | 30[c] | 0 | 30[c] | 0 | 30[c] | 0 |
|  |  | L.T. Incentive | 30[c] | 0 | 30[c] | 12 | 30[c] | 14 |
| Manager | L | Annual bonus | 40[c] | 0 | 40[c] | 0 | 50[c] | 0 |
|  |  | L.T. Incentive | 35[c] | 0 | 35[c] | 14 | 35[c] | 16 |
| Manager | M | Annual bonus | 50[c] | 0 | 50[c] | 0 | 50[c] | 0 |
|  |  | L.T. Incentive | 50[c] | 0 | 50[c] | 20 | 50[c] | 46 |
| Manager | N | Annual bonus | — | — | 35[a] | 60 | 35[a] | 0 |
|  |  | L.T. Incentive | 40[a] | 39 | 40[a] | 37 | 40[a] | 36 |
| Manager | O | Annual bonus | 40[a] | 40 | 40[a] | 68 | 40[a] | 0 |
|  |  | L.T. Incentive | 25[a] | 24 | 25[a] | 23 | 25[a] | 23 |
| Manager | P | Annual bonus | 20[a] | 20 | 20[a] | 34 | 20[a] | 0 |
|  |  | L.T. Incentive | 20[a] | 19 | 20[a] | 18 | 20[a] | 18 |

[a]Worth                               SBU
[b]Hotel Telecom Services              SBU
[c]Hospitality Equipment Services      SBU
[d]Duckworth Industries                SBU

operation of the annual incentive plan of Worth in 1992. In many ways Worth's performance in 1992 was improved over that of 1991.

|  | WORTH CORP. | |
| --- | --- | --- |
|  | 1991 | 1992 |
| Return on gross performing assets | 23.6% | 23.9% |
| Sales growth | 13.9 | (2.3) |

The return on gross performing assets had increased, but sales had declined slightly (versus a 10% goal and a minimum 5% sales growth requirement to achieve any annual incentive plan payment). The sales decline was caused by the loss of a very large customer buying a product with commodity-type profit margins. Most of the lost sales in 1992 had been replaced by new customers purchasing proprietary products at higher margins. The change in customer mix was good for enhancing long-run shareholder value, but Worth's management failed to achieve any annual incentive bonus as a result of the change given the structure of the existing annual incentive plan (**Exhibit 6**).

Near the close of fiscal 1992 Mr. John Duckworth began reading a book entitled *The Quest for Value* by G. Bennett Stewart. The Stewart book outlined a management incentive plan that promised to link management pay directly to the creation of long-run economic value for shareholders. Implementation of the plan required the services of Stern Stewart & Co., a financial consulting firm.

The economic value-added (EVA) compensation system developed by Stern Stewart would require (1) considerable data analysis and (2) some reorienting in thinking about how to approach the business going forward for Duckworth's senior management. The EVA system was predicated on the following logic:

1. Economic value for shareholders is created when a firm earns a rate of return on invested capital which exceeds the cost of capital. The economic value-added in a particular year should equal the product of:
   i) The average capital employed during the year multiplied by
   ii) The spread separating the cost of capital from the return on capital earned during the year.
2. The economic value-added during a year can be calculated for each business unit. The management of each unit can be directly compensated for their success in adding economic value via a compensation formula that automatically adjusts the baseline for calculating next year's bonus to reflect the actual performance of the prior year.

### The Key Drivers of Economic Value-Added

**Exhibit 11** shows a calculation of the economic value-added by the Worth division of Duckworth Industries from 1988 through 1992. It also shows the *forecasted* economic value-added for the period 1993–1997.

The key variables in determining the economic value-added by a business unit were:

1. Net operating profit after taxes (NOPAT)— **Exhibit 11**, Line 9. This excludes corporate overhead, and capitalizes R&D expenses and then amortizes them over three years. NOPAT excludes non-economic noncash charges.[1]
2. Average capital—**Exhibit 11**, Line 15. This excludes construction in progress, and assumes FIFO inventory valuation and the add-back of bad debt reserves. Non-economic non-cash writeoffs are added back to average capital.[2]
3. Cost of capital—**Exhibit 11**, Line 17. This is determined annually for each business unit by using an assumed capital structure and riskiness factor ($\beta$ value) for peer group firms comparable to each business unit. The formula for calculating capital cost was tied to the yield on 30-year Treasury obligations plus a risk premium.

[1]Items such as the one-time writeoff of a divested business would be a non-economic non-cash charge. Items such as depreciation or the amortization of debt discount would be economic non-cash charges.
[2]This was designed to prevent managers from escaping responsibility for poor prior investment decisions by simply divesting the poor performing assets.

**EXHIBIT 11** Worth Corporation Summary of Historical and Projected Operating Performance ($000's)

| LINE # | | HISTORY | | | | | FORECAST | | | | |
| --- | --- | --- | --- | --- | --- | --- | --- | --- | --- | --- | --- |
| | | 1988 | 1989 | 1990 | 1991 | 1992 | 1993 | 1994 | 1995 | 1996 | 1997 |
| | **Operating Results** | | | | | | | | | | |
| 1 | Revenue | $47,255 | $54,615 | $57,125 | $65,035 | $63,565 | $69,500 | $76,100 | $83,330 | $91,250 | $99,915 |
| 2 | % Growth | 15.0% | 15.6% | 4.6% | 13.9% | (2.3%) | 9.3% | 9.5% | 9.5% | 9.5% | 9.5% |
| 3 | −Cost of Sales | 34,985 | 40,305 | 41,760 | 46,020 | 42,025 | 47,355 | 51,950 | 56,915 | 62,415 | 68,445 |
| 4 | % Sales | 74.0% | 73.8% | 73.1% | 70.8% | 66.1% | 68.1% | 68.3% | 68.3% | 68.4% | 68.5% |
| 5 | −SG&A | 6,620 | 6,700 | 6,905 | 6,905 | 8,585 | 9,695 | 10,865 | 11,715 | 12,680 | 13,585 |
| 6 | % Sales | 14.0% | 12.3% | 12.1% | 10.6% | 13.5% | 13.9% | 14.3% | 14.1% | 13.9% | 13.6% |
| 7 | −Cash Taxes | $2,280 | $1,965 | $2,615 | $3,500 | $3,650 | $4,225 | $4,855 | $5,310 | $5,785 | $6,215 |
| 8 | % Operating Income | 40.4% | 25.8% | 30.9% | 28.9% | 28.2% | 33.9% | 36.5% | 36.1% | 35.8% | 34.8% |
| 9 | NOPAT net op prof after taxes | $3,370 | $5,645 | $5,840 | $8,615 | $9,305 | $8,225 | $8,430 | $9,390 | $10,370 | $11,670 |
| | **Capital** | | | | | | | | | | |
| 10 | Net Accounts Receivable | $5,310 | $4,855 | $ 5,460 | $5,525 | $ 6,060 | $ 6,185 | $ 6,760 | $ 7,395 | $ 8,090 | $ 8,850 |
| 11 | Inventory | 2,865 | 2,965 | 3,360 | 3,865 | 4,020 | 4,030 | 4,260 | 4,585 | 4,945 | 5,325 |
| 12 | PP&E | 5,540 | 9,415 | 13,775 | 13,505 | 12,180 | 19,465 | 21,555 | 21,825 | 20,915 | 21,200 |
| 13 | Other Assets | 620 | 350 | 1,455 | 1,565 | 3,765 | 3,210 | 2,450 | 1,800 | 1,245 | 1,185 |
| 14 | −NIBCL's[a] | (10,775) | (9,790) | (11,545) | (10,025) | (13,125) | (9,940) | (10,860) | (12,040) | (13,360) | (14,725) |
| 15 | Capital | $3,555 | $7,795 | $12,505 | $14,440 | $12,900 | $22,945 | $24,165 | $23,560 | $21,830 | $21,835 |
| | **Operating Analysis** | | | | | | | | | | |
| 16 | NOPAT/Avg Cap (r) | 51.4% | 99.5% | 57.5% | 63.9% | 68.1% | 45.9% | 35.8% | 39.3% | 45.7% | 53.5% |
| 17 | −Cost of Capital (c) | 13.0% | 12.6% | 12.7% | 12.4% | 12.2% | 12.2% | 12.2% | 12.2% | 12.2% | 12.2% |
| 18 | Spread (r − c) | 38.4% | 86.9% | 44.8% | 51.5% | 55.9% | 33.7% | 23.6% | 27.2% | 33.5% | 41.3% |
| 19 | × Average Capital | $6,550 | $5,675 | $10,150 | $13,470 | $13,670 | $17,925 | $23,555 | $23,865 | $22,695 | $21,830 |
| 20 | Economic Value Added | $2,515 | $4,935 | $4,550 | $6,945 | $7,640 | $6,045 | $5,565 | $6,485 | $7,605 | $9,010 |

[a]*Noninterest-bearing current liabilities.*

**EXHIBIT 12**  Worth Corporation

## INPUT TABLE

| LINE # | | 1993 | 1994 | 1995 | 1996 | 1997 |
|---|---|---|---|---|---|---|
| | Bonus Pool Characteristics | | | | | |
| 1 | Target Bonus | 37% | 37% | 37% | 37% | 37% |
| 2 | Base Salary (000) | $1,710 | $1,795 | $1,885 | $1,980 | $2,075 |
| 3 | # of Units (000) | 630 | 660 | 695 | 730 | 765 |
| | Bonus Calculation Framework | | | | | |
| 4 | Baseline EVA (000) | $6,045 | | | | |
| 5 | Annual Target Adjustment Factor | 50% | | | | |
| 6 | Base Unit Value | $ 1.00 | $ 0.80 | $ 0.80 | $ 0.80 | $ 0.80 |
| | EVA Bonus Sensitivity Factor | | | | | |
| 7 | EVA Bonus Sensitivity Factor (000) | $1,625 | | | | |

## CURRENT BONUS CALCULATION

| LINE # | | 1993 | 1994 | 1995 | 1996 | 1997 | AVERAGE |
|---|---|---|---|---|---|---|---|
| | Performance Unit Value | | | | | | |
| 8 | EVA (000) | $6,045 | $5,565 | $6,485 | $7,605 | $9,010 | $6,940 |
| 9 | − Baseline EVA (000) | $6,045 | $6,045 | $5,805 | $6,145 | $6,875 | $6,180 |
| 10 | = EVA vs Baseline EVA (000) | $ 0 | ($ 480) | $ 680 | $1,460 | $2,135 | $ 760 |
| 11 | / EVA Bonus Sensitivity Factor (000) | $1,625 | $1,625 | $1,625 | $1,625 | $1,625 | $1,625 |
| 12 | = Performance Unit Value | $ 0.00 | ($ 0.29) | $ 0.42 | $ 0.90 | $ 1.31 | $ 0.47 |
| | Total Unit Value | | | | | | |
| 13 | Performance Unit Value | $ 0.00 | ($ 0.29) | $ 0.42 | $ 0.90 | $ 1.31 | $ 0.47 |
| 14 | + Base Unit Value | $ 1.00 | $ 0.80 | $ 0.80 | $ 0.80 | $ 0.80 | $ 0.84 |
| 15 | = Total Unit Value | $ 1.00 | $ 0.51 | $ 1.22 | $ 1.70 | $ 2.11 | $ 1.31 |
| | Current Bonus | | | | | | |
| 16 | Total Unit Value | $ 1.00 | $ 0.51 | $ 1.22 | $ 1.70 | $ 2.11 | $ 1.31 |
| 17 | # of Units (000) | 630 | 660 | 695 | 730 | 765 | 695 |
| 18 | Current Bonus Earned (000) | $ 630 | $ 335 | $ 850 | $1,240 | $1,620 | $ 935 |

## PAST BONUS IF SYSTEM HAD BEEN IN PLACE PRIOR 5 YEARS

| LINE # | | 1988 | 1989 | 1990 | 1991 | 1992 | AVERAGE |
|---|---|---|---|---|---|---|---|
| | Current Bonus | | | | | | |
| 19 | Total Unit Value | $1.00 | $ 2.29 | $1.31 | $ 2.53 | $ 2.09 | $ 1.84 |
| 20 | # of Units (000) | 695 | 720 | 720 | 740 | 530 | 680 |
| 21 | Current Bonus Earned (000) | $ 695 | $1,645 | $ 945 | $1,875 | $1,115 | $1,255 |

## *The Mechanism for Calculating Incentive Compensation*

Stern Stewart recommended a mechanism for linking economic value-added in a business unit during a given year to the incentive compensation paid to management in that year.

*First*, a bonus target was established. At Worth this might equal 37% of base pay (**Exhibit 12**, Line 1). Bonus units (like phantom stock) would be assigned to each manager in an amount such that if the bonus unit was valued at $1.00, the desired level of bonus would be earned by the manager (**Exhibit 12**, Line 3).

*Second*, a baseline EVA level was established (**Exhibit 12**, Line 4). At the end of each year the baseline EVA for the *following* year would change by one-half of the difference between the actual EVA achieved and the baseline EVA for the prior year (**Exhibit 12**, Lines 8–10). This made the system "self-adjusting." If EVA performance improved each year, the new base would click up by one-half the amount of the improvement. If EVA performance deteriorated for several years, the base level would decline so that the targets would not be so far away as to be unreachable in ensuing years.

*Third*, a base unit value was established for each ensuing year (**Exhibit 12**, Lines 6 and 14). This base unit value defined, to a large degree, how much of the target bonus could be earned by just maintaining the existing level of business performance. If EVA hit exactly the baseline EVA each year, and the base unit value was set at $1.00, then exactly the target bonus would be earned each year. In the case of Worth, after the first year the base unit value dropped to $.80. This meant that simply repeating the EVA baseline performance after 1993 would produce only 80% of the targeted bonus.

*Fourth*, a bonus sensitivity factor (**Exhibit 12**, Lines 7 and 11) was established which could either add to or subtract from the base unit value to create a total unit value. In the Worth example, the bonus sensitivity factor was set at $1,625,000. In any year that EVA varied from the baseline EVA, the amount of the gap was divided by $1,625,000, and the resulting amount (called the *performance* unit value, **Exhibit 12**, Lines 12 and 13) was added to the *base* unit value to determine the *total* unit value (**Exhibit 12**, Line 15). In order to earn one times the target bonus *solely* from the performance unit factor, management of the business unit had to beat the baseline EVA by the amount of the bonus sensitivity factor.

As indicated in **Exhibit 12**, if Worth hit the forecasted level of EVA in each year, Worth's management would earn the following percentage of their target bonus in each of the next five years.[3]

|  | % OF TARGET BONUS EARNED |
|---|---|
| 1993 | 100% |
| 1994 | 51 |
| 1995 | 122 |
| 1996 | 170 |
| 1997 | 211[3] |

As indicated in **Exhibits 13–16**, if the Hotel Telecom Services and Hospitality Equipment Services business units hit their forecasted level of EVA in each year, Hotel Telecom's and Hospitality Equipment's managements would earn the following percentage of their targeted bonus in each of the next five years (**Exhibits 14** and **16**, Line 15).

---

[3]Bonuses up to two times the target bonus were paid immediately. One-third of the amount over this maximum was also paid in cash. Remaining amounts were allocated to a "bonus bank" to be paid out in the future. Negative charges for deteriorating performance reduced the bonus bank. Negative charges could even create a negative balance in the bonus bank which would have to be overcome in order to resume bonus payments in future years.

**EXHIBIT 13**  Hotel Telecom Services, Summary of Historical and Projected Operating Performance ($000s)

| LINE # | | HISTORY | | | | | FORECAST | | |
|---|---|---|---|---|---|---|---|---|---|
| | | 1989 | 1990 | 1991 | 1992 | 1993 | 1994 | 1995 | 1996 | 1997 |
| | **Operating Results** | | | | | | | | | |
| 1 | Revenue | $29,115 | $32,540 | $29,980 | $32,285 | $46,600 | $55,920 | $60,115 | $64,625 | $69,470 |
| 2 | % Growth | NMF | 11.8% | (7.9%) | 7.7% | 44.3% | 20.0% | 7.5% | 7.5% | 7.5% |
| 3 | − Cost of Sales | 20,750 | 24,120 | 22,395 | 24,730 | 36,150 | 43,435 | 46,735 | 50,205 | 54,005 |
| 4 | % of Sales | 71.3% | 74.1% | 74.7% | 76.6% | 77.6% | 77.7% | 77.7% | 77.7% | 77.7% |
| 5 | − SG&A | 5,610 | 5,475 | 5,560 | 5,820 | 7,935 | 9,150 | 9,820 | 10,550 | 11,320 |
| 6 | % of Sales | 19.3% | 16.8% | 18.5% | 18.0% | 17.0% | 16.4% | 16.3% | 16.3% | 16.3% |
| 7 | − Cash Taxes | $ 455 | $ 1,000 | $ 700 | $ 500 | $ 815 | $ 1,060 | $ 1,135 | $ 1,235 | $ 1,325 |
| 8 | % Operating Income | 16.5% | 33.9% | 34.5% | 28.9% | 32.4% | 31.8% | 31.8% | 31.9% | 31.9% |
| 9 | NOPAT | $ 2,300 | $ 1,950 | $ 1,325 | $ 1,230 | $ 1,700 | $ 2,275 | $ 2,425 | $ 2,640 | $ 2,825 |
| | **Capital** | | | | | | | | | |
| 10 | Net Accounts Receivable | $ 3,370 | $ 3,240 | $ 3,935 | $ 4,365 | $ 6,115 | $ 7,265 | $ 7,805 | $ 8,385 | $ 9,010 |
| 11 | Inventory | 4,525 | 4,145 | 4,570 | 6,245 | 7,120 | 8,520 | 9,150 | 9,820 | 10,550 |
| 12 | PP&E | 1,365 | 1,250 | 1,355 | 1,525 | 1,520 | 1,405 | 1,395 | 1,255 | 1,085 |
| 13 | Goodwill | 4,395 | 4,395 | 4,395 | 4,400 | 4,400 | 4,400 | 4,400 | 4,400 | 4,400 |
| 14 | Other Assets | 230 | 715 | 1,250 | 1,935 | 290 | 320 | 330 | 345 | 360 |
| 15 | − NIBCL's[a] | (4,720) | (3,860) | (4,630) | (5,490) | (5,575) | (6,985) | (7,505) | (8,085) | (8,685) |
| 16 | Capital | 9,170 | 9,890 | 10,891 | 12,975 | 13,870 | 14,920 | 15,570 | 16,115 | 16,710 |
| | **Operating Analysis** | | | | | | | | | |
| 17 | NOPAT/Avg Cap (r) | 22.3% | 20.5% | 12.8% | 10.3% | 12.7% | 15.8% | 15.9% | 16.7% | 17.2% |
| 18 | − Cost of Capital (c) | 13.1% | 13.2% | 12.9% | 12.7% | 12.7% | 12.7% | 12.7% | 12.7% | 12.7% |
| 19 | Spread (r − c) | 9.2% | 7.3% | (0.1%) | (2.4%) | 0.0% | 3.1% | 3.2% | 4.0% | 4.5% |
| 20 | × Average Capital | $10,345 | $ 9,530 | $10,390 | $11,935 | $13,420 | $14,395 | $15,245 | $15,840 | $16,410 |
| 21 | Economic Value Added | $ 950 | $ 695 | ($ 10) | ($ 280) | $ 0 | $ 450 | $ 495 | $ 630 | $ 745 |

[a]*Noninterest-bearing current liabilities.*

**EXHIBIT 14** Hotel Telecom Services

## INPUT TABLE

| LINE # | | 1993 | 1994 | 1995 | 1996 | 1997 | |
|---|---|---|---|---|---|---|---|
| | Bonus Pool Characteristics | | | | | | |
| 1 | Target Bonus | 38% | 38% | 38% | 38% | 38% | |
| 2 | Base Salary (000) | $ 905 | $ 950 | $1,000 | $1,050 | $1,100 | |
| 3 | # of Units (000) | 345 | 360 | 380 | 400 | 420 | |
| | Bonus Calculation Framework | | | | | | |
| 4 | Baseline EVA (000) | ($140) | | | | | |
| 5 | Annual Target Adjustment Factor | 50% | | | | | |
| 6 | Base Unit Value | $0.25 | $0.25 | $ 0.25 | $ 0.25 | $ 0.25 | |
| | EVA Bonus Sensitivity Factor | | | | | | |
| 7 | = EVA Bonus Sensitivity Factor (000) | $ 700 | | | | | |

## CURRENT BONUS CALCULATION

| LINE # | | 1993 | 1994 | 1995 | 1996 | 1997 | AVERAGE |
|---|---|---|---|---|---|---|---|
| | Performance Unit Value | | | | | | |
| 8 | EVA (000) | $   0 | $ 450 | $ 495 | $ 630 | $ 745 | $ 465 |
| 9 | − Baseline EVA (000) | ($ 140) | ($ 570) | $ 190 | $ 340 | $ 485 | $ 160 |
| 10 | = EVA vs Baseline EVA (000) | $ 140 | $ 520 | $ 305 | $ 290 | $  25 | $ 300 |
| 11 | / EVA Bonus Sensitivity Factor (000) | $ 700 | $ 700 | $ 700 | $ 700 | $ 700 | $ 700 |
| 12 | = Performance Unit Value | $0.20 | $0.74 | $0.44 | $0.41 | $0.37 | $0.43 |
| | Total Unit Value | | | | | | |
| 13 | Performance Unit Value | $0.20 | $0.74 | $0.44 | $0.41 | $0.37 | $0.43 |
| 14 | + Base Unit Value | $0.25 | $0.25 | $0.25 | $0.25 | $0.25 | $0.25 |
| 15 | = Total Unit Value | $0.45 | $0.99 | $0.69 | $0.66 | $0.62 | $0.68 |
| | Current Bonus | | | | | | |
| 16 | Total Unit Value | $0.45 | $0.99 | $0.69 | $0.66 | $0.62 | $0.68 |
| 17 | # of Units (000) | 345 | 360 | 380 | 400 | 420 | 380 |
| 18 | Current Bonus Earned (000) | $ 155 | $ 360 | $ 260 | $ 265 | $ 260 | $ 260 |

## PAST BONUS IF SYSTEM HAD BEEN IN PLACE PRIOR 4 YEARS

| LINE # | | 1989 | 1990 | 1991 | 1992 | AVERAGE |
|---|---|---|---|---|---|---|
| | Current Bonus | | | | | |
| 19 | Total Unit Value | $1.27 | $0.39 | ($0.68) | ($ .60) | $0.08 |
| 20 | # of Units (000) | 50 | 150 | 325 | 340 | 215 |
| 21 | Current Bonus Earned (000) | $  60 | $  60 | ($ 225) | ($205) | ($  78) |

**EXHIBIT 15**  Hospitality Equipment Service Co., Summary of Historical and Projected Operating Performance ($000s)

| LINE # | | HISTORY | | | | | | FORECAST | | | |
|---|---|---|---|---|---|---|---|---|---|---|---|
| | | 1988 | 1989 | 1990 | 1991 | 1992 | 1993 | 1994 | 1995 | 1996 | 1997 |
| | **Operating Results** | | | | | | | | | | |
| 1 | Revenue | $24,770 | $28,670 | $26,555 | $28,525 | $26,720 | $29,220 | $31,410 | $33,765 | $36,300 | $39,020 |
| 2 | % Growth | 49.2% | 15.8% | (7.4%) | 7.4% | (6.3%) | 9.4% | 7.5% | 7.5% | 7.5% | 7.5% |
| 3 | − Cost of Sales | 18,560 | 21,545 | 19,545 | 20,955 | 14,305 | 21,190 | 22,500 | 24,170 | 25,965 | 27,895 |
| 4 | % Sales | 74.9% | 75.1% | 73.6% | 73.5% | 72.2% | 72.5% | 71.6% | 71.6% | 71.5% | 71.5% |
| 5 | − SG&A | 5,765 | 6,100 | 7,240 | 6,495 | 7,135 | 7,065 | 7,480 | 7,950 | 8,455 | 8,985 |
| 6 | % Sales | 23.3% | 21.3% | 27.3% | 22.8% | 26.7% | 24.2% | 23.8% | 23.5% | 23.3% | 23.0% |
| 7 | − Cash Taxes | $ 275 | $ 440 | $ 55 | $ 420 | $ 320 | $ 420 | $ 545 | $ 615 | $ 690 | $ 780 |
| 8 | % Operating Income | 62.0% | 43.0% | (23.7%) | 38.8% | 113.3% | 43.6% | 38.0% | 37.2% | 36.7% | 36.4% |
| 9 | NOPAT | $ 170 | $ 585 | ($ 290) | $ 660 | ($ 35) | $ 545 | $ 885 | $ 1,035 | $ 1,190 | $ 1,365 |
| | **Capital** | | | | | | | | | | |
| 10 | Net Accounts Receivable | $ 2,655 | $ 3,775 | $ 3,075 | $ 3,525 | $ 3,010 | $ 3,660 | $ 6,288 | $ 4,220 | $ 4,530 | $ 4,865 |
| 11 | Inventory | 2,830 | 3,420 | 4,115 | 3,205 | 3,105 | 3,365 | 3,560 | 3,815 | 4,085 | 4,380 |
| 12 | PP&E | 545 | 965 | 815 | 515 | 360 | 950 | 1,160 | 1,370 | 1,580 | 1,790 |
| 13 | Other Assets | 535 | 355 | 335 | 835 | 850 | 675 | 770 | 805 | 805 | 810 |
| 14 | − NIBCL's[a] | (4,295) | (4,845) | (4,095) | (3,250) | (4,045) | (3,295) | (3,520) | (3,805) | (4,110) | (4,440) |
| 15 | Capital | $ 2,270 | $ 3,675 | $ 4,250 | $ 4,825 | $ 3,280 | $ 5,355 | $ 5,900 | $ 6,405 | $ 6,890 | $ 7,400 |
| | **Operating Analysis** | | | | | | | | | | |
| 16 | NOPAT/Avg Cap (r) | 7.8% | 19.7% | (7.3%) | 14.5% | (0.9%) | 12.6% | 15.7% | 16.8% | 17.9% | 19.1% |
| 17 | − Cost of Capital (c*) | 13.4% | 13.4% | 13.4% | 13.4% | 13.4% | 13.5% | 13.5% | 13.5% | 13.5% | 13.5% |
| 18 | Spread (r − c*) | (5.6%) | 6.3% | (20.7%) | 1.1% | (14.3%) | (1.0%) | 2.2% | 3.3% | 4.4% | 5.5% |
| 19 | × Average Capital | $ 2,155 | $ 2,970 | $ 3,960 | $ 4,535 | $ 4,055 | $ 4,315 | $ 5,625 | $ 6,150 | $ 6,645 | $ 7,145 |
| 20 | Eonomic Value Added | ($ 120) | $ 185 | ($ 820) | $ 50 | ($ 580) | ($ 40) | $ 125 | $ 205 | $ 290 | $ 395 |

**EXHIBIT 16**  Hospitality Equipment Service Co.

## INPUT TABLE

| LINE # | | 1993 | 1994 | 1995 | 1996 | 1997 |
|---|---|---|---|---|---|---|
| | Bonus Pool Characteristics | | | | | |
| 1 | Target Bonus | 42% | 42% | 42% | 42% | 42% |
| 2 | Base Salary (000) | $ 705 | $740 | $775 | $815 | $855 |
| 3 | # of Units (000) | 300 | 315 | 330 | 345 | 365 |
| | Bonus Calculation Framework | | | | | |
| 4 | Baseline EVA (000) | ($ 310) | | | | |
| 5 | Annual Target Adjustment Factor | 50% | | | | |
| 6 | Base Unit Value | $ 0.25 | $0.25 | $0.25 | $0.25 | $0.25 |
| | EVA Bonus Sensitivity Factor | | | | | |
| 7 | = EVA Bonus Sensitivity Factor (000) | $ 500 | | | | |

## CURRENT BONUS CALCULATION

| LINE # | | 1993 | 1994 | 1995 | 1996 | 1997 | AVERAGE |
|---|---|---|---|---|---|---|---|
| | Performance Unit Value | | | | | | |
| 8 | EVA (000) | ($  40) | $ 125 | $ 205 | $ 290 | $ 395 | $ 195 |
| 9 | − Baseline EVA (000) | ($ 310) | ($ 175) | ($  25) | $  90 | $ 190 | ($  45) |
| 10 | = EVA vs Baseline EVA (000) | $ 270 | $ 300 | $ 230 | $ 200 | $ 205 | $ 240 |
| 11 | / EVA Bonus Sensitivity Factor (000) | $ 500 | $ 500 | $ 500 | $ 500 | $ 500 | $ 500 |
| 12 | = Performance Unit Value | $0.54 | $0.60 | $0.46 | $0.40 | $0.41 | $0.48 |
| | Total Unit Value | | | | | | |
| 13 | Performance Unit Value | $0.54 | $0.60 | $0.46 | $0.40 | $0.41 | $0.48 |
| 14 | + Base Unit Value | $0.25 | $0.25 | $0.25 | $0.25 | $0.25 | $0.25 |
| 15 | = Total Unit Value | $0.79 | $0.85 | $0.71 | $0.65 | $0.66 | $0.73 |
| | Current Bonus | | | | | | |
| 16 | Total Unit Value | $0.79 | $0.85 | $0.71 | $0.65 | $0.66 | $0.73 |
| 16 | # of Units (000) | 300 | 315 | 330 | 345 | 365 | 330 |
| 18 | Current Bonus Earned (000) | $ 235 | $ 265 | $ 235 | $ 225 | $ 240 | $ 240 |

## PAST BONUS IF SYSTEM HAD BEEN IN PLACE PRIOR 5 YEARS

| LINE # | | 1988 | 1989 | 1990 | 1991 | 1992 | AVERAGE |
|---|---|---|---|---|---|---|---|
| | Current Bonus | | | | | | |
| 19 | Total Unit Value | $0.71 | $1.10 | ($1.34) | $1.20 | ($0.54) | $0.22 |
| 20 | # of Units (000) | 285 | 525 | 315 | 335 | 255 | 345 |
| 21 | Current Bonus Earned (000) | $ 205 | $ 575 | ($ 425) | $ 405 | ($ 140) | $ 125 |

| | % OF TARGET BONUS EARNED | |
|---|---|---|
| | HOTEL TELECOM | HOSPITALITY EQUIPMENT |
| 1993 | 45% | 79% |
| 1994 | 99 | 85 |
| 1995 | 69 | 71 |
| 1996 | 66 | 65 |
| 1997 | 62 | 66 |

According to Bennett Stewart, the beauty of the EVA incentive compensation system was that it was "A self-motivated, self-adjusting corporate governance system that linked capital budgeting and strategic investment decisions to the compensation system."

From John Duckworth's perspective, not only were the interests of management and shareholders aligned, but in addition the bogeys for determining bonus compensation would not have to be renegotiated each year. What had been two plans (one annual plan and a long-term plan) could be combined into *one* plan that paid on annual results but was designed to build long-term shareholder value. The system was like a self-winding watch. You set it once and it might keep going, all by itself, for quite some time.

# 14

# Formal Models in Budgeting and Incentive Contracts

## ISSUES AND TERMS IN FORMAL INCENTIVE MODELS
### Wealth, Leisure, and Risk Attitudes

In Chapter 13, we explored the types of incentive contracts used by organizations. Building on this institutional base, contemporary research in organizational economics, finance, and accounting has developed theoretical insights about how contracts can be constructed to motivate managers to act in the best interests of the company's owners. The research consists of formal economic and mathematical models of the behavior of individuals. The research models the relationship between the owners, or principals, and their managers, or agents. Both principals and agents are assumed to be rational economic-maximizing individuals. They pursue their specified individual objectives within the organizational setting and the terms of the contractual relationship. Specifically, owners are interested solely in the expected monetary return that will be generated from their investments in the firm, and managers value both their **wealth** and their **leisure**.

The analysis assumes that managers prefer more wealth to less but that the marginal utility, or satisfaction, of wealth decreases as more wealth is accumulated. Therefore, managers display **risk aversion**, which leads them to value the outcomes from a risky investment as less than its expected, or actuarial, value. Owners, however, are assumed to be **risk-neutral**: They value investments at their expected value.

For example, consider a large company, with shares widely dispersed among individual shareholders, who are also well diversified through investments in many other companies. We would expect that the individual shareholder would evaluate investments on an expected-value (i.e., risk-neutral) basis. Individual managers, however, responsible for making large risky investments, would be concerned about how negative outcomes would affect their compensation or opportunities for advancement. Because managers cannot diversify away from the consequences of bad outcomes, they are risk-averse and may turn down risky projects that have positive expected values. The difference in risk attitude between managers and owners creates one source of conflict between the two groups.

Managers are also assumed to value their leisure. *Leisure* is defined as the opposite of the effort that managers put into the firm. That is, managers who work hard sacrifice leisure in return for increasing the value of the firm. Leisure is a generic concept that also includes the manager's consumption of perquisites or benefits. Examples of perquisites are company cars, lavish offices, first-class travel, and other nonmonetary benefits. Such perquisites divert the owners' capital away from productive investments in the firm and into the managers' consumption. Leisure could also represent time spent by senior managers on prestigious or personally remunerative external activities, such as boards of directors and trusteeships, that provide them with visibility and status but little in direct return to their companies.

Thus, owners hire managers (buy the managers' time) and also supply capital to the firm. Managers split their time between leisure and productive time and deploy the owners' capital between productive investments and personal perquisites. The agency literature attempts to design incentives for managers to mitigate excess consumption of leisure and perquisites.

Note that we are not speaking of illegal theft as monitored by law-enforcement agents or auditors. We are concerned with a more subtle theft, of time (the manager does not work when or as hard as he is supposed to) and capital (the manager spends more money than necessary to accomplish assigned managerial tasks).

## Individual Honesty and the Role of Contract Monitoring

Many readers of this agency paradigm comment, "The agency literature involves fraud and theft. I believe that most people are honest. Therefore, the agency literature is cynical and irrelevant." But extensive evidence exists of efforts in the world around us to monitor behavior and provide disincentives for engaging in effort diversion and time theft.

A second common observation is: "Even if I grant that some people will shirk their assigned duties or will spend more money than they should on their personal consumption, I can always observe and discipline this behavior." **Monitoring** involves observing people to determine whether they have lived up to the provisions of a contract. If the job is well defined, monitoring is fairly easy. We can simply measure outputs. Like Frederick Taylor, we can assess the performance of a manual task by measuring the amount of work done or the amount of output created. However, if the job is more complicated, measuring output may not be realistic because of the possibility of many intervening variables between input and output.

For example, suppose we decided to assess the performance of a neurosurgeon by observing the patient six months after the operation. Consider the problems with a rule that assesses the neurosurgeon as having done a bad job if the patient dies or has suffered a disability as the result of the operation. For example, the outcome—patient disabled—could have occurred because the patient's condition was very poor before the surgeon's intervention and it was only the surgeon's great skill that prevented death, or the unhappy outcome could have occurred because of a patient condition that was not serious, coupled with an incompetent surgeon. The intervening variable—the unobserved state of the environment (the patient's condition)—makes it difficult to infer inputs (the neurosurgeon's skill, effort, and care put into the procedure) from outputs (the patient's condition after the operation). Therefore, we have an outcome that is jointly determined by the manager (the surgeon) and the environment (the patient's condition at the time of the operation). Any given outcome can result from different combinations of the environment and the manager's skill and effort.

In general, inputs are related to the amount of effort and the quality of effort or skill. The agency literature has focused on the first aspect, namely, checking up on the withholding of effort. This withholding is called **shirking**. Measurement, or monitoring, of inputs is introduced to verify that the conditions of the contract have been met: The manager has delivered the required amount of time and has not shirked.

It seems reasonable to conclude that the lack of time clocks for managers implies that shirking, at least overt shirking related to staying away from work, cannot be the crucial issue in manager-owner conflicts. The shirking, however, may be more subtle. Recall from the discussion in Chapter 7 that we create decentralized organizations to allow managers the opportunity to specialize in terms of both action (the skill component) and information. Developing the market and technological information to accomplish these tasks successfully may require managers to leave their comfortable offices (and homes) to travel to diverse operating sites and to spend considerable amounts of their time in settings where they can accumulate relevant market, technological, and competitive information. In this case, shirking would involve not investing sufficient time and energy to develop the information required to be successful in the job and being prepared with an alibi if bad outcomes occur: "I did my best. This bad outcome resulted from events beyond my control."

## Choosing the Right Manager and the Role of Information

Owners must be concerned with managers' skills. The difficulty of selecting managers with the appropriate skills for a required task is called the **adverse selection** problem. When a managerial contract is offered, it will appeal only to managers who have opportunities that are equal to or lower than the skill levels and compensation level envisioned in the contract of employment. Therefore, unless carefully designed, the contract will encourage people who are not qualified for the position to apply for the job. Moreover, once selected and installed in jobs, incumbent managers may not invest enough to keep their skills up to the level required for satisfactory job performance.

Because of the differences in information and skills between the owners and the manager, the owners can never be certain about how managerial effort and skill contributed to actual outcomes. This information difference, or **information asymmetry**, brought about by differences in skills, specialization, and the limited ability of owners to monitor the amount and quality of the manager's inputs, creates problems in contracting between owners and managers. The information asymmetry prevents the imposition of the obvious contract: namely, to pay the manager a salary and to verify that the manager's inputs were as specified in the contract of employment. The principal paying a salary under conditions in which the agent's input cannot be verified creates a situation, called **moral hazard**, wherein the manager is motivated to renege on the contractual terms. *Moral hazard* is a general term that was first used in the medical insurance literature to describe a situation in which the provisions of a contract may motivate someone to act in a way that is prejudicial or unintended by the contract.[1]

Information asymmetry presents additional problems because the best information available for planning and control is in the hands of the controlled (the managers) and not in the hands of the controller (the owners). Moreover, managers are not motivated to disclose their private information for fear that it might be used against them. Managers' reluctance to disclose their specialized local information is called **information impactedness** and has led to interest in designing innovative schemes to encourage managers to reveal what they actually believe or know.

When inputs (managerial effort and ability) cannot be measured, the only variable available for constructing an incentive contract is the output: the consequences of managers' decisions, efforts, and skills. But a contract that provides rewards based on outputs imposes undesirable risk on the manager. Managers invest effort (for which they have disutility, relative to leisure, by assumption) to improve the firm's return. The managers' efforts combine with factors outside the managers' control to determine the actual outcome. One can think of the manager's effort affecting the mean of the distribution that will generate the actual result, but not the actual realization from this distribution. A manager may think, "Wait a minute here. I might work hard (by sacrificing leisure) and then have all my hard work wiped out by something beyond my control like a general downturn in the economy or industry."

Therefore, managers face a gamble, or risk, when deciding whether to invest some of their leisure for a chance at increased outcomes (or, for that matter, by sacrificing perquisites for income-generating investments). In making this tradeoff, managers will prefer a different allocation of effort or perquisite consumption than risk-neutral owners would select. The owners, because of their risk neutrality, should absorb all the risk in the firm. But by rewarding managers on the basis of actual outcomes, owners end up imposing risk on risk-averse managers because the owners do not have the same information available to them as the managers. The contract is inefficient, because owners, willing to bear risk without cost, must provide additional compensation to managers to bear risk because of the owners' inability to observe the managers' information, actions, and abilities.

## Balancing Incentive and Return Considerations

In designing an optimal incentive contract for the manager, we must make compromises between the desirability of having the owner bear all the risk in the firm and the necessity of imposing risk on the manager to minimize shirking and overconsumption of perquisites. For this reason, contracts requiring managers to bear risk are called **second-best** solutions to the incentive contracting, or motivation, problem. These contracts are second best because an economic loss is created by the owners' inability to monitor inputs; therefore owners cannot verify that managers have lived up to the terms of the employment contract and pay them with a fixed (nonrisky) wage.

Any output (such as profit or product quality or customer satisfaction) that we can observe and that is correlated *in any way* with managerial effort can provide a useful basis for structuring incentives. Moreover, the more closely the outcome measure reflects (that is, is correlated with) the input of the manager, the more valuable the measure is in an incentive contract.[2] This, of course, is the reason for tying executive compensation to stock options or for providing rewards based on reported profit.

Many variations have been created from this basic theme in the agency literature. First, to control for the adverse selection problem in hiring, we try to structure contracts that weed out people who are not qualified. As one example, research suggests offering salespeople contracts that provide high rewards for high sales achievement and low or no rewards for selling nothing. Such a contract would attract people who know (or believe) that they have strong selling skills and would help to eliminate unqualified applicants for a selling job. But by tying compensation solely to sales results achieved, we impose risk, created by factors beyond selling effort and ability, on the salesperson. Therefore, we have to offer a higher expected-cost contract to compensate the salesperson for absorbing this risk. Thus, we overcome the adverse selection problem but at the expense of having to offer additional expected compensation.

To avoid the imposition of risk on the manager, we might determine whether the outcome provides any indication of the manager's input. If the manager's input can be inferred exactly from the output, then a simple wage/penalty scheme can be used. For example, suppose that when a purchasing manager does not perform effectively one time in 100 poor-quality materials will be purchased. Moreover, the poor-quality materials can be purchased only when the purchasing manager is not doing the contracted job. The employment contract in this case is simple: The wage is paid unless poor-quality materials are purchased. If poor-quality materials are purchased, the manager is penalized, perhaps fired. If the penalty is large enough and can be enforced, shirking can be eliminated entirely.

These are the broad insights that have emerged from the agency literature. The theory attempts to explain or predict contracts observed in practice, but we must be cautious in interpreting the results literally. The conclusions have been derived from models with restrictive and perhaps unrealistic assumptions. The literature's main contribution has been to provide us with a framework for thinking about incentive contracts and to point out relevant issues on risk sharing and observability that we might be less sensitive to without the formal analysis.

## PROBLEMS OF OBTAINING INFORMATION FOR STANDARDS AND BUDGETS

Standards and budgets occupy a prominent place in the literature of cost accounting, management control, and organization theory. Standard-setting and budgeting activities are so pervasive in management teaching and practice that we tend to accept them without considering the fundamental forces that make these activities desirable. In an ideal world of certainty, costless information, and observability, and unbounded computational capacity, a central decision maker can make globally optimal decisions and can direct subordinates (local managers) to implement centrally determined plans. In this setting, there would seem to be little role for budgets.

In the real world, however, local managers are given considerable decision-making authority. Profit-sharing incentive contracts may be instituted to motivate the managers to make decisions that are in the firm's best interests, as described above and in Chapter 13. But, as we have seen, simple profit-sharing contracts introduce uncertainty into the managers' compensation functions, and managers may take actions (such as lowering output levels) to compensate for this uncertainty. Such risk-avoiding behavior is not generally desirable for the firm as a whole or for its shareholders. We must attempt to design the most efficient contracts to balance the conflicts between managers and owners.

## Using Information for Rewards and Control—The Moral Hazard Problem

Conflicts can arise in even simple situations. Consider a salesperson who is asked by the sales manager to provide an estimate of expected sales in the upcoming period. The sales manager will use the estimate to plan production and marketing efforts and as the basis for the compensation plan. More specifically, the salesperson is paid a base salary and a commission on sales in excess of a target amount. The sales manager will use the estimate of sales potential to set the target level of sales that the salesperson must attain before commissions are paid. In this situation, almost all salespersons tend to understate the assessed sales potential. The problem is not limited to sales. A production manager may understate the potential output from an assembly line so that, if something goes wrong, she will still have a good chance of attaining the production quota.

The misrepresentation of private information occurs because of two critical conditions: (1) The subordinate has information, by virtue of specialization, that the superior requires for planning purposes; and (2) the information is used both for planning and for control purposes. These problems are another example of the moral hazard problem; in this case, the manager (or subordinate) is motivated by the structure of the control or evaluation system to misrepresent private information.[3] The condition for this moral hazard situation arises whenever the manager's information or actions are not directly observable by the manager's superiors.

Moral hazard is not necessarily the consequence of a poorly designed control system. In fact, because of the specialization sought by decentralization, and the need for specialist information in control, moral hazard is almost guaranteed in a decentralized firm that attempts to assess individual contributions to the firm.

## Moral Hazard and Information Impactedness

The existence of moral hazard creates the information impactedness situation, described earlier, whenever available, valuable information does not flow as required in the firm. As another example of information impactedness, consider a situation in which a manager knows that she has made a bad decision but refuses to correct the situation because doing so would make the bad decision obvious to all. On the other hand, leaving the existing decision unchanged may cause damage to the firm but not harm the manager's reputation (or compensation), because no one else will recognize that a bad decision has been made.

Information impactedness arises when local managers possess valuable, perhaps unique, information about their local environment but do not convey it truthfully. We are not suggesting that managers are evil or indifferent to the overall performance of the firm. We are suggesting that when managers are evaluated and promoted on the basis of comparisons of their performance with a standard, we should not expect managers to act contrary to their own self-interest when asked to provide information on the appropriate level of the standard. Their self-interest may cause them to strategically manipulate their information and intentions. Because of inherent uncertainty and the costliness of observation, owners will rarely be able to detect whether an unexpected outcome was due to prior misrepresentation of information or an unusually good or bad outcome.

Information impactedness problems can be mitigated by basing rewards on companywide rather than individual performance. In this way, managers have more motivation to share information and cooperate. But, when managerial rewards are based on overall rather than individual performance, managers will not capture the full gains from their individual efforts, information acquisition, and decision making. As a consequence, they will reduce their efforts along those dimensions—the practice of free-riding described in Chapter 13. Many firms base rewards on individual performance. Apparently, the motivational benefits provided by measuring and rewarding individual behavior outweigh the potential costs of information impactedness and risk-avoiding behavior.

## THE AGENCY MODEL

To bring this discussion into focus consider the following example that illustrates the problem of choosing an incentive compensation plan that the owner (or principal) will find superior to a pure wage contract.

### The Setting

Suppose that the principal, who is risk-neutral, is dealing with an agent who is risk-averse and whose utility for wealth can be modeled by the negative exponential utility function with risk aversion parameter $r = -0.0001$. That is, this manager's utility[4] for wealth ($w$) can be written

$$U[w] = -\exp^{rw}$$

Both the principal and the agent agree that the prospects facing the firm depend jointly on the actions taken by the agent (the act which can be high or low) and an event (the state of nature, which can be favorable or unfavorable) that is outside the agent's control.

When the agent's effort is high (which we will denote as $H$) he devotes considerable time and effort to develop information and skills and refrains from excess consumption of perquisites that would reduce the organization's asset base and its earnings power. Effort level low (which we will denote as $L$) occurs when the agent puts less work into the firm while consuming more perquisites.[5]

The agent can earn a wage of $10,000 working outside the firm. We will call this wage $m$, the market wage. Moreover, the agent experiences a personal cost, which is expressed in dollar terms as $15,000, for providing a high level of effort (which we will denote as $ch$) and $5,000 for providing a low level of effort (which we will denote as $cl$).[6] The manager suffers no psychic cost from contracting with the principal to provide one level of effort and then providing another (i.e. lying).

An unfavorable state means that the general conditions facing the firm are adverse; in the unfavorable state, a given action by the agent produces a lower financial return to the organization than in the favorable state.

There are two possible results from the agent's actions and the random state of nature: a return of $50,000 (called the high outcome) or a return of $20,000 (called the low outcome). The following are the probabilities of the high and low outcomes given the underlying agent effort level.

| LEVEL OF EFFORT | HIGH OUTCOME | LOW OUTCOME |
| --- | --- | --- |
| High | 0.9 | 0.1 |
| Low | 0.2 | 0.8 |

The agent's activities and the state of nature are such that they are unobservable, or observable only at a prohibitive cost, to the principal. Therefore, faced with any outcome, high or low, the principal is unable to know which effort level the agent provided.

## The Motivational Problem: Why a Flat Wage Will Not Do

In terms of the discussion preceding this section we have the conditions that create the problem of moral hazard. The principal has no way of enforcing a flat wage contract of $25,000 ($10,000 for the opportunity cost and $15,000 for the high level of effort), for a high level of effort that will be paid whatever outcome occurs. The agent will sign this contract and then renege by providing a low level of effort. The agent's reward or utility from this contract will be

$$\text{Utility} = -\exp^{-0.0001*(25000-5000)} = -0.135$$

which is higher than the utility of $-0.368$ corresponding to the market wage of $10,000. This is the gain from shirking. The principal's expected return from this contract will be

$$\text{Expected return} = (0.2 * 50,000) + (0.8 * 20,000) - 25,000 = 1,000$$

## The Principal's Problem: How to Tie Reward to Performance

The principal wants to see if she can increase her expected reward by tying the agent's reward to the outcome. The principal's problem is to find the lowest-cost pay for performance scheme that motivates the agent to provide the level of effort that the principal thinks best benefits the firm.[7]

The compensation package the principal offers the agent must reflect two constraints. First, compensation package must provide a return that is no less than what the agent can earn outside the firm. This is called the **individual rationality** (IR) condition or constraint. Second, the compensation package must provide the agent with a return from providing the desired level of effort that is no less than the expected return from a lower level of effort. This is called the **incentive compatibility** (IC) condition or constraint.

If it is in the principal's best interests to contract for the lowest level of effort, the problem is trivial. In that case, the principal will pay the agent a flat wage of $15,000, and the agent will supply low level of effort. The agent is not motivated to provide more than what is contracted. The more interesting problem is when the principal's best interests require contracting for the high level of agent effort.[8]

In this case, the principal wants to minimize the expected compensation paid to the agent subject to giving the agent a compensation package that at least matches the outside opportunities (*IR*) and that motivates the agent to deliver the high rather than the low level of effort (*IC*).

If we write *rh* as the compensation paid to the agent if the outcome is high, and *rl* as the compensation paid to the agent if the outcome is low, we can write the principal's problem as follows:

$$\text{Minimize } (0.90 * rh) + (0.10 * rl)$$
$$\text{Subject to: EU}[w|H] \geq \text{EU}[w|L] \qquad IC$$
$$\text{EU}[w|H] \geq \text{EU}[m] \qquad IR$$

where

1. EU[$w|H$] is the agent's expected utility under the compensation package of providing the high level of effort. In this case EU[$w|H$] equals $(0.9 * [ -\exp^{r(rh-ch)}]) + (0.1 * [-\exp^{r(rl-ch)}])$

2. EU[$w|L$] is the agent's expected utility under the compensation package of providing the low level of effort. In this case EU[$w|L$] equals $(0.2* [-\exp^{(rh-cl)}]) + (0.8 * [-\exp^{r(rl-cl)}])$

3. EU[$m$] is the agent's expected utility of the market wage. In this case, EU[$w$] equals $-\exp^{rw}$

Recall that we are designing a compensation package that guarantees that the agent will supply a high level of effort, so we use the outcome probabilities associated with the effort level's being high.

We can solve[9] this problem to find that the optimal solution is $rh$ = \$27,816.59 and $rl$ = \$13,339.76. Note that the principal's expected return is

$$\text{Expected return} = [0.9 * (50,000 - 27,816.59)] + [0.1 * (20,000 - 13,339.76)] = \$20,631$$

That is considerably higher than the \$1,000 return expected under the flat wage contract. Moreover, we can verify that the expected utility provided by this compensation package exactly equals the utility of the market wage and is such that the agent's utility of providing the high level of effort equals that of providing the low level of effort, and we invoke the assumption that the agent, when indifferent, will choose not to shirk.[10]

Note that the expected compensation given this solution is \$26,368.91 ([0.9 * 27,816.59] + [0.1 * \$13,339.76]). The difference of \$1,368.91 between \$25,000 and \$26,368.91 is the risk premium that the principal must pay the agent to bear the risk imposed on the agent to provide for incentive compatibility. The risk premium plus the \$15,000 the principal must pay the agent to provide the high level of effort is the total agency cost.

As the agent's risk aversion falls (that is, goes to zero), the risk premium falls as the agent's expected compensation converges on \$25,000, as shown in Exhibit 14-1.

The expected return from the organization before the agent's compensation is \$47,000 ([0.9 * 50,000] + [0.1 * 20000]). If the agent were risk-neutral, the optimal solution would be for the agent to rent the organization from the principal for \$22,000 and bear all the organization's risk.

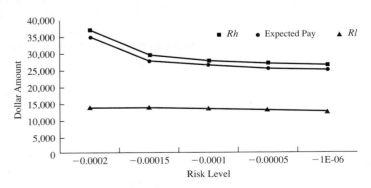

**EXHIBIT 14-1  The Effect of Risk**

## ELICITING HONEST REVELATION OF PRIVATELY HELD BELIEFS

Organizations decentralize to allow managers to develop specialist information. When planners want information to develop companywide plans, they face the problem of eliciting this information since it is often used for both planning and control purposes. That is, the information is often simultaneously used in planning and also to evaluate the manager's subsequent performance.

The central planners of the Soviet Union devised and apparently implemented a system of bonuses that rewarded both accurate forecasts and outstanding performance.[11] Independently and outside the Soviet Union, an essentially identical scheme was advocated for eliciting accurate forecasts in a sales organization and for a budget-forecasting system.[12] The scheme provided penalties for managers who set output targets so low that the budget was easily achieved. Also, it provided an incentive for managers, after achieving the budgeted performance, to put out even more effort to exceed the budget. The scheme motivated people to disclose their information truthfully in the process of target setting and then, once the target was set, to work to achieve or better the target.

With the forecast incentive scheme, the top management establishes a basic bonus pool, $B_0$, and specifies three positive parameters: $\alpha$, $\beta$, and $\gamma$. The manager first declares a targeted or budgeted output level $y_h$, which increases the bonus pool by the amount of $\beta y_h$. This factor provides the manager with an incentive to declare a higher, rather than a lower, budgeted output level. If the actual output level, $y$, exceeds the budgeted level, $y_h$, an additional bonus of $\alpha(y - y_h)$ is paid. This bonus component motivates the manager to exceed budgeted performance after the budgeted target has been established. But $\alpha$ is set less than $\beta$, so that if output is going to be high, it is better to declare this fact in the budget than to realize it by exceeding the budget. If the actual output level, $y$, is less than budget, a penalty of $\gamma(y_h - y)$ is subtracted from the bonus. In this case, $\gamma$ is set larger than $\beta$, so that the manager receives no benefit from inflating the budget, only to be disappointed later. In summary, the incentive properties of this mechanism require that $0 < \alpha < \beta < \gamma$.

Formally, if $B$ is the actual bonus paid to the manager, the plan can be described by

$$B = \begin{cases} B_0 + \beta y_h + \alpha(y - y_h) \text{ if } y \geq y_h \\ B_0 + \beta y_h - \gamma(y_h - y) \text{ if } y < y_h \end{cases} \tag{1}$$

with $0 < \alpha < \beta < \gamma$. As an example of how this incentive scheme operates, Exhibit 14-2 displays the bonus, $B$, as a function of $y_h$ and $y$ when $B_0 = 100$, $\alpha = 0.2$, $\beta = 0.4$, and $\gamma = 0.6$.

For any given value of actual output, $y$, in Exhibit 14-2 (reading along a row), the highest bonus is achieved when the forecast $y_h$, equals $y$. That is, the largest bonuses appear along the main diagonal. If the manager knows for certain what the actual output will be, she can maximize her bonus by issuing a forecast equal to this actual amount. Any other forecast will decrease the bonus below the maximum achievable level. Looking down a column reveals that once a forecast $y_h$ is issued, the manager will always prefer more output to less output. Thus, there is an incentive for the manager to produce the maximum output regardless of the forecast. Also, the parameters have been established so

**EXHIBIT 14-2**  Truth-Inducing Budget-Based Contract

$$B = \begin{cases} 100 + 0.4\,y_h + 0.2(y - y_h) & \text{if } y \geq y_h \\ 100 + 0.4\,y_h - 0.6(y_h - y) & \text{if } y < y_h \end{cases}$$

| ACTUAL OUTPUT, $Y$ | 50 | 60 | 70 | 80 | 90 | 100 | 110 | 120 |
|---|---|---|---|---|---|---|---|---|
| 50 | 120 | 118 | 116 | 114 | 112 | 110 | 108 | 106 |
| 60 | 122 | 124 | 122 | 120 | 118 | 116 | 114 | 112 |
| 70 | 124 | 126 | 128 | 126 | 124 | 122 | 120 | 118 |
| 80 | 126 | 128 | 130 | 132 | 130 | 128 | 126 | 124 |
| 90 | 128 | 130 | 132 | 134 | 136 | 134 | 132 | 130 |
| 100 | 130 | 132 | 134 | 136 | 138 | 140 | 138 | 136 |
| 110 | 132 | 134 | 136 | 138 | 140 | 142 | 144 | 142 |
| 120 | 134 | 136 | 138 | 140 | 142 | 144 | 146 | 148 |

that not achieving the forecasted output is penalized more heavily than output in excess of the forecast is rewarded. Note also that, for any budgeted output, rewards are increasing in the actual output.

The key to obtaining all these desirable properties in the incentive scheme is to ensure that $0 < \alpha < \beta < \gamma$. Planners using this incentive device developed a rule of thumb that $\beta$ should be at least 30% larger than $\alpha$ and that $\gamma$ should be at least 30% larger than $\beta$.

## The Role of Uncertainty in Belief Elicitation Models

When we speak of exceeding the budget in this model, we introduce the prospect of uncertainty, which we have not formally developed. Uncertainty is important, because it introduces two dimensions that are not apparent in the certainty model: (1) the possibility of managerial risk aversion, which we will ignore for the moment, and (2) the need to further restrict the relationship among the model parameters. Note that this model really makes little sense without some form of uncertainty. If the controller knew that the manager knew, with certainty, what the result would be, the incentive scheme would simply be to penalize the manager heavily for not disclosing during the planning stage what turned out to have actually happened. Therefore, the certainty case is both trivial and unrealistic. Assume, therefore, that the manager does not know for sure what the outcome will be but does have beliefs about what will happen.

Using equation [1], and assuming that the manager can express her uncertainty about the outcome $y$ in terms of a cumulative probability distribution, $F(y)$, we can construct the manager's expected return problem as choosing the communicated target $y_h$ when the realized value of $y$ is not known for sure. We can show that the manager's expected return is maximized under this scheme when the target communicated has the following property:

$$F(y_h) = \frac{\beta - \alpha}{\gamma - \alpha} \qquad \qquad [2]$$

where the function F represents the cumulative distribution of the manager's assessed distribution for the outcome, $y$. Equation [2] states that the manager's target output is a function of the values of the parameters of the incentive model as well as her beliefs about the probabilistic nature of the outcome. If we want the mean of the manager's distribution of $y$ communicated as $y_h$, then the parameters of the model will be chosen so that

$$0.5 = \frac{\beta - \alpha}{\gamma - \alpha}$$

or

$$\gamma = 2\beta - \alpha \qquad [3]$$

This result imposes an additional constraint on the values of the model parameters.

To illustrate, return to the example in Exhibit 14-2 and assume that the manager believes that actual output can assume any value on the interval 50 to 120, with all outcomes equally likely. In this case, the manager believes that the mean of the distribution of outcome is 85. With $\alpha = 0.2$, $\beta = 0.4$, and $\gamma = 0.6$, as in the previous example, the budgeted output, or target $y_h$, that will be communicated by the manager should satisfy:

$$F(y_h) = \frac{\beta - \alpha}{\gamma - \alpha} = \frac{0.4 - 0.2}{0.6 - 0.2} = \frac{1}{2}$$

That is, the manager chooses a budget target $y_h$ with the property that the probability is one-half that the actual outcome will be less than, or equal to, the budget. In our numerical example, she will choose 85 as the budget [85 = 50 + 1/2 * (120 − 50)].

Suppose we use the Soviet rule of setting $\beta$ 30% larger than $\alpha$. Therefore, $\beta = 1.3\alpha$. Now using the $\gamma = 2\beta - \alpha$ rule, we have

$$\gamma = 2(1.3\alpha) - \alpha = 1.6\alpha$$

So, if we set $\alpha = 0.2$, we have $\beta = 1.3 * 0.2 = 0.26$ and $\gamma = 1.6 * 0.2 = 0.32$. Now,

$$F(y_h) = \frac{\beta - \alpha}{\gamma - \alpha} = \frac{0.26 - 0.20}{0.32 - 0.20} = \frac{1}{2}$$

and the value of $y_h$ that would be chosen is 85 [since 85 = 50 + 0.5 * (120 − 50)]. Note that the same incentive to communicate the mean has been achieved but with parameters that are much closer together.

In summary, the bonus forecasting incentive system given by equation [1] and illustrated in Exhibit 14-2 produces the desirable incentives of rewarding accurate forecasts and encouraging greater rather than lesser output. The parameters $\alpha$, $\beta$, and $\gamma$ can be set on the basis of the relative values of accurate forecasts, the benefits of output in excess of the forecast, and the costs of not achieving the forecasted output level.

## Limitations of the Truth-Inducing Budget Scheme

The forecasting incentive scheme provides an attractive but imperfect mechanism for eliciting realistic forecasts. It is a costly mechanism, since real resources (cash payments to managers) are being transferred based on a forecast, $y_h$, rather than on the basis of actual output, but it does serve to reward managers for both information skill or knowledge (the forecast) and for performance (the outcome). The cost of operating this scheme seems necessary and even desirable if resource allocation and coordination decisions are to be based on budgeted output levels.

We mentioned briefly the rule of thumb that Soviet planners have used to define the relative values of $\alpha$, $\beta$, and $\gamma$, but this discussion raises the issue of how planners should choose the absolute levels of $B_0$, $\alpha$, $\beta$, and $\gamma$, the components of the incentive scheme. Compensation experts appear to agree that a person's basic market wage should not be at risk. Therefore the fixed or certain part of the compensation should reflect the individual's market wage. The fixed part of the compensation equals the $B_0$ component and the portion of the $\beta y_h$ component. To illustrate, suppose that the planner or controller sets a target, $y_t$, based on past experience and revises the bonus scheme as follows.

$$B = \begin{Bmatrix} B_0 + \beta(y_h - y_t) + \alpha(y - y_h) \text{ if } y \geq y_h \\ B_0 + \beta(y_h - y_t) - \gamma(y_h - y) \text{ if } y < y_h \end{Bmatrix}$$

The motivational properties of this revised scheme are the same as those of the original. Therefore, specifying a target $y_t$ has the same effect as adjusting the fixed wage. That effect is to determine whether the overall compensation package is acceptable to the individual. However, it has no effect on the output or prediction levels.

The advantage of the revised scheme is that it sets a target, often called a *bogey*, that taxes away the portion of the bonus that reflects an average level of performance and bases the bonus on an above-average level of performance. Therefore, it would be desirable to set $\alpha$ at a level thought to encourage the additional level of effort that would cause performance to rise above the target or average level of performance. The values of $\beta$ and $\gamma$ would then follow using the 30% rule discussed earlier. Presumably this rule reflects the experience of the planners in determining the sharing rules that provide the appropriate motivation to work harder without giving away too much to the employee. The problem with this adjustment is that the planner, strictly speaking, must guess at the target level used to tax away the easy returns.

The scheme does have some other major limitations. First, multiperiod gaming effects exist that are not captured in the simple one-period incentive scheme. For example, the manager may believe that the fixed portion of compensation, or equivalently the target level of output, in the subsequent period will be a function of the budgeted and actual output levels in the current period. This ratchet effect is a well-known budgeting procedure, particularly in governmental organizations.[13] If the ratchet effect is a plausible assumption, the manager, when determining what the current forecast and actual output should be, will try to solve a multiperiod optimization problem based on expectations of how current forecasts and actual output will affect future bonus pools. If this occurs, the one-period properties described above (for example, optimal forecast equals expected output) will not be valid. To avoid these complications, the manager must be convinced that any current communication will not affect the setting of future standards or bonus pools or that the adjustments will occur so far into the future that when they are discounted they will effectively be ignored.

A second problem arises from risk aversion on the part of the manager in the presence of uncertainty, conditions not formally treated with our simple formulation. The piecewise linear-sharing rules, given by the compensation scheme in equation [1], will not yield the equation [2] result that we derived under conditions of risk neutrality. With risk aversion, the budget chosen by the manager will reflect, in addition to the parameters already discussed, the manager's attitude toward risk. In general, however, we would expect that if equation [3] were used to set the parameters of the incentive scheme, the risk-averse manager would set a target such that the probability exceeds 0.50 and that the target would be achieved.

More important is the third limitation: If real resources are to be transferred among divisions (or among firms in the economy) on the basis of the forecasts, an incentive still exists to misrepresent forecasts. When headquarters allocates resources to divisions on the basis of forecasts, divisions may be motivated to conceal certain production or profit opportunities.[14]

## Truth-Inducing Schemes for Resource Allocation Decisions

Some research has been carried out to devise truth-inducing incentive mechanisms when two or more divisions are competing for the firm's common scarce resources (such as capital and computing facilities). In this situation, a central planner acquires a resource centrally (the motivation may be economies of scale in management and operation of the resource or a desire to tightly control the resource) and then allocates the capacity to the individual managers each period. To undertake the resource allocation, the central planner relies on forecasts, provided by the division managers, of the return that they can earn from using the centrally supplied resource. In a system in which managers are rewarded based on divisional profitability and divisional profitability does not reflect the cost of the centrally held resources that they use, the managers are motivated to overstate the return that the resource can provide in order to obtain as much of the centrally controlled resource as possible. Therefore, the objective in designing an incentive plan is to find an alternative performance measure that will not provide an incentive to overstate the return from divisional use of the resource.

The Groves mechanism[15] to obtain truthful forecasts computes a performance measure for Division $i$ based on the actual realized profits in Division $i$ plus the forecasted profits of the other divisions at their actual allocated resource levels. We will not work through the proof, but it can be shown that if divisions attempt to maximize their Groves measures, then:

1. Each division will attempt to maximize its actual profits, since the Groves measure is strictly increasing in the division's profits.
2. Each division is best off sending an accurate forecast independent of what any other division sends or how it believes any other division is computing its forecast.
3. Each division's performance measure will be independent of the realized (actual) profits or operating efficiency of the other divisions.

Thus, this measure seems to have the desirable properties we would prefer to see in a performance measure. The Groves mechanism achieves its desirable properties by using a combination of realized division profits and a profit-sharing scheme based on expected corporate profits. The form of the incentive scheme is

$$\text{Reward} = a + k\,(Q + R)$$

where $a$ is any constant, which can be construed as a wage; $k$ is any constant (lying between 0 and 1), which can be construed as a profit share; $Q$ is the *expected* profit of all the other divisions in the firm (given the final allocation of the centrally held resource); and $R$ is the *realized* profit of the manager's division. Note that $Q + R$ equals the expected total corporate profits of all the divisions plus the variance of the manager's divisional profit. Therefore, we can write this reward function as

$$\text{Manager's reward} = \text{wage} +$$
$$k\,(\text{firm's total expected profits} + \text{variance in manager's division})$$

If the division reward were based solely on realized division profits ($R$), each division manager would be motivated to distort the communicated information about the value of allocating the common resources to himself. The manager treats the allocated resource as a free good and wants to have as much of its capacity as he can. Eliminating this tendency is the portion ($Q$) of the reward function relating to corporate profitability. This term forces the manager to consider all uses of the centrally held resource and, in effect, charges the manager with the opportunity cost of the resource (reflecting its use in other divisions) when the resource is allocated to the manager's division. This term ($Q$) represents the sum of the profit expectations of all the other divisions conditioned on an optimal centrally determined resource-allocation decision and the prior information of the central agent. Because the reward function for each division represents overall corporate profits, the incentive for divisional honesty in communicating its opportunity set dominates the incentive for false reporting, and all divisions report truthfully. Finally, no division need be concerned, ex post, about efficiency or forecasting variances in other divisions, since such variances are allocated solely to the responsible division.

An element of noncontrollability still remains, because the evaluation of a division depends on forecasts produced by other divisions. But this interdependency seems inevitable because of the divisional competition for the common resource. The noncontrollable aspect may even be desirable in this setting, since it highlights the interdependence among the operating divisions and, therefore, the need for the divisions to work together for their overall benefit.

Unfortunately, the Groves scheme is cumbersome to implement in practice because the parameters $a$ and $b$ of the Groves model must be specified before any type of communication takes place. Therefore, the resulting managerial compensation could be very large, insignificant, or even negative.[16]

A second shortcoming of the Groves scheme is the assumption that all managers are risk-neutral. If any of the managers is risk-averse or prefers leisure to working, the properties of the scheme are lost. For example, suppose a risk-neutral manager believes that another manager is highly risk-averse. Because of the nature of the manager's risk aversion, that manager will request lower amounts of the centrally held resource than if he had been risk-neutral. The risk-neutral manager in the second division, sensing this effect, will understate his opportunities to cause more of the centrally held resource to be allocated to the first division in order to correct for that manager's risk aversion. When this type of manipulation starts to happen, the desirable properties of the Groves mechanism vanish as each manager second-guesses the decisions and actions of all the other managers.

## THE ROLE OF INSURANCE

We have seen that uncertainty, in the form of noncontrollable random outcomes, makes it difficult to develop local performance measures for the managers of decentralized units. Uncertainty leads managers to engage in risk-avoiding behavior that may not be optimal for the overall firm. It also hinders contractual arrangements between units that interact with each other and leads to a demand for subjective information to develop budgets for performance appraisal.

A thoughtful reader may wonder whether some form of insurance contract might be developed to reduce the adverse effects of uncertainty. After all, on a personal level, we purchase insurance to limit the negative financial consequences from uncertain events such as death, illness, or accidents. Why cannot such arrangements be developed for commercial transactions within a firm? If local managers could purchase insurance to protect themselves (or their divisions) from the adverse consequences of uncertainty, deleterious risk-avoiding behavior could be eliminated.

Unfortunately, good reasons can be provided for why insurance against uncertain events is not readily available for local managers. Two factors introduced earlier in the chapter, moral hazard and adverse selection, make it difficult to offer reasonably priced insurance in this situation. Moral hazard creates the problem of distinguishing between genuine risks (such as adverse outcomes caused by exogenous random events) and failures to take the best action to avoid the event being insured against. Once the insured manager is protected from the negative consequences of events such as sales declines, delivery delays, or uncertain product quality, the manager's incentive to exert a maximum effort to overcome normal commercial difficulties is greatly reduced. We do not want the managers, because they are insured against these events, to accept such commercial difficulties passively. We want them to do whatever they can to reach their sales targets, expedite deliveries, or improve the quality of their products.

Moral hazard arises in personal insurance when people with automobile insurance drive less carefully or when people with full medical insurance coverage forego health-building activities or demand excessive amounts of medical care. Because of moral hazard, the insurer must insure not only against random factors causing losses but also against the expected reduction in effort to avoid the insured event by the insured.

Adverse selection problems also limit the role for insurance to reduce the consequences of uncertainty within the firm. In general, the insured knows its own risks better than the insurer. The insurer may set rates on an overall fair actuarial basis after observing many similar events. High-risk units will find it profitable to purchase this insurance, but low-risk units will find the insurance too expensive. The actual experience for the insurer will therefore have a higher incidence of claims than had been expected when rates were initially set. When rates are raised to reflect the higher-than-expected losses, more lower-risk units will withdraw from the insurance contract. Thus, because of the inequality of information between the insured and the insurer, many units will have risks that are inadequately covered. Both moral hazard and adverse selection are caused by limited observability (or as we have called it earlier, private or asymmetric information).

Limited observability will be characteristic of most activities within a firm, so insurance arrangements are unlikely to be developed to eliminate the unfavorable consequences of uncertainty. Devices such as flexible budgets and annual budgeted performance can be viewed as limited forms of insurance to shield managers from some uncontrollable factors, but a significant degree of uncertainty in evaluating managerial performance is unavoidable if incentives for excellent performance are to be part of the managers' compensation arrangement.

## SUMMARY

Many solutions have been proposed to determine optimal contracts between managers and their superiors in the presence of private (asymmetric) information and diverse risk attitudes. Agency theory attempts to design efficient and effective incentive schemes to motivate decentralized managers to act in the best interests of the owners. The optimal contracts under these conditions require that managers bear more risk, by sharing in the outcomes from their actions, than what would otherwise be required or desirable. Because risk-averse managers have to be compensated for the risk bearing that has been imposed on them for motivational purposes, the owners of the firm suffer economic losses. Moreover, because managers are put in situations in which they must bear risk, the managers may make decisions that reflect risk attitudes different from those of the owners and may be motivated to misrepresent the information they have about local markets, technologies, and opportunities.

Researchers have studied a number of incentive systems that have been developed in practice. The most interesting of these is the incentive system used in the former Soviet centrally controlled economy. The Groves mechanism represents an alternative approach to incentive contracting in a situation in which the decision makers control both the level of effort and the level of investment in their respective divisions.

In general, these incentive contracting devices focus on situations in which the manager, by virtue of skill and specialized knowledge, is best able to determine the appropriate course of action in the firm. The problem is that a manager may pursue a personal agenda when making decisions that clashes with the owners' objectives. This dichotomy is possible because the owners are unable to determine, because of the difficulty of auditing managerial actions and the impossibility of auditing managerial beliefs, whether the manager's decisions are in their best interests. The objective in incentive contracting is to choose an incentive contract that aligns the interests of the owner and managers.

## ENDNOTES

1. For example, in the medical insurance literature, researchers were concerned whether medical insurance would cause the insured to act more recklessly since risks of injury would now be covered.

2. Note that, in the limit, if the measure is perfectly correlated with the manager's input, we are back to imposing no risk on the manager because we can always infer the manager's input from the output.

3. In general, this literature assumes that people suffer no personal costs from guile or lying. Even if people do suffer personal costs from lying, the substantive results of this literature remain unchanged.

4. Those unfamiliar with the notion of utility can think of utility as an index of the desirability of a particular level of wealth. Exponential utility models an individual with constant aversion to risk where aversion to risk is the willingness to sell the rights to a gamble for less than its expected value. The difference between the monetary value of a gamble to the risk-averse person and the expected value is called the risk premium and is a function of the individual's aversion to risk. For negative exponential utility, the parameter $r$ captures all that is relevant about the person's risk attitude than is constant for all levels of wealth. Risk aversion falls as the value of $r$, the risk parameter, approaches zero.

5. A more realistic analysis would treat agent effort as a continuous variable. However, we have simplified the agent's action choices for the insight the resulting simplification provides without changing the basic nature of the results that follow.

6. That is to say, the agent values the loss of personal time, the mental stress of providing effort, and the value of perquisites foregone as $15,000 for providing the high level of effort relative to the outside employment opportunity.

7. Note that the principal may prefer the high level of effort, the low level of effort, or may prefer not to contract with the agent at all (that is, to liquidate the firm).

8. The reader can verify that for this problem the principal's best interests are served by contracting for the high level of agent effort, which is the contract we will discuss.

9. You can solve this problem using a nonlinear program. Alternatively, your instructor can provide you with an Excel worksheet (**amach14.xls**) provided by the authors that solves this problem using Excel's solver algorithm. This compensation package results in a net (after paying the agent) expected return to the principal of $20,631. Using the same approach, you can show that the principal's net expected return from contracting with the agent to supply a low level of effort is $14,627.

10. If you find this latter assumption disagreeable, add one cent to the agent's compensation in either outcome and the agent will strictly prefer to provide a high level of effort.

11. This system is described in M. L. Weitzman, "The New Soviet Incentive Model," *Bell Journal of Economics* (Spring 1976), pp. 251–57. Extensions to the basic model have been provided by V. Snowberger, "The New Soviet Incentive Model: Comment," *Bell Journal of Economics* (Autumn 1977), pp. 591–600; and M. L. Weitzman, "The 'Ratchet Principle' and Performance Incentives," *Bell Journal of Economics* (Spring 1980), pp. 302–08. Criticisms of the Soviet incentive system are presented in M. Loeb and W. A. Magat, "Soviet Success Indicators and the Evaluation of Divisional Management," *Journal of Accounting Research* (Spring 1978), pp. 1–28.

12. See J. Gonik, "Tie Salesmen's Bonuses to Their Forecasts," *Harvard Business Review* (May–June 1978); and Y. Ijiri, J. C. Kinary, and F. B. Putney, "An Integrated Evaluation System for Budget Forecasting and Operating Performance with a Classified Budgeting Bibliography," *Journal of Accounting Research* (Spring 1968), pp. 1–28.

13. See Weitzman, 'Ratchet Principle' and Performance Incentives."

14. See Loeb and Magat, "Soviet Success Indicators" and L. P. Jennergren, "On the Design of Incentives in Soviet Firms—A Survey of Some Research," *Management Science* (February 1980), pp. 193–97.

15. This class of performance measures was first formally described in T. Groves, "Incentives in Teams," *Econometrica* (July 1973), pp. 617–31. It is also featured in Loeb and Magat, "Soviet Success Indicators" and Groves and M. Loeb, "Incentives in a Divisionalized Firm," *Management Science* (March 1979), pp. 221–30.

16. The motivational properties of the Groves mechanism do not change if a constant is added to the basic model or if the basic equation is multiplied by a constant.

---

### ■ *PROBLEMS*

---

### 14-1 Effect of the Profit-Sharing Parameter on the Selection of a Risky Project

Many incentive contracts reward people with bonuses if performance exceeds a target level or bogey but do not penalize performance that falls below the target. That is, the incentive scheme is

$$\begin{cases} \text{Wage} + a*(\text{performance} - \text{target}) & \text{if performance} > \text{target} \\ \text{Wage} & \text{if performance} \leq \text{target} \end{cases}$$

where $a$ is number between 0 and 1.

#### Required

(1) What are the likely behavioral consequences of this type of reward system?
(2) What modifications would you make to this type of reward system, and why? Alternatively, why would you leave it as it is?

### 14-2 Design of the Optimal Incentive Contract When Employee Is Work-Averse

Helmut Paris, the owner of a small farming operation is pondering the current employment contract between himself and his sole employee, Gary Drumbo.

Gary operates a small farm owned by Helmut. The farm is located some distance from Helmut, who, therefore, has no opportunity to observe Gary's activities. The farm's total output, $X$, is a function of Gary's level of effort, $a$, and a combination of outside, uncertain events, $\theta$, such as sun, rain, and pests, over which Gary has no control.

Helmut and Gary have studied the production function and found that it has the form:

$$X = a + \theta$$

where $\theta$ is thought to take on values lying between zero and $b$.

Helmut makes decisions using the expected value decision-making criterion, whereas Gary is both risk- and effort-averse. That is, Gary suffers a personal cost when exerting effort.

This admission has prompted Helmut to offer Gary a share in output "to motivate Gary to provide higher effort." After some haggling, Gary has agreed to provide 100 units of effort in exchange for a salary of $1,000 and 10% of the farm's output, which will be accurately measured by a third party at the end of the growing season.

Although the matter has not been discussed, if Gary is caught supplying fewer than

100 units of *a* he will face immediate dismissal. Dismissal will result in irreparable damage to his reputation, thereby impairing future employment opportunities, so Gary will avoid putting himself in danger of dismissal at any cost.

### Required

(1) Do you think that this contract will achieve its intention of motivating "more effort" from Gary?

(2) Suppose that Gary and Helmut agree on a contract that pays $1,000 plus 10% of any output that is in excess of a target that is set equal to the average yield in surrounding farm properties. Would that condition change Gary's behavior?

(3) Ignore the variation in Requirement 2. What will happen if Gary is risk-neutral and effort-averse? Can you think of a better contract than the existing one?

(4) Ignore the variation in Requirement 2. How does the situation in the original contract change if *X* is of the form $X = a\theta$?

## 14-3    *Effect of Observability on the Form of an Employment Contract*

Fred Principal of Swissvale Investments is considering an investment in a farming venture in the country of Markovia.

The plan is to grow and harvest Gronk, a revolutionary natural food highly prized by distance runners for its sustenance attributes. The climatic conditions and soil of southwestern Markovia are unique and are the only known conditions under which Gronk can be produced.

Gronk-growing technology is well understood. Gronk production depends on weather conditions and the effort of the farmer in the growing season and hence is subject to uncertainty.

Markovia is a new and remote country that is virtually inaccessible to outsiders. Although Markovia has a well-established legal system, commercial development is backward.

Moral Hazard, a Markovian farmer and promoter, has invited Fred and other investors to invest in Gronk farming. Moral would farm the Gronk, sell the product, and distribute the proceeds to investors.

Fred, and all other potential investors, are risk-neutral. Moral is risk-averse.

### Required

(1) If no other information is available, what is Fred's best course of action regarding this opportunity?

(2) Suppose Fred discovers that Markovia has a well-established and reputable public accounting profession. How, if at all, would this information affect your response to Requirement 1?

(3) What further information, if any, might Fred seek beyond the information that a public accountant might supply?

## 14-4    *Incentives for Distorting Information*

HS Construction specializes in renovations and new home construction. For incentive purposes, the company is organized on a profit-center basis with two profit centers: the renovation division and the new home division.

The critical resource of the firm is its skilled carpenters. Because there is a shortage of carpenters, HS Construction has a policy of hiring all carpenters at the corporate level and then assigning carpenters to one of the two profit centers. The union rate for carpenters is $26.00 per hour, and, at this price, the managers of the two profit centers have a joint demand for carpenters that is far in excess of the available supply.

Given this situation, the company is faced with the problem of how to ration the available supply of carpenters. The operation of each of the profit centers is subject to some uncertainty, so ex ante managerial claims regarding carpenter productivity are difficult to evaluate ex post. Consequently, the controller is reluctant to base allocations on a priori assertions by the divisional managers.

In the renovation division, the return ($\pi_1$) received per carpenter hour ($q_1$) is

$$\pi_1 = 600 - 0.18q_1$$

In the new home construction division, the return is

$$\pi_2 = 300 - 0.07q_2$$

Suppose the controller successively announces prices the divisions will pay per carpenter hour and the division managers respond with demand at that price. The controller seeks to equate demand and the supply of carpenter hours which is 2,000. Divisions will be assessed a charge against profits equal to the amount bid for the labor used. All managers are risk-neutral.

### Required

(1)  Suppose both divisions respond honestly to the controller's price bids:
   (a)  How many carpenter hours will be allocated to each division?
   (b)  What price will clear this market?
   (c)  What will be the profit reported by each division?
(2)  Suppose the manager of the renovation division intends to respond honestly to the controller's bids. The manager of the new construction division knows this and also knows the renovation division's return function. Show that there is an incentive for the manager of the new construction division to be dishonest. (Hint: How would a manager behave to produce a transfer price of $0?)
(3)  Can you suggest a method for solving the problem raised in Requirement 2?
(4)  Under what circumstances will the solution proposed in Requirement 3 not have the desired motivational consequences?

## 14-5  Groves Mechanism: Applications and Limitations

For Susan Martin, President of Elmira Nursery, the crucial weekly operating decision is allocating the firm's 10 gardeners to the firm's two operating divisions, Commercial and Nursery. No other gardeners can be hired.

The Commercial division solicits contracts for landscaping and garden maintenance. It is widely known that its return is fixed and contracts reflect market conditions. Shawn Dempsey, the manager of this division, knows that this division can keep all 10 of the firm's ten gardeners fully occupied at a net profit to the firm of $50 per gardener hour.

The Nursery division consists of a greenhouse operation that grows plants and shrubs for the commercial market. Its return is uncertain and depends on volatile market conditions. Karen Barton, the manager of this division, believes that, in the current market, the distribution of net profit per gardener hour is uniform over the interval $40 to $55. This belief is held privately by Karen and is not known to the other members of the senior management team at Elmira Nursery.

### Required
### Consider each question separately.

(1) Suppose Karen's compensation is a function of the reported weekly profits of the Nursery division. Suppose further that Susan allocates gardeners to divisions based on the expected returns estimated by the division managers. If Karen is an expected-value decision maker, show that this organization structure will motivate Karen to lie about her division's expected return per gardener hour.

(2) Suppose now that Karen's compensation is a function of the reported weekly profits of Elmira Nursery. If Karen is an expected-value decision maker, is there any motivation for Karen to lie about her division's expected return per gardener hour? Explain the dysfunctional consequences of this reward mechanism if the divisional return can be influenced by managerial competence.

(3) Suppose Susan has decided to use the Groves mechanism to allocate the gardeners to the two divisions in her business. For Elmira Nursery, the Groves measure for the Nursery division would have the form

$$G_N = \pi_N^A(X_N) + \pi_C^F(X_c) - K_N$$

where $\pi_N^A(X_N)$ = actual weekly profits for the Nursery division, with $X_N$ gardeners allocated to this division

$\pi_C^F(X_C)$ = forecasted weekly profits for the Commercial division, with $X_C$ gardeners allocated to this division

$K_N$ = a constant independent of the Nursery division's forecasted or actual profits

How would use of the Groves measure improve the information elicited from Karen and Shawn?

(4) Suppose further that Susan wishes to make $G_N$ relevant to Karen by incorporating it into Karen's compensation function. Karen's compensation will be

$$y_E = W_E + kG_N$$

where $y_E$ = Karen's total compensation

$W_E$ = Karen's fixed wage

$K$ = a fixed positive constant

$G_N$ = the Groves measure for the Nursery division

Note that $EG_N$ represents, apart from the scalar $K_N$, *expected* corporate profits so that Karen's expected return is a wage plus a share of expected corporate profits. Assume that Karen could earn $550 per week in a comparable job outside the firm. Show that a compensation policy based on $y_E$ is unlikely to be optimal. Is $G_N$ a reasonable basis to use for compensating divisional managers?

(5) Return to the original data of this problem but assume now that the net profit per gardener in the Commercial division is only $47 per hour. Karen has the same beliefs as before but is risk-averse. Karen's utility for wealth, and therefore her compensation ($y_E$) is given by

$$U(y_E) = -\exp\left[\frac{-y_E}{500}\right]$$

where $y_E = \$500 + 0.1G_N$.

$K_N$ is set equal to the profit of the firm if the Nursery division received no gardeners; that is, $K_N = (\$47/\text{hour})(10 \text{ gardeners})(40 \text{ hours/week}) = 18,800$.

Suppose Susan is risk-neutral. What is the optimal allocation of gardeners from Susan's point of view? Show that Karen will lie about her beliefs in this case so that all gardeners will be allocated to the Commercial division. What are the implications of this result?

(6) Assume the same data as in Requirement 5 with the following exception. Karen's utility function is

$$U(y_E, X_N) = E(y_E) - 0.1X_N$$

where $X_N$ is the number of gardeners assigned to the Nursery division. In other words, Karen is risk-neutral but suffers a loss of well-being (or utility) when she is assigned workers to supervise.

Show that, in this case, Karen will lie about her prospects and all gardeners will be assigned to the Commercial division. What are the implications of this result?

## 14-6    *The Effect of a Skill Parameter in Formulating an Incentive Plan*

Outport Fishery Products is a large integrated fish-products company. The company operates its own fleet of fishing trawlers, whose catches are processed in one of the company's 11 processing plants. The final products are sold internationally under the company's brand name Bye-the-Sea.

Because of the demand for sea products and the limitations on the amount of fish that can be caught and processed, the company can sell as much fish as it can produce.

Many of the processing plants are located in depressed areas, and employment in the plants is highly valued. One of the most prestigious and skilled plant jobs is filleting, the process that separates the flesh of the fish from the bones. In filleting, the two fillets (one from each side) must be removed from the spine of the fish in whole pieces, because whole fillets command a large premium over broken pieces. Also, the cut separating the flesh from the bone should be deep enough that a minimal amount of flesh is left on the bone, yet shallow enough so that no bones remain in the fillet. Leaving flesh on the bone results in a loss of salable product. Leaving bones in the fillet requires indirect labor to remove the bones from the fillet. For this reason, the skill exercised in the filleting operation is a significant determinant of the value of the final product that is derived from a given catch (the others are the size of each fish and the species of fish). Skilled filleters are highly paid.

### Required

How would you evaluate the performance of the filleters, and how would you pay them?

### *14-7*   *Setting the Parameters of the Soviet Incentive System*

In the former Soviet Union a central planning authority controlled production in the manufacturing enterprises. In order to plan and coordinate aggregate production in the economy, the central planning authority requires forecasts from the enterprise managers about the production possibilities during the upcoming planning period. At first, managers were rewarded based on their ability to live up to production quotas that were, for the most part, based on the production forecasts of the managers themselves.

In response to evidence that enterprise managers built slack into forecasts of production possibilities, a new Soviet Incentive Plan was implemented. This plan provided a means of eliminating slack from forecasts by changing the basis of the rewards received by the enterprise managers.

The details of this plan were discussed in the chapter.

#### *Required*

(1) Explain why the ranking of the order of the three parameters of the Soviet Incentive model is important.

(2) What relationship must exist among the three parameters of the incentive equation of the Soviet Incentive model in order to motivate the manager to set a planned target that equals the manager's expectation of the mean value of production?

(3) In applying the scheme, the central planners committed to changing the parameters of the incentive plan only every five years. Why is this characteristic important, and how would the properties of the incentive scheme be changed if the parameters of the incentive scheme were changed annually? What implications does this observation have for target setting in participative budgeting schemes in general?

(4) Explain how the properties of the Soviet Incentive model would change if managers were risk-averse. (This question requires the use of differential calculus and a basic knowledge of the properties of utility theory.)

### *14-8*   *Incentive Considerations in Allocating a Scarce Resource*

The Brantford Corporation has 500 units of capacity available for production during the upcoming period. This capacity is to be distributed between the two major divisions in the company: the Commercial Controls Division and the Computer Division. Each division uses one unit of capacity to make one unit of output.

The managers of each division view the demand for the products of the two divisions. Only the division's manager knows the demand facing that division.

The contribution margin provided by each Commercial Controls Division product is $250,000, and the division manager believes that the total demand for the Commercial Controls Division products will be somewhere between 500 and 800 units, with each value on this interval equally likely.

The contribution margin provided by each Computer Division product is $320,000, and the division manager believes that the total demand for the Computer Division products will be somewhere between 0 and 500 units, with each value on this interval equally likely.

Because of production line setups and tooling, once the capacity is assigned to one division at the start of the production period, it cannot be transferred for the other division to use if the demand on the facility turns out to be less than the amount allocated. The managers of the two divisions have been asked to submit their requirements for use of the capacity during the upcoming period.

### *Required*

(1)   What level of capacity will each manager request if each manager's bonus is based solely on the manager's ability to meet the production plan for the allocated capacity? What is the expected contribution margin associated with this assignment of capacity?

(2)   What level of capacity will each manager request if each manager's bonus is based on the contribution margin generated by the capacity allocated to that manager's division and the managers are not assigned a charge for the capacity allocated to their respective divisions? What is the expected contribution margin associated with this assignment of capacity?

(3)   What level of capacity will each manager request if each manager's bonus is based on the contribution margin associated with the capacity that is earned by the company? What is the expected contribution margin associated with this assignment of capacity?

(4)   What do the results to Requirements 1, 2, and 3 imply about the design of incentive schemes in decentralized organizations? Why might these results be misleading?

## *14-9*     *The Revelation Principle in Budget Setting*

Kentville Orchards grows and sells a wide variety of fruits. Norm Wilson, the vice president-controller of Kentville Orchards, is responsible for all aspects of budgeting and forecasting in the firm. Norm has become both disillusioned and dissatisfied with the traditional approach that Kentville Orchards has taken to budgeting. Norm summarized his concerns as follows:

> The traditional approach, where we set budget objectives and then evaluate performance relative to those objectives, is not working well. First, the budget is focusing attention on the wrong things. The managers are interested in making short-run profit as large as possible and are not doing things to improve long-run profitability. Second, I do not think that the model of evaluating performance based on profits has the scope to evaluate the jobs that the managers are doing. Their jobs are much more complicated than a simple profit measure implies, and we need a more accurate picture of how well they are doing. Finally, the existing system is motivating the managers to build slack into both their standards and performance targets so that they can make budget and earn bonuses. As a result, our forecasting system is unable to predict either sales levels or input usage accurately.

Norm went on to indicate that he was considering recommending to the senior management committee at Kentville Orchards that the current budgeting system be replaced with a new system using participative budgeting techniques. Specifically, the new system would require that the objectives for each management job in the organization be defined relative to the organization's strategic goals by negotiations between the job's incumbent and the incumbent's supervisor. From these general objectives, specific performance objectives would be set for each job each year through negotiations between the incumbent and the incumbent's supervisor. The objectives would be multidimensional and would include performance objectives for all attributes of the job that are considered important.

The annual evaluation would reflect two dimensions of performance appraisal. First, the incumbent would be evaluated for innovation in developing ways of carrying out assigned responsibilities. Second, the incumbent's performance would be evaluated relative to the targets that were negotiated with the supervisor. Norm summarized his feelings as follows:

> The only thing that is holding me back is that I do not think that the proposed changes go far enough. The proposed system deals with the problem of inadequate performance measurement but still provides managers with incentives to understate their potential, since their performance will be evaluated relative to the targets that each manager negotiates with his supervisor. Moreover, the planned system, like the old system, still has the aspect of checking up on people rather than relying on them to do their jobs. Perhaps we should go even further and implement the proposed system but evaluate managers only on their ability to be innovative in undertaking the tasks that they have been assigned. If they are not evaluated relative to the targets that they set jointly with their supervisors, they will be motivated not to understate their potential. The bottom line is that I think that we should get rid of the concept of standards altogether, irrespective of who sets the standards. As a result of eliminating the concept of standards, the budget will serve to communicate and coordinate rather than be a threat and a means of checking up on the managers.

### Required

Evaluate the initial proposal for the revision of the budgeting system as well as the proposal that would eliminate the use of standards.

## 14-10    *Individual Rewards versus Group Rewards*

Lake Erie Steel Products Limited is a large integrated steel-products firm producing a full line of steel products that are sold internationally.

The company is organized on a profit center basis, with the major primary profit centers being the coal-mining operations, the iron ore-mining operations, and the scrap steel operations. The major manufacturing profit centers are hot-rolled products, cold-rolled products, and shaped products. The major finishing profit centers are fastener products, tube products, and specialty products.

The company has implemented a market-based transfer pricing system for every product that has a well-organized external market. This segment accounts for about 75% of the transfers that take place between the profit centers. The balance of transferred products are priced using a transfer price that consists of fixed fee plus standard variable cost.

The transfer pricing system is used to evaluate profit center performance along two dimensions. First, the profit center's controllable margin is used as an assessment of the performance of the manager. Second, the profit center's profit is used to evaluate the on-going decision to continue the operations of the profit center or to abandon the profit center.

All the employees in the organization except the chairman, president, and vice presidents participate in the corporate profit-sharing plan. (The excepted individuals participate in a stock option plan and a bonus system that focuses on accomplishing strategic performance objectives.) The pool available for bonuses is based on corporate earnings and equals 10% of all corporate earnings in excess of the target level of earnings that is established for any particular year.

The senior management committee evaluates the performance of each profit center relative to its financial *and* operating goals. The overall performance of the profit center is rated as poor, acceptable, or outstanding. Performance values of 0, 0.25, and 1 are assigned to each of these qualitative ratings, respectively. Therefore, an overall profit center performance that is rated as acceptable is assigned a performance value of 0.25.

Next, the employee's supervisor rates the individual performance of each employee. (In the case of the profit center manager, the evaluation is done by the vice president to whom the manager reports.) The employee's performance is evaluated relative to the objectives that the employee and his supervisor established for each job. There are, by design, exactly four attributes of each employee's job that are measured and evaluated. None of the four attributes is a financial measurement. The overall performance of the employee is rated as poor, acceptable, or outstanding and is assigned the corresponding performance value of 0, 0.25, or 1, respectively.

The following sequence of calculations is then undertaken:

1. Sum the employee's profit center performance rating and the individual's personal performance rating to determine the employee's aggregate performance measure.
2. Multiply each employee's aggregate performance measure by the employee's wages to determine the employee's weighted wages.
3. Sum the weighted wages of all the employees who are participants in the profit-sharing plan to compute a sum of weighted wages.
4. Divide the bonus pool available by the sum of weighted wages to determine the bonus per dollar of weighted wage.
5. Determine each employee's bonus by multiplying the employee's weighted wage by the bonus per dollar of weighted wage.

This calculation had resulted, on average, of bonuses of 18% of wages to be paid during the last five years.

### Required

Evaluate this incentive scheme, discussing your impressions of its positive and negative aspects.

## 14-11  *Agency Theory Considerations in Choosing a Wage*

Conestogo Farms produces ginseng. The farm is owned by an absentee landlord who hires a manager to grow and harvest the crop. The market wage for hired help is $40,000 per season.

The ginseng output is determined by two factors: the weather, which is a random factor that cannot be controlled, and the manager's care level, which can be high or low. The manager suffers a personal cost of $10,000 for putting in a low level of care and $25,000 for putting in a high level of care. The landlord can observe neither the weather conditions nor the manager's care level. Only the crop outcome can be observed.

There are two possible crop outcomes: good or bad. The following table shows the probability of good and bad outcomes, for high and low care levels.

|  | CARE LEVEL HIGH | CARE LEVEL LOW |
|---|---|---|
| Probability of good crop outcome | 0.85 | 0.25 |
| Probability of bad crop outcome | 0.15 | 0.75 |

The landlord has decided that she would like to motivate the manager to provide a high level of care. The manager has a utility for wealth that can be modeled as negative exponential with a risk parameter equal to $-0.0001$.

### Required

How should the landlord pay the manager to ensure that the manager provides a high level of care?

## 14-12    *Designing an Incentive Scheme to Attract the Target Manager*

Scharl Construction does house framing. The owner, Holly Scharl, wants to hire a carpenter. The work is unsupervised, so Holly wants to make sure that she hires the right kind of person.

There are two grades of carpenters: qualified and unqualified. The difference between the two grades is reflected in the amount of work they do during a shift, which results in a high or low level of output. Output is also affected by the quality of the raw materials and whether there are delays caused by weather or late deliveries of supplies, neither of which Holly can observe because she is not on site. The result is that it is impossible to infer, from the output level, whether the carpenter was qualified or unqualified.

The following table indicates the probability of a high or low level of output for the two types of workers.

|  | OUTPUT IS HIGH | OUTPUT IS LOW |
|---|---|---|
| Carpenter is qualified | 0.9 | 0.1 |
| Carpenter is unqualified | 0.2 | 0.8 |

Holly wants to hire a qualified carpenter. However, although the carpenter knows whether he is qualified or unqualified, he has no way of proving it to Holly. Qualified carpenters require a market wage of $15,000 for the time period that Herman is considering; unqualified carpenters command a market wage of $8,000. Holly knows that the wealth preferences of all carpenters can be modeled by a negative exponential utility function. The risk-aversion parameter for qualified carpenters is $-0.0001$ and for unqualified carpenters is $-0.00005$.

## Required

(1) Given these circumstances, devise an incentive plan for Holly that will ensure that she hires a qualified carpenter.

(2) Suppose that the market wage for an unqualified carpenter is $5,000 instead of $8,000. How would this difference change the incentive plan that you devised in Requirement 1? Explain the change.

(3) Suppose that Kathy Investigations can do a background check on any prospective carpenter and verify that carpenter's qualification with 100% accuracy. What is the maximum that Kathy should be willing to pay Kathy Investigations to supply a qualified carpenter? You can assume that Kathy Investigations will act honestly in its dealings with Kathy.

# Index